eBook and Digital Course Materials for

Directions
e-Book and Digital Course Materials

Anthropology
What Does It Mean to Be Human?

FIFTH EDITION

ROBERT H. LAVENDA
EMILY A. SCHULTZ

Carefully scratch off the silver coating to see your personal redemption code.

This code can be used only once and cannot be shared!

If the code has been scratched off when you receive it, the code may not be valid. Once the code has been scratched off, this access card cannot be returned to the publisher. You may buy access at **www.oup.com/he/lavenda5e**.

The code on this card is valid for 2 years from the date of first purchase. Complete terms and conditions are available at **learninglink.oup.com**.

Access length: 6 months from redemption of the code.

VIA OXFORD **learning link**

> Visit **www.oup.com/he/lavenda5e**

> Select the edition you are using and the student resources for that edition.

> Click the link to upgrade your access to the student resources.

> Follow the on-screen instructions.

> Enter your personal redemption code when prompted.

VIA YOUR SCHOOL'S LEARNING MANAGEMENT SYSTEM

> Log in to your instructor's course.

> When you click a link to a protected resource, you will be prompted to register for access.

> Follow the on-screen instructions.

> Enter your personal redemption code when prompted.

For assistance with code redemption or registration, please contact customer support at **learninglink.support@oup.com**.

OXFORD
UNIVERSITY PRESS

anthropology

anthropology

what does it mean to be human?

FIFTH EDITION

Robert H. Lavenda
St. Cloud State University

Emily A. Schultz
St. Cloud State University

New York   Oxford
OXFORD UNVIERSITY PRESS

Oxford University Press is a department of the University of Oxford. It furthers the University's objective of excellence in research, scholarship, and education by publishing worldwide. Oxford is a registered trade mark of Oxford University Press in the UK and certain other countries.

Published in the United States of America by Oxford University Press 198 Madison Avenue, New York, NY 10016, United States of America.

For titles covered by Section 112 of the US Higher Education Opportunity Act, please visit www.oup.com/us/he for the latest information about pricing and alternate formats.

Library of Congress Cataloging-in-Publication Data

Names: Lavenda, Robert H., author. | Schultz, Emily A. (Emily Ann), author.
Title: Anthropology : what does it mean to be human? / Robert H. Lavenda, St. Cloud State University, Emily A. Schultz, St. Cloud State University.
Description: Fifth edition. | New York : Oxford University Press, [2021] | Includes bibliographical references and index. | Summary: "This is a general, four fields, anthropology textbook"—Provided by publisher.
Identifiers: LCCN 2020025285 | ISBN 9780197534434 (paperback) | ISBN 9780197534465 (ebook)
Subjects: LCSH: Anthropology—Textbooks.
Classification: LCC GN25 .L38 2021 | DDC 301—dc23
LC record available at https://lccn.loc.gov/2020025285

9 8 7 6 5 4 3 2 1
Printed by Quad/Graphics, Inc., Mexico

In memory of Beatrice G. Schultz,
Violet H. Lavenda, George Lavenda,
and Henry W. Schultz

Brief Contents

Contents

**CHAPTER 3   What Can the Study of Primates Tell Us
about Human Beings?   63**

CHAPTER 4   What Can the Fossil Record Tell Us about Human Origins? 97

CHAPTER 5 How Does the Evolutionary Study of Human Variation Undermine Notions of Biological Race? 145

CHAPTER 6 How Do We Know about the Human Past? 171

CHAPTER 11 Why Do Anthropologists Study Economic Relations? 343

CHAPTER 12   How Do Anthropologists Study Political Relations?   369

CHAPTER 13 What Can Anthropology Teach Us About Sex, Gender, and Sexuality? 401

CHAPTER 14 Where Do Our Relatives Come from and Why Do They Matter? 429

CHAPTER   15   What Can Anthropology Tell Us About Social Inequality?   477

Boxes

Preface

This book emerged out of our increasing dissatisfaction with all the available general anthropology texts. We found that they either overwhelmed beginning students with detail and the sheer volume of material or provided overly brief introductions that failed to convey the richness of the field. We therefore set out to write a book that introduces this broad field concisely yet thoroughly, providing diverse perspectives and examples to foster not only an appreciation of anthropology but also a deeper engagement with it—one that helps students better understand themselves and the world around them. We (and our students) needed a general anthropology text that struck the right balance; fit into a 15-week semester; and came with a complete package of ancillary materials including quizzes, exams, suggested videos, and supplemental readings.

Throughout the process of writing the first edition and revising for subsequent editions, two central questions have guided our decisions on what material to include. First, what is the essential material that a balanced introduction to four-field anthropology must cover? Second, how much detail on any particular topic could we include without overwhelming beginning students? Most general anthropology textbooks are essentially cultural anthropology textbooks that have bulked up, but we decided to start anew and build a general anthropology text chapter by chapter. We address the central issues of the discipline, highlighting the controversies and commitments that shape contemporary anthropology and that make it interesting and exciting.

Approach

This book may be concise, but we cover the field effectively and in a way that we think is intellectually honest. We take a question-oriented approach that illuminates major concepts for students and shows them the relevance of anthropology in today's world. Structuring each chapter around an important question and its subquestions, we explore what it means to be human, incorporating answers from all four major subfields of anthropology—biological anthropology, archaeology, linguistic anthropology, and cultural anthropology—as well as from applied anthropology. We have made every effort to provide a balanced perspective, both in the level of detail we present and in our coverage of the major subfields.

The questioning approach not only sparks curiosity but also orients students' reading and comprehension of each chapter, highlighting the concepts every student should take away from a general anthropology course. For example, students need to know about evolutionary theory; human variation; and the biological, social, and cultural critique of the concept of race since knowledge in these areas is one of the great achievements of the discipline of anthropology. No other discipline (and possibly no other course) will teach about these matters the way anthropologists do. Students need to know about the fossil evidence for the evolution of *Homo sapiens*, which they are not likely to learn about elsewhere. Students need to know what archaeology can tell us about the human past, as well as what ethnography can teach us about social complexity and inequality. They need to know that culture isn't just the Festival of Nations and unusual foods and interesting traditional costumes. They need to know about language and the central role of learning in human development. They need to understand the wellsprings of human creativity and imagination. It is valuable for them to see the panoply of forms of human relatedness and how people organize themselves. They need to know about globalization from the bottom up and not just the top down. They need to see how all the subfields of anthropology together can provide important, unique insights into all these topics and so many more and how anthropology can provide a vital foundation for their university education.

The world we face as anthropologists has changed dramatically in the last quarter century, and anthropology has changed, too. We have always felt it necessary to present students with a view of what contemporary anthropologists are doing; we therefore address the most current issues in the field and have thoroughly updated the text accordingly for this edition. Your students will take away from the book an appreciation of how these areas of specialization have developed over time and how they contribute to our understanding of the world in the twenty-first century.

Organization

Divided into 16 chapters and 4 modules, this book is the ideal length for one semester. After Chapter 1, which introduces the entire field, 6 chapters are devoted to biological anthropology and archaeology: evolutionary theory (Chapter 2); the primates (Chapter 3); the fossil record and human origins (Chapter 4); human variation (and why anthropologists reject the concept of biological race); (Chapter 5); the human past (Chapter 6); and the first farmers, cities, and states (Chapter 7). Topics in cultural and linguistic anthropology are covered in chapters on culture (Chapter 8); language (Chapter 9); symbolic practices (Chapter 10, covering play, art, myth, ritual, and religion); economics (Chapter 11); politics (Chapter 12); sex, gender, and sexuality (Chapter 13); forms of relatedness, including kinship, marriage, and friendship (Chapter 14); social inequality and human rights (Chapter 15, covering class, caste, race, ethnicity, and human rights and sovereignty); and applied anthropology (covering medical anthropology and development anthropology, Chapter 16). In addition, brief methodological modules after Chapters 1, 3, 8, and 9 discuss anthropology, science, and storytelling; dating methods for paleoanthropology and archaeology; ethnographic methods; and the components of language. Throughout the book, we pay special attention to issues of power and inequality in the contemporary world.

Key Features

- **We take an explicitly global approach throughout the text.** We highlight ways that the post-Cold War global spread of capitalism has drastically reshaped the local contexts in which people everywhere live their lives.

- **We incorporate current anthropological approaches to power and inequality throughout the text.** We explore how power is manifested in different human societies, how it permeates all aspects of social life, and how it is deployed, resisted, and transformed. We discuss issues of trauma, social suffering, and human rights.

- **Material on gender and feminist anthropology is featured both in its own chapter and throughout the text.** In addition to a chapter devoted to gender, discussions of gender are tightly woven into the fabric of the book, and include (e.g.) material on gender and feminist archaeology, controversies over female genital cutting, supernumerary sexes and genders, varieties of human sexual practices, language and gender, gay marriage, women and colonialism, gender issues in Islam in Europe, Nuer women marriage, and contemporary forms of social inequality.

- **"In Their Own Words."** New voices, including those of indigenous peoples, anthropologists, and nonanthropologists, are presented in the text in commentaries called "In Their Own Words." These short commentaries provide alternative perspectives—always readable and sometimes controversial—on topics featured in the chapter where they appear.

- **"EthnoProfiles."** These text inserts provide a consistent, brief information summary for each society discussed at length in the text. They emerged from our desire as teachers to supply our students with basic geographical, demographic, and political information about the peoples anthropologists have worked with. Each EthnoProfile also contains a map of the area in which the society is found. They are not intended to be a substitute for reading ethnographies, nor are they intended to reify or essentialize the "people" or "culture" in question. Their main purpose is simply to provide a consistent orientation for readers, though of course it is becoming more and more difficult to attach peoples to particular territories in an era of globalization. How does one calculate population numbers or draw a simple map to locate a global diaspora? How does one construct an EthnoProfile for overseas Chinese or trans-border Haitians? We don't know how to answer these questions, which is why EthnoProfiles for those groups are not included in the textbook.

- **"Anthropology in Everyday Life."** Following the suggestions of reviewers, we have provided selections on anthropology in practice throughout the text; topics include agricultural development, archaeology and community engagement, anthropology and advertising, Human Terrain Teams, and forensic anthropology and human rights, among others.

- Additional learning aids. Key terms are boldfaced in the text and defined in a running glossary on the page where they appear, in addition to in a glossary at the back of the text. Each chapter ends with a list of the key terms in alphabetical order with page references, a numbered chapter summary, review questions, and annotated suggested readings. Maps are featured extensively throughout the text.

- **Use of citations and quotations.** In our discussions, we have tried to avoid being omniscient narrators by making use of citations and quotations in order to indicate where anthropological ideas come from. In our view, even first-year students need to know that an academic discipline like anthropology is constructed by the work of many people; no one, especially not textbook authors, should attempt to impose a single voice on the field. We have avoided, as much as we could, predigested statements that students must take on faith. We try to give them the information that they need to see where particular conclusions come from. In our experience, students appreciate being taken seriously.

• **Supplemental chapter materials provide flexibility for instructors.** As we considered how to create a new book for this course, we realized we would have to omit material that you may want your students to know about or that might interest them. To offer you flexibility, we decided to include some of that material on the accompanying website (www.oup.com/he/lavenda5e). Each entry ranges in length from one or two paragraphs to about three pages and can easily be used either for lecture topics or as handouts. For example, if you'd like to stress the different routes that led to the rise of civilization, you could assign the reading about the rise of civilization in Mesopotamia to supplement the textbook's discussion of the rise of civilization in the Andes. If you're looking for more examples to illustrate ritual and cultural patterns in the United States, you could assign the selection on children's birthday parties in the United States. The bulk of the supplemental chapter material on the Instructor's website is linked to the cultural chapters, and many entries are additional ethnographic examples.

What's New in the Fifth Edition?

There are many changes, both large and small, in the fifth edition:

• Chapter 1 now includes a discussion of the roots of anthropological scholarship around the world. We also incorporate material about the relational approach to development and growth, exploring what it would mean to consider members of our species as "biosocial becomings." This relational approach links productively with discussions in earlier editions of the text that address efforts by theoretical biologists to articulate an expanded evolutionary synthesis that includes ontogeny. It also connects with recent work in multispecies ethnography, which reconsiders longstanding human relations with other species. This reconsideration, in turn, has prompted new ways of understanding the domestication of plants and animals (more fully addressed in Chapter 6). Our introductory remarks about globalization now include two anthropological accounts of immigration at the southern border of the United States. One is Seth Holmes's account of Triqui migrants from Oaxaca, Mexico, who work in the strawberry fields of Washington state; the other is Jason de Leon's "Undocumented Migration Project."

Among its many strengths, de Leon's work offers a fresh understanding of the contributions four-field, holistic anthropology can make, not only to our understanding of life and death in the Sonoran Desert, but also throughout the world at a politically fraught moment in history.

• Chapter 2 includes an expanded discussion of the history of evolutionary theory, from Darwin through the modern synthesis to current efforts to expand the synthesis. Such expansion would include, among other topics, processes of ontogeny and niche construction, both of which link productively to new descriptions of human development and evolution as relational processes of members of "biosocial becoming."

• Chapter 3 includes information from comparative DNA analyses showing repeated instances of interbreeding between different species of primates. The chapter now includes a new "In Their Own Words" contribution by Tim Flannery, who discusses how widespread interbreeding appears to be among other species. The "In Their Own Words" discussion of chimpanzee tourism has been updated with new information about an ongoing project begun in the 1980s by Jane Goodall and her associates to protect chimps and the Gombe forest, while involving local residents in chimpanzee conservation.

• Module 2 on dating methods points out how information from electron spin resonance and thermoluminescence helped secure the date of 300,000 years ago for the Jebel Irhoud fossils. Discussion of climate fluctuation now mentions niche construction and the Anthropocene.

• Chapter 4 connects species selection to discussions of multilevel selection that are proposed for inclusion in an extended evolutionary synthesis. The chapter now contains new information about controversial 7-million-year old fossils assigned *Graecopithecus*, which some suggest could be ancestral to all later hominins. We update the age of the earliest reliable instances of *H. sapiens* to 300,000 years ago, based on fossils from Jebel Irhoud, Morocco. We discuss new footprints from the UK assigned to *H. antecessor*. We describe how increasing information from ancient DNA has supported the view that our species' ancestry is mixed, complicating older, more linear accounts of human origins. This is illustrated by new information about Neandertals and their contemporaries. We highlight new work suggesting that the Neandertals were far less numerous than anatomically modern *H. sapiens* and could easily have been absorbed into that larger population via inbreeding.

- Chapter 5 has a new title: "How Does the Evolutionary Study of Human Variation Undermine Notions of Biological Race?" This title makes more prominent what has always been the key theme of this chapter on human variation. We have expanded our discussion of epigenetic inheritance, and "The molecularization of race" is now the final subsection of the chapter. Previous discussions in this chapter concerning development and evolution are now explicitly connected to new discussions in previous chapters about "biosocial becoming."

- Chapter 6 includes a new discussion of recent arguments by anthropologists and others about the Anthropocene, and we consider how thinking in terms of the Anthropocene may affect archaeological interpretations of the deep past. We use James Scott's provocative account in *Against the Grain* to reconsider how to identify subsistence strategies; and we also discuss Scott's critical discussion of what anthropologists might mean when they speak about bands, tribes, chiefdoms, and states. We present Scott's own analysis of domestication, which he links explicitly to niche construction, and which resonates with other recent anthropological discussions of domestication and multispecies relations. We confirm the reburial in 2017 of the remains of Kennewick Man/the Ancient One.

- Chapter 7 builds on the reconsideration of subsistence strategies, domestication, and niche construction, and multispecies connections presented in Chapter 6. We highlight new work that emphasizes relational connections between humans, other species, and particular features of the wider environment. We reprise the new understandings of domestication presented in earlier chapters, including the connection between domestication, the emergence of social complexity, and the Anthropocene.

- Chapter 8. "Why Is the Concept of Culture Important?" We now begin by presenting culture from a point of view that emphasizes biosocial becoming, a move that makes explicit many of the emphases that have always been central to this chapter. We expand our discussion of ethnocentrism, including insights from Ghassan Hage about the otherness that always dwells within us. We have updated our discussion of female genital cutting in Sudan to include recent research by Janice Boddy. Her discussion, which illustrates the effect of a variety of globalization processes on men and women from Hofriyat, is now followed by our discussion of Kiowa Christianity. Together, these materials demonstrate clearly to students that thinking of "cultures" as separate, self-contained entities is no longer mainstream among cultural anthropologists.

- Module 3 "On Ethnographic Methods". A new addition to our discussion of anthropology and ethics is material from Katherine Verdery's path-breaking reflection on her fieldwork in Romania during the Cold War, *My Life As a Spy* (2018).

- Chapter 10. We now include a discussion of anthropological approaches to secularism alongside our discussion of anthropological discussions of religion. We also include new material on the "anthropology of ontology," illustrated by the ethnographic work of Marisol de la Cadena among the *runakuna* of highland Peru. Finally, we update our discussion of shamans by including new understandings of Amazonian shamanism influenced by the anthropology of ontology, citing the work of Eduardo Viveiros de Castro. We discuss how the anthropology of ontology challenges the traditional anthropological notion of "worldview" as too weak to capture the different "worlding" practices enacted by different human groups.

- Chapter 11. "Why Do Anthropologists Study Economic Relations?" The chapter now incorporates the revised discussion of subsistence strategies presented in earlier chapters.

- Chapter 12. "How Do Anthropologists Study Political Relations?" This chapter updates several case studies from earlier editions, including the latest elections in Fiji and the politics of migration in Europe and in the United States. We note the end of resistance to eviction in Bangkok in May 2018. We note new forms of resistance by CONAIE in Ecuador in 2019.

- Chapter 15 "What Can Anthropology Tell Us about Social Inequality?" We update the number of countries that had ratified CEDAW by November 2019.

- Chapter 16. This chapter has a new title "What is Applied Anthropology?" Based on recommendations by reviewers, we now supplement a discussion of medical anthropology with a new discussion of development anthropology.

Teaching and Learning Support

Oxford University Press offers students and instructors a comprehensive teaching and learning package of support materials for adopters of *Anthropology: What Does It Mean to Be Human? 5e.*

Oxford Learning Link

Oxford Learning Link at www.oup.com/he/lavenda5e is a convenient, instructor-focused single destination for resources to accompany *Anthropology: What Does It Mean to Be Human?*. Accessed online through individual user accounts, Oxford Learning Link provides instructors with access to up-to-date ancillaries while guaranteeing the security of grade-significant resources. In addition, it allows OUP to keep instructors informed when new content becomes available.

Oxford Learning Link for *Anthropology: What Does It Mean to Be Human?* includes a variety of materials to aid in teaching:

- Digital copy of the **Instructor's Manual**, which includes:
  - Discussion Questions
  - Critical Thinking Questions
  - Activities and Assignments
  - Supplemental Materials
  - Film Suggestions and Questions
  - PowerPoint Lecture Slides
- A computerized **Test Bank** formatted according to Bloom's Taxonomy, which includes:
  - Multiple-Choice Questions
  - True/False Questions
  - Short-Answer Questions
  - Essay Questions
- **Learning Management System Integration:** OUP offers the ability to integrate OUP content into currently supported versions of Canvas, D2L, or Blackboard. Contact your local rep or visit https://learninglink.oup.com/integration for more information.

Digital Learning Tools

Anthropology: What Does It Mean to Be Human? comes with an extensive array of digital learning tools to ensure your students get the most out of your course.

Enhanced eBook: The enhanced eBook provides students with a versatile, accessible, online version of the textbook, with embedded video clips and accompanying assessment questions, as well as self-assessment quizzes after each main heading and at the end of each chapter. The eBook reader also provides functionality that will help students be more effective in their study time—for instance, bookmarking, highlighting, note taking, and search tools. Every new copy of the print text includes access to the eBook. The eBook is also available for separate purchase, either online or through campus bookstores.

Online Study Tools: Many additional online study tools are available at www.oup.com/he/lavenda5e for the student's self-paced learning and assessment. For each chapter, these include:

- **Flashcards** to assist students in studying and reviewing key terms
- **Suggestions for Further Reading**
- **Web Links**
- **Chapter Summaries**
- **Study Skills Guide** filled with hints and suggestions on improving study skills, organizing information, writing exam essays, and taking multiple-choice exams

Acknowledgments

Our thanks to our editor at Oxford, Sherith Pankratz. It continues to be a pleasure to work with her as well as with the production department. Assistant Editors, Olivia Clark and Grace Li have been wonderful in keeping track of and organizing all the details involved with a project of this magnitude.

Once again, we are amazed at how much time and effort reviewers put into their task. The many reviewers for this project have contributed significantly to both the shape and the details of the book. We hope they can see where we have taken their advice, and we would like them to know that we carefully thought through every suggestion, even the ones we decided we could not follow. So, our thanks to the reviewers for this edition:

Jenna Andrews-Swann, Georgia Gwinnett College

Susan Bird, Wayne State College

Steve Dasovich, Lindenwood University

Marni Finkelstein, Pace University

Susan Krook, Normandale Community College

Carmen Laguer Díaz, Valencia College

Jon K. Loessin, Wharton County Junior College

Kathe Managan, University of Louisiana-Lafayette

Jayur Mehta, Florida State University

Kristen Ogilvie, University of Alaska, Anchorage

Jessica L. Skinner, College of Lake County

Mary Vermilion, Saint Louis University

Our sincere thanks also to our supplement author, Jennifer Wies, Ball State University who created high-quality additional resources specifically for this text.

This book is dedicated to the memory of our parents. Relatedness remains important in human societies, and as we grow older, we better understand why. So we also recognize our children, Daniel and Rachel, whose lives have been bound up with our books in so many ways, not the least of which are our hopes that they and their generation will find something of value in the anthropological approach.

anthropology

1

What is anthropology?

This chapter introduces the field of anthropology. We look at what anthropology is and explore its different subfields. We touch on anthropology's key concept, culture, as well as its key research method, fieldwork. We conclude with a discussion of the ways anthropological insights are relevant in everyday life.

CHAPTER OUTLINE

LEARNING OBJECTIVES

- Define "anthropology" and describe the unique characteristics of the disciplines (holism, comparison, and evolution).
- Identify the culture concept and how culture is used and applied in anthropology.

- Explain the history and meaning of anthropology as cross-disciplinary.
- Describe the four subfields (biological anthropology, cultural anthropology, linguistic anthropology, and archaeology), including areas of similarities and differences between them.

- Articulate the definition for and value of applied anthropology.
- Define the area of medical anthropology and explain its importance for the practice of anthropology.
- Apply anthropology to contemporary social issues to express the promise of anthropology.

Children gathered on a school playground with a Maasai instructor.

In early 1976, the authors of this book traveled to northern Cameroon, in western Africa, to study social relations in the town of Guider, where we rented a small house. In the first weeks we lived there, we enjoyed spending the warm evenings of the dry season reading and writing in the glow of the house's brightest electric fixture, which illuminated a large, unscreened veranda. After a short time, however, the rains began, and with them appeared swarms of winged termites. These slow-moving insects with fat, two-inch abdomens were attracted to the light on the veranda, and we soon found ourselves spending more time swatting at them than reading or writing. One evening, in a fit of desperation, we rolled up old copies of the international edition of *Newsweek* and began an all-out assault, determined to rid the veranda of every single termite.

The rent we paid for this house included the services of a night watchman. As we launched our attack on the termites, the night watchman suddenly appeared beside the veranda carrying an empty powdered milk tin. When he asked if he could have the insects we had been killing, we were a bit taken aback but warmly invited him to help himself. He moved onto the veranda, quickly collected the corpses of fallen insects, and then joined us in going after those termites that were still airborne. Although we became skilled at thwacking the insects with our rolled-up magazines, our skills paled beside those of the night watchman, who simply snatched the termites out of the air with his hand, squeezed them gently, and dropped them into his rapidly filling tin can. The three of us managed to clear the air of insects—and fill his tin—in about 10 minutes. The night watchman

thanked us and returned to his post, and we returned to our books.

The following evening, soon after we took up our usual places on the veranda, the watchman appeared at the steps bearing a tray with two covered dishes. He explained that his wife had prepared the food for us in exchange for our help in collecting termites. We accepted the food and carefully lifted the lids. One dish contained *nyiri*, a stiff paste made of red sorghum, a staple of the local diet. The other dish contained another pasty substance with a speckled, salt-and-pepper appearance, which we realized was termite paste prepared from the insects we had all killed the previous night.

The night watchman waited at the foot of the veranda steps, an expectant smile on his face. Clearly, he did not intend to leave until we tasted the food his wife had prepared. We looked at each other. We had never eaten insects before or considered them edible in the North American, middle-class diet we were used to. To be sure, "delicacies" like chocolate-covered ants exist, but such items are considered by most North Americans to be food fit only for eccentrics. However, we understood the importance of not insulting the night watchman and his wife, who were being so generous to us. We knew that insects were a favored food in many human societies and that eating them brought no ill effects (Figure 1.1). So we reached into the dish of *nyiri*, pulling off a small amount. We then used the ball of *nyiri* to scoop up a small portion of termite paste, brought the mixture to our mouths, ate, chewed, and swallowed. The watchman beamed, bid us goodnight, and returned to his post. We looked at each other in wonder. The sorghum paste had

FIGURE 1.1 Many people around the world eat insects. Here, a restaurant worker in Bangkok, Thailand, prepares grubs for cooking.

a grainy tang that was rather pleasant. The termite paste tasted mild, like chicken, not unpleasant at all.

Not long afterward, we received a package from our family in the United States that contained, among other treats, a bag of commercial chocolate chip cookie mix. The kitchen of the house we were renting had an oven; eager to enjoy this quintessential North American treat, we baked the cookies and offered them to one of our field assistants. He politely tasted the cookies, but declined a second serving with the explanation that they were just too sweet for him.

What Is Anthropology?

This anecdote is not just an encounter about our field assistant and us; it also illustrates some of the central elements of the anthropological experience. Anthropologists want to learn about as many different human ways of life as they can. The people they come to know are members of their own society or live on a different continent, in cities or in rural areas. Their ways of life may involve patterns of regular movement across international borders, or they may make permanent homes in the borderlands themselves. Archaeologists reconstruct ancient ways of life from traces left behind in the earth that are hundreds or thousands of years old; anthropologists who strive to reconstruct the origin of the human species itself make use of fossil remains that reach back millions of years into the past. Whatever the case may be, anthropologists are sometimes exposed to practices that startle them. However, as they take the risk of getting to know such ways of life better, they are often treated to the sweet discovery of familiarity. Still, the response of our field assistant to the chocolate chip cookies is a valuable reminder that encounters with the unfamiliar can also sometimes be "too sweet." One of the strengths of anthropology comes precisely from unexpected insights that emerge from such encounters, when we and the people with whom we work discover that we can connect with one another in sometimes surprising ways, even though such connections may at times be awkward (Tsing 2005). In this book, we share aspects of the anthropological experience in the hope that you may come to find pleasure, insight, and self-recognition from an involvement with the unfamiliar.

Anthropology can be defined as the study of human nature, human society, and the human past (Greenwood and Stini 1977). It is a scholarly discipline that aims to describe in the broadest possible sense what it means to be human. Anthropologists are not alone in focusing their attention on human beings and their creations. Human biology, literature, art, history, linguistics, sociology, political science, economics—all these scholarly disciplines and many more—concentrate on one or another aspect of human life. Anthropologists are convinced, however, that explanations of human activities will be superficial unless they acknowledge that human lives are always entangled in complex patterns of work and family, power and meaning.

What is distinctive about the way anthropologists study human life? As we shall see, anthropology is holistic, comparative, field based, and evolutionary. First, anthropology emphasizes that all aspects of human life intersect with one another in complex ways. They shape one another and become integrated with one another over time. Anthropology is thus the integrated, or *holistic*, study of human nature, human society, and the human past. **Holism** has long been central to the anthropological perspective and remains the feature that draws together anthropologists whose specializations might otherwise divide them.

Second, in addition to being holistic, anthropology is a discipline interested in **comparison**. Generalizing about human nature, human society, and the human past requires evidence from the widest possible range of human societies. It is not enough, for example, to observe only our own social group, discover that we do not eat insects, and conclude that human beings as a species do not eat insects. When we compare human diets in different societies, we discover that insect eating is quite common and that our North American aversion to eating insects is nothing more than a dietary practice specific to our own society.

Third, anthropology is also a field-based discipline. That is, for almost all anthropologists, the actual practice of anthropology—its data collection—takes place away from the office and in direct contact with the people, the sites, or the animals that are of interest. Whether they are biological anthropologists studying chimpanzees in Tanzania, archaeologists excavating a site high in the Peruvian Andes, linguistic anthropologists learning an unwritten language in New Guinea, or cultural anthropologists studying ethnic identity in West Africa or small-town festivals in Minnesota, anthropologists are in direct contact with the sources of their data. For most anthropologists, the richness and complexity of this immersion

anthropology The study of human nature, human society, and the human past.

holism A characteristic of the anthropological perspective that describes, at the highest and most inclusive level, how anthropology tries to integrate all that is known about human beings and their activities.

comparison A characteristic of the anthropological perspective that requires anthropologists to consider similarities and differences in as wide a range of human societies as possible before generalizing about human nature, human society, or the human past.

in other patterns of life is one of our discipline's most distinctive features. Field research connects anthropologists directly with the lived experience of other people or other primates or with the material evidence that they have left behind. Academic anthropologists try to intersperse field research with the other tasks they perform as university professors. Other anthropologists—applied anthropologists—regularly spend most or all of their time carrying out field research. All anthropology begins with a specific group of people (or other animals, such as primates) and always comes back to them as well.

Finally anthropologists are interested in documenting and explaining change over time in the human past; this is why **evolution** is at the core of the anthropological perspective. Anthropologists examine the *biological evolution* of the human species, which documents change over time in the physical features and life processes of human beings and of our ancestors. Topics of interest include both human origins and genetic variation and inheritance in living human populations. If evolution is understood broadly as change over time, then human societies and cultures may also be understood to have evolved from prehistoric times to the present.

Anthropologists have long been interested in *cultural evolution*, which concerns change over time in beliefs, behaviors, and material objects that shape human development and social life. Early discussions of cultural evolution in anthropology emphasized a series of universal stages. However, this approach has been rejected by contemporary anthropologists who talk about cultural evolution, like William Durham (1991) and Robert Boyd (e.g., Richerson and Boyd 2005). Theoretical debates about culture change and about whether it ought to be called "cultural evolution" are very lively right now, not only in anthropology but also in related fields like evolutionary biology and developmental psychology. In the midst of this debate, one of anthropology's most important contributions to the study of human evolution remains the demonstration that biological evolution is not the same thing as cultural evolution. Distinction between the two remains important as a way of demonstrating the fallacies and incoherence of arguments claiming that everything people do or think can be explained biologically, for example, in terms of "genes" or "race" or "sex."

evolution A characteristic of the anthropological perspective that requires anthropologists to place their observations about human nature, human society, or the human past in a temporal framework that takes into consideration change over time.

culture Sets of learned behavior and ideas that human beings acquire as members of society together with the material artifacts and structures that human beings create and use. Human beings use culture to adapt to and transform the world in which they live.

What Is the Concept of Culture?

A consequence of human evolution that had the most profound impact on human nature and human society was the emergence of **culture**, which can be defined as sets of learned behavior and ideas that human beings acquire as members of society together with the material artifacts and structures that human beings create and use. Our cultural heritage allows humans to adapt to and transform the world around us through our interactions with material structures and objects in the communities where we live, through the connections we form with other people and other living organisms, through the actions and skills of our individual bodies, and through the ideas and values of our minds. The cultural heritage of the human species is both meaningful and material, and it makes us distinctive among living creatures.

Human beings are more dependent than any other species on learning for survival because we have no instincts that automatically protect us and help us find food and shelter. Instead, we have come to use our large and complex brains to learn from other members of society what we need to know to survive. Learning is a primary focus of childhood, which is longer for humans than for any other species.

From the anthropological perspective, the concept of *culture* is central to explanations of why human beings are what they are and why they do what they do. Anthropologists are frequently able to show that members of a particular social group behave in a particular way *not* because the behavior was programmed by their genes, but because they observed other people and copied what they did. For example, North Americans typically do not eat insects, but this behavior is not the result of genetic programming. Rather, North Americans have been told as children that eating insects is disgusting, have never seen any of their friends or family eat insects, and do not eat insects themselves. As we discovered personally, however, insects can be eaten by North Americans with no ill effects. This difference in dietary behavior can be explained in terms of culture rather than biology.

However, to understand the power of culture, anthropologists must also know about human biology. Anthropologists in North America traditionally have been trained in both areas so that they can understand how living organisms work and better evaluate how biology and culture contribute to different forms of human behavior. Indeed, most anthropologists reject explanations of human behavior that force them to choose either biology or culture as the unique cause. Instead, they emphasize that human beings are **biocultural organisms**. Our biological makeup—our brain, nervous system, and anatomy—is the outcome of developmental processes to which our genes and cellular chemistry contribute in fundamental ways. It also makes us organisms capable of creating and using culture. Without these biological endowments, human culture as we know it would not exist. At the same time, our survival as biological organisms depends on learned ways of thinking and acting that help us find food, shelter, and mates and that teach us how to rear our children. Our biological endowment, rich as it is, does not provide us with instincts that would automatically take care of these survival needs. Human biology makes culture possible; human culture makes human biological survival possible.

To understand the power of culture, anthropologists are also paying increasing attention to **material culture** in the lives of biocultural human organisms. Many cultural anthropologists, including ourselves, have traditionally emphasized the way people's dealings with artifacts are shaped by the cultural meanings they attach to those artifacts. This emphasis has seemed particularly necessary in the face of the widespread assumptions in our own North American society that material objects have obvious functional meanings that are the same for everyone, everywhere. But cultural anthropologists have found repeatedly that the same object can mean different things to different people. Just consider the varied meanings attached to assault weapons or the "morning after pill" in the recent history of the United States.

All the same, innovative theories of materiality developed in fields called *cyborg anthropology* and science studies have provided cultural anthropologists with new ways of conceptualizing relations between persons and things, enabling new connections between work in cultural anthropology and archaeology—a field with long experience in dealing with, and thinking about, material culture (see Chapters 6 and 7). Other examples illustrating these new approaches will be found throughout this book. Many examples center on human experiences with new kinds of things—computers, cell phones, the Internet—that are increasingly central to the lives of people all over the world. For instance, persons who play online video games seem to join with the technology and the other players to form a seamless hybrid entity; or the technology that links us to friends on social media disappears from our awareness. This is a phenomenon that anthropologist Daniel Miller calls *the humility of things*: "objects are important, not because they are evident and physically constrain or enable, but quite the opposite. It is often precisely because we do not see them" (2010, 50). The merging of persons and things is sometimes a source of pleasure, as when we do our holiday shopping on the Internet; but it can also be troubling when we realize that our web-surfing activities are being tracked by commercial web bots or by government entities like the National Security Agency. For these and other reasons, we agree with Daniel Miller that "the best way to understand, convey, and appreciate our humanity is through attention to our fundamental materiality" (2010, 4). And this means taking material culture seriously.

What Makes Anthropology a Cross-Disciplinary Discipline?

The roots of anthropological scholarship go back many centuries. According to Aleksandar Boškovic′ and Thomas Hylland Eriksen, European voyages of exploration in the fifteenth and sixteenth centuries stimulated a variety of efforts to make sense of different ways of life, with implications for Europeans' own understandings of themselves (2010, 2). They also conclude that "just as anthropology never had a single point of origin, it also never had a single stream of development and this becomes, perhaps, more pronounced than ever in our "post-colonial" or "post-industrial" times" (2010, 2). Boškovic′ and Eriksen trace the ways that historical developments and global politics have encourage or discouraged the development of anthropological research in different times and places. They document a contrast between anthropologies of the "centers" (North America, Western Europe, Japan) and "peripheries" (Eastern Europe, Africa, Latin America, Siberia, southern China), with the former locations historically enjoying greater support for research and publication. In some parts of the world, anthropological interest has been stimulated by foreign anthropologists; in other cases, foreign and local anthropologists have collaborated with one another; and in still other cases, the development of local anthropological work has been hampered by lack of financial and institutional support. However, the eleven case studies in their volume make it clear that "there is no such thing as 'peripheral anthropology,' but many, arising from highly distinct historical circumstances, and functioning under extremely different institutional, financial, and intellectual conditions" (2010, 9).

Because of its diversity, anthropology does not easily fit into any of the standard academic classifications. The discipline is usually listed as a social science, but it spans the natural sciences and the humanities as well.

biocultural organisms Organisms (in this case, human beings) whose defining features are codetermined by biological and cultural factors.

material culture Objects created or shaped by human beings and given meaning by cultural practices.

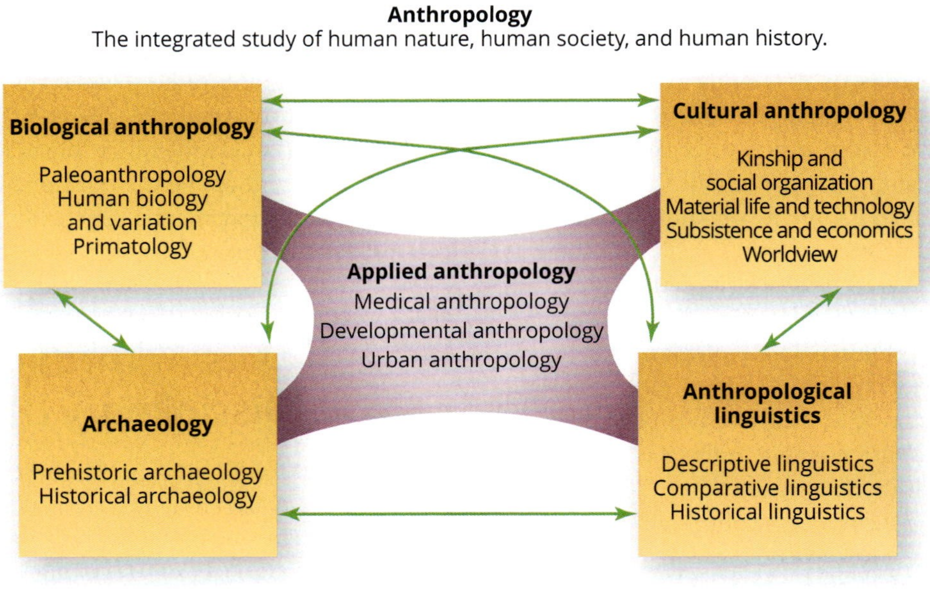

Anthropology
The integrated study of human nature, human society, and human history.

Biological anthropology

Paleoanthropology
Human biology
and variation
Primatology

Cultural anthropology

Kinship and
social organization
Material life and technology
Subsistence and economics
Worldview

Applied anthropology
Medical anthropology
Developmental anthropology
Urban anthropology

Archaeology

Prehistoric archaeology
Historical archaeology

Anthropological linguistics

Descriptive linguistics
Comparative linguistics
Historical linguistics

FIGURE 1.2   In the United States, anthropology is traditionally divided into four specialties: biological anthropology, cultural anthropology, anthropological linguistics, and archaeology. Applied anthropology draws on information provided by the other four specialties.

What it is *not*, as we will see, is the study of the "exotic," the "primitive," or the "savage," terms that anthropologists reject. Figure 1.2 brings some order to the variety of interests found under the anthropological umbrella.

Traditionally, North American anthropology has been divided into four subfields: *biological anthropology, cultural anthropology, linguistic anthropology,* and *archaeology.* Because of their commitment to holism, many anthropology departments try to represent most or all of the subfields in their academic programs. Many North American anthropologists, however, associate holistic four-field North American anthropology with the successful repudiation of nineteenth-century scientific racism by Franz Boas and other early twentieth-century anthropologists. They also value four-field anthropology as a protected "trading zone" within which anthropologists are encouraged to bring together fresh concepts and knowledge from a variety of research traditions. North American anthropologist Rena Lederman (2005), for example, has stressed that four-field anthropology does not insist on a single way of bringing the subfields together.

Anthropological holism is attractive even to those who were not trained in North America. British anthropologist Tim Ingold (1994), for example, argues, "The best anthropological writing is distinguished by its receptiveness to ideas springing from work in subjects far beyond its conventional boundaries, and by its ability to connect these ideas in ways that would not have occurred to their originators, who may be more enclosed in their particular

disciplinary frameworks" (xvii). We share the views of Lederman and Ingold: trained in holistic, four-field anthropology, we continue to value the unique perspective it brings to the study of human nature, human society, and the human past. Indeed, as the organizers of a recent anthropological conference observed, "Even those who were the least persuaded that the traditional four-field organization of American anthropology was still viable (if it ever was) came away with a strong sense that the subfields had a great deal to say to one another and indeed needed one another" (McKinnon and Silverman 2005, viii).

Biological Anthropology

Since the nineteenth century, when anthropology was developing as an academic field, anthropologists have studied human beings as living organisms to discover what makes us different from or similar to other animals. Early interest in these matters was a byproduct of centuries of exploration. Western Europeans had found tremendous variation in the physical appearance of peoples around the world and had long tried to make sense of these differences. Some researchers developed a series of elaborate techniques to measure different observable features of human populations—including skin color, hair type, body type, and so forth—hoping to find scientific evidence that would allow them to classify all the peoples of the world into a set of unambiguous categories based on distinct sets of biological attributes. Such categories were called **races**, and many scientists were convinced that clear-cut criteria for racial classification

---

races Social groupings that allegedly reflect biological differences.

Anthropology as a Vocation

Listening to Voices

James W. Fernandez (PhD, Northwestern University) is a professor of anthropology at the University of Chicago. He has worked among the Fang of Gabon and among cattle keepers and miners of Asturias, Spain. This is an excerpt from an essay about the anthropological vocation.

For me, the anthropological calling has fundamentally to do with the inclination to hear voices. An important part of our vocation is "listening to voices," and our methods are the procedures that best enable us to hear voices, to represent voices, to translate voices.

By listening carefully to others' voices and by trying to give voice to these voices, we act to widen the horizons of human conviviality. If we had not achieved some fellow feeling by being there, by listening carefully and by negotiating in good faith, it would be more difficult to give voice in a way that would widen the horizons of human conviviality. Be that as it may, the calling to widen

horizons and increase human conviviality seems a worthy calling—full of a very human optimism and good sense. Who would resist the proposition that more fellow feeling in the world is better than less, and that to extend the interlocutive in the world is better than to diminish it?

At the same time, there is a paradox here, one that demands of us a sense of proportion. Although the anthropologist is called to bring diverse people into intercommunication, he or she is also called to resist the homogenization that lies in mass communication. We are called by our very experience to celebrate the great variety of voices in the human chorus. The paradox is that we at once work to amplify the scale of intercommunication—and in effect contribute to homogenization—while at the same time we work to insist on the great variety of voices in communication. We must maintain here too a sense of proportion. We must recognize the point at which wider and wider cultural intercommunication can lead to dominant voices hidden in the homogenizing process. Human intercommunication has its uses and abuses.

Source: Fernandez 1990, 14–15.

---

would be discovered if careful measurements were made on enough people from a range of different populations.

European scientists first applied racial categories to the peoples of Europe itself, but their classifications soon included non-European peoples, who were coming under increasing political and economic domination by expanding European and European American capitalist societies. These peoples differed from "white" Europeans not only because of their darker skin color but also because of their unfamiliar languages and customs. In most cases, their technologies were also no match for the might of the West. In the early eighteenth century, the European biologist Carolus Linnaeus (Carl von Linné, 1707–1778) classified known human populations into four races (American, European, Asian, and Negro) based on skin color (reddish, white, yellow, and black, respectively). Linnaeus also connected racial membership with the mental and moral attributes of group members. Thus, he wrote, Europeans were "fickle, sanguine, blue-eyed, gentle, and governed by laws," whereas Negros were "choleric, obstinate, contented, and regulated by custom" and Asians were "grave, avaricious, dignified, and ruled by opinion" (Molnar 2001, 5–6).

In the nineteenth century, influential natural scientists such as Louis Agassiz, Samuel George Morton, Francis Galton, and Paul Broca assumed that biological races were real and that they could be ranked in a hierarchy. They then embarked on a program of scientific research (sometimes called *scientific racism*) that sought material evidence that would define racial boundaries and explain why the racial hierarchy existed. For instance, they ranked different populations of the world in terms of brain size; they found the brains of "white" Europeans and North Americans to be larger and saw the other races as representing varying grades of inferiority, with Africans ranked at the bottom (Gould 1996). These findings were used to justify the familiar social practices we now call **racism**: the systematic oppression of members of one or more socially defined "races" by another socially defined "race" that is justified in terms of the supposed inherent biological superiority of the rulers and the supposed inherent biological inferiority of those they rule.

---

racism The systematic oppression of one or more socially defined "races" by another socially defined "race" that is justified in terms of the supposed inherent biological superiority of the rulers and the supposed inherent biological inferiority of those they rule.

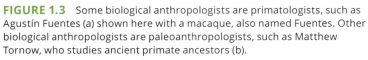

FIGURE 1.3 Some biological anthropologists are primatologists, such as Agustín Fuentes (a) shown here with a macaque, also named Fuentes. Other biological anthropologists are paleoanthropologists, such as Matthew Tornow, who studies ancient primate ancestors (b).

Biological or physical anthropology as a separate discipline had its origins in the work of scholars like these, whose training was in some other discipline, often medicine. Johann Blumenbach (1752–1840), for example, whom some have called the "father of physical anthropology," was trained as a physician. Blumenbach identified five different races (Caucasoid, Mongoloid, American, Ethiopian, and Malayan), and his classification was influential in the later nineteenth and twentieth centuries (Molnar 2001, 6). He and his contemporaries assumed that the races of "mankind" (as they would have said) were fixed and unchanging subdivisions of humanity.

However, as scientists learned more about biological variation in human populations, some of them came to realize that traits traditionally used to identify races, such as skin color, did not correlate well with other physical and biological traits, let alone mental and moral traits. Indeed, scientists could not even agree about how many human races there were or where the boundaries between them should be drawn.

By the early twentieth century, some anthropologists and biologists were arguing that "race" was a cultural label invented by human beings to sort people into groups and that races with distinct and unique sets of biological attributes simply did not exist. Anthropologists like Franz Boas, for example, who in the early 1900s founded the first department of anthropology in the United States, at Columbia University, had long been uncomfortable with racial classifications in anthropology. Boas and his students devoted much energy to debunking racist stereotypes, using both their knowledge of biology and their understanding of culture. As the discipline of anthropology developed in the United States, students were trained in both human biology and human culture to provide them with the tools to fight racial stereotyping. After World War II, this position gained increasing strength in North American anthropology, under the forceful leadership of anthropologist Sherwood Washburn. The "new" physical anthropology Washburn developed at the University of California, Berkeley, repudiated racial classification and shifted attention to patterns of variation and adaptation within the human species as a whole. This shift in emphasis led many of Washburn's followers to define their specialty as **biological anthropology**, a move that highlighted their differences with the older "physical anthropology" devoted to racial classification.

Some biological anthropologists work in the fields of **primatology** (the study of the closest living relatives of human beings, the nonhuman primates), **paleoanthropology** (the study of fossilized bones and teeth of our earliest ancestors), and human skeletal biology (measuring and comparing the shapes and sizes—or morphology—of bones and teeth using skeletal remains from different human populations) (see Figure 1.3). Newer specialties focus

biological anthropology (or physical anthropology) The specialty of anthropology that looks at human beings as biological organisms and tries to discover what characteristics make them different from other organisms and what characteristics they share.

primatology The study of nonhuman primates, the closest living relatives of human beings.

paleoanthropology The search for fossilized remains of humanity's earliest ancestors.

on human adaptability in different ecological settings, on human growth and development, or on the connections between a population's evolutionary history and its susceptibility to disease. Forensic anthropologists use their knowledge of human skeletal anatomy to aid law enforcement and human rights investigators. Some molecular anthropologists knowledgeable about the chemical properties and processes that characterize the human immune system were able to contribute to research on the virus that causes HIV/AIDS. Analytic techniques, such as biostatistics, three-dimensional imaging, and electronic communication and publishing, have transformed the field (Boaz and Wolfe 1995; Weinker 1995). Even more revolutionary has been the recent development of techniques for extracting ancient biomolecules from fossils. *Ancient DNA (aDNA)* extracted from fossil bones can reveal a range of information about the individual from whom it came, such as the individual's sex and its relationships to other populations in the past and present. Entire genomes of fossilized individuals, such as Neanderthals, have been reconstructed, providing dazzling new windows on migrations and contacts among ancient populations, as well as their connections to living populations (see Chapter 5). Ancient molecules can also be recovered, not only from fossilized bones, but also from ancient artifacts. For example, casein, a protein found in milk, leaves residues in the containers people used to store milk products such as cheese, which provides information about ancient dietary practices. This kind of information is of interest both to paleoanthropologists and to archaeologists, creating new opportunities for them to collaborate in reconstructing the human past (Brown and Brown 2013). In all these ways, biological anthropologists can illuminate what makes human beings similar to and different from one another, other primates, and other forms of life.

Whether they study human biology, primates, or the fossils of our ancestors, biological anthropologists clearly share many methods and theories used in the natural sciences—primarily biology, ecology, chemistry, and geology. What tends to set biological anthropologists apart from their nonanthropological colleagues is the holistic, comparative, and evolutionary perspective that has been part of their anthropological training. That perspective reminds them always to consider their work as only part of the overall study of human nature, human society, and the human past.

Cultural Anthropology

The second specialty within anthropology is **cultural anthropology**, which is sometimes called *sociocultural anthropology*, *social anthropology*, or *ethnology*. By the early

twentieth century, anthropologists realized that racial biology could not be used to explain why everyone in the world did not dress the same, speak the same language, pray to the same god, or eat insects for dinner. About the same time, anthropologists such as Margaret Mead were showing that the biology of sexual difference could not be used to predict how men and women might behave or what tasks they would perform in any given society. Anthropologists concluded that something other than biology had to be responsible for these variations. They suggested that this "something else" was culture.

Many anthropologists did significant research throughout the twentieth century that demonstrated why human cultural practices could not be reduced to "racial" difference. They also argued that culturally shaped **gender** roles considered appropriate for males or females in a given society could not be reduced to (or predicted by) the biological **sex** of an individual, whether determined by anatomy, physiology, or chromosomes. Today, anthropologists, along with others, call into question the assumption that human beings come in two (and only two) biological sexes and that gender roles are built on those two sexes. As anthropologist Keridwen Luis puts it, "We cannot understand our bodies except through culture; therefore, there is no pregendered body and there *is* no 'raw' precultural body or body experience. While biological bodies undoubtedly exist—we are not brains in jars—how we interpret, understand, and experience those bodies is culturally shaped" (2018, Loc 3616).

By the latter part of the twentieth century, anthropologists also regularly distinguished between the biological **sex** of an individual and the culturally shaped **gender** roles considered appropriate for each sex in a given society. As we shall see throughout the text, attention to gender has become an integral part of all anthropological work.

Because people everywhere use culture to adapt to and transform everything in the wider world in which they live, the field of cultural anthropology is vast. Cultural anthropologists tend to specialize in one or another domain of human cultural activity (Figure 1.4). Some study the ways particular groups of human beings organize themselves to carry out collective tasks, whether

cultural anthropology The specialty of anthropology that shows how variation in the beliefs and behaviors of members of different human groups is shaped by sets of learned behaviors and ideas that human beings acquire as members of society—that is, by culture.

gender The cultural construction of beliefs and behaviors considered appropriate for each sex.

sex Observable physical characteristics that distinguish two kinds of humans, females and males, needed for biological reproduction.

FIGURE 1.4 Cultural anthropologists talk to many people, observe their actions, and participate as fully as possible in a group's way of life. Here, Sri Lankan anthropologist Arjun Guneratne converses with some of his consultants in Nepal.

economic, political, or spiritual. This focus within cultural anthropology bears the closest resemblance to the discipline of sociology, and from it has come the identification of anthropology as one of the social sciences.

Sociology and anthropology developed during the same period and share similar interests in social organization. What differentiated anthropology from sociology was the anthropological interest in comparing different forms of human social life. In the racist framework of nineteenth and early twentieth-century European and North American societies, some people viewed sociology as the study of "civilized" industrial societies and labeled anthropology as the study of all other societies, lumped together as "primitive." Today, by contrast, anthropologists are concerned with studying *all* human societies, and they reject the labels *civilized* and *primitive* for the same reason they reject the notion of biological race. Contemporary anthropologists do research in urban and rural settings around the world and among members of all societies, including their own.

Anthropologists discovered that people in many non-Western societies do not organize bureaucracies or churches or schools, yet they still manage to carry out

successfully the full range of human activity because they developed institutions of relatedness that enabled them to organize social groups through which they could live their lives. One form of relatedness, called *kinship*, links people to one another on the basis of birth, marriage, and nurturance. The study of kinship has become highly developed in anthropology and remains a focus of interest today. In addition, anthropologists have described a variety of forms of social groups organized according to different principles, such as secret societies, age sets, and numerous forms of complex political organization, including states. In recent years, cultural anthropologists have studied contemporary issues of gender and sexuality, transnational labor migration, urbanization, globalization, the post-Cold War resurgence of ethnicity and nationalism around the globe, and debates about human rights.

Cultural anthropologists have investigated the patterns of material life found in different human groups. Among the most striking are worldwide variations in clothing, housing, tools, and techniques for getting food and making material goods. Some anthropologists specialize in the study of technologies in different societies or in the evolution of technology over time. Those interested in material life also describe the natural setting for which technologies have been developed and analyze the way technologies and environments shape each other. Others have investigated the way non-Western people have responded to the political and economic challenges of colonialism and the capitalist industrial technology that accompanied it.

Cultural anthropologists, no matter what their area of specialization, ordinarily collect their data during an extended period of close involvement with the people in whose language or way of life they are interested.

This period of research, called **fieldwork**, has as its central feature the anthropologists' involvement in the everyday routine of those among whom they live. People who share information about their culture and language with anthropologists have traditionally been called **informants**; however, some anthropologists prefer to describe these individuals as *respondents*, *collaborators*, *teachers*, or simply *"the people I work with"* because such terms emphasize a relationship of equality and reciprocity. Fieldworkers gain insight into another culture by participating with members in social activities and by observing those activities as outsiders. This research method, known as *participant observation*, is central to cultural anthropology.

Cultural anthropologists write about what they have learned in scholarly articles or books and sometimes document the lives of the people they work with on film or video. An **ethnography** is a description of "the customary social behaviors of an identifiable group of people" (Wolcott 1999, 252–53); **ethnology** is the comparative

---

fieldwork An extended period of close involvement with the people in whose language or way of life anthropologists are interested, during which anthropologists ordinarily collect most of their data.

informants People in a particular culture who work with anthropologists and provide them with insights about their way of life. Also called consultants, respondents, teachers, or friends.

ethnography An anthropologist's written or filmed description of a particular culture.

ethnology The comparative study of two or more cultures.

study of two or more such groups. Thus, cultural anthropologists who write ethnographies are sometimes called *ethnographers*, and anthropologists who compare ethnographic information on many different cultural practices are sometimes called *ethnologists*. But not all anthropological writing is ethnographic. Some anthropologists specialize in reconstructing the history of our discipline, tracing, for example, how anthropologists' fieldwork practices have changed over time and how these changes may be related to wider political, economic, and social changes within the societies from which they came and within which they did their research.

People everywhere are increasingly making use of material goods and technologies produced outside their own societies. Anthropologists have been able to show that, contrary to many expectations, non-Western people do not slavishly imitate Western ways. Instead, they make use of Western technologies in ways that are creative and often unanticipated but that make sense in their own local cultural context. These forms of cultural exchange were powerfully accelerated after the end of the Cold War in 1989, when advances in the technologies of communication, manufacturing, and transportation seemed to dissolve, or at least seriously reduce, previous barriers of space and time. All parts of the world were drawn into these processes of **globalization**: the reshaping of local conditions by powerful global forces on an ever-intensifying scale. Globalization suggests a world full of movement and mixture, contacts and linkages, and persistent cultural interaction and exchange (Inda and Rosaldo 2002, 2). Some people have clearly benefitted from globalization, whereas others have suffered, and people everywhere struggle to respond to effects of globalization that seem impossible to manage. In a globalized world, it is no longer possible to presume that peoples and cultures are firmly attached to specific geographical locations. As a result, for many years, cultural anthropologists have been increasingly attentive to the experiences of refugees and migrants. For instance, they have traced ongoing connections between migrants and those they leave behind, showing how the money and goods they send back keep families and communities alive back home. In some cases, leaving the home community to work elsewhere becomes an expectation, with one generation of migrants following another, hoping to amass enough wealth to allow them to eventually return home for good.

With the intensification of human population movements stimulated by globalization, the stakes for those seeking to migrate have escalated. In recent years, the borders of Western Europe and the United States have become political flashpoints, pitting people fleeing economic marginalization and political violence

who want to get in against local populations trying to keep them out. In 2016, for example, presidential candidate Donald Trump characterized undocumented immigrants and asylum seekers crossing the southern border of the United States as dangerous invaders who needed to be stopped, making a campaign promise to build a wall along the border with Mexico and to make Mexico pay for it. Since his election, the Trump administration's immigration policies at the border have become increasingly restrictive, challenging both federal laws protecting undocumented migrants and international agreements protecting the rights of asylum seekers. But policies designed to restrict immigration and deport those seeking to enter the United States without documentation were not invented by the Trump administration. Anthropologist Jason de Leon reports that "In the Obama era of mass deportations, close to 2 million people were removed from the country through fiscal year 2013" (2015, 3).

Ethnographic methods have allowed anthropologists to provide fine-grained accounts of the experiences of individuals and groups caught up in the crosswinds of migration. Seth Holmes, for example, spent five years following indigenous Triqui migrants from Oaxaca, Mexico, as they moved from Washington State to California harvesting produce. He worked alongside them in the fields and traveled with them from state to state. He spent time in their home community in Mexico. And he eventually accompanied some of them as they attempted to cross back into the United States to resume their seasonal work. Among other things, Holmes's ethnography illuminates the bitter paradoxes of the system of labor migration with which the migrants and their employers contend: "Systems of labor migration involve economic forces inviting and even requiring the cheap labor of migrants at the same time that political forces ban migrants from entering the country" (2013, 13). Despite the dangers and setbacks associated with clandestine border crossings, the Triqui individuals Holmes knew managed eventually to cross successfully and resume their migrant labor circuit, year after year. Although policymakers might insist that their migration is purely voluntary, this was not the way Holmes's Triqui companions understood their situation: "Rather, they have told me repeatedly that they are forced to migrate in order for themselves and their families to survive" (2013, 17–18).

Two decades into the twenty-first century, it would be difficult to find any research projects by contemporary cultural anthropologists that do not in some way acknowledge the ways in which global processes affect the local communities where they work. Indeed, global

---

globalization The reshaping of local conditions by powerful global forces on an ever-intensifying scale.

flows of technologies and commodities have pushed ethnographers to expand their ethnographic focus to topics and settings that are unprecedented from the perspective of research undertaken during most of the twentieth century. Especially striking has been the move of cultural anthropologists into fields like computer engineering or into ethnographic settings like scientific laboratories or the Internet. As we noted earlier, this interest has also stimulated new approaches to material culture, especially the ways human beings and their computerized devices connect with each other.

Cybernetics was an early name given to those technologies that connected people and machines in this intimate way, and it influenced the thinking of Donna Haraway, a biologist and radical feminist, who published "A Cyborg Manifesto" in 1991. The image of the cyborg—an organism–machine hybrid—was popularized in science fiction, but Haraway pointed out that, for good or for ill, such hybrids were all around us, from cybernetically advanced weapons systems to laboratory rats with implanted cyber-control devices. Although many people are troubled by the notion of organism–machine hybrids, Haraway urged her readers to embrace the image of the cyborg as new model for challenging rigid social, political, and economic boundaries that have been used to separate people by gender, sexuality, class, and race, boundaries proclaimed by their defenders to be "natural." Haraway's work attracted the attention of a wide range of scholars in many disciplines, including anthropology. **Cyborg anthropology** refers to ethnographic research that focuses on human–machine hybrids that blur boundaries between nature and culture, the living and the nonliving. Haraway's cyborg insights also contributed to the development of the interdisciplinary field of **science studies**, which explores the interconnections among sociocultural, political, economic, and historic conditions and practices that make scientific research both possible and successful. Cyborg thinking reinforced work by scholars like Bruno Latour, who undertook ethnographic fieldwork in scientific laboratories, following practicing scientists engaging in skillful work with different kinds of material apparatus, and later following them outside laboratories as they sought various kinds of support for their work (e.g., Latour and Woolgar 1986) (see Module 1). But cyborg

thinking has also been taken up successfully by anthropologists who explore the many other ways that material culture and nonhuman organisms are deeply entangled with human cultural meanings, beliefs, and values and practices. Models from science studies and cyborg anthropology allow for fresh understandings of human beings as biocultural hybrids, enmeshed with living and nonliving features of their material worlds, including artifacts of their own manufacture. These models resonate with the approach of anthropologist Tim Ingold, who has long emphasized that human beings do not exist apart from the rest of "nature," but rather are part of the natural world alongside other living things and the soil and water and sunlight on which we all depend. Our growth and development, as much as those of our living companions, depend on the relations we build with one another. Precisely because of this interrelatedness, no account of human evolution is complete if it does not pay attention to processes of development and growth (or *ontogeny*) in accounting for change over time. Ingold's integration of developmental and evolutionary processes has been echoed in the work of other evolutionary theorists who also insist on the central role played by developmental processes in organismic evolution (Oyama et al. 2001; West-Eberhard 2003).

This relational approach has gained increasing anthropological support in the past decade (e.g., Schultz 2009; Fuentes 2013). It is explored in a recent collection of articles edited by Ingold and Gisli Pálsson, entitled *Biosocial Becomings: Integrating Social and Biological Anthropology* (2013). In his own contribution, Ingold urges humans "to think of ourselves not as *beings* but as *becomings*—that is, not as discrete and pre-formed entities but as trajectories of movement and growth" (Ingold 2013, 8). He adds, "*The domains of the social and the biological are one and the same.* But . . . we are not reducing the social to the biological, or vice versa. The life of a becoming (which is also, the becoming of a life) could be compared to a hempen rope, twisted from multiple strands. . . . Like the rope, the becoming is biological all the way up, and social all the way down" (Ingold 2013, 9; emphasis in original).

The fruitfulness of adopting the approach endorsed by Ingold and Pálsson can be seen in recent research that anthropologists call *multispecies ethnography*: investigating the varied relationships that specific human groups have developed with specific populations of other species in particular times and places. This ethnographic work highlights animal-human relations that involve more mutuality and less human control than usually assumed in many discussion of animal or plant domestication. It also draws attention to the crucial roles played by particular landscapes and specific forms of material

---

cyborg anthropology A form of anthropological analysis based on the notion of animal–machine hybrids, or cyborgs, that offers a new model for challenging rigid social, political, or economic boundaries that have been used to separate people by gender, sexuality, class, and race, boundaries proclaimed by their defenders as "natural."

science studies Research that explores the interconnections among sociocultural, political, economic, and historic conditions and practices that make scientific research both possible and successful.

culture in stabilizing relationships between humans and other species. Examples of such work can be found in the edited volume *Domestication Gone Wild: Politics and Practices of Multispecies Relations* (Swanson et al. 2018). Included are ethnographic accounts ranging from a study of the mutual involvement of humans and birds in falcon breeding in Britain, to human reliance on the relations between "wild" and "domesticated" dogs in Aboriginal Australia and Mongolia, to the human building of nesting houses to attract eider ducks in Norway. Regarding the latter example, Marianne Elisabeth Lien writes, "Neither domesticated nor wild, the eider ducks on the Vega islands alert us to how subtle and repeated encounters between humans and animals have come to shape more-than-human worlds in mutual processes of biosocial becoming (Ingold and Pálsson 2013). These relations are always uncertain, open-ended and potentially transformative and hence might inspire us to think domestication differently" (Swanson et al. 2018, 121). As we will see in Chapter 7, research of this kind has indeed influenced the way some archaeologists and other scholars are reconsidering how to interpret the beginnings of animal and plant domestication in human history. In general, it helps to keep in mind Ghassan Hage's observation: "capture is not domestication, and even domestication itself can never be a total process" (Hage 2015, Loc 924–5).

As cultural anthropologists have become increasingly aware of the sociocultural influences that stretch across space to affect local communities, they have also become sensitive to those that stretch over time. As a result, many contemporary cultural anthropologists make serious efforts to place their cultural analyses in detailed historical context. Cultural anthropologists who do comparative studies of language, music, dance, art, poetry, philosophy, religion, or ritual often share many of the interests of specialists in the disciplines of fine arts and humanities.

Linguistic Anthropology

Perhaps the most striking cultural feature of our species is **language**, which we can provisionally define as the system of arbitrary symbols humans use to communicate about all areas of our lives, from material to spiritual, and to encode our experience of the world and of one another. **Linguistic anthropology** therefore studies language, not only as a form of symbolic communication but also as a major carrier of important cultural information. Indeed, linguistic anthropologists understand language broadly, insisting that words and sentences cannot be understood apart from the social and cultural

FIGURE 1.5 Professor of Anthropology and Linguistics H. Samy Alim (second from left) leads a graduate seminar at Stanford University.

contexts in which they are uttered; and, conversely, that the study of language in its contexts of use is a particularly useful way to investigate social and cultural aspects of human society. Many early anthropologists were the first people to transcribe non-Western languages and to produce grammars and dictionaries of those languages. Contemporary linguistic anthropologists and their counterparts in sociology (called *sociolinguists*) study the way language differences correlate with differences in gender, race, class, or ethnic identity (Figure 1.5). Some have specialized in studying what happens when speakers are fluent in more than one language and must choose which language to use under what circumstances. Others have written about what happens when speakers of unrelated languages are forced to communicate with one another, producing languages called *pidgins*. Some linguistic anthropologists study sign languages. Others look at the ways children learn language or the styles and strategies followed by fluent speakers engaged in conversation. More recently, linguistic anthropologists have paid attention to the way political ideas in a society contribute to people's ideas of what may or may not be said and the strategies speakers devise to escape these forms of censorship. Some take part in policy discussions about literacy and language standardization and address the challenges faced by speakers of languages that are being displaced by international languages of commerce and technology such as English.

In all these cases, linguistic anthropologists try to understand language in relation to the broader cultural, historical, or biological contexts that make it possible.

language The system of arbitrary symbols used to encode one's experience of the world and of others.

linguistic anthropology The specialty of anthropology concerned with the study of human languages.

Because highly specialized training in linguistics as well as anthropology is required for people who practice it, linguistic anthropology has long been recognized as a separate subfield of anthropology. Contemporary linguistic anthropologists continue to be trained in this way, and many cultural anthropologists also receive linguistics training as part of their professional preparation.

Archaeology

Archaeology, another major specialty within anthropology, is a cultural anthropology of the human past involving the analysis of material remains. Through archaeology, anthropologists discover much about human history, particularly about the long stretch of time before the development of writing, which some have called "prehistory," but which others prefer to describe as "deep history. Archaeologists look for evidence of past human cultural activity, such as postholes, garbage heaps, and settlement patterns. Depending on the locations and ages of sites they are digging, archaeologists may also have to be experts on stone-tool manufacture, metallurgy, or ancient pottery. Because archaeological excavations frequently uncover remains such as bones or plant pollen, archaeologists often work in teams with other scientists who specialize in the analysis of these remains.

Archaeologists' findings complement those of paleoanthropologists. For example, archaeological information about successive stone-tool traditions in a particular region may correlate with fossil evidence of prehistoric occupation of that region by ancient human populations. Archaeologists can use dating techniques to establish ages of *artifacts*, portable objects modified by human beings. They can create distribution maps of cultural artifacts that allow them to make hypotheses about the ages, territorial ranges, and patterns of sociocultural change in ancient societies. Tracing the spread of cultural inventions over time from one site to another allows them to hypothesize about the nature and degree of social contact between different peoples in the past. The human past that they investigate may be quite recent: some contemporary archaeologists dig through layers of garbage deposited by human beings within the last two or three decades, often uncovering surprising information about contemporary consumption patterns.

archaeology A cultural anthropology of the human past involving the analysis of material remains left behind by earlier societies.

applied anthropology Subfield of anthropology in which anthropologists use information gathered from the other anthropological specialties to solve practical cross-cultural problems.

FIGURE 1.6 Members of the Argentine Forensic Anthropologists Team work on the biggest dictatorship-era mass grave to date, where around 100 suspected victims of the 1976–1983 military junta were buried in a local cemetery in Córdoba, 800 km (500 miles) northwest of Buenos Aires.

Applied Anthropology

Applied anthropology is the subfield of anthropology in which anthropologists use information gathered from the other anthropological specialties to propose solutions to practical problems (Figure 1.6). Some may use a particular group of people's ideas about illness and health to introduce new public health practices in a way that makes sense to and will be accepted by members of the group. Other applied anthropologists may use knowledge of traditional social organization to ease the problems of refugees trying to settle in a new land. Still others may use their knowledge of traditional and Western methods of cultivation to help farmers increase their crop yields. Given the growing concern throughout the world with the effects of different technologies on the environment, this kind of applied anthropology holds promise as a way of bringing together Western knowledge and non-Western knowledge to create sustainable technologies that minimize pollution and environmental degradation. Some applied anthropologists have become management consultants or carry out market research, and their findings may contribute to the design of new products.

In recent years, some anthropologists have become involved in policy issues, participating actively in social processes that attempt to shape the future of those among whom they work (Moore 2005, 3), and this has involved a change in their understanding of what applied anthropology is. Les W. Field (2004), for example, has addressed the history of applied anthropology on Native American reservations—"Indian Country"—in the United States. He observes that by the end of the twentieth century, a major transformation had occurred, "from applied anthropology in Indian Country to applications of anthropological tools in Indian country to accomplish tribal goals" (472). This often draws anthropologists into work in the legal arena, as when, for example, they have lent their expertise to arguments in favor of legislation mandating the repatriation of culturally significant artifacts and tribal lands in North America, or to efforts by tribal groups to reclaim official government-recognized status (Field 2004), or to defending indigenous land rights in Latin America (Stocks 2005).

Although many anthropologists believe that applied work can be done within any of the traditional four fields of anthropology, increasing numbers in recent years have come to view applied anthropology as a separate field of professional specialization (see Figure 1.2). The Society for Applied Anthropology has many active members and organizes its own professional meetings. More and more universities in the United States have begun to develop courses and programs in a variety of forms of applied anthropology. Anthropologists who work for government agencies or nonprofit organizations or in other nonuniversity settings often describe what they do as the *anthropology of practice*. In the twenty-first century, it has been predicted that more than half of all new PhDs in anthropology will become practicing anthropologists rather than take up positions as faculty in university departments of anthropology.

Medical Anthropology

Some areas of applied anthropology have attracted greater numbers of practitioners than others. Perhaps the most rapidly growing branch of applied anthropology is **medical anthropology**, which has offered new ways to link methods and findings from biological and cultural anthropology. Medical anthropology concerns itself with human health—the factors that contribute to disease or illness and the way that human populations deal with disease or illness (Baer et al. 2003, 3). Medical anthropologists begin with the recognition that Western *biomedicine* is based on

specific cultural assumptions: for example, that diseases are caused by material factors located inside individual bodies (microorganisms, parasites, tumors), and that treatment of diseases will involve intervention in individual bodies (ingesting medicines or undergoing surgery). Biomedical understandings, however, often do not mesh well with different ideas about health and illness held by people of different cultural backgrounds. Medical anthropologists have done important work to bridge these differences. Because of their holistic training in anthropology, they have also been vocal in pointing out how various forms of suffering and disease cannot be explained by focusing on individual bodies alone. For example, Seth Holmes, the anthropologist who has studied migrant farmworkers from Oaxaca, Mexico, is also a medical anthropologist. His work with migrants was motivated not simply to document migration itself, but also to study the toll migration takes on the bodies and minds of migrants. He writes: "I used the classic anthropological research method of participant observation in order to understand the complicated issues of immigration, social hierarchy, and health" (2013, 3). He uses his research to reveal how "the social and economic histories of people not only reshape their bodies over time but also shape the perceptions of those bodies in such a way as to establish their ethnicity" but also "to show that illness is often the manifestation of structural, symbolic, and political violence, as well as, at times, resistance and rebellion" (2013, 28).

Development Anthropology

Efforts by governments and nongovernmental organizations (NGOs) to improve the quality of life of marginalized populations is also the concern of practitioners of **development anthropology**. "Development" in this context comes from longstanding discussions contrasting the standard of living provided in the wealthiest "developed" countries of the world (such as the United States and European nations) and the standard of living in the poorer "underdeveloped" countries of the world, many of them former colonies of European empires. Since these empires were dissolved in the middle of the twentieth century, development anthropologists have used their knowledge and expertise concerning ecological, agricultural, or environmental matters to help better the economic

---

medical anthropology The specialty of anthropology that concerns itself with human health—the factors that contribute to disease or illness and the ways that human populations deal with disease or illness.

development anthropology Efforts by governments and nongovernmental organizations (NGOs) to improve the quality of life of marginalized populations.

FIGURE 1.7 Medical anthropologist Andrea Wiley is shown here in a high-altitude setting in the Himalayas of Ladakh (India), where she studied maternal and child health.

circumstances of those with whom they work. For many developmental anthropologists, the challenge is to find ways of bringing together Western and non-Western understandings and skills to create sustainable technologies that minimize pollution and environmental degradation while raising incomes and improving the quality of life.

The globalizing flows of people, wealth, commodities, images, and ideologies that were set in motion in the late twentieth century were driven by the spread of capitalism to territories where it had been forbidden during the Cold War. This widening acceptance of capitalist business practices offered many new opportunities for firms in Western capitalist countries to seek out business partners in places outside Europe or North America who were also looking for partners in the West. Such conditions drew many anthropologists with regional cultural expertise to become involved in forms of cultural translation that helped potential business partners to find one another and work successfully with one another, even when their previous understandings about the appropriate ways to engage in business were not the same. Over time, different forms of anthropological involvement with businesses of various kinds has led to the emergence of a significant area of applied anthropology, sometimes called *business anthropology*. Although it may seem quite different from the work of medical anthropology or development anthropology, the kinds of research that business anthropologists undertake can be quite surprising, challenging preconceptions,

or stereotypes. We will explore some of these areas of applied anthropology in greater depth in Chapter 16.

The Promise of Anthropology

The relationships between the various subfields of anthropology have changed over time. In the early years of the twenty-first century, some anthropologists were convinced that attempts to keep the subfields together would fail. Today, however, in the context of globalization, new theoretical developments, new research topics, and new kinds of collaboration are bringing the subfields together again in powerful ways.

One of the most remarkable examples of what this can look like is the long-term "Undocumented Migration Project" developed by Jason de Leon, an anthropologist at the University of Michigan. His book, *The Land of Open Graves*, addresses "the violence and death that border crossers face on a daily basis as they attempt to enter the United States by walking across the vast Sonoran Desert of Arizona" (2015, 3). De Leon's research focuses on the effects of a strategy called Prevention Through Deterrence (PTD), first implemented by the federal government in 1994, "that largely relies on rugged and desolate terrain to impede the flow of people from the south" (2015, 9). By deliberately funneling people through the Sonoran Desert, he argues, "nature has been conscripted by the Border Patrol to act as an enforcer while simultaneously providing this federal agency with plausible deniability regarding blame for any victims the desert may claim" (2015, 29–30).

But how could a federal agency "conscript" the desert in this way? De Leon answers this question by drawing on a theory developed by science studies scholars Michel Callon and John Law. As we noted earlier, science studies explains how scientific and technological achievements depend not on individual human genius alone but on the stabilization of networks of heterogeneous elements, living and nonliving, human and non-human. As De Leon explains, Callon and Law's theory shows how "people or objects don't act in isolation, but instead have complex relationships at different moments across time and space that sometimes create things or make things happen" (2015, 39). In the case of the PTD program, "our gaze must widen to include all of the components—human, animal, mineral, weather pattern, and so forth—that make up a hybrid system" (2015, 40). Such an approach, he finds, meshes well with the multifield anthropological approach (2015, 14):

> This book draws on a four-field anthropology—that is ethnography, archaeology, forensic science, and linguistics—in the name of enhancing our understanding of the process of undocumented desert migration. In many ways, the [Undocumented Migration Project] is intended to challenge preconceived notions about what a holistic anthropology can look like and how it can be deployed in politically hostile terrain.

De Leon chose not to accompany migrants attempting to cross the border, but he did gather many kinds of evidence that provided insight into the nature of their experiences. First, he conducted ethnographic interviews, in Spanish and English, with individuals on both sides (and several sites) along the southern border—an ethnographic practice called *multisited fieldwork*. Next, he and his colleagues engaged in an "archaeology of the contemporary," collecting and studying artifacts left behind in the desert by migrants. Although some observers regard these items as "trash," the Bibles, photographs, letters, and other items left in makeshift shrines were not considered trash by the migrants. "In the context of migration, archaeology can get at elements of the process that are overshadowed by exceptional incidents of trauma or violence, and can help decenter the story away from the perspective of outside observers, such as journalists who shadow border crossers" (2015, 170).

Finally, survey research in the Sonoran Desert reveals more than the material culture left behind by migrants; sometimes human remains are also found. De Leon and his team discovered the body of a woman who had died trying to make the crossing. De Leon describes his response to the discovery: "This is a crime scene and I don't want to destroy any evidence . . . This is what 'Prevention Through Deterrence' looks like" (2015, 212, 213). Expertise from biological anthropology (especially forensic anthropology) made it possible to determine how long ago the woman died. De Leon and his team worked with the medical examiner in the county where the woman's body was found in order to figure out who she was and where she came from, eventually locating her family of origin in Ecuador, arranging for her remains to be returned there, and learning more about the circumstances that propelled her to migrate in the first place. His team's later efforts to locate another member of her family who also set out to cross the Sonoran Desert, however, were unsuccessful.

De Leon's work provides a powerful illustration of the complex interconnections that shape the contemporary globalized world. Anthropologists experience both the rewards and risks of getting to know how people live (and sometimes how they die). For over a century, anthropological work has helped to dispel many harmful stereotypes that sometimes make cross-cultural contact dangerous or impossible. Studying anthropology may help prepare you for some of the shocks you will encounter in dealing with people who look different from you, speak a different language, or do not agree that the world works exactly the way you think it does. Anthropology can equip you to deal with people with different cultural backgrounds in a less threatened, more tolerant manner. At the same time, cross-cultural encounters offer many unfamiliar pleasures and rewards. It is likely that you will one day encounter a situation in which none of the old rules seem to apply. As you struggle to make sense of what his happening, what you learned in anthropology class may help you relax and try something new. If you do so, perhaps you too will discover the rewards of an encounter with the unfamiliar that is at the same time unaccountably familiar. We hope you will savor the experience.

What Can You Learn from an Anthropology Major?

The Career Development Center at SUNY Plattsburgh developed a document that highlights what students typically learn from a major in anthropology.

1. Social agility

   In an unfamiliar social or career-related setting, you learn to quickly size up the rules of the game. You can become accepted more quickly than you could without this anthropological skill.

2. Observation

   You must often learn about a culture from within it, so you learn how to interview and observe as a participant.

3. Analysis and planning

   You learn how to find patterns in the behavior of a cultural group. This awareness of patterns allows you to generalize about the group's behavior and predict what they might do in a given situation.

4. Social sensitivity

   Although other people's ways of doing things may be different from your own, you learn the importance of events and conditions that have contributed to this difference. You also recognize that other cultures view your ways as strange. You learn the value of behaving toward others with appropriate preparation, care, and understanding.

5. Accuracy in interpreting behavior

   You become familiar with the range of behavior in different cultures. You learn how to look at cultural causes of behavior before assigning causes yourself.

6. Ability to appropriately challenge conclusions

   You learn that analyses of human behavior are open to challenge. You learn how to use new knowledge to test past conclusions.

7. Insightful interpretation of information

   You learn how to use data collected by others, reorganizing or interpreting the data to reach original conclusions.

8. Simplification of information

   Because anthropology is conducted among publics as well as about them, you learn how to simplify technical information for communication to nontechnical people.

9. Contextualization

   Although attention to details is a trait of anthropology, you learn that any given detail might not be as important as its context and can even be misleading when the context is ignored.

10. Problem solving

    Because you often function within a cultural group or act on culturally sensitive issues, you learn to approach problems with care. Before acting, you identify the problem, set your goals, decide on the actions you will take, and calculate possible effects on other people.

11. Persuasive writing

    Anthropologists strive to represent the behavior of one group to another group and continually need to engage in interpretation. You learn the value of bringing someone else to share—or at least understand—your view through written argument.

12. Assumption of a social perspective

    You learn how to perceive the acts of individuals and local groups as both shaping and being shaped by larger sociocultural systems. The perception enables you to "act locally and think globally."

Source: Omohundro 2000.

Chapter Summary

1. Anthropology aims to describe in the broadest sense what it means to be human. The anthropological perspective is holistic, comparative, and evolutionary and has relied on the concept of culture to explain the diversity of human ways of life. Human beings depend on cultural learning for successful biological survival and reproduction, which is why anthropologists consider human beings biocultural organisms. Anthropology is also a field-based discipline. In the United States today, anthropology is considered to have five major subfields: biological anthropology, archaeology, cultural anthropology, linguistic anthropology, and applied anthropology.

2. Biological anthropology began as an attempt to classify all the world's populations into different races. By the early twentieth century, however, most anthropologists had rejected racial classifications as scientifically unjustifiable and objected to the ways in which racial classifications were used to justify the social practice of racism. Contemporary anthropologists who are interested in human biology include biological anthropologists, primatologists, and paleoanthropologists.

3. Cultural anthropologists study cultural diversity in all living human societies, including their own. Linguistic anthropologists approach cultural diversity by relating varied forms of language to their cultural contexts. Both gather information through fieldwork, by participating with their informants in social activities, and by observing those activities as outsiders. Today, some of them carry out research in fields like computer engineering or in ethnographic settings such as scientific laboratories or the Internet. They publish accounts of their research in ethnographies. Archaeology is a cultural anthropology of the human past, with interests ranging from the earliest stone tools to twenty-first-century garbage dumps. Applied anthropologists use information from the other anthropological specialties to solve practical cross-cultural problems.

4. In contemporary anthropology, science studies has influenced work in all subfields of anthropology, offering fresh ways to reconsider what it means for anthropology to be a holistic discipline. One powerful illustration of what this makes possible is Jason De Leon's Undocumented Migration Project.

For Review

1. What is anthropology, as defined in the text?
2. What are the four distinctive approaches anthropologists take to the study of human life?
3. How do anthropologists define culture?
4. What makes anthropology a cross-disciplinary discipline?
5. Describe the main subfields of modern anthropology.
6. What are some of the main topics of interest in biological anthropology?
7. What are some of the main topics of interest in cultural anthropology?
8. Summarize the difference between ethnography and ethnology.
9. What do linguistic anthropologists try to learn about human languages?
10. What are some of the things archaeologists study?
11. How is applied anthropology connected to the other branches of anthropology?
12. North American anthropology has long claimed to be a holistic discipline. What does this mean?

Key Terms

anthropology 5
applied anthropology 16
archaeology 16
biocultural organisms 7
biological anthropology (or physical anthropology) 10
comparison 5
cultural anthropology 11
culture 6
cyborg anthropology 14
ethnography 12
ethnology 12
evolution 6
fieldwork 12
gender 11
globalization 13
holism 5
informants 12
language 15
linguistic anthropology 15
material culture 7
medical anthropology 17
paleoanthropology 10
primatology 10
races 8
racism 9
science studies 14
sex 11

Suggested Readings

Ashmore, Wendy, and Robert J. Sharer. 2013. *Discovering our past: A brief introduction to archaeology*, 6th ed. New York: McGraw-Hill. *An engaging introduction to the techniques, assumptions, interests, and findings of modern archaeology.*

Besteman, Catherine, and Hugh Gusterson, eds. 2005. *Why America's top pundits are wrong: Anthropologists talk back*. Berkeley: University of California Press. *According to the editors, "pundits" are media personalities—conservative and liberal—who lack authoritative knowledge on important issues but whose confident, authoritative, and entertaining pronouncements attract large audiences, especially when they defend simplified views of issues that reinforce rather than challenge popular prejudices. Twelve anthropologists offer critical assessments of the writings of pundits Samuel Huntington, Robert Kaplan, Thomas Friedman, and Dinesh D'Sousa and also explore questionable popular accounts of the origins of racial inequality and sexual violence.*

Feder, Kenneth L. 2014. *Frauds, myths and mysteries: Science and pseudoscience in archaeology*, 8th ed. New York: McGraw-Hill. *An entertaining and informative exploration of fascinating frauds and genuine archaeological mysteries that also explains the scientific method.*

Ingold, Tim. 2018. *Anthropology: Why it Matters*. Cambridge, England: Polity Press. *Tim Ingold's brief volume elaborates on the position articulated in* Biosocial Becomings, *making a case for a holistic anthropology that evades the traps posed by the past history of our discipline and promotes a version of anthropology that is equal to the serious challenges of our present-day world.*

Kidder, Tracy. 2004. *Mountains beyond mountains: The quest of Dr. Paul Farmer, a man who would cure the world*. New York: Random House. *Kidder follows Dr. Farmer, an anthropologist and physician, relating his efforts to enlist powerful funders, the World Health Organization, and ordinary people in neglected communities in a quest to bring the best modern medicine to those who need it most.*

Relethford, John. 2013. *The human species: An introduction to biological anthropology*, 9th ed. New York: McGraw-Hill. *An excellent, clear introduction to biological anthropology.*

Strang, Veronica. 2009. *What anthropologists do*. Oxford: Berg. *Written for students, this book provides illustrations of many ways anthropology is being used in everyday life.*

 Visit our online resource center for further reading, web links, free assessments, flashcards, and videos. www.oup.com/he/lavenda5e

"Things are similar: this makes science possible. Things are different: this makes science necessary" (Levins and Lewontin 1985, 141). Many anthropologists claim that their attempts to explain human nature, human society, and the human past are scientific. A scientific approach is what distinguishes the ethnographer from the tourist, the archaeologist from the treasure hunter. But scientists are clearly not the only people who offer explanations for the intriguing and often contradictory features of our world. People in all societies tell stories about why we are the way we are and why we live the way we do. What makes these nonscientific explanations different from the scientific explanations of an anthropologist?

Scientific and Nonscientific Explanations

In some respects, scientific and nonscientific explanations of the way the world works have much in common. For one thing, scientists today are more aware than ever before of the fact that scientific theorizing is a form of storytelling (Landau 1984). Like the tales collected by anthropologists from peoples all over the world, scientific theories offer narrative accounts of how things got to be the way they are.

Consider the following two extracts taken from longer narratives. The first is from the Amazon and is part of the creation story of the Desana (Tukano) people (Figure M1.1):

> The sun created the Universe and for this reason he is called Sun Father (*pagé abé*). He is the father of all the Desana. The Sun created the Universe with the power of his yellow light and gave it life and stability. From his dwelling place, bathed in yellow reflections, the Sun made the earth, with its forests and rivers, with its animals and plants. The Sun planned his creation very well, and it was perfect.
>
> The world we live in has the shape of a large disk, an immense round plate. It is the world of men and animals, the world of life. While the dwelling place of the Sun has a yellow color, the color of the power of the Sun, the dwelling place of men and animals is of a red color, the color of fecundity and of the blood of living beings. Our earth is *maria turí*, and is called the "upper level" (*vekámaha turí*) because below is another world, the "lower level" (*dohkámaha turí*). The world below is called *Ahpikondia*, Paradise. Its color is green, and the souls of those who were good Desana throughout their life go there. . . . Seen from below, from Ahpikondia, our earth looks like a large cobweb. It is transparent, and the Sun shines light through it. The threads of this web are like the rules that men should live by, and they are guided by these threads, seeking to live well, and the Sun sees them. . . .
>
> The Sun created the animals and the plants. To each one he assigned the place he should live. He made all of

FIGURE M1.1   Desana (Tukano) man playing panpipes.

> the animals at once, except the fish and the snakes; these he made afterward. Also, together with the animals, the Sun made the spirits and the demons of the forest and the waters.
>
> The Sun created all of this when he had the yellow intention—when he caused the power of his yellow light to penetrate, in order to form the world from it. (Reichel-Dolmatoff 1971, 24–25)

The second extract comes from an American work on modern physics:

> At the start of the lepton era the universe is one ten-thousandth of a second old, the temperature is 1 trillion Kelvin (1012 K) and each cubic centimeter of the cosmic quantum soup weighs about a thousand tons. The universe consists of a mixture of approximately equal numbers of photons, electrons, electron neutrinos, muons, muon neutrinos, some other particles like pions . . . and their antiparticles, plus a

relatively small "contamination" of equal numbers of protons and neutrons which are no longer in equilibrium with the other particles. . . .

As the temperature falls from its value at the beginning of the lepton era, the production threshold for the muons is crossed. All the muons and antimuons now annihilate into electrons, positrons and muon and electron neutrinos. Any excess charge of the muons can be passed on to the electrons. . . . For this reason no muons survive the muon slaughter. . . .

At the end of the lepton era all the heavy leptons, muons and tauons have disappeared, while hordes of neutrinos flood the universe but no longer interact with anything. Photons, electrons and antielectrons are still in equilibria, creating and destroying one another. When the temperature falls below the production threshold to create electron–positron pairs, most of the pairs annihilate into photons. This temperature threshold marks the beginning of the photon era. . . .

At the first second (which marks the beginning of the photon era, which goes on to last for 300,000 years), the temperature of the photons was 10 billion Kelvin and the density of the radiation about 100 kilograms (about 220 pounds) per cubic centimeter—a very thick viscous fluid of light. (Pagels 1985, 250–53)

Both the Desana story and the scientific story might be called **myths**—as long as we use this term the way anthropologists use it. For anthropologists, myths are stories that recount how various aspects of the world came to be the way they are. The power of myths comes from their ability to make life meaningful for those who accept them. The truth of myths seems self-evident because they effectively integrate personal experiences with a wider set of assumptions about the way society, or the world in general, operates. In everyday speech, by contrast, the term *myth* is used to refer to a story that is false. To be sure, origin myths like the Desana tale contain marvelous and fantastic elements that stretch the credulity of ordinary sensible folk. Still, the anthropological understanding of myth does not assume that myths are necessarily false. Stories that survive to become myths usually connect in important ways with everyday human experiences in a particular society. But what about stories that recount events that we could never experience personally, such as the origin of the universe? If we study a variety of origin myths from different cultural traditions, we learn that many of these stories differ substantially from one another. Since nobody alive today was around when the world began or when our ancestors first walked its surface, how could we ever find out what actually happened?

For increasing numbers of people over the past few centuries, the answer to this question has lain with science. The growth of modern science in western Europe and its spread throughout the world are largely a result of scientists' belief that the answers to the history of the world could be found in the world itself if only people looked at the world in a new way. This new perspective claimed that "the world of phenomena is a consequence of the regular operation of repeatable causes and their repeatable effects, operating roughly along the lines of known physical law" (Lewontin 1983, xxvi). Scientists believed that remarkable new insights about the universe, the objects in it, and even ourselves could be gained if we carried out observations according to a new set of rules.

These rules were first set on a firm foundation by Isaac Newton (Figure M1.2). A pious Christian, Newton did not doubt that God had created the universe, yet he believed that the universe God had created was orderly, that the movements of objects within it were constrained by laws discoverable by human reason, and that those laws could be precisely described using the language of mathematics. Newton's approach gained followers because it was extremely successful at describing and predicting, exactly as it had promised. Moreover, different observers could independently test the descriptions and predictions, and scientific knowledge could grow as the verified predictions were retained and the unverified predictions were discarded. Most fatefully, the new, scientifically verified knowledge about nature's laws could be put to work to transform nature in unprecedented ways. It appeared that human desires could be satisfied through scientific mastery of the material world. For many people, the practical application of scientific discoveries in astronomy, navigation, and industry became the clinching proof of scientific superiority.

Niles Eldredge and Ian Tattersall (1982), two prominent evolutionary biologists, have written that science is "storytelling, albeit of a special kind. **Science** is the invention of explanations about what things are, how they work, and how they came to be. There are rules, to be sure: for a statement to be scientific, we must be able to go to nature and assess how well it actually fits our observations of the universe" (1). Indeed, these rules give science its particular dynamic because science is firmly and explicitly committed to open-ended self-correction. If ideas about the way the world works can be shown *not* to fit our observations of the universe, then the scientist must reject those ideas, regardless of the consequences, and invent better ones.

---

myths Stories that recount how various aspects of the world came to be the way they are. The power of myths comes from their ability to make life meaningful for those who accept them. The truth of myths seems self-evident because they effectively integrate personal experiences with a wider set of assumptions about the way society, or the world in general, must operate.

science The invention of explanations about what things are, how they work, and how they came to be that can be tested against evidence in the world itself.

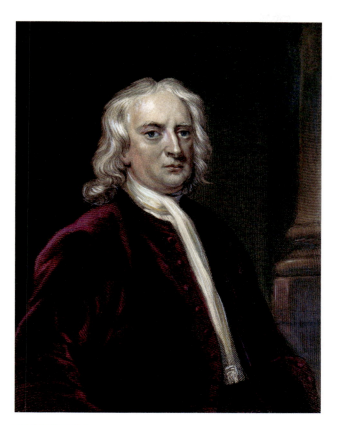

FIGURE M1.2   One of the founders of the new worldview of science, Sir Isaac Newton (1642–1727), made major contributions to mathematics, optics, and experimental investigation.

Scientists believe that the answers to questions about how the world works can be found by going to the world itself. Put another way, science is *empirical*, based on concrete experience and observation. Scientists have never been content to observe the world without getting their hands dirty. Scientific theories must build on and be tested against direct physical contact with real objects in the world. Of course, scientists did not invent trial-and-error experimentation with the material world; that activity lies behind the technical achievements of all human societies. Nevertheless, scientific research has taken experimentation to a new level of complexity. Using elaborate tools that are themselves the product of previous scientific work, scientists have engaged in increasingly refined experimental manipulation of material objects and processes in the world. One result of this activity has been the production of more sophisticated stories about the way the world works. The success and persuasive power of evolutionary biology, for example, are due in no small measure to the fact that scientists have been able to generate new evidence about the living world, reinterpret old evidence, and produce a new story that remains richer, more comprehensive, and more fruitful than any of its rivals.

Some Key Scientific Concepts

The first step in understanding scientific stories is to master a few key concepts that are part of every scientist's vocabulary. In this section, we introduce some terms you will encounter frequently as you read this book. Special attention must be paid to the way scientists define these terms because they are also often used in everyday speech with rather different meanings. Six terms are particularly important: assumptions, evidence, hypotheses, testability, theories, and objectivity.

Assumptions   **Assumptions** are basic, unquestioned understandings about the way the world works. Under ordinary circumstances, most human beings do not question whether the sun will come up in the morning; it is taken for granted. If you want to go birdwatching tomorrow, you might be concerned about how cold it will be or whether it will rain, but you need not worry whether the sun will rise.

Everybody, scientist or not, operates on the basis of assumptions. Scientists are particularly concerned about the assumptions they bring to their observations of the natural world because the significance of what they see and measure is never obvious. If their observations are guided by incorrect assumptions about the way the world works, their measurements will be meaningless and the conclusions they draw from those measurements will be misleading.

Evidence   In science, **evidence** refers to what we can see when we examine a particular part of the world with great care. The structures and processes of living cells as revealed under the microscope, the systematic distribution of related species of birds in neighboring geographical regions, the different kinds of bones found together again and again in the same geological strata—these are examples of the kinds of evidence scientists use to support theories of biological evolution. There are two different kinds of evidence: material and inferred.

Material evidence   consists of things—material objects—themselves, information recorded about them, or scientific measurements made of them. In the study of human origins, for example, bones and stones are the most conspicuous forms of material evidence (Figure M1.3a) but so are careful records (including photographs) of other material objects recovered from the site of an excavation. The precise geological layering at a site is an important form of material evidence but so are objects at a site (e.g., certain kinds of rocks or baked

assumptions   Basic, unquestioned understandings about the way the world works.

evidence   What is seen when a particular part of the world is examined with great care. Scientists use two different kinds of evidence: material and inferred.

FIGURE M1.3 That particular material features, such as this pot (**a**), are found in an archaeological site and that the people of Bali perform a certain dance (**b**) are material facts, verifiable by inspection. How or why the pot came to be here and what it was used for or what this dance means may be far from obvious and must be inferred.

clay) that can be subjected to forms of laboratory analysis that yield reliable information about the dates when they formed. For cultural anthropologists, ritual performances observed and transcribed in the field constitute material evidence (Figure M1.3b). Material evidence is ordinarily what scientists mean when they refer to "the facts" or "the data."

Material evidence has two striking attributes. First, "the facts" can be inspected by anyone who wants to examine them. Like cowpats in a pasture, the facts exist in their own right, and their existence, shape, and position cannot be ignored by people who wish to walk through the particular field and keep their shoes clean. Second, the facts cannot speak for themselves. That a particular accumulation of bones and stones was found at a certain place in an archaeological site and that certain people perform a particular ritual are material facts verifiable by inspection. How or why the bones and stones got there or what the ritual means may be far from obvious. This leads to the second kind of evidence used by scientists: the interpretation put on material evidence.

Inferred evidence is material evidence plus interpretation. As one paleoanthropologist observes, "We can all see a bone and know it is a bone, but what it is 'evidence' for depends upon one's interpretation" (Clarke 1985, 176–77). Interpretation begins with the simple description of individual objects or events and is followed by the description of patterns of distribution of similar objects and events. The final stage of interpretation consists of elaborate explanatory frameworks that link many different objects or events to one another by drawing on findings from many different fields of knowledge. The connection between material evidence and inferred evidence is an intimate one. Several scientists examining the same material evidence frequently emphasize different descriptions and construct different explanations of what it is and how it got there. Rather than the facts speaking for themselves, the observers speak to one another about the facts in an attempt to make sense of them.

For example, the discovery of ancient hominin bones on the Indonesian island of Flores in 2003 sparked much debate among paleontologists (Figure M1.4). The bones are tens of thousands of years old and look human but are unusually small. Some paleontologists have argued that the bones belonged to modern humans who suffered from a disease that reduced their stature. Other paleontologists insist that the bones show no morphological signs of such disease and that they most likely represent a previously undiscovered species of *Homo*. Further, they argue that this species evolved to have a small stature in response to selective pressures associated with living on an island, a phenomenon known as *insular dwarfing*. Others prefer to withhold judgment until more fossil evidence is available.

As you will see, scientific debate about evolution has long involved just this sort of interpretive dialogue. But it is important to remember that the debates about interpretation would be pointless without something to interpret. Science is more than just "the data," but it can never get too far away

FIGURE M1.4 Ancient hominin bones from the Indonesian island of Flores (the skull is pictured above, between a *Homo erectus* skull on the left and a modern human skull on the right) have been the subject of much debate among paleontologists.

from the data before it is not science anymore. The data are the pretext and the context for debate among observers. The data, in their stubborn materiality, set limits to the kinds of interpretation that are scientifically plausible.

Hypotheses   Scientists state their interpretations of data in the form of **hypotheses**, which are statements that assert a particular connection between fact and interpretation, such as "The bones found at the Hadar site in Ethiopia belonged to an extinct form of primate that appears ancestral to modern human beings." Hypotheses are also predictions about future data based on data already in hand. On the basis of the Hadar findings, paleoanthropologists might hypothesize as follows: "Bones similar to those found at Hadar are likely to be found in geological strata of the same age elsewhere in eastern Africa." Indeed, hypotheses of the latter kind have guided paleoanthropologists in their search for fossils of human ancestors. The impressive collections of fossils of all kinds that have been amassed over the past couple of centuries show just how successful such hypotheses have been in guiding scientific discovery.

Testability   **Testability** is the scientific requirement that a hypothesis must be matched against evidence to see whether it is confirmed or refuted. That is, our assertion about the connection between fact and interpretation must be subject to testability if it is to be regarded as a scientific hypothesis.

How might we test the hypothesis about the bones from the Hadar site? The first step would be to make sure the bones were not simply those of a modern primate that had recently died. If examination of the bones revealed them to be permeated by mineral deposits, making them hard and stone-like, we would be justified in concluding that they were very

old because such a process takes a long time. The next step might be to compare the fossil bones with the bones of living primates, human and nonhuman, to see how they matched. If the bones from Hadar appeared more similar to the bones of humans than to the bones of monkeys or apes, we would be justified in concluding that we had found the bones of an organism ancestral to modern humans. Our confidence in the correctness of the original hypothesis would increase, especially if a number of experts in primate anatomy agreed.

Why would the experts not simply claim, however, that the fossils from Hadar belonged to a human being just like ourselves who happened to have lived and died millions of years ago? What would lead them to conclude that these fossils belonged to a primate *ancestral* to modern human beings? The answer to this question depends on just how similar to modern human bones the Hadar fossils appeared to be. Paleoanthropologists would be justified in assigning the bones from Hadar to an ancestor of modern humans if the bones, although clearly humanlike, nevertheless differed in some significant respect from the bones of modern human beings. If the bones were significantly smaller than those of modern human beings, if the teeth were significantly larger in proportion to the jaw, if the skull were significantly smaller, if the arm bones were relatively longer in proportion to the leg bones, if the finger and toe bones appeared curved—all these traits would suggest strongly that the bones from Hadar, although humanlike, did not belong to a modern human being.

In addition, if the same geological strata yielding the Hadar bones produced the fossils of other organisms that were equally unlike the bones of living animals, we might well conclude that we had discovered the remains of more than one extinct animal species. The plausibility of our original hypothesis about the bones from the Hadar site would be further strengthened.

Some hypotheses, however, may not be subject to testability. That is, there may be no way, even in principle, to find evidence in nature that could show a hypothesis to be false. As a result, even if such a hypothesis were correct, it could not be considered a scientific hypothesis. Suppose someone were to hypothesize that all of the fossils from the Hadar site (together with all the objects in every geological layer on the surface of the earth) had been placed in the ground 10,000 years ago by aliens from another planet. These aliens had the desire and the skill to trick us about the history of life on earth. Is such a hypothesis testable? What sort of evidence could nature give us that would either confirm or refute such a hypothesis?

hypotheses Statements that assert a particular connection between fact and interpretation.

testability The ability of scientific hypotheses to be matched against evidence to see whether they are confirmed or refuted.

Certainly, if we found the remains of sophisticated technological devices alongside the fossil bones, we would instantly suspect that the site was very odd. Our suspicion might be confirmed if laboratory analysis reported that these devices were constructed using materials and engineering principles unknown on earth. Our suspicion would deepen if the remains of similar devices began to appear regularly in paleontological digs, and it would become more than suspicion if datable remains from every site, analyzed by a variety of laboratory techniques, consistently turned out to be around 10,000 years old! But what if no such material evidence were ever found? What if nothing in any archaeological site suggested the presence of high technology, alien or otherwise? What if the objects recovered from digs turned out to vary in age in a manner consistent with the geological layers in which they were found? What if only a few sites could be reliably dated to 10,000 years ago and many more could be reliably dated to either older or more recent times?

Perhaps diehard supporters of the alien story might offer a new hypothesis. They might claim that the aliens were so amazingly skilled that they were able to arrange the pattern of burial so as to trick us into thinking we were observing a series of deposits laid down over time. The aliens were so fiendishly clever that they were able to chemically treat the objects they buried in a way that would make them yield misleading dates—a pattern of misleading dates—whenever they were subjected to laboratory analysis!

We now have a new alien hypothesis to consider, but this time we cannot call it a scientific hypothesis. The first version of the alien hypothesis was not confirmed: it was tested against nature and did not match. But there is no way of testing the new hypothesis that aliens carried out this massive task of rearranging the layers in the earth's crust and tampering with its contents. If scientists objected that the bones and stones in their laboratories showed no evidence of chemical tampering, a defender of the new hypothesis could reply that this demonstrated how adept the aliens were at covering their tracks. Indeed, any evidence offered by a scientist to refute the new hypothesis would simply be interpreted by supporters as another part of the alien scheme to deceive earthlings.

In the absence of any evidence to support it and the presence of overwhelming evidence against it (all the patterned geological deposits with older or younger dates, cross-checked by more than one dating method), the new alien hypothesis holds no scientific interest. This does not mean that scientists have proved beyond question that aliens never visited our planet or buried fake fossils in our soil; it does mean, however, that the alien hypothesis need not be taken seriously by scientists. Under these circumstances, to continue to support the alien hypothesis would be to leave the realm of science and enter the realm of science fiction.

Theories   In everyday speech, we frequently use the word *theory* to refer to an explanation that is as likely to be false as it is to be true. Indeed, we tend to invent "theories" in the absence of evidence. This is why we often plead, "It's just a theory," to defend ourselves against critics who demand that we produce evidence to back up our claims. In science, the contrary is true. Scientists speak of a **scientific theory** only when they are able to link up a series of testable hypotheses in a coherent manner to explain a body of material evidence. Scientific theories are the combined result of sifting data, testing hypotheses, and imagining how all the resulting information might be put together in an enlightening way. Scientific theories are taken seriously because they account for a wide range of material evidence in a coherent, persuasive manner even though their hypotheses remain open to testing and possible falsification. The most powerful theories in science, such as the theory of relativity or the theory of evolution, are valued not just because they explain more of the material evidence than their competitors but also because their central hypotheses are open to testing and potential falsification—and yet, after repeated tests, they have never been disconfirmed.

It is often the case that the same body of material evidence, interpreted in different ways, gives rise to rival theories. Scientists have long been involved in a lively dialogue with one another about the meaning of material evidence, as well as about what should count as material evidence in the first place. This scientific give and take helps refine and strengthen some theories over time while exposing the weaknesses of others. Areas in which scientists agree at one period, however, may be reopened for debate at a later time, when new material evidence or a new hypothesis, or both, arises. As scientists compare their theories not only with nature but also with the theories of their rivals, their understanding is deepened, and their theories are revised.

Objectivity   One reason scientific findings are highly respected is that they are considered objective. But what do we mean when we speak of "objectivity"? The meaning of this concept in Western thought has varied over time, but by the nineteenth century, **objectivity** had acquired the meaning many people associate with it today: a judgment about some feature of the world that is free of individual idiosyncrasies (Daston 1999, 111). Western science has traditionally emphasized the demands that objectivity places on individual

---

scientific theory A coherently organized series of testable hypotheses used to explain a body of material evidence.

objectivity The separation of observation and reporting from the researcher's wishes.

scientists. From this point of view, objectivity can be defined as "the separation of observation and reporting from the researcher's wishes" (Levins and Lewontin 1985, 225). Because theories are rooted in material evidence, new material evidence can tip the balance in favor of one theory over its alternatives or expose all current theories as inadequate. Scientific researchers who faithfully report results even when these results undermine their own pet hypotheses would be viewed as objective in this individual sense.

But scientific objectivity may also be understood as an attribute of communities of scientists, not just of individual researchers. Most historians and philosophers of science recognize that science as it developed in Western Europe has always been a social activity. The testability of scientific hypotheses, for example, makes sense only when we understand that an individual's work is carried out in a scientific community whose members share their work, in the form of public presentations or articles in professional journals. Members of the same scientific community scrutinize each other's stories about nature, testing to see if they are confirmed or disconfirmed, in a process called "peer review." Public evaluation of scientists' work ideally appeals to the same standards for everyone, and members of the community are expected to be responsive to the observations of all knowledgeable critics (Figure M1.5). As philosopher of science Helen Longino (1990) emphasizes, responsiveness to other members of a scientific community "does not require that individuals whose data and assumptions are criticized recant. . . . What is required is that community members pay attention to the critical discussion taking place and that the assumptions that govern their group activity remain logically sensitive to it" (78).

Longino (1990) adds that criticism cannot go on indefinitely if scientific research is to achieve its goals. Scientists become impatient if their detractors repeat the same criticisms over and over but never develop an alternative research program of their own that produces rich new evidence in support of their own views (Longino, 79). In part, this is because scientists are often unwilling to give up on even an inadequate research program until they find an alternative that somehow works better than what they already have. This unsatisfactory state of affairs regularly provokes the development of new approaches in science that produce new evidence, thus allowing critics to do more than merely point out the deficiencies of other scientists' work. The history of paleoanthropology is full of lively debates that have produced new theories, new evidence, and new research techniques (such as those associated with dating ancient fossils and artifacts or recovering ancient biomolecules such as DNA). These have enormously increased our understanding of the complex evolutionary history of our species and our closest relatives.

Scholars like Helen Longino and Lorraine Daston have been part of an important multidisciplinary effort over the past quarter century to rethink traditional assumptions about what science is and how it works. By the 1980s, these theorists (anthropologists among them) had produced a large body of work known as **science studies**, which explores the interconnections among the sociocultural, political, economic, and historic conditions that make scientific research both possible and successful. As we observed in Chapter 1, science studies has provided a stronger, more nuanced account of how science is done and why it succeeds (or fails), primarily by drawing attention to people, technology, and institutions whose activity is essential for the success of science but that are regularly downplayed or ignored in standard accounts of the scientific method.

One innovation of science studies that is important for anthropology was *laboratory ethnography*. One of the first laboratory ethnographers was Bruno Latour, who carried out fieldwork at the Salk Institute in Southern California in the 1970s (Latour and Woolgar 1986). Laboratory fieldwork involves following scientists as they go about their everyday laboratory activities and brings to light the range of embodied skills that scientists in certain fields must master if they are effectively to operate the often-elaborate technological apparatuses that make successful research possible. In addition, Latour and others revealed the significance of a range of "nonscientific" institutions and individuals *outside* the laboratory whose support was essential if "strictly scientific" research projects *inside* the laboratory were to continue (Latour and Woolgar 1986; Latour 1987). Successful directors of laboratories, for example, must wear many hats: not only must they be able to secure proper working conditions for their scientific staff, but also they must cultivate good relationships with university administrators; laboratory instrument makers; government funding agencies; and, increasingly, private industry. These days, some scientists even run their own companies.

Recent successful laboratory ethnographies undertaken by anthropologists can be found in the 2014 volume *Mestizo Genomics: Race Mixture, Nation, and Science in Latin America*, edited by Peter Wade, Carlos López Beltrán, Eduardo Restrepo, and Ricardo Ventura Santos (2014b). Three of the four editors of this collection are anthropologists, and the fourth is a historian of science. The chapters in the volume are based on laboratory ethnographies carried out in genetics laboratories in Mexico, Brazil, and Colombia, countries whose populations have often been considered to be the product of "race mixture" between European conquistadors, enslaved

---

science studies Research that explores the interconnections among the sociocultural, political, economic, and historic conditions that make scientific research both possible and successful.

FIGURE M1.5   There is an important social aspect to science. It is not just that scientists work in teams, but they also meet regularly to discuss and debate their research, informally as conference goers seek food (**a**) or formally as bioanthropologist Jonathan Marks presents his research (**b**). Increasingly, collaborations take shape in a variety of forms online, from blogs and podcasts to open-source, peer-reviewed publications of cutting-edge research. Some of these initiatives can be seen with a visit to the website of the American Anthropological Association, https://www.americananthro.org/. As we will see, online activity has become a recognized area of ethnographic research in anthropology.

Africans, and Indigenous peoples. In each country, ethnographers worked closely with scientists in different laboratories and were able to show (among other things) how scientists' relationships outside the laboratory (e.g., with members of local populations from which they desired to obtain genetic samples) affected the kind of science carried out inside the laboratory. The scientists' initial concern to identify genes that put different populations at risk for genetic diseases became aligned with the concern of national governments to accord official political recognition to different ethnic and racial groups within each country. Finally, the authors explore a paradox in the ways the results of this research were received by different audiences: "while [the patterns scientists discovered] appear nonracial to genetic experts, [they] might look a lot like race to nonexperts in genetics . . . reinforcing commonsense understandings of human diversity as divided up into continent-shaped groups" (Wade et al. 2014a, 2).

Many anthropologists value science studies for having provided a more accurate, if less exalted, view of the complex alliances and entanglements that produce scientific outcomes. The legacy of science studies in anthropology has inspired anthropologists such as primatologists who work with other species (e.g., Fuentes 2012) as well as archaeologists and

other anthropologists interested in material culture, from clothing to computers to art objects and ancient artifacts (e.g., Miller 2005; Hodder 2012). Historian of science Steven Shapin encapsulates the science studies perspective in the title of a recent collection of his essays: *Never Pure: Historical Studies of Science as If It Was Produced by People with Bodies, Situated in Time, Space, Culture, and Society, and Struggling for Credibility and Authority* (2010). The title of Shapin's book also highlights the way science studies draws attention to the people with bodies who were involved with science and technology as researchers, as research subjects, or in other vital supporting roles. As we observed in Chapter 1, anthropological research such as the Undocumented Migration Project illustrates how theories from science studies can suggest innovative ways to bring various subfields of anthropology into closer collaboration. We will present additional examples of such collaboration in subsequent chapters.

To evaluate the scientific stories told about human origins, people must become more knowledgeable about the kinds of material evidence and the interpretations of that evidence that scientists use. This book deals with both matters. The next two chapters provide an overview of the basic elements of modern evolutionary theory and the evidence that evolutionary biologists have collected to support their hypotheses. Subsequent chapters will discuss, step by step, the way scientific inquiry into the biology of living primates, the analysis of fossils, the interpretation of archaeological remains, and the study of a wide range of contemporary human societies has provided a vast body of evidence in support of an evolutionary story about human origins, the origin of culture, and the development of human cultural diversity.

nonhuman organisms, and technical apparatus in the course of scientific research has inspired anthropologists from many subfields to revise our understanding of relationships between nature and culture, people and artifacts, and people and other living species. It has also inspired creative rethinking of how the subfields of anthropology might be brought together.

Module Summary

1. Anthropologists regularly claim that their attempts to explain human nature, human society, and the human past are scientific. Scientists are not the only people to tell stories about the way the world works. But scientific stories are different from other stories because they must be open to testing that will confirm or refute them. Stories about the material world that are not open to this kind of testing cannot be considered scientific.

2. Scientists use the term *theory* in a way that is different from everyday, nonscientific usage. Well-confirmed scientific theories are taken very seriously by scientists because they account for a wide range of material evidence in a coherent, persuasive manner, although they remain open to testing and possible refutation. The most powerful scientific theories are those whose key hypotheses have been tested repeatedly and have never been disconfirmed.

3. Over the past quarter century, many anthropologists and other scholars have become involved in the interdisciplinary field of science studies, which subjects scientific laboratories and their activities to ethnographic investigation, and have shown how successful science in action differs from traditional idealized accounts of scientific research. Science studies research highlighting the productive interconnections among human beings,

For Review

1. According to the text, what is science?

2. How does science differ from myth?

3. Why must scientists be particularly concerned about the assumptions they bring to their observations of the natural world?

4. Explain the difference between material and inferred evidence.

5. Why does a hypothesis need to be testable to be considered scientific?

6. What are scientific theories, and why are they taken seriously even when their hypotheses remain open to testing?

7. What is objectivity?

8. Summarize the discussion in the text about scientific communities.

Key Terms

assumptions 25	science 24
evidence 25	science studies 29
hypotheses 27	scientific theory 28
myths 24	testability 27
objectivity 28	

Why is evolution important to anthropologists?

This question is fundamental to contemporary anthropology and is a topic of great significance in wider scientific discussions. In this chapter, we will look at how the living world was understood before the nineteenth century; where Darwin's ideas came from; how they have been further elaborated since his time; and why evolutionary theory continues to be our most powerful tool for understanding biological processes today.

CHAPTER OUTLINE

LEARNING OBJECTIVES

- Describe the characteristics of evolutionary theory and why it is important for the discipline of anthropology.

- Explain the different sources of evidence used by anthropologists to explain evolution.

- Compare and contrast the historical views of the natural world that predated Darwin's theory of natural selection.

- Identify the historical development of the concept of natural selection and how this concept is similar to and different from previous views of the natural world.

- Describe the historical context for the emergence of biologists' knowledge of genes and the field of genetics.

- Discuss the basic concepts in contemporary genetics and how they serve as building blocks for the field of genetics.

- Compare and contrast genotype and phenotype and how these two concepts relate to the norm of reaction.

- Describe the emergence of the modern evolutionary synthesis and our contemporary understanding of evolution.

Galapagos Darwin finch in the Galápagos Islands, Ecuador.

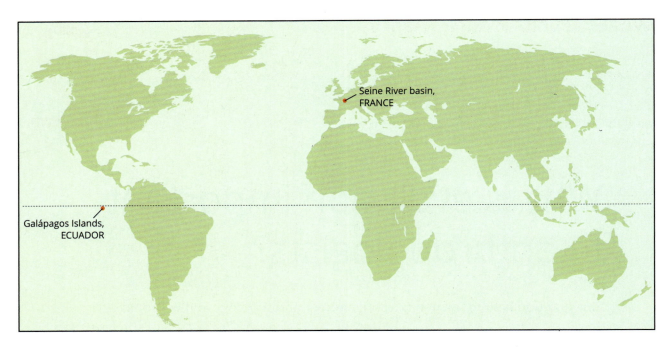

FIGURE 2.1   Major locations discussed in Chapter 2.

Philosopher of science Philip Kitcher (1982) has suggested that successful scientific theories are testable, unified, and fruitful. A theory is testable when its hypotheses can be independently matched up against nature. A theory is unified when it offers just one or a few basic problem-solving strategies that make sense of a wide range of material evidence. And a theory is fruitful when its central principles suggest new and promising possibilities for further research. The modern theory of biological evolution possesses all three characteristics. Evolutionary hypotheses are highly testable in a number of ways. As we shall see, material evidence from widely diverse sources has consistently fit evolutionary predictions. Because it is based on a few central concepts and assumptions, the evolutionary research program is also highly unified. Charles Darwin's *On the Origin of Species by Means of Natural Selection* appeared in 1859. As Kitcher (1982, 48) puts it, Darwin "gave structure to our ignorance." After that date, biologists could borrow Darwin's methods to guide them in new and promising directions. The study of life has not been the same since. As we begin our study of human evolution, you may be surprised at the number of terms and concepts that you are learning from biology, genetics, and ecology. The theory of evolution has engaged the efforts of many scientists for more than 150 years. Evolutionary theory today is powerful, multistranded, and (like all good science) still a work in progress. Although Charles Darwin and Alfred Russel Wallace may have had the first word in the construction of this theory, they have not had the last word. Indeed, several decades after 1859, once scientists began investigating the properties of chromosomes and genes, many of them became convinced that

genetics, and not natural selection, would explain how evolution worked. By the 1930s, however, some biologists persuaded by the power of natural selection joined forces with other biologists knowledgeable about genetics; together, they negotiated what came to be called the *modern evolutionary synthesis*. Those who adopted the synthesis agreed to narrow the focus of evolutionary research and theorizing to natural selection on genes in populations of organisms. Thus was born the discipline of *population biology*, which developed formal mathematical theorizing about the consequences of natural selection on genes. By the end of the twentieth century, however, new theories and new data raised evolutionary questions that the Modern Synthesis seemed ill-equipped to address. As a result, in recent years, many evolutionary theorists have been calling for an expanded evolutionary synthesis that would incorporate these new insights and data. This is why it is problematic today to presume that evolutionary theory has to do only with Darwin's original claims about natural selection. As biological anthropologist Agustín Fuentes observes, it is incorrect to equate evolutionary theory in biology or anthropology with the views of Darwin alone: "current evolutionary theory is well past the basic contributions of Darwin and there is a growing pattern amongst evolutionary biologists to use the terms 'multiple processes of evolution' and 'evolutionary theory' rather than 'Darwinian evolution'" (Fuentes 2013, 43, n3). And so, complicated as it may be to understand the arguments made by modern evolutionary biologists and anthropologists, we must learn the language of evolution. The payoff will be a nuanced view of what the theory of evolution is really about and how powerful it really is.

What Is Evolutionary Theory?

At its most basic, **evolutionary theory** claims that living species can change over time and give rise to new kinds of species, with the result that all organisms ultimately share a common ancestry. Because of this common ancestry, information about biological variation in finches or genetic transmission in fruit flies can help us understand the roles of biological variation and genetics in human evolution.

Nearly forty years ago, Niles Eldredge and Ian Tattersall (1982) observed that evolution "is as highly verified a thesis as can be found in science. Subjected to close scrutiny from all angles for over a century now, evolution emerges as the only naturalistic explanation we have of the twin patterns of similarity and diversity that pervade all life" (2). Steven Stanley (1981) stated that "the theory of evolution is not just getting older, it is getting better. Like any scientific concept that has long withstood the test of time, this one has suffered setbacks, but, time and again, has rebounded to become richer and stronger" (xv). Two decades into the twenty-first century, these evaluations still hold: evolutionary thinkers remain convinced that the story they propose to tell about the history of life on earth is more persuasive than any of its rivals. To what do they owe this sense of confidence?

What Material Evidence Is There for Evolution?

Two kinds of material evidence have been particularly important in the history of evolutionary theory: material evidence of change over time and material evidence of change across space. Geological research led to the discovery of the fossil record—the remains of life forms that had been preserved in the earth for a long time. When scientists compared these fossils with each other and with living organisms, they noted that the living organisms were quite different from the fossilized organisms. This was material evidence of change over time, or **evolution**, in the kinds of organisms that have lived on the earth. Any persuasive biological theory would have to find a way to explain this material evidence.

Equally important material evidence for evolutionary theory came from the study of living organisms. Darwin himself was most interested in explaining the spatial distributions of living species of organisms. In one of his best-known studies, Darwin noted that neighboring geographic areas on the islands of the Galápagos Archipelago were inhabited by species of finch different from the finch species found on the Ecuadorian mainland. At the same time, the various Galápagos species resembled one another closely and resembled mainland finch species

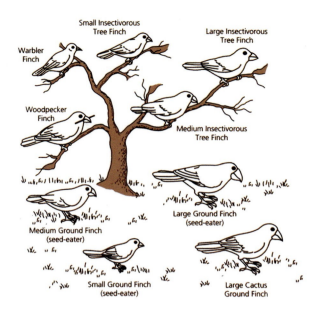

FIGURE 2.2 Charles Darwin and Alfred Russel Wallace explained the pattern of distribution of living species of organisms (such as the various species of finches living on the Galápagos Islands) by arguing that all the variants had evolved from a single ancestral species.

(Figure 2.2). Species distribution patterns of this kind suggested change over space, which, again, any persuasive biological theory would have to explain.

In the centuries before Darwin, however, the fossil record was mostly unknown, and many of those concerned with biology did not see the pattern of distribution of living species as evidence for past change. To understand why Darwin's ideas had such a powerful impact requires an understanding of pre-Darwinian views of the natural world (Table 2.1).

Pre-Darwinian Views of the Natural World

In the Western societies of antiquity, the Greeks thought the world had been, and would be, around forever; in the Judeo-Christian tradition, it was thought that the world was young and would end soon. Both traditions saw the world as fixed and unchanging.

Essentialism

If the world does not change, then the various forms of life that are part of that world also do not change. We can trace this view back to the ancient Greek philosopher

---

evolutionary theory The set of testable hypotheses that assert that living organisms can change over time and give rise to new kinds of organisms, with the result that all organisms ultimately share a common ancestry.

evolution The process of change over time.

TABLE 2.1 Pre-Darwinian Views of the Natural World

VIEW	KEY FEATURES
Essentialism	Each "natural kind" of living thing is characterized by an unchanging core of features and separated from all other natural kinds by a sharp break.
Great Chain of Being	Based on three principles: 1. *Continuity:* Attributes of one kind of organism always overlap to some extent with the attributes of organisms closest to it in the classification. 2. *Plentitude:* A world of organisms created by a benevolent God can have no gaps but must include all logically conceivable organisms. 3. *Unilinear gradation:* All organisms can be arranged in a single hierarchy based on various degrees to which they depart from divine perfection.
Catastrophism	The notion that natural disasters, such as floods, are responsible for the extinction of species, which are then replaced by new species.
Uniformitarianism	The belief that the same gradual processes of erosion and uplift that change the earth's surface today had been at work in the past. Thus, we can use our understanding of current processes to reconstruct the history of the earth.
Transformational evolution	Assuming essentialist species and a uniformly changing environment, Lamarck (1744–1829) argued that individual members of a species transform themselves in identical ways to adapt to commonly experienced changes in the environment. To explain why, Lamarck invoked (1) the law of use and disuse and (2) the inheritance of acquired characters.

Plato. A central element of Plato's philosophy was a belief in an ideal world of perfect, eternal, unchanging forms that exist apart from the imperfect, changeable, physical world of living things. Plato believed that these two worlds—ideal and material—were linked; and that every ideal form, the ideal form of "cowness," for instance, was represented in the physical, material world by a number of imperfect but recognizable real cows of varying sizes, colors, temperaments, and so on. When observers looked at real cows and saw their similarities despite all this variation, Plato believed that what they were really seeing was the ideal form, or essence, of "cowness" that each individual cow incarnated.

According to Plato, all living things that share the same essence belong to the same "natural kind;" and there are many natural kinds in the world, each of which is the result of the imperfect incarnation in the physical world of one or another eternal form or ideal ("cowness," "humanness," "ratness," and the like). This view is called **essentialism**. For essentialists, as Ernst Mayr (1982) explained, "each species is characterized by its unchanging essence . . . and separated from all other species by a sharp discontinuity. Essentialism assumes that the diversity of inanimate as well as of organic nature is

the reflection of a limited number of unchanging universals. . . . All those objects belong to the same species that share the same essence" (256). That essence is what made every individual cow a cow and not, say, a deer.

The Great Chain of Being

Greek ideas were adopted and adapted by thinkers in the Judeo-Christian religious tradition. By the Middle Ages, many scholars thought they could describe the organizing principles responsible for harmony in nature. According to Arthur Lovejoy ([1936] 1960), they reasoned as follows: the ancient Greek philosopher Aristotle suggested that kinds of organisms could be arranged in a single line from most primitive to most advanced. He further argued that the attributes of one kind of organism always overlap to some extent with the attributes of organisms closest to it in the classification, so that the differences between adjacent organisms were slight. Together, these ideas constituted a principle of continuity. Logically implied by the principle of continuity is the principle of plenitude, or fullness, which states that a world of organisms created by a benevolent God can have no gaps but must include all logically conceivable organisms. Finally, the ancient philosophers' assumption that God alone is self-sufficient and perfect implied that each of God's creatures must lack, to a greater or lesser degree, some part of divine perfection. As a result,

essentialism The belief, derived from Plato, in fixed ideas, or "forms," that exist perfect and unchanging in eternity. Actual objects in the temporal world, such as cows or horses, are seen as imperfect material realizations of the ideal form that defines their kind.

the various kinds of organisms can be arranged in a single hierarchy, or unilinear gradation, like a ladder or a chain, based on the degrees to which they depart from the divine ideal.

When the notion of unilinear gradation was combined with the notions of continuity and plenitude, the result was called the **Great Chain of Being**, a comprehensive framework for interpreting the natural world. This framework suggested that the entire cosmos was composed "of an immense, or of an infinite, number of links . . . every one of them differing from that immediately above and that immediately below it by the 'least possible' degree of difference" (Lovejoy [1936] 1960, 59). Degrees of difference were understood in theological terms to be degrees of excellence. Creatures farthest away from divine perfection were lowest in the hierarchy, whereas creatures most like God (such as the angels) ranked highest. Human beings occupied a unique position in the chain. Their material bodies linked them to other material beings, but unlike other material creatures, they also possessed souls and were thereby linked to the spiritual realm by a God who had created them in his image.

For several hundred years—from the Middle Ages through the eighteenth century—the Great Chain of Being was the framework in the Western world within which all discussions of living organisms were set. As late as the mid-eighteenth century, Carolus Linnaeus (1707–1778), the father of modern biological **taxonomy** (or classification), operated within this framework. Linnaeus was committed to an essentialist definition of natural kinds. He focused on what modern taxonomists call the **genus** (plural *genera*) (see Figure 2.3) and used the morphology of reproductive organs to define the "essence" of a genus (Mayr 1982, 178). (The term **species**, which modern biologists assign to subpopulations of the same genus that share certain specific attributes, was used more loosely in the past by essentialists and by nonessentialists.) Essentialists like Linnaeus knew that individuals sometimes differ markedly from what is considered "normal" for others of their kind. But these deviations were still thought of as accidents, or "degradations," that could not affect the unity of the natural kind.

Catastrophism and Uniformitarianism

The unprecedented social and scientific changes brought about by the eighteenth-century Enlightenment in Europe gradually raised doubts about the Great Chain

of Being. The principle of continuity was criticized by the French scientist Georges Cuvier (1769–1832), a pioneer in modern anatomy who also carried out some of the first important excavations of fossils in the Seine River basin near Paris. He was a firm believer in the essentialist definition of natural kinds, but his anatomical studies convinced him that there were only four natural categories of living things. Each category was excellently adapted to its way of life but had no connection to any of the others. Cuvier's studies of the fossil record convinced him that, over time, some species had been abruptly wiped out and replaced, equally abruptly, by new species from somewhere else. Cuvier employed the French term *revolution* to describe these, although this term was translated into English as "catastrophe." Hence, the term **catastrophism** came to refer to the notion that natural disasters, such as floods, are responsible for the extinction of some natural kinds, which are later replaced by new natural kinds.

In some ways, Cuvier's ideas were perfectly traditional: he did not reject the essentialist understanding of species and never suggested that new species were simply old species that had changed. Yet, his idea that some species might disappear in mass extinctions was quite radical because, according to Judeo-Christian theology, God had created all possible forms of life only once. In the same way, Cuvier's assertion in 1812 that there were no connections whatsoever among the four basic categories of living things seriously undermined the principle of unilinear gradation. That is, if the four categories had nothing in common with one another, then they could not be arranged in a simple chain of natural kinds, each precisely placed between the one slightly less advanced and the one slightly more advanced. Ernst Mayr (1982, 201) concluded that this argument dealt the Great Chain of Being its death blow.

But the Great Chain of Being did not die gently because its principles had become inextricably intertwined with Judeo-Christian beliefs about the natural world. By

Great Chain of Being A comprehensive framework for interpreting the world, based on Aristotelian principles and elaborated during the Middle Ages, in which every kind of living organism was linked to every other kind in an enormous, divinely created chain. An organism differed from the kinds immediately above it and below it on the chain by the least possible degree.

taxonomy A classification; in biology, the classification of various kinds of organisms.

genus The level of the Linnaean taxonomy in which different species are grouped together on the basis of their similarities to one another.

species (1) For Linnaeus, a Platonic "natural kind" defined in terms of its essence. (2) For modern biologists, a reproductive community of populations (reproductively isolated from others) that occupies a specific niche in nature.

catastrophism The notion that natural disasters, such as floods, are responsible for the extinction of species, which are then replaced by new species.

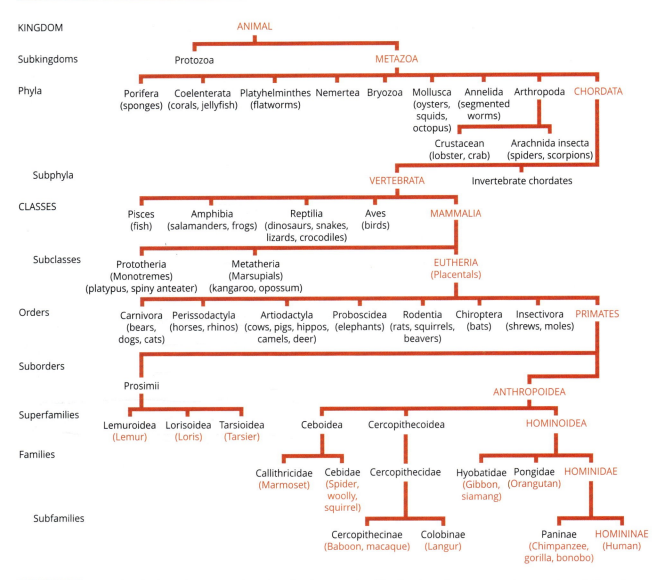

FIGURE 2.3 A modern biological taxonomy based on the Linnaean classification (popular names are in parentheses). Organisms sharing structural similarities are still grouped together, but their similarities are understood to be the result of common ancestry, indicated by the horizontal line connecting them. Thus, Paninae (chimpanzees, gorillas, and bonobos) and Homininae (human beings) all share a recent common ancestor.

the late eighteenth and early nineteenth centuries, one result of this process of amalgamation was the development of an approach arguing that the perfection of each organism's adaptation could only be the result of intentional design by a benevolent creator. One group of thinkers, known as "catastrophists," modified Cuvier's theory and argued that the new species that replaced old ones had been specially created by God. Others subscribed to a position known as **uniformitarianism,**

which stressed nature's overall harmonious integration as evidence for God's handiwork. These "uniformitarians" criticized the ideas of Cuvier and the catastrophists. God might allow the world to change, they admitted, but a benevolent God's blueprint for creation could not include sharp breaks between different forms of life and the abrupt disappearance of species through extinction. The uniformitarian position gained powerful support from the book *Principles of Geology* by Charles Lyell (1797–1875), published between 1830 and 1833. Lyell argued that the same gradual processes of erosion and uplift that change the earth's surface today had also been at work in the past. Assuming the uniformity of these processes, he contended that our understanding of

uniformitarianism The notion that an understanding of current processes can be used to reconstruct the past history of the earth, based on the assumption that the same gradual processes of erosion and uplift that change the earth's surface today had also been at work in the past.

current processes could be used to reconstruct the past history of the earth.

The quarrel between catastrophists and uniformitarians has often been portrayed as a conflict between narrow-minded dogmatism (identified with the catastrophists) and open-minded, empirical science (identified with the uniformitarians). But, as Stephen Jay Gould (1987) demonstrated, this portrayal misrepresents the nature of their disagreement. Both Cuvier and Lyell were empirical scientists: the former, a leading anatomist and excavator of fossils; the latter, a fieldworking geologist. Both confronted much of the same material evidence; however, as Gould points out, they interpreted that evidence in very different ways. Catastrophists were willing to accept a view of earth's history that permitted ruptures of harmony to preserve their belief that history, guided by divine intervention, was going somewhere. By contrast, the harmonious, nondirectional view of the uniformitarians was rooted in their belief that time was cyclic, like the changing seasons. Uniformitarians promoted the view that God's creation was the "incarnation of rationality"—that is, that God's creation unfolded in accordance with God's laws, without requiring subsequent divine intervention or a fixed historical trajectory.

Transformational Evolution

Thus, by the early years of the nineteenth century, traditional ideas about the natural world had been challenged by new material evidence and conflicting interpretations of that evidence. In the ferment of this period, the French naturalist Jean-Baptiste de Monet de Lamarck (1744–1829) grappled with the inconsistencies described above, dealing the first serious blow against essentialism (Figure 2.4). Lamarck wanted to preserve the traditional view of a harmonious living world. One of the most serious challenges to that view was the problem of extinction. How could perfectly adapted creatures suddenly be wiped out, and where did their replacements come from? Some suggested that the extinctions were the result of Noah's flood, but this could not explain how aquatic animals had become extinct. Others suggested that extinctions were the result of human hunting, possibly explaining why mastodons no longer roamed the earth. Some hoped that natural kinds believed to be extinct might yet be found inhabiting an unexplored area of the globe.

Lamarck suggested an original interpretation of the material evidence that had been used to argue in favor of extinction. Noticing that many fossil species bore a close resemblance to living species, he suggested in 1809 that perhaps fossil forms were the ancestors of living forms.

FIGURE 2.4 Jean-Baptiste de Monet de Lamarck. Lamarck wanted to preserve the traditional view of a harmonious living world, but his interpretation of the evidence of fossils eventually undermined exactly the view he was trying to defend.

Fossil forms looked different from their descendants, he believed, because ancestral features had been modified over time to suit their descendants to changing climate and geography. Such a process would prove that nature was harmonious after all—that, although the world was a changing world, living organisms possessed the capacity to change along with it.

Many elements of the Great Chain of Being could be made to fit with Lamarck's scheme. Lamarck believed that once a natural kind had come into existence, it had the capacity to evolve over time into increasingly complex (or "perfect") forms. This could happen, Lamarck suggested, because all organisms have two attributes: (1) the ability to change physically in response to environmental demands and (2) the capacity to activate this ability whenever environmental change makes the organism's previous response obsolete. Otherwise, the resulting lack of fit between organisms and environment would create disharmony in nature. Lamarck never suggested that a species might adapt to change by splitting into two or more new species; rather, every member of every species is engaged in its own individual adaptive transformation over time. This is why Lamarckian evolution has also been called **transformational evolution**.

Lamarck proposed two "laws" to explain how such transformation occurs. First, he said, an organ is strengthened by use and weakened by disuse (an early statement of "use it or lose it"). If environmental changes cause members of a species to rely more heavily on some organs than on others, the former will become enhanced and the latter reduced. But the law of use and disuse had evolutionary consequences, Lamarck argued, because the physical result of use or disuse could be passed from one generation to the next. This is Lamarck's second law, the law of inheritance of acquired characteristics.

Consider the following example: modern pandas possess an oversized, elongated wrist bone that aids them in stripping bamboo leaves, their favorite food, from bamboo stalks (Figure 2.5). This bone has been called the panda's "thumb," although pandas retain all five digits on each paw. Had Lamarck known about the panda's thumb, he might have explained its origin as follows: suppose that pandas originally had wrist bones like other bears. Then the environment changed, obliging pandas to become dependent on bamboo for food. Pandas, unable to survive on bamboo unless they found an efficient way to strip the leaves off the stalk, were forced to use their forepaws more intensively (the law of use and disuse) to remove enough bamboo leaves to satisfy their appetite. Continual exercise of their wrists caused the wrist bone to enlarge and lengthen into a shape resembling a thumb. After acquiring "thumbs" through strenuous activity, pandas gave birth to offspring with elongated wrist bones (the law of inheritance of acquired characters). Thus, Lamarck's laws could explain how each species builds up new, more complex organs and attains, over many generations, increasingly higher levels of "perfection."

Because transformational evolution works through the efforts of individual members of a species, what would prevent different individuals from transforming themselves in different directions? Part of the answer is that Lamarck expected a changing environment to affect all individuals of the same species in the same way, leading to identical responses in terms of use and disuse. But the rest of the answer lies with the fact that Lamarck still accepted the view that every individual member of a species was identical in essence to every other member. Only if this were so could all members

FIGURE 2.5 Lamarckian transformational evolution and Darwinian variational evolution offer two different explanations for how the panda got its "thumb." The thumb is actually an elongated wristbone that aids pandas in stripping bamboo leaves, their favorite food, from bamboo stalks.

of the same species respond in the same ways to the same environmental pressures and retain their species identity over time.

Lamarck's transformational theory of biological evolution was rejected by biologists in the early twentieth century, when geneticists were able to demonstrate that neither the law of use and disuse nor the law of inheritance of acquired characters applied to genes. In the early nineteenth century, however, Lamarck's speculations opened the door for Darwin.

What Is Natural Selection?

Lamarck had argued that a species could vary over time. Contemporaries of Lamarck, observing living organisms in the wild in Europe, the Americas, Africa, and Asia, had demonstrated that species could vary over space as well. Where did all this mutually coexisting but previously unknown living variation come from?

---

transformational evolution Also called *Lamarckian evolution*, it assumes essentialist species and a uniform environment. Each individual member of a species transforms itself to meet the challenges of a changed environment through the laws of use and disuse and the inheritance of acquired characters.

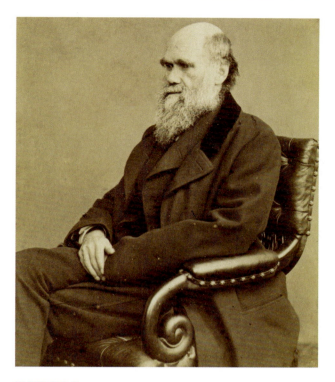

FIGURE 2.6 Charles Darwin (1809–1882).

The mystery of geographical variation in living organisms was particularly vexing to Charles Darwin (1809–1882, Figure 2.6) and Alfred Russel Wallace (1823–1913), whose field observations made it impossible to ignore. Wallace reasoned that the relationship between similar but distinct species in the wild could be explained if all the similar species were related to one another biologically—that is, if they were considered daughter (or sibling) species of some other parental species. Darwin, comparing the finches on the Galápagos Islands with finches on the Ecuadorian mainland, reasoned that the similarities linking the finches could be explained if all of them had descended from a single parental finch population. Both men concluded independently that similar species must descend from a common ancestor, meaning that any species might split into a number of new species given enough time. But how much time? In the 1650s, James Ussher, the Anglican archbishop of Ireland, used information in the Bible to calculate that God created the earth on October 23, 4004 BC, a date that was still widely accepted in the nineteenth century. Charles Lyell and other geologists, however, claimed that the earth was much more than 6,000 years old (indeed, it is about 4.5 billion years old). If the geologists were right, there had been ample time for what Darwin called "descent with modification" to have produced the high degree of species diversity we find in the world today.

Darwin had refrained from publishing his work on evolution for years but was moved to action when Lyell warned him that Wallace was ready to publish his ideas. As a result, Darwin and Wallace first published their views in a scientific paper carrying both their names. Darwin became better known than Wallace in later years, in part because of the mass of material evidence he collected in support of his theory together with his refined theoretical interpretations of that evidence.

The theory of **common ancestry**—"the first Darwinian revolution" (Mayr 1982, 116)—was in itself scandalous because it went far beyond Lamarck's modest suggestion that species can change without losing their essential integrity. Not only did Darwin propose that similar species can be traced to a common ancestor, but also he offered a straightforward, mechanistic explanation of how such descent with modification takes place. His explanation, the theory of **natural selection**, was "the second Darwinian revolution." That natural selection remains central to modern evolutionary theory is testimony to the power of Darwin's insight because it has been tested and reformulated for more than 150 years and remains the best explanation we have today for the diversity of life on earth.

Charles Darwin's theory of evolution was possible only because he was able to think about species in a new way. Although Lamarck had begun to do this when he suggested that species could change, Darwin completed the job. If organisms could change, then they did not have a fixed essence. This, in turn, meant that variation—or differences—among individual members of a species might be extremely important.

Thus, Darwin turned the essentialist definition of *species* on its head. He argued that the important thing about individual members of a species is not what they have in common but how they are different. The Darwinian theory of evolution by natural selection argued that variation, not a unitary essence, is the ground condition of life. This is why it is called **variational evolution**, in contrast to the transformational evolution of Lamarck (see, e.g., Lewontin 1982). The idea of variational evolution depends on what Ernst Mayr (1982) calls "population thinking"—that is, seeing the populations that make

common ancestry Darwin's claim that similar living species must all have had a common ancestor.

natural selection A two-step, mechanistic explanation of how descent with modification takes place: (1) every generation, variant individuals are generated within a species because of genetic mutation, and (2) those variant individuals best suited to the current environment survive and produce more offspring than other variants.

variational evolution The Darwinian theory of evolution, which assumes that variant members of a species respond differently to environmental challenges. Those variants that are more successful ("fitter") survive and reproduce more offspring who inherit the traits that made their parents fit.

up a species as composed of biological individuals whose differences from one another are genuine and important.

Population Thinking

Darwin combined this new view of species with other observations about the natural world. Consider, for example, frogs in a pond. Nobody would deny that new frogs hatch from hundreds of eggs laid by mature females every breeding season, yet the size of the population of adult frogs in a given pond rarely changes much from one season to the next. Clearly, the great potential fertility represented by all those eggs is never realized or the pond would shortly be overrun by frogs. Something must keep all those eggs from maturing into adults. Darwin (following Thomas Malthus) attributed this to the limited food supply in the pond, which means that the hatchlings are forced to struggle with one another for food and that the losers do not survive to reproduce. Darwin wondered what factors determined which competitors win and which lose. Pointing to the variation among all individuals of the species, he argued that those individuals whose variant traits better equip them to compete in the struggle for existence are more likely to survive and reproduce than those who lack such traits. Individuals who leave greater numbers of offspring are said to have superior **fitness**.

Such an argument makes no sense, of course, unless species are understood in variational terms. For an essentialist, the individual members of a species are identical to one another because they share the same essence; it makes no difference which or how many of them survive and reproduce. From an essentialist point of view, therefore, competition can only occur between different species because only the differences between entire species (not between a species' individual members) matter. Once we think of a species in variational terms, however, the notion that competition for resources "is 'dog eat dog' rather than 'dog eat cat'" begins to make sense (Depew and Weber 1989, 257).

When Darwin interpreted his observations, he came up with the following explanation of how biological evolution occurs. Levins and Lewontin (1985, 31ff.) summarize his theory in three principles and one driving force that sets the process in motion:

1. The principle of variation. No two individuals in a species are identical in all respects; they vary in such features as size, color, and intelligence.

2. The principle of heredity. Offspring tend to resemble their parents.

3. The principle of natural selection. Different variants leave different numbers of offspring.

The driving force, Darwin suggested, was the struggle for existence. In a later edition of *On the Origin of Species*, he borrowed a phrase coined by sociologist Herbert Spencer and described the outcome of the struggle for existence as "survival of the fittest."

Natural Selection in Action

To illustrate the operation of natural selection, let us return to the problem of how pandas got their "thumbs." Lamarck would explain this phenomenon by arguing that individual pandas all used their wrists intensively to obtain enough bamboo leaves to survive, causing their wrist bones to lengthen, a trait they passed on to their offspring. Darwin, by contrast, would explain this phenomenon by focusing attention not on individual pandas, but on a *population* of pandas and the ways in which members of that population differed from one another. He would argue that originally there must have been a population of pandas with wrist bones of different lengths (the principle of variation). Because offspring tend to resemble their parents, pandas with long wrist bones gave birth to offspring with long wrist bones and pandas with short wrist bones gave birth to offspring with short wrist bones (the principle of heredity). When the climate changed such that pandas became dependent on bamboo leaves for food, pandas with wrist bones of different lengths had to compete with one another to get enough leaves to survive (the struggle for existence).

Note that, in this example, "the struggle for existence" does not imply that the pandas were necessarily *fighting* with one another over access to bamboo. The pandas with long wrist bones functioning as "thumbs" for stripping bamboo stalks were simply more successful than pandas who lacked such a "thumb"; that is, in this new environment, their elongated wrist bones made them fitter than pandas with short wrist bones. Thus, pandas in the population with "thumbs" survived and left more offspring than did those without "thumbs." As a result, the proportion of pandas in the population with elongated wrist bones in the next generation was larger than it had been in the previous generation and the proportion of pandas in the population with short wrist bones was smaller. If these selective pressures were severe enough, pandas with short wrist bones might not leave any offspring at all, resulting at some point in a population made up entirely of pandas with "thumbs."

---

fitness A measure of an organism's ability to compete in the struggle for existence. Those individuals whose variant traits better equip them to compete with other members of their species for limited resources are more likely to survive and reproduce than individuals who lack such traits.

In Darwinian terms, adaptation has been traditionally understood as the process by which an organism "is engineered to be in harmony with the natural environment" as a result of natural selection (Little 1995, 123). However, this concept contains ambiguities that can confuse the *process* of adaptation with its *outcomes* (also often called "adaptations"). In 1982, paleontologists Stephen Jay Gould and Elisabeth Vrba helped to resolve this confusion by distinguishing among aptation, adaptation, and exaptation. An **aptation** refers to any useful feature of an organism, regardless of its origin. An **adaptation** refers to a useful feature of an organism that was shaped by natural selection for the function it now performs. An **exaptation**, by contrast, refers to a useful feature of an organism that was originally shaped by natural selection to perform one function but later reshaped by different selection pressures to perform a new function.

The distinction between adaptation and exaptation is important because mistaking one for the other can lead to evolutionary misinterpretations. For example, it has been standard practice to explain an organism's current form (e.g., an insect's wing shape) as an adaptation for the function it currently carries out (i.e., flight). This kind of explanation, however, raises problems. If insect wings evolved gradually via natural selection, then the first modest appendages on which selection would operate could not have looked like—or worked like—the wings of living insects. As a result, those early appendages could not have been used for flying. But what adaptive advantage could something that was not yet a wing confer on insect ancestors? Gould and Vrba showed that appendages that were not yet wings could have been adaptive for reasons having nothing to do with flying. For example, the original adaptive function of insect appendages was body cooling, but these appendages were later exapted for the function of flying, once they had reached a certain size or shape (Figure 2.7). Specialists in human evolution like Ian Tattersall (2012, 44) use the concepts of adaptation and exaptation to explain some of the twists and turns in human evolutionary history.

Darwin's theory of evolution by natural selection is elegant and dramatic. As generations of biologists have tested its components in their own research, they have come to examine it critically. For example, much debate has been generated about the concept of fitness. Some people have assumed that the biggest, strongest, toughest individuals must be, by definition, fitter than the smaller, weaker, gentler members of their species. Strictly speaking, however, Darwinian, or biological, fitness is nothing more (and nothing less) than an individual's ability to survive and leave offspring. There is no such thing as "absolute" fitness. In a given environment,

FIGURE 2.7 How did wings evolve for flight? Gould and Vrba (1982) suggest that appendages on early insects were for body cooling but later exapted for flying once they had reached a certain size or shape.

those who leave more offspring behind are fitter than those who leave fewer offspring behind. But any organism that manages to reproduce in that environment is fit. As geneticist Richard Lewontin put it, "In evolutionary terms, an Olympic athlete who never has any children has a fitness of zero, whereas J. S. Bach, who was sedentary and very much overweight, had an unusually high Darwinian fitness by virtue of his having been the father of twenty children" (1982, 150).

Clearly, evolutionary theory has been challenged to show that biological heredity operates to produce ever-renewing variation and to explain how such variation is generated and passed on from parents to offspring.

---

aptation The shaping of any useful feature of an organism, regardless of its origin.

adaptation The shaping of useful features of an organism by natural selection for the function they now perform.

exaptation The shaping of a useful feature of an organism by natural selection to perform one function and the later reshaping of it by different selection pressures to perform a new function.

Darwin's original formulation of the theory of evolution by natural selection was virtually silent about these matters. Darwin was convinced on the basis of considerable evidence that heritable variation must exist, but he and his colleagues were completely ignorant about the sources of variation. Not until the beginning of the twentieth century did knowledge about these matters begin to accumulate, and not until the 1930s did a new evolutionary synthesis of Darwinian principles and genetics become established.

How Did Biologists Learn about Genes?

Offspring tend to look like their parents, which suggests that something unchanging is passed on from one generation to the next. At the same time, offspring are not identical to their parents, which raises the possibility that whatever the parents pass on may be modified by environmental forces. Whether biological inheritance was stable or modifiable, or both, challenged Darwin and his contemporaries.

In the absence of scientific knowledge about heredity, Darwin and many of his contemporaries adopted a theory of heredity that had roots in antiquity: the theory of pangenesis. **Pangenesis** was a theory of inheritance in which multiple particles from both parents blended in their offspring. That is, it claimed that an organism's physical traits are passed on from one generation to the next in the form of distinct particles. Supporters of pangenesis argued that all the organs of both mother and father gave off multiple particles that were somehow transmitted, in different proportions, to each of their offspring. For example, suppose that a child resembled her father more than her mother in a particular trait (say, hair color). Pangenesis explained this by arguing that the child had received more "hair color particles" from her father than from her mother. The particles inherited from both parents were believed to blend in their offspring. Thus, the child's hair color would be closer to her father's shade than to her mother's.

---

pangenesis A theory of heredity suggesting that an organism's physical traits are passed on from one generation to the next in the form of multiple distinct particles given off by all parts of the organism, different proportions of which get passed on to offspring via sperm or egg.

Mendelian inheritance The view that heredity is based on nonblending, single-particle genetic inheritance.

principle of segregation A principle of Mendelian inheritance in which an individual gets one particle (gene) for each trait (i.e., one-half of the required pair) from each parent.

principle of independent assortment A principle of Mendelian inheritance in which each pair of particles (genes) separates independently of every other pair when germ cells (egg and sperm) are formed.

Mendel's Experiments

The notion of particulate inheritance was already common in the middle of the nineteenth century when the Austrian monk Gregor Mendel (1822–1884) began conducting plant-breeding experiments in the garden of his monastery. His great contribution was to provide evidence in favor of nonblending, single-particle inheritance, called **Mendelian inheritance**. When Mendel crossed peas with strikingly different traits, some of those traits did not appear in offspring of the first generation (F1) (see Figure 2.8). They did, however, reappear in their original form in the next generation (F2). Had the particles blended, all the offspring of plants with red flowers and plants with white flowers should have been some shade of pink, but this did not happen, providing strong evidence that the particles responsible for the trait did not blend in offspring but remained discrete.

When Mendel carefully counted the number of offspring in the F2 generation that showed each trait, he consistently came up with a 3:1 ratio of one form to the other, a factor nobody before him had noticed. This ratio recurred whenever Mendel repeated his experiments. If pangenesis were correct, no such ratios would have occurred because each individual would have inherited an unpredictable number of particles from each parent. However, the 3:1 ratio made excellent sense if, as Mendel assumed, each individual inherited only one particle from each parent (Mayr 1982, 721).

The results of his breeding experiments suggested to Mendel something else as well—that the particle responsible for one form of a particular trait (e.g., flower color) could be present in an organism but go unexpressed. Those particles whose traits are expressed in an organism are said to be *dominant*; those whose traits are not expressed are said to be *recessive*. (We now know that sometimes both traits can be expressed, in which case they are said to be *codominant*.) Mendel thus concluded that the particles responsible for a particular trait, such as the pea's flower color, occur in pairs. An individual gets one particle for each trait (i.e., one-half of the pair) from each parent. This is the **principle of segregation**. Mendel further argued that each pair of particles separates independently of every other pair when what he called "germ cells" (egg and sperm) are formed. This is the **principle of independent assortment**. As a result, each sperm and ovum is virtually guaranteed to be different from all others produced by an individual because the collection of particles that each contains will be distinct. Moreover, the pairs of particles that come together in any individual offspring are random, depending on which egg and which sperm happened to unite to form that individual.

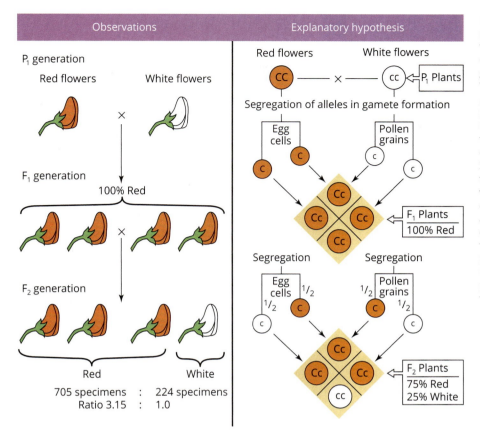

Observations	Explanatory hypothesis

FIGURE 2.8 Mendel crossbred peas with red flowers and peas with white flowers (the parental, or Pl, generation). This produced a generation (F1) of only red flowers. When Mendel crossed red-flowered peas from the F1 generation, they produced the F2 generation of peas in which there were approximately three red-flowered plants for every one plant with white flowers. This 3:1 ratio of red to white flowers, together with the reappearance of white flowers, could be explained if each plant had two genetic factors and the factor for red flowers was dominant. Only a plant with two factors for white flowers would produce white flowers, whereas red flowers would appear in every plant that had at least one factor for red.

The Emergence of Genetics

Mendel's insights were ignored for nearly 35 years until three biologists rediscovered them at the beginning of the twentieth century, resulting in an explosion of research and vast growth of scientific knowledge about heredity. The British scientist William Bateson coined the term **genetics** in 1908 to describe the new science being built on Mendelian principles. He invented the term **homozygous** to describe a fertilized egg that receives the same particle from both parents for a particular trait and the term **heterozygous** to describe a fertilized egg that receives a different particle from each parent for the same trait. In 1909, the Danish geneticist W. L. Johannsen suggested the term **gene** to refer to the particle itself. Although genes occur in pairs in any individual, geneticists discovered that there might be many more than two forms of a given gene. Bateson used the term **alleles** to refer to all the different forms that a particular gene might take.

At first, nobody knew what physical structures corresponded to the genes and alleles they had been describing. However, advances in cell biology led some scientists to suggest that the **chromosomes** in the cell nucleus might play an important role. These sets of paired bodies were easy to see under the microscope because they accepted a colored stain very well (hence

their name, from Greek, meaning "colored bodies"). Animals of different species have different numbers of chromosomes (humans have 46), but all chromosomes are found in pairs (humans have 23 pairs).

What Are the Basics of Contemporary Genetics?

Biologists learned that living cells undergo two different kinds of division. The first kind, **mitosis**, is simply the way cells make copies of themselves (Figure 2.9a).

---

genetics The scientific study of biological heredity.

homozygous Describes a fertilized egg that receives the same particle (or allele) from each parent for a particular trait.

heterozygous Describes a fertilized egg that receives a different particle (or allele) from each parent for the same trait.

gene Portion or portions of the DNA molecule that code for proteins that shape phenotypic traits.

alleles All the different forms that a particular gene might take.

chromosomes Sets of paired bodies in the nucleus of cells that are made of DNA and contain the hereditary genetic information that organisms pass on to their offspring.

mitosis The way body cells make copies of themselves. The pairs of chromosomes in the nucleus of the cell duplicate and line up along the center of the cell. The cell then divides, each daughter cell taking one full set of paired chromosomes.

FIGURE 2.9 Cells divide in two different ways: (a) in mitosis, ordinary body cells double the number of chromosomes they contain before dividing so that each daughter cell carries a full copy of the genetic information in the mother cell; (b) meiosis occurs only when sex cells (sperm or eggs) are produced. In meiosis, each daughter cell retains only half the genetic material of the mother cell; the other half will be supplied when sperm and egg join in fertilization.

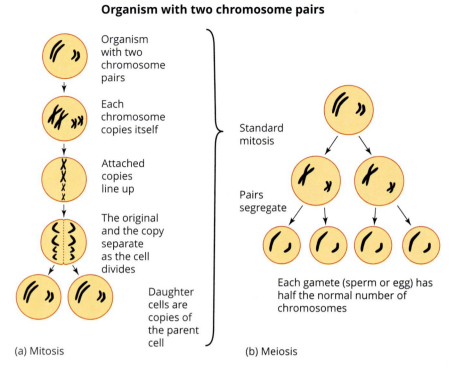

Organism with two chromosome pairs

Organism with two chromosome pairs

Each chromosome copies itself

Attached copies line up

The original and the copy separate as the cell divides

Daughter cells are copies of the parent cell

(a) Mitosis

Standard mitosis

Pairs segregate

Each gamete (sperm or egg) has half the normal number of chromosomes

(b) Meiosis

The process is different, however, when the sex cells (sperm and eggs) are formed. This process is **meiosis**, or reduction division (Figure 2.9b).

The behavior of the chromosomes during meiosis intrigued geneticists. Slides of cells made at different stages in the process showed that chromosomes obey the principles of segregation and independent assortment, just like Mendelian genes. This fact led geneticists, early in the twentieth century, to hypothesize that genes and chromosomes are connected. The first real test of this hypothesis came when a number of geneticists looked at the ratio of males to females among the offspring of sexually reproducing species. They found that this 1:1 ratio is the same as "the ratio resulting from the cross of a heterozygote (*Aa*) and a homozygous recessive (*aa*).

Mendel himself had already suggested this possibility" (Mayr 1982, 750).

A gene was understood as a unit occupying a particular position, or **locus** (plural, *loci*), on the chromosome. Early geneticists discovered that frequently one trait appears in an organism only when another trait is also present. This discovery suggested that the genes responsible for those traits must, for some reason, always be passed on together, a phenomenon called **linkage**. We now know that linkage occurs when genes for different traits occur on the same chromosome (Figure 2.10a). However, in some cases, the expected linkages do not occur. Geneticists eventually discovered that part of a chromosome can break off and reattach itself to a different chromosome during meiosis, a phenomenon known as **crossing over**, or incomplete linkage (Figure 2.10b).

Genes and Traits

Geneticists originally thought (and many nonscientists still believe) that one gene equals one trait. Sometimes a single allele does appear to govern a single physical trait. This may be true of many physical traits that show **discontinuous variation**, that is, sharp breaks from one individual to the next. Recall that the flowers on Mendel's pea plants were either red or white; they did not come in various shades of pink. This observation led Mendel to conclude that a single dominant

---

meiosis The way sex cells make copies of themselves, which begins like mitosis, with chromosome duplication and the formation of two daughter cells. However, each daughter cell then divides again without chromosome duplication and, as a result, contains only a single set of chromosomes rather than the paired set typical of body cells.

locus A portion of the DNA strand responsible for encoding specific parts of an organism's biological makeup.

linkage An inheritance pattern in which unrelated phenotypic traits regularly occur together because the genes responsible for those co-occurring traits are passed on together on the same chromosome.

crossing over The phenomenon that occurs when part of one chromosome breaks off and reattaches itself to a different chromosome during meiosis; also called *incomplete linkage*.

discontinuous variation A pattern of phenotypic variation in which the phenotype (e.g., flower color) exhibits sharp breaks from one member of the population to the next.

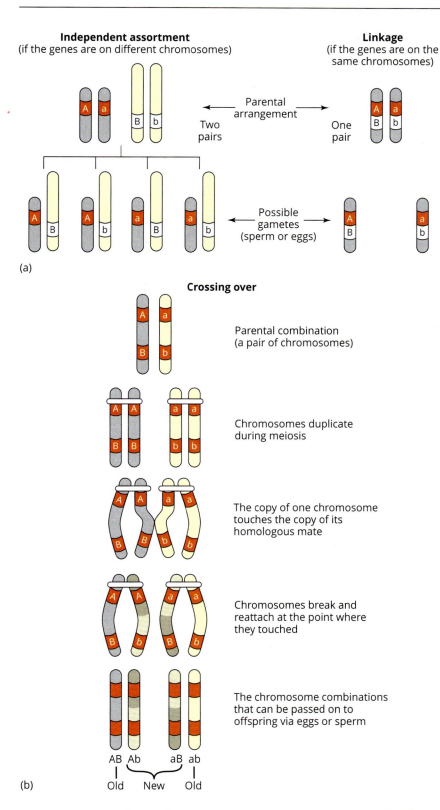

Independent assortment
(if the genes are on different chromosomes)

Linkage
(if the genes are on the same chromosomes)

Parental arrangement

Two pairs

One pair

Possible gametes
(sperm or eggs)

(a)

Crossing over

Parental combination
(a pair of chromosomes)

Chromosomes duplicate
during meiosis

The copy of one chromosome
touches the copy of its
homologous mate

Chromosomes break and
reattach at the point where
they touched

The chromosome combinations
that can be passed on to
offspring via eggs or sperm

AB Ab   aB ab
| | | |
Old   New   Old

(b)

FIGURE 2.10 The principle of independent assortment predicts that genetic factors on different chromosomes will not be passed on together; each will be passed on to a different sex cell during meiosis. (a) Linkage predicts that genetic factors on the same chromosome will tend to be passed on together because it is the chromosomes that separate during meiosis, not individual genes. (b) The predictions about independent assortment and linkage do not hold if chromosomes cross over prior to meiosis. When this occurs, chromosomes break and reattach to their mates, leading to new combinations of genes on each chromosome that can then be passed on to offspring.

particle (or two identical recessive particles) determines flower color.

Early research, however, showed that one gene–one trait was too simplistic an explanation for many hereditary traits. Sometimes many genes are responsible for producing a single trait, such as skin color (Figure 2.12); such traits are thus said to be the result of **polygeny**. Traits like skin color in human beings are different from

traits like flower color in Mendel's peas because they show **continuous variation**. That is, the expression of the trait grades imperceptibly from one individual to

polygeny The phenomenon whereby many genes are responsible for producing a phenotypic trait, such as skin color.

continuous variation A pattern of variation involving polygeny in which phenotypic traits grade imperceptibly from one member of the population to another without sharp breaks.

ANTHROPOLOGY *in Everyday Life*

Investigating Human-Rights Violations and Identifying Remains

In Argentina, between 1976 and 1983, more than 10,000 people disappeared during the "dirty war" waged by the Argentine military government against supposed subversives. A not-for-profit nongovernmental organization called the Equipo Argentino de Antropología Forense (EAAF, Argentine Forensic Anthropology Team; Figures 1.6 and 2.11) was established in 1984 to investigate the cases of the disappeared. This organization, which notable anthropologist Clyde Snow helped found, has gone on to investigate human-rights violations in more than forty countries—from Bolivia, Bosnia, and Brazil to Guatemala, Venezuela, Kosovo, and Zimbabwe. They have also trained similar forensic teams in Chile, Guatemala, Peru, and elsewhere. The EAAF takes a multidisciplinary approach to its work, drawing on both forensic and cultural anthropology, archaeology, dental analysis, human genetics, pathology, ballistics, and computer science.

FIGURE 2.11 Members of the Argentine Forensic Anthropology Team excavating in the Avellaneda cemetery, sector 134, where Karina's family was secretly buried.

Their formal mission includes six objectives:

1. Apply forensic scientific methodology to the investigation and documentation of human-rights violations.

2. Give testimony of our findings in trials and other judicial inquiries in human-rights cases.

3. Provide identification of the victims, providing closure for victims' families.

4. Train new teams in other countries where investigations into human-rights violations are necessary.

5. Conduct seminars on the applications of forensic science to the investigation of human-rights violations in cooperation with human-rights organizations, judicial systems, and forensic institutes.

6. Collect and analyze scientific evidence of massive human-rights violations, providing data to reconstruct the often distorted or hidden histories of repressive regimes (Doretti and Snow 2009, 306).

One example of their work, which Doretti and Snow (2009) call the Manfil Case, illustrates both the multidisciplinary skills of the EAAF and the profound human drama that human-rights violations generate. In 1991, the EAAF team was working in Sector 134, a small, walled-off area inside a huge municipal cemetery in Avellaneda, a suburb of Buenos Aires, Argentina. One day, an eighteen-year-old woman named Karina Manfil approached them and informed them of her search for her family, who had disappeared fifteen years earlier during a death-squad raid on their home on October 27, 1976. Someone had told her that her parents and little brother might be buried in Sector 134.

At that time, the EAAF had been working in Sector 134 for three years using their regular four-step approach: (1) historical research, (2) collection of antemortem (predeath) data, (3) archaeology, and (4) laboratory analysis (Doretti and Snow 2009, 308). In conducting historical research, they collected information from written records and through interviews with witnesses toward the goal of answering questions such as "Why was the grave made, and how long was it used to bury bodies? Who made the grave? How was it made? How many people may be buried there?" (308). The researchers discovered that the death squads who operated during the dirty war had created a network of clandestine detention centers (CDCs) throughout the country and that CDCs tended to use the same cemetery for disposing of the remains of their victims. This meant that the remains of people who were swept up together in raids (members of the same political party, student group, union, or occupation) at times ended up in the same cemetery, sometimes in the same grave. This pattern also applied to families who were arrested together.

Once the historical investigation gave some sense of who might be buried in the Avellaneda cemetery, the team collected antemortem data—such as age at death, sex, height, handedness, dental work, and any old injuries—through interviews with family members, doctors, and dentists. As DNA testing became more sophisticated, they also took DNA samples from relatives. They could then apply these data to the analysis of skeletal material recovered.

Third, the team used archaeological techniques to excavate the cemetery. In Sector 134, they found nineteen mass graves, eleven single burials, and more than 300 bullets. In the mass graves, the number of skeletons ranged from ten to twenty-eight. Nearly all had been buried without clothing or jewelry. Laboratory analysis, the fourth step in EAAF's approach, indicated the remains of 324 individuals—104 more than cemetery records indicated. About three-quarters of the skeletons were male, about a third elderly, but most of the female skeletons were of women who were between the ages of 21 and 35 at the time of death. The elderly seemed to have died of natural causes. Almost all of the much larger group of younger individuals (male and female) had died of gunshot wounds.

Through their work, the EAAF team who took on Karina's quest were able to reconstruct what had happened on the night of October 27. A joint police-army death squad had broken into the Manfil family's third-floor apartment, where most of the family members were asleep: 35-year-old Carlos Manfil, a politically active member of the party that had been overthrown by the military; his 28-year-old wife, Angélica; and three of their four children—Carlitos, age 9; Karina herself, age 4; and 6-month-old Cristian. Also asleep in the apartment were guests of the Manfils: Rosario Ramírez, her husband José Vega, and their two children. As the attack began, 9-year-old Carlitos leaned out the window to see what was happening and was shot in the forehead. The other children hid under the bed and were wounded when the attackers sprayed the room with bullets.

The EAAF team determined that Karina's mother, Angélica, was killed inside the apartment. The other three adults tried to escape by climbing down the drainpipes. Carlos Manfil and Rosario Ramirez fell, fracturing their legs, and were shot and killed on the spot. Karina, her infant sibling Cristian, and the two Vega children, apparently overlooked by the death squad, were the only survivors. José Vega escaped but was caught about a year later and disappeared. The bodies of Carlos and Angélica, their son Carlitos, and Rosario Ramirez were not returned to their families; and the families were not even informed of their deaths. Some family members heard rumors that they were buried in Sector 134. The team interviewed family members about the antemortem details of the people who had disappeared and searched the official records, where they discovered the death certificates that showed that the bodies had, in fact, been buried in Sector 134.

The only skeleton of a young boy recovered from this sector had a gunshot entrance wound in the frontal bone of the skull. The archaeological records showed that this particular skeleton came from a mass grave containing several adult skeletons, including three that matched the sex, age, height, and dental information that family members had provided about Carlos, Angélica, and Rosario. The male and one of the females had perimortem (meaning from around or at the time of death) fractures of the long bones of the legs. In 1991, the EAAF group found a file on the Manfil case from a military court that included an autopsy report, which described gunshot wounds and leg fractures corresponding to those of the skeletons.

The EAAF team felt that they could provisionally identify the skeletons but were not yet able to make a positive identification. So they sent bone samples to a lab at Oxford University, where nuclear DNA was extracted; and they sent teeth from each skull, along with blood samples from family members, to a lab at the University of California Berkeley for mitochondrial DNA (mtDNA) testing. By August 1992, the geneticists had connected the DNA of two of the skeletons—those of Carlitos and his mother, Angélica. Furthermore, the mtDNA testing of a tooth from the skeleton believed to be Angélica's matched the mtDNA from the blood of her daughter Karina; and the mtDNA of the male presumed to be Carlos Manfil matched mtDNA from the blood of his mother. The genetic analyses confirmed the historical and anthropological results, and the Argentine Federal Court of Appeals accepted the EAAF report on the Manfil case, releasing the remains to the family. This case marked the first time that the court had accepted DNA evidence for skeletal identification. It took several more years to locate relatives of Rosario Ramirez, but once found, DNA analysis established a positive identification of the remaining skeleton. "In December 1992, Karina's sixteen-year quest finally ended when she was able to inter the long-lost bones of her father, mother, and little brother Carlitos in a modest family crypt. Ironically, it stands in the cemetery of Avellaneda, not far from Sector 134" (Doretti and Snow 2009, 311).

Despite the difficulty in resolving such cases, the EAAF continues its work. They point out that their work benefits from the four-field anthropological approach: their skills as biological anthropologists are complemented by their training in archaeology, which allows them to excavate properly and to interpret the burials they find, and their training in cultural anthropology, which provides them "with some insight and sensitivity in dealing with families and communities oppressed by the violence" (Doretti and Snow 2009, 329). The EAAF's website is www.eaaf.org.

FIGURE 2.12 Skin color in human populations shows continuous variation, that is, different skin shades grade imperceptibly into one another without sharp breaks. Geneticists have shown that such continuous variation is produced by polygeny, the interaction of many genes to produce a single, observable trait.

another, without sharp breaks. The discovery of polygenic inheritance showed that Mendelian concepts could be used to explain discontinuous and continuous variation alike.

Perhaps even more surprising than polygenic activity was the discovery that a single gene may affect more than one trait, a phenomenon called **pleiotropy**. For example, the *S* allele that gives human red blood cells increased resistance to malarial parasites also reduces the amount of oxygen these cells

can carry (Rothwell 1977, 18). Similarly, the allele that causes the feathers of chickens to be white also works to slow down their body growth (Lerner and Libby 1976). The discovery of pleiotropy showed that genes do not produce traits in isolation. Many geneticists came to focus attention on what the Russian geneticist Sergei Chetverikov called the "genetic milieu," investigating the effects that different genes could have on one another (Figure 2.13). For example, Theodosius Dobzhansky was able to demonstrate that "certain genes or chromosomes could convey superior fitness in some combinations, and be lethal in combination with other chromosomes" (Mayr 1982, 580).

---

pleiotropy The phenomenon whereby a single gene may affect more than one phenotypic trait.

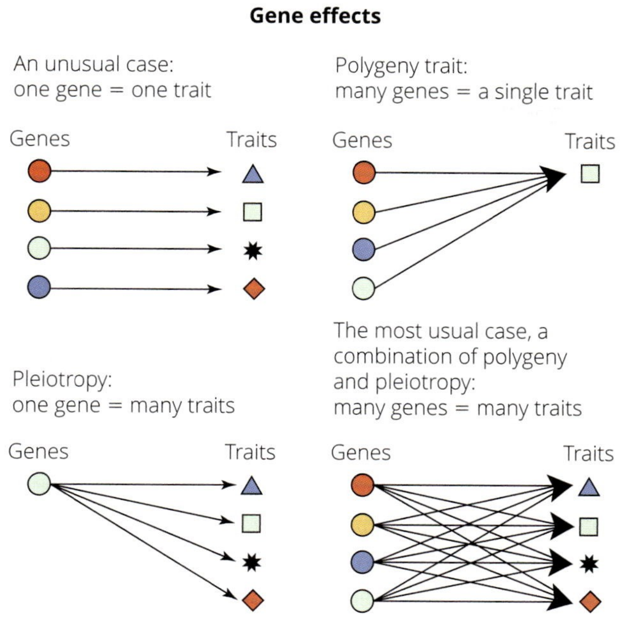

Gene effects

An unusual case:
one gene = one trait

Genes   Traits

Polygeny trait:
many genes = a single trait

Genes   Traits

The most usual case, a
combination of polygeny
and pleiotropy:
many genes = many traits

Pleiotropy:
one gene = many traits

Genes   Traits

Genes   Traits

FIGURE 2.13 Only rarely is a single physical trait the result of the action of a single gene. Many traits are the result of gene interaction, involving polygeny or pleiotropy or, as is usually the case, both.

Mutation

Early in the twentieth century, geneticists discovered that very occasionally a new allele can result when the old form of a gene suddenly changes (or undergoes a **mutation**) but that otherwise, genes are stable. Mutation thus explains how genetic inheritance can be unchanging and still produce the variation that makes evolutionary change possible (Mayr 1982, 755). Being part of a process of stable inheritance means, however, that the occurrence of genetic mutations is random with respect to the adaptive challenges facing the organism in which it occurs: mutations do not occur because the organism "needs" them. Thus, modern geneticists rejected Lamarckian transformational evolution because it assumes a theory of modifiable inheritance. That is, to put it in modern terms, Lamarck assumed that information about the adaptive needs of an organism can somehow be fed back directly into the eggs or sperm cells of that organism, reshaping the information they contain, thereby allowing an adaptation to be passed on to offspring.

Modern genetics, by contrast, assumes that, apart from mutation, genes are inherited unchanged from parent organisms and that it is impossible for an organism's experiences or "needs" to feed back and reshape the genetic information in the sex cells. Natural selection can act only on randomly produced variation, which makes evolution by natural selection a two-step process. First, random genetic variation is produced. Second, those organisms whose variant traits better equip them to meet

environmental challenges survive and produce more off-spring than those whose traits equip them less well. The modern evolutionary synthesis of the 1930s and 1940s had barely come into existence when the basic structure of chromosomes was discovered in the 1950s.

It is important to emphasize that, from the point of view of modern population biology, *individual organisms* do not evolve genetically According to the modern evolutionary synthesis, individual organisms are stuck with the genes they are born with. An individual's genes can be altered only by mutations (or the interventions of genetic engineering). However, the *populations* to which individuals belong *can evolve* as each generation contributes different numbers of offspring to the generation that comes after it. Put another way, from a Darwinian perspective, the only *biological* effect an individual can have on its population's evolution is in terms of the *number of offspring* that it bequeaths to the next generation. More (or fewer) offspring mean more (or fewer) copies of parental genes in the next generation. This is why population biologists traditionally track evolutionary change by measuring changes in gene frequencies in populations over time.

DNA and the Genome

The modern evolutionary synthesis of the 1930s and 1940s had barely come into existence when the basic structure of chromosomes was discovered in the 1950s, greatly expanded our understanding of genetic mutation. We now know that chromosomes are made up largely of long molecules of deoxyribonucleic acid, or **DNA**, parts of which are used by living cells as templates for the construction, or *synthesis*, of proteins that make up most of the tissues and organs of any living organism. The DNA molecule, assembled in the shape of a double helix, resembles a twisted ladder, the rungs of which are made up of chemical components called "bases." Although there are many bases, DNA ordinarily makes use of only four: guanine, cytosine, adenine, and thymine. Each rung of the DNA ladder is made up of two of these bases: guanine always links to cytosine, and adenine always links to thymine. Faithful copies of DNA molecules are made when chromosomes are copied prior to mitosis or meiosis. The biochemical machinery of the cell breaks the chemical bonds holding the bases together,

---

mutation The creation of a new allele for a gene when the portion of the DNA molecule to which it corresponds is suddenly altered.

DNA (deoxyribonucleic acid) The structure that carries the genetic heritage of an organism as a kind of blueprint for the organism's construction and development.

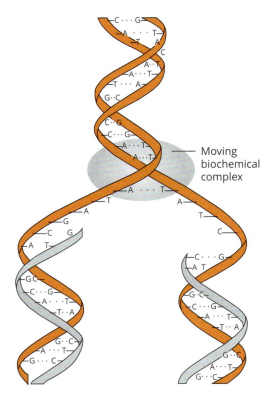

Moving biochemical complex

FIGURE 2.14 For DNA to replicate, a biochemical complex moves along the molecule and "unzips" the double helix, and two complete copies are rebuilt from appropriate molecules floating in the nucleus. Adenine (A) always attracts thymine (T), and cytosine (C) always attracts guanine (G).

and the DNA ladder splits apart, like a zipper unzipping (Figure 2.14). The absent half of each separated strand of DNA is then rebuilt from appropriate complementary bases that float freely within the nucleus of a cell. When this process is complete, two identical copies of the same DNA molecule are produced.

The sum total of all the genetic material in the cell nucleus is called the **genome**. We know today that the human genome contains approximately 20,000 genes, but these account for less than 2% of the entire genome. Geneticists know that some noncoding DNA in the genome is involved in regulatory functions, but we remain ignorant of the functions played by much of it.

Discovery of the structure and operation of DNA solidified the rejection of Lamarckian views by geneticists. At the same time, knowledge of DNA explained what mutations were: changes in the structure of the DNA molecule. Cosmic radiation, heat, and chemicals can all alter the structure of DNA; when these alterations occur in the sex cells, they can be passed on to offspring.

Mutations can be harmful or helpful, but they may also have no effect at all. Mutations that neither help

nor harm an organism are called "neutral" mutations. Molecular biologists have found an enormous amount of variation in those portions of the DNA molecule involved in protein synthesis, much of which appears to be neutral, although this is controversial.

When segments of the DNA molecule are required for particular cellular processes, parts of the cellular machinery enter the cell nucleus, unwind the relevant portion of a chromosome, and make copies of (or *transcribe*) relevant portions of the DNA molecule. These transcriptions are then transported into the cytoplasm of the cell and used to construct proteins, molecules that are basic to an organism's life processes (Figure 2.15). But this process is far from simple. Ironically perhaps, the more molecular biologists have learned about the way DNA functions in cells, the more difficult it has become for them to provide an unambiguous definition of what a "gene" is and what it does. As biologist Henry Plotkin (2003) observes, until the 1950s, geneticists assumed that genes occupied discrete positions on chromosomes, "like beads on a string."

This image has had to be radically revised. Genes, it turns out, are structurally complex, almost messy. They are smeared across chromosomes, with large reaches of DNA not coding for anything as far as currently known. Genes also form complex families of spatially widespread units. . . . Far from being rather dull, inert, passive stores of information, genes interact in dynamic ways with other cellular molecules, including their own products. (38)

Many popular accounts of genes portray DNA as an all-powerful "master molecule" that determines an organism's physical appearance, with the added assumption that unless genes mutate, new physical traits will never appear. This is incorrect. Biologist Mary Jane West-Eberhard (2003) points out that most of the genetic variation in multicellular organisms comes from the shuffling of existing genetic sequences at different stages of the developmental process, rather than from mutation (334). Moreover, when more and more different developmental events become dependent on the same DNA sequences, these sequences become more resistant to evolutionary change, a phenomenon known as generative entrenchment (West-Eberhard 2003, 326; Wimsatt and Schank 1988). For these reasons, many biologists argue that an exclusive focus on the role of DNA in evolution must give way to a more complex view that situates genes as one component in the biological processes of living cells, playing different roles at different stages in the life cycles of developing organisms and in the evolutionary histories of living species. This is why developmental biologist Anne Fausto-Sterling urges us not to "get stuck trying to divide nature from nurture,"

genome The sum total of all the genetic information about an organism, carried on the chromosomes in the cell nucleus.

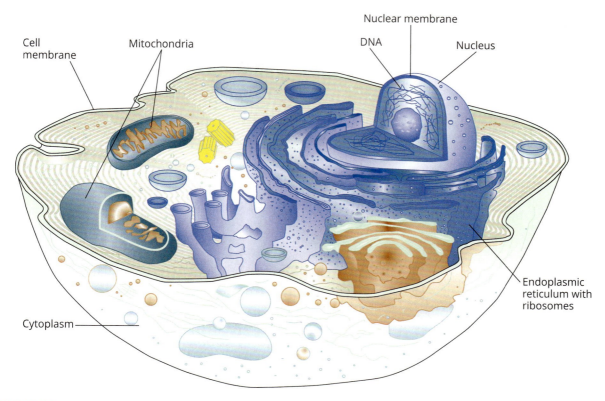

FIGURE 2.15   A nucleated cell is a complex system involving many components. DNA replication and protein synthesis are cellular processes that both involve and affect many cellular components.

and never to forget "that living bodies are dynamic systems that develop and change in response to their social and historical contexts" (2012, xii). In other words, we should "think developmentally and appreciate biological diversity," remembering above all that "bodies are not bounded" (2012, xxi, 119). These observations resonate well with the relational approach to human biology, development, and evolution described in Chapter 1 in which Tim Ingold argues that humans need to be understood as "biosocial becomings"—"not as discrete and pre-formed entities but as trajectories of movement and growth" (Ingold 2013, 8).

Genotype, Phenotype, and the Norm of Reaction

Geneticists realized long ago that the molecular structure of genes (or **genotype**) had to be distinguished from the observable, measurable, overt characteristics of an organism that genes help to produce (its **phenotype**). For example, the sequences of bases on a stretch of DNA (genotypes) are used by living cells to assemble strings of amino acids that bond to form proteins (phenotypes), but bases are not the same thing as protein molecules. How does a genotype get realized in a

phenotype? The question is not idle because fertilized eggs do not turn into organisms in a vacuum. Living organisms grow in a physical environment that provides them with nourishment, protection, and other vital resources to support their development over time until they are mature and able to reproduce their own offspring. Without the raw materials for protein synthesis supplied by the ovum, and later by food, genotypes can do nothing. At the same time, just as one gene does not equal one trait; different genotypes may be associated with the same phenotype. Mendel first showed this when he was able to demonstrate the existence of recessive genes. That is, red flowers could be produced by homozygous dominant parents (i.e., both red) as well as by heterozygous parents (i.e., one red and one white), but only one in every four offspring of heterozygous parents would have the chance of producing white flowers (i.e., if it received a recessive white gene from each parent). Nevertheless, individuals with the same genotype—twins, for example, or cuttings from a single plant or cloned animals—may also develop a range of different phenotypes.

genotype   The genetic information about particular biological traits encoded in an organism's DNA.

phenotype   The observable, measurable overt characteristics of an organism.

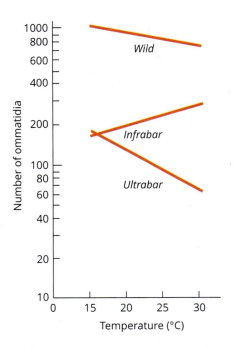

FIGURE 2.16 Each genotype has its own norm of reaction, specifying how the developing organism will respond to various environments. How many eye cells (*ommatidia*) a fruit fly develops depends both on that fly's genotype and on the environmental temperature at which development takes place. Not only does the same genotype produce different phenotypes at different temperatures, but also different genotypes may produce the same phenotype at the same temperatures (Levins and Lewontin 1985, 91).

To understand how we get from an organism's genotype to its phenotype, we must consider both genotype and phenotype in relation to the environment in which that organism developed. Biologists compare the phenotypic outcomes of organisms with the same genotype in different environments and with different genotypes in the same environment, and they plot these outcomes on what is called a **norm of reaction**. Levins and Lewontin (1985) define the norm of reaction as "a table or graph of correspondence between the phenotypic outcome of development and the environment in which the development took place. Each genotype has its own norm of reaction, specifying how the developing organism will respond to various environments. In general, a genotype cannot be characterized by a unique phenotype" (90–91).

Figure 2.16 shows the norms of reaction for three different genotypes for a particular trait in *Drosophila*, the fruit fly. The genotype in question controls the number of ommatidia, or light-receptor cells, that a particular individual will have in its compound eye. Flies carrying the Wild genotype usually have about 1,000 ommatidia in

norm of reaction A table or graph that displays the possible range of phenotypic outcomes for a given genotype in different environments.

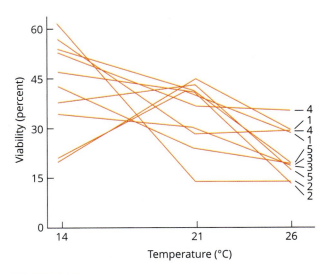

FIGURE 2.17 Comparison of norms of reaction for variant fruit fly genotypes in variant environments shows two things: (1) some genotypes always do better than others at any temperature, and (2) no single genotype does better than all the rest at every temperature. Such evidence argues against the concept of a single, ideal genotype that is supposed to be produced deterministically by the genes (Levins and Lewontin 1985, 92).

their eyes, whereas those with the Ultrabar and Infrabar genotypes have far fewer. However, as the graph shows, the number of ommatidia a fly develops depends not only on that fly's genotype but also on the environment (in this case, the temperature) at which development takes place—that is, the same genotype produces different phenotypes at different temperatures.

Figure 2.16 demonstrates yet another surprising fact about the relationship of genes to the environment: at about 15°C, both Ultrabar and Infrabar genotypes develop about the same number of ommatidia! In other words, different genotypes may also produce the same phenotype in a particular environment. This fact illustrates what Levins and Lewontin (1985) call the "many-to-many relationship among gene and organism" (94) and shows that the fitness of a particular genotype can vary depending on the environment. Figure 2.17 displays norms of reaction for the survival at different temperatures of immature fruit flies with different genotypes, all of which were taken from natural populations. As the graph illustrates, some genotypes always do better than others at any given temperature, but there is no single genotype that does better than all the rest at every temperature. The complexity of the relationship among genes, organism, and environment does not mean "that the organism is infinitely plastic, or that any genotype can correspond to any phenotype. Norms of reaction for different genotypes are different, but it is the norms of reaction that are the proper object of study for developmental biologists rather than some ideal organism that is supposed to be produced deterministically by the genes" (Levins and Lewontin 1985, 94).

The principles apply to humans as well. Different genotypes can produce the same phenotype in some environments, and the same genotype can produce different phenotypes in different environments. Despite very different genotypes, the eyes of newborn babies all tend to be the same color, as does hair color as we age. Indeed, the phenotype of a single individual can vary markedly from one environment to the next. As Richard Lewontin pointed out four decades ago, "People who 'tend to be fat' on 5,500 calories a day 'tend to be thin' on 2,000. Families with both 'tendencies' will be found living in the same towns in Northeastern Brazil, where two thirds of the families live on less than what is considered a minimum subsistence diet by the World Health Organization" (1982, 20). So, what is it about the "environments" of these families that is responsible for their varying caloric intakes? If bodies are unbounded dynamic systems that develop and change in response to their social and biological contexts, answers to this question will require greater attention to the specific features of the wider social and biological contexts in which these families, and other human groups, move and grow.

Niche Construction

One promising source of insight into the social and biological contexts in which humans (and other organisms) move and grow has been proposed by evolutionary theorists who look not only at how organism's phenotypes are shaped by environments but also *how organisms shape the environments in which they develop.* In their book *Niche Construction,* F. John Odling-Smee, Kevin Laland, and Marcus Feldman (2003) build on a concept first suggested by Richard Lewontin (1991) and argue that organisms play two roles in evolution: carrying genes and interacting with environments.

> Specifically, organisms interact with environments, take energy and resources from environments, make micro- and macrohabitat choices with respect to environments, construct artifacts, emit detritus and die in environments, and by doing all these things, modify at least some of the natural selection pressures in their own and in each other's local environments. This second role for phenotypes in evolution is not well described or understood by evolutionary biologists and has not been subject to a great deal of investigation. We call it "niche construction." (Odling-Smee et al. 2003, 1)

Niche construction is understood to occur either when an organism actively perturbs the environment or when it actively moves into a different environment

FIGURE 2.18 Many species, including beavers, construct key features of their own ecological niches. Beaver dams modify selection pressures experienced by beavers, but they also alter selection pressures experienced by neighboring species whose own niches are altered by the presence of the beaver dam in their habitats.

(Odling-Smee et al. 2003, 41). If the physical, environmental consequences of niche construction are erased between generations, this process can have no long-term effects on evolution. But if these consequences endure, they feed back into the evolutionary process, *modifying the selection pressures* experienced by subsequent generations of organisms (Figure 2.18). Odling-Smee et al. (2003) provide numerous examples taken from all taxonomic groups of living organisms, including blue-green algae, earthworms, dam-building beavers, burrowing rodents, and nest-building birds (50–115). Their most controversial proposal is that niche construction be incorporated into evolutionary theory as an additional adaptive process alongside natural selection, and that nongenetic "legacies of modified natural selection

niche construction When organisms actively perturb the environment in ways that modify the selection pressures experienced by subsequent generations of organisms.

How Living Organisms Construct Their Environments

Geneticist Richard Lewontin rejects the notion that living organisms are passively molded by the "environment," thereby challenging us to rethink exactly what an environment is.

We must replace the adaptationist view of life with a constructionist one. It is not that organisms find environments and either adapt themselves to the environments or die. They actually *construct* their environment out of bits and pieces. In this sense, the environment of organisms is coded in their DNA, and we find ourselves in a kind of reverse Lamarckian position. Whereas Lamarck supposed that changes in the external world would cause changes in the internal structures, we see that the reverse is true. An organism's genes, to the extent that they influence what that organism does in its behavior, physiology, and morphology, are at the same time helping to construct an environment. So, if genes change in evolution, the environment of the organism will change, too.

Consider the immediate environment of a human being. If one takes motion pictures of a person, using schlieren optics that detect differences in the refractive index of the air, one can see that a layer of warm, moist air completely surrounds each one of us and is slowly rising from our legs and bodies and going off the top of our heads. In fact, every living organism, including trees, has this boundary layer of warm air that is created by the organism's metabolism. The result is that we are encapsulated in a little atmosphere created by our own metabolic activities. One consequence is what is called the wind-chill factor. The reason that it gets much colder when the wind blows across us is because the wind is blowing away the boundary layer and our skins are then exposed to a different set of temperatures and humidities. Consider a mosquito feeding on the surface of the human body. That mosquito is completely immersed in the boundary layer that we have constructed. It is living in a warm, moist world. Yet one of the most common evolutionary changes for all organisms is a change in size, and over and over again organisms have evolved to be larger. If the mosquito species begins to evolve to a larger size, it may

in fact find itself with its back in the "stratosphere" and only up to its knees in the warm, moist boundary layer while it is feeding. The consequence will be that the mosquito's evolution has put it into an entirely different world. Moreover, as human beings early in their evolution lost hair and the distribution of sweat glands over their bodies changed, the thickness of the boundary layer changed and so changed the microworld that they carry with them, making it rather less hospitable for fleas, mosquitoes, and other parasites that live on hairy animals. The first rule of the real relation between organisms and environment is that environments do not exist in the absence of organisms but are constructed by them out of bits and pieces of the external world.

The second rule is that the environment of organisms is constantly being remade during the life of those living beings. When plants send down roots, they change the physical nature of the soil, breaking it up and aerating it. They exude organic molecules, humic acids, that change the soil's chemical nature as well. They make it possible for various beneficial fungi to live together with them and penetrate their root systems. They change the height of the water table by removing water. They alter the humidity in their immediate neighborhood, and the upper leaves of a plant change the amount of light that is available to the lower leaves. When the Canadian Department of Agriculture takes weather records for agricultural purposes, they do not set up a weather station in an open field or on the roof of a building. They take measurements of temperature and humidity at various levels above the ground in a field of growing plants because the plants are constantly changing the physical conditions that are relevant to agriculture. Moles burrow in the soil. Earthworms through their castings completely change the local topology. Beavers have had at least as important an effect on the landscape in North America as humans did until the beginning of the last century. Every breath you take removes oxygen and adds carbon dioxide to the world. Mort Sahl once said, "Remember, no matter how cruel and nasty and evil you may be, every time you take a breath you make a flower happy."

Source: Lewontin 1991, 112–14.

pressures" be recognized in addition to the genetic legacies passed on in the egg and sperm. In their view, a suitably extended evolutionary theory would recognize both niche construction and natural selection as evolutionary processes contributing together to the dynamic adaptive match between organisms and environments (Odling-Smee et al. 2003, 2–3).

Taking niche construction into account encourages biologists to look at organisms in a new way. Rather than picturing them as passively staying in place, subject to selection pressures they cannot affect, organisms are now seen as sometimes capable of actively intervening in their evolutionary fate by *modifying the environment:* Odling-Smee et al. (2003) predict that "those members of the population that are least fit relative to the imposed selective regime will be the individuals that exhibit the strongest evidence for niche construction" (298). Alternatively, organisms that *move into a new environment* with different selection pressures can no longer be automatically identified as the unquestionable losers in evolutionary competition in their former environment. Niche construction portrays all organisms (not just human organisms) as active agents living in environments that are vulnerable to the consequences of their activities, contributing in potentially significant ways to the evolutionary histories of their own and other species.

According to Odling-Smee et al. (2003), acknowledging niche construction as an adaptive process offers a way to link evolutionary theory and ecosystem ecology, and it also alters the relationship between evolutionary theory and the human sciences (3). Odling-Smee and colleagues regard human beings as "virtuoso niche constructors" (367), and their arguments offer resources to anthropologists who insist that any evolutionary explanation of change in human societies must make room for **human agency**: the way people struggle, often against great odds, to exercise some control over their lives. At the same time, niche construction theorists remind us that humans are not the only agents at work: other organisms and the nonliving ecological artifacts they (and we) have created (nests, burrows, the ozone hole) also play roles in shaping evolutionary outcomes. The agency of organisms as niche constructors matters in evolution "because it introduces feedback into the evolutionary dynamic [which] significantly modifies the selection pressures [on organisms]" (Odling-Smee et al. 2003, 2; see also Deacon 2003). As we will see in later chapters, we as humans are never free to do exactly as we please but always have options for action. And the actions we choose to undertake can sometimes reshape the selective pressures we experience, exactly as niche construction theorists would predict.

What Does Evolution Mean?

Ever since Darwin, evolutionary theory has been subjected to repeated testing. The outcomes of those tests have sometimes led to modifications of the theory, as happened when the modern evolutionary synthesis selection was negotiated in the middle of the twentieth century. Scholars and scientists active in the field acknowledge that a phenomenon as complex as evolution requires theoretical pluralism—that is, the recognition that a variety of processes operating at different levels work together to produce the similarities and differences that characterize the living world. Evolutionary theorists Peter Richerson, Robert Boyd, and Joseph Henrich concede this when they observe that "any sentence that starts with 'evolutionary theory predicts' should be regarded with caution" (2003, 366). Now, at the beginning of the twenty-first century, increasing numbers of evolutionary theorists are arguing that new research and new data have proliferated to the point where an expanded evolutionary synthesis is needed (Figure 2.19). Among the supporters of an expanded synthesis are many anthropologists who are persuaded that this new work helps strengthen our own analyses of human evolution.

For example, niche construction was originally proposed by evolutionary theorists who borrowed mathematical methods from population biologists, and yet it is quite apparent that niche construction theory fits uncomfortably (if at all) within the current configuration of the modern evolutionary synthesis. At the same time, niche construction has been taken up by anthropologists who are less concerned about mathematical models than they are attracted to the conceptual insights offered by niche construction. In Philip Kitcher's (1982) phrasing, niche construction gives structure to our ignorance. For instance, as originally formulated, niche construction acknowledges the importance not simply of biological factors (such as genes), or cultural factors (such as ideas in people's heads), but also of nonliving ("abiotic") material artifacts that are produced by niche-constructing organisms and that regularly outlast them. This triple formulation destabilizes rigid binaries between biology and culture and resonates both with science studies formulations of heterogeneous networks and with relational evolutionary thinking that focuses on processes of biosocial becoming. For instance, archaeologist Nicole Boivin (2008) combines insights from science studies scholars, the writings of Tim Ingold, and

---

human agency The way people struggle, often against great odds, to exercise some control over their lives.

FIGURE 2.19 The scope of evolutionary theory has broadened and deepened over time. Evolutionary theorists Massimo Pigliucci and Gerd Müller represent these changes in this graphic. Darwin's original views are within the inner oval; the features added by the Modern Synthesis are encompassed within the middle oval; and new developments in evolutionary biology that may presage a new, extended synthesis, are included in the outermost oval.

Source: Pigliucci and Müller, 2010.

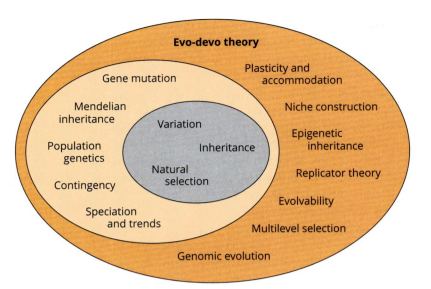

niche construction theory in her analysis of the impact of things on human thought, society, and evolution.

For his part, Kevin Laland, one of the original architects of niche construction theory, has collaborated with archaeologist Michael O'Brien (Laland and O'Brien 2010). Laland has also called into question traditional assumptions about genes as master molecules, acknowledging that developmental biologists find this assumption to be "inconsistent with the dynamic, reciprocal nature of development and inheritance," which their research has produced (2017, 334, n 1). And biological anthropologist Agustín Fuentes, elaborating a relational approach to human evolution (2013), emphasizes the importance both of niche construction and of multiple inheritance theory, developed by Eva Jablonka and Marion Lamb (2005). Jablonka and Lamb argue for the recognition of four primary modes of inheritance in evolutionary theory: (1) genetic inheritance; (2) epigenetic inheritance (such as nongenetic changes in cellular structures that can be passed along in cell lineages when cells divide); (3) behavioral inheritance, involving learning from others; and (4) symbolic inheritance, associated with human language and unique to our species. If you look again at Figure 2.19, you will see that epigenetic inheritance and niche construction are both listed as components of the proposed extended evolutionary synthesis.

Finally, there is an unavoidable intersection between the processes identified by niche construction theory and other discussions of the ways human activities have reshaped the earth over thousands of years, creating a new, identifiable geological epoch that is being called the Anthropocene. Laland makes this connection explicit (2017, 235, 263), as have anthropologists like Gisli Pálsson, who writes that "during the current age of the Anthropocene, practically everything 'natural' on planet Earth is undergoing change as a result of human impact.

It now seems clear that 'natural' climate has much to do with 'artificial' human services and goods—and it is rapidly changing. . . . Thus, growing awareness of environmental epigenetic processes independent of the genetic code necessarily complicates the classic differentiation between 'nature's handiwork' and the 'artificial' products of human creativity" (2013, 236-37).

Differences in approach definitely remain, but some evolutionary theorists inside and outside anthropology are making strong efforts, however partial or awkward, to bridge these differences. To quote Gisli Pálsson again, "The point is not to silence other voices or to establish a new elite, but to open up an innovative space for theoretical developments that take the merging of the biological and the social for granted" (2013, 248).

Life has a comprehensible history for modern evolutionists. How it is likely to change next, however, cannot be predicted with any certainty because random factors continue to play an important evolutionary role. Human biologists have been forced to rethink the place of their own species in the web of life. Unquestionably, the result has been to dislodge human beings from the center. Moreover, once we consider our own species alongside other species whose comings and goings have been so well documented in the fossil record, we cannot avoid grappling with the following well-known facts:

> The only certainty about the future of our species is that it is limited. Of all the species that have ever existed 99.999% are extinct. The average lifetime of a carnivore genus is only 10 million years, and the average lifetime of a species is much shorter. Indeed, life on earth is nearly half over: Fossil evidence shows that life began about 3 billion years ago, and the sun is due to become a red giant about 4 billion years from now, consuming life (and eventually the whole earth) in its fire. (Lewontin 1982, 169)

Who knows? Perhaps we will find a way to spread beyond our solar system, and our descendants may escape the grim fate that awaits our planet in 4 billion years—or even sooner, given current scientific predictions about the rate and consequences of climate change. In the meantime, we remain on earth, searching for answers about who we are and how we are to live our lives.

Chapter Summary

1. Evolutionary theory is a testable, unified, and fruitful scientific theory. Charles Darwin and Alfred Russel Wallace laid its foundations with their theory of natural selection in 1859, but since then evolutionary theory has expanded far beyond those foundations. At the end of the nineteenth century, it seemed that genetics might displace the role of natural selection in evolutionary theory, but natural selection and genetics were brought together in the modern evolutionary synthesis of the 1930s and 1940s. Since that time, many new findings and theoretical developments have led theoretical biologists to call for an expanded evolutionary synthesis that would incorporate these new materials.

2. Before Darwin, European thinkers divided living things into natural kinds, each of which was thought to have its own unchanging essence. The Great Chain of Being was understood as God's creation, naturally harmonious and without gaps, and it inspired Linnaeus's important eighteenth-century taxonomy of living organisms.

3. In the nineteenth century, catastrophism and uniformitarianism undermined the Great Chain of Being. Catastrophism was based on the ideas of Georges Cuvier, who argued that some species had become extinct in massive natural disasters, after which new species were introduced from elsewhere. Uniformitarianism was promoted by geologist Charles Lyell, who argued that the same processes of erosion and uplift that can be observed to change the earth's surface today had been at work in the past. Uniformitarianism implied that changes in life forms were as gradual and reversible as changes in the earth's surface.

4. Lamarck tried to preserve the view of a harmonious Great Chain of Being by claiming that fossil species had not become extinct. Lamarck argued that individual members of a species are all able to transform themselves in the same way when facing the same environmental pressures. Lamarckian transformational evolution has been rejected by contemporary evolutionary researchers. In contrast to Lamarck, Darwin and Wallace concluded that the similarities shared by distinct living species could be explained if all such species had descended from a single parental species that had lived in the past. In addition, Darwin proposed that such "descent with modification" could occur as a result of the straightforward, mechanistic process of natural selection.

5. Darwin's theory of evolution by natural selection (or variational evolution) was based on the principle of variation, the principle of heredity, and the principle of natural selection. Variational evolution was driven by what Darwin called the "struggle for existence" between individuals of the same species to survive and reproduce. In a given environment, those variant individuals who survive and leave greater numbers of offspring are said to have greater fitness than other members of their species who leave fewer offspring. There is no such thing as "absolute" fitness. Today, evolutionists recognize four evolutionary processes, including natural selection, that can determine which variant individuals in a population will leave greater numbers of offspring than others.

6. Evolutionary theorists use the concept of adaptation to refer both to a process of mutual adjustment between organisms and their environments and to the phenotypic features of organisms that are produced by this process. Reconstructing accurate evolutionary histories of organisms requires distinguishing adaptations from exaptations.

7. Darwin did not know why offspring tend to resemble their parents, nor did he understand how variation was introduced into populations. Answers to these questions were developed in the field of genetics. Genes are associated with particular portions of the DNA molecules located on the chromosomes in the cell nucleus. The machinery of the cell uses DNA to synthesize proteins necessary for life processes and makes it possible for chromosomes to be copied before cells divide. Gene interaction helps explain how continuous traits, such as skin color or hair color, are the result of unchanging inheritance. Different genotypes may produce the same phenotype, and the same genotype may produce different phenotypes, depending on the kinds of environments

in which organisms possessing these genotypes live and grow. That is, each genotype has its own norm of reaction.

8. The study of evolution in contemporary biology is very lively. Modern biologists agree that life on earth has evolved, but they have different views about how evolutionary processes work. Many evolutionary thinkers are increasingly convinced that a phenomenon as complex as biological evolution requires theoretical pluralism. Current advances in evolutionary theory incorporate developmental processes, niche construction, and multiple inheritance systems in addition to genes. These advances have led many theoretical biologists to propose expanding the modern evolutionary synthesis of the 1930s and 1940s.

For Review

1. Define evolution.
2. Explain the kinds of material evidence that have been important in the development of evolutionary theory.
3. Define essentialism and the Great Chain of Being.
4. Explain the difference between transformational (Lamarckian) evolution and variational (Darwinian) evolution.
5. Describe the basic principles and driving force of natural selection.
6. Distinguish among aptation, adaptation, and exaptation.
7. Why is variation so important in evolutionary theory?
8. Explain nonblending, single-particle inheritance (Mendelian inheritance).
9. What is the difference between discontinuous and continuous variation?
10. Explain how, from a Darwinian perspective, it is populations (not individual organisms) that can evolve.
11. How does the modern evolutionary synthesis differ from Darwin's original account of evolution by natural selection?
12. What are the differences between genotype and phenotype, and why are they important?
13. What is a norm of reaction? Explain its significance for the evolution of human populations.
14. Summarize the main claims of niche construction theory. Why do evolutionary theorists argue that it belongs in an extended evolutionary synthesis?

Key Terms

adaptation   43
alleles   45
aptation   43
catastrophism   37
chromosomes   45
common ancestry   41
continuous variation   47
crossing over   46
discontinuous
   variation   46
DNA   51
essentialism   36

evolution   35
evolutionary theory   35
exaptation   43
fitness   42
gene   45
genetics   45
genome   52
genotype   53
genus   37
Great Chain of Being   37
heterozygous   45
homozygous   45

human agency   57
linkage   46
locus   46
meiosis   46
Mendelian
   inheritance   44
mitosis   45
mutation   51
natural selection   41
niche construction   55
norm of reaction   54
pangenesis   44

phenotype   53
pleiotropy   50
polygeny   47
principle of independent
   assortment   44
principle of
   segregation   44
species   37
taxonomy   37
transformational
   evolution   40
uniformitarianism   38
variational evolution   41

Suggested Readings

Ayala, Francisco J., and John C. Avise, eds. 2014. *Essential readings in evolutionary biology.* Baltimore: Johns Hopkins University Press. *This book is a bit challenging for students new to evolutionary biology, but it is a marvelous compendium of forty-eight excerpts by influential evolutionary thinkers, from Darwin until the present day, including theoretical developments connected with the rise of genetics, the negotiation of the evolutionary synthesis, the discovery of the structure of DNA, and more.*

Gould, Stephen Jay. 1987. *Time's arrow, time's cycle: Myth and metaphor in the discovery of geological time.* Cambridge, MA: Harvard University Press. *A fascinating account of the historical and cultural context out of which catastrophism and uniformitarianism were forged in the nineteenth century.*

Gould, Stephen Jay. 1996. *Full house: The spread of excellence from Plato to Darwin.* New York: Harmony Books. *An eloquent and entertaining defense of the view that human beings were not the end point of biological evolution and that bacteria are more properly regarded as the dominant life forms on earth.*

Ingold, Tim, and G. Pálsson, eds. 2013. *Biosocial Becomings: Integrating Social and Biological Anthropology.* Cambridge: Cambridge University Press. *Ingold, Pálsson, and other contributors to this volume describe the limitations of so-called "Darwinian" or "neo-Darwinian" attempts to account for human evolution. More than critique, however, the contributors provide examples of the fresh insights afforded by new evolutionary approaches that rely on a relational perspective, one that recognizes the entanglement of humans with other forms of life in ongoing processes of movement and growth. The authors write with a lively awareness of contemporary contexts shaped by capitalist globalization, in the shadow of the Anthropocene.*

Kevles, Daniel J., and Leroy Hood. 1992. *The code of codes: Scientific and social issues in the Human Genome Project.* Cambridge, MA: Harvard University Press. *This edited collection contains a wide range of articles by geneticists, molecular biologists, biochemists, historians of science, and social scientists who examine the prospects and consequences of mapping all the genes in the human body. The book offers a range of opinions on how fully we will know what it means to be human if we learn one day all there is to know about our genes.*

Lewontin, Richard. 1991. *Biology as ideology: The doctrine of DNA.* New York: Harper Perennial. *The text of this book began as a series of radio broadcasts for the Canadian Broadcasting Company and is supplemented with an article Lewontin published in the* New York Review of Books. *Lewontin's accessible and hard-hitting essay addresses excessive claims that are sometimes made in the name of human genetics and offers incisive criticism of current efforts by geneticists to map all the genes in the human body.*

Lewontin, Richard. 2001. *The triple helix: Gene, organism, and environment.* Cambridge, MA: Harvard University Press. *Lewontin reminds biologists not to forget the role of organisms and environment in discussions of evolution; these are often ignored in discussions that attribute everything to genes.*

Lovejoy, Arthur O. (1936) 1960. *The Great Chain of Being.* New York: Harper Torchbooks. *Originally published in 1936, this classic is as fresh and relevant as anything being written about evolution today. A marvelously clear and detailed account of pre-Darwinian thinking about life on earth.*

Marks, Jonathan. 1995. *Human biodiversity.* New York: Aldine. *Marks is a biological anthropologist with a strong commitment to a biocultural approach to human nature. This book is an excellent introduction to biological anthropology.*

 Visit our online resource center for further reading, web links, free assessments, flashcards, and videos. www.oup.com/he/lavenda5e

What can the study of primates tell us about human beings?

Our closest animal relatives are the primates. This chapter introduces you to the richness and variety of primate ways of life and provides an overview of primate evolution. Primates are fascinating in their own right but also can help us understand more about what it means to be human.

CHAPTER OUTLINE

What Are Primates?

How Do Biologists Classify Primates?

How Many Categories of Living Primates Are There?

What Is Ethnoprimatology?

Are There Patterns in Primate Evolution?

How Do Paleoanthropologists Reconstruct

Primate Evolutionary History?

Chapter Summary

LEARNING OBJECTIVES

- Explain what the category of primates includes, and describe the relationships between human and nonhuman primates.
- Describe how biologists classify primates using taxonomy.
- Identify the tremendous diversity among the many categories of living primates, their similarities and differences, and corresponding ecological niches.
- Explain the theoretical and methodological characteristics of the field of ethnoprimatology.
- Discuss common patterns in the evolutionary developments among and between primates.
- Apply the field of paleontology to efforts to reconstruct primate evolutionary history.

Primatologist Jane Goodall interacts with a chimpanzee.

Human beings are primates, and the evolution of human beings constitutes one strand of the broader evolutionary history of the primate order. Because knowledge of living primate species offers important clues to their evolutionary past, this chapter begins with an overview of what we know about living nonhuman primates. After all, in addition to the evolutionary history they share with humans, living nonhuman primates have a fascinating evolutionary history of their own.

What Are Primates?

Western Europeans first learned about African apes in the seventeenth century. Ever since, these animals have been used as a mirror to reflect on and speculate about human nature. But the results of this exercise have been contradictory. The physical characteristics that humans share with other primates have led many observers to assume that these primates also share our feelings and attitudes. This is called **anthropomorphism**, the attribution of human characteristics to nonhuman animals. In the twentieth century alone, Westerners vacillated between viewing primates as innocent and comical versions of themselves (Curious George) and as brutish and degraded versions of themselves (King Kong; Figure 3.1). When studying nonhuman primates, we must remain aware of how our own human interests can distort what we see (Haraway 1989). If you think humans are basically kind and generous, nonhuman primates will look kind and generous; if you think humans are basically nasty and selfish, nonhuman primates will look nasty and selfish. Primatologists have an obligation to avoid either romanticizing or demonizing primates if they are to understand these animals in their own right.

How Do Biologists Classify Primates?

The first step in understanding primates is to address the variety they exhibit. Primatologists, like other biologists, turn for assistance to modern biological **taxonomy**, the foundations of which were laid by Linnaeus in the eighteenth century. Today, taxonomists group organisms together on the basis of morphological traits, behavioral traits, and geographical distribution (Mayr 1982, 192). The laboratory technique of DNA hybridization allows

FIGURE 3.1   In the West, nonhuman primates are often portrayed in ways that embody human fears and anxieties. In the 1930s, the giant ape in the original *King Kong* (a) embodied a racial threat to the power of white males and the sexual virtue of white females. Since that time, the popularization of Jane Goodall's chimpanzee research and Dian Fossey's gorilla research, as well as worries about the extinction of wild ape populations, seems to have reshaped the recent remake of *King Kong* (b) in which the white human heroine and the giant ape become allies in an effort to evade greedy, abusive, and exploitative white males.

researchers to combine single strands of DNA from two species to see how closely they match. When human DNA is combined with the DNA of other primates, they all match very closely, with the closest match being between humans and chimpanzees. As we will see in Chapter 4, these kinds of comparisons no longer are limited to the DNA of living primates. New laboratory techniques that permit the recovery of ancient DNA from fossilized bones tens of thousands of years old are making it possible to reconstruct evolutionary continuity and divergence as measured in similarities and differences in the DNA of living species and their extinct relatives (Brown and Brown 2013).

---

anthropomorphism   The attribution of human characteristics to nonhuman animals.

taxonomy   A biological classification of various kinds of organisms.

Taxonomists classify organisms by assigning them to groups and arranging the groups in a hierarchy based on the seven levels originally recognized by Linnaeus: kingdom, phylum, class, order, family, genus, and species. Biologists continue to assign Latin names to species (e.g., *Homo sapiens*). The species name consists of (1) a generic name (always capitalized) that refers to the genus in which the species is classified and (2) a specific name that identifies particular species (any distinguishing name will do, including the Latinized name of the person who first identified the species). Genus and species names are always italicized. The taxonomy recognized by modern biologists is an *inclusive hierarchy*. That is, related lower groups are combined to make higher groups: related species make up a genus, related genera make up a family, and so on. Each species—and each set of related species grouped at any level of the hierarchy—is called a **taxon** (plural, *taxa*). For example, *H. sapiens* is a taxon, as is Hominoidea (the superfamily to which humans and apes belong) and Mammalia (the class to which primates and all other mammals belong).

Contemporary taxonomies are designed to reflect the evolutionary relationships that modern biologists believe were responsible for similarities and differences among species, and taxonomists debate which kinds of similarities and differences they ought to emphasize. Traditional evolutionary taxonomies focused on the **morphology** of organisms—the shapes and sizes of their anatomical features—and related these to the adaptations the organisms had developed. Organisms that seemed to have developed similar adaptations at a similar level of complexity in similar environments were classified together in the same evolutionary *grade*. Primates are classified into four evolutionary grades: the least complex grade is represented by prosimians ("premonkeys") and includes lemurs, lorises, and tarsiers; anthropoids (monkeys, apes, and humans) represent a more advanced grade; followed by the hominoids (apes and humans); the most advanced grade is the hominins (humans). The lesser apes (gibbons and siamangs) are distinguished from the great apes (gorillas, chimpanzees, and orangutans) on the grounds that the great apes had achieved a more complex adaptation than the lesser apes. For the same reason, the great apes were grouped together on the grounds that their adaptations were more similar to one another than any of them were to human beings.

The traditional approach to taxonomy has much to recommend it—especially to paleontologists, because fossils are often so few and so incomplete that any classification more precise than "grade" is likely to be misleading. As we will discuss in Chapter 5, paleontologists face numerous challenges in the systematic classification of fossil organisms that biologists studying living species usually do not encounter. Paleontologists realize that adaptive morphological similarity by itself is not a foolproof indicator of evolutionary relatedness. This is because similarity can arise in one of two ways. Sometimes, members of different species have inherited common features from a common ancestor (a phenomenon called **homology**); in other cases, members of different species have common features, but do not share a recent common ancestor (a phenomenon called **homoplasy**). Homoplasy is the result of convergent, or parallel, evolution, as when two species with very different evolutionary histories develop similar physical features as a result of adapting to a similar environment. Examples include wings in birds and in bats and long, hydrodynamic body shapes in fishes and in whales.

To avoid confusing homology with homoplasy, some twentieth-century taxonomists developed an alternative taxonomic method called *cladistics* that is based on homology alone (i.e., on evolutionary relatedness alone). Cladistics attempts to reconstruct the degrees of similarity and difference that result from **cladogenesis** (the formation of one or more new species from an older species). First, cladists must distinguish between homologous and analogous physical traits, focusing on homologous traits only. Then, they must determine which of the homologous traits shared by a group of organisms belonged to the ancestral population out of which they all evolved. These are called "primitive traits."

To trace later evolutionary developments, cladists identify phenotypic features shared by some, but not all, of the descendant organisms. A group of organisms possessing such a set of shared, derived features constitutes a natural group called a clade that must be recognized in the taxonomy. Finally, if cladists find derived features that are unique to a given group, this too requires taxonomic recognition. A group of organisms sharing a set of unique, derived features that sets them apart from other such groups within the same genus would qualify as a species (Figure 3.2). This way of defining species exemplifies the Phylogenetic Species Concept, to be discussed in Chapter 5. In recent years, cladistic methods have been widely adopted by primatologists and

---

taxon Each species, as well as each group of related species, at any level in a taxonomic hierarchy.

morphology The physical shape and size of an organism or its body parts.

homology Genetic inheritance resulting from common ancestry.

homoplasy Convergent, or parallel, evolution, as when two species with very different evolutionary histories develop similar physical features as a result of adapting to a similar environment.

cladogenesis The birth of a variety of descendant species from a single ancestral species.

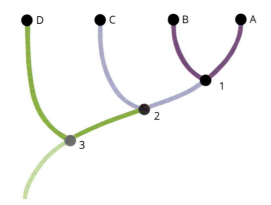

FIGURE 3.2 This cladogram shows the relationships among four hypothetical species. A, B, C, and D are assigned separate species status on the basis of unique, derived traits. A and B together possess shared, derived traits not found among C or D, indicating that A and B share a recent common ancestor (1). A, B, and C together possess shared, derived traits that distinguish them from D, indicating that they, too, share a common—but more distant—ancestor (2). A, B, C, and D are grouped together for analysis on the basis of shared, primitive traits common to them all or shared, derived traits that distinguish their common ancestor (3) from an out-group not shown in the cladogram.

human paleontologists, and the following discussion uses cladistic categories. (To explore these matters further, check out the evolution website at the University of California, Berkeley: https://evolution.berkeley.edu/evolibrary/article/evo_04

How Many Categories of Living Primates Are There?

Nonhuman primates are found today in all the major rain forests of the world, except those in New Guinea and northeastern Australia. Some species, such as the Japanese macaque, have moved out of the tropics and into temperate climates. Primates are unusual, however, because, unlike most mammalian groups, their many and varied species are nearly all found in the tropics. Primates are studied in laboratories, in captive populations in zoos or research facilities, and in the wild. Primatologists must gather and compare information from all these settings to construct a picture of primate life that does justice to its richness and diversity.

And primate life is tremendously diverse. Different species live in different habitats, eat different kinds of food, organize themselves into different kinds of social

configurations, and observe different patterns of mating and raising offspring. In light of all this diversity, most primatologists would probably caution against taking any single primate species as a model of early human social life (Cheney et al. 1987, 2). Alison Jolly (1985) points out that any species' way of life—what it eats and how it finds mates, raises its young, relates to companions, and protects itself from predators—defines that species' **ecological niche**. And, she adds, "With primates, much of the interest lies in guessing how our ancestors evolved from narrow confinement in a particular niche into our present cosmopolitan state."

Strepsirrhines

Strepsirrhini include lemurs and lorises (see Figures 3.3 and 3.4), the prosimians that have a *rhinarium*, or upper lip, attached to the gums by a web of skin. Other shared, derived features that unite Strepsirrhines include the *tooth comb* (forward-tilting lower incisors and canine teeth used for grooming), a *grooming claw* on the second digit of their feet, and an ankle bone (or *talus*) that flares to the side (Fleagle 2013, 57). Strepsirrhine **dentition** (the sizes, shapes, and number of their teeth) displays the dental formula 2.1.3.3 (i.e., each side of both upper and lower jaws has two incisors, one canine, three premolars, and three molars). Females have a bicornate ("two-horned") uterus and a primitive form of placenta in which the blood of the mother and the blood of the fetus are more separated from one another than they are in other primates. Ancient and contemporary DNA comparisons indicate that all the Madagascar species (including the mouse lemur, the smallest living primate) form a clade separate from lorises and galagos, although more detailed relations among many species remain unclear (Fleagle 2013, 82).

Today lemurs are found only on the island of Madagascar, off the east coast of Africa, where they were isolated from competition from later-evolving primate species on the African mainland. They have been classified into 2 superfamilies, 5 families, and 15 *genera* (plural of genus) (Fleagle 2013, 5). There is evidence that different species of brown lemur are able to successfully interbreed with one another, although they have different numbers of chromosomes; different species of sportive lemurs are also able to interbreed despite chromosome differences that distinguish them (Fleagle 2013, 63, 67).

Humans first arrived in Madagascar about 2000 years ago, and it appears that they were responsible for the extinction of a number of large-bodied lemur species, either by hunting or by destruction of their habitats (Fleagle 2013, 73).

---

ecological niche Any species' way of life: what it eats and how it finds mates, raises its young, relates to companions, and protects itself from predators.

dentition The sizes, shapes, and number of an animal's teeth.

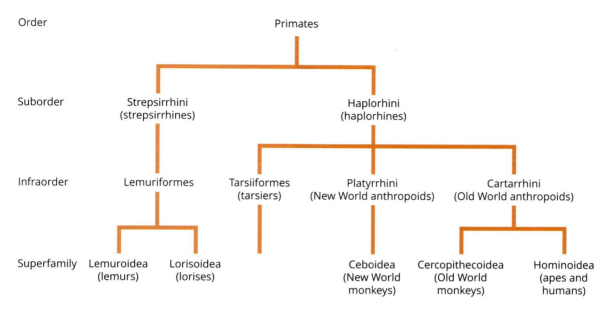

Order			Primates			

Suborder — Strepsirrhini (strepsirrhines) — Haplorhini (haplorhines)

Infraorder — Lemuriformes — Tarsiiformes (tarsiers) — Platyrrhini (New World anthropoids) — Cartarrhini (Old World anthropoids)

Superfamily — Lemuroidea (lemurs) — Lorisoidea (lorises) — Ceboidea (New World monkeys) — Cercopithecoidea (Old World monkeys) — Hominoidea (apes and humans)

FIGURE 3.3 Cladistic taxonomy of the primates (Relethford 1996, 175). Compare this taxonomy of the primates with the traditional taxonomy in Figure 2.3. Where are the similarities? Where are the differences? Reasoning behind the construction of different biological taxonomies will be taken up again in Chapter 5.

FIGURE 3.4 Lemurs are native only to the island of Madagascar, off the east coast of Africa. They managed to avoid competition from later-evolving monkeys and apes in Africa thanks to their geographical isolation.

Lorises are found in Africa and Asia, and their close relatives, the galagos, are found in Africa. These groups all share the same three strepsirrhine features as lemurs, but in addition possess features in their cranium that differentiate them from lemurs. Both groups live in trees and are **nocturnal** (active at night), but differ in their characteristic styles of movement: lorises are slow climbers, whereas galagos are leapers (Fleagle 2013, 78).

Haplorhines

Haplorhini includes tarsiers and anthropoids, primates whose upper lips are not attached to their gums. Some taxonomies emphasize the features all Haplorhini share and recognize three Haplorhini infraorders: Tarsiiformes (tarsiers), Platyrrhini (New World anthropoids), and Catarrhini (Old World anthropoids) (see Figure 3.3). Other taxonomists, who judge that anthropoids have more in common with each other than they do with tarsiers, treat Haplorhini and Anthropoidea as semi-orders, place Tarsiiformes in Haplorhini, and classify Platyrrhini and Catarrhini as two infraorders in Anthropoidea (see Table 3.1).

Tarsiers Tarsiers are small nocturnal primates (Figure 3.5) that eat only animal food, such as insects, birds, bats, and snakes. Tarsiers used to be grouped with lemurs and lorises, but cladists have argued persuasively that they belong in the same clade as anthropoids. This is because they share a number of derived traits with the

nocturnal Describes animals that are active during the night.

IN THEIR OWN WORDS

Interbreeding

Increasingly refined techniques for analyzing and comparing the genomes of organisms, both living and fossilized, have produced results that calls into question the widespread assumption that interbreeding among closely related species is unlikely, if not impossible. Fleagle's discussion of the long history of such interbreeding among species of brown lemurs in Madagascar is just one example of a growing catalogue of instances. In his recent survey of the geological and biological history of Europe, paleontologist Tim Flannery highlights just how widespread cross-species interbreeding is.

Advances in DNA analysis, particularly in the study of ancient DNA, are unlocking a hitherto unsuspected aspect of hybridization (or *metissage* as the French might call it). It is increasingly shown to have been important in the origination of species, and in helping species adapt, with many examples coming from Europe. But perhaps most strikingly hybridization has been a very important influence on human evolution in Europe. We often think of hybrids as something inferior—a sort of bastard or mongrel type. Pejorative associations of the word "hybrid" were particularly common in the first half of the twentieth century, when misguided ideas about genetics made purity of race a dangerously attractive concept. . . .

The idea that species are discrete entities—carriers of a unique genetic inheritance, is deeply embedded within us, perhaps reflecting some sense of a perfect, pre-human world, so hybrids can threaten our sense of order. They certainly complicate the work of taxonomists, some defying easy classification and threatening the Linnaean system of classification that has ruled biology for more than 250 years.

Yet we have long known that hybridization is widespread. By 1972, about 600 kinds of mammal hybrid had been identified (many from zoos or other captive situations. By 2005 it was estimated that 25% of plant species, and 10% of animal species, were involved in hybridization. Over the last few years, research into ancient DNA has revealed that such figures are gross underestimates, even for wild species living in nature. Two recent studies, one involving bear species and the other elephants, illustrate what is being learned.

The six bear species living today (polar, brown, Asiatic black, American back, sloth and sun) have evolved from a common ancestor over the last five million years. While they remain very different in appearance and ecology, DNA analysis reveals an astonishing degree of hybridization in their lineage. . . . The researchers concluded that hybridization between various bear species has been going on for millions of years so that when the crosses between bear species are included on the bear family tree, the diagram looks more like a family network.

The history of hybridization among elephants is, if anything, even more astonishing. A recent study by the Harvard-based palaeogeneticist Eleftheria Palkopoulou and her colleagues, which includes the three living species (African, African forest, and Asiatic) and three extinct kinds (European straight-tusked, woolly mammoth, and American mastodon), revealed that elephants have hybridized throughout most of their history. Indeed, some extinct elephants result from such extensive hybridization that they are not easily classifiable in the Linnaean system. . . .

Were hybridization extensive enough, life would become one undifferentiated mass. So why do species exist? It turns out that there are mechanisms (known as species isolating mechanisms) that make the production of hybrids difficult. It is rare for an individual to overcome these barriers, but among the millions of individuals that comprise a species it is common for enough hybrids to be produced to allow genes to flow between species. Some species' isolating mechanisms are behavioral—such as possession of a particular mating call, which only females of a given species will respond to—or a preference for reproducing at a particular time of the year. Others, such as penis size or shape, are physical. But there are also genetic and epigenetic barriers. Sometimes genetic factors prevent a viable embryo from forming. But they can also result in most first-generation hybrid individuals being infertile, or having low fertility. In a phenomenon known as Haldane's rule, this is particularly true for male hybrids among mammals. But if first generation hybrids do manage to produce some offspring, the next generation of the has improved fertility—though usually only with one or the other species (but not both) involved in the original cross. All of these barriers tend to limit, but not eliminate entirely, the flow of genes from one species to another.

(Flannery 2018, 154–156).

TABLE 3.1 Classification of *Homo sapiens*

Kingdom	Animal
Phylum	Chordata
Class	Mammalia (mammals)
Order	Primates (primates)
Semi-order	Haplorhini
Suborder	Anthropoidea
Infraorder	Catarrhini
Superfamily	Hominoidea
Family	Hominidae
Subfamily	Homininae
Genus	*Homo*
Species	*Homo sapiens*

A modern biological classification of our species, *Homo sapiens*, using Linnaean principles, based on Fleagle (2013, 5).

FIGURE 3.5 Although tarsiers used to be grouped together with lemurs and lorises on phenetic grounds, cladists point out that tarsiers share a number of derived traits with the anthropoids.

anthropoids, including dry noses, detached upper lips, a similarly structured placenta (and heavier infants), and a structure in their skulls called the "postorbital partition" (Bearder 1987; Aiello 1986). Tarsier body morphology—a tiny body and enormous eyes and feet—is quite distinctive. Tarsier dentition is also unusual: tarsiers have no tooth comb, but resemble lemurs and lorises in the upper jaw (2.1.3.3), although not the lower jaw (1.1.3.3). In other respects, tarsier tooth morphology resembles that of anthropoids (Fleagle 2013, 85).

Anthropoids Anthropoids include New World monkeys, Old World monkeys, apes, and humans. New World monkeys are called *platyrrhines*, a term referring to their broad, flat noses; Old World monkeys, apes, and humans are called *catarrhines* in reference to their downward-pointing nostrils (Figure 3.6). Platyrrhines (Figure 3.7) also differ from catarrhines in dentition: the platyrrhine dental formula is 2.1.3.3, whereas the catarrhine dental formula is 2.1.2.3. Some platyrrhines have **prehensile**, or grasping, tails, whereas no catarrhines do. Finally, all platyrrhines are tree dwellers, whereas some catarrhine species live permanently on the ground. John Fleagle (2013, 90) reminds us that all these anthropoid features did not appear at once, but evolved in a piecemeal fashion over millions of years.

New World monkeys are the only clade of anthropoids in Central and South America; neither apes nor strepsirrhines are found there. It happens that some New World monkeys have evolved lemur-like adaptations,

and some have evolved ape-like adaptations, but other adaptations are unique (Fleagle 2013, 92). Platyrrhini are classified into 2 superfamilies, 7 subfamilies, and 18 genera (Fleagle 2013, 5). Titi monkeys are the least specialized of all New World monkeys and may bear the closest resemblance to the earliest platyrrhines (Fleagle 2013, 93). Capuchins (or organ-grinder monkeys) are well known outside their habitats in the South American rainforest. Some populations in open habitats in Brazil have been observed walking on their hind legs and using tools to break open palm nuts (Fleagle 2013, 104). Owl monkeys, found throughout South America, are the only nocturnal anthropoid species (Fleagle 2013, 106). The largest New World monkeys are atelids like the spider monkey, which have prehensile tails. Their tails function much like a fifth limb, helping them to suspend themselves in the trees. These are the New World monkeys whose adaptations most resemble those of Old World apes (Fleagle 2013, 98). Overall, the adaptive diversity of New World monkeys is impressive. There is no evidence

---

prehensile The ability to grasp, with fingers, toes, or tail.

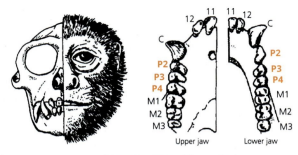

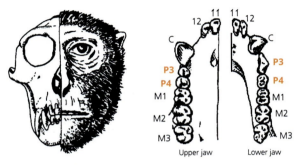

FIGURE 3.6 New World monkeys, such as the capuchin, have flat noses with nostrils pointing sideways and three premolars (P2, P3, and P4). By contrast, Old World anthropoids, including Old World monkeys such as the macaque, have noses with downward-pointing nostrils and only two premolars (P3 and P4).

FIGURE 3.7 A well-known species of New World monkeys is the spider monkey. This monkey was photographed in the Guatemalan rain forest.

of hybridization among species of New World monkeys (Fleagle 2013, 116).

Old World monkeys include two major groups: the colobines and the cercopithecines. *Colobines*, including the langurs of Asia (Figure 3.8) and the red colobus monkeys of Africa, are all **diurnal** (active during the day) and primarily adapted to arboreal life, although they have been observed to travel on the ground between tracts of forest. Colobines have four-chambered stomachs, presumably an adaptation to a heavy diet of leaves (Struhsaker and Leland 1987). Sorting out the phylogenetic connections among colobines in Africa and Asia has been difficult; it appears that much hybridization has occurred among them in the past (Fleagle 2013, 135). Indeed, hybridization seems to have happened regularly among many Old World monkey species, which makes it difficult for taxonomists to agree about how to classify them (Fleagle 2013, 148). *Cercopithecines* include some species adapted to live in the trees and others adapted to live on the ground. Those species living in forests, such as African guenons, are often found in one-male breeding groups; females remain in the groups where they were born, whereas males ordinarily transfer out

at puberty. Groups of more than one species are often found feeding and traveling together (Cords 1987).

Ground-dwelling cercopithecines include several species of baboons, perhaps the best known of all Old World monkeys. Hamadryas baboons (*Papio hamadryas*) and gelada baboons (*Theropithecus gelada*) are found in Africa (Figure 3.9). Although they belong to different genera, they both live in social groups that possess a single breeding male. However, this superficial similarity turns out to be the result of very different social processes. Hamadryas males build up their one-male units by enticing females away from other units or by "adopting" immature females and caring for them until they are ready to breed. They carefully police the females in their units, punishing those that stray with a ritualized neck bite. In addition, hamadryas males thought to be kin form bonds to create a higher-level social unit known as a "clan." Several one-male units, several clans, and some individual males congregate in a band to forage together; and three or four bands may sleep together at night in a troop. By contrast, gelada baboons construct their one-male units on a core of strongly bonded

diurnal Describes animals that are active during the day.

FIGURE 3.8 Gray langurs are Old World colobine monkeys. Some primatologists have described events in which all-male langur groups "invade" one-male langur groups. Invading males have been reported to deliberately kill unweaned offspring of resident females. Whether this behavior should be interpreted as adaptive or maladaptive has been one of the great controversies of contemporary primatology.

female relatives that are closely influenced by the dominant female and that stay together even if the male of their group is removed (Stammbach 1987).

The most widely distributed primate genus in the world is *Macaca*—or the macaques—of which there are 20 species, ranging from Gibraltar and North Africa to Southeast Asia. All macaque species live in large multimale groups with complex internal social structures. They do well in a wide variety of habitats and have been especially successful living in habitats disturbed by human populations, with whom they have a long history of interaction in many parts of the world (Fleagle 2013, 123).

Hominoidea is the superfamily of catarrhines that includes apes and humans (see Table 3.1). Apes can be distinguished from Old World monkeys by morphological features such as dentition (reduced canine size, changes in jaw shape and molar shape) and the absence of a tail. Traditional taxonomies divide living apes into three grades, or families: the lesser apes (gibbons and siamangs), the great apes (orangutans, gorillas, and chimpanzees), and the hominids (humans). As we noted earlier, this taxonomic judgment was based on the differences in the kinds of adaptations each grade of anthropoid had developed. In recent years, however, many cladists have argued that classification within the great ape and human categories must be revised to reflect the results of biochemical and DNA testing, which show that humans and African apes (gorillas and chimpanzees) are far more closely related to one another than they are to orangutans. Moreover, because chimpanzees and humans share more than 98% of their DNA, more and more taxonomists have concluded that these genetic

FIGURE 3.9 Both hamadryas baboons (a) and gelada baboons (b) are ground-dwelling Old World cercopithecine monkeys. Although both species live in social groups with a single breeding male, hamadryas groups are created when the male entices females away from other groups; whereas gelada groups construct their one-male units on a core of closely related females.

similarities require placing chimpanzees and humans together in the same family, Hominidae; humans and their immediate ancestors are then grouped into a subfamily called Homininae and are called **hominins** (Goodman et al. 1990). This usage, now adopted by many leading authorities (e.g., Klein 2009, 74–75; Stringer and Andrews 2005, 16), will be followed in this book.

However, some biological anthropologists object that using genetics alone to determine taxonomy ignores important evolutionary information. For instance, emphasizing the genetic similarities between chimps and humans ignores wide adaptive differences between these taxa that illustrate Darwinian "descent with modification." These differences help explain why chimps and other apes are on the verge of extinction, largely as a consequence of human adaptive success. Biological anthropologist Jonathan Marks (2013) asks

> Who would say "nature" is reducible to "genetics" (aside from self-interested geneticists)? Certainly not the evolutionary "synthetic theorists" of the mid-twentieth century (Huxley 1947, Simpson 1949). If "evolution" refers to the naturalistic production of difference, then to say that we are apes is equivalent to denying that we have evolved. Or to put it another way, if evolution is descent with modification, then our ape identity implies descent without modification. (251)

Both traditionalists and cladists agree that gibbons (Figure 3.10) belong in their own family, Hylobatidae. Gibbons, the smallest of the apes, are found in the tropical rain forests of southeastern Asia. Most primate species show **sexual dimorphism** in size; that is, individuals of one sex (usually the males) are larger than individuals of the other sex. Gibbons, however, show no sexual dimorphism in size, although in some species, males and females have different coat colors. Gibbons are monogamous, neither male nor female is consistently dominant, and males contribute a great deal of care to their offspring. Gibbon groups usually comprise the mated pair and one or two offspring, all of whom spend comparatively little time in social interactions with one another. Gibbon pairs defend their joint territory, usually by vocalizing together to warn off intruders but occasionally with physical encounters. Establishing a territory appears to be difficult for newly mated pairs, and there is some evidence that parents may assist offspring in this effort. Evidence also suggests that some young male gibbons inherit the territory of their parents by pairing with their widowed mothers, although these pairs do not seem to breed (Leighton 1987).

Orangutans (Figure 3.11) are found today only in the rain forests of Sumatra and Borneo in southeastern

FIGURE 3.10   Gibbons are the smallest of the apes. Unlike most primate species, gibbons are monogamous; and male and female gibbons show no sexual dimorphism in size.

Asia. Their dentition is different from that of chimpanzees and gorillas. Orangutans are an extremely solitary species whose way of life has made them difficult to study in the wild. Adult female orangutans and their offspring occupy overlapping ranges that also overlap the ranges of more than one male. Orangutan males come in two different adult forms, unflanged and flanged. Unflanged males are the size of females, whereas flanged males grow protruding fleshy jowls, called flanges, and may be twice as large. Some orangutan populations have been documented demonstrating cultural differences in tool use and vocalization (Fleagle 2013, 158–59).

There are five living subspecies of gorillas, all of which are found in Africa: the western lowland gorilla, the Cross River gorilla, Grauer's gorilla, the Bwindi gorilla, and the mountain gorilla. The rarest subspecies, the mountain gorilla, is probably the best known, thanks to the work of Dian Fossey (Figure 3.12), whose experiences have been popularized in books and film. Mountain gorillas eat mostly leaves. Like the New World howler monkeys, both male and female gorillas transfer out

hominins   Humans and their immediate ancestors.

sexual dimorphism   The observable phenotypic differences between males and females of the same species.

IN THEIR OWN WORDS

The Future of Primate Biodiversity

In a recent collection presenting the latest research on primates, Karen Strier writes about one of the most critical concerns for all who work with primates: conservation. Carl Zimmer then takes up the story

"Between the inevitable effects of global warming on the world's endangered ecosystems and the ongoing expansion of human populations in and around the world's biodiversity hotspots, it is difficult to foresee how the future of primates—and other animals—that are threatened with extinction can be protected. Global losses of biodiversity and ecosystem changes are predicted to occur by 2050, and major primate extinctions may occur even sooner than this because rates of deforestation in countries such as Indonesia and Madagascar are so high. . . .

There is no question that human pressures are accelerating the extinction risks for many primate taxa. Whether through direct actions, such as unsustainable hunting and habitat destruction, or indirect activities, such as the far-reaching effects of atmospheric pollution on global climate, the impact of humans on other primates today is much greater than it has been in the past. . . . Yet, despite the depressing forecast for primates, increased awareness about the status of the world's endangered primates has fueled intensified international conservation efforts. It is too soon to tell whether these efforts will ultimately succeed in securing the futures of all endangered taxa, but there is no doubt that they are helping gain essential time in what for many primates is now an urgent race against extinction."

Ten years after Strier published her warning, matters have not improved. On January 18, 2017, science writer Carl Zimmer of the *New York Times* reported that "a team of 31 primatologists has analyzed every known species of primate to judge how they are faring. The news for man's closest animal relatives is not good. Three-quarters of primate species are in decline, the researchers found, and about 60% are now threatened with extinction. From gorillas to gibbons, primates are in significantly worse shape now than in recent decades because of the devastation from agriculture, hunting and mining."

Echoing the findings of ethnoprimatologists, the researchers Zimmer interviewed reported mixed outcomes, depending on the primate species; for example, generalist species that do well in a range of habitats are doing better than species that are dependent on highly specific resources. The decrease in primate numbers, however, affects more than the survival of individual species. Scientists now know that the activities of primate species keep tropical forests healthy. Zimmer quotes one of the coauthors of the study, biological anthropologist Katherine C. MacKinnon, who observed that "People used to think of primates as icing on the cake, as not being vital for ecosystems. . . . But now we know they are."

Some conservation efforts have been successful. For example, Anthony Rylands, another coauthor of the study, told Zimmer about a project to conserve golden lion tamarins, whose numbers were greatly reduced when the coastal forests of Brazil were cut down to make way for agriculture. Begun in 1983, the project has succeeded in preserving a small, stable population of this species in the wild. Still, conservation faces severe challenges: as Rylands pointed out, "the immensity of the destruction of tropical forests makes it very difficult."

Sources: Strier 2007, 506; Zimmer 2017.

---

of the group in which they were born before they start breeding. The transfer, which does not appear forced, may occur more than once in a female's life. An adult female gorilla may produce three surviving offspring in her lifetime. Gorillas are highly sexually dimorphic, and the dominant male often determines group activity and the direction of travel. Immature gorillas are attracted to dominant males, who ordinarily treat them with tolerance and protect them in dangerous situations (Stewart and Harcourt 1987; Whitten 1987).

Chimpanzees (*Pan troglodytes*) are probably the most studied of all the apes (Figure 3.13). Jane Goodall and her associates in Gombe, Tanzania, have followed some chimpanzee groups for 50 years. Other long-term field research on chimpanzees has been carried out elsewhere in eastern and western Africa as well (Boesch-Achermann and Boesch 1994). In recent years, a second species belonging to the genus *Pan*, *Pan paniscus*, known as the "pygmy chimpanzee" or bonobo (Figure 3.14), has received increasing attention, both in the wild and in captivity. Bonobos are found only in central Africa south of the Zaire River and may number fewer than 100,000; forest destruction, human predation, and capture for illegal sale all threaten their survival (de Waal 1989, 177). The two species differ morphologically: bonobos have less rugged builds, shorter upper limbs, and longer lower

FIGURE 3.11 Orangutans are an extremely solitary species that lives deep in the rain forests of Sumatra and Borneo.

FIGURE 3.12 The mountain gorilla of central Africa is the rarest of the living species of gorilla found in Africa.

limbs than chimpanzees and sport a distinctive coiffure. Both species share a fluid social structure; that is, temporary smaller groups form within the framework of a larger community (de Waal 1989, 180; Nishida and Hiraiwa-Hasegawa 1987, 172). Their patterns of social interactions differ, however. Bands of unrelated adult males are common among chimpanzees but rare among bonobos. Bonds formed between unrelated females are

FIGURE 3.13 Chimpanzees are probably the most studied of all the apes.

relatively weak among chimpanzees but strong among bonobos. Bonds between the sexes are much stronger among bonobos as well. This means that female bonobos play a more central role in their society than female chimpanzees play in theirs (de Waal 1989, 180).

Chimpanzees and bonobos eat both plant and animal foods. Indeed, one of Goodall's famous early discoveries was that chimpanzees deliberately make tools to help them find food. They have been observed preparing sticks to fish for insects in termite mounds or anthills, using leaf sponges to obtain water from tree hollows, and using rocks to smash open nuts. Indeed, patterns of tool use seem to vary regionally, suggesting the existence of separate cultural traditions in different chimpanzee groups. Male chimpanzees have been observed hunting for meat and sharing their kill with other members of the group; interestingly, forest-dwelling chimpanzees are more likely to hunt in groups, presumably because the foliage makes their prey harder to secure (Boesch-Achermann and Boesch 1994).

Bonobos have never been observed using tools (Nishida and Hiraiwa-Hasegawa 1987, 166). However, the sexual life of chimpanzees cannot compare with the highly eroticized social interactions typical of bonobos. Bonobo females are able and willing to mate during much of their monthly cycle, but researchers have also observed a high degree of mounting behavior and sexual play between all members of bonobo groups, young and old, involving individuals of the same sex and of the opposite sex. Studying a captive colony of bonobos in the San Diego Zoo, Frans de Waal and his assistants observed

FIGURE 3.14 Social interactions among bonobos are highly eroticized, apparently to manipulate social relationships rather than to increase reproductive rates. Female bonobos play a more central role in their society than female chimpanzees play in theirs.

600 mounts, fewer than 200 of which involved sexually mature individuals. Although this might be a function of life in captivity, it does not appear to be contradicted by data gathered in the wild. Nishida and Hiraiwa-Hasegawa (1987), who refer to material gathered under both conditions, conclude that elaborate bonobo sexual behavior is "apparently used to manipulate relationships rather than to increase reproductive rates" (173); de Waal (1989) agrees, suggesting that "conflict resolution is the more fundamental and pervasive function of bonobo sex" (212). Wolfe (1995) notes that same-sex mounting behavior has been observed in 11 different primate species.

When we try to summarize what makes primate life unique, we are struck by its flexibility, resilience, and creativity. Primates can get by under difficult circumstances, survive injuries, try out new foods or new social arrangements, and take advantage of the random processes of history and demography to do what none has done before (Jolly 1985, 80–81, 242, 319). Simplistic models of primate behavior assuming that all primates are fundamentally alike, with few behavioral options, are no longer plausible. Mary Ellen Morbeck (1997) observes that "Most current models are inadequate when applied to the complex lives of large-bodied, long-lived, group-living mammals, primates, and humans with big brains and good memories" (14). Overall, it seems quite clear that flexibility is the hallmark of primate adaptations.

What Is Ethnoprimatology?

More than 30 years ago, in *Primate Visions* (1989), Donna Haraway showed how human ambivalence about race and gender had shaped much traditional Western scientific thinking about nonhuman primates. Today, many primatologists are focusing their research on the complex and often contradictory interconnections between human and nonhuman primates. As a result, they increasingly insist that field studies of primates must be connected with conservation activities that take into consideration the welfare not only of the animals themselves but also of the ecosystems and human communities with which they are inextricably interconnected (e.g., Strier 1997; Jolly 2004; SAGA [Support for African/Asian Great Apes] 2005; see the In Their Own Words feature, "The Future of Primate Biodiversity"). These concerns have become central to a new specialty within primatology that is called *ethnoprimatology*.

Ethnoprimatology has been defined as the "theoretically and methodologically interdisciplinary study of the multifarious interactions and interfaces between humans and other primates" (Fuentes 2012, 102). As Agustín Fuentes explains, humans and other primates have long coexisted successfully in many global settings, but human activities now threaten the survival of many primate species in the wild. Indeed, ethnoprimatologists call into question the very notion of "the wild," given mounting knowledge that human niche construction is responsible for vast modifications of the living and nonliving world. As noted in Chapter 2, some scientists argue that this human-generated (or *anthropogenic*) environmental modification has been extensive enough to initiate a new geological epoch, which they call the *Anthropocene*: "the current geological epoch wherein anthropogenic agency is one of the prominent forces affecting global landscapes and climates" (Fuentes 2012, 102).

To study human–primate interactions in the Anthropocene requires reconfiguring the focus of primatological field research and broadening the kinds of questions researchers ask. For instance, if we all live in the Anthropocene, ethnoprimatologists must give up on the idea that there are any settings on the planet where primates are able to live beyond the influences of human activity. Acknowledging these multiple entanglements means that ethnoprimatologists must also explore a range of issues that go beyond their traditional focus on predator–prey relations. Overall, "Ethnoprimatology rejects the idea that humans are separate from natural ecosystems and mandates that anthropological and multiple stakeholder approaches be included in behavioral ecological and conservation research on other primates" (Fuentes 2012, 102; see the In Their Own Words feature, "The Future of Primate Biodiversity").

Fuentes, a biological anthropologist, was an early advocate of ethnoprimatological research, which now involves field primatologists, primate conservationists, and sociocultural anthropologists interested in human–animal interactions. These concerns have led to the writing of multispecies ethnographies in which relations of humans to nonhuman others are a central concern (Haraway 2008; Kirksey and Helmreich 2010). Ethnoprimatology is also beginning to have an impact on other disciplines, such as *anthrozoology*: a field in which

veterinarians, public health researchers, psychologists, and psychiatrists study a variety of human–animal interactions; it even promises to engage members of the animal welfare movement who in the past have been critical of the work of primatologists (Fuentes 2012, 104).

In some parts of the world, human relations with nonhuman primates have provoked conflict. Early ethnoprimatological studies focused on situations where crops planted by humans were subject to raiding by primates living in nearby forests. Other studies look at the increasing importance of primates as tourist attractions. In recent decades, ethnoprimatological research projects have been undertaken in a number of sites in Southeast Asia and Africa. Some ethnoprimatological research projects are multisited undertakings, similar to multisited projects that have become common in ethnographic research on human populations. For example, macaques are found in parts of Europe, Africa, and Asia and have established a variety of long-standing relationships with local human populations in a range of types of human settlements. Comparison of the similarities and differences in these relationships across different sites allows ethnoprimatologists to document successes and challenges faced

IN THEIR OWN WORDS

Gombe, Tanzania, in the Twenty-First Century

In the 1960s, when Jane Goodall began research on the chimpanzees of Gombe, their closest human neighbors were African villagers and Goodall's research team. By the late 1980s, human encroachment on chimpanzee territory had become an everyday fact of life, with negative consequences. The chimps had become world-famous, and Gombe was being inundated by "the most intrepid tourists who find their own way there, on foot or by water taxi, camp on the beach, and attempt to make their own arrangements with the underpaid park staff" (Brooks and Smith 1991, 14). A major concern was the health of the chimpanzees, who are susceptible to human diseases: numerous Gombe chimpanzees had died from polio in 1966 and from a respiratory infection in 1988. But other threats came from poachers and dealers hoping to sell chimps as "bushmeat" or as medical research subjects, and from growing populations of human settlers who cut down forest to expand their farms.

In the late 1980s, Goodall and her associates began a series of interventions at Gombe, aiming to protect the chimps and the forest while also drawing local residents into chimpanzee conservation and improving their livelihoods. An ongoing chimpanzee tourism project was one outcome. In September 2019, Jane Goodall described the outcomes of some of the other

interventions to reporter David Gelles at the New York Times, https://www.nytimes.com/2019/09/12/business/jane-goodall-corner-office.html?searchResultPosition=1:

"When we went to find out about the chimps' problems in Gombe, Tanzania, we also learned about the suffering of the people—poverty, lack of health care and education. They needed to find ways that they could make a living without cutting down the last trees in their desperate effort to either grow food or make charcoal.

So we set up micro credit, based on the work of Muhammad Yunus, and we quickly saw the effect on the women. We then got money for scholarships to keep girls in school, during and after puberty. We started restoring fertility to the overused farmland, bringing in better health education and family planning information.

Now they love us, and they have agreed to put up a buffer zone between Gombe and the villages, and now they're creating corridors for the Gombe isolated chimps to interact with other chimpanzee groups. And if you fly over Gombe today, there are no bare hills anymore."

You can learn more about ongoing projects at Gombe through The Jane Goodall Institute: https://www.janegoodall.org.uk/chimpanzees/protecting-chimpanzees/13-protection

by all parties to these encounters. For instance, ongoing multiple encounters between humans and nonhuman primates seem to have shaped the evolution and transmission of disease-causing microorganisms, relationships that are increasingly affected by human migration and tourism (Gumert et al. 2011; Radhakrishna et al. 2013).

How have different primate populations fared in their encounters with humans? The great apes seem to face the greatest threats: gorillas, chimpanzees, and orangutans all require large areas of forest to meet their dietary needs and reproduce at slow rates. They are threatened by forest destruction by human settlement and logging, as well as by hunters who capture infants for the exotic pet trade or prize the flesh of these animals as "bushmeat." By comparison, macaques and baboons seem able to coexist with humans on much better terms. These monkeys are generalist foragers who seem to thrive in areas disturbed by human settlement and are becoming important draws for tourists in Southeast Asia and South Africa (Fuentes 2012, 111).

In many situations, Fuentes argues, "ethnoprimatological projects provide a particularly robust arena for the (re) integration of sociocultural and biological perspectives in anthropology" (2012,106). This reintegration of perspectives is clear in situations where ethnoprimatologists work with conservationists and local communities to find ways of managing human–nonhuman primate relations more successfully. Indeed, Fuentes (2012) reports, programs of this kind "that incorporate anthropological orientations and multistake-holder approaches show the most potential, although in some cases it appears that the human social and economic crises will overwhelm attempts to find sustainable solutions that benefit alloprimates as well as humans" (109–10).

Are There Patterns in Primate Evolution?

How do we begin to trace evolutionary developments within the primate order? The first step is to create a framework for comparison. For example, to trace the evolution of the mammalian skeleton, paleontologists collect samples of fossil mammal bones that span a long stretch of geological time, and they distinguish the bones of the animal's head—the skull, or **cranium** (plural, *crania*), and lower jaw, or **mandible**—from the rest of the animal's bones, its **postcranial skeleton**. Homologous bones of different ages can then be compared for similarities and differences. The fossilized and living species grouped together in the primate order share no single attribute that sets all of them apart from other living creatures (Figure 3.15). What does distinguish primates, living and extinct, are three different sets of features: ancestral characteristics (often called "primitive characteristics"), past evolutionary trends, and unique

features. In addition, primates are unusual because they are "distinguished mainly by a tendency to retain specific parts that other animals have lost during their evolution" (Klein 2009, 68). This is why primates are often described as *generalized* organisms.

Ancestral characteristics that primates inherited from earlier, nonprimate, mammalian ancestors appear in their generalized postcranial skeletons. These characteristics include the following:

- The presence of five digits on the hands and feet
- The presence of the clavicle, or collar bone, allowing for flexibility in the shoulder joint
- The use of the palms of the hand and foot (rather than the toes) for walking, called *plantigrade locomotion*

W. E. LeGros Clark (1963) identified four evolutionary trends that can be traced across the primate order since the first primates evolved away from their primitive mammalian ancestors:

1. An increase in brain size, relative to body size, and an increase in the complexity of the neocortex (or new brain)
2. A reduction of both the projection of the face and the reliance on the sense of smell
3. An increasing dependence on the sense of sight, resulting in the relocation of the eyes onto the same plane on the front of the face so that the visual field of each eye overlaps, producing depth perception (or **stereoscopic vision**; Figure 3.16)
4. A reduction in the number of teeth

Some scholars have suggested two additional evolutionary trends: an increasing period of infant dependence and a greater dependence on learned behavior.

Finally, primates' unique prehensile morphological features include the following:

1. Opposable thumbs and great toes (i.e., the thumb is opposite the other fingers and can be "opposed to" the other fingers for grasping)
2. Nails rather than claws on at least some digits
3. Pads at the tips of fingers and toes that are rich in nerve endings
4. Dermal ridges, or friction skin, on the digits, soles, palms, and underside of prehensile tails

---

cranium The bones of the head, excluding the jaw.

mandible The lower jaw.

postcranial skeleton The bones of the body, excluding those of the head.

stereoscopic vision A form of vision in which the visual field of each eye of a two-eyed (binocular) animal overlaps with the other, producing depth perception.

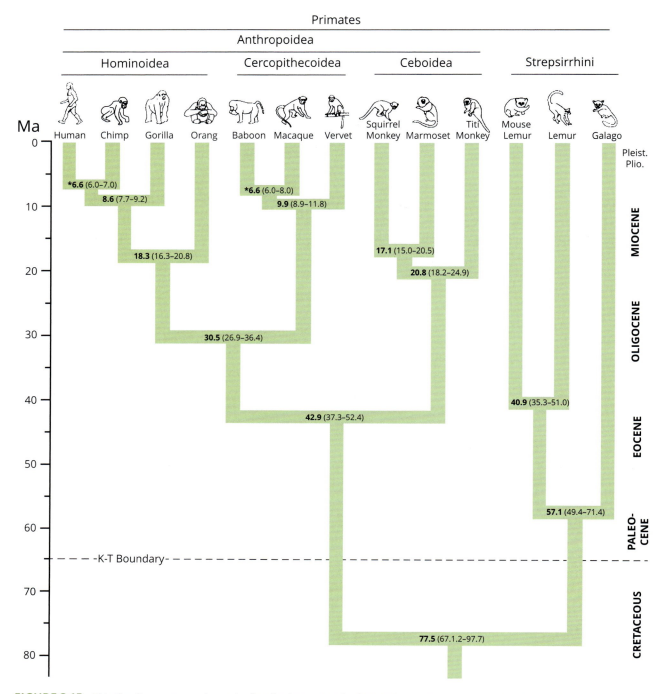

FIGURE 3.15 This timeline arranges the major fossil primate taxa by date and geological epoch and indicates estimated divergence dates in millions of years.

LeGros Clark (1963) argued that primate evolutionary trends and unique features were the outcome of an arboreal adaptation—that is, adaptation to life in the trees. In his view, creatures with excellent grasping abilities, acute binocular vision, and a superior brain are well suited to an arboreal habitat. However, many other organisms (e.g., squirrels) have adapted to life in the trees without having evolved such traits. Matt Cartmill (1972) offered the "visual predation hypothesis." He suggested that many of these traits derive from an ancestral adaptation to feeding on insects at the ends of tree branches

in the lower levels of tropical forests. Selective pressure for improved vision resulted from the fact that these ancestral primates fed at night and relied on sight to locate their prey. More recently, Robert Sussman (1991) and Katherine Milton (1993) have argued that switching from insect predation to consumption of edible plant parts set the stage for future primate evolution leading to grasping hands, visual acuity (including color vision), larger brains, and increased behavioral flexibility.

It is important to remember that while past evolutionary trends apply to the primate order as a whole,

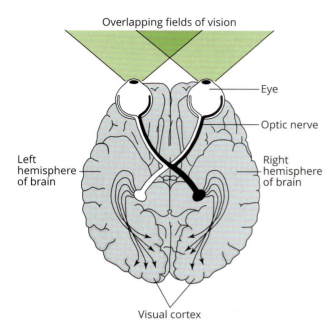

FIGURE 3.16 Stereoscopic vision. The fields of vision overlap, and the optic nerve from each eye travels to both hemispheres of the brain. The result is true depth perception.

all primate species were not affected by these trends in the same way. R. D. Martin (1986, 13) pointed out that lessened reliance on smell probably only developed in primates that were diurnal rather than those that were nocturnal (active at night). Some living primates are still nocturnal and continue to rely heavily on a well-developed sense of smell. These matters continue to be debated, but, as Fleagle concludes, "Unfortunately, until we have a better fossil record . . . the details of primate origins will remain hidden" (Fleagle 2013, 225).

How Do Paleoanthropologists Reconstruct Primate Evolutionary History?

The following survey of primate evolution is organized in terms of the five geological divisions, or epochs, recognized in the Tertiary period of the geological era called the Cenozoic. The Cenozoic began 65 million years ago (mya), about the same time as the primates did.

Primates of the Paleocene

The Paleocene lasted from about 65 to 55 mya. Evidence about early primate evolution in this period is growing, but remains complex and subject to debate. Based on DNA evidence from living mammals, it now seems that primates, tree shrews, and so-called "flying lemurs" (gliding mammals from Southeast Asia with tooth combs) are more closely related to one another than they are to

other mammals. All three have been placed together into the superorder Euarchonta, which also includes a group of Paleocene fossils known as *plesiadapiforms* (Fleagle 2013, 212). Plesiadapiforms were numerous, varied, and successful during the Paleocene and early Eocene of Europe and North America (Fleagle 2013, 213–14). But taxonomists disagree about their connection to primates, and the relation of Euarchonta to primates remains unclear (Fleagle 2013, 224). The best current candidate for the oldest probable primate is *Altiatlasius*, whose fragmentary fossils have been found in late Paleocene deposits in North Africa. Too little is known about *Altiatlasius*, however, to relate it clearly to later primate taxa; indeed, exactly where the first primates evolved is still unknown (Rose 1994; Fleagle 2013, 231).

Primates of the Eocene

The first undisputed primates appeared during the Eocene epoch, which lasted from about 55 to about 38 mya. Most of the fossils are jaws and teeth; but skulls, limb bones, and even some nearly complete skeletons have also been recovered. The best-known Eocene primates fall into two basic groups. The first group, *adapids*, look a lot like living lemurs. However, a number of morphological features—dentition in particular—distinguish them from their modern counterparts. Eocene adapids had four premolars, whereas modern lemurs have only three; and their lower incisors and canines were generalized, whereas modern lemurs possess a specialized tooth comb. The second group, the *omomyids*, resembles living tarsiers (Figure 3.17). Most omomyids were much smaller than adapids. Adapted for climbing, clinging, and leaping, omomyids appear to have been nocturnal, feeding on insects, fruit, or gum (Rose 1994). A tiny primate from the Early Eocene of Mongolia called *Altanius orlovi* may be ancestral to both adapoids and omomyoids (Fleagle 2013, 231). Linking later omomyoid fossils to living tarsiers, however, is not straightforward because different features evolved at different times, and parallel evolution seems to have been common. "Nevertheless, omomyoids, tarsiers and anthropoids all share a number of features that lead almost all researchers to group them together in the semi-order Haplorhini" (Fleagle 2013, 256). Currently, taxonomists are working to reconcile contradictions between older biomolecular estimates of the period that strepsirrhines split from haplorhines with more recent dates provided from the fossil record (Fleagle 2013, 259).

The early ancestors of later anthropoids began to appear in the period of transition between the late Eocene and early Oligocene, perhaps 44 to 40 mya (Martin 1993; Simons and Rasmussen 1994). The parapithecoids are the most primitive early anthropoid group from this period, with a dental formula of 2.1.3.3., which, as we saw, is

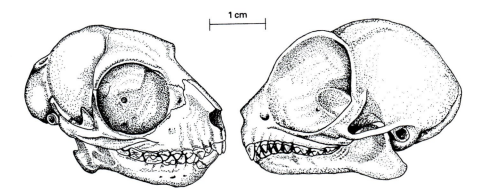

FIGURE 3.17   The fossil omomyid *Necrolemur* (left) belongs to the superfamily Omomyoidea, thought to be ancestral to the modern tarsier (right).

found in platyrrhines (Fleagle 2013, 267). However, parapithecoids may well not be direct ancestors of New World monkeys because this and other shared attributes may be primitive traits retained from earlier ancestors (Fleagle 2013, 273). We still do not know how the earliest platyrrhines reached the New World (Fleagle 2013, 291).

Primates of the Oligocene

The Oligocene epoch lasted from about 38 to about 23 mya. Temperatures cooled and environments dried out. Those adapids whose ancestors made it to the island of Madagascar unwittingly found a safe refuge from evolutionary competition elsewhere and evolved into modern lemurs. Elsewhere, the early anthropoids and their descendants flourished.

Oligocene layers at the Fayum, in Egypt, dating from between 35 and 31 mya, have long been our richest source of information about anthropoid evolution. The best represented group of early anthropoids is the *propliopithecids*, which were larger than the parapithecids and had the 2.1.2.3 dental formula characteristic of all later catarrhines. However, many features of their anatomy are more primitive than those found in Old World monkeys and apes (Fleagle 2013, 273).

Aegyptopithecus zeuxis, the largest of the Oligocene anthropoideans, is well known from numerous fossilized teeth, skulls, and limb bones and appears ancestral to later Old World anthropoids, or *catarrhines* (Figure 3.18). *A. zeuxis* lived 35 mya and looked very much like a primitive monkey (Simons 1985, 40). The bones of its lower jaw and upper cranium are fused along the midlines, and the eye orbits are closed off from the brain by a bony plate. Nevertheless, its limb bones show none of the features that allow modern apes to hang upright or swing from the branches of trees. Its cranium also shows some primitive characteristics: its brain was smaller, its snout projected more, its eye orbits did not face as fully to the front, and its ear was not as fully developed. Propliopithecids

FIGURE 3.18   *Aegyptopithecus zeuxis* is the largest of the Oligocene fossil anthropoids and may be ancestral to all catarrhines (Old World monkeys, apes, and humans).

like *A. zeuxis* have long been described as primitive apes; but recent work suggests that the anatomical traits they share with apes are primitive catarrhine traits, rather than shared, derived ape specializations (Fleagle 2013, 276).

A. zeuxis had two premolars (a diagnostic catarrhine [Old World anthropoid] feature), and it also had Y-5 molars. A *Y-5 molar* is a tooth with five cusps that are separated by a "Y"-shaped furrow (Figure 3.19). Later Old World monkeys (cercopithecoids) have *bilophodont molars* with four cusps arranged in pairs, each of which is joined by a ridge of enamel called a "loph." Early Miocene fossils, 17–19 million years old, of undoubted cercopithecoid monkeys have molars with a fifth cusp and incomplete lophs. Thus, "the bilophodont teeth of Old World monkeys are derived from an ancestor with more ape-like teeth" (Fleagle 2013, 348); and the Y-5 pattern was primitive for all Old World anthropoids, making *A. zeuxis* and other Oligocene catarrhines likely ancestors of both Old World monkeys and hominoids (apes and humans) (Fleagle 2013, 273; Stringer and Andrews 2005, 84).

The earliest known hominoid fossils date from the middle to late Oligocene (29 mya) and come from

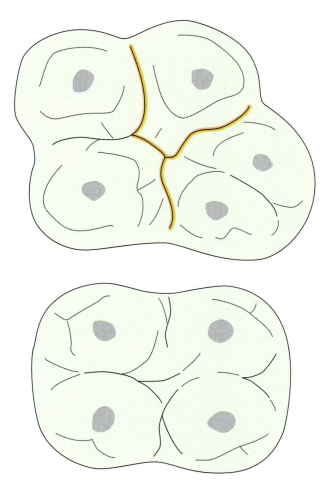

FIGURE 3.19   The upper molar shows the characteristic *Y*-5 pattern of apes and humans; the lower molar exhibits the bilophodont pattern of Old World cercopithecoid monkeys. Current evidence suggests that the Y-5 molar was primitive for all Old World anthropoids and that the bilophodont molar of the cercopithecoids developed later.

western Saudi Arabia and northern Kenya (Fleagle 2013, 313). It was during the Miocene, however, that hominoid evolution took off.

Primates of the Miocene

The Miocene lasted from about 23 to about 5 mya. Between 18 and 17 mya, the continents finally arrived at their present positions, when the African plate (which includes the Arabian Peninsula) contacted the Eurasian plate. This helps explain why fossil hominoids from the early Miocene (about 23–16 mya) have been found only in Africa. More recent fossil hominoids have been found from western Europe to China, presumably because their ancestors used the new land bridge to cross from Africa into Eurasia. During the middle Miocene (about 16–10 mya), hominoid diversity declined. During the late Miocene (about 9–5 mya), cercopithecoid monkeys became very successful; many hominoid species became extinct; and the first members of a new lineage, the hominins, appeared.

In the early Miocene, eastern Africa was covered with tropical forest and woodland. One well-known collection of early Miocene primate fossils has been assigned to the hominoid genus *Proconsul*. The best evidence, including a nearly complete skeleton, exists for the smallest species, *Proconsul heseloni* (formerly *P. africanus*) (Figure 3.20), which was about the size of a modern gibbon (Klein 2009, 117). *Proconsul heseloni* is very apelike in its cranium, teeth, and shoulder and elbow joints. However, its long trunk, arm, and hand resemble those of modern monkeys. It appears to have been a fruit-eating, tree-dwelling, four-footed (four-handed?) protoape that may have lacked a tail. Some argue that it is also generalized enough in its morphology to have been ancestral to later hominoids, including modern apes and human beings, although this is debated (Fleagle 1995). *Proconsul* and other early Miocene hominoids were confined to Africa and the Arabian Peninsula.

Most taxonomists agree, however, that *P. heseloni* and other early-Miocene hominoids were outside the modern hominoid clade (Fleagle 2013, 320). They also retained many primitive catarrhine features lost by later cercopithecoid monkeys, showing that "Old World monkeys are a very specialized group of higher primates" (Fleagle 2013, 322).

The land bridge connecting Africa to Eurasia was formed during the middle Miocene (16–10 mya). The earliest fossils assigned to the modern hominoid clade first date to the middle and late Miocene (10–5 mya) and come mostly from Africa, although one genus, *Kenyapithecus*, is also represented by a second species from Turkey (Fleagle 2013, 320). Once hominoids made it out of Africa, they experienced a rapid radiation throughout many parts of the Old World, and their fossils remain difficult to classify (Fleagle 2013, 326). Unfortunately, very

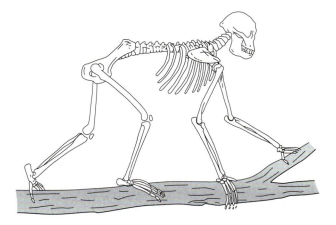

FIGURE 3.20   *Proconsul*, perhaps the best known of the earliest African hominoids. Some argue that *Proconsul* is generalized enough in its morphology to have been ancestral to later hominoids, including modern apes and human beings, although this is debated.

few African hominoid fossils of any kind date from the late Miocene (10–5 mya) or early Pliocene (5–2.5 mya) (Benefit and McCrossin 1995, 251).

In the absence of hard data, attempts to identify either the last common ancestor of the African apes and human beings or the earliest ancestors of chimpanzees and gorillas must be based on educated speculation (Stringer and Andrews 2005, 114). Nevertheless, we know that it was during the late Miocene that the first ancestors in our own lineage appeared. Tracing their evolutionary history is the topic of the next chapter.

Chapter Summary

1. If we avoid anthropomorphism, careful comparison between human beings and other primate species offers enormous insight into our evolutionary past. Primatologists attempt to make sense of primate diversity by creating a primate taxonomy. Traditional taxonomies of primates compared the phenotypes and adaptations of primates and recognized four primate grades. Cladistic taxonomies ignore adaptation and the fossil record and classify organisms only on the basis of homologous evolutionary traits found in living species. Many primatologists combine features of both kinds of taxonomies to demonstrate relations of evolutionary relatedness between species.

2. Strepsirrhines include lemurs and lorises. Haplorhines include tarsiers and anthropoids. Anthropoids include New World and Old World forms. New World monkeys evolved separately from Old World anthropoids and differ from them in nose shape and the number of premolars; in addition, some New World monkeys evolved prehensile tails. All New World monkey species are tree dwellers.

3. Old World anthropoids include species of monkeys and apes, as well as human beings: all share the same nose shape and the same number of premolars. Apes are distinguished from Old World monkeys by dentition, skeletal shape and size, and the absence of a tail. The African apes are far more closely related to one another than they are to gibbons or orangutans, and human beings are more closely related to chimpanzees than to any other ape species. Chimpanzees deliberately make simple tools to help them find food. Bonobos, or pygmy chimpanzees, are known for their highly eroticized social interactions and for the central role females play in their society.

4. Primates show at least six evolutionary trends of their own and four unique features associated with prehensility. These evolutionary trends have not affected all primate species in the same way.

5. Paleontologists assign primate fossils to various categories after examining and comparing cranial and postcranial skeletal material. They have concluded that the first undisputed primates appeared during the Eocene. The best-known Eocene primates are the adapids, which resemble living lemurs, and the omomyids, which resemble living tarsiers. Anthropoideans, ancestral to all later monkeys, apes, and humans, appeared in the late Eocene and are known from sites in northern Africa and Asia. Some Oligocene primate fossils look like possible ancestors to modern New World anthropoids; others, like *Aegyptopithecus zeuxis*, appear ancestral to all later Old World anthropoids.

6. The first hominoids that evolved in Africa during the early Miocene are very diverse. One of the best-known examples is *Proconsul*, which is generalized enough to have been ancestral to later apes and human beings. During the middle Miocene, hominoids rapidly spread and diversified, and their fossils are found from Europe to eastern Asia. In the late Miocene, many hominoid species became extinct. Paleoanthropologists agree that chimpanzees, gorillas, and human beings shared a common ancestor in the late Miocene.

For Review

1. Summarize the discussion of taxonomy at the beginning of the chapter.
2. Distinguish between homology and homoplasy.
3. What are clades? Illustrate with examples.
4. Summarize the features used to distinguish different kinds of primates from each other. What is distinctive about the anthropoids?
5. Discuss the differences and similarities of chimpanzees and bonobos.

6. What are primate ancestral characteristics? Evolutionary trends? Unique morphological features?

7. What adaptive explanations do paleoanthropologists give for the unique features of primates?

8. Prepare a table or chart that displays what is currently known about key developments in primate evolution, from the Paleocene to the Miocene.

Key Terms

anthropomorphism 64	ecological niche 66	morphology 65	stereoscopic vision 77
cladogenesis 65	hominins 72	nocturnal 67	taxonomy 64
cranium 77	homology 65	postcranial skeleton 77	taxon 65
dentition 66	homoplasy 65	prehensile 69	
diurnal 70	mandible 77	sexual dimorphism 72	

Suggested Readings

All the World's Primates. http://www.alltheworldsprimates.org. *This website, which describes itself as "the comprehensive online resource for primate information," provides information on all primate species currently recognized by the International Union for Conservation of Nature. It also presents contributions by researchers on living and fossil primates, including Jane Goodall, Richard Leakey, and John Fleagle.*

Campbell, Christina, Agustín Fuentes, Katherine MacKinnon, Melissa Panger, and Simon Bearder. 2011. *Primates in perspective,* 2nd ed. New York: Oxford University Press. *A comprehensive overview of the primates and what we know about them.*

de Waal, Frans. 2003. *My family album: Thirty years of primate photography.* Berkeley: University of California Press. *In addition to being an influential primatologist, de Waal is a superb photographer. These images are an excellent visual introduction to the various primate species he has studied.*

Fleagle, John G. 2013. *Primate adaptation and evolution,* 3rd ed. Amsterdam: Elsevier. *The third edition of a detailed, up-to-date, and engaging introduction to primatology. The chapters cover both living primates and the fossil record of primate evolution, including that of Homo sapiens. It also addresses current issues in primate conservation.*

Fossey, Dian. 1983. *Gorillas in the mist.* Boston: Houghton Mifflin. *Dian Fossey's account of research among the mountain gorillas of Rwanda over a 13-year period; includes many color photographs. Fossey was murdered at her field station in 1985. This book inspired a major motion picture of the same name.*

Goodall, Jane. 1986. *The chimpanzees of Gombe: Patterns of behavior.* Cambridge, MA: Harvard University Press. *This volume presents the results of a quarter of a century of scientific research among chimpanzees in Gombe, Tanzania.*

Goodall, Jane. 1999. *Jane Goodall: 40 years at Gombe.* New York: Stewart, Tabori and Chang. *After 1986, Jane Goodall shifted the emphasis of her work from scientific observation to rescuing and rehabilitating laboratory animals and working for environmental causes, as have many primatologists concerned about threats to the continued viability of the species they have studied.*

Haraway, Donna. 1989. *Primate visions.* New York: Routledge. *This volume, a major landmark in primate studies, contains a series of essays by a feminist historian of science who describes the way Western cultural assumptions about gender, race, and nature have shaped American primatology. Chapters discussing how collections were made for the American Museum of Natural History and the symbolic significance of white female primatologists should be of particular interest to beginning students.*

International Union for Conservation of Nature. http://www.iucnredlist.org. *The International Union for Conservation of Nature (IUCN) manages a website that contains updated lists of endangered animal species, estimating the degree of endangerment and explaining the sources of endangerment. Entering "Primates" into their search engine brings up a list of endangered primate species. It also provides a wealth of information about the taxonomic status of primate species, their life histories, their habitats, and where their populations can be found.*

Smuts, Barbara, Dorothy Cheney, Robert Seyfarth, and Richard Wrangham, eds. 1987. *Primate societies.* Chicago: University of Chicago Press. *This volume is a classic, comprehensive survey of research on primates from all over the world and includes articles by 46 contributors.*

 Visit our online resource center for further reading, web links, free assessments, flashcards, and videos. www.oup.com/he/lavenda5e

The people who study the human and pre-human past—paleoanthropologists and archaeologists—are vitally concerned with accurately determining when the organisms whose fossils they find actually lived and at what point in time artifacts were made. Without firm dates, paleoanthropologists cannot accurately reconstruct the path of extinction and speciation that led to modern humans; and, as we will see in Chapters 6 and 7, archaeologists cannot accurately trace cultural development. Fortunately, a number of scientific procedures, developed over the past century or so, can aid paleoanthropologists and archaeologists in assigning dates to fossils and artifacts. The following discussion relies primarily on Richard Klein's discussion (2009; Chapter 2).

Relative dating methods identify a particular object as being older or younger in relation to some other object and arrange material evidence in a linear sequence so that we know what came before what (Klein 2009, 22–24). By themselves, however, relative dating methods cannot tell us how long ago a sequence began or how long each stage in the sequence lasted. For such information, we must turn to **numerical (or "absolute") dating** methods, which use laboratory treatment or analysis of various items recovered from an excavation. These techniques can tell us how many years ago a rock layer was formed, a piece of clay was fired, or an animal died (Klein 2009, 33–54).

Numerical dates are sometimes called "absolute dates." Strictly speaking, this term is not accurate because numerical dates always have a margin of error (sometimes in hundreds or thousands of years), ordinarily expressed as plus or minus a certain number of years. The precision of a numerical date depends on the quality of the sample being analyzed and the method of analysis. Nevertheless, because the time frame within which scientists work ordinarily involves thousands or millions of years, the margins of error for most numerical dates are impressively small, explaining why most geologists, paleontologists, and archaeologists continue to call them absolute dates.

In any case, experienced paleontologists and archaeologists rarely rely on only one dating method. Professional practice demands using as many different dating methods, both relative and numerical, as can be applied to any recovered material. When the same materials are subjected to a series of independent analyses and the resulting dates reinforce one another, scholars are increasingly confident of the accuracy of the data.

Relative Dating Methods

Stratigraphic Superposition   The oldest and most venerable of all dating techniques, stratigraphic superposition interprets what we find when we dig deeply into the earth and look at a wall of the resulting hole, which tends to resemble a layer cake of rocks and soil of different color and composition (Figure M2.1). Geologists reason that, other things being equal, things on the bottom are older than things on the top. When applied to soil layers, or strata (singular **stratum**), this so-called **law of superposition** states that layers lower down must be older than the layers above them. If so, then objects embedded in lower layers must be older than those in upper layers, whether these objects are fossils or artifacts fashioned by human hands.

Superposed layers of rock rarely remain undisturbed forever. Sometimes old rocks are crosscut by other geological features, as when molten lava forces its way through fractures in several superposed layers on its way to the surface. The intruding features must be younger than the layers of rock they cut across, a deduction called the **law of crosscutting relationships**. In addition, periods of uplift and subsidence in the earth's crust have sometimes tilted or twisted large sections of layered rock from a horizontal to a vertical position (Figure M2.2). These rearranged rock layers (*unconformities*) may be exposed to erosion for a considerable period of time before new layers of sediment begin to collect and bury them again.

The pattern of stratigraphic superposition in a given rock column tends to be distinctive, something like a fingerprint. As a result, geologists are often able to correlate deposits at one site with those at another site when those deposits have the same distinctive pattern. This enables them to generalize about what was happening geologically over wider regions and longer periods of time.

Typological Sequences   Classifying fossils or artifacts into a series of types on the basis of their similarities and differences is a time-honored and very useful form of relative dating. Those objects that look most alike are grouped together, compared to other objects of similar kinds (often recovered from other excavations), and ordered in a chronological or developmental sequence. If at least one end of the typological

---

relative dating methods   Dating methods that arrange material evidence in a linear sequence, each object in the sequence being identified as older or younger than another object.

numerical (or "absolute") dating   Dating methods based on laboratory techniques that assign age in years to material evidence.

stratum   Layer; in geological terms, a layer of rock and soil.

law of superposition   A principle of geological interpretation stating that layers lower down in a sequence of strata must be older than the layers above them; and, therefore, that objects embedded in lower layers must be older than objects embedded in upper layers.

law of crosscutting relationships   A principle of geological interpretation stating that where old rocks are crosscut by other geological features, the intruding features must be younger than the layers of rock they cut across.

sequence can be anchored by a numerical date, the sequence then becomes a powerful tool for understanding evolutionary change, even in the absence of fossil evidence.

Certain kinds of fossil evidence can provide an extremely helpful framework for the relative dating of other fossils or of the artifacts associated with them. As we saw, scientific confidence in the law of superposition increased when geologists found that not only rock layers but also the fossils they contained could be systematically correlated. Two kinds of fossil species are most useful for relative dating: those that spread out quickly over a large area following the widespread extinction of their parent species and those that evolved so rapidly that a fossil representing any evolutionary stage is a good indicator of the relative age of other fossils found in association with it. Relative dating that relies on patterns of fossil distribution in different rock layers is called **biostratigraphic dating** (Klein 2009, 24–33).

For paleoanthropologists, the most useful biostratigraphic patterns deal with regions and periods of time in which human beings, or our ancestors, were evolving. Although biostratigraphy can establish only relative dates, its correlations are indispensable for cross-checking dates provided by numerical methods. For example, fossils of the one-toed horse played an important role in the 1970s when paleoanthropologists were attempting to assign firm dates to important hominin fossil-bearing layers at the eastern African site of Koobi Fora. The potassium-argon dating method (see the section "Isotopic Methods") yielded a date for the Koobi Fora site that would have made it over half a million years older than a site only 100 km north, in the lower Omo River valley, yet the biostratigraphy of these two sites was identical. The paleoanthropologists reasoned that either the one-toed horse had appeared at Koobi

Fora over half a million years earlier than it had in the Lower Omo, or something was wrong with the potassium-argon dates. Eventually, they determined that the potassium-argon date for Koobi Fora was 700,000–600,000 years too early (Klein 2009, 38). This is exactly what can happen if paleoanthropologists give too much importance to a single, "absolute" date.

Archaeologists also use typological sequences based on collections of artifacts. Artifacts that look alike are assumed to have been made at the same time, which allows archaeologists to arrange them in a linear order, a technique called **seriation**. Seriation can only indicate patterns of change; some other source of information must be used to anchor one end of the series in time. *Contextual seriation*, based on changes in artifact styles, is most successfully applied to artifacts like pottery, whose stylistic features are visible and highly modifiable. At the end of the nineteenth century, archaeologist Sir Flinders Petrie used contextual seriation to analyze variations in the pottery recovered from predynastic burials at Diospolis Parva in Upper Egypt. Petrie had no method to assign firm dates to these burials, so he devised a relative chronology in the following way. All the contents of each grave were written on a separate sheet of paper. Then, Petrie moved the sheets around until he had a sequence in which as many similar artifacts as possible were arranged as closely as possible to one another. Then, he created a relative chronology based on stylistic changes in the artifacts they contained (Figure M2.3).

---

biostratigraphic dating A relative dating method that relies on patterns of fossil distribution in different rock layers.

seriation A relative dating method based on the assumption that artifacts that look alike must have been made at the same time.

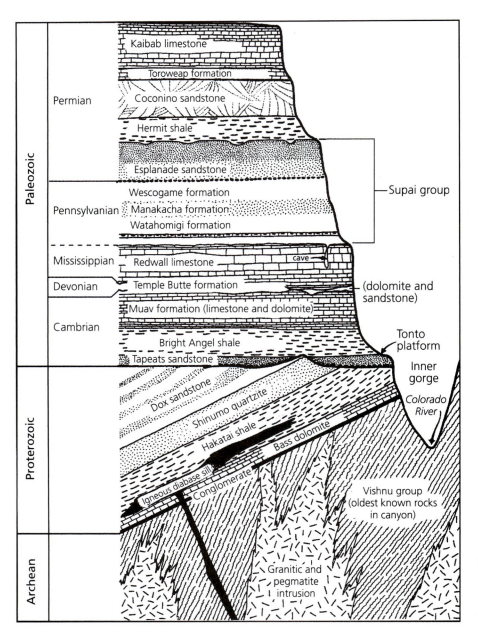

FIGURE M2.2 Geological analysis of one wall of the Grand Canyon yields evidence of superposition (e.g., Coconino sandstone lies atop Hermit shale and is thus younger), unconformities (e.g., the Paleozoic and Proterozoic strata), and crosscutting relationships (e.g., granitic and pegmatitic intrusions into the Vishnu group).

Later research confirmed that Petrie's relative sequence was very close to the actual historical sequence.

Artifacts and structures from a particular time and place in a site are called an **assemblage**. *Frequency seriation* measures changes in artifact percentages from one undated assemblage

to another. Archaeologists assume that different proportions of artifact styles in an assemblage are a measure of popularity, that all styles gain and lose popularity over time, and that styles popular at one site should also be popular at contemporary sites nearby. When the frequencies of different artifacts from a series of assemblages are plotted on a graph, and sites containing the styles in similar frequencies are kept together, the result, once again, is a relative chronology of assemblages

---

assemblage Artifacts and structures from a particular time and place in an archaeological site.

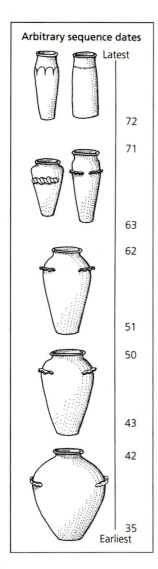

Arbitrary sequence dates

Latest

72

71

63

62

51

50

43

42

35

Earliest

FIGURE M2.3 Contextual seriation is a time-honored and very useful form of relative dating. The classic use of seriation in archaeology is attributed to Sir Flinders Petrie, who used it at the end of the nineteenth century to analyze variations in pottery recovered from predynastic burials in Egypt.

based on the rising and falling frequencies of the different styles. Frequency seriation has been used by archaeologists to arrange a number of undated pottery assemblages into relative sequences that have been confirmed by stratigraphic sequences from excavations (Renfrew and Bahn 2004, 128).

Obsidian hydration is a relative dating method based on the principle that when obsidian (volcanic glass that can be made into extremely sharp tools) is fractured, it starts to absorb water along the newly exposed surface, forming a hydration layer. This hydration layer gets thicker over time and can be measured. Every time obsidian breaks, the hydration

process begins anew on the freshly revealed surface. If the rate of hydration is constant, then it should be possible to tell how long it has been since the obsidian was fractured, either naturally or by someone making a tool out of it. Unfortunately, the hydration rate of obsidian is not uniform throughout the world—different kinds of obsidian have different hydration rates, and the atmospheric temperature at the time the obsidian surface is revealed also affects the hydration rate. However, correlation maps of climate and hydration rates have been prepared, and several researchers are working on how to distinguish among different kinds of obsidian. But where these limitations can be controlled, obsidian hydration can be very helpful to archaeologists: it can be used for dates from 7.8 mya to the present, it is relatively inexpensive, and it can be used to trace the trade routes of obsidian in the past. The technique has been quite helpful in Mesoamerica, where Ann Corinne Freter and her colleagues, for example, were able to analyze an abundant collection of obsidian artifacts at Copán and plot changing settlement patterns over time with great accuracy (Fagan and DeCorse 2005, 161).

Numerical (or Absolute) Dating Methods

Numerical (or absolute) dating methods are valuable because they anchor a series of fossils dated by relative methods to a numbered date, a fixed point in time that can be used to estimate rates of evolution. Perhaps best known are **isotopic dating** methods, which are based on knowledge about the rate at which various radioactive isotopes of naturally occurring elements transform themselves into other elements by losing subatomic particles. This process is called *decay*, and the rate of decay of a given radioactive isotope is measured in terms of its *half-life*, or the time it takes for half of the original radioactive sample to decay into the nonradioactive end product. Rates of decay make useful atomic clocks because they are unaffected by other physical or chemical processes. Moreover, because each radioactive element has a unique half-life, we can cross-check dates obtained by one isotopic method with those obtained by another. As geologists Sheldon Judson and Marvin Kauffman (1990) conclude, "The fact that several clocks regularly agree indicates that radio-active dating is self-consistent and reassures us that we are measuring real ages" (146).

Geologists using isotopic dating methods to determine the ages of rocks generally agree that the earth is about 4.6 billion years old. Paleoanthropologists are most interested in only a tiny fraction of all that geological time, perhaps the last

isotopic dating Dating methods based on scientific knowledge about the rate at which various radioactive isotopes of naturally occurring elements transform themselves into other elements by losing subatomic particles.

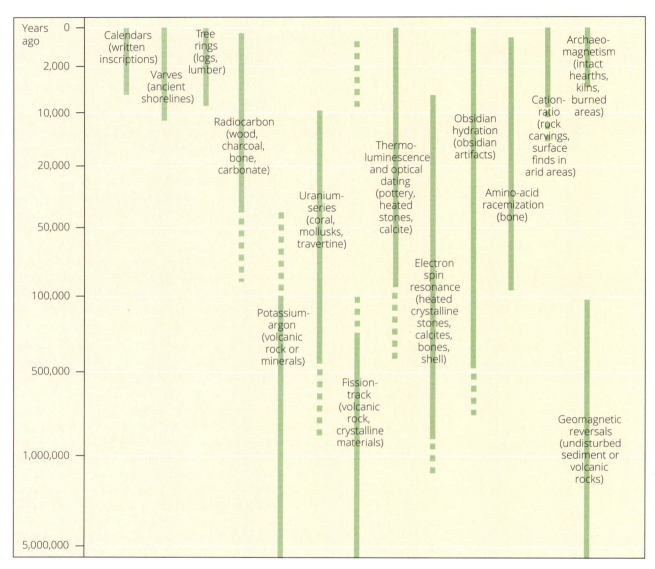

FIGURE M2.4   Chronometric dating methods can be used to anchor a series of fossils or artifacts dated by relative methods to a fixed point in time. This chart summarizes some of the most important chronometric methods, showing the spans of time and materials for which each is applicable. (Adapted from Renfrew and Bahn 2008, 133.)

65 million years, the period during which nonhuman primates and then human beings evolved. Archaeologists focus on an even narrower slice: the last 2.5 million years.

Isotopic Methods   Described below are several reliable isotopic dating methods. A more complete list of numerical dating methods, with the periods for which dates are the most accurate, appears in Figure M2.4.

Potassium-Argon Dating   Potassium is one of the most commonly occurring elements in the earth's crust. One isotope of potassium that occurs in relatively small quantities is radioactive potassium 40, which decays at a known rate into

argon 40. During volcanic activity, very nearly all of the argon 40 in molten lava escapes, resetting the atomic clock to zero. Potassium, however, does not escape. As lava cools and crystallizes, any argon 40 that collects in the rock can only have been produced by the decay of potassium 40. The date of the formation of the volcanic rock can then be calculated, based on the half-life of potassium 40, which is 1.3 billion years.

The potassium-argon method is accurate for dates from the origin of the earth up to about 100,000 years ago. This method is valuable to paleoanthropologists because it can date volcanic rock formed early in the evolutionary history of nonhuman primates and human beings and thus any fossils found in or under volcanic rock layers themselves.

Fortunately, volcanic activity was common during these periods in areas like eastern Africa, where many important fossils of early human ancestors have been found.

Potassium-argon dating has two main limitations. First, it can be used only on volcanic rock. Second, its margin of error is about ±10%. A volcanic rock dated by the potassium-argon technique to 200,000 years ago ±10% could have been formed anywhere from 220,000 to 180,000 years ago. Nevertheless, no other technique yet provides more accurate dates for the periods in which early hominin evolution occurred. Since the late 1980s, a variant called the 40Ar/39Ar method has been developed, which produces more precise dates using samples as small as a single grain of volcanic rock. The 40Ar/39Ar method was able to determine that the ash layer beneath the oldest hominin fossils at Aramis, in Ethiopia, was actually 4.4 million years old, after separating out 23.6 million-year-old volcanic grains that were intrusions (Klein 2009, 37).

Fission-Track Dating   A recently developed technique, fission-track dating is also based on the decay of radioactive material in rock. Many minerals, natural glasses such as obsidian, and manufactured glasses contain uranium 235 and small quantities of radioactive uranium 238. Occasionally, atoms of uranium 238 split in half. During this spontaneous fission, the two halves of the atom fly apart violently, leaving tracks in the mineral. The older the material, the more uranium 238 atoms split and the more tracks are found. If the rock is heated, however, the fission tracks are erased, resetting the radioactive clock to zero.

To calculate the age of a rock using the fission-track technique, two counts of fission tracks must be made. The first count identifies the number of tracks formed naturally by uranium 238. In the next step, to determine how much uranium was in the sample to begin with, the sample is irradiated to induce fission in the uranium 235, and the resulting tracks are counted to calculate the amount of uranium 235. Because the naturally occurring ratio of uranium 238 to uranium 235 in rock is known, the count of uranium 235 indirectly measures the original quantity of uranium 238. Because the fission rate of uranium 238 is also known, the date of the sample can now be calculated based on the ratio of uranium 238 tracks to the quantity of uranium 238 the sample is thought to have originally contained.

The range of dates from the fission-track technique overlaps the range from the potassium-argon method: from about 300,000 to some 2.5 billion years ago. Fission-track dating can be used where the potassium-argon method cannot be applied and can also provide a second opinion on materials already dated by the potassium-argon method. Paleontologists and archaeologists have applied fission-track dating to sites where volcanic rock layers lie above or below sediments containing hominin fossils, especially in eastern Africa (Klein 2009, 38).

Uranium-Series Dating   This dating method is based on two facts. First, when uranium 238, uranium 235, and thorium 232 decay, they produce intermediate radioactive isotopes until eventually they transform into stable isotopes of lead. Second, uranium is easily dissolved in water; as it decays, the intermediate isotopes it produces tend to solidify, separate out of the water, and mix with salts that collect on the bottom of a lake or sea. Using their knowledge of the half-lives of uranium isotopes and their intermediate products, scientists can date soil deposits that formed in ancient lake or sea beds.

Uranium-series evidence can be used to date broad climatic events, such as glaciations, that may have affected the course of human evolution. But it also allows paleoanthropologists to date inorganic carbonates, such as limestones, that accumulate in cave, spring, and lake deposits where hominin fossils are sometimes found. Uranium-series dating is significant because it is useful for dating many important archaeological sites that contain inorganic carbonates and because it provides dates for periods of time not covered well by other dating methods—particularly the period between 150,000 and 350,000 years ago, when *Homo sapiens* first appeared (Klein 2009, 38–41). At present, uranium-series dating is particularly useful for the period 50,000–500,000 years ago (see Figure M2.4).

Radiocarbon Dating   Radiocarbon dating may be the method of absolute dating best known to nonanthropologists. The method is based on four assumptions: (1) that the amount of radioactive carbon 14 in the atmosphere has remained constant over time, (2) that radioactive and nonradioactive carbon mix rapidly so that the ratio of one to the other in the atmosphere is likely to be the same everywhere, (3) that radioactive carbon is just as likely as nonradioactive carbon to enter into chemical compounds, and (4) that living organisms are equally likely to take radioactive carbon and nonradioactive carbon into their bodies.

If these assumptions hold, then we can deduce that equal amounts of radioactive and nonradioactive carbon are present in all living tissues. Once an organism dies, however, it stops taking carbon into its system, and the radioactive carbon 14 in its remains begins to decay at a known rate. The half-life of carbon 14 is 5,730 years, making radiocarbon dating extremely useful for dating the remains of organisms that died as long ago as 30,000–40,000 years. Samples older than about 40,000 years usually contain too little carbon 14 for accurate measurement. However, a refinement in radiocarbon technology called accelerator mass spectrometry (or AMS) solves that problem in part for smaller samples. AMS counts the actual atoms of carbon 14 in a sample. Charcoal, for example, can be reliably dated to 55,000 years ago using AMS (Klein 2009, 46; Figure M2.5).

FIGURE M2.5   The University of Arizona accelerator mass spectrometry lab is a center for the dating of organic materials that are 50,000–80,000 years old.

Radiocarbon dating is not flawless. Evidence shows that the amount of carbon 14 in the earth's atmosphere fluctuates periodically as a result of such factors as solar activity, changes in the strength of the earth's magnetic field, and changes in the amount of carbon dioxide dissolved in the world's oceans. Scientists are also concerned that an organism's tissues can become contaminated by carbon from outside sources either before or after death; this problem is particularly acute in very old samples analyzed by AMS. If undetected, any of these factors could yield inaccurate radiocarbon dates. AMS dating of bone samples targets collagen molecules. Together with improved cleaning routines, ultrafiltration screens out low-quality bone samples and produces purer collagen samples using extremely fine filters to remove contaminants that coarser filters cannot capture. As a consequence, older AMS dates can be accurately calculated (Higham et al. 2006). Ancient charcoal samples submitted for radiocarbon dating also are pretreated before undergoing the procedure, but acid-base wet oxidation (ABOX) removes more contaminants than previous pretreatments, especially when performed under conditions that isolate the process from the atmosphere (Bird et al. 1999).

Scientists have discovered that radiocarbon dates for samples less than about 7,500 years old differ from their true ages anywhere from 1 to 10%. Fortunately, radiocarbon dates can be corrected by dendrochronology over roughly the same 7,000-year time span. Most archaeologists use radiocarbon dates corrected by dendrochronology, or tree-ring dating (see Figure M2.6), to convert radiocarbon years into calendar years, assigning dates in "radiocarbon years" rather than in calendar solar years. Radiocarbon years are indicated when they are followed by the letters B. P., meaning "before present"; for purposes of calibration, "present" was established as 1950. In addition, radiocarbon ages are always given with a plus-or-minus range, reflecting the statistical uncertainties of the method (e.g., 14,000 ± 120 years ago; Klein 2009, 45).

Thermoluminescence   If a natural substance is exposed to radiation emitted by naturally occurring radioactive isotopes of uranium, thorium, and potassium, the electrons released become trapped in the crystal structure of the irradiated substance. If the irradiated substance is subsequently heated, however, the trapped electrons will be released together with a quantity of light directly in proportion to their number. The light released in this process is called *thermoluminescence*.

If we know the amount of radiation our sample receives per year, heat it up, and measure the amount of thermoluminescence released, then we can calculate the number of years since the sample was last heated. This is a handy way of determining the date when ancient pottery fragments were last fired, when burnt-flint artifacts were last heated, or even when naturally occurring clays were heated accidentally by a fire burning above them. The accuracy of this method may be questioned if it can be determined either that trapped electrons sometimes escape without being heated or that radiation doses are not constant.

Electron Spin Resonance (ESR)   This method is based on the fact that tooth enamel in a living organism is free of uranium but begins to absorb uranium after burial. Dates are determined by estimating background radioactivity, measuring the amount of uranium in the enamel of a fossilized tooth, and then determining the rate at which the uranium accumulated in the tooth after burial. ESR dates are often used to cross-check dates provided by thermoluminescence, but sometimes ESR dates do not match up very well. It may be that the process of uranium uptake is more complicated than previously understood and that a variety of factors can affect the level of uranium that actually accumulates in tooth enamel at a particular site. According to Klein, both luminescence dates and ESR dates are affected by site-specific factors that may interfere with their degree of accuracy. ESR dates, in particular, must be evaluated with great care (Klein 2009, 47–48).

Techniques like thermoluminescence and ESR are valuable because, like the uranium-series method, they use materials other than bones or charcoal to yield reliable dates for the troublesome gap between the limits of the radiocarbon method and the potassium-argon methods—between 40,000 and 100,000–300,000 years ago (Fagan 1991, 64; Klein 2009, 35). As we will see in Chapter 4, this is the period when our

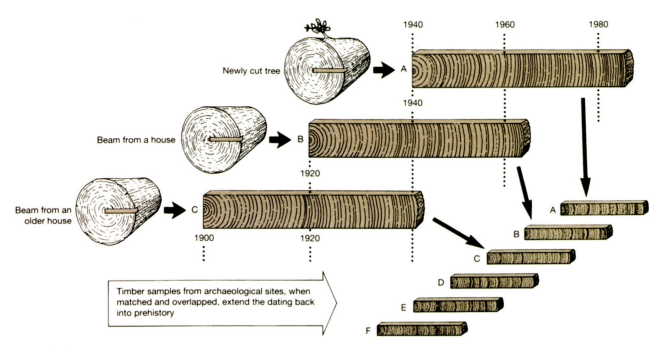

FIGURE M2.6 Trees with annual growth rings are similar to rock layers in that their distinctive sequences can be correlated across sites to yield an uninterrupted chronology that may go back hundreds or thousands of years. Researchers use this master chronology to assign chronometric dates to wood recovered from archaeological sites. *Acknowledgments:* Original drawn by Simon S. S. Driver, based on other sources (Renfrew and Bahn 2008, 139).

own species emerged, when we coexisted, and occasionally exchanged genes with, Neandertals. Paleoanthropologist Chris Stringer, a specialist in this period, has been involved with the development and refinement of such techniques. He recently observed that "As with radiocarbon dating, procedures have continuously been refined, so that now even single grains of sand can be dated by luminescence. Equally in the case of ESR . . . we have moved to a situation in which, using the microscopic technique of laser ablation, it is now possible to directly date a tiny area of fossil tooth enamel" (Stringer, 2012, 44); indeed, "the potential of ESR to match the ability of AMS radiocarbon in directly dating human fossils is at last being realized" (47).

Nonisotopic Methods   Unlike isotopic techniques, **nonisotopic dating** methods do not use rates of nuclear decay to provide numerical dates of materials recovered from excavations.

Dendrochronology   Dendrochronology yields numerical dates for trees and objects made of wood. A crosscut section of a mature tree exposes a series of concentric rings, which normally accumulate one per year over the tree's life.

(Old trees do not need to be cut down to recover the tree-ring chronology they contain; instead, scientists bore long, thin holes into their trunks and remove samples that preserve the sequence.) Tree rings are thicker in wet years and thinner in dry years. The pattern of thick and thin rings is similar for all trees growing in the same habitat over many years. The older the tree, the more growth rings it has and the more complete is its record of the growth pattern for the locality. Clearly, only trees with seasonal growth patterns can be used successfully in dendrochronology—those that grow all year round, such as those in tropical rain forests, do not produce variable ring patterns.

Tree rings are similar to rock layers because scientists can use their distinctive sequences to correlate different sites with one another. Figure M2.6 shows how the tree-ring sequences from three old trees cut down at different times can be cross-correlated to yield an uninterrupted chronology that covers 100 years. Scientists use this master chronology to match wood recovered from archaeological sites against the appropriate sequence to determine when a tree lived and when it

---

nonisotopic dating Dating methods that assign age in years to material evidence but not by using rates of nuclear decay.

was cut down. Tree-ring chronologies based on the California bristlecone pine extend more than 8,000 years into the past. In Europe, chronologies based on oak trees go back to about 6,000 years ago (Renfrew and Bahn 2008, 139).

Amino Acid Racemization (AAR)   This method is based on the fact that amino acids in proteins can exist in two mirror-image forms, left-handed (L amino acids) and right-handed (D amino acids). Usually, only L amino acids are found in living organisms, but after the organism dies, they are converted into D amino acids. The rate of conversion is different for each amino acid and depends on a variety of factors, including the surrounding temperature, moisture, and acidity level. If those levels can be determined since the time the specimen died, the ratio of D to L forms can be used to calculate how long ago death occurred. Amino acid racemization has proved most accurate when dating fossilized shells (Klein 2009, 50).

Paleomagnetism   This dating method is based on the discovery that the earth's magnetic poles have not always been where they are today, perhaps because of shifting currents within the earth's molten core. A magnet points north during some periods of earth history, south during others. Sometimes a past polarity shift lasted for a long period, called a *chron*; at other times, shifts alternated repeatedly for short intervals, called *subchrons*. Changes in polarity are preserved in volcanic rocks or rocks composed of fine-grained sediments that settled slowly. When volcanic rocks cool or sediments settle, their particles align themselves toward the current magnetic pole and retain this pattern. By examining geologic cores to map the positions and deduce the time of particular changes in polarity, geologists have been able to create a master chronology of paleomagnetic shifts that covers the past 5 million years.

Boundary dates between chrons are better established than boundary dates between subchrons; but because all paleomagnetic dates are less precise than other numerical dating methods, paleomagnetism looks more like a form of relative dating than a form of numerical dating. However, paleomagnetism is extremely valuable because, unlike other dating methods, it has the potential to provide a temporal framework within which geological, climatological, and evolutionary events can be related on a worldwide scale. It is particularly helpful to paleoanthropologists because the human line evolved during the last 5 million years. Paleomagnetic dates can be used to cross-check dates for important sites and to provide a general time frame for sites undatable by other means (Klein 2009, 51–54).

The Molecular Clock   The concept of a molecular clock is based on the assumption that genetic mutations accumulate in DNA at a constant rate. This is most accurately measured in DNA that is unlikely to experience natural selection, such as mitochondrial DNA (mtDNA). Geneticists compare the genes of different living species (or the proteins produced by those genes), measure the degree of genetic (or protein) differences among them, and deduce the length of time since they all shared a common ancestor.

This dating method begins as a form of cladistic analysis. However, it can be converted into a numerical dating method if other numerical techniques tell us when the fossil ancestors of one of the living species being compared first appeared (Ruvolo and Pilbeam 1986, 157). For example, "if a fossil (geological) date of 25 mya for the divergence of Old World monkeys from apes is assumed, recently developed DNA hybridization data imply that the human and chimpanzee lines split about 5.5 mya and that the gorilla lineage became distinct about 7.7 mya, the gibbon lineage about 16.4 mya, the orangutan lineage about 12.2 mya, and (by definition) the line leading to Old World monkeys about 25 mya" (Klein 1989, 28). When this series of dates was first suggested, it contradicted dates for the divergence of primate species established on other grounds. However, new fossils and further research appear to vindicate the chronology suggested by the molecular clock.

Not all paleoanthropologists accept the validity of this technique. Some question the key assumption that genetic mutations accumulate at a constant rate; others point out that the accuracy of the molecular clock depends on the accuracy of some other numerical method used to date the presumed fossil ancestors of one of the species being compared. If the original numerical date is wrong or if variation in a population's DNA has been affected by evolutionary forces other than mutation (genetic drift, e.g.), the molecular clock will provide a series of erroneous dates for later species' divergences (see, e.g., Thorne and Wolpoff 1992; Templeton 1993). Klein (2009), however, observes that recent African fossil finds "now support the 8- to 5-Ma molecular estimate for African ape and human divergence, and few specialists now ignore the molecular clock" (94). However, as we will see, even if the molecular clock is a problematic dating method, DNA and other biomolecules recovered from fossils are now used to inform paleoanthropologists about many other features of extinct human organisms and their ways of life (K. A. Brown and T. A. Brown 2013).

Modeling Prehistoric Climates

Much of the geological data that provide primate paleontologists with dates for their fossils and archaeologists with dates for their artifacts also provide information about the environment in which those fossil organisms and the

TABLE M2.1 The Major Divisions of Geological Time Relevant to Paleoanthropologists

ERA	PERIOD	EPOCH	MILLION YEARS AGO (MYA)	IMPORTANT EVENTS
	Quaternary	Recent	.01	Modern genera of animals
Cenozoic		Pleistocene	2	Early humans and giant mammals now extinct
		Pliocene	5.1	Anthropoid radiation and culmination of mammalian speciation
		Miocene	25	
	Tertiary	Oligocene	38	
		Eocene	54	Expansion and differentiation of mammals
		Paleocene	65	

Source: Price and Feinman 2001, 27.

artifacts' makers once lived (Table M2.1). In recent years, information about ancient climates and climate changes has accumulated and aided primate paleontologists and archaeologists in better reconstructing the various selective pressures under which prehistoric nonhuman primate and human populations would have lived. Evidence for major fluctuations in ancient climates has been incorporated into the theory of punctuated equilibrium, discussed in Chapter 4.

A major source of information on past climate comes from the contents of cores drilled into the ocean floor or into glaciers (Figure M2.7). Deep sea sediments are especially reliable because their deposition shows fewer interruptions than do dry land deposits, and they rarely experience erosion (Klein 2009, 59). Ocean water contains two different isotopes of oxygen, the lighter 16O and the heavier 18O. The lighter isotopes are taken out of ocean water when glaciers form but return to it when glaciers melt. Furthermore, oxygen is incorporated into the skeletons of microscopic marine organisms called *foraminifera*. For millions of years, foraminifera have been settling on the ocean bottom after they die, which means that those collected in ocean cores can be analyzed to see which isotope of oxygen they contain. Foraminifera with 18O in their skeletons must have lived and died when glaciers took up 16O, whereas those with 16O must have lived and died when glaciers were not present. Oxygen isotope curves can be plotted to trace climate changes over the past 2.3 million years. Isotope sequences can be correlated with paleomagnetic

reversals, and the forams themselves can be dated by carbon 14. The result is a powerful worldwide chronology of climate change within which biological evolutionary events may be contextualized (Potts 1996, 50–51; Renfrew and Bahn 2004, 130).

Scientists do not fully understand the causes of climatic fluctuations but suspect that they are connected with such phenomena as changes in the shape and position of the continents, the tilt of the earth's axis, sunspot activity, the shape of the earth's orbit around the sun, and volcanic activity (Potts 1996). Debate continues about whether some of these fluctuations correlate with evolutionary events: the temperature drop around 15 mya seems to coincide with the diversification of hominoids in Africa and Asia, whereas the development of a drier, more seasonal climate between 10 and 5 mya may be connected with widespread hominoid extinctions and the appearance of the first human ancestors (Vrba et al. 1995). Data on climate also show that human prehistory for the past million years developed during periods of intense glaciation interrupted by periods of warmer climate. Different interpretations of these climatic fluctuations affect the way paleoanthropologists model the selective pressures that eventually gave rise to our own species some 200,000 years ago. They also affect explanations of major shifts in cultural adaptation (such as the domestication of plants and animals and the adoption of a sedentary life) that closely followed the retreat of the last glaciers some 12,000 years ago. We will explore these matters more fully in Chapter 6.

FIGURE M2.7 Ice cores can provide information about the sequences of changing climate over extended periods of time. They are carefully extracted from glaciers (a) and stored in temperature-controlled rooms (b) until they can be analyzed.

Module Summary

1. Scientific dating methods assist paleoanthropologists and archaeologists in their work. Relative dates indicate which objects are older or younger in a given sequence. Numerical dates identify how many years ago a rock layer was formed, a piece of clay was fired, or a living animal died. Paleoanthropologists and archaeologists ordinarily use as many dating methods as possible to assign reliable dates to the objects they recover.

2. Stratigraphic superposition underlies all relative and numerical dating methods. Scientists can cross-correlate strata from different locations to generalize about what was happening geologically over wider regions and longer periods of time. These correlations apply not only to the rock layers themselves but also to the fossils or artifacts they contain. Biostratigraphic dating uses the fossils of widespread or rapidly evolving species to date the relative age of other fossils associated with them.

3. Numerical (or "absolute") dating methods can anchor a series of fossils dated by relative methods to a fixed point in time. Isotopic dating methods are based on scientific knowledge about the rate at which various radioactive isotopes of naturally occurring elements transform themselves into other elements by losing subatomic particles. Nonisotopic dating methods that do not involve radioactive decay include paleomagnetism and the molecular clock.

4. Paleontologists have drawn on climatic data to better reconstruct the various selective pressures under which prehistoric nonhuman primate and human populations would have lived. Between 1.6 mya and 12,000 years ago, temperatures plunged and ice sheets expanded and contracted during the Pleistocene. Some of these climatic fluctuations appear to correlate to evolutionary events and changes in human cultural adaptation.

For Review

1. What is the difference between relative dating methods and numerical dating methods?

2. Explain stratigraphic superposition and the law of crosscutting relationships.

3. What is seriation? What is the difference between contextual seriation and frequency seriation?

4. List the main forms of relative dating discussed in the text.

5. What are the isotopic methods of dating discussed in the text?

6. What are the nonisotopic methods of dating?

7. Why are climatic data useful to paleontologists?

Key Terms

assemblage   86

biostratigraphic
  dating   85

isotopic dating   87

law of crosscutting
  relationships   84

law of superposition   84

nonisotopic dating   91

numerical (or "absolute")
  dating methods   84

relative dating
  methods   84

seriation   85

stratum   84

What can the fossil record tell us about human origins?

Anthropology has made major contributions to our understanding of human biological and cultural evolution. This chapter tells the story of what we have learned from fossils, stone tools, and other cultural remains from the appearance of our earliest known ancestors about 6 million years ago through the appearance of modern *Homo sapiens* about 300,000 years ago.

CHAPTER OUTLINE

What Is Macroevolution?
Who Were the First Hominins (6–3 mya)?
How Can Anthropologists Explain the Human Transition?

What Do We Know about Early *Homo* (2.4–1.5 mya)?
Who Was *Homo erectus* (1.8–1.7 mya to 0.5–0.4 mya)?

How Did *Homo sapiens* Evolve?
Chapter Summary

LEARNING OBJECTIVES

- Describe the process of macroevolution and distinguish this concept from other evolutionary concepts.
- Describe major evolutionary trends that resulted in *Homo sapiens* and anatomically modern humans as evidenced by fossil records.

- Describe the characteristics of the Neandertals and how they are situated in evolutionary history.
- Explain evidence for cultural patterns during the Middle Paleolithic, Stone Age, Upper Paleolithic, and Late Stone Age
- Discuss the cultural diversity evidenced during the Upper

Paleolithic and Late Stone Age
- Recognize the migration patterns of modern Homo sapiens during the Late Pleistocene
- Summarize two million years of human evolution using key concepts such as social and cognitive skills and ecological niches.

The discovery of a new hominin species, Homo naledi, *is revealed to the public in Johannesburg, South Africa, in 2015.*

TABLE 4.1 Models of Macroevolution		
	PHYLETIC GRADUALISM	**PUNCTUATED EQUILIBRIA**
Macroevolution	A uniform process, the eventual outcome of microevolution, given enough time	*Different* from microevolution, not a uniform process
Motor of speciation	The result of *anagenesis*, the gradual transformation of one species into another species	The result of *cladogenesis*, the rapid production of multiple new species alongside parent species
Species boundary	Species boundaries are arbitrary	Species boundaries are real
Consequences	No sharp breaks in fossil record between old and new species	Speciation achieves the shifting of "genetic and morphological centers of gravity of parent and daughter species" such that "each species is now free to accumulate more variation and hence more potential species differences" (Tattersall 1998, 163)

Chapter 2 presented some of the central concepts of modern evolutionary theory, and Chapter 3 used some of these concepts to locate human beings within the primate order. In this chapter, we turn to a consideration of the fossil evidence that provides evidence for the evolutionary history of our species, highlighting the ways in which that history differed from that of our closest primate relatives. As such, this chapter will be adopting the perspective of **macroevolution**, which focuses on long-term evolutionary changes, especially the origins of new species and their diversification across space and time over millions of years. Spanning many generations and the growth and decay of many different ecological settings, macroevolution is measured in geological time. **Microevolution**, by contrast, devotes attention to short-term evolutionary changes that occur within a given species over relatively few generations. It is measured in what is sometimes called "ecological time," or the pace of time as experienced by organisms living and adapting to their ecological settings. The study of microevolutionary processes affecting the human species will be the topic of Chapter 5.

What Is Macroevolution?

Macroevolution studies evolution at or above the species level over extremely long stretches of geological time and is concerned with tracing (and explaining) the

extinction of old species and the origin of new species. Evidence for these processes comes from close study of fossils and of the comparative anatomy of living organisms. As we shall see, the way we understand macroevolution shapes our understanding of human evolution.

Until the 1970s, most evolutionary biologists were more or less convinced that the problems of macroevolution had been solved in a satisfactory manner by Darwin himself. Darwin claimed, and neo-Darwinians agreed, that macroevolution—the origin of new species—is simply what happens when microevolution continues over a long enough period of time (Table 4.1). Such a view seemed plausible because, as we have seen, all these evolutionary thinkers assumed that over time, genetic and environmental changes are inevitable. Mutation (if unchecked by natural selection) inevitably changes a species' physical attributes over time in the same way that the natural environment, perpetually subject to uniformitarian processes of erosion and uplift, never remains constant. Evolution was thought to occur when independent processes of genetic change and environmental change intersect in the phenotypes of organisms living in a particular habitat.

In his final formulation of the theory of natural selection, Darwin argued that there is no such thing as a fixed species, precisely because evolution is gradual. And evolution is gradual because environments change slowly. Lamarck's concept of long-term evolutionary change was also gradualistic, except that he pictured *individual members* of a long-lived natural kind (and their offspring) tracking the changing environment over a long period of time. For Darwin, however, *a species* gradually transforms itself over time into a new species, a process called **anagenesis**, although the actual boundary between species can never be detected but only

---

microevolution A subfield of evolutionary studies that devotes attention to short-term evolutionary changes that occur within a given species over relatively few generations of ecological time.

macroevolution A subfield of evolutionary studies that focuses on long-term evolutionary changes, especially the origins of new species and their diversification across space and over millions of years of geological time.

anagenesis The slow, gradual transformation of a single species over time.

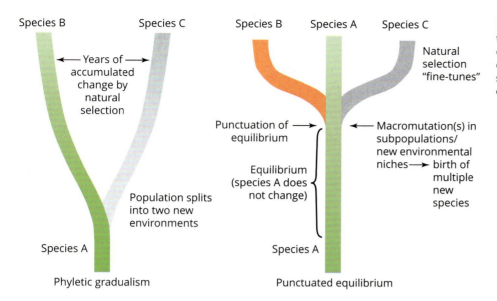

FIGURE 4.1   Research and theories about punctuated equilibria have challenged the common neo-Darwinian understanding of speciation by means of phyletic gradualism.

drawn arbitrarily. Darwin's theory of the origin of new species is called **phyletic gradualism** (Figure 4.1).

Arguing for phyletic gradualism made a lot of sense in Darwin's day, given the kind of opposition he faced, and it has many defenders today. But some biologists have argued that phyletic gradualism does not explain a number of things that evolutionary theory must explain. In particular, it cannot explain the fact that a single fossil species often seems to have given birth to a number of descendant species, a process called *cladogenesis*. What about those breaks in the fossil record that led Cuvier to argue that old species disappeared and new species appeared with what, from the point of view of geological time, was extreme rapidity? Is this just the result of poor preservation of intermediate forms, or do new species arise suddenly without having to go through any drawn-out intermediate stages? Or do the fossils that we thought represented intermediate stages in the anagenesis of a single species actually belong to several different species that resulted from the process of cladogenesis?

In the early 1970s, these problems led evolutionists Stephen Jay Gould and Niles Eldredge to propose that the rate and manner of evolutionary change may differ at the level of genes, of organisms, and of species. They argued that patterns in the fossil record (including the patterns Cuvier had recognized) suggest that phyletic gradualism might not explain all cases of evolutionary change. Between the breaks in the fossil record, many fossil species show little—if any—change for millions of years. Moreover, it is often the case that new species appear in the fossil record alongside their unchanged ancestors (Eldredge and Tattersall 1982, 8). We observe this phenomenon when we compare ourselves to the other living primates (see Chapter 3). Gould and Eldredge (1977) contended that evolutionary change

is not a uniform process but rather that most of evolutionary history has been characterized by relatively stable species coexisting in equilibrium (plural, *equilibria*). Occasionally, however, that equilibrium is punctuated by sudden bursts of speciation, when extinctions are widespread and many new species appear. This view is called the theory of **punctuated equilibrium** (see Figure 4.1). Gould and Eldredge claimed "that speciation is orders of magnitude more important than phyletic evolution as a mode of evolutionary change" (116).

But if phyletic gradualism is not the rule, where do new species come from? Gould and Eldredge (1977) argue that drastic changes in the natural environment trigger extinction and speciation by destroying habitats and breaking reproductive communities apart. When this happens, the populations that remain have both a radically modified gene pool and the opportunity to construct a new niche in a radically modified environment. When adaptive equilibria are punctuated this way, speciation is still thought to require thousands or hundreds of thousands of years to be completed. From the perspective of ecological time, the process still appears "gradual"; but from the perspective of geological time, speciation appears "rapid" when compared to the long periods of stasis that precede and follow it.

Research and theorizing about punctuated equilibria have challenged the common neo-Darwinian understanding of speciation by means of anagenesis.

phyletic gradualism   A theory arguing that one species gradually transforms itself into a new species over time, yet the actual boundary between species can never be detected and can only be drawn arbitrarily.

punctuated equilibrium   A theory claiming that most of evolutionary history has been characterized by relatively stable species coexisting in an equilibrium that is occasionally punctuated by sudden bursts of speciation, when extinctions are widespread and many new species appear.

Punctuationists view speciation as the outcome of clado-genesis, which had always been recognized as part of the neo-Darwinian synthesis but had never been given the important role that punctuationists assign it. Punctuationists also reject neo-Darwinian descriptions of speciation as the outcome of changing gene frequencies, insisting that speciation itself triggers adaptive change (Eldredge and Tattersall 1982, 62). Finally, punctuationists propose that natural selection may operate among variant, related species within a single genus, family, or order: a process called **species selection**. Just like natural selection among individuals of the same species, however, species selection is subject to random forces. Some species flourish simply because they tend to form new species at a high rate. Sometimes, however, none of the variant species is able to survive in the changed environment, and the entire group—genus, family, or order—may become extinct (Stanley 1981, 187–88). If speciation events occur rapidly in small, isolated populations, punctuationists predict that fossil evidence of intermediate forms between parent species and descendant species may not survive or may be hard to find, although occasionally paleontologists might get lucky (see also Eldredge 1985). If, as Darwin suggested, variation within populations provides the raw material on which natural selection can work, then it makes sense to examine how it might operate not only on populations of *genes*, but also populations of *individual organisms* and populations of *species*. If you look again at Figure 2.19, you will see that *multilevel selection* of exactly this kind has been proposed for inclusion in an extended evolutionary synthesis.

Geneticists have not yet been able to pinpoint the genetic changes involved in speciation, but one hypothesis links speciation to mutations in genes involved in the timing of interrelated biological processes, which have major pleiotropic effects. Ernst Mayr (1982, 605–6) argued, however, that only a few such mutations might be sufficient if the population undergoing speciation was small and isolated, involving few reproducing individuals and thus subject to the force of genetic drift. This is, in fact, the sort of speciation scenario the punctuationists also imagine, the setting in which cladogenesis has long been presumed to occur. As Steven Stanley (1981) observed, "It is estimated that 98 or 99% of the protein structures of humans and chimpanzees are the same! Clearly, evolution is reshaping animals in major ways without drastically remodeling the genetic code" (127).

Thinking about evolution in terms of punctuated equilibria fundamentally restructures our view of life. As Stanley (1981) explains, "the punctuational view implies, among other things, that evolution is often ineffective at perfecting the adaptations of animals and plants; that there is no real ecological balance of nature; that most large scale evolutionary trends are not produced by the gradual reshaping of established species, but are the net result of many rapid steps of evolution, not all of which have moved in the same direction" (5). He later observes that the theory of punctuated equilibrium "accentuates the unpredictability of large-scale evolution" and interprets speciation as "a kind of experimentation, but experimentation without a plan" (181).

Needless to say, these suggestions remain highly controversial. Many modern evolutionary biologists are convinced that phyletic gradualism is well supported by the fossil records of many species. Punctuationists and gradualists have argued vehemently about whether our own species, *Homo sapiens*, is the product of phyletic gradualism or of a punctuated equilibrium. The debate between gradualists and punctuationists has triggered a close re-examination of biological ideas about macro-evolution that promises to increase our understanding in unanticipated ways.

What Is Hominin Evolution?

About 10 mya, when the Miocene epoch was drawing to a close, grasslands increased at the expense of forests, and many species of hominoids became extinct throughout Europe, Asia, and Africa. Some African hominoids seem to have adapted to the changed conditions by spending more time on the ground, a move that apparently exposed them to new selective pressures favoring **bipedalism**—walking on two feet rather than four. *Hominins* (bipedal hominoids) first appeared in Africa at the end of the Miocene or beginning of the Pliocene, between 10 and 5 mya.

As we saw in Chapter 3, contemporary taxonomists classify the African great apes and humans together as *hominids*; within the hominid category, they separate out humans and their bipedal ancestors, who are classified together as *hominins*. Within the hominin category, a further distinction is also commonly made between recent hominin species assigned to the genus *Homo* and earlier hominin species assigned to such genera as *Ardipithecus*, *Australopithecus*, or *Paranthropus*. Several authorities informally refer to all the earlier hominins as "australo-piths" (Tattersall 2012; Klein 2009, 131), and that is what we will do here.

Fossil hominins are grouped together with living human beings because of a set of skeletal features that

---

species selection A process in which natural selection is seen to operate among variant, related species within a single genus, family, or order.

bipedalism Walking on two feet rather than four.

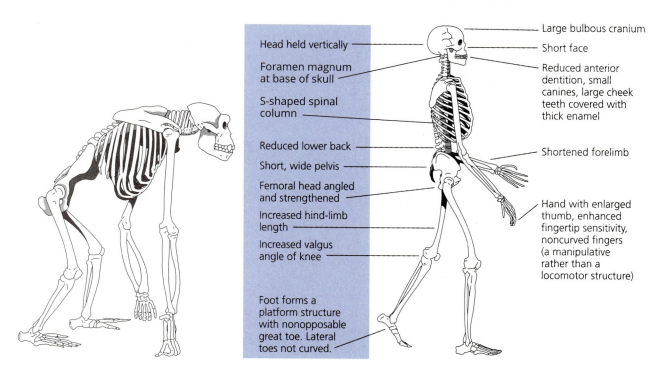

FIGURE 4.2 Apes (*left*) are adapted anatomically for a form of quadrupedal locomotion called knuckle walking, although they often stand upright and occasionally may even walk on their hind limbs for short distances. A human skeleton (*right*) shows the kinds of reshaping natural selection performed to produce the hominid anatomy, which is adapted to habitual bipedalism.

TABLE 4.2	Four Major Trends in Hominin Evolution	
TREND	**DEVELOPMENT**	**DATES**
Bipedalism	Evidence of bipedalism marks the appearance of the hominin line.	Between 10 and 5 mya
Distinctive dentition	The development of huge cheek teeth (molars) and much smaller front teeth was characteristic of the australopiths.	4 to 2 mya
Expanded brain	Brain expansion beyond 400 to 500 cm³ of the australopiths was characteristic of genus *Homo*.	Beginning 2.4 mya
Culture	Greater reliance on learned patterns of behavior and thought, on tools, and on language became important for *Homo*.	Beginning 2.5 mya

indicate habitual bipedalism, a feature that seems to be the first of our distinctive anatomical traits to have appeared (Figure 4.2). Hominin evolution has also been marked by additional evolutionary changes in dentition. Finally, some developed an expanded brain and ultimately came to depend on tools and language—that is, on culture—for their survival (Table 4.2). These developments did not occur all at once but were the result of **mosaic evolution** (different traits evolving at different rates). This is the reason anthropologists speak of human *origins* when describing the evolution of our species.

Who Were the First Hominins (6–3 mya)?

The Origin of Bipedalism

The skeletons of all primates allow upright posture when sitting or swinging from the branches of trees. Many primates often stand upright and occasionally walk on

mosaic evolution A phenotypic pattern that shows how different traits of an organism, responding to different selection pressures, may evolve at different rates.

their hind limbs for short distances. Because bipedalism requires upright posture, primates have already, so to speak, taken a step in the right direction. Put another way, we could say that hominoid morphology for upright posture that evolved in an arboreal context was exapted for hominin bipedalism in a terrestrial context.

What sort of selective pressures might have favored bipedal locomotion in hominoids? To answer this question, paleoanthropologists examine the advantages bipedalism would have conferred. Moving easily on the ground might have improved hominoids' ability to exploit food resources outside the protective cover of the shrinking Miocene forests. Upright posture would have made it easier for them to spot potential predators in open country, and skillful bipedal locomotion would have made it easier for them to escape. Finally, walking upright simultaneously reduces the amount of skin surface exposed to the sun, allows greater distances to be covered (albeit at slow speeds), and is more energy efficient (Day 1986, 189; Foley 1995, 143).

Michael Day (1986) suggests that this greater stamina may have permitted bipedal hominins to become "endurance hunters," slowly tracking game over long distances as they moved into the previously vacant ecological niche of daylight hunting (190). However, endurance walking would have been equally important in enabling the first hominins to cover long distances between widely scattered sources of plant food or water. Indeed, the teeth of these hominins suggest that they were probably **omnivorous**, not carnivorous; that is, they ate a wide range of plant and animal foods. Equipped with just a simple digging stick, their diet might have included "berries, fruits, nuts, buds, shoots, shallow-growing roots and tubers, fruiting bodies of fungi, most terrestrial and the smaller aquatic reptiles, eggs, nesting birds, some fish, mollusks, insects, and all small mammals, including the burrowing ones. This diverse diet . . . is very close to that of the Gombe National Park chimpanzees . . . and living gatherer/hunters" (Mann 1981, 34). As the forests retreated, and stands of trees became smaller and more widely scattered, groups of bipedal hominins appear to have ranged over a variety of environments (Isaac and Crader 1981, 89; see also Freeman 1981, Mann 1981). They would have been able to carry infants, food, and eventually tools in their newly freed hands (Lewin 1989, 67–68).

The oldest known hominin fossils come from Africa (Figure 4.3), some dating back into the Miocene. The oldest remains are fragmentary, however, and their significance for later hominin evolution is still being debated. The most noteworthy of these finds are *Sahelanthropus*

tchadensis, from Chad, in central Africa (6–7 million years old) (Brunet et al. 2002); *Orrorin tugenensis* from Kenya (6 million years old) (Senut et al. 2001); and *Ardipithecus kadabba* (5.8–5.2 million years old) and *Ardipithecus ramidus* (5.8–4.4 million years old) (White et al. 2009; Haile-Selassie et al. 2004; Haile-Selassie 2001; White et al. 1994). After 15 years of reconstruction and analysis, Tim White and his colleagues formally announced the discovery of "Ardi," a relatively complete skeleton of *Ar. ramidus*, which apparently could walk bipedally on the ground, although in a manner different from later australopiths and members of the genus *Homo* (see Figure 4.4). Most paleoanthropologists have traditionally viewed bipedal locomotion as an adaptation to life in open African grasslands called *savanna*. However, *Ar. ramidus* apparently lived in a wooded environment. Richard Potts, an expert in ancient environments, reviewed evidence about the environment in which *Ar. ramidus* would have lived at the two Ethiopian sites, Aramis and Gona, where its fossils were found. He also looked at biomolecular information about the kinds of plants *Ar. ramidus* ate, based on analysis of teeth from five different fossil individuals. Potts (2012) concluded that "combined evidence from the two sites thus appears to indicate a certain degree of spatial and possibly temporal variability in the proportion of grass versus trees" (157). Potts also expressed concern that "the term savanna can be interpreted too broadly; it is, in fact, defined so variably in time and space that it is almost useless when examining habitat-specific versus habitat variability explanations of human evolution" (158).

Other very early fragments of fossil hominins include two lower jaws and an arm bone from Kenya, ranging in age between 5.8–5.6 and 4.5 mya. Some fragmentary remains from Ethiopia and Kenya are between 4.5 and 3.8 million years old (Boaz 1995, 35; Foley 1995, 70). A mandible found in Greece in 1944 and a tooth found in Bulgaria in 2012 were recently re-examined together by an international team of paleoanthropologists who suggested that these remains belonged to an ancient hominin, *Graecopithecus*, which would have lived in southern Europe some 7 million years ago and which could have been ancestral to all later hominins (Fuss et al. 2017, Begun 2018). Another team reported the discovery of a set of late Miocene footprints in Crete, which they suggest may have been made by *Graecopithecus* (Gierliński et al. 2017). However, these *Graecopithecus* finds are few, worn, and fragmentary; and claims about their hominin status remain very controversial (Barras 2017).

By contrast, given the rich collection of hominin fossil remains that have been found in Africa, most paleoanthropologists continue to view Africa as the location where the first hominins evolved. The earliest direct

---

omnivorous Eating a wide range of plant and animal foods.

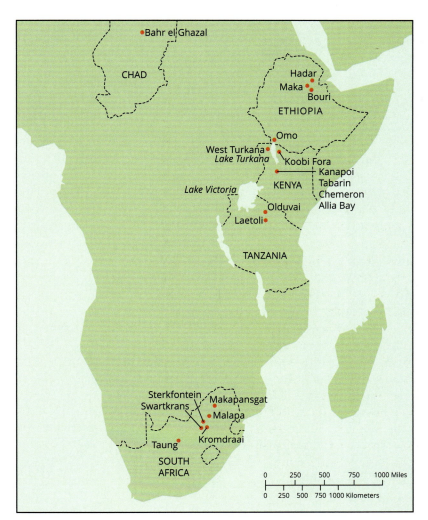

FIGURE 4.3 Major sites in eastern and southern Africa from which fossils of australopiths and early *Homo* have been recovered.

evidence of hominin bipedalism is 3.6 million years old. It comes from a trail of footprints that extends over 70 feet, preserved in a layer of hardened volcanic ash laid down during the middle Pliocene at the site of Laetoli, Tanzania (Figure 4.5). When compared to footprints made by modern apes and human beings, experts agree that the Laetoli prints were definitely produced by hominin bipedal locomotion (Day 1985, 92; 1986, 191; Feibel et al. 1995).

Most early hominin fossils showing skeletal evidence of bipedalism have been placed in the genus *Australopithecus*. The oldest of these is *Australopithecus anamensis*, whose fossils come from Kanapoi and Allia Bay in Kenya. *Au. anamensis* dates from 4.2 to 3.9 mya. *Au. anamensis* shows that bipedality had evolved at least a few hundred thousand years before the previous date of 3.6 mya provided by the Laetoli footprints (Leakey et al. 1995).[1]

---

[1]Leakey and colleagues (2001) have also described a 3.4 million-year-old eastern African fossil said to possess a series of derived features not found in other australopiths, thus justifying its being placed in a separate genus, *Kenyanthropus platyops*, although this interpretation is controversial.

The remaining early hominin fossils have been assigned to the species *Australopithecus afarensis*. Fossils assigned to this taxon have also been found at Laetoli and in a region of Ethiopia known as the Afar Depression—hence the species name "afarensis" (see Figure 4.3). These fossils, which are quite numerous, range between 3.9 and 3.0 million years of age (Johanson and Edey 1981, Kimbel et al. 1994, White et al. 1993). The famous *Au. afarensis* fossil Lucy (named after the Beatles song "Lucy in the Sky with Diamonds"; Figure 4.6) was found 40% intact and undisturbed where she had died, which allowed Donald Johanson and his colleagues to reconstruct her postcranial skeleton in great detail. The first fairly complete adult skull of *Au. afarensis*, found in the early 1990s, confirmed its small-brained, apelike features. The 0.9 million-year age range of these Hadar fossils suggests a period of prolonged evolutionary stasis within *Au. afarensis*.

Some features of the skeleton of *Au. afarensis* reveal its adaptation to habitual bipedalism, especially when

---

Australopithecus The genus in which taxonomists place most early hominins showing skeletal evidence of bipedalism.

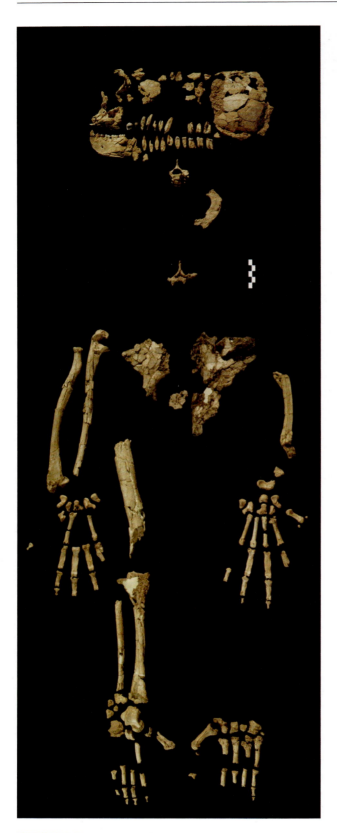

FIGURE 4.5   The earliest evidence of hominin bipedalism comes from the 3.6 million-year-old fossil footprints preserved in hardened volcanic ash at Laetoli, Tanzania.

FIGURE 4.4   The fossils of *Ardipithecus ramidus*, pictured above, have been interpreted as belonging to a bipedal hominoid living in a forested environment, which challenges the traditional notion that bipedalism evolved in an open, savannah environment.

we compare it to the skeletons of modern humans and apes. The spinal column of a chimpanzee joins its head at the back of the skull, as is normally the case in quadrupedal animals. This is revealed by the position of a large hole, the *foramen magnum*, through which the spinal cord passes on its way to the brain. The ape pelvis is long and broad, and the knee is almost directly in line with the femur (or thigh bone) and therefore ill-adapted to support the ape's center of gravity when it tries to move on its hind legs. As a result, when apes walk bipedally, they appear to waddle in an awkward attempt to stay upright. Finally, the great toe of the ape foot diverges like a thumb from the rest of the digits, a feature that allows apes to use their feet for grasping but inhibits their ability to use this toe for the "push-off" so important for effective bipedalism.

By contrast, the modern human head balances on the top of the spinal column. The foramen magnum

IN THEIR OWN WORDS

Finding Fossils

Searching for remains of the human past is not glamorous work. As he relates the experiences of Alemayehu, one of the most successful fossil hunters on his team, Donald Johanson reveals both the extraordinary discipline required for the search and the near delirium that ensues when the search is successful.

One day Alemayehu found a small piece of a lower jaw with a couple of molars in it. They were bigger than human molars, and he told me that he had a baboon jaw with funny big teeth.

"You think this is a baboon?" I asked him.

"Well, with unusually large molars."

"It's a hominid."

The knee joint of the year before had proved the existence of hominids at Hadar. Everyone had been sanguine about finding more of them in 1974. In fact, the French had been so eager that they had gone rushing out to survey on the very first day, leaving it to the Americans to put up the tents. But after weeks of searching without results, that ardor had dimmed somewhat. Now it flared again, but in no one more than Alemayehu himself.

It is impossible to describe what it feels like to find something like that. It fills you right up. That is what you are there for. You have been working and working, and suddenly you score. When I told Alemayehu that he had a hominid, his face lit up and his chest went way out. Energized to an extraordinary degree, and with nothing better to do in the late afternoons, Alemayehu formed the habit of poking quietly about for an hour or so before dark. He chose areas close to camp because, without the use of a Land-Rover, they were easy to get to. He refrained from saying—although I feel sure that this was a factor in his choice of places to survey—that he had begun to realize that he was a more thorough and more observant

surveyor than some of the others who were doing that work.

The day after he found the hominid jaw, Alemayehu turned up a complete baboon skull. I had it on the table for a detailed description the next afternoon when Alemayehu burst into camp.

His eyes were popping. He said he had found another of those things. After having seen one, he was sure this was another human jaw. I dropped the baboon skull and ran after Alemayehu, forgetting that I was barefoot. I began to cut my feet so badly on the gravel that I was forced to limp back to my tent to put on shoes. Guillemot and Petter, who were with me, kept going. When I rejoined them, it was in a little depression just a few hundred yards beyond the Afar settlement. Guillemot and Petter were crouching down to look at a beautiful fossil jaw sticking out of the ground. Guillemot ruefully pointed out his own footprints, not ten feet away, where he had gone out surveying that first morning in camp and seen nothing.

A crowd of others arrived and began to hunt around feverishly. One of the French let out a yell—he had a jaw. It turned out to be a hyena, an excellent find because carnivores are always rare. But after that, interest dwindled. It began to get dark. The others drifted back to camp. I stopped surveying and was about to collect Alemayehu's jaw when I spotted Alemayehu struggling up a nearby slope, waving his arms, completely winded.

"I have another," Alemayehu gasped. "I think, two."

I raced over to him. The two turned out to be two halves. When I put them together, they fitted perfectly to make a complete palate (upper jaw) with every one of its teeth in position: a superb find. Within an hour Alemayehu had turned up two of the oldest and finest hominid jaws ever seen. With the addition of the partial jaw of a few days before, he has earned a listing in the *Guinness Book of World Records* as the finder of the most hominid fossils in the shortest time.

Source: Johanson and Edey 1981, 172–73.

---

in humans is located directly beneath the skull rather than at its back. The basin-shaped human pelvis is the body's center of gravity, supporting and balancing the torso above it. Finally, the bones of human legs have a knock-kneed appearance, with the femur pointing inward toward the knee joint at the *valgus angle*. As a result, humans can easily transfer their center of

gravity directly over the stepping foot in the course of bipedal walking.

The skeleton of *Au. afarensis* more closely resembles that of modern humans than that of apes. As Figure 4.7 shows, the great toe does not diverge from the rest of the digits on the foot, the femur bends inward toward the knee joint at the valgus angle, and the pelvis is short

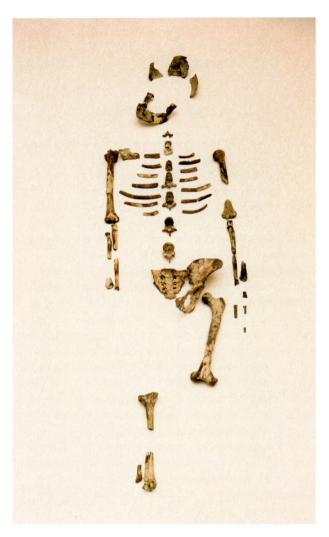

FIGURE 4.6 40% of Lucy's bones were found undisturbed, and her remains included much of her postcranial skeleton.

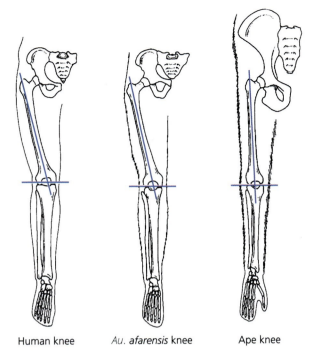

Human knee   *Au. afarensis* knee   Ape knee

FIGURE 4.7 The bones of human legs have a somewhat knock-kneed appearance, with the femur pointing inward toward the knee joint at the valgus angle. This allows human beings to easily transfer the center of gravity directly over the foot in the course of bipedal walking. Ape femurs do not angle inward in this manner, so apes waddle when they try to walk bipedally. Because *Au. afarensis* is humanlike in its valgus angle and in the shape of its pelvis, we conclude that, like us, it walked bipedally.

Changes in Hominin Dentition

Once the first australopiths ventured regularly down from the trees and into a variety of new habitats, they presumably began to rely on new food sources. Their new diet appears to have created a set of selective pressures that led to important changes in hominin dentition, first evident in the teeth of *Au. afarensis*. To assess the importance of these changes, it helps to compare the teeth of *Au. afarensis* with those of modern apes and humans.

A striking feature of ape dentition is a "U"-shaped dental arch that is longer front to back than it is side to side. By contrast, the human dental arch is parabolic, or gently rounded in shape and narrower in front than in back. Apes have large, sexually dimorphic canine teeth that project beyond the tooth row. In addition, they possess a *diastema* (plural, *diastemata*), or space in the tooth row for each canine of the opposite jaw to fit into when the jaws are closed. Human canine teeth do not project beyond the tooth row and show little sexual dimorphism, and humans have no diastemata. Ape teeth show functional specialization, with biting incisors, shearing canines, and grinding molars. In addition, the incisors

and basinlike. In addition, the skull of *Au. afarensis* is balanced on the top of the spinal column, as shown by the position of its foramen magnum. Nevertheless, elements of the postcranial skeleton of *Au. afarensis* clearly recall its recent ape ancestry (Figure 4.8). It has longer arms, in proportion to its legs, than any other hominin. Also, the bones of its fingers and toes are slightly curved, and the toes are much longer, resembling the finger and toe bones of apes. Because these features are related to the typical tree-climbing adaptation of most hominoids, some paleoanthropologists have concluded that *Au. afarensis* must have had significant tree-climbing ability along with bipedalism (Susman et al. 1985; Lewin 1989, 77; Klein 2009, 213). A 3.5 million-year-old australopith fossil found in Chad, in central Africa, is contemporaneous with *Au. afarensis*. Called *Australopithecus bahrelghazali*, this specimen extends the range of australopiths far beyond southern and eastern Africa (Brunet et al. 1995).

FIGURE 4.8   Although *Au. afarensis* was humanlike in some respects, in other respects its skeleton retained adaptations to life in the trees.

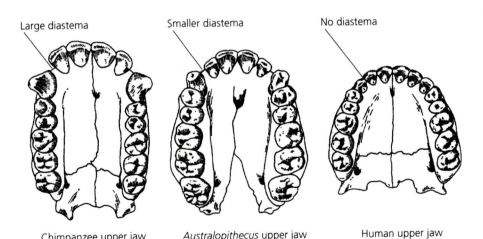

Chimpanzee upper jaw   *Australopithecus* upper jaw   Human upper jaw

FIGURE 4.9   The upper jaw of *Au. afarensis* shows some apelike features, but its dentition shows signs of change in the direction of smaller front teeth and large cheek teeth that would appear fully developed in later australopith species.

are about the same size as the molars, and the canines are the largest teeth of all. Functional specialization in human teeth is very different. Humans have canines and incisors that are similar in shape and much smaller than their molars.

How does *Au. afarensis* compare? As Figure 4.9 shows, the *Au. afarensis* dental arcade is "U"-shaped, like that of the apes. Its canines, although relatively smaller than those of apes, still project somewhat; and 45% of

the *Au. afarensis* specimens examined have diastemata (Lewin 1989, 70). Although *Au. afarensis* canines were getting smaller, *Au. afarensis* molars were getting larger, marking the beginning of an evolutionary trend toward smaller front teeth and enormous cheek teeth that appear, fully developed, among australopiths that flourished a million years after *Au. afarensis*. The increase in the size of later australopith molars is greater than would be expected if it were merely the result of a larger-bodied

FIGURE 4.10   Two-million-year-old bipedal hominins with small front teeth and large cheek teeth fall into two major categories. (a) Gracile australopiths (such as this specimen of *Au. africanus* from Sterkfontein, South Africa) have smaller, more lightly built faces; (b) Robust australopiths (such as this specimen from Swartkrans, South Africa) have more rugged jaws, flatter faces, truly enormous molars, and sagittal crests.

hominin having proportionately larger teeth. Thus, paleoanthropologists deduce that the enlarged molars were produced by natural selection (McHenry 1985, 179). Some experts argue that this dental pattern is an effective adaptation to grassland diets consisting of coarse vegetable foods. Because projecting canine teeth prevent the side to side jaw movement that grinding tough foods requires, natural selection may have favored australopiths whose canines did not project beyond the tooth row.

Who Were the Later Australopiths (3–1.5 mya)?

Fossils of 3 million-year-old australopiths with small front teeth and large cheek teeth were found first in southern Africa and later in eastern Africa, beginning in the 1920s and 1930s. Some of them possessed the typical late-australopith enlargement of the cheek teeth, but their faces were small and lightly built; they were classified together as *Australopithecus africanus* and came to be known as the "gracile australopiths" (Figure 4.10a). *Au. africanus* lived between 3 and 2 mya. Other australopith fossils with more rugged jaws, flatter faces, and enormous molars have been assigned to the species *Paranthropus robustus*, and they are called the "robust australopiths" (Figure 4.10b). *P. robustus* lived between 2 and 1.5 mya.

Both gracile and robust australopith fossils show the same adaptation to bipedalism found in *Au. afarensis*. The foramen magnum of both forms was directly underneath the skull, and the size of the braincase (or **cranial capacity**) in both forms ranged between 400 and 550 cubic centimeters. Despite such small brains, australopiths living at Swartkrans in present-day South Africa 1.5 mya apparently controlled fire and used it to cook meat (Brain and Sillen 1988). Whether they had hands capable of making stone tools is unclear (Lewin 1989, 83; McHenry and Berger 1998). Robust australopiths in southern Africa may have used fragments of bone and animal horn as digging tools (Tattersall 1998, 125). Some research suggests that australopiths resemble apes in the timing of tooth eruption and the patterns of surface wear on teeth (Lewin 1989, 71, 73).

It turns out that the striking morphological differences between gracile and robust australopiths have to do almost exclusively with their chewing anatomy. To begin with, selection seems to have favored large molars to grind tough plant foods. But large molars are ineffective without jaws massive enough to absorb the shock of grinding and muscles large enough to move the jaws. The robust australopiths had the flattest faces because their cheekbones had expanded the most, to accommodate huge jaw muscles that attached to bony crests along the midlines of their skulls.

All australopith fossils from southern Africa have been recovered from limestone quarries or limestone caves. Unfortunately, none of the deposits from which

cranial capacity   The size of the braincase.

FIGURE 4.11 The "Zinjanthropus" skull, classified as *Paranthropus boisei*. When the potassium-argon method was used in 1959 to date the volcanic rock lying above the sediment in which this fossil was found, the date of 1.75 million years stunned the scientific community.

these fossils came can be dated by traditional numerical methods, but newer uranium-series and paleomagnetic techniques are more promising. Dating is much easier at eastern African sites like Olduvai Gorge, Tanzania, where volcanic rock layers can be dated using isotopic methods (Figure 4.11). Since 1959, eastern Africa has become the most important source of hominin fossils in the world.

How Many Species of Australopith Were There?

How many australopith species (and genera) ought to be recognized continues to be debated. Fleagle (2013) counts six species of *Australopithecus* that are generally recognized and observes that "more are probably waiting to be uncovered" (365; see Table 4.3). It now appears that robust australopiths go back some 1.75 million years in southern Africa and perhaps 2.5 million years in eastern Africa, becoming extinct between 1.2 and 0.7 mya.

Gracile australopiths apparently flourished between 3 and 2 mya, in both southern and eastern Africa,

TABLE 4.3 Increase in Cranial Capacity in Hominins

HOMININ	DATE RANGE (YEARS)	CRANIAL CAPACITY (CM³)
Sahelanthropus tchadensis	6–7 million	350
Orrorin tugenensis	6 million	[a]
Ardipithecus ramidus	4.4–5.8 million	[a]
Australopithecus anamensis	4.2–3.9 million	[a]
Australopithecus afarensis	3.9–3.0 million	375–550
Australopithecus africanus	3–2 million	420–500
Australopithecus bahrelgazali	3.5–3 million	[a]
Australopithecus sediba	1.95–1.78 million	420
Australopithecus garhi	2.5 million	[a]
Paranthropus aethiopicus	2.6–2.3 million	410
Paranthropus robustus	2.0–1.5 million	530
Paranthropus boisei	2.1–1.1 million	530
Homo habilis	2.4–1.5 million	500–800
Homo naledi	indirect evidence	465–560
Homo georgicus	1.8 million–900,000	600–680
Homo erectus	1.8 million	750–1,225
Homo ergaster	1.8 million–300,000	910
Homo antecessor	1.6 million	[a]
Homo heidelbergensis	780,000	1,200
Homo neanderthalensis	500,000	1,450
Denisovans	230,000–30,000	[a]
Homo sapiens	?–41,000–? 300,000–present	1,350

[a]Unknown at present.

suggesting an early divergence between the robust and gracile australopith lineages. In 1999, the 2.5 million-year-old fossil of a gracile australopith, called *Australopithecus garhi*, was found in Ethiopia (Asfaw et al. 1999). Not only did *Au. garhi* appear morphologically distinct from other gracile australopiths of roughly the same age, but also it was found in association with primitive stone tools 2.5 to 2.6 million years old (De Heinzelin et al. 1999). The greatest confusion surrounds those gracile fossils dated to about 2 mya. Perhaps most intriguing are the fossils of *Australopithecus sediba*, found at the site of Malapa in South Africa, and dated to between 1.95 and 1.78 mya (Berger et al. 2010). These fossils show a mix of features: their cranial capacity resembles that of *Au. africanus*, whereas their teeth and long thumb bones resemble those of early *Homo*. Fleagle (2013) concludes that "Overall, *Au. sediba* seems to be intermediate between fossils currently classified as *Australopithecus* and those attributed to early *Homo*, and researchers differ on which genus is more appropriate" (368–69).

How Can Anthropologists Explain the Human Transition?

By 2 mya, bipedal hominins with specialized teeth and expanded brains were walking the open environment of the east African savanna. At least some of them made artifacts out of wood, stone, and bone and used fire. Some observers have concluded that meat eating led to a need for stone tools to kill and butcher animals and that stone-tool manufacture led natural selection to favor hominins with expanded brains. This is the "man the hunter" story about human origins and purports to explain nearly every physical and behavioral trait that makes humans human as the outcome of our ancestors' devotion to hunting. In 1968, for example, anthropologists Sherwood Washburn and C. S. Lancaster concluded that "the biological bases for killing have been incorporated into human psychology" (1968, 299–300). This story seemed to be supported by early primatological work reporting that savanna baboons lived by a rigid hierarchy in a closed society: large males with huge canines dominated much smaller females and juveniles. As primatologist Linda Fedigan (1986) observed, this model of human origins "can be said to have been traditional and consistent with contemporary role expectations for Western men and women" (39). For those who saw such role expectations as natural rather than culturally imposed, the baboon model was highly persuasive.

Such a story is exciting, and it fits in well with many traditional Western views of human nature.

But it quickly ran into trouble, both because anthropologists could not agree about how to define "hunting" and because ethnographic fieldwork showed that plant food gathered by women was more important to the survival of foraging peoples than was meat hunted by men (Fedigan 1986, 33–34). For many anthropologists, the Ju/'hoansi people of southern Africa provide helpful insights concerning the social and economic life of the first hominins (see Chapter 11, "EthnoProfile 11.4: Ju/'hoansi (!Kung)"). Richard Lee, an ethnographer who has worked among the Ju/'hoansi since the 1960s, suggested that several "core features" of Ju/'hoansi society may have characterized the first hominin societies: a flexible form of kinship organization that recognized both the male and the female lines, group mobility and a lack of permanent attachment to territory, small group size (25–50 members) with fluctuating group membership, equitable food distribution that leads to highly egalitarian social relations, and a division of labor that leads to sharing (Lee 1974; Lee and DeVore 1968). In addition, women in foraging societies appear to arrange their reproductive lives around their productive activities, giving birth on average to one child every 3–4 years (Fedigan 1986, 49). More recently, Fuentes, Wyczalkowski, and MacKinnon (2010) have argued that niche construction through cooperation may well have distinguished the lineage *Homo* from the beginning, likely contributing to our ancestors' ability to out-compete the late australopiths whose members appear to have lacked this vital social feature.

In sum, ethnographic evidence suggested that females played active roles in the adaptations of our early hominin ancestors. Some feminist anthropologists used this evidence to construct stories of human evolution that stressed the importance of "woman the gatherer" in which the key tools for human adaptation were digging sticks, slings to carry infants, and containers for gathered foods—all of which, they suggest, were probably invented by women. Rather than use an Old World monkey as a primate model, they used the chimpanzee. Jane Goodall's early reports from Gombe, in Tanzania, suggested that chimpanzee females were not constrained within a rigid hierarchy or dominated by aggressive males; they were active and mobile, feeding themselves and their young, and spending most of their lives apart from their mates. Their closest bonds were with their offspring, and the mother–infant group was the most stable feature of chimpanzee society. Perhaps the first human food sharing was between women and their children; perhaps even hunters would have most likely shared food with their mothers and siblings rather than with their mates. This "woman the gatherer" account—no less extremist than the "man the hunter" scenario—tested earlier assumptions about the foundations of human society and found them wanting.

All reconstructions of the lives of ancestral hominins, however, are tempered with the realization that the key features of contemporary human behavior did not all appear at the same time. As in the case of our skeletal morphology, human behavior also appears to be the product of mosaic evolution.

What Do We Know about Early *Homo* (2.4–1.5 mya)?

About 2.5–2 mya, the drying trend that had begun in Africa in the Late Miocene became more pronounced, possibly causing a wave of extinction as well as the appearance of new species. During this period, the gracile australopiths disappeared by either evolving into or being replaced by a new kind of hominin.

Expansion of the Australopith Brain

Whereas the brains of all australopith species varied within the range of 400–550 cm³, the new hominins had brains over 600 cm³. Were these merely advanced gracile australopiths, or did they belong to a new species or even a new genus? For Louis Leakey, who discovered at Olduvai in 1963 a skull with a cranial capacity of 680 cm³, the answer was clear. He asserted that the skull belonged to the genus **Homo** and named it *Homo habilis*—"handy man." Eventually, Leakey and his allies discovered more fossils that were assigned to *H. habilis*. But some paleoanthropologists believed that these fossils showed too much internal variation for a single species, and they proceeded to sort the fossils into new categories.

How Many Species of Early *Homo* Were There?

How do paleoanthropologists decide if a gracile fossil younger than 2 million years should be placed in the genus *Homo*? The key criterion is still cranial capacity. In general, the cranial capacities of these early *Homo* fossils range from 510 to 750 cm³. Larger brains resided in larger, differently shaped skulls. Compared to the more elongated australopith cranium, the cranium of early *Homo* has thinner bone and is more rounded; the face is flatter and smaller in relation to the size of the cranium; and the teeth and jaws are less rugged, with a more parabolic arch. Most significantly, early *Homo*'s expansion in brain size was not accompanied by a marked increase

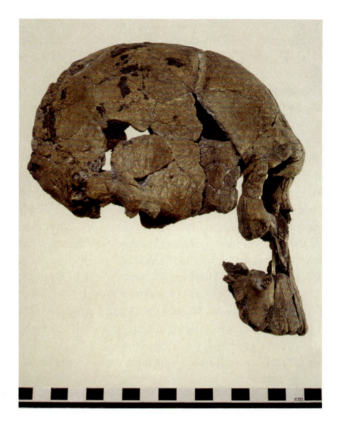

FIGURE 4.12 Perhaps the best-known fossil of early *Homo* is KNM-ER 1470, found by Richard Leakey and his team near Lake Turkana in northern Kenya.

in body size, meaning that the enlarged brain was a product of natural selection (Figure 4.12). We know little about the postcranial morphology of any early *Homo* species.

Our understanding of the early *Homo* fossil record was enriched and complicated by two new finds in 2015, one from South Africa and one from Ethiopia. The fossils that received the most publicity came from Rising Star Cave in South Africa, where paleontologists announced the discovery of a rich trove of hominin fossils that they argued were distinct from other early species of *Homo* previously identified (Dirks et al. 2015). Called *Homo naledi*, these fossils had small cranial capacities comparable to those of australopiths (between 465 and 560 cm³). Other features of their anatomy, however, more closely resembled fossils assigned to early *Homo*. The sediments that yielded these fossils have not permitted scientists to assign them a firm geological date, although estimates of their age may be made indirectly. For instance, based on morphological comparisons of *H. naledi* with other, well-dated fossils assigned to early *Homo*, paleoanthropologists who have worked directly with the

Homo The genus to which taxonomists assign large-brained hominins 2 million years old and younger.

H. naledi fossils believe that they are about 1.8–2 mya (Dirks et al. 2015; Thackeray 2015). Chris Stringer, who was not part of this team, concluded that *H. naledi* appeared to most closely resemble early *Homo erectus* fossils from Dmanesi, Georgia, which is also thought to be about 1.8–2 mya (Stringer 2015). Other paleoanthropologists have disagreed with these estimates. For example, paleoanthropologists concluded that *H. naledi* was more likely to be around 900,000 years old, based on sophisticated statistical analysis, comparing measurements of *H. naledi*'s skull and teeth with comparable measurements taken from other fossil hominins and living African apes (Dembo et al. 2016). In response, members of the original team have emphasized that the morphological relations between *H. naledi* and other early *Homo* fossils cannot be discounted, regardless of how old *H. naledi* turns out to be (Hawks and Berger 2016).

The second early *Homo* find of 2015 came from the Ledi-Geraru in the Afar region of Ethiopia (Villmoare et al. 2015). This find consisted of a single lower jawbone with teeth, but Villmoare and his colleagues argue that it displays morphological features associated with *Homo*. Most exciting was the age of this fossil, which dates to between 2.8 and 2.75 mya—some 400,000 years earlier than previously known fossils of early *Homo*.

Today, it is widely believed that several species belonging to the genus *Homo* coexisted in eastern Africa in the early Pleistocene (Tattersall 2012, 88–89; Fleagle 2013, 376). The remains of *Homo naledi* and the Ledi Geraru find further complicate our understanding of the origin of our own genus. While the species of early *Homo* listed in Table 4.2 have all gained some measure of acceptance, some paleoanthropologists are convinced that the category "early *Homo*" is far too inclusive and that a more precise list of derived morphological traits unique to the genus *Homo* needs to be formulated, even though experts disagree about just which traits ought to be included on that list (Schwartz and Tattersall 2015). This debate is likely to continue for some time.

Earliest Evidence of Culture: Stone Tools

Stone tools are the most enduring evidence we have of culturally created human artifacts. Ian Tattersall (1998) emphasizes that the earliest hominins who made

identifiable stone tools "*invented* efficient toolmaking from materials they consciously chose" (57), something different from what any living apes have ever been observed to do. The oldest undisputed stone tools come from the Ethiopian site of Gona and are from 2.6 mya (Semaw 2000); other early tools, found at Hadar in Ethiopia, are at least 2.5 million years old (Semaw et al. 1997; Detleinzelin et al. 1999). The oldest stone tools found in association with a fossil human ancestor also come from Ethiopia and date to 2.33 mya (Kimbel et al. 1994). Other similar tools, dating from 2.5–2 mya, have been found elsewhere in eastern and southern Africa. For the most part, these tools consist of *cores* (tennis ball-sized rocks with a few flakes knocked off to produce cutting edges) and *flakes* (chipped-off pieces of rocks that may or may not have been used as small cutting tools). This style of stone toolmaking is called the **Oldowan tradition** after the Olduvai Gorge, where the first specimens were found (Figure 4.13). But in 2015, paleoanthropologists working in West Turkana, Kenya, reported the discovery stone tools 3.3 million years old that are different enough from Oldowan tools to have been given their own name: *Lomekwian* (Harmand et al. 2015). Prior to these finds, members of early *Homo* had been considered the makers of the first stone tools, which were understood to be Oldowan tools. If the claims about Lomekwian tools are confirmed, however, they will demonstrate toolmaking by hominins living *before* the appearance of the

FIGURE 4.13 An Oldowan chopper with flakes removed from one side (or face).

Oldowan tradition A stone-tool tradition named after the Olduvai Gorge (Tanzania), where the first examples of these tools were found. The earliest Oldowan tools are 2.6 million years old and were found in Gona, Ethiopia. Until recently, Oldowan tools were considered the oldest stone tools made by hominins, although this status is now claimed by Lomekwian tools, found in West Turkana, Kenya. (Lomekwian tools are stylistically different, and they are 3.3 million years old.)

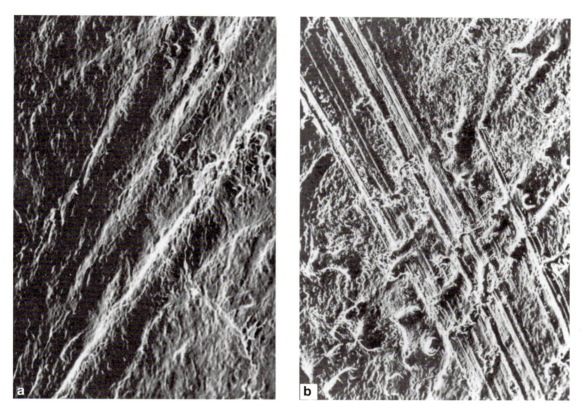

FIGURE 4.14 The scanning electron microscope allows taphonomists to distinguish between different kinds of marks on bones: (a) Hyena tooth marks on modern bones; (b) V-shaped stone-tool cut marks on modern bones.

genus *Homo*. Who the makers of these tools were is not known, but they seem to have possessed less advanced stone-knapping skills than the makers of Oldowan tools. One possible candidate is a poorly known hominin called *Kenyanthropus platyops*, whose 3.5 mya old remains have been found near West Turkana itself (Leakey et al. 2001). Another possible candidate is *Au. afarensis*, who was living 3.39 mya in the same Middle Awash region of Ethiopia where bones *older* than 3.39 mya have been found; these bones are said to display cut marks made by stone tools (McPherron et al. 2010). Scholarly discussion surrounding these recent finds has just begun.

In the meantime, Oldowan tools still remain the best documented and best understood early stone tools in the hominin evolutionary record. In what follows, therefore, we will discuss what paleoanthropologists have learned about Oldowan tools.

Oldowan tools are extremely simple and seem indistinguishable from stones that have lost a few flakes through perfectly natural means. Given this simplicity, how can paleoanthropologists conclude that they are dealing with deliberately fashioned artifacts rather than objects modified by natural processes? Answers to such questions come from paleoanthropologists who specialize in **taphonomy**, the study of the various processes that bones and stones undergo in the course of

becoming part of the fossil and archaeological records (Brain 1985). Taphonomists using a scanning electron microscope (SEM) can examine stones and bones for evidence of human activity. Stones used as tools, for example, have characteristic wear patterns along their flaked edges. Flaked rocks that lack wear patterns are not usually considered tools unless they are unmistakably associated with other evidence of human activity.

Paleoanthropologists Pat Shipman, Rick Potts, and Henry Bunn examined bones for marks of butchery by early hominids. Shipman learned how modern hunters butcher animals and discovered that carnivore tooth marks and stone cut marks on fresh bone look very different under the SEM (Figure 4.14). Shipman and an assistant used the SEM to examine more than 2,500 2 million-year-old fossil bones from Bed I at Olduvai. They found (1) that fewer than half of the cut marks seemed to be associated with meat removal; (2) that the stone-tool cut marks and carnivore tooth marks showed basically the same pattern of distribution; (3) that nearly three-quarters of the cut marks occurred on bones with little meat, suggesting they resulted from skinning; and (4) that in 8 of 13 cases where cut marks

taphonomy The study of the various processes that objects undergo in the course of becoming part of the fossil and archaeological records.

and tooth marks overlapped, the cut marks were on top of the tooth marks. Taken together, these patterns suggested to Shipman and her colleagues that, rather than hunting for meat, the Olduvai hominins regularly scavenged carcasses killed by carnivores, taking what they could get (Shipman 1984). Numerous mammalian bones dated to 2.58–2.1 mya, with cut marks indicating butchery, have recently been found at Gona, Ethiopia (Dominguez-Rodrigo et al. 2005). It is now widely accepted that scavenging for meat was more likely than hunting among early hominins.

Taphonomists have also re-examined data from eastern African sites once thought to have been home bases, where tools were kept and to which early hominins returned to share meat. They found no convincing evidence of hearths or shelters or other structures that are found at the campsites of later human groups. In some cases, they concluded that the site in question was a carnivore lair or simply a location beside a body of water that attracted many different kinds of animals, some of whose remains ended up buried there. Modern human foragers who hunt for meat never use the same kill site for very long, leading taphonomists to conclude that their hominin ancestors probably did not do so either. In some cases, both hominins and carnivores may have used a site, and the problem lies in determining which group of animals was responsible for which bones. Finally, it is important to remember how small and scattered these ancient hominin populations were (Tattersall and DeSalle 2011, 75–76), which makes their traces even harder to find.

The home-base hypothesis for ancient collections of tools and bones has thus been called into question. Rick Potts, however, has offered his "stone cache hypothesis" to explain how stones and bones might have accumulated at Olduvai 2 mya. Using a computer simulation, he found that the most efficient way for early hominins to get stones and animal carcasses together would be to cache (or hide) stones at various spots in areas where they hunted and bring carcasses to the nearest cache for processing. Early hominins might have created the first stone caches accidentally but would have returned to them regularly whenever stone tools were needed, thus reconstructing their niche by creating a collection of stones and animal parts. In Potts's view, stone cache sites could turn into home bases once hominins could defend these sites against carnivores. He hypothesizes that this new way of using the landscape could have created the conditions favoring selection for "a large bodied, diurnal, sweaty, long-distance walking hominid" like *Homo erectus* (Potts 1993, 65).

Homo erectus The species of large-brained, robust hominins that lived between 1.8 and 0.4 mya.

Who Was *Homo erectus* (1.8–1.7 mya to 0.5–0.4 mya)?

Fossils of early *Homo* disappear around the beginning of the Pleistocene, about 1.8 mya, by either evolving into or being replaced by large-brained, robust hominins called **Homo erectus** (Figure 4.15). *H. erectus* seems to have coexisted in eastern Africa with the robust australopithecines until between 1.2 and 0.7 mya, when the australopiths became extinct, and was the first hominin species to migrate out of Africa, apparently shortly after it first appeared. A collection of cranial and postcranial hominin fossils found in the Republic of Georgia (part of the former Soviet Union) date to 1.8 mya and appear to represent an early *Homo erectus* population of this kind. Five adult crania from this population showed a range of phenotypic variation that may have characterized early populations of *H. erectus* in general (Lordkipanidze et al. 2013). One of these crania belonged to an individual who had lost all his teeth long before he died. Tattersall (2012, 123) interprets this individual's survival as evidence of support from other members of his social group. Rocks yielding *H. erectus* fossils from Java have been dated to 1.8 and 1.7 mya; and Chinese fossils, including the famous specimens from Zhoukoudian near Beijing, are from 700,000–900,000 to 250,000 years old. No agreed-upon *H. erectus* fossils have been found in western Europe, although artifacts have been found at European sites that date from the time when *H. erectus* was living in Africa and Asia (Browne 1994; Boaz 1995, 33; Klein 2009, 367).

The earliest known African *H. erectus* fossil (sometimes called *H. ergaster*) is of a boy found at the Nariokotome III site, on the west side of Lake Turkana in 1984 (Figure 4.16). Dated to 1.7 mya, the Turkana boy is the most complete early hominin skeleton ever found and different from other *H. erectus* specimens in several ways. First, the boy was taller: it was estimated that he would have been more than six feet tall had he reached adulthood. Such a tall, slim body build, found in some indigenous eastern African peoples today, is interpreted as an adaptation to tropical heat. From this, it has been argued that the Turkana boy's body was cooled by sweating and "may thus have been the first hominin species to possess a largely hairless, naked skin" (Klein 2009, 326). Second, the size and shape of the Turkana boy's thoracic canal are less developed than our own. Nerves passing through this bony canal control muscles used for breathing, and modern human speech makes special demands on these muscles. It appears that neural control over breathing was less developed in *H. erectus*, casting doubt on their ability to speak (Walker 1993).

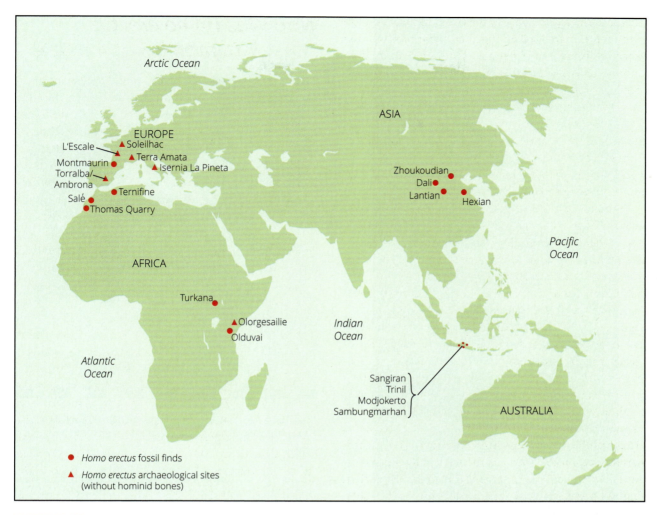

FIGURE 4.15 The major sites where *H. erectus* fossils or evidence of *H. erectus* settlement (without human fossils) have been found.

Third, the Turkana boy looks very different from Javanese *H. erectus* specimens. Some argue that if *H. erectus* was living in Java at the same time that the Turkana boy was living in eastern Africa, they probably belonged to separate species. Thus, paleoanthropologists have reconsidered the possible taxonomic relationships among the various fossils traditionally assigned to *H. erectus*, and they have devised new evolutionary trees (see Figure 4.31).

Morphological Traits of *H. erectus*

Morphological traits traditionally used to assign fossils to *H. erectus* involve its cranium, its dentition, and its postcranial skeleton. The cranial capacity of *H. erectus* averages around 1,000 cm³ (Figure 4.17), a significant advance over early *Homo*, for whom cranial capacity ranged from 610 to 750 cm³. In addition, the skull of *H. erectus* possesses a number of distinctive morphological features, including heavy brow ridges, a five-sided cranial profile (when viewed from the rear), and a bony protuberance at the rear of the skull called a "nuchal

crest." The molars of *H. erectus* are reduced in size, and the jawbones less robust than those of early *Homo*. In addition, the wear patterns on teeth are different from those found on the molars of early *Homo*. The enamel of *H. erectus* is heavily pitted and scratched, suggesting that its diet was significantly different from that of previous hominins, whose tooth enamel was much smoother.

The postcranial skeleton of *H. erectus* is somewhat more robust than modern human skeletons but is otherwise like our own (see Figure 4.16). In addition, sexual dimorphism is much reduced in *H. erectus*; males are only 20–30% larger than females. Reduced sexual dimorphism in primates is often thought to indicate reduced competition for mates among males and to be associated with monogamy and male contributions to the care of offspring. What reduced sexual dimorphism may have meant for *H. erectus*, however, is still an open question.

An assemblage of bones discovered on the Indonesian island of Flores in 2003, called *Homo floresiensis*, may have belonged to a so-called dwarf form of

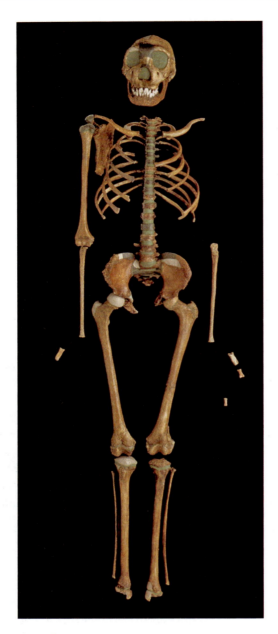

FIGURE 4.16   The most complete *H. erectus* (or *H. ergaster*) skeleton ever discovered is KNM-WT 15000 from Kenya. Believed to have been a 12-year-old boy, this fossil includes a nearly complete postcranial skeleton.

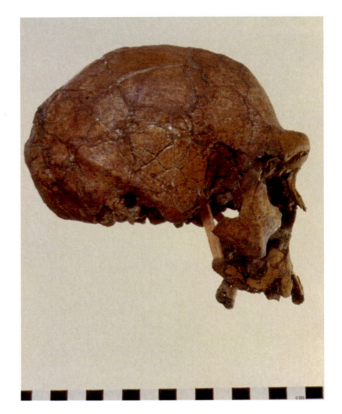

FIGURE 4.17   This *H. erectus* fossil (ER 3733) from Lake Turkana, in Kenya, has a cranial capacity of about 850 cm³.

Homo erectus (Brown et al. 2004; Morwood et al. 2004; Lahr and Foley 2004). When biologists speak of "dwarf" forms of large mammals, they are describing normally proportioned but considerably smaller varieties of mammalian species that have frequently evolved on islands. Most of the bones ranged from between 38,000 and 13,000 years of age. It appears that, apart from its small stature, *H. floresiensis* used stone tools and fire like other populations of *H. erectus* and hunted dwarf elephants

on the island. Since its discovery, some scholars have argued that small stature and other unusual features of the skeleton of *H. floresiensis* suggest that the bones belonged to modern *H. sapiens* individuals suffering from a pathology such as microcephaly or, more recently, endemic cretinism (e.g., Oxnard et al. 2010). These views have been systematically challenged by others (e.g., Falk et al. 2009). Unless and until more and better preserved bones are found, it does not appear that these disagreements will be resolved. It has been proposed that *H. floresiensis* may have close affinities to the earliest *Homo* populations to have left Africa (Tattersall 2012, 133; Fleagle 2013, 382). In any case, the status of *H. floresiensis* does not affect our overall understanding of human evolutionary patterns (Klein 2009, 724).

The Culture of *H. erectus*

Traditionally, the appearance of *H. erectus* in the fossil record has been linked to the appearance of a new stone-tool tradition in the archaeological record: the **Acheulean tradition**. Acheulean stone tools come in a variety of forms, but the Acheulean biface, or "hand ax," is the most characteristic (Figure 4.18). Acheulean bifaces are shaped from stone cores perhaps twice the size of Oldowan cores. Acheulean tools replaced Oldowan

Acheulean tradition   A Lower Paleolithic stone-tool tradition associated with *Homo erectus* and characterized by stone bifaces, or "hand axes."

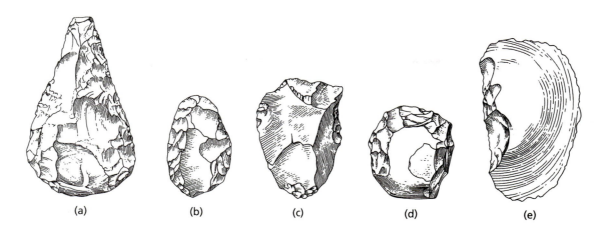

FIGURE 4.18 Although the biface, or "hand ax" (a), is the best-known tool from the Acheulean tradition, other core tools—such as scrapers (b), choppers (c and d), and cleavers (e)—have also been found. For reasons that are not well understood, large bifaces are rarely found in otherwise similar Asian assemblages.

tools in the archaeological record shortly after the appearance of *H. erectus*. Archaeologists traditionally assign the Acheulean tradition and the Oldowan tradition to a single period known as the Lower Paleolithic in Europe and the **Early Stone Age (ESA)** in Africa.

In recent years, the clear-cut association of Acheulean tools with *H. erectus* has been questioned. First, researchers have found African stone-tool assemblages between 1.5 and 1.4 million years old that contain both Oldowan and larger biface tools, but it is not known which hominins made and used these tools. Second, typical Acheulean tools continue to appear in African sites containing fossils of early *H. sapiens* over a million years later. The conclusion seems to be that there is no one-on-one correspondence between a particular stone-tool tradition and a particular hominin species. Put another way, more than one hominin species may have made and used tools that we assign to a single archaeological culture.

The Acheulean tradition in Africa and Europe changed very little over a period of slightly more than a million years, disappearing about 200,000 years ago. As long as 1 million years ago, however, stone-tool assemblages found in eastern Asia were quite different, reflecting adaptations to the very different environments invaded by *H. erectus* and its descendants (Klein 2009, 281). The best-known stone-tool assemblages associated with *H. erectus* in China lack large bifaces and consist mostly of flakes. Although bifaces have been found in other east Asian early Paleolithic sites, they are few in number, more crudely made than Acheulean bifaces, and more recent in date (around 200,000 years old) (Klein 2009, 386–87). Brian Fagan (1990, 119) pointed out that areas in which large bifaces are rare coincide

roughly with the distribution of bamboo and other forest materials in Asia. He argued that bamboo would have made excellent tools capable of doing the work performed elsewhere by stone bifaces.

H. erectus also used fire, the best evidence for which comes from the site of Gesher Benot Ya'akov in Israel (780,000 years ago) and Zhoukoudian, China, and Europe (between 670,000 and 400,000 years ago) (Klein 2009, 412–13). Burned cobbles and bones from a southern African site suggest that African *H. erectus* (*H. ergaster*) may have had intermittent control of fire a million years earlier than this (Tattersall 2012, 111–12).

H. erectus the Hunter?

Some paleoanthropologists claimed that *H. erectus* was primarily a hunter of big game, based on the fact that the bones of animals such as elephants and giant baboons were found in association with Acheulean tools in such important sites as Zhoukoudian. However, taphonomists question the assumption that *H. erectus* hunters killed the animals whose bones have been found together with Acheulean tools. As Lewis Binford and C. K. Ho (1985) have shown, doubts about how to interpret the bone assemblages from Zhoukoudian were raised almost as soon as the site was excavated. It is extremely difficult to determine whether elephant or baboon bones got into the caves as the result of carnivore or human activity. Although evidence of fire was found at Zhoukoudian, Binford and Ho called for a thorough re-examination of claims connecting fire to human activities in the caves;

Early Stone Age (ESA) The conventional name given to the period when Oldowan and Acheulean stone-tool traditions flourished in Africa.

and they found no evidence to support the idea that *H. erectus* used fire to cook meat.

Many of the *H. erectus* skulls found in Zhoukoudian lacked faces and parts of the cranial base. Some scholars interpret the skull damage as evidence that *H. erectus* practiced cannibalism. However, other scholars propose that hyena activity and the compacting of natural cave deposits are more reasonable, if less lurid, explanations for the condition of those skulls.

Earlier in the chapter, we discussed the hypothesis that bipedal locomotion enabled endurance walking and daylight hunting among the australopiths. Recent research has suggested that *endurance running* may also have played a crucial role in the evolution of later hominins, linking the emergence of new forms of hunting with the appearance of *Homo erectus*. Biological anthropologist Daniel Lieberman and human biologist Dennis Bramble point out that endurance running is not found among primates other than humans and that the distinctive characteristics of human endurance running are unusual among mammals in general. For example, many people are aware that most mammals can outsprint human beings, but they may not realize that humans can outrun almost all other mammals (sometimes even horses) for marathon-length distances (Lieberman and Bramble 2007, 289). Lieberman and Bramble argue that endurance running could have been a very powerful adaptation to the environments in which later hominins such as *Homo erectus* were living (see later discussion in this chapter).

Three sets of adaptations make human endurance running possible: *energetics* (the flow and transformation of energy), *stabilization* (how the body keeps from falling), and *temperature regulation* (maintaining body temperature within limits). Human energetic adaptations include tendons and ligaments in the legs and feet that are absent or very much smaller in other primates. These anatomical structures store energy and then push the body forward in a gait that is fundamentally different from the mechanics of walking. Human stabilization adaptations affect the center of mass and balance during running. These adaptations include a ligament that helps keep the head stable during running and an enlarged *gluteus maximus* (the muscle that makes up the distinctively large human buttocks). The *gluteus maximus*, which hardly contracts during level walking, contracts strongly during running, stiffening the torso and providing a counterbalance to the forward tilt of the trunk.

Human temperature regulation adaptations address what Lieberman and Bramble (2007, 289) consider the biggest physiological challenge that runners face: muscle activity generated by running generates as much as ten times more heat than does walking. Most mammals stop

galloping after short distances because they cannot cool their body temperature fast enough to prevent *hyperthermia*, or overheating. "Humans, uniquely, can run long distances in hot, arid conditions that cause hyperthermia in other mammals, largely because we have become specialized sweaters" (Lieberman and Bramble 2007, 289). Humans have less body hair and many more sweat glands than do other mammals, which allows for effective body cooling through evapotranspiration. By contrast, other mammals cool down by panting, which requires them to slow down from a gallop, if not stop running altogether.

When and why did humans become good at running long distances? Lieberman and Bramble (2007) argue that running emerged long after bipedal walking evolved—about 2 million years ago, at the time of the transition to *Homo erectus*. They argue that endurance running made scavenging meat and especially hunting of medium- to large-sized mammals increasingly successful. They also argue that it made persistence hunting possible: long-distance hominin runners forced prey animals to run at speeds that they could not endure for long, driving the animals to hyperthermia. The animals could then be killed by the only weapons available to hominins such as *H. erectus*—simple stone tools and sharpened, untipped, thrusting spears.

Biological anthropologist Richard Wrangham has suggested that the transition to *H. erectus* was pushed by the control of fire, which led to an increasing reliance on cooked food. In his view, cooking was of major importance in human evolution: "The newly delicious cooked diet led to their evolving smaller guts, bigger brains, bigger bodies, and reduced body hair" (Wrangham 2009, 194), as well as smaller teeth, since cooked foods are softer than raw foods. For Wrangham, the things that separate humanity from the other primates are the consequences of cooking.

What Happened to *H. erectus*?

H. erectus has long been seen as a logical link between more primitive hominins and our own species, *H. sapiens*. When paleoanthropologists assumed that evolution proceeded in a gradualistic manner, getting from *H. erectus* to *H. sapiens* seemed unproblematic. But thinking of speciation in terms of punctuated equilibria changes things. On the one hand, Richard Klein (2009) concludes that "*H. ergaster* and *H. erectus* resembled each other closely, and reasonable specialists can disagree on whether they can be separated" (329). On the other hand, Ian Tattersall (2009) contrasts the fossil record in Asia with the fossil record in Africa during the crucial period between 2 and 1.5 million years ago. During this period, he says, Africa "seems to have been

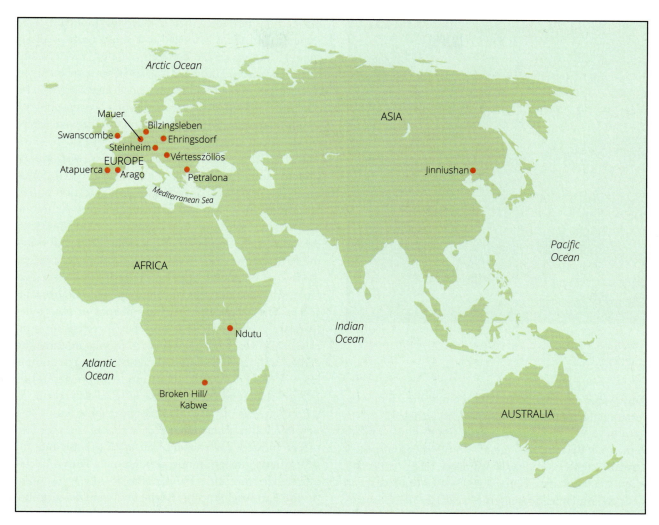

FIGURE 4.19 The major sites providing fossils assigned to archaic *H. sapiens.*

a hotbed of evolutionary experimentation," producing a variety of species of early *Homo*, one of which was *H. ergaster*; whereas Asian fossils assigned to *Homo erectus* show much greater morphological similarity, suggesting little or no evolutionary experimentation (Tattersall 2009, 240). Phyletic gradualists could argue that very little change in *H. erectus* morphology is still more than no change at all; some trends, such as a slight increase in cranial capacity from earlier to later *H. erectus* skulls, support their argument. If, however, regional populations of *H. erectus* are better understood as separate species, this argument requires revision.

Still, the scope of evolutionary adaptation attained by *H. erectus* surpassed that of earlier *Homo* species such as *H. habilis*. The postcranial skeleton of *H. erectus* was essentially modern in form, and its brain was considerably larger than that of its precursors. These features apparently allowed populations of *H. erectus* to make more elaborate tools and to move successfully into arid, seasonal environments in Africa and cooler climates in

Eurasia. As best we can tell now, it was from among these populations that the first members of our own species, *H. sapiens*, issued forth.

How Did *Homo sapiens* Evolve?

What Is the Fossil Evidence for the Transition to Modern *H. sapiens*?

The relatively rich and reasonably uniform fossil record associated with *H. erectus* disappears after about 500,000 years ago, to be replaced by a far patchier and more varied fossil record. Some 30 sites in Africa, Europe, and Asia have yielded a collection of fossils sometimes called early or **archaic *Homo sapiens*** (Figures 4.19 and 4.20). Most of

---

archaic *Homo sapiens* Hominins dating from 500,000 to 200,000 years ago that possessed morphological features found in both *Homo erectus* and *Homo sapiens.*

FIGURE 4.20 Fossils assigned to archaic *H. sapiens* include the Broken Hill skull, from Kabwe, Zambia.

these fossils consist of fragmented crania, jaws, and teeth. Postcranial bones thought to belong to archaic *H. sapiens* are robust, like those of *H. erectus*, but they are difficult to interpret because they are few in number and poorly dated and show considerable variation. Interpreting variation is particularly problematic when only a few specimens are available for analysis (Hager 1997). Arguments about interpretations of these fossils have grown heated at times, precisely because their resolution has implications for the way we understand not just the fate of *H. erectus* but also the birth of our own species.

Paleoanthropologist Günter Bräuer used cladistic methods to compare all the skulls from Africa that had been assigned to archaic *H. sapiens*. Bräuer (1989, 132) argued that his morphological analysis showed that modern *H. sapiens* evolved from *H. erectus* only once, in Africa, and that the period of transition from archaic *H. sapiens* to modern *H. sapiens* was slow, taking some tens of thousands of years. Such a conclusion might be interpreted as an argument for the evolution of modern *H. sapiens* as a result of phyletic gradualism. But is a period of tens of thousands of years relatively long or relatively short, geologically speaking? G. Philip Rightmire favors a punctuationist analysis of the evolution of modern *H. sapiens*. That is, he regards *H. erectus* "as a real species, stable during a long time period" (Rightmire 1995, 487; see also Rightmire 1990). The appearance of modern *H. sapiens* would have followed the punctuation of this equilibrium some 300,000 years ago.

Paleoanthropologist Ian Tattersall also favors a punctuationist explanation for the origins of *H. sapiens*,

but he does not agree that all regional populations assigned to *H. erectus* belonged to a single species. All archaic *H. sapiens* fossils between 600,000 and 200,000 years of age, from Europe, Africa, and China, are included by Tattersall in the fossil species *Homo heidelbergensis*; he describes *H. heidelbergensis* as the first "cosmopolitan" hominin species, and he locates its origin somewhere within early African *Homo* (Tattersall 2012, 135–36). Tattersall also believes that *H. heidelbergensis* was responsible for a number of cultural innovations dated to this time period: shelter construction, domestication of fire, fabrication of spears, and the prepared-core technique of stone-tool manufacture (Tattersall 2012, 138–41). In the mid-1990s, moreover, paleoanthropologists working in limestone caves in the Sierra de Atapuerca, Spain, discovered fragments of hominin bones and teeth that are nearly 800,000 years old (Bermúdez de Castro et al. 1997). They argue that it is an offshoot of *H. ergaster* (African *H. erectus*) and may be ancestral to both *H. heidelbergensis* and *H. sapiens*. Not only are these the earliest well-dated hominin fossils ever found in Europe, but they also display a mix of modern and *erectus*-like features that do not match those of *H. heidelbergensis*. As a result, the Spanish scholars assigned these fossils to a new species, *Homo antecessor* (*antecessor* is Latin for "explorer, pioneer, early settler," an appropriate name for the earliest known hominin population in Europe). A set of fossilized footprints found at the site of Happisburgh, on the East Anglian coast of the UK, were dated to between 1 and 1.78 million years old and have also been assigned to *H. antecessor* (Ashton et al. 2014). Other paleoanthropologists seem willing to accept *H. antecessor* as a valid species but believe that not enough evidence yet exists to link it firmly to other species that came before or after it.

The same team of Spanish paleontologists also discovered hominin fossils at Atapuerca that appear to represent a very early stage in Neandertal evolution (Arsuaga et al. 1993). In 2007, improved uranium-series dating methods showed that these fossils were at least 530,000 years old (Tattersall 2012, 156).

Today, most experts place the African and European fossils once classified as "archaic *Homo sapiens*" into the species *H. heidelbergensis*. Originating in Africa some 600,000 years ago, it "may lie close to the origin of the European and African lineages that led to the Neanderthals and modern humans, respectively" (Tattersall 2009, 281). This conclusion is based on the judgment that these fossils all show derived morphological features not present in *H. erectus*, but none shows any of the derived features that are distinctive of either Neandertals or modern humans (Stringer and Andrews 2005, 150–51). *H. heidelbergensis* "could have emerged in the same kind of rapid burst that may have produced *H. ergaster* a million years earlier" (Klein 2009, 433).

Where Did Modern *H. sapiens* Come from?

In the last decade of the twentieth century, paleoanthropologists primarily relied on fossils of archaic *H. sapiens* to formulate arguments about the origins of our own species. Two main positions were staked out. On one side were those who thought of speciation in terms of punctuated equilibrium. They hypothesized that *H. erectus* was a single, long-lived species that had initially spread throughout the entire Old World. However, only one regional population of *H. erectus*, probably located in Africa, was thought to have undergone a rapid spurt of evolution to produce *H. sapiens* around 200,000–100,000 years ago, and this new species was thought to have moved out of Africa, replacing any remaining populations of *H. erectus*, and repopulating the globe. This scenario was called the "out of Africa" or **replacement model**.

However, the replacement model was challenged by paleoanthropologists who agreed that the first species of *Homo* to leave Africa was *H. erectus* but who detected distinct physical differences in the fossils of *H. erectus* found in different regions of the Old World. They interpreted these regional differences as the result of adaptation to regional selection pressures. Over time, a complex pattern of gene flow would have spread any advantageous adaptations arising in one regional population to all the others, while preventing regional populations from evolving into separate species. This scenario was usually called the **regional continuity model** (e.g., Thorne and Wolpoff 1992)

Yet still other paleoanthropologists viewed both scenarios as problematic, either because they simplified the fossil record (Aiello 1993) or because they overlooked the possibility that regional populations in anatomically modern humans might have been the result of several different migrations out of Africa by phenotypically different populations at different times and using different routes (Lahr and Foley 1994). In 2001, biological anthropologist John Relethford proposed a compromise: the *mostly out of Africa model*. Relethford agreed that the fossil evidence suggested an African origin for modern human *anatomy*, but he argued that this did not mean that the entire contents of the modern human *gene pool* were exclusively from Africa as well.

Recognition that the gene pool of our ancestors is indeed mixed has come from recent research and recovery of ancient DNA, which we will be looking at shortly. As we saw in Chapter 3, the genomes of many species, both living and fossilized, are being sequenced and compared, and the significance of hybridity within their evolutionary histories is becoming clear. And this history of mixing includes *Homo sapiens*. Chris Stringer, the paleoanthropologist who long defended the replacement model, now acknowledges both that dispersal events back "into Africa" played a role in our species' early history and that anatomically modern humans interbred with Neandertals in Europe (2012). But in order to better understand what he and other paleoanthropologists were arguing about, we need to take a closer look at perhaps the best known archaic human population in the world: the Neandertals.

Who Were the Neandertals (130,000–35,000 Years Ago)?

Neandertals get their name from the Neander Tal ("Neander Valley"), in Germany, where a fossil skullcap and some postcranial bones were discovered in 1856. Thereafter, paleoanthropologists used the name Neandertal to refer to other fossils from Europe and western Asia that appeared to belong to populations of the same kind (Figure 4.21). The first Neandertals appeared about 130,000 years ago. The youngest known Neandertal fossil, from France, is about 35,000 years old; and another, from Spain, may be even younger, at 27,000 years of age (Hublin et al. 1996). After this date, Neandertals disappear from the fossil record.

Because numerous cranial and postcranial bones have been recovered, paleoanthropologists have been able to reconstruct Neandertal morphology with some confidence (Figure 4.22). Neandertals were shorter and more robust than modern *H. sapiens*, with massive skulls, continuous brow ridges, and protruding, chinless faces. Neandertal teeth are larger than those of modern human populations and have enlarged pulp cavities and fused roots, a condition known as *taurodontism*. Unlike modern human beings, Neandertal lower jaws possess a gap behind the third molar called a *retromolar space*, which results from the extreme forward placement of teeth in the jaw. This forward placement and the characteristic wear

---

replacement model The hypothesis that only one subpopulation of *Homo erectus*, probably located in Africa, underwent a rapid spurt of evolution to produce *Homo sapiens* 200,000 to 100,000 years ago. After that time, *H. sapiens* would itself have multiplied and moved out of Africa, gradually populating the globe and eventually replacing any remaining populations of *H. erectus* or their descendants.

regional continuity model The hypothesis that evolution from *Homo erectus* to *Homo sapiens* occurred gradually throughout the entire traditional range of *H. erectus*.

Neandertals An archaic species of *Homo* that lived in Europe and western Asia 130,000–35,000 years ago.

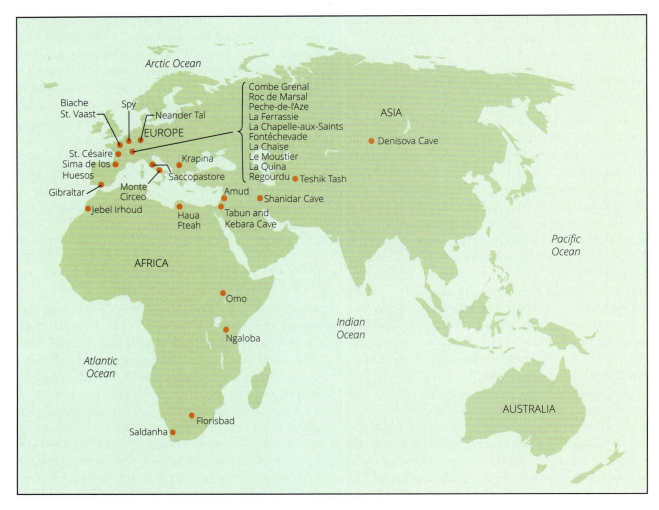

FIGURE 4.21   Major Neandertal sites, indicating the concentration of these hominins in Europe and southwestern Asia. Note also the location of Denisova Cave in Russian Siberia, where Pleistocene fossils with DNA distinct from Neandertals were recovered. Mitochondrial DNA recovered from a fossil hominin from Sima de los Huesos in northern Spain shows connections to the mtDNA of the Denisovan fossils. These data suggest more population movement and mixing among Pleistocene hominins than previously suspected.

patterns on Neandertal incisors suggest that Neandertals regularly used their front teeth as a clamp (Stringer and Andrews 2005, 155; Klein 2009, 461).

The average Neandertal cranial capacity (1,520 cm³) is actually larger than that of modern human populations (1,400 cm³); however, the braincase is elongated, with a receding forehead, unlike the rounded crania and domed foreheads of modern humans. Fossilized impressions of Neandertal brains appear to show the same pattern of difference between the left and right halves (*brain asymmetry*) that is found in modern human brains. Among other things, this suggests that Neandertals were usually right-handed. Brain asymmetries are not unique to modern human beings—or even to primates. H. L. Dibble (1989) argues that we cannot conclude that Neandertal brains functioned like ours simply because we share the same pattern of brain asymmetries. If Neandertal and anatomically modern human

populations descended from the same ancestral group (i.e., some form of archaic *H. sapiens*), then it is likely that both groups inherited similarly functioning brains.

Neandertal postcranial skeletons are not significantly different from those of modern human beings, but the pelvis and femur are quite distinct (Aiello 1993, 82). Neandertal robusticity and the markings for muscle attachment on their limbs suggest that they were heavily muscled. Differences in the Neandertal hand suggest to paleoanthropologists that it had an unusually powerful grip. Some paleoanthropologists explain Neandertal robusticity as an adaptation to the stress of glacial conditions in Europe. Neandertals who lived in the far milder climate of western Asia were equally robust, however, making this explanation not entirely convincing. The Neandertal pubic bone is longer and thinner than that of modern human beings. Erik Trinkaus (1984) concluded that the Neandertal birth canal was larger as well;

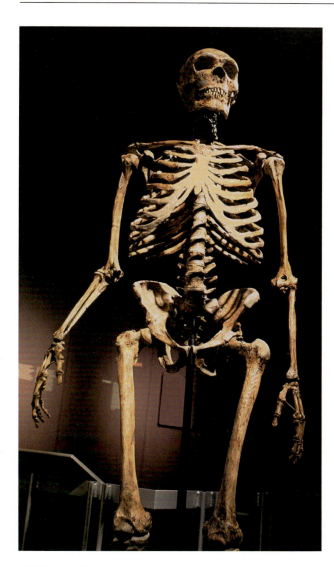

FIGURE 4.22   A recent reconstruction of a Neandertal skeleton.

but B. O. Arensburg (1989), another Neandertal expert, found no evidence for a larger birth canal. He related the length of the Neandertal pubic bone to posture and locomotion. More recently, Holly Dunsworth and Leah Eccleston have argued that "childbirth is a much more dynamic process than can be reconstructed from bones alone, so the hominin fossil record provides limited and tenuous information" (2015, 60). First, humans give birth to large fat babies, which increases difficulties in childbirth, and this trend may have began before the appearance of the genus *Homo*. Second, "primate birth is a social event" (2015, 59), even for nonhuman primates like bonobos, which do not possess the features of pelvic anatomy and infant size that make human birthing difficult. In short, "fossils may be blinding us to other significant contributors to childbirth difficulty," many of which may be related to the social and personal circumstances under which human women give birth (Dunsworth and

Eccleston 2015, 60). These circumstances were seriously reshaped with the adoption of agriculture, which altered nourishment and growth patterns for human mothers and fetuses; "it is likely that there was never more childbirth difficulty than there is now and in recent history" (2015, 60).

The morphological differences that distinguish modern humans from Neandertals are not considered to be greater than the differences that distinguish two subspecies within some species of mammals. Moreover, as we shall see, genetic information from ancient DNA indicates not only that Neandertals apparently exchanged genes with a previously unknown "Denisovan" population in Russian Siberia, but also that ancient mtDNA from the Denisovans appears closely related to ancient mtDNA from a fossil from Sima de los Huesos in Spain (Meyer et al. 2014). It seems clear that mobility and interbreeding among ancient hominin populations were much greater than suspected, and they are reconsidering how boundaries between fossil species ought to be understood.

What Do We Know about Middle Paleolithic/Middle Stone Age Culture?

Late archaic human populations in Europe, Africa, and southwestern Asia are associated with a new stone-tool tradition, the **Mousterian tradition**, named after the cave in Le Moustier, France, where the first samples of these tools were discovered. Mousterian tools are assigned to the Middle Paleolithic, whereas similar tools from Africa are assigned to the **Middle Stone Age (MSA)**. They differ from the Lower Paleolithic/ESA tools in that they consist primarily of flakes, not cores. Many Mousterian flakes, moreover, were produced by the Levallois technique of core preparation. The earliest MSA tool industries in Africa are probably about 200,000 years old. The earliest Mousterian industries of Europe may be equally old, but dating is far less certain because radiometric techniques cannot provide reliable dates for this period. Although Neandertals were responsible for Mousterian tools in western Europe, similar tools were made by non-Neandertal populations elsewhere (Mellars 1996, 5).

Despite differing names and a distribution that covers more than one continent, most Mousterian/MSA stone-tool assemblages are surprisingly similar, consisting of flake tools that were retouched to make scrapers

Mousterian tradition A Middle Paleolithic stone-tool tradition associated with Neandertals in Europe and southwestern Asia and with anatomically modern human beings in Africa.

Middle Stone Age (MSA) The name given to the period of Mousterian stone-tool tradition in Africa, 200,000–40,000 years ago.

IN THEIR OWN WORDS

Bad Hair Days in the Paleolithic

Modern (Re)Constructions of the Cave Man

Judith Berman has written about how Paleolithic human beings have been visually stereotyped in Western culture since the end of the nineteenth century.

The Cave Man looks as he does because he is a representation of our ideas about human nature and human origins. His image is not necessarily based on scientific data, but is rather anchored in and entwined with other tremendously puissant representations deriving from pagan and Judeo-Christian traditions. We are readily convinced of the "truth" of Cave Man images because they seem "natural" or familiar to us; in fact, they draw on a set of conventionalized observations about the origins and natural history of humans.

Hairstyles are a clue to where on the evolutionary tree an artist or illustrator places his or her subject. Certainly a thick coat of body hair and ungroomed head hair puts an ancestor a great distance from modern humans (although we have no data on when a hairy coat was lost), while most Neanderthals have longer and untidier hair than Upper Paleolithic humans. Now these may be perfectly accurate representations of our ancestors, but we have no data on this subject until the Upper Paleolithic. Hair is our marker of evolutionary position; the further away from our animal origins, the more it is under control. (In many of the pictorial histories of humankind, later humans leave the Paleolithic behind, put on good Neolithic cloth coats, invent headbands and pageboys, and settle down on their farms.)

So far, we have delineated some of the natural history of the convention of the Cave Man and have examined the significance of his hair. But why should this Cave Man matter so to us? The Cave Man is a representation of our ancestors; the fact of evolution forces us to acknowledge that the Cave Man resides within each of us. He is our animal, primitive self, before the limits of society.

Source: Berman 1999, 297.

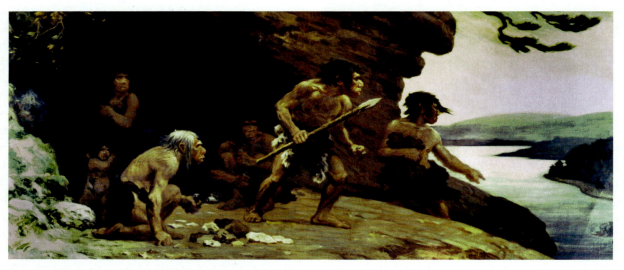

Charles R. Knight's 1921 painting of Neandertals for the American Museum of Natural History in New York City follows the convention Judith Berman describes, giving them ungroomed head hair to mark their great distance from modern humans.

(a) (b) (c) (d) (e)

FIGURE 4.23 Mousterian tools were primarily flake tools, commonly produced by the Levallois technique of core preparation.

and points (Figure 4.23). Flint was the stone of choice in Europe and southwestern Asia, but quartzite and some volcanic rock types were widely used in Africa, where flint is absent. Most Mousterian/MSA sites are rock shelters located near what were once sources of fresh water. The rock shelters were probably living sites because many contained hearths as well as stone tools. Interestingly, Mousterian sites found in the European part of the former Soviet Union appear to be the earliest hominin sites that exist in these areas. This might mean that Neandertals were the first hominins capable of settling areas with such a cold, harsh climate.

Mousterian/MSA tools are more varied than the Lower Paleolithic/ESA tools that preceded them. Archaeologists have offered three different explanations for the variation found in western Europe. François Bordes identified five major Mousterian variants and thought they represented five different cultural traditions. Lewis and Sally Binford countered that what Bordes had identified were actually varied tool kits that a single group of people might have used to perform different functions or to carry out different tasks at different times of the year. Both these interpretations were rejected by H. L. Dibble and Nicolas Rolland, who saw the "variety" of Mousterian assemblages as a by-product of other factors, such as periodic resharpening (which changed the shapes of tools and reduced their size until they were discarded) or the different kinds of stone the toolmakers had used (see Mellars 1996). Archaeologist Paul Mellars reviewed the evidence for each of these arguments, and he concluded that Bordes's original interpretation is the most plausible. Each Mousterian variant has a distinct pattern of spatial and chronological distribution, and some industries are characterized by specific tools that do not occur in the other variants. For Mellars (1996), this shows "a real element of cultural patterning" (355).

What other cultural remains are there from the Middle Paleolithic? In western Europe, Neandertals left

traces of hearths, although their sites were not centered around hearths, as is typical of the Upper Paleolithic. The evidence for stone walls is ambiguous, but there is good evidence for pits and even a posthole, especially at Combe-Grenal in France, where Bordes excavated (Mellars 1996, 295). Moreover, we know that Neandertals deliberately buried their dead, often with arms and legs folded against their upper bodies. A number of the most famous Neandertal finds, such as La Ferrassie in France and Shanidar Cave in Iraq, are grave sites. Many paleoanthropologists interpret deliberate burials as evidence for the beginnings of human religion. Accumulations of bear skulls found at some European sites have been interpreted as collections Neandertals made for use in a "cave bear cult." Flower pollen scattered over the Shanidar burial was interpreted as the remains of flowers mourners had placed on the grave. Fragments of natural red or black pigments were interpreted as possible ritual cosmetics. However, taphonomic analyses question these interpretations. For example, the cave bear skulls may simply have accumulated where cave bears died; flower pollen was found throughout the Shanidar site and may have been introduced by burrowing rodents; red and black pigments may have been used to tan hides or change the color of objects. Klein points out that Neandertals made no formal bone artifacts, and he has argued that some so-called Neandertal art objects may be **intrusions** from later deposits; that is, they may be artifacts made by more recent populations that accidentally found their way into Neandertal strata as the result of natural forces (Klein 2009, 528). But this explanation cannot be extended to paintings found in Spanish caves that are at least 65,000 years old, squarely within the time period that Neandertals flourished in Europe (Hoffman, D. L. et al. 2018). Moreover, the anatomically modern peoples who came after the Neandertals left a

intrusions Artifacts made by more recent populations that find their way into more ancient strata as the result of natural forces.

profusion of decorative objects made of bone, ivory, antler, and shell (Mellars 1996; Stringer and Andrews 2005, 212ff.; Klein 2009, 660ff.). Tattersall proposes that "the physical origin of our species lay in a short-term event of major developmental reorganization, even if that event was likely driven by a rather minor structural innovation at the DNA level" (2012, 207). Tattersall thinks this reorganization event probably occurred within a small, isolated African Pleistocene population and that it took a while for subsequent generations to gain awareness of the new potentials for language and symbolic thought that it made possible. That is, for Tattersall (2012), language and symbolic thought are best understood as exaptations: "In the case of *Homo sapiens* the potential for symbolic thought evidently just lurked there, undetected, until it was released by a stimulus that must necessarily have been a cultural one—the biology, after all, was already in place" (211).

A very different kind of evidence may illustrate the humanity of the Neandertals. All the data indicate that Neandertals lived hard lives in a difficult habitat, and many Neandertal bones show evidence of injuries, disease, and premature aging. To survive as long as they did, the individuals to whom these bones belonged would have needed to rely on others to care for them (Chase 1989, 330). As Klein (2009) observes, "group concern for the old and sick may have permitted Neandertals to live longer than any of their predecessors, and it is the most recognizably human, nonmaterial aspect of their behavior that can be directly inferred from the archaeological record" (585).

Did Neandertals Hunt?

Archaeologists in Germany and Britain have discovered wooden spears that date to the period when Neandertals were the only hominins in Europe (Klein 2009, 404–05). In addition, several Mousterian stone points show what appears to be impact damage, suggesting use as a weapon. Animal remains at some sites in France and on the island of Jersey suggest that Neandertals collectively drove the animals over cliffs or engaged in other kinds of mass-killing strategies (Mellars 1996, 227–29). Archaeologists have also found the bones of hoofed mammals such as deer, bison, and wild species of oxen, sheep, goats, and horses at Eurasian Mousterian sites. As in other cases, however, it is often difficult—particularly at open-air sites—to tell how many of these bones are the remains of Neandertal meals and how many got to the site some other way. Furthermore, at some Eurasian and African sites, the bones of elephants and rhinoceros were used as building materials and their flesh may not have been eaten.

What about the flesh of other Neandertals? As we saw in our discussion of *H. erectus*, claims that one or another hominin species practiced cannibalism are made from time to time, often on the basis of equivocal evidence. Sometimes the evidence is more straightforward—for example, at Gran Dolina in Spain, where butchered human bones were found together in 800,000-year-old deposits associated with *H. antecessor* (Fernandez-Jalvo et al. 1999). Persuasive evidence of cannibalism in association with Neandertals has been reported from the 100,000-year-old site of Moula Guercy, in France (Defleur et al. 1993, 1999) and from the 49,000-year-old site of El Sidron, in Spain (Lalueza-Fox et al. 2005, 2010; Rosas et al. 2006). In both sites, the bones of a number of individuals show unmistakable signs of cut marks that indicated some or all of the following: the deliberate cutting apart of bodies, the cutting away of muscles, or the splitting of bones to extract marrow. The question is how to interpret these findings. Middle Paleolithic archaeologist Richard Klein suggests that these remains might reflect a response to nutritional stress rather than a regular dietary practice. He also suggests that in some cases, the damage to human bones may have been the work of carnivores that feasted on human bodies they had dug out of graves, which still happens in Africa today (Klein 2009, 574–75). Biological anthropologist Jonathan Marks reminds us that numerous contemporary human groups remove flesh from the bones of the dead, not to consume it but as part of a mortuary ritual. Making sense of these remains is complex because what it means to be human seems to ride in the balance: if Neandertals ate one another, they would appear "behaviorally nonhuman (since the consumption of human flesh lies on the symbolic boundary of human behavior)," whereas mortuary defleshing of the dead "symbolically renders them as more human, since it invokes thought and ritual" (Marks 2009, 225).

P. G. Chase argued that Neandertals were skilled hunters of large game and that their diet does not seem to have differed much from that of the modern people who eventually replaced them. He described the changes that set anatomically modern people apart from Neandertals in terms that highlighted the particular way in which they constructed their niches; that is, he emphasized the way moderns used symbolic thought and language to transform "the intellectual and social contexts in which food was obtained" (Chase 1989, 334).

What Do We Know about Anatomically Modern Humans (200,000 Years Ago to Present)?

During the period when classic Neandertal populations appeared in Europe and western Asia, a different kind of hominin appeared to the south that possessed an anatomy like that of modern human beings. They had an average cranial capacity of more than 1,350 cm³, domed foreheads, and round braincases. These early modern people also had flatter faces than Neandertals, usually with distinct chins. Their teeth were not crowded into the front of their jaws, and they lacked retromolar spaces. The postcranial skeleton of these **anatomically modern human beings** was much more lightly built than that of the Neandertals. In Europe, where the fossil record is fullest, their skeletons gradually became smaller and less robust for about 20,000 years after they first appeared. Many paleoanthropologists believe that these changes were a byproduct of niche construction, as anatomically modern human beings increasingly dependent on culture buffered themselves from selection pressures that favored physical strength.

Experts long thought that anatomically modern humans first appeared about 40,000 years ago in Europe. However, discoveries in recent years have profoundly altered our understanding of modern human origins. It is now accepted that the earliest documented evidence for the appearance of anatomically modern humans is around 300,000 years old, from the site of Jebel Irhoud, in Morocco (Richter, D. et al. 2017; see Figure 4.25). Newly discovered hominin skeletal material (Hublin et al. 2017) included a tooth that was dated using both uranium series and electron spin resonance techniques, and fire-heated flint artifacts associated with the hominin fossils were dated using thermoluminescence. Together, these materials suggest a date of 315,000 (±34,000) years ago, a date that is also consistent with biostratigraphic dates obtained from rodent fossils at the site (Geraads, D. et al. 2013). Other fossils assigned to early anatomically modern *Homo sapiens* have been found elsewhere in Africa. Two sites in Ethiopia produced important finds: fossils from Omo Kibish have been dated to 195,000 years ago and fossils from Herto to between 154,000 and 160,000 years ago. At Klasies River Mouth Cave in southern Africa, modern human fossils too old to be accurately dated by radiocarbon methods were cross-dated using paleoclimatic and biostratigraphic methods, as well as uranium-series dating and electron spin resonance. They were assigned an age of between 74,000 and 60,000 years ago, although some experts are not convinced by the cross-dating. Bone harpoons found at a site in Katanda, Congo, were dated to more than 70,000 years of age using thermoluminescence and electron spin resonance. If this date stands, it would reinforce the hypothesis that anatomically modern *H. sapiens* first made Upper Paleolithic-style tools in Africa thousands of years before moving into Europe (Brooks and Yellen 1992). It is possible, however, that these bone tools are intrusions (Klein 2009, 527–28).

As we noted in Module 2, dating methods such as thermoluminescence and electron spin resonance have offered important ways of obtaining dates for crucial finds in hominin evolutionary history that are found in strata when other methods cannot be used. Their reliability has been questioned, but they have been refined and are providing firmer dates for the earliest fossils of anatomically modern humans, especially when more than one method can be used to cross-check results from the others. For example, until recently, archaeologists could only assign relative dates to southwestern Asian Middle Paleolithic archaeological sites, based on changes in the stone-tool assemblages they contained. Especially tricky were sites in Israel where Mousterian tools were found in association both with Neandertal bones at Kebara and Tabun and with anatomically modern human bones at Qafzeh (Bar-Yosef 1989, 604; Mellars and Stringer 1989, 7). In the 1990s, thermoluminescence, uranium-series dating, and electron spin resonance were added to rodent biostratigraphy and sedimentary data to date both the Neandertal remains and the modern human remains. This effort yielded dates of 90,000 years and older for both sets of fossils. In 2018, a fossilized jaw and teeth found at Misliya Cave, Israel, assigned to anatomically modern humans, and associated with a Middle Stone Age stone tool technology, was dated to 177,000 to 194,000 years ago. Once again, this was achieved by cross-dating using thermoluminescence on burned flints, uranium series analysis of the dentine and crust from the jaw, and combined uranium-series and electron spin resonance dating of the tooth enamel. (Hershkovitz, I. et al. 2018). Chris Stringer (2012), who has been closely involved with this work over the years, reports that "Continuing dating work using all the available techniques now suggests that the Skhul and Qafzeh people actually range from about 90,000 to 120,000 years old, while the Tabun Neanderthal is most likely about 120,000 years old. So the emerging scenario is one where populations apparently ebbed and flowed in the region" (47).

In sum, although not all experts are convinced (Callaway, 2017), many do accept that the Jebel Irhoud fossils belong to anatomical moderns, and that anatomically modern humans appeared much earlier than previously thought in Africa and southwest Asia. These early anatomical moderns also apparently used the same stone-tool technologies long associated with Neandertals. Furthermore, some paleoanthropologists

---

anatomically modern human beings Hominin fossils assigned to the species *Homo sapiens* with anatomical features similar to those of living human populations: short and round skulls, small brow ridges and faces, prominent chins, and light skeletal build.

have concluded that "The emergence of our species and of the Middle Stone Age appear to be close in time, and these data suggest a larger scale, potentially pan-African, origin for both" (Richter et al. 2017, 293). Or, as Hublin et al. put it, "the evolutionary processes behind the emergence of *H. sapiens* involved the whole African continent" (2017, 289). This assessment was endorsed by the paleoanthropologists who reanalyzed the Apidima fossils from Greece, found in the 1970s, but recently virtually reconstructed and dated using uranium series radiometric methods (Harvati et al. 2019). One fossil cranium, called Apidima 1, is described as possessing a mixture of primitive and modern features, especially a rounded cranium that is "consistent with a taxonomic attribution to early modern humans;" and its age of over 210,000 years old suggests that "early modern humans dispersed out of Africa starting much earlier, and reaching much further, than previously thought" (Harvati et al. 2019, 504). This skull fragment was found isolated from any material culture or other contextual data, which leaves a number of paleoanthropologists skeptical about its attribution (Aschenbach 2019). But its age and geographical location is consistent with the pattern suggested by the Jebel Irhoud finds and those from Skhul, Qafzeh, and Misliya caves in Israel; namely, "multiple dispersals of early modern humans out of Africa, [which] highlight the complex demographic processes that characterized Pleistocene human evolution and modern human presence in southeast Europe" (Harvati et al. 2019, 500).

Klein (2009) hypothesizes that "the Skhul/Qafzeh people were simply near modern Africans who extended their range slightly to the northeast during the relatively mild and moist conditions of the Last Interglacial, between 127 and 71 [thousand years] ago" (606). In any case, for at least 45,000 years, Neandertals and moderns apparently lived side by side or took turns occupying southwestern Asia. If Neandertals and anatomically modern human beings were contemporaries, then Neandertals cannot be ancestral to moderns as the regional continuity theorists argue.

What Can Genetics Tell Us about Modern Human Origins?

You will recall from Module 2 that geneticists claimed to be able to construct a molecular clock based on the mutation rate in human DNA. (In fact, they chose to focus on mtDNA, which is found in the mitochondria of cells, outside the nucleus, and is only transmitted along the female line—unlike eggs, sperm are cell nuclei and only carry nuclear DNA.) The results of their initial analysis suggested that the ancestors of modern humans originated in Africa some 100,000–200,000 years ago (Cann et al. 1987; Wilson and Cann 1992). An early study of the pattern of DNA variation in the Y (i.e., the male) chromosome of different regional human populations also suggested an African origin for modern *H. sapiens* (Rouhani 1989, 53). Since that time, information about the DNA of many living species, not just our own, has grown at an impressive rate, as will be discussed in Chapter 5.

But most exciting of all has been the invention of techniques that can successfully remove ancient DNA

FIGURE 4.24   Fossils of anatomically modern human beings have been recovered from these Old World and New World sites.

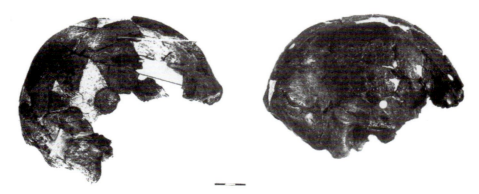

FIGURE 4.25   The earliest anatomically modern human fossils known come from the Ethiopian site of Omo Kibish and are 195,000 years old.

from bones that are tens of thousands of years old. Again, these operations have been performed on the bones of many extinct species, but the successes achieved using bone from Neandertals and their contemporaries has been dazzling. In 1997, molecular geneticists working in the laboratory directed by Svante Pääbo at the Max Planck Institute for Evolutionary Anthropology in Leipzig, Germany, extracted a sequence of mtDNA with 378 base pairs from the original 1856 Neandertal-type specimen. They compared the Neandertal sequence with 994 human mtDNA lineages taken from a worldwide sample of living human populations. They concluded that Neandertal females contributed no mtDNA to modern human populations and reaffirmed that the ancestor of the mtDNA pool of contemporary humans lived in Africa (Krings et al. 1997). Shortly thereafter, they concluded that the last common mtDNA ancestor of Neandertals and modern humans lived approximately half a million years ago (Krings et al. 1999).

However, Krings and his colleagues noted that their results tell us nothing about whether Neandertals contributed *nuclear* genes (i.e., from the chromosomes in our cell nuclei) to modern populations.

More recent work has begun to answer this question. A major breakthrough was the publication of a draft Neandertal nuclear genome (Green et al. 2010). Green and his colleagues in the Leipzig lab extracted nuclear DNA from 21 Neandertal bones from Vindija, Croatia, and found that 1% to 4% of the genomes of modern non-Africans contained Neandertal sequences, but that no sequences from modern humans appeared in the Neandertal genome. They concluded, therefore, that most genetic variation in modern humans outside Africa originated with our anatomically modern ancestors. Finally, because they thought the Neandertal genome was equally distant from the genomes of modern individuals from around the world, they concluded that the inbreeding between modern humans and Neandertals probably took place in southwest Asia, before modern

humans spread out and diversified throughout the Old World. These results do not support the regional continuity model but would be consistent with the mostly out of Africa model. Back in Chapter 3, we noted the increasing evidence of cross-species interbreeding throughout the history of life in many species, including mammals, other primates, and even ourselves. Here we can consider more fully the consequences of ancient DNA analysis for our interpretations of human evolutionary history. Svante Pääbo and his colleagues extracted both mtDNA and nuclear DNA from two tiny fossils found at Denisova Cave in Siberia. When the Denisova sequences were compared with those of Neandertal and modern sequences, three key findings emerged: (1) although they lived between 400,000 and 30,000 years ago, the **Denisovans** were genetically distinct from Neandertals; (2) the Denisovans and Neandertals shared a common ancestor who had left Africa nearly half a million years ago; and (3) the Denisovan genome was very similar to the genome of modern humans from New Guinea. Pääbo and his colleagues concluded that the Denisovan and Neandertal populations must have split apart after leaving Africa; but that about 50,000 years ago, the Denisovans interbred with anatomically modern humans, who took some Denisovan DNA with them when they moved into South Asia. And as we saw earlier, connections exist between the mtDNA from a 300,000-year-old fossil hominin from Spain and the Denisovans from Russian Siberia. Although the Denisovan genome has been reconstructed, so far no fossils of the Denisovan skeleton are known, apart from the original Denisovan finger bone and a recently discovered jawbone and teeth from Xuchang,

Denisovans a population of Pleistocene hominins known only from ancient DNA recovered from two tiny 41,000-year-old fossils deposited in Denisova Cave, Russian Siberia. Denisovans and Neandertals are thought to share a common ancestor that left Africa 500,000 years ago. Parts of the Denisovan genome resemble the genomes of modern humans from New Guinea.

China, which have been identified as Denisovan (Chen et al. 2019).

The collection and analysis of ancient DNA has become increasingly detailed and sophisticated. When such data are compared with genome data collected from living human populations all over the world, it is sometimes possible to tell whether genetic variants found in living human populations were part of the gene pool of these ancient populations. For example, the *FOXP2* gene found in living human populations has been implicated in our ability to speak and use language. A variant of this gene has been recovered from Neandertal bones in Spain, suggesting that limits on Neandertal language ability may have been less severe than once thought (Krause et al. 2007). In addition, a variant of the *MC1R* gene, which affects skin pigmentation in modern human populations, has been recovered from Neandertal bones in Spain and Italy; tests on its functioning suggest that Neandertals had light skin and red hair (Lalueza-Fox et al. 2007).

This new genetic evidence is exciting and accumulating at an impressive rate. Still, some perspective is called for. Jonathan Marks (2011) reminds us that "while our DNA matches that of a chimpanzee at over the 98% level, it matches the DNA of the banana the chimpanzee is eating at over the 25% level. Yet there is hardly any way we can imagine ourselves to be over one-quarter banana—except in our DNA" (139). So what does it mean to share 1% to 4% of our genome with Neandertals? Many paleontologists and archaeologists are likely to be cautious about endorsing the DNA evidence until it is backed up by additional fossil evidence; as Klein (2009) observes, studies of genetic diversity are "a useful and independent means of assessment" of proposed models of human evolution, but "[t]he fossil record must be the final arbiter" (631) when it comes to evaluating such models.

What Do We Know about the Upper Paleolithic/Late Stone Age (40,000?–12,000 Years Ago)?

Middle Paleolithic/MSA tools disappear in Africa and southwestern Asia by 40,000 years ago at the latest and in Europe after about 35,000 years ago. What replaces them are far more elaborate artifacts that signal the beginning of the **Upper Paleolithic** in Europe and southwestern Asia and the **Late Stone Age (LSA)** in Africa.

The stone-tool industries of the Upper Paleolithic/LSA are traditionally identified by the high proportion of blades they contain when compared with the Middle Paleolithic/MSA assemblages that preceded them. A **blade** is defined as any flake that is at least twice as long as it is wide. Blades have traditionally been associated with anatomically modern humans, who have been given credit for the development of the various cultures of the Upper Paleolithic. Indeed, the discovery of an MSA stone-tool industry in southern Africa that may be as much as 90,000 years old—the Howieson's Poort Industry (Figure 4.26)—has been viewed by some anthropologists as indirect evidence for the presence of anatomically modern humans in southern Africa at the same time (see Stringer 1989). However, Ofer Bar-Yosef and Steven L. Kuhn (1999) challenged this understanding of blades. Bar-Yosef and Kuhn identify over a dozen sites in western Eurasia and Africa that contain Middle Paleolithic or MSA stone-tool assemblages rich in blades. Drawing on their expertise in stone-tool manufacture, they point out that blades are not necessarily more difficult to make than Acheulean bifaces, nor are they necessarily superior to flakes for all purposes: after all, the very effective modern hunting and gathering peoples known in recent historical times did not use blades. Probably, blade technologies were invented again and again. There is no need to suppose that Neandertals or *H. heidelbergensis* were incapable of making blades and, therefore, no grounds for assuming that the presence of blades indicates the presence of anatomically modern humans.

At the same time, they note the rapid spread of blade-based technologies in the Upper Paleolithic/LSA, and this is a new development. During the Upper Paleolithic, blades were also regularly attached to wood, bone, antler, or ivory to form **composite tools** such as bows and arrows. Bar-Yosef and Kuhn note that composite tools require interchangeable parts, so the efficient production of standardized blades would have been advantageous and would have encouraged the spread of blade-production techniques that allowed toolmakers better control over the sizes and shapes of the blades they produced. Bar-Yosef and Kuhn (1999) conclude that Upper Paleolithic reliance on blades might ultimately have been a historical accident, but "if proliferation of blade and bladelet technologies during the Upper Paleolithic is in fact linked to composite tool manufacture, it may also reflect the emergence of novel and highly significant patterns of social and economic cooperation within human groups" (323).

Upper Paleolithic/Late Stone Age (LSA) The name given to the period of highly elaborate stone-tool traditions in Europe in which blades were important, 40,000–10,300 years ago.

blades Stone tools that are at least twice as long as they are wide.

composite tools Tools such as bows and arrows in which several different materials are combined (e.g., stone, wood, bone, ivory, antler) to produce the final working implement.

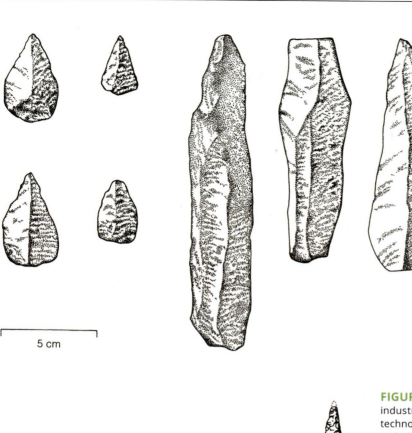

5 cm

FIGURE 4.26 Klasies River Mouth Cave in South Africa yielded both fossils of anatomically modern human beings and blade tools, which are the characteristic tools of the European Upper Paleolithic and the African Late Stone Age.

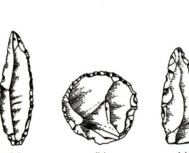

(a)   (b)   (c)   (d)   (e)

FIGURE 4.27 Upper Paleolithic stone-tool industries in Europe were fully developed blade technologies that show considerable stylistic variation over time. Tools a, b, and c are from the Perigordian culture, a variety of the Gravettian; tool d is from the Aurignacian; and tool e is from the Solutrean.

Indeed, Upper Paleolithic/LSA people clearly had a new capacity for cultural innovation. Although Mousterian/MSA tool types persist with little change for more than 100,000 years, several different Upper Paleolithic/LSA tool traditions replace one another over the 20,000 years or so of the Upper Paleolithic/LSA. Each industry was stylistically distinct and possessed artifact types not found in the others (Figure 4.27). For the earliest anatomically modern people to abandon the Mousterian/MSA culture that had served them well for so long, something important must have happened. Many experts believe this something was a reorganization of the brain, producing the modern capacity for culture. This anatomical change, if it occurred, has left no fossil evidence. However, as knowledge about the genomes of living humans, other primates, and fossil hominins accumulates, it may become increasingly possible to find

and date key mutations associated with brain expansion or language ability (Klein 2009, 638ff.; Tattersall 2009, 243–44). For the present, such a change must be inferred from the cultural evidence produced by anatomically modern humans after about 40,000 years ago.

What Happened to the Neandertals?

The first appearance of Upper Paleolithic culture in Europe is important because of what it can tell us about the fate of the Neandertals. In this search for answers, the Châtelperronian and Aurignacian industries have attracted the most attention.

Châtelperronian assemblages from France, 35,000–30,000 years old, contain a mixture of typical Mousterian backed knives and more advanced pointed cutting tools called "burins." They also contain bone tools and pierced animal teeth. Other mixed assemblages similar to the Châtelperronian have been found in Italy, central and northern Europe, and southern Russia (Mellars 1996, 417–18). Aurignacian assemblages, 34,000–30,000 years old, are Upper Paleolithic blade assemblages. We know that Neandertals were capable of making Châtelperronian tools because two Neandertal skeletons were found in 32,000-year-old Châtelperronian deposits at St. Césaire, France (Mellars 1996, 412ff.). Some archaeologists argue, however, that Neandertals may have borrowed elements of Upper Paleolithic technology from a culturally more advanced population of outsiders. For example, deposits found in some cave sites in southwestern France and northern Spain show Châtelperronian layers on top of some Aurignacian layers, suggesting that two different cultural groups coexisted and occupied the same caves at different times (Mellars 1996, 414). These archaeologists believe that anatomically modern people invented the Aurignacian industry in southwestern Asia and brought it with them when they migrated into central and western Europe 40,000–35,000 years ago. The skeletons of anatomically modern human beings begin to appear at European sites about this time, when the ice sheets had begun to melt and the climate was improving. For many archaeologists, the arrival in Europe of both modern human beings and Aurignacian culture during the same time period seems too well correlated to be an accident. No Aurignacian assemblages have been found in eastern Europe, which suggests that the Upper Paleolithic developed differently there (Klein 2009, 586–88, 605).

Even if European Neandertals borrowed Upper Paleolithic technology from southwestern Asian immigrants, they were gone a few thousand years later. What happened to them? There is no evidence that the replacement of Neandertals by modern people involved conquest and extermination, although this has been proposed from time to time. In light of recent evidence of mobility and mixing among various populations of Neandertals, Denisovans, and anatomically modern humans during the Pleistocene, a more likely hypothesis might be that European Neandertals disappeared because they evolved into anatomically modern people, developing Aurignacian culture as they did so, in line with the regional continuity model. This hypothesis, however, runs afoul of the fact that Neandertals and moderns apparently originated on different continents and coexisted in southwestern Asia for 45,000 years, both of them making and using Mousterian tools. European Neandertals may have disappeared as they interbred with the in-migrating modern people and as their descendants adopted Aurignacian culture. Rasmus Nielsen and his colleagues remind us that Neandertals probably made up no more than a tenth of the human

population on earth at the time when they encountered anatomically modern humans, which makes such absorption plausible (Nielsen et al. 2017). If this happened, then contemporary European populations might be expected to share morphological and genetic traits with Neandertals. As we saw earlier, morphological evidence for such inbreeding during the Pleistocene is stronger for populations in eastern Europe and western Asia than for the classic Neandertals of western Europe. Evidence from ancient DNA also shows that Neandertals did interbreed with other non-Neandertal populations during the Pleistocene, and Neandertal genes make up 1% to 4% of our modern nuclear genome. However, Y-chromosome DNA recently extracted from a Neandertal skeleton is distinct from all known modern human Y-chromosome lineages, which suggests that this lineage has gone extinct. If so, its disappearance could be due to genetic drift, but the researchers also suggest another possibility: that genetic incompatibilities in the genomes of male fetuses with Neandertal fathers and anatomically modern human mothers rendered these fetuses unviable or infertile. If this second possibility were the case, it might have contributed to reproductive isolation between Neandertals and anatomically modern humans (Mendez et al. 2016).

Information from ancient and modern genomes, advanced mathematical models, and increasingly sophisticated computerized technology are contributing to new interpretations of our species' past. For example, Aurélian Mounier and Marta Lahr embrace the more complex view of movement and mixing in the ancestry of modern humans that we have been reviewing here, highlighting the range of morphological variability found in the fossil crania that have been proposed as belonging to early anatomically modern humans. They developed mathematical modeling formulas and computational methods to generate a "virtual" last common ancestor (vLCA) of all anatomically modern humans, and then compared this virtual LCA with genuine fossils that have been identified as anatomically modern. The closest matches were fossils from east and southern Africa, leading them to conclude that these populations contributed the most to our ancestry (2019). Another recent study examined ancient DNA samples from 51 anatomically modern humans, from 45,000 years old to 7,000 years old, obtained from a range of sites in western Europe, central Europe, and Asia (Fu et al. 2016). Early samples included between 3 and 6% Neandertal DNA, but in later samples, the portion of Neandertal DNA had decreased to about 2%; this was interpreted as the result of natural selection removing Neandertal alleles from the gene pool. The patterns of migration

FIGURE 4.28 Upper Paleolithic stoneworkers developed bone-, antler-, and ivory-working techniques to a high degree, as shown by these objects from Europe.

and interbreeding reflected in the samples are complex. One explanation might be that these patterns reflect the movements of European and Asian populations into southeastern Europe or west Asia during the last Ice Age, where they met and interbred. After the ice began to melt, the mixed population of their descendants may then have expanded, moving back into Europe. "These results document how population turnover and migration have been recurring themes of European pre-history" (Fu et al. 2016, 200).

How Many Kinds of Upper Paleolithic/ Late Stone Age Cultures Were There?

Although blades are the classic tools of Upper Paleolithic/ LSA culture, other tool types appear that are not found in Mousterian/MSA assemblages, such as endscrapers,

burins, and numerous artifacts of bone, ivory, and antler (Figure 4.28). Brian Fagan (1990) called this technological explosion the "Swiss army knife effect": "like its modern multipurpose counterpart, the core and blade technique was a flexible artifact system, allowing Upper Paleolithic stoneworkers to develop a variety of subsidiary crafts, notably bone and antler working, which likewise gave rise to new weapons systems and tailored clothing" (157).

As we saw earlier, the most distinctive Upper Paleolithic artifacts are composite tools, such as spears and arrows, made of several different materials. The oldest undisputed evidence of wooden bows and arrows in Europe dates from 12,000–11,000 years ago; however, bows and arrows may have been used as long as 20,000 years ago in Africa and Eurasia, where researchers have found indirect evidence in the form of stone points, backed bladelets, and bone rods resembling arrow shafts (Klein 2009, 679–80). Archaeologists have also found the skeletons of fur-bearing animals whose remains suggest they were captured for their skins, not for food; pointed bone tools that were probably used to sew skins together (the oldest eyed needles appeared between 35,000 and 28,000 years ago); and the remains of tailored clothing in Upper Paleolithic burials dating from between 26,000 and 19,000 ya (Klein 2009, 673).

Evidence for regular hunting of large game is better at Upper Paleolithic sites than at sites from earlier periods, especially in Europe and Asia. In addition to hunting tools, researchers have found the bones of mammoth, reindeer, bison, horse, and antelope, animals that provided not only meat but also ivory, antler, and bone. Some animals were hunted, but not for food. The mammoth, for instance, supplied bones used for building shelters. Fresh bone and animal droppings were also probably burned as fuel. The Upper Paleolithic way of life probably resembled that of contemporary foragers. Consequently, plant foods probably formed a larger part of the diet than meat. Reliance on plant foods was probably greater among those living in warmer areas of Africa and southwestern Asia, whereas those living in the cooler climates of eastern Europe and northern Asia may have relied more on animals for food.

The richness and sophistication of Upper Paleolithic culture is documented in many other ways. Upper Paleolithic burials are more elaborate than Mousterian/MSA burials, and some of them contain several bodies (Klein 2009, 690–91). Some Upper Paleolithic sites have yielded human bones that have been shaped, perforated, or burned or that show cut marks suggesting defleshing. Again, some paleoanthropologists conclude that Upper Paleolithic peoples may have been cannibals. However, the shaped or perforated bones may have been trophies or mementos of individuals who had died for other reasons; the burned bones may be the remains of deliberate cremation or accidental charring under a hearth; and the flesh may have been removed from human bones after death for ritual purposes, a practice documented in modern ethnographic literature.

The most striking evidence for a modern human capacity for culture comes from Upper Paleolithic/LSA art. In Africa, ostrich-eggshell beads date to 38,000 years ago, while animal paintings on rocks date to at least 19,000 and possibly 27,500 years ago. Fire-hardened clay objects shaped like animals or human beings, dating to about 28,000–27,000 years ago, were recovered at a Gravettian site in the former Czechoslovakia. This and other Gravettian sites in western and central Europe have yielded human figurines, some of which depict females with exaggerated breasts and bellies, thought to have been made between 27,000 and 20,000 years ago (see Figure 4.28). More than 200 caves in southern France and northern Spain, including Lascaux and Altamira, contain spectacular wall paintings or engravings (Figure 4.29); other painted caves exist in Italy, Portugal, and the former Yugoslavia; spectacular wall art from rock shelters in northern Australia may be especially old (Renfrew and Bahn 2004, 523). The European paintings portray a number of animal species now extinct and were probably painted between 15,000 and 11,000 years ago, during Magdalenian times. New techniques now permit archaeologists to analyze the recipes of pigments used to make these wall images, whereas accelerator mass spectrometry can be used to date the charcoal used to make other drawings (Conkey 1993). As a result, archaeologists are increasingly able to determine when images were painted and whether all the images in a particular cave were painted at the same time. How to interpret these images continues to be debated (Guthrie 2005; Clottes et al. 2016).

Where Did Modern *H. sapiens* Migrate in Late Pleistocene Times?

Upper Paleolithic peoples were more numerous and more widespread than previous hominins. In Europe, according to Richard Klein, Upper Paleolithic sites are more numerous and have richer material remains than do Mousterian sites. Skeletons dating from this period show few injuries and little evidence of disease or violence, and they possess relatively healthy teeth. The presence of skeletons belonging to older or incapacitated individuals at Upper Paleolithic sites suggests that these people, like the Neandertals, cared for the old and sick. Analysis indicates that the life expectancy of Upper Paleolithic people was greater than that of the Neandertals and little different from that of contemporary foragers (Klein 2009, 695ff.).

Archaeologists have found amber, seashells, and even flint in Upper Paleolithic/LSA sites located tens to hundreds of kilometers away from the regions where these items occur naturally. They must have been deliberately transported to these sites, suggesting that Upper Paleolithic peoples, like contemporary foragers, participated in trading networks. However, no evidence of such social contacts exists for earlier times. Perhaps the linguistic and cultural capacities

Women's Art in the Upper Paleolithic?

In a 1996 article in American Anthropologist, *Catherine Hodge McCoid and LeRoy D. McDermott propose that the so-called Venus figures of the early Upper Paleolithic might be more successfully understood as women's art rather than as sex objects made from a male point of view.*

Since Édouard Piette (1895) and Salomon Reinach (1898) first described the distinctive small-scale sculptures and engravings of human figures found in the rock shelters and caves of southern France, several hundred more European Upper Paleolithic figures have been identified. The earliest of these, the so-called Stone Age Venuses or Venus figurines, constitute a distinctive class and are among the most widely known of all Paleolithic art objects. As a group they have frequently been described in the professional and popular literature. Most of the figures are about 150 mm in height and depict nude women usually described as obese.

In spite of many difficulties in dating, there is a growing belief that most of these early sculptures were created during the opening millennia of the Upper Paleolithic (circa 27,000–21,000 BC) and are stylistically distinct from those of the later Magdalenian. These first representations of the human figure are centered in the Gravettian or Upper Perigordian assemblages in France and in related Eastern Gravettian variants, especially the Pavlovian in the former Czechoslovakia, and the Kostenkian in the former Soviet Union.

Most Pavlovian-Kostenkian-Gravettian (PKG) statuettes are carved in stone, bone, and ivory, with a few early examples modeled in a form of fired loess (Van-diver et al. 1989). Carved reliefs are also known from four French Gravettian sites: Laussel, La Mouthe, Abri Pataud, and Terme Pialet. These images show a formal concern with three-dimensional sculpted masses and have the most widespread geographical distribution of any form of prehistoric art. . . . While considerable variation occurs among PKG figurines, claims of true diversity ignore a central tendency that defines the group as a whole. The overwhelming majority of these images reflect a most unusual anatomical structure, which André Leroi-Gourhan (1968) has labeled the "lozenge composition." What makes this structural formula so striking is that it consists of a

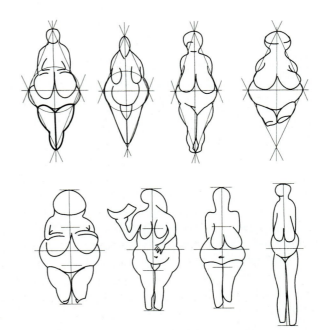

The PKG "lozenge composition." PKG images routinely elevate both the vertical midpoint and greatest width of the female body, and most make what should be one-half of the body closer to one-third. (Figures redrawn and simplified based on information in Leroi-Gourhan 1968.)

recurring set of apparent departures from anatomical accuracy [see figure]. The characteristic features include a faceless, usually downturned head; thin arms that either disappear under the breasts or cross over them; an abnormally thin upper torso; voluminous, pendulous breasts; large fatty buttocks and/or thighs; a prominent, presumably pregnant abdomen, sometimes with a large elliptical navel coinciding with the greatest physical width of the figure; and often oddly bent, unnaturally short legs that taper to a rounded point or disproportionately small feet. These deviations produce what M. D. Gvozdover (1989, 79) has called "the stylistic deformation of the natural body." Yet these apparent distortions of the anatomy become apt renderings if we consider the body as seen by a woman looking down on herself. Comparison of the figurines with photographs simulating what a modern woman sees of herself from this perspective reveals striking correspondences. It is possible that since these images were discovered, we have simply been looking at them from the wrong angle of view.

(continued on next page)

IN THEIR OWN WORDS

Women's Art in the Upper Paleolithic? *Continued*

Although it is the center of visual self-awareness, a woman's face and head are not visible to her without a reflecting surface. This may explain why—although there are variations in shape, size, and position in the heads of these pieces—virtually all are rendered without facial features and most seem to be turned down, as is necessary to bring the body into view. A woman looking down at herself sees a strongly foreshortened view of the upper frontal surface of the thorax and abdomen, with her breasts looming large. Such a perspective helps to explain the apparently voluminous size and distinctive pendulous elongation routinely observed in the breasts of the figurines. Viewed in this way, the breasts of the figurines possess the natural proportions of the average modern woman of childbearing age [see photographs]. Even pieces such as the one from Lespugue, in which the breasts seem unnaturally large, appear naturalistic when viewed from above.

Other apparent distortions of the upper body undergo similar optical transformations from this perspective. For example, the inability to experience the true thickness of the upper body may account for the apparently abnormal thinness seen in the torsos of many figurines. Several figurines also have what seem to be unnaturally large, elliptical navels located too close to the pubic triangle. In a foreshortened view, however, the circular navel forms just such an ellipse, and when pregnant, a woman cannot easily see the space below the navel. Thus, when viewed as women survey themselves, the apparent anatomical distortions of the upper body in these figurines vanish [see photographs].

Similarly, as a woman looks down at the lower portion of her body, those parts farthest away from the eyes look smallest. A correct representation of the foreshortened lower body would narrow toward the feet, thus explaining the small size of the feet in these figurines. It is also true that, for a pregnant woman, inspection of the upper body terminates at the navel with the curving silhouette of the distended abdomen [see photo on left]. Without bending forward, she cannot see her lower body. Thus for a gravid female, the visual experience of her body involves two separate views whose shared boundary is the abdomen at the level of the navel, which is also the widest part of the body in the visual field. The apparent misrepresentation of height and width in the figurines results from the visual experience of this anatomical necessity. The location of the eyes means that for an expectant mother the upper half of the body visually expands toward the abdomen, whereas the lower half presents a narrow, tapering form. Efforts to represent the information contained in these two views naturally resulted in the lozenge compositional formulation, which others have seen as anatomically "incorrect" proportions [see figures].

The idea that women sought to gain and preserve knowledge about their own bodies provides a direct and parsimonious interpretation for general as well as

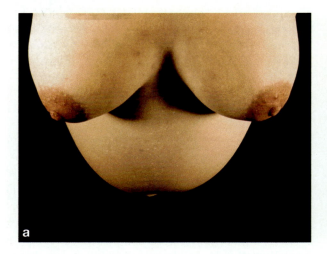

(a) View of her own upper body by a 26-year-old female who is five months pregnant and of average weight; (b) view of the upper body of the Willendorf figurine from same perspective used at left.

(continued on next page)

IN THEIR OWN WORDS

idiosyncratic features found among female representations from the middle European Upper Paleolithic. The needs of health and hygiene, not to mention coitus and childbirth, ensure that feminine self-inspection actually occurred during the early Upper Paleolithic. Puberty, menses, copulation, conception, pregnancy, childbirth, and lactation are regular events in the female cycle and involve perceptible alterations in bodily function and configuration (Marshack 1972). Mastery and control of these processes continues to be of fundamental importance to women today. It is possible that the emergence and subsequent propagation of these images across Europe occurred precisely because they played a didactic function with actual adaptive consequences for women. . . .

. . . These Upper Paleolithic figurines were probably made at a time when there was similarly significant population increase along with cultural and economic restructuring. The early to middle Upper Paleolithic was characterized by productive changes that harnessed energy and by reproductive changes that helped make possible the population expansion and technological changes that followed in the later European Upper Paleolithic. Could women have made a recognizable contribution to the fluorescence of art and technology seen in the opening millennia of this era? Anything they did to improve their understanding of reproduction and thereby reduce infant and maternal mortality would clearly have contributed to this productive and reproductive change. Perhaps the figurines served as obstetrical aids, the relative sizes of the abdomens helping women to calculate the progress of their pregnancies. . . .

Theoretically, if these figurines were used to improve reproductive success, keep more women alive and healthy, and produce healthier children, then natural selection would have been acting directly on the women who made and/or used them. If these Upper Paleolithic figures are naturalistic, accurate self-representations made by women, then it is reasonable to speculate that they might have had such direct, pragmatic purposes.

Source: McCoid and McDermott 1996.

FIGURE 4.29 Upper Paleolithic cave paintings, like this one from Lascaux, France, have been dated to between 15,000 and 11,000 years ago.

of fully modern humans were necessary before they could develop.

Eastern Asia and Siberia

Physically and culturally modern human beings were the first hominins to occupy the coldest, harshest climates in Asia. Upper Paleolithic blade industries developed in central Asia about 40,000–30,000 years ago (Fagan 1990, 195). The oldest reliable dates for human occupation in Siberia are between 35,000 and 20,000 years ago (Klein 2009, 673). Alaskan and Canadian sites with Upper Paleolithic artifacts similar to those of northeast Siberia date to between 15,000 and 12,000 years ago. Artifacts from one of these sites, Bluefish Caves, may even be 20,000 years old. Between 25,000 and 14,000 years ago, land passage south would have been blocked by continuous ice. By 14,000 years ago, conditions for southward migration would have improved considerably.

The Americas

Genetic studies strongly support an Asian origin for Native American populations (Stringer and Andrews 2005, 198; Klein 2009, 707). The earliest known skeletal remains found in the Americas are between 11,000 and 8,000 years old, and their morphological variation suggests that the Americas may have been colonized more than once (Stringer and Andrews 2005, 198–99; Klein 2009, 707). The strongest archaeological evidence of human presence in the Americas comes after 14,000 years ago. The first anatomically modern human beings in North America, called "Paleoindians," apparently were

FIGURE 4.30 Stone tools made by Paleoindian peoples have been found at sites that provide the oldest reliable dates for human occupation in North America. The Clovis point pictured here was probably hafted to a shaft to make a spear.

successful hunting peoples. The oldest reliable evidence of their presence comes from sites dated between 11,500 and 11,000 years ago, which contain stone tools called Clovis points (Figure 4.30). Meadowcroft Rockshelter in Pennsylvania may represent an early Clovis site (Adovasio et al. 1978; Stringer and Andrews 2005, 197). Clovis points were finely made and probably attached to shafts to make spears. Rapidly following the Clovis culture were a series of different stone-tool cultures, all of which were confined to North America. Some experts believe that Paleoindian hunting coupled with postglacial climatic changes may have brought about the extinction of mammoth, camel, horse, and other big game species in North America, but evidence is inconclusive (Meltzer 2015).

In 1997, the "Clovis barrier" of 11,200 years was finally broken when a group of archaeologists and other scientists formally announced that the South American site of Monte Verde, in Chile, was 12,500 years old (Suplee 1997; Dillehay 2000). Because it was covered by a peat bog shortly after it was inhabited, Monte Verde contained many well-preserved organic remains, including stakes lashed with knotted twine, dwellings with wooden frames, and hundreds of tools made of wood and bone. Thomas Dillehay (2000) argues that evidence

from Monte Verde shows that the people who lived there were not big game hunters but rather generalized gatherers and hunters. A lower level at the same site, dated to 33,000 years ago, is said to contain crude stone tools. If the 33,000-year-old Monte Verde artifacts are genuine, they remain puzzling. First, these artifacts are few and extremely crude. Second, the dearth of sites in the Americas of such great age suggests that, if human beings were in the Americas 30,000 years ago, they were very thinly scattered compared to populations in Eurasia and Africa at the same period. Finally, blood group and tooth shape evidence supports the idea that the ancestors of indigenous peoples of the Americas migrated into North America from Asia. If the makers of 33,000-year-old Monte Verde artifacts also came from Asia, archaeologists must explain how these people could have reached South America from Siberia by that date. Possibly, they traveled over water and ice, but how they got to South America remains a mystery.

In 2011, evidence for pre-Clovis occupations in North America was found at the Debra L. Friedkin site near Austin, Texas: more than 15,000 artifacts assigned to the Buttermilk Creek Complex, dating between 13,200 and 15,000 years ago, were discovered in soil beneath a Clovis assemblage (Waters et al. 2011). The archaeologists who discovered the tools view them as potentially representing the technology from which Clovis was developed; other archaeologists remain unconvinced.

Perhaps ancient DNA analysis may help resolve some of these questions, even as it opens up entirely new sets of questions. Ancient mitochondrial DNA and Y chromosome DNA were extracted from the skeleton of a male infant found in association with Clovis artifacts and buried around 12,600 years ago. The DNA evidence showed that this skeleton, known as Anzick-1, belonged to a population more closely related to populations from Central and South America than anywhere else (Rasmussen et al. 2014, 227–28). In 2015, Rasmussen and his colleagues also published results of ancient DNA analysis on skeletal material taken from the controversial 8,500-year-old fossil known as Kennewick Man (or the Ancient One), found in the state of Washington in 1996 (Rasmussen et al. 2015). As we will see in Chapter 6, control over the remains of Kennewick Man had become a focus of sharp debate among archaeologists, members of local indigenous tribes, and the Army Corps of Engineers. After negotiations with all interested parties, Rasmussen and his team performed a DNA analysis that showed Kennewick Man to be closely related to Native American populations from Central and South America, as was the Anzick-1 individual. However, Kennewick Man showed closer affinity than the Anzick-1 individual to geographically closer tribes of the Pacific Northwest of North America. Ancient DNA studies are bound to be controversial, but there is no question that they are forming an important component of scientific efforts to answer questions about ancient human migrations all over the world.

Australasia

Anatomically modern human beings first arrived in Australia between 60,000 and 40,000 years ago, at a time when lower sea levels had transformed the Malayan Archipelago into a land mass called Sunda and when Australia was linked to New Guinea in a second land mass called Sahul. Nevertheless, the migrants would still have had to cross 30–90 km of open water. Presumably, they used watercraft, but finding the remains of boats or the sites where they landed along the now sunken continental shelf is unlikely. Modern people spread throughout the Australian interior by 25,000–20,000 years ago. They may have been connected to widespread extinctions of grass-eating marsupials in Australia between 40,000 and 15,000 years ago (Klein 2009, 714ff.).

Two Million Years of Human Evolution

By 12,000 years ago, modern human beings had spread to every continent except Antarctica, a fact that we take for granted today but that could not have been predicted 2 mya in Africa, when the first members of the genus *Homo* walked the earth. In fact, the more we learn about hominins and their primate ancestors, the more zigs and zags we perceive in our own past. Our species' origin must be regarded as "an unrepeatable particular, not an expected consequence" (Gould 1996, 4). Some paleoecologists have concluded that "human features may not be adaptations to some past environment, but exaptations . . . accidental byproducts of history, functionally disconnected from their origins" (Foley 1995, 47). For example, Rick Potts (1996) argues that, rather than "survival of the fittest" (i.e., of a species narrowly adapted to a specific environment), modern *H. sapiens* better illustrates "survival of the generalist" (i.e., of a species that had the plasticity, the "weedlike resilience," to survive the extremes of the rapidly fluctuating climate of the Ice Ages).

In other words, our ancestors' biological capacity to cope with small environmental fluctuations was exapted to cope with larger and larger fluctuations. In Potts's view, selection for genes favoring open programs of behavior "improve an organism's versatility and response to novel conditions" (Potts 1996, 239).

Archaeologist Clive Gamble (1994) believes that the human social and cognitive skills that allowed our ancestors to survive in novel habitats were exapted by *H. sapiens* to colonize the world: "We were not adapted for filling up the world. It was instead a consequence of changes in behavior, and exaptive radiation produced by the cooption of existing elements in a new framework of action" (182). Gamble is sensitive to the way humanly constructed niches modified the selection pressures our ancestors faced: he argues that all the environments of Australia could never have been colonized so rapidly without far-flung social networks that enabled colonizers to depend on one another in time of need. He sees the colonization of the Pacific as a deliberate undertaking, showing planning and care (Gamble 1994, 241; see also Dillehay 2000).

The role of niche construction is also implicated in the approach of Richard Klein (2009), who lists a series of "related outcomes of the innovative burst behind the out of Africa expansion" (742) that are detectable in the archaeological record after 50,000 years ago—ranging from standardization and elaboration of artifacts to evidence for increasing elaboration of a built environment (with campsites, hearths, dwellings, and graves) to evidence of elaborate trading networks, ritual activity, and successful colonization of challenging cold climates.

Paleoanthropologists, archaeologists, and geneticists have assembled many of the pieces of the human evolutionary puzzle, but many questions remain. Experts differ, for example, on how to reconstruct the human family tree. Figure 4.31 shows one recent attempt to summarize what is known (and what remains to be established) about the evolution of human beings. Because new data and interpretations appear in the news almost daily, you may want to find out how much this summary has been modified by the time you read this book! Another knotty problem concerns how we interpret mounting evidence that human biology and human culture evolved at different rates. Finally, within a few thousand years after the glaciers retreated, human groups in Asia and the Americas were settling in villages and domesticating plants and animals. Why they should have done so at this particular time is addressed in Chapter 6.

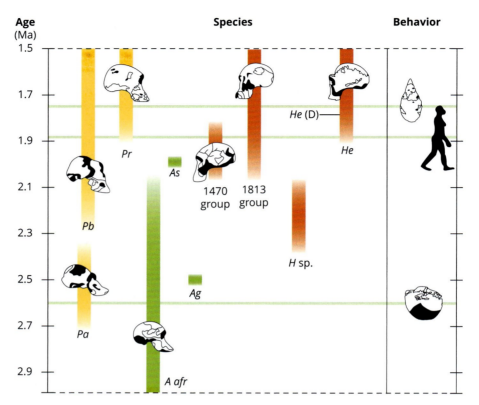

FIGURE 4.31 Timelines for hominin evolution. This image shows one recent attempt to depict the relationships among various groups of hominin fossils, showing the periods in the past for which they are well attested and placing them alongside the time-lines for the best-known early stone-tool traditions. From left to right, the timelines depict the periods when the following fossil groups flourished: (1) *P. aethiopicus* (*Pa*), *P. boisei* (*Pb*), and (2) *P. robustus* (*Pr*) the robust australopiths; (3) the gracile australopith *Australopithecus africanus* (*A afr*); and (4) and (5) *Australopithecus sediba* (*As*) and *A. garhi*. The next four timelines to the right of these represent different subgroups of early members of the genus *Homo*, which emerge between 2.5 and 2.3 million years ago; this appearance is indicated by the timeline labeled "*H. sp.*" This side of the image attempts to sort different groups of "early *Homo*" fossils into distinct subgroups, "1470 group" (AKA *Homo habilis*) and the "1813 group" (AKA *Homo rudolfensis*), on the basis of a new analysis of their distinctive morphological traits. The rightmost timeline groups together fossils assigned to *Homo erectus* (*He*); the callout labeled "*He* (D)" indicates the appearance of the *H. erectus* fossils from Dmanisi, Georgia. The cell to the right of the species timelines juxtaposes timelines associated with the appearance of the two best-attested stone-tool traditions associated with early hominins: Oldowan at the bottom (between 2.5 and 2.7 million years ago) and Acheulean at the top (after about 1.9 million years ago). Juxtaposing the timelines for fossils and for stone tools leaves open the question of which earlier hominin species might have given rise to later hominin species, as well as which of these species might have made or used the stone tools.

Chapter Summary

1. Bipedal hominoids that appeared in Africa at the end of the Miocene are known as hominins and are placed in the same lineage as living human beings. Bipedalism may have been favored by natural selection in hominoids exploiting food resources on the ground, outside the protection of forests. Their diet was probably omnivorous; and they could carry infants, food, and tools in their newly freed hands. The earliest hominin skeletal fossils are 6–7 million years old. The best-known early hominin fossils are 2–3 million years younger and have been placed in the genus *Australopithecus*. The earliest direct evidence of hominin bipedalism is a 3.6

million-year-old trail of fossilized footprints found in Laetoli, Tanzania.

2. Hominin adaptations apparently led to changes in dentition. The teeth of australopiths show an evolutionary trend toward smaller front teeth and enormous cheek teeth. This dental pattern is interpreted as an adaptation to diets of coarse vegetable foods that required grinding. Fossils of hominins between 3 and 2 million years old with this dental pattern have been found at southern and eastern African sites and have been classified in two groups: the gracile australopiths and the robust australopiths.

Robust australopiths had more rugged jaws, flatter faces, and larger molars than the gracile forms. Apart from differences in dentition, the gracile and robust australopiths had similar postcranial skeletons and chimpanzee-sized cranial capacities.

3. The first members of the genus *Homo* appeared about 2.5 mya. Many paleontologists believe that more than one species belonging to *Homo* may have coexisted in eastern Africa in the early Pleistocene alongside the eastern African robust australopiths.

4. Fossils of early *Homo* disappear about 1.8 mya, by either evolving into or being replaced by *Homo ergaster*, the first member of the genus *Homo* to spread out of Africa, giving rise to *Homo erectus* populations in Asia. The cranium of *H. erectus* averages around 1,000 cm³, within the lower range of modern human beings. *H. erectus* may have been, to some extent, capable of speech. Wear patterns on teeth suggest that *H. erectus* had a diet different from that of previous hominins. The postcranial skeleton of *H. erectus* is more robust than that of modern humans and shows a marked reduction in sexual dimorphism. *H. erectus* was probably not primarily a hunter of big game, nor is there any evidence that *H. erectus* might have practiced cannibalism.

5. The oldest undisputed stone tools, classified in the Oldowan tradition, were found in Ethiopia, date to at least 2.5 mya, and may have been made by early *Homo*. Acheulean bifaces are associated with *H. erectus*. In recent years, however, archaeologists have concluded that it is misleading to associate individual stone-tool traditions with only one hominin species. Some archaeologists have suggested that bamboo was available for toolmaking in those areas in Asia where Acheulean bifaces are lacking. Oldowan and Acheulean traditions are usually grouped together in a single period known as the Lower Paleolithic in Europe and the Early Stone Age in Africa.

6. Between 500,000 and 200,000 years ago, *H. erectus* fossils disappear form the fossil record, to be replaced by fossils that show a mosaic of features found in *H. erectus* and *H. sapiens*. How to classify these fossils has been debated. Many paleontologists classify these fossils as *Homo heidelbergensis;* some have been classified as *H. antecessor*. Recent advances in analysis and comparison of ancient DNA from some of these fossils with the modern human genome has revealed evidence of movement and mixing of populations that challenge rigid interpretations of species boundaries among these groups.

7. Neandertals in Europe flourished between 130,000 and 35,000 years ago. They were shorter and more robust than anatomically modern *H. sapiens*. Their molars showed taurodontism, their jaws possessed retromolar spaces, and they may have habitually used their incisors as a clamp. Their average cranial capacity was larger than that of modern human populations, although their skull was shaped differently. Neandertal fossils are typically associated in Europe with the Mousterian stone-tool tradition. Similar tools, found in southwestern Asia and Africa, have all been assigned to the Middle Paleolithic/Middle Stone Age, which probably began at least 200,000 years ago. Ancient DNA recovered from hominin fossils in Denisova Cave did not belong to Neandertals, but to a previously unknown population with which Neandertals interbred.

8. Neandertals and moderns apparently lived side by side in southwestern Asia for at least 45,000 years, and both populations used the same kinds of Mousterian tools. Ancient DNA studies have shown that modern humans share from 1% to 4% of their nuclear genome with Neandertals. It is becoming increasingly clear that our species emerged from movement and mixing of several closely related populations of ancient humans in the Pleistocene.

9. By 40,000 years ago in southwestern Asia and 35,000 years ago in Europe, Mousterian/Middle Stone Age tools are replaced by far more elaborate artifacts that signal the beginning of the Upper Paleolithic/Late Stone Age. Upper Paleolithic people made many different stone tools as well as tools and ornaments out of bone, ivory, and antler; composite tools, such as spears and arrows; and clothing from animal fur. They regularly hunted large game and used bones from animals such as mammoths to construct dwellings and to burn as fuel. Upper Paleolithic burials were far more elaborate than Middle Paleolithic burials. Cave paintings and personal ornaments offer the most striking evidence in the Upper Paleolithic for the modern human capacity for culture.

10. Some Upper Paleolithic assemblages, like the Châtelperronian industry from France, contain a mixture of typical Mousterian tools and more elaborate cutting tools, bone tools, and pierced animal teeth. Paleoanthropologists disagree about what these mixed assemblages represent. Some interpret the Châtelperronian industry as evidence that Neandertals gradually invented Upper

Paleolithic tools on their own. Others argue that Châtelperronian Neandertals borrowed Upper Paleolithic techniques from in-migrating modern people who already possessed an Upper Paleolithic technology called the Aurignacian. Current understandings of Neandertals portray them as more culturally capable than older views allowed. There is no evidence of conquest or extermination of Neandertals by newcomers. Rather, evidence of movement and mixing at the end of the Ice Age suggest that Neandertals were absorbed into the much larger populations of anatomically modern humans with which they interbred.

11. Upper Paleolithic peoples show few signs of injury or disease, and their life expectancy was longer than that of Neandertals. Upper Paleolithic peoples apparently constructed niches that allowed them to participate in widespread trading networks. Anatomically modern people with Upper Paleolithic cultures were the first humans to migrate into the northernmost regions of Asia and into the New World, arriving at least 12,000 years ago, possibly earlier. It seems likely that the New World was populated by more than one wave of immigrants from Siberia. Anatomically modern people first arrived in Australia between 60,000 and 40,000 years ago, probably by boat.

For Review

1. Define bipedalism and explain its importance in human evolution.
2. What is distinctive about the evolution of dentition in hominins?
3. Explain the differences between robust and gracile australopiths.
4. Summarize the different arguments for explaining the evolutionary transition from early hominins to the genus *Homo*.
5. List what paleoanthropologists and archaeologists know about early *Homo* species.
6. Define taphonomy and explain why it is important for paleoanthropologists who study bones and stone tools.
7. Summarize what is known about *Homo erectus*, morphologically and culturally.
8. Describe the argument that emphasizes the importance of endurance running in human evolution.
9. What is the fossil evidence for the evolutionary transition to modern *Homo sapiens*?
11. Make a chart of the different *Homo* species currently identified, including the periods in which they lived, where they were found, and other distinctive anatomical features they display, such as brain size.

12. What is the "mostly out of Africa" model of the origin of modern *Homo sapiens*? What evidence do biological anthropologists use to defend this model? How does this model contrast with the earlier "replacement" model and the "regional continuity" model?
13. Summarize what biological anthropologists know about the Neandertals, Denisovans, and other archaic populations of early humans. What recent research and discoveries have complicated older views of the relations between Neandertals and anatomically modern humans? How do paleoanthropologists now understand the origins of our species?
14. What happened to the Neandertals?
15. How do archaeology and biological anthropology contribute to our understanding of the evolution of a modern human capacity for culture?
16. Summarize anthropological evidence used to support current arguments concerning the peopling of the Americas.
17. Compare and contrast phyletic gradualism and punctuated equilibria.
18. Define cladogenesis and explain how evolutionary biologists use it to develop taxonomies of species.

Key Terms

Acheulean tradition 116	cranial capacity 108	Middle Stone Age (MSA) 123	punctuated equilibrium 99
anagenesis 98	Denisovans 129	mosaic evolution 101	regional continuity model 121
anatomically modern human beings 127	Early Stone Age (ESA) 117	Mousterian tradition 123	replacement model 121
archaic *Homo sapiens* 119	*Homo* 111	Neandertals 121	species selection 100
Australopithecus 103	*Homo erectus* 114	Oldowan tradition 112	taphonomy 113
bipedalism 100	intrusions 125	omnivorous 102	Upper Paleolithic/Late Stone Age (LSA) 130
blades 130	macroevolution 98	phyletic gradualism 99	
composite tools 130	microevolution 98		

Suggested Readings

Dahlberg, Frances, ed. 1981. *Woman the gatherer.* New Haven: Yale University Press. *A classic collection of essays challenging the "man the hunter" scenario using bioanthropological data and ethnographic evidence from four different foraging societies.*

Flannery, Tim (with Luigi Boitani). 2018. *Europe: A Natural History.* New York: Atlantic Monthly Press. *Flannery's 100-million-year survey of the geological and biological history of the European continent is brief, and his interpretations of human origins in relation to the continent are occasionally controversial. On the other hand, a genuine strength of the book is its sheer scope, helping widen the context in which we compare our own species' evolutionary history with that of other organisms on a changing earth over millions of years, beginning at a point when the continent of Europe we know today was a tropical archipelago. His discussion of the role hybridity has played in the history of our own and other species is exemplary*

Gamble, Clive. 1994. *Timewalkers.* Cambridge, MA: Harvard University Press. *Gamble argues that our species' ability to colonize the world was the result of exaptation of attributes we evolved for other purposes. Usefully read in conjunction with the Potts volume listed below.*

Kennis and Kennis Reconstructions. http://www.kenniskennis.com *The achievements of the Kennis brothers in reconstructing the appearance of Neandertals and other fossil hominins are extraordinary. The brothers are sticklers for scientific accuracy, yet their imaginative sensibilities allow them to create sculptures that appear plausibly lifelike.*

Lee, Richard, and Irven DeVore, eds. 1968. *Man the hunter.* New York: Aldine. *The classic collection of articles that undergirded the "man the hunter" scenario of human origins—and paradoxically offered evidence for its critique.*

Lewin, Roger. 1999. *Human evolution: An illustrated introduction,* 5th ed. Boston: Blackwell. *A highly readable introduction to human evolution. Lewin, a science journalist, has worked closely with Richard Leakey and cowritten three books about human origins with him.*

Morell, Virginia. 1996. *Ancestral passions: The Leakey family and the quest for humankind's beginnings.* New York: Simon & Schuster. *A biography of the Leakey family over several generations that brilliantly contextualizes their contributions to paleoanthropology.*

Pääbo, Svante. 2014. *Neanderthal man.* New York: Basic Books. *Svante Pääbo is the director of the Department of Genetics at the Max Planck Institute for Evolutionary Anthropology in Leipzig, Germany. This volume is an engaging account of his personal and professional life, centering on how he and his team of scientists succeeded in sequencing Neandertal mitochondrial DNA, the first draft Neanderthal genome, and the Denisovan genome, thereby revolutionizing the study of extinct human populations. Among other things, Pääbo's professional history illustrates the science-studies point that cutting-edge science within the laboratory depends on the laboratory director's skills outside the laboratory, securing the necessary funds, staffing, materials, and equipment. In the twenty-first century, these negotiations are global in scope, and Pääbo's skills have been masterful.*

Potts, Rick. 1996. *Humanity's descent.* New York: William Morrow. *A survey of human evolution in which evidence is presented that the great flexibility of modern Homo sapiens resulted from selection for the ability to survive wide fluctuations in environments rather than adaptation to any single environment. Usefully read in conjunction with the Gamble volume above.*

Shreeve, James. 1995. *The Neandertal enigma.* New York: Avon Books. *A science journalist's account of the controversy between replacement and regional continuity theorists, all of whom we meet in this engaging volume.*

Stringer, Chris. 2012. *Lone survivors.* New York: Holt. *Stringer is best known for proposing that our species had a recent origin in Africa some 200,000 years ago, after which we moved out of Africa and eventually replaced earlier populations of hominins. This volume contains his current views about evolution of Homo sapiens—the "lone survivors" of millions of years of hominin evolution—and also discusses his involvement with scientists who have developed new and reliable dating methods for the earliest fossils of modern humans.*

Tattersall, Ian. 2012. *Masters of the planet.* New York: Palgrave-Macmillan. *An up-to-date account of human evolutionary history, anchored in the hominin fossil record, as interpreted by a distinguished paleoanthropologist.*

Wrangham, Richard. 2009. *Catching fire: How cooking made us human.* New York: Basic Books. *Wrangham, a biological anthropologist, makes a provocative case for the key role played by cooked food in the evolutionary success of humans.*

 Visit our online resource center for further reading, web links, free assessments, flashcards, and videos. www.oup.com/he/lavenda5e

How does the evolutionary study of human variation undermine notions of biological race?

Not everyone looks the same. Why is that? Does it make a difference? Do the differences cluster together? In this chapter, we will look at the way evolutionary theory explains patterns of human biological variation. In particular, we will show why anthropologists have concluded that these patterns cannot be explained by the concept of biological "race."

CHAPTER OUTLINE

What Is Microevolution?

Can We Predict the Future of Human Evolution?

Chapter Summary

LEARNING OBJECTIVES

- Define microevolution and explain its key concepts.
- Define the characteristics of a species and the processes that contribute to speciation, including molecularization.
- Describe the four evolutionary processes and how they contribute

to the modern evolutionary synthesis.
- Identify microevolution and how these processes contribute to human variation.
- Explain how multiple genes, natural selection, and phenotypic traits relate in ways that

are adaptive for the organisms in which they are found.
- Analyze how phenotype, the environment, and culture interact in the microevolutionary process.
- Apply the concept of human evolution to determine models of change for the future.

What Is Microevolution?

In Chapter 2, we saw how in the 1930s and 1940s, biologists and geneticists worked to formulate a new way of thinking about evolution that combined Darwinian natural selection and Mendelian ideas about heredity. Until recently, this approach (called the "modern evolutionary synthesis") has dominated research and thinking in biology. Chapter 2 also discussed new directions in evolutionary theorizing that have challenged, expanded, and enriched this neo-Darwinian research program, much the way the formulators of the modern synthesis had earlier challenged, expanded, and enriched the contributions made by Darwin, Mendel, and other early evolutionary thinkers.

As we saw, one of the challenges faced by all evolutionary theorists has been how to connect **macroevolution** (the vast patterns of evolutionary change revealed by the fossil record) with the **microevolution** (the more intimate, localized evolutionary changes that take place from one generation to the next within particular species of living organisms). We saw how phyletic gradualists interpreted the connection as unproblematic, viewing macroevolutionary patterns as the inevitable outcomes of microevolution, given enough time. By contrast, punctuationists pointed to evidence showing that macroevolutionary change was not always gradual, and bursts of new speciation often alternated with long periods of evolutionary stasis. Paleoanthropologists have had to take into account the outsized role that culture (in the form of tools and language) began playing in our lineage's evolutionary history millions of years before *Homo sapiens* appeared some 300,000 years ago. Recently, the sequencing of the genomes of living species, together with the recovery of ancient DNA from fossils, has permitted new comparisons within and across taxonomic categories, pointing to past instances of interbreeding and hybridization across species boundaries as an important microevolutionary process with macroevolutionary consequences.

In anthropology, perhaps the most significant contribution of microevolutionary studies has been (and continues to be) the way they undermine the nineteenth-century anthropological concept of "biological race." This concept had been challenged by Franz Boas and his colleagues and students prior to the formulation of the evolutionary synthesis in the 1930s and 1940s. After World War II, and the exposure of the horrors resulting from Nazi "race science," anthropologists like Sherwood Washburn took decisive steps to reject the old, race-based physical anthropology and to replace it with a "new physical anthropology" or "biological anthropology." Research in biological anthropology took for granted the common membership of all human beings in a single species, and addressed human variation using concepts and methods drawn from the modern evolutionary synthesis (Strum et al. 1999).

In this chapter, we will focus on how microevolutionary studies, rooted in the modern synthesis, approach patterns of similarity and difference within our own species, *Homo sapiens*. In order to do this, we will begin with a discussion of how evolutionary biologists understand the concept of *species*. We will see how microevolutionary research permitted scientists to account for many patterns of phenotypic variation *within* our species in terms of natural selection on the gene pools of human populations living in different geographic and ecological settings. We review the key evolutionary processes that show how environment and genetic inputs together contribute to specific phenotypic traits over the life course. We also show how microevolutionary work of this kind demonstrated that different phenotypic traits did not cluster in the ways predicted by the biological race concept. Instead, individual traits showed gradually shifting frequencies from population to population across geographic space—patterns called *clines*. When clinal maps for different traits were compared, it became instantly obvious that they did *not* cluster in overlapping patterns as the biological race concept had presumed. We review new findings that stress the openness of developing organisms to environmental inputs that are enlarging the way the concept of adaptation can be understood.

And yet the concept of race has not disappeared from contemporary discussions of human variation. And so we look at some of the factors that have, in recent years, revived discussions that connect race and biology—the so-called *molecularization of race*. This revival followed the sequencing of the human genome, and was encouraged by the connections some geneticists, physicians, and others have tried to make between genes, race, and disease. We will show how anthropologists have responded to this revival by emphasizing processes of *biosocial or biocultural becoming* over the course of human development, showing "how race *becomes* biology through the embodiment of social inequality" (Gravlee 2013, 22).

What Is a Species?

A key innovation of the modern evolutionary synthesis was its focus on the importance of natural selection on genetic variation within individual populations of a species. But how do evolutionary biologists define a species? As it happens, evolutionary biologists have proposed alternative definitions of **species** that attempt to respect the purpose of Darwinian taxonomy, which is to represent scientists' best current understanding of the relationships between and among organisms. As biological anthropologist John Fleagle points out, "Most biologists agree that a species is a distinct segment of an evolutionary lineage, and many of the differences among species concepts reflect attempts to find criteria that can be used to identify species based on different types of information" (Fleagle 2013, 2). Neo-Darwinians defined a species as "a reproductive community of populations (reproductively isolated from others) that occupies a specific niche in nature" (Mayr 1982, 273). This definition, commonly referred to as the *Biological Species Concept*, has been useful to field biologists studying populations of living organisms. However, this definition of species has been less useful for scientists studying fossils. In fact, Fleagle notes that the Biological Species Concept has even been losing favor among field biologists because "as more and more 'species' have been sampled genetically, it has become clear that *hybridization* between presumed species has been very common in primate evolution" (Fleagle 2013, 1; see also Stringer 2012, 34).

Many taxonomists working with living primates prefer to use the *Phylogenetic Species Concept*, which identifies species on the basis of a set of unique features (morphological or genetic) that distinguish their members from other, related species, based on cladistic analysis. Contemporary paleoanthropologists also often rely on this concept of species, as we saw in Chapter 4, although they also sometimes apply a *Phenetic Fossil Species Concept*. Users of the Phenetic Fossil Species Concept first attempt to calculate the measurable morphological differences between living species. They then assume that similar degrees of morphological difference may also be used to distinguish species in the fossil record. Fleagle observes that this concept can be a useful way to sort fossils in a continuously changing lineage "in which the endpoints may be very different but individual samples overlap" (2013, 2).

Evolutionary biologists normally subdivide species into *populations* that are more or less scattered, although the separation is not complete. That is, populations of the same species (or individual members of those populations) may be separated at one time, but may merge together again, and successfully reproduce,

at a later time. Evolutionary theorists Ian Tattersall and Rob DeSalle describe this process of species differentiation and reintegration as *reticulation* (Tattersall and DeSalle 2011, 50). As we saw in Chapter 4, for instance, the current view is that regional populations of early *Homo sapiens* in southern Africa, eastern Africa, and northern Africa reticulated with one another over several hundred thousand years prior to the emergence of anatomically modern humans at the end of the Ice Age. Similar processes of reticulation would have linked anatomically modern humans with Neandertals and Neandertals with Denisovans, producing the mixed genomes revealed by ancient DNA analysis. They emphasize that reticulation takes place *within species* and that the "resulting weblike pattern of relationships is very different from the dichotomous pattern among species" on which the Phylogenetic Species Concept is based (Tattersall and DeSalle 2011, 50). Similarly, prior to the rise of the great ancient civilizations, the human species was made up of widely scattered populations. Those populations living in North America had been separated from populations in Europe for thousands of years, until the European explorations of the Americas began in the fifteenth century. However, when Europeans and the native peoples of North America did come into contact, they were able to interbreed and produce viable, fertile offspring. From the perspective of the Biological Species Concept, this ability to interbreed and produce fertile offspring indicates that members of these different populations belong to the same reproductive community and hence the same species. Proponents of the Phylogenetic Species Concept can specify the set of unique features that distinguish all successfully interbreeding populations of the human species from populations of other, related species.

Finally, Darwinian population thinking requires biologists to recognize the distinctiveness of each individual *organism* that belongs to a particular population of a given species. It is variation among individual organisms in particular populations, in particular environmental circumstances, that engenders the Darwinian struggle for existence. To follow arguments made by evolutionary biologists, therefore, these three nesting concepts—*species* made up of *populations* made up of *organisms*—must be kept distinct from one another. It is also important to remember that even if individual *organisms* from *populations* of different *species* occasionally mate with one

---

species A distinct segment of an evolutionary lineage. Different biologists, working with living and fossil organisms, have devised different criteria to identify boundaries between species.

IN THEIR OWN WORDS

Have We Ever Been Individuals?

Evolutionary biologists committed to the Modern Evolutionary Synthesis, interested in carrying out microevolutionary studies of natural selection on genes, have worked hard to clarify distinctions between species, populations of a particular species, and organisms that belong to such populations. Now, the seemingly self-evident, taken-for-granted boundary distinguishing one individual organism from another is not looking so self-evident after all—even among mammalian species, such as ourselves. Recent research is showing that it is incorrect to assume that each biological individual (such as an individual human organism) is also a genetic individual; that is, in possession of just a single genome. On the contrary, each human organism contains within it multiple communities of different species of microbes, each with its own separate genomes, living with us in a mutually beneficial association called symbiosis. Biologists Lynn Chiu and Scott Gilbert explain that 90% of the cells in mammalian bodies belong to populations of different species of microbes that affect a range of chemical processes supporting our ongoing health and well-being. Some of these microbes contribute to our digestive processes; others to the construction of our bodies; others to our brain function; still others keep our immune system operating properly. And these symbiotic relationships are ancient. As Chiu and Gilbert put it, "Development is a multi-species project. The mammalian body requires its symbionts; it is not constructed properly if it does not have them" (2015, 193).

For these reasons, biologists suggest that the proper term to identify organisms such as ourselves is not "individual" but rather "holobiont," a label that acknowledges the fact that each of us contains within ourselves multiple communities of symbionts of different species. Thinking of organisms as holobionts reshapes the way we think about not only our relation to other organisms but also the way we understand our own life cycles. In particular, Chiu and Gilbert argue that thinking of humans as holobionts reshapes our understanding of what happens when we reproduce. We can no longer consider human reproduction to involve only a male individual and a female individual, whose individual genetic endowments are joined to produce an individual offspring. Rather, we need to reconceptualize human reproduction as "holobiont birth" in which individual persons and their symbiotic communities are all involved. Thus, they write, "There is never an autonomous mammal. . . . Symbiosis is a necessary condition for continued life. From the symbiotic perspective, birth is a transition from one symbiotic state to another. Remarkably, this transition appears to be mediated by the mother" (Chiu and Gilbert 2015, 195). Indeed, they identify four processes through which "the mother creates conditions suitable for her own reproduction and the reproduction of symbiotic microbes" (2015, 196): the physiology of the pregnant women, including hormone levels, modify populations of helpful microbes in her gut and vagina; the mother transfers helpful bacteria to her fetus during gestation; further helpful bacteria are transferred to the infant during vaginal birth; and additional helpful bacteria are transferred to nursing infants via the mother's milk.

Recognizing the symbiotic relationships that characterize holobionts cannot be missed unless biologists pay close attention to developmental processes over time. In the case of holobiont birth, paying attention to processes requires rethinking the relationship between the human host and the multiple symbiotic communities of bacteria that live within it. That is, it is incorrect to conceive of the host as a static, self-interested, independent "habitat" colonized by static, self-interested, independent species. Rather, from the perspective of biological process, it becomes clear that different symbionts provide different niches for one another over time; that symbionts therefore support the ongoing life processes of one another. Even though each individual symbiont does not support every other symbiont all of the time, the overall network of interactions among all symbionts together supports and sustains the ongoing life process of the holobiont.

And this has implications for how we understand human reproduction. Rather than conceiving of the relationship between father, mother, and offspring (or between their genes) as competition for limited resources, the birth of the holobiont highlights the heterogeneous connections among host, symbionts, and offspring. As Chiu and Gilbert conclude,

The past decade has brought about remarkable new discoveries about relationships between and within organisms. One of the most revolutionary of these discoveries has been the importance of symbiotic signals used to build, maintain, and protect a holobiont. Developmental symbiosis merges embryology and ecology in interspecies webs of mutual and reciprocal communication. Birth is seen not as the origin of a new individual, but as the perpetuation of these organizing webs of signals between animals and microbes. (2015, 205)

TABLE 5.1   Example of Allele Frequency Computation

Imagine you have just collected information on *MN* blood group genotypes for 250 humans in a given population. Your data are as follows:
Number of *MM* genotype = 40
Number of *MN* genotype = 120
Number of *NN* genotype = 90
The allele frequencies are computed as follows:

GENOTYPE	NUMBER OF PEOPLE	TOTAL NUMBER OF ALLELES	NUMBER OF *M* ALLELES	NUMBER OF *N* ALLELES
MM	40	80	80	0
MN	120	240	120	120
NN	90	180	0	180
Total	250	500	200	300

The relative frequency of the *M* allele is computed as the number of *M* alleles divided by the total number of alleles: 200/500 = 0.4.
The relative frequency of the *N* allele is computed as the number of *N* alleles divided by the total number of alleles: 300/500 = 0.6.
As a check, note that the relative frequencies of the alleles must add up to 1.0 (0.4 + 0.6 = 1.0).

Source: Relethford 1996, 66.

---

another, such matings do not necessarily dissolve the species boundary. For instance, horses and donkeys can interbreed to produce mules; but mules are infertile, so the species boundary between horses and donkeys is unaffected by these matings.

Neo-Darwinians were also concerned about the genetic makeup of species. They introduced the concept of the **gene pool**, which includes all of the genes in the bodies of all members of a given species (or a population of a species). Using mathematical models, evolutionary theorists can estimate the **gene frequency** of particular genes—that is, the frequency of occurrence of gene variants or alleles within a particular gene pool. Measuring the stability or change of gene frequencies in populations over time allowed geneticists to trace short-term evolutionary change in a new field called **population genetics**. Once population geneticists had identified a target population, they analyzed its gene pool by calculating the frequencies of various alleles within that gene pool and trying to figure out what would happen to those frequencies if the carriers of the various alleles were subjected to particular selection pressures (Table 5.1). Some evolutionary geneticists tested these predictions on such organisms as fruit flies, but others concentrated on human beings.

The ability of human beings from anywhere in the world to interbreed successfully is one measure of membership in a single species. Comparing our genotypes provides additional evidence of our biological closeness. As we have seen, most alleles come in a range of different forms (i.e., are **polymorphous**), and known polymorphous variants fall into one of two groups. The first group, *polymorphic alleles*, accounts for most genetic variation across populations. Populations differ not because they have mutually exclusive sets of alleles but because they possess different *proportions* of the same set of alleles. An example is the ABO blood groups: the polymorphic alleles *A*, *B*, and *O* are found in all human populations, but the frequency of each allele differs from population to population. The second group, *private polymorphisms*, includes alleles that are found in the genotypes of some, but usually not all, members of a particular population. One example is a genetically determined blood cell antigen known as the "Diego antigen." The Diego antigen occurs only in Asian and African populations, but 60 to 90% of the members of the populations where it is found do not have it (Marks 1995, 165).

gene pool All the genes in the bodies of all members of a given species (or a population of a species).

gene frequency The frequency of occurrence of the variants of particular genes (i.e., of alleles) within the gene pool.

population genetics A field that uses statistical analysis to study short-term evolutionary change in large populations.

polymorphous Describes alleles that come in a range of different forms.

This work leads to the inescapable conclusion that *the traditional Western concept of "race" makes no sense in terms of genetics.* Evolutionary geneticist Richard Lewontin demonstrated more than four decades ago that more genetic variation could be found *within* conventionally identified racial groups than could be found *between* them (Lewontin 1972). These results, based on population thinking, make it clear that "humankind . . . is not divided into a series of genetically distinct units" (Jones 1986, 324). Ian Tattersall and Rob DeSalle remind us that Lewontin's claims have successfully withstood attempts to invalidate them experimentally for over forty years (2011, 141). The boundaries said to define human races do not reflect any deep underlying biological differences between particular human populations; rather, human races have been culturally imposed in shifting and unstable clusters of alleles (Marks 1995, 117).

It turns out that genetic variation in human populations is mostly a matter of differences in the relative proportions of the same sets of alleles. In fact, the distribution of particular phenotypes shifts gradually from place to place across populations as the frequencies of some alleles increase, whereas others decrease or stay the same. Moreover, the distributions of some traits (like skin color) do not match the distributions of other traits (like hair type). Such a pattern of gradually shifting frequency of a phenotypic trait from population to population across geographic space is called a **cline**. Clines can be represented on maps such as that presented later in Figure 5.4, which shows the gradually shifting distribution of differences in human skin color from the equator to the poles.

Phenotypic contrasts are greatest when people from very different places are brought together and compared while ignoring the populations that connect them (Marks 1995, 161). This is what happened when Europeans arrived in the New World, conquered the indigenous peoples, and imported Africans to work as slaves on their plantations. But if you were to walk from Stockholm, Sweden, to Cape Town, South Africa (or from Singapore to Beijing, China), you would perceive gradual changes in average skin color as you moved from north to south (or vice versa). Evolutionary biologists explain this pattern as a consequence of natural selection: individuals in tropical populations with darker skin pigmentation had a selective advantage in equatorial habitats over individuals with light pigmentation.

This may explain the fair skin Neandertals apparently had. By contrast, populations farther away from the equator faced less intense selection pressure for darkly pigmented skin and perhaps even selective pressures in favor of lighter skins. But *different* selection pressures would have been at work on other traits within the same population, such as stature or hair type, which is why the geographical distributions of these traits do *not* match up neatly with the distribution of skin pigmentation. To make things even more complex, different genes may be involved in the production of similar phenotypic traits in different populations: for example, although different ancestral populations of humans living near the equator have dark skin, the identity and the number of alleles involved in the production of this phenotypic trait may be different in different populations.

Evidence for this gradual geographical intergradation of human phenotypes led biological anthropologist Frank Livingstone to declare in 1964 that "There are no races, there are only clines" (279). Clinal variation explains why people searching for "biological races" have never been able to agree on how many there are or how they can be identified. *Clines are not groups.* The only group involved in clinal mapping is the entire human species. Each cline is a map of the distribution of a *single* trait. Why not, therefore, superimpose a grid over a particular geographical region, and then sample individuals randomly from the grid squares? As Peter Wade and his colleagues point out, "Starting with a grid tends to produce gradients or clines of gradual variation and reduces the impression of located genetic populations; the absence of boundaries suggests the continuous movement and biological mixture of peoples between populations" (2014a, 23). Although many people think that human population movement and mixture is relatively recent, we saw in Chapter 4 that studies of ancient DNA now suggest that human populations have been moving and mixing with one another for hundreds of thousands of years, if not longer (Bolnick et al. 2016, 328). And modern clinal mapping reveals similar patterns of movement and mixture.

Biologists might compare the clinal maps of trait A and trait B to see if they overlap and, if so, by how much. But the more clines they superimpose, the more obvious it becomes that the trait distributions they map *do not coincide* in ways that neatly subdivide into distinct human subpopulations; that is, clinal distributions are *not concordant.* Since the biological concept of "race" predicts exactly such overlap, or concordance, it cannot be correct. In other words, *clinal analysis tests the*

---

cline A pattern of gradually shifting frequency of a phenotypic trait from population to population across geographic space.

biological concept of "race" and finds nothing in nature to match it. And if biological races cannot be found, then the so-called races identified over the years can only be symbolic constructs, based on cultural elaboration of a few superficial phenotypic differences—skin color, hair type and quantity, skin folds, lip shape, and the like. In short, early race theorists "weren't extracting races from their set of data, they were imposing races upon it" (Marks 1995, 132).

The Four Evolutionary Processes

What controls the patterns of gene frequencies that characterize a given population? As we have seen, **natural selection** among variant traits is responsible for evolutionary changes in organisms, and **mutation** is the ultimate (and constant) source of new variation. These two important evolutionary processes shape the histories of living organisms; however, they are not the only processes in the natural world that can alter gene frequencies.

Most genetic variation results from mixing already existing alleles into new combinations. This variation is the natural result of chromosomal recombination in sexually reproducing species. However, gene frequencies can be drastically altered if a given population experiences a sudden expansion resulting from the in-migration of outsiders from another population of the species, which is called **gene flow**. A population that is unaffected by mutation or gene flow can still undergo **genetic drift**—random changes in gene frequencies from one generation to the next. Genetic drift may have little effect on the gene frequencies of large, stable populations, but it can have a dramatic impact on populations that are suddenly reduced in size by disease or disaster (the *bottleneck effect*) or on small subgroups that establish themselves apart from a larger population (the *founder effect*). Both of these effects accidentally eliminate large numbers of alleles.

Therefore, the modern evolutionary synthesis recognizes four evolutionary processes: mutation, natural selection, gene flow, and genetic drift. Chance plays a role in each. The occurrence of a mutation is random, and there is no guarantee that a useful mutation will occur when it is needed; many mutations are neutral, neither helping nor harming the organisms in which they occur. Nor is there any way to predict the factors that make population migrations possible or to foresee the natural accidents that diminish populations. Unpredictable changes in the environment can modify the selection pressures on a given population, affecting its genetic makeup. Moreover, as we saw in Chapter

2, *niche construction*—the enduring consequences of efforts organisms make to modify the environments in which they live—can sometimes alter the selection pressures they, their descendants, and other neighboring organisms experience in those environments. As we shall see, control of fire and the invention of clothing made it possible for early humans to colonize cold environments that were inaccessible to earlier ancestors, who lacked these cultural skills. Niche construction of this kind buffers us from experiencing some selection pressures, but it simultaneously exposes us to others. Indeed many scientists, including anthropologists, have concluded that niche construction by humans has resulted in a number of far-reaching, human-made environmental threats including pollution, environmental destruction, rising global temperatures, and increasing levels of species extinctions. As we will examine more fully in Chapter 7, many scientific observers have concluded that we need to recognize a new geological epoch, called the *Anthropocene*, in which the major influence on climate and the environment has been human activity.

In addition, our species faces intense selection pressures from disease organisms that target our immune systems (Farmer 2003; Leslie and Little 2003). Evidence that microorganisms are a major predatory danger to humans comes from research on the connection between infectious diseases and polymorphic blood groups (i.e., blood groups that have two or more genetic variants within a population). Biological anthropologists James Mielke, Lyle Konigsberg, and John Relethford (2011) point out, for example, that the diseases human beings have suffered from have not always been the same. When our ancestors were living in small foraging bands, they were susceptible to chronic parasitic infections, such as pinworms, or diseases transmitted from animals. After the domestication of plants and animals, however, human diets changed, settled life in towns and cities increased, and

---

natural selection A two-step, mechanistic explanation of how descent with modification takes place: (1) every generation, variant individuals are generated within a species as a result of genetic mutation; and (2) those variant individuals best suited to the current environment survive and produce more offspring than other variants.

mutation The creation of a new allele for a gene when the portion of the DNA molecule to which it corresponds is suddenly altered.

gene flow The exchange of genes that occurs when a given population experiences a sudden expansion caused by in-migration of outsiders from another population of the species.

genetic drift Random changes in gene frequencies from one generation to the next caused by a sudden reduction in population size as a result of disaster, disease, or the out-migration of a small subgroup from a larger population.

sanitation worsened. Populations expanded, individuals had more frequent contact with one another, and the stage was set for the rise and spread of *endemic* diseases (i.e., diseases particular to a population) that could persist in a population without repeated introduction from elsewhere. As a result,

> the increase in endemic diseases started to apply selective pressures that were different from those exerted by chronic diseases. These diseases usually select individuals out of the population before they reach reproductive age. Differential mortality (natural selection) based on genetic variation in the blood types would be expected to influence genetic polymorphisms. Thus recurrent epidemics of diseases such as smallpox, cholera, plague, and measles, which swept through continents, undoubtedly contributed to the shaping of the genetic landscape. (Mielke et al. 2011, 105–06)

Several evolutionary processes may affect a population at the same time. For example, a rare, helpful allele (say, one that increased resistance to a disease like malaria) might appear in a population through mutation. If malaria were an environmental threat to that population, we would expect natural selection to increase the frequency of this new allele. But suppose a natural disaster like an earthquake struck the population and many people died. If the new allele were still very rare, it might be completely lost if its few carriers were among those who perished (genetic drift). Alternatively, the frequency of a harmful new allele might increase in subsequent generations if its carriers survived such a disaster

and if they introduced the new allele into a larger population through inbreeding (gene flow). Niche construction could also be implicated if, for example, gene flow were enabled or intensified as a result of persisting, environment-modifying activities of the populations exchanging genes.

Measuring the interaction among these evolutionary processes allows population geneticists to predict the probable effects of inbreeding and outbreeding on a population's gene pool. Inbreeding tends to increase the proportion of homozygous combinations of alleles already present in a population. If some of these alleles are harmful in a double dose, inbreeding increases the probability that a double dose will occur in future generations and thus decrease fitness. If helpful combinations of alleles occur in an inbreeding population, their proportions can increase in a similar way.

At the same time, inbreeding over several generations tends to reduce genetic variation. Natural selection on genes has a better chance of shaping organisms to changed environments if it has a wider range of genetic variation to act on. Perhaps for this reason, mating with individuals from outgroups is widely observed in the animal kingdom. Monkeys and apes, for example, regularly transfer into a new social group before they begin to reproduce (Figure 5.1). Human beings ordinarily do the same thing, except that our reproductive practices are shaped by culture; people in different societies draw the boundaries around in-groups and out-groups differently. In one society, the children of brothers and sisters may be considered members of the same family and, thus, off limits for marriage; in another, they

FIGURE 5.1 Monkeys and apes regularly transfer into a new social group before they reproduce.

TABLE 5.2 Effects of the Four Evolutionary Processes on Variation within and between Populations

EVOLUTIONARY PROCESS	VARIATION WITHIN POPULATIONS	VARIATION BETWEEN POPULATIONS
Mutation	Increases	Increases
Gene flow	Increases	Decreases
Genetic drift	Decreases	Increases
Natural selection	Increases *or* decreases	Increases *or* decreases

may be considered members of different "families" and, thus, ideal marriage partners. However, cultural rules forbidding *incest*, or sexual relations with close kin, do not always succeed in preventing such relations from occurring.

Table 5.2 summarizes the effects of the four standard evolutionary processes on gene frequencies within and between populations.

Microevolution and Patterns of Human Variation

Gene Flow   As we have seen, phenotypic variation in different human populations does not require different alleles for different populations; rather, the variation we find mostly involves differences in the proportions of the same sets of alleles common to the human species as a whole. Therefore, genetic relationships between interbreeding human groups are best understood in terms of gene flow between superficially distinct populations whose gene pools already overlap considerably. For example, we know that individuals from European and African populations have interbred considerably since Europeans brought the first Africans to the New World as slaves. Similar processes have mixed the genes of these and other in-migrating populations with the genes of indigenous American populations. These are examples of gene flow among populations of a single species that had experienced relative isolation in the past but that continued to exchange enough genes often enough with neighboring populations to prevent speciation.

Accidents of geography and history had allowed for relative isolation between these populations prior to the European voyages of exploration in the fifteenth century. From the fifteenth century on, similar chance factors brought them together. Moreover, the way in which reproductive isolation ended was powerfully shaped by the social and cultural forces that brought Europeans to the New World in the first place, structured their relationships with the indigenous peoples, and led them to enslave Africans. Similar cultural forces continue to affect the degree to which different human populations in the Americas remain reproductively isolated or exchange genes with other populations.

Genetic Drift   One kind of genetic drift, the founder effect, occurs when a small subgroup of a larger population becomes isolated for some reason, taking with it unrepresentative proportions of the alleles from the larger population's gene pool. One of numerous examples of genetic drift that have occurred in human history began early in the nineteenth century when British soldiers occupied the island of Tristan da Cunha in the Atlantic Ocean. Eventually, the soldiers withdrew, leaving only a single married couple who were later joined by a few other settlers. Throughout the nineteenth century, the population of Tristan da Cunha never grew much beyond 100 individuals. This tiny population was later reduced even more, once in the late 1850s by the out-migration of 70 inhabitants and again in 1885 by the drowning of all but 4 adult males (only one of whom contributed genes to the next generation). Over the twentieth century, the population grew to as many as 270 people, all of whom owe an enormous proportion of their genes to a very few individuals. It was calculated that nearly a third of those living on the island in 1961 had genes contributed by just 2 members of the original founding population (Roberts 1968; Underwood 1979).

Mutation and Natural Selection   Mutation is responsible for variant alleles that may be present at a single locus. Some of these mutant alleles are mobilized during development to help produce specific physical traits. When a trait proves helpful, evolutionary theory predicts that the frequency of the alleles involved in its production will be increased by natural selection. Perhaps the most famous instance of microevolution of such a trait by means of natural selection concerns a variant of hemoglobin, one of the proteins in red blood cells.

In many human populations, only one allele—hemoglobin A (*HbA*)—is present. In other populations, however, mutant forms of hemoglobin A may also be present. One such mutant allele, known as *HbS*, alters the structure of red blood cells, distorting them into a characteristic sickle shape and reducing their ability to carry oxygen (Figure 5.2). When individuals inherit the *HbS* allele from both parents, they develop sickle cell anemia. About 85% of those with the *HbS/HbS* genotype do not survive to adulthood and, hence, do not reproduce. Although many people in the United States think that sickle cell anemia affects only people with ancestors who came from Africa, in fact many people in India, Saudi Arabia, and Mediterranean countries such as Turkey, Greece, and Italy also suffer from the disease.

Because the *HbS* allele seems to be harmful, we would expect it to be eliminated through natural selection. But in some populations of the world, it has a frequency of up to 20% in the gene pool. Why should that be? Geneticists might have concluded that this high frequency was the result of genetic drift if it were not for the fact that the areas with a high frequency of *HbS* are also areas where the mosquito-borne malaria parasite is common. There is, in fact, a connection. People exposed to malaria have a better chance of resisting the parasite if their hemoglobin genotype is *HbA/HbS* rather than the normal *HbA/HbA*. This is an example of what geneticists

call a "balanced polymorphism" in which the heterozygous genotype is fitter than either of the homozygous genotypes. In Mendelian terms, we would say that the *HbA* and *HbS* alleles are codominant, with the result that a single *HbS* allele changes the structure of red blood cells enough to inhibit malarial parasites but not enough to cause sickle cell anemia.

The rise of malarial infection in human beings appears to have begun only a few thousand years ago (Livingstone 1958). Before that time, the people who lived where malaria is now found gathered and hunted wild foods for a living. This way of life kept forests intact, leaving few open areas where water could collect and malaria-carrying mosquitoes could breed in large numbers. As these inhabitants began to cultivate plants for food, however, they needed to clear large tracts of forest for their fields, creating large open spaces where rainwater could collect in stagnant pools, providing ideal breeding conditions for mosquitoes. And as the population of cultivators grew, so grew the number of hosts for the malaria parasite.

If the *HbS* allele first appeared in the populations of gatherers and hunters, it probably had a low frequency. But once cultivation began, land was cleared, water accumulated in open spaces, and the number of malaria-infested mosquitoes increased, selection pressures changed. At that point, individuals with the *HbA/HbS* genotype were fitter because they had a greater probability of surviving and reproducing than individuals with *HbA/HbA* or *HbS/HbS*. As a result, the frequency of *HbS* increased in the population, despite the fact that in a double dose, it was generally lethal. This example also illustrates the way niche construction can reshape the selection pressures that a population experiences. In this case, a switch from one pattern of human food getting to another created new niches for humans, mosquitoes, and malaria parasites, simultaneously reshaping the selection pressures experienced by all three populations (Odling-Smee et al. 2003). Indeed, niche construction may also be implicated in discussions of gene flow and genetic drift since in both cases activities undertaken by particular human populations may alter their respective niches in persistent ways, thereby altering the selection pressures that each population subsequently experiences.

Adaptation and Human Variation

One of the breakthroughs of modern genetics was the discovery of *gene interaction*. That is, a single gene may contribute to the production of more than one phenotypic feature (*pleiotropy*), and many genes regularly

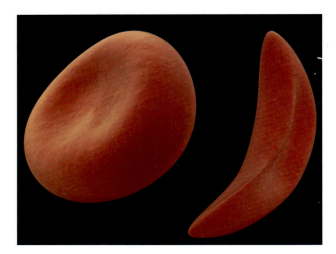

FIGURE 5.2   Normal red blood cells are easily distinguished from the distorted, "sickled" red blood cells. Sickled red blood cells carry less oxygen than do normal red blood cells, but they resist malarial parasites more successfully.

combine forces (*polygeny*), helping to produce a single phenotypic feature. Pleiotropy and polygeny help explain how it is that genes, which are discrete, could influence phenotypic traits such as body size or skin color, which show continuous gradations. Traits that are the product of multiple genes offer multiple and varied opportunities for natural selection to shape phenotypic traits in ways that are adaptive for the organisms in which they are found.

In discussions of gene action, biologists commonly distinguish between genes of major effect and polygenes of intermediate or minor effect. A *gene of major effect* is a gene at one locus whose expression has a critical effect on the phenotype. The *HbS* allele that produces the sickling trait in red blood cells is an example of a gene of major effect. But phenotypic traits that depend on one or a few genes of major effect are rare. The evolution of a phenotypic trait may begin with selection on genes of major effect, but the products of such genes may be pleiotropic, producing adaptive as well as harmful consequences for the organism. Further selection on multiple *polygenes of intermediate or minor effect* that also affect the trait, however, may modify or eliminate those harmful consequences (West-Eberhard 2003, 101–04). Finally, because gene expression does not take place in an environmental vacuum, many phenotypic traits in organisms are even more finely tuned for their adaptive functions by inputs from environmental factors such as nutrients, temperature, humidity, altitude, or day length. Human phenotypic traits such as body size or skin color, for example, are the outcome of complex interactions among multiple gene products and environmental influences throughout the life cycle.

Many students of human genetics have devoted attention to the way natural selection may mold complex human phenotypic traits, better adapting human populations to their specific environments. More recently, developmental biologists have been able to show how the responsiveness of organisms to their environments also contributes to the abilities of those organisms to adapt to their environments. A fertilized human egg (or zygote) has its own phenotype, and the zygote's phenotype can respond to environmental influences—such as those encountered in a woman's uterus—*even before its own genes are active*. This responsiveness is called **phenotypic plasticity**: "the ability of an organism to react to an environmental input with a change in form, state, movement, or rate of activity" (West-Eberhard 2003, 35). Because all living organisms exhibit phenotypic plasticity, it is *incorrect* to assume that genes "direct" the development of organisms or "determine" the

FIGURE 5.3 Changes in environment can have major effects on phenotype. Generational differences in height are often connected with changes in diet.

production of phenotypic traits. Indeed, much of the "action" that goes into producing adult organisms with distinctive phenotypes goes on during development (Figure 5.3).

It is important to stress that acknowledging the phenotypic plasticity of organisms has nothing to do with Lamarckian ideas of use and disuse and the inheritance of acquired characteristics, neither of which is accepted by modern evolutionary biologists. As West-Eberhard (2003) points out,

> There is no hint of direct (Lamarckian) influence of environment on genome in this scheme—it is entirely consistent with conventional genetics and inheritance. By the view adopted here, evolutionary change depends upon the genetic component of phenotypic variation screened by selection, whether phenotypic variants are genetically or environmentally induced. It is the genetic *variation* in a response (to mutation

phenotypic plasticity Physiological flexibility that allows organisms to respond to environmental stresses, such as temperature changes.

or environment) that produces a response to selection and cross-generational, cumulative change in the gene pool. (29)

Some of the most exciting work in evolutionary biology today involves linking new understandings about developmental influences on phenotypes with understandings of traditional evolutionary processes like mutation, gene flow, genetic drift, and natural selection (Oyama et al. 2001; Gould 2002; West-Eberhard 2003).

As we saw earlier, **adaptation** as a *process* refers to the mutual shaping of organisms and their environments. However, the term *adaptation* can also be used to refer to the *phenotypic traits* that are the outcome of adaptive processes. As Zaneta Thayer and Amy Non explain,

> Humans must adapt to multiple timescales of evolutionary change. . . . Very stable environmental trends can be accommodated through natural selection, the slowest mechanism of genetic change. Immediate, minute-to-minute fluctuations in the environment, such as changes in temperature, are accommodated via homeostatic processes, including changes in blood flow. At a more intermediate level on the timescale of months to years, organisms adapt to environmental conditions via developmental plasticity. (2015, 727–28)

The sickling trait in hemoglobin described in the previous section is a classic example of a genetic adaptation produced by natural selection, in response to environmental conditions that stabilized in regions where tropical forests were cleared for farming several thousand years ago, creating expanded breeding grounds for mosquitos carrying the malaria parasites and thereby increasing human exposure to the parasites. In this case, the form of the hemoglobin molecule is the phenotypic product of a single-locus gene of major effect. Most human phenotypic traits, however, are the product of pleiotropy, polygeny, and inputs from the environment.

The shivering response in humans illustrates adaptation to the brief timescale of minute-to-minute fluctuations in the environment, a response in human beings sometimes called "short-term **acclimatization**." Human beings are warm-blooded organisms who need to maintain a constant internal body temperature to

function properly. When the surrounding temperature drops, however, and threatens to cool our internal organs below this threshold temperature (roughly 98.6° Fahrenheit), this temperature drop triggers a twitching response in the muscles that surround our vital organs as a way of generating heat. If we are able to increase our body temperature above the threshold—by going indoors, putting on clothes, or moving closer to the fire—the shivering stops.

Other forms of acclimatization take shape over more intermediate timescales. Such adaptations emerge over the course of many months or years, as human phenotypic plasticity is shaped by inputs from the particular environments within which individuals develop. That is, physiological or morphological changes resulting from developmental plasticity are *not* a consequence of genetic variation. Put another way, "developmental plasticity allows one genotype to give rise to multiple phenotypes in response to variation in the environment in which an organism develops" (Thayer and Non 2015, 728). For example, some environments in which human populations live, such as the highlands of the Andes Mountains in South America, are characterized by *hypoxia*; that is, less oxygen is available to breathe than at lower altitudes. Studies have shown that people who grow up in high altitudes adapt to lower oxygen levels by developing greater chest dimensions and lung capacities than do people living at low altitudes. These changes—sometimes called "developmental acclimatization"—are a consequence of human phenotypic plasticity and occur when the human body is challenged by a low level of oxygen in the environment. Studies have shown that individuals who were not born in such an environment increased in chest dimensions and lung capacity the longer they lived in such an environment and the younger they were when they moved there (Greska 1990).

One kind of biological mechanism that seems to allow environmental stresses to mold phenotypic plasticity are called *epigenetic marks*. Epigenetic marks are "chemical modifications to DNA that are associated with changes in the way genes are expressed or turned on, and are essential for normal development in mammals" (Thayer and Non 2015, 725). As we saw in Chapter 2, epigenetic inheritance of such marks constitutes one of the dimensions of biological inheritance (in addition to behavioral inheritance and symbolic inheritance) that "go beyond" genetic inheritance, and that have been proposed for incorporation into an extended evolutionary synthesis (see Figure 2.19). Epigenetic marks are fully compatible with the Darwinian foundations of contemporary

---

adaptation (1) The mutual shaping of organisms and their environments; (2) the shaping of useful features of an organism by natural selection for the function they now perform (see Chapter 2).

acclimatization A change in the way the body functions in response to physical stress.

evolutionary theory, and "can only occur in interaction with the underlying genetic variation that is available" (2015, 725).

One kind of epigenetic mark is called *DNA methylation*. Methylation chemically modifies a portion of the DNA molecule in a way that reduces the level of gene product produced by a particular gene, "and its influence is dependent on the genetic context within which the methylation occurs" (Thayer and Non, 2015, 723). Unlike DNA itself, methylation and other epigenetic marks "are sensitive to environmental exposures throughout growth and development, [and] they represent a prime candidate mechanism underlying developmental plasticity" (2015, 728).

Skin Color Skin color is a highly visible, complex, continuous phenotypic trait in human populations. Variation in skin color seems to be the product of a few genes of major effect, additional polygenes of intermediate or minor effect, and input from the environment. As Nina Jablonski (2004) writes, "determination of the relative roles of variant genes and varying environments has proven extremely challenging" (613); and it is not clear how many alleles are involved or whether identical genes are responsible for the dark skin of apparently unrelated human populations (Marks 1995, 167–68). Biological anthropologists agree that skin color is adaptive and related to the degree of ultraviolet radiation

(UVR) that human populations have experienced in particular regions of the globe.

It is important to emphasize that "similar skin colors have evolved independently in human populations inhabiting similar environments," making skin color "useless as a marker for membership in a unique group or 'race'" (Jablonski 2004, 615). Indeed, some of the most striking features of human skin are clearly consequences of developmental and phenotypic plasticity: variations in skin thickness are a function of age and history of sun exposure; the outer layers of the skin in darkly pigmented or heavily tanned people have more, and more compact, cell layers, making the skin more effective as a barrier to sun damage. The overall intensity of skin color is thus determined by a combination of morphological, physiological, environmental, and developmental factors. When the intricate articulation of these factors is destabilized, the outcome can be anomalous skin conditions such as *albinism* (an absence of pigmentation), abnormally intense pigmentation, or a patchy spotting of light and dark skin (Jablonski 2004, 590).

Human skin color exhibits clinal variation, with average pigmentation growing gradually lighter in populations that live closer to the poles (Figure 5.4). The pigments in human skin (melanins) protect the skin against sunburn by absorbing and scattering UVR and by protecting DNA from damage that can lead to

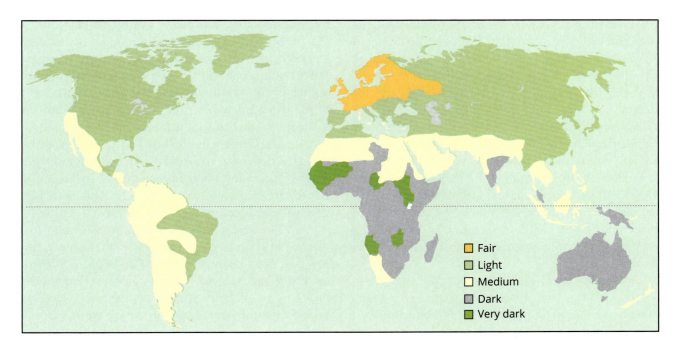

Fair
Light
Medium
Dark
Very dark

FIGURE 5.4 When the unexposed skin of indigenous peoples is measured and mapped according to the degree of pigmentation, skin shades tend to grow progressively lighter the farther one moves from the equator.

cancer (Jablonski 2004, 590). Of course, as humans we risk sun damage to the skin because we do not grow fur coats, like our closest primate relatives. Dark fur coats can actually protect primates from tropical heat by absorbing short-wave radiation (UVA) near the surface of the coat and reflecting much long-wave radiation (UVB) away before it reaches the skin. These advantages of fur, however, are reduced if the fur is wet with sweat, which can happen if the temperature rises or the organism's activity level increases. Under these conditions, "thermal sweating as a method of cooling becomes more important" and it is "greatly facilitated by the loss of body hair" (Jablonski 2004, 599). It is now hypothesized that the last common ancestor of humans and chimpanzees probably had light skin covered with dark hair, like other Old World primates. However, the loss of hair created new selection pressures in favor of increasingly darker skin, such that by 1.2 mya, early members of the genus *Homo* would have had darkly pigmented skin (Rogers et al. 2004). In addition, contemporary human populations all seem to show sexual dimorphism in skin color, "with females being consistently lighter than males in all populations studied" (Jablonski and Chaplin 2000; Jablonski 2004, 601).

Exposure of human skin to solar radiation has complex and contradictory consequences. Too much sunlight produces sunburn, and UVB destroys a B vitamin, folic acid, which is a crucial factor in healthy cell division. At the same time, solar radiation also has positive consequences: UVA stimulates the synthesis of vitamin D in human skin. Vitamin D is crucial for healthy bone development and other cellular processes. According to Jablonski and Chaplin (2000), these selective pressures have produced two opposing clines of skin pigmentation. The first cline grades from dark skin at the equator to light skin at the poles and is an adaptive protection against sun damage. The second cline grades from light pigmentation at the poles to dark pigmentation at the equator and is an adaptive response favoring vitamin D production. In the middle of these two clines, they argue, natural selection favored populations with enhanced phenotypic plasticity who could tan more easily during hot, sunny seasons but easily lose their tans in seasons when temperature and sunlight levels decreased.

Jablonski (2004) concludes that "the longer wavelengths of UVR . . . have been the most important agents of natural selection in connection with the evolution of skin pigmentation" (604). At the same time, because people have always migrated, different populations vary in the numbers of generations exposed to the selective pressures of any single regime of solar radiation.

Human cultural practices (wearing clothes, using sun block, staying indoors) have shaped the levels of pigmentation and levels of vitamin D production in particular individuals or populations. Gene flow following the interbreeding of human populations with different selective histories would further complicate the relationship between the skin colors of their offspring and selection pressures imposed by local levels of solar radiation.

Many of these factors may explain why the skin colors of the native people of South America are lighter than those of native populations in Asia or Europe who live at similar latitudes. Most anthropologists estimate these populations migrated from the Old World perhaps 10,000–15,000 years ago, which means they have had far less time to experience the selective pressures associated with local solar radiation levels anywhere on the continent. In addition, these migrants were modern humans with many cultural adaptations to help them modify the negative effects of solar radiation, including both protective clothing and a vitamin D–rich diet. Obtaining vitamin D from food rather than sunlight has thus altered selection pressures that otherwise would have favored lighter skin. Thus, the darker skin pigmentation of circumpolar peoples may be the consequence of selection pressures for darker skin as a protection against solar radiation reflected from snow and ice (Jablonski 2004, 612).

Intelligence   Intelligence may be the most striking attribute of human beings. However, attempts to define and measure "intelligence" have a long history of controversy. Is intelligence a single, general, unitary "thing" that people have more or less of? If not, what attributes and skills ought to count? Psychologist Howard Gardner (2000) points out that "every society features its ideal human being" (1). In his view, "the intelligent person" in modern Western societies has been exemplified by individuals who could do well at formal schooling and succeed in commerce. It is perhaps not surprising, then, that tests developed in Western societies purporting to measure individuals' intelligence quotient (IQ) traditionally have equated high scores on verbal and mathematical reasoning with high intelligence.

But these are not the only areas in which humans display differing levels of ability or skill. Gardner, for example, has long argued that in addition to linguistic and logico-mathematical intelligence, human beings possess different types of intelligence, including bodily–kinesthetic intelligence (displayed by exceptional athletes and dancers), interpersonal or intrapersonal intelligence (displayed by individuals with exceptional understanding of social relations or their own psyches), musical intelligence, spatial intelligence, and naturalist intelligence (which attunes us to plants and animals in the world around us). In Gardner's view, these types of intelligence can probably be enhanced in all individuals, given the right kind of environmental support. Indeed, even linguistic intelligence and logico-mathematical intelligence require the proper environmental support—long-term training and practice in rich cultural settings—to produce the highest levels of achievement.

Because the definition of *intelligence* is so controversial and because not all forms of intelligence are equally rewarded in the United States, great controversy results when attempts to measure intelligence are applied not only to individuals but also to entire social groups, defined on the basis of gender, class, or "race." In 2005, the former president of Harvard University was subjected to strong criticism when he acknowledged that fewer women than men become scientists and suggested, in the face of massive evidence to the contrary, that perhaps this meant that women simply had less "intrinsic aptitude" for science and engineering than men (https://www.harvard.edu/president/speech/2005/remarks-nber-conference-on-diversifying-science-engineering-workforce). Controversies have been as great or greater when ideas about intelligence have been linked to ideas about race. In the United States, as we have seen, people tend to assign each other to "races" on the basis of phenotypic criteria like skin color. Such "races" are then often regarded as different natural kinds, each sharing its own biological essence. From this assumption, it is a short step to conclude that differences between races must include differences in intelligence. Some scientists have devised IQ tests that they claim can measure intelligence, the results of such testing repeatedly showing that the average IQ score for African Americans is below that of European Americans, which is below that of Asian Americans.

Do IQ scores show that racial differences in intelligence are clear-cut and genetically determined? They do not. First, the idea that races are natural kinds assumes that racial boundaries are clear and that traits essential to racial identity (e.g., skin color) are discrete and nonoverlapping. However, we have seen that skin color is a continuously varying phenotypic trait, both among members of the so-called racial groups and the boundaries of those groups. Particular shades of skin color cannot be assigned exclusively to particular socially defined races, nor can they be used to infer any other so-called racial attribute, such as intelligence or athletic ability.

Second, it is far from clear that there is a single, accurately measurable substance called "intelligence" that some people have more of than others. Performing well on paper-and-pencil tests tells us nothing about problem-solving skills and creativity, which might equally deserve to be called "intelligence." Third, even if intelligence is such a measurable substance, we do not know that IQ tests actually measure it. People can score badly on an IQ test for many reasons that have nothing to do with intelligence: they may be hungry or ill or anxious, for example. When different social groups within a society consistently score differently as groups, however, we may suspect that the test itself is to blame. Arguing that IQ tests measure cultural knowledge, not intelligence, many critics contend that the vocabulary items used on IQ tests reflect experiences typical of European American, middle-class culture. People from different cultural backgrounds do poorly on the test because their experiences have not provided them with the knowledge being tested.

Indeed, many studies have shown that how an individual will do on an IQ test is more accurately predicted by social class and educational background than by "race." When African Americans and European Americans are matched in terms of these factors, the differences in average IQ scores disappear (Molnar 1992). The results of these studies are not new. On the contrary, studies like these demonstrate repeatedly that IQ scores are not phenotypic traits uniquely determined by genes but that they are powerfully affected by a range of environmental factors over the course of the human life cycle. Or as Greg Downey and Daniel Lende put it, "humans' capacity for thought and meaning making emerges equally from social and individual sources, built of public symbol, evolutionary endowment, social scaffolding, and private neurological achievements" (2012, 23–24).

The Molecularization of Race?

During the 1960s and 1970s, anthropologists and others explained that there was no biological basis for race; in other words, all humans are part of a single species. Although there is internal variation within the species, it does not easily fall into the cultural categories of "race" developed in the United States. In the past thirty years, however, we have witnessed in the United States and elsewhere a resurgence of attempts to explain group differences in terms of race. Sometimes it is the powerful who engage in such practices, in controversial books such as *The Bell Curve* (Herrnstein and Murray 1994). Sometimes, however, it is members of politically and economically marginalized groups who do so, as a calculated move in political struggles with those who dominate them.

Perhaps no more complicated set of questions has been raised about race in the twenty-first century than those that have emerged following the completion of the Human Genome Project (HGP) in 2003. The goals of the project were as follows:

- to identify all of the approximately 20,000–25,000 genes in human DNA
- to determine the sequences of the 3 billion chemical base pairs that make up human DNA
- to store this information in databases
- to improve tools for data analysis
- to transfer related technologies to the private sector
- to address the ethical, legal, and social issues that may arise from the project (http://www.ornl.gov/sci/techresources/Human_Genome/home.shtml)

As anthropologist Nadia Abu El-Haj (2007) has shown, some molecular biologists quickly mobilized the information produced by the HGP to attempt to develop forms of medical treatment based on the identification of genes associated with particular diseases. Some formed private biomedical research companies that promised to help create a future of *personalized medicine*: therapies based on knowledge of individuals' genomes that were precisely tailored to a particular individual's degree of genetic risk for a particular disease.

In recent years, the cost of sequencing individual genomes has been dropping; in 2011, Tattersall and DeSalle predicted that "with the $1000 genome on the horizon, we will soon have the ultimate tool for individualized medicine" (2011, 184). However, the cost has been high enough that many researchers have used genetic data from other members of populations to which an individual belongs as a surrogate, or stand-in, for that individual's particular genome. For example, if your mother's brother suffers from a particular disease with a genetic component, researchers may conclude that you and other biological relatives have an increased risk for that disease. That is, your biological family becomes a surrogate, or stand-in, for genetic risk factors that potentially are faced by individual family members. As Abu El-Haj explains, some biomedical researchers in the United States use "racial" groups as surrogates for individuals who consider themselves members of such groups. The thinking is that if a genetic disease marker shows up in the genomes of some people said to be members of a particular "race," then this may be an indication that other people classified in the same "race" might also be at risk for the disease.

Does this pragmatic use of race in medical research mean that the researchers are committed to the doctrines associated with scientific racism? Abu El-Haj (2007, 284) says no, for two reasons. First, the old race concept focused on the classification of *phenotypes*, whereas the new race concept classifies *genotypes*. The transition from a phenotypic to a genotypic view of race came about, she says, as a consequence of changing historical understandings of sickle cell disease in the United States. In the first part of the twentieth century, sickle cell anemia was identified as a disease of "black" people—of African Americans. But later, as we will shortly discuss, research in population genetics traced its cause to molecular genes: the presence of an abnormal "sickling" hemoglobin allele at a particular locus on a chromosome. "At the meeting point between these two definitions of the disease . . . the commitment to race as a molecular attribute took form," leading over time to "the correlation of disease risk and racial difference" (Abu El-Haj 2007, 287).

Second, nineteenth-century race science aimed to discover how many races existed and to assign all individuals to their "true race." The commercial technologies used by biomedical researchers regularly distinguish human populations in terms of the continents from which their ancestors presumably came. But all these technologies assume that everyone has a mixed ancestry of some kind; the goal is to measure how much of which ancestry markers are present in each population, thereby determining the degree of risk that members of that population face for genetic diseases associated with particular ancestries. As Abu El-Haj says, ancestry markers "are not used to discover one's 'true' race. . . . Instead, ancestry markers are used, for example, to understand the Puerto Rican population's risk for asthma" (2007, 288). That is, if genome analysis determined that some ancestral population contributed genes to contemporary Puerto Rican populations that enhanced their risk for developing asthma, this information would be crucial in devising personalized drugs precisely keyed to individuals with different risks for asthma.

Third, Abu El-Haj (and others) have pointed out that many African Americans view medical research and drug trials in which they are involved to be nothing less than a form of long-overdue biomedical justice. Anthropologist John Hartigan recently reviewed studies showing that, starting in the 1980s, the US government began to respond to pressure from racial minorities protesting the fact that most medical research focused on white males only. The exclusion of groups like African Americans in such research, however, was the result of "reforms in the 1970s to counter researchers' excessive reliance on 'vulnerable populations' such as women and prisoners" (Hartigan 2013, 9–10). One notorious example was African Americans' past participation in the Tuskegee Study of Untreated Syphilis in the Negro Male, conducted between 1932 and 1972. According to the website for the Centers for Disease

Control and Prevention (http://www.cdc.gov/tuskegee/timeline.htm), a review panel set up in 1972 found that participants in this study

> had agreed freely to be examined and treated. However, there was no evidence that researchers had informed them of the study or its real purpose. In fact, the men had been misled and had not been given all the facts required to provide informed consent.
>
> The men were never given adequate treatment for their disease. Even when penicillin became the drug of choice for syphilis in 1947, researchers did not offer it to the subjects. The advisory panel found nothing to show that subjects were ever given the choice of quitting the study, even when this new, highly effective treatment became widely used.

All these matters came together in the contentious and much-analyzed example of BiDil, a medication designed to treat African Americans suffering from heart disease. On its website (which has since been taken down), NitroMed, the original manufacturer of BiDil, described this drug as "a fixed-dose combination medicine consisting of isosorbide dinitrate and hydralazine hydrochloride. It is approved by the FDA for the treatment of heart failure in self-identified African American patients when added to standard heart failure medicines" (http://www.bidil.com/pnt/questions.php#1). FDA approval, the site reported, was based on the results of the African-American Heart Failure Trial (or A-HeFT), which "studied 10,050 self-identified African American patients with heart failure: It is the largest number of African American patients ever studied in a major heart failure trial. . . . A-HeFT was started on May 29, 2001, and the study was halted early in July 2004 due to a significant survival benefit seen with BiDil as compared to standard therapy alone" (http://www.bidil.com/pnt/questions.php#2).

The original BiDil website also listed a series of "common questions" people ask about BiDil, including the following: "What about claims that BiDil is a 'race drug'?" The site's answer included the following excerpt from a 2007 article by the FDA doctors who approved the drug:

> Only African American patients were studied in A-HeFT, so the FDA approval for BiDil is for "self-identified African American patients with heart failure" only. There is insufficient clinical trial data to draw any conclusions about the effects of BiDil in other populations. . . .
>
> Not understanding the reasons for the difference in treatment effect by race did not justify withholding the treatment from those who could benefit from it. . . . Race or ethnicity is clearly a highly imperfect description of the genomic and other physiological

characteristics that cause people to differ, but it can be a useful proxy for those characteristics until the pathophysiological bases for observed racial differences are better understood. (http://www.bidil.com/pnt/questions.php#9)

As these excerpts show, neither NitroMed nor the FDA endorsed nineteenth-century American racial categories. They emphasized that the drug trial showing the effectiveness of BiDil involved only "self-identified" African American subjects, which the FDA agrees is a "highly imperfect" but "useful proxy" for whatever factors are responsible for the observed "racial differences." However, BiDil quickly became the center of a controversy that ended in commercial failure for NitroMed in 2008. In 2011, BiDil was purchased by Arbor Pharmaceuticals, which was still marketing the drug in June 2020 (http://bidil.com).

Ann Pollock, who provides a detailed analysis of the BiDil controversy, points out that none of those involved disputed BiDil's efficacy: it worked. Rather, the challenge was to bring the drug to market in a way that would simultaneously address the needs of different stakeholders with an interest in African American heart failure. That is, the FDA, NitroMed, and the Association of Black Cardiologists (ABC) (who carried out the original A-HeFT trials) shared "an interest in health disparities, the deluge of data around African American responses to ACE inhibitors, and the increasing capacity of African American cardiologists to do clinical trials" (Pollock 2012, 162). In Pollock's view,

> In the lead-up to BiDil, there was alignment of interests by NitroMed and ABC, but they were not necessarily seeing BiDil as a solution to the same problem. For NitroMed, the principal problem was how to get approval for the drug combination in a way that would be profitable. . . . For ABC, the problem was and is more diffuse: how to get the funding to run trials and thus participate in the production of evidence-based medicine, and how to find solutions for black morbidity and mortality from heart failure. (2012, 162–63)

The current situation is perplexing, to say the least: such notions as race and "genetics" and "biology" are still with us, but their meanings appear to have changed, producing consequences that seem to be both positive and negative. Some observers suspect that this kind of research will only give the older racial classifications a new lease on life. John Hartigan (2013) argues, however, that although biomedical research of this kind "seems to affirm that 'biological differences' are a more powerful explanation for health disparities than are social factors," the situation is better understood as "the outcome of various ways in which people struggle to contend with the significance of race in multiple social and biological registers simultaneously, often in contradictory manners" (10).

One way to disentangle these matters may be to follow the suggestion of anthropologist Clarence Gravlee and examine more closely a widespread tendency, found among medical researchers and ordinary citizens alike, to equate genetics with biology in discussions of race and disease. Gravlee (2013) rightly points out that everyone agrees that race cannot be defined in terms of genetics, as we saw previously. And anthropologists and other social scientists are also well aware of the sociocultural and historical factors in the United States and elsewhere that have created the conditions of racism with which African Americans and other nonwhite groups must contend. However, "the claim that race is not biology unwittingly perpetuates genetic determinism because it tacitly reduces biology to genetics. The more we appreciate the complexity of human biology beyond the genome, the sooner we can explain how race *becomes* biology through the embodiment of social inequality" (Gravlee 2013, 22).

Gravlee (2013) reminds us that many discussions of possible links between race and genetics use "the concept of biology and genetics interchangeably, often pitting these concepts against socioeconomic factors. . . . The implication is that the mere observation of biological differences is sufficient evidence of a genetic one" (30). Instead, he argues, we need to stop using biology as a synonym for genetics and "to pay as much attention to the meaning of biology as we have paid to the meaning of race" (32). Since the deciphering of the human genome, scientists are increasingly learning that many factors other than genes contribute to disease. At the same time, biological theorists have begun to pay closer attention to the factors that affect the health of developing organisms throughout their life course. As we saw earlier, these factors include phenotypic plasticity (see Figure 2.19), a phenomenon, Gravlee reminds us, that Boas was insightfully investigating a century ago.

These considerations have led Gravlee to develop a model of the phenotype that pays attention to a hierarchy of causal influences that shape it over time. As a developing organism encounters these influences (which may have individual, cultural, or historical sources), the organism's responses become *embodied* in the organism's physiology in ways that shape the biological functioning of individual human bodies. "Most relevant," Gravlee (2013) writes, "is the evidence that racism at multiple levels of analysis has direct and indirect effects on health" (33). If we argue that "race is not biology," however, and equate biology with genetics, we blind ourselves "to the biological consequences of race

and racism," leaving ourselves "without a constructive framework for explaining biological differences between racially defined groups" (Gravlee 2013, 34).

Gravlee's (2013) approach brings together what anthropologists have learned about "race": first, race does not line up with patterns of genetic variation in human populations; second, race is a sociocultural and historical construct that shapes the circumstances of people's lives; and third, awareness of the consequences for health of living under racist conditions constitutes "a mandate for ethnographic research on the social reality of race and racism . . . to identify . . . the experiences and exposures that shape the emergence and persistence of racial inequalities in health" (41).

Gravlee and his colleagues used this approach to carry out research in Puerto Rico, attempting to explain why darker skin pigmentation was associated with higher blood pressure. They discovered that skin color had two dimensions that needed to be distinguished: "the phenotype of skin pigmentation and the cultural significance of skin color as a criterion of social status" (Gravlee 2013, 38). Measurement of skin pigmentation was carried out using the method of reflectance spectrometry, which reliably estimates the concentration of melanin in the skin. Measurement of the cultural relationship between skin color and social status required ethnographic methods. This "biocultural" (or "biosocial") approach revealed that Puerto Ricans with darker skins and higher socioeconomic status actually experienced higher blood pressure than other Puerto Ricans. This was interpreted as resulting from the fact that such individuals were likely to experience more intense racism as their social status increased, thereby producing increasingly frustrating social interactions that contributed to higher blood pressure (Gravlee 2013, 38). When Gravlee (2013) and his colleagues later included genetic-based estimates of African ancestry, they found that

> adding sociocultural data to the model revealed a statistically significant association between blood pressure and a particular candidate gene for hypertension—an association that was not evident in the analysis including only African ancestry and standard risk factors. This finding suggests that taking culture seriously may both clarify the biological consequences of social inequalities and empower future genetic association studies. (39)

Biocultural or biosocial approaches like that of Gravlee and his colleagues demonstrate, in the words of Greg Downey and Daniel Lende, how "social differences can become biology because they shape the emerging nervous system" (2012, 31). As Downey and Lende explain, "the predominant reason that culture becomes embodied . . . is that neuroanatomy inherently makes experience material" (2012, 37). Ultimately, they conclude, "The material environment, both natural and artificial, provides structure and information to the growing organism while being incorporated with its inherited biological legacy" (2012, 44). This is an excellent decription of what Ingold, Pálsson, and their collaborators call "biosocial becoming" (Ingold and Pálsson 2013).

Phenotype, Environment, and Culture

In recent years, many evolutionary biologists and biological anthropologists have recognized that trying to attribute every phenotypic trait of an organism to adaptation is problematic. Sometimes an adaptive explanation seems transparently obvious, as with body shape in fish and whales or wing shape in bats and birds, which equips these animals for efficient movement through water and air. Other times, adaptive explanations are less obvious, or even contrived. As we saw in Chapter 2, the wings of contemporary insects are better understood as an exaptation, when appendages that evolved as an adaptation to one set of selective pressures began at some point to serve an entirely different function.

In other words, the trait an organism possesses today may not be the direct result of adaptation but, instead, may be the byproduct of some other feature that was being shaped by natural selection. It may also be the consequence of random effects. Jonathan Marks (1995) has observed, for example, that anthropologists have tried, without notable success, to offer adaptive explanations for the large, protruding brow ridges found in populations of human ancestors. He suggests that brow ridges might well have appeared "for no reason at all—simply as a passive consequence of growing a fairly large face attached to a skull of a small frontal region" (Marks 1995, 190).

We must also remember that phenotypes are shaped by environment as well as by genes. For example, some have argued that slow growth in height, weight, and body composition and delayed onset of adolescence among Guatemalan Mayan children constitute a genetic adaptation to a harsh natural environment. However, by comparing measurements of these traits in populations of Mayans who migrated to the United States with those in Guatemala, Barry Bogin was able to disprove these claims because "the United States–living Maya are significantly taller, heavier and carry more fat and muscle mass than Mayan children in Guatemala" (Bogin 1995, 65). Similarly, other biological anthropologists working in the Andean highlands have refuted the hypothesis that hypoxia is responsible for poor growth among some indigenous populations (Leonard et al. 1990; de

Meer et al. 1993). They point out that the genetic explanation fails to consider the effects on growth of poverty and political marginalization.

At the beginning of the twenty-first century, it has become fashionable for many writers, particularly in the popular media, to treat genes as the ultimate explanation for all features of the human phenotype. Given the great achievements by molecular biology that followed the discovery of the structure of the DNA molecule, this enthusiasm is perhaps understandable. But discussions of human adaptive patterns that invoke natural selection on genetic variation *alone* are extremely unsatisfactory. For one thing, they mischaracterize the role genes play in living organisms. Speaking as if there were a separate gene "for" each identifiable phenotypic trait ignores pleiotropy and polygeny, as well as phenotypic plasticity. It also ignores the contribution of the other classic evolutionary processes of genetic drift and gene flow, as well as the influences of historical and cultural factors on human development (as in the case of the Mayan migrants). Researchers in the HGP originally expected that, given our phenotypic complexity, the human genome would contain at least 100,000 genes; today, we know that the actual number is more like 20,000, only twice as many as the roundworm *Caenorhabditis elegans*, one of the simplest organisms that exists (http://www.genome.gov/). Clearly, the number of genes possessed by an organism is not coupled in any straightforward way to its phenotypic complexity.

The gene-centered approach gained considerable influence in anthropology after 1975 because of the widespread theoretical impact of a school of evolutionary thought called "sociobiology." Sociobiology attracted some anthropologists who proposed explanations of human adaptations based on sociobiological principles. Other anthropologists have been highly critical of sociobiology. However, after four decades, some proposals emerging from this debate have come a long way toward meeting the objections of sociobiology's original critics.

It is important to understand that much of this research is based on **formal models**. These models are "formal" because scientists use the tools of formal logic or mathematics to find answers to particular questions about the evolution of human behavior. For example, evolutionary psychologists typically assume that the psychological abilities possessed by modern human beings are adaptations that were shaped by specific environmental challenges early in our species' evolutionary history. They employ formal psychological tests on contemporary human subjects to demonstrate the presence

formal models Mathematical formulas to predict outcomes of particular kinds of human interactions under different hypothesized conditions.

of these abilities and then use logical deduction to "reverse engineer" from these contemporary abilities back to the hypothetical selective pressures that would have shaped these abilities. By contrast, scientists who study gene-culture coevolution, cultural group selection, or niche construction use mathematical formulas originally developed by population biologists to predict outcomes of particular kinds of human interactions under different hypothesized conditions. Computers allow them to simulate, for example, what happens when certain behavioral patterns are repeated for many generations. The researchers then examine the reports of ethnographers or other social scientists to see if any of the outcomes produced by their mathematical calculations match the actual behavior patterns found in real human societies.

No beginning anthropology textbook can offer an in-depth introduction to formal modeling of human biological and cultural evolutionary processes (Table 5.3). But students should be aware of this dynamic and contentious field of research in which anthropologists, biologists, ecologists, psychologists, and other scientists collaborate. Students should also be aware that many anthropologists—cultural anthropologists in particular—are highly critical of formal models, especially formal models of cultural evolution. They point out that formal modeling cannot work unless actual human interactions, which are messy and complex, are tidied up and simplified so that they can be represented by variables in mathematical equations. Reverse engineering has also been criticized for being overly reliant on logical deduction, rather than empirical evidence, in the generation of hypotheses about the human past. Critics argue that these approaches produce nothing more than cartoon versions of everyday life that often reveal systematic Western ethnocentric bias.

In our view, the perspective with the most promise is that of niche construction, which articulates in unusually clear language a point of view many anthropologists and others have held for a very long time. And they are not the only ones. As ecologist Richard Levins and biologist Richard Lewontin pointed out in 1985,

> [using] cultural mechanisms to control our own temperature has made it possible for our species to survive in almost all climates, but it has also created new kinds of vulnerability. Our body temperature now depends on the price of clothing or fuel, whether we control our own furnaces or have them set by landlords, whether we work indoors or outdoors or leave places with stressful temperature regimes. . . . Thus our temperature regime is not a simple consequence of thermal needs but rather a consequence of social and economic conditions. (259)

Can We Predict the Future of Human Evolution?

Current arguments among evolutionary biologists illustrate their varied attempts to grasp the meaning of evolution. How we classify the natural world matters not only to scientists, who want to be sure their classifications match what they find when they go to nature, but also to nonscientists. How we make sense of evolution is important because people of all societies see a connection between the way they make sense of the natural world and the way they make sense of their own lives. Many people believe that human morality is, or ought to be, based on what is natural. For such people, evolutionary interpretations of nature can be threatening even if they portray a natural world that is orderly. If nature's order is dog eat dog, and if human morality must be based on nature's order, then survival at any cost must be morally correct because it is "natural." This is clearly why many people found the more extreme claims of human sociobiology so repugnant. For those who want to root compassion and generosity in human nature, sociobiology offers a portrait of human nature in which such behavior has little or no value.

But perhaps the uncontrolled and uncontrollable pursuit of food and sex is no more natural in our species than sharing, compassion, and nonviolent resolution of differences. As we saw in Chapter 3, many primatologists have evidence to show that, most of the time, most apes and monkeys do not live by the "law of the jungle." The law of the jungle is not a law after all.

Human beings, like all living organisms, are subject to evolutionary processes. Like other organisms, our species shares a gene pool whose different combinations, together with environmental input over the course of a lifetime, produce a range of different human phenotypes that develop over their lifetimes, incorporating a certain range of adaptive responses. But we are not like other organisms in all respects, and this is what makes the study of human nature, human society, and the human past necessary. To adapt to our environments—to make a living and replace ourselves—we have options that do not exist for other organisms: cultural adaptations that are passed on by learning, even when there is no biological reproduction (see Figure 5.5).

The rich heritage of human culture is the source of much wisdom to guide us in our moral dealings with one another. The more we learn about biology, however, the more we realize that neither genotypes nor phenotypes nor environmental pressures provide obvious answers to our questions about how to live. If anything, "nature" offers us mixed messages about what is, or is not, likely to promote survival and reproduction.

TABLE 5.3 Formal Models in the Study of Human Biological and Cultural Evolution	
THEORETICAL PERSPECTIVE	**KEY FEATURES**
Sociobiology	• Defined by E. O. Wilson (1980), one of its founders, as "the systematic study of the biological basis of all social behavior" (322). Originally focused on explaining the evolution of *altruism*—the willingness to give up benefits for oneself to help someone else—sociobiologists argued that altruism makes sense if we pay attention not to individuals but to the genes they carry. • Organisms share the most genes with their close relatives; therefore, sociobiologists hypothesize, natural selection will preserve altruistic behaviors if the altruists sacrifice themselves for close kin, a concept known as *kin selection*. Some anthropologists adopted the sociobiological approach to human societies, whereas others viewed sociobiology as a pernicious perspective that threatened to resurrect nineteenth-century racism.
Behavioral ecology	• A school of thought based on sociobiological reasoning that accepts the importance of natural selection on human adaptations, but rejects sociobiology's genetic determinism. Behavioral ecologists accept the view that human adaptations depend on cultural learning rather than on genetic control, but they insist that the cultural behavior human beings develop is closely circumscribed by the selection pressures imposed on us by the ecological features of the environments in which human populations have lived (see Cheverud 2004; Sussman and Garber 2004).
Evolutionary psychology	• Like earlier sociobiologists, evolutionary psychologists insist that human adaptations are phenotypes under close genetic control. Unlike earlier sociobiologists, however, evolutionary psychologists do not invoke natural selection on genes to explain human behavior patterns as adaptations to present-day conditions. Rather, they argue that natural selection on human genes was most significant millions of years ago, in the environment in which our ancestors lived when they were first evolving away from the other African apes (called the "environment of evolutionary adaptedness," or EEA). • Evolutionary psychologists argue that natural selection in the EEA produced a human brain consisting of a set of sealed-off "mental modules," each of which was designed by natural selection to solve a different adaptive problem (see Barkow et al. 1992).
Gene–culture coevolution	• An analysis of the origin and significance of culture in human evolution that is critical of standard sociobiological accounts. The version developed by Robert Boyd and Peter Richerson (1985) argues that human behavior is shaped by two inheritance systems, one genetic and one cultural. Cultural traits are passed on by learning, not via the chromosomes; but since these traits vary, are passed on from individual to individual, and confer differential fitness on those who use them, they can undergo natural selection (76). • The two inheritance systems are interconnected: human biological evolution creates the possibility for cultural creativity and learning, whereas human cultural traditions created the environment that allows human biological processes to continue, even as culture creates selection pressures of its own that shape human biological evolution. This is why the process is called gene-culture *coevolution* (see also Cavalli-Sforza and Feldman 1981; Durham, 1991).
Cultural group selection	• Sociobiologists argue that group selection cannot occur as the outcome of natural selection operating on genes unless group members are biological kin who share genes (see *kin selection* above). If group members do not share genes, the good of the individual and the good of the group no longer coincide; this means that individuals who sacrificed themselves for other group members would take their "group selection" genes with them to the grave. • But if behaviors are shaped by cultural inheritance rather than genetic inheritance (as in gene–culture coevolution), this argument may not hold. When the forces of cultural learning are powerful enough, the fitness of an individual may come to depend on the behaviors of other individuals in a local group. This is known as cultural group selection. Once the forces of cultural transmission take hold, it is usually easier and cheaper to behave the way the group dictates than it is to strike out on one's own (D. S. Wilson 2002; Richerson and Boyd 2005).
Niche construction	• Odling-Smee, Laland, and Feldman (2003) argue that human evolution depends not just on our genetic heritage and our cultural heritage but also on an additional heritage of modified selection pressures that we pass on to our descendants in the form of a constructed niche. They use the concept of "artifact" to represent these environmental modifications: artifacts include birds' nests and rodents' burrows as well as human artifacts like clothing and furnaces. Odling-Smee et al. argue that their "triple-inheritance" theory offers a more satisfactory explanation of the evolutionary histories of organisms than do accounts focusing on genes and culture alone.

FIGURE 5.5 An individual may have high cultural fitness and no genetic fitness at all. Here, a religious teacher who is celibate (thereby reducing her genetic fitness to zero) passes cultural knowledge to a new generation of other people's offspring.

And in any case, with the development of culture, for good or for ill, human beings have long been concerned not only with survival and reproduction but also with what it takes to lead a meaningful life. Physical life and a meaningful life usually, but not always, go together. This paradox has been part of the human condition for millennia and is likely to remain with us long after our contemporary scientific debates have become history.

Chapter Summary

1. The evolutionary synthesis of the 1930s and 1940s combined Darwinian natural selection with Mendelian ideas about heredity. One result was a distinction between macroevolutionary studies, focusing on the fossil record, and microevolutionary studies, focusing on short-term changes within populations of a species from one generation to the next. In anthropology, perhaps the most significant contribution of microevolutionary studies (and the population genetics to which it gave rise) has been (and continues to be) the way they undermine the nineteenth-century anthropological concept of "biological race."

2. Evolutionary biologists distinguish between species, populations that make up a species, and individual organisms that make up a population. Different kinds of evolutionary studies define species in different ways. Population genetics adopts the biological species concept and focuses on living populations of reproductively isolated species, concentrating on the population's gene pool, estimating the frequency of occurrence of different alleles

of a particular gene, and predicting how those gene frequencies might be affected by different selection pressures.

3. Human population genetics has shown that different human populations from all over the world share basically the same range of genotypic variation, no matter how different from one another they may appear phenotypically. These findings reinforce the claims of biological anthropologists that the concept of "race" is biologically meaningless: different phenotypic traits do not in fact cluster together in populations, as the biological race concept assumes. Rather, the clinal distribution of any individual phenotypic trait can be traced across geographical space, from population to population, as its frequency increases or decreases.

4. Population genetics explains phenotypic patterns as consequences of natural selection favoring particular traits in particular environments. They show how the four evolutionary processes of natural selection, mutation, gene flow, and genetic drift can lead to changes in gene frequencies in a population

over time. Sometimes one evolutionary process may work to increase the frequency of a particular allele while a different process is working to decrease its frequency. Inbreeding over several generations can be harmful because it decreases genetic variation and increases the probability that any alleles for deleterious traits will be inherited in a double dose, one from each parent.

5. Natural selection seems to have molded many complex human phenotypic traits, better adapting human populations to their environments. Anthropologists have studied how variation in traits such as skin color appear to have been shaped by natural selection. Anthropologists have also shown how variation in IQ test scores reflect variations in social class and educational background rather than "race."

6. Despite the efforts by population biologists and others to demonstrate that there is no scientific basis for the category of "biological race," there has been a resurgence in the United States and elsewhere in recent decades to explain group differences in terms of race. Much of this renewed interest in race has come from advances in molecular biology that resulted in decoding the human genome. Biomedical research firms have attempted to find ways of using knowledge of an individual's genome to predict that individual's degree of risk for particular diseases. However, researchers have often used genetic data from other members of populations to which an individual belongs as stand-ins for the individual in question. Some biomedical researchers use "racial" groups as standings for individuals who consider themselves members of such groups. This has proved controversial because self-identified group affiliation is no guarantee of close genetic relatedness, as we have seen.

7. Anthropologist Nadia Abu El-Haj argues that the pragmatic use of race in medical research is different from the so-called "scientific racism" of the late nineteenth and early twentieth centuries. First, the old race concept focused on the classification of phenotypes, whereas the new race concept classifies genotypes. Second, nineteenth-century race science aimed to discover how many races existed and to assign all individuals to their "true race"; whereas the new race concept looks at genetic ancestry markers in order to understand a particular

population's risk for a given disease. The goal would then be to develop drugs keyed to individuals with different risks for that disease.

8. Abu El-Haj and others also argue that many African Americans view medical research and drug trials in which they are involved to be nothing less than a form of long-overdue biomedical justice. Between 1932 and 1972, for example, African American men who participated in the notorious Tuskegee Study of Untreated Syphilis in the Negro Male were never told of the study's true purpose; were denied treatment with penicillin in 1947 even when it was shown to be highly effective against syphilis; and were never given the choice to leave the study. This history was implicated in the controversy over BiDil, a drug promoted in the early 2000s to treat heart failure in self-identified African American patients. Although nobody disputed that the drug worked, the FDA (which approved the drug), NitroMed (which marketed the drug), and the Association of Black Cardiologists (who carried out the original drug trials with African American patients) saw BiDil as a solution to different problems: effective treatment for heart failure, marketing a drug that would make a profit, and increasing the capacity of African American cardiologists to do clinical trials, respectively.

9. In the early twenty-first century, notions such as race and "genetics" and "biology" are still with us, but their meanings appear to have changed, producing consequences that seem to be both positive and negative. One way to disentangle these matters has been proposed by anthropologist Clarence Gravlee, who has emphasized the importance of not equating biology with genetics. Biology includes much more than genetics, such as organismic growth and development over time, which is shaped by various environmental inputs. Gravlee and his colleagues showed a relationship in Puerto Rico between skin color and social status. This biocultural approach revealed that Puerto Ricans with darker skins and higher socioeconomic status actually experienced higher blood pressure than other Puerto Ricans.

10. Many evolutionary biologists and biological anthropologists recognize that trying to attribute every phenotypic trait of an organism to adaptation is problematic. Some traits may not be the result of adaptation but the byproduct of some other feature

that was shaped by natural selection—or even the consequence of random effects.

11. Gene-centered explanations of human evolution gained considerable influence in anthropology after 1975 because of the widespread theoretical impact of a school of evolutionary thought called "sociobiology." Sociobiologists used formal mathematical models borrowed from population genetics and game theory to back up some of their claims. However, critics have also used formal models to challenge sociobiological principles. The most influential critical models include those of gene-culture coevolution, cultural group selection, and niche construction. In our view, the perspective with the most promise is that of niche construction.

For Review

1. Distinguish between microevolution and macroevolution.
2. How is a species defined in your text?
3. Explain what a cline is and why it is important.
4. Explain what is meant by the "molecularization of race."
5. What are the four evolutionary processes discussed in the text?
6. Describe how natural selection explains why a high proportion of the sickling allele is maintained in certain human populations and not others.
7. What is phenotypic plasticity, and why is it important?
8. Explain the difference between short-term acclimatization and developmental acclimatization.
9. Summarize the discussion of skin color in the text.
10. Why do anthropologists and many other scholars insist that IQ is not determined by genes alone?
11. Explain why natural selection on genetic variation alone is not sufficient to explain the range of human adaptive patterns revealed by archaeology, ethnography, and history.
12. What are formal models?

Key Terms

acclimatization 156	gene flow 151	macroevolution 146	phenotypic plasticity 155
adaptation 156	gene frequency 149	microevolution 146	polymorphous 149
cline 150	gene pool 149	mutation 151	population genetics 149
formal models 163	genetic drift 151	natural selection 151	species 147

Suggested Readings

Gould, Stephen Jay. 1989. *Wonderful life: The Burgess Shale and the nature of history*. New York: Norton. *In this now-classic account of the discovery and interpretation of an important paleontological site, Gould analyzes what it tells us about the nature of evolution and sciences that study history.*

Marks, Jonathan. 2011. *The alternative introduction to biological anthropology*. New York: Oxford University Press. *An up-to-date introduction to the subfield, raising critical issues in the field that are often sidestepped in introductory textbooks. Especially strong on the value of the anthropology of science for biological and cultural anthropology.*

Marks, Jonathan, 2017. *Is science racist? (Debating race)*. Cambridge, UK: Polity Press. *In this volume, Marks focuses both on the eugenic race science of the early twentieth century and on the genomic science in the early twenty-first century, demonstrating how both endeavors are based on the mistaken assumption that race is a natural category, despite the fact that this assumption has no evidence to back it up.*

Mielke, James H., Lyle W. Konigsberg, and John H. Relethford. 2011. *Human biological variation*, 2nd ed. New York: Oxford University Press. *Provides a thorough and contemporary view of our biological diversity. Integrates real-world examples on interesting topics, including genetic testing, lactose intolerance, dyslexia, IQ, and homosexuality.*

Relethford, John H. 2013. *The human species: An introduction to biological anthropology*, 9th ed. New York: McGraw-Hill. *A fine introduction to modern biological anthropology, with up-to-date reviews of current research on human* variation as well as chapters on primatology and human evolution. *Comes with a related web page.*

Robins, A. H. 1991. *Biological perspectives on human pigmentation.* Cambridge: Cambridge University Press. *A concise survey of what is known about the biological factors responsible for human pigmentation as well as the possible evolutionary significance of variation in pigmentation in different human populations.*

Stanley, Steven. 1981. *The new evolutionary timetable.* New York: Basic Books. *A classic, accessible introduction (by a punctuationist) to the debate between phyletic gradualists and punctuationists.*

Stinson, Sara, Barry Bogin, and Dennis O'Rourke, eds. 2012. *Human biology: An evolutionary and biocultural perspective,* 2nd ed. Malden, MA: Wiley Blackwell. *The essays in this collection cover a range of topics of interest to contemporary biological anthropologists, including genetic variation, human adaptability, human biology and health, the human life course, and the dynamics of human populations.*

Visit our online resource center for further reading, web links, free assessments, flashcards, and videos. www.oup.com/he/lavenda5e

6

How do we know about the human past?

In this chapter, you will learn about how archaeologists reveal the remains of past human societies and interpret what they find. We look at the increasingly important question of who owns the past. We examine some newer approaches to archaeological research and interpretation. And we conclude by considering how archaeological evidence is being used to argue that we now live in a geological epoch called the Anthropocene, in which human activities have become the primary influence on climate and the environment.

CHAPTER OUTLINE

What Is Archaeology?
How Do Archaeologists Interpret the Past?

Whose Past Is It?
How Is the Past Being Plundered?

What Are the Critical Issues in Contemporary Archaeology?
Chapter Summary

LEARNING OBJECTIVES

- Describe the field of archaeology and the major methodological techniques that archaeologists utilize, including surveys, excavation, and digital tools.
- Summarize the approaches that archaeologists use for interpreting the past and the corresponding evidence.

- Explain evidence for variation in subsistence strategies and cultural and social structures through time and across cultures.
- Discuss challenges for determining who has claims to and ownership of the past, and how those challenges have been addressed through time.

- Identify threats to preserving evidence for understanding the past and examples of how the past is being plundered.
- Analyze critical issues in contemporary archaeology, including patterns related to gender, collaborative approaches, and cosmopolitan archaeology.

Archaeological excavations in Downtown Beirut, Lebanon, that show continuous occupation from prehistoric times to the present day.

Anthropologists who study the human past are of different kinds. As we have seen, paleoanthropologists study the hominin fossil record, from its earliest beginnings through the appearance of our own species. Although archaeologists also sometimes study human skeletal remains, **archaeology** focuses primarily on the **archaeological record**—material evidence of human modification of the physical environment. Beginning with humble stone tools, the archaeological record encompasses many classes of artifacts (pottery, metalwork, textiles, and other technological developments) and nonportable material culture (architecture, irrigation canals, and ancient farm fields). This is why archaeology is sometimes called "the past tense of cultural anthropology" (Renfrew and Bahn 2008, 12). Archaeology makes many contributions to anthropology. Although it may not supply the kind of ethnographic details that are revealed by research among living groups, it does provide great time depth and reveals evidence of past forms of human culture that would otherwise be unknown.

What Is Archaeology?

Archaeologists study the material remains left by our ancestors to interpret cultural variation and cultural change in the human past. What kinds of analytical tools do archaeologists use? Renfrew and Bahn (2008, 17) suggest that four kinds of objectives have guided archaeology at different times over its history. First came traditional approaches that focused on *reconstructing the material remains* of the past by putting together pots, reassembling statues, and restoring houses. Later came the goal of *reconstructing the lifeways*—the culture—of the people who left those material remains. Since the 1960s, however, a third objective has been *explaining the cultural processes* that led to ways of life and material cultures of particular kinds. This has been the focus of what came to be known as *processual archaeology*.

Processual archaeologists "sought to make archaeology an objective, empirical science in which hypotheses about all forms of cultural variation could be tested" (Wenke 1999, 33). They integrated mathematics into

their work, using statistics to analyze the distribution of artifacts at a site, the transformations of artifact usage over time, or the dimensions of trade networks. Their interest in human adaptations to various environments in the course of cultural evolution led to an interest in the field of *cultural ecology* in which cultural processes must be understood in the context of climate change, the variability of economic productivity in different environments, demographic factors, and technological change. As a general rule, processual archaeologists downplayed explanations in which people play an active role as agents who are conscious to a greater or lesser degree of what is happening around them and whose activities contribute to cultural maintenance or change.

In recent years, however, archaeologists have begun to ask different questions—leading to a fifth kind of objective. Many have concluded that processual archaeology neglected human agency and the power of ideas and values in the construction of ancient cultures. A variety of new approaches, which are sometimes called *postprocessual* or *interpretive archaeology*, stress the symbolic and cognitive aspects of social structures and social relations. Some postprocessual archaeologists focus on power and domination in their explanations of certain aspects of the archaeological record; they draw attention to the ways that archaeological evidence may reflect individual human agency and internal contradictions within a society. Other postprocessual archaeologists point out that similar-looking features can mean different things to different people at different sites, which is why it can be seriously misleading to assume that all cultural variation can be explained in terms of universal processes like population growth or ecological adaptation. (We will look at varieties of postprocessual archaeology at the end of this chapter.) At the same time, increasingly precise archaeological methods and subtle archaeological theorizing are worthless if there is nothing left to study. By the twenty-first century, the looting and destruction of archaeological sites had reached crisis proportions. Archaeologists have come to recognize that stewardship of the remains of the human past may be their most pressing responsibility (Fagan and DeCorse 2005, 25).

Archaeologists identify the precise geographical locations of the remains of past human activity from local **sites** of human habitation to the wider regions in which these sites were once embedded. Archaeologists pay attention not only to portable **artifacts** of human manufacture but also to nonportable remnants of material culture, such as house walls or ditches, which are called **features**. They note the presence of other remains, such as plant residues or animal bones connected with food provisioning, which are not themselves artifacts but appear to be the byproducts of human activity (these are

---

archaeology A cultural anthropology of the human past focusing on material evidence of human modification of the physical environment.

archaeological record All material objects constructed by humans or near-humans revealed by archaeology.

site A precise geographical location of the remains of past human activity.

artifacts Objects that have been deliberately and intelligently shaped by human or near-human activity.

features Nonportable remnants from the past, such as house walls or ditches.

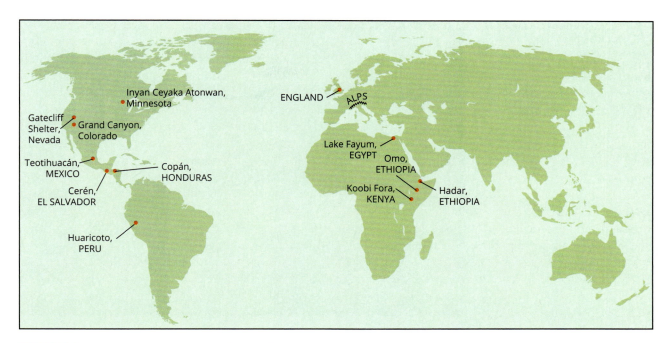

FIGURE 6.1 Major locations discussed in Chapter 6.

sometimes called *ecofacts*). When archaeologists study sites through survey or excavation, they carefully record the immediate *matrix* (e.g., gravel, sand, or clay) in which the object is found and its *provenance* (sometimes spelled *provenience*), which is the precise three-dimensional position of the find within the matrix. They also record exactly where each kind of remain is found, along with any other remains found near it and any evidence that the site may have been disturbed by natural or human intervention. Sometimes they do small-scale excavation, using a shovel to dig small pits over a large area. This strong emphasis on the *context* in which artifacts are found makes scientific archaeology a holistic undertaking. Archaeological sites are important scientifically if they contain evidence that answers key questions about human migration or settlement in certain places at particular times, even when the sites themselves yield none of the elaborate artifacts valued by museums and private collectors.

Archaeologists must know what to look for to identify sites and the remains that can serve as evidence. They have to think about the kinds of human behavior past populations are likely to have engaged in and what telltale evidence for that behavior might have been left behind. Sometimes the artifacts themselves tell the story: a collection of blank flint pieces, partly worked flint tools, and a heap of flakes suggest that a site was used for flint-tool manufacture. Other times, when archaeologists are unclear about the significance of remains, they use a method called **ethnoarchaeology**, which is the study of the way present-day societies use artifacts and structures

and how these objects become part of the archaeological record. Archaeologists studying how contemporary foraging people build traditional shelters—what kinds of materials are employed and how they are used in construction—can predict which materials would be most likely to survive in a buried site and the patterns they would reveal if they were excavated. If such patterns turn up in sites used by prehistoric foragers, archaeologists will already have important clues to their interpretation.

However, archaeologists must not overlook the possibility that a variety of natural and human forces may have interfered with remains once they are left behind at a site. An important source of information about past human diets may be obtained from animal bones found in association with other human artifacts; but just because hyena bones, stone tools, and human bones are found together does not in itself mean that the humans ate hyenas. Careful study of the site may show that all these remains came together accidentally after having been washed out of their original resting places by flash flooding. As we saw in the Chapter 4, being able to tell when processes like this have or have not affected the formation of a particular site is the focus of *taphonomy*.

Even in ideal situations, where a site has lain relatively undisturbed for hundreds, thousands, or millions of years, not all kinds of important human activity may be represented by preserved remains. Wood and plant

ethnoarchaeology The study of the way present-day societies use artifacts and structures and how these objects become part of the archaeological record.

FIGURE 6.2 One of the most spectacular archaeological discoveries in recent years was the so-called Ice Man. He froze to death in an Alpine glacier more than 5,000 years ago. His remains were exposed only in 1991 as the glacier melted.

fibers decay rapidly, and their absence at a site does not mean that its human occupants did not use wooden tools. The earliest classification of ancient human cultural traditions in Europe was based on stone, bronze, and iron tools, all of which can survive for long periods. Baked clay, whether in the form of pottery, figurines, or naturally occurring deposits that were accidentally burned in a fire, is also quite durable. Fire also renders plant seeds virtually indestructible, allowing important dietary clues to survive.

Extreme climates can enhance artifact preservation. Hot, dry climates, such as those in Egypt or northern Chile, hinder decay. Sites in these regions contain not only preserved human bodies but also other organic remains such as plant seeds, baskets, cordage, textiles, and artifacts made of wood, leather, and feathers. Cold climates provide natural refrigeration, which also hinders decay. Burial sites in northern or high-mountain regions with extremely low winter temperatures may never thaw out once they have been sealed, preserving even better than dry climates the flesh of humans and animals, plant remains, and artifacts made of leather and wood. This is well illustrated by the spectacular 1991 discovery of the so-called Ice Man, who had frozen to death in an Alpine glacier 5,300–5,200 years ago (Figure 6.2). Eyes, brain, and intestines were preserved in his dried-up body, together with his clothing, the wooden handles of his flint knife and copper ax head, an unstrung bow, two arrows, and a dozen extra shafts (Sjovold 1993).

As we saw in Chapter 4, ancient DNA can survive for tens of thousands of years in bones, teeth, or hair preserved in permafrost or in cool caves; and laboratory analyses are revealing information about the genomes of extinct species, including hominins. Techniques have also been developed to extract proteins and fats from archaeological remains. Collagen protein from bones can be used to identify species to which ancient bones belonged, and the ratio between stable isotopes of carbon and nitrogen in bone collagen can indicate the amount of meat in the human diet (Brown and Brown 2013, 162). Ancient fat molecules can also be recovered from ceramic fragments or other materials and can be analyzed as biomarkers of leaf wax, muscle, or milk residues, again providing insights about past diets (K. A. Brown and T. A. Brown 2013, 162).

Occasionally, archaeological sites are well preserved as a result of natural disasters, such as volcanic eruptions (Figure 6.3). Similarly, mudslides may cover sites and protect their contents from erosion, whereas waterlogged sites free of oxygen can preserve a range of organic materials that would otherwise decay. Peat bogs are exemplary airless, waterlogged sites that have yielded many plant and animal remains, including artifacts made of wood, leather, and basketry as well as the occasional human body. Log pilings recovered from Swiss lakes have been useful both for reconstructing ancient sunken dwellings and for establishing tree-ring sequences in European dendrochronology.

Surveys

Sometimes research takes archaeologists or paleontologists to museums, where scholars with new theories, new evidence, or new or more sophisticated techniques can reexamine fossils or artifacts collected years earlier to gain new insights. Often, the research problem requires a trip to the field. Traditionally, this meant surveying the region in which promising sites were likely to be found and

FIGURE 6.3 Some archaeological sites are well preserved as a result of natural disasters. This adobe house in Cerén, El Salvador (a), was buried under several layers of lava following a series of volcanic eruptions. Sometimes organic remains leave impressions in the soil where they decayed. These remains of a corn crib and ears of corn from Cerén (b) are actually casts made by pouring dental plaster into a soil cavity.

then excavating the most promising of them—literally digging up the past. As archaeologists have increasingly come to recognize, however, excavations cost a lot of money and are inevitably destructive. Fortunately, nondestructive, remote-sensing technologies have improved significantly in recent years. **Survey** archaeology can now provide highly sophisticated information about site types, their distribution, and their layouts, all without a spadeful of earth being turned (Figure 6.4). Surveys have other advantages as well, as archaeologists Colin Renfrew and Paul Bahn remind us: "Excavation tells us a lot about a little of a site, and can only be done once, whereas survey tells us a little about a lot of sites, and can be repeated" (2008, 79). As the kinds of questions archaeologists ask have changed, larger regions—entire landscapes, contrasting ecological zones, trading zones, and the like—are increasingly of interest. And for this kind of research, surveys are crucial.

Surveys can be as simple as walking slowly over a field with eyes trained on the ground. They are as important to paleontologists as to archaeologists. For example, paleontologist Donald Johanson and his colleagues discovered the bones of "Lucy" when they resurveyed a locality in the Hadar region of Ethiopia that had yielded nothing on previous visits (see Chapter 5). Between the previous visit and that one, the rainy season had come and gone, washing away soil and exposing Lucy's bones. Had Johanson or his colleagues not noticed those bones at that time, another rainy season probably would have washed away Lucy's remains (Johanson and Edey 1981). Of course, Johanson and his team were not in Hadar accidentally; they had decided to look for sites in areas that seemed promising for good scientific reasons. Archaeologists ordinarily decide where to do their field surveys based on previous work, which can give them

clues about where they will most likely find suitable sites. Local citizens in the region who may know of possible sites are also important sources of information.

Aerial surveys can be used for mapping purposes or to photograph large areas whose attributes may suggest the presence of otherwise invisible sites. For example, when contemporary crops are planted in fields that were once used for other purposes, seeds sown over features such as buried walls or embankments will show growth patterns different from the plants around them, casting a shadow that is easily seen in aerial photographs (Figure 6.5). Black-and-white aerial photography is the oldest and cheapest form of aerial reconnaissance and provides the highest image resolution. Infrared photography and remote-sensing techniques using false-color, heat-sensitive, or radar imaging can sometimes produce better results. In 1983, for example, archaeologists used false-color Landsat imagery to discover a vast, previously unknown network of ancient Mayan fields and several other important sites in Yucatán, Mexico. Archaeologists continue to experiment with satellite imaging technology, which is developing at an extraordinary rate. However, the resolution of images from satellites is not yet as good as that of conventional aerial photography, and satellite images can be extremely expensive.

Another remote-sensing technology called LiDAR (light detecting and ranging) uses laser beams to penetrate heavy forest vegetation, providing high-resolution images of hidden archaeological features like ancient roads or settlements. LiDAR surveys in Central America "demonstrate that some ancient Mesoamerican sites are far more extensive and complex than was thought

survey The physical examination of a geographical region in which promising sites are most likely to be found.

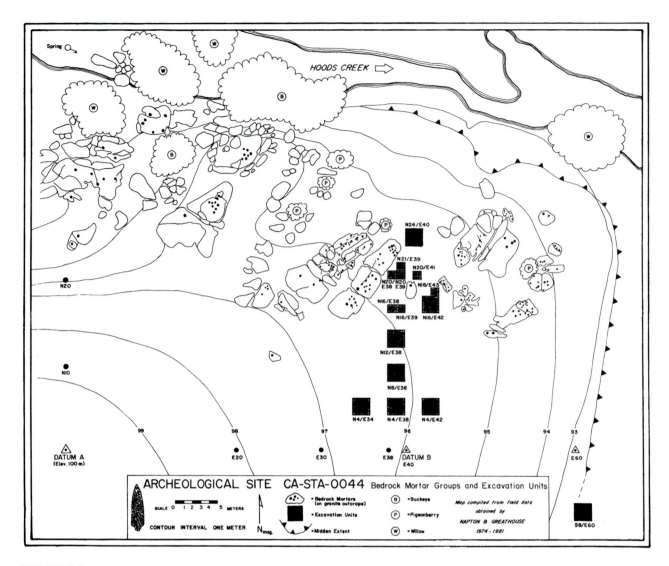

FIGURE 6.4 The final map representing an archaeological site usually combines several kinds of information. This map of a site in California includes cartographic data, data from aerial photography, and data photographed on the site itself.

possible following popular sociopolitical models" (Chase et al. 2012, 12,918; see also Preston 2013).

Thanks to modern technology, archaeologists can also learn a lot about what is beneath a site's surface without actually digging. Some machines can detect buried features and gravitational anomalies using echo sounding or by measuring the electrical resistivity of the soil. Magnetic methods can detect objects made of iron or baked clay, and metal detectors can locate buried metal artifacts. In recent years, ground-penetrating radar (GPR) has become more readily available for archaeological use. GPR reflects pulsed radar waves off features below the surface. Because the radar waves pass through different kinds of materials at different rates, the echoes that are picked up reflect back changes in the soil and sediment encountered as well as the depth at which those changes are found. Advances in data processing

and computer power make it possible to produce large three-dimensional sets of GPR data that can be used effectively to produce three-dimensional maps of buried archaeological remains. GPR is very useful when the site to be studied is associated with people who forbid the excavation of human remains.

Geographic information systems (GIS) is also becoming increasingly important in archaeological research. A GIS is a "computer-aided system for the collection, storage, retrieval, analysis, and presentation of spatial data of all kinds" (Fagan and DeCorse 2005, 188). In essence, a GIS is a database with a map-based interface. Anything that can be given a location in space—information about topography, soil, elevation, geology, climate, vegetation, water resources, site location, and field boundaries, as well as aerial photos and satellite images—is entered into the database, and maps can be generated with the

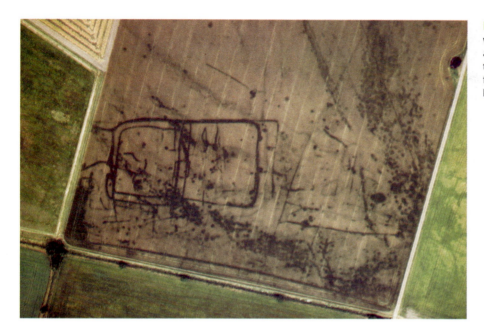

FIGURE 6.5 From the air, buried walls, ditches, and other features of a site may be more easily revealed than from the ground. Here, buried features became visible as the barley in this field grew.

information the researcher wants. At the same time, statistical analysis can be done on the database, allowing archaeologists to generate new information and to study complex problems of site distribution and settlement patterns over a landscape. GIS is being used to construct predictive models as well. That is, if certain kinds of settlement sites are found in similar places (close to water, sheltered, near specific food sources), then a GIS for an area can make it possible to predict the likelihood of finding a site at a particular location whose environmental characteristics are in the database. For archaeologists, the drawback to this kind of predictive modeling is a tendency to place a very heavy weight on the environmental features as determining human settlement patterns. It is easy to measure, map, and digitize features of the natural environment. Social and cultural modifications or interpretations of the environment, however, are equally important but more difficult to handle using GIS methods.

Archaeological Excavation

When archaeologists or paleoanthropologists need to know "a lot about a little of a site," as Renfrew and Bahn (2008) put it, excavation is necessary. **Excavation** is the systematic uncovering of archaeological remains through removal of the deposits of soil and other material covering and accompanying them (Renfrew and Bahn 2008, 580). It is important to remember that excavation is a form of destruction; and a site, once excavated, is gone forever. Archaeologists today will excavate only a small part of a site on the assumption that future archaeologists will have better techniques and different questions if they return to the same site. Some sites are shallow,

with only one or a few levels. Other sites, especially deposits in caves that were used for centuries by successive human groups or urban sites going back thousands of years, are far more complex. In either case, however, excavators keep track of what they find by imposing on the site a three-dimensional grid system that allows them to record stratigraphic associations.

As Renfrew and Bahn (2008, 107) point out, a multilayered site contains two kinds of information about human activities: contemporary activities that take place horizontally in space and changes in those activities that take place vertically over time. Artifacts and features associated with one another in an undisturbed context provide evidence for contemporary activities. As excavators uncover one stratum after another in sequence, they gradually reveal evidence for changes in human activities over time (Figure 6.6). The more levels of occupation at a site, the more likely it is that some of the levels will have been disturbed by subsequent humans, other animals, or natural forces. It then becomes the excavator's job to determine the degree of disturbance that has occurred and its effect on the site.

Only on shallow sites are archaeologists likely to expose an entire occupation level; this procedure is prohibitively expensive and destructive on large, multileveled sites. Archaeologists often use statistical sampling techniques to choose which portions of large, complex sites to excavate, aiming for a balance between major features and outlying areas (see Figure 6.4).

---

excavation The systematic uncovering of archaeological remains through removal of the deposits of soil and other material covering them and accompanying them.

FIGURE 6.6 Graduate and undergraduate students work to excavate a series of stair-step units at the Paleoindian Hudson Meng site (25SX115), Sioux County, Nebraska. All artifacts and features are recorded photographically and in writing, as are the stratigraphic layers that are exposed.

As the excavation proceeds, researchers record photographically and in writing all artifacts and features discovered and the stratigraphic layers exposed. Such record keeping is especially important for structures that will be destroyed as digging continues. Loose soil is sifted to recover tiny artifacts such as stone flakes or remains of plants or animals. Flotation methods allow archaeologists to separate light plant matter that will float, such as bits of wood, leaves, fibers, some seeds, stems, and charcoal, from heavier items that sink, such as rocks, sand, bones, pottery, and chipped stone. Everything is labeled and bagged for more detailed analysis in the laboratory.

Work on an archaeological dig ranges from the backbreaking shifting of dirt to the delicate brushing away of soil from a key fossil or artifact. Each dig brings special challenges. Archaeologist Robert Wenke (1999) describes his team's daily routine during the first 3 months of a 6-month field season as they searched for evidence for the emergence of agriculture after 7000 BCE at a site on the southern shore of the Fayum lake in Egypt:

> We began by making a topological map of the area we intended to work in. We then devised a sampling program and collected every artifact in the sampling units

defined, that is, in the hundreds of 5 × 5 meter squares in our study area. The average temperature during much of this work was over 40°C (104°F), and by midday the stone tools were often so hot we would have to juggle them as we bagged them. Afternoons were spent sorting, drawing, and photographing artifacts, drinking warm water, and drawing each other's attention to the heat. (84)

Most of the labor of cleaning, classifying, and analyzing usually takes place in laboratories after the dig is over and frequently requires several years to complete. Researchers clean the artifacts well enough for close examination—but not so well that possible organic residues (grain kernels inside pots, traces of blood on cutting edges) are lost. They then classify the artifacts according to the materials out of which they are made, their shapes, and their surface decoration, if any, and arrange them in typologies, using ordering principles similar to those employed for fossil taxonomies. Once the artifacts are classified, researchers analyze records from the dig for patterns of distribution in space or time. It is important to underline that individual records of the excavation—notebooks, drawings, plots of artifact distributions, photographs, and computer data—are as much part of the results of the excavation as the materials excavated.

Archaeologist Ian Hodder has argued that archaeology would benefit if discovery were not separated from interpretation in this way. For this reason, he advocates "interpretation at the trowel's edge": that is, "bringing forward interpretation to the moment of discovery" (Hodder 2010, 12) by making it possible for analytic specialists and interested groups of various kinds to converse with excavators working in the trenches, and by building specialist labs on the site itself. For instance, over a three-year period, a group of anthropologists, philosophers, and theologians were brought to the Neolithic site of Çatalhöyük, Turkey, where Hodder directs research. "The dialogue between different specialists in religion in the context of grappling with the data from a particular archaeological site has opened up new lines of inquiry and new perspectives on religion and its origins" (Hodder 2010, 27; see the box feature "Anthropology *in Everyday Life*: Archaeology as a Tool of Civic Engagement").

The artifacts and structures from a particular time and place in a site are called an *assemblage*. Cultural change at a particular site may be traced by comparing assemblages from lower levels with those found in more recent levels. When surveys or excavations at several sites turn up the same assemblages, archaeologists refer to them as an "archaeological culture." Such groupings can be very helpful in mapping cultural similarities and differences over wide areas during past ages.

The pitfall, however, which earlier generations of archaeologists did not always avoid, is to assume that archaeological cultures necessarily represent real social groups that once existed. As Hodder demonstrated in 1982, archaeological cultures are the product of scientific analysis. Hodder's ethnoarchaeological research among several contemporary ethnic groups in eastern Africa showed that artifact distributions do sometimes coincide with ethnic boundaries when the items in question are used as symbols of group identity. He found, for example, that the ear ornaments worn by women of the Tugen, Njemps, and Pokot groups were distinct from one another and that women from one group would never wear ear ornaments typical of another. However, other items of material culture, such as pots or tools, which were not used as symbols of group identity, were distributed in patterns very different from those typical of ear ornaments. Such artifact distribution patterns could be misinterpreted by future researchers and result in a misleading archaeological culture.

Questions about the correspondences between archaeological cultures and present-day cultures are important to archaeologists because they would like to use archaeological evidence to explain cultural variation and cultural change over time. Burning questions for many prehistoric archaeologists concern when and why small bands of foragers decided to settle down and farm for a living; and why some of these settlements grew large and complex and came to dominate their neighbors, whereas others did not. Patterned distributions of artifacts offer clues about groups of people who might have been responsible for these developments (as we will see in Chapter 7); however, we need to remember the risks of associating these distributions too literally with real past societies.

Archaeology and Digital Heritage

We noted earlier that advances in data processing and computer power had improved the quality of data obtained by archaeologists from ground-penetrating radar and GIS; in fact, computerization and digital information storage have become important in all areas of contemporary archaeology. In recent decades, a digital revolution has swept individuals and institutions into a global digital mediascape, and some archaeologists have begun to reflect on the challenges and the opportunities associated with these changes. Cutting-edge digital technology offers the "the potential of connecting data to spatial coordinates, fleshing out site and landscape, and rendering simulated pasts in photographic detail, all on the scale of world-building—as complete a model of the past as possible; a '**digital heritage**'" (Olsen et al.

2012, 88). However, Olsen and his colleagues emphasize that these dazzling possibilities must not blind archaeologists to the fact that the creation and management of digital heritage depends on the successful negotiation among archaeologists, digital experts, and various communities for whom the digital heritage is meaningful; it also involves serious tinkering with the hardware and software to make online access to digital heritage sites as unproblematic as possible. Olsen and his colleagues describe this as the hard work of mediation; that is, of "work done in the spaces between old things and the stories they hold in the present" (89).

Digital documentation and storage requires decisions to be made concerning what to keep and what to discard, which was also the case with traditional management and preservation of archaeological materials. However, archaeologists who digitize their archives have often found it difficult to connect different kinds of digital records with one another. Often this is because different digital technologies operate according to different data standards. Olsen and his colleagues (2012) argue that data standards are necessary, but that archaeologists must be mindful of the choices they make in setting up such standards: "just as there is a reality that standards and knowledge infrastructures strive to maintain, there is a politics of memory that they render invisible" (108). Digital media make it possible to connect "analog" hand-drawn maps and sketches of artifacts with digitized maps and photographs, linking them back to the original artifacts in storerooms and sites in the environment. However, most archaeologists "often only get one chance at translating the things and their relations that are displaced by excavation" (Olsen et al. 2012, 110). Moreover, preserving connections between digital and analog materials depends on preserving "our ability to retrace the linkages" between one and the other (Olsen et al. 2012, 111). One way archaeologists are working to resolve these issues is the digital archaeological record, which aims at "broadening the access to a wide variety of archaeological data" by establishing standards for digital systems of archaeological data storage and retrieval (https://www.tdar.org/why-tdar/access/).

On the positive side, current digital media enable more extensive forms of interaction with varied forms of archaeological data than were possible in the past. For example, an important area of contemporary archaeology in the United States involves the identification and documentation of traditional cultural property (TCP) sites affiliated with Native American or Native Hawaiian

digital heritage Digital information about the past available on the Internet. It can include a range of materials from digitized documents and photographs to images of artifacts to video and sound recordings.

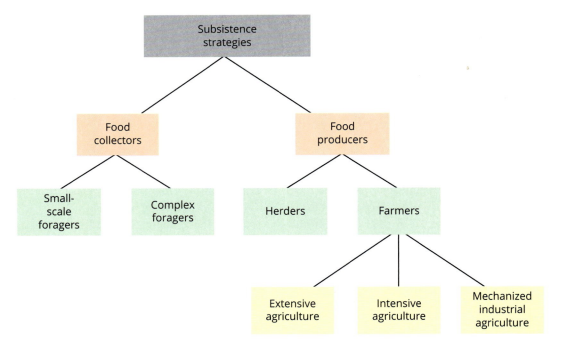

FIGURE 6.7 This is a conventional taxonomy of human subsistence strategies. What does such a taxonomy emphasize? What does it leave out?

groups. Olsen and his colleagues point out that digitally documented data about TCP sites is much richer than traditional written documentation, bringing together maps, photographs, video excerpts, and handwritten notes. Indeed, "Without digitally-mediated engagements with sites such as TCPs it would be difficult to register those very qualities that define them as significant" (Olsen et al. 2012, 129).

At the same time, concern remains about the sustainability of digital formats currently in use. In addition, as digital heritage resources become increasingly accessible on the Internet, via open-source and Creative Commons agreements, outside groups are permitted to engage with digital heritage sites, and some may challenge the authority of archaeological interpretations. But such engagements can be a source of strength, not merely a threat (see the box feature "Anthropology *in Everyday Life* in Chapter 7, Çatalhöyük in the Twenty-First Century," for a comparable example). Olsen and his colleagues (2012) conclude: "Just as analog media in deteriorating archives require attention, the networks constituting digital information and documents and sustaining their preservation require curatorial work to maintain. This creates new responsibilities for sustaining our digital heritage, new rules for manifesting the past . . .

a combination of practices that are orderly and consistent as well as open and creative (134).

How Do Archaeologists Interpret the Past?

What Are Subsistence Strategies?

Human beings construct their ecological niches by inventing ways of using their relationships with one another, with other organisms, and with other features of the physical environment to make a living. *Subsistence* is the term often used to refer to the satisfaction of the most basic material survival needs: food, clothing, and shelter. The different ways that people in different societies go about meeting subsistence needs are called **subsistence strategies**.

Nineteenth-century anthropologists were curious about the range of ways in which different human societies secured their subsistence, and they collected a vast amount of detailed information from the accounts of travelers, merchants, missionaries, and colonial administrators. In an effort to organize this vast amount of data, subsequent generations of anthropologists devised a typology of subsistence strategies that gained wide acceptance over the course of the twentieth century (Figure 6.7). The basic division is between food collectors, or *foragers* (those who gather, fish, or hunt), and food producers

---

subsistence strategies Different ways that people in different societies go about meeting their basic material survival needs.

FIGURE 6.8 Extensive agriculture, sometimes known as *swidden* or *slash-and-burn horticulture*, requires a substantial amount of land, since soils are exhausted within a couple of years and may require as many as 20 years to lie fallow before they can be used again.

(those who depend on domesticated plants or animals or both). The strategies followed by food collectors depend on the richness of the environments in which they live. Small-scale food collectors live in harsher environments and are likely to change residence often in search of resources, as the Ju/'hoansi traditionally did (see Chapter 11, "EthnoProfile 11.4: Ju/'hoansi (!Kung)"). By contrast, complex food collectors live in environments richly endowed with dependable food sources and may even, like the indigenous peoples of the northwest coast of North America, build settlements with permanent architecture. Food producers may farm exclusively or herd exclusively or do a little of both. Those who depend on herds are called *pastoralists*. As can be seen in Figure 6.7, conventional classifications of herding peoples allot them a somewhat marginal status alongside farmers, a judgment reflecting the perceptions of settled peoples.

Traditional classifications of subsistence strategies involving dependence on domesticated plants acknowledge a range of variation (see Figure 6.7). Some farmers depend primarily on human muscle power plus a few simple tools such as digging sticks or hoes or machetes. They clear plots of uncultivated land, burn the brush, and plant their crops in the ash-enriched soil that remains. Because this technique exhausts the soil after two or three seasons, the plot must then lie fallow for several years as a new plot is cleared and the process repeated. This form of cultivation is called *extensive agriculture*, emphasizing the extensive use of land as farm plots are moved every few years (see Figure 6.8). Other farmers use plows, draft animals, irrigation, fertilizer, and the like. Their method of farming—known as *intensive*

agriculture—brings much more land under cultivation at any one time and produces significant crop surpluses. Finally, *mechanized industrial agriculture* is found in societies in which farming or animal husbandry has become organized along industrial lines. Agribusiness "factories in the field" or animal feedlots transform food production into a large-scale, technology-dependent industry of its own.

What Are Bands, Tribes, Chiefdoms, and States?

Early anthropologists wanted not only to sort out subsistence strategies; they also wanted to classify and map the range of variation in forms of human society over time. They especially wanted to explain cultural and social change over time, and, in particular, to account for the origin of the state. The American Lewis Henry Morgan, for example, was struck by certain patterns he found in which particular forms of social and political organization seemed regularly to correlate with particular forms of economic and technological organization, which he called "the arts of subsistence." Morgan's book *Ancient Society*, published in 1877, summarized the basic orientation of what became known as *unilineal cultural evolutionism*: "The latest investigations respecting the early condition of the human race are tending to the conclusion that man-kind commenced their career at the bottom of the scale and worked their way up from savagery to civilization through the slow accumulations of experimental knowledge" (Morgan [1877] 1963, 3).

By the early twentieth century, the extravagant claims of some unilineal schemes of cultural evolutionism

TABLE 6.1 Formal Categories Used by Anthropologists to Classify the Forms of Human Society

CATEGORY	DESCRIPTION
Band	A small, predominantly foraging society of 50 or fewer members that divides labor by age and sex only and provides relatively equal access for all adults to wealth, power, and prestige.
Tribe	A farming or herding society, usually larger than a band, that relies on kinship as the framework for social and political life; provides relatively egalitarian social relations but may have a chief who has more prestige (but not more power or wealth) than others. Sometimes called a *rank society*.
Chiefdom	A socially stratified society, generally larger than a tribe, in which a chief and close relatives enjoy privileged access to wealth, power, and prestige and which has greater craft production but few full-time specialists.
State	An economic, political, and ideological entity invented by stratified societies; possesses specialized government institutions to administer services and collect taxes and tributes; monopolizes use of force with armies and police; possesses high level and quality of craft production. Often developed writing (particularly in early states).
Empire	Forms when one state conquers another.

led most anthropologists to abandon such theorizing. Key critics in Britain were social anthropologists A. R. Radcliffe-Brown and Bronislaw Malinowski. Radcliffe-Brown argued that the evidence about social forms in past periods of human history was so incomplete that all such schemes amounted to little more than guesswork. Malinowski and his students used detailed ethnographic information to explode popular stereotypes about so-called savage peoples. In the United States, Franz Boas was highly critical of the racist assumptions in unilineal evolutionary schemes. He and his students worked to reconstruct the histories of indigenous North American societies. They were struck by the links among neighboring societies, especially by the ways in which people, ideas, rituals, and material artifacts regularly flowed across porous social boundaries. Boas was quick to note that if borrowing, rather than independent invention, played an important role in cultural change, then any unilineal evolutionary scheme was doomed.

After World War II, mindful of this critique, a new generation of archaeologists and cultural anthropologists in North America worked to construct models of cultural evolution that would avoid problematic assumptions about race and progress, while still capturing key turning points in social change. By the 1960s, they

had produced economic and political classifications of human social forms that mapped onto each other in interesting ways. As archaeologist Matthew Johnson (1999) summarizes,

> Cultural anthropologists Elman Service and Morton Fried . . . have been particularly influential on archaeologists. Service gives us a fourfold typology ranging along the scale of simple to complex of band, tribe, chiefdom, and state. Fried offers an alternative [political] scheme of egalitarian, ranked, stratified and state [societies]. . . . Both start and stop at the same point (they start with "simple" gatherer–hunter societies, though their definitions of such societies differ, and end with the modern state). They both also share a similar methodology. (141; see also Wenke 1999, 340–44; Table 6.1)

The **band** is the characteristic form of social organization found among foragers. Foraging groups are small, usually numbering no more than 50 people, and labor is divided ordinarily on the basis of age and sex. All adults in band societies have roughly equal access to whatever material or social valuables are locally available, which is why anthropologists call them "egalitarian" forms of society. A society identified as a **tribe** is generally larger than a band, and its members usually farm or herd for a living. Social relations in a tribe are still relatively egalitarian, although there may be a chief who speaks for the group or organizes certain group activities. The chief often enjoys greater prestige than other individuals, but this prestige does not ordinarily translate into greater power or wealth. Social organization and subsistence activities are usually carried out according to rules of kinship (see Chapter 12).

band The characteristic form of social organization found among foragers. Bands are small, usually no more than 50 people, and labor is divided ordinarily on the basis of age and sex. All adults in band societies have roughly equal access to whatever material or social valuables are locally available.

tribe A society that is generally larger than a band, whose members usually farm or herd for a living. Social relations in a tribe are still relatively egalitarian, although there may be a chief who speaks for the group or organizes certain group activities.

FIGURE 6.9 Members of the Oruro, Bolivia, devil sodality dance.

However, many societies of foragers, farmers, and herders have developed what Elman Service (1962) called "pantribal sodalities" (113). **Sodalities** are "special-purpose groupings" that may be organized on the basis of age, sex, economic role, and personal interest. "[Sodalities] serve very different functions—among them police, military, medical, initiation, religious, and recreation. Some sodalities conduct their business in secret, others in public. Membership may be ascribed or it may be obtained via inheritance, purchase, attainment, performance, or contract. Men's sodalities are more numerous and highly organized than women's and, generally, are also more secretive and seclusive in their activities" (Hunter and Whitten 1976, 362). Sodalities create enduring diffuse solidarity among members of a large society, in part because they draw their personnel from a number of "primary" forms of social organization, such as lineages (Figure 6.9).

The **chiefdom** is the first human social form to show evidence of permanent inequalities of wealth and power, in addition to inequality of **status**, or position in society. Ordinarily, only the chief and close relatives are set apart from the rest of society; other members continue to share roughly similar social status. Chiefdoms are generally larger than tribes and show a greater degree of craft production, although such production is not yet in the hands of full-time specialists. Chiefdoms also exhibit a greater degree of hierarchical political control, centered on the chief and relatives of the chief, based on their great deeds. Archaeologically, chiefdoms are interesting because some apparently remained as they were and then disappeared, whereas others went on to

develop into states. A **state** is defined as a stratified society that possesses a territory that is defended from outside enemies with an army and from internal disorder with police. States, which have separate governmental institutions to enforce laws and to collect taxes and tribute, are run by an elite who possesses a monopoly on the use of force.

Are the Categories of Band, Tribe, Chiefdom, and State Still of Value to Anthropologists?

Table 6.1 summarizes the standard categories that anthropologists have used to classify forms of human society, taking into consideration subsistence strategies and forms of social and political organization. Today, however, when archaeologists or cultural anthropologists use these categories in their work, they are making no claims about a particular society's place in a series of universal stages of cultural evolution. As we shall see in Chapter 7, most archaeologists who use this general evolutionary

sodalities Special-purpose groupings that may be organized on the basis of age, sex, economic role, and personal interest.

chiefdom A form of social organization in which a leader (the chief) and close relatives are set apart from the rest of the society and allowed privileged access to wealth, power, and prestige.

status A particular social position in a group.

state A stratified society that possesses a territory that is defended from outside enemies with an army and from internal disorder with police. A state, which has a separate set of governmental institutions designed to enforce laws and to collect taxes and tribute, is run by an elite that possesses a monopoly on the use of force.

scheme to help them interpret their findings reject the lockstep determinism that gave nineteenth-century cultural evolutionism such a bad name. Usually, anthropologists employ these terms as nothing more than a useful shorthand way of sketching a society's overall contours.

However, given this history, does it make sense for anthropologists to continue to use these terms at all? After all, attempting to squeeze complex human subsistence strategies and social arrangements into four stereotypical categories leads to serious misunderstandings about how human subsistence strategies work. Moreover, the conventional sequence of band-tribe-chiefdom-state seems to embody a view of human cultural history that leaves no room for openness and contingency in human affairs, implicitly suggesting that human cultural development moves on rails toward a predestined outcome. For example, James Scott has recently objected to the simplistic and misleading ways in which modes of subsistence are typically discussed:

> Domestication, in light of the deep history and massive effects of these practices, needs to be seen far more expansively than mere planting and pastoralism. Since the dawn of the species, Homo sapiens has been domesticating whole environments, not just species. The preeminent tool for this, before the Industrial Revolution, was not the plough so much as fire. The domestication of whole environments in turn made possible the other adaptive advantage of our species, namely high rates of reproduction, making us the world's most successful invasive mammal. . . . Whether we wish to call it niche construction, domestication of the environment, landscape modification, or the human management of ecosystems, it is clear on a long view that much of the world was shaped by human activity (anthropogenic) well before the first societies based on fully domesticated wheat, barley, goats and sheep appear in Mesopotamia. This is why, finally, the conventional "subspecies" of subsistence modes— hunting, foraging, pastoralism, and farming—make so little historical sense. The same people have practiced all four, sometimes in a single lifetime; the activities can and have been combined for thousands of years, and each of them bleeds imperceptibly into the next along a vast continuum of human rearrangements of the natural world. (Scott 2017, 70–71).

Let us return to our earlier discussion of pastoralists, which tends, as we saw, to marginalize them. Today, new high-tech analytic methods, coupled with new efforts to compare the archaeologies of pastoral peoples from different parts of the world, are altering this understanding, "replacing cultural stereotypes with a diverse range of material evidence that has revealed how ancient pastoral nomads lived, organized, and fully participated

in many of the traditions we refer to as 'civilization'" (Honeychurch and Makarewicz 2016, 342). For example, the traditional question in past research on pastoralism has been the origin of animal domestication, but the newer work is investigating "subsequent processes involving enhancement of livestock management strategies, which contributed to the emergence of more intensive forms of pastoralism and pastoral nomadism" (Honeychurch and Makarewicz 2016, 343).

Comparative work carried out in different regions and landscapes now shows that "Mobile herding, in its various expressions, is but one possible outcome of the long-term processes of coevolution and cocommunity between animals and human beings initiated with if not before, the domestication of wild animals" (Honeychurch and Makarewicz 2016, 343). Incorporation of herd animals into subsistence practices probably emerged more than once, taking on different patterns in different landscapes. In the millennia following domestication, mobility and settled life existed side by side, and might be taken up by members of the same community at different times, as we will see in Chapter 7. In addition, skills and knowledge in herd management practices improved over time, and it can be seen in material remains of houses, corrals, deliberately constructed mounds of stone, landscape modifications such as dams or storage spaces for water, and rock carvings. People with herds also developed craft skills that allowed them to transform animal products like wool or leather into high-value goods. Overall, households with herds seem to have maintained a "multi-resource and multi-purpose pastoralism," which afforded an impressive degree of productive flexibility. Hence, Honeychurch and Makarewicz conclude that their "nomadic" movements "may not have been principally an adaptation to a marginal environment but instead a flexible response" (2016, 344–47). Archaeologists now contribute to contemporary efforts by ethnographers and others to defend the rights of indigenous herders, highlighting the roles they have long played in managing grasslands and demonstrating that the so-called pastoral nomad is "an innovative social agent, an architect of political complexity, and a modern-day actor who is well-suited to the contemporary globalized world" (Honeychurch and Makarewicz 2016, 352).

Perhaps speaking about bands, tribes, and chiefdoms may continue to be of value to archaeologists who think of them as points on a continuum, recognizing that a single social group may move back and forth between more than one of these forms over time. We have seen that ethnoarchaeology rests explicitly on the notion that archaeological remains from the deep past may bear a strong resemblance to features of material culture known from recent or contemporary living societies, providing suggestions about how to interpret how past human groups organized themselves or made a living. Most anthropologists would probably agree that knowledge about human cultural prehistory is important in helping us understand what it means to be human, even if our more immediate research interests do not focus on prehistory itself. For example, knowledge that gender relations in band societies tend to be egalitarian and that humans and their ancestors apparently lived in bands for most of evolutionary history has been important to feminist anthropologists; knowledge that nation-states and empires are recent developments in human history that came about as a result of political, technological, and other sociocultural processes undermines the assumptions of scientific racism.

At the same time, anthropologists may continue to be interested in why certain kinds of developments came about in one place and time rather than another. Archaeologists notice that there were numerous settled villages in southwest Asia 10,000 years ago, but only a few of them became cities or city-states. Some band-living hunter–gatherers settled down to become farmers or animal herders in some times and places; some of their neighbors, however, managed to find a way to continue to survive by gathering and hunting in bands right up until the end of the twentieth century. Indeed, in parts of the world, like Afghanistan, tribal organizations continue to thrive, and attempts to establish centralized states regularly fail. Might these categories retain value if we subject them to critique and put them to work in unconventional ways? James Scott urges to do exactly this by thinking "against the grain;" that is, reconsidering what counts as failure and what counts as success when trying to make sense of evidence about patterns of social change in the distant past. Scott reminds us that those who were designated "barbarians" by ancient settled societies include people like foragers living in bands, herders living in tribes—indeed, anyone who was not subject to control by rulers of states that depended on settled grain agriculture and the labor of peasants. Scott upends standard cultural evolutionary accounts that culminate in the state, and takes the perspective of the so-called "barbarians." The earliest states were unstable and limited in their ability to extend their control, he argues, creating the conditions for a "golden age of barbarians" (2017, 223).

> States were juicy sites for plunder and tribute. Just as the state required a sedentary grain-growing population for its predations, so did this concentration of settled people, with their train, livestock, manpower and goods, serve as a site of extraction for more mobile predators. When the predator's mobility was enhanced by camels, horses, stirrups, or swift boats of shallow draft, the range and effectiveness of their raids was greatly extended. . . . And here we should recall that virtually all of our knowledge of barbarian "threats" comes from state sources—sources that might well have self-interested reasons to downplay or more likely, to overdramatize the threat and to define the term "barbarian" narrowly or widely. (2017, 223–224)

This suggests, in turn, that "tribes begin where states end" (Scott 2017, 236). "Given what we now know, it would be more accurate to say that states preceded tribes and, in fact, largely invented them as an instrument of rule" (2017, 236). It also suggests that we need to reconsider what we mean by "adaptation" when looking at how a society makes a living. For example, critical medical anthropologist Merrill Singer pointed out some years ago that "various practices that biocultural anthropologists have traditionally called 'adaptations' might better be analyzed as social adjustments to the consequences of oppressive sociopolitical relationships" (Singer 1998, 115). Gavin Smith and R. Brooke Thomas also draw attention to situations where "social relations compromise people's options" for attaining biological well-being and cultural satisfaction but where people do not passively accept this situation and choose instead to "try to escape or change those relations"; Smith and Thomas call these practices "adaptations of resistance" (1998, 466).

Archaeology, history, and ethnography can help explain why these developments have (or have not) occurred by seeking to identify social structural elements and cultural practices that may enhance, or impede, the transformation of one kind of social form into another. Nor is classification an end in itself. Today's archaeologists do not see the categories of band, tribe, chiefdom, and state as eternal forms through which all societies are fated to pass. Instead, these are understood as theoretical constructs based on available evidence and subject to critique. Their main value comes from the way in which they give structure to our ignorance.

Whose Past Is It?

As a social science discipline, archaeology has its own theoretical questions, methodological approaches, and history. In recent years, archaeologists have explicitly had to come to terms with the fact that they are not the only people interested in what is buried in the ground, how it got there, how it should be interpreted, and to whom it belongs. In some cases, archaeological sites have come to play an important role in identity formation for people who see themselves as the descendants of the builders of the site. Machu Picchu in Andean Peru, the Pyramids in Egypt, the Acropolis in Athens, Great Zimbabwe in Zimbabwe, and Masada in Israel are just a few examples of ancient monuments that have great significance for people living in modern states today. The meanings people take from them do not always coincide with the findings of current archaeological research. At the same time, these sites, and a great many others, have become major tourist destinations. Geographically remote Machu Picchu, for example, now receives about 300,000 tourists per year, a number that is both impressive and worrisome, since the constant movement of tourists may be doing permanent damage to the site (Figure 6.10). Nations, regions, and local communities have discovered that the past attracts tourists and their money, which can provide significant income in some parts of the world. The past may even be mobilized by the entertainment industry: for example, increasingly popular "time capsule" sites invite tourists to visit places where local people wear costumes and carry out the occupations associated with a "re-created" past way of life.

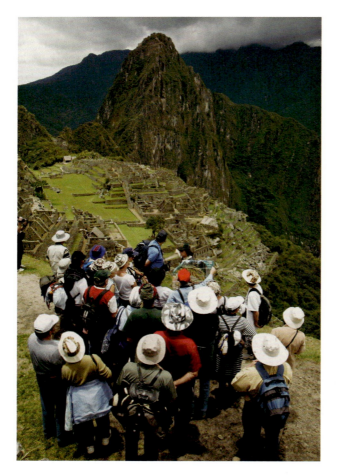

FIGURE 6.10 Although Machu Picchu is a spectacular example of human ingenuity and achievement, it has had to endure increasing pressure from visitors who come to admire it. The Peruvian government has proposed closing the Inca trail during the rainy season to protect the sites.

Nevertheless, not all peoples welcome either archaeologists or tourists. For example, as former colonies became independent states, their citizens became interested in uncovering their own past and gaining control over their heritage. This has often meant that the artifacts discovered during archaeological research must stay in the country in which they were found. In addition, citizens of these states are now asking museums in Western countries to return cultural property—substantial quantities of material artifacts—removed long ago by colonizers. There seems to be little question that objects of special religious or cultural significance should be returned to the places from which they were taken. Some objects, for example, were considered sacred by their makers and were not intended for public view but have been openly displayed in public museums for many years. Is displaying such objects in public, even among people who do not believe in their sacredness, disrespectful to their makers? Is it just another way of representing the political power of the current owners? Renfrew and Bahn (2004, 552) suggest that the matter may be more complex:

> [One can] ask whether the interest of the great products of human endeavor does not in fact transcend the geographical boundaries of modern-day nationalism. Does it make sense that all the Paleolithic handaxes and other artifacts from Olduvai Gorge or Olorgesaillie in East Africa should remain confined within the bounds of the modern nations where they have been found? Should we not all be able to benefit from the insights they offer? And is it not a profound and important experience to be able, in the course of one day in one of the world's great museums, to be able to walk from room to room, from civilization to civilization, and see unfolded a sample of the whole variety of human experience?

But artifacts are not all that have come out of the ground over the course of a century and a half of archaeological research. Human skeletal material has also been found, usually recovered from intentional burials. For archaeologists and biological anthropologists, this skeletal material offers important data on past patterns of migration, disease, violence, family connections, social organization and complexity, technology, cultural beliefs, and many other phenomena. Constantly improving analytical techniques are increasing the quality of data that can be extracted from skeletal remains, making this material even more valuable. Yet, these may be the remains of ancestors of peoples now living in the area from which the bones were removed, peoples who do not believe that the dead should be disturbed and have their bones analyzed.

This has been a particularly important issue for archaeology in the United States because most of the collections of skeletal materials (and sacred objects) came from Native American populations. Many, although not all, Native Americans are deeply angered by the excavation of indigenous burials. That the bones of their ancestors end up in museums, laboratories, and universities embodies for them the disrespect and domination that has been the lot of indigenous Americans since Europeans first arrived. Thus, their objections have both religious and political dimensions. These objections were recognized in the Native American Graves Protection and Repatriation Act (NAGPRA), passed by the US Congress in 1990.

First, NAGPRA requires all federal agencies and institutions that receive federal funds to inventory all American Indian and Native Hawaiian human remains in their possession, as well as funerary objects, sacred objects, and "objects of cultural patrimony." These institutions must establish whether these remains or objects have a connection with any living indigenous groups. Should a connection be found, the institutions are required to notify the appropriate American Indian or Native Hawaiian group and offer to return, or "repatriate," the materials in question. In addition, if indigenous groups believe that they have a connection to remains held by an institution, they may request repatriation of those remains, even if the institution is not convinced by their claims (Figure 6.11).

Second, NAGPRA protects American Indian graves and cultural objects on all federal and tribal lands (it does not extend protection to sites on private lands). The act also requires that anyone carrying out archaeological research on federal or tribal lands must consult with the Native American people who are affiliated or may be affiliated with those lands regarding the treatment and disposition of any finds.

NAGPRA has made it necessary for archaeologists to take seriously the rights and attitudes of native peoples toward the past. Although this has led to disagreements, it has also led to compromise, collaboration, and recognition of shared concerns. As Fagan and DeCorse (2005) put it, "no archaeologist in North America, and probably elsewhere, will be able to excavate a prehistoric or historic burial without the most careful and sensitive preparation. This involves working closely with native peoples in ways that archaeologists have not imagined until recently. Nothing but good can come of this" (504).

Among the positive consequences of NAGPRA have been cooperative agreements with Native American groups that are interested in developing their own museums and archaeological and historical research programs. In other cases, tribal councils or other representatives have been willing to allow archaeologists and biological anthropologists to study excavated bones or to make extremely accurate copies of them before returning them for reburial. Attempts are being made to establish working relationships based on mutual respect for the positions of all sides—respectful treatment of the ancestors and sacred objects as well as the concerns of science and education. The situation remains uncertain, however. Changes in tribal council membership can lead to changes of policy positions regarding archaeology.

One case that has involved extensive legal action is that of Kennewick Man (also called the Ancient One), an 8,500-year-old skeleton found in the state of Washington in 1996, six years after the passage of NAGPRA (Figure 6.12). Since initial examination

FIGURE 6.11 Ceremony for reburial of remains of Eyak Indians in Cordova, Alaska. The bones were released by the Smithsonian Institution under NAGPRA.

FIGURE 6.12   Biological anthropologist Douglas Owsley, of the Smithsonian Institution, examining various features of the right femur of the Kennewick Man skeleton to try to determine the original position of the body in the ground.

seemed to indicate that the remains belonged to a nineteenth-century white settler, scholars were surprised when the skeleton received a radiocarbon date of 9300 B. P. More study seemed essential to resolve the matter, but the US Army Corps of Engineers intended to return the remains to the Umatilla tribe for reburial. Eight anthropologists sued the Corps of Engineers for permission to study the bones, contending that the bones could not be linked to any living tribe. The Umatilla insisted, however, that their traditions held that they had occupied the land from the beginning of time, which meant that the bones belonged to one of their ancestors and should be returned to them. In 2002, a magistrate found in favor of the scientists, but four tribes and the US Department of the Interior appealed the decision. In February 2004, a US court of appeals upheld the magistrate's decision, and a 10-day study of the skeletal remains was carried out in July 2005. Since 1998, the remains have been kept at the Burke Museum of Science on the campus of the University of Washington in Seattle, Washington, under control of the US Army

Corps of Engineers (https://www.burkemuseum.org/news/ancient-one-kennewick-man).

In the years since the discovery of the Kennewick skeleton, much has changed in the relations between archaeologists and Native American peoples. As we noted in Chapter 4, the development of ancient DNA analysis has made possible the tracing of past population movements and mixtures in many parts of the world, including the Americas. An important milestone was the analysis of the genome of the Anzick-1 child, the age of which was dated to around 12,600 years old. This burial was found on private land and therefore not covered by NAGPRA; but as we saw, the researchers still checked to verify that no indigenous group had claimed the remains. The researchers also personally contacted representatives of nine Native American tribes living near the Anzick site to explain their research, and they encountered no objections. Some tribal members did ask that the remains be reburied, and Rasmussen and his colleagues reported that the Anzick family is working to honor this request (Rasmussen et al. 2014, 228). On December 16, 2016, President Obama signed legislation, known as the WIIN Act, that would supersede the NAGPRA process. According to the website, the WIIN Act "prompts The Army Corps of Engineers to transfer control of the remains to the Washington State Department of Archaeology and Historic Preservation (DAHP) within 90 days of December 16, 2016, on the condition that DAHP return the remains to the claimant tribes." On February 17, 2017, the remains of Kennewick Man/the Ancient One were reburied in the presence of members of five Columbia Plateau tribes, including the Umatilla (Cary 2017).

Indigenous people in the United States are not the only ones concerned with the disposition of human remains unearthed by archaeologists and others. In Australia, Aboriginal people have successfully pressed for the return of the remains of their ancestors, remains that were often collected unethically, sometimes through grave robbing and even murder. In recent years, the Australian government has established programs for the repatriation of cultural material and human remains that are held in Australian museums or other institutions and has worked to secure the repatriation of Aboriginal remains from outside Australia. The Australian Archaeological Association has supported these initiatives.

According to the Australian government:

The aim of the program is to repatriate all ancestral remains and secret sacred objects from the eligible museums to their communities of origin. The four specific objectives are to: identify the origins of all ancestral remains and secret sacred objects held in the museums where possible; notify all communities who have ancestral remains and secret sacred objects held in the museums; arrange for repatriation where and when it is requested; appropriately store ancestral remains and secret sacred objects held in the museums at the request of the relevant community. (Department of Communications, Information Technology, and the Arts 2005)

How Is the Past Being Plundered?

Many people in the world were shocked and appalled in March 2001, when the extremist Taliban government of Afghanistan decided to destroy the Bamiyan Buddhas, two giant sculptures carved into the face of a cliff about 1,500 years ago (Figure 6.13). Although almost no Buddhists live in Afghanistan today, these sculptures had long been part of the cultural heritage of the Afghan people. Despite world condemnation of this decision

that included a delegation from the Islamic Conference representing 55 Muslim nations, the Taliban insisted that these human images were impious and destroyed them, along with even older objects in the national museum. This act shocked many people, perhaps not only because it seemed so narrow-minded and thoughtless but also because the statues were irreplaceable examples of human creative power. To make sense of such destruction, anthropologists speak of *heritage regimes* in which material remains like the Bamiyan Buddhas are seen to be entangled in political and economic activities, primarily as these are managed by nation-states (Geismar 2015, 72). Defenders of the continued protection of the Buddhas accept the appropriateness of a heritage regime in which such material objects are seen to be as universally valuable and deserving of protection, either by nation-states or by international organizations like UNESCO. However, Geismar explains that the Taliban followers who destroyed the Buddhas may be understood as participating in an *antiheritage movement*, which "negates the very idea of heritage itself" (Geismar 2015, 80). Therefore, their destruction of the Buddhas

a

b

FIGURE 6.13 (a, b) Many people in the world were shocked when the Taliban leaders of Afghanistan blew up the 1,500-year-old statues of the Buddha despite worldwide requests to save these examples of the heritage of the Afghan people.

IN THEIR OWN WORDS

Rescue Archaeology in Europe

In the United States, Cultural Resources Management (CRM) archaeology plays an important role in carrying out research on archaeological sites threatened by road building or other infrastructure projects. In Europe, these issues are the focus of a field originally called "rescue archaeology" after World War II, but that has been called "preventive archaeology" since 1979. The term comes from the French archéologie préventive, which aims to prevent the destruction of archaeological sites (analogous to the way that "preventive medicine" aims to prevent outbreaks of dangerous disease). The term originated in France but is now used in scientific policy debates throughout Europe. Preventive archaeology was inspired by CRM in the United States, but developed differently in different parts of Europe. In the following excerpt from his essay "Rescue Archaeology: A European View," French archaeologist Jean-Paul Demoule explains how changing political and economic policies in France and other European countries in recent years undermined previous understandings about the role of the state in the protection of archaeological heritage.

The gradual introduction of a competitive market for preventive archaeology was initially undertaken without real debate, some countries not being immediately affected, while others considered it an inevitable fate (Oebbecke 1998). However, discussion on the issue has gradually been mobilized, especially across multiple European agencies or programs. Two conceptions compete, reflecting two visions of the state. On one hand, in the tradition of the Enlightenment and the French Revolution, the nation is a community of citizens, united by a common destiny, and which manages goods and services, among other elements. On the other hand, there is only a multitude of individuals; consumers, with no links to one another, who choose to buy or not buy goods and services from producers in competition.

For partisans of private, commercial archaeology, developers are clients, for whom they need to be as efficient as possible. This is why preventive archaeology is often referred to as developer-led archaeology (Bradley et al. 2010) or developer-funded archaeology, as if it were the developer who decided on the excavation. This view has created a kind of archaeology that has allowed for unprecedented development of the production of archaeological data, the end result of which is sometimes viewed as a gold rush. At the same time, in an attempt to regulate the market of archaeology, it is considered appropriate that archaeologists organize themselves in professional associations, along the model of the Register of Professional Archaeologists in the United States. This is, in fact, the case in the United Kingdom with the Institute for Archaeologists (formerly the Institute of Field Archaeology; http://www.archaeologists.net). A code of ethics is supposed to define the rights and duties of these archaeologists, including respect for the basic rules of scientific research (http://www.concernedhistorians.org/content/ethicarcha.html). A public authority is also to define standards (see Willems & Brand 2004) and exercise quality control. However, this practice is complicated by the fact that control of archaeological work a posteriori is hardly possible because the excavated site no longer exists. This overall vision thus underpins the organization of archaeology in a number of European countries, and it has been explicitly defended in various articles (e.g., Thomas 2002; Wheaton 2002; Carver 2007; Aitchison 2009; van den Dries 2011, among others).

For those who oppose the development of private commercial archaeology, developers are not clients. They are companies whose projects are often designed to make money and who endanger the archaeological heritage of a nation's citizens. This is why they must pay a tax, designed to help compensate for the destruction and to preserve a part of the archaeological information. It is therefore the state—as an emanation of the community of citizens—that must organize these preventive excavations through public research institutions responsible for defining national research programs and publishing the results of the excavations. In fact, the development of preventive archaeology is due to the reinforcement of state legislation and has nothing to do with the interests of private companies to carry out the work. The codes of ethics have no binding value (and mainly concern a Protestant cultural ethos).

The notion of commercial competition in archaeology is based on a fundamental misunderstanding. In fact, developers do not want to buy the best archaeology possible but seek only the company that will release their land as soon as possible at the least cost. If competition exists in the scientific field, it is to produce not the cheapest

IN THEIR OWN WORDS

research possible, but instead the best research possible. And if private research exists in general, the quality of its production (a drug, an aircraft, a weapon, etc.) can be controlled a posteriori. Furthermore, private research tends to focus on more profitable products. This is why private pharmaceutical research, for example, focuses on the profitable diseases of rich countries—at the expense of unprofitable diseases in poor countries.

Note as well that the excavations of private companies are rarely published adequately, if at all. Moreover, in the United States, for example, the private archaeologists of Cultural Resource Management, which account for perhaps more than 50% of the ~12,000 professional archaeologists in the country, very rarely attend scientific meetings such as the Annual Meeting of the Society for American Archaeology. The term professional archaeologist, which private archaeologists give themselves, is also questionable because it implies that academic archaeologists are not professionals. Furthermore, the purely economic logic of private archaeological companies makes them sensitive to economic fluctuations. As such, hundreds of British archaeologists have lost their jobs because of the global financial crisis that started in the fall of 2008, as have 80% of private Irish archaeologists and a significant number in Spain (Schlanger and Aitchison 2010). In contrast, national public institutions allow for the practice of homogeneous scientific standards for the study and publication of excavations, and they offer a guarantee of employment. This is why the model of private commercial archaeology has been criticized by a number of archaeologists

(Cumberpatch and Blinkhorn 2001; Demoule 2002a,b, 2011; Chadwick 2003; Kristiansen 2009; Schlanger and Salas Rossenback 2010). In any case, it seems impossible to separate the real practices of archaeology from their ideological backgrounds (Pluciennik 2001, Hamilakis and Duke 2007, Kolen 2010, Bernbeck and McGuire 2011). The economic crisis since 2008 has demonstrated both the weakness of a model based solely on the market and the need for state regulations. Moreover, some economists had already announced these weaknesses before the crisis (Stiglitz 2003), and as early as 2004, the European Union had become aware of the limits of the market for public services of general interest (Green Pap. 2004). . . .

For the past four decades, thanks to preventive archaeology and growing legislative protection, Europe has experienced an unprecedented explosion of knowledge about its own past. . . . This explosion of data has also revolutionized the very approach to archaeology: it is no longer the study of isolated sites, but the study of whole territories, something that has been enabled by excavation prior to major development projects. . . . Nevertheless, a certain number of essential questions concerning preventive archaeology are still under debate. . . . The ability of preventive archaeology to produce compelling and useful knowledge for our reflection on trajectories of the past, as well as on the futures of human societies, supports its existence and the efforts made for its continued practice.

Source: Demoule 2012, 618–22.

cannot simply be reduced to an extreme form of Islamic iconoclasm. Rather, Geismar insists, this destructive action is better viewed as an effort by the Taliban in particular to install "a politics around the governance of culture at the center of its own regime" (Geismar 2015, 80). She cites a Taliban representative who argued that "the Buddhas were destroyed in the wake of a UNESCO visit to Kabul, which made clear that the international community was prepared to spend money to preserve heritage but not to support starving Afghans in the region" (Geismar 2015, 80–81).

These Taliban actions are unusually blatant and violent, but antiheritage resistance comes in a variety of forms. For example, many family members of individuals who died in the attacks on the World Trade Center on September 11, 2001, struggled with government officials about how that event should be memorialized in the

September 11 Memorial and Museum. Geismar quotes Chip Colwell-Chanthaponh, who criticized the museum not only for failing to consult with the families of the victims but also for engaging in questionable practices in its management of the victims' remains (Geismar 2015, 81).

Nevertheless, destruction of the human past on a much greater scale goes on every day as a consequence of land development, agriculture, and looting for sale to collectors. The construction of roads, dams, office buildings, housing developments, libraries, subways, and so on has enormous potential to damage or destroy evidence of the past. As mechanized agriculture has spread across the world, the tractors and deep plows tear across settlement sites and field monuments. Although construction, development, and agriculture cannot be stopped, they can be made more sensitive to the potential damage they can do.

Unfortunately, such cannot be said for looting and the market in stolen antiquities. There is nothing really new about looting—the tombs of the pharaohs of Egypt were looted in their own day—but the scale today surpasses anything that has come before. It is safe to say that any region of the world with archaeological sites also has organized looting, and the devastation looters leave behind makes any scientific analysis of a site impossible. We have seen how important it is for archaeologists to record the precise placement of every object they excavate. When that context is destroyed, so is the archaeological value of a site. "In the American Southwest, 90% of the Classic Mimbres sites (c. 1000 C.E.) have now been looted or destroyed. In southwestern Colorado, 60% of prehistoric Anasazi sites have been vandalized. Pothunters work at night, equipped with two-way radios, scanners, and lookouts. They can be prosecuted under the present legislation only if caught red-handed, which is almost impossible" (Renfrew and Bahn 2008, 563). Looters steal to make money. Buyers, including museums and private collectors, have been willing to overlook the details of the process by which ancient objects come into their hands. Although museum owners have taken some steps to make sure that they purchase (or accept as gifts) only objects that have been exported legally from their countries of origin, private collectors remain free to feed on the illegal destruction of the heritage of the world's people (Figure 6.14).

In the United States, one sign of progress has been a series of legislative actions at the federal, state, and local levels that require the consideration of environmental and cultural factors in the use of federal, state, or local funds for development. At the most basic level, projects involving federal land or federal funds (highway funds, e.g.) must file an Environmental Impact Assessment, which includes attention to cultural resources—the material record of the human past—located in affected sites. To meet this federal requirement, the archaeological specialty of cultural resources management (CRM) was developed. CRM is an attempt to ensure that cultural resources threatened by projects are properly managed—"recorded, evaluated, protected, or, if necessary, salvaged" (Fagan and DeCorse 2005, 483). CRM is a multimillion-dollar undertaking; the major source of employment for archaeologists; and is practiced by private companies, federal agencies, universities, and individuals. The legal grounds for CRM developed out of a concern with conservation, rather than research. Over time, however, it has become clear that CRM archaeology contributes in a very significant way not just to the preservation of the past but also to basic archaeological research and theory. In this way,

FIGURE 6.14   The looting of archaeological sites continues to be a serious problem because the heritage of the world's people is destroyed.

we see again how archaeologists have become the stewards of the past, a task that will require great energy and all of their skill.

What Are the Critical Issues in Contemporary Archaeology?

As we have seen, contemporary social issues lead archaeologists to rethink how they study the human past. We now consider three examples of contemporary archaeology that illustrate these developments.

Archaeology and Gender

By the 1980s, awareness of the unequal treatment of women in modern European and American societies had led archaeologists (both women and men) to examine why women's contributions had been systematically written out of the archaeological record. Building on anthropological studies of living people, **feminist archaeology** rejected biological determinism of sex roles, arguing that cultural and historical factors were responsible for how a society allocated tasks and that this allocation could change over time. The goal was to develop a view of the past that "replaces focus on remains with a focus on people as active social agents" (Conkey and Gero 1991, 15).

Feminist archaeology did not depend on new technological breakthroughs in excavation methods to pursue this goal. Rather, using what they already knew about living human societies, together with available historical documents, feminist archaeologists asked new kinds of questions. For example, Joan Gero (1991) drew attention to male bias in discussions of the oldest, best-known collections of human artifacts: stone tools. Gero showed how traditional archaeological discussion of stone-tool technologies focused on highly formalized, elaborately retouched, standardized core tools. This focus, together with the assumption that such tools were made by men to hunt with, turns men and their activities into the driving force of cultural evolution. It simultaneously downplays or ignores the far more numerous flake tools that were probably made and used by women in such tasks as processing food or working wood and leather. Gero cited ethnographic and historical reports that describe women as active makers of stone tools, including more elaborate core tools, exposing as false the supposition that women are not strong or smart enough to produce them.

Gero then applied her findings to her analysis of a multilayered site at Huaricoto in highland Peru. The lowest occupation level at Huaricoto dates from a period in which the site was a ceremonial center visited by foragers who apparently made elaborate biface (two-sided) core tools out of imported stone in a workshop on the site. The most recent occupation level dated from a later period, when the site was no longer a ritual center but had become a residential settlement whose inhabitants used many flake tools made of local stone for a variety of subsistence tasks. Gero pointed out that "the flake tool performs many of the same actions unceremoniously that bifaces perform in a ritualistic setting" (1991, 184). She suggests that the change from ceremonial center to village settlement probably involved a shift not in the use of stone tools but rather in their social significance: male status may have been connected with stone-tool production during the early period but had probably become connected with some other kind of prestige goods instead (perhaps ceramics or textiles) by the later period. Stone tools continued to be made and used, but they were utilitarian flake tools, and their makers and users were most likely women.

Insights from feminist archaeology inform more recent work in **gender archaeology**, which "addresses the needs of contemporary gender studies for an understanding of how people come to understand themselves as different from others; how people represent these differences; and how others react to such claims" (Joyce 2008, 17). Contemporary gender studies asks, for example, why archaeologists often assume that the meanings of artifacts from all societies across space and over time should be interpreted in terms of a universal male–female gender binary. As Rosemary Joyce (2008) observes, "The experiences of people in the contemporary world are actually a good deal more varied than those expected under the normative two-sex/two-gender model" (18). Gender archaeologists have found that new questions can be asked about variation in sex, gender, and other kinds of human difference in past societies if attention shifts away from the universals and focuses instead on detailed contextual features of specific archaeological sites.

Focusing on site-specific details affects the kinds of interpretations that archaeologists make. First, the meaning of a common artifact, whether found in a household rubbish dump or in a burial site, cannot be assumed to remain unchanging over time. This insight was central to Gero's reinterpretation of stone tools and their use at Huaricoto. Gero's approach also illustrates a second point: archaeological analyses that focus on the highly elaborated artifact can downplay or ignore patterns that would be visible if all relevant artifacts, ordinary and extraordinary, are considered. Joyce (2008) argues that Paleolithic figurines depicting females with exaggerated breasts and bellies have been misunderstood. Because of a widely shared assumption that *all* figurines depicting human females had to be "fertility symbols," archaeologists have tended to ignore other contemporary figurines that did not easily fit such an interpretation. For example, the 30,000-year-old central European Paleolithic site of Dolní Věstonice yielded figurines representing animals and human males as well as human females; moreover, the only figurines depicted wearing woven clothing were some of the female figurines (Figure 6.15). Since most female and all male figurines lacked any representation of clothing, archaeologists now suggest that the female figurines with clothing represent a few women at this time and place who "gained individual status from their skill at producing textiles" (Joyce 2008, 15). This interpretation is strengthened by evidence from contemporary burials that clothing of men and women

---

feminist archaeology A research approach that explores why women's contributions have been systematically written out of the archaeological record and suggests new approaches to the human past that include such contributions.

gender archaeology Archaeological research that draws on insights from contemporary gender studies to investigate how people come to recognize themselves as different from others, how people represent these differences, and how others react to such claims.

FIGURE 6.15   Sculpture head of woman, Dolní Věstonice. The Dolní Věstonice site in the Czech Republic has yielded extensive numbers of figures, some of which seem to represent women of status.

was not differentiated by gender and did not resemble the images of clothing portrayed on figurines (Joyce 2008, 15).

Third, Joyce stresses the need for archaeologists to think of material artifacts "as having had lives of their own . . . made, used, and discarded, and during which people's experiences and associations with them would have varied" (2008, 28). Focusing on the social lives of individual artifacts shifts attention away from artifacts to the individuals who made those artifacts and highlights the variety of motivations they may have had for making them the way they did. It also draws attention to the likelihood that all images were not accepted at face value but instead offered "a means for the circulation of propositions that might be contested" (Joyce 2008, 16). As a result, the same images might well have meant different things to different members of the social group that produced or used them. This approach provides "a critical basis for challenges to orthodox interpretations that might otherwise ignore complexities in human societies now as much as in the past" (16, 17).

historical archaeology   The study of archaeological sites associated with written records, frequently the study of post-European contact sites in the world.

The value of such an approach is displayed in the work of bioarchaeologist Sandra Hollimon, who was faced with interpreting remains of Chumash burials in California. As Joyce explains, contemporary Chumash culture traditionally recognized a third gender—"two-spirited" men whose status is neither male nor female. Moreover, as is the case in a number of Native American societies, such two-spirited individuals were often skilled craftspeople who were given baskets in exchange for their work. Hollimon first expected that the graves of two-spirited individuals would stand out from the graves of women or other men because they would contain male skeletons accompanied by baskets. It turned out, however, that baskets were found together with the skeletal remains of both women and men. This prompted Hollimon to wonder if gender distinctions were not important in Chumash mortuary practices. She looked for other patterns of difference in the remains and discovered a typically female form of spinal arthritis in the skeletons of two young males. This form of arthritis was associated with regular use of digging sticks, typically women's work, but also the work of two-spirited men.

These two particular male skeletons had been buried both with digging stick weights and with baskets, which strengthened the conclusion that they belonged to two-spirited males. However, digging sticks and baskets were tools traditionally associated with Chumash *undertakers*, who could be either two-spirited men or postmenopausal women. Hollimon concluded that the *status* of undertaker apparently was more significant in Chumash burial practices than the *gender* of the individual being buried. "In Chumash society, these people helped the spirits of the dead make the transition to their next stage of life. To be able to do this, they needed a special spiritual status. This special status was limited to those whose sexual activity could not lead to childbirth" (Joyce 2008, 60). The lesson is clear: "not finding three burial patterns led to a realization that sex may not have been the most significant basis for the identity of these people. . . . Genders were not permanent categorical identities, but rather distinctive performances related to sexuality that could change over a person's life" (61).

Collaborative Approaches to Studying the Past

Janet Spector was one of the first archaeologists in the United States to initiate a collaborative research project with the descendants of the people who once occupied the sites she excavated. Her work in Minnesota is an example of **historical archaeology** (Figure 6.16)—the study (in this case) of post-European contact sites in North America. Like other feminist archaeologists,

Archaeology as a Tool of Civic Engagement

Barbara J. Little and Paul A. Shackel (2007) use the term *civic engagement* to refer to an important direction in contemporary archaeology. Civic engagement in archaeology refers to involvement and participation in public life, especially in directing people's attention to "the historical roots and present-day manifestations of contemporary social justice issues." Civic engagement also refers to connecting archaeologists and the work they do to the communities that are connected in one way or another to archaeological sites and the history they embody (46).

One example of civic engagement comes from Virginia and the site of one of the most famous episodes in US popular history—the arrival in 1607 of English colonists who founded Jamestown and the supposed interactions of Chief Powhatan, John Smith, and Pocahontas. Martin Gallivan and Daniehalle Moretti-Langholtz (2007) have been involved with the first archaeological excavation at Werowocomoco, the site of the Powhatan chiefdom. This research has shed light on the history of Native life at the site from its founding in about 1200 CE to its abandonment by Powhatan in 1609 because the English colonists were too close. The research has been strongly engaged with the wider communities of Virginia, especially Native communities. The history of Native peoples in Virginia is a troubled one in which the more prominent biracial divide between whites and African Americans seemed to overwhelm the Native presence. Indeed, in 1924, people of Native descent were defined by the Racial Integrity Act legally as "colored persons," the same category used for people of African descent. Interracial marriage was prohibited, and Native children were forced to attend schools for "colored persons."

> The sting of the Racial Integrity Act, which remained in force until 1968, is still felt in Virginia's indigenous community. Native people were denied the right to self-identify as Native people, making it impossible for them to enter the civic arena as representatives of their respective communities. Despite the fact that the Pamunkeys and Mattaponis had long-held reservation lands within the commonwealth, official state policy maintained that there were no longer indigenous Indians in Virginia. (Gallivan and Moretti-Langholtz 2007, 54)

Finally, during the 1980s, eight Indian tribes were recognized by the Virginia Commonwealth; and when NAGPRA became law in 1990, representatives of the tribes worked closely with archaeologists in the reburial of remains that had been held in collections.

Engagements of this kind with descendant communities served as the foundations of the Werowocomoco research project: "from its inception, the WRG [Werowocomoco Research Group] has worked toward a model of archaeological research on Native sites in the Chesapeake that includes close Native collaboration at every stage" (Gallivan and Moretti-Langholtz 2007, 58). Indeed, when the WRG found the site they believed to be Werowocomoco, they requested a meeting with the Virginia

Council on Indians to ensure that tribal leaders would have the information about the site and the excavation before it was announced to the public. Members of the WRG met privately with the tribal chiefs to introduce them to the research team and the owner of the property on which the site had been found. They also outlined a long-term plan to study the site with the close involvement of the Native communities. A visit to the site was scheduled, and a Native advisory board was established. Tribal representatives presented their perspectives on the site and its history. "Though these perspectives varied, several tribal leaders expressed a powerful connection to Werowocomoco as the historic center of the Powhatan chiefdom and as a modern place for renewing Virginia Indians' influence on representations of the Native past. Others encouraged us to pursue research that focuses on the power and social complexity of the Powhatan chiefdom during the years prior to 1607" (Gallivan and Moretti-Langholtz 2007, 59–60).

The research team shares all information with the advisory board, including minutes from meetings and financial reports. In recent years, some Virginia Indians have gotten involved in the excavations themselves. Among other things, this has had the effect of enabling one member of the Pamunkey Tribal Council to have a better understanding of the archaeological research process when evaluating CRM proposals made to the tribe. On days set aside for public visitation, partners from the Pamunkey tribe speak with visitors about the excavations and about their feelings regarding archaeological research involving their ancestors (Gallivan and Moretti-Langholtz 2007, 61).

But many archaeologists involved with community engagement want to go beyond public outreach. As archaeologists engage with a wide range of publics and present their research, new topics and ways of discussing old topics may emerge, and some of those discussions may contradict existing historical narratives. "Taking archaeological practice from civic engagement and toward social justice, conceived of as equity, honesty, and tolerance across segments of a society, represents a difficult challenge that we have not begun to master" (Gallivan and Moretti-Langholtz 2007, 61). Gallivan and Moretti-Langholtz think that the research at Werowocomoco has the potential to expand the restrictive narratives about Native peoples in Virginia that have dominated public and academic discourse and to challenge the received stories of the past. Their research alone was not sufficient to push this transformation; but by giving descendant populations a central role in the recovery of the history of their ancestors, it opened a place for new discussions regarding the Native past. Such discussions may help create an indigenous archaeology, one in which Native peoples "become full partners in representations concerning their past" (Gallivan and Moretti-Langholtz 2007, 62). This is a route for archaeology to follow in contributing to social justice in the wider societies in which archaeologists work. ■

FIGURE 6.16   Historical archaeologists, shown here excavating in the Roman Forum, supplement written documents with records of settlement patterns, structures, and artifacts, which reveal valuable information about the past that was never written down.

Spector (1993) wanted to shift attention from the artifacts to the people who made them, from a preoccupation with active men and passive women to a more realistic assessment of active women and men and from a focus on the remains as evidence of European contact to what these remains suggested about "Indian responses or resistance to European expansion and domination" (6).

In 1980, Spector and her team began to dig at a site near Jordan, Minnesota, known by the Dakota as *Inyan Ceyak Atonwan*, or "Village at the Rapids." She examined historical documents that referred to the site for clues about what tasks were carried on by men and women at the site as a guide to what kinds of material remains to look for. After several seasons, concerned that her work might be meaningless or offensive to the Dakota, Spector met a Dakota man who was a descendant of a man named Mazomani, one of the original inhabitants of the Village at the Rapids. Eventually, other descendants of Mazomani visited the site. By the 1985–1986 season, Dakota and non-Dakota were collaborating in teaching Dakota language, oral history, ethnobotany, ecology, and history at the site while digging continued. A Dakota elder conducted a pipe ceremony at the site

shortly before the field season began, which symbolized for Spector the Dakota people's permission to work there (Spector 1993).

Since the early 1980s, collaborative archaeological research of this kind has become increasingly common. Renfrew and Bahn (2008), for example, report on a multidisciplinary research project inside Kakadu National Park in the Northern Territory of Australia that began in 1981. Archaeologists wanted to learn more about the earliest occupation of tropical Australia, which began more than 23,000 years ago, and Kakadu National Park was an ideal place to look: the park contains a number of rockshelters filled with rich material traces of ancient human occupation, including rock paintings as old as those found in European caves such as Lascaux. Archaeologists wanted to build on previous work and to test the proposal made by an earlier researcher, George Chaloupka, who argued that the rock art in the region reflected changes in the environment triggered by rising sea levels (Renfrew and Bahn 2008, 521).

But Rhys Jones, the team leader from the Australian National University, knew that the site was legally owned by the local Aborigine community, whose permission would be needed before any excavation could begin. The Aborigine community was willing to give permission for the project, but they wanted to ensure that the dig was carried out in a way that was responsible and respectful. They insisted that one member of the community supervise the project, primarily "to protect the diggers from doing something that could bring practical or ritual danger: the totemic geography of a region contains some 'dangerous places,' into which archaeologists might stray through ignorance" (Renfrew and Bahn 2008, 521). The archaeologists also had to agree to complete work at one site before moving on to another and to return all disturbed areas to the condition in which they had been prior to the excavation. But Aboriginal involvement in the project did not stop there. "Senior Aborigine men representing the relevant groups accompanied the team on field trips and carefully monitored the excavations, while trainee Aboriginal rangers helped in the laboratory, and were instructed in archaeological procedures" (Renfrew and Bahn 2008, 522). When the project was completed, the researchers did indeed find evidence that verified Chaloupka's hypothesis, but two other findings were perhaps even more exciting. The first was the discovery of plant remains as much as 6,000 years old, preserved thanks to the unusual microclimate present in one rockshelter. The second came from a second rockshelter and consisted of pieces of red ochre, a pigment used by ancient human populations in many parts of the world. These pieces were 53,000 years old, had been worked by hand, and might have been the sources of pigment for some of the rock art. Renfrew and Bahn (2008) judge this project "very successful" (528), and one measure of its success was the way it provided a model—as did Spector's work—of finding a way to do archaeology while working together with an indigenous community that had its own stake in the way the project was carried out, as well as in the outcome.

Cosmopolitan Archaeologies

A variety of far-reaching changes have swept the world since the end of the Cold War in 1989. As we will see in later chapters, these changes have affected the way all anthropologists do research, and archaeologists are no exception. Collaborative projects between local communities and archaeologists have become increasingly common in recent years, but these collaborations themselves have been affected by a number of broader changes. For example, global tourism has mushroomed, and huge numbers of tourists from all over the world now want to visit archaeological sites such as Machu Picchu or Kakaku National Park, both of which have been named UNESCO World Heritage Sites.

As we saw in the case of Machu Picchu, a lot of money can be made managing flows of wealthy tourists to well-known cultural heritage sites (see Figure 6.10). When tourist traffic threatens to destroy such sites, therefore, it is not merely the ruins themselves that are at stake; so are the livelihoods of local people and governments. Moreover, powerless minorities with traditional connections to these sites frequently find themselves shoved aside as national and international institutions step in and take over. In the past, most archaeologists tried to do their research while avoiding local legal and political involvements, hoping to achieve "a 'do no harm' model of coexistence" (Meskell 2009, 5). Today, many archaeologists have adopted the view that their first obligation should be to those local (and often marginalized) people with traditional connections to the archaeological sites where they work. But more and more archaeologists are finding that this kind of single-minded commitment is increasingly problematic because they and their local allies must find a way to deal with a range of other local and global stakeholders who have their own, often conflicting, ideas about how cultural heritage should be managed.

Like many contemporary cultural anthropologists (see Chapter 8), some archaeologists have been moved by these struggles to question a view of the world that divides it up into a patchwork quilt of distinct, neatly bounded "cultures," each of which embodies a unique heritage that must be protected from change at all costs. Again, like many of their cultural anthropologist colleagues, these archaeologists have concluded that the only way forward is to cultivate a "cosmopolitan" point of view. For many cultural anthropologists, **cosmopolitanism** means being able to move with ease from one cultural setting to another. Cultural anthropologists regularly develop cosmopolitan skills and awareness as they move in and out of fieldwork situations. Moreover, people everywhere—tourists, immigrants, or refugees, for example—have crafted a variety of different kinds of cosmopolitan skills to cope successfully with movement from one cultural setting to another. These movements have become the focus of new "multisited" forms of ethnographic research.

For archaeologists, adopting a cosmopolitan orientation means giving up universalistic assumptions about the meaning of the past. It means acknowledging, for example, that preservation of material artifacts may in fact sometimes go against the wishes of local groups with close connections to those artifacts. Dealing with such challenges means that cosmopolitan

cosmopolitanism Being able to move with ease from one cultural setting to another.

archaeologists will no longer be able to avoid involvement in legal and political debates about the future of cultural heritage, even as they come to recognize that their views may carry less weight than the views of other stakeholders. "Cosmopolitans suppose . . . that all cultures have enough overlap in their vocabulary of values to begin a conversation. Yet counter to some universalists, they do not presume they can craft a consensus" (Meskell 2009, 7).

Archaeologist Chip Colwell-Chanthaphonh, for example, has asked, "Can the destruction of heritage ever be ethically justified? If so, by what principle, why, and under what conditions?" He speaks of "the preservation paradox"—that is, "the concept of preservation is itself culturally conceived," with the result that "one group's notion of cultural preservation can be another group's notion of cultural destruction" (2009, 143). Colwell-Chanthaphonh describes disagreements about the ethics of preservation of artifacts valued in different ways by different groups in the American Southwest. Commitment to a "salvage ethic" led nineteenth-century collectors to "rescue" sculptures that the Zuni purposefully left to deteriorate in sacred shrines. "This is the core of the salvage ethic, the urge to 'preserve' objects by physically protecting them. But for the Zunis, such acts that aspired to cultural preservation were in fact acts of cultural destruction" (Colwell-Chanthaphonh 2009, 146).

Conflict over whether to preserve or to destroy ancient rock carvings is an issue that divides the Navajo people and the Hopi people, both of whom have lived in the American Southwest for a very long time. Hopi people wish to preserve these rock carvings, which they regard as "monuments to Hopi history, proof of ancestral homelands and clan migrations" (Colwell-Chanthaphonh 2009, 149). Navajo people, however, regard all ruins from the past, including these rock carvings, as products of human evil or the activity of witches. Contact with the rock carvings is believed to cause sickness or other misfortunes, and curing ceremonies involve the destruction of the carvings. These days, moreover, the Hopi and Navajo peoples are far from being the only groups who assign meaning to carvings and ancient ruins in the American Southwest (Figure 6.17). As Colwell-Chanthaphonh points out,

> The ancient ruins of Chaco Canyon in New Mexico are at once a Hopi ancestral site, a locus of Navajo spiritual power, a ritual space for New Agers, an archaeological and scientific resource, a National Historical Park of the United States, and a UNESCO World Heritage Site. . . . Clearly, in anthropological as much as ethical terms, such a complex convergence of people, communities, and institutions cannot be reduced to just intra-nationalist, nationalist, or internationalist

FIGURE 6.17 Preservation and use of material artifacts or ruins, such as the ruins at Chaco Canyon in New Mexico, can be complicated by the range of different and sometimes opposed interests that different groups bring to them.

> claims. The key ethical problem . . . is not so much categorizing rights but trying to illuminate the relationships. (2009, 151)

This is the reason a cosmopolitan approach appeals to him: "we must develop a sophisticated understanding of how heritage works from the individual level, to the community, to the nation and beyond it. . . . A just solution cannot simply pick out the rights of one group but must instead interweave these multiple values" (2009, 152). Colwell-Chanthaphonh recommends what he calls "the principle of complex stewardship": that is, "we should maximize the integrity of heritage objects for the good of the greatest number of people, but not absolutely" (160). To maximize the integrity of heritage objects would support those who want objects preserved. Concern for the good of the greatest number, however, would mean that the positions of other stakeholders with different views would also be included and might carry great weight, especially if they outnumbered the preservationists. Even then, however, the majority position might not necessarily carry the day because special consideration would need to be given to those whose ancestors made the objects or who are closely connected to them in other ways. The principle of complex stewardship is not a ready-made solution to disputes about the management of cultural heritage; rather, it is "a frame archaeologists can use to begin deliberations on ethical predicaments" (Colwell-Chanthaphonh 2009, 161). Finding solutions, for cosmopolitans, involves negotiations whose outcome cannot be predicted in advance.

Chapter Summary

1. By the end of the last Ice Age, cultural variation, not biological species differences, distinguished human populations from one another. Archaeologists interpret cultural variation and cultural change in the human past. Archaeology has changed focus over time, from reconstructing material remains or lifeways of past human groups to explaining the cultural processes that led to particular kinds of material culture to emphasizing the role of human agency and the power of ideas and values in the construction of past cultures.

2. Archaeologists trace patterns in past human cultures by identifying sites and regions of human occupation and by recovering artifacts, features, and other remains of human activity from these sites. In all cases, they are concerned with recording information about the context in which these remains are found.

3. The survival of archaeological remains depends on what they were made of and the conditions they experienced over time. Very dry and very cold climates and oxygen-free, waterlogged settings preserve many organic remains that would decay under other circumstances. Natural catastrophes, such as mudslides and lava flows, sometimes bury sites and preserve their contents remarkably well. Ethnoarchaeology and taphonomy are two methods archaeologists use to help them interpret the meaning of the remains they find.

4. Before archaeologists begin their work, they survey the region they are interested in. Surveys, whether on the ground or from the air, can yield important information that cannot be gained from excavations. Excavations are done when archaeologists want to know a lot about a little of a site. The style of excavation depends on the kind of site being excavated. As the excavation proceeds, archaeologists keep careful records to preserve contextual information. Much of the final analysis of the remains is carried out in laboratories, but some archaeologists promote the integration of discovery and analysis by bringing theorists to excavations in progress to engage in "interpretation at the trowel's edge." Storage and retrieval of archaeological data in digital databases presents challenges and also offers rich possibilities.

5. Artifacts and structures from a particular time and place in a site are grouped together in assemblages; similar assemblages from many sites are grouped together in archaeological cultures. Archaeological cultures are constructed by archaeologists to reflect patterns in their data, so they cannot be assumed to represent specific ethnic groups that existed in the past. Archaeologically reconstructed societies are classified using a taxonomy of forms of human society that was developed in conjunction with cultural anthropologists in the middle of the twentieth century. Its major categories are bands, tribes, chiefdoms, and states. In recent years, some anthropologists have objected that these categories seem too stereotyped and appear to imply a universal direction to cultural change that does not accurately reflect the archaeological record. However, these categories can still help us make sense of the archaeological and historical record when put to work in unconventional ways.

6. In recent years, many archaeologists have rethought their traditional methods. Feminist archaeologists explored why women's contributions have been systematically written out of the archaeological record. Gender archaeologists have questioned the assumption that a male–female gender division is universal and have asked instead how variation in sex, gender, and other kinds of difference can be inferred from archaeological remains of past societies. Collaborative forms of archaeological research have increasingly involved cooperation between scientists and members of groups with past or current connections to the sites under investigation. In recent years, however, archaeological sites and artifacts have become

Chapter Summary *(continued)*

the target of claims by a number of additional groups, including local and national governments, international institutions such as UNESCO, and tourists. These groups do not always agree about the value of cultural heritage preservation or about who has the right to decide the fate

of remains from the past. Many archaeologists have concluded that it is vital to develop a cosmopolitan understanding of the claims of these varied stakeholders and to promote conversations among them, even if achieving consensus may not be possible.

For Review

1. What do archaeologists do?
2. Compare and contrast survey archaeology and excavation.
3. What kinds of questions do archaeologists ask about the human past, and what kinds of evidence do they look for to answer these questions?
4. List the different human subsistence strategies presented in the text. How have cultural anthropologists and archaeologists contributed to the identification of these strategies? What are the limitations of traditional taxonomies of these strategies?
5. Make a table of the characteristics of bands, tribes, chiefdoms, and states. How have cultural anthropologists and archaeologists together made use of these categories in their work? How do they help? What are their drawbacks? What does it mean to think "against the grain" about these categories?

6. Who owns the past? In your answer, draw on the discussion of various answers to this question presented in the chapter.
7. What is NAGPRA, and why are its requirements so important to archaeologists?
8. Explain why the looting of archaeological sites is so problematic for archaeological attempts to reconstruct the human past.
9. Using case studies in which gender considerations inform archaeological work, describe feminist archaeology.
10. What are collaborative approaches to studying the past? Illustrate your answers with examples from the text.
11. What does it mean to speak of a "cosmopolitan" orientation in archaeology? Refer in your answer to the example given in the text.

Key Terms

archaeological record   172
archaeology   172
artifacts   172
band   182
chiefdom   183

cosmopolitanism   197
digital heritage   179
ethnoarchaeology   173
excavation   177
features   172
feminist archaeology   193

gender archaeology   193
historical archaeology   194
sites   172
sodalities   183
state   183

status   183
subsistence strategies   180
survey   175
tribe   182

Suggested Readings

Cary, Annette. 2017. *Tri City Herald, Tribes return ancient Kennewick Man to the ground.* https://www.tri-cityherald.com/news/local/article133780309.html

Fagan, Brian. 2012. *Archaeology: A brief introduction,* 11th ed. Englewood Cliffs, NJ: Prentice Hall. *The latest edition of a brief, classic introductory archaeology text.*

Feder, Kenneth L. 2014. *Frauds, myths, and mysteries: Science and pseudoscience in archaeology,* 8th ed. New York:

McGraw–Hill. *Feder shows how scientific archaeological methods can be used to expose dubious claims about the past.*

Hodder, Ian (ed.). 2010. *Religion in the emergence of civilization: Çatalhöyük as a case study.* Cambridge, UK: Cambridge University Press. *Hodder has directed the ongoing excavation of the Neolithic site of Çatalhöyük in Turkey for a number of years. This edited collection consists of essays written by a group of anthropologists, philosophers, and theologians who* visited the site for three summers between 2006 and 2008, engaging with excavators in "interpretation at the trowel's edge." Their interactions produced fresh perspectives on the role of religious ritual in the emergence of the first complex societies in Anatolia (Turkey) and the Middle East.

Joyce, Rosemary A. 2008. *Ancient bodies, ancient lives: Sex, gender, and archaeology.* New York: Thames & Hudson. *A sophisticated yet accessible introduction to gender archaeology. Highly recommended.*

Price, T. Douglas, and Anne Birgitte Gebauer. 2002. *Adventures in Fugawiland: Computer simulation in archaeology,* 3rd ed. New York: McGraw–Hill. *This simulation, for Windows PC only, gives users "hands-on" experience in basic archaeological field techniques.*

Renfrew, Colin, and Paul Bahn. 2016. *Archaeology: Theories, methods, and practice,* 7th ed. New York: Thames & Hudson. *The latest edition of a voluminous, profusely illustrated, up-to-date introduction to all facets of modern archaeology.*

Scott, James. 2017. *Against the Grain: A deep history of the earliest states.* New Haven: Yale University Press. *Scott brings together work by anthropologists and other scholars to argue against interpretations of the ancient human past that still presume a universal linear directionality culminating in state societies. Scott's critical discussion of traditional classifications by anthropologists of subsistence strategies and forms of human society is incisive and insightful.*

 Visit our online resource center for further reading, web links, free assessments, flashcards, and videos. www.oup.com/he/lavenda5e

7

Why did humans settle down, build cities, and establish states?

Modern human beings took what appear in retrospect to have been three majors steps that profoundly transformed the lives of their descendants: some of them settled in one place for extended periods of time; some of them later began to intervene in the reproductive cycle of plants and animals, while the habitat in which they lived produced domestication and agriculture; and perhaps about 7,500 years ago, a few peoples in the world independently developed social systems characterized by structural complexity and status inequality. In this chapter, we survey what anthropological research can tell us about the causes and consequences of these developments.

CHAPTER OUTLINE

LEARNING OBJECTIVES

- Explain how human social structures and imagination relate to and entangle with aspects of the material world.
- Describe the process and benefits of plant cultivation, identifying challenges and opportunities presented by this form of subsistence.
- Define animal domestication and describe how anthropologists explain the emergence of this form of subsistence.
- Describe the history of domestication, cultivation, and sedentism in Southwest Asia and how this history intersects with domestication elsewhere in the world.
- Analyze the positive and negative consequences of domestication and sedentism from selected examples.
- Recognize the types of evidence for social complexity as found in the archaeological record, including evidence for the emergence of stratification.
- Apply anthropological concepts to the rise of complex societies such as the Andean Civilization.

The Acropolis Museum in Athens, Greece, is built over an archaeological site.

Today, many of us take settled life and dependence on agriculture for granted, but anthropologists argue that this was neither an easy nor an inevitable outcome of human history. In this chapter, we provide an overview of what anthropologists are able to say about the changes in human subsistence patterns, especially the factors responsible for the domestication of plants and animals. We then consider the impact of human dependence on culturally constructed agricultural niches for subsequent developments in human history, such as the formation and growth of permanent settlements, the emergence of craft specialization, social stratification, writing, and other developments traditionally associated with "complex societies."

How Is the Human Imagination Entangled with the Material World?

As our discussion in Chapter 6 suggests, anthropologists have challenged widely accepted ideas about the direction and meaning of developments in human societies over the last several thousand years. The evidence provided by archaeologists has played a central role, offering fresh insights into the ways the material things they unearth were once connected to past human projects. For example, conventional discussions of the emergence of social complexity often begin with the assumption that humans and things are separate, self-contained entities. Some accounts present things (such as tool technologies) as powerful material entities that push humans to act in ways they are helpless to resist. Other accounts present things as lumps of inert matter that humans may bend to their will. However, many contemporary archaeologists and anthropologists find both these views unsatisfactory. They argue that humans and things are not separate and self-contained, but instead are always connected in the ongoing processes of life in a material world. Archaeologist Ian Hodder, for example, emphasizes not only that humans depend on things, but that "our dependence on things does itself depend—not just on the things themselves, but also on the ways in which we want to interact with them" (2012, 20). And things do not simply bend to our will. They have physical and chemical properties of their own that we must respect if we wish to relate successfully with them. Hodder refers to these properties as constituting

"the objectivity of things—the fact that they stand up against us" (2012, 40–41).

The things in question may also be living things, nonhuman as well as human. Recall the observations in Chapter 6 by archaeologists who study pastoral societies: "Mobile herding, in its various expressions, is but one possible outcome of the long-term processes of coevolution and co-community between animals and human beings initiated with if not before, the domestication of wild animals" (Honeychurch and Makarewicz 2016, 343). Indeed, a good place to study the relationship between humans and things is to consider what happens when humans bring living and nonliving things together in order to make a living. It turns out that people can make a living in much the same way in different environments or in different ways in the same environment. People work in factories in the tropical coastlands of Nigeria and in the bitter cold of Siberia in Russia; in Papua New Guinea, similar environments are used for gardening by some people, whereas others have established huge plantations. Our study therefore requires us to pay attention to factors that do not depend on the natural environment alone: features of a group's cultural tradition, for example, or external influences resulting from unpredictable historical encounters with other human groups. In sum, documenting and accounting for major transformations in human material adaptations require attention to ecological, economic, and sociocultural factors; as Hodder says " Doing things with things is always embedded in human sociality" (2012, 44).

As we have seen, paleoanthropologists and archaeologists combine their knowledge with that of other scientific specialists to reconstruct earlier modes of human life. Based on these reconstructions, we can say that our ancestors lived by gathering and hunting, at a band level of social organization, for most of human prehistory. But about 10,000 years ago, at the end of the Pleistocene, the last ice sheets retreated, sea levels rose, winds shifted, and environments changed. Humans responded to these changes by systematically interfering with the reproduction of other species to suit them better to human purposes. This process is called **domestication**, and it occurred independently in seven different areas of the world between 10,000 and 4,000 years ago (Smith 1995a, 12–13).

However, defining domestication in this way may be too narrow. In Chapter 6, we quoted James Scott who concluded, upon reviewing the work of archaeologists, that "Since the dawn of the species, *Homo sapiens* has been domesticating whole environments, not just species" (Scott 2017, 70; italics added). Ian Hodder makes a similar point when he explains why he refuses to separate natural and cultural thing interactions in his own

---

domestication Human interference with the reproduction of another species, with the result that specific plants and animals become more useful to people and dependent on them.

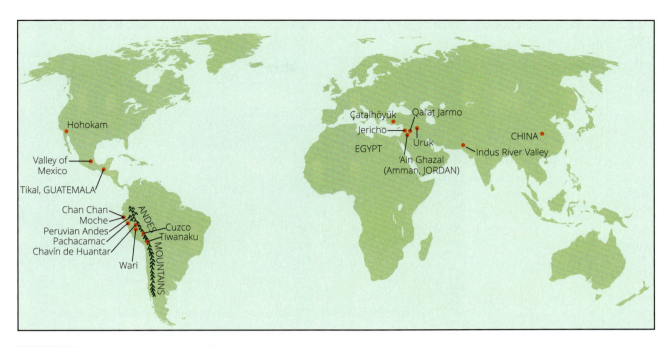

FIGURE 7.1 Major locations discussed in Chapter 7.

work. To be sure, he tells us, there are physical, geological, and chemical thing–thing dependences that exist apart from humans, or in ecosystems; indeed,

> Since the spread of modern humans, many ecosystems have been affected by human presence and many 'natural' dependences are influenced by human-induced hunting, burning, of the landscape, or intensive gathering and fishing. So rather than separated natural and culture thing interactions, I will simply explore the processes by which things depend on other things (2012, 42).

The influences to which Hodder points are now being seen by some scientists, including anthropologists, as having inaugurated a new geological epoch called the Anthropocene. We will consider their claims shortly. At this point, however, we would like to begin by looking more closely at the ways anthropologists have drawn on concepts taken from the discipline of ecology in order to gain insight to the ways humans initiate or respond to environmental changes. To appreciate the ways human beings responded to these environmental and ecological changes, anthropologists have needed to draw on concepts taken from the discipline of ecology. To begin with, ecologists are not content to speak vaguely of "the environment" when they discuss the relations that species develop with each other and with the material world in which they live. Rather, they look for patterns in these relations in specific geographic settings. Traditionally, a population of a species is said to have adapted to a particular local physical environment, or *habitat*, when

it has found a place, or *niche*, for itself in the local community of organisms within that habitat. An **ecological niche** includes the space the population occupies and what it eats. Broader definitions also include how different populations relate to one another and the impact of their activities on the community (Figure 7.2). Many contemporary ecologists would argue that niches are best defined in terms of the activities of a particular species, including the space, time, and resources that a population utilizes on a daily or seasonal basis (Odling-Smee et al. 2003, 39).

Traditional ecological studies of animal populations in particular habitats have explained the social organization of that population's members—a troop of baboons, for example—by conceiving of space, time, and resources as limiting factors to which that population must adapt if it is to survive and reproduce successfully. Biologists studying changing adaptations over time convert this ecological niche concept into an **evolutionary niche** concept by treating "the niche of any population as the sum of all the natural selection pressures to which the population is exposed . . . that part of its niche from which it is actually earning its living, from which it is not excluded by other organisms, and in which it is either able to exclude other organisms or

evolutionary niche Sum of all the natural selection pressures to which a population is exposed.

ecological niche Any species' way of life: what it eats and how it finds mates, raises its young, relates to companions, and protects itself from predators.

FIGURE 7.2 Broader definitions of ecological niches include the interactions of different species sharing the same habitat.

to compete with coexisting organisms" (Odling-Smee et al. 2003, 40). Two further ecological concepts are needed to describe the dynamics relating organisms to their niches: morphological *features*, a term ecologists apply to the phenotypic traits or characteristics of organisms, and environmental *factors*, a term that refers to subsystems of the organism's environment. "Thus, natural selection can be described as promoting a matching of features and factors" (Odling-Smee et al. 2003, 41).

Ordinarily, ecologists and evolutionary biologists assume that environmental factors are more powerful than morphological features of organisms: that is, natural selection involves an organism's adaptation *to* the environment. Ever since Darwin, it has been clear that this process of adaptation has played a powerful role in the evolution of life on Earth. However, as we noted in earlier chapters and as the notion of ecological niche implies, organisms are not passive occupants of rigid environmental slots. Their activities regularly modify the factors in their habitats, as when birds build nests, gophers dig burrows, or beavers build dams. Moreover, these environmental modifications can be passed on to their descendants (or to other organisms living in their local communities). As we saw in Chapter 2, this process is called **niche construction**. To qualify as niche construction, the modifications made by organisms to their environments must persist and/or accumulate over time to affect selection pressures. The legacy of altered environments with modified

selection pressures is what Odling-Smee et al. (2003) call an "ecological inheritance" (42).

How widely the process of niche construction can be successfully applied throughout the living world is controversial. But it makes excellent sense of the history of human adaptations. For example, Odling-Smee et al. argue that the effects of niche construction (or its absence) should be visible when we consider the morphologies of organisms living in particular habitats. If niche construction is absent, we should expect to find that successful organisms have adapted to their environments through modifications of their phenotypes. However, if niche construction has been present in evolution, organisms should show less phenotypic change in response to environmental changes. That is, the organisms modify their selective environments in ways that buffer them against selection for morphological changes. And they argue that this is exactly what we seem to find in hominin evolutionary history (Odling-Smee et al. 2003, 348–50). People who live in extremely cold climates do not adapt by growing fur—they modify their environment by making clothing, building shelters, and heating them.

As we saw in Chapter 6, the archaeological record documents a changing legacy of human modifications to environments that, at certain points, also allowed our ancestors to make a successful living in geographical regions of the world that previously had been impenetrable to them. Particularly in the past 300,000 years, we see minor morphological change in the hominin line accompanied by dramatic elaboration of human means of environmental modification. It is within this context that questions about transitions in human adaptive patterns are most fruitfully addressed.

niche construction When an organism actively perturbs the environment or when it actively moves into a different environment, thereby modifying the selection pressures it is subject to.

Is Plant Cultivation a Form of Niche Construction?

For many years, scholars have argued about the extent to which plant domestication was accidental or intentional. Biologist David Rindos, for example, suggests that domestication could have occurred without people's full awareness of what they were doing. Reminding us that human beings are just another animal species that eats plants, Rindos argues that the relationship between humans and plants is no different in principle from the relationship between a species of ant and a species of acacia. The ants live inside enlarged thorns on acacia trees. They consume a sugary substance produced at the base of the acacia leaves, and they feed modified leaf tips to their larvae. But the ants also eat other insects that would otherwise attack acacia leaves. Ant activity is so beneficial to the acacia trees that "when ants were experimentally removed from acacias, the plants were severely attacked and all died within a year" (Rindos 1984, 102).

The unintended, mutually beneficial effects of acacia trees and ants on each other modify the natural selection pressures each species experiences; this is what biologists call *mutualism*. Examples of multispecies mutualism illustrate the important fact that species need not be related to one another only as predators and prey. Indeed, mutualistic species together achieve higher biological fitnesses than either could have achieved on its own. At the same time, to focus narrowly on the mutualistic *species* themselves neglects the wider environmental context within which both species must make a living. Rindos's example must invoke that context to explain why acacia trees did so poorly when the ants were removed. It is not simply that these two species lived together in a non-predatory manner; rather, each species served to modify significantly the ecological niche of the other species, buffering it from selective pressures that it would otherwise have been exposed to.

Clearly, ants and acacia trees were able to develop this relationship without conscious planning. But does this mean, as Robert Wenke (1999) quipped, that "people have proved to be excellent devices for cereals to conquer the world" (271)? Some feminist archaeologists were wary of this way of approaching plant domestication by humans. First, to argue that domestication was an unconscious process overlooks the fact that human beings of the late Pleistocene were fully modern and bright enough to understand cause and effect concerning their livelihood. Thus, they surely selected deliberately those plants that were easier to harvest, more nourishing, and tastier. In this view, humans actively intervened in the gene pool of the wild plants; domestication was

conscious, not unconscious. Second, women in contemporary foraging societies are primarily responsible for gathering wild plants, which makes women likely candidates for the first human ancestors to have experimented with plant domestication. To assume, therefore, that plant domestication was a passive, unconscious process looks like the imposition of a crude sexist stereotype on the subsistence behaviors of our ancestors. Third, paying attention only to the plants and the people ignores the kinds of *environmental modifications* needed to make plant domestication successful, which clearly depended on conscious, active human intervention.

Some archaeologists have tried to fill in this gap. T. Douglas Price and Anne Birgitte Gebauer, for example, distinguish between domestication and cultivation. *Domestication* is human interference with the reproduction of another species, with the result that specific plants and animals become both more useful to people and dependent on them. It modifies the genotypes and phenotypes of plants and animals as they become dependent on humans. *Cultivation*, by contrast, is a deliberate cultural process involving the activities of preparing fields, sowing, weeding, harvesting, and storing and that requires a new way of thinking about subsistence and new technology to bring it about (Price and Gebauer 1995, 6). That is, habitats suitable for domesticated species must be carefully constructed and maintained for the domesticated species to mature and be harvested successfully. Indeed, the same process is required for successful animal domestication.

From this perspective, **agriculture** is best understood as the systematic modification of "the environments of plants and animals to increase their productivity and usefulness" (Wenke 1999, 270). Price and Gebauer call this systematically modified environment (or constructed niche) the **agroecology**, which becomes the only environment within which the plants (or animals) can flourish (Figure 7.3). Bruce Smith emphasizes that activities that led to domestication were conscious, deliberate, active attempts by foraging peoples to "increase both the economic contribution and the reliability of one or more of the wild species they depended on for survival, and thus reduce risk and uncertainty" (1995a, 16). Such activities include burning off vegetation to encourage preferred plants that thrive in burned-over landscapes or to attract wild animals that feed on such plants (Figure 7.4). These are

---

agriculture The systematic modification of the environments of plants and animals to increase their productivity and usefulness.

agroecology The systematically modified environment (or constructed niche) that becomes the only environment within which domesticated plants can flourish.

FIGURE 7.3 Industrial agriculture converts acres of habitat into a uniform agroecology for growing commercial crops like wheat.

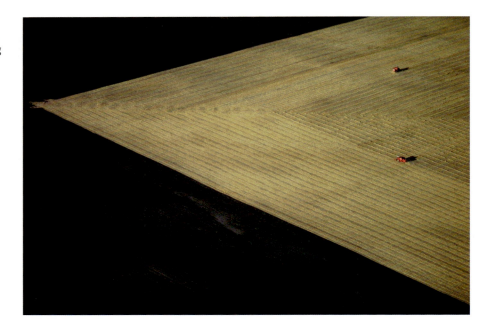

FIGURE 7.4 In Australia, hunter–gatherers burn vegetation to encourage the growth of plants.

clear examples of niche construction. The ancestors of domesticated seed plants like wheat were weedy generalists that, in addition to their dietary appeal, thrived in disturbed environments. Such attributes made them prime candidates for domestication.

More recently, some anthropologists have argued that niche construction theory can clarify relationships between people, plants, and animals that emerge in processes of domestication. Melinda Zeder, for example, suggests that such relationships are best understood as *coevolutionary* and that "niche-construction plays a role in each of three distinctive pathways that humans, plants and animals follow into domestication" (2016, 328). First, humans engage in ecosystem engineering to modify the conditions of growth for plants. Second, plants and animals enter into relations with humans in order to take advantage of opportunities offered by human-engineered environments. Third, humans may begin interfering with the reproduction of plants and animals to suit them better to human purposes (Zeder 2016, 328). The third step is what has traditionally been understood by "domestication," but the degree of control humans exercise in this coevolutionary network of relations can vary. Zeder points to research suggesting that "species with high degrees of genetic variation, especially those that display plasticity in the expression of phenotypic traits, are thought to be more likely to respond to changes in selective environments caused by niche construction" (2016,

Is Plant Cultivation a Form of Niche Construction?   **209**

329). Zeder concludes that the study of domestication promises to clarify issues in contemporary evolutionary theory, "exploring the role of acquired behaviors and cultural transmission in the profound evolutionary changes that transformed both plant and animal domesticates and human domesticators" (2016, 341).

To better understand how domestication and agriculture developed, both must be distinguished from **sedentism**, which is the process of increasingly permanent human habitation in one place and contrasts with the less permanent, more nomadic patterns of habitation experienced by earlier hominins. But people do not have to become farmers to become sedentary. The sedentary adaptations of the indigenous people of the northwest coast of North America depended not on agriculture but on seasonally abundant salmon runs, which could be "harvested" as regularly as crops but involved minimal ecological interference and no processes of domestication.

Sedentism is probably more usefully understood as a consequence of humans choosing to depend on resources in particular kinds of constructed niches. Sedentism is a key element that modifies the selection pressures of those who come to depend on subsistence resources in a fixed location, be it a riverbank or a cultivated field or a pasture. Human beings who farm for a living may buffer themselves against periodic famine and be able to support larger populations. At the same time, they make themselves vulnerable to a variety of new selection pressures brought about by sedentary life: exposure to threats from agricultural pests and thieves, as well as disease organisms that breed and spread more successfully among settled people than they do among nomads. James Scott argues that "Sedentism alone, well before widespread cultivation of domesticated crops, created conditions of crowding that were ideal 'feedlots' for pathogens" (2017, 100). As we saw, the clearing of forest by the first farmers in West Africa apparently created ecological conditions favoring larger pools of standing water, which were the ideal breeding grounds for malaria-carrying mosquitoes. This, in turn, created a new selection pressure in favor of the sickle cell allele, which offers heterozygous carriers some protection against malaria (Odling-Smee et al. 2003, 251).

What obstacles faced those who first interfered in the life cycle of wild plants? If the plant was a grass, like wheat, they had to cope with that plant's reproductive pattern. The wheat kernel, both domesticated and wild, is attached to the cereal shaft by a spikelet called the "rachis" (Figure 7.5). In wild wheat, the rachis becomes extremely brittle as the kernel ripens, and the kernels on any stem ripen from bottom to top over a week or two. As each kernel ripens, the rachis can be broken by

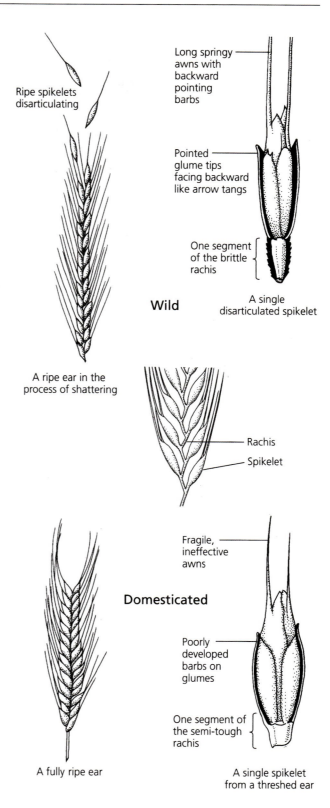

FIGURE 7.5 Wheat kernels form within spikelets that attach to the plant by a structure called the "rachis." The rachis of wild wheat is brittle, which aids the dispersal of seeds in the wild. The rachis of domesticated wheat is not brittle, and spikelets remain attached to the ear during harvest. (B. Smith 1995a, 73)

sedentism The process of increasingly permanent human habitation in one place.

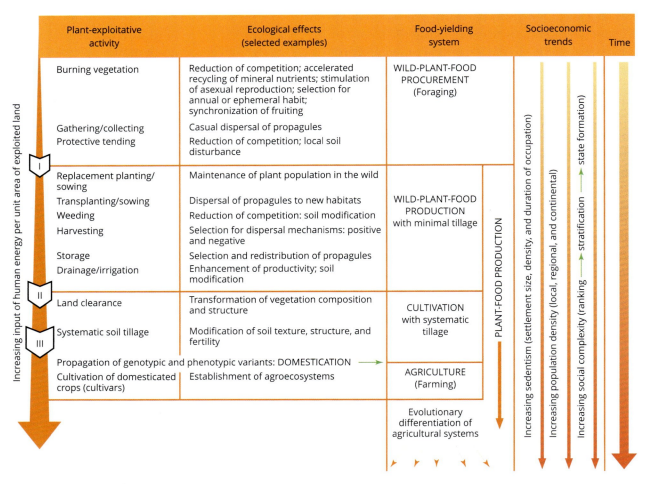

FIGURE 7.6 The four major food-yielding systems according to David Harris. Energy-input/energy-output ratios jump sharply where wild plant-food production begins, where cultivation begins, and where agriculture begins. (The *propagules* referred to in the second column are the forms by which plants are reproduced—seeds, shoots, and so on.) (Harris 1989, 17)

an animal walking through the stand of wheat or even by a gust of wind, dispersing the kernel into the air and eventually onto the ground. Wild wheat has two rows of kernels on each stalk. Because the kernels ripen at different times, the seeds have a greater chance of scattering in different directions and not all landing at the foot of the parent plant in a clump. The kernel of wild wheat is enclosed in a tough outer husk called a "glume," which protects the kernel from frost and dehydration and allows it to remain viable for as long as 20 years in the ground.

To be used successfully by human beings, wheat would require a much less brittle rachis, seed heads that mature at the same time, and a softer glume. It would also require a larger, more easily visible seed head (in terms of both kernel size and number of kernel rows on a stalk). Plants with these variations would have had a selective advantage once human beings began to eat them. As the genes responsible for these traits increased in the wheat plant population—changes that, given plant genetics, might have taken very few generations—the

plants would have contributed more and more to the human diet. The earliest domesticated wheat shows precisely these evolutionary trends, including six rows of kernels on a stalk rather than two.

The constructed niches favorable for agriculture have also varied over time and space in several important ways, and they did not appear overnight. David Harris (1989, 17) provides a useful overview of these patterns and classifies the relationships between plants and people into four major food-yielding systems: (1) wild plant-food procurement, (2) wild plant-food production, (3) cultivation, and (4) agriculture (Figure 7.6). Harris notes that there are three points at which the amount of energy people put into plant-food activities increases sharply: (1) where wild plant-food production begins, (2) where cultivation begins, and (3) where agriculture begins (Figure 7.6). In Harris's classification, agriculture (or farming) depends on cultivation with systematic tillage. And although Harris's chart does not make this explicit, the stabilization of systematic tillage, cultivation, and farming sooner or later come to involve the construction of fields and storage facilities, and to depend on animal labor as well as human labor. Domesticated animals are central to pastoral forms of subsistence. So what can archaeologists tell us about the deep history of human-animal co-community and the origins of animal domestication?

How Do Anthropologists Explain the Origins of Animal Domestication?

Animal domestication can be defined as "the capture and taming by human beings of animals of a species with particular behavioral characteristics, their removal from their natural living area and breeding community, and their maintenance under controlled breeding conditions for mutual benefits" (Bökönyi 1989, 22). This definition views animal domestication as a consequence of people's attempts to control the animals they were hunting, which assumes active human intervention in selecting which animals to domesticate and how to domesticate them. Animals are more mobile than plants, and although culling wild herds can induce some changes in the gene pool, it is only by confining animals or maintaining them in captivity that human beings can directly intervene in their breeding patterns. As we saw earlier, however, Zeder and others have begun to draw attention to the forms of mutualism between humans and animals that lay at the heart of domestication (Zeder 2016, 328), contributing to an emerging field of *social zooarchaeology* that draws attention to the animal side of human-animal mutualism (Honeychurch and Makarewicz, 2016, 350). The work of archaeologist Kristin Armstrong Oma (2010) exemplifies this approach. She argues that the design of Scandinavian Bronze Age longhouses suggests that people and animals were able to live together in intimacy because herd animals were sentient beings willing to extend to human beings the forms of social trust they already extended to other members of their herd. Even as this kind of mutualism bound humans and animals closely together, however, the relationship was not one of equals, for humans might always choose to act in ways that favored their interests over those of their animals.

Thus, Bökönyi's phrase "maintaining them in captivity" is not an innocent phrase. As work in social zooarchaeology suggests, humans have engineered a range of different environments to attract sentient animals of different species, with differing degrees of success. These environmental modifications may range from protecting selected animals from other predators to supplying them with food and water to close monitoring of their life cycles, from birth to slaughter, under highly artificial conditions. And again, human commitment to the construction of niches favorable to domesticated animals simultaneously modifies the selection pressures humans experience: dependence on a reliable supply of meat and skins may mean that a human group is obliged to follow a herd wherever it chooses to go or to modify their own adaptations seasonally to move herds to reliable supplies of water and forage. Such movements will make humans vulnerable to negative as well as positive encounters with other habitats and other species, including other human beings, with whom they will have to come to terms if their pastoral adaptation is to succeed. Not all people are pleased when herders pasture their animals in areas where cultivated plants are growing.

Animal domestication is difficult to measure with precision in the archaeological record. Wenke (1999) identifies four main classes of evidence used by archaeologists to assess animal domestication. First, the presence of an animal species outside its natural range may indicate herding. For example, because the southern Levant (the coastal area at the eastern end of the Mediterranean Sea; see Figure 7.7) is outside the area in which wild sheep evolved, scholars say that sheep remains found there constituted evidence of herding: the sheep must have been brought into the area by people. For such an argument to be effective, we must be sure we know precisely what the natural range of the wild species was.

Second, morphological changes occur in most animal populations as domestication progresses. Wenke and Olszewski (2007, 253) point out that the shape and size of sheep horns reflect the process of domestication. Wild sheep have larger, stronger horns than do domesticated sheep. In wild sheep, large horns are connected with the breeding hierarchies that males establish through fighting. The selective pressure for these horns relaxed as sheep were domesticated, so horn size and shape changed.

Third, the abrupt population increase of some species relative to others at a site is often taken as evidence of domestication. About 9,000 years ago in southwestern Asia, the makeup of animal-bone assemblages changes. The nearly total domination of gazelle bones gives way, and the percentage of sheep and goat bones increases dramatically.

Fourth, the age and sex of the animals whose bones are fossilized are used to infer the existence of animal domestication. Researchers assume that numerous remains of immature or juvenile herd animals, especially males, represent human involvement with the herd. Why? In the wild, animals killed for meat come from a much wider age range; there is no emphasis on younger,

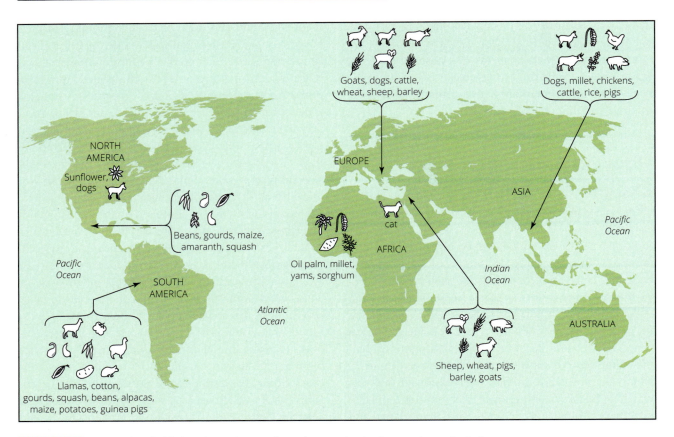

FIGURE 7.7 A map of probable locations where various plants and animals were domesticated.

especially younger male, animals. Also, human beings who manage herds kill immature males more readily than females because only a small number of males are required for reproduction, whereas larger numbers of females provide more offspring, more milk, and other products such as dung, wool, and hair. Analyses of the age and sex structure of animal remains help to establish the function of a domesticated herd: a meat herd contains a lot of adolescent and young adult animals, whereas a dairy herd consists mostly of adult females.

The earliest known domesticated animal was the dog, for which there is Old World evidence from a Magdalenian cave site in northern Spain as old as 16,000 years. Clearly, there were significant mutual advantages for both dogs and human beings to team up in the hunt. The first barely domesticated wolves must have been fearsome companions for Paleolithic hunters, but eventually the human–dog relationship became a very close one. The earliest undisputed evidence of dog domestication was found at a 14,700-year-old site in Germany, in a grave containing two human skeletons and the jawbone of a dog. Mitochondrial DNA analysis identified the dog remains as belonging to an ancestor of contemporary dogs (Morey 2010; Thalmann 2013; Giemsch and Feine 2015; Figure 7.8).

It seems that other animals were domesticated to provide food rather than to help get food McCorriston and Hole (1991) argue that people in different areas experimented with animals found around them to determine which ones were both desirable as food and amenable to human control. Both sheep and goats were relatively harmless, gregarious herd animals that had multiple uses for human beings and were found seasonally in the same locales as the ripening plants that people wanted to harvest.

However, the evidence, as summarized by McCorriston and Hole, puts sheep and goats in different ecological zones of northern Mesopotamia, and it is likely that their distribution did not overlap much, if at all (Figures 7.7 and 7.8). In other words, sheep and goats were domesticated separately and at different times. The earliest evidence for goat herding is about 11,000–10,000 years before the present, in a narrow zone along the front of the Zagros Mountains. The earliest sites for domesticated sheep were perhaps in central Anatolia (the Asian part of modern Turkey). The evidence for two other major Old World animal domesticates, cattle and pigs, is much more difficult to come by but seems to point to multiple domestication sites for cattle from China to western Europe beginning

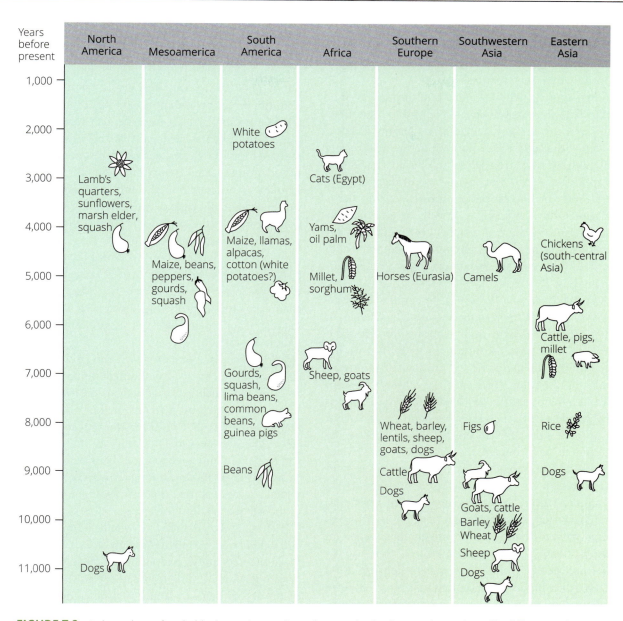

FIGURE 7.8 A chronology of probable dates when various plants and animals were domesticated in different regions.

sometime after 11,000 years ago. Domesticated pig bones have been found throughout southwestern Asia as far back as 8,000 years.

As mentioned above, wild-hunted and domesticated-herded are but extreme ends of a continuum of animal-human-environmental relationships. Jarman and his associates (1982, 51-54) outlined six stages in these relationships, although in light of our previous discussion, the term "stages" is misleading. There is no necessary directionality to these forms of human-herd co-communities. Each point identified on the continuum identifies looser or tighter entanglements between humans and herds, any of which may be maintained indefinitely. The loosest form is *random hunting* in which hunters make no attempt to control herds but hunt animals as they find them. *Controlled hunting* involves the selective hunting of herds—killing young males, for example. This is the beginning of regular human intervention in the herd species' gene pool. *Herd following* ties specific herds and specific groups of people together: as the herd moves from place to place, the people also move. *Loose herding* involves human effort to control the movements of the herd. They move the herd at various times of the year, ensuring that all of the animals move safely at the same time, while actively intervening in the herd's gene pool through selective breeding and culling. *Close herding* is the most familiar practice in much of the United States and western Europe. The animals' mobility is limited, and their gene pool is actively managed. The most intensive control in all aspects of the animals' lives is found in *factory farming*: in some cases, animals never leave the building or feedlot in which they are raised.

Some animals that were hunted in the past, even in a controlled way, resisted human attempts to exert fuller control over them. The gazelle is a good example: there is evidence that controlled hunting about 9,500 years ago in southwestern Asia led to significant changes in the gazelle gene pool, but there is no evidence of any tighter forms of domestication. Clearly, culling herds of certain kinds of animals . . . affects the gene pool in ways that demonstrate that people have an influence on animals even if the animals are not fully domesticated. Thus, herd following shades almost imperceptibly into loose herding.

Richard Meadow (1989, 81), by contrast, has argued that herding represents a complete change in human attitudes toward and relationships with animals. At the very least, the human focus shifts from the hunted animal to the principal product of the living animal—its offspring. This shift, he suggests, is connected to a major shift in worldview that was involved in the other cultural processes—sedentism and plant cultivation—of post-Pleistocene southwestern Asia: the development of a concern for property and its maintenance over time. Meadow argues that this change in focus was essential for the development of herding as a social and cultural phenomenon and for the development of social complexity. But herding itself had to undergo changes before this could happen, as Adam Allentuck (2015) shows for the eastern coast of the Mediterranean Sea (called the Levant). Between 4500 and 3100 BCE, a major shift occurred in this region, from exploitation of herds for *primary products* such as meat, bone, and hide, to a focus on renewable *secondary products* such as milk or fiber (for textiles), or muscle power (for pulling plows or carrying loads). "People would have formed distinctive relationships with specialized livestock animals, as each of the secondary products developed independently in different places and at different times" (Allentuck 2015, 99). These changes both extended the lives of the herd animals and increased the mutual dependencies connecting herds and herders, freeing "human labor for agricultural expansion, craft specialization and large-scale building projects" (2015, 99). Developments such as these provided a rich scaffold for the subsequent development of social complexity in the Levant.

broad-spectrum foraging   A subsistence strategy based on collecting a wide range of plants and animals by hunting, fishing, and gathering.

Was There Only One Motor of Domestication?

About 10,000 years ago, after nearly 4 million years of hominin evolution and more than 100,000 years of successful foraging by *H. sapiens*, human beings living in distant and unconnected parts of the world nearly simultaneously developed subsistence strategies that involved domesticated plants and animals. Why? Some scholars have sought a single, universal explanation that would explain all original cases of domestication. Thus, it has been argued that domestication is the outcome of population pressure as the increasing hunting-and-gathering human population overwhelmed the existing food resources. Others point to climate change or famine as the postglacial climate got drier. Increasing archaeological research has made it clear, however, that the evidence in favor of any single-cause, universally applicable explanation is weak.

Some scholars have proposed universally applicable explanations that take several different phenomena into account. One such explanation, called **broad-spectrum foraging**, is based on a reconstruction of the environmental situation that followed the retreat of the most recent glaciers. The very large animals of the Ice Age began to die out and were replaced by increased numbers of smaller animals. As sea levels rose to cover the continental shelves, fish and shellfish became more plentiful in the warmer, shallower waters.

The effects on plants were equally dramatic as forests and woodlands expanded into new areas. Consequently, these scholars argue, people had to change their diets from big game hunting to broad-spectrum foraging for plants and animals by hunting, fishing, and gathering. This broadening of the economy is said to have led to a more secure subsistence base, the emergence of sedentary communities, and a growth in population. In turn, population growth pressured the resource base of the area, and people were forced to eat "third-choice" foods, particularly wild grain, which was difficult to harvest and process but which responded to human efforts to increase yields. Although the broad-spectrum foraging argument seems to account for plant domestication in the New World, the most recent evidence from ancient southwestern Asia does not support it. There is also evidence for the development of broad-spectrum gathering in Europe, but domestication did not follow. Rather, domesticated crops were brought into Europe by people from southwestern Asia, where a broad-spectrum revolution had not occurred.

A very different kind of argument came from Barbara Bender (1977), who suggested that before farming began there was competition between local groups to achieve dominance over each other through feasting and the expenditure of resources on ritual and exchange, engaging in a kind of prehistoric "arms race." To meet increasing demands for food and other resources, land use was intensified, and the development of food production followed. This argument emphasizes social factors, rather than environmental or technical factors, and takes a localized, regional approach. It is supported by ethnographic accounts concerning competitive exchange activities, such as the *potlatch* of the indigenous inhabitants of the northwest coast of North America. These people were foragers in a rich environment that enabled them to settle in relatively permanent villages without farming or herding. Competition among neighboring groups led to ever more elaborate forms of competitive exchange, with increasingly large amounts of food and other goods being given away at each subsequent potlatch. As suggestive as Bender's argument is, however, it is difficult to find evidence for competitive feasting in archaeological remains.

Recently, archaeologists have avoided grand theories claiming that a single, universal process was responsible for domestication wherever it occurred. Many prefer to take a regional approach, searching for causes particular to one area that may or may not apply to other areas. Currently, the most powerful explanations seem to be *multiple strand theories* that consider the combined local effect of climate, environment, population, technology, social organization, and diet on the emergence of domestication. The multiple strand approach is well illustrated in an article by McCorriston and Hole (1991), and their work forms the basis for the following case study of domestication in ancient southwestern Asia.

How Did Domestication, Cultivation, and Sedentism Begin in Southwest Asia?

Southwestern Asian domestication is thought to have begun about 12,500 years ago with the Natufian foragers, who relied on the intensive exploitation of wild cereals (notably wild wheat and barley), nuts (especially acorns, pistachios, and almonds), and wild game (especially gazelle and red deer) (Belfer-Cohen 1991, 167; Figures 7.7 and 7.8). Because of the climatic and ecological changes in the world that followed the retreat of the glaciers, the Natufians were able to exploit what were, at first, increasingly rich supplies of wild cereals and large herds of gazelle, which made sedentism possible. Although many Natufian sites are small hunting camps,

researchers have discovered at least two dozen Natufian villages, or base camps, that reached a size of 1,000 m² (about a quarter of an acre) and beyond (Belfer-Cohen 1991, 176–77). Henry (1989, 218) estimates that the Natufian hamlets ranged from 40 to 150 people; they were five to ten times larger than the mobile foraging camps of the peoples who preceded them.

That these early Natufian villages were more than just campsites is revealed in their architecture (Figure 7.9). Natufian houses were dug partially into the ground and had walls of stone and mud with some timber posts and probably roof beams. At the Mallaha site, archaeologists found plaster-lined storage pits in the houses. Archaeologists infer that such buildings, which required a considerable amount of labor and material to build, were not constructed for brief residence only. Archaeologists also found massive stone mortars used to grind seeds. The implication is that people could not have transported such heavy utensils, nor would they have invested the time and effort to make them if they were going to abandon them after one season's use. In addition, the remains of migratory birds and a great number of young gazelle bones indicate year-round hunting from the hamlets because migratory birds fly over the area during different seasons and young gazelles are born at one time only during the year.

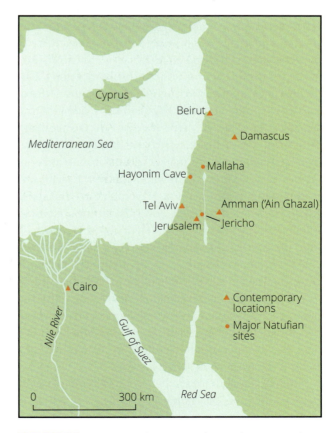

FIGURE 7.9 Major Natufian sites in the southern Levant in relation to other contemporary features.

Finally, artistic production among the Natufians was high. Anna Belfer-Cohen and others suggest that artistic activity may be viewed as indirect evidence for a sedentary way of life that forces people to interact regularly with others who are not closely related to them. In these situations, the production of such objects as personal ornaments helps to create a sense of identity among smaller groups while allowing them to participate in a larger society (Belfer-Cohen 1988, 1991; Lewis-Williams 1984). Elaborate ritual and ceremonial activities would also have soothed interactions and reduced tensions in increasingly large communities where cooperation was essential (Henry 1989, 206).

Natufian Social Organization

Information about social organization from the archaeological record is indirect, but Donald Henry (1989) believes that over time, Natufian society developed social divisions with unequal access to wealth, power, and prestige. That is, Natufian society showed **social stratification**, an important sign of social complexity. His evidence comes from Natufian burials.

In early Natufian times, the dead were buried together in small groups, which Henry believes corresponded to subgroups of a larger community. There is evidence that relatives lived in the same area for several generations. For example, nearly half the skeletons recovered from the Hayonim Cave site showed evidence of the genetically recessive trait, *third-molar agenesis* (failure of the third molars, or wisdom teeth, to develop). This trait occurs at much lower frequencies—on the order of 0–20%—in other human populations. Evidence from six other Natufian sites revealed the normal frequency of third-molar agenesis, suggesting that the group that lived at Hayonim Cave mated with other members of their own group rather than with outsiders. It seems this mating pattern continued at Hayonim Cave for about 1,000 years (Henry 1989, 208). These group burials sometimes included dentalium shell headdresses, which were decorative and valuable objects with no identifiable practical use (Figure 7.10). In other cases, elaborate grave goods were buried with children. Both these burial practices indicate the differentiation of subgroups and inherited status differences. These group burials suggest that in early Natufian times, social position depended on which group a person belonged to, rather than on a community-wide set of social standards.

In late Natufian times, there were still differences in grave goods from one burial to the next, but the dead

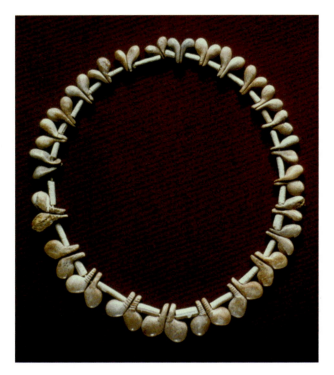

FIGURE 7.10 A Natufian collar from El Wad with 25 fragments of dentalia separating a type of bone bead. This collar was found in a male burial site.

were buried individually in cemeteries. The new pattern suggests that the old boundaries around descent groups had been destroyed and replaced by a new pattern in which resources were controlled by an entire community and stratification was community wide. Some people now coordinated activities for the group as a whole and had come to occupy high-status positions that crosscut subgroup boundaries. For these reasons, Henry suggests that Natufian social organization had come to resemble what is called a "chiefdom" in anthropological literature. *Chiefdoms*, you will recall, are societies in which a leader (the chief) and close relatives are set apart from the rest of the society and allowed privileged access to wealth, power, and prestige.

Natufian Subsistence

The Natufians obtained 98% of their meat protein from red deer, wild sheep, and wild goats, but especially from gazelles, whose bones make up 40–80% of all the animal bones recovered from Natufian sites. Henry (1989, 91) believes entire herds of gazelle were hunted communally in game drives. Woodlands were burned to promote the growth of young plants, attractive to gazelle and deer. Henry points out that the increased attention to gazelles, wild grains, and nuts also represented specialization of subsistence activities by Natufian foragers. They were *complex foragers*, who lived in areas of abundant resources

---

social stratification A form of social organization in which people have unequal access to wealth, power, and prestige.

that may have appeared inexhaustible (Price and Gebauer 1995, 7), making them different from *generalized foragers*, who live in less generous environments and cope with shortages by diversifying their subsistence activities.

Unfortunately for the Natufians, the choices they made were destabilizing in the long run. They fed an increasingly large population by intensively exploiting small areas. By settling down, they gave up mobility, the key to the long-term success of a foraging life. The short-term stability and security of sedentism and intensive collection increased the rigidity of their society, making it vulnerable to disruptive environmental changes. And changes came about 10,500 years ago: the shallow interior lakes of the southern Levant were drying up, and the Mediterranean woodlands on which they depended had shrunk to one-half the area they had covered 2,000 years earlier. Natufians in the southern part of the region abandoned their settlements and returned to simple foraging, developing what archaeologists refer to as the "Harifian culture." In the central core of the Natufian area, however, the people tried to keep the cereal plants growing in areas that were no longer ideal for them.

The first evidence for domesticated cereals in this core Natufian area dates to about 10,300 years ago. Both wheat and barley were found at Jericho and barley alone at other sites. For archaeologists, domesticated plants signal the end of the Paleolithic and the beginning of the **Neolithic**. This transition from the Natufian culture is marked in the southern Levant by the appearance of a culture called the "Pre-Pottery Neolithic A" (PPNA), in which cultivation was practiced but pottery had not yet been invented. PPNA Jericho was much larger than the preceding Natufian settlement, with a surface area of about 2.5 hectares (about 6 acres) and perhaps 300 or more inhabitants (Smith 1995a, 3). Henry (1989) suggests that this was a result of the concentration of populations from smaller, more numerous hamlets in a setting where "large tracts of arable land, suitable for hoe cultivation, adjoined year-round water sources" (53–54).

Jericho was located on the edge of an *alluvial fan* (a fan-shaped accumulation of sediment from flowing water at the mouth of a ravine) on a permanent stream, near hills rich in gazelle, wild grains, and nuts. The stream provided clear drinking water, whereas the alluvial fan provided mud for bricks, and its regular floods provided rich soil for plants. By about 9,300 years ago, the inhabitants of Jericho had built a stone wall, 3 meters thick, 4 meters high, and perhaps 700 meters in circumference (Figure 7.11). The wall, it is now thought, was erected as protection from the floods; similar protections from flooding are found at other PPNA sites, although none is as elaborate as the wall of Jericho (Bar-Yosef and Kislev 1989, 635).

FIGURE 7.11   By about 9,300 years ago, the inhabitants of Jericho had built a stone wall, probably to protect the settlement from yearly flooding.

Trade was also significant in PPNA Jericho. Obsidian is an extremely sharp and highly prized volcanic glass that is found in relatively few places worldwide (Figure 7.12). Anatolia, in modern Turkey, contained the major sites for obsidian in Neolithic southwestern Asia. Archaeologists have found Anatolian obsidian in Jericho, some 700 kilometers (430 miles) from Anatolia; it is unlikely that residents traveled that distance to get it themselves. Jericho also contained marine shells from the Mediterranean Sea and the Black Sea as well as *amulets* (charms against evil or injury) and greenstone beads. These objects suggest not just trade from village to village but also trade between the settled farmers and the foraging peoples living in the semiarid regions or higher areas.

Beginning about 9,500 years ago, the PPNA culture was replaced by the Pre-Pottery Neolithic B (PPNB) culture, which represents the rapid expansion of agriculture. Although there are but a handful of PPNA sites, all in a small area around Jericho, there are more than 140 PPNB sites, many of which are very large and some of which are found in Anatolia and the Zagros Mountains. As the new farming technology moved north and east, it was adapted to fit local circumstances. At some point, farmers met herders from the Zagros Mountains and north Mesopotamia who had domesticated sheep and goats, animals that were well known in their wild state

Neolithic   The "New Stone Age," which began with the domestication of plants 10,300 years ago.

Çatalhöyük in the Twenty-First Century

Archaeology began as an antiquarian pursuit in Europe and the United States and only in the past century or so was transformed into a professionalized scholarly discipline. Today, professional archaeology is changing again, in ways that bring it to the public in a variety of unprecedented ways. Many of these changes are connected with the spread of neoliberal capitalism after the end of the Cold War. As Demoule describes (see the box feature "In Their Own Words: Rescue Archaeology in Europe," Chapter 6), these changes led to pressures on national governments to reduce budgets, such that archaeologists have had to secure funding in new ways, often from private business firms. At the same time, legislation like NAGPRA now requires archaeologists to take into consideration the concerns of descendants of indigenous peoples whose heritage is affected by archaeological research. Finally, residents of the communities where archaeological sites are located, or outside groups with their own interests in such sites, may also insist that their voices be heeded as research is undertaken.

These concerns are all magnified when the site in question has a high profile, such as the 9,000-year-old Neolithic site of Çatalhöyük in south-central Turkey. Archaeologist Ian Hodder of Stanford University is the current director of an ongoing research project at Çatalhöyük that began in 1993, some three decades after the site had first been discovered and excavated by James Mellaart. In *The Leopard's Tale* (2006), Hodder describes the project, which is more ambitious than much previous archaeological research, in Turkey and elsewhere.

When Hodder sought to reopen excavations at Çatalhöyük, the Turkish Ministry of Culture and Tourism was in charge of protecting and preserving the site. "One central aim of the project, developed in consultation with Turkish officials, is to provide Turkish Ministry of Culture and Tourism with a well-planned heritage site. This was certainly one of the main reasons that led to the decision to allow renewed work at the site in the 1990s" (Hodder 2006, 37). Heritage sites are designed to attract tourists, but a well-planned heritage site takes into consideration the concerns of a range of other stakeholders. As Hodder (2006) has written, "we need to look at the discovery of the site and the various communities to whom it has become important" (13). Hodder describes these communities as "fellow travelers."

Some fellow travelers are archaeologists: Mellaart and his team from the 1960s (and the results they produced), Turkish archaeologists (and their universities); excavation teams from several different countries who dig at the site today; and many specialized researchers who analyze human remains, animal remains and plant remains, stone tools, and pottery that have been recovered from the digs. Hodder includes as fellow travelers other anthropologists whose ethnographic research provides ethnoarchaeological clues for interpreting remains at the site, especially its art. Indeed, artists are fellow travelers at Çatalhöyük, including some who contribute new approaches to scientific illustration, a number of examples of which are published in *The Leopard's Tale*.

Some fellow travelers are Turkish citizens, from the residents of local communities, to representatives of regional and national government; others are visiting international diplomats and dignitaries like the Prince of Wales. Fellow travelers include representatives of the national and international press, who visit the site regularly. "Underlying all this for Turkey is the reputation of the site as the origin of Anatolian civilization, expressed clearly in the main museum in Turkey in Ankara, and in numerous publications" (Hodder 2006, 32). Hodder (2006) insists that it is his ethical duty to respond to the concerns of local politicians "not simply because of responsibility towards one's hosts, but also because the politicians use the distant past to make claims about origins and identities. . . . The site and the data that are made known by the archaeologist will be used in one way or another to support political claims—in my view it is unethical for the archaeologists to wash their hands of this process and to remain disengaged" (36–37).

Another group of fellow travelers are low-income residents of nearby communities, many of whom hope that the site and its visitors may provide economic benefits. Some local community members are employed at the site, one opened a café near the site, and local women are permitted to sell embroidered cloth there. "We have started, in consultation with local groups, to develop a Çatalhöyük brand and to undertake craft production and training at the site. . . . The project has also contributed to the digging of a new well and the provision of a new water supply. It has helped to persuade regional officials to build a new school in the village and it has contributed a

throughout the area. The agriculturalists adopted these herding techniques, which spread quickly and were incorporated into the agricultural life of the entire region. By 8,000 years ago, the farmers in southwestern Asia practiced a mixed agricultural strategy, incorporating grains and livestock.

Domestication Elsewhere in the World

The conditions under which domestication began varied around the world. In highland Mexico, for example, the predomestication population was relatively stable, and sedentism had not yet occurred. There are no indications of the kinds of long-term shifts in resource library to the village" (Hodder 2006, 37). Local farmers have contributed their knowledge of the local landscape. "They do not have some privileged knowledge based on cultural continuity. To claim that would be to 'museumize' the local communities. They are heavily involved in global processes (and some have lived as guest workers in Germany)" (Hodder 2006, 39).

Çatalhöyük was declared a World Heritage Site by UNESCO in 2012 (http://whc.unesco.org/en/list/1405), a status that certifies its importance around the globe and attracts the interest of private corporations, fellow travelers willing to fund the ongoing research. Many other fellow travelers are tourists from within and outside Turkey, including some who consider the site the center of a Neolithic Goddess cult. As Hodder (2006) observes, "It is not possible for archaeologists to contribute to the religious view that the Goddess is present at Çatalhöyük. But it is possible to try to respond to those women's groups that want to know about the role of women at the site. . . . Many followers of the Goddess have engaged in dialogue and have been able to see that new evidence can be incorporated into a revised perspective . . . one in which women were powerful for reasons other than mothering and in which some equality existed in practice" (39–40).

Hodder believes that negotiating with all these different kinds of fellow travelers is unavoidable in a globalized world. "At times the interactions may be difficult, and the travelers may feel the need to part company. I am very aware at Çatalhöyük that there are many tensions. . . . These can all be difficult interactions, but in the end the ethical responsibility is to use the specialist archaeological and conservation knowledge to respond to the interests of one's fellow travelers" (Hodder 2006, 42).

How do these negotiations affect the scholarly work of archaeology done at the site? Being able to mobilize so many diverse allies to fund the research has permitted the archaeologists and other scientific specialists to use the most up-to-date techniques of survey, excavation, and analysis, much of which is carried out in laboratories built on the site. It has made possible the construction of shelters to protect and preserve open parts of the site, both for the archaeologists and for the visitors.

But the project has been innovative theoretically as well, especially in the way it has responded to a series of issues raised by science-studies scholars concerned about the practice of scientific research. One issue has to do with *reflexivity:* the researchers' need to step back and reflect on their own research and the context within which it is being carried out (see "Module 3: On Ethnographic Methods"). The Çatalhöyük project has a team devoted to "reflexive methodology," which involves ethnographic research both in the local communities (to address local people's interest and concerns) and in the trenches themselves (to focus on the scientific practice of archaeology). A second issue of concern to science-studies scholars is the traditional separation of excavation and analysis (what philosophers of science call the "context of discovery" and the "context of justification"). Hodder and his colleagues have moved to close this gap by building their own laboratories on the site and by bringing theorists to engage with excavators at work in the trenches, a practice Hodder calls "*interpretation at the trowel's edge*" (see pages 1-31). Hodder (2010) believes that "dialogue between different specialists in religion in the context of grappling with the data from a particular archaeological site has opened up new lines of inquiry and new perspectives on religion and its origins. The data from the site have acted as a player in the dialogue, bringing different perspectives together and forcing engagement between them. The end result is a coherent overview incorporating new perspectives on the role of religion in the early development of complex societies" (27).

Finally, Hodder and his colleagues are particularly mindful of the opportunities and challenges of living in a digitized world. Digital technologies for data storage, publication, and communication are central to the functioning of the Çatalhöyük project and have yielded a state-of-the-art website (http://www.catalhoyuk.com/). The majority of the videos, images, and texts accessible via this website are licensed with a Creative Commons license, which allows the free distribution of copyrighted materials. Reflexivity about the use of digital media has also been part of the project, making it a case study of the kinds of human–machine connections central to cyborg anthropology.

A visit to the Çatalhöyük website may be the ideal illustration of twenty-first-century anthropology—or anthropological archaeology—in everyday life because it allows you to take a virtual tour around the East Mound, among other things. You will also find links to materials about the site on Facebook, Twitter, YouTube, Vimeo, and Tumblr. ■

density in Mexico that were characteristic of the eastern Mediterranean. As noted earlier, many scholars agree that broad-spectrum foraging was practiced prior to the transition to domestication in highland Mexico and elsewhere in the New World. The mix of crops characteristic of New World domestication also was different. In Mesoamerica, maize and squash appear between 5,000 and 4,000 years ago, with beans appearing about 2,000 years ago (Smith 1995a). In South America, maize appears between 4,000 and 3,000 years ago but was only one of several domesticates. In other areas of South America, soil conditions, altitude, and climate favored

FIGURE 7.12 The distribution of obsidian in Neolithic southwestern Asia from sources in Anatolia (west) and Armenia (east). Obsidian is an extremely sharp and highly prized volcanic glass. Obsidian was traded widely and has been found as far as 500 miles away from its source.

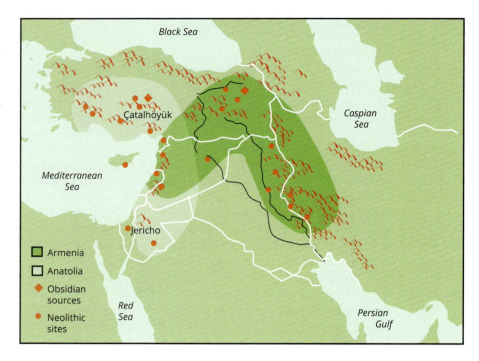

root crops—manioc or potatoes—as well as beans and quinoa (a high-altitude grain), which were of greater importance. Animal domestication was far less important in the Americas than it was in the Old World, largely because of the absence of large, domesticable animals. The Andean llama is the largest animal domesticated in the New World.

Some plants and animals were also domesticated on other continents. Goosefoot, marsh elder, sunflowers, and squash were all domesticated in eastern North America (Smith 1995a, 189–90). A variety of crops, including coffee, millet, okra, and sorghum, were domesticated in different parts of Africa. A large number of important plant domesticates came from eastern Asia, including rice, yam, tea, sugarcane, garlic, onion, apple, and carrot. Archaeologists are coming to agree that complex foragers living in areas of relatively abundant resources were probably responsible for domestication wherever it developed (Price and Gebauer 1995, 7; Smith 1995a, 213). Rich and complex archaeological and genetic evidence from specific areas of the world downplays single-cause explanations of domestication and stresses the need to consider each domestication event in its own terms. Melinda A. Zeder and Bruce D. Smith (2009) are impressed by abundant and varied data from southwestern Asia showing that during several thousand years prior to the appearance of agriculture, "people appear to have been auditioning a wide variety of region-specific plants and animals for leading roles as domesticated resources in the absence of population increase or resource imbalance" (683). In eastern North America, the evidence is similar: climate change at the end of the Pleistocene

occurred 5,000 years before initial plant domestication, 6,200 years before the development of a complex of domesticated crops, and 8,500 years before the key shift to maize agriculture. Thus, climate change is "a necessary precondition rather than a central causal variable," and there is no evidence for population pressure during the 2,000 years or so when plants were first being domesticated and the crop complex was first being organized (Zeder and Smith 2009, 686).

Zeder and Smith insist that this evidence is best understood in terms of niche construction: humans "were actively, and with deliberate intent, shaping adaptive niches with the conscious goal of enhancing the density and productivity of desired resources" (688). Related concerns appear in the work of archaeologists who have adopted from cultural anthropology *theories of practice* that, like niche construction, "examine how humans create macroscale features such as traditions or sociopolitical institutions (structures) through their own daily actions" (Bruno 2009, 703). Bruno also emphasizes the importance for archaeologists of *historical ecology*, which also "focuses on how long-term, accumulative human activities cause observable changes in the natural environment thus creating a 'landscape'" (704). To the extent that the process of niche construction is understood as a form of practical activity and that engineered environments/humanly shaped landscapes are understood as the outcomes of such practical activity, both approaches point in the same direction (Schultz 2009). Their incorporation into anthropological theories of cultural transitions such as the origins of agriculture or social complexity promises to shed important new light on these developments.

What Were the Consequences of Domestication and Sedentism?

Constructed agricultural niches, within which domesticated plants and animals could thrive, promoted sedentism and transformed human life in ways that still have repercussions today. First, land was no longer a free good, available to anyone; it was transformed into particular territories, collectively or individually owned, on which people raised crops and flocks. Thus, sedentism and a high level of resource extraction (whether by complex foraging or farming) led to concepts of property that were rare in previous foraging societies. Graves, grave goods, permanent housing, grain-processing equipment, and the fields and herds connected people to places. The human mark on the environment was larger and more obvious following sedentization and the rise of farming: people built terraces or walls to hold back floods, transforming the landscape in more dramatic ways. Second, settling down affected female fertility and contributed to a rise in population. In foraging societies, a woman's pregnancies tend to be spaced 3–4 years apart because of an extended period of breastfeeding. That is, children in foraging societies are weaned at 3 or 4 years of age but still nurse whenever they feel like it, as frequently as several times an hour (Shostak 1981, 67; Figure 7.13). This nursing stimulus triggers the secretion of a hormone that suppresses ovulation (Henry

1989, 41). Henry summarizes the effects of foraging on female fertility:

> It would appear then that a number of interrelated factors associated with a mobile foraging strategy are likely to have provided natural controls on fertility and perhaps explain the low population densities of the Paleolithic. In mobile foraging societies, women are likely to have experienced both long intervals of breastfeeding by carried children as well as the high energy drain associated with subsistence activities and periodic camp moves. Additionally, their diets, being relatively rich in proteins, would have contributed to maintaining low fat levels, thus further dampening fecundity. (1989, 43)

With complex foraging and increasing sedentism, these brakes on female fecundity would have been eased. This is not to say that a sedentary life is physically undemanding. Farming requires its own heavy labor, from both men and women. The difference seems to be in the kind of physical activity involved. Walking long distances while carrying heavy loads and children was replaced by sowing, hoeing, harvesting, storing, and processing grain. A diet increasingly rich in cereals would have significantly changed the ratio of protein to carbohydrate in the diet. This would have changed the levels of prolactin, increased the positive energy balance, and led to more rapid growth in the young and an earlier age for first menstruation. The ready availability of ground cereals would have enabled mothers to feed their infants soft, high-carbohydrate porridges and gruels. The analysis of infant fecal material recovered from the Wadi Kubbaniya site in Egypt seems to demonstrate that a similar practice was in use with root crops along the Nile at what may have been a year-round site by 19,000 years before the present (Hillman 1989, 230).

The influence of cereals on fertility was observed by Richard Lee (1992) among settled Ju/'hoansi, who had recently begun to eat cereals and experienced a marked rise in fertility (see Chapter 11, "EthnoProfile 11.4: Ju/'hoansi (!Kung)"). Renee Pennington (1992) notes that the increase in Ju/'hoansi reproductive success also seems to be related to a reduction in infant and child mortality rates. But diets based on high-carbohydrate grains are, perhaps surprisingly, less nutritious than the diets of hunters and gatherers. Skeletons from Greece and Turkey in late Paleolithic times indicate an average height of 5 feet 9 inches for men and 5 feet 5 inches for women. With the adoption of agriculture, the average height declined sharply; by about 5,000 years ago, the average man was about 5 feet 3 inches tall and the average woman about 5 feet. Even modern Greeks and Turks

FIGURE 7.13 Ju/'hoansi mothers and children. Until recently, Ju/'hoansi women used to walk more than 1,500 miles per year with children and other burdens on their backs. Children nursed for several years.

are still not, on average, as tall as the late Paleolithic people of the same region.

In the short term, agriculture was probably developed in ancient southwestern Asia, and perhaps elsewhere, to increase food supplies to support an increasing population at a time of serious resource stress. Because the agroecology created an environment favorable to the plants, farmers were able to cultivate previously unusable land. When such vital necessities as water could be brought to the land between the Tigris and Euphrates rivers in Mesopotamia, for example, land on which wheat and barley was not native could support dense stands of the domesticated grains. The greater yield of domesticated plants per unit of ground also led to a greater proportion of cultivated plants in the diet, even when wild plants were still being eaten and were as plentiful as before. But as cultivated plants took on an increasingly large role in prehistoric diets, people became dependent on plants, and the plants in turn became completely dependent on the agroecology created by the people (Figure 7.14). According to Richard Lee (1992, 48), the Ju/'hoansi, who live in the Kalahari Desert, use more than 100 plants (14 fruits and nuts; 15 berries; 18 species of edible gum; 41 edible roots and bulbs; and 17 leafy greens, beans, melons, and other foods). By contrast, modern farmers rely on no more than 20 plants, and of those, 3—wheat, maize, and rice—feed most of the world's people. Historically, only one or two grain crops were staples for a specific group of people. If hail, floods, droughts, infestations, frost, heat, weeds, erosion, or other factors destroyed the crop or reduced the harvest, the risk of starvation increased. Deforestation, soil loss, silted streams, and the loss of many native species followed domestication. In the lower Tigris–Euphrates Valley, irrigation water used by early farmers carried high

levels of soluble salts, poisoning the soil and making it unusable to this day (Figure 7.15).

New features of the agroecology also created new opportunities for the spread of disease. As we saw earlier, in sub-Saharan Africa, the clearing of land for farming created standing water, which provided an excellent environment for malaria-carrying mosquitoes. As increasing numbers of people began to live near each other in relatively permanent settlements, the disposal of human (and eventually animal) waste also became increasingly problematic. Food storage was a key element in agroecological niches, but stored grains attracted pests, like rats and mice, which coevolved with the domesticated crops that attracted them. Some of these pests also spread disease-causing microorganisms that thrived in human, animal, and plant wastes. The larger the number of people living very near each other, the greater the likelihood of communicable disease transmission: by the time one person recovers from the disease, someone else reaches the infectious stage and can reinfect the first; as a result, the disease never leaves the population. Finally, the nutritional deficiencies of an agricultural diet may have reduced people's resistance to disease. Foragers could just walk away from disease, reducing the likelihood that it would spread, but this option is closed for

FIGURE 7.14 (*Left*) Corn as far as the eye can see: monocropping can provide enormous yields but exposes the field to risk. (*Right*) Rwandan man tending his intercropped banana and coffee farm, where the plants provide nutrients for one another and lower the risk of catastrophic losses.

FIGURE 7.15 The lower Tigris–Euphrates Valley; irrigation water used by early farmers carried high levels of soluble salts, poisoning the soil and making it unusable to this day.

settled people. Thus, increased exposure to epidemic disease was a major consequence of the modified selection pressures to which human populations became vulnerable as a consequence of their ancestors' construction of agroecological niches.

Maintaining an agroecology that will support domesticated plants and animals requires much more labor than does foraging. People must clear the land, plant the seeds, tend the young plants, protect them from predators, harvest them, process the seeds, store them, and select the seeds for planting the next year; similarly, people must tend and protect domesticated animals, cull the herds, shear the sheep, milk the goats, and so on. This heavy workload is not divided up randomly among members of the population. Increasing dependence on agriculture by increasing numbers of people produced an increasingly complex division of labor, which set the stage for the emergence of complex hierarchical societies with different forms of social inequality.

Insight into the processes producing these changes is offered by economic anthropologist Rhoda Halperin (1994). Borrowing concepts from the economic historian Karl Polanyi, Halperin argues that every economic system can be analyzed in terms of two kinds of movements: *locational movements,* or "changes of place," and

IN THEIR OWN WORDS

The Food Revolution

Although dietary quality declined for the earliest full-time farmers, later contact and trade among different farming societies enriched diets everywhere. Over the past 500 years, as Jack Weatherford emphasizes, foods domesticated in the New World have played a particularly important role in the "food revolution."

On Thanksgiving Day, North Americans sometimes remember the Indians who gave them their cuisine by dining on turkey with cornbread stuffing, cranberry sauce, succotash, corn on the cob, sweet potato casserole, stewed squash and tomatoes, baked beans with maple syrup, and pecan pie. Few cooks or gourmets, however, recognize the much broader extent to which American Indian cuisine radically changed cooking and dining in every part of the globe from Timbuktu to Tibet. Sichuan beef with chilies, German chocolate cake, curried potatoes, vanilla ice

cream, Hungarian goulash, peanut brittle, and pizza all owe their primary flavorings to the American Indians.

The discovery of America sparked a revolution in food and cuisine that has not yet shown any signs of abating. Tomatoes, chilies, and green peppers formed the first wave of American flavorings to circle the globe, but the American Indian garden still grows a host of plants that the world may yet learn to use and enjoy. These plants may have practical uses, such as providing food in otherwise unusable land or producing more food in underused land. They also vary the daily diets of people throughout the world and thereby increase nutrition. Even in this high-tech age, the low-tech plant continues to be the key to nutrition and health. Despite all the plant improvements brought about by modern science, the American Indians remain the developers of the world's largest array of nutritious foods and the primary contributors to the world's varied cuisines.

Source: Weatherford 1988, 115.

appropriational movements, or "changes of hands." In her view, ecological relationships that affect the economy are properly understood as changes of place, as when people must move into the grasslands, gather mongongo nuts, and transport them back to camp. Economic relationships, by contrast, are more properly understood as changes of hands, as when mongongo nuts are distributed to all members of the camp, whether or not they helped to gather them. Thus, ecological (locational) movements involve transfers of energy; economic (appropriational) movements, by contrast, involve transfers of rights (Halperin 1994, 59). Analyzed in this way, people's rights to consume mongongo nuts cannot be derived from the labor they expended to gather them.

Another way of seeing the difference is to pay attention to the connection between food storage and food sharing. An ecologist might argue that those who gather mongongo nuts have no choice but to share them out and consume them immediately because they have no way to store this food if it is not eaten. Anthropologist Tim Ingold (1983) agreed that the obligation to share would make storage unnecessary, but he also pointed out that sharing with others today ordinarily obligates them to share with you tomorrow. Put another way, sharing food can be seen not only as a way of avoiding spoilage but also as a way of storing up IOUs for the future.

Once societies develop ways to preserve and store food and other material goods, however, new possibilities open up. Archaeological evidence indicates that the more food there is to store, the more people invest in storage facilities (e.g., pits, pottery vessels) and the more quickly they become sedentary. Large-scale food-storage techniques involve a series of "changes of place" that buffer a population from ecological fluctuations for long periods of time. But techniques of food storage alone predict nothing about the "changes of hands" that food will undergo once it has been stored. Food-storage techniques have been associated with all subsistence strategies, including that of complex food collectors. This suggests that economic relations of consumption, involving the transfer of rights in stored food, have long been open to considerable cultural elaboration and manipulation (Halperin 1994, 178).

When people started planting grain, they could not have anticipated all of the problems to come. Initially, agriculture had several apparent advantages, the foremost of which was that farmers could extract far more food from the same amount of territory than could foragers. Put another way, to feed the same number of

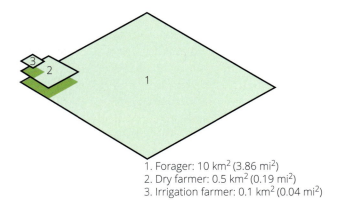

1. Forager: 10 km² (3.86 mi²)
2. Dry farmer: 0.5 km² (0.19 mi²)
3. Irrigation farmer: 0.1 km² (0.04 mi²)

FIGURE 7.16 Each square shows the proportionate amount of land needed to feed a single individual using three different food-getting strategies.

people, a dry farmer needs 20 times less land than a forager, and an irrigation farmer needs 100 times less land (Figure 7.16). Foragers know that they will find enough food to eat, but they never know how much of any given food resource they will find or exactly when or where they will find it. By contrast, farmers can predict, with a given amount of seed—and favorable conditions—the approximate size of a harvest. Herders can predict how many lambs they will have in the spring based on the number of rams and ewes in their herds. Sedentism and a fairly reliable and predictable domesticated food supply provided new opportunities for social complexity.

How Do Anthropologists Define Social Complexity?

Early Neolithic farming and herding societies differed little from the foraging societies they replaced. For the Natufians, foraging continued to be important alongside cultivation for many generations. In the same way, the social organization of these societies differed little from that of foraging societies; although people began to settle in permanent villages, archaeological evidence suggests that no great differences in wealth, power, or prestige divided villagers initially. Put another way, these early farming villages continued to practice **egalitarian social relations**. Things began to change, however, beginning about 5,000 years ago in southwestern Asia and shortly thereafter in Egypt, the Indus Valley (India), China, Mesoamerica (Valley of Mexico), and the Andes (Peru; see Figure 7.1). These six regions of the globe were the first to invent, essentially independently, a new way of organizing society called social stratification, which, as we saw earlier, was based on the assumption that different groups in society were entitled to different amounts of wealth, power, and prestige.

---

egalitarian social relations Social relations in which no great differences in wealth, power, or prestige divide members from one another.

A move from egalitarian forms of social organization to social stratification involves the development of social complexity. Social stratification was made possible when societies produced amounts of food that exceeded the basic subsistence needs of the population. Storage of **surplus production** and control over its distribution made it possible for some members of a society to stop producing food altogether and to specialize in various occupations (e.g., weaving, pot making) or in new social roles (e.g., king, priest). In some cases, **occupational specialization** also created a wide gulf between most of society's members and a new social **class** of rulers who successfully claimed the bulk of this new wealth as their due. Societies set up in this way could support many more people than could the village societies that preceded them, not only because they successfully produced, stored, and distributed more food but also because they invented new ways of organizing people to carry out many new tasks. As a result, anthropologists refer to these as the first **complex societies** to appear in the archaeological record.

Why Is It Incorrect to Describe Foraging Societies as "Simple"?

Although the concept of a complex society seems straightforward enough, anthropologists must define this expression carefully to avoid misunderstanding. It is common to assume that the opposite of complex is simple, yet foraging and farming societies are not "simple" societies. As we saw, not even all foragers were alike; and in any case, foragers had to file away in their minds an enormously complex amount of information about different varieties of plants, seasonal habits of animals, details of kinship, and nuances of their religion and art. It was the comparatively simple technology of foragers— based on wood, stone, and bone tools that could be easily made by everyone—that was very different from the more complex technology that had to be developed and mastered to build massive pyramids, weave cloth, or smelt and mold metals such as copper, tin, and iron. These activities not only required highly specialized knowledge of architecture, textiles, and metallurgy but also presupposed a form of social organization that permitted some members of society to become highly specialized in certain activities while other members carried out different tasks.

Differences in technology and social organization say nothing about the complexity of the minds of the people involved. However, such differences strongly shaped the scale and texture of life in the two kinds of society. Setting up a temporary camp in a foraging society involved fewer options and fewer decisions, in terms

of technology and social organization, than did the construction of a pyramid. Pyramid building required more than architectural skill; suitable materials had to be found, quarried, or produced and transported to the site. Additionally, suitable workers had to be found, trained, supervised, fed, and lodged for the duration of construction, which may have taken decades. Finally, all these specialized activities had to occur in the right order for the project to be successfully completed. Not only would a foraging band—some 50 individuals of all ages—have been too small to carry out such a project, but also their traditional egalitarian social relations would have made the giving and taking of orders impossible. Indeed, the whole idea of building massive pyramids would have probably seemed pointless to them.

A society that not only wants to build pyramids but also has the material, political, and social means to do so is clearly different from a foraging band or a Neolithic farming village. For archaeologist T. Douglas Price (1995), a complex society has "more parts and more connections between parts" (140). Anthropologist Leslie White (1949) spoke in terms of a major change in the amount of energy a society can capture from nature and use to remodel the natural world to suit its own purposes. The members of foraging bands also depended on energy captured from the natural world but on a scale vastly smaller than that required to build pyramids. Archaeologist Robert Wenke (1999) emphasizes that, in complex societies, "the important thing is that the ability and incentive to make these investments are radically different from the capacities of Pleistocene bands, in that they imply the ability of some members of society to control and organize others" (348).

What Is the Archaeological Evidence for Social Complexity?

How do archaeologists recognize social and cultural complexity when they see it? Important clues are certain kinds of remains that begin to appear in the

---

surplus production The production of amounts of food that exceed the basic subsistence needs of the population.

occupational specialization Specialization in various occupations (e.g., weaving or pot making) or in new social roles (e.g., king or priest) that is found in socially complex societies.

class A ranked group within a hierarchically stratified society whose membership is defined primarily in terms of wealth, occupation, or other economic criteria.

complex societies Societies with large populations, an extensive division of labor, and occupational specialization.

FIGURE 7.17 Monumental modern architecture: the Petronas Towers dwarf the surrounding city of Kuala Lumpur, Malaysia.

FIGURE 7.18 Among the most widespread indicators of early social complexity are the remains of monumental architecture, such as the Temple of the Great Jaguar at the Mayan site of Tikal, Guatemala.

archaeological record after about 5,000 years ago. Among the most widespread indicators of social complexity are the remains of **monumental architecture**. Contemporary monumental architecture includes such structures as the Eiffel Tower in Paris, France; the Mall of America in Bloomington, Minnesota; and the Petronas Towers in Kuala Lumpur, Malaysia (Figure 7.17). Ancient monumental architecture included public buildings, private residences, tombs, settlement walls, irrigation canals, and so on. Together with monumental architecture, however, archaeologists usually find evidence of technologically simpler constructions. Assemblages that demonstrate such architectural variability contrast with those from earlier periods, when dwellings were simpler and more uniform, and monumental structures were absent.

Everywhere it is found, the earliest monumental architecture consists of raised platforms, temples, pyramids, or pyramidlike structures (Figure 7.18). Different building techniques were used to construct these monuments in different areas, and the structures did not all serve the same purpose. Therefore, archaeologists have long rejected the notion that all pyramid-building societies derived from ancient Egypt. Rather, the cross-cultural similarities of these structures appear to have a more practical explanation. None of the architects in the earliest complex societies knew how to build arches and barrel vaults. Moreover, in places like the Maya lowlands in modern Central America, builders had to work without metal, winches, hoists, or wheeled carts. Under these circumstances, the only tall structures they could have built were such basic geometric forms as squares, rectangles, and pyramids (Wenke 1999, 577).

Among the monumental structures built in the earliest complex societies were tombs. Differences in the size and construction of burials parallel differences in the size and construction of residences, and both suggest the emergence of a stratified society. Graves that are larger and built of more costly materials often contain a variety of objects, called **grave goods**, that were buried with the corpse. Smaller, modest graves occurring in the same assemblage and containing few or no grave goods provide evidence for social stratification. The number and quality of grave goods found with a corpse give clues as to just how highly stratified a society was. Many of the grave goods recovered from rich tombs are masterpieces of ceramics, metallurgy, weaving, and other crafts, indicating that the society had achieved a high degree of technological skill and, thus, a complex division of labor.

Archaeologists often recover evidence of complex occupational specialization directly from a site. They search for **concentrations of particular artifacts** that may indicate what sort of activity was carried out in each area. Archaeologists can distinguish garbage dumps from, say, areas where people lived, which would have

monumental architecture Architectural constructions of a greater-than-human scale, such as pyramids, temples, and tombs.

grave goods Objects buried with a corpse.

concentrations of particular artifacts Sets of artifacts indicating that particular social activities took place at a particular area in an archaeological site when that site was inhabited in the past.

been kept free of refuse. Similarly, broken pots or kilns found evenly distributed throughout a settlement might suggest that pottery was made by individual families. However, considerable evidence of pottery manufacture concentrated within a particular area strongly suggests the existence of a potter's workshop and, thus, occupational specialization. Remains of the tools used to make artifacts—potter's wheels, spindle whorls, or slag, for example—often provide important information about the degree to which craft technology developed at a particular time and place.

The emergence of complex societies seems connected almost everywhere with a phenomenal explosion of architectural and artistic creativity. Although anthropologists admire the material achievements of these ancient societies, many are struck by the "wasteful" expenditure of resources by a tiny ruling elite. Why, for example, did virtually every original complex society build monumental architecture? Why did they not invest their increasing technological and organizational power in less elaborate projects that might have benefited the ordinary members of society? Why were masterpieces of pottery, metallurgy, and weaving often hoarded and buried in the tombs of dead rulers instead of being more widely available? These excesses apparently did not develop in the early Harappan civilization of the Indus Valley, but they are so widespread elsewhere that the questions remain important.

Archaeologist Michael Hoffman, an expert on prehistoric Egypt, proposed that the key to understanding the first complex societies lies in their social organization. For the first time in human history, societies had been formed in which tremendous power was concentrated in the hands of a tiny elite—who undoubtedly found their privileges challenged by their new subjects. Under such circumstances, the production of monumental architecture and quantities of luxury goods served as evidence of the elite's fitness to rule. Hoffman prefers to call these objects "powerfacts" rather than "artifacts" because their role was to demonstrate the superior power of the rulers (Hoffman 1991, 294; Hayden 1995, 67; Figure 7.19).

So far, we have described the kinds of archaeological remains that suggest that a site was once part of a complex society. But complex societies ordinarily consisted of a number of settlements organized in a hierarchy. Consequently, archaeologists survey the region to determine how any given site compares to other simultaneously occupied settlements in the same area. (See Chapter 6 for a discussion of survey techniques.) The most common and helpful surface artifacts recovered during such surveys are often pieces of broken pots called **sherds**. Different kinds of sherds found on a site's

FIGURE 7.19 A "powerfact" from the tomb of Tutankhamen. A collar found around the neck is composed of gold, colored glass, and obsidian. There are 250 inlaid segments, and each claw is grasping a *shen*, a symbol of totality.

surface provide a rough inventory of the different cultural traditions followed by inhabitants over time. When the survey is completed, archaeologists tabulate and map the percentages of different kinds of sherds. A series of maps showing the distribution of each particular kind of pottery illustrates the degree to which settlement size and population changed over time. When researchers are able to accurately associate the different kinds of pottery with the stratigraphy of well-excavated sites in the region, they can devise a portrait of settlement patterns over time. Systematic survey and mapping work in southern Iraq permitted Robert Adams and Hans Nissen to show how the small, scattered settlements that prevailed in the countryside of ancient Mesopotamia around 8,000 years ago were gradually abandoned over the centuries, such that by about 5,200 years ago virtually everyone was living in a handful of large settlements, which Adams and Nissen (1972) call "cities."

Why Did Stratification Begin?

As we saw in Chapter 6, archaeologists typically organize their findings using a set of four categories that serve as benchmarks in the history of human social organization. These categories—bands, tribes, chiefdoms, states—were developed together with cultural anthropologists and rest on insights derived from the study of living and historically documented societies of different kinds together with the material remains they all tend to leave behind (Wenke 1999, 340–44).

sherds Pieces of broken pots.

As we have seen, our ancestors apparently lived in foraging *bands* until some 10,000 years ago, when the last ice sheets melted, after which they began to experiment with new subsistence strategies and forms of social organization. Those who came to farm or herd for a living were able to support larger populations and are classified as *tribes*. Societies classified as tribes are enormously varied. Morton Fried (1967) preferred to call a society of this kind a "rank" society. Elman Service (1962), who was attempting to identify key turning points in the course of human prehistory, viewed tribes as a transitional form rather than a well-defined societal type. The ambiguity of terms like *rank society* or *tribe* has led some archaeologists to substitute the term *transegalitarian society* to describe all societies that are neither egalitarian nor socially stratified (Hayden 1995, 18). Seemingly poised between equality and hierarchy, transegalitarian societies have flourished at various times and places up to the present day, and they do not appear necessarily to be on the way to becoming anything else in particular.

Unlike a transegalitarian society, the *chiefdom* is an example—indeed, the earliest clear example—of a socially stratified society, as we saw among the southern Natufians. Ordinarily, only the chief and close relatives are set apart and allowed privileged access to wealth, power, and prestige; other members of the society continue to share roughly similar social status. Chiefdoms are generally larger than tribes and show a greater degree of craft production, although such production is not yet in the hands of full-time specialists. Chiefdoms also exhibit a greater degree of hierarchical political control, centered on the chief, relatives of the chief, and their great deeds. Archaeologically, chiefdoms are interesting because some, such as the southern Natufians, apparently remained as they were and then disappeared, whereas others went on to develop into states.

The *state* is a stratified society that possesses a territory that is defended from outside enemies with an army and from internal disorder with police. States, which have separate governmental institutions to enforce laws and to collect taxes and tribute, are run by an elite that possesses a monopoly on the use of force. In early states, government and religion were mutually reinforcing: rulers were often priests or were thought to be gods themselves. State societies are supported by sophisticated food-production and food-storage techniques. Craft production is normally specialized and yields a dazzling variety of goods, many of which are refined specialty items destined for the ruling elite. Art and architecture also flourish, and writing frequently has developed in state societies. Shortly after the appearance of the first state in an area, other states usually develop

nearby. From time to time, one might conquer its neighbors, organizing them into a vaster political network called an *empire*.

Monumental public buildings of a religious or governmental nature, highly developed crafts (e.g., pottery, weaving, and metallurgy), and regional settlement patterns that show at least three levels in a hierarchy of social complexity are all archaeological evidence of a state. Interstate conflict is suspected when towns and cities are surrounded by high walls and confirmed by artifacts that served as weapons, by art depicting battle, and by written documents that record military triumphs. Because writing developed in most of the early states, various inscriptions often provide valuable information on social organization that supplements the archaeologist's reconstructions.

Archaeologists assume regional integration when they find unique styles in architecture, pottery, textiles, and other artifacts distributed uniformly over a wide area; such evidence is called a *cultural horizon*. For archaeologists, the term *civilization* usually refers to the flowering of cultural creativity that accompanies the rise of state societies and persists for a long time. Widespread uniformity in material culture, however, need not imply a single set of political institutions. Archaeologists who wish to speak of a state or empire, therefore, require additional evidence, such as a hierarchy of settlement patterns or written records that spell out centralized governmental policies. Cultural change in all early complex societies tended to alternate between periods of relative cultural uniformity and political unity and periods of regional differentiation and lack of political integration.

We should note that the preceding categories and the framework for cross-cultural comparison that they provide have been critiqued in recent years. Postprocessual archaeologists like Shanks and Tilley (1987), for example, argue that traditional comparisons of ancient "state" societies pay too much attention to environmental and technological similarities while ignoring or dismissing the significance of the distinct cultural patterns of meanings and values that made each of these ancient civilizations unique. Other archaeologists, however, maintain that the similarities among ancient civilizations are just as striking as their cultural differences and require explanation (Trigger 1993). Although this debate continues, many archaeologists have tried to strike a balance, acknowledging the overall descriptive value of a formal category like "state" but carrying out research projects that highlight the cultural variation to be found among societies grouped together as "states" (Wenke 1999, 346).

How Can Anthropologists Explain the Rise of Complex Societies?

Given that humans lived in foraging bands for most of their history and that, in some parts of the world, village farming remained a stable, viable way of life for hundreds or thousands of years, it is not obvious why complex societies should ever have developed at all. Over the years, anthropologists have proposed a number of explanations. Some of their hypotheses (like some designed to explain our ancestors' turn to domestication or sedentism) argue for a single, uniform cause, or prime mover, that triggered the evolution of complex society worldwide. Indeed, as we will see, many of these prime movers are the same factors suggested to explain the development of domestication and sedentism.

For a long time, scholars thought that the domestication of plants and sedentary life in farming villages offered people the leisure time to invent social and technological complexity. This explanation is questionable, however, because many farming societies never developed beyond the village level of organization. In addition, social complexity apparently can develop without the support of a fully agricultural economy, as among the Natufians. Finally, ethnographic research has shown that foraging people actually have more leisure time than most village farmers.

Other scholars suggest that social complexity depended on arid or semiarid environments (Figure 7.20).

The first complex societies in Egypt, Mesopotamia, and the Indus Valley were located in dry regions crossed by a major river, which provided water for intensified agricultural production following the construction of irrigation canals. The apparent connection between farming in an arid environment, the need for irrigation water, and the rise of complex societies led Karl Wittfogel (1957) to hypothesize that complex societies first developed to construct and maintain large irrigation systems. Wittfogel argued that these irrigation systems could not have functioned without a ruling elite to direct operations. Thus, he sees the development of what he calls *hydraulic agriculture* as the key to the evolution of complex society. This hypothesis, although suggestive, has also been called into question. First, societies such as the Hohokam of the American Southwest apparently operated an extensive irrigation system without developing social stratification or cultural complexity (Wenke 1999, 356). Second, the sorts of complex irrigation systems Wittfogel had in mind—those requiring a bureaucracy—appear late in the archaeological record of several early civilizations, long after the first appearance of monumental architecture, cities, and other signs of social complexity (see, e.g., Adams 1981, 53). Irrigation may have played a role in the development of complex societies, but it was apparently not the single prime mover that brought them into existence.

Because many early groups of village farmers never developed a high degree of social complexity, archaeologists see its appearance more as the exception, not the rule. Some suggest that population pressure was the

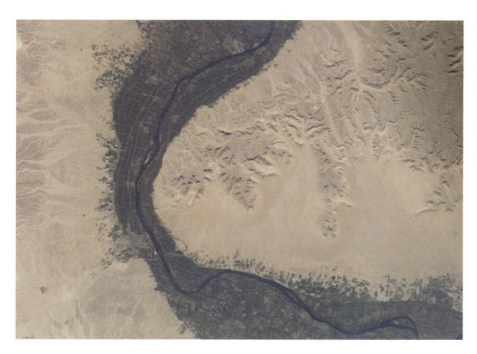

FIGURE 7.20 The civilization of ancient Egypt was supported by agricultural practices that relied on the regular flooding pattern of the Nile River. In this photograph taken from the Space Shuttle, the wide, dark band crossing the light desert region is the cultivated floodplain of the Nile. The river itself is the very dark, narrow line snaking its way through this cultivated area.

decisive force: if the food supply could not keep up with a growing population, social chaos would have resulted unless someone were able to exercise power to allocate resources and keep the peace. This scenario is rejected, however, by those who argue that social inequality developed in societies where resources were abundant and opportunistic individuals could gain power using surpluses to indebt others to them through competitive feasting or control of labor (Arnold 1995; Hayden 1995). Also, archaeological evidence from more than one part of the world shows that population pressure was not a problem when social complexity first appeared. Some archaeologists now suggest that human societies were able to limit population growth if they chose to do so, whether by migration, infanticide, abortion, contraception, or late marriage. Finally, the greatest decline in fertility in the modern Western world did not occur among the hungry, nor was it triggered by the invention of new birth-control technology: it was the well-fed, middle-class families in capitalist societies who began to have fewer children, not the poverty-stricken workers. The forces that change reproductive rates are far more complex than a simple population-pressure model would allow.

If population pressure did not undermine the egalitarian social relations of village farmers, perhaps conflict with other villagers was to blame. If all available farmland were settled, for example, making it impossible for people to move away at times of conflict, the only solution, apart from chaos, would have been to establish rules to resolve conflicts, thus leading to the development of more complex political structures (Nissen 1988, 60–61). Sooner or later, however, if chaos could not be contained, warfare might have broken out between neighboring villages. Indeed, Brian Hayden suggests that power-seeking individuals might well have manipulated such tensions, using economic surpluses to settle conflicts and amassing personal wealth and power in the process. This could not occur, in his view, until people became willing to accept bloodwealth, a crucial innovation not found in egalitarian societies (Hayden 1995, 32). **Bloodwealth** is economic surplus, paid by perpetrators to compensate their victims for their loss. If bloodwealth payments disproportionately favored some individuals or groups over others, their social relations would no longer be egalitarian.

Warfare, population pressure, and arid environments all play roles in Robert Carneiro's (1970) theory of the rise of the first states in Peru, Mesopotamia, and Egypt and of later, secondary states elsewhere. In Carneiro's scheme, population pressure would have led to increasing conflict between neighboring villages once it was no longer possible for villagers to cultivate new lands. This situation, which he calls *environmental circumscription*, might have been especially likely in early farming societies that grew up along river valleys running through deserts, such as those in Mesopotamia, Egypt, and coastal Peru. When the desert barrier halted village expansion, new farmlands could be obtained only by taking them away from other villages by force. Carneiro's theory has stimulated much discussion. However, the role he assigns to population pressure is open to the criticism raised earlier, and many archaeologists still have not found evidence that would confirm or refute Carneiro's hypotheses.

Clearly, any force that could destroy the egalitarian relations that prevailed in farming societies for hundreds or thousands of years would have had to be very powerful. In this connection, David Webster (1975) suggested that the turning point came in farming societies that were chiefdoms. You will recall that chiefdoms possess a limited form of social stratification that sets the chiefly line above other members of society, who continue to enjoy social equality reinforced by kinship. If warfare in such a society undermined the old relations of kinship, people might eventually be desperate for social order and accept social stratification if that restored stability.

All the prime movers discussed so far involve technological, economic, environmental, or biological factors that would have forced societies into complexity no matter what their previous cultural traditions might have been. Realizing that these external factors were less powerful than once believed, many anthropologists turned their attention to internal, sociocultural factors that might have led to the rise of social complexity: recall Barbara Bender's theory about the origin of domestication, which has inspired Brian Hayden, among others. During the 1960s and 1970s, some anthropologists were influenced by the work of Karl Marx and his followers, who argued that attempts to resolve contradictions that develop within a particular form of social organization can lead to profound social change. Marxian analysis might suggest, for example, that external trade in luxury items by the leaders of early chiefdoms may have generated conflict between the chief's family (whose interests were served by trade) and the common people (whose interests were undermined by it) (Kipp and Schortman 1989). Such a conflict of interests might eventually have thrown a chiefdom completely out of equilibrium, leading to the kind of social transformation suggested by Webster (1975).

Written documents, when available, can sometimes provide enough detailed insight into social organization to identify social hierarchies and trace their

---

bloodwealth Material goods paid by perpetrators to compensate their victims for their loss.

IN THEIR OWN WORDS

The Ecological Consequences of Social Complexity

Many people have tried to ascribe both the rise and decline of early complex societies to factors rooted in the natural environment. Dan and Prudence Rice argue that a closer look at Mesoamerica suggests that things were never that simple.

It is apparent that the Maya initiated practices to reduce the regionwide processes of nutrient loss, deterioration of soil structure, destabilization of water flows, soil erosion, and loss of productive components of their environment. The results of the Maya "experiment" demonstrate that tropical forests are neither zones of unbounded fertility nor homogeneous zones in which cultivation redundancy is in order. Theirs was a multihabitat and multitechnology system that was labor intensive, a system that relied on a primary motivation for increased production—a growing population—as the source of energy to run the system. Relatively speaking, it was an ecologically efficient regime that met increased demands for production through increased labor intensity and an increased agricultural land base.

The Maya adapted to the tropical forest environment over a long period, and a key to their success was undoubtedly the opportunity for sustained experimentation and evaluation. In the Yaxha-Sacnab basins, the environmental strains caused by soil depletion and alteration of the lacustrine ecosystem developed slowly, in tandem with low rates of population growth, too slowly to act as a

mechanism to reduce overall population increase until at least Late Classic times. This statement is not meant to suggest that the Maya did not suffer constraints. Their growth, expansion, and intensification forced the Maya to consider more closely the processes of degradation. No data exist at present, however, indicating that the Maya agricultural system had reached its productive limits or that reduced productivity caused the civilization's "collapse." Certainly, some habitats or technologies were more vulnerable to strain than others, and the circumstantial juxtaposition of degradation and cultural decline in the Yaxha-Sacnab basins is theoretically enticing. But Maya responses to production problems were not only technological but social, religious, and political, and effective maintenance of an agro-economic infrastructure depended on cultural forces in addition to environmental ones. Both require further investigation.

The unresolved issue of the Maya "collapse" and the long-term success of the Maya civilization may foster spurious—and dangerous—complacency toward future economic development of the tropics if the relative rates of change are not kept in perspective. Current population trends in tropical areas engender a real sense of urgency about the work ahead. Tropical environments such as the Petén must be evaluated before modern populations obscure the details of ecosystem history so that pertinent information on successful, long-term adaptive strategies can be made available while it still might have some impact on future land use.

Source: Rice and Rice 1993.

development over time. But for ancient complex societies that lacked writing—and this includes all six of the first such societies—the Marxian approach is exceedingly difficult to apply to archaeological materials. Many of the remains of the earliest complex societies are incomplete and could be compatible with more than one form of social organization. Indeed, any theory, Marxian or not, that seeks to explain the rise of a complex society in terms of social relations, political culture, or religious beliefs faces the same problem. However important they may have been, such phenomena do not fossilize and cannot be reliably inferred on the basis of archaeological data alone, an uncomfortable fact that continues to frustrate archaeologists trying to reconstruct prehistory.

Anthropologists cannot offer a single, sweeping explanation of cultural evolution, although this was their hope at the end of the nineteenth century. But their attempts to test various hypotheses that promise such explanations have led to a far richer appreciation of the complexities of social and cultural change. Archaeologist Robert Wenke observed that "cultural evolution is not a continuous, cumulative, gradual change in most places. 'Fits and starts' better describes it" (1999, 336). He further emphasized the remarkable adaptability of cultural systems, noting in a discussion of Mesoamerica that environmental and ecological analyses can only explain so much: "once we get beyond this simple ecological level of analysis, we encounter a welter of variability in socio-political forms, economic histories, settlement patterns, and the other elaborations of these complex societies" (1999, 609).

More recently, however, increasing attention has shifted to the intensive, cumulative *effects* of the emergence and spread of domestication, sedentism, social hierarchies, and states. Many observers are now speaking of the **Anthropocene**, a new geological epoch that marks the point at which human activities became decisive in shaping the climate and the environment on earth. As anthropologist Heather Anne Swanson observes, "In the Anthropocene, humans are no longer creatures who merely alter regional ecologies; rather, through fossil fuel consumption, global climate change, and mass species extinctions, humans trump even the glaciers in their planetary effects. . . . At the same time . . . the Anthropocene is also a call to recognize that while human influence is ubiquitous, people are thoroughly dependent on multispecies arrangements that far exceed their control" (2018, 143).

James Scott also speaks of the Anthropocene, arguing that evidence traditionally interpreted to support universal cultural evolutionary sequences of improvement may tell a rather different story when read "against the grain" (Scott 2017). Provocatively, Scott argues "that domestication ought to be understood in an expansive way, as the ongoing effort of *Homo sapiens* to shape the entire environment to its liking (2017, 19; italics added). Notably, Scott situates his analysis within the framework of niche construction. According to Scott, "Long before the more explosive and recent 'thick' Anthropocene," human niche construction initiated a "thin" Anthropocene when our ancestors used fire to remodel the landscape some 400,000 years ago—later intensifying our mark on the landscape about 12,000 ears ago, when our ancestors developed ways of life based on the domestication of plants and animals and permanent settlement on the land. A decisive shift took place around 4,000 years after than, when some of our ancestors invented the institution of the state (2017, 3).

Using Neolithic Mesopotamia as his example, Scott emphasizes how activities involved in human niche construction expanded as our ancestors entered into coevolutionary relationships not only with grains such as wheat and animals such as sheep, goats, and chickens, but also with scavengers and parasites and microbes that found places within a new settled ecosystem, which some archaeologists have come to call the *domus*, or household (e.g., Hodder 1990). Scott describes the early

domus as a "multispecies resettlement camp" that promoted new alliances and adjustments among the humans and nonhumans who now had to find a way to live together. That is, his interpretation echoes the work of those anthropologists who regard domestication as a process that evolutionary biologists describe as *mutualism*, which acknowledges the active contributions of both human and nonhuman partners (2017, 73).

Reliance on domesticated grains and animals (and the modified environments they required) eventually produced a qualitative change in human subsistence practices. This has traditionally been described by anthropologists as a move from forms of extensive agriculture like swiddening to forms of intensive agriculture incorporating fixed fields and the use of draft animals to pull plows. When this occurs, Scott argues, "the term 'domestication'—from 'domus,' or household—needs to be taken rather literally. The domus was a unique and unprecedented concentration of tilled fields, seed and plant stores, people, and domestic animals, all coevolving with consequences no one could have foreseen" (2017, 73). Importantly, successfully managing the heterogeneous components on which intensive agriculture depended created the conditions for the development of more complex human forms of social life. What Scott calls "the late Neolithic grain and manpower module" became the base on which the first states were erected (2017, 116). In his view, if the key attributes of the first states were "territoriality and a specialized state apparatus: walls, tax collection, and officials," then such states were present in Mesopotamia by 3200 BCE (2017, 118).

Scott emphasizes that the domesticated grains on which states came to rely not only were sources of food, but they were better suited than root crops for "concentrated production, tax assessment, appropriation, cadastral survey, storage and rationing. On suitable soil, wheat provides the agro-ecology for dense concentrations of human subjects" (2017, 21). In the context of a state, niche construction takes the form of what Scott calls "state landscaping," which involves the building and maintenance of infrastructure like irrigation canals and new fields (but also leads to deforestation and the degradation of soil and water). State institutions are a success when they are able to manage relations among plants, animals, and the human populations required to perform agroecological labor, but they are vulnerable to social breakdown in the face of epidemic disease, raiding, and warfare (2017, 23). Over time, these processes generate non-linear trajectories that Scott prefers to call *deep history* rather than prehistory or cultural evolution. The rest of this chapter offers a sample of some of that variability, examining comparative evidence bearing on the deep history of the first complex societies in South America.

Anthropocene A new geological epoch that marks the point at which human activities became decisive in shaping the climate and the environment on earth.

Andean Civilization

The Andean region of South America gave birth to a rich, complex, and varied civilization that culminated in the Inka Empire, the largest political system to develop in the New World before the arrival of Europeans. The very richness and complexity of this civilization, however, coupled with insufficient funding for archaeological research, has meant that only the barest outlines of its development can be traced (Table 7.1).

The geography of the Andes is distinctive and had an important influence on the development of local complex societies. This is a region of young, steep-sided mountains and volcanoes. Along the Pacific can be found deserts on which rain has not fallen for centuries as well as a narrow, lowland coastal strip covered with lush greenery that is supported not by rain but by fog rising from the ocean. This is the zone of the *lomas*, or fog meadows, which is crossed by over two dozen short rivers flowing from the highlands. The western edge of the loma lowlands rises abruptly through several climatic zones to the highlands, or *sierra*, of the Andes Mountains. Rolling grassland areas between 3,900 and 5,000 meters form a zone called the *puna*, the highest level suitable for human habitation. Finally, the eastern slopes of the Andes descend into the humid tropical forests of the Amazon headwaters, a zone called the *selva*. In recent years, mounting evidence suggests that farming cultures in the tropical forest contributed many of the domesticated plants that later became indispensable to Andean agriculture (Chauchat 1988; Raymond 1988; Rick 1988).

The presence of humans in South America before 15,000 years ago is still being debated, but bands of foragers were definitely living along the Peruvian coast between 14,000 and 8,000 years ago and in the sierra between 11,000 and 10,000 years ago. Lowland groups took advantage of the unique upswelling of the cold coastal current—which kept nutrients for ocean-dwelling organisms close to the surface—to exploit a bounty of marine food resources. Between about 5,000 and 4,000 years ago, quinoa, guinea pigs, potatoes, and camelids (llamas and alpacas) were domesticated in the highlands. Neither the coastal foragers nor the earliest highland farmers made pottery, however. By 3,200 years ago, the first maize appears on the Ecuadorian coast (Smith 1995a, 157, 181).

On the Peruvian coast, between 5,000 and 4,500 years ago, villagers began to construct multiroomed buildings, which were later filled in to form pyramid-shaped mounds. Complexes of platforms, pyramids, and raised enclosures first appeared after 4,000 years ago at sites like El Paraíso on the coast and Kotosh in the highlands. There is evidence that the early coastal mound builders were not farmers, but villagers who relied on food from the sea. Possibly the first mound builders in the highlands were not farmers either, but highland settlements soon became dependent on the cultivation of maize and other crops. Between 3,800 and 2,900 years ago, the number of sites with monumental architecture increased in the coastal valleys, as did the proportion of cultivated plants in the coastal diet, which suggests that irrigation agriculture had become important in coastal economies. There is also evidence during this period of increasing contact between coastal and highland settlements: the "U"-shaped plan of coastal ceremonial sites began to appear in the highlands, while llamas became important, economically and ritually, on the coast (Pineda 1988).

These early developments toward social complexity appeared among peoples with distinct cultural

TABLE 7.1	Cultural Periods of Andean Civilization			
TIME SCALE	**SELECTED CULTURE**			**PERIOD/HORIZON**
1500	Inka			Late Horizon
1250	Chimú			Late Intermediate period
1000 750		Wari	Tiwanaku	Middle Horizon
500 CE	Moche			Early Intermediate period
BCE				
500 1000		Chavín		Early Horizon
2000				Initial period
4000 6000	Paijan			Preceramic period
8000 10,000		Luz		Lithic period

traditions. However, between 2,900 and 2,200 years ago, a single cultural tradition with its own styles of art, architecture, and pottery spread rapidly throughout central and northern Peru. This phenomenon is called the Chavín Horizon, and the period in which it occurred is usually called the Early Horizon because this was the first time in Andean history that so many local communities had adopted a single cultural tradition (Figure 7.21). Much is obscure about the Chavín period. It does not seem that Chavín culture spread by conquest, nor did it totally replace the local traditions of those who adopted it; but its appearance was accompanied by a new level of social and economic interaction between previously isolated local societies.

Most experts agree that the spread of Chavín culture was connected with the spread of a religious ideology, sometimes called the Chavín cult. Richard Berger (1988) suggests that this may have been a regional cult that was voluntarily adopted by a number of different ethnic groups, perhaps a forerunner of the cult of Pachacamac that flourished in sixteenth-century Peru. The Chavín

FIGURE 7.21 Chavín culture spread widely during the Early Horizon in Peru (900–200 BCE). The monumental sculpture illustrated here is the Lanzón in the Old Temple at the ceremonial complex of Chavín de Huantar.

cult got its name from the highland ceremonial center Chavín de Huantar, which was important toward the end of the Early Horizon. The flowering of pottery, metallurgy, and textile production that marks the Chavín Horizon may have been encouraged by a religious elite eager to enhance its status among its new followers.

The Chavín cult and the regional integration that went with it fell apart after 2,200 years ago. Although this development led to the reemergence of village life in some regions, complex society did not collapse everywhere. During the Early Intermediate period (200 BCE–600 CE), separate cultural groups followed their own paths. On the coast, more than a dozen new regional states appeared, but only a few are well known archaeologically. The Moche state, for example, encompassed several river valleys on the north coast and continued the earlier pattern connecting religion, monumental architecture, and rich grave goods. The largest structures in ancient Peru that were built of sun-dried bricks (or adobe) were constructed in the Moche Valley during the Early Intermediate period, as was an elaborate system for the distribution of water. The Moche also developed a distinctive art style that appeared in ceramics, textiles, and wall paintings (Figure 7.22).

On the south coast, a complex society centered in the Nazca Valley produced monumental pyramids, terraced hills, burial areas, and walled enclosures, as well as elaborate pottery and textiles. It also produced the famous Nazca lines, monumental markings that were made by brushing away the dark, upper layer of the desert surface to expose the lighter soil beneath (Figure 7.23). The earliest markings are drawings of animals and supernatural figures, also found on textiles, whereas later markings are mostly straight lines. The exact significance of the Nazca lines is unclear. Similar structures are known elsewhere in Peru, and many experts suspect that the lines may have been memorial markers or part of a calendrical system. There is no evidence whatsoever that they were built as landing strips for aliens from outer space.

In the Andean highlands, many small, independent societies developed during the Early Intermediate period. Of these, perhaps the most significant was the tradition that grew up in the basin of Lake Titicaca in the southern highlands. Titicaca basin culture possessed distinctive traditions in architecture, textiles, and religious art that heavily influenced later complex societies in the region (Conklin and Moseley 1988).

After 600 CE, the cultural fragmentation of the Early Intermediate period was reversed in two regions of Peru. A complex society called Tiwanaku (sometimes spelled *Tiahuanaco*) began to spread the Titicaca basin culture throughout the southern highlands of the Andes. In the central highlands and central coast, a second complex society known as Wari (sometimes spelled *Huari*) extended its influence. Both these regional powers were named after large prehistoric cities that presumably served as their capitals. The period during which these two states spread their cultural and political influence (600–1000 CE) is called the Middle Horizon of Andean cultural evolution.

Wari and Tiwanaku share some common cultural attributes, but archaeologists have difficulty deciphering the nature of their relationship with each other. Tiwanaku had a religiously oriented ruling hierarchy; Wari did not. The architecture of Wari administrative centers lacks residences, storehouses, and community kitchens, which were built in Tiwanaku provincial settlements for members of the religious bureaucracy. William Isbell (1988) connects the administrative structure of Wari to an earlier, nonhierarchical form of social organization that had flourished in the Ayacucho Valley during the Early Intermediate period. In that system, highland communities founded colonies in the different ecological zones that ranged between the highlands and the coast, thus providing the highland communities and their various colonies with a full range of products from each zone. This distinctive Andean pattern of niche construction, which integrates economic resources from a variety of environments, is called the *vertical archipelago system*.

Isbell thinks that the rulers of Wari adopted the form of centralized, hierarchical government from Tiwanaku but not the religious ideas that went with it. Wari then used these centralized political structures to transform the egalitarian vertical archipelago system of the Early Intermediate period into a socially stratified system of wealth collection for the state (Isbell 1988, 182). Archaeological evidence for state-sponsored feasting in return for collective labor on state land may have

FIGURE 7.22 Ceramics were developed to a high level of sophistication in early states, as shown by this stirrup-spout portrait jar produced by the Moche civilization, which flourished in northern Peru between 250 and 500 CE. It is important to note that pottery was also made and used by people who were not settled, full-time farmers.

FIGURE 7.23 Image of a monkey revealed through aerial photograph in the Nazca Valley of Peru.

been found at the Middle Horizon site of Jargampata, located 20 kilometers from Wari. Both the vertical archipelago system and the facilities for state-sponsored feasts for laborers on state land were later incorporated into the society of the Inkas. Isbell (1988) also thinks that the Inka administrative system, involving regional capitals linked by highways with way stations for runners, may have first developed in Wari.

After about 1000 CE, Wari and Tiwanaku declined, ushering in the Late Intermediate period, which lasted until the rise of the Inkas in 1476 CE It was during the Late Intermediate period that the pilgrimage center of Pachacamac on the central coast became fully established (Keatinge 1988). Independent regional states with distinct cultures emerged in half a dozen areas of Peru, the best known of which is the Chimú state, Chimor, on the north coast. The capital of the Chimú state, Chan Chan, is located in the Moche Valley. Chimú administered a complex irrigation system in a number of adjacent river valleys. Most of the farmers of the Chimú state appear to have lived in cities. Although the connection between hydraulic agriculture and state power seems clear in the case of Chimú, other large valleys on the central and south coast were equally well suited to hydraulic agriculture but never produced equally centralized states (Parsons and Hastings 1988).

Both Chan Chan, the Chimú capital, and Cuzco, the Inka capital, were located in areas that lay on the border between spheres of cultural and political influence during the Middle Horizon. The rise of Cuzco began in Late Intermediate times, when kingdoms that descended from Tiwanaku and Wari began to fight with one another. Warfare continued until the 1460s, when the Inkas, whose empire had begun only 20 years earlier, subdued neighboring states and brought them into their expanding empire (Parsons and Hastings 1988). By 1476, the Inkas put down the last of a series of internal rebellions, firmly establishing their empire of Tawantinsuyu, which means "world of four quarters." When the Spanish arrived in 1525, the Inka Empire stretched from present-day Colombia to central Chile, from the Pacific coast to the rain forests of the eastern Andean slopes (Wenke 1999, 640).

During the period of Inka dominance from 1476 to 1525, known as the Late Horizon, the Inkas built on the achievements of hundreds of years of Andean civilization. They further developed the vertical archipelago system; expanded the road system; and built new monumental palaces, temples, storage facilities, barracks, and way stations on highways. They maintained control of their vast empire through military force by moving large sections of the population from one region to another for political reasons and by continuing to recruit labor for state projects in return for state-sponsored feasting. Unlike Chimú, which was largely urban, the Inka Empire was based in rural villages. Society was organized in large kin groups called *ayllu*, which were then grouped

together into higher-level units. But the administrative system was not identical in all regions of the empire: in places like Chan Chan, the Inkas made use of preexisting administrative structures; but in areas where centralized administration did not exist, such as Huánuco Pampa in the central highlands, they built new administrative centers from the ground up (Morris 1988).

The Andes are so ecologically diverse and so much data remain unrecovered that it may seem hazardous to speculate about the rise of complex society here. If the first complex societies on the Peruvian coast were based on a steady supply of food from the sea, rather than agriculture, the notion that village agriculture must precede the rise of social complexity is dealt a blow. Moreover, the fact that these first complex coastal societies were without pottery was no more a barrier to development than was the fact that the early Andean states, up to and including the Inkas, were without a written language (Figure 7.24). Carneiro's (1970) environmental circumscription hypothesis seems suggestive when we consider the rise of the first multivalley states on the coast during the Early Intermediate period; but the constant warfare required for his scheme does not become significant until much later, long after complex states had already emerged. Hydraulic agriculture was clearly important to the rise of the Chimú state, yet it emerged hundreds of years after the first complex societies on the coast. Even if hydraulic agriculture had been important during the Late Intermediate period, as we saw in comparing the Chimú with their neighbors, it cannot explain why people living in similar ecological settings in nearby valleys did not produce similar states. Much work remains to be done, but none of the current gaps in our knowledge detracts from the dazzling achievements of this unique civilization.

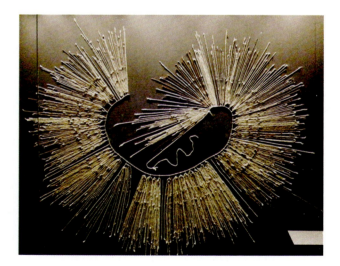

FIGURE 7.24 The indigenous civilizations of the Andes never developed systems of writing but were able to record important information using the *quipu*, a system of knotted strings. Based on a decimal system, quipu knots were coded by size, location, relative sequence, and color.

Chapter Summary

1. About 10,000 years ago, the retreat of the last glaciers marked the end of the Pleistocene. Earth's climate changed significantly, affecting the distribution of plants and animals and transforming the ecological settings in which human beings made their livings. Soon thereafter, humans began to develop new ways of adapting by intervening in these changed environmental settings to create new niches for themselves. But archaeologists increasingly understand that human and nonhuman features of these settings are not separate and self-contained, but instead are always interconnected in the ongoing processes of life in a material world. In the case of our own species, these processes include human social and cultural processes.

2. Plant and animal domestication are usefully understood as forms of niche construction. Not only did human beings interfere with the reproduction of local species, to make them more useful for human purposes, but also they remodeled the environmental settings in which plants were grown or animals were fed and watered. When the invention of agriculture is viewed as niche construction, there is no question that it involved conscious human choice. Intelligent human beings consciously chose to domesticate wild plants that were easy to harvest, nourishing, and tasty; but they also had to consciously create the tools and plan the activities that would make cultivation of a domestic crop possible and successful.

3. The niches human beings construct to exploit plants are not all the same. Anthropologists have identified four major ways in which humans relate to plant species: wild plant-food procurement, wild plant-food production, cultivation, and agriculture. In each successive form, the amount of energy people apply to get food from plants increases, but the energy they get back from plants increases even more.

4. Animal domestication apparently developed as people consciously attempted to control the animals that they were hunting to intervene in their breeding patterns. Archaeological evidence for animal domestication may be indicated in one of four ways: when an animal species is found outside its natural range, when animal remains show morphological changes that distinguish them from wild populations, when the numbers of some species at a site increase abruptly relative to other species, and when remains show certain age and gender characteristics. The earliest animal domesticated, some 16,000 years ago, was the dog. Although archaeologists can pinpoint the regions where goats were domesticated, the earliest sites for domesticated sheep are not clear. It seems that cattle and pigs were domesticated at different sites in the Old World. Animal domestication seems to have been slower and less important in the New World than it was in the Old World.

5. The niches humans have constructed that involve close relations to others to make use of animals vary. They include random hunting, controlled hunting, herd following, loose herding, close herding, and factory farming. There is no necessary directionality to these forms of human–herd co-community. Each point identified on the continuum identifies looser or tighter entanglements between humans and herds, any of which may be maintained indefinitely. Some archaeologists argue that once humans domesticated animals, their focus shifted from dead animals to their living offspring, which may have triggered concern for private property.

6. Scholars have suggested different factors responsible for plant and animal domestication; none alone is entirely satisfactory. Today, most archaeologists prefer multiple strand theories that focus on the particular (and often different) sets of factors that were responsible for domestication in different places. One good example of a multiple strand approach to domestication is shown by recent studies of the Natufian cultural tradition in southwestern Asia, which developed about 12,500 years ago. Post-Pleistocene human niches involving sedentism and domestication had both positive and negative consequences for human beings who came to depend on them. By the time farmers became fully aware of agriculture's drawbacks, their societies had probably become so dependent on it that abandoning it for some other subsistence strategy would have been impossible.

7. Neolithic farming villages were basically egalitarian societies, like the foraging societies that had preceded them. However, beginning about 5,000 years ago in southwestern Asia and shortly thereafter in Egypt, the Indus Valley (India), China, Mesoamerica (Valley of Mexico), and the Andes (Peru), humans independently developed social stratification. Social stratification occurred when surplus food production made it possible for some members of society to stop producing food altogether and to specialize in various occupations. A wide gulf developed between most of society's members and a new social class of rulers who controlled most of the wealth. It appears that social complexity first appeared among complex foragers who lived in environments with abundant resources.

(continued on next page)

Chapter Summary *(continued)*

8. Archaeological evidence of social complexity includes the remains of monumental architecture, elaborate burials alongside much simpler burials, and concentrations of particular artifacts in specific areas of an archaeological site that might indicate occupational specialization. Complex societies are also normally made up of a number of settlements organized in a hierarchy: state organization is suspected when regional settlement patterns show at least three levels in the settlement hierarchy. Art and written inscriptions may provide further information about ancient social organization. Cultural change in all early complex societies tended to alternate between periods of relative cultural uniformity and political unity and periods of regional differentiation and lack of political integration.

9. Anthropologists have devised a number of different hypotheses to explain why complex societies developed. Frequently, the hypothesis places emphasis on a single cause, or "prime mover." Although some of these causes were important in some places, they were not all important everywhere. Attempts to test these hypotheses about prime movers have led to a rich appreciation of the complexities of social and cultural change in prehistory. However, the cumulative effects of these processes have led many observers to speak of the Anthropocene, a new geological epoch that marks the point at which human activities became decisive in shaping the climate and the environment on earth. The Anthropocene demonstrates how the rise of complex human societies is implicated in resource depletion, species extinctions, and climate change. It also illustrates how dependent humans are on other living and nonliving resources for our own survival.

10. Andean civilization developed in a distinctive geographical setting. Foragers were living on the coast and in the sierra of the Andes Mountains between 14,000 and 8,000 years ago. The first monumental architecture appeared after 4,000 years ago. Irrigation agriculture became important along the coast between 3,800 and 2,900 years ago. Numerous independent states rose and fell on the coast and in the highlands until the rise of the Inka Empire in the late 1400s. During Inka times, the achievements of earlier states were consolidated and expanded. When the Spanish arrived in 1525, the Inka Empire stretched from present-day Colombia to central Chile, from the Pacific coast to the rain forests of the eastern Andean slopes.

11. The Andes are so diverse ecologically and so much information remains uncovered that it seems hazardous to speculate about the causes for the rise of complex societies there. Village agriculture was not responsible for the rise of complexity on the Peruvian coast. Environmental circumscription may explain the rise of the first states on the coast in the Early Intermediate period, but warfare and hydraulic agriculture did not become important until long after complex states had emerged. The most puzzling question is why people living in similar ecological settings in nearby valleys did not produce similar states.

For Review

1. What are ecological and evolutionary niches?
2. Why is domestication not the same as agriculture? Illustrate your answer with examples from the text.
3. Explain the basic points of animal domestication.
4. What are the different explanations offered by archaeologists for the domestication of plants and animals by humans?
5. Summarize the discussion of the beginning of domestication in Southwest Asia. According to James Scott, what roles were played by "multispecies resettlement camps" in this process? How did they undergird the "the late Neolithic grain and manpower module" that Scott views as responsible for the earliest Mesopotamian states?
6. Who were the Natufians? What does archaeological research tell us about the processes of plant and animal domestication in Natufian society?
7. Summarize the key consequences of domestication and sedentism for human ways of life.
8. What is social complexity? What is the archaeological evidence for social complexity?

9. What were the world's first complex societies and where were they located?

10. What connections do archaeologists see between sedentism and the beginning of social stratification? Illustrate with examples.

11. What are the different explanations archaeologists offer for the beginning of complex societies?

12. Summarize the discussion in the text concerning the rise of social complexity in the Andes.

Key Terms

anthropocene 232
agriculture 207
agroecology 207
bloodwealth 230
broad-spectrum foraging 214
class 225

complex societies 225
concentrations of particular artifacts 226
domestication 204
ecological niche 205

egalitarian social relations 224
evolutionary niche 205
grave goods 226
monumental architecture 226
Neolithic 217

niche construction 206
occupational specialization 225
sedentism 209
sherds 227
social stratification 216
surplus production 225

Suggested Readings

Chang, K. C. 1986. *The archaeology of ancient China*, 4th ed. New Haven, CT: Yale University Press. *A fascinating account of the rise of social complexity in China by one of the most distinguished interpreters of Chinese civilization in the United States.*

Henry, Donald. 1989. *From foraging to agriculture: The Levant at the end of the Ice Age*. Philadelphia: University of Pennsylvania Press. *A detailed, well-illustrated discussion of the archaeology of ancient southwestern Asia at the time of the emergence of agriculture. Particularly good on cultural variation.*

Hoffman, Michael. 1991. *Egypt before the pharaohs: The prehistoric foundations of Egyptian civilization*. Austin: University of Texas Press. *A highly readable account of the important developments in prehistoric Egypt that made the civilization of the pharaohs possible.*

Price, T. Douglas, and Gary M. Feinman, eds. 1995. *Foundations of social inequality*. New York: Plenum. *A fascinating collection of scholarly articles exploring the various factors responsible for institutionalizing social inequality in the first complex societies.*

Price, T. Douglas, and Anne Birgitte Gebauer, eds. 1995. *Last hunters, first farmers*. Santa Fe, NM: SAR Press. *A collection of scholarly articles exploring, among other topics, the importance of complex foraging societies in the process of domestication.*

Scott, James. 2017. *Against the Grain: A deep history of the earliest states*. New Haven: Yale University Press. *Scott brings together work by anthropologists and other scholars to argue against interpretations of the ancient human past that still presume a universal linear directionality culminating in state societies. Scott's critical discussion of traditional classifications by anthropologists of subsistence strategies and forms of human society is incisive and insightful, as is his account of the role of niche construction in the rise of the state, and his overall arguments relating to the origins of what is called the Anthropocene.*

Swanson, Heather Anne, Marianne Elisabeth Lien, and Gro B. Ween. 2018. *Domestication gone wild: Politics and practices of multispecies relations*. Durham: Duke University Press. *This collection of essays by different anthropologists pushes our understanding of what kinds of interspecies relations might count as domestication and how these forms of domestication may differ from the forms of grain and animal domestication responsible for the first states. These studies also draw attention to the negative legacy of human-instigated, state-sponsored grain agriculture through out the world, which has led many observers to describe our current geological epoch as the Anthropocene.*

Smith, Bruce D. 1995. *The emergence of agriculture*. New York: Scientific American Library. *An accessible, beautifully illustrated discussion of domestication throughout the world.*

Soustelle, Jacques. 1961. *Daily life of the Aztecs on the eve of the Spanish conquest*. Stanford, CA: Stanford University Press. *A classic text that attempts to reconstruct for modern readers exactly what the title claims.*

Wenke, Robert, and Deborah Olszewski. 2006. *Patterns in prehistory: Humankind's first three million years*, 5th ed. New York: Oxford University Press. *An excellent, up-to-date, and highly readable account of the rise of social complexity in Mesopotamia, Egypt, the Indus Valley, China, Mesoamerica, and the Andes as well as a chapter on early cultural complexity in pre-European North America.*

 Visit our online resource center for further reading, web links, free assessments, flashcards, and videos. www.oup.com/he/lavenda5e

Why is the concept of culture important?

In this chapter, you will examine in greater detail the concept of culture, one of the most influential ideas that anthropologists have developed. We will survey different ways that anthropologists have used the culture concept to expose the fallacies of biological determinism. We will also discuss the reasons why some anthropologists believe that continuing to use the culture concept today may be a problem.

CHAPTER OUTLINE

LEARNING OBJECTIVES

- Define the anthropological concept of culture and how it is used in anthropology.
- Explain the relationship between the anthropological concepts of culture, history, and agency and how they are reconciled to explain human behavior.
- Describe approaches employed by anthropologists to explain

- responses to cultural differences and how they are applied to anthropological research.
- Apply the concept of cultural relativism to controversial cultural practices, such as genital cutting.
- Determine the scope of application for the culture concept and its possibilities and limitations for explaining everything.

- Explain challenges to understanding cultural change in the context of cultural authenticity using the example of the Kiowa of North America.
- Apply anthropological concepts to understand culture and the promise of the anthropological perspective.

A Sami man with his dog on a snowmobile in Lapland, Sweden.

Anthropologists have long argued that the human condition is distinguished from the condition of other living species by *culture*. Other living species learn, but the extent to which human beings depend on learning is unique in the animal kingdom. Because our brains are capable of open symbolic thought and our hands are capable of manipulating matter powerfully or delicately, we interact with the wider world in a way that is distinct from that of any other species.

How Do Anthropologists Define Culture?

In Chapter 1 we defined **culture** as patterns of learned behavior and ideas that human beings acquire as members of society, together with the material artifacts and structures humans create and use. Culture is not reinvented by each generation; rather, we learn it from other members of the social groups we belong to, although we may later modify this heritage in some way. Children use their own bodies and brains to explore their world. But from their earliest days, other people are actively working to steer their activity and attention in particular directions. Consequently, their exploration of the world is not merely trial and error. The path is cleared for them by others who shape their experiences. Two terms in the social sciences refer to this process of culturally and socially shaped learning. The first, **socialization**, is the process of learning to live as a member of a group. This involves mastering the skills of appropriate interaction with others and learning how to cope with the behavioral rules established by the social group. The second term, **enculturation**, refers to the cognitive challenges facing human beings who live together and must come to terms with the ways of thinking and feeling considered appropriate to their respective cultures.

Historically, generations of anthropologists and other social scientists have stressed the importance of socialization and enculturation processes, because these processes have been regularly downplayed or ignored by those who chose to reduce patterned variations in human behavior to "biological race" or genetic endowment.

culture Sets of learned behaviors and ideas that humans acquire as members of society. Humans use culture to adapt to and transform the world in which they live.

socialization The process by which human beings as material organisms, living together with other similar organisms, cope with the behavioral rules established by their respective societies.

enculturation The process by which human beings living with one another must learn to come to terms with the ways of thinking and feeling that are considered appropriate in their respective cultures.

As we discussed in Chapter 5, however, more persuasive explanations for patterns of social and cultural variation require acknowledging how biological, social, cultural, political, and other factors intertwine over time, in the course of human development, in particular times and places. Gisli Pálsson reminds us that "humans may usefully be regarded as fluid beings, with flexible, porous boundaries; they are necessarily embedded in relations, which may be called 'biosocial;' and their essence is best rendered as something constantly in the making" (2013a, 39). In this process, we incorporate lessons about how to adjust the biosocial (or biocultural) relations in which we live, responding more or less successfully to the demands we encounter in our regular dealings with others. But this is an open process, never closed down once and for all, as long as we are alive.

So culture is *shared* as well as *learned*. But many things we learn, such as table manners and what is good to eat and where people are supposed to sleep, are never explicitly taught but rather are absorbed in the course of daily practical living. French anthropologist Pierre Bourdieu called this kind of cultural learning *habitus*, and it is heavily influenced by our interactions with material culture. According to Daniel Miller (2010), Bourdieu's theory "gives shape and form to the idea that objects make people. . . . We walk around the rice terraces or road systems, the housing and gardens that are effectively ancestral. These unconsciously direct our footsteps, and are the landscapes of our imagination, as well as the cultural environment to which we adapt" (53). The cultural practices shared within social groups always encompass the varied knowledge and skills of many different individuals. For example, space flight is part of North American culture, and yet no individual North American could build a space shuttle from scratch in his or her backyard.

Human cultures also appear *patterned*; that is, related cultural beliefs and practices show up repeatedly in different areas of social life. For example, in North America, individualism is highly valued; and its influence can be seen in child-rearing practices (babies are expected to sleep alone, and children are reared with the expectation that they will be independent at the age of 18), economic practices (individuals are urged to get a job, to save their money, and not to count on other people or institutions to take care of them; many people would prefer to be in business for themselves; far more people commute to work by themselves in their own cars than carpool), and religious practices (the Christian emphasis on personal salvation and individual accountability before God). Cultural patterns can be traced through time: That English and Spanish are widely spoken in North America, whereas Fulfulde (a language spoken in West Africa) is not, is connected to the colonial conquest and domination of North America by speakers of English and Spanish in past centuries. Cultural patterns also vary across space: in the United States, for example, the English of New York City differs from the English of Mississippi in style, rhythm, and vocabulary ("What? You expect me to schlep this around all day? Forget about it!" is more likely to be heard in the former than the latter!).

It is this patterned cultural variation that allows anthropologists (and others) to distinguish different "cultural traditions" from one another. But separate cultural traditions are often hard to delineate. That is because, in addition to any unique elements of their own, all contain contradictory elements, and they also share elements with other traditions. First, customs in one domain of culture may contradict customs in another domain, as when religion tells us to share with others and economics tells us to look out for ourselves alone. Second, people have always borrowed cultural elements from their neighbors, and many increasingly refuse to be limited in the present by cultural practices of the past. Why, for example, should literacy not be seen as part of Ju/'hoansi culture once the children of illiterate Ju/'hoansi foragers learn to read and write (see Chapter 11, "EthnoProfile 11.4: Ju/'hoansi (!Kung)")? Thus, cultural patterns can be useful as a kind of shorthand, but it is important to remember that the boundaries between cultural traditions are always fuzzy. Ultimately, they rest on someone's judgment about how different one set of customs is from another set of customs. As we will see shortly, these kinds of contradictions and challenges are not uncommon, leading some anthropologists to think of culture not in terms of specific customs but in terms of rules that become

IN THEIR OWN WORDS

The Paradox of Ethnocentrism

Ethnocentrism is usually described in thoroughly negative terms. As Ivan Karp points out, however, ethnocentrism is a more complex phenomenon than we might expect.

Anthropologists usually argue that ethnocentrism is both wrong and harmful, especially when it is tied to racial, cultural, and social prejudices. Ideas and feelings about the inferiority of blacks, the cupidity of Jews, or the lack of cultural sophistication of farmers are surely to be condemned. But can we do without ethnocentrism? If we stopped to examine every custom and practice in our cultural repertoire, how would we get on? For example, if we always regarded marriage as something that can vary from society to society, would we be concerned about filling out the proper marriage documents, or would we even get married at all? Most of the time we suspend a quizzical stance toward our own customs and simply live life.

Yet many of our own practices are peculiar when viewed through the lenses of other cultures. Periodically, for over fifteen years, I have worked with and lived among an African people. They are as amazed at our marriage customs as my students are at theirs. Both American students and the Iteso of Kenya find it difficult to imagine how the other culture survives with the bizarre, exotic practices that are part of their respective marriage customs. Ethnocentrism works both ways. It can be practiced as much by other cultures as by our own.

Paradoxically, ethnographic literature combats ethnocentrism by showing that the practices of cultures (including our own) are "natural" in their own setting. What appears natural in one setting appears so because it was constructed in that setting—made and produced by human beings who could have done it some other way. Ethnography is a means of recording the range of human creativity and of demonstrating how universally shared capacities can produce cultural and social differences.

This anthropological way of looking at other cultures—and, by implication, at ourselves—constitutes a major reason for reading ethnography. The anthropological lens teaches us to question what we assume to be unquestionable. Ethnography teaches us that human potentiality provides alternative means of organizing our lives and alternative modes of experiencing the world. Reading ethnographies trains us to question the received wisdom of our society and makes us receptive to change. In this sense, anthropology might be called the subversive science. We read ethnographies in order to learn about how other peoples produce their world and about how we might change our own patterns of production.

Source: Karp 1990, 74–75.

FIGURE 8.1 Of all living organisms, humans are the most dependent on learning for their survival. From a young age, girls in northern Cameroon learn to carry heavy loads on their heads and also learn to get water for their families.

"established ways of bringing ideas from different domains together" (Strathern 1992, 3).

So far we have seen that culture is learned, shared, and patterned. Cultural traditions are also reconstructed and enriched, generation after generation, primarily because human biological survival depends on culture. Thus, culture is also *adaptive*. Human newborns are not born with "instincts" that would enable them to survive on their own. On the contrary, they depend utterly on support and nurturance from adults and other members of the group in which they live. It is by learning the cultural practices of those around them that human beings come to master appropriate ways of thinking and acting that promote their own survival as biological organisms Moreover, as can be seen in Figure 8.1, appropriate ways of thinking and acting are always scaffolded by artifacts and features of a particular local setting. In the 1970s, for example, young girls in Guider, Cameroon, promoted their own and their families' welfare by fetching water for their mothers, who were forbidden by propriety from leaving their household compounds alone during the day. The presence in town of public water spigots, only a few years old at the time, lightened the chore of bringing water back to homes that did not have plumbing. Imported metal basins and pails were more reliable than large calabashes for carrying water, especially for young water carriers who had mastered the impressive skill of balancing heavy loads on their heads (sometimes atop a flat fabric pad). Public spigots, together with recycled

symbol Something that stands for something else.

metal containers, a pole, and rope, also afforded young men the opportunity to earn money by selling their services to residents who could not rely on young relatives to bring water to them. In such ways do tradition and innovation shape each other over time, mediated by material culture.

Finally, culture is *symbolic*. A **symbol** is something that stands for something else. The letters of an alphabet, for example, symbolize the sounds of a spoken language. There is no necessary connection between the shape of a particular letter and the speech sound it represents. Indeed, the same or similar sounds are represented symbolically by very different letters in the Latin, Cyrillic, Hebrew, Arabic, and Greek alphabets, to name but five. Even the sounds of spoken language are symbols for meanings a speaker tries to express. The fact that we can translate from one language to another suggests that the same or similar meanings can be expressed by different symbols in different languages. But language is not the only domain of culture that depends on symbols. Everything we do in society has a symbolic dimension, from how we conduct ourselves at the dinner table to how we bury the dead. It is our heavy dependence on symbolic learning that sets human culture apart from the apparently nonsymbolic learning on which other species rely.

Human culture, then, is *learned, shared, patterned, adaptive,* and *symbolic.* And the contemporary human capacity for culture has also evolved, over millions of years. Culture's beginnings can perhaps be glimpsed among Japanese macaque monkeys who invented the custom of washing sweet potatoes and among wild chimpanzees who invented different grooming postures or techniques to crack open nuts or to gain access to termites or water (Boesch-Achermann and Boesch 1994; Wolfe 1995, 162–63). Our apelike ancestors surely shared similar aptitudes when they started walking on two legs some 6 million years ago. By 2.5 million years ago, their descendants were making stone tools. Thereafter, our hominin lineage gave birth to a number of additional species, all of whom depended on culture more than their ancestors had. Thus, culture is not something that appeared suddenly, with the arrival of *Homo sapiens.* By the time *Homo sapiens* appeared some 300,000 years ago, a heavy dependence on culture had long been a part of our evolutionary heritage.

Thus, as Rick Potts puts it, "an evolutionary bridge exists between the human and animal realms of behavior. . . . Culture represents continuity" (1996, 197). Potts proposes that modern human symbolic culture and the social institutions that depend on it rest on other, more basic abilities that emerged at different times in our evolutionary past (Figure 8.2). Monkeys and apes possess

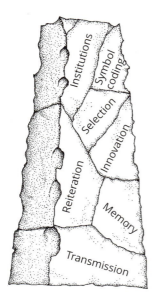

FIGURE 8.2 The modern human capacity for culture did not appear all at once; rather, the various pieces that make it up were added at different times in our evolutionary past.

many of these abilities to varying degrees, which is the reason they may be said to possess simple cultural traditions. Certainly our earliest hominin ancestors were no different.

Apes apparently also possess a rudimentary capacity for *symbolic coding*, or symbolic representation, something our ancestors undoubtedly possessed as well. But new species can evolve new capacities not found in their ancestors. This occurred in the human past when our ancestors first developed a capacity for *complex symbolic representation*, including the ability to communicate freely about the past, the future, and the invisible. This ability distinguishes human symbolic language, for example, from the vocal communication systems of apes (see Chapter 9). Biological anthropologist Terrence Deacon argues that evolution produced in *Homo sapiens* a brain "that has been significantly overbuilt for learning symbolic associations" such that "we cannot help but see the world in symbolic categories" (1997, 413, 416). Complex symbolic representation apparently was of great adaptive value for our ancestors. It created selective pressures that increased human symbolic capacities over time. Put another way, culture and the human brain *coevolved*, each furnishing key features of the environment to which the other needed to adapt (Odling-Smee 1994; Deacon 1997, 44). As we saw in earlier chapters, one component of this coevolving complex was surely material culture, which reshaped the environments to which our ancestors were adapting via a process of *niche*

IN THEIR OWN WORDS

Culture and Freedom

Finding a way to fit human agency into a scientific account of culture has never been easy. Hoyt Alverson describes some of the issues involved.

One's assumptions concerning the existence of structure in culture, or the existence of freedom in human action, determine whether one believes that there can be a science of culture or not. Note that the possibility of developing a science of culture has nothing to do with the use of mathematics, the precision of one's assertions, or the elegance of one's models. If a phenomenon actually has structure, then a science of that phenomenon is at least conceivable. If a phenomenon exhibits freedom and is not ordered, then a science of that phenomenon is inconceivable. The human sciences, including anthropology, have been debating the issue of structure versus freedom in human cultural behavior for the past two hundred years, and no resolution or even consensus has emerged.

Some persuasive models of culture, and of particular cultures, have been proposed, both by those working with scientific, universalist assumptions, and by those working with phenomenological, relativistic assumptions.

To decide which of these approaches is to be preferred, we must have a specific set of criteria for evaluation. Faced with good evidence for the existence of both structure and freedom in human culture, no coherent set of criteria for comparing the success of these alternative models is conceivable. The prediction of future action, for example, is a good criterion for measuring the success of a model that purports to represent structure: it must be irrelevant to measuring the success or failure of a model that purports to describe freedom. For the foreseeable future, and maybe for the rest of time, we may have to be content with models that simply permit us to muddle through.

Source: Alverson 1990, 42–43.

construction. From nest-building birds to dam-building beavers, many species have altered the natural selection pressures to which they are exposed. They may do this by altering social relations, by modifying material features of the ecological settings in which they live, or both. Theorists of niche construction agree that human beings are "virtuoso niche constructors" (Odling-Smee et al. 2003, 367). When human matter-manipulating skills are considered together with human symbolic abilities, the unprecedented features of human niches constructed over time become more comprehensible. We have used our complex abilities to create what Potts calls *institutions*—complex, variable, and enduring forms of cultural practice that organize social life. The material buttressing of cultural institutions over time—through customs like the exchange of valuable goods or material construction of permanent and symbolically distinctive dwellings, agricultural fields, irrigation canals, and monumental architecture—is also unique to our species. As a result, for *H. sapiens*, culture is not only central to our adaptation, but also has become "the predominant manner in which human groups vary from one another . . . it *swamps* the biological differences among populations" (Marks 1995, 200).

Culture, History, and Human Agency

The human condition is rooted in time and shaped by history. As part of the human condition, culture is also historical, being worked out and reconstructed in every generation. Culture is central to human biosocial becoming. Our biocultural heritage has produced a living species that uses culture to manage biological and individual limitations and is even capable of studying itself and its own biocultural evolution.

This realization, however, raises another question: Just how free from limitations are humans? Opinion in Western societies often polarizes around one of two extremes: Either we have *free will* and may do just as we please or our behavior is completely determined by forces beyond our control. Many social scientists, however, are convinced that a more realistic description of human freedom was offered by Karl Marx (1963), who wrote, "Men make their own history, but they do not

make it just as they please; they do not make it under circumstances chosen by themselves, but under circumstances directly encountered, given and transmitted by the past" (15). That is, people regularly struggle, often against great odds, to exercise some control over their lives. Human beings active in this way are called *agents* (Figure 8.3). Human agents cannot escape the cultural and historical context within which they act. However, they must frequently select a course of action when the "correct" choice is unclear and the outcome uncertain. Some anthropologists even liken human existence to a mine field that we must painstakingly try to cross without blowing ourselves up. It is in such contexts, with their ragged edges, that human beings exercise their **human agency** by making interpretations, formulating goals, and setting out in pursuit of them.

Efforts to understand the multiple factors and complex processes that feed into human biosocial becoming has deep roots in anthropology. Over a century ago, anthropologists like Franz Boas and his students attempted to characterize these interconnections using the biological term **holism**, which took the single-celled organism as its model: Figure 2.15 suggests why this model inspired them. A single-celled organism persists by absorbing nutrients, expelling waste, and receiving stimuli through the cell wall; yet within the wall, no sharp boundaries separate the various components and processes that keep this organism alive. From a holistic

FIGURE 8.3 People regularly struggle, often against great odds, to exercise some control over their lives. During the "Dirty War" in Argentina in the 1970s and early 1980s, women whose children had been disappeared by secret, right-wing death squads began, at great personal risk, to stand every Thursday in the Plaza de Mayo, the central square of Buenos Aires, with photographs of their missing children. Called the Mothers of Plaza de Mayo, they continue their weekly vigil today. They were a powerful rebuke to the dictatorship and to subsequent governments that were not forthcoming about providing information about the disappeared.

human agency The exercise of at least some control over their lives by human beings.

holism Perspective on the human condition that assumes that mind and body, individuals and society, and individuals and the environment interpenetrate and even define one another.

IN THEIR OWN WORDS

Human-Rights Law and the Demonization of Culture

Sally Engle Merry is Professor of Anthropology at New York University.

Why is the idea of cultural relativism anathema to many human-rights activists? Is it related to the way international human-rights lawyers and journalists think about culture? Does this affect how they think about anthropology? I think one explanation for the tension between anthropology and human-rights activists is the very different conceptions of culture that these two groups hold. An incident demonstrated this for me vividly a few months ago. I received a phone call from a prominent radio show asking if I would be willing to talk about the recent incident in Pakistan that resulted in the gang rape of a young woman, an assault apparently authorized by a local tribal council. Since I am working on human rights and violence against women, I was happy to explain my position that this was an inexcusable act, that many Pakistani feminists condemned the rape, but that it was probably connected to local political struggles and class differences. It should not be seen as an expression of Pakistani "culture." In fact, it was the local Islamic religious leader who first made the incident known to the world, according to news stories I had read.

The interviewer was distressed. She wanted me to defend the value of respecting Pakistani culture at all costs, despite the tribal council's imposition of a sentence of rape. When I told her that I could not do that, she wanted to know if I knew of any other anthropologists who would. I could think of none, but I began to wonder what she thought about anthropologists.

Anthropologists, apparently, made no moral judgments about "cultures" and failed to recognize the contestation and changes taking place within contemporary local communities around the world. This also led me to wonder how she imagined anthropologists thought about culture. She seemed to assume that anthropologists viewed culture as a coherent, static, and unchanging set of values. Apparently cultures have no contact with the expansion of capitalism, the arming of various groups by transnational superpowers using them for proxy wars, or the cultural possibilities of human rights as an emancipatory discourse. I found this interviewer's view of culture wrongheaded and her opinion of anthropology discouraging. But perhaps it was just one journalist, I thought.

However, the article "From Skepticism to Embrace: Human Rights and the American Anthropological Association" by Karen Engle in *Human Rights Quarterly* (23: 536–60) paints another odd portrait of anthropology and its understanding of culture. In this piece, a law professor talks about the continuing "embarrassment" of anthropologists about the 1947 statement of the AAA (American Anthropological Association) Executive Board, which raised concerns about the Universal Declaration of Human Rights. Engle claims that the statement has caused the AAA "great shame" over the last fifty years (p. 542). Anthropologists are embarrassed, she argues, because the statement asserted tolerance without limits. While many anthropologists now embrace human rights, they do so primarily in terms of the protection of culture (citing 1999 AAA Statement on Human Rights at www.aaanet.org). Tensions over how to be a cultural relativist and still make overt political judgments that the 1947 Board confronted remain. She does acknowledge that not all anthropologists think about culture this way. But relativism, as she describes it, is primarily about tolerance for difference and is incompatible with making moral judgments about other societies.

But this incompatibility depends on how one theorizes culture. If culture is homogenous, integrated and consensual, it must be accepted as a whole. But anthropology has developed a far more complex way of understanding culture focusing on its historical production, its porosity to outside influences and pressures, and its incorporation of competing repertoires of meaning and action. Were this conception more widely recognized within popular culture as well as among journalists and human-rights activists, it could shift the terms of the intractable debate between universalism and relativism. Instead, culture is increasingly understood as a barrier to the realization of human rights by activists and a tool for legitimating noncompliance with human rights by conservatives.

One manifestation of the understanding of culture prevalent in human-rights law is the concept of harmful traditional practices. Originally developed to describe female genital mutilation or cutting, this term describes practices that have some cultural legitimacy yet are designated harmful to women, particularly to their health. In 1990, the committee monitoring the Convention on the Elimination of All Forms of Discrimination Against Women

(continued on next page)

IN THEIR OWN WORDS

Human-Rights Law and the Demonization of Culture *Continued*

(CEDAW), an international convention ratified by most of the nations of the world, said that they were gravely concerned "that there are continuing cultural, traditional and economic pressures which help to perpetuate harmful practices, such as female circumcision," and adopted General Recommendation 14, which suggested that state parties should take measures to eradicate the practice of female circumcision. Culture equals tradition and is juxtaposed to women's human rights to equality. It is not surprising, given this evolving understanding of culture within human-rights discourse, that cultural relativism is seen in such a negative light. The tendency for national elites to defend practices oppressive to women in the name of culture exacerbates this negative view of culture.

Human-rights activists and journalists have misinterpreted anthropology's position about relativism and difference because they misunderstand anthropology's position about culture. Claims to cultural relativism appear to be defenses of holistic and static entities. This conception of culture comes from older anthropological usages, such as the separation of values and social action advocated in the 1950s by Talcott Parsons. Since "culture" was defined only as values, it was considered inappropriate to judge one ethical system by another one. For Melville Herskovits, the leader of the AAA's relativist criticism of the Universal Declaration of Human Rights in 1947, cultural relativism meant protecting the holistic cultures of small communities from colonial intrusion (AAA 1947 Statement, AA 49: 539–43).

If culture is understood this way, it is not surprising that cultural relativism appears to be a retrograde position to human-rights lawyers. Nor is it puzzling that they find anthropology irrelevant. As human-rights law demonizes culture, it misunderstands anthropology as well. The holistic conception of culture provides no space for change, contestation or the analysis of the links between power, practices and values. Instead, it becomes a barrier to the reformist project of universal human rights. From the legal perspective on human rights, it is the texts, the documents and compliance that matter. Universalism is essential while relativism is bad. There is a sense of moral certainty which taking account of culture disrupts. This means, however, that the moral principle of tolerance for difference is lost.

When corporate executives in the U.S. steal millions of dollars through accounting fraud, we do not criticize American culture as a whole. We recognize that these actions come from the greed of a few along with sloppy institutional arrangements that allow them to get away with it. Similarly, the actions of a single tribal council in Pakistan should not indict the entire culture, as if it were a homogeneous entity. Although Pakistan and many of its communities have practices and laws that subordinate women, these are neither homogeneous nor ancient. Pakistan as a "culture" can be indicted by this particular council's encouragement to rape only if culture is understood as a homogeneous entity whose rules evoke universal compliance. Adopting a more sophisticated and dynamic understanding of culture not only promotes human-rights activism, but also relocates anthropological theorizing to the center of these issues rather than to the margins, where it has been banished.

Source: Merry 2003.

perspective, attempts to divide reality into mind and matter are unsuccessful because of the complex nature of reality, which resists isolation and dissection.

A holistic approach to the human condition based on a modular, multicellular organism might make more sense for holobionts such as ourselves (see "In Their Own Words: Have We Ever Been Individuals?," Chapter 5). The emphasis however, is still to highlight the absence of sharp boundaries separating mind, body, symbionts, and components of the wider social, cultural, and ecological settings in which we find ourselves. Indeed, individuals and societies, my ideas and your ideas, their traditions and our traditions interpenetrate and even define each other. Humans are closed off from the wider world in some ways, by how our cells, tissues, and organs are bound together. But we are open to the world in other ways: we breathe, eat, harbor colonies of intestinal bacteria to aid our digestion, excrete waste products, and learn from experience (see Deacon 2003, 296–97). Similarly, a society is not just the sum of its individual members; people in groups develop dynamic relationships that facilitate collective actions impossible for individuals to bring about on their own. And cultural traditions are not just a list of beliefs, values, and practices; rather, different dimensions of cultural activity, such as economics and politics and religion, are knotted together in complex ways. To understand any human community requires untangling those cultural threads to reveal the full range of factors that shape particular cultural practices in that community. Nor are the paths those threads might trace in the future fully predictable ahead of time. Tim Ingold puts it this way: "Humanity . . . does not come with the territory, from the mere fact of species membership or from having been born into a particular culture or society. It is rather something we have continually to work at, and for which, therefore, we bear responsibility. . . . Life is a task, and it is one in which we have, perpetually, never-endingly and collaboratively, to be creating ourselves" (2013, 8).

Human beings who develop and live together in groups shaped by cultural patterns are deeply affected by shared cultural experiences. They become different from what they would have been had they matured in isolation; they also become different from other people who have been shaped by different social and cultural patterns. Social scientists have long known that human beings who grow up isolated from meaningful social interactions with others do not behave in ways that appear recognizably human. As anthropologist Clifford Geertz observed long ago, such human beings would be neither failed apes nor "natural" people stripped of their veneer of culture; they would be "mental basket cases" (1973, 40). Social living and cultural sharing are necessary for individual human beings to develop what we recognize as a *human* nature.

One useful way of thinking about the relationships among the parts that make up a whole is in terms of **coevolution**. A coevolutionary approach to the human condition emphasizes that human organisms, their physical environments, and their symbolic practices *codetermine* one another; with the passage of time, they can also *coevolve* with one another. A coevolutionary view of the human condition also sees human beings as organisms whose bodies, brains, actions, and thoughts are equally involved in shaping what they become. Coevolution produces a human nature connected to a wider world and profoundly shaped by culture. These connections make us vulnerable over the course of our lives to influences that our ancestors never experienced. The open, symbolic, meaning-making properties of human culture make it possible for us to respond to those influences in ways that our ancestors could not have anticipated.

Why Do Cultural Differences Matter?

The same objects, actions, or events frequently mean different things to people with different cultures. In fact, what counts as an object or event in one tradition may not be recognized as such in another. This powerful lesson of anthropology was illustrated by the experience of some Peace Corps volunteers working in southern Africa.

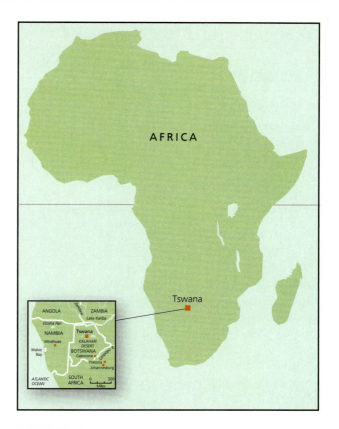

FIGURE 8.4 Location of Tswana. For more information, see "EthnoProfile 8.1: Tswana."

In the early 1970s, the Peace Corps office in Botswana was concerned by the number of volunteers who seemed to be "burned out," failing in their assignments, leaving the assigned villages, and increasingly hostile to their Tswana hosts. (See Figure 8.4 and "EthnoProfile 8.1: Tswana.") The Peace Corps asked American anthropologist Hoyt Alverson, who was familiar with Tswana culture and society, for advice. Alverson (1977) discovered that one major problem the Peace Corps volunteers were having involved exactly this issue of similar actions having very different meanings. The volunteers complained that the Tswana would never leave them alone. Whenever they tried to get away and sit by themselves for a few minutes to have some private time, one or more Tswana would quickly join them. This made the Americans angry. From their perspective, everyone is entitled to a certain amount of privacy and time alone. To the Tswana, however, human life is social life; the only people who want to be alone are witches and the insane. Because these young Americans did not seem to be either, the Tswana who saw them sitting alone naturally assumed that there had been a breakdown in hospitality and that the volunteers

coevolution The dialectical relationship between biological processes and symbolic cultural processes, in which each makes up an important part of the environment to which the other must adapt.

EthnoProfile 8.1

Tswana

Region: Southern Africa

Nation: Botswana

Population: 1,200,000 (also 1,500,000 in South Africa)

Environment: Savanna to desert

Livelihood: Cattle raising, farming

Political organization: Traditionally, chiefs and headmen; today, part of a modern nation-state

For more information: Comaroff, Jean. 1985. *Body of power, spirit of resistance: The culture history of a South African people.* Chicago: University of Chicago Press.

FIGURE 8.5 For Tswana, human life is social life. It was difficult for Peace Corps volunteers from the United States accustomed to having "private time" to adjust to Tswana practices.

would welcome some company. Here, one behavior—a person walking out into a field and sitting by himself or herself—had two very different meanings (Figure 8.5).

From this example we can see that human experience is inherently ambiguous. Even within a single cultural tradition, the meaning of an object or an action may differ, depending on the context. Quoting philosopher Gilbert Ryle, anthropologist Clifford Geertz (1973, 6) noted that there is a world of difference between a wink and a blink, as anyone who has ever mistaken one for the other has undoubtedly learned. To resolve the ambiguity, experience must be interpreted, and human beings regularly

turn to their own cultural traditions in search of an interpretation that makes sense. They do this daily as they go about life among others with whom they share traditions. Serious misunderstandings may arise, however, when individuals confront the same ambiguous situation without realizing that their cultural ground rules differ.

What Is Ethnocentrism?

Ethnocentrism is the term anthropologists use to describe the opinion that one's own way of life is natural or correct, indeed the only way of being fully human. As long as we are among people who share our way of life, this may seem unproblematic, even comforting. As Sarah Mahler points out (2012), the skills and knowledge we adopt from those who nurture us shapes the cultural "comfort zones" we come to take for granted. But the limits of our cultural comfort zones are tested when we encounter others whose beliefs or actions differ from our own. Often enough, such encounters leave us "discomforted," but as Mahler observes, culture is something we do, not just something we possess. Consequently, as we come to appreciate cultural diversity, we can expand our comfort zones and learn new ways of doing culture.

At the same time, ethnocentrism can turn into a form of defense against the inevitable tension that cultural discomfort can produce when people with different backgrounds come into contact. It reduces the other way of life to a version of one's own. Sometimes we correctly identify meaningful areas of cultural overlap. But other times, we are shocked by the differences we encounter. We may conclude that if our way is right, then their way can only be wrong. (Of course, from their perspective, our way of life may seem to be a distortion of theirs.)

The members of one society may go beyond merely interpreting another way of life in ethnocentric terms. They may decide to do something about the discrepancies they observe. They may conclude that the other way of life is wrong but not fundamentally evil and that the members of the other group need to be converted to their own way of doing things. If the others are unwilling to change their ways, however, the failed attempt at conversion may enlarge into an active dualism: us versus them, civilization versus savagery, good versus evil. The ultimate result may be war and *genocide*—the deliberate attempt to exterminate an entire group based on race, religion, national origin, or other cultural features.

Is It Possible to Avoid Ethnocentric Bias?

One way to address this question is to view relationships between individuals with different cultural backgrounds as

ethnocentrism The opinion that one's own way of life is natural or correct and, indeed, the only true way of being fully human.

not being fundamentally different from relationships between individuals with very similar cultural backgrounds (we pursue this further in Chapter 14). Even people with little in common can learn to get along, even if it is not always easy. Like all human relationships, they affect all parties involved in the encounter, changing them as they learn about each other. People with a cultural background very different from your own may help you see possibilities for belief and action that are drastically at odds with everything your tradition considers possible. As Ghassan Hage puts it, "Such difference disorients us to begin with, and in the process of helping us reorient ourselves within it and in relation to it, anthropology widens our sphere of what is socially and culturally possible" (2015, Loc 925). We discover, according to Hage, that "Our otherness is always dwelling within us; there is always more to us than we think, so to speak. Anthropology . . . works critically through a comparative act that constantly exposes us to the possibility of being other than what we are (Hage 2015, Loc 943). By becoming aware of these unsuspected possibilities, you become a different person. People from cultural backgrounds different from yours are likely to be affected in the same way.

Learning about other cultures is at once enormously hopeful and immensely threatening; once it occurs, we can no longer claim that any single culture has a monopoly on truth. Although this does not mean that the traditions in question must therefore be based entirely on illusion or falsehood, it does mean that the truth embodied in any cultural tradition is bound to be partial, approximate, and open to further insight and growth.

What Is Cultural Relativism?

Anthropologists must come to terms with the tensions produced by cultural differences as they do their fieldwork. One result has been the formulation of the concept of cultural relativism. Definitions of cultural relativism have varied as different anthropologists have tried to draw conclusions based on their own experience of other ways of life. For example, **cultural relativism** can be defined as "understanding another culture in its own terms sympathetically enough so that the culture appears to be a coherent and meaningful design for living" (Greenwood and Stini 1977, 182). According to this holistic definition, the goal of cultural relativism is to promote understanding of cultural practices, particularly of those that an outsider finds puzzling, incoherent, or morally troubling. These practices range from trivial (like eating insects) to horrifying (like genocide), but most are likely to be located somewhere between these extremes.

How Can Cultural Relativity Improve Our Understanding of Controversial Cultural Practices?

Rituals initiating girls and boys into adulthood are widely practiced throughout the world. In some parts of Africa, this ritual includes genital cutting (Figure 8.6). For example, ritual experts may cut off the foreskins of the penises of adolescent boys, who are expected to endure this operation without showing fear or pain. In the case of girls, ritual cutting may involve little more than nicking the clitoris with a knife blade to draw blood. In other cases, however, the surgery is more extreme. The clitoris itself may be cut off (or *excised*), a procedure called *clitoridectomy*. In some parts of eastern Africa, however, the surgery is even more extreme: The labia are excised along with the clitoris, and remaining skin is fastened together, forming scar tissue that partially closes the vaginal opening. This version is often called *pharaonic circumcision* or *infibulation*. When young women who have undergone this operation marry, they may require further surgery to widen the vaginal opening. Surgery may be necessary again to widen the vaginal opening when a woman gives birth; and after she has delivered her child, she may expect to be closed up again. Many women who have undergone these procedures repeatedly can develop serious medical complications involving the bladder and colon later in life.

FIGURE 8.6 Among many East African people, including the Maasai, female genital cutting is an important part of the transformation of girls into women. These young women are recovering from the operation. Maasai women are proud of their new status as adults.

cultural relativism Understanding another culture in its own terms sympathetically enough so that the culture appears to be a coherent and meaningful design for living.

The removal of the male foreskin—or *circumcision*—has long been a familiar practice in Western societies, not only among observant Jews, who perform it for religious reasons, but also among physicians, who have encouraged circumcision of male newborns as a hygienic measure. The ritual practice of female genital cutting, by contrast, has been unfamiliar to most people in Western societies until recently.

Genital Cutting, Gender, and Human Rights

In 1978, radical feminist Mary Daly (1978) grouped "African female genital mutilation" together with practices such as foot binding in China and witch burning in medieval Europe and labeled all these practices patriarchal "Sado-Rituals" that destroy "the Self-affirming being of women." Feminists and other cultural critics in Western societies spoke out against such practices in the 1980s. In 1992, African American novelist Alice Walker published a best-selling novel *Possessing the Secret of Joy* in which the heroine is an African woman who undergoes the operation, suffers psychologically and physically, and eventually pursues the female elder who performed the ritual on her. Walker also made a film, called *Warrior Marks*, that condemned female genital cutting. Although many Western readers continue to regard the positions taken by Daly and Walker as formidable and necessary feminist assertions of women's resistance against patriarchal oppression, other readers—particularly women from societies in which female genital cutting is an ongoing practice—have responded with far less enthusiasm.

Does this mean that these women are in favor of female genital cutting? Not necessarily; in fact, many of them are actively working to discourage the practice in their own societies. But they find that when outsiders publicly condemn traditional African rituals like clitoridectomy and infibulation, their efforts may do more harm than good. Women anthropologists who come from African societies where female genital cutting is traditional point out that Western women who want to help are likely to be more effective if they pay closer attention to what the African women themselves have to say about the meaning of these customs: "Careful listening to women helps us to recognize them as political actors forging their own communities of resistance. It also helps us to learn how and when to provide strategic support that would be welcomed by women who are struggling to challenge such traditions within their own cultures" (Abusharaf 2000).

A better understanding of female genital cutting is badly needed in places like the United States and the European Union, where some immigrants and refugees from Africa have brought traditions of female genital cutting with them. Since the mid-1990s, growing awareness and public condemnation of the practice have led to the passage of laws that criminalize female genital cutting in 19 African states and 11 industrialized nations, including the United States and Canada (http://reproductiverights.org/en/document/female-genital-mutilation-fgm-legal-prohibitions-worldwide). Nonprofit legal advocacy organizations such as the Center for Reproductive and Legal Rights consider female genital cutting (which they call *female genital mutilation*, or FGM) a human rights violation. They acknowledge: "Although FGM is not undertaken with the intention of inflicting harm, its damaging physical, sexual, and psychological effects make it an act of violence against women and children" (http://reproductiverights.org/en/document/female-genital-mutilation-fgm-legal-prohibitions-worldwide). Some women have been able successfully to claim asylum or have avoided deportation by claiming that they have fled their home countries to avoid the operation. However, efforts to protect women and girls may backfire badly when immigrant or refugee mothers in the United States who seek to have their daughters ritually cut are stigmatized in the media as "mutilators" or "child abusers" and find that this practice is considered a felony punishable by up to five years in prison (Abusharaf 2000). Indeed, as we will see in Chapter 14, such efforts can backfire even when members of the receiving society attempt to be culturally sensitive.

Genital Cutting as a Valued Ritual

Female genital cutting is clearly a controversial practice about which many people have already made up their minds. In such circumstances, is there any role to be played by anthropologists? Abusharaf thinks there is. She writes, "Debates swirling around circumcision must be restructured in ways that are neither condemnatory nor demeaning, but that foster perceptions illuminated by careful study of the nuanced complexities of culture" (Abusharaf 2000, 17).

One ethnographic study that aims to achieve these goals has been written by Janice Boddy, a cultural anthropologist who has carried out field research since 1976 in the Muslim village of Hofriyat in rural northern Sudan, where female genital surgery is traditionally performed in childhood. She writes that "nothing . . . had adequately prepared me for what I was to witness" when she first observed the operation; nevertheless, "as time passed in the village and understanding deepened I came to regard this form of female circumcision in a very different light" (Boddy 1997, 309). Circumcisions in Hofriyat were traditionally performed on both boys and girls, but the ritual had a different meaning for boys than it did for girls. Once circumcised, a boy takes a step toward manhood, but a girl will not become a woman until she marries. Female circumcision is required, however, to make a girl marriageable, making it possible for her "to use her one great gift, fertility" (Boddy 1997, 310).

In Hofriyat, female circumcision traditionally involved infibulation, the most extreme version of genital cutting. Among the justifications offered for infibulation, Boddy found that preserving chastity and curbing female sexual desire made the most sense in rural northern Sudan, where women's sexual conduct is the symbol of family honor. In practical terms, infibulation ensures "that a girl is a virgin when she marries for the first time" (Boddy 1997, 313). Women who undergo the procedure do indeed suffer a lot, not only at the time of circumcision, but whenever they engage in sexual intercourse, whenever they give birth, and, over time, as they become subject to recurring urinary infections and difficulties with menstruation. What cultural explanation could make all this suffering meaningful to women?

The answer lies in the connection rural northern Sudanese villagers make between the infibulated female body and female fertility. Boddy believes that the women she knew equated the category of "virgin" more with fertility than with lack of sexual experience and believed that a woman's virginity and her fertility could be renewed and protected by the act of reinfibulation after giving birth. Women she knew described infibulated female bodies as clean and smooth and pure (Boddy 1997, 313). Boddy concluded that the ritual was best understood as a way of socializing female fertility "by dramatically de-emphasizing their inherent sexuality" (314) and turning infibulated women into potential "mothers of men" (314). This means they are eligible, with their husbands, to found a new lineage section by giving birth to sons. Women who become mothers of men are more than mere sexual partners or servants of their husbands and may attain high status, with their name remembered in village genealogies.

Boddy discovered that the purity, cleanliness, and smoothness associated with the infibulated female body are also associated with other activities, concepts, and objects in everyday village customs. For example, Boddy discovered that "clean" water birds, "clean food" such as eggs, ostrich eggshells, and gourds shaped like ostrich eggshells, all were associated with female fertility. Indeed, "the shape of an ostrich egg, with its tiny orifice, corresponds to the idealized shape of the circumcised woman's womb" (Boddy 1997, 317). Fetching water is traditionally considered women's work, and the ability of an object to retain moisture is likened to its ability

to retain fertility. A dried egg-shaped gourd with seeds that rattle inside it is like the womb of an infibulated woman that contains and mixes her husband's semen with her own blood. The traditional house in Hofriyat itself seems to be a symbol for the womb, which is called the "house of childbirth" (321). In the same way that the household enclosure "protects a man's descendants, so the enclosed womb protects a woman's fertility . . . the womb of an infibulated woman is an oasis, the locus of appropriate human fertility" (321).

Evidence like this leads Boddy to insist that, for the women of Hofriyat, pharaonic circumcision is "an assertive symbolic act." The experience of infibulation, as well as other traditional curing practices, teaches girls to associate pure female bodies with heat and pain, making them meaningful. Such experiences become associated with the chief purpose women strive for—to become mothers of men—and the lesson is taught to them repeatedly in a variety of ways when they look at waterbirds or eggs or make food or move around the village. Boddy's relativistic account demonstrates how the meanings associated with female infibulation are reinforced by so many different aspects of everyday life that girls who grow up, marry, and bear children in Hofriyat come to consider the operation a dangerous but profoundly necessary and justifiable procedure that enables them to help sustain all that is most valued in their own world.

Culture and Moral Reasoning

A relativistic understanding of female genital cutting, therefore, accomplishes several things. It makes the practice comprehensible and even coherent. It reveals how a physically dangerous procedure can appear perfectly acceptable—even indispensable—when placed in a particular context of meaning. It can help us see how some of the cultural practices that we take for granted, such as the promotion of weight loss and cosmetic surgery among women in our own society, are equally dangerous—from "Victorian clitoridectomy" (Sheehan 1997) to twenty-first century cosmetic surgery. In the March 1, 2007, issue of the *New York Times*, for example, reporter Natasha Singer (2007) observes, "Before braces, crooked teeth were the norm. Is wrinkle removal the new orthodontics?" (E3). Media and marketing pressure for cosmetic treatments that stop the visible signs of aging bombard middle-aged women. People are living longer, and treatments like Botox injections are becoming more easily available, with the result that "the way pop culture perceives the aging face" is changing, leaving women "grappling with the idea of what 60 looks like" (Singer 2007, E3). Moreover, pressure to undergo antiaging treatments, including plastic surgery, is not simply a matter of vanity. "At the very least, wrinkles are being repositioned as the new gray hair—another means to judge attractiveness, romantic viability, professional competitiveness and social status" (Singer 2007, E3). Singer quotes a 33-year-old real estate broker who has had Botox injections, chemical peels, and laser treatments who said, "If you want to sell a million-dollar house, you have to look good . . . and you have to have confidence that you look good" (E3). In Sudan, people say that virgins are "made, not born" (Boddy 1997, 313); perhaps in the United States, youth is also made, not born. In the United States today, the media message to women is that success in life requires not an infibulated body, but a face that never ages. In both cases, cultural practices recommend surgical intervention in the female life cycle to render permanent certain aspects of youthful female bodies that are otherwise transient (fertility and unlined faces, respectively).

Did Their Culture Make Them Do It?

Do these examples imply that women support "irrational" and harmful practices simply because "their culture makes them do it?" For some people, this kind of explanation is plausible, even preferable, to alternative explanations, because it absolves individual people of blame. How can one justify accusing immigrant African women of being mutilators or abusers of children and throw them into prison if they had no choice in the matter, if their cultures conditioned them into believing that female circumcision was necessary and proper and they are powerless to resist?

Nevertheless, such an explanation is too simplistic to account for the continued practice of infibulation in Hofriyat. First, the villages of northern Sudan are not sealed off from a wider, more diverse world. Northern Sudan has experienced a lively and often violent history as different groups of outsiders, including the British, have struggled to control the land. Boddy describes the way rural men regularly leave the village as migrant workers and mix with people whose customs—including sexual customs—are very different from the ones they left behind; and outsiders, like anthropologists, also may come to the village and establish long-lasting relationships with those whom they meet. Second, Boddy's account makes clear that the culture of Hofriyat allows people more than one way to interpret their experiences. For example, she notes that although men in Sudan and Egypt are supposed to enjoy sexual intercourse with infibulated women more than with noninfibulated women; in fact, these men regularly visit brothels where they encounter prostitutes who have not undergone the surgery.

Third, and perhaps most significantly, Boddy observes that a less radical form of the operation began to gain acceptance after 1969, and "men are now marrying—and what is more, saying that they prefer to marry—women who have been less severely mutilated" (Boddy 1997, 312), at least in part because they find sexual relations to be more satisfying. Finally, as these observations also show, Boddy's account emphatically rejects the view that women or men in Hofriyat are passive beings, helpless to resist cultural indoctrination. As Abusharaf (2000, 18) would wish, Boddy listened to women in Hofriyat and recognized them "as political actors forging their own communities of resistance." Specifically, Boddy showed how increasing numbers of women (and men) continued to connect female genital cutting with properly socialized female fertility—but they no longer believed that infibulation was the only procedure capable of achieving that goal.

Understanding something is not the same as approving of it or excusing it. People everywhere may be repelled by unfamiliar cultural practices when they first encounter them. Sometimes when they understand these practices better, they change their minds. They may conclude that the practices in question are more suitable for the people who employ them than their own practices would be. They might even recommend incorporating practices from other cultures into their own society. But the opposite may also be the case. It is possible to understand perfectly the cultural rationale behind such practices as slavery, infanticide, headhunting, and genocide—and still refuse to approve of these practices. Insiders and outsiders alike may not be persuaded by the reasons offered to justify these practices, or they may be aware of alternative arrangements that could achieve the desired outcome via less drastic methods. In fact, changing practices of female circumcision in Hofriyat seem to be based precisely on the realization that less extreme forms of surgery can achieve the same valued cultural goals. This should not surprise us: it is likely that any cultural practice with far-reaching consequences for human life will have critics as well as supporters within the society where it is practiced. This is certainly the case in the United States, where abortion and capital punishment remain controversial issues.

A sensitive ethnographic account of a controversial cultural practice, like Boddy's account of infibulation in Hofriyat, will address both the meaningful dimensions of the practice and the contradictions it involves. As Boddy (1997) concludes,

Those who work to eradicate female circumcision must, I assert, cultivate an awareness of the custom's local significances and of how much they are asking people to relinquish as well as gain. The stakes are high and it is hardly surprising that efforts to date have met with little success. It is, however, ironic that a practice that—at least in Hofriyat—emphasizes female fertility at a cultural level can be so destructive of it physiologically and so damaging to women's health overall. That paradox has analogies elsewhere, in a world considered "civilized," seemingly far removed from the "barbarous East." Here too, in the west from where I speak, feminine selfhood is often attained at the expense of female well-being. In parallels like these there lies the germ of an enlightened approach to the problem. (322)

Since she made these observations, Boddy has returned to Hofriyat several times. By 2016, she says, many of the families she knew had given up female genital cutting entirely. The reasons are complex. Part of the explanation is the success of public education campaigns in which respected leaders have argued against the practice. Families are now aware that many Islamic scholars do not consider female genital cutting to be a religious obligation. Change also has been promoted by processes of globalization. An oil boom, which brought local prosperity, allowed some families from Hofriyat to move to the Sudanese capital of Khartoum and to send their daughters to school. Indeed, more young women are now going to university than young men, and educated young women are sometimes able to elude family pressure to marry. But global digital technology has also had a powerful effect. Mobile phones allow people of all ages to communicate more freely and more privately than in the past, and young men and women have taken advantage of this. Thanks to the Internet, Western Internet pornography has become popular among both women and men in Sudan. Such pornography features images of naked women with smooth, hairless genitalia, which is increasingly becoming a feminine ideal in the West. Ironically, the desired look is not that different from the desired traditional outcome sought from female genital cutting in Hofriyat in the past. But unlike these "customary" forms of female genital cutting that have been condemned in the West, the new forms of female genital surgery (called "labiaplasties") are expensive and much sought after by women who want their genitalia to look like that of women in porn films. Meanwhile, in Sudan, Boddy heard gossip about urban husbands, familiar with the images of women in pornography, who did not like the look of their uncut wives and sent them home to be cut in the traditional way. Boddy is troubled by "the convergences and contradictions outlined here. For they expose the multiple ways that techniques and concepts of the gendered body linked to global neoliberalism saturate the most intimate levels of human life in the twenty-first century, no matter who we are or where we live" (2016).

Cultural relativism makes moral reasoning more complex. It does not, however, require us to abandon every value our own society has taught us. Every cultural tradition offers more than one way of evaluating experience. Exposure to the interpretations of an unfamiliar culture forces us to reconsider the possibilities our own tradition recognizes in a new light and to search for areas of intersection as well as areas of disagreement. What cultural relativism does discourage is the easy solution of refusing to consider alternatives from the outset. It also does not free us from sometimes facing difficult choices between alternatives whose rightness or wrongness is less than clear-cut. In this sense, "cultural relativism is a 'toughminded' philosophy" (Herskovits 1973, 37).

Does Culture Explain Everything?

We believe that our view of the concept of culture as presented in this chapter is widely shared among contemporary cultural anthropologists. Nevertheless, in recent years, the concept of culture has been critically reexamined as patterns of human life have undergone major dislocations and reconfigurations. The issues are complex and are more fully explored in later chapters, but we offer here a brief account to provide some historical context.

For at least the past 50 years, many anthropologists have distinguished between Culture (with a capital *C*) and cultures (plural with a lowercase *c*). *Culture* has been used to describe an attribute of the human species as a whole—its members' ability, in the absence of highly specific genetic programming, to create and to imitate patterned, symbolically mediated ideas and activities that promote the survival of our species. By contrast, the term *cultures* has been used to refer to particular, learned *ways of life* belonging to specific groups of human beings. Given this distinction, the human species as a whole can be said to have Culture as a defining attribute, but actual human beings would only have access to particular human cultures—either their own or other people's.

It is the plural use of cultures with a lowercase c that has been challenged. The challenge may seem puzzling, however, because many anthropologists have viewed the plural use of the culture concept not only as analytically helpful but also as politically progressive. Their view reflects a struggle that developed in nineteenth-century Europe: supporters of the supposedly progressive, universal civilization of the Enlightenment, inaugurated by the French Revolution and spread by Napoleonic conquest, were challenged by inhabitants of other European nations, who resisted both Napoleon and the

Enlightenment in what has been called the Romantic Counter-Enlightenment. Romantic intellectuals in nations like Germany rejected what they considered the imposition of "artificial" Enlightenment *civilization* on the "natural" spiritual traditions of their own distinct national *cultures* (Kuper 1999; Crehan 2002).

This political dynamic, which pits a steamroller civilization against vulnerable local cultures, carried over into the usage that later developed in anthropology, particularly in North America. The decades surrounding the turn of the twentieth century marked the period of expanding European colonial empires as well as westward expansion and consolidation of control in North America by European settlers. At that time, the social sciences were becoming established in universities, and different fields were assigned different tasks. Anthropology was allocated what Michel-Rolph Trouillot (1991) has called "the savage slot"—that is, the so-called "primitive" world that was the target of colonization. Anthropologists thus became the official academic experts on societies whose members suffered racist denigration as "primitives" and whose ways of life were being undermined by contact with Western colonial "civilization."

Anthropologists were determined to denounce these practices and to demonstrate that the "primitive" stereotype was false. Some found inspiration in the work of the English anthropologist E. B. Tylor, who, in 1871, had defined "culture or civilization" as "that complex whole which includes knowledge, belief, art, morals, law, custom, and any other capabilities and habits acquired by man as a member of society" ([1871] 1958, 1). This definition had the virtue of blurring the difference between "civilization" and "culture," and it encouraged the view that even "primitives" possessed "capabilities and habits" that merited respect. Thus, in response to stereotypes of "primitives" as irrational, disorganized, insensitive, or promiscuous, anthropologists like Franz Boas and Bronislaw Malinowski were able to show that, on the contrary, so-called "primitives" possessed "cultures" that were reasonable, orderly, artistically developed, and morally disciplined. The plural use of culture allowed them to argue that, in their own ways, "primitives" were as fully human as "civilized" people.

By the end of the twentieth century, however, some anthropologists became concerned about the way the plural concept of culture was being used. That is, the boundary that was once thought to protect vulnerability was starting to look more like a prison wall, condemning those within it to live according to "their" culture, just as their ancestors had done, like exhibits in a living museum, whether they wanted to or not. But if some group members criticize a practice, such as female

FIGURE 8.7   A McDonald's in Guangzhou, China.

genital cutting, that is part of their cultural tradition, does this mean that the critics are no longer "authentic" members of their own culture? To come to such a conclusion overlooks the possibility that alternatives to a controversial practice might already exist *within* the cultural tradition and that followers of that tradition may *themselves* decide that some alternatives make more sense than others in today's world. The issue then becomes not just which traditions have been inherited from the past—as if "authentic" cultures were monolithic and unchanging—but rather, which traditional practices *ought* to continue in a contemporary world— and who is entitled to make that decision.

Cultural Change and Cultural Authenticity

It is no secret that colonizing states have regularly attempted to determine the cultural priorities of those whom they conquered. Sending missionaries to convert colonized people to Christianity is one of the best known practices of Western cultural imperialism. In

North America, in the 1860s, for example, escalating struggles between settlers and Native American groups led federal policymakers to place federal Indian policy in the hands of Christian reformers "who would embrace the hard work of transforming Indians and resist the lure of getting rich off the system's spoils" (Lassiter et al. 2002, 22). And although missionaries were initially resisted, eventually they made many converts, and Christianity remains strong among indigenous groups like the Comanches and Kiowas today. But how should this religious conversion be understood?

Doesn't the fact that Kiowas are Christians today show that federal officials and missionaries succeeded in their policies of Western Christian cultural imperialism? Maybe not: "Taking the 'Jesus Way' is not necessarily the story of how one set of beliefs replace another one wholesale or of the incompatibility of Kiowa practices with Christian ones. Rather, it is a more complex encounter in which both sides make concessions" (Lassiter et al. 2002, 19). True, missionaries arrived as the buffalo were disappearing and Kiowa people were being confined to reservations; and in 1890, the US government used military force to put an end to the Kiowa Sun Dance, the centerpiece of Kiowa ceremonies. And yet, Lassiter et al. tells us, "For many Kiowas—as for Indian people generally—Christianity has been, and remains, a crucially important element in their lives as Native people. Its concern for community needs, its emphasis on shared beliefs, and its promise of salvation have helped to mediate life in a region long buffeted by limited economic development, geographic isolation, and cultural stress" (18).

One reason it succeeded was that missionaries did not insist that the Kiowa give up all traditional ways (Lassiter et al. 2002, 53). Prominent individuals adopted Christianity, and Kiowa converts were trained to become missionaries and ministers, which proved attractive (Lassiter et al. 2002, 57; Figure 8.8). Especially persuasive were women missionaries who "lived in the Kiowa camps, ate their food, and endured the privations of life on the plains with impressive strength" (Lassiter et al. 2002, 59). Missionaries, in turn, actively sought to adapt Christian practices to traditional Kiowa ways. For example, "Missions were historically located in and around established camps and communities," with the result that "churches were the natural extension of traditional Kiowa camps" and eventually took their place at the center of Kiowa life (Lassiter et al. 2002, 61). "People would often camp on the grounds or stay with relatives for weeks at a time. . . . Services with Kiowa hymns and special prayers often extended into the evening" (62). It might be as accurate to say that the Kiowa "Kiowanized" Christianity, therefore, as

FIGURE 8.8 Among the Kiowa, prominent individuals, like Chief Lone Wolf, adopted Christianity and invited missionaries to train Kiowa ministers.

it would be to say that missionaries "Christianized" the Kiowa. One of Lassiter's Kiowa collaborators, Vincent Bointy, insists that Christianity is not the same as "the white man's way" and explains that "the elders didn't say 'Christian.' . . . They said 'this is the way of God'" (Lassiter et al. 2002, 63). Kiowa identity and Christian values are so closely intertwined for Bointy that "he believes that he can express the power of Christianity better in Kiowa than in English." And this is why Kiowa hymns are so important. Unlike other Kiowa songs, Kiowa hymns are sung in the Kiowa language, which is spoken less and less in other settings. Kiowa hymns "give life to a unique Kiowa experience, preserve the language, and affirm an ongoing (and continually unfolding) Kiowa spirituality. Indeed, Kiowa Indian hymns are as much Kiowa (if not more) as they are Christian" (Lassiter 2004, 205).

The way in which Kiowa Christians have been able to transform what began as an exercise in cultural imperialism into a reaffirmation of traditional Kiowa values challenges the presumption that "authentic cultures" never change. Such an inflexible concept of culture can accommodate neither the agency of Kiowa Christians nor the validity of the "ongoing" and "continually unfolding" cultural traditions they produce.

The Promise of the Anthropological Perspective

The anthropological perspective on the human condition is not easy to maintain. It forces us to question the commonsense assumptions with which we are most comfortable. It only increases the difficulty we encounter when faced with moral and political decisions. It does not allow us an easy retreat because once we are exposed to the kinds of experience that the anthropological undertaking makes possible, we are changed. We cannot easily pretend that these new experiences never happened to us. There is no going back to ethnocentrism when the going gets rough, except in bad faith. So anthropology is guaranteed to complicate your life. Nevertheless, the anthropological perspective can give you a broader understanding of human nature and the wider world—of society, culture, and history—and thus help you construct more realistic and authentic ways of coping with those complications.

Chapter Summary

1. Anthropologists have argued that culture distinguishes the human condition from the condition of other living species. Human culture is learned, shared, patterned, adaptive, and symbolic. It did not emerge all at once but evolved over time.

2. Many anthropologists have long thought holistically about human culture. Anthropological holism argues that objects and environments interpenetrate and even define each other. Thus, the whole is more than the sum of its parts. Human beings and human societies are open systems that cannot be reduced to the parts that make them up. The parts and the whole mutually define, or codetermine, each other and coevolve. This book adopts a coevolutionary approach to human nature, human society, and the human past. Human beings depend on symbolic cultural understandings to help them resolve the ambiguities inherent in everyday human experience.

3. Anthropologists believe that ethnocentrism can be countered by a commitment to cultural relativism, an attempt to understand the cultural underpinnings of behavior. Cultural relativism does not require us to abandon every value our society has taught us; however, it does discourage the easy solution of refusing to consider alternatives from the outset. Cultural relativism makes moral decisions more difficult because it requires us to take many things into account before we make up our minds.

4. Human history is an essential aspect of the human story. Culture is worked out over time and passed on from one generation to the next. The cultural beliefs and practices we inherit from the past or borrow from other people in the present make some things easier for us and other things more difficult. At the same time, culture provides resources human beings can make use of in the pursuit of their own goals. Thus, the anthropological understanding of human life recognizes the importance of human agency.

5. Many anthropologists have criticized use of the term *cultures* to refer to particular, learned ways of life belonging to specific groups of human beings. Critics argue that this way of talking about culture seems to endorse a kind of oppressive cultural determinism. Supporters, however, argue that in some cases, this version of the culture concept can be used to defend vulnerable social groups against exploitation and oppression by outsiders.

6. In recent years, cultural anthropologists who follow the vast contemporary population movements of migrants, refugees, and tourists have begun to study processes of cultural mixing that appears to reflect new forms of multicultural consciousness.

For Review

1. What are the five key attributes of human culture that are highlighted in this chapter?

2. What are complex symbolic representation and institutions, and why are they especially important to human culture?

3. What is human agency? How does attention to human agency affect the way anthropologists interpret cultural phenomena?

4. What do anthropologists mean by holism?

5. Describe the problems US Peace Corps volunteers were having in Botswana and the explanation that was provided by anthropologist Hoyt Alverson.

6. Explain ethnocentrism and cultural relativism.

7. Summarize in your own words how cultural relativity can improve outsiders' understanding of a cultural practice that is unfamiliar and disturbing to them, such as female genital cutting.

8. Distinguish between Culture (with a capital C) and cultures (plural with a lowercase c). What does this difference reflect for anthropologists?

9. Summarize the case study on Kiowa Christianity. What does this case study reveal about human cultural processes?

Key Terms

coevolution 249	enculturation 242	holism 246	socialization 242
cultural relativism 251	ethnocentrism 250	human agency 246	symbol 244
culture 242			

Suggested Readings

Gamst, Frederick, and Edward Norbeck. 1976. *Ideas of culture: Sources and uses.* New York: Holt, Rinehart & Winston. *A useful collection of important articles about culture. The articles are arranged according to different basic approaches to culture.*

Geertz, Clifford. 1973. Thick description: Towards an interpretive theory of culture *and* The impact of the concept of culture on the concept of man. In *The interpretation of cultures.* New York: Basic Books. *Two classic discussions of culture from a major figure in American anthropology. These works have done much to shape the discourse about culture in anthropology.*

Kuper, Adam. 1999. *Culture: The anthropologists' account.* Cambridge, MA: Harvard University Press. *A critical history of the use of the culture concept in anthropology, which traces its links to earlier Western ideas about culture and analyzes the work of several late twentieth-century anthropologists who made the concept central to their scholarship. Based on his experience with the abuse of the culture concept in apartheid South Africa, Kuper recommends that anthropologists drop the term entirely from their professional vocabulary.*

Voget, Fred. 1975. *A history of ethnology.* New York: Holt, Rinehart & Winston. *A massive, thorough, and detailed work. For the student seeking a challenging read.*

 Visit our online resource center for further reading, web links, free assessments, flashcards, and videos. www.oup.com/he/ lavenda5e

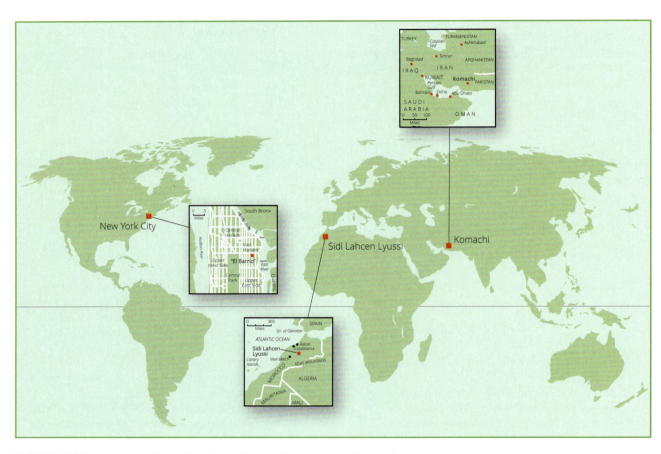

FIGURE M3.1   Locations of societies whose EthnoProfiles appear in Module 3.

A Meeting of Cultural Traditions

Ethnographic **fieldwork** is an extended period of close involvement with the people whose way of life interests an anthropologist. This is the period in which anthropologists collect most of their data. Fieldwork deliberately brings together people from different cultural backgrounds, an encounter that makes misunderstandings, understandings, and surprises likely. It is nevertheless through such encounters that fieldwork generates much of what anthropologists come to know about people in other societies.

Gathering data while living for an extended period in close contact with members of another social group is called **participant observation**. Cultural anthropologists also gather data by conducting interviews and administering surveys, as well as by consulting archives and previously published literature relevant to their research. But participant observation, which relies on face-to-face contact with people as they go about their daily lives, was pioneered by cultural anthropologists and remains characteristic of anthropology as a discipline. Participant observation allows anthropologists to interpret what people say and do in the wider context of social interaction and cultural beliefs and values. Sometimes they administer questionnaires and psychological tests as part of their fieldwork, but they would never rely solely on such methods because, by themselves, the information they produce cannot be contextualized and may be misleading. Participant observation is perhaps the best method available to scholars who seek a holistic understanding of culture and the human condition.

fieldwork An extended period of close involvement with the people in whose language or way of life anthropologists are interested, during which anthropologists ordinarily collect most of their data.

participant observation The method anthropologists use to gather information by living as closely as possible to the people whose culture they are studying while participating in their lives as much as possible.

Classic Single-Sited Fieldwork

For most cultural anthropologists, ethnographic fieldwork is the key experience that characterizes the discipline. Anthropologists sometimes gain field experience as undergraduates or early in their graduate studies by working on research projects or in field schools run by established anthropologists. An extended period of fieldwork is the final phase of formal anthropological training, but most anthropologists hope to incorporate additional periods of field research into their subsequent careers.

Beginning anthropologists usually decide during graduate school where and on what topic they wish to do their research. These decisions are based on their interests, their readings, the courses they have taken, the interests of their professors, and current debates in cultural anthropology. Success depends on being able to obtain both permission to work in a particular place in the form of approvals from academic and governmental offices in the host country and the funds to support one's research. Getting grants from private or government agencies involves, among other things, persuading them that your work will focus on a topic of current interest within anthropology and is connected to their funding priorities. As a result, "field sites end up being defined by the crosshatched intersection of visa and clearance procedures, the interests of funding agencies, and intellectual debates within the discipline and its subfields" (Gupta and Ferguson 1997, 11). Because there is a great demand for grants, not all topics of current interest can be funded, so some anthropologists pay for their research themselves by getting a job in the area where they want to do fieldwork or by supplementing small grants out of their own pockets.

Classic cultural anthropological fieldwork emphasized working "abroad"—that is, doing fieldwork in societies that were culturally and geographically distant from that of the ethnographer. This orientation bears undeniable traces of its origins under European colonialism, but it continues to be a valuable means of drawing attention to ways of life and parts of the world that elite groups in powerful Western nations have traditionally dismissed and marginalized. It also forces the fieldworker to recognize differences that might not be so obvious at home. More recent discussions of anthropological fieldwork have drawn attention to the significance of working "at home"—including paying attention to the forms of social differentiation and marginalization present in the society to which the ethnographer belongs. This orientation has the virtue of emphasizing ethnographers' ethical and political accountability to those among whom they work, especially when the anthropologists are themselves members of the groups they study. Such an orientation incorporates traditions of anthropological research that have developed in countries like Mexico, Brazil, India, and Russia, where fieldwork at home has long been the norm. At the beginning of the twenty-first century, these developments are helping to create "decolonized anthropology in a deterritorialized world" that will be enriched by varied contributions of anthropologists trained in different traditions, working at home and abroad.

How Do Anthropologists Think about the Ethics of Their Work?

Ethnographic fieldwork practice was developed and regularized during the decades before World War II, both in the United States and the United Kingdom, by anthropologists such as Bronislaw Malinowski, Franz Boas, and their students and colleagues. Here, we will provide a brief history of how members of the American Anthropological Association (AAA) have addressed the ethics associated with anthropological fieldwork. A series of informative documents that trace these developments can be accessed via the AAA website (http://www.americananthro.org/) under the tab "Learn and Teach," which links to a further tab, "Methods and Ethics," which opens links to the *Ethics Handbook*, to an ethics blog, and to "Anthropological Research Methods," this provides links to a variety of electronic documents relating to research design and data collection methods, data analysis resources, and data analysis tools.

The *Handbook on Ethical Issues in Anthropology*, originally published in 1987, contains a series of chapters that trace the development and transformation of ethical reflection by American anthropologists, from the early twentieth century through the last years of the Cold War. In their introductory chapter, coeditors Joan Cassell and Sue-Ellen Jacobs observe that "in the field, especially, situations may be so complex, involve so many parties and so much factionalism, that it becomes difficult to decide what must be done." They also point out that "to improve the ethical adequacy of anthropological practice, we must consider not only exceptional cases but everyday decisions, and reflect not only upon the conduct of others but also upon our own actions." Chapter 1 (by Murray L. Wax) traces ethical concerns of anthropologists from the late nineteenth century through World War II and into the beginning of the Cold War. In the early twentieth century, under the influence of Boas, Wax observes that "Insofar as 'ethics' were topics of serious concern among fieldworking anthropologists, the central issues were relativism and intervention." The "intervention" they objected to came from colonial powers, businessmen or missionaries who threatened to damage the harmony of integrated individual cultures. Fieldworkers also struggled with their relationships with their informants: "many felt constrained by the methodological ideal of the natural scientist, who was intrinsically detached from the objects of study."

During World War II, in the face of fascism, many anthropologists viewed working for the US government as a way to continue these ethical commitments. In the 1950s and 1960s, however, Cold War politics changed attitudes. In particular, one Cold War US government proposal, Project Camelot, recommended that anthropologists and other social scientists be enlisted to collect field data that could be useful for government intelligence purposes. When this plan became publicly known in 1965, an enormous scandal ensued, and the project was formally cancelled. However, as Wax notes, this scandal, as well as later conflict over the war in Vietnam, led to the view of many anthropologists that to be "ethical" meant to refuse to accept funding or employment by any agencies of the US government.

As James N. Hill discusses in Chapter 2, outrage over these matters led in the late 1960s to the creation of the first AAA code of ethics as well as to the formation of the AAA Committee on Ethics (COE). The 1970s and 1980s were years when the attention to reflexivity and the critique of positivist "natural science" gained ground among many anthropologists. The AAA COE (officially called the "Principles of Professional Responsibility") has been revised periodically, most recently in 2012. The AAA COE still exists, but Hill notes that, after the Vietnam War ended, its focus changed, as "the entire issue of secret and clandestine research passed (temporarily?) into history." By the early 1980s, the COE was considering whether it ought to be involved in the ethical resolution of employment grievances involving AAA members, but these efforts were viewed as ineffectual, and adjudication on such matters was no longer considered appropriate for the COE. At the end of the 1980s, Hill concluded that the most important task of the COE was educational, and he pointed to the valuable contributions of the "Ethical Dilemmas" columns that have been published regularly in the *Anthropology Newsletter* since the 1970s.

Chapters 3 and 4 of the *Handbook* are collections of case studies from this column during the years when Sue-Ellen Jacobs and Joan Cassell served as editors. Chapter 3 includes 12 case studies published under Jacobs's editorship. Each case study was based on a specific problem communicated to her by anthropologists that involved a particular ethical issue. Readers were then invited to solve these dilemmas, drawing on the Principles of Professional Responsibility or other ethics-related resolutions passed by the members of the AAA. The last three cases, however, focused on ethical matters that arose between anthropologists. Chapter 4 includes an additional 12 ethical dilemmas, presented under Cassell's editorship in a changed format: each case study is followed by a series of questions to the reader about possible responses, and these questions are followed by responses from anthropologists or ethicists asked by Cassell to offer their views. In chapter 5, Jacobs shares her experiences teaching ethics in anthropological fieldwork classes; and in chapter 6, Cassell suggests how anthropologists might organize a workshop on ethical problems encountered in fieldwork settings.

In retrospect, many of the ethical dilemmas presented in the *Handbook* reflect the concerns of Cold War anthropology, published two years before the fall of the Berlin Wall, in a world without the Internet. But other cases show the growing importance of applied anthropology, especially medical anthropology, dealing with ethical dilemmas encountered

by ethnographers who were now working alongside medical professionals with training and ethical perceptions often quite different from their own (see chapter 15). The inclusion of responses to these dilemmas by professionals from other disciplines helped raise the level of ethical discussion to a new level of sophistication, offering a new appreciation of the ethical complexities engendered by fieldwork in new places.

With the end of the Cold War, the global spread of capitalism, and the increase in global movements of wealth and things, people, and ideas (see chapter 13), the context for ethical reflection in anthropology changed again. Transformed theoretical understandings about culture had undermined previous assumptions about the harmonious integration of different cultures. Multisited ethnography was emerging, and ethnographers increasingly found themselves working with groups of informants who were differently situated, both socially and geographically, from one another. Anthropologists also became increasingly involved in social media; and when the website of the AAA was upgraded in 2012, a new ethics blog (http://ethics.americananthro.org/about/) became available. Sponsored by the AAA Committee on Ethics, the site describes itself as "a new type of ethics blog post—a short description of an ethics issue related to anthropology that is appearing in the news and other online media, accompanied by links to original source material."

The site provides a list of topical keywords that link to previous posts, as well as links to archives dating back to November 2012. It also links to a full-text version of the 2012 Principles of Professional Responsibility (or "Ethics Statement"). The ethics statement includes seven principles: Do No Harm; Be Open and Honest Regarding Your Work; Obtain Informed Consent and Necessary Permissions; Weigh Competing Ethical Obligations Due Collaborators and Affected Parties; Make Your Results Accessible; Protect and Preserve Your Records; and Maintain Respectful and Ethical Professional Relationships. The blog posts sometimes comment on these principles, raising questions of their applicability in the twenty-first century; for instance, one recent post pointed out that the first principle—Do No Harm—provides no guidance to the many anthropologists involved in advocacy work. The fourth principle clearly addresses ethical challenges presented to ethnographers working in a globalizing post–Cold War world: although the primarily ethical obligations are said to be to research participants and vulnerable populations, the legitimacy of obligations to students, colleagues, employers, and funders is clearly acknowledged, as are the challenges in balancing the competing obligations to a range of stakeholders. Some of the elaborations of each principle clearly reflect wisdom gleaned from the earlier "ethical dilemmas" discussions, which have become only more important in the twenty-first century for applied anthropologists working with professionals in other fields. Indeed, links to some of their professional codes of ethics are provided on the website.

Many contemporary ethical challenges facing anthropologists in the twenty-first century are quite different from those that led to the formulation of the first code of ethics nearly 50 years ago. Yet for some anthropologists who began their careers that long ago, perhaps especially those who found ways to carry out fieldwork "behind the Iron Curtain," the end of the Cold War brought to light disconcerting information about how their research had been understood, especially by the national governments that had permitted them to carry out fieldwork. Anthropologist Katherine Verdery, who began a quarter-century of ethnographic fieldwork in Romania in 1973, was shocked to discover, after the end of the Communist regime, that the Securitate (or secret police) had considered her a spy almost from the beginning, and over the years had assembled nearly 3,000 pages of surveillance data about her. The first entries began in the 1970s, when she began her dissertation field research on village life in rural Transylvania. She had purchased a new motorbike, decided to take a ride in the hills to find a research site, and was pulled over by a policeman. In her ignorance, she had ridden straight into a military base. Worried initially that things would go very badly, she was surprised when the attitude of the officer who interviewed her seemed to change. He urged her to proceed with her research, insisting that the region would be ideal. Despite misgivings, she followed his suggestion. "And so began my life as a spy" (Verdery 2018, 3).

Working through the pages of her security file, Verdery discovered that she has a "secret double" whose nefarious intentions toward the Romanian regime were fleshed out over time, under the cover of nine different pseudonyms. In the 1970s, her desire to do research near the military base led the Romanian security apparatus to infer that she must be spying for the US military. In the 1980s, working in a different location, they inferred that she was actually spying for Hungarians in the United States. In the late 1980s, she herself was spied on in Baltimore, Maryland, at Johns Hopkins University, apparently because of her connections with certain Romanian dissidents. Initially, her reaction was one of befuddlement:

> When I read their descriptions of myself as a spy, I began to wonder whether I really *was* one. How much of the practice of anthropology resembles spying? Then I ask myself whether the unattractive portrait they paint of me might actually be true, or at least have something to it. . . . Far from being intriguing additions to my repertoire, my doubles have unmoored my self-perception. (2018, 7–8)

She observed that "Nothing in my graduate school training had prepared me for this. Virtually every one of the scholars was assumed to be a spy. . . . I and other Americans are regularly referred to as 'CIA agents.' Therefore, in the Securitate's view, 'spy' was the default identity for Western scholars" (2018, 15). We now know, Verdery reminds us, that many people working in the US embassy probably *were* involved in US intelligence operations; and that in those years, many cultural organizations *were* backed by the CIA, even if the personnel who worked for the organizations had no inkling of this connection. And, of course, the US government had similar suspicions about the motives of scholars from Soviet bloc countries who came to the United States for research and study (2018, 16).

What raised the suspicions of the Securitate about Verdery's "real" reasons for being in Romania? First, she claimed to be an ethnographer, but Romanian ethnographers at the time did short bursts of research in groups, and wrote up their findings collectively. By contrast, Verdery engaged in classic Euro-American, single-site fieldwork for over a year, which looked more like what intelligence officers did. Second, her friends in the village immediately suspected she was a spy because she didn't dress like a foreigner, but chose to dress as the villagers did. Thus, she seemed to be hiding her presence in the village while asking questions of informants, also just as intelligence officers did (2018, 17). Verdery's intention was to be completely transparent in all her dealings with Romanians, not imagining how odd this would appear to those living in a surveillance state governed by secrecy. Looking back, she marvels at how naïve and ethnocentric she was "to imagine that 'transparency' would be a value for a communist intelligence service. How little I knew" (2018, 23). In choosing to write about these matters today, Verdery wanted to come to terms with her double revealed in the security files, but she also wanted to use these materials to explore how the secret police operated in communist Romania: "exploring these files helps to decompose the monolithic 'totalitarian' identity of the Securitate and in the process to bring together the fragments that constitute my own" (2018, 29).

As James Hill anticipated, the original worry about anthropologists being drawn into "secret and clandestine research" has not gone away. In the years following the terrorist attacks of September 11, 2001, the US government once again became involved in military conflicts abroad, and controversy erupted once again about whether anthropologists should get involved.

Anthropologists were particularly concerned about the Human Terrain System, a US Army program that hired civilian anthropologists to become part of small units of five people embedded with US combat brigades in Iraq and Afghanistan. These teams were intended to provide relevant sociocultural information about the particular neighborhood and village communities in which the US military was operating. Backed by an elaborate 24-hour research center in the United States, the Human Terrain System was an attempt to improve relations between US military personnel and Iraqis and Afghans they might encounter, to report on development needs, and to recommend culturally relevant strategic advice. The hope was that if US military forces had some understanding of the social and cultural context they were part of, there would be a reduction in misunderstandings and unintentional insults and ultimately less bloodshed. This program was instantly controversial: was this an appropriate use of anthropological knowledge?

A number of anthropologists were concerned that the integrity of the discipline would be compromised by anthropologists serving in military units, almost like spies. Anthropologist Hugh Gusterson was quoted as saying, "'The prime directive is you do no harm to informants.' . . . Data collected by [Human Terrain Team] members can also be accessed by military intelligence operatives who might use the same information for targeting Taliban operatives" (Caryl 2009). Indeed, it might be used to target supposed Taliban sympathizers. As Gusterson puts it, "The product generated by the Human Terrain Teams is inherently double-edged" (Caryl 2009). The interest of the military unit may not be the same as the interest of the anthropologist or other social scientist embedded in a team. To whom would the anthropologist complain if his or her research were being used for purposes to which he or she objected?

Echoing Project Camelot, the Human Terrain System undermines the integrity of all other anthropological research, which depends on the trust anthropologists develop with the people with whom they work. If some anthropologists are working for the US military, how can people be sure that a person claiming to be an anthropologist in their community is not also working for the US military?

Although the Human Terrain Teams project was ended in September 2014, the questions it raised are still significant: Should anthropologists work for military organizations? Is it better to stand on the sidelines and criticize or to enter into an organization to try to effect change and improve the work and risk being co-opted? Indeed, given Katherine Verdery's experiences, even field research with no ostensible connection to military intelligence may be understood far differently by other interested parties. Who "owns" anthropological knowledge? These are not simple issues. What would you do?

What Is Participant Observation?

Participant observation requires living as closely as possible to the people whose culture you are studying. As Katherine Verdery's experience illustrates, Euro-American fieldwork has long been based on classic, long-term, single-site research projects. Although this has not been the model followed by ethnographers in all parts of the world, even in Euro-American contexts, it still

remains a goal for many social and cultural anthropologists. Anthropologists who work among remote peoples in rain forests, deserts, or tundra may need to bring along their own living quarters. In other cases, an appropriate house or apartment in the village, neighborhood, or city where the research is to be done becomes the anthropologist's home. In any case, living conditions in the field can themselves provide major insights into the culture under study. This is powerfully illustrated by the experiences of Charles and Bettylou Valentine, whose field site was a poor neighborhood they called "Blackston," located in a large city in the northern United States (see "EthnoProfile M3.1: Blackston"). The Valentines lived for the last field year on one-quarter of their regular income; during the final 6 months, they matched their income to that of welfare families:

> For five years we inhabited the same decrepit rat- and roach-infested buildings as everyone else, lived on the same poor quality food at inflated prices, trusted our health and our son's schooling to the same inferior institutions, suffered the same brutality and intimidation from the police, and like others made the best of it by some combination of endurance, escapism, and fighting back. Like the dwellings of our neighbors, our home went up in flames several times, including one disaster caused by the carelessness or ill will of the city's "firefighters." For several cold months we lived and worked in one room without heat other than what a cooking stove could provide, without hot water or windows, and with only one light bulb. (C. Valentine 1978, 5)

Not all field sites offer such a stark contrast to the middle-class backgrounds of many fieldworkers, and indeed some can be almost luxurious. But physical and mental dislocation

---

EthnoProfile M3.1

Blackston

Region: North America

Nation: United States

Population: 100,000

Environment: Urban ghetto

Livelihood: Low-paying, full-time and temporary jobs, welfare

Political organization: Lowest level in a modern nation-state

For more information: Valentine, Bettylou. 1978. *Hustling and other hard work*. New York: Free Press.

and stress can be expected anywhere. People from temperate climates who find themselves in the tropics have to adjust to the heat; fieldworkers in the Arctic have to adjust to the cold. In hot climates especially, many anthropologists encounter plants, animals, insects, and diseases with which they have had no previous experience. In any climate, fieldworkers need to adjust to local water and food.

In addition, there are the cultural differences—which is why the fieldworkers came. Yet the immensity of what they will encounter is difficult for them to anticipate. Initially, just getting through the day—finding a place to stay and food to eat—may seem an enormous accomplishment, but there are also data to gather, research to do! Sometimes, however, the research questions never become separate from the living arrangements. Philippe Bourgois, who studied drug dealers in East Harlem in New York City, had to learn to deal not only with the violence of the drug dealers but also with the hostility and brutality that white police officers directed toward him, a white man living in *El Barrio* (see "EthnoProfile M3.2: *El Barrio*"; Figure M3.2). His experiences on the street pressed

EthnoProfile M3.2

El Barrio

Region: North America

Nation: United States (New York City)

Population: 110,000

Environment: Urban ghetto

Livelihood: Low-paying, full-time and temporary jobs, selling drugs, welfare

Political organization: Lowest level in a modern nation-state

For more information: Bourgois, Philippe. 1995. *In search of respect: Selling crack in El Barrio*. New York: Cambridge University Press.

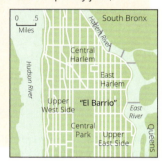

FIGURE M3.2 *El Barrio*, the part of New York City in which Philippe Bourgois did his research, is a socially complex, dynamic urban neighborhood.

FIGURE M3.3   Multisited field research is increasingly important in contemporary anthropology. As part of her research in Bolivia, Michelle Bigenho played violin with an ensemble in La Paz (*left*) and spent time in participant observation—here helping with planting—while studying music in the small town of Yura (*right*).

him to consider how the situation he was studying was a form of what he calls "inner-city apartheid" in the United States (Bourgois 1995, 32).

Multisited Fieldwork

In many ways, Bourgois's fieldwork in Spanish Harlem was very much in keeping with the fieldwork tradition inherited from Malinowski and Boas. That is, he engaged in what remains the most common mode of fieldwork in anthropology: "the intensively-focused-upon single site of ethnographic observation and participation" (Marcus 1995, 96). Much valuable work continues to be done in this mode. But changes in the world in the past 40 years have led many anthropologists to undertake fieldwork projects that include more than a single site.

Multisited fieldwork focuses on cultural processes that are not contained by social, ethnic, religious, or national boundaries; and the ethnographer follows the process from site to site, often doing fieldwork at sites and with persons who traditionally were never subjected to ethnographic analysis. As Marcus (1995) describes it, "Multi-sited research is

designed around chains, paths, threads, conjunctions, or juxtapositions of locations" as ethnographers trace "a complex cultural phenomenon . . . that turns out to be contingent and malleable as one traces it" (105–6). Multisited ethnographers follow people, things, metaphors, plots, and lives (Marcus 1995, 107). Examples of this kind of ethnography will appear throughout the book, but here is one to start:

Michelle Bigenho (2002) was interested in "authenticity" in Bolivian musical performances and in how Bolivian identities and music were connected. Studying this topic took her to Bolivia for two years plus several subsequent summers, where she performed with one musical ensemble in La Paz, studied a nongovernmental organization in La Paz dedicated to cultural projects related to music, and worked in two highland indigenous communities in the south. She also traveled to France to perform at an international folk festival with the Bolivian ensemble in which she played (Figure M3.3). This kind of topic could not have been pursued except as multisited ethnography. As she herself puts it, "I moved through multiple places to conduct research on the narratives of Bolivian nations as experienced through several music performance contexts" (Bigenho 2002, 7).

multisited fieldwork   Ethnographic research on cultural processes that are not contained by social, ethnic, religious, or national boundaries, in which the ethnographer follows the process from site to site, often doing fieldwork at sites and with persons who traditionally were never subjected to ethnographic analysis.

Collecting and Interpreting Data

Fieldwork is not just participating and observing—it also involves writing. It seems as though fieldworkers always have a notebook somewhere handy and, whenever possible, jot

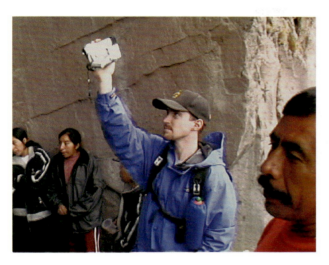

FIGURE M3.4 Anthropologists use different technologies for different research purposes. Anthropologist Ryan Cook videotapes the spectators and ritual performers at the Popocatepetl volcano in Mexico.

down notes on what they are seeing, hearing, doing, or wondering. These days, laptops, digital cameras, video cameras, and digital recorders are usually considered essential to accurate recording of what the ethnographer is learning (Figure M3.4). We cannot really trust our memories to keep track of the extraordinary range of information that comes at us in the field, so effective note taking is required. But note taking is not sufficient. The quickly jotted scrawls in notebooks must be turned into field notes; and as a result, anthropologists spend a lot of their time in front of their computers, writing as complete and coherent a set of notes as possible. Most ethnographers try to write up field notes on a daily basis and also try to code the information so that they can find it later. There are very useful field manuals for neophyte ethnographers to consult to assist them in developing workable and straightforward coding systems (e.g., Bernard 2011; DeWalt and DeWalt 2011).

As fieldworkers type up their notes, places for further inquiry become plain, and a back-and-forth process begins. The ethnographer collects information, writes it down, thinks about it, analyzes it, and then takes new questions and interpretations back to the people with whom he or she is working to see if these questions and interpretations are more accurate than the previous ones.

The Dialectic of Fieldwork: Interpretation and Translation

Fieldwork in cultural anthropology is a risky business. Fieldworkers not only risk offending their informants by misunderstanding their way of life but also face the shock of the unfamiliar

and their own vulnerability. Indeed, they must embrace this shock and cultivate this vulnerability if they are to achieve any kind of meaningful understanding of their informants' culture.

In the beginning, fieldworkers can be reassured by some of the insights that anthropological training provides. Since all human beings are members of the same biological species, ethnographers can expect to find in all human groups the same range of variation with regard to such human potentialities as intelligence. This can fortify them against ethnocentric impulses by recalling "that if what we observe appears to be odd or irrational, it is probably because we do not understand it and not because it is a product of a 'savage' culture in which such nonsense is to be expected" (Greenwood and Stini 1977, 185).

Anthropologist Michael Agar uses the expression "rich points" for those unexpected moments when problems in cross-cultural understanding emerge. Rich points may be words or actions that signal the gaps between the local people's out-of-awareness assumptions about how the world works and those of the anthropologist. For Agar, rich points are the raw material of ethnography, challenging researchers but also offering opportunities for insight. As he says, "it is this distance between two worlds of experience that is exactly the problem that ethnographic research is designed to locate and resolve" (Agar 1996, 31). Ethnographers work hard to situate rich points within the local cultural world, continually testing their interpretations in a variety of settings, with different people, to see if those interpretations are or are not confirmed.

Interpreting Actions and Ideas How does one go about interpreting the actions and ideas of other human beings? Paul Rabinow addressed this problem in a book based on reconsideration of his own fieldwork experiences. In *Reflections on Fieldwork in Morocco* (1977), Rabinow suggested that what goes on in ethnographic research is interpretation. As we come to grasp the meaning of the other's cultural self, we simultaneously learn something of the meaning of our own cultural identity.

The gulf between self and other may seem unbridgeable in the context of cross-cultural ethnography. Yet, anthropologists and informants engaged in participant observation share at least one thing: the fieldwork situation itself. They are in physical proximity, observing and discussing the same material objects and activities. At first, they may talk past one another as each describes these activities from a different perspective using a different language. However, all cultures and languages are open enough to entertain a variety of viewpoints and a variety of ways to talk about them. Continued discussion allows anthropologists and informants to search for ways to communicate about what is going on around them. Any overlap or intersection that promotes

FIGURE M3.5   Daniel Bradburd and Komachi camels packed for moving.

mutual understanding, however small, can form the foundation on which anthropologist and informant may build a new, intersubjective, symbolic language of their own. This process of building a bridge of understanding between self and other is what Rabinow (1977, 39) refers to as the **dialectic of fieldwork**. Both fieldworker and informant may begin with little or nothing in the way of shared experience that could allow them to figure one another out with any accuracy. But if they are motivated to make sense of one another and willing to work together, steps toward valid interpretation and mutual understanding can be made.

For example, traditional fieldwork often begins with collecting data on how people in the local community believe themselves to be related to each other. A trained anthropologist comes to the field with knowledge of a variety of possible forms of social organization in mind. These ideas derive in part from the anthropologist's own personal experiences of social relations, but they will also be based on research and theorizing about social relations by other anthropologists. As the fieldworker begins to ask questions about social relations, he or she may discover that the informants have no word in their language that accurately conveys the range of meaning carried by a term like *kinship* or *ethnic group*. This does not mean that the anthropologist must give up. Rather, the anthropologist must enter into the dialectic process of interpretation and translation.

In the dialectic of fieldwork, both anthropologist and informant are active agents. Each party tries to figure out what the other is saying. For example, the anthropologist asks about

---

dialectic of fieldwork   The process of building a bridge of understanding between anthropologists and informants so that each can begin to understand the other.

reflexivity   Critically thinking about the way one thinks, reflecting on one's own experience.

EthnoProfile M3.3

Komachi (mid-1970s)

Region: Southwest Asia

Nation: Iran

Population: 550

Environment: Varied—mountain valleys, lowland wooded areas

Livelihood: Nomadic herders

Political organization: Part of modern nation-state

For more information: Bradburd, Daniel. 1998. *Being there: The necessity of fieldwork.* Washington, DC: Smithsonian Institution Press.

"ethnic groups" using a term in the informants' language that seems close to "ethnic group" in meaning. Informants then try to interpret the anthropologist's question in a way that makes sense. That is, each informant has to be reflexive, thinking about how people in his or her society think about the topic that they believe is addressed by the anthropologist's question. This thinking about thinking is called **reflexivity**. Having formulated an answer, informants respond in terms they think the anthropologist will understand. Now it is the anthropologist's turn to interpret this response, to decide if it makes sense and carries the kind of information he or she was looking for.

If there is goodwill on the part of both, each party also tries to provide responses that make sense to the other. That is, anthropological fieldwork is also translation, and translation is a complicated and tricky process, full of false starts and misunderstandings. As time passes, each participant learns more about the other: the anthropologist gains skill at asking questions that make sense to the informant, and the informant becomes more skilled at answering those questions in terms relevant to the anthropologist. The validity of this ongoing translation is anchored in the setting of ongoing cultural activities in which both anthropologist and informant are participant observers. Out of this mutual effort comes knowledge about the informant's culture that is meaningful to both anthropologist and informant. This is new cultural knowledge, a hybrid product of common understandings that emerges from the collaboration of anthropologist and informant.

Informants are equally involved in this dialogue and may end up learning as much or more about anthropologists as anthropologists learn about them. But it is important to emphasize that in field situations, the dialogue is initiated by anthropologists. Anthropologists come to the field with their own sets of questions, which are determined not by the field situation but by the discipline of anthropology itself (see Karp and Kendall 1982, 254). Furthermore, when anthropologists are finished with a particular research project, they are often free to break off the dialogue with informants and resume discussions with fellow professionals. The only links between these two sets of dialogues—between particular anthropologists and the people with whom they work and among anthropologists in general—are the particular anthropologists themselves.

In recent years, members of indigenous societies have begun to speak powerfully on their own behalf as political advocates for their people, as lawyers, as organizers, and as professionals. Language and other barriers often prevent many such individuals from speaking to an audience of professional scholars on complex topics, nor are their interests necessarily the same as those of professional scholars. Fieldwork thus involves differences of power and thereby places a heavy burden of responsibility on ethnographers. They are accountable not only to their informants but also to the discipline of anthropology, which has its own theoretical and practical concerns and ways of reasoning about ethnographic data. For these reasons, Arjun Appadurai has called for a "deparochialization of the research ethic" that would involve collaboration with colleagues outside the United States such as grassroots activists, who often lack the kinds of institutional resources and professional experience that scholars in the United States take for granted. With the right support, such colleagues could become equal partners in "a conversation about research" in which they "bring their own ideas of what counts as new knowledge" as well as their own ideas of how to measure the researcher's accountability to those among whom they work (Appadurai 2002, 281). Luke Eric

Lassiter's work with Kiowa elders, discussed in Chapter 8, is a successful example of such collaboration.

Anthropologists feel strongly that their informants' identities should be protected. The need for protection is all the greater when informants belong to marginal and powerless groups that might suffer retaliation from more powerful members of their society. However, because some informants wish to express their identity and their ideas openly, anthropologists have experimented with forms of ethnographic writing in which they serve primarily as translators and editors of the voices and opinions of individual informants (e.g., Keesing 1982; Shostak 1981). Increasingly, anthropologists working in their own societies write about their fieldwork both as observers of others and as members of the society they are observing (e.g., Foley 1989; Kumar 1992).

The Dialectic of Fieldwork: An Example

Daniel Bradburd wrote about the give and take of cross-cultural learning in his discussion of fieldwork among the Komachi, a nomadic people in Iran with whom he and his wife, Anne Sheedy, lived in the mid-1970s (see Figure M3.5 and "EthnoProfile M3.3: Komachi (mid 1970s)." Bradburd had gone to Iran to study the process of active decision-making among nomadic herding people, and he was therefore quite interested in when people would move their camps and why they would do it. His first experience with moving was not what he had expected. After a month in one place, he started to hear talk about moving. Why? he asked. To be closer to the village and because the campsite was dirty. When? Soon. When is soon? When Tavakoli comes. This answer made no sense until further questioning revealed that Tavakoli was the son of the leader of the camp.

Eventually, their hosts told them that the move would be the next day; but when the next day came, there were no signs of activity in the camp. Finally, when it became clear that they would not be moving that day, Bradburd began asking why they had not moved. The answer was *ruz aqrab*. When they looked up *aqrab* in the dictionary, the answer made even less sense than the previous one: they were not moving because it was the day of the scorpion.

> As was often the case, we felt as though we had moved one step forward and two steps back. We had an answer, but we hadn't the faintest idea what it meant. We were pretty certain it didn't have anything to do with real scorpions, because we hadn't seen any. We were also pretty certain that we hadn't heard any mention of them. So back we trudged to Qoli's tent, and we started asking more questions. Slowly it became clear. The scorpion was not a real, living one; it was the constellation Scorpio, which Qoli later pointed out to us on the horizon. (Bradburd 1998, 41)

FIGURE M3.6 Paul Rabinow's reflections on his fieldwork experiences in a Moroccan village much like this one led him to reconceptualize the nature of anthropological fieldwork.

EthnoProfile M3.4

Sidi Lahcen Lyussi

Region: Northern Africa

Nation: Morocco

Population: 900

Environment: Mountainous terrain

Livelihood: Farming, some livestock raising

Political organization: Village in a modern nation-state

For more information: Rabinow, Paul. 1977. *Reflections on fieldwork in Morocco.* Berkeley: University of California Press.

After more questioning and more thinking, Bradburd and Sheedy finally concluded that the Komachi believed it was bad luck to undertake a new activity on days when it appeared that Scorpio would catch the rising moon. On checking back with their informants, they found that their conclusion was correct, but they were still puzzled. On the day that they had been told the move would be the next day, the Komachi in their camp had been fully aware that Scorpio and the rising moon would be in conjunction the next day. Eventually, Bradburd and Sheedy decided that "ruz aqrab" was a reasonable excuse for not moving, but they never did figure out the real reason for not moving that day. In fact, over the course of many such experiences, Bradburd and Sheedy came to realize that the Komachi did not have specific reasons for not moving. Rather, they still had one or another thing to do where they were, the weather was uncertain, the route to take was not clear yet, and so on. As a result of Bradburd's questions and the Komachi's responses, his interpretations and their responses to those, he gradually concluded that the Komachi decision-making process was an attempt to minimize the risks they had to take. Rather than being heroic nomads, masters of their fate, the Komachi made decisions only when they had to.

The Effects of Fieldwork

Fieldwork changes both anthropologists and informants. What kinds of effects can the fieldwork experience have on informants? Anthropologists have not always been able to report on this. In some cases, the effects of fieldwork on informants cannot be assessed for a long time. In other cases, it becomes clear in the course of fieldwork that the anthropologist's presence and questions have made the informants aware of their own cultural selves in new ways that are both surprising and uncomfortable. This was the case for Katherine Verdery, for example, who only became aware many years later of the ongoing pressures placed by the Securitate on people she worked with in Romania in the 1970s and 1980s. During her dissertation fieldwork, for instance, she had been puzzled when the head of the first family with whom she lived arranged for her to move into the household of his brother instead. When she read her Securitate file, she learned that the head of the first family was a member of the Communist Party, and Party members were exempt from surveillance by the secret police. In order for the Securitate to continue to keep an eye on her, therefore, it was decided to have her to live with the brother's family, who was not a Party member. "I did not realize it at the time, of course, but learning it now makes clear that there were limits to Securitate surveillance" (2018, 54). As her own personal network of friends expanded, they developed knowledge about her that countered rumors that she was a spy. Even so, she later learned that her telephone calls had been tapped, her mail intercepted, and her room searched. The Securitate also occasionally arranged for her to meet people designed to influence her views or become part of her intimate circle of friends.

When her file disclosed that some close friends had been recruited as informers, Verdery found it "truly distressing. It produced a reorganization of my entire affective landscape" (2018, 197). She came to realize, however, that most of her informers worked very hard to keep their reports minimal and uninformative. She also insists that "My relations with various Romanians who arguable 'broke my trust' have to be placed in the context of the larger set of relationships in which they are embedded, which these people may be trying to shelter when they agree to inform on me. For me to see their abandonment as betrayal would be to insist that I be more important to them than those others" (2019, 227). The Securitate, she argues, "had a flair for detecting people who were fearful and were thus especially vulnerable to recruitment" (2019, 233). One of her friends found recruitment so distressing that she vowed to give up her friendship with Verdery, telling her years later "What a lot of harm you caused me!" (2019, 238). Verdery's most important conclusion from this conversation was "that the Securitate's methods changed how people related to themselves and altered their relationships with others. . . . Securitate practices subverted positive sentiment and turned it into guilt, rejection and avoidance, making me feel *guilty* for having loved my friends and for not protecting them enough" (2019, 239).

What are the consequences of fieldwork for the fieldworker? As Verdery's account makes painfully clear, much more than the anthropologist's personality is responsible. Establishing rapport with the people being studied is jointly achieved by anthropologists and those with whom they work. Acceptance

is problematic, rather than ensured, even for the most gifted fieldworkers, perhaps especially when they are outsiders with no personal ties to the community in which they will do their research. As Ivan Karp and Bonnie Kendall cautioned in 1982, it is not just naïve to think that the locals will accept you as one of them without any difficulty; it is also bad science.

As he reflected on his own fieldwork in Morocco, Rabinow recalled some cases in which his informants' new reflexivity led to unanticipated consequences (Figure M3.6). One key informant, Malik, agreed to help Rabinow compile a list of landholdings and other possessions of the villagers of Sidi Lahcen Lyussi (see "EthnoProfile M3.4: Sidi Lahcen Lyussi"). As a first step in tracing the economic status of the middle stratum in society, Rabinow suggested that Malik list his own possessions. Malik appeared to be neither rich nor poor; in fact, he considered himself "not well off." "As we began to make a detailed list of his possessions, he became touchy and defensive. . . . It was clear that he was not as impoverished as he had portrayed himself. . . . This was confusing and troubling for him. . . . Malik began to see that there was a disparity between his self-image and my classification system. The emergence of this 'hard' data before his eyes and through his own efforts was highly disconcerting for him" (Rabinow 1977, 117–18).

Malik's easy understanding of himself and his world had been disrupted, and he could not ignore the disruption. He would either have to change his self-image or find some way to assimilate this new information about himself into the old self-image. In the end, Malik managed to reaffirm his conclusion that he was not well off by arguing that wealth lay not in material possessions alone. Although he might be rich in material goods, his son's health was bad, his own father was dead, he was responsible for his mother and unmarried brothers, and he had to be constantly vigilant to prevent his uncle from stealing his land (Rabinow 1977, 117–19).

What are the consequences of fieldwork for the fieldworker? Graduate students in anthropology who have not yet been in the field sometimes develop an idealized narrative about fieldwork: at first, the fieldworker is a bit disoriented and potential informants are suspicious, but uncertainty soon gives way to understanding and trust as the anthropologist's good intentions are made known and accepted. The fieldworker succeeds in establishing rapport. In fact, the fieldworker becomes so well loved and trusted, so thoroughly accepted, that he or she is incorporated as an equal and allowed access to cultural secrets. Presumably, all this happens as a result of the personal attributes of the fieldworker. If you have what it takes, you will be taken in and treated like one of the family. If this does not happen, you are obviously cut out for some other kind of work.

But much more than the anthropologist's personality is responsible for successful fieldwork. Establishing rapport with the people being studied is an achievement of anthropologist and informants together. Acceptance is problematic, rather than ensured, even for the most gifted fieldworkers. After all, fieldworkers are usually outsiders with no personal ties to the community in which they will do their research.

The preceding accounts illustrate what Paul Rabinow calls the "shock of otherness." Fieldwork institutionalizes this shock. Having to anticipate **culture shock** at any and every turn, anthropologists sometimes find that fieldwork takes on a tone that is anything but pleasant and sunny. For many anthropologists, what characterizes fieldwork, at least in its early stages, is anxiety—the anxiety of an isolated individual with nothing familiar to turn to, no common sense on which to rely, and no relationships that can be taken for granted. There is a reason anthropologists have reported holing up for weeks at a time reading paperback novels and eating peanut butter sandwiches. One of us (E. A. S.) recalls how difficult it was every morning to leave the compound in Guider, Cameroon. Despite the accomplishments of the previous day, she was always convinced that no one would want to talk to her *today* (see Chapter 15, "EthnoProfile 15.2: Guider").

Good ethnography should allow readers to *experience* the informants' full humanity. This privileged position, the extraordinary opportunity to experience "the other" as human beings while learning about their lives, is an experience that comes neither easily nor automatically. It must be cultivated, and it requires cooperation between and effort from one's informants and oneself. We have made an important first step if we can come to recognize, as Paul Rabinow (1977) did, that "there is no primitive. There are other [people] living other lives" (151).

Multisited ethnography can complicate the picture by simultaneously offering rich, fieldwork-based portraits of other people living other lives as variously situated as AIDS patients and corporate managers and by demonstrating, moreover, that members of these groups share important cultural commitments. In the best ethnographic writing, we can grasp the humanity—the greed, compassion, suffering, pleasure, confusions, and ambivalences—of the people who have granted the anthropologist the privilege of living with them for an extended period of time. Because of such experiences, it may

become more natural for us to talk about cultural differences by saying "not 'they,' not 'we,' not 'you,' but some of us are thus and so" (W. C. Smith 1982, 70).

The Production of Anthropological Knowledge

Anthropologist David Hess (1997) defines **fact** as a widely accepted observation, a taken-for-granted item of common knowledge (101–2). Ethnographers' field notebooks will be full of facts collected from different informants, as well as facts based on their own cultural experiences and professional training. But what happens when facts from these various sources contradict one another?

Facts turn out to be complex phenomena. On the one hand, they assert that a particular state of affairs about the world is true. On the other hand, reflexive analysis has taught us that *who* tells us that *x* is a fact is an extremely important thing to know. This is because, as we saw in Module 1, facts do not speak for themselves. They speak only when they are interpreted and placed in a context of meaning that makes them intelligible. What constitutes a cultural fact is ambiguous. Anthropologists and informants can disagree; anthropologists can disagree among themselves; informants can disagree among themselves. The facts of anthropology exist neither in the culture of the anthropologist nor in the culture of the informant. "Anthropological facts are cross-cultural, because they are made across cultural boundaries" (Rabinow 1977, 152). In short, facts are not just out there, waiting for someone to come along and pick them up. They are made and remade (1) in the field, (2) when fieldworkers reexamine field notes and reflect on the field experience at a later time, and (3) when the fieldworkers write about their experiences or discuss them with other anthropologists.

For Daniel Bradburd, fieldwork begins with "being there." But simply being there is not enough. As Bradburd (1998) puts it, "my experiences among the Komachi shaped my understanding of them, and that part of field experience consists of a constant process of being brought up short, of having expectations confounded, of being forced to think very hard about what is happening, right now, with me and them, let alone the thinking and rethinking about those experiences when they have—sometimes mercifully—passed" (161–62). After all, fieldwork is field*work*—there are notes to be taken, interviews to be carried out, observations to make, interpretations to be made. There is also the transformation of the experiences of being there into what Bradburd calls "elements of an understanding that is at once incomplete and impossible to complete, but also wonderfully capable

---

culture shock The feeling, akin to panic, that develops in people living in an unfamiliar society when they cannot understand what is happening around them.

fact A widely accepted observation, a taken-for-granted item of common knowledge. Facts do not speak for themselves but only when they are interpreted and placed in a context of meaning that makes them intelligible.

of being improved" (164). According to Harry Wolcott (1999), it is what ethnographers *do* with data—"making considered generalizations about how members of a group tend to speak and act, warranted generalizations appropriate for collectivities of people rather than the usual shoot-from-the-hip stereotyping adequate for allowing us to achieve our individual purposes" (262)—that makes fieldwork experience different from just experience and turns it into doing ethnography.

Multisited fieldwork elaborates on and further complicates this experience because it involves being "here and there." In the course of the movement from site to site, new facts come into view that would otherwise never be known, adding a further layer to the thinking and rethinking that all fieldwork sets in motion. What happens if you find that your activism in support of the urban poor at one site works against the interests of the indigenous people you have supported at a different site? "In conducting multi-sited research," Marcus (1995) says, "one finds oneself with all sorts of cross-cutting commitments" that are not easily resolved (113).

Anthropological Knowledge as Open-Ended

Cultivating reflexivity allows us to produce less distorted views of human nature and the human condition, yet we remain human beings interpreting the lives of other human beings. We can never escape from our humanity to some point of view that would allow us to see human existence and human experience from the outside. Instead, we must rely on our common humanity and our interpretive powers to show us the parts of our nature that can be made visible.

If there truly is "no primitive," no subsection of humanity that is radically different in nature or in capacity from the anthropologists who study it, then the ethnographic record of anthropological knowledge is perhaps best understood as a vast commentary on human possibility. As with all commentaries, it depends on an original text—in this case, human experience. But that experience is ambiguous, speaking with many voices, capable of supporting more than one interpretation. Growth of anthropological knowledge is no different, then, from the growth of human self-understanding in general. It ought to contribute to the domain of human wisdom that concerns who we are as a species, where we have come from, and where we may be going.

Like all commentaries, the ethnographic record is and must be unfinished: human beings are open systems, human history continues, and problems and their possible solutions change. There is no one true version of human life. For anthropologists, the true version of human life consists of all versions of human life. This is a sobering possibility.

It makes it appear that "the anthropologist is condemned to a greater or lesser degree of failure" (Basham 1978, 299) in even trying to understand another culture. Informants would equally be condemned to never know fully even their own way of life. But total pessimism does not seem warranted. We may never know everything, but it does not follow that our efforts can teach us nothing. "Two of the fundamental qualities of humanity are the capacity to understand one another and the capacity to be understood. Not fully certainly. Yet not negligibly, certainly. . . . There is no person on earth that I can fully understand. There is and has been no person on earth that I cannot understand at all" (W. C. Smith 1982, 68–69).

Moreover, as our contact with the other is prolonged and as our efforts to communicate are rewarded by the construction of intersubjective understanding, we can always learn more. Human beings are open organisms, with a vast ability to learn new things. This is significant, because even if we can never know everything, it does not seem that our capacity for understanding ourselves and others is likely to be exhausted soon. This is not only because we are open to change but also because our culture and our wider environment can change, and all will continue to do so as long as human history continues. The ethnographic enterprise will never be finished, even if all nonindustrial ways of life disappear forever, all people move into cities, and everyone ends up speaking English. Such a superficial homogeneity would mask a vast heterogeneity beneath its bland surface. In any case, given the dynamics of human existence, nothing in human affairs can remain homogeneous for long.

Module Summary

1. Anthropological fieldwork has traditionally involved participant observation, extended periods of close contact at a single site with members of another society. Anthropologists were expected to carry out research in societies different from their own; but in recent years, increasing numbers have worked in their own societies. Each setting has its own advantages and drawbacks for ethnographers.

2. Many contemporary anthropologists have begun to carry out fieldwork in a number of different sites. Such multisited fieldwork is usually the outcome of following cultural phenomena wherever they lead, often crossing local, regional, and national boundaries in the process. Such fieldwork allows anthropologists to understand better many cultural processes that link people, things, metaphors, plots, and lives that are not confined to a single site.

3. Contemporary ethnographers still take field notes by hand, but most also rely on electronic forms of data collection, including laptop computers, digital cameras, video cameras, and digital recorders. Because all this information needs to be organized and interpreted, ethnographers tack back and forth between their various sources of data, seeking feedback whenever possible from the people among whom they work before finally writing up and publishing their findings in ethnographies.

4. When human beings study other human beings, scientific accuracy requires that they relate to one another as human beings. Successful fieldwork involves anthropologists who think about the way they think about other cultures. Informants also must reflect on the way they and others in their society think and try to convey their insights to the anthropologist. This is basic to the reflexive approach to ethnographic research, which sees participant observation as a dialogue about the meaning of experience in the informant's culture. Fieldworkers and informants work together to construct an intersubjective world of meaning.

5. Taking part in ethnographic fieldwork has the potential to change informants and researchers in sometimes unpredictable ways. In some cases, anthropologists have worked with their informants to bring about social changes, although not all anthropologists agree that this is appropriate. In other cases, anthropologists argue that their main task is to figure out and explain to others how people in particular places at particular moments engage with the world.

6. Because cultural meanings are intersubjectively constructed during fieldwork, cultural facts do not speak for themselves. They speak only when they are interpreted and placed in a context of meaning that makes them intelligible. Multisited fieldwork complicates this because it involves the anthropologist in crosscutting commitments in different contexts, where the same cultural facts may be differently understood or valued.

7. The ethnographic record of anthropological knowledge is perhaps best understood as a vast unfinished commentary on human possibility. We will surely never learn all there is to know, but we can always learn more.

For Review

1. Explain the basic elements of ethnographic fieldwork.

2. Describe multisited fieldwork and explain why many anthropologists undertake it.

3. What is the dialectic of fieldwork, and why is it important for ethnographic research?

4. Using the examples in the text, explain how ruptures of communication in fieldwork may turn out to have positive consequences for the ethnographer.

5. What are some of the ways that fieldwork may affect informants?

6. What are some of the ways that fieldwork affects the researcher?

7. What is the importance of "being there" for ethnographic fieldwork?

8. In your view, what are the strengths and weaknesses of ethnographic fieldwork?

Key Terms

culture shock 272	multisited fieldwork 266
dialectic of fieldwork 268	participant observation 260
fact 272	reflexivity 268
fieldwork 260	

Suggested Readings

Bernard, H. Russell. 2011. *Research methods in anthropology*, 5th ed. Lanham, MD: AltaMira Press. *An enduring classic of methods books, detailed and thorough.*

Bigenho, Michelle. 2002. *Sounding indigenous: Authenticity in Bolivian musical performance.* New York: Palgrave Macmillan. *A recent multisited ethnography that follows Bolivian and non-Bolivian members of a Bolivian musical ensemble through different settings on more than one continent, chronicling varied understandings of what counts as "indigenous" Bolivian music.*

Bradburd, Daniel. 1998. *Being there: The necessity of fieldwork.* Washington, DC: Smithsonian Institution Press. *An engaging personal study of how the many seemingly small details of experience during field research add up to anthropological understanding.*

Lévi-Strauss, Claude. 1974. *Tristes tropiques.* New York: Pocket Books. *Originally published in French in 1955, this book (with an untranslatable title) is considered by some the greatest book ever written by an anthropologist (although not necessarily a great anthropology book). This is a multifaceted work about voyaging, fieldwork, self-knowledge, philosophy, and much more. It is a challenging read in some places but highly rewarding overall.*

Rabinow, Paul. 1977. *Reflections on fieldwork in Morocco.* Berkeley: University of California Press. *An important, brief, powerfully written reflection on the nature of fieldwork. Very accessible and highly recommended.*

Valentine, Bettylou. 1978. *Hustling and other hard work.* New York: Free Press. *An innovative, provocative, and now classic study of African American inner-city life. Reads like a good novel.*

Verdery, Katherine. 2018. *My Life as a Spy: Investigations in a Secret Police File.* Durham, NC: Duke University Press.

Why is understanding human language important?

Only human beings have symbolic language, and it is so deeply part of our lives that we rarely even think about how unusual it is. In this chapter, you will learn about what makes human symbolic language different from other forms of animal communication. You will also explore its deep connections to other symbolic dimensions of social and cultural life, including the ways your patterns of thought, your sense of self, and even your personality are shaped by experiences in different kinds of symbolically shaped settings.

CHAPTER OUTLINE

What Makes Language Distinctively Human?

How Are Language and Culture Related?

What Does It Mean to "Learn" a Language?

What Happens When Languages Come into Contact?

What Does Linguistic Inequality Look Like?

How Have Language Ideologies Been at Work in Studies of African American Speech?

What Is Raciolinguistics?

What Is Lost If a Language Dies?

How Are Language and Truth Connected?

Chapter Summary

LEARNING OBJECTIVES

- Describe the features that makes language a distinctively human trait.
- Explain how language and culture are related in terms of how people talk about their experiences.
- Explain what it means to learn a language in terms of how context affects language, how language affects how we see the world, and the study of both pragmatics and ethnopragmatics.
- Analyze the effects of what happens when languages come into contact, including pidgin and creole languages.
- Interpret the processes that result in linguistic inequality and what linguistic inequality looks like.
- Define raciolinguistics and provide examples of transracialization.
- Analyze the factors that result in language death and what is lost when languages die.
- Describe the connection between language, truth, and the human experience.

Communication takes many forms, including sign language.

As we saw in Chapter 3, primates depend on learned behavior to survive, and some primate species appear to have developed their own cultural traditions. Primates also communicate with one another in a variety of ways, most obviously by relying on vocal calls to alert one another about significant aspects of their environment, from presence of food to the threat of a predator. In the past, some anthropologists hypothesized that human language was simply an elaboration of the call system of our ancestors, but this hypothesis proved to be incorrect, as we shall see.

In Chapter 8, we defined a **symbol** as something that stands for something else. Human symbolic language is perhaps the clearest illustration of the central role played by symbols in all of human culture. Indeed, it is the dependence of human language on symbols that makes it such a flexible and creative system of communication—and far more powerful than any primate call system could ever be. So when anthropologists talk about human language, they always mean human *symbolic* language. This is why we define **language** as the system of arbitrary symbols human beings use to encode and communicate about their experience of the world and of one another. The role played by symbols in human language sets it apart from the apparently nonsymbolic communication systems of other living species. Symbolic language has also made many singular human achievements possible. And yet, language is double-edged: it allows people to communicate with one another, but it also creates barriers to communication. There are some 3,000 mutually unintelligible languages spoken in the world today (Figure 9.1). This chapter explores the ambiguity, limitations, and power of human language and its connections to other forms of human symbolic activity.

What Makes Language Distinctively Human?

In 1966, the anthropological linguist Charles Hockett listed 16 different *design features* of human language that, in his estimation, set it apart from other forms of animal communication. Six of these design features seem especially helpful in defining what makes human language distinctive: openness, displacement, arbitrariness, duality of patterning, semanticity, and prevarication.

Openness indicates that human language is productive. Speakers of any given language not only can create new messages but also can understand new messages created by other speakers. Someone may have never said to you "Put this Babel fish in your ear," but knowing English, you can understand the message. Openness might also be defined as "the ability to understand the same thing from different points of view" (Ortony 1979, 14). In language, this means being able to talk about the same experiences from different perspectives, to paraphrase using different words and various grammatical constructions. Indeed, it means that the experiences themselves can be differently conceived, labeled, and discussed. In this view, no single perspective would necessarily emerge as more correct in every respect than all others.

The importance of openness for human verbal communication is striking when we compare, for example, spoken human language to the vocal communication systems (or *call systems*) of monkeys and apes. Biological anthropologist Terrence Deacon (1997) pointed out that, in addition to spoken symbolic language, modern human beings possess a set of six calls: laughing, sobbing, screaming with fright, crying with pain, groaning, and sighing. Building on these insights, linguistic anthropologist Robbins Burling (2005) emphasizes the difference between call systems and symbolic language: "Language . . . is organized in such utterly different ways from primate or mammalian calls and it conveys such utterly different kinds of meanings, that I find it impossible to imagine a realistic sequence by which natural selection could have converted a call system into a language. . . . We will understand more about the origins of language by considering the ways in which language differs form the cries and gestures of human and nonhuman primates than by looking for ways in which they are alike" (16). In Deacon's view, human calls appear to have *coevolved alongside* symbolic language, together with gestures and the changes in speech rhythm, volume, and tonality that linguists call *speech prosody*. This would explain why calls and speech integrate with one another so smoothly when we communicate vocally with one another.

Nonhuman primates can communicate in rather subtle ways using channels of transmission other than voice. However, these channels are far less sophisticated than, say, American Sign Language. Burling points out that human sign languages share all the features of spoken human language, except for the channel of communication, which is visual rather than auditory. Ape call systems, by contrast, contain between 15 and 40 calls, depending on the species. And the calls are produced only when the animal finds itself in a situation including

---

symbol A mode of signification in which the sign bears no intrinsic connection to that which it represents. Symbols embody the design feature of arbitrariness.

language The system of arbitrary symbols human beings use to encode and communicate about their experience of the world and one another.

by George Herriman

FIGURE 9.1 In 1918, Krazy Kat asks the question, "Why is 'lenguage'?"

such features as the presence of food or danger; friendly interest and the desire for company; or the desire to mark a location or to signal pain, sexual interest, or the need for maternal care. If the animal is not in the appropriate situation, it does not produce the call. At most, it may refrain from uttering a call in a situation that would normally trigger it. In addition, nonhuman primates cannot emit a signal that has some features of one call and some of another. For example, if the animal encounters food and danger at the same time, one of the calls takes precedence. For these reasons, the call systems of nonhuman primates are said to be *closed* when compared to open human languages.

Closed call systems also lack *displacement*, our human ability to talk about absent or nonexistent objects and past or future events as easily as we discuss our immediate situations. Although nonhuman primates clearly have good memories, and some species, such as chimpanzees, seem to be able to plan social action in advance (such as when hunting for meat), they cannot use their call systems to discuss such events.

Closed call systems also lack *arbitrariness*, the fact that there is no universal, necessary link between particular linguistic sounds and particular linguistic meanings. For example, the sound sequence /*boi*/ refers to a "young male human being" in English but means "more" or "many" in Fulfulde, a major language in northern Cameroon. One aspect of linguistic creativity is the free, creative production of new links between sounds and meanings. Thus, arbitrariness and openness imply each other: if all links between sound and meaning are open, then any particular links between particular sounds and particular meanings in a particular language must be arbitrary. In nonhuman primate call

systems, by contrast, links between the sounds of calls and their meanings appear fixed, and there is no easy slippage between sounds and what they stand for from one population to the next.

Arbitrariness is evident in the design feature of language *duality of patterning*. Human language, Hockett claimed, is patterned on two different levels: sound and meaning. On the first level, the arrangement of the small set of meaningless sounds (or *phonemes*) that characterize any particular language is not random but systematically patterned to create meaning-bearing units (or *morphemes*): in English, the final /*ng*/ sound in *song*, for example, is never found at the beginning of a sound sequence, although other languages in the world do allow that combination. The result is that from any language's set of phonemes (in English, there are some 36 phonemes), a very large number of correctly formed morphemes can be created. On the second level of patterning, however, the rules of **grammar** allow for the arrangement and rearrangement of these single morphemes into larger units—utterances or sentences—that can express an infinite number of meanings ("*The boy bit the dog*" uses the same morphemes as "*The dog bit the boy*," but the meaning is completely different). Since Hockett first wrote, many linguists have suggested that there are more than just two levels of patterning in language—that there are levels of morphemes, of sentence structure (*syntax*), meaning (*semantics*), and use (*pragmatics*). In each case, patterns that characterize one level cannot be reduced to the patterns of any other level but can serve as resources for the construction of more comprehensive levels. For example,

---

grammar A set of rules that aim to describe fully the patterns of linguistic usage observed by speakers of a particular language.

units at the level of sound, patterned in one way, can be used to create units of meaning (or morphemes) at a different level, patterned in a different way. Morphemes, in turn, can be used to create units at a different level (sentences) by means of syntactic rules that are different from the rules that create morphemes, and syntactic rules are again different from the rules that combine sentences into discourse. Ape call systems, by contrast, appear to lack multilevel patterning of this kind (Wallmann 1992).

Arbitrariness shows up again in the design feature of *semanticity*—the association of linguistic signals with aspects of the social, cultural, and physical world in which the speakers live. (Semanticity is not the same thing as semantics, which refers to the formal study of meaning relations within a particular language.) People use language to refer to, and make sense of, and talk about objects and processes in their world. Think about the specialized vocabulary used by baseball fans in the United States as they dispute the way an umpire has called a pitch: for instance, was it "high and inside" or was it "right over the plate?" Any linguistic description of reality is bound to be somewhat arbitrary because all linguistic descriptions are selective, highlighting some features of the world and downplaying others. Each speaker links the same words to the world in different ways.

Perhaps the most striking consequence of linguistic openness is the design feature *prevarication*. Hockett's (1966, 10) remarks about this design feature deserve particular attention: "Linguistic messages can be false, and they can be meaningless in the logician's sense." In other words, not only can people use language to lie, but also utterances that seem perfectly well formed grammatically may yield nonsense. An example is this sentence invented by linguist Noam Chomsky: "Colorless green ideas sleep furiously" (1957, 15). This is a grammatical sentence on one level—the right kinds of words are used in the right places—but on another level, it contains multiple contradictions. The ability of language users to prevaricate—to make statements or ask questions that violate convention—is a major consequence of open symbolic systems. Apes using their closed call systems can neither lie nor formulate theories.

How Are Language and Culture Related?

Human language is a biocultural phenomenon. The human brain and the anatomy of the mouth and throat make language a biological possibility. At the same time,

no human language can be restricted only to the sounds that come out of people's mouths. Languages are clearly cultural products embedded in meanings and behavioral patterns that stretch beyond individual bodies, across space, and over time. Anthropologists have long been particularly attentive to the multiple powerful dimensions of language, especially when ethnographic fieldwork in societies presented them with the challenge of learning unwritten languages without formal instruction. At the same time, anthropologists who transcribed or tape-recorded speech could lift it out of its cultural context to be analyzed on its own. Their analyses revealed grammatical intricacies and complexities suggesting that language might be a good model for the rest of culture. It also became obvious that the way people use language provides important clues to their understanding of the world and of themselves. Indeed, some theories of culture are explicitly based on ideas taken from **linguistics**, the scientific study of language.

As with the culture concept, the concept of "language" has regularly involved a distinction between *Language* and *languages*. *Language* with a capital *L* (like *Culture* with a capital *C*) has often been viewed as an abstract property belonging to the human species as a whole, not to be confused with the specific *languages* of concrete groups of people. This distinction initially enabled the recognition that all human groups possessed fully developed *languages* rather than "primitive," "broken," or otherwise defective forms of vocal communication. Today, however, linguistic anthropologists realize that totalizing views of "languages" can be as problematic as totalizing views of "cultures." The difficulties associated with demarcating the boundaries between one language and another or with distinguishing between dialects and languages become particularly obvious in studies of pidgins and creoles, as we will see.

But drawing boundaries around particular languages are only one challenge. Attempting to define what language can be used for—the functions it performs—can also be a point of debate. Many philosophers and linguists—indeed, many ordinary speakers—view language as primarily a vehicle for information transfer about some state of affairs in the world. And speakers certainly do use language for this purpose: Hockett's design feature of *semanticity* points to this possibility, as we saw. But this *referential* function is only one way to make use of language. At least since the work of Russian linguist Roman Jakobson (1960), linguistic anthropologists have insisted that language must be seen as *multifunctional*. Other functions of language recognized by Jakobson included the *expressive* function (which conveys the speaker's feelings); the *conative* function (which shapes the message for its recipient); the *poetic* function

linguistics The scientific study of language.

(which involves word play with elements of the message itself); the *phatic* function (which uses speech to reinforce ongoing communicative links between conversational partners); and the *metalinguistic* function (which demonstrates our ability to talk about the way we talk, demonstrating the operation of human reflexivity in the way we monitor our speech and that of other people).

For example, I may use the *referential* function of language to attach the English word "thunderstorm" to features of the physical world. If I say to you, "I am sorry that the thunderstorm interrupted your picnic," I am using the *expressive* function of language to let you know how I feel, and also perhaps using the *conative* function of language to indicate that I sympathize with your disappointment. On the other hand, it may be that my comment about the thunderstorm is only small talk about the weather, intended to keep you involved in an ongoing conversation with me, which is a *phatic* use of language. Should I add the observation that "Perhaps 'thunderstorm' is not the correct word to describe the weather, considering how little rain fell," I would be showing reflexive awareness of my own speech, making use of the *metalinguistic* function. As linguistic anthropologist Laura Ahearn explains, "All functions are always present in each speech event, Jakobson argues, but in certain cases, one function may predominate over all the others" (2017, 21–22).

If we take a broad view of *human communication* as the transfer of information from one person to another, it immediately becomes clear that humans can communicate without the use of spoken words. People communicate with one another nonverbally all the time, sending messages with the clothes they wear, the way they walk, or how long they keep other people waiting for them. Studies of this multidimensional communication are usually called *semiotics*, which refers to the study of meaningful signs and their use. In recent years, linguistic anthropologists have been attracted by the rich and suggestive approach to semiotics developed by the American pragmatic philosopher Charles Sanders Peirce. Especially important has been Peirce's distinction between three modes of signification: (1) *iconicity*, a mode of signification in which the sign (or **icon**) *looks like* that which it represents (e.g., the stylized image of a moving watch face or hourglass that appears on your computer screen indicates the passage of time while an operation is being performed); (2) *indexicality*, a mode of signification in which the sign (or **index**) *points to*, or is *beside*, or is *causally linked to* that which it signifies (e.g., the verbal expression "y'all," which indexes, or points to, the speech that is characteristic of a particular region of the United States); and (3) *symbolism*, a mode of signification in which the sign (or symbol) bears no intrinsic

connection to that which it represents. As we observed earlier, symbols exhibit the design feature of arbitrariness; that is, there is no necessary link between, say, the pattern of stars and stripes on the flag of the United States of America and the territorial unit for which it stands. Thus, arbitrary links between symbols and what they signify must be learned.

One key strength of Peirce's modes of signification is that they provide the theoretical apparatus needed to investigate the operations of semanticity; that is, for analyzing how language gets outside our heads and into the world. As anthropologist Webb Keane observes, Peirce's "three part model of the sign included the objects of signification" (2003, 413). This differentiates Peirce's semiotics from the work of the influential linguist Ferdinand de Saussure (2013), whose two-part model of the arbitrary link between *sound image* and *meaningful concept* was located entirely *inside* the brain and was deliberately cut off from the wider world. Peirce's three-part model of the sign, moreover, is not limited to language but can also encompass meaningful relations conveyed by material objects and relations in the world. And because Peirce's signs continually generate new signs as they are drawn into relations with one another, Keane views Peirce's theoretical framework as a valuable way of tracing the meaningful connections between words *and* things that are at the core of human cultural relations. That is, "the Peircean model of the sign . . . can be taken to entail sociability, struggle, historicity, and contingency. . . . Peirce offers a way of thinking about the logic of signification that displays its inherent vulnerability to causation and contingency, as well as its openness to further causal consequences, without settling for the usual so-called 'materialist' reductionisms" (Keane 2003, 413). The possibilities opened up by Peircean semiotics have been taken up not only by linguistic anthropologists (e.g., Silverstein 1976) but also by cultural anthropologists like Keane who study material culture, as well as by some archaeologists (e.g., Preucel 2010).

The symbolic nature of human language makes it a flexible and creative system of communication. The role played by symbols in human language sets it apart from the apparently nonsymbolic communication systems of other living species. As noted earlier, when anthropologists talk about human language, they always mean human *symbolic* language.

Many people often equate language with *spoken* language (speech), but it is important to distinguish *language* from *speech*. It is also important to remember

---

icon A sign that looks like that which it represents.

index A sign that points to, or is beside, or is causally linked to that which it signifies.

FIGURE 9.2 Locations of societies whose EthnoProfiles appear in Chapter 9.

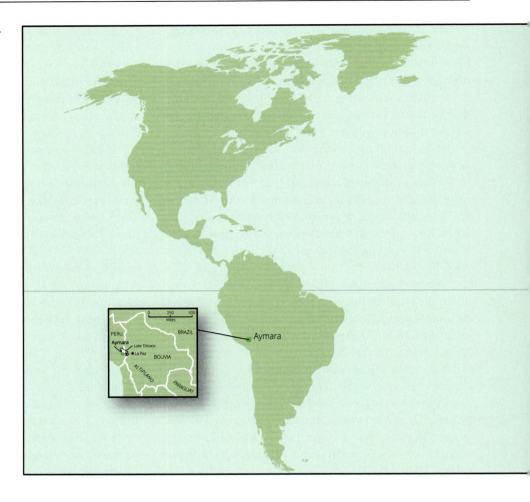

that English can be communicated in writing, Morse code, or American Sign Language, to name just three nonspoken media. Nevertheless, all human linguistic communication, regardless of the medium, depends on more than words alone. Native speakers of a language share not just vocabulary and grammar but also a number of assumptions about how to speak that may not be shared by speakers of a different language. Students learning a new language discover early on that word-for-word translation from one language to another does not work. Sometimes there are no equivalent words in the second language; but even when there appear to be such words, a word-for-word translation may not mean in language B what it meant in language A. For example, when English speakers have eaten enough, they say "I'm full." This may be translated directly into French as "Je suis plein." To a native speaker of French, this sentence (especially when uttered at the end of a meal) has the nonsensical meaning "I am a pregnant [male] animal." Alternatively, if uttered by a man who has just consumed a lot of wine, it means "I'm drunk."

Learning a second language is often frustrating and even unsettling; someone who once found the world simple to talk about suddenly turns into a babbling fool. Studying a second language, then, is less a matter of learning new labels for old objects than it is of learning how to identify new objects that go with new labels. The student must also learn the appropriate contexts in which different linguistic forms may be used: a person can be "full" after eating in English but not in French. Knowledge about context is cultural knowledge.

How Do People Talk about Experience?

Each natural human language is adequate for its speakers' needs, given their particular way of life. Speakers of a particular language tend to develop larger vocabularies to discuss those aspects of life that are of importance to them. The Aymara, who live in the Andes of South America, have invented hundreds of different words for the many varieties of potato they grow (Figure 9.2 and see "EthnoProfile 9.1: Aymara"). By contrast, speakers of English have created an elaborate vocabulary for discussing computers. However, despite differences in vocabulary and grammar, all natural human languages ever studied by linguists prove to be equally complex. Just as there is no such thing as a primitive human culture, there is no such thing as a primitive human language.

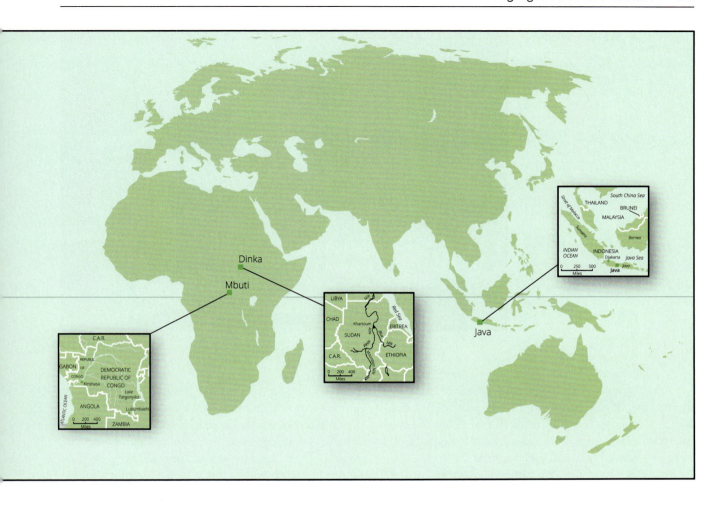

EthnoProfile 9.1

Aymara

Region: South America

Nation: Bolivia, Peru, Chile

Population: 2,000,000

Environment: High mountain lake basin

Livelihood: Peasant farmers

Political organization:
Preconquest state societies
conquered first by Inkas and
later by Spanish; today, part
of a modern nation-state

For more information:
Miracle, Andrew. 1991.
Aymara joking behavior. *Play
and Culture* 4(2):144–52.

Traditionally, languages are associated with concrete groups of people called *speech communities*. But, as Laura Ahearn points out, "complications set in . . . once we start trying to specify exactly what we mean by 'speech'

and by 'community'" (2017, 120). As Ahearn observes, the definitions of these terms have varied over time; they have varied among formal linguists, sociolinguists, and linguistic anthropologists; and today there is still no overall agreement as to how narrowly or how widely these terms should be specified. In part, the answer depends on whether the research is primarily focused on a particular *language* or on the particular *group of people* who happen to speak that language (or languages). According to Ahearn, "Within linguistic anthropology, the most influential alternative to 'speech community' is the notion of 'community of practice'" (2017, 132). Especially influential has been a definition of *community of practice* devised by linguistic anthropologists Penelope Eckert and Sally McConnell-Ginet:

> A community of practice is an aggregate of people who come together around mutual engagement in an endeavor. Ways of doing things, ways of talking, beliefs, values, power relations—in short, practices—emerge in the course of this mutual endeavor. As a social construct, a community of practice is different from the traditional community, primarily because it is defined simultaneously by its membership and by the practice in which that membership engages. (1992, 464)

FIGURE 9.3 Him'be boi 'don nder luumo.

Ahearn argues that the great advantage of thinking about a speech community as a community of practice is that it supports forms of research that "illustrate the emergent nature of communities and the inseparability of language from actual social contexts" (2017, 133). Such studies reveal the way different members of the community make use of linguistic resources in different ways. Consequently, there is a tension in language between diversity and commonality. Individuals and subgroups attempt to use the varied resources of a language to create unique, personal voices or ways of speaking. These efforts are countered by pressures to negotiate shared codes for communication within larger social groups. In this way, language patterns are produced, imitated, or modified through the activity of speakers.

There are many ways to communicate our experiences, and there is no absolute standard favoring one way over another. Some things that are easy to say in language A may be difficult to say in language B, yet other aspects of language B may appear much simpler than equivalent aspects of language A. For example, English ordinarily requires the use of determiners (*a, an, the*) before nouns, but this rule is not found in all languages. Likewise, the verb *to be*, called the "copula" by linguists, is not found in all languages, although the relationships we convey when we use *to be* in English may still be communicated. In English, we might say "There *are* many people in the market." Translating this sentence into Fulfulde, the language of the Fulbe of northern Cameroon, we get "Him'be boi 'don nder luumo," which, word for word, reads "people-many-there-in-market" (Figure 9.3). No single Fulfulde word corresponds to the English *are* or *the*.

Differences across languages are not absolute. In Chinese, for example, verbs never change to indicate tense; instead, separate expressions referring to time are used. English speakers may conclude that Chinese speakers cannot distinguish among past, present, and future. This structure seems completely different from English structure. But consider such English sentences as "Have a hard day at the office today?" and "Your interview go well?" These abbreviated questions, used in informal English, are very similar to the formal patterns of Chinese and other languages of southeastern Asia (Akmajian et al. 2017).

This kind of overlap between two very different languages demonstrates at least four things. First, it shows the kind of cross-linguistic commonality that forms the foundation both for learning new languages and for translation. Second, it highlights the variety of expressive resources to be found in any single language. We learn that English allows us to use either tense markers on verbs (*-s, -ed*) or unmarked verbs with adverbs of time (*have + today*). Third, we learn that the former grammatical pattern is associated with formal usage, whereas the latter is associated with informal usage. Fourth, it shows that the same structures can have different functions in different languages. As the linguistic anthropologist Elinor Ochs observed long ago, most cross-cultural differences in language use "turn out to be differences in *context* and/or *frequency of occurrence*" (1986, 10).

Cultural Translation

Linguistic translation is complicated and beset with pitfalls, as we have seen. Cultural translation, as David Parkin describes, requires knowledge not only of different grammars but also of the various different cultural contexts in which grammatical forms are put to use.

Cultural translation, like translation from one language to another, never produces a rendering that is semantically and stylistically an exact replica of the original. That much we accept. What is not often recognized, perhaps not even by the translators themselves, is that the very act of having to decide how to phrase an event, sentiment, or human character engages the translator in an act of creation. The translator does not simply represent a picture made by an author. He or she creates a new version, and perhaps in some respects a new picture—a matter that is often of some great value.

So it is with anthropologists. But while this act of creation in reporting on "the other" may reasonably be regarded as a self-sustaining pleasure, it is also an entry into the pitfalls and traps of language use itself. One of the most interesting new fields in anthropology is the study of the relationship between language and human knowledge, both among ourselves as professional anthropologists and laypeople and among peoples of other cultures. The study is at once both reflexive and critical.

The hidden influences at work in language use attract the most interest. For example, systems of greetings have many built-in elaborations that differentiate subtly between those who are old and young, male and female, rich and poor, and powerful and powerless. When physicians discuss a patient in his or her presence and refer to the patient in the third-person singular, they are in effect defining the patient as a passive object unable to enter into the discussion. When anthropologists present elegant accounts of "their" people that fit the demands of a convincing theory admirably, do they not also leave out [of] the description any consideration of the informants' own fears and feelings? Or do we go too far in making such claims, and is it often the anthropologist who is indulged by the people, who give him or her the data they think is sought, either in exchange for something they want or simply because it pleases them to do so? If the latter, how did the anthropologist's account miss this critical part of the dialogue?

Source: Parkin 1990, 290–91.

What Does It Mean to "Learn" a Language?

Years ago studies of child language amounted to a list of errors that children make when attempting to gain what Chomsky (1965) calls **linguistic competence**, or mastery of adult grammar. For some time, however, linguists who study children's verbal interactions in social and cultural contexts have drawn attention to what children can do very well. "From an early age they appear to communicate very fluently, producing utterances which are not just remarkably well-formed according to the linguist's standards but also appropriate to the social context in which the speakers find themselves. Children are thus learning far more about language than rules of grammar. [They are] acquiring communicative competence" (Elliot 1981, 13).

Communicative competence, or mastery of adult rules for socially and culturally appropriate speech, is a term introduced by American anthropological linguist Dell Hymes (1972). As an anthropologist, Hymes objected to Chomsky's notion that linguistic competence consisted only of being able to make correct judgments of sentences grammaticality (Chomsky 1965, 4). Hymes observed that competent adult speakers do more than follow grammatical rules when they speak. They are also able to choose words and topics of conversation appropriate to their social position, the social position of the person they are addressing, and the social context of interaction.

linguistic competence A term coined by linguist Noam Chomsky to refer to the mastery of adult grammar.

communicative competence A term coined by anthropological linguist Dell Hymes to refer to the mastery of adult rules for socially and culturally appropriate speech.

How Does Context Affect Language?

Anthropologists are very much aware of the influence of context on what people choose to say. For example, consider the issue of using personal pronouns appropriately to address another person you are speaking to. In English, the problem almost never arises because native speakers address all people as "you." But any English speaker who has ever tried to learn French has worried about when to address an individual using the second-person plural (*vous*) and when to use the second-person singular (*tu*). To be safe, most students use *vous* for all individuals because it is the more formal term and they want to avoid appearing too familiar with native speakers whom they do not know well. But if you are dating a French person, at which point in the relationship does the change from *vous* to *tu* occur, and who decides? Moreover, sometimes—for example, among university students—the normal term of address is *tu* (even among strangers); it is used to indicate social solidarity. Native speakers of English who are learning French wrestle with these and other linguistic dilemmas. Rules for the appropriate use of *tu* and *vous* seem to have nothing to do with grammar, yet the choice between one form and the other indicates whether the speaker is someone who does or does not know how to speak French.

But French seems quite straightforward when compared with Javanese in which all the words in a sentence must be carefully selected to reflect the social relationship between the speaker and the person addressed (see "EthnoProfile 9.2: Java"). In the 1950s, when Clifford Geertz first did fieldwork in Java, he discovered that it was impossible to say anything in Javanese without also communicating your social position relative to the person to whom you are speaking. Even a simple request—like "Are you going to eat rice and cassava now?"—required that speakers know at least five different varieties of the language to communicate socially as well as to make the request (Figure 9.4). This example illustrates the range of diversity present in a single language and how different varieties of a language are related to different subgroups within the speech community.

How Does Language Affect How We See the World?

During the first half of the twentieth century, two American anthropological linguists, Edward Sapir and Benjamin Whorf, observed that the grammars of

---

EthnoProfile 9.2

Java

Region: Southeastern Asia

Nation: Indonesia

Population: 120,000,000

Environment: Tropical island

Livelihood: Intensive rice cultivation

Political organization: Highly stratified state

For more information: Geertz, Clifford. 1960. *The religion of Java.* New York: Free Press.

---

different languages often described the same situation in different ways. They concluded that language has the power to shape the way people see the world. This claim has been called the **linguistic relativity principle**, or the "Sapir–Whorf hypothesis." This principle has been highly controversial because it is a radical proposition that is difficult to test and, when it has been tested, the results have been ambiguous.

The so-called strong version of the linguistic relativity principle is also known as *linguistic determinism*. It is a totalizing view of language that reduces patterns of thought and culture to the grammatical patterns of the language spoken. If a grammar classifies nouns in male and female gender categories, for example, linguistic determinists claim that speakers of that language are forced to think of males and females as radically different kinds of beings. By contrast, a language that makes no grammatical distinctions on the basis of gender supposedly trains its speakers to think of males and females as exactly the same. If linguistic determinism is correct, then a change in grammar should change thought patterns: if English speakers replaced *he* and *she* with a new, gender-neutral, third-person, singular pronoun, such as *te*, then, linguistic determinists predict, English speakers would begin to treat men and women as equals.

There are a number of problems with linguistic determinism. In the first place, there are languages such as Fulfulde in which only one third-person pronoun is used for males and females (*o*); however, male-dominant social patterns are quite evident among Fulfulde speakers. In the second place, if language determined thought in this way, it would be impossible to translate from one language to another or even to learn another language with a different grammatical

---

linguistic relativity principle A position, associated with Edward Sapir and Benjamin Whorf, that asserts that language has the power to shape the way people see the world.

Speaking to persons of:	Level	"Are	you	going	to eat	rice	and	cassava	now?"	Complete sentence
Very high position	3a	menapa	pandjenengan	badé	dahar	sekul	kalijan	kaspé	samenika	Menapa pandjenengan badé dahar sekul kalijan kaspé samenika?
High position	3	menapa	sampéjan	badé	neda	sekul	kalijan	kaspé	samenika	Menapa sampéjan badé neda sekul kalijan kaspé samenika?
Same position, not close	2	napa	sampéjan	adjéng	neda	sekul	lan	kaspé	saniki	Napa sampéjan adjéng neda sekul lan kaspé saniki?
Same position, casual acquaintance	1a	apa	sampéjan	arep	neda	sega	lan	kaspé	saiki	Apa sampéjan arep neda sega lan kaspé saiki?
Close friends of any rank; also to lower status (basic language)	1	apa	kowé	arep	mangan	sega	lan	kaspé	saiki	Apa kowé arep mangan sega lan kaspé saiki?

FIGURE 9.4   The dialect of nonnoble, urbanized, somewhat educated people in central Java in the 1950s (Geertz 1960).

structure. Because human beings do learn foreign languages and translate from one language to another, the strong version of the linguistic relativity principle cannot be correct. Third, even if it were possible to draw firm boundaries around speech communities (which it is not), every language provides its native speakers with alternative ways of describing the world. Finally, in most of the world's societies, people learn to speak more than one language fluently. Yet people who grow up bilingual do not also grow up unable to reconcile two contradictory views of reality. Indeed, bilingual children ordinarily benefit from knowing two languages, do not confuse them, can switch readily from one to another, and even appear to demonstrate greater cognitive flexibility on psychological tests than do monolinguals (Elliot 1981, 56) (Figure 9.5).

In the face of these objections, other researchers offer a "weak" version of the linguistic relativity principle that rejects linguistic determinism but continues to claim that language shapes thought and culture. Thus, grammatical gender might not determine a male-dominant social order, but it might facilitate the acceptance of such a social order because the grammatical distinction between *he* and *she* might make separate and unequal

FIGURE 9.5   Canada is officially a bilingual country, and signs are in both French and English.

gender roles seem "natural." In the United States, however, changing views of sex, gender, and sexuality are leading many English speakers to challenge this standard male–female linguistic binary for the third person singular. Indeed, even if *formal* grammarians insist that an unknown third-person singular should be designated "he," *informal* English usage has long permitted alternatives such as "they" or "you" in such contexts. This usage history suggests that "they" may also have the best chance of displacing "he" and "she" as pronouns of reference for individuals who declare themselves *nonbinary*, refusing to be classified as either male or female, even though several other alternatives have also been proposed (see Chapter 13). Because many native speakers of English also are strong promoters of gender equality, however, the shaping power of grammar would seem far too weak to merit any scientific attention.

Neither Sapir nor Whorf favored linguistic determinism. Sapir argued that language's importance lies in the way it directs attention to some aspects of experience rather than to others. He was impressed by the fact that "it is generally difficult to make a complete divorce between objective reality and our linguistic symbols of reference to it" (Sapir [1933] 1966, 9, 15). Whorf's views have been more sharply criticized by later scholars. His discussions of the linguistic relativity principle are complex and ambiguous. At least part of the problem arises from Whorf's attempt to view grammar as the linguistic pattern that shapes culture and thought. Whorf's contemporaries understood grammar to refer to rules for combining sounds into words and words into sentences. Whorf believed that grammar needed to be thought of in broader terms (Schultz 1990), but he died before working out the theoretical language to describe such a level.

In recent years, interest in the "Whorfian question" has been revived, and scholars have recognized that there are several different ways to ask about the relationship of language to thought. Especially exciting is the new perspective that comes from focusing on the influence of language in pragmatic contexts of use. Dan Slobin's "thinking for speaking" hypothesis, for example, suggests that the influence of linguistic forms on thought may be greatest when people prepare to speak to others on a specific topic in a specific setting. "One fits one's thoughts into available linguistic forms. . . . 'Thinking for speaking' involves picking those characteristics that (a) fit some conceptualization of the event, and (b) are readily encodable in the language" (Slobin 1987, 435). Slobin points out that related challenges are faced by speakers involved in "thinking for writing" or "thinking for translating." Thinking for translating is especially intriguing, particularly when translators must render features that are grammatically encoded in one language into a second language in which they are not encoded, or vice versa (Slobin 2003).

For example, an English speaker who is trying to say "I like fast food" in Spanish will have to use a passive encoding—*me gusta la comida rápida* ("fast food pleases me."). This encoding is not easy for many English speakers to learn, precisely because it is not the standard English way to encode the thought.

Dedre Gentner and Susan Goldin-Meadow (2003) point out that some researchers still take a traditional Whorfian approach, viewing language as a lens through which people view the world. Others think of language as a tool kit, a set of resources that speakers make use of to build more elaborate conceptual structures. Still others think of language as a category maker, influencing the way people classify experiences and objects in the world. They note that the research that produces the most consistent evidence of the influence of language on thought comes from those who view language as a tool kit—that is, as a set of resources that speakers make use of for conceptual or communicative purposes (Gentner and Goldin-Meadow 2003, 10). Nevertheless, they emphasize that defining the research question in such variable ways means that "we are unlikely to get a yes-or-no answer to the whole of Whorf's thesis. But if we have delineated a set of more specific questions for which the answer is no to some and yes to others, we will have achieved our goal" (12).

Pragmatics: How Do We Study Language in Contexts of Use?

Pragmatics can be defined as the study of language in the context of its use. Each context offers limitations and opportunities concerning what we may say and how we may say it. Everyday language use is thus often characterized by a struggle between speakers and listeners over definitions of context and appropriate word use. Linguistic anthropologist Michael Silverstein (1976; 1985) was one of the first to argue that the referential meaning of certain expressions in language cannot be determined unless we go beyond the boundaries of a sentence and place the expressions in a wider context of use. Two kinds of context must be considered. *Linguistic context* refers to the other words, expressions, and sentences that surround the expression whose meaning we are trying to determine. The meaning of *it* in the sentence "I really enjoyed it" cannot be determined if the sentence is considered on its own. However, if we know that the previous sentence was "My aunt gave me this book," we have a linguistic context that allows us to deduce that *it* refers to *this book. Nonlinguistic context* consists of objects and activities that are present in the situation of speech at the same time we are speaking. Consider the sentence "Who is that standing by the door?" We need to inspect the actual physical context at the moment this sentence is uttered to find the door and the person standing by the door and thus give a referential meaning to the words

---

pragmatics The study of language in the context of its use.

FIGURE 9.6   To answer the question "What is that on the door?" requires that we examine the actual physical context at the moment we are asked the question to try to determine what "that" refers to. Is it the locks? the door handles? the studs on the door? Also, what part of the structure is the "door"?

who and *that*. Furthermore, even if we know what a door is in a formal sense, we need the nonlinguistic context to clarify what counts as a door in this instance (e.g., it could be a rough opening in the wall) (Figure 9.6).

By going beyond formal grammatical analysis, pragmatics directs our attention to **discourse**, understood as a stretch of speech longer than a sentence united by a common theme. Discourse may be a series of sentences uttered by a single individual or a series of rejoinders in a conversation among two or more speakers. Many linguistic anthropologists accept the arguments of M. M. Bakhtin (1981) and V. N. Voloshinov (see, e.g., Voloshinov [1926] 1987) that the series of verbal

exchanges in conversation is the primary form of discourse. In this view, the speech of any single individual, whether a simple *yes* or a book-length dissertation, is only one rejoinder in an ongoing dialogue.

When Michael Silverstein and his colleagues considered pragmatics and discourse from the point of view of the multifunctionality of language—particularly in terms of reflexive metalinguistic commenting on our own language production—they became interested in metapragmatic discourse as well: that is, in reflexive commentary concerning language in the context of use (Silverstein 1993). We will explore these matters more closely when we address the topic of language ideologies.

Ethnopragmatics

Linguistic anthropologists pay attention not only to the immediate context of speech, linguistic and nonlinguistic, but also to broader contexts that are shaped by unequal social relationships and rooted in history (Hill and Irvine 1992; Brenneis and Macauley 1996). Alessandro Duranti (1994) calls this **ethnopragmatics**, "a study of language use which relies on ethnography to illuminate the ways in which speech is both constituted by and constitutive of social interaction" (11). Such a study focuses on *practice*, human activity in which the rules of grammar, cultural values, and physical action are all conjoined (Hanks 1996, 11). Such a perspective locates the source of meaning in everyday routine social activity, or *habitus*, rather than in grammar. As a result, phonemes, morphemes, syntax, and semantics are viewed as *linguistic resources* people can make use of, rather than rigid forms that determine what people can and cannot think or say (see Module 4).

If mutual understanding is shaped by shared routine activity and not by grammar, then communication is possible even if the people interacting with one another speak mutually unintelligible languages. All they need is a shared sense of "what is going on here" and the ability to negotiate successfully who will do what (Hanks 1996, 234). Such mutually coengaged people shape *communicative practices* that involve spoken language but also include values and shared habitual knowledge that may never be put into words. Because most people in most societies regularly engage in a wide range of practical activities with different subgroups, each one will also end up knowledgeable about a variety

discourse   A stretch of speech longer than a sentence united by a common theme.

ethnopragmatics   The study of language use that relies on ethnography to illuminate the ways in which speech is both constituted by and constitutive of social interaction.

of different communicative practices and the linguistic habits that go with them. For example, a college student might know the linguistic habits appropriate to dinner with parents, to the classroom, to worship services, to conversations in the dorm with friends, and to a part-time job in a restaurant. Each set of linguistic habits that student knows is called a *discourse genre*. Because our student simultaneously knows a multiplicity of different discourse genres that can be chosen when speaking, this linguistic knowledge is characterized by what Bakhtin called *heteroglossia* (Bakhtin 1981).

For Bakhtin, heteroglossia is the normal condition of linguistic knowledge in any society with internal divisions. Heteroglossia describes a coexisting multiplicity of linguistic norms and forms, many of which are anchored in more than one social subgroup. Because we all participate in more than one of these subgroups, we inevitably become fluent in many varieties of language, even if we speak only English! Our capacity for heteroglossia is an example of linguistic openness: it means that our thought and speech are not imprisoned in a single set of grammatical forms, as linguistic determinists have argued. Indeed, if our college student reflects on the overlap as well as the contrasts between the language habits used in the dorm with those used in the restaurant, that student might well find themselves raising questions about what words really mean. To the extent, however, that habitual ways of speaking are deeply rooted in everyday routine activity, they may guide the way that student typically thinks, perceives, and acts. And to that extent, the linguistic relativity hypothesis may be correct—not on the level of grammatical categories but on the level of discourse (Hanks 1996, 176, 246; Schultz 1990).

What Happens When Languages Come into Contact?

In local communities where they know each other well, speakers and listeners are able, for the most part, to draw on knowledge of overlapping language habits to converse or argue about moral and political issues. This may still be the case, to some extent, when communities of speakers who engage regularly with one another in practical activities do not all speak the same languages,

---

pidgin A language with no native speakers that develops in a single generation between members of communities that possess distinct native languages.

---

or speak them equally fluently. Sometimes, however, potential parties to a verbal exchange find themselves sharing little more than physical proximity to one another. Such situations arise when members of communities with radically different language traditions and no history of previous contact with one another come face to face and are forced to communicate. There is no way to predict the outcome of such enforced contact on either speech community, yet from these new shared experiences, new forms of practice, including a new form of language—pidgin—may develop.

"When the chips are down, meaning is negotiated" (Lakoff and Johnson 1980, 231). The study of pidgin languages is the study of the radical negotiation of new meaning, the production of a new whole (the pidgin language) that is different from and reducible to none of the languages that gave birth to it. The shape of a pidgin reflects the context in which it arises—generally one of colonial conquest or commercial domination. Vocabulary is usually taken from the language of the dominant group, making it easy for that group to learn. The system of pronunciation and sentence structure may be similar to the subordinate language (or languages), however, making it easier for subordinated speakers to learn. Complex grammatical features marking the gender or number of nouns or the tenses of verbs tend to disappear (Holm 1988).

What Is the Difference between a Pidgin and a Creole?

Pidgins are traditionally defined as reduced languages that have no native speakers. They develop, in a single generation, between groups of speakers that possess distinct native languages. When speakers of a pidgin language pass that language on to a new generation, linguists have traditionally referred to the language as a *creole*. As linguists studied pidgins and creoles more closely, they discovered that the old distinction between pidgins and creoles did not seem to hold up. In the Pacific, for example, linguists have discovered pidgin dialects, pidgin languages used as main languages of permanently settled groups, and pidgins that have become native languages. Moreover, creolization can take place at any time after a pidgin forms, creoles can exist without having been preceded by pidgins, pidgins can remain pidgins for long periods and undergo linguistic change without acquiring native speakers, and pidgin and creole varieties of the same language can coexist in the same society (Jourdan 1991, 192ff.). In fact, it looks as if heteroglossia is as widespread among speakers of pidgins and creoles as among speakers of other languages.

How Is Meaning Negotiated?

More information has been gathered about the historical and sociocultural contexts within which pidgins first formed. Here, as elsewhere in linguistic anthropology, the focus has turned to communicative practice. From this perspective, creolization is likely when pidgin speakers find themselves in new social contexts requiring a new language for *all* the practical activities of everyday life; without such a context, it is unlikely that creoles will emerge. Accordingly, a pidgin is now defined as a secondary language in a speech community that uses some other main language, and a creole is understood as a main language in a speech community, whether or not it has native speakers (Jourdan 1991, 196).

Viewing pidgin creation as a form of communicative practice means that attention must be paid to the role of pidgin creators as agents in the process (Figure 9.7). As we negotiate meaning across language barriers, it appears that all humans have intuitions about which parts of our speech carry the most meaning and which parts can be safely dropped. Neither party to the negotiation, moreover, may be trying to learn the other's language; rather, "speakers in the course of negotiating communication use whatever linguistic and sociolinguistic resources they have at their disposal, until the shared meaning is established and conventionalized" (Jourdan 1991, 200).

What Does Linguistic Inequality Look Like?

Pidgins and creoles turn out to be far more complex and the result of far more active human input than we used to think, which is why they are so attractive to linguists and linguistic anthropologists as objects of study. Where they coexist, however, alongside the language of the dominant group (e.g., Hawaiian Pidgin English and English), they are ordinarily viewed as defective and inferior languages. Such views can be seen as an outgrowth of the situation that led to the formation of most of the pidgins we know about: European colonial domination. In a colonial or postcolonial setting, the language of the colonizer is often viewed as better than pidgin or creole languages, which are frequently thought to be broken, imperfect versions of the colonizer's language. The situation only worsens when formal education, the key to participation in the European-dominated society, is carried out in the colonial language. Speakers of pidgin who remain illiterate may never be able to master the colonial tongue and may find themselves effectively barred from equal participation in the civic life of their societies.

FIGURE 9.7   Tok Pisin, a pidgin language that developed in New Guinea following colonization by English speakers, has become a major medium of communication in New Guinea. The news in Tok Pisin is available on the Internet at http://www.radioaustralia.net.au/tokpisin/

What Is Language Ideology?

Building on earlier work on linguistic inequality, linguistic anthropologists in recent years have developed a focus on the study of **language ideology**—ways of representing the intersection "between social forms and forms of talk" (Woolard 1998, 3). Although the study of language ideology discloses speakers' sense of beauty or morality or basic understandings of the world, it also provides evidence of the ways in which our speech is always embedded in a social world of power differences. Language ideologies are markers of struggles between social groups with different interests, revealed in what people say and how they say it. The way people monitor their speech to bring it into line with a particular language ideology illustrates that language ideologies are "active and effective . . . they transform the material reality they comment on" (Woolard 1998, 11). In settings with a history of colonization, where groups with different power and different languages coexist in tension, the study of language ideologies has long been significant (Woolard 1998, 16). The skills of linguistic anthropologists especially suit them to study language ideologies because their linguistic training allows them to describe precisely the linguistic features (e.g., phonological, morphological, or syntactic) that become the focus of ideological attention, and their training in cultural analysis allows them to explain how those linguistic features come to stand symbolically for a particular social group.

language ideology A marker of struggles between social groups with different interests, revealed in what people say and how they say it. To employ a language ideology is to make value judgments about other people's speech in a context of domination and subordination.

How Have Language Ideologies Been at Work in Studies of African American Speech?

In the 1960s, some psychologists claimed that African American children living in urban areas of the northern United States suffered from linguistic deprivation. They argued that these children started school with a limited vocabulary and no grammar and thus could not perform as well as Euro-American children in the classroom—that their language was unequal to the challenges of communication. Sociolinguist William Labov (1972) and his colleagues found such claims incredible and undertook research of their own, which demonstrated two things. First, they proved that the form of English spoken in the inner city was not defective pseudolanguage. Second, they showed how a change in research setting permitted inner-city African American children to display a level of linguistic sophistication that the psychologists had never dreamed they possessed.

When African American children were in the classroom (a Euro-American–dominated context) being interrogated by Euro-American adults about topics of no interest to them, they said little. This did not necessarily mean, Labov argued, that they had no language. Rather, their minimal responses were better understood as defensive attempts to keep threatening Euro-American questioners from learning anything about them. For the African American children, the classroom was only one part of a broader racist culture. The psychologists, because of their ethnocentrism, had been oblivious to the effect this context might have on their research.

Reasoning that reliable samples of African American speech had to be collected in settings where the racist pressure was lessened, Labov and his colleagues conducted fieldwork in the homes and on the streets of the inner city. They recorded enormous amounts of speech in African American English (AAE) produced by the same children who had had nothing to say when questioned in the classroom. Labov argued that AAE was a variety of English that had certain rules not found in Standard English. This is a strictly linguistic difference: most middle-class speakers of Standard English would not use these rules, but most African American speakers of AAE would. However, neither variety of English should be seen as "defective" as a result of this difference. This kind of linguistic difference, apparent when speakers of two varieties converse, marks the speaker's

membership in a particular speech community. Such differences distinguish the language habits of most social subgroups in a society, like that of the United States, that is characterized by heteroglossia.

From the perspective of communicative practice, however, AAE is distinctive because of the historical and sociocultural circumstances that led to its creation. For some time, linguists have viewed AAE as one of many creole languages that developed in the New World after Africans were brought there to work as slaves on plantations owned by Europeans. Dominant English-speaking elites have regarded AAE with the same disdain that European colonial elites have accorded creole languages elsewhere. Because African Americans have always lived in socially and politically charged contexts that questioned their full citizenship, statements about their language habits are inevitably thought to imply something about their intelligence and culture. Those psychologists who claimed that inner-city African American children suffered from linguistic deprivation, for example, seemed to be suggesting either that these children were too stupid to speak or that their cultural surroundings were too meager to allow normal language development. The work of Labov and his colleagues showed that the children were not linguistically deprived, were not stupid, and participated in a rich linguistic culture. But this work itself became controversial in later decades when it became clear that the rich African American language and culture described was primarily that of adolescent males. These young men saw themselves as bearers of authentic African American language habits and dismissed African Americans who did not speak the way they did as "lames." This implied that everyone else in the African American community was somehow not genuinely African American, a challenge that those excluded could not ignore. Linguists like Labov's team, who thought their work undermined racism, were thus bewildered when middle-class African Americans, who spoke Standard English, refused to accept AAE as representative of "true" African American culture (Morgan 1995, 337).

From the perspective of linguistic anthropology, this debate shows that the African American community is not homogeneous, linguistically or culturally, but is instead characterized by heteroglossia (Figure 9.8). At a minimum, language habits are shaped by social class, age cohort, and gender. Moreover, members of all of these subgroups use both Standard English and AAE in their speech. Morgan reports, for example, that upper middle-class African American students at elite colleges who did not grow up speaking AAE regularly

IN THEIR OWN WORDS

Varieties of African American English

The school board of Oakland, California, gained national attention in December 1996 when its members voted to recognize Ebonics as an official second language. What they called Ebonics is also known as Black English Vernacular (BEV), Black English (BE), African American English Vernacular (AAEV), and African American English (AAE). The school board decision generated controversy both within and outside the African American community because it seemed to be equating Ebonics with other "official second languages," such as Spanish and Chinese. This implied that Standard English was as much a "foreign language" to native speakers of Ebonics as it was to native speakers of Spanish and Chinese and that Oakland school students who were native speakers of Ebonics should be entitled not only to the respect accorded native Spanish- or Chinese-speaking students but also, perhaps, to the same kind of funding for bilingual education. The uproar produced by this dispute caused the school board to amend the resolution a month later. African American linguistic anthropologist Marcyliena Morgan's commentary highlights one issue that many disputants ignored: namely, that the African American community is not monoglot in Ebonics but is in fact characterized by heteroglossia.

After sitting through a string of tasteless jokes about the Oakland school district's approval of a language education policy for African American students, I realize that linguists and educators have failed to inform Americans about varieties of English used throughout the country and the link between these dialects and culture, social class, geographic region and identity. After all, linguists have been a part of language and education debates around AAE and the furor that surrounds them since the late 1970s. Then the Ann Arbor school district received a court order to train teachers on aspects of AAE to properly assess and teach children in their care.

Like any language and dialect, African American varieties of English—ranging from that spoken by children and some adults with limited education to those spoken by adults with advanced degrees—are based on the cultural, social, historical and political experiences shared by many US people of African descent. This experience is one of family, community and love as well as racism, poverty and discrimination. Every African American does not speak AAE. Moreover, some argue that children who speak the vernacular typically grow up to speak both AAE as well as mainstream varieties of English. It is therefore not surprising that the community separates its views of AAE, ranging from loyalty to abhorrence, from issues surrounding the literacy education of their children. Unfortunately, society's ambivalent attitudes toward African American students' cognitive abilities, like Jensen's 1970s deficit models and the 1990s' *The Bell Curve*, suggest that when it comes to African American kids, intelligence and competence in school can be considered genetic.

African American children who speak the vernacular form of AAE may be the only English-speaking children in this country who attend community schools in which teachers not only are ignorant of their dialect but refuse to accept its existence. This attitude leads to children being marginalized and designated as learning disabled. The educational failure of African American children can, at best, be only partially addressed through teacher training on AAE. When children go to school, they bring not only their homework and textbooks but also their language, culture and identity. Sooner rather than later, the educational system must address its exclusion of cultural and dialect difference in teacher training and school curriculum.

Source: Morgan 1997, 8.

adopt many of its features and that hip-hop artists combine the grammar of Standard English with the phonology and morphology of AAE (Morgan 1995, 338). This situation is not so paradoxical if we recall, once again, the politically charged context of African American life in the United States. African Americans both affirm and deny the significance of AAE for their identity, perhaps because AAE symbolizes both the oppression of slavery and the resistance to that oppression (Morgan 1995, 339).

FIGURE 9.8 The language habits of African Americans are not homogeneous but vary according to gender, social class, region, and situation.

What Is Raciolinguistics?

Over 40 years ago, Claudia Mitchell-Kernan described African Americans as "bicultural" and struggling to develop language habits that could reconcile "good" English and AAE (1972, 209). That struggle continues at the beginning of the twenty-first century, but the arena of struggle has expanded and become more complex. For linguistic anthropologist H. Samy Alim and others, this new complexity was indexed by the 2008 election of President Barack Obama, the United States' "first 'Black-language-speaking' president" (2016a, 1). As Alim notes, the metalinguistic commentary that surrounded the way Barack Obama talks "revealed much about language and racial politics in the United States" (2016a, 1). Alim and Geneva Smitherman explored this commentary in *Articulate While Black: Barack Obama, Language, and Race in the U.S.* (Alim and Smitherman 2012), a book that critically examines the attention paid to the ways commentators, black and white, dissected President Obama's speech. Their analysis pointed to a deeper philosophical question: "What does it mean to speak as a racialized subject in contemporary America? This is the central concern of raciolinguistics" (Alim 2016a, 1). **Raciolinguistics** involves theorizing race and language together, a project "that is dedicated to bringing to bear the diverse methods of linguistic analysis to ask and answer critical questions about the relations between language, race, and power across diverse ethnoracial contexts and societies" (2016a, 3).

As Alim points out, the founders of North American Anthropology, Franz Boas and Edward Sapir, insisted nearly a century ago that there was no evidence to support the ranking either of peoples ("races") or of languages on a universal scale of superiority and inferiority. In the decades since, however, anthropologists have struggled with how to insist simultaneously that race is not real biologically, but that it is very real socially, culturally, and historically. In 2008, Alim and other linguistic anthropologists launched "a focused, collective effort to theorize race and ethnicity within and across language studies." Their volume, *Raciolinguistics: How Language Shapes Our Ideas about Race*, contains 18 chapters that emphasize "both the central role that language plays in racialization and . . . the enduring relevance of race and racism in the lives of People of Color" (Alim 2016a, 3). The raciolinguistic framework allows Alim and his colleagues to consider how global immigration flows, which are altering the demographic profiles of the United States and other countries, reveal both old and new challenges at the intersection of race, ethnicity, and language (Alim 2016a, 7).

By the end of the twentieth century, the black–white divide that has traditionally been central to racial discourse in the United States had become more complex to acknowledge the racialization of Native Americans, Latinos, and Asian Americans; however, ongoing immigration from many continents have made clear-cut racial divides even harder to identify. H. Samy Alim has proposed coping with this state of affairs from a raciolinguistic perspective that he calls *transracialization*. For example, the election of Barack Obama as president produced a "colorblind" discourse among "white" Americans claiming that Obama's election meant that race no longer mattered in the United States, that the country had become "postracial." However, in the summer of 2015, critical scholars and theorists of race were drawn into a heated debate concerning news reports about Rachel Dolezal, a woman whose parents were "white," but who had successfully passed as "black" for several years, and who described herself as "transracial" (https://www.nytimes.com/2015/06/13/us/rachel-dolezal-naacp-president-accused-of-lying-about-her-race.html; https://www.nytimes.com/2015/06/17/us/rachel-dolezal-nbc-today-show.html). Alim comments: "Despite the fact that Dolezal indeed crossed over into blackness . . . we need a focused interrogation of what it means to be *transracial*. Can someone be transracial?" (2016b, 34). Alim argued that any answer to this question could not simply leave racial groupings, however defined, unchanged.

> Thinking transracially, as opposed to postracially, we can move beyond attempt[s] to demonstrate our loyalty and belonging to particular racial categories and

raciolinguistics Theorizing race and language together by drawing on "diverse methods of linguistic analysis to ask and answer critical questions about the relation between languages, race, and power across diverse ethnoracial contexts and societies" (Alim 2016a, 3).

work toward problematizing the very process of racial categorization itself . . . transracialization is not simply how race is coded and decoded across "different" racial formations but also about *resisting codifications*. . . . The transracial subject is transgressive because crossing borders becomes central to disrupting race. (2016b, 35)

Alim reflected on his own experience as a person of color who has been racialized in a variety of different ways. He found that both language and phenotype were involved, but "with language being, usually, the more malleable . . . I describe nine moments of racial translation across at least five 'language varieties,' in five days and three countries by one speaker (me)" (2016b, 38). The first occurred when a cab driver picked him up at his home in the San Francisco Bay Area to take him to the airport and asked him in an "Indian" (i.e., South Asian) accent if he were "Indian." Later on a plane to Paris, he met a man whom he had raced as "white," but who identified himself as Native American, and who asked him if his name "Samy" was short for "Osama"; apparently taking Alim for an Algerian, the man explained that he had an Algerian friend who had shortened his name in this way. Alim chatted with two women, one of whom he thought was "Asian"; the other he inferred was "Latina." When it came out during the conversation that Alim spoke Spanish, the Latina woman turned to him and asked if he was Mexican, adding that she was Mexican but unfortunately could not speak Spanish. On a later flight from Paris to Berlin, the flight attendants occasionally addressed him in a language that he knew was not Arabic (a language he also speaks), but that might have been Turkish, given the large number of Turks who live in Berlin. Once in Berlin, he went to an Italian restaurant, where he was greeted by the cook whom Alim assumed was Italian but who spoke to him in German. When Alim answered in English, the cook responded in Italian-accented English, asking if Alim were "American Latino. Español." Alim replied in Spanish, the cook responded in the Spanish of a nonnative speaker, and "while the food was cooking, we continued to chit-chat in our new lingua franca . . . and I wondered what my Italian former sister-in-law's family would make of the whole exchange!" (2016b, 39–41).

Alim had not yet reached the conference, or embarked on his return trip to the United States, where even more attempts by others to classify him (and of him to classify them) would ensue. However, all these encounters, he insists, involved raciolinguistic classifications: people moved back and forth between phenotype and language and back again in the effort to settle on a classification, however temporary. For people of color like Alim, as he says, "the same phenotype can be raced in different ways" (2016b, 42), and a key contributor is

the language (or languages) one happens to be speaking. The radical potential of transracialization, as Alim sees it, comes from playing with the ambiguity of phenotype and language(s) to expose racializing processes while at the same time resisting efforts to be assigned to any single, exclusive, category (2016b, 45).

What Is Lost If a Language Dies?

At the beginning of the twenty-first century, many anthropologists and linguists have become involved in projects to maintain or revive languages with small numbers of native speakers. These languages are in danger of disappearing as younger people in the speech community stop using the language or never learn it in the first place. Communities concerned about language revitalization can range from Irish speakers in the United Kingdom to Kiowa speakers in Oklahoma to users of indigenous sign languages in Australia.

And the threats to these languages range widely as well. They include the spread of "world" languages like English and the marginalization of one dialect in favor of a neighboring dialect. They also include support for a "national" sign language in Thailand instead of local, "indigenous" sign languages used by small communities, and (as is the case in places like the United States, Australia, and Norway) the spread of technologies that can "save" people from being deaf (Walsh 2005). How seriously different "small languages" are endangered depends on what counts as small and how imminent the threat is perceived to be—and experts can differ in their evaluation of these matters.

Linguistic anthropologists have paid particular attention to indigenous languages spoken by small communities who have experienced a history of colonization by outsiders and who are minorities within states where colonial languages dominate. At the same time, as Michael Walsh explains, indigenous language situations are not all alike. In Guatemala, for example, "Mayan languages are spoken among a majority of the populations, and the languages are all closely related; so it is possible to have a more unified approach to Mayan language revitalization. Mayas in Guatemala are now using their languages in schools, and they are taking steps toward gaining official recognition of their languages" (Walsh 2005, 296). Sometimes, however, colonial borders separate members of an indigenous language community, meaning that speakers on one side of the border may be better supported in their language revitalization efforts than speakers on the other side of

Language Revitalization

Many linguists and linguistic anthropologists who specialize in the study of the indigenous languages of North America are increasingly involved in collaborating with the speakers of those languages to preserve and revive them in the face of threatened decline or extinction with the spread of English. Leanne Hinton is a linguist at the University of California, Berkeley, who has worked for many years to help revitalize the languages of the indigenous peoples of California (Table 9.1, Figure 9.9). In 1998, she wrote:

Of at least 98 languages originally spoken in what are now the political confines of the state, 45 (or more) have no fluent speakers left, 17 have only one to five speakers left, and the remaining 36 have only elderly speakers. Not a single California Indian language is being used now as the language of daily communication. The elders do not in actuality speak their language—rather, they remember how to speak their language. (Hinton 1998, 216)

FIGURE 9.9   A map of indigenous languages of California prior to western European settlement. From California Indian Library Collections, Ethnic Studies Library, University of California, Berkeley.

TABLE 9.1   California Languages and Their Classification (adapted from Hinton 1998, 83–85)

STOCK	FAMILY/BRANCH	LANGUAGES IN CALIFORNIA
Hokan		Chimariko*
		Esselen*
		Karuk
		Salinan*
		Washo
	Shastan	Shasta,* New River Shasta,* Okwanuchu,* Konomihu*
	Palaihnihan	Achumawi (Pit River), Atsugewi (Hat Creek) (<5)
	Yanan	Northern Yana,* Central Yana,* Southern Yana,* Yahi*
	Pamoan	Northern (<5), Northeastern,* Eastern (<5), Central, Southeastern (<5), Southern (<5), Kashaya Pomo
	Yuman	Quechan, Mojave, Cocopa, Kumeyaay, Ipai, Tipai
	Chamashan	Obispeño,* Barbareño,* Ventureño,* Purisimeño,* Ynezeño,* Island*
Penutian	Costanoan (Ohlone)	Karkin,* Chochenyo,* Tamyen,* Ramaytush,* Awaswas,* Chalon,* Rumsen,* Mutsun*
	Wintun	Wintu, Nomlaki,* Patwin (<5)
	Maiduan	Maidu (<5), Konkow (<5), Nisenan (<5)
	Miwokan*	Lake Miwok (<5), Coast Miwok (<5), Bay Miwok,* Saclan,* Plains Miwok (<5), Northern Sierra Miwok, East Central Sierra Miwok, West Central Sierra Miwok, Southern Sierra Miwok
	Yokutsan	Choynumni, Chukchansi, Dumna (<5), Tachi (<5), Wukchumi, Yowlumni, Gashowu (<5) (at least 6 other extinct Yokutsan major dialects or languages)*
	Klamath-Modoc	Klamath, Modoc (<5)
Algic		Yurok
		Wiyot*
Na-Dené	Athabascan	Tolowa (<5), Hupa, Mattole,* Wailaki-Nongatl-Lassik-Sinkyone-Cahtco* (a group of related dialects, all without known speakers)
Uto-Aztecan	Numic	Mono, Owens Valley Paiute, Northern Paiute, Southern Paiute, Shoshoni, Kawaiisu, Chemehuevi
	Takic	Serrano, Cahuilla, Cupeño (<5), Luiseño, Ajachemem* (Juaneño), Tongva* (Gabrielino), Tataviam,* San Nicolas,* Kitanemuk,* Vanyume*
		Tubatulabal
Yukian		Yuki,* Wappo

*Starred languages have no known fluent native speakers (although some of them have semi-speakers). Languages with five or fewer speakers are marked "(<5)" (Hinton 1998, 217).

Source: Hinton, Leanne. 1998. Language loss and revitalization in California: Overview. In Blum, Susan (ed.), *Making Sense of Language*. New York: Oxford University Press, 216–22.

(continued on next page)

Language loss began with the arrival of European American settlers in the nineteenth century, especially in connection with the California Gold Rush. In later years, indigenous Californians were subjected to a range of disruptive and oppressive practices that undermined their cultures and reduced their numbers severely. By the 1870s, populations began to increase again, but the possibilities of preserving indigenous language and culture were bleak: most tribes had no land base, their children had been sent to boarding schools to forget indigenous traditions, and most California Indians were forced to find work in the wider, English-speaking society. "Thus, California Indians are now immersed in English. There is little or no space in the present-day way of life for the use of indigenous languages" (Hinton 1998, 218).

Recent decades have brought change, however. In the 1970s, government funds became available to support bilingual education programs for some indigenous groups. By the 1990s, laws such as the Native American Languages Act were providing additional funds for such projects. But private individuals were also attempting language revival outside these settings. In 1997, a new journal called *News from Native California* helped connect members of California tribes with one another, and a main focus of their interest became language revitalization. A few years later, the Native California Network was formed to fund projects related to traditional culture, and language became its focus as well. This network gave birth to the Advocates for Indigenous California Language Survival (AICLS), an organization that has brought many California language activists together over the years. AICLS sponsors a range of workshops and other programs that are concerned in one way or another with language revitalization.

One of the major successes of this organization has been the Master-Apprentice Language Learning Program with which Hinton has been involved. As the AICLS website explains,

An elder and a younger tribal member who are committed to learning the language are trained in one-on-one immersion techniques. The trained team members are then paid stipends so that they can devote the 10 to 20 hours per week necessary to do the work.

Key to the program is the concept that the team live their daily lives together in the language. The teams keep journals and AICLS monitors them by phone and site visits. (http://www.aicls.org/)

In addition to these formal programs, many informal efforts have been made to devise new writing systems for indigenous languages; to write books and educational materials in indigenous languages; and to offer language classes, immersion camps, or other gatherings in which students can practice their new language skills.

Those who participate in these language revitalization programs do not end up speaking their heritage languages exactly the way they used to be spoken by their ancestors. As Hinton notes, "Learners have an accent and exhibit many grammatical simplifications and influences from English, their dominant language" (Hinton 1998, 220). Although this is disappointing to some, others are determined to do the best they can under the circumstances. "A number of learners have expressed the notion that even if the future of their language takes on a pidginized form, the social value of using their language far exceeds the detriments of the change" (Hinton 1998, 220). ■

the border. Examples include Ojibwe speakers (who are better supported in Canada than in the United States) and Quichua speakers (who receive different levels of support in Ecuador, Bolivia, and Peru) (Walsh 2005, 296). And sometimes the ethnolinguistic practices of speakers can interfere with language retention: among Ilgar speakers in northern Australia, for example, conversation between opposite-sex siblings is forbidden. This means that a man finds himself "talking his mother tongue to people who don't speak it, and not talking it with the couple of people who do" (Evans 2001, 278, as cited in Walsh 2005, 297).

Attempts to implement language revitalization have met with mixed success. Methods that work for literate groups (e.g., French speakers in Quebec) may be inappropriate for programs of language revival among speakers of languages that lack a long tradition of literacy, which is often the case with indigenous languages

in the Americas and Australia (Figure 9.10). In some cases, where prospects for revitalization are poor, it has been suggested that the functions of the endangered language can be transferred to a different language. This is a well-known phenomenon in the case of colonial languages like Spanish and English, which have all experienced "indigenization" as the communities who adopt them tailor them to fit their own local communicative practices. Other scholars have pointed out that language loss is nothing new. In the ancient world, for example, the spread of Latin led to the extinction of perhaps 50 of the 60 or so languages spoken in the Mediterranean prior to 100 BCE. However, the extension of Latin into ancient Europe also led to the birth of the Romance languages, some of whose native speakers (e.g., the French) express concern that the survival of their mother tongue is also threatened by the spread of global English (Walsh 2005; Sonntag 2002). New languages emerging from the

FIGURE 9.10 Students at Waadookodaading, an Ojibwe language immersion charter school in Hayward, Wisconsin, where they are taught culture and language. The school is part of a program to revive the language by immersing children in their native language.

processes of pidginization and creolization also continue to appear. For example, Copper Island Aleut is a hybrid of Russian and Aleut (Walsh 2005, 297).

Maintaining or reviving endangered languages faces many obstacles, not the least of which is the concern of many parents who care less about preserving their dying language than they do about making sure their children become literate in a world language that will offer them a chance at economic and social mobility. Some indigenous groups are concerned that loss of language will mean loss of access to traditional sources of religious power, which can only be addressed in the traditional tongue. Yet other indigenous speakers would not like to see what was once a fully functioning mode of communication reduced to nothing but ceremonial use. Clearly, language endangerment is a very delicate topic of discussion. This is unfortunate, in Walsh's view, since practical solutions require "frank and forthright discussions of the issues . . . and good clear statements of advice" (2005, 308). But Walsh also believes that concerned people who want to save their languages ought to try to do what they can and not wait until scholarly experts arrive at a consensus.

How Are Language and Truth Connected?

For the late Thomas Kuhn, a philosopher of science, metaphor lay at the heart of science. He argued that changes in scientific theories were "accompanied by a change in some of the relevant metaphors and in corresponding

parts of the network of similarities through which terms attach to nature" (1979, 416). Kuhn insisted that these changes in the way scientific terms link to nature are not reducible to logic or grammar. "They come about in response to pressures generated by observation or experiment"—that is, by experience and context. And there is no neutral language into which rival theories can be translated and subsequently evaluated as unambiguously right or wrong (416). Kuhn asks the question, "Is what we refer to as 'the world' perhaps a product of mutual accommodation between experience and language?"

If our understanding of reality is the product of a dialectic between experience and language (or, more broadly, culture), then ambiguity will never be permanently removed from any of the symbolic systems that human beings invent. Reflexive consciousness makes humans aware of alternatives. The experience of doubt, of not being sure what to believe, is never far behind.

This is not merely the experience of people in Western societies. When E. E. Evans-Pritchard lived among the Azande of Central Africa in the early twentieth century, he found that they experienced a similar form of disorientation (see Chapter 10, "EthnoProfile 10.6: Azande"). The Azande people, he wrote, were well aware of the ambiguity inherent in language, and they exploited it by using metaphor (what they called *sanza*) to disguise speech that might be received badly if uttered directly. For example, "A man says in the presence of his wife to his friend, 'Friend, those swallows, how they flit about in there.' He is speaking about the flightiness of his wife and in case she should understand the allusion, he covers himself by looking up at the swallows as he makes his seemingly innocent remark" (Evans-Pritchard 1963, 211). Evans-Pritchard later observed that sanza "adds greatly to the difficulties of anthropological inquiry. Eventually the anthropologist's sense of security is undermined and his confidence shaken. He learns the language, can say what he wants to say in it, and can understand what he hears, but then he begins to wonder whether he has really understood . . . he cannot be sure, and even they [the Azande] cannot be sure, whether the words do have a nuance or someone imagines that they do" (228). However much we learn about language, we will never be able to exhaust its meanings or circumscribe its rules once and for all. Human language is an open system, and as long as human history continues, new forms will be created and old forms will continue to be put to new uses.

Chapter Summary

1. Symbolic language is a uniquely human faculty that both permits us to communicate with one another and sets up barriers to communication. The anthropological study of languages reveals the cultural factors that shape language use. Human symbolic language is also multifunctional, capable of performing many roles in speech events besides reference. In every language, there are many ways to communicate our experiences, and there is no absolute standard favoring one way over another. Individual efforts to create a unique voice are countered by pressures to negotiate a common code within a larger speech community.

2. Of Charles Hockett's 16 design features of language, 6 are particularly important: openness, arbitrariness, duality of patterning, displacement, semanticity, and prevarication. Among other things, Charles Peirce's three-part theory of signs provides tools for explaining how human speakers link symbolic language to the wider world outside their heads.

3. Early linguistic anthropologists like Edward Sapir and Benjamin Whorf suggested that language has the power to shape the way people see the world. This is called the "linguistic relativity principle." How this shaping process works is still investigated by some linguistic anthropologists, who argue that linguistic relativity should not be confused with linguistic determinism, which they reject.

4. Ethnopragmatics locates linguistic meaning in routine practical activities, which turn grammatical features of language into resources people can use in their interactions with others. It pays attention both to the immediate context of speech and to broader contexts that are shaped by unequal social relationships and rooted in history.

5. Because linguistic meaning is rooted in practical activity, which carries the burden of meaning, different social groups engaged in different activities generate different communicative practices. The linguistic habits that are part of each set of communicative practices constitute discourse genres. People normally command a range of discourse genres, which means that each person's linguistic knowledge is characterized by heteroglossia.

6. The study of pidgin languages is the study of the radical negotiation of new meaning. Pidgin languages exhibit many of the same linguistic features as nonpidgin languages. Studies of African American English illustrate the historical circumstances that can give rise to creoles and provide evidence of the ways in which human speech is always embedded in a social world of power differences.

7. Language ideologies are unwritten rules shared by members of a speech community concerning what kinds of language are valued. Language ideologies develop out of the cultural, social, and political histories of the groups to which they belong. Knowing the language ideology of a particular community can help listeners make sense of speech that otherwise would seem inappropriate or incomprehensible to them.

8. The design features of human language, particularly openness, seem to characterize human thought processes in general. The work of psychological anthropologists on human perception, cognition, and practical action overwhelmingly sustains the view that human psychological processes are open to a wide variety of influences.

For Review

1. What are the three reasons given in the text to explain why language is of interest to anthropologists?

2. Distinguish among language, speech, and communication.

3. Summarize the key points for each of the six design features of language discussed in the text (openness, displacement, arbitrariness, duality of patterning, semanticity, and prevarication).

4. What is the difference between closed call systems and open symbolic languages?

5. Describe the differences between linguistic competence and communicative competence.

6. Why do linguistic anthropologists emphasize the importance of context in language use?

7. What is the linguistic relativity principle? Summarize the problems with linguistic determinism and describe the steps that contemporary linguists and linguistic anthropologists have taken to address these problems.

8. Explain the differences between pidgins and creoles.

9. Summarize the research done by William Labov and subsequent scholars on African American speech patterns.

10. What is language ideology? Summarize the case studies in this section of the text that analyze the language ideology of specific speech communities.

11. What is language revitalization? What are some of the difficulties in implementing language revitalization?

Key Terms

communicative competence 285
discourse 289
ethnopragmatics 289
grammar 279

icon 281
index 281
language 278
language ideology 291

linguistic competence 285
linguistic relativity principle 286
linguistics 280

pidgin 290
pragmatics 288
raciolinguistics 294
symbol 278

Suggested Readings

Akmajian, A., R. Demers, A. Farmer, and R. Harnish. 2017. *Linguistics*, 7th ed. Cambridge, MA: MIT Press. *A fine introduction to the study of language as a formal system.*

Blum, Susan, ed. 2008. *Making sense of language: Readings in culture and communication*, 2nd ed. New York: Oxford University Press. *An engaging and accessible collection of original essays by a wide range of scholars, inside and outside anthropology, past and present, who explore the many dimensions of human language.*

Brenneis, Donald, and Ronald K. S. Macauley (eds.). 1996. *The matrix of language*. Boulder, CO: Westview Press. *A wide-ranging collection of essays by anthropologists studying linguistic habits in their sociocultural contexts.*

Burling, Robbins. 2005. *The talking ape*. Oxford: Oxford University Press. *A lively, up-to-date introduction for nonspecialists to the nature and evolution of human language, written by a distinguished linguistic anthropologist.*

Smitherman, Geneva. 1977. *Talkin and testifyin: The language of black America*. Detroit, MI: Wayne State University Press. *An engaging introduction to Black English Vernacular, for native and nonnative speakers alike, with exercises to test your mastery of African American English.*

 Visit our online resource center for further reading, web links, free assessments, flashcards, and videos. www.oup.com/he/lavenda5e

Linguistic anthropologists are trained in cultural anthropology but must also master the finer points of language structure, which is the focus of formal linguistics. This module offers brief introductions to four key areas of specialization in formal linguistics: phonology, morphology, syntax, and semantics.

Linguistic study involves a search for patterns in the way speakers use language; linguists aim to describe these patterns by reducing them to a set of rules called a **grammar**. As Edward Sapir (1921) once commented, however, "all grammars leak" (38). Over time, linguists came to recognize a growing number of language components; each new component was an attempt to plug the "leaks" in an earlier grammar, to explain what had previously resisted explanation. The following discussion pinpoints the various leaks linguists have recognized (as well as their attempts to plug the leaks) and demonstrates how culture and language influence each other.

Phonology: Sounds

The study of the sounds of language is called **phonology**. The sounds of human language are special because they are produced by a set of organs, the speech organs, that belong only to the human species (Figure M4.1). The sounds that come out of our mouths are called *phones*, and they vary continuously in acoustic properties. However, speakers of a particular language hear that language's variant phones within a particular range as functionally equivalent sounds (e.g., we hear different pronunciations of the word *pecan* as meaning the same thing).

Part of the phonologist's job is to map out possible ways that human beings use speech organs to create the sounds of language. Another part is to examine individual languages to discover the particular sound combinations they contain and the patterns into which those sound combinations are organized. No language makes use of all the many sounds the human speech organs can produce, and no two languages use exactly the same set. American English uses only 38 sounds. Most work in phonology has been done from the perspective of the speaker, who produces, or articulates, the sounds of language using the speech organs. Although all languages rely on only a handful of what are called *phonemes*—classes of functionally equivalent sounds—no two languages use exactly the same set. Furthermore, different speakers of

the same language often differ from one another in the way their phonemes are patterned, producing "accents," which constitute one kind of variety within a language. This variety is not random; the speech sounds characteristic of any particular accent follow a pattern. Speakers with different accents are usually able to understand one another in most circumstances, but their distinctive articulation is a clue to their ethnic, regional, or social class origins.

Morphology: Word Structure

Morphology, the study of how words are put together, developed as a subfield of linguistics as soon as linguists realized that the rules they had devised to explain sound patterns in language could not explain the structure of words. What is a word? English speakers tend to think of words as the building blocks of sentences and of sentences as strings of words. But words are not all alike: some words (e.g., *book*), cannot be broken down into smaller elements; others (e.g., *bookworm*) can. The puzzle becomes more complex when we try to translate words from one language into another. Sometimes expressions that require only one word in one language require more than one word in another (e.g., *préciser* in French is *to make precise* in English). Other times, we must deal with languages whose utterances cannot easily be broken down into words at all. Consider the utterance *nikookitepeena* from Shawnee (an indigenous North American language), which translates into English as "I dipped his head in the water" (Whorf 1956, 172). Although the Shawnee utterance is composed of parts, the parts do not possess the characteristics we attribute to words in, say, English or French (Table M4.1). To make sense of the structure of languages such as Shawnee, anthropological linguists needed a concept that could refer to both words (like those in the English sentence given) and the parts of an utterance that could not be broken down into words. This need led to the development of the concept of *morphemes*, traditionally defined as "the minimal units of meaning in a language." The various parts of a Shawnee utterance or an English word can be identified as morphemes. Describing minimal units of meaning as morphemes, and not as words, allows us to compare the morphology of different languages. Morphemic patterning in languages such as Shawnee may seem hopelessly complicated to native English speakers, yet the patterning of morphemes in English is equally complex. Why is it that some morphemes can stand alone as words (e.g., *sing, red*) and others cannot (*-ing, -ed*)? What determines a word boundary in the first place? Words, or the morphemes they contain, represent the fundamental point at which the arbitrary pairing of sound and meaning occurs.

grammar A set of rules that aim to describe fully the pattern of linguistic usage observed by speakers of a particular language.

phonology The study of the sounds of language.

morphology In linguistics, the study of the minimal units of meaning in a language.

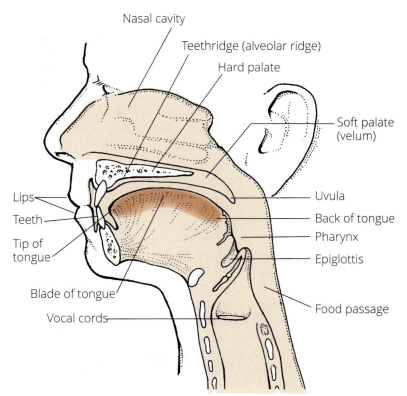

Nasal cavity

Teethridge (alveolar ridge)

Hard palate

Soft palate (velum)

Lips

Teeth

Tip of tongue

Blade of tongue

Vocal cords

Uvula

Back of tongue

Pharynx

Epiglottis

Food passage

TABLE M4.1	Morphemes of Shawnee Utterance and Their Glosses			
NI	**KOOKI**	**TEPE**	**EN**	**A**
I	immersed in water	point of action at head	by hand action	cause to him

Syntax: Sentence Structure

A third component of language is **syntax**, or sentence structure. Linguists such as Noam Chomsky began to study syntax when they discovered that morphological rules alone could not account for certain patterns of morpheme use. In languages such as English, for example, rules governing word order cannot explain what is puzzling about the following English sentence: "Smoking grass means trouble." For many native speakers of American English, this sentence exhibits what linguists call *structural ambiguity*. That is, we must ask ourselves what *trouble* means here: is it the act of smoking grass (marijuana) or observing grass (the grass that grows on the prairie) that is giving off smoke? In the first reading, *smoking* is a verb functioning as a noun; in the second, it is a verb functioning as an adjective. We can explain the ambiguity by assuming that

a word's role in a sentence depends on sentence structure and not on the structure of the word itself. Thus, sentences can be defined as ordered strings of words, and those words can be classified as parts of speech in terms of the function they fulfill in a sentence. But these two assumptions cannot account for the ambiguity in a sentence such as "The father of the girl and the boy fell into the lake." How many people fell into the lake? Just the father, or the father and the boy? Each reading of the sentence depends on how the words of the sentence are grouped together. Linguists discovered numerous other features of sentence structure that could not be explained in terms of morphology alone, leading to a growth of interest in the study of

syntax The study of sentence structure.

syntactic patterns in different languages. Although theories of syntax have changed considerably since Chomsky's early work, the recognition that syntax is a key component of human language structure remains central to contemporary linguistics.

Semantics: Meaning

For many years, linguists avoided **semantics**, the study of meaning, because *meaning* is a highly ambiguous term. What do we mean when we say that a sentence means something? We may be talking about what each individual word in the sentence means, or what the sentence as a whole means, or what I mean when I utter the sentence, which may differ from what someone else would mean even if uttering the same sentence.

In the 1960s, however, formal semantics took off when Chomsky argued that grammars needed to represent all of the linguistic knowledge in a speaker's head and that word meanings were part of that knowledge. Formal semanticists focused attention on how words are linked to one another within a language, exploring relations such as *synonymy*, or "same meaning" (e.g., *old* and *aged*); *homophony*, or "same sound, different meaning" (e.g., *would* and *wood*); and *antonymy*, or "opposite meaning" (e.g., *tall* and *short*). They also defined words in terms of denotation, or what they referred to in the "real world."

The denotations of such words as *table* or *monkey* seem fairly straightforward, but this is not the case with such words as *truth* or *and*. Moreover, even if we believe a word can be linked to a concrete object in the world, it may still be difficult to decide exactly what the term refers to. (Anthropological linguist Charles Hockett elaborated on this issue in describing the *semanticity* feature of human language.) Suppose we decide to find out what *monkey* refers to by visiting the zoo. In one cage, we see small animals with grasping hands feeding on fruit. In a second cage are much larger animals that resemble the ones in the first cage in many ways, except that they have no tails. And in a third cage are yet other animals who resemble those in the first two cages except that they are far smaller and use their long tails to swing from the branches of a tree. Which of these animals are monkeys? To answer this question, the observer

must decide which features of similarity or difference are important and which are not. Having made this decision, it is easier to decide whether the animals in the first cage are monkeys and whether the animals in the other cages are monkeys as well.

But such decisions are not easy to come by. Biologists have spent the past 300 years or so attempting to classify all living things on the planet into mutually exclusive categories. To do so they have had to decide which traits matter out of all the traits that living things exhibit. They have therefore constructed meaning in the face of ambiguity.

Formal linguistics, on the other hand, tries to deal with ambiguity by eliminating it, by "disambiguating" ambiguous utterances. To find a word's "unambiguous" denotation, we might consult a dictionary. According to the *American Heritage Dictionary*, for example, a pig is "any of several mammals of the family *Suidae*, having short legs, cloven hoofs, bristly hair, and a cartilaginous snout used for digging." A formal definition of this sort indirectly relates the word *pig* to other words in English, such as *cow* and *chicken*.

To complicate the matter, however, words also have *connotations*, additional meanings that derive from the typical contexts in which they are used in everyday speech. In the context of antiwar demonstrations in the 1960s, for example, a *pig* was a police officer. From a denotative point of view, to call police officers *pigs* is to create ambiguity deliberately, to muddle rather than to clarify. It is an example of **metaphor**, a form of figurative or nonliteral language that violates the formal rules of denotation by linking expressions from unrelated semantic domains. Metaphors are used all the time in everyday speech. Does this mean, therefore, that people who use metaphors are talking nonsense? What can it possibly mean to call police officers *pigs*?

We cannot know until we place the statement into some kind of context. If we know, for example, that protesters in the 1960s viewed the police as the paid enforcers of racist elites responsible for violence against the poor and that pigs are domesticated animals, not humans, who are often viewed as fat, greedy, and dirty, then the metaphor "police are pigs" begins to make sense. This interpretation, however, does not reveal the meaning of the metaphor for all time. In a different context, the same phrase might be used, for example, to distinguish the costumes worn by police officers to a charity function from the costumes of other groups of government functionaries. Our ability to use the same words in different ways (and different words in the same way) is the hallmark of the *openness* feature of language (Hockett 1966), and

---

semantics The study of meaning.

metaphor A form of figurative or nonliteral language that violates the formal rules of denotation by linking expressions from unrelated semantic domains.

formal semantics is powerless to contain it. Much of the referential meaning of language escapes us if we neglect the context of language use.

For Review

Prepare a chart listing the components of language identified by linguists and explain the significance of each component.

Key Terms

grammar   302

metaphor   304

morphology   302

phonology   302

semantics   304

syntax   303

10

How do we make meaning?

Human beings are creative, not just in their use of language, but also in a variety of symbolic forms. We look at several different kinds of creative symbolic forms in this chapter, including play, art, myth, ritual, and religion. But human cultural creativity is never entirely unconstrained. You will also learn about how symbolic forms are shaped by power relations in different social settings.

CHAPTER OUTLINE

What Is Play?
What Is Art?
How Does Hip-Hop Become Japanese?
What Is Ritual?

How Are Symbolic Practices and Society Related?
What Is Religion?
Two Case Studies

How Are Symbolic Practices Used as Instruments of Power?
Chapter Summary

LEARNING OBJECTIVES

- Explain the making of meaning through play and the effects of play on the human experience.
- Describe the human practice of making art as a mechanism for making meaning and how art is contested in human societies.
- Define the anthropological concepts of myth and ritual, and how they reflect and shape society and help humans think about their world.

- Define the anthropological concept of symbols and how they are negotiated in human societies.
- Discuss how anthropologists define religion and how religion is interrelated with communication and social organizations.
- Compare the Azande and Contemporary Evangelists to understand how religion is interrelated with other aspects of culture.

- Analyze how different human societies cope with change by creating new interpretations of the world around them.
- Examine how symbolic practices are used as instruments of power when different worldviews coexist.

Building on the discussion of language and symbolism from Chapter 9, this chapter looks at human play, art, myth, ritual, and religion—dimensions of human experience in which the interplay of openness and creativity encounters rules and constraints, enabling people to produce powerful and moving symbolic practices that transform the character of human life.

What Is Play?

In Chapter 9, we explored the concept of "openness" in relation to language and cognition. *Openness* was defined as the ability to talk or think about the same thing in different ways and different things in the same way. If we expand openness to include all behavior—that is, the ability not just to talk or think about but also to *do* the same thing in different ways or different things in the same way—we begin to define **play**. All mammals play, and humans play the most and throughout their lives.

Robert Fagen (1981, 1992, 2005) looks at play as a product of natural selection that may have significant fitness value for individuals in different species. Play gives young animals (including young human beings) the exercise they need to build up the skills necessary for physical survival as adults: fighting, hunting, or running away when pursued. Play may be important for the development of cognitive and motor skills and may be connected with the repair of developmental damage caused by either injury or trauma. It may also communicate the message "all's well," signaling "information about short-term and long-term health, general well-being, and biological fitness to parents, littermates, or other social companions" (Fagen 1992, 51). In species with more complex brains, playful exploration of the environment aids learning and allows for the development of behavioral versatility. Fagen (2005) suggests that play reflects natural selection for unpredictability. That is, to be able to produce unpredictable behaviors can be advantageous for an intelligent species faced with unanticipated adaptive challenges.

play A framing (or orienting context) that is (1) consciously adopted by the players; (2) somehow pleasurable; and (3) systemically related to what is nonplay by alluding to the nonplay world and by transforming the objects, roles, actions, and relations of ends and means characteristic of the nonplay world.

metacommunication Communication about the process of communication itself.

framing A cognitive boundary that marks certain behaviors as "play" or as "ordinary life."

reflexivity Critical thinking about the way one thinks; reflection on one's own experience.

How Does Play Encourage Reflexivity?

Moving from everyday reality to the reality of play requires a radical transformation of perspective. To an outside observer, the switch from everyday reality to play reality may go undetected. However, sometimes the switch can have serious consequences for other people and their activities. In this case, play and nonplay must be signaled clearly so that one is not mistaken for the other.

According to Gregory Bateson (1972), shifting into or out of play requires **metacommunication**, or communication about communication. Metacommunication provides information about the relationship between communicative partners. In play there are two kinds of metacommunication. The first, called **framing**, sends a message that marks certain behaviors either as play or as ordinary life. Dogs, for example, have a *play face*, a signal understood by other dogs (and recognizable by some human beings) indicating a willingness to play. If dogs agree to play, they bare their fangs and one animal attacks the other, but bites become nips. Both dogs have agreed to enter the *play frame*, an imaginative world in which bites do not mean bites. Within the play frame, a basic element of Western logic—that *A* = *A*—does not apply; the same thing is being treated in different ways. Human beings have many ways of marking the play frame: a smile, a particular tone of voice, a referee's whistle, or the words "Let's pretend." The marker says that "everything from now until we end this activity is set apart from everyday life." The second kind of metacommunication involves **reflexivity**. Play offers us the opportunity to think about the social and cultural dimensions of the world in which we live. By suggesting that ordinary life can be understood in more than one way, play can be a way of speculating about what can be rather than about what should be or what is (Handelman 1977, 186). When we say that jokes keep us from taking ourselves too seriously, for example, we are engaging in reflexive metacommunication. Joking allows us to consider alternative, even ridiculous, explanations for our experience.

What Are Some Effects of Play?

Helen Schwartzman (1978, 232–45) has demonstrated how play, through satire and clowning, may allow children to comment on and criticize the world of adults. A powerful example of this kind of commentary is described by anthropologist Elizabeth Chin, who studied African American girls and their dolls in Newhallville, a working-class and poor neighborhood in New Haven, Connecticut. Although "ethnically correct" dolls are on the market, very few of the girls had them because they cost too much. The poor children Chin knew in

Newhallville had white dolls. But in their play, these girls transformed their dolls in a powerful way by giving them hairstyles like their own. The designers gave the dolls smooth, flowing hair to be brushed over and over again and put into a ponytail. But the girls' dolls had beads in their hair, braids held at the end with twists of aluminum foil or barrettes, and braids that were themselves braided together (Chin 1999, 315). As Chin observed, "In some sense, by doing this, the girls bring their dolls into their own worlds, and whiteness here is not absolutely defined by skin and hair, but by style and way of life. The complexities of racial references and racial politics have been much discussed in the case of black hair simulating the look of whiteness; what these girls are creating is quite the opposite: white hair that looks black" (315). It is not that the girls did not realize that their dolls were white; it is that through their imaginative and material work they were able to integrate the dolls into their own world. The overt physical characteristics of the dolls—skin color, facial features, hair—did not force the girls into treating the dolls in ways that obeyed the boundaries of racial difference. Their transformative play does not make the realities of poverty, discrimination, and racism disappear from the worlds in which they live; but Chin points out that "in making their white dolls live in black worlds, they . . . reconfigure the boundaries of race" and in so doing "challenge the social construction not only of their own blackness, but of race itself as well" (318) (Figure 10.1).

What Is Art?

In Western societies, art includes sculpture, drawing, painting, dance, theater, music, and literature, as well as such similar processes and products as film, photography, mime, mass media production, oral narrative, festivals, and national celebrations. These are the kinds of objects and activities that first caught the attention of anthropologists who wanted to study art in non-Western societies. Whether non-Western peoples referred to such activities or products as "art," however, is a separate question. People everywhere engage in these kinds of playful creativity, yet activities defined as art differ from free play because they are circumscribed by rules. Artistic rules direct particular attention to, and provide standards for evaluating, the *form* of the activities or objects that artists produce.

Is There a Definition of Art?

Anthropologist Alexander Alland (1977) defines **art** as "play with form producing some aesthetically successful transformation-representation" (39). For Alland, *form* refers to the rules of the art game: the culturally appropriate restrictions on the way this kind of play may be organized in time and space. We can also think about form in terms of style and media. A *style* is a schema (a distinctive patterning of elements) that is recognized within a culture as appropriate to a given medium. The media themselves in which art is created and executed are culturally recognized and characterized (Anderson 1990, 272–75). A painting is a form: it is two-dimensional; it is done in the medium of paint (oil, acrylic, water color, etc.); it is intentionally made; it represents or symbolizes something in the world outside the canvas, paper, or wood on which it is created. There are different kinds of paintings as well. There is the painting form called "portrait"—a portrait depicts a person, it resembles the person in some appropriate way, it is done with paint, it can be displayed, and more.

By "aesthetic," Alland (1977, xii) means appreciative of, or responsive to, form in art or nature. "Aesthetically successful" means that the creator of the piece of art (and possibly its audience) responds positively or negatively to it ("I like this," "I hate this"). Indifference is the sign of something that is aesthetically unsuccessful. It is

FIGURE 10.1   Play enables this girl in Guider, Cameroon, to incorporate her European doll into the world she knows.

art "Play with form producing some aesthetically successful transformation-representation" (Alland 1977, 39).

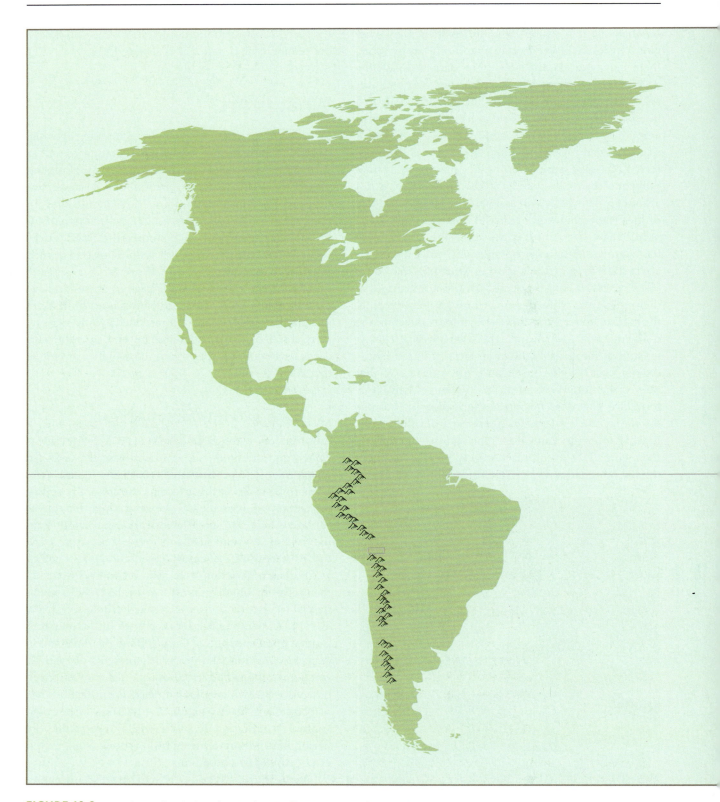

FIGURE 10.2 Locations of societies whose EthnoProfiles appear in Chapter 10.

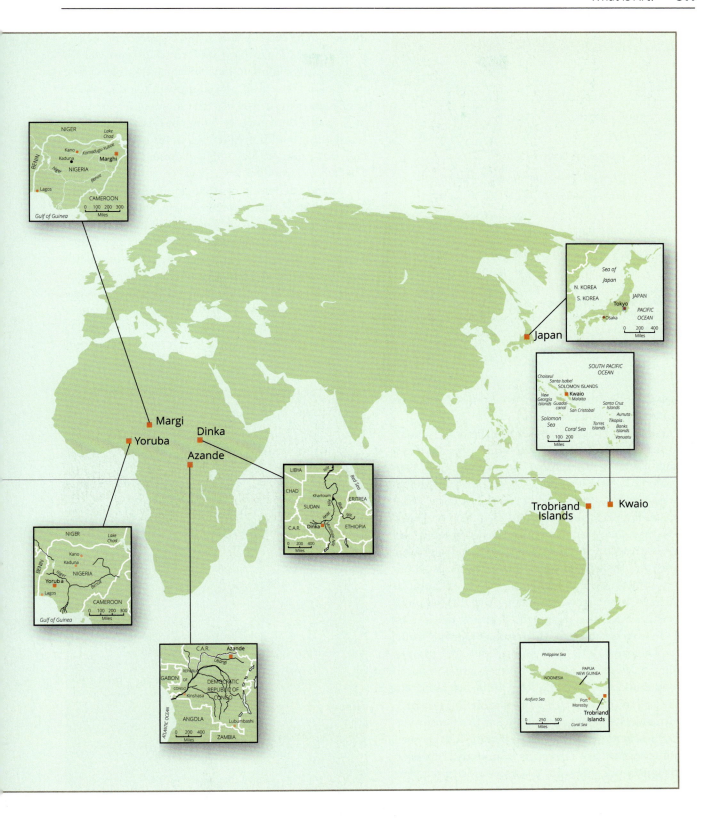

EthnoProfile 10.1

Margi

Region: Western Africa

Nation: Nigeria

Population: 100,000 to 200,000 (1960s)

Environment: Mountains and plains

Livelihood: Farming, selling surplus in local markets

Political organization: Traditionally, kingdoms; today, part of a modern nation-state

For more information: Vaughan, James. 2006. *The Mandara Margi: A society living on the verge.* http://www.indiana.edu/~margi/

the hero in his work; but he is also transforming a three-dimensional human form into a two-dimensional flat puppet made of buffalo hide, in which the colors, style, inclination of the head, and adornment stand for the internal state of the hero at a specific moment (Figure 10.3). At the same time, he is carrying out this work more or less skillfully and is representing in his work the meanings that Arjuna carries for his Javanese audience (see Chapter 9, "EthnoProfile 9.2: Java").

Alland's definition of art attempts to capture something universal about human beings and cultural creativity. Similarly, anthropologist Shelly Errington (1998) observes that all human cultures have "'symbolic forms': artifacts, activities, or even aspects of the landscape that humans view as densely meaningful" (84). One dramatic example in the United States that demonstrates the power of art as a densely meaningful landscape is the Vietnam Veterans Memorial in Washington, DC (Figure 10.4). This work by architect Maya Lin not only

probably the case that the aesthetic response is a universal feature in all human societies.

Aesthetic value judgments guide the artist's choice of form and material; they also guide the observers' evaluations. This implies that art involves more than just objects. V. N. Voloshinov ([1926] 1987) argues that art is a creative "event of living communication" (107) involving the work, the artist, and the artist's audience. Artists create their works with an audience in mind, and audiences respond to these works as if the works were addressed to them. Sometimes their response is enthusiastic; sometimes it is highly critical. In addition, if aesthetic creation involves more than just the end product, such as a painting or a poem, attention needs to be paid to the *process* through which some product is made. James Vaughan (1973, 186) pointed out, for example, that in the 1960s, the Margi of northeastern Nigeria do not appreciate a folktale as a story per se but rather enjoy the *performance* of it (see "EthnoProfile 10.1: Margi").

To understand what Alland means by "transformation-representation," we can recall that the link between a symbol and what it represents is arbitrary. This separation makes possible what Jakobson called the poetic function of language. But *all* symbols can be separated from the object or idea represented and appreciated for their own sake. They may also be used to represent a totally different meaning. Because transformation and representation depend on each other, Alland (1977, 35) suggests that they be referred to together (i.e., as transformation-representation). When a Javanese leather-puppet maker makes a puppet of the great mythic hero Arjuna, for example, he is representing the traditional form of

FIGURE 10.3 One of the great mythic heroes of Javanese wajang is represented here in a beautifully painted, flat, leather shadow puppet. The color of the image, the angle of the head, the shape of the eye, the position of the fingers, and the style, color, and quantity of clothing all represent the inner state of the hero.

FIGURE 10.4   The Vietnam Veterans Memorial is a powerfully affecting work of art that speaks directly to central issues in the culture of the United States.

has impressed art critics but also continues to have a profound aesthetic and emotional impact on hundreds of thousands of people who visit it each year. The memorial continues to draw offerings by visitors, not just wreaths or flowers but also messages of all kinds remembering those memorialized and even communicating with them. Letters from friends and families, a hand-lettered sign from a long-ago high school class in a small Indiana town, tracings of names, intensely private grief, and respectful silence in its presence are all testimony to the success of this piece of art.

"But Is It Art?"

Many people—anthropologists included—have resisted the notion that art is only what a group of Western experts define as art. To highlight the ethnocentrism of Western art experts, they have stressed that the division into categories of art and nonart is not universal. In many societies, there is no word that corresponds to "art," nor is there a category of art distinct from other human activities. On the other hand, convinced that all people were endowed with the same aesthetic capacities, anthropologists felt justified in speaking of art and of

artists in non-Western societies. Their goal was to recognize a fully human capacity for art in all societies but to redefine art until it became broad enough to include on an equal basis aesthetic products and activities that Western art experts would qualify, at best, as "primitive," "ethnic," or "folk" art.

For example, some anthropologists focused on the evaluative standards that artists use for their own work and other work in the same form and how these may differ from the standards used by people who do not themselves perform such work. Anthony Forge (1967), for example, noted that Abelam carvers in New Guinea discuss carvings in a language that was more incisive than that of noncarvers. Forge and other anthropologists pointed out that artists in traditional non-Western societies created objects or engaged in activities that reinforced the central values of their culture. Thus, their work helped to maintain the social order, and the artists did not see themselves as (nor were they understood to be) avant-garde critics of society as they often are in modern Western societies. Forge (1967) reported that Abelam artworks are statements about male violence and warfare, male nurturance, and the combination of the two. These statements about the nature of men and their culture are not made by other means of communication, such as speech. At the same time, he insisted that these statements were essential to Abelam social structure.

Recent work in the anthropology of art, however, has prompted many anthropologists to rethink Forge's position. They have turned their attention to the way certain kinds of material objects made by tribal peoples flow into a global art market, where they are transformed into "primitive" or "ethnic" art. Some anthropologists, like Shelly Errington (1998), point out that even in the West, most of the objects in fine arts museums today, no matter where they came from, were not intended by their makers to be "art." They were intended to be, for example, masks for ritual use; paintings for religious contemplation; reliquaries for holding the relics of saints, ancestor figures, furniture, jewelry boxes, architectural details, and so on. They are in fine arts museums today because at some point they were claimed to be art by someone with the authority to put them in the museum (Figure 10.5).

For these reasons, Errington (1998) distinguishes "art by intention" from "art by appropriation." Art by intention includes objects that were made to be art, such as Impressionist paintings. Art by appropriation, however, consists of all the other objects that "became art" because at a certain moment certain people decided that they belonged to the category of art. Because museums, art dealers, and art collectors are found everywhere in the world today, it is now the case that potentially any material object crafted by human hands can be appropriated by these institutions as "art."

To transform an object into art, Errington argues, it must have *exhibition value*—someone must be willing to display it. Objects that somehow fit into the Western definition of art will be selected for the art market as "art." Looking at the collection of objects that over the years have been defined as "art," Errington (1998) sees that the vast majority show certain elements to be embedded rather deeply in the Western definition of art: the objects are "portable (paintings, preferred to murals), durable (bronze preferred to basketry), useless for practical purposes in the secular West (ancestral effigies and Byzantine icons preferred to hoes and grain grinders), [and] representational (human and animal figures preferred to, say, heavily decorated ritual bowls)" (116–17). In other words, for Errington, art requires that someone *intend* that the objects be art, but that someone does not have to be the objects' creator.

It can be fruitful to talk about art as a kind of play. Like play, art presents its creators and participants with alternative realities, a separation of means from ends, and the possibility of commenting on and transforming the everyday world. In today's global art market, however, restrictions of an entirely different order also apply. Errington (1998) observes that the people who make "primitive art" are no longer "tribal" but have become

> modern-day peasants or a new type of proletariat. . . . They live in rain forests and deserts and other such formerly out-of-the-way places on the peripheries . . . within national and increasingly global systems of buying and selling, of using natural and human resources, and of marketing images and notions about products. Some lucky few of them make high ethnic art, and sell it for good prices, and obtain a good portion of the proceeds. Others make objects classed as tourist or folk art, usually for much less money, and often through a middleperson. (268)

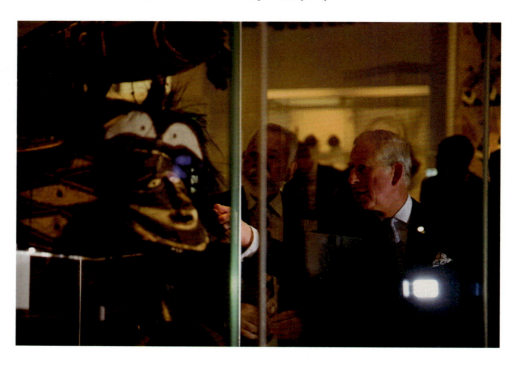

FIGURE 10.5 Non-Western sculpture is transformed into art when it is displayed like Western art in a museum and viewed by a public that has the opportunity to look at it intensively (in this case, by Prince Charles).

IN THEIR OWN WORDS

Tango

Anthropologist Julie Taylor describes the traditional cultural understandings that inform the contexts in which the Argentine tanguero, or tango-man, dances the tango.

Traditionally, Argentines will not dance to a tango that is sung. If they danced they could not attend properly to the music and lyrics, or hear their own experience and identity revealed in the singer's and musicians' rendering of quintessential Argentine emotions. The singer of the tango shares his personal encounter with experiences common to them all. He does not need bold pronouncement or flamboyant gesture. His audience knows what he means and his feelings are familiar ones. They listen for the nuances—emotional and philosophical subtleties that will tell them something new about their guarded interior worlds.

When they dance to tangos, Argentines contemplate themes akin to those of tango lyrics, stimulating emotions that, despite an apparently contradictory choreography, are the same as those behind the songs. The choreography also reflects the world of the lyrics, but indirectly. The dance portrays an encounter between the powerful and completely dominant male and the passive, docile, completely submissive female. The passive woman and the rigidly controlled but physically aggressive man contrast poignantly with the roles of the sexes depicted in the tango lyrics. This contrast between two statements of relations between the sexes aptly mirrors the insecurities of life and identity.

An Argentine philosophy of bitterness, resentment, and pessimism has the same goal as a danced statement of machismo, confidence, and sexual optimism. The philosopher elaborates his schemes to demonstrate that he is a man of the world—that he is neither stupid nor naive. In the dance, the dancer acts as though he has none of the fears he cannot show—again proving that he is not *gil*. When an Argentine talks of the way he feels when dancing a tango, he describes an experience of total aggressive dominance over the girl, the situation, the world—an experience in which he vents his resentment and expresses his bitterness against a destiny that denied him this dominance. Beyond this, it gives him a moment behind the protection of this facade to ponder the history and the land that have formed him, the hopes he has treasured and lost. Sábato echoes widespread feeling in Argentina when he says "Only a gringo would make a clown of himself by taking advantage of a tango for a chat or amusement."

While thus dancing a statement of invulnerability, the somber tanguero sees himself, because of his sensitivity, his great capacity to love, and his fidelity to the true ideals of his childhood years, as basically vulnerable. As he protects himself with a facade of steps that demonstrate perfect control, he contemplates his absolute lack of control in the face of history and destiny. The nature of the world has doomed him to disillusionment, to a solitary existence in the face of the impossibility of perfect love and the intimacy this implies. If by chance the girl with whom he dances feels the same sadness, remembering similar disillusion, the partners do not dance sharing the sentiment. They dance together to relive their disillusion alone. In a Buenos Aires dance hall, a young man turned to me from the fiancee he had just relinquished to her chaperoning mother and explained, "In the tango, together with the girl—and it does not matter who she is—a man remembers the bitter moments of his life, and he, she, and all who are dancing contemplate a universal emotion. I do not like the woman to talk to me while I dance tango. And if she speaks I do not answer. Only when she says to me, 'Omar, I am speaking,' I answer, 'And I, I am dancing.'"

Source: Taylor 1987, 484–85.

Others fulfill orders from elsewhere, "producing either masses of 'folk art' or expensive handmade items designed by people in touch with world taste and world markets" (269). Errington points out the bitter irony that international demand for "exotic" objects is growing at the very moment when the makers of these objects are severely threatened by international economic policies and resource-extraction projects that impoverish them and undermine the ways of life that give the objects they make their exotic allure. It should also be noted that what counts as fashionable decoration this year—"world taste"—may be out of fashion next year, leaving the producers with very little to fall back on.

"She's Fake": Art and Authenticity

Michelle Bigenho is an anthropologist and violinist whose multisited ethnography, mentioned in Module 3, "On Ethnographic Methods," examines music performance in Bolivia, in part through her experiences performing with Música de Maestros (Figure 10.6). This ensemble performs the works of master Bolivian composers of the past and attempts to recreate accurate performances of contemporary original music that they have studied in the countryside (Bigenho 2002, 4). The ensemble included both classically trained and traditionally trained musicians, and three were foreigners: a Japanese who played the Andean flute; a Cuban who played violin; and Bigenho, from the United States, who also played violin. Along with a local dance ensemble, the musicians were invited to represent Bolivia in a folklore festival in France. As the bands were lining up, a member of the Belgian delegation walked over to Bigenho and announced, in French, "She's fake." The Belgian woman then "pointed to one of the Bolivian dancers dressed in her dancing costume with her long fake braids worked into her short brown hair. As she pointed, she said, 'She's real'" (Bigenho 2002, 88).

In this way, Bigenho raises the issue of the connection between "authenticity" and so-called folk art. How do the images that people in dominant nations have of "folk" or indigenous peoples affect the production and circulation of indigenous art? Can a Bolivian band include musicians from Japan, Cuba, and the United States and still be Bolivian? And who gets to decide what is authentic? Bigenho discusses a kind of authenticity that she calls "unique authenticity," which refers to the individual artist's new, innovative, and personal production,

such as the original compositions of creative musicians. Unique authenticity is "the founding myth of modern concepts of authorship and copyright" (Bigenho 2002, 20). It concerns who owns cultural products and raises the issue of whether it is possible to talk about collective creation and ownership of the music of a community, a people, or an ethnic group.

Bigenho came face to face with this issue when she compiled a cassette of music from one of the villages where she worked. While the villagers recognized that the music they played was composed by individuals, they felt strongly that ownership of the music was collective. In doing so, they moved from uniquely authentic individual compositions—intellectual property—to collective ownership of a "culturally authentic representation": cultural property (Bigenho 2002, 217). She discussed with the villagers how to register the copyright on the cassette. When Bigenho went to La Paz to register the copyright, however, she found that it was impossible to register the cassette under collective authorship or ownership. Ironically, *she* as the compiler could register the work but the people who created the work could not, unless they were willing to be recognized as individuals. According to Bolivian law, the music on the cassette was legally folklore, "the set of literary and artistic works created in national territory by unknown authors or by authors who do not identify themselves and are presumed to be nationals of the country, or of its ethnic communities, and that are transmitted from generation to generation, constituting one of the fundamental elements of traditional cultural patrimony of the nation" (Bigenho 2002, 221). As a result, the music was part of the "national patrimony" and belonged to the nation-state. Given the context of

FIGURE 10.6 Música de Maestros in costume performing in a folklore festival in France.

Bolivian cultural and ethnic politics, Bigenho reports that the villagers decided to try to gain visibility and connections as a collective indigenous entity, which they believed would provide them with possible economic advantages; whether this belief was accurate remains to be seen. But similar struggles over the relationship between art and authenticity can be found all over the world.

How Does Hip-Hop Become Japanese?

An opposite case—where global popular culture is subject to pressures from the local situation into which it is adopted—comes from anthropologist Ian Condry's work on Japanese hip-hop. Starting in mid-1995, Condry spent a year and a half studying hip-hop in Japan, which began there in the 1980s and continues to develop. It seems to be an example of the expansion of a popular culture form from the United States into another part of the world, but Condry shows how Japanese artists and fans have adapted hip-hop so that it is Japanese (Figure 10.7).

On the face of it, the Japanese hip-hop scene looks very similar to that of the United States: "It is more than a little eerie to fly from New York to Tokyo and see teenagers in both places wearing the same kinds of fashion characteristic of rap fans: baggy pants with boxers on display, floppy hats or baseball caps, and immaculate space-age Nike sneakers" (Condry 2001, 373). But the similarities disguise some important differences—most Japanese rappers and fans only speak Japanese, they live

at home with their parents, and they are the products of the Japanese educational system. Their day-to-day world is Japanese.

Moreover, to understand hip-hop in Japan requires understanding where the rap scene in Japan is located. For Tokyo, this site (Condry uses the Japanese word *genba* for the "actual site") is the network of all-night clubs, where the show starts at midnight and ends at 5:00 a.m., when the trains start to run again. The largest of these clubs can accommodate over 1,000 people on the weekend. Condry describes one of the bigger clubs, called "Harlem":

> On the wall behind the DJ stage, abstract videos, *anime* clips, or edited Kung Fu movies present a background of violence and mayhem, albeit with an Asian flavor. Strobe lights, steam, and moving spotlights give a strong sense of the space, and compound the crowded, frenetic feeling imposed by the loud music. The drunken revelry gives clubs an atmosphere of excitement that culminates with the live show and the following freestyle session. (Condry 2001, 376–77)

But it is not only the music that matters. People circulate through the club, sometimes making contact, sometimes doing business (promoters, magazine writers, or record company representatives are also often there), just being part of the scene. Condry notes that he found that the time between 3:00 and 4:00 a.m. was best for his fieldwork because the clubbers had exhausted their supplies of stories and gossip and were open to finding out what he was up to (see "EthnoProfile 10.2: Japan").

One striking experience that Condry observed was of a concert right after the New Year. "I was surprised to see all the clubbers who knew each other going around

FIGURE 10.7 Japanese hip-hop artists perform at the Moshi Moshi Nippon Festival in Tokyo, Japan. While the hip-hop scene in Japan may look similar to that in the United States, Ian Condry directs attention to some significant differences.

EthnoProfile 10.2

Japan

Region: Northeastern Asia

Nation: Japan

Population: 118,000,000

Environment: Temperate climate

Livelihood: Full range of occupations to be found in a core industrial nation-state

Political organization: Highly urbanized nation-state

For more information: Kondo, Dorinne K. 1990. *Crafting selves: Power, gender, and discourses of identity in a Japanese workplace.* Chicago: University of Chicago Press.

and saying the traditional New Year's greeting in very formal Japanese: 'Congratulations on the dawn of the New Year. I humbly request your benevolence this year as well.' There was no irony, no joking atmosphere in these statements" (Condry 2001, 380). As he remarks, "Japanese cultural practices do not disappear" just because people seem to conform to the style of global hip-hop. In the same way, the topics addressed in the lyrics speak in some way to the concerns of the listeners, ridiculing school and television or celebrating video games and young men's verbal play. Most striking, perhaps, is the repeated theme that youth need to speak out for themselves. Rapper MC Shiro of Rhymester remarked, "If I were to say what hip-hop is, it would be a 'culture of the first person singular.' In hip-hop, . . . rappers are always yelling, 'I'm this'" (Condry 2001, 383). While this may not appear to be the edgy, tough lyrics of US rap, in the Japanese context, where the dominant ideology is that the harmony of the group should come before individual expression, the idea that people should speak for themselves is powerful. This process of localizing the global is one that many anthropologists are now studying.

myths Stories that recount how various aspects of the world came to be the way they are. The power of myths comes from their ability to make life meaningful for those who accept them. The truth of myths seems self-evident because they effectively integrate personal experiences with a wider set of assumptions about how the world works.

What Is Myth?

We have suggested that play lies at the heart of human creativity. However, because the openness of play seems random and thus just as likely to undermine the social order as to enhance it, societies tend to surround play with cultural rules, channeling it in directions that appear less destructive. Rules designed to discipline artistic expression are one result of this channeling process. As we have seen, artists in various media are permitted a wide range of expression as long as they adhere to rules governing the form that expression takes. Societies differ in how loose or strict the rules of artistic form may be. Artists who challenge the rules, however, are often viewed negatively by those in power, who believe they have the right to restrict artistic expressions that question social, religious, or sexual precepts that ought not to be questioned.

In fact, all societies depend on the willingness of their members to not question certain assumptions about the way the world works. Because the regularity and predictability of social life might collapse altogether if people were free to imagine and act on their own understandings of the world, most societies find ways to restrict the available options through the use of myth. As we saw in Module 1, "Anthropology, Science, and Storytelling," many people take the word *myth* to mean something that is false. But for anthropologists, **myths** are stories that recount how various aspects of the world came to be the way they are. The power of myths comes from their ability to make life meaningful for those who accept them. The truth of myths seems self-evident because they do such a good job of integrating personal experiences with a wider set of assumptions about how the world works. As stories that involve a teller and an audience, myths are products of high verbal art (and increasingly of cinematic art). Frequently, the official myth-tellers are the ruling groups in society: the elders, the political leaders, the religious specialists. They may also be considered master storytellers. The content of myths usually concerns past events (usually at the beginning of time) or future events (usually at the end of time). Myths are socially important because, if they are taken literally, they tell people where they have come from and where they are going and, thus, how they should live right now (Figure 10.8).

Societies differ in the degree to which they permit speculation about key myths. In complex Western societies such as that of the United States, many different groups, each with its own mythic tradition, often live side by side. Ironically, Americans' rights to do so without state interference are guaranteed in mythic statements

FIGURE 10.8   A vase painting illustrating part of the Popul Vuh, the Mayan creation story.

from documents crafted at the time of this country's founding. Consider the "self-evident" truths proclaimed in the US Declaration of Independence: "that all men are created equal, that they are endowed by their Creator with certain inalienable rights, that among these rights are life, liberty, and the pursuit of happiness." Despite the imperfect realization of these rights over the centuries, Americans still appeal to the self-evident truths enshrined in the Declaration of Independence in ongoing struggles to establish the equality of all citizens under the law. That is, US citizens are striving to bring their lived reality in line with the Declaration's mythic proclamation, the truth of which remains unquestioned.

Myths and related beliefs that are taken to be self-evident truths are sometimes codified in an explicit manner. When this codification is extreme and deviation from the code is treated harshly, we sometimes speak of **orthodoxy** (or "correct doctrine"). Societies differ in the degree to which they require members to adhere to orthodox interpretations of key myths. But even societies that place little emphasis on orthodoxy are likely to exert some control over the interpretation of key myths because myths have implications for action. They may justify past action, explain present action, or generate future action. To be persuasive, myths must offer plausible explanations for our experience of human nature, human society, and human history.

The success of Western science has led many members of Western societies to dismiss nonscientific myths as flawed attempts at science or history. Only recently have some scientists come to recognize the similarities between scientific and nonscientific storytelling about such events as the origin of life on earth. Scientific stories about origins, *origin myths*, must be taken to the natural world to be matched against material evidence;

the success of this match determines whether they are accepted or rejected. By contrast, nonscientific origin myths get their vitality from how well they match up with the social world.

How Does Myth Reflect—and Shape—Society?

Early in the twentieth century, anthropologist Bronislaw Malinowski introduced a new approach to myth. He believed that to understand myths we must understand the social context in which they are embedded. Malinowski argued that myths serve as "charters" or "justifications" for present-day social arrangements. In other words, a myth operates much like the Declaration of Independence. That is, the myth contains some "self-evident" truth that explains why society is as it is and why it cannot be changed. If the social arrangements justified by the myth are challenged, the myth can be used as a weapon against the challengers.

Malinowski's famous example is of the origin myths of the Trobriand Islanders ([1926] 1948; see "EthnoProfile 10.3: Trobriand Islanders"). Members of every significant kinship grouping knew, marked, and retold the history of the place from which their group's ancestress and her brother had emerged from the depths of the earth. These origin myths were set in the time before history began. Each ancestress-and-brother pair brought a distinct set of characteristics that included special objects and knowledge, as well as various skills, crafts, spells, and the like. On reaching the surface, the pair took possession of the land. That is why, Malinowski was

orthodoxy "Correct doctrine"; the prohibition of deviation from approved mythic texts.

EthnoProfile 10.3

Trobriand Islanders

Region: Oceania

Nation: Papua New Guinea

Population: 8,500 (1970s)

Environment: Tropical island

Livelihood: Yam growing

Political organization:
Traditionally, chiefs and others of rank; today, part of a modern nation-state

For more information:
Weiner, Annette. 1988. *The Trobrianders of Papua New Guinea*. New York: Holt, Rinehart and Winston.

told, the people on a given piece of land had rights to it. It is also why they possessed a particular set of spells, skills, and crafts. Because the original sacred beings were a woman and her brother, the origin myth could also be used to endorse present-day membership in a Trobriand clan, which depends on a person's ability to trace kinship links through women to that clan's original ancestress. A brother and a sister represent the prototypical members of a clan because they are both descended from the ancestress through female links. Should anyone question the wisdom of organizing society in this way, the myth could be cited as proof that this is indeed the correct way to live.

In Trobriand society, Malinowski found, clans were ranked relative to one another in terms of prestige. To account for this ranking, Trobrianders referred to another myth. In the Trobriand myth that explains rank, one clan's ancestor, the dog, emerged from the earth before another clan's ancestor, the pig, thus justifying ranking the dog clan highest in prestige. To believe in this myth, Malinowski asserted, is to accept a transcendent justification for the ranking of clans. Malinowski made it clear, however, that if social arrangements change, the myth changes too—to justify the new arrangements. At some point, the dog clan was replaced in prominence by the pig clan. This social change resulted in a change in the mythic narrative. The dog was said to have eaten food that was taboo. In so doing, the dog gave up its claim to higher rank. Thus, to understand a myth and its transformations, one must understand the social organization of the society that makes use of it.

Do Myths Help Us Think?

Beginning in the mid-1950s, a series of books and articles by the French anthropologist Claude Lévi-Strauss (1967) transformed the study of myth. Lévi-Strauss argues that myths have meaningful structures that are worth studying in their own right, quite apart from the uses to which the myths may be put. He suggested that myths should be interpreted the way we interpret musical scores. In a piece of music, the meaning emerges not just from the melody but also from the harmony. In other words, the structure of the piece of music, the way in which each line of the music contributes to the overall sound and is related to other lines, carries the meaning.

For Lévi-Strauss, myths are tools for overcoming logical contradictions that cannot otherwise be overcome. They are put together in an attempt to deal with the oppositions of particular concern to a particular society at a particular moment in time. Using a linguistic metaphor, Lévi-Strauss argues that myths are composed of smaller units—phrases, sentences, words, relationships—that are arranged in ways that give both a linear, narrative (or "melodic") coherence and a multilevel, structural (or "harmonic") coherence. These arrangements represent and comment on aspects of social life that are thought to oppose each other. Examples include the opposition of men to women; opposing rules of residence after marriage (living with the groom's father or the bride's mother); the opposition of the natural world to the cultural world, of life to death, of spirit to body, of high to low, and so on.

The complex syntax of myth works to relate those opposed pairs to one another in an attempt to overcome their contradictions. However, these contradictions can never be overcome; for example, the opposition of death to life is incapable of any earthly resolution. But myth can transform an insoluble problem into a more accessible, concrete form. Mythic narrative can then provide the concrete problem with a solution. For example, a culture hero may bridge the opposition between death and life by traveling from the land of the living to the land of the dead and back. Alternatively, a myth might propose that the beings who transcend death are so horrific that death is clearly preferable to eternal life. Perhaps a myth describes the journey of a bird that travels from the earth, the home of the living, to the sky, the home of the dead. This is similar to Christian thought, where the death and resurrection of Jesus may be understood to resolve the opposition between death and life by transcending death.

From this point of view, myths do not just talk about the world as it is but also describe the world as it might be. To paraphrase Lévi-Strauss, myths are good to think with; mythic thinking can propose other ways to live our lives. Lévi-Strauss insists, however, that the alternatives that myths propose are ordinarily rejected as impossible. Thus, although myths allow for play with self-evident truths, this play remains under strict control.

Is Lévi-Strauss correct? There has been a great deal of debate on this issue since the publication in 1955 of his article "The Structural Study of Myth" (see Lévi-Strauss 1967). But even those who are most critical of his analyses of particular myths agree that mythic structures are meaningful because they display the ability of human beings to play with possibilities as they attempt to deal with basic contradictions at the heart of human experience.

For Malinowski, Lévi-Strauss, and their followers, those who believe in myths are not conscious of how their myths are structured or of the functions their myths perform for them. More recent anthropological thinking takes a more reflexive approach. This research recognizes that ordinary members of a society often *are* aware of how their myths structure meaning, allowing them to manipulate the way myths are told or interpreted to make an effect, to prove a point, or to buttress a particular perspective on human nature, society, or history.

What Is Ritual?

Play allows unlimited consideration of alternative perspectives on reality. Art permits consideration of alternative perspectives, but certain limitations restricting the form and content are imposed. Myth aims to narrow radically the possible perspectives and often promotes a single, orthodox perspective presumed to be valid for everyone. It thus offers a kind of intellectual indoctrination. But because societies aim to shape action as well as thought to orient all human faculties in the approved direction, art, myth, and ritual are often closely associated with one another. In this section, we will look at ritual as a form of action in a variety of societies.

How Can Ritual Be Defined?

For many people in Western societies, rituals are presumed to be religious—for example, weddings, Jewish bar mitzvahs, Hmong sacrifices to the ancestors, or the Catholic Mass. For anthropologists, however, rituals also include practices such as scientific experiments, college graduation ceremonies, procedures in a court of law, and children's birthday parties.

To capture this range of activities, our definition of **ritual** has four parts. First, ritual is a repetitive social practice composed of a sequence of symbolic activities in the form of dance, song, speech, gestures, the manipulation of certain objects, and so forth. Second, it is set off from the social routines of everyday life. Third, rituals in any culture adhere to a characteristic, culturally defined schema. This means that members of a culture can tell that a certain sequence of activities is a ritual even if they have never seen that particular ritual before. Fourth, ritual action is closely connected to a specific set of ideas that are often encoded in myth. These ideas might concern, for example, the relationship of human beings to the spirit world, how human beings ought to interact with one another, or the nature of evil. The purpose for which a ritual is performed guides how these ideas are selected and symbolically enacted. What gives rituals their power is that the people who perform them assert that the authorization for the ritual comes from outside themselves—from the state, society, a divine being, god, the ancestors, or "tradition." They have not made up the ritual themselves; rather, it connects them to a source of power that they do not control but that controls them.

How Is Ritual Expressed in Action?

A ritual has a particular sequential ordering of acts, utterance, and events: that is, ritual has a *text*. Because ritual is action, however, we must pay attention to the way the ritual text is performed. The performance of a ritual cannot be separated from its text; text and performance shape each other. Through ritual performance, the ideas of a culture become concrete, take on a form, and, as Bruce Kapferer (1983) puts it, give direction to the gaze of participants. At the same time, ritual performers are not robots but active individuals whose choices are guided but not rigidly dictated by previous ritual texts; ritual performance can serve as a commentary on the text and even transform it. For example, Jewish synagogue ritual following the reading from the Torah (the five books of Moses, the Hebrew Bible) includes lifting the Torah scroll, showing it to the congregation, and then closing it and covering it. In some synagogues, a man and a woman, often a couple, are called from the congregation to lift and cover the Torah: the man lifts it and, after he seats himself, the woman rolls the scroll closed, places the tie around it, and covers it with the mantle that protects it. One of the authors once observed a performance of this ritual in which the woman lifted the Torah and

---

ritual A repetitive social practice composed of a sequence of symbolic activities in the form of dance, song, speech, gestures, or the manipulation of objects; set off from the social routines of everyday life; adhering to a culturally defined ritual schema; and closely connected to a specific set of ideas that are often encoded in myth.

the man wrapped it; officially, the ritual text was carried out, but the performance became a commentary on the text—on the role of women in Judaism, on the Torah as an appropriate subject of attention for women as well as for men, on the roles of men and women overall, and so on. The performance was noteworthy—indeed, many of the regular members of the congregation seemed quite surprised—precisely because it violated people's expectations and in so doing directed people's attention toward the role of men and women in religious ritual at the end of the twentieth century as well as toward the Torah as the central symbol of the Jewish people.

What Are Rites of Passage?

Graduating from college, getting married, joining the military, and other "life cycle" rituals share certain important features, most notably that people begin the ritual as one kind of person (e.g., student, single, recruit), and by the time the ritual is over, they have been transformed into a different kind of person (e.g., graduate, spouse, soldier). These rituals are called **rites of passage**. At the beginning of the twentieth century, the Belgian anthropologist Arnold Van Gennep noted that certain kinds of rituals around the world had similar structures. These were rituals associated with the movement (or passage) of people from one position in the social structure to another. They took place at births, initiations, confirmations, weddings, funerals, and the like (Figure 10.9).

Van Gennep (1960) found that all these rituals began with a period of *separation* from the old position and from normal time. During this period, the ritual passenger leaves behind the symbols and practices of his or her previous position. For example, military recruits leave their families behind and are moved to a new place. They are forced to leave behind the clothing, activities, and even the hairstyle that marked who they were in civilian life.

The second stage in rites of passage involves a period of *transition* in which the ritual passenger is neither in the old life nor yet in the new one. This period is marked by rolelessness, ambiguity, and perceived danger. Often, the person involved is subjected to ordeal by those who have already passed through. In the military service, this

is the period of basic training in which recruits (not yet soldiers but no longer civilians) are forced to dress and act alike. They are subjected to a grinding-down process, after which they are rebuilt into something new.

During the final stage—*reaggregation*—the ritual passenger is reintroduced into society in his or her new position. In the military, this involves graduation from basic training and a visit home, but this time as a member of the armed forces, in uniform and on leave—in other words, as a new person. Other familiar rites of passage in youth culture in the United States include high school graduation and the informal yet significant ceremonies associated with the twenty-first birthday, both of which are understood as movements from one kind of person to another.

The work of Victor Turner greatly increased our understanding of rites of passage. Turner concentrated on the period of transition, which he saw as important both for the rite of passage and for social life in general. Van Gennep (1960) referred to this part of a rite of passage as the "liminal period," from the Latin *limen* ("threshold"). During this period, the individual is on the threshold, betwixt and between, neither here nor there, neither in nor out. Turner notes that the symbolism accompanying the rite of passage often expresses this ambiguous state. **Liminality**, he tells us, "is frequently likened to death, to being in the womb, to invisibility, to darkness, to bisexuality, to the wilderness, and to an eclipse of the sun or moon" (Turner 1969, 95). People in the liminal state tend to develop an intense comradeship with each other in which their nonliminal distinctions disappear or become irrelevant. Turner calls this kind of social relationship communitas, which is best understood as an unstructured or minimally structured community of equal individuals.

Turner (1969) contends that all societies need some kind of **communitas** as much as they need structure. Communitas gives "recognition to an essential and generic human bond, without which there could be no society" (97). That bond is the common humanity that underlies all culture and society. However, periods of communitas (often in ritual context) are brief. Communitas is dangerous, not just because it threatens structure but also because it threatens survival itself. During the time of communitas, the things that structure ensures—production of food and physical and social reproduction of the society—cannot be provided. But someone always has to take out the garbage and clean up after the party. Thus, communitas gives way again to structure, which in turn generates a need for a new release of communitas. The feeling of communitas can also be attained by means of play and art. Indeed, it may well be that for people in contemporary nation-states,

---

rite of passage A ritual that serves to mark the movement and transformation of an individual from one social position to another.

liminality The ambiguous transitional state in a rite of passage in which the person or persons undergoing the ritual are outside their ordinary social positions.

communitas An unstructured or minimally structured community of equal individuals found frequently in rites of passage.

IN THEIR OWN WORDS

Video in the Villages

Patricia Aufderheide describes how indigenous peoples of the Amazonian rain forest in Brazil have been able to master the video camera and use it for their own purposes.

The social role and impact of video is particularly intriguing among people who are new to mass-communications technologies, such as lowlands Amazonian Indians. One anthropologist has argued persuasively that a naive disdain for commercial media infuses much well-meaning concern over the potential dangers of introducing mass media and that "indigenous media offers a possible means—social, cultural, and political—for reproducing and transforming cultural identity among people who have experienced massive political, geographic, and economic disruption." . . . In two groups of Brazilian Indians, the Nambikwara and the Kayapo, this premise has been tested.

The Nambikwara became involved with video through Video in the Villages, run by Vincent Carelli at the Centro de Trabalho Indigenista in São Paulo. This project is one example of a trend to put media in the hands of people who have long been the subjects of ethnographic film and video. . . . While some anthropologists see this resort as a "solution" to the issue of ethnographic authority, others have focused on it as part of a struggle for indigenous rights and political autonomy. . . . Many of the groups Carelli has worked with have seized on video for its ability to extensively document lengthy rituals that mark the group's cultural uniqueness rather than produce a finished product. . . .

Carelli coproduced a project with a Nambikwara leader, documenting a cultural ritual. After taping, the Nambikwara viewed the ritual and offered criticisms, finding it tainted with modernisms. They then repeated the ritual in traditional regalia and conducted, for the first time in a generation, a male initiation ceremony—taping it all. (This experience is recounted in a short tape, *Girls' Puberty Ritual*, produced by Carelli with a Nambikwara leader for

outsiders.) Using video reinforced an emerging concept of "traditional" in contrast to Brazilian culture—a concept that had not, apparently, been part of the Nambikwara's repertoire before contact but that had practical political utility.

The Kayapo are among the best-known Brazilian Indians internationally, partly because of their video work, promoted as a tool of cultural identification by the anthropologist who works most closely with them. Like other tribes such as the Xavante who had extensive contact with Brazilian authorities and media, the Kayapo early seized on modern media technologies. . . . Besides intimidating authorities with the evidence of recording equipment . . . the Kayapo quickly grasped the symbolic expectations of Brazilian mass media for Indians. They cannily played on the contrast between their feathers and body paint and their recording devices to get coverage. Even staging public events for the purpose of attracting television crews, they were able to insert, although not ultimately control, their message on Brazilian news by exploiting that contrast. . . . Using these techniques, Kayapo leaders became international symbols of the ironies of the postmodern age and not incidentally also the subjects of international agitation and fundraising that benefited Kayapo over other indigenous groups and some Kayapo over others.

Kayapo have also used video to document internal cultural ceremonies in meticulous detail; to communicate internally between villages; to develop an archive; and to produce clips and short documentaries intended for wide audiences. Their video work, asserts anthropologist Terence Turner, has not merely preserved traditional customs but in fact transformed their understanding of those customs as customs and their culture as a culture. Turner also found that video equipment, expertise, and products often fed into existing factional divisions. Particular Kayapo leaders used the equipment in their own interests, sometimes as a tool to subdue their enemies, sometimes as evidence of personal power.

Source: Aufderheide 1993, 587–89.

the experience of communitas comes through the climactic winning moments of a sports team; attendance at large-scale rock concerts; or participation in mass public events like Carnival in Rio de Janeiro, the Greenwich Village Halloween parade, or Mardi Gras in New Orleans.

How Are Play and Ritual Complementary?

How does the logic of ritual differ from the logic of play? Play and ritual are complementary forms of metacommunication (Handelman 1977). The movement from

FIGURE 10.9 Rites of passage are rituals that enable people to move from one position in the social structure to another. (a) In June 2004, an Apache girl, accompanied by her godmother and a helper, moves into adulthood through the Sunrise Dance. (b) In May 2011, a group of Harvard students moves into a new part of their lives as law school graduates following Commencement.

nonplay to play is based on the premise of metaphor ("Let's make believe"); the movement to ritual is based on the premise of literalness ("Let's believe"). From the perspective of the everyday social order, the result of these contrasting premises is the "inauthenticity" of play and the "truth" of ritual.

Because of the connection of ritual with self-evident truth, the metacommunication of the ritual frame ("This is ritual") is associated with an additional metacommunication: "All messages within this frame are true." It is ritual that asserts *what should be* to play's *what can be*. The

orthopraxy "Correct practice"; the prohibition of deviation from approved forms of ritual behavior.

ritual frame is more rigid than the play frame. Consequently, ritual is the most stable liminal domain, whereas play is the most flexible. Players can move with relative ease into and out of play, but such is not the case with ritual.

Finally, play usually has little effect on the social order of ordinary life. This permits play a wide range of commentary on the social order. Ritual is different: its role is explicitly to maintain the status quo, including the prescribed ritual transformations. Societies differ in the extent to which ritual behavior alternates with everyday, nonritual behavior. When nearly every act of everyday life is ritualized and other forms of behavior are strongly discouraged, we sometimes speak of **orthopraxy** ("correct practice"). Traditionally observant Jews and Muslims, for

EthnoProfile 10.4

Yoruba

Region: Western Africa

Nation: Nigeria

Population: 40,000,000

Environment: Coastal and forest

Livelihood: Farming, commerce, modern professions

Political organization:
Traditionally, kingdoms; today, part of a modern nation-state

For more information:
Bascom, William. 1969. *The Yoruba of southwestern Nigeria.* New York: Holt, Rinehart and Winston.

example, lead a highly ritualized daily life, attempting from the moment they awaken until the moment they fall asleep to carry out even the humblest of activities in a manner that is ritually correct. In their view, ritual correctness is the result of God's law, and it is their duty and joy to conform their every action to God's will.

Margaret Drewal argues that, at least among the Yoruba, play and ritual overlap (see "EthnoProfile 10.4: Yoruba"). Yoruba rituals combine spectacle, festival, play, sacrifice, and so on and integrate diverse media—music, dance, poetry, theater, sculpture (Drewal 1992, 198). They are events that require improvisatory, spontaneous individual moves; as a result, the mundane order is not only inverted and reversed but also may be subverted through power play and gender play. For example, when Drewal carried out her research in the late twentieth century, she learned that gender roles are rigidly structured in Yoruba society. Yoruba rituals, however, allow some cross-dressing by both men and women, providing institutionalized opportunities for men and women to cross gender boundaries and to express the traits that the Yoruba consider characteristic of the opposite sex, sometimes as parody but sometimes seriously and respectfully (Drewal 1992, 190).

How Are Symbolic Practices and Society Related?

Our previous discussions of language, play, art, myth, and ritual provided an overview of some of the ways

human beings use culture to construct rich understandings of everyday experiences. In this section, we build on those insights and describe how human beings use cultural creativity to make sense of the wider world on a more comprehensive scale as they construct encompassing pictures of reality called **worldviews**.

What Are Symbols?

As they develop complex understandings of themselves and the wider world, people regularly devise symbols to organize this knowledge. As we saw earlier, a symbol—such as a word, an image, or an action—is something that stands for something else. Symbols signal the presence and importance of given domains of experience.

Some symbols, which anthropologist Sherry Ortner calls summarizing symbols, sum up, express, or represent for people "in an emotionally powerful . . . way what the system means to them" (1973, 1339). To many people, for example, the American flag stands for the American way (Figure 10.10). But the American way is a complex collection of ideas and feelings that includes such things as patriotism, democracy, hard work, free enterprise, progress, national superiority, apple pie, and motherhood. As Ortner points out, the flag focuses our attention on all these things at once. It does not encourage us, say, to reflect on how the American way affects non-Americans. But the symbolic power of the flag is double-edged. For some people, Americans included, this same flag stands for imperialism, racism, opposition to the legitimate struggle of exploited peoples, and support for right-wing dictatorships. Perhaps stranger still, for many Americans, the flag sums up all these things at once, contradictory though they are!

What Ortner calls elaborating symbols are essentially analytic. They allow people to sort out and label complex and undifferentiated feelings and ideas into comprehensible and communicable language and action. Elaborating symbols provide people with categories for thinking about how their world is ordered. For the Dinka, a cattle-herding people of eastern Africa, cattle are a key elaborating symbol (see Figure 10.11 and "EthnoProfile 10.5: Dinka"). According to Godfrey Lienhardt, in the middle of the twentieth century, cattle provided the Dinka with most of the metaphors they used for thinking about and responding to experience. For instance, Dinka perceptions of color, light, and shade were connected to the colors they saw in cattle. They even likened how their society was put together to how a bull is put together (Lienhardt 1961; Ortner 1973).

---

worldviews Encompassing pictures of reality created by the members of societies.

FIGURE 10.10   For US citizens, the flag of the United States is a summarizing symbol that brings together and evokes for them a range of images and emotions, positive and negative, about their country.

FIGURE 10.11   For pastoral people such as the Dinka and their neighbors the Nuer, cattle are elaborating symbols of paramount power.

What Is Religion?

For many readers of this text, the most familiar form of worldview is probably religion. The anthropological concept of religion, like many analytic terms, began as a description of a certain domain of Western culture. As a result, it has been very difficult for anthropologists to settle on a definition of religion that is applicable in all human societies. Scholars have often argued that a religion differs from other kinds of worldviews because it assumes the existence of a supernatural domain: an invisible world populated by one or more beings who are more powerful than human beings and able to influence events in the "natural" human world. The problem with

this definition is that the distinction between "natural" and "supernatural" was originally made by nonreligious Western observers to distinguish the real "natural" world from what they took to be the imaginary "supernatural" world. Many anthropologists who study different religious traditions believe that it is less distorting to begin with their informants' statements about what exists and what does not. In this way, they are in a better position to understand the range of forces, visible and invisible, that religious devotees perceive as being active in their world.

For these reasons, John Bowen has proposed that anthropologists approach religion in a way that begins broadly but that allows for increasing specificity as we

EthnoProfile 10.5

Dinka

Region: Eastern Africa

Nation: Sudan

Population: 2,000,000

Environment: Savanna

Livelihood: Principally cattle herding, also agriculture

Political organization: Traditionally, egalitarian with noble clans and chiefs; today, part of a modern nation-state

For more information: Deng, Francis Madeng. 1972. *The Dinka of the Sudan.* New York: Holt, Rinehart and Winston.

learn more about the details of particular religious traditions. Bowen (2008) defines **religion** as "ideas and practices that postulate reality beyond that which is immediately available to the senses" (4). In individual societies, this may take the shape of beliefs in spirits and gods, in impersonal forces that affect the world, in the correct practice of ritual, or in the awareness that their ancestors continue to be active in the world of the living. It is important to note that this definition encompasses both practices and ideas; religions involve actions as well as beliefs (Figure 10.12). Indeed, anthropologist A. F. C. Wallace (1966) proposed a set of "minimal categories of religious behavior" that describe many of the practices usually associated with religions. Several of the most important are as follows:

1. *Prayer.* Where there are personified cosmic forces, there is a customary way of addressing them, usually by speaking or chanting out loud. Often, people pray in public, at a sacred location, and with special apparatus: incense, smoke, objects (e.g., rosary beads or a prayer wheel), and so on (Figure 10.12a).

2. *Physiological exercise.* Many religious systems have methods for physically manipulating psychological states to induce an ecstatic spiritual state. Wallace suggests four major kinds of manipulation: (1) drugs; (2) sensory deprivation; (3) mortification of the flesh by pain, sleeplessness, and fatigue; and (4) deprivation of food, water, or air. In many societies, the experience of ecstasy, euphoria, dissociation, or hallucination seems to be a goal of religious effort (Figure 10.12b).

3. *Exhortation.* In all religious systems, certain people are believed to have closer relationships with the invisible powers than others, and they are expected to use those relationships in the spiritual interests of others. They give orders, they heal, they threaten, they comfort, and they interpret.

4. *Mana.* Mana refers to an impersonal superhuman power that is sometimes believed to be transferable from an object that contains it to one that does not. The laying on of hands, in which the power of a healer enters the body of a sick person to remove or destroy an illness, is an example of the transmission of power. In Guider, Cameroon, some people believe that the ink used to copy passages from the Qur'an has power (see Chapter 15, "EthnoProfile 15.2: Guider"). Washing the ink off the board on which the words are written and drinking the ink transfer the power of the words into the body of the drinker. All these examples illustrate the principle that sacred things are sometimes to be touched so that their power may be transferred to human beings.

5. *Taboo.* Objects or people that may not be touched are taboo. Some people believe that the cosmic power in such objects or people may "drain away" if touched or may injure the toucher. Many religious systems have taboo objects. Traditionally, Catholics were not to touch the Host during communion. Jews may not touch the handwritten text of the biblical scrolls. In ancient Polynesia, commoners could not touch the chief's body; even an accidental touch resulted in the death of the commoner. Food may also be taboo; many societies have elaborate rules concerning the foods that may or may not be eaten at different times or by different kinds of people.

6. *Feasts.* Eating and drinking in a religious context is very common. The Holy Communion of Catholics and Protestants is a meal set apart by its religious context. The Passover Seder for Jews is another religious feast. For the Huichol of Mexico, the consumption of peyote is set apart from other meals by its religious context. Even everyday meals may be seen to have a religious quality if they begin or end with prayer.

7. *Sacrifice.* Giving something of value to the invisible forces or their agents is a feature of many religious systems. This may be an offering of money, goods, or services. It may also be the immolation of animals or, very rarely, human beings. Sacrifices may be made in thanks to the cosmic forces in hopes of influencing them to act in a certain way or simply to gain general religious merit.

---

religion "Ideas and practices that postulate reality beyond that which is immediately available to the senses" (Bowen 2008).

FIGURE 10.12 (a) The joint pilgrimage by Hindu worshipers to the Ganges River illustrates the social nature of religion. (b) This participant in the Hindu Thaipusam ritual pilgrimage in Singapore in 2004 has agreed to carry a kavadi for religious benefit. Kavadi can weigh 60 pounds (27 kg).

How Do Anthropologists Understand the Relations between Religion and Secularism?

The European Enlightenment of the eighteenth century gave birth to a new worldview that has come to be called "**secularism**," and the spread of this worldview has had repercussions across the globe. Secularism is usually defined as the separation of religion and state, and is commonly understood as the Enlightenment solution to the bloody and irresolvable European wars of religion that followed the Protestant Reformation. The development of secular ideas and practices profoundly transformed the religions and political institutions that had dominated European society in the Middle Ages. Earlier generations of anthropologists took secularism for granted, as the expected outcome of cultural evolution, but no longer. Some have taken secularism itself as a focus of ethnographic and historical research.

According to Susan Harding, "Anthropologists of secularism . . . focus . . . on the complex of practices that define and evaluate *what counts as religion* within nation-states" (2019, 51). Talal Asad, for instance, argues that secularism is "not a simple matter of absence of 'religion' in the public life of the modern nation-state. For even in modern secular countries the place of religion varies" (Asad 2003, 5–6). Rather, he tells us that European secularism presupposed specific post-Reformation concepts of "religion," of "the state," as well as a notion of

secular citizenship that owes much to the notion of individual agency developed in Protestant theology. Asad reminds us that religious disputes in the Reformation and wars of religion concerned questions of doctrinal *orthodoxy*—that is, correct religious *beliefs*. In European secularism, thus, "religion" is defined primarily in terms of the beliefs to which its adherents choose to commit themselves as individuals. This concept of individual agency was itself the product of Protestant theology, and became absolutely crucial to the successful functioning of democratic government and the capitalist market. Similarly, the secular "state" is always understood to be the modern nation-state with a capitalist economy. It is from these understandings of religion and state that the Enlightenment concept of citizenship develops: just as independent, self-motivating individuals were responsible before God; in their role as citizens of a liberal secular state, they were individually responsible before the law. Thus, secular citizenship is supposed to "transcend the different identities built into class, gender, and religion, replacing conflicting perspectives by unifying experience. In a sense, this transcendent mediation *is* secularism" (Asad 2003, 5). These notions were spread by European colonial conquest and Christian missionizing, and have formed part of the ideologies of nation-states that emerged around the world after the end of colonialism in the middle of the twentieth century.

But not all those living in nation-states today are able to fit their own religious practices into this secular understanding of religion. Asad shows how the assumptions of Western secularism about religion, the state, and the individual can challenge some Muslims' understandings about how their religious practices should

Secularism : The separation of religion and state, including a notion of secular citizenship that owes much to the notion of individual agency developed in Protestant theology.

relate to social and political organization. First, religion in the secular state is supposed to be defined in terms of beliefs; second, religious rituals are supposed to be observed in private, or in special settings like churches, synagogues, or mosques; and third, religion is viewed as a matter of individual faith, and is not supposed to be imposed by the state. Rather, an individual's overarching identity as a state-recognized secular citizen is supposed to rise above all other personal identity claims, including religious identity.

In contrast to this, Asad writes, Islam is one of "many traditions attribute to the living human body the potential to be shaped (the power to shape itself) for good or ill. . . . The living body's materiality is regarded as an essential means for cultivating what such traditions define as virtuous conduct and for discouraging what they consider as vice. The role of fear and hope, of felicity and pain, is central to such practices . . . the more one exercises a virtue the easier it becomes . . . the more one gives into vice, the harder it is to act virtuously" (2003, 89–90). Islamic religious traditions are rooted in such forms of disciplined religious practice, which cannot be reduced to a list of religious beliefs. Moreover, successful cultivation of correct practice is thought to depend on living within a community of like-minded practitioners that acts to reinforce the desired habits of obedience. Finally, Asad observes that "For many Muslims minorities (though by no means all) being Muslim . . . is being able to live as autonomous individuals in a collective life that extends beyond national borders" (2003, 180). But if this is the case, then correct Muslim practice would appear to be incompatible with secular citizenship.

Thus, the concept of religion developed in the modern West, and deployed by anthropologists and others, is far from an innocent concept. Susan Harding observes that "Turning other people's lived traditions into beliefs also renders those traditions dispensable," (2019, 50). It is in an effort to ensure that this does not happen that many anthropologists today may continue to use the term "religion," but have, like John Bowen, shifted their emphasis away from beliefs to focus on forms of ritual practice.

What is the Anthropology of Ontology?

Like the anthropology of secularism, what Susan Harding calls the "anthropology of ontology" originated in a critique of how Western ideas about the world had come to dominate anthropological thinking, not only about what counted as religion, but also more broadly, what counted as "reality." In Western philosophy, "ontology" is the field of inquiry concerning what does and does not

exist in "reality," and modern philosophers have insisted that there is only one such reality: physical, material and the same for everyone everywhere. Traditional anthropology has not questioned these ontological claims, while nevertheless insisting that this single universal reality can be, and has been, made meaningful to different peoples in multiple, different ways. This is, after all, the basis of cultural relativism and the description of different cultural worldviews.

Anthropologists of ontology, however, go further than this, "adding that 'reality' is plural. The anthropological concept of ontology refers to a multiplicity of modes of existence, of worlds, that are enacted in and embodied through social practices" (Harding 2019, 46). Sociocultural anthropologists Martin Holbraad and Morten Axel Pederson have argued that this new commitment to the existence of multiple realities is best understood as an effort to *intensify* the commitment to reflexivity in anthropology. To make their point, they draw attention to a key feature of ethnographic fieldwork: experiencing what Michael Agar (1996) called "rich points," and what Holbraad and Pederson call "a-ha! moments" (2017, 1). Encountering rich points can utterly challenge the ethnographer's taken-for-granted assumptions about the way the world works. For example, indigenous *runakuna* in Peru apparently regard Andean mountain peaks like Ausangate as living beings who monitor and intervene in human affairs, who may be addressed through appropriate rituals, and with whom bargains may be struck (de la Cadena 2015). But these runakuna assumptions are flatly contradicted by Western ontological views of mountains as "really" nothing more than inert matter. Anthropologists have long recognized that a rich point of this kind *relativizes* Western claims about mountains and also pushes ethnographers into more *reflexive* awareness of ontological commitments about mountains that they have always accepted but must now consider anew.

Upon reflection, an ethnographer might conclude that although "we know" that mountains are inert matter, indigenous Andean peoples "believe" that they are living beings involved in human affairs. But what would it mean to do *more* than this, to *intensify* our anthropological commitment to reflexivity? According to Holbraad and Pederson, it means to take anthropology's relativizing rich points and a-ha! moments and "to *run with them*. Instead of encasing them within generalizing theories about culture, society, human nature, and so forth, of trying to explain them away with a good dose of common sense, this way of thinking in anthropology seeks deliberately to take these moments as far as they will go, making fully virtue of their capacity to stop thinking in its tracks, unsettling what we think we know in favour of what we may not even have imagined" (2017, 2). To continue the previous Andean example, this would mean rethinking, from top to bottom, what mountains are—but this time beginning with the ontological assumptions of *runakuna*, attempting to provide an anthropological account of mountain peaks like Ausangate that might have been developed by *runakuna* anthropologists, rather than by Euro-Americans. This is what de la Cadena attempts in her ethnography *Earth Beings* (2015), exposing in the process just how tricky translation becomes when the ethnographer is not free to ignore (or to dismiss as mere "beliefs") the foundational ontological principles of the people with whom she is working.

But what would be the *value* of stopping our thinking in its tracks, of unsettling what we think we know in favor of what we may not even have imagined? For anthropologists of ontology, this slowing down and shaking up of our though processes promises to bring us closer toward finding *ways of making a world that do not depend on Western ontology and the capitalist modernity that has produced the ravages of the Anthropocene.* This systematic, principled search for other ontologies, other ways of "worlding," may disclose alternative ways to build a new future for the earth and all its inhabitants (not just humans) before it is too late. Not all anthropologists are persuaded by these arguments; many prefer to continue to analyze worldviews as cultural constructions placed on a single "real world." For Ghassan Hage, however, and others like him, the anthropology of ontology offers "the critical anthropological gaze that captures the existence of other spaces or realities" (Hage 2015, Loc 1488–1497). Hage argues that the anthropology of ontology has the potential to recommit our discipline to a radical search for alternative ways of living in the future, "summarized in the formula: we can be other than what we are" (2015, Loc 242).

The anthropology of ontology also has implications for how anthropologists talk about "religion." Marisol de la Cadena draws attention to the way traditional anthropological ways of writing about Andean "religion" have excluded or truncated elements of indigenous ontology that contradict or exceed what Westerners accept as actually existing in the world, and this has implications for how anthropologists identify what counts as religion. Again, a key example concerns alternative answers to the question, *What is Ausangate?* Western observers and indigenous Andeans alike would be able to identify Ausangate as a mountain peak near Cuzco. But how do we deal with the Western insistence that it is nothing more than inert matter, in the face of indigenous

Andeans insistence that Ausangate (and other peaks) are alive, aware, and involved in human affairs? Do these Andeans hold a "religious belief" that Ausangate is a living "earth being"—or is that just the awkward and partly misleading Western translation? Is it the best Westerners can do, given their unquestioned Enlightenment commitment to an ontology in which mountains are *not* alive, *not* aware, and *not* consciously involved in human affairs? As de la Cadena writes, "Practices with earth beings . . . can be identified as religious, but they cannot be reduced to such, for the notion of religion may not contain all that they are" (2015, 207–208).

How Do People Communicate in Religion?

Maintaining contact with cosmic powers can be a tremendously complex undertaking. It is not surprising, therefore, that some societies have developed complex social practices to ensure that it is done properly. In other words, religion becomes institutionalized. Social positions are created for specialists who supervise or embody correct religious practice.

Anthropologists have identified two broad categories of religious specialists: shamans and priests. A **shaman** is a part-time religious practitioner who is believed to have the power to contact invisible powers directly on behalf of individuals or groups. Shamans are often thought to be able to travel to the cosmic realm to communicate with the beings or forces that dwell there. They often plead with those beings or forces to act in favor of their people and may return with messages for them. The Ju/'hoansi, for example, recognize that some people are able to develop an internal power that enables them to travel to the world of the spirits—to enter "half death"—to cure those who are sick (see Chapter 11, "EthnoProfile 11.4: Ju/'hoansi (!Kung)").

In many societies, the training that a shaman receives is long and demanding and may involve the use of powerful psychotropic substances. Repeatedly entering altered states of consciousness can produce long-lasting effects on shamans themselves, and shamans may be viewed with suspicion or fear by others in the society. This is because contacting cosmic beings to persuade them to heal embodies dangerous ambiguities: someone who can contact such beings for positive benefits may also be able to contact them to produce negative outcomes like disease or death.

The term *shaman* comes from the Tungus of eastern Siberia, where, at a minimum, it referred to a religious specialist who has the ability to enter a trance through which he or she is believed to enter into direct contact with spiritual beings and guardian spirits for

shaman A part-time religious practitioner who is believed to have the ability to contact invisible powers directly on behalf of individuals or groups.

the purposes of healing, fertility, protection, and aggression in a ritual setting (Bowie 2006, 175; Hultkrantz 1992, 10). The healing associated with Siberian shamanism was concerned with the idea that illness was caused by soul loss and healing through recovery of the soul (Figure 10.13). Thus, the shaman was responsible for dealing with spirits that were, at best, neutral, and at worst, actively hostile to human beings. The shaman could travel to the spirit world to heal someone by finding the missing soul that had been stolen by spirits. But a shaman who was jealous of a hunter, for example, was believed to be able to steal the souls of animals so that the hunter would fail. In these societies, shamans are dangerous.

Shamanic activity takes place in the trance séance, which can be little more than a consultation between shaman and patient, or it can be a major public ritual, rich in drama. Becoming a shaman is not undertaken for personal development. In the societies in which shamanism is important, it is said that the shaman has no choice but to take on the role; the spirits demand it. It can take a decade or more to become fully recognized as

a shaman, and it is assumed that the shaman will be in service to the society (for good or ill) for the rest of his or her life.

The anthropology of ontology has refreshed some old anthropological understandings about shamans. This has gone furthest in the work of anthropologists working the Amazon of South America. Perhaps most influential has been the Brazilian anthropologist Eduardo Viveiros the Castro, who, we could say, took what he learned about shamanic practices among the Amazonian Arawaté people and ran with them. To understand shamanism beginning with Arawaté ontology is to acknowledge, first of all, that the Arawaté take for granted that all animals (especially large prey species like jaguars) are just as much human persons as are the Arawaté themselves. But different outward bodies (jaguar, peccary, Arawaté) activate this underlying universal humanity in different ways. Shamans are significant in this world because they have the power to detect the humanity under the animal clothing; indeed, a shaman can put on the skin of an animal like a jaguar and transform himself into a jaguar, without coming to harm. Put another way, shamans have the power to mediate between Arawaté and jaguars without being turned into the jaguar's prey. For Viveiros de Castro, these features of Amazonian cosmology "are not are not cultural representations of reality. He wants us to understand them not as epistemology but as ontology, as ways Amazonians understand what counts as the world, that is, what things really *are*" (Harding 2019, 47). For a Western outsider, a glimpse of this Amazonian cosmos suggests a possibly superior way of relating to what Westerners consider nonhuman animals. Perhaps it might also suggest a way of negotiating the horrors of the Anthropocene. As Hage put it, it offers a valuable illustration of one way that we might be other than what we are.

The other traditional category of religious specialists identified by anthropologist is the priest. A **priest** is skilled in the practice of religious rituals, which are carried out for the benefit of the group or individual members of the group. Priests do not necessarily have direct contact with cosmic forces. Often their major role is to mediate such contact by ensuring that the required ritual activity has been properly performed. Priests are found in hierarchical societies, and they owe their ability to act as priests to the hierarchy of the religious institution (Figure 10.14). Status differences separating rulers and subjects in such societies are reflected in the unequal relationship between priest and laity.

FIGURE 10.13 Using smoke from a juniper twig, Siberian shaman Vera heals a patient possessed by evil spirits.

priest A religious practitioner skilled in the practice of religious rituals, which he or she carries out for the benefit of the group.

FIGURE 10.14 The complex organization of the Roman Catholic Church was illustrated at the inauguration mass for Pope Francis in 2013.

Two Case Studies

We have been discussing how worldviews are constructed, but most of us encounter them fully formed, both in our own society and in other societies. We face a rich tapestry of symbols, rituals, and everyday practices linked to one another in what often appears to be a seamless web. Where do we begin to sort things out?

Coping with Misfortune: Witchcraft, Oracles, and Magic among the Azande

Anthropologist E. E. Evans-Pritchard, in his classic work *Witchcraft, Oracles, and Magic among the Azande* ([1937] 1976), showed how Azande beliefs and practices concerning witchcraft, oracles, and magic were related to one another (see "EthnoProfile 10.6: Azande"). He describes how Azande in the 1920s used witchcraft beliefs to explain unfortunate things that happened to them and how they employed oracles and magic to exert a measure of control over the actions of other people. Evans-Pritchard was impressed by the intelligence, sophistication, and skepticism of his Azande informants. For this reason, he was all the more struck by their ability to hold a set of beliefs that many Europeans would regard as superstitious.

Azande Witchcraft Beliefs The Azande Evans-Pritchard knew believed that *mangu* (translated by Evans-Pritchard as **witchcraft**) was a substance in the body of witches,

---

EthnoProfile 10.6

Azande

Region: Central Africa

Nation: Sudan, Democratic Republic of the Congo (Zaire), Central African Republic

Population: 1,100,000

Environment: Sparsely wooded savanna

Livelihood: Farming, hunting, fishing, chicken raising

Political organization: Traditionally, highly organized, tribal kingdoms; today, part of modern nation-states

For more information: Evans-Pritchard, E. E. (1937) 1976. *Witchcraft, oracles, and magic among the Azande*, abridged ed., prepared by Eva Gillies. Oxford: Oxford University Press.

---

generally located under the sternum.[1] Being a part of the body, the witchcraft substance grew as the body grew; therefore, the older the witch, the more potent his or her witchcraft. The Azande believed that children inherited

---

[1]Beliefs and practices similar to those associated with Azande *mangu* have been found in many other societies, and it has become traditional in anthropology to refer to them as "witchcraft." This technical usage must not be confused with everyday uses of the word in contemporary Western societies, still less with the practices of followers of movements like Wicca, which are very different.

---

witchcraft The performance of evil by human beings believed to possess an innate, nonhuman power to do evil, whether or not it is intentional or self-aware.

witchcraft from their parents. Men or women might be witches. Men practiced witchcraft against other men, women against other women. Witchcraft worked when its "soul" removed the soul of a certain organ in the victim's body, usually at night, causing a slow, wasting disease. Suffering such a disease was therefore an indication that an individual had been bewitched.

Witchcraft was a basic concept for the Azande, one that shaped their experience of adversity. All deaths were caused by witchcraft and had to be avenged by **magic**. Other misfortunes were also commonly attributed to witchcraft unless the victim had broken a taboo, had failed to observe a moral rule, or was believed to be responsible for his or her own problems. Suppose I am an incompetent potter and my pots break while I am firing them. I may claim that witchcraft caused them to break, but everyone will laugh at me because they know I lack skill. Witchcraft was believed to be so common that the Azande were neither surprised nor awestruck when they encountered it. Rather, their usual response was anger.

To the Azande, witchcraft was a completely natural explanation for events. Consider the classic case of the collapsing granary. Azandeland is hot, and people seeking shade often sit under traditional raised granaries, which rest on logs. Termites are common in Azandeland, and sometimes they destroy the supporting logs, making a granary collapse. Occasionally, when a granary collapses, people sitting under it are killed. Why does this happen? The Azande are well aware that the termites chew up the wood until the supports give way, but to them that is not answer enough. Why, after all, should that particular granary have collapsed at that particular moment? To skeptical observers, the only connection is coincidence in time and space. Western science does not provide any explanation for why these two chains of causation intersect. But the Azande did: witchcraft caused the termites to finish chewing up the wood at just that moment, and that witchcraft had to be avenged by magic.

Dealing with Witches   To expose the witch, the Azande consulted **oracles** (invisible forces to which people address questions and whose responses they believe to be truthful). Preeminent among these was the poison oracle. The poison was a strychnine-like substance imported into Azandeland. The oracle "spoke" through the effect the poison had on chickens. When witchcraft was suspected, a relative of the afflicted person took some young chickens into the bush along with a specialist in administering the poison oracle. This person fed poison to one chicken, named a suspect, and asked the oracle to kill the chicken if that person were the witch. If the chicken died, a second chicken was fed poison, and

the oracle was asked to spare the chicken if the suspect just named was indeed the witch. Thus, the Azande double-checked the oracle carefully; a witchcraft accusation was not made lightly.

People did not consult the oracle with a long list of names. They needed only to consider those who might wish them or their families ill: people who had quarreled with them, who were unpleasant, who were antisocial, or whose behavior was somehow out of line. Indeed, witches were always neighbors because neighbors were the only people who know you well enough to wish you and your family ill.

Once the oracle identified the witch, the Azande removed the wing of the chicken and had it taken by messenger to the compound of the accused person. The messenger presented the accused witch with the chicken wing and said that he had been sent concerning the illness of so-and-so's relative. "Almost invariably the witch replies courteously that he is unconscious of injuring anyone, that if it is true that he has injured the man in question he is very sorry, and that if it is he alone who is troubling him then he will surely recover, because from the bottom of his heart he wishes him health and happiness" (Evans-Pritchard [1937] 1976, 42). The accused then called for a gourd of water, took some in his mouth, and sprayed it out over the wing. He said aloud, so the messenger could hear and repeat what he said, that if he was a witch he was not aware of it and that he was not intentionally causing the sick man to be ill. He addressed the witchcraft in him, asking it to become cool, and concluded by saying that he made this appeal from his heart, not just from his lips (42).

People accused of witchcraft were usually astounded; no Azande thought of himself or herself as a witch. However, the Azande strongly believed in witchcraft and in the oracles; and if the oracle said someone was a witch, then it must be so. The accused witch was grateful to the family of the sick person for being informed. Otherwise, if the accused had been allowed to murder the victim, all the while unaware of it, the witch would surely be killed later by vengeance magic. The witchcraft accusation carried a further message: the behavior of the accused was sufficiently outside the bounds of acceptable Azande behavior to have marked him or her as a potential witch. Only the names of people who you suspected of wishing you ill were submitted to the oracle. The accused witch, then, was being told to change his or her behavior.

---

magic A set of beliefs and practices designed to control the visible or invisible world for specific purposes.

oracles Invisible forces to which people address questions and whose responses they believe to be truthful.

Are There Patterns of Witchcraft Accusation?

Compared with the stereotypes of Euro-American witchcraft—old hags dressed in black, riding on broomsticks, casting spells, causing milk to sour or people to sicken—Azande witchcraft seems quite tame. People whose impression of witchcraft comes from western European images may believe that witchcraft and witch-hunting tear at the very fabric of society. Yet, anthropological accounts like Evans-Pritchard's suggest that practices such as witchcraft accusation can sometimes keep societies together. Anthropologist Mary Douglas (1970, xxvi–xxvii) looked at the range of witchcraft accusations worldwide and discovered that they fell into two basic types: in some cases, the witch is an evil outsider; in others, the witch is an internal enemy, either the member of a rival faction or a dangerous deviant. These different patterns of accusation perform different functions in a society. If the witch is an outsider, witchcraft accusations can strengthen in-group ties. If the witch is an internal enemy, accusations of witchcraft can weaken in-group ties; factions may have to regroup, communities may split, and the entire social hierarchy may be reordered. If the witch is a dangerous deviant, the accusation of witchcraft can be seen as an attempt to control the deviant in defense of the wider values of the community. Douglas concluded that how people understand witchcraft is based on the social relations of their society.

Coping with Misfortune: Listening for God among Contemporary Evangelicals in the United States

Anthropologist T. M. Luhrmann spent several years studying the beliefs and practices of Vineyard Christian Fellowship evangelical churches in Chicago and California. Luhrmann (2012) notes that the Vineyard movement came out of the turmoil and spiritual ferment of the 1960s and early 1970s, as some people were searching for a more direct experience of God. Specifically, when they prayed to God, they expected an answer. Luhrmann's research was designed to address a significant issue in the study of religion—how might one know that God exists? "I set out many years ago to understand how God becomes real for modern people. I chose an example of the style of Christianity that would seem to make the cognitive burden of belief most difficult: the evangelical Christianity in which God is thought to be present as a person in someone's everyday life, and in which God's supernatural power is thought

to be immediately accessible by that person" (Luhrmann 2012, xix). The people in the churches she attended were generally middle class, college educated, and typically white, although there were some very wealthy and very poor people and many members of minority groups who belonged.

One of the striking characteristics of the church, in fact, is that congregants expect to experience God immediately, directly, and personally. Members of the church told her that God is an intimate friend who wants to know everything about them, who is as concerned with the clothing they wear as he is with matters of life and death. For these Christians, God is transformed into someone with whom members of the church have a relationship. That relationship is cultivated through prayer, the act of talking with God; and for the members of the Vineyard, prayer was a skill that, Luhrmann points out, must be learned (Luhrmann 2012, 47; see also discussion of hearing God's voice in Chapter 14). For members of the church, prayer is modeled on the idea of a conversation between friends, and the hardest part of prayer training was learning to hear God's part of the communication.

The Vineyard Christian Fellowship fosters an intense individuality among its congregants, who were taught that God was to be addressed and listened to individually. God is an all-good, all-powerful, all-knowing friend. He will care for those who seek him and who learn to pray to him. He loves them unconditionally and answers prayers; but if this is so, how does this understanding of God explain why bad things happen in the world? Evil is a fundamental problem for all religions, because part of being human is suffering, often unjustly. Theologians use the term *theodicy* to describe the field of study that proposes answers to the problem of evil. Luhrmann points out that theologians have proposed three general solutions: (1) evil is the lack of God's goodness, and humans create it when they do not choose God; (2) the world will be good in the end, even if it isn't now; and (3) although it may not look like it to us right now, we live in the best of all possible worlds (2012, 268). So how does the Vineyard Church explain human suffering? According to Luhrmann, "Churches like the Vineyard handle the problem of suffering with a fourth solution: they ignore it. Then they turn the pain into a learning opportunity. When it hurts, you are supposed to draw closer to God. . . . When God is very close and very powerful and always very loving, there is no easy explanation when he does not deliver" (2012, 260). Luhrmann adds that modern believers don't need religion to explain misfortune, or indeed anything else. "They have plenty of scientific accounts for why the

For All Those Who Were Indian in a Former Life

Andrea Smith challenges members of the New Age movement who, in her view, trivialize the situation of women like herself "who are Indian in this life."

The New Age movement completely trivializes the oppression we as Indian women face: Indian women are suddenly no longer the women who are forcibly sterilized and tested with unsafe drugs such as Depo Provera; we are no longer the women who have a life expectancy of 47 years; and we are no longer the women who generally live below the poverty level and face a 75% unemployment rate. No, we're too busy being cool and spiritual.

This trivialization of our oppression is compounded by the fact that nowadays anyone can be Indian if s/he wants to. All that is required is that one be Indian in a former life, or take part in a sweat lodge, or be mentored by a "medicine woman," or read a how-to book.

Since, according to this theory, anyone can now be "Indian," then the term Indians no longer regresses specifically to those people who have survived five hundred years of colonization and genocide. This furthers the goals of white supremacists to abrogate treaty rights and to take away what little we have left. When everyone becomes "Indian," then it is easy to lose sight of the specificity of oppression faced by those who are Indian in this life. It is no wonder we have such a difficult time finding non-Indians to support our struggles when the New Age movement has completely disguised our oppression.

The most disturbing aspect about these racist practices is that they are promoted in the name of feminism. Sometimes it seems that I can't open a feminist periodical without seeing ads promoting white "feminist" practices with little medicine wheel designs. I can't seem to go to a feminist conference without the woman who begins the conference with a ceremony being the only Indian presenter. Participants then feel so "spiritual" after this opening that they fail to notice the absence of Indian women in the rest of the conference or Native American issues in the discussions. And I certainly can't go to a feminist bookstore without seeing books by Lynn Andrews and other people who exploit Indian spirituality all over the place. It seems that, while feminism is supposed to signify the empowerment of all women, it obviously does not include Indian women.

If white feminists are going to act in solidarity with their Indian sisters, they must take a stand against Indian spiritual abuse. Feminist book and record stores should stop selling these products, and feminist periodicals should stop advertising these products. Women who call themselves feminists should denounce exploitative practices wherever they see them.

Source: A. Smith 1994, 71.

---

world is as it is and why some bodies rather than others fall ill" (2012, 295).

But if prayer is not intended to find answers to suffering, then what do these congregants get from it? According to Luhrmann, what they get is God's role as a friend to help them through a difficult time. Members of the Vineyard do not generally speculate about why there is evil or misfortune. They turn to God as they would turn to a powerful and especially trusted friend to help them deal with pain or unhappiness, and God's friendship becomes its own reward. In other words, "People stay with this God not because the theology makes sense but because the practice delivers emotionally" (Luhrmann 2012, 268). So far, this seems to be a theology of the individual—"me and my relationship with God"—but Luhrmann points out that the congregational community is essential to the development of these individual relationships: "It takes a great deal of work for the community to teach people to develop these apparently private and personal relationships with God. . . . At the Vineyard, the community stood in for God when God seemed distant and particularly when he seemed unreal" (279). Thus, although the religious beliefs of these US evangelicals offer no cause for misfortune, their religious *practice* does offer a solution for misfortune: to strengthen their personal relationship with God with the aid of their community. "They want to hold on to hope, despite their doubt. They care about transforming their own suffering, not about explaining why suffering persists. Their faith is practical, not philosophical" (Luhrmann 2012, 299).

How Do People Cope with Change?

Drastic changes in experience lead people to create new interpretations that will help them cope with the changes. Sometimes the change is an outcome of local or regional struggles. The Protestant Reformation, for example, adapted the Christian tradition to changing social circumstances in northern Europe during the Renaissance by breaking ties to the pope, turning church lands over to secular authorities, allowing clergy to marry, and so forth. Protestants continued to identify themselves as Christians, although many of their religious practices had changed.

In Guider, Cameroon, lone rural migrants to town frequently abandoned their former religious practices and took on urban customs and a new identity through conversion to Islam. However, similar conflicts between new and old ways do not everywhere lead to religious conversion. Sometimes the result is a creative synthesis of old religious practices and new ones, a process called **syncretism**. Under the pressure of Christian missionizing, indigenous people of Central America identified some of their own pre-Christian, personalized superhuman beings with particular Catholic saints. Similarly, Africans brought to Brazil identified Catholic saints with African gods to produce the syncretistic religion Candomblé.

Anthropologists have debated the nature of syncretistic practices, noting that, whereas some may be viewed as a way of resisting new ideas imposed from above, others may be introduced from above by powerful outsiders deliberately making room for local beliefs within their own more encompassing worldview. The Romans, for example, made room for local deities within their imperial pantheon, and post–Vatican II Catholicism explicitly urged non-European Catholics to worship using local cultural forms (Stewart and Shaw 1994).

When groups defend or refashion their own way of life in the face of outside encroachments, anthropologists sometimes describe their activities as **revitalization**—a deliberate, organized attempt by some members of a society to create a more satisfying culture (Wallace 1972, 75). Revitalization arises in times of crisis, most often among groups who are facing oppression and radical transformation, usually at the hands of outsiders (e.g., colonizing powers). Revitalization movements engage in a "politics of religious synthesis" that produces a range of outcomes (Stewart and Shaw 1994). Sometimes syncretism is embraced. Other times it is rejected in favor of **nativism**, or a return to the old ways. Some nativistic movements expect a messiah or prophet, who will bring back a lost golden age of peace, prosperity, and harmony, a process often called *revivalism, millenarianism,* or *messianism.*

A classic New World example of a millenarian movement is the Ghost Dance movement among indigenous peoples of the Great Plains of the United States in the late 1880s to 1890. When the buffalo were exterminated, indigenous Plains dwellers lost their independence and were herded onto reservations by numerically superior and better-armed Euro-Americans. Out of this final crisis emerged Wovoka, a prophet who taught that the existing world would soon be destroyed and that a new crust would form on the earth. All settlers and indigenous people who followed the settlers' ways would become buried. Those indigenous people who abandoned the settlers' ways, led pure lives, and danced the Ghost Dance would be saved. As the new crust formed, the buffalo would return, as would all the ancestors of the believers. Together, all would lead lives of virtue and joy.

Because the world was going to change by itself, violence against the oppressors was not a necessary part of the Ghost Dance. Nevertheless, the movement frightened settlers and the US Army, which suspected an armed uprising. Those fears and suspicions led to the massacre at Wounded Knee in which the cavalry troopers killed all the members of a Lakota (Sioux) band, principally women and children, whom they encountered off the reservation.

Nativistic movements, however, may represent resistance to, rather than escape from, the outside world, actively removing or avoiding any cultural practices associated with those who seek to dominate them. One such "antisyncretistic" group is the Kwaio, living on the island of Malaita in the Solomon Islands (see "EthnoProfile 10.7: Kwaio"). When Roger Keesing lived among them in the late twentieth century, he observed that almost all their neighbors had converted to Christianity, and that the nation of which they are a part is militantly Christian. Members of other groups wore clothing, worked on plantations or in tourist hotels, attended schools, and lived in cities. The Kwaio refused all this: "Young men carry bows and arrows; girls and women, nude except for customary ornaments, dig taro in forest gardens; valuables made of strung shell beads are exchanged at mortuary feasts; and priests sacrifice pigs to the ancestral spirits on whom prosperity and life itself depend" (Keesing 1982, 1).

---

syncretism The synthesis of old religious practices (or an old way of life) with new religious practices (or a new way of life) introduced from outside, often by force.

revitalization A conscious, deliberate, and organized attempt by some members of a society to create a more satisfying culture in a time of crisis.

nativism A return to the old ways; a movement whose members expect a messiah or prophet who will bring back a lost golden age of peace, prosperity, and harmony.

IN THEIR OWN WORDS

Custom and Confrontation

In the following passage, the late Roger Keesing recorded the words of one of his Kwaio informants, Dangeabe'u, who defends Kwaio custom.

The government has brought the ways of business, the ways of money. The people at the coast believe that's what's important, and tell us we should join in. Now the government is controlling the whole world. The side of the Bible is withering away. When that's finished, the government will rule unchallenged. It will hold all the land. All the money will go to the government to feed its power. Once everything—our lands, too—are in their hands, that will be it.

I've seen the people from other islands who have all become Christians. They knew nothing about their land. The white people have gotten their hands on their lands. The whites led them to forget all the knowledge of their land, separated them from it. And when the people knew nothing about their land, the whites bought it from them and made their enterprises. . . .

That's close upon us too. If we all follow the side of the Bible, the government will become powerful here too, and will take control of our land. We won't be attached to our land, as we are now, holding our connections to our past. If the government had control of our land, then if we wanted to do anything on it, we'd have to pay them. If we wanted to start a business—a store, say—we'd have to pay the government. We reject all that. We want to keep hold of our land, in the ways passed down to us.

Source: Keesing 1992, 184.

EthnoProfile 10.7

Kwaio

Region: Oceania (Melanesia)

Nation: Solomon Islands (Malaita)

Population: 7,000 (1970s)

Environment: Tropical island

Livelihood: Horticulture and pig raising

Political organization: Traditionally, some men with influence but no coercive power; today, part of a modern nation-state

For more information: Keesing, Roger. 1992. *Custom and confrontation: The Kwaio struggle for cultural autonomy.* Chicago: University of Chicago Press.

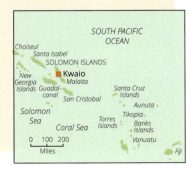

Keesing (1992) later admitted that he did not know exactly why the Kwaio responded in this way. He suspected that precolonial social and political differences between the Kwaio and their coastal neighbors influenced later developments. The colonial encounter itself was certainly relevant. In 1927, some Kwaio attacked a British patrol, killing the district officer and 13 Solomon Island troops. The subsequent massacre of many Kwaio by a police force made up of other Malaitans, followed by marginalization and persecution by the colonial government, also clearly contributed to Kwaio resistance.

It is important to emphasize that the Kwaio maintained their old ways deliberately, in the face of alternatives; their traditional way of life is therefore lived in a modern context. "In the course of anticolonial struggle, 'kastomu' (custom) and commitment to ancestral ways have become symbols of identity and autonomy" (Keesing 1992, 240). In the eyes of the Kwaio, the many Solomon Islanders who became Christianized and acculturated lost their cultural ties and thereby their ties to the land and to their past, becoming outsiders in their own homeland. Maintaining traditional ways was thus a form of political protest. From this perspective, many contemporary antisyncretistic movements in the world, from fundamentalism of various religions to movements for national identity and cultural autonomy, can be understood as having aims similar to those of the Kwaio, sparked by many of the same forces.

How Are Symbolic Practices Used as Instruments of Power?

Within any particular cultural tradition, different worldviews often coexist. How then does a particular picture of reality become the "official" worldview for a given society? And once that position is achieved, how is it maintained? To be in the running for the official picture of reality, a worldview must be able, however minimally, to make sense of some people's personal and social experiences. Sometimes, however, it may seem to some members of society that barely credible views of reality have triumphed over alternatives that seem far more plausible. Thus, something more than persuasive ability alone must be involved, and that something is power. Powerless people may be unable to dislodge the official worldview of their society. They can, however, refuse to accept the imposition of someone else's worldview and develop an unofficial worldview based on metaphors that reflect their own condition of powerlessness (Scott 1990).

How can worldviews be mobilized as instruments of power and control? First, a religious symbol can be invoked as a guarantee of self-evident truths when people in power seek to eliminate or impose certain forms of conduct. Holy books, like the Qur'an, may be used in this way. For example, a legal record from Guider, Cameroon, indicates that a son once brought suit against his father for refusing to repay him a certain amount of money. The father claimed that he had paid. Both father and son got into an increasingly heated argument in which neither would give ground. Finally, the judge in the case asked the father to take a copy of the Qur'an in his hand and swear that he was telling the truth. This he did. The son, however, refused to swear on the Qur'an and finally admitted that he had been lying. In this case, the status of the Qur'an as the unquestioned word of God, which implied the power of God to punish liars, controlled the son's behavior.

Second, a symbol may be under the direct control of a person wishing to affect the behavior of others. Consider the role of official interpreters of religious or political ideology, such as priests or kings. Their pronouncements define the bounds of permissible behavior. As Roger Keesing (1982) points out:

> Senior men, in Melanesia as elsewhere in the tribal world, have depended heavily on control of *sacred knowledge* to maintain their control of earthly politics. By keeping in their hands relations with ancestors and other spirits, by commanding magical knowledge, senior men could maintain a control mediated by the

supernatural. Such religious ideologies served too, by defining rules in terms of ancient spirits and by defining the nature of men and women in supernatural terms, to reinforce and maintain the roles of the sexes—and again to hide their nature. (219)

Keesing's observations remind us that knowledge, like power, is not evenly distributed throughout a society. Different kinds of people know different things. In some societies, what men know about their religious system is different from what women know, and what older men know may be different from what younger men know. Keesing (1982, 14) suggested that men's control over women and older men's control over younger men are based on differential access to knowledge. It is not just that these different kinds of people know different things; rather, the different things they know (and do not know) enable them (or force them) to remain in the positions they hold in the society (Figure 10.15).

FIGURE 10.15 Senior Dogon men carrying out fox trail divination. The knowledge and skills of elderly men, based on experience gained over a lifetime, provide their interpretations with an authority that those of people with less experience would not have.

Worldviews represent comprehensive ideas about the structure of the world and the place of one's own group, or one's own self, within that world. The ethnographic record offers a broad array of different worldviews, each testifying to the imaginative, meaning-making cultural capacity of humans. We have seen, however, that the influence of particular worldviews is shaped by power relations in a society. We have also seen that some anthropologists now suggest that the notion of "worldview" is insufficiently powerful to grasp the different "worlding" practices that different human groups enact.

All these ethnographic materials provoke reflection, and they are closely tied to everyday social practices. As a result, they are heavily implicated in how we understand our relations with others—human and nonhuman, living or nonliving. And if those relations lead to crisis—for example, in the form of the Anthropocene—humans respond by, among other things, seeking a way of making the crisis appear meaningful and therefore manageable. We are meaning-making, meaning-using, meaning-dependent organisms; and that is nowhere more clear than when a meaningful way of life is under assault.

Chapter Summary

1. Play is a generalized form of behavioral openness: the ability to think about, speak about, and do different things in the same way or the same thing in different ways. Play can also be thought of as a way of organizing activities. We put a frame that consists of the message "This is play" around certain activities, thereby transforming them into play. Play also permits reflexive consideration of alternative realities by setting up a separate reality and suggesting that the perspective of ordinary life is only one way to make sense of experience. The functions of play include exercise, practice for the real world, increased creativity in children, and commentary on the real world.

2. Art is a kind of play that is subject to certain culturally appropriate restrictions on form and content. It aims to evoke a holistic, aesthetic response from the artist and the observer. It succeeds when the form is culturally appropriate for the content and is technically perfect in its realization. Aesthetic evaluations are culturally shaped value judgments. We recognize art in other cultures because of its family resemblance to what we call art in our own culture. Although people with other cultural understandings may not have produced art by intention, we can often successfully appreciate what they have created as art by appropriation. These issues are addressed in ethnographic studies that call into question received ideas about what counts as "authentic" art.

3. Myths are stories whose truth seems self-evident because they do such a good job of integrating personal experiences with a wider set of assumptions about the way the world works. The power of myths comes from their ability to make life meaningful for those who accept them. As stories, myths are the products of high verbal art. A full understanding

of myth requires ethnographic background information.

4. Ritual is a repetitive social practice composed of sequences of symbolic activities such as speech, singing, dancing, gestures, and the manipulation of certain objects. In studying ritual, we pay attention not just to the symbols but also to how the ritual is performed. Cultural ideas are made concrete through ritual action. Rites of passage are rituals in which members of a culture move from one position in the social structure to another. These rites are marked by periods of separation, transition, and reaggregation. During the period of transition, individuals occupy a liminal position. All those in this position frequently develop an intense comradeship and a feeling of oneness, or communitas.

5. Ritual and play are complementary. Play is based on the premise "Let us make believe," whereas ritual is based on the premise "Let us believe." As a result, the ritual frame is far more rigid than the play frame. Although ritual may seem overwhelming and all-powerful, individuals and groups can sometimes manipulate ritual forms to achieve nontraditional ends.

6. In recent years anthropologists have become aware of how the Western idea of "religion," defined as a system of beliefs, is highly ethnocentric, rooted in Protestant Reformation of Christianity and the growth of the European secular state. These days, anthropologists who study "religion" tend to shift their emphasis to the importance of ritual practices instead of beliefs. Some anthropologists have studied the way secularism in modern nation-states is a way of defining what counts as a legitimate form of religion, and what does not. Anthropologists of ontology have found notions of religion and worldview too weak to capture the radical differences that characterize other

(continued on next page)

Chapter Summary *(continued)*

people's ways of making their worlds. Seeking out these alternative ontologies is valued as ways of finding other ways to live that might help us cope from the ravages of the Anthropocene.

7. Anthropological studies of religion tend to focus on the social institutions and meaningful processes with which they are associated. Some have also focused on the ways drastic changes in people's experiences lead them to create new meanings to explain the changes and to cope with them. This can be accomplished through elaboration of the old system to fit changing times, conversion to a new worldview, syncretism, revitalization, or resistance.

8. Because religious knowledge is not distributed evenly among the members of societies, those who control such knowledge may use it as an instrument of power to control other members of society. Two traditionally recognized kinds of religious specialists are shamans and priests, each of which is understood to possess particular skills and knowledge that allows them to mediate connections between cosmic forces and human communities. Recent work in the anthropology of ontology, focusing on small-scale societies in the Amazon, has refreshed our understanding of what a shaman can be.

For Review

1. Take the definition of play in the running glossary and explain the importance of each feature of this complex definition.

2. What are the consequences of play for animals?

3. What is metacommunication?

4. How does the case study by Elizabeth Chin about African American girls and their dolls in New Haven, Connecticut, illustrate the importance of play for understanding human symbolic practices?

5. What are the main components of the definition of art offered in the text, and why is each component important?

6. Distinguish "art by intention" from "art by appropriation."

7. What argument is made in the text concerning the role of "authenticity" in art? How does the case study illustrate these points?

8. What are myths?

9. Compare Malinowski's view of myth with the view of Claude Lévi-Strauss.

10. Explain the significance of each of the major components of the definition of ritual given in the text.

11. How may a child's birthday party be understood as a ritual?

12. Describe each stage of a rite of passage.

13. How are play and ritual complementary?

14. List A. F. C. Wallace's minimal categories of religion and define and illustrate each of them.

15. Explain the differences anthropologists recognize between shamans and priests.

16. Compare the Azande and the US evangelicals with regard to the way members of each group explain misfortune.

17. What is syncretism?

18. Explain how worldviews can be used as instruments of power.

19. How do anthropological studies of secularism lead anthropologists who study religion to rethink what a "religion" is?

20. Why do anthropologists of ontology argue that studies of "religion" and "worldview" are insufficiently reflexive? How do they argue that the anthropology of ontology can push beyond the claims of cultural relativism to show us more radical ways of being other than we are? Why do they consider this to be urgent work?

Key Terms

art 309	myths 318	priest 331	secularism 328
communitas 322	nativism 336	reflexivity 308	shaman 330
framing 308	oracles 333	religion 327	syncretism 336
liminality 322	orthodoxy 319	revitalization 336	witchcraft 332
magic 333	orthopraxy 324	rite of passage 322	worldviews 325
metacommunication 308	play 308	ritual 321	

Suggested Readings

Alland, Alexander. 1977. *The artistic animal.* New York: Doubleday Anchor. *An introductory look at the biocultural bases for art. This work is well written, clear, and fascinating.*

Bowen, John. 2008. *Religions in practice: An approach to the anthropology of religion,* 4th ed. Needham Heights, MA: Allyn & Bacon. *An up-to-date introduction of the anthropology of religion focusing on religious practice and interpretation, with a wide range of case studies.*

De la Cadena, Marisol. 2015. *Earth beings: Ecologies of practice across Andean worlds.* Durham, NC: Duke University Press. *This rich, complex text directly addresses issues of incommensurability across cultural worlds, and the sometimes surprising partial connections that may be forged across the gap. De la Cadena, a Peruvian anthropologist, set out to write a historical account of the abolition of the hacienda system in 1960s Peru, from the point of view of an indigenous man, Mariano Turpo, who had played an active role in those events. Achieving her goal, however, meant setting aside a box of archived documents and listening to Mariano's own narrative in which the earth being Ausangate played a central role. Later, de la Cadena worked with Nazario Turpo, Mariano's son, who became internationally famous as an Andean shaman, and she accompanied him when he went to Washington, DC, to advise on Andean indigenous cultures for the National Museum of the American Indian. De la Cadena's "co-labor" with Mariano and Nazario Turpo illustrates the riches that may be found when a cultural anthropologist deploys the anthropology of ontology with skill and insight.*

Errington, Shelly. 1998. *The death of authentic primitive art and other tales of progress.* Berkeley: University of California Press. *A sharp and witty book about the production, distribution, interpretation, and selling of "primitive art."*

Evans-Pritchard, E. E. (1937) 1976. *Witchcraft, oracles, and magic among the Azande,* abridged ed., prepared by Eva Gillies. Oxford: Oxford University Press. *An immensely influential and readable anthropological classic.*

Keesing, Roger. 1992. *Custom and confrontation: The Kwaio struggle for cultural autonomy.* New York: Columbia University Press. *Based on 30 years of research, Keesing's final book provides a clear, readable, and committed discussion of Kwaio resistance.*

Lambek, Michael. 2008. *A reader in the anthropology of religion,* 2nd ed. Malden, MA: Blackwell. *An excellent collection of classic and contemporary readings in the anthropology of religion.*

Schwartzman, Helen. 1978. *Transformations: The anthropology of children's play.* New York: Plenum. *A superlative work that considers how anthropologists have studied children's play, with some insightful suggestions about how they might do this in the future.*

Turner, Victor. 1969. *The ritual process.* Chicago: Aldine. *An important work in the anthropological study of ritual, this text is an eloquent analysis of rites of passage.*

Vogel, Susan. 1997. *Baule: African art/Western eyes.* New Haven, CT: Yale University Press. *A book of extraordinary photographs and beautifully clear text, this work explores both Baule and Western views of Baule expressive culture.*

 Visit our online resource center for further reading, web links, free assessments, flashcards, and videos. www.oup.com/he/lavenda5e

11

Why do anthropologists study economic relations?

All human groups must organize themselves to make available to their members the material things they need for survival, such as food, shelter, and clothing. This chapter explores the variety of economic patterns human societies have developed over the millennia. It also draws attention to the way large-scale connections forged by trade or conquest continue to shape—and be reshaped by—the local economic practices of societies throughout the world.

CHAPTER OUTLINE

How Do Anthropologists Study Economic Relations?

How Do Anthropologists Study Production, Distribution, and Consumption?

How Are Goods Distributed and Exchanged?

Does Production Drive Economic Activities?

Why Do People Consume What

They Do?

The Anthropology of Food and Nutrition

Chapter Summary

LEARNING OBJECTIVES

- Describe how anthropologists study human economic relations and address connections between culture and livelihood and self-interest, institutions, and morals.

- Explain the ways that anthropologists study production, distribution, and consumption in diverse human societies.

- Discuss how goods are distributed and exchanged in human societies, including systems of capitalism, different modes of exchange, and reciprocity.

- Articulate the relationship between production and economic activities via the concepts of labor and production and how this

relationship corresponds with conflict.

- Examine why people consume what they do according to internal and external explanations and the patterns therein.

- Identify the main ideas of the area of anthropology examining food and nutrition.

A woman sells strings of marigolds at the Mullik Ghat flower market in Kolkata, India.

Human beings are material organisms, and the seemingly endless meaningful ways we can imagine to live must always come to terms with the material realities of day-to-day existence. Culture contributes to the way human beings organize their social lives to meet such challenges. **Social organization** can be defined as the patterning of human interdependence in a given society through the actions and decisions of its members. This chapter and Chapters 12 and 13 that follow will explore the ways anthropologists have investigated differences in human social organization in three key domains: economic relations, political relations, and more intimate forms of human relatedness associated with kin and families. The variation these forms of human social organization display across space and over time is truly remarkable, but that does not mean that people are free to do or be whatever they like. Rather, the adaptive flexibility of long-lived, large-brained, social animals such as ourselves develops over the life cycle in response to a range of sometimes unpredictable experiences. This kind of developmental response would be impossible if human behavior were rigidly programmed by genes, firmly circumscribed by environments, or strictly limited by technologies.

How Do Anthropologists Study Economic Relations?

Over fifty years ago, I. M. Lewis (1967, 166ff.) observed that the northern Somalis and the Boran Galla lived next to each other in semiarid scrubland and even herded the same animals (goats, sheep, cattle, camels) (see "EthnoProfile 11.1: Somalis [Northern]" and "EthnoProfile 11.2: Boran"). Despite these similarities, the Somali and the Boran were quite different in social structure: The Boran engaged in much less fighting and feuding than the Somali; Boran families split up to take care of the animals, whereas the Somali did not; and lineage organization was less significant among the Boran. Economic and political anthropologists have attempted to explain why this should be.

What Are the Connections between Culture and Livelihood?

Although our physical survival depends on our making adequate use of the resources around us, our culture tells us which resources to use and how to use them.

social organization The patterning of human interdependence in a given society through the actions and decisions of its members.

economic anthropology The part of the discipline [of anthropology] that debates issues of human nature that relate directly to the decisions of daily life and making a living.

As we saw in Chapters 6 and 7, the subsistence strategies humans have devised are complex and involve, to one degree or another, modifying material settings in ways that enhance the success of these strategies. Economic anthropologists have attempted to explain the many variations in human livelihood that anthropologists have found in different societies. Richard Wilk (1996) has defined **economic anthropology** as "the part of the discipline that debates issues of *human nature* that relate directly to the decisions of daily life and making a living" (xv).

In ordinary conversation, when we speak of making a living, we usually mean doing what is necessary to obtain the material things—food, clothing, shelter—that sustain human life. As Chris Hann and Kevin Hart remind us (2011), "Ultimately, economic anthropology addresses questions of human nature and well-being, questions that have preoccupied every society's philosophers from the beginning" (x).

Self-Interest, Institutions, and Morals

Wilk and Cliggett (2007) argue that it is possible to identify three theoretical camps in economic anthropology, each of which depends on a different set of assumptions about human nature, and that the "real heat and argument in economic anthropology comes from underlying disagreements over these starting assumptions" (40).

EthnoProfile 11.2

Boran

Region: Eastern Africa

Nation: Kenya and Ethiopia

Population: 80,000 (1970s)

Environment: Adequate rangeland, scrub, and desert

Livelihood: Herding of cattle by preference, also sheep and goats

Political organization: Traditionally, a kinship-based organization with a set of six elders who have certain responsibilities for maintaining order; today, part of a modern nation-state

For more information: Baxter, P. T. W., and Uri Almagor, eds. 1978. *Age, generation and time*. New York: St. Martin's Press.

The first model Wilk and Cliggett (2007) identify is the *self-interested model:* This model of human nature originated during the Enlightenment and is based on the assumption that individuals are first and foremost interested in their own well-being, that selfishness is natural. Economists since Adam Smith have argued that people's resources (e.g., money) are not and never will be great enough for them to obtain all the goods they want. This view of economy also assumes that economic analysis should focus on *individuals* who must maximize *utility* (or satisfaction) under conditions of scarcity. An economizing individual sets priorities and allocates resources rationally according to those priorities. Economic anthropologists who accept the self-interest model of human behavior should therefore investigate the different priorities set by different societies and study how these priorities affect the maximizing decisions of individuals.

Other economic anthropologists, however, are committed to the *social model* of human nature. This means that they pay attention to "the way people form groups and exercise power" (Wilk and Cliggett 2007, 42). This view of human nature assumes that people ordinarily identify with the groups to which they belong and, in many cases, cannot even conceive of having a self with interests that diverge from the interest of the group. This view of human nature suggests that economics ought to focus on **institutions**—stable and enduring cultural

practices that organize social life—not on individuals. From an institutional point of view, a society's economy consists of the culturally specific processes its members use to provide themselves with material resources. Therefore, economic processes cannot be considered apart from the cultural institutions in which they are embedded (Halperin 1994).

Wilk and Cliggett's third model of human nature is the *moral model.* Economic anthropologists committed to a moral model of human nature assume that people's motivations "are shaped by culturally specific belief systems and values . . . guided by a culturally patterned view of the universe and the human place within it" (Wilk and Cliggett 2007, 43). People are socialized and enculturated into these values and practices over a lifetime, such that they will experience distress and conflict if tempted to make decisions—including economic decisions—that are contrary to their internalized morality. From the point of view of the moral model, "modern society is one that has lost the morality and ethics that guided behavior in traditional cultures, replacing them with amoral selfishness" (Wilk and Cliggett 2007, 44). Wilk and Cliggett are unwilling to take any one model as a fact and are more interested in paying close ethnographic attention to the particularities of real human beings in real sociocultural settings. "The problem is explaining why people are guided sometimes by one set of motivations and at other times by others.. . . By suspending our preconceptions about human nature, we can give more direct attention to this fundamental question, which forms the basis of each culture's practical ethics and its distinction between moral and immoral" (Wilk and Cliggett 2007, 46). This concern can also be seen in Hann and Hart's insistence that economic anthropologists focus on *persons* (rather than abstract calculating individuals), "whose preferences and choices are sometimes shaped by calculation, but usually also by the familial, social, and political contexts in which human beings are enmeshed or embedded" (2011, 9).

How Do Anthropologists Study Production, Distribution, and Consumption?

Anthropologists generally agree that economic activity is usefully subdivided into three distinct phases: production, distribution, and consumption. Production

---

institutions Complex, variable, and enduring forms of cultural practices that organize social life.

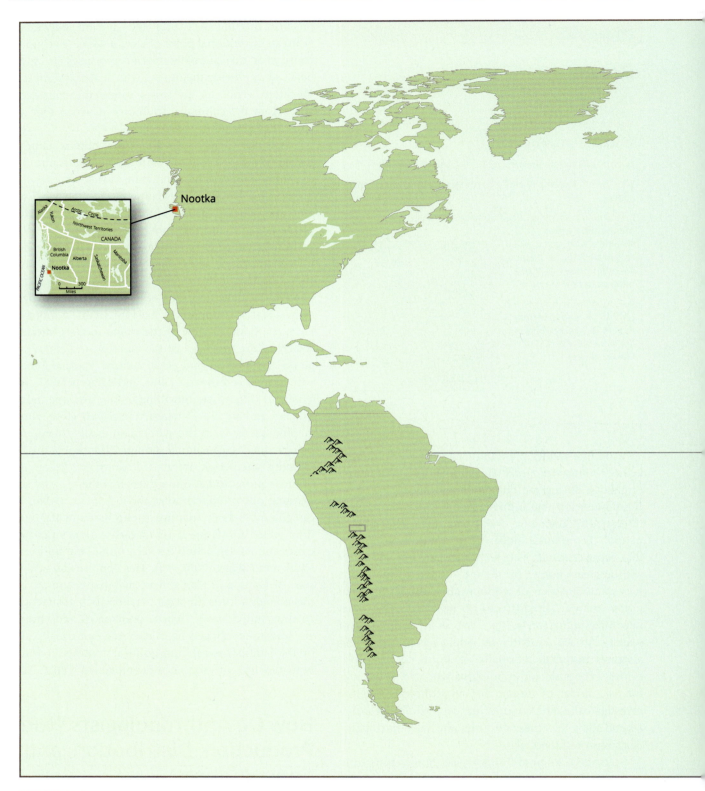

FIGURE 11.1 Locations of societies whose EthnoProfiles appear in Chapter 11.

involves transforming nature's raw materials into products useful to human beings. Distribution involves getting those products to people. Consumption involves using up the products—for example, by eating food or wearing clothing. When analyzing economic activity in a particular society, however, anthropologists differ in the importance they attach to each phase. For example, the distributive process known as *exchange* is central to the functioning of capitalist free enterprise. Some anthropologists have assumed that exchange is equally central to the functioning of all economies and have tried to explain the economic life of non-Western societies in terms of exchange. Anthropologists influenced by the work of Karl Marx, however, have argued that exchange cannot be understood properly without first

studying the nature of *production*. They point out that production shapes the context in which exchange can occur, determining which parties have how much of what kind of goods to exchange. Other anthropologists have suggested that neither production nor exchange patterns make any sense without first specifying the *consumption* priorities of the people who are producing and exchanging. Consumption priorities, they argue, are certainly designed to satisfy material needs. But the recognition of needs and of appropriate ways to satisfy them is shaped by historically contingent cultural patterns. Finally, as noted in Chapter 7, many would agree that patterns of production, exchange, and consumption are seriously affected by the kind of *storage* in use in a particular society (Figure 11.2).

FIGURE 11.2 A seventeenth-century drawing of storage warehouses built at the height of the Inka empire (below). At right, the plan of Huánuco Pampa shows the location of these storage warehouses. Some anthropologists argue that food storage practices buffer a population from ecological fluctuations, making possible considerable cultural manipulation of the economic relations of consumption.

How Are Goods Distributed and Exchanged?

Capitalism and Neoclassical Economics

The discipline of economics was born in the late 1700s, during the early years of the Industrial Revolution in western Europe. At that time, such thinkers as Adam Smith and his disciples struggled to devise theories to explain the profound changes in economic and social life that European societies had recently begun to experience.

Capitalism differed in many ways from the feudal economic system that had preceded it, but perhaps the most striking difference was how it handled distribution. Feudal economic relations allotted goods and services to different social groups and individuals on the basis of status, or position in society. Because lords had high status and many obligations, they had a right to more goods and services. Peasants, with low status and few rights, were allowed far less. This distribution of goods was time honored and not open to modification. The customs derived from capitalist economic relations, by contrast, were considered "free" precisely because they swept away all such traditional restrictions. As we shall see in our discussion of "Sedaka" Village, Malaysia, capitalism also swept away traditional protections (see Chapter 12, "EthnoProfile 12.1: 'Sedaka' Village"). In any case, distribution under capitalism was negotiated between buyers and sellers in the market.

Capitalist market exchange of goods for other goods, for labor, or (increasingly) for cash was an important development in Western economic history. It is not surprising, therefore, that Western economic theory was preoccupied with explaining how the capitalist market worked. Markets clearly had a new, decisive importance in capitalist society, which they had not possessed in feudal times. Toward the end of the nineteenth century, the views of early economic thinkers like Adam Smith were transformed into **neoclassical economics**, which remains the foundation of formal economics today. As Hann and Hart explain, neoclassical economics "still celebrated the market as the main source of increased economic welfare; but it replaced the classical view of economic value as an objective property of produced commodities, to be struggled over by the different classes, with a focus on the subjective calculations of individuals seeking to maximize their own utility" (2011, 37). This was a key turning point in the history of economics that produced the divergent theoretical positions, identified by Wilk and Cliggett, about which economists and economic anthropologists continue to disagree today.

What Are Modes of Exchange?

Some anthropologists argued that taking self-interested, materialistic decision-making in the capitalist market as the prototype of human rationality was ethnocentric. They pointed out that the capitalist market is a relatively recent cultural invention in human history. Western capitalist societies distribute material goods in a manner that is consistent with their basic values, institutions, and assumptions about human nature. So too non-Western, noncapitalist societies might be expected to have devised alternative modes of exchange that distribute material goods in ways that are in accord with their basic values, institutions, and assumptions about human nature. Anthropologists differed, however, in their attempts to characterize these differences. In the early twentieth century, for example, French anthropologist Marcel Mauss ([1950] 2000) contrasted noncapitalist **gift exchanges** (which are deeply embedded in social relations and always require a return gift) with impersonal **commodity exchanges** typical of the capitalist market (in which goods are exchanged for cash and exchange partners need have nothing further to do with one another). For other anthropologists, however, Mauss's binary division seemed to exclude too much variation. For example, Marshall Sahlins (1972) drew on the work of economic historian Karl Polanyi (e.g., 1957) to propose that three **modes of exchange** could be identified historically and cross-culturally: reciprocity, redistribution, and market exchange.

The most ancient mode of exchange was **reciprocity**. Reciprocity is characteristic of egalitarian societies, such as the Ju/'hoansi once were (see "EthnoProfile 11.4: Ju/'hoansi (!Kung")). Sahlins identified three kinds of reciprocity. *Generalized reciprocity* is found when those who exchange do so without expecting an immediate return and without specifying the value of the return. Everyone assumes that the exchanges will eventually balance out. Generalized reciprocity is often said to characterize the exchanges that ideally occur between parents

---

neoclassical economics A formal attempt to explain the workings of capitalist enterprise, with particular attention to distribution.

gift exchanges Noncapitalist forms of economic exchange that are deeply embedded in social relations and always require a return gift.

commodity exchanges Impersonal economic exchanges typical of the capitalist market in which goods are exchanged for cash and exchange partners need have nothing further to do with one another.

modes of exchange Patterns according to which distribution takes place: reciprocity, redistribution, and market exchange.

reciprocity The exchange of goods and services of equal value. Anthropologists distinguish three forms of reciprocity: *generalized*, in which neither the time nor the value of the return is specified; *balanced*, in which a return of equal value is expected within a specified time limit; and *negative*, in which parties to the exchange hope to get something for nothing.

"So Much Work, So Much Tragedy . . . and for What?"

Angelita P. C. (the author's surnames were initialed to preserve her anonymity) describes traditional labor for farmers' wives in Costa Rica during the 1930s. Her account was included in a volume of peasant autobiographies published in Costa Rica in 1979.

The life of farmers' wives was more difficult than the life of day laborers' wives; what I mean is that we work more. The wife of the day laborer, she gets clean beans with no rubbish, shelled corn, pounded rice, maybe she would have to roast the coffee and grind it. On the other hand, we farm wives had to take the corn out of the husk, shuck it; and if it was rice, generally we'd have to get it out of the sack and spread it out in the sun for someone to pound it in the mortar. Although we had the advantage that we never lacked the staples: tortillas, rice, beans, and sugar-water. When you had to make tortillas, and that was every day, there were mountains of tortillas, because the people who worked in the fields had to eat a lot to regain their strength with all the effort they put out. And the tortilla is the healthiest food that was eaten—still is eaten—in the countryside. Another thing we had to do often was when

you'd get the corn together to sell it, you always had to take it off the cob and dry it in the sun: the men spread it out on a tarp, maybe two or three sackfuls, and they would go and bring the corn, still in the husks, up from the corn-field or the shack where it was kept. Well, we women had to guard it from the chickens or the pigs that were always in the house, but the rush we had when it started to rain and the men hadn't gotten back! We had to fill the sacks with corn and then a little later haul it in pots to finish filling them; that's if the rain gave us time. If not, all of us women in the house would have to pick up the tarps—sometimes the neighbor-women would get involved in all the bustle— to carry the corn inside. We looked like ants carrying a big worm! The thing was to keep the corn from getting wet.

It didn't matter if you threw out your spine, or if your uterus dropped, or you started hemorrhaging, or aborted, but since none of that happened immediately, it was the last thing we thought of. So much work, so much tragedy and that was so common that it seemed like just a natural thing, and for what? To sell corn at about 20 colones or at most at 24 colones per fanega [about 3 bushels] of 24 baskets! What thankless times for farm people!

Source: *Autobiografías campesinas.* 1979. Vol. 1. Heredia, Costa Rica: Editorial de la Universidad Nacional, 36 (translation from the original Spanish by Robert H. Lavenda).

and their children. In the United States, for example, parents ordinarily do not keep a running tab on what it costs them to raise their children and then present their children with repayment schedules when they reach the age of 18. The expectation is that children will eventually reciprocate by meeting the needs of their aged parents as best they can, whatever those needs turn out to be. *Balanced reciprocity* is found when those who exchange expect a return of equal value within a specified time limit (e.g., when cousins exchange gifts of equal value with one another at Christmastime). Lee (1992, 103) notes that the Ju/'hoansi distinguish between barter, which requires an immediate return of an equivalent,

and *hxaro*, which is a kind of generalized reciprocity that encourages social obligations to be extended into the future. Finally, *negative reciprocity* is an exchange of goods and services in which at least one party attempts to get something for nothing without suffering any penalties. These attempts can range from haggling over prices to outright seizure, as with cattle rustling.

Redistribution, the second mode of exchange, requires some form of centralized social organization. Those who control the central position receive economic contributions from all members of the group. It is then their responsibility to redistribute the goods they receive in a way that provides for every member of the group. The Internal Revenue Service is probably the institution of redistribution that people in the United States know best. A classic anthropological example of redistribution is the *potlatch* of the indigenous peoples of the Northwest coast of North America. In the highly stratified fishing

redistribution A mode of exchange that requires some form of central-ized social organization to receive economic contributions from all members of the group and to redistribute them in such a way as to provide for every group member.

FIGURE 11.3 Shirts for sale at the market in Guider, Cameroon. Markets can be found in many societies, but capitalism links markets to trade and money in a unique way.

EthnoProfile 11.3

Nootka

Region: North America

Nation: Canada (Vancouver Island)

Population: 6,000 (1970s)

Environment: Rainy, relatively warm coastal strip

Livelihood: Fishing, hunting, gathering

Political organization: Traditionally, ranked individuals, chiefs; today, part of a modern nation-state

For more information:
Rosman, Abraham, and Paula G. Rubel. 1971. *Feasting with mine enemy: Rank and exchange among northwest coast societies.* New York: Columbia University Press.

and gathering society of the Nootka, for example, nobles sought to outdo one another in generosity by giving away vast quantities of objects during the potlatch ceremony (see "EthnoProfile 11.3: Nootka"). The noble who gave the potlatch accumulated goods produced in one village and redistributed them to other nobles attending the ceremony. When the guests returned to their own villages, they in turn redistributed the goods among their followers.

Market exchange, invented in capitalist society, is the most recent mode of exchange, according to Polanyi (1977) (Figure 11.3). Polanyi was well aware that trade, money, and market institutions had developed independently of one another historically. He also knew that they could be found in societies outside the West. The uniqueness of capitalism was how all three institutions were linked to one another in the societies of early modern Europe.

According to Polanyi (1977), different modes of exchange often coexist within a single society, although he argued that only one functions as the society's overall mode of economic integration. The United States, for example, is integrated by the market mode of exchange, yet redistribution and reciprocity have not disappeared. Within the family, parents who obtain income from the market redistribute that income, or goods obtained with that income, to their children. Generalized reciprocity also characterizes much exchange within the family: as noted earlier, parents regularly provide their children with food and clothing without expecting any immediate return; and children regularly feel obligated to do what they can to meet the needs of their parents as they age.

The Maisin and Reciprocity

John Barker (2016) has studied the Maisin of Collingwood Bay, Papua New Guinea, for many years. Part of his research has looked at the way in which

---

market exchange The exchange of goods (trade) calculated in terms of a multipurpose medium of exchange and standard of value (money) and carried out by means of a supply–demand–price mechanism (the market).

reciprocity forms the social structure of the Maisin and how the cash economy and the reciprocity economy have affected each other.

Barker notes that Maisin society is based on reciprocity. A steady give and take of gifts, labor, and advice should characterize the relationship of close relatives. The Maisin do not keep track of what each person gives, gets, or is owed. Rather, people demonstrate their mutual trust and support by allowing things to balance out over time. This is what we have just referred to as *generalized* reciprocity. This kind of sharing is what the Maisin refer to as *marawa-wawe*, which translates as "love, peace, or social amity," and is a Maisin central value (Barker 2016, 50). It represents the way family and close friends should treat each other. "Indeed, it is what makes family and close friends." It is at this level that the obligation to reciprocate is most strongly felt. Barker distinguishes three different types of relationship at this level: sisters and brothers and wives and husbands employ complementary reciprocity, with each making distinct contributions to the household. Their exchanges denote separate if not equal status. Parents and children, and older and younger siblings engage in asymmetrical reciprocity—the elder should take care of the child or younger sibling by providing general food and good advice, and the child or younger sibling should listen respectfully and obey the parents' or older siblings' wishes. Over the course of a lifetime, children should return the original gifts of food or support to bring the relationship into balance. Exchange among members of different households, clan mates, and friends is symmetrical, such that the exchange is more or less in balance. This marks their equivalence.

The circle of neighbors and relatives in which the steady give and take is found tends not to extend much beyond nearby households that usually belong to close relatives. While these circles overlap, forming what Barker calls a dense interwoven exchange network, they do not form a unitary system. Rather, the more distant people are in terms of relatedness and residence, the harder it is to create the easy give and take of the inner circle. Exchanges are far less frequent, more carefully organized, and are recognized as balanced. This is *balanced* reciprocity.

As one moves from trusted family and close friends to increasingly distant exchange partners, one reaches the edges of social relationships, marked by *negative* reciprocity. Negative reciprocity in the Maisin world occurs between parties that have little or no social connection and so have no moral obligation to each other. They are strangers or nearly so. They are also potential antagonists, targets for barter rather than exchange, and for stealing rather than giving.

As Barker (2016) puts it:

Reciprocity lies at the heart of the Maisin subsistence economy, but it should be clear by now that it is neither simple nor limited to the business of moving items between producers and consumers. Reciprocity provides the key means by which the Maisin create and sustain social relationships. The constant give-and-take of daily exchanges embodies an essential assumption that social relationships cannot be taken for granted. They must be created, affirmed, reproduced, and modified through giving and receiving. (54)

But there is more to the story. As well as growing their own food and building their own houses out of material from the forest, since the 1890s, the Maisin have simultaneously lived in a world of cash and commodities, a world with different rules and a different moral logic. Over the years, Barker tells us, villagers have become increasingly dependent on purchased commodities, ranging from clothing or fish hooks to soccer balls and cigarettes, travel to visit relatives in town, or school fees for their children (2016, 56–57). Although villagers complain about the problems money brings, no one wants to return to a time when people relied on local resources alone.

Opportunities for earning money locally are limited; the best and most reliable source of money now is remittances from relatives who are working elsewhere, either in Papua New Guinea or in another country. Villagers expect that their relatives who find work outside the village will "not forget" the people at home. "While life in the towns is expensive, most employed Maisin routinely put aside part of their salaries to assist their rural relatives in medical emergencies, bride wealth exchanges, funerals, and local business start-ups. They accommodate relatives visiting from the village and send them home with parcels of clothing and other goods" (Barker 2016, 58). They do this because they have been brought up in a world based on reciprocal exchange, and because their rural relatives regularly remind them of the debt owed to those who brought them up. They also do it in order to leave open the possibility of being able to retire in their native village. By helping their rural relatives, they are assisting the people who care for the land and protect their property rights. As of 2016, almost all adult Maisin have lived for a time—and in many cases, a long time—in their towns, either working or visiting employed relatives.

There appears to be a conflict between a "traditional" economic system built on reciprocal exchange and a "modern" one, based on money and commodities. The conflict can be seen as between an egalitarian system, in which there are no permanent ranked socioeconomic classes based on unequal access to wealth and prestige. Money can disrupt the obligation to return a gift, in part because it can be hidden. "At a deeper level, money and markets imply a different type of morality, one focused on the individual who through hard work, good luck, or a combination of both succeeds on his or her own merits, with no help from others. Thus the introduction of money can be understood as the main engine of a series of transformations—for reciprocity between people to transactions mediated by abstract markets in which value is set; from self-reliance to dependence upon wages paid by employers; from a relatively egalitarian to an economically stratified society; from a moral emphasis upon one's kin and community to the celebration of the self-reliant individual" (Barker 2016, 60–61).

Although there are indications of a market-oriented change in Maisin society, Barker observed that at every stage, Maisin have used their assumptions about reciprocity and morality to shape their understanding and use of money. The requirement to reciprocate remains strong and public. Indeed, employed Maisin often complained privately to Barker about the pressure they receive from villagers to share their cash. Yet most people share what they have because it is the normal thing to do. Those who have more take pleasure and pride in demonstrating their generosity. The subsistence, reciprocity-based economy is actually being subsidized by the cash economy.

Barker concludes his discussion of the interacting economic systems by noting that in recent years, the Maisin have become more tolerant of the inequalities money creates. Some households are better off than others. Villagers have become accustomed to using money in the village. Even so, reciprocity remains central to both the Maisin economy and moral system. "There is no hunger in Maisin communities; the requirement to share, to support others, is too compelling. Maisin are keenly aware of the dangers money can bring or the threat it represents to their ancestral way of life. They need money; there is no turning back. Yet, at least for the time being, the Maisin appear to have been more or less successful in balancing the opposed logic of gift and commodity systems of value" (2016, 63–64).

Does Production Drive Economic Activities?

Some economic anthropologists have argued that production is the driving force behind economic activity, creating supplies of goods that must accommodate people's demand, thereby determining levels of consumption. Anthropologists who take this view borrow their perspective, as well as many key concepts, from the works of Karl Marx. They argue that studying production explains important economic processes ignored by views that emphasize market exchange as the driving force of economic activity.

Labor

Labor is perhaps the most central Marxian concept these anthropologists have emphasized. **Labor** is the activity linking human social groups to the material world around them: human beings must actively struggle together to transform natural substances into forms they can use. Human labor is therefore always *social* labor. Marx emphasized the importance of human physical labor in the material world, especially in the production of food, clothing, shelter, and tools. But Marx also recognized the importance of mental or cognitive labor: human intelligence allows us to reflect on and organize productive activities in different ways.

Modes of Production

Marx attempted to classify the ways different human groups carry out production. Each way is called a **mode of production**. Anthropologist Eric Wolf (1982) defined a mode of production as "a specific, historically occurring set of social relations through which labor is deployed to wrest energy from nature by means of tools, skills, organization, and knowledge" (75). Tools, skills, organization, and knowledge constitute what Marx called the **means of production**. The social relations linking human beings who use a given means of production within a particular mode of production are called the **relations of production**. That is, different productive tasks (clearing the bush, planting, harvesting, etc.) are assigned to different social groups, which Marx called **classes**, all of which must work together for production to be successful. Wolf notes that Marx speaks of at least eight different

---

labor The activity linking human social groups to the material world around them; from the point of view of Karl Marx, labor is therefore always social labor.

mode of production A specific, historically occurring set of social relations through which labor is deployed to wrest energy from nature by means of tools, skills, organization, and knowledge.

means of production The tools, skills, organization, and knowledge used to extract energy from nature.

relations of production The social relations linking the people who use a given means of production within a particular mode of production.

classes Ranked groups within a hierarchically stratified society whose membership is defined primarily in terms of wealth, occupation, or other economic criteria.

ANTHROPOLOGY *in Everyday Life*

Producing Sorghum and Millet in Honduras and the Sudan

Applied anthropologists carry out much work in international development, often in agricultural programs. The US Agency for International Development (AID) is the principal instrument of US foreign development assistance. One direction taken by AID in the mid-1970s was to create multidisciplinary research programs to improve food crops in developing countries. An early research program dealt with sorghum and millet, important grains in some of the poorest countries in the world (Figure 11.4). This was the International Sorghum/Millet Research Project (INTSORMIL). Selected American universities investigated one of six areas: plant breeding, agronomy, plant pathology, plant physiology, food chemistry, and socioeconomic studies.

Anthropologists from the University of Kentucky, selected for the socioeconomic study, used ethnographic field research techniques to gain firsthand knowledge of the socioeconomic constraints on the production, distribution, and consumption of sorghum and millet among limited-resource agricultural producers in the western Sudan and in Honduras. They intended to make their findings available to INTSORMIL as well as to scientists and government officials in the host countries. They believed sharing such knowledge could lead to more effective research and development. This task also required ethnographic research and anthropological skill.

The principal investigators from the University of Kentucky were Edward Reeves, Billie DeWalt, and Katherine DeWalt. They took a holistic and comparative approach, called *Farming Systems Research* (FSR). This approach attempts to determine the techniques used by farmers with limited resources to cope with the social, economic, and ecological conditions under which they live. FSR is holistic because it examines how the different crops and livestock are integrated and managed as a system. It also relates farm productivity to household consumption and off-farm sources of family income (Reeves et al. 1987, 74). This is very different from the traditional methods of agricultural research, which grow and test one crop at a time in an experiment station. The scientists at INTSORMIL are generally acknowledged among the best sorghum and millet researchers in the world, but their expertise comes from traditional agricultural research methods. They have spent little time working on the problems of limited-resource farmers in Third World countries.

The anthropologists saw their job as facilitating "a constant dialog between the farmer, who can tell what works best given the circumstances, and agricultural scientists, who produce potentially useful new solutions to old problems" (Reeves et al. 1987, 74–75). However, this was easier said than done in the sorghum/millet project. The perspectives of farmers and scientists were very different from one another. The anthropologists found themselves having to learn the languages and the conceptual systems of both the farmers and the scientists for the two groups to be able to communicate.

The anthropologists began research in June 1981 in western Sudan and in southern Honduras. They were in the field for 14 months of participant observation and in-depth interviewing, as well as survey interviewing of limited-resource farmers, merchants, and middlemen. They discovered that the most significant constraints the farmers faced were uncertain rainfall, low soil fertility, and inadequate labor and financial resources (Reeves et al. 1987, 80). Equally important

modes of production in his own writings, although he focused mainly on the capitalist mode.

Wolf (1982) found the concept of mode of production useful and suggests that three modes of production have been particularly important in human history: (1) a *kin-ordered mode* (Figure 11.5) in which social labor is deployed on the basis of kinship relations (e.g., husbands/fathers clear the fields, the whole family plants, mothers/wives weed, children keep animals out of the field); (2) a *tributary mode* "in which the primary producer, whether cultivator or herdsman, is allowed access to the means of production while tribute [a payment of goods or labor] is exacted from him by political or military means" (Wolf 1982, 79); and (3) the *capitalist mode*, which has three main features—the means of production are private property owned by members of the capitalist class, workers must sell their labor power to the capitalists to survive, and surpluses of wealth are produced that capitalists may retain as profit or reinvest in production to increase output and generate further surpluses and higher profits.

The kin-ordered mode of production is found among foragers and those farmers and herders whose political organization does not involve domination by one group. The tributary mode is found among farmers or herders living in a social system that is divided into classes of rulers and subjects. Subjects produce both for themselves and for their rulers, who take a certain proportion of their subjects' produce or labor as tribute. The capitalist mode, the most recent to develop, can be found in the industrial societies of North America and western Europe beginning in the seventeenth and

FIGURE 11.4 INTSORMIL has been involved in the improvement of the cultivation of sorghum and millet. This is sorghum.

were the social and cultural systems within which the farmers were embedded. Farmers based their farming decisions on their understanding of who they were and what farming meant in their own cultures.

As a result of the FSR group's research, it became increasingly clear that "real progress in addressing the needs of small farmers in the Third World called for promising innovations to be tested at village sites and on farmers' fields under conditions that closely approximated those which the farmers experience" (Reeves et al. 1987, 77). Convincing the scientists and bureaucrats of this required the anthropologists to become advocates for the limited-resource farmers. Bill DeWalt and Edward Reeves ended up negotiating INTSORMIL's contracts with the Honduran and Sudanese governments and succeeded in representing the farmers. They had to learn enough about the bureaucracies and the agricultural scientists so they could put the farmers' interests in terms the others could understand.

As a result of the applied anthropologists' work, INTSORMIL scientists learned to understand how small farmers in two countries made agricultural decisions. They also learned that not all limited-resource farmers are alike.

The INTSORMIL staff was so impressed that it began funding long-term research directed at relieving the constraints that limited-resource farmers face. Rather than trying to develop and then introduce hybrids, INTSORMIL research aimed to modify existing varieties of sorghum. The goal is better-yielding local varieties that can be grown together with other crops.

In summary, Reeves et al. point out that without the anthropological research, fewer development funds would have been allocated to research in Sudan and Honduras. More important, the nature of the development aid would have been different. ◼

FIGURE 11.5 This drawing from 1562 shows Native American men breaking the soil and Native American women planting, a gender-based division of labor.

IN THEIR OWN WORDS

Solidarity Forever

Anthropologist Dorinne Kondo, who worked alongside Japanese women in a Tokyo sweets factory, describes how factory managers, almost despite their best efforts, managed to engender strong bonds among women workers.

Our shared exploitation sometimes provided the basis for commonality and sympathy. The paltry pay was often a subject of discussion.. . . My co-workers and I were especially aware, however, of the toll our jobs took on our bodies. We constantly complained of our sore feet, especially sore heels from standing on the concrete floors. And a company-sponsored trip to the seashore revealed even more occupational hazards. At one point, as we all sat down with our rice balls and our box lunches, the part-timers pulled up the legs of their trousers to compare their varicose veins. In our informal contest, Hamada-san and Iida-san tied for first prize. The demanding pace and the lack of assured work breaks formed another subject of discussion. At most of the factories in the neighborhood where I conducted extensive interviews, work stopped at ten in the morning and at three in the afternoon, so workers could have a cup of tea and perhaps some crackers. Nothing of the sort occurred at the Satō factory, although the artisans were, if the pace of work slackened, able to escape the workroom, sit on their haunches, and have a smoke, or grab a snack if they were out doing deliveries or running up and down the stairs to the other divisions.

Informal restrictions on the part-timers' movement and time seemed much greater. Rarely, if ever, was there an appropriate slack period where all of us could take a break. Yet our energy, predictably, slumped in the afternoon. After my first few months in wagashi, Hamadasan began to bring in small containers of fruit juice, so we could take turns having a five-minute break to drink the juice and eat some seconds from the factory. Informal, mutual support enabled us to keep up our energies, as we each began to bring in juice or snacks for our tea breaks.

The company itself did nothing formally in this regard, but informal gestures of thoughtfulness and friendliness among co-workers surely redounded to the company's benefit, for they fostered our sense of intimacy and obligation to our fellow workers. The tea breaks are one example, but so are the many times we part-timers would stop off at Iris, our favorite coffee house, to sip banana juice or melon juice and trade gossip. We talked about other people in the company, about family, about things to do in the neighborhood. On one memorable occasion, I was sitting with the Western division part-timers in a booth near the window. A car honked as it went by, and Sakada-san grimaced and shouted loudly, "Shitsurei yarō—rude bastard!" The offender turned out to be her husband. In subsequent weeks, Sakada-san would delight in recounting this tale again and again, pronouncing shitsurei yarō with ever greater relish, and somehow, we never failed to dissolve in helpless laughter.

Source: Kondo 1990, 291–92.

---

eighteenth centuries. The concept of mode of production thus draws attention to many of the same features of economic life highlighted in traditional anthropological discussions of subsistence strategies. Yet, the concept emphasizes forms of social and political organization as well as material productive activities and shows how they are interconnected. That is, the kin-ordered mode of production is distinctive as much for its use of the kinship system to allocate labor to production as for the kind of production undertaken, such as farming. In a kin-ordered mode of production, the *relations of kinship* serve as the *relations of production* that enable a particular *mode of production* to be carried out. Farm labor

organized according to kin-ordered relations of production, where laborers are relatives to whom no cash payment is due, is very different from farm labor organized according to capitalist relations of production, where laborers are often nonrelatives who are paid a wage.

What Is the Role of Conflict in Material Life?

Anthropologists traditionally have emphasized the important links between a society's organization (kinship groups, chiefdom, state) and the way that society meets its subsistence needs, either to demonstrate the stages of cultural evolution or to display the functional inter-relationships between a society's parts. In both cases, however, the emphasis of the analysis has been on the harmonious fashion in which societies operate. For some observers, this carried the additional message that social harmony was "natural" and should not be tampered with. Social change was possible, but it would take place in an orderly fashion, in the fullness of time, according to laws of development beyond the control of individual members of society.

Many anthropologists, however, have not been persuaded that social organization is naturally harmonious or that social change is naturally orderly. They find the Marxian approach useful precisely because it treats conflict and disorder as a natural part of the human condition. The concept of mode of production makes a major contribution to economic anthropology precisely because it acknowledges that the potential for conflict is built into the mode of production itself. And the more complex and unequal is the involvement of different classes in a mode of production, the more intense is the struggle between them likely to be. The links between economic and political relations become particularly obvious and must be addressed (see Chapter 12).

Why Do People Consume What They Do?

Consumption usually refers to the using up of material goods necessary for human survival. These goods include—at a minimum—food, drink, clothing, and shelter; they can and often do include much more. Until quite recently, the study of consumption by economists and others has been much neglected, especially when compared to distribution or production. It seemed clear either that people consume goods for obvious reasons (i.e., because they need to eat and drink to survive) or that they consume goods as a result of idiosyncratic personal preferences (e.g., "I like the flavor of licorice and so I eat a lot of it, but my neighbor hates the flavor and would never put it into his mouth"). In either case, studying consumption seemed unlikely to reveal any interesting cultural patterns. As we will see below, however, anthropologists have always noticed striking differences in consumption patterns in different societies that seemed hard to reconcile with accepted economic explanations. Historically, anthropologists have taken three basic approaches to account for these patterns: (1) the internal explanation, (2) the external explanation, and (3) the cultural explanation.

The Internal Explanation: Malinowski and Basic Human Needs

The internal explanation for human consumption patterns comes from the work of Bronislaw Malinowski. Malinowski's version of functionalist anthropology explains social practices by relating them to the basic human needs that each practice supposedly fulfills. Basic human needs can be biological or psychological. Whatever their origin, if these needs go unmet, Malinowski argued, a society might not survive. Malinowski proposed a list of basic human needs, which includes nourishment, reproduction, bodily comforts, safety, movement, growth, and health. Every culture responds in its own way to these needs with some form of the corresponding institutions: food-getting techniques, kinship, shelter, protection, activities, training, and hygiene (Malinowski 1944, 91).

Malinowski's approach had the virtue of emphasizing the dependence of human beings on the physical world to survive. In addition, Malinowski was able to show that many customs that appear bizarre to uninitiated Western observers make sense once it is seen how they help people satisfy their basic human needs. However, Malinowski's approach fell short of explaining why all societies do not share the same consumption patterns. After all, some people eat wild fruit and nuts and wear clothing made of animal skins, others eat bread made from domesticated wheat and wear garments woven from the hair of domesticated sheep, and still others eat millet paste and meat from domesticated cattle and go naked. Why should these differences exist?

The External Explanation: Cultural Ecology

A later generation of anthropologists was influenced by evolutionary and ecological studies. They tried to answer this question with an external explanation for the diversity of human consumption patterns. As we saw in earlier chapters, ecology has to do with how living species relate to one another and the physical environment. To explain patterns of human consumption (as well as production and distribution), cultural ecologists have often turned to the resources available in the particular habitats exploited by particular human groups. Hence, the particular consumption patterns found in a particular society cannot depend just on the obvious, internal

---

consumption The using up of material goods necessary for human survival.

IN THEIR OWN WORDS

Questioning Collapse

Since the late 1990s, geographer Jared Diamond has published two books that have enjoyed wide popular success, Guns, Germs, and Steel: The Fates of Human Societies *(1997) and* Collapse: How Societies Choose to Fail or Succeed *(2005). At the same time, some anthropologists— including those who admire Diamond's achievements—are concerned by the selective way in which he makes use of anthropological data to support his arguments. These issues are explored in* Questioning Collapse: Human Resilience, Ecological Vulnerability, and the Aftermath of Empire *(2009), a recent volume of essays edited by Mesoamerican archaeologist Patricia A. McAnany and Near Eastern archaeologist Norman Yoffee.*

What's the Beef between Scholars and Popular Writers?

Among the issues we wanted to explore in our AAA [American Anthropological Association] symposium and in our subsequent seminar were the reasons for the incredible success of Jared Diamond's books. After all, Diamond is a professor of geography at UCLA, not an anthropologist, archaeologist, or historian. He obviously reads prolifically the obscure (to most laypersons and students) publications of historians, archaeologists, and sociocultural anthropologists and can present their research with verve and clarity and as important knowledge for a larger public. In *Guns, Germs, and Steel*, Diamond confronts racist views of the past that claim that Western superiority is due to the genes and genius of Westerners. In *Collapse* he warns of real and potential environmental destruction in the present by arguing that past societies and cultures collapsed because they damaged their environments. His successful writing style of distilling simple points from complex issues is a remarkable gift; it is no wonder that his books win prizes and are used in classrooms.. . .

In this book most of the chapters are critical of Diamond's stories. This is why the AAA session was organized in the first place. Whereas we are indebted to Diamond for drawing together so much material from our own fields of research and for emphasizing how important anthropological and historical knowledge is for the modern world, as scholars we want to get things right. We also want to write in such a way that the public can grasp not only the significance of research findings but also how we do research and why we think that some stories are right,

whereas others are not as right or are incomplete and still others are dead wrong.

Thanks to Diamond's provoking inquiries and more generally those of the popular media, we focus this book on several questions: (1) Why do we portray ancient societies—especially those with indigenous descendants—as successes or failures, both in scholarship and in the popular media? We want to get the story of social change right, and descendants of the ancient societies we study demand it. (2) How do we characterize people who live today in the aftermath of empires? Today's world is the product of past worlds, and the consequences of the past cannot be ignored. (3) How are urgent climatic and environmental issues today similar to those faced by our ancestors? Can we learn from the past? . . .

The Question of Societal Collapse

Over two decades ago the sociologist Shmuel Eisenstadt wrote that societal collapse seldom occurs if collapse is taken to mean "the complete end of those political systems and their accompanying civilizational framework." Indeed, studying collapse is like viewing a low-resolution digital photograph: it's fine when small, compact, and viewed at a distance but dissolves into disconnected parts when examined up close. More recently, Joseph Tainter, after a search for archaeological evidence of societal "overshoot" and collapse, arrived at a conclusion similar to Eisenstadt's: there wasn't any. When closely examined, the overriding human story is one of survival and regeneration. Certainly crises existed, political forms changed, and landscapes were altered, but rarely did societies collapse in an absolute and apocalyptic way. Even the examples of societal collapse often touted in the media—Rapa Nui (Easter Island), Norse Greenland, Puebloan U.S. Southwest, and the Maya Lowlands—are also cases of societal resilience when examined carefully, as authors do in the chapters in this book (see Figure 11.6). Popular writers' tendency to approach the past in terms of a series of societal failures and collapses—while understandable in terms of providing drama and mystery—falls apart in light of the information and fresh perspectives presented in this book.

Abandoned ruins—the words themselves evoke a romantic sense of failure and loss to which even archaeologists—most of whom are reared in the Western tradition—are not immune. But why is it that when we visit Stonehenge we don't feel a twinge of cultural loss, but simply a sense that things were very different 5,000 years ago? Is it because Stonehenge is somehow part of *our* civilization? On the other hand, the Great Houses of Chaco Canyon, the soaring pyramids of ancestral Maya cities, the

IN THEIR OWN WORDS

FIGURE 11.6   One case study by Jared Diamond that has been criticized by anthropologists is that of Rapa Nui (Easter Island), where enormous human figures were carved between the years 1250 and 1500.

fallen colossal heads of Rapa Nui tend to invoke a sense of mysterious loss and cultural failure, and a notion that something must have gone terribly wrong environmentally. For many of us these places and people are not part of the Western experience. Moreover, descendant communities—in all three cases—live marginalized on the edge of nation-states without the resources and connections to worldwide media that are needed to tell their own story, at least to an English-speaking audience. Might these abandoned places, in many cases, be just as accurately viewed as part of a successful strategy of survival, part of human resilience? . . . Abandonment also can be read as indicative of opportunity elsewhere and of the societal flexibility to seize that opportunity. . . .

Although it would be wonderful to feel that scholarly understanding of abandonment stood outside contemporary social concerns, it is pretty clear that today's worries about the future make their way into our explanations of the past. . . . Historians and archaeologists, who are not immune to seeing the past through modern lenses, try to test the relevance of their ideas by looking for multiple lines of evidence that point to the same conclusion.

In our chapters we hold interpretations of past environmental abuse up to critical scrutiny for two reasons. First, because the fit between ideas and evidence is never straightforward. Second (and for better or worse), humans have a long history of both interacting assertively with their environments and coalescing into fragile political groups that fission easily. Archaeologists such as Sander van der Leeuw have shown that landscape alteration has occurred in human societies since the end of the Pleistocene (Ice Age), 10,000 years ago. It is not difficult to find evidence of preindustrial landscape alteration . . . but it is another

matter altogether to link that evidence in a convincing and rigorous fashion to site abandonment or changes in political forms. The notion that the present recapitulates the past is not necessarily true. We ask how long human societies have possessed the technological ability to profoundly change and destroy their environment and bring down their societies.

In concluding comments to this book and elsewhere, J. R. McNeill amasses a formidable body of evidence suggesting that the human ability to impact environment on a global scale is newfound and cannot be pushed back beyond the Industrial Revolution of the 1800s. . . .

Choice and Geographic Determinism

In his book on societal collapse, Jared Diamond proposes that societies choose to succeed or fail. On the other hand, in *Guns, Germs, and Steel*, there was no choice: today's inequalities among modern nation-states are argued to be the result of geographic determinism. In the first scenario, societies (or power brokers within societies) make the decisions that result in long-term success or failure. . . . At the root of this thesis is the modern neoliberal theory of self-interested motivation as well as the assumption of unconstrained and rational choice. . . . Many economists view the motivational assumptions of self-interest and rational choice as lacking explanatory power, even when applied to Western societies. When applied globally and into deep time, this theory has particular difficulties. . . .

If we are to understand global events today, we must perceive that the basis of intentionality and motivation can differ profoundly across the globe. . . . For those of us studying early states, archaeologists and historians alike, it isn't easy to discern intentions and their effects in the remote past. . . . Many current global inequalities indisputably are the product of historical colonialism and its enduring legacy. . . .

If one takes a long view, as archaeologists and historians are wont to do, then the situation in the year 2009 seems less the manifestation of a geographic destiny than it is a temporary state of affairs. Can anyone say that the present balance of economic and political power will be the same in 2500 as it is today? For example, in the year 1500 some of the most powerful and largest cities in the world existed in China, India, and Turkey. In the year 1000, many of the mightiest cities were located in Peru, Iraq, and Central Asia. In the year 500 they could be found in central Mexico, Italy, and China. In 2500 BCE, the most formidable rulers lived in Iraq, Egypt, and Pakistan. What geographic determinism can account for this? Is history a report card of success or failure?

Source: McAnany and Yoffee 2009, 4–10.

hunger drive, which is the same for all people everywhere; instead, people depend on the particular external resources present in the local habitat to which their members must adapt.

How Is Consumption Culturally Patterned?

Why do people X raise peanuts and sorghum? The internal, Malinowskian explanation would be to meet their basic human need for food. The external, cultural ecological explanation would be because peanuts and sorghum are the only food crops available in their habitat that, when cultivated, will meet their subsistence needs. Both these answers sound reasonable, but they are also incomplete. To be sure, people must consume something to survive, and they will usually meet this need by exploiting plant and animal species locally available. However, Malinowski and many cultural ecologists seem to assume that patterns of consumption are dictated by an iron environmental necessity that permits only narrow adaptive options. They further seem to assume that human beings are by and large powerless to modify what the environment offers (at least, it is sometimes implied, until the invention of modern technology).

But we have seen that human beings (along with many other organisms) are able to construct their own niches, buffering themselves from some kinds of selection pressures while exposing themselves to other kinds. This means that human populations, even those with foraging technologies, are not passive in the face of environmental demands. On the contrary, people have the agency to produce a range of cultural inventions—tools, social relations, domesticated crops, agroecologies. Or as Marshall Sahlins (1976) put it, human beings are *human* "precisely when they experience the world as a concept (symbolically). It is not essentially a question of priority but of the unique quality of human experience as meaningful experience. Nor is it an issue of the reality of the world; it concerns *which worldly dimension becomes pertinent*, and in what way, to a given human group" (142; emphasis added). Because human beings construct their own niches, they construct their patterns of consumption as well.

What Is the Original Affluent Society? Many Westerners long believed that foraging peoples led the most miserable of existences, spending all their waking hours in a food quest that yielded barely enough to keep them alive. To test this assumption in the field, Richard Lee went to live among the Dobe Ju/'hoansi, a foraging people of southern Africa (see "EthnoProfile 11.4: Ju/'hoansi"). Living in the central Kalahari Desert

EthnoProfile 11.4

Ju/'hoansi (!Kung)

Region: Southern Africa

Nation: Botswana and Namibia

Population: 45,000

Environment: Desert

Livelihood: Hunting and gathering

Political organization:
Traditionally, egalitarian bands; today, part of modern nation-states

For more information: Lee, Richard B. 1992. *The Dobe Ju/'hoansi*, 2nd ed. New York: Holt, Rinehart and Winston.

of southern Africa in the early 1960s, the Ju/'hoansi of Dobe were among the few remaining groups of San still able to return to full-time foraging when economic ties to neighboring herders became too onerous. Although full-time foraging has been impossible in the Dobe area since the 1980s, and the Ju/'hoansi have had to make some difficult adjustments, Lee documented a way of life that contrasts vividly with their current settled existence.

Lee accompanied the Ju/'hoansi as they gathered and hunted in 1963, and he recorded the amounts and kinds of food they consumed. The results of his research were surprising. It turned out that the Ju/'hoansi provided themselves with a varied and well-balanced diet based on a selection from among the food sources available in their environment. At the time of Lee's fieldwork, the Ju/'hoansi classified more than 100 species of plants as edible, but only 14 were primary components of their diet (Lee 1992, 45ff.). Some 70% of this diet consisted of vegetable foods; 30% was meat. Mongongo nuts, a protein-rich food widely available throughout the Kalahari, alone made up more than one-quarter of the diet. Women provided about 55% of the diet, and men provided 45%, including the meat. The Ju/'hoansi spent an average of 2.4 working days—or about 20 hours—per person per week in food-collecting activities. Ju/'hoansi bands periodically suffered from shortages of their preferred foods and were forced to consume less desired items. Most of the time, however, their diet was balanced and adequate and consisted of foods of preference (Lee 1992, 56ff.; Figure 11.7).

Marshall Sahlins coined the expression "the original affluent society" to refer to the Ju/'hoansi and other

FIGURE 11.7 Ju/'hoansi women returning from foraging with large quantities of mongongo nuts.

foragers like them. In an essay published in 1972, Sahlins challenged the traditional Western assumption that the life of foragers is characterized by scarcity and near-starvation (see Sahlins 1972). **Affluence**, he argued, is having more than enough of whatever is required to satisfy consumption needs. There are two ways to create affluence. The first, to *produce much*, is the path taken by Western capitalist society; the second, to *desire little*, is the option, Sahlins argues, that foragers have taken. Put another way, the Ju/'hoansi foragers used culture to construct a niche within which their wants were few but abundantly fulfilled by their local environment. Moreover, it is not that foragers experience no greedy impulses; rather, according to Sahlins, affluent foragers live in societies whose institutions do not reward greed. Sahlins concluded that, for these reasons, foragers cannot be considered poor, although their material standard of living is low by Western measures.

Original affluent foraging societies emphasize the longstanding anthropological observation that the concept of economic "needs" is vague (Douglas and Isherwood 1979). Hunger can be satisfied by beans and rice or steak and lobster. Thirst can be quenched by water or beer or soda pop. In effect, human beings in differently constructed niches define needs and provide for their satisfaction according to their own *cultural* logic, which is reducible to neither biology nor psychology nor ecological pressure. In every case, the human need for food is met but selectively, and the selection humans make carries a social message. But what about cases of consumption that do not involve food and drink?

Banana Leaves in the Trobriand Islands Anthropologist Annette Weiner traveled to the Trobriand Islands in the 1970s, more than half a century after Malinowski carried out his classic research there (see Chapter 10, "EthnoProfile 10.3: Trobriand Islanders"). To her surprise, she discovered a venerable local tradition involving the accumulation and exchange of banana leaves, which were known locally as "women's wealth" (Figure 11.8). Malinowski had never described this tradition, although there is evidence from photographs and writing that it was in force at the time of his fieldwork. Possibly, Malinowski overlooked these transactions because they are carried out by women, and Malinowski did not view women as important actors in the economy. However, Malinowski might also have considered banana leaves an unlikely item of consumption because he recognized as "economic" only those activities that satisfied biological survival needs, and banana leaves are inedible. Transactions involving women's wealth, however, turn out to be crucial for the stability of Trobrianders' relationships to their relatives.

---

affluence The condition of having more than enough of whatever is required to satisfy consumption needs.

FIGURE 11.8 In the Trobriand Islands, women's wealth, made from banana leaves, is displayed during a funeral ritual called the *sagali*, which serves to reaffirm the status of the women's kinship group. Here a woman prepares the leaves with a design.

Banana leaves might be said to have a "practical" use because women make skirts out of them. These skirts are highly valued, but the transactions involving women's wealth more often involved the bundles of leaves themselves. Why bother to exchange great amounts of money or other goods to obtain bundles of banana leaves? This would seem to be a classic example of irrational consumption. Yet, "as an economic, political, and social force, women's wealth exists as the representation of the most fundamental relationships in the social system" (Weiner 1980, 289).

Trobrianders are *matrilineal* (i.e., they trace descent through women; see Chapter 14), and men traditionally prepare yam gardens for their sisters. After the harvest, yams from these gardens are distributed by a woman's brother to her husband. Weiner's research suggested that what Malinowski took to be the *redistribution* of yams, from a wife's kin to her husband, could be better understood as a *reciprocal exchange* of yams for women's wealth. The parties central to this exchange are a woman, her brother, and her husband. The woman is the person through whom yams are passed from her own kin to her

husband and through whom women's wealth is passed from her husband to her own kin.

Transactions involving women's wealth occurred when someone in a woman's kinship group died. Surviving relatives must "buy back," metaphorically speaking, all the yams or other goods that the deceased person gave to others during his or her lifetime. All the payments must be made in women's wealth. Each payment marks a social link between the deceased and the recipient, and the size of the payment marks the importance of their relationship.

The dead person's status, as well as the status of her or his family, depends on the size and number of the payments made; and the people who must be paid can number into the hundreds. Women make women's wealth themselves and exchange trade store goods to obtain it from other women; but when someone in their matrilineage dies, they collect it from their husbands. Indeed, a woman's value is measured by the amount of women's wealth her husband provides. Furthermore, "if a man does not work hard enough for his wife in accumulating wealth for her, then her brother will not increase his labor in the yam garden. . . . The production in yams and women's wealth is always being evaluated and calculated in terms of effort and energy expended on both sides of production. The value of a husband is read by a woman's kin as the value of his productive support in securing women's wealth for his wife" (Weiner 1980, 282).

Weiner argues that women's wealth upholds the kinship arrangements of Trobriand society. It balances out exchange relationships between lineages linked by marriage, reinforces the pivotal role of women and matriliny, and publicly proclaims, during every funeral, the social relationships that make up the fabric of Trobriand society. The system had been stable for generations, but Weiner suggested that it could collapse if cash ever became widely substitutable for yams. Under such conditions, men might buy food and other items on the market. If they no longer depended on yams from their wives' kin, they might refuse to supply their wives' kin with women's wealth. This had not yet happened at the time of Weiner's research, but she saw it as a possible future development.

How Is Consumption Being Studied Today?

The foregoing examples focus attention on distinctive consumption practices in different societies and demonstrate that the Western market is not the measure of all things. These studies also encourage respect for alternative consumption practices that, in different times

Fake Masks and Faux Modernity

Christopher Steiner addresses the perplexing situation all of us face in the contemporary multicultural world: given mass reproduction of commodities made possible by industrial capitalism, how can anybody distinguish "authentic" material culture from "fake" copies? The encounter he describes took place in the Ivory Coast, western Africa.

In the Plateau market place, I once witnessed the following exchange between an African art trader and a young European tourist. The tourist wanted to buy a Dan face mask which he had selected from the trader's wooden trunk in the back of the market place. He had little money, he said, and was trying to barter for the mask by exchanging his Seiko wrist watch. In his dialogue with the trader, he often expressed his concern about whether or not the mask was "real." Several times during the bargaining, for example, the buyer asked the seller, "Is it really old?" and "Has it been worn?" While the tourist questioned the trader about the authenticity of the mask, the trader, in turn, questioned the tourist about the authenticity of his watch. "Is this the real kind

of Seiko," he asked, "or is it a copy?" As the tourist examined the mask—turning it over and over again looking for the worn and weathered effects of time—the trader scrutinized the watch, passing it to other traders to get their opinion on its authenticity.

Although, on one level, the dialogue between tourist and trader may seem a bit absurd, it points to a deeper problem in modern transnational commerce: an anxiety over authenticity and a crisis of misrepresentation. While the shelves in one section of the Plateau market place are lined with replicas of so-called "traditional" artistic forms, the shelves in another part of the market place—just on the other side of the street—are stocked with imperfect imitations of modernity: counterfeit Levi jeans, fake Christian Dior belts, and pirated recordings of Michael Jackson and Madonna. Just as the Western buyer looks to Africa for authentic symbols of a "primitive" lifestyle, the African buyer looks to the West for authentic symbols of a modern lifestyle. In both of their searches for the "genuine" in each other's culture, the African trader and the Western tourist often find only mere approximations of "the real thing"—tropes of authenticity which stand for the riches of an imagined reality.

Source: Steiner 1994, 128–29.

---

and places, have worked as well as or better than capitalist markets to define needs and provide goods to satisfy those needs. But many anthropologists also draw attention to the way in which the imposition of Western colonialism has regularly undermined such alternatives, attempting to replace them with new needs and goods defined by the capitalist market. This helps explain why, as Daniel Miller (1995) summarized, "much of the early literature on consumption is replete with moral purpose" (144–45), emphasizing the ways in which vulnerable groups have resisted commodities or have developed ritual means of "taming" them, based on an awareness at some level of the capacity of those commodities to destroy. At the beginning of the twenty-first century, however, the consumption of market commodities occurs everywhere in the world. Moreover, not only are Western commodities sometimes embraced by those we might have expected to reject them (e.g., video technology by indigenous peoples of the Amazon), but this embrace frequently involves making use of these

commodities for local purposes, to defend or to enrich local culture, rather than to replace it (e.g., the increasing popularity of sushi in the United States).

Daniel Miller therefore urged anthropologists to recognize that these new circumstances require that they move beyond a narrow focus on the destructive potential of mass-produced commodities to a broader recognition of the role commodities play in a globalizing world. But this shift does not mean that concern about the negative consequences of capitalist practices disappears. In a global world in which everyone everywhere increasingly relies on commodities provided by a capitalist market, Miller believes that critical attention must be refocused on "inequalities of access and the deleterious impact of contemporary economic institutions on much of the world's population" (1995, 143).

Coca-Cola in Trinidad   The change of focus promoted in Miller's writing about anthropological studies of consumption is nowhere better in evidence than in his own research on the consumption of Coca-Cola in Trinidad (Miller 1998). He points out that for many observers of global consumption, Coca-Cola occupies the status of a *meta-symbol*: "a symbol that stands for the debate about the materiality of culture" (Miller 1998, 169). That is, Coca-Cola is often portrayed as a Western/American commodity that represents the ultimately destructive global potential of all forms of capitalist consumption. Extracting profits from dominated peoples by brainwashing them into thinking that drinking Coke will improve their lives, the powerful controllers of capitalist market forces are accused of replacing cheaper, culturally appropriate, locally produced, and probably more nutritious beverages with empty calories. Based on his own fieldwork, however, Miller is able to show that this scenario grossly misrepresents the economic and cultural role that Coca-Cola plays in Trinidad, where it has been present since the 1930s.

First, Coca-Cola is not a typical example of global commodification because it has always spread as a franchise, allowing for flexible arrangements with local bottling plants. Second, the bottling plant that originally produced Coca-Cola in Trinidad was locally owned (as is the conglomerate that eventually bought it). Third, apart from the imported concentrate, the local bottler was able to obtain all the other key supplies needed to produce the drink (e.g., sugar, carbonation, bottles) from local, Trinidadian sources. Fourth, this bottling company exports soft drinks to other islands throughout the Caribbean, making it an important local economic force that accounts for a considerable proportion of Trinidad's foreign exchange earnings. Fifth, the bottler of Coca-Cola also bottled other drinks

and has long competed with several other local bottling companies. Decisions made by these companies, rather than by Coca-Cola's home office, have driven local production decisions about such matters as the introduction of new flavor lines. Sixth, and perhaps most importantly, Coca-Cola has long been incorporated into a set of local, Trinidadian understandings about beverages that divides them into two basic categories: "red sweet drinks" and "black sweet drinks." In this framework, Coke is simply an up-market, black, sweet drink, and it has traditionally been consumed, like other black sweet drinks, as a mixer with rum, the locally produced alcoholic beverage. Finally, the Trinidadian categories of "sweet drinks" do not correspond to the Coca-Cola company's idea of "soft drinks," a distinction that has baffled company executives. For example, executives were taken by surprise when Trinidadians objected to attempts to reduce the sweetness of Coca-Cola and other beverages since this did not correspond to the trend they were familiar with from the United States, where taste has shifted away from heavily sugared soft drinks in recent years (Figure 11.9).

Beverage consumption in Trinidad is connected with ideas of cultural identity. "Red sweet drinks" have been associated with the Trinidadian descendants of indentured laborers, originally from the Indian subcontinent, and "black sweet drinks" with Trinidadian descendants of enslaved Africans. But this does not mean that the drinks are consumed exclusively by members of those communities. On the contrary, at the end of the twentieth century, both kinds of sweet drink make sense as elements in a more complex image of what it meant to be Trinidadian: "a higher proportion of Indians drink

FIGURE 11.9 The soft drink market in Trinidad is both complex and idiosyncratic, reflecting Trinidadian understandings of beverage categories.

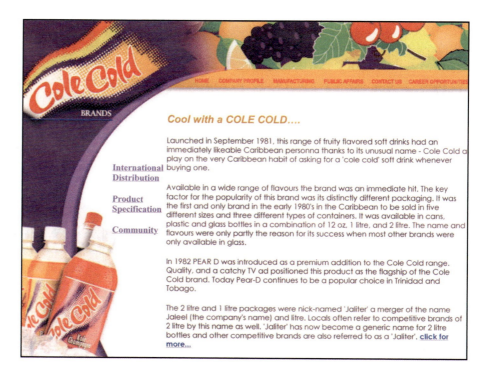

Cool with a COLE COLD....

Launched in September 1981, this range of fruity flavored soft drinks had an immediately likeable Caribbean personna thanks to its unusual name - Cole Cold a play on the very Caribbean habit of asking for a 'cole cold' soft drink whenever buying one.

Available in a wide range of flavours the brand was an immediate hit. The key factor for the popularity of this brand was its distinctly different packaging. It was the first and only brand in the early 1980's in the Caribbean to be sold in five different sizes and three different types of containers. It was available in cans, plastic and glass bottles in a combination of 12 oz, 1 litre, and 2 litre. The name and flavours were only partly the reason for its success when most other brands were only available in glass.

In 1982 PEAR D was introduced as a premium addition to the Cole Cold range. Quality, and a catchy TV ad positioned this product as the flagship of the Cole Cold brand. Today Pear-D continues to be a popular choice in Trinidad and Tobago.

The 2 litre and 1 litre packages were nick-named 'Jaliter' a merger of the name Jaleel (the company's name) and litre. Locals often refer to competitive brands of 2 litre by this name as well. 'Jaliter' has now become a generic name for 2 litre bottles and other competitive brands are also referred to as a 'Jaliter'. **click for more...**

Colas, while Kola champagne as a red drink is more commonly drunk by Africans. Many Indians explicitly identify with Coke and its modern image," whereas "In many respects the 'Indian' connoted by the red drink today is in some ways the Africans' more nostalgic image of how Indians either used to be or perhaps still should be" (Miller 1998, 180). There was no simple connection between the political parties that different segments of the Trinidadian population support and the owners of different local bottling companies producing red or black sweet drinks. Finally, the Trinidadians Miller knew emphatically did *not* associate drinking Coke with trying to imitate Americans. "Trinidadians do not and will not choose between being American and being Trinidadian. Most reject parochial nationalism or neo-Africanized roots that threaten to diminish their sense of rights of access to global goods, such as computers or blue jeans. But they will fiercely retain those localisms they wish to retain, not because they are hypocritical but because inconsistency is an appropriate response to contradiction" (Miller 1998, 185). Miller concluded, therefore, that it is a serious mistake to use Coca-Cola as a meta-symbol of the evils of commodity consumption. Miller's conclusion is reinforced by studies of consumption that focus on the many ways in which global commodities are incorporated into locally defined cultural practices.

The Anthropology of Food and Nutrition

One of the most recent areas of anthropological specialization centers on studies of food and nutrition. For some time, biological anthropologists have carried out cross-cultural comparisons of nutrition and growth in different societies; and anthropologists, such as Daniel Miller, have written detailed studies of particular local or ethnic food habits. Today, however, the anthropology of food and nutrition is increasingly concerned with the way the global capitalist food market works, favoring the food security of some consumers over others. At the same time, exploring links between food and culture in a globally complex world exposes changing understandings of fatness and thinness, and it reveals the many ways different kinds of food and cooking can be embraced by different groups in society to bolster their gender, sexual, racial, ethnic, class, or national identities.

Carole Counihan is a pioneering anthropologist of food and nutrition whose work was initially inspired by a feminist desire to give an ethnographic voice to women. She found that food was an aspect of culture that many women used to express themselves when other avenues were blocked. Beginning in 1970, she lived and worked in Italy for fourteen years. During this time, she developed a "long term relationship with a Florentine I call Leonardo," and most of the data for her book *Around the Tuscan Table: Food, Family, and Gender in Twentieth-Century Florence* (Counihan 2004) comes "from fifty-six hours of food-centered life histories tape-recorded in Italian with Leonardo's twenty-three living relatives in 1982–84" (2).

Counihan began collecting food-centered life histories from women but eventually collected them from men as well. Because these life histories came from individuals from different generations, they reflected historical changes in the political economy of food that had shaped the lives of her interview subjects over time. For example, situating the food memories of the oldest members of her sample required reconstructing the traditional *mezzadria* sharecropping system in Tuscany. This system was based on large landholdings worked by peasant laborers whose households were characterized by a strict division of labor by gender: the patriarch (male head of the family) managed food production in the fields, and his wife supervised food preparation for the large extended family. The *mezzadria* system would disappear in the early twentieth century, but it constituted the foundation of Tuscan food practices that would follow.

Counihan's interviewees ate a so-called "Mediterranean" diet consisting of "pasta, fresh vegetables, legumes, olive oil, bread, and a little meat or fish" (Counihan 2004, 74) (Figure 11.10). Food was scarce in the first part of the twentieth century but more abundant after World War II. "This diet, however, was already being modified by the postmodern, ever-larger agro-food industry that continued to grow in 2003, but which Florentines and other Italians shaped by alternative food practices" (Counihan 2004, 4).

The postwar capitalist market also drew younger Florentines into new kinds of paid occupations, which led to modifications of the earlier gendered division of labor, without eliminating it entirely. Counihan describes the struggles of Florentines of her generation, especially women, who needed to work for wages but who were still expected to maintain a household and a paying job at the same time and who often could not count on assistance from their husbands with domestic chores, including cooking. Counihan is especially critical about Italian child-rearing practices that allow boys to grow up with no responsibilities around the house, learning to expect their sisters (and later their wives) to take care of them, explaining away their incompetence at housekeeping tasks as a natural absence of talent or interest. She also describes men who cook on a regular basis but who often do not take on the tasks of shopping for ingredients or cleaning up and who tend to dismiss cooking as easy, thereby diminishing the status of work that has long been central to Florentine women's sense of self-worth.

FIGURE 11.10 Tuscan women making pasta in a farm kitchen.

Food-centered life histories from Counihan's oldest interviewees traced nearly a century of changing Tuscan food practices and revealed, surprisingly, older people's nostalgia for the more constrained patterns of food consumption in their youth. "When my older subjects were young before and during the second world war, consumption was highly valued because it was scarce and precarious. Yet their children, born after the war in the context of the Italian economic miracle, grew up in a world where consumption was obligatory, taken for granted, and essential to full personhood—a transformation lamented by older people" (Counihan 2004, 5).

Even as Counihan's research documents continuities in Tuscan diet and cuisine, it also demonstrates the way deeply rooted consumption practices were upended by the Italian state under Mussolini in the 1920s and 1930s and by the international cataclysm of World War II. Anthropologists have long argued that economic life cannot be considered apart from political relations in any society.

Chapter Summary

1. Contemporary cultural anthropologists are interested in how cultures change, but they are suspicious of evolutionary schemes that give the impression that social arrangements could not have been—or could not be—other than the way they are. They also point out that no society anywhere is static. The power that human beings have to reproduce or to change their social organization is an important focus of anthropological study. Anthropological approaches can provide insights often overlooked by other disciplines.

2. Human economic activity is usefully divided into three phases—production, distribution, and consumption—and is often shaped in important ways by storage practices. Formal neoclassical economic theory developed in Europe to explain how capitalism works, and it emphasizes the importance of market exchange. Economic anthropologists showed that noncapitalist societies regularly relied on nonmarket modes of exchange, such as reciprocity and redistribution, which still play restricted roles in societies dominated by the capitalist market.

3. Marxian economic anthropologists view production as more important than exchange in determining the patterns of economic life in a society. They classify societies in terms of their modes of production. Each mode of production contains within it the potential for conflict between classes of people who receive differential benefits and losses from the productive process.

4. In the past, some anthropologists tried to explain consumption patterns in different societies either by arguing that people produce material goods to satisfy basic human needs or by connecting consumption patterns to specific material resources available to people in the material settings where they lived. Ethnographic evidence demonstrates that both these explanations are inadequate because they ignore how culture defines our needs and provides for their satisfaction according to its own logic.

5. Particular consumption preferences that may seem irrational from the viewpoint of neoclassical economic theory may make sense when the wider cultural practices of consumers are taken into consideration. In the twenty-first century, those whom Western observers might have expected to reject Western market commodities often embrace them, frequently making use of them to defend or enrich their local culture rather than to replace it. In a global world in which everyone everywhere increasingly relies on commodities—including food—provided by a capitalist market, some anthropologists focus on inequalities of access and the negative impact of contemporary economic institutions on most of the world's population.

For Review

1. Explain the connection between culture and livelihood.
2. Describe each of the three models presented by Wilk and Cliggett.
3. Define production, distribution, and consumption.
4. What is neoclassical economics?
5. Describe each of the three modes of exchange.
6. What is a mode of production? What are the three modes of production that Eric Wolf found useful?
7. Explain how conflict is built into the mode of production.
8. Define consumption. Summarize each of the explanations offered in the text for human consumption patterns.
9. Explain the significance of food storage and food sharing in economic activity.
10. What are the key elements in Marshall Sahlins's argument about "the original affluent society"?
11. The text offers two case studies about the cultural construction of human needs—the original affluent society and banana leaves in the Trobriand Islands. Explain how each of these illuminates the cultural construction of human needs.
12. Summarize Miller's argument about the significance of Coca-Cola in Trinidad.
13. Discuss the connections between gender and food in Italy, as presented by Carole Counihan.

Key Terms

affluence 361
classes 353
commodity exchanges 349
consumption 357
economic anthropology 344
gift exchanges 349
institutions 345
labor 353
market exchange 351
means of production 353
mode of production 353
modes of exchange 349
neoclassical economics 349
reciprocity 349
redistribution 350
relations of production 353
social organization 344

Suggested Readings

Counihan, Carole. 2004. *Around the Tuscan table.* New York: Routledge. *Food-centered life histories allow Counihan to recreate a century of changing food practices—and social relations—in central Italy. Counihan analyzes the historically changing foodways of Tuscany to reveal changes in Tuscan (and Italian) understandings of gender and family relations.*

Counihan, Carole, and Penny van Esterik, eds. 2008. *Food and culture: A reader,* 2nd ed. New York: Routledge. *A collection of classic and recent essays on a range of topics currently investigated by anthropologists who study the anthropology of food and nutrition.*

Douglas, Mary, and Baron Isherwood. 1996. *The world of goods: Towards an anthropology of consumption,* rev. ed. New York: Routledge. *A discussion of consumption, economic theories about consumption, and what anthropologists can contribute to the study of consumption.*

Ensminger, Jean, ed. 2002. *Theory in economic anthropology.* Walnut Creek, CA: AltaMira Press. *An introductory volume that addresses the contributions that economic anthropology can make to understanding a globalized world economy.*

Lee, Richard. 2002. *The Dobe Ju/'hoansi,* 3rd ed. Belmont, CA: Wadsworth. *This highly readable ethnography contains important discussions about foraging as a way of making a living and traces political and economic changes in Ju/'hoansi life since Lee began fieldwork in Dobe in the 1960s.*

Sahlins, Marshall. 1972. *Stone Age economics.* Chicago: Aldine. *A series of classic essays on economic life, written from a substantivist position. Includes "The Original Affluent Society."*

Wilk, Richard, and Lisa Cliggett. 2007. *Economies and cultures.* Boulder, CO: Westview. *A current, accessible, "theoretical guidebook" to the conflicting views of human nature that underlie disputes in economic anthropology.*

Williams-Forson, Psyche, and Carole Counihan, eds. 2011. *Taking food public: Redefining foodways in a changing world.* London: Routledge. *This collection of essays, co-edited by American studies scholar Psyche Williams-Forson and anthropologist Carole Counihan, illustrate a variety of ways in which food is taking on new roles in different communities as processes of globalization challenge earlier identities and practices. The politics of food production, consumption, and exchange are explored, as are the meanings carried by such activities in specific cultural settings. This is a rich and provocative collection that succeeds in challenging many stereotypes about food and those who grow, prepare, distribute, and consume it.*

 Visit our online resource center for further reading, web links, free assessments, flashcards, and videos. www.oup.com/he/lavenda5e

12

How do anthropologists study political relations?

Human societies are able to organize human interdependency successfully only if they find ways to manage relations of power among the different individuals and groups of which they are composed. In this chapter, we survey approaches anthropologists take to the study of political relations in different societies.

CHAPTER OUTLINE

How Are Culture and Politics Related?

How Do Anthropologists Study Politics?

How Do Anthropologists Study Politics of the Nation-State?

What Happens to Citizenship in a Globalized World?

Global Politics in the Twenty-First Century

Chapter Summary

LEARNING OBJECTIVES

- Explain how culture and politics are related according to the domain of political anthropology.
- Compare the different concepts and methods that anthropologists use to study politics.

- Apply the anthropological study of politics to acts of coercion, domination, biopower, and governmentality found across different cultures.
- Describe the ways that anthropologists study politics in nation-states, including the example of Fiji.

- Define and describe globalization and how the processes therein affect the operations of nation-states.
- Analyze what happens to citizenship in a globalized world and the ways that humans negotiate and embrace citizenship in the contemporary context.

Protesters demonstrate against President Donald Trump's travel ban at San Francisco City Hall in February 2017.

Anthropologists have long been interested in the role of power in human societies. Why are members of some societies able to exercise power on roughly equal terms, whereas other societies sharply divide the powerful from the powerless? In societies where access to power is unequal, how can those with little power gain more? What, in fact, is power?

Human societies are able to organize human interdependency successfully only if they find ways to manage relations of power among the different individuals and groups they comprise. **Power** may be understood broadly as "transformative capacity" (Giddens 1979, 88). When the choice affects an entire social group, scholars speak of *social power*. In this chapter, you will learn about the approaches anthropologists take to the study of political relations in different societies. Eric Wolf (1994) describes three different modes of social power: the first, *interpersonal power*, involves the ability of one individual to impose his or her will on another individual; the second, *organizational power*, highlights how individuals or social units can limit the actions of other individuals in particular social settings; and the third, *structural power*, organizes social settings themselves and controls the allocation of social labor. To lay bare the patterns of structural power requires paying attention to the large-scale and increasingly global division of labor among regions and social groups, the unequal relations between these regions and groups, and the way these relations are maintained or modified over time. For example, today clothing is manufactured in factories in Indonesia or El Salvador, Romania or China, for markets in Europe, the United States, and Japan: this is an example of structural power. People are hired to work long hours for low wages in unpleasant conditions to make clothing that they cannot afford to buy, even if it were available for sale in the communities where they live (Figure 12.1).

How Are Culture and Politics Related?

The study of social power in human society is the domain of **political anthropology**. In an overview, Joan Vincent argues that political anthropology continues to be vital because it involves a complex interplay among ethnographic fieldwork, political theory, and critical reflection on political theory (Vincent 2002, 1). Vincent divides the history of political anthropology into three phases. The first phase, from 1851 to 1939, she considers the "formative" era in which basic orientations and

some of the earliest anthropological commentaries on political matters were produced. The second phase, from 1942 to about 1971, is the classic era in the field. It is most closely associated with the flourishing of British social anthropology rooted in functionalist theory and produced well-known works by such eminent figures as E. E. Evans-Pritchard, Max Gluckman, Fredrik Barth, and Edmund Leach. This phase developed in the context of the post–World War II British Empire through the period of decolonization in the 1950s and 1960s. Topics of investigation during this period were also the classic topics of political anthropology: the classification of preindustrial political systems and attempts to reconstruct their evolution; displaying the characteristic features of different kinds of preindustrial political systems and demonstrating how these functioned to produce political order; studying local processes of political strategizing by individuals in non-Western societies (see, e.g., Lewellen 2003). Decolonization drew attention to emerging national-level politics in new states and the effects of "modernization" on the "traditional" political structures that had formerly been the focus of anthropological investigation. The turbulent politics of the 1960s and early 1970s, however, called this approach into question.

Beginning in the 1960s, political anthropologists developed new ways of thinking about political issues and new theoretical orientations to guide them, inaugurating in the 1970s and 1980s a third phase in which the anthropology of politics posed broader questions about power and inequality (Vincent 2002, 3). Under conditions of globalization, anthropologists interested in studying power have joined forces with scholars in other disciplines who share their concerns and have adopted ideas from influential political thinkers such as Antonio Gramsci and Michel Foucault to help them explain how power shapes the lives of those among whom they carry out ethnographic research. The cross-cultural study of political institutions reveals the paradox of the human condition. On one hand, open cultural creativity allows humans to imagine worlds of pure possibility; on the other hand, all humans live in material circumstances that make many of those possibilities profoundly unrealistic. We can imagine many different ways to organize ourselves into groups; but, as Marx pointed out long ago, the past weighs like a nightmare on the brain of the living—and the opportunity to remake social organization is ordinarily quite limited.

As we have seen, human beings actively work to reshape the environments in which they live to suit themselves. Because the resources available in any environment can be used to sustain more than one way of life, however, human beings must choose which aspects of the material world to depend on. This is why, inevitably, questions about human economic activity are

---

power Transformative capacity; the ability to transform a given situation.
political anthropology The study of social power in human society.

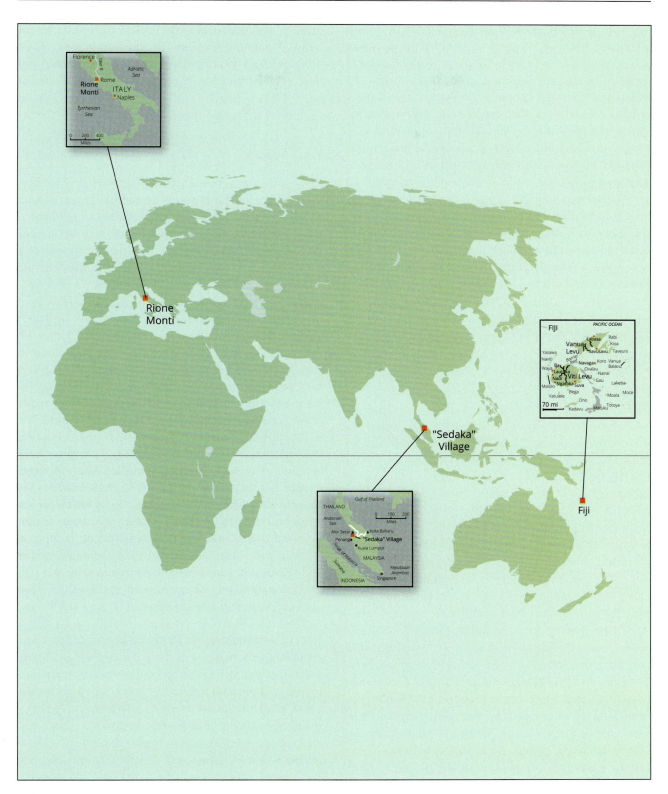

FIGURE 12.1 Location of societies whose EthnoProfiles appear in Chapter 12.

intimately intertwined with questions about the distribution of power in society. Some archaeologists have argued, as we saw in Chapter 7, that population growth is a constant aspect of the human condition that determines forms of social organization. However, as Marshall

Sahlins pointed out long ago (1976, 13), population pressure determines nothing more than the number of people that can be supported when the environment is used in a particular way. Members of a society can respond to that pressure in any of various ways: they can try to get along on less, intensify food production by inventing new technology, reduce their numbers by inventing new social practices (infanticide or other forms of birth control), or migrate elsewhere. Indeed, the manner in which a group might choose to implement any of these options is equally undetermined by population pressure. Which members of the group will have to do with less? Which members will control technological innovation? Who will be expected to migrate? And will the ultimate decision be imposed by force or voluntarily adopted?

The answers offered to these questions by members of any particular society describe the niche they have constructed for themselves. By building social and political alliances and mobilizing technology and material resources to make a living, ways of life are scaffolded and sustained over time.

How Do Anthropologists Study Politics?

Political anthropologists were first strongly influenced by earlier Western thinkers who had assumed that the state was the prototype of "civilized" social power. For them, the absence of a state could mean only *anarchy*, disorderly struggles for power among individuals—what the English philosopher Thomas Hobbes (1588–1679) called the "war of all against all." This view assumes that power is best understood as physical force, or *coercion*. A fistfight might be seen as a typical, "natural" manifestation of attempts by individuals to exercise physical coercion. Although states that monopolize the use of force often perpetrated injustice or exploitation as a side effect, Hobbes and others viewed this as the necessary price for social order. Their assumption was that cooperative social living is not natural for human individuals because they are born with **free agency**—instincts that lead them to pursue their own self-interest above everything else and to challenge one another for dominance.

Discussions of power as coercion tend to see political activity as competition between individual free agents over political control. When free agents make decisions, no larger groups, no historical obligations, no collective beliefs can or ought to stand in their way. For some, cultural evolution took a giant leap forward when our ancestors first realized that sticks and stones could be used as weapons not only against nonhuman predators but also especially against human enemies. In this

view, human history is a chronicle of the production of better and better weapons. The civilizations we are so proud of have been born and sustained in violence. But this is not the only way to understand human agency, as we will see.

Is Political Power Nothing More Than Coercion?

Early anthropologists such as Lewis Henry Morgan showed that kinship institutions could organize orderly social life in societies without states, and his observations were confirmed by later political anthropologists, such as E. E. Evans-Pritchard, based on his work among the Azande. Evans-Pritchard's description of social life among the Azande ([1937] 1976) in no way resembled a war of all against all, although the Azande lived in a stateless society and held a complex set of beliefs about witchcraft, oracles, and magic (see Chapter 10, "EthnoProfile 10.6: Azande"). Evans-Pritchard observed that Azande people discussed witchcraft openly, and if they believed they were bewitched, they were likely to be angry rather than afraid. This kind of attitude made sense because most Azande subscribed to a worldview in which witchcraft had a meaningful place. In addition, they did not feel helpless because their society also supplied them with practical remedies, like vengeance magic, that they could use to defend themselves if they thought they had been bewitched. Here, we see an example of what Wolf called organizational power that does not depend on state coercion. Instead, it depends on *persuasion*. Scaffolded by particular social institutions and practices, the belief system continues to appear natural and rational to members of the society; this is why ordinary, rational people support it.

How Do Anthropologists Study Resistance to Coercion?
What happens, however, if members of a society decide that the institutions and practices endorsed by their leaders are coercive, rather than legitimate? What if they decided to take action to overturn such coercion? History is full of examples of people rising up against their rulers, resisting coercion, and struggling to create new social relations that would provide greater freedom and justice. Indeed, stories about the founding of modern nation-states like France and the United States often begin precisely with revolutionary accounts of successful resistance to oppression. The framework of analysis in which such accounts are located is dualistic: rulers monopolize power and those who are ruled struggle against that monopoly in order to wrest power away from the rulers.

In the 1960s and 1970s, many anthropologists and others were convinced that efforts by peasants and other

free agency The freedom of self-contained individuals to pursue their own interests above everything else and to challenge one another for dominance.

subordinated groups were the first wave of a new series of large-scale uprisings that would successfully resist coercive oppression and remake unjust social relations in many parts of the world. When these expectations were not met, however, attention turned to smaller scale forms of resistance that demonstrated ongoing efforts by oppressed peoples to push back against coercion, sometimes in unlikely ways. In the mid-1980s, for example, political scientist and ethnographer James Scott published findings based on 2 years of ethnographic research among peasant rice farmers in a Malaysian village called "Sedaka" (a pseudonym; see "EthnoProfile 12.1: 'Sedaka' Village"). He had learned that poor Malaysian peasants were at the bottom of a social hierarchy dominated locally by rich farmers and nationally by a powerful state apparatus. According to Scott, these peasants were not kept in line by some form of state-sponsored terrorism; rather, the context of their lives was shaped by what he called "routine repression": "occasional arrests, warnings, diligent police work, legal restrictions, and an Internal Security Act that allows for indefinite preventive detention and proscribes much political activity" (1987, 274).

Scott quickly realized that the poor peasants of "Sedaka" were not about to rise up against their oppressors. But this was not because they accepted their poverty and low status as natural and proper. For one thing, organized overt defense of their interests was difficult because local economic, political, and kinship ties generated conflicting loyalties. For another, the peasants knew that overt political action in the context of routine repression would be foolhardy. Finally, they had to feed their families. Their solution was to engage in what Scott called "everyday forms of peasant resistance": this included "foot dragging, dissimulation, desertion, false compliance, pilfering, feigned ignorance, slander, arson, sabotage, and so forth" (1987, xvi). These actions may have done little to alter the peasants' situation in the short run; however, Scott argued, in the long run they had the potential to be more effective than overt rebellion in undercutting state repression.

Scott argued that "The struggle between rich and poor in Sedaka is not merely a struggle over work, property rights, grain, and cash. It is also a struggle over the appropriation of symbols, a struggle over how the past and present shall be understood and labeled, a struggle to identify causes and assess blame" (1987, xvii). According to Scott, when peasants criticize rich landowners or rich landowners find fault with peasants, the parties involved are not just venting emotion. Instead, each side is simultaneously constructing a worldview. Rich and poor alike are offering "a critique of things as they are as well as a vision of things as they should be . . . [they] are writing a kind of social text on the subject of

EthnoProfile 12.1

"Sedaka" Village

Region: Southeastern Asia

Nation: Malaysia

Population: 300

Environment: Lush paddy land

Livelihood: Rice cultivation

Political organization: Village within a modern nation-state

For more information: Scott, James. 1987. *Weapons of the weak*. New Haven, CT: Yale University Press.

human decency" (Scott 1987, 23). Scott (1990) refers to such peasant-formulated critiques and visions as **hidden transcripts**: private accounts of their oppression, and alternatives to it, developed by dominated groups outside the public political arena. These hidden accounts contrast with the views that dominated peoples routinely express in public contexts that do not challenge the legitimacy of the dominant political order. The existence of hidden transcripts shows that even though thought alone may not be able to alter the *fact* of material coercion, it still has the power to transform the *meaning* of material coercion for those who experience it. Poor peasants formulating hidden transcripts are exercising their human reflexive awareness, investing their experiences with meanings of their own choosing.

For Scott, the contrast between the worldview of the state and the worldview of peasants in "Sedaka" was revealed during the introduction of mechanized rice harvesting. Traditionally, rice harvesting had been manual labor. It regularly allowed poor peasants to earn cash and receive grain from their employers as a traditional form of charitable gift (Figure 12.2). In the late 1970s, however, the introduction of combine harvesters eliminated the rich farmers' need for hired labor, a loss that dealt poor families a severe economic blow. When the rich and poor talked about the harvesters, each side offered a different account of their effect on economic life in the village.

hidden transcripts Private accounts of their oppression and alternatives to it developed by dominated groups outside the public political arena. These hidden accounts contrast with the views dominated peoples express in public political contexts that do not challenge the legitimacy of the dominant political order.

IN THEIR OWN WORDS

Protesters Gird for Long Fight over Opening Peru's Amazon

Latin American Indigenous people have been organizing in recent years to protect their lands, sometimes from agricultural invasion, sometimes against oil exploration and drilling, sometimes to assert land claims. These are not always peaceful. Simon Romero reports for the New York Times, June 12, 2009 (Andrea Zarate contributed reporting from Lima, Peru).

Iquitos, Peru—Faced with a simmering crisis over dozens of deaths in the quelling of indigenous protests last week, Peru's Congress this week suspended the decrees that had set off the protests over plans to open large parts of the Peruvian Amazon to investment. Senior officials said they hoped this would calm nerves and ease the way for oil drillers and loggers to pursue their projects.

But instead, indigenous groups are digging in for a protracted fight, revealing an increasingly well-organized movement that could be a tinderbox for President Alan García. The movement appears to be fueled by a deep popular resistance to the government's policies, which focused on luring foreign investment, while parts of the Peruvian Amazon have been left behind.

The broadening influence of the indigenous movement was on display Thursday in a general strike that drew thousands of protesters here to the streets of Iquitos, the largest Peruvian city in the Amazon, and to cities and towns elsewhere in jungle areas. Protests over Mr. García's handling of the violence in the northern Bagua Province last Friday also took place in highland regions like Puno, near the Bolivian border, and in Lima and Arequipa on the Pacific coast.

"The government made the situation worse with its condescending depiction of us as gangs of savages in the forest," said Wagner Musoline Acho, 24, an Awajún Indian and an indigenous leader. "They think we can be tricked by a maneuver like suspending a couple of decrees for a few weeks and then reintroducing them, and they are wrong."

The protesters' immediate threat—to cut the supply of oil and natural gas to Lima, the capital—seems to have subsided, with protesters partly withdrawing from their occupation of oil installations in the jungle. But as anger festers, indigenous leaders here said they could easily try to shut down energy installations again to exert pressure on Mr. García.

Peruvian indigenous leaders Alberto Pizango (R) and Servando Puerta Pena (L) at a press conference in Lima, Peru, in June 2009, requesting an investigation of the clashes in the north of the country that left an undetermined number of people dead.

Another wave of protests appears likely because indigenous groups are demanding that the decrees be repealed and not just suspended. The decrees would open large jungle areas to investment and allow companies to bypass indigenous groups to obtain permits for petroleum exploration, logging and building hydroelectric dams. A stopgap attempt to halt earlier indigenous protests in the Amazon last August failed to prevent them from being reinitiated more forcefully in April.

The authorities said that nine civilians were killed in the clashes that took place last Friday on a remote highway in Bagua. But witnesses and relatives of missing protesters contend that the authorities are covering up details of the episode, and that more Indians died. Twenty-four police officers were killed on the highway and at an oil installation.

Indigenous representatives say at least 25 civilians, and perhaps more, may have been killed, and some witnesses say that security forces dumped the bodies of protesters into a nearby river. At least three Indians who were wounded said they had been shot by police officers as they waited to talk with the authorities.

"The government is trying to clean the blood off its hands by hiding the truth," said Andrés Huaynacari Etsam, 21, an Awajún student here who said that five of his relatives had been killed on June 5 and that three were missing.

Senior government officials repudiate such claims. "There is a game of political interests taking place in which some are trying to exaggerate the losses of life for their own gain," said Foreign Minister José García Belaunde.

He said the ultimate aim of the protesters was to prevent Peru from carrying out a trade agreement with the United States, because one of the most contentious of the decrees that were suspended on Thursday would bring Peru's rules for investment in jungle areas into line with the trade agreement.

"But," Mr. García Belaunde insisted, "the agreement is not in danger."

Still, the government's initial response to the violence seems to have heightened resentment. A television commercial by the Interior Ministry contained graphic images of the bodies of some police officers who were killed while being held hostage by protesters. The commercial said that the killings were proof of the "ferocity and savagery" of indigenous activists, but an uproar over that depiction forced the government to try to withdraw the commercial.

The authorities are struggling to understand a movement that is crystallizing in the Peruvian Amazon among more than 50 indigenous groups. They include about 300,000 people, accounting for only about 1% of Peru's population, but they live in strategically important and resource-rich locations, which are scattered throughout jungle areas that account for nearly two-thirds of Peru's territory.

So far, alliances have proved elusive between Indians in the Amazon and indigenous groups in highland areas, ruling out, for now, the kind of broad indigenous protest movements that helped oust governments in neighboring Ecuador and Bolivia earlier in the decade.

In contrast to some earlier efforts to organize indigenous groups, the leaders of this new movement are themselves indigenous, and not white or mestizo urban intellectuals. They are well organized and use a web of radio stations to exchange information across the jungle. After one prominent leader, Alberto Pizango, was granted asylum in Nicaragua this week, others quickly emerged to articulate demands.

"There has been nothing comparable in all my years here in terms of the growth of political consciousness among indigenous groups," said the Rev. Joaquín García, 70, a priest from Spain who arrived in Iquitos 41 years ago and directs the Center of Theological Studies of the Amazon, which focuses on indigenous issues.

"At issue now," he said, "is what they decide to do with the newfound bargaining power in their hands."

Source: Romero 2009.

Scott tells us that both sides agreed that using the machines hurt the poor and helped the rich. When each side was asked whether the benefits of the machines outweighed their costs, however, consensus evaporated. The poor offered practical reasons against the use of combine harvesters: they claimed that the heavy machines were inefficient and that their operation destroyed rice paddies. They also offered moral reasons: they accused the rich of being "stingy," of ignoring the traditional obligation of rich people to help the poor by providing them with work and charity. The rich denied both the practical and the moral objections of the poor. They insisted that using harvesters increased their yield. They accused the poor people of bad faith. They claimed that the poor suffered because they were bad farmers and lazy, and they attributed their own success to hard work and prudent farm managements.

Rich farmers, on the other hand, would never have been able to begin using combine harvesters without the outside assistance of both the national government and the business groups that rented the machines to them at harvest time. Poor peasants were aware of this, yet they directed their critique at the local farmers and not at the government or outside business organizations. After all, the rich farmers "are a part of the community and therefore *ought* not to be indifferent to the consequences of their acts for their neighbors" (Scott 1987, 161). The stinginess of the rich did not just bring economic loss; it also attacked the social identity of the poor, who vigorously resisted being turned into nonpersons. The poor insisted on being accorded the "minimal cultural decencies in this small community" (Scott 1987, xvii). The only weapon they controlled in this struggle was their ability, by word and deed, to undercut the prestige and the reputation of the rich. This strategy worked in "Sedaka" because rich local famers were not ready to abandon the traditional morality that had regulated relations between rich and poor; they still cared what other villagers thought of them. A shrewd campaign of character assassination might have caused at least some of the rich to hesitate before ignoring their traditional obligations to the poor, which would have helped the poor defend their claims to citizenship in the local community. Scott was convinced that if the wider political

FIGURE 12.2 Until recently, rice harvesting in rural Malaysia was manual labor that regularly allowed poor peasants to earn cash and receive grain from their employers as a traditional form of charitable gift.

arena changed in the future, such that routine repression disappeared, many of the poor peasants he knew might well engage in open active rebellion.

Are There Limitations to Analyzing Power in Terms of Domination and Resistance?

Scott's studies of domination and the arts of resistance have become classics in anthropology for a reason: they move beyond crude understandings of political coercion as nothing but the exercise of brute force; they address the role of meaning and morality in political struggles; and they reveal nuanced interpretations that members of oppressed groups are able to offer concerning their situation in the world. At the same time, some political anthropologists who admire studies of this kind nevertheless have suggested that continuing to describe political struggles in such dualistic terms is limiting in its own way. Anthropologist Lila Abu-Lughod, for example, was concerned that "despite the considerable theoretical sophistication of many studies of resistance . . . they do not explore as fully as they might the implications of the forms of resistance that they locate. There is perhaps a tendency to romanticize resistance," she concluded, which could

lead anthropologists to give insufficient attention to the complexity and variety of ways in which power operates (Abu-Lughod 2016, 37).

Abu-Lughod was among those who drew attention to political theorists like Pierre Bourdieu, Antonio Gramsci, and Michel Foucault, whose work offered ways for political anthropologists to rethink the ways they conceptualized power. These writings, she argued, emphasize "the importance of ideological practice in power and resistance, and works to undermine distinctions between symbolic and instrumental, behavioral and ideological, and cultural, social and political processes" ([1990] 2016: 37). As we saw, Scott's analysis of the peasants' struggle against local landowners in Sedaka village undermined precisely these kinds of distinctions: both sides offered both practical and moral reasons to defend themselves. Indeed, Scott himself had been influenced by the work of Antonio Gramsci who, among other things, offered a fresh view of how cultural understandings could play a role, not only in consolidating power from above, but also in resisting domination from below. Gramsci's perspective can be approached by considering two of his key concepts: domination and hegemony.

What Are Domination and Hegemony?

Earlier in the chapter, we noted that anthropologists and others have offered different answers to the question of why people submit to institutionalized power. On one hand, they may have been coerced and fear punishment if they refuse to submit. On the other hand, they may submit because they believe that the power structures in their society are legitimate, given their understandings about the way the world works. What could lead people to accept coercion by others as legitimate (Figure 12.3)? A worldview that justifies the social arrangements under which people live is sometimes called an **ideology**. Karl Marx argued that rulers consolidate their power by successfully persuading their subjects to accept an ideology that portrays domination by the ruling class as legitimate; dominated groups who accept the ruling class ideology were said to suffer from false consciousness. The concept of *false consciousness* is problematic, however, since it views people as passive beings lacking reflexivity and incapable of withstanding ideological indoctrination. As we discussed in Chapter 8, this is not a plausible view of human nature.

More promising is the approach taken by Antonio Gramsci (1971). Writing in the 1930s, Gramsci pointed out that coercive rule—what he called **domination**—is expensive and unstable. Rulers do better if they can persuade the dominated to accept their rule as legitimate, both by providing some genuine material benefits to their subjects and by using schools and other cultural institutions to disseminate an ideology justifying their rule. If they achieve all this—while also ensuring that none of these concessions seriously undermines their privileged position—they have established what Gramsci called **hegemony.** Hegemony is never absolute but always vulnerable to challenges: struggles may develop between rulers trying to justify their domination and subordinate groups who exercise agency by challenging "official" ideologies and practices that devalue or exclude them. Hegemony may be threatened if subordinate groups maintain or develop alternative, or *counterhegemonic*, cultural practices. Successful hegemony, by contrast, involves linking the understandings of dominant and subordinate groups into what appears to be mutual accommodation. Gramsci's contrast between domination (rule by coercive force) and hegemony (rule by persuasion) was central to his own analysis of the exercise of power (Crehan 2002, 153).

James Scott found the concepts of hegemony (and counterhegemony) to be helpful in his effort to explain key features of the struggle between peasants and landowners in "Sedaka" village. The hidden transcripts to which he refers are the raw materials out of which peasants are able to fashion a counterhegemonic critique of

FIGURE 12.3   Prior to colonial conquest by outsiders, Muslim emirs from northern Cameroon had coercive power.

their situation, demonstrating that they are not suffering from false consciousness. Thus, if peasants refrain from engaging in public political critique, this is not because they have been brainwashed, but because they are choosing to remain silent in the face of routine repression. Many anthropologists find the concept of hegemony attractive because it draws attention to the central role of cultural beliefs and symbols in struggles to consolidate social organization and political control. Although originally developed to analyze how states exercise power, anthropologists have found Gramsci's concepts helpful in studying the exercise of power in societies with and without traditional state institutions. In attempting to extend Gramsci's insights into nonstate settings, anthropologists are able to avoid some of the implausible

ideology A worldview that justifies the social arrangements under which people live.

domination Coercive rule.

hegemony The persuasion of subordinates to accept the ideology of the dominant group by mutual accommodations that nevertheless preserve the rulers' privileged position.

accounts of power that depend on fear of punishment or false consciousness. In place of such arguments, attention can be drawn to the verbal dexterity and personal charisma of leaders with limited coercive force at their disposal who can nonetheless persuade others to follow them by skillfully aligning shared meanings, values, and goals with a particular interpretation of events or proposed course of action.

Consider, for example, the Azande belief that people use witchcraft only against those they envy. The psychological insight embodied in this belief makes it highly plausible to people who experience daily friction with their neighbors. At the same time, however, this belief makes it impossible to accuse Azande chiefs of using witchcraft against commoners—because, as the Azande themselves told Evans-Pritchard, why would chiefs envy their subjects? In this way, hegemonic ideology deflects challenges that might be made against those in power.

In his own writings, Gramsci did not fully develop the concept of hegemony, which has led to disagreement about what exactly he meant by this concept. Anthropologists Jean and John Comaroff, however, have chosen to take this as an opportunity to combine his insights about ideology and hegemony with their own reflections on the connection between culture and power. From their perspective, power has two forms: (1) an *agentive mode* in which human beings are able to wield power in specific historical situations, and (2) a *nonagentive mode* in which power is hidden in the forms of everyday life, and not easily challenged, because these forms are assumed to come from the gods or the ancestors or some other nonhuman source and may not be questioned. Yet, as they point out, "the silent power of the sign, the unspoken authority of habit, may be as effective as the most violent coercion in shaping, directing, even dominating social thought and action" (Comaroff and Comaroff 1991, 22).

The Comaroffs' research shows how, from the beginning of the nineteenth century, the Tswana of southern Africa experienced a series of profound changes as they encountered European missionaries and merchants and settlers. Over this period, the Tswana were in some cases targets of explicit ideological power that entered culture in the agentive mode: for example, they were targets for conversion to Christian religious practices and for participation in the growing market economy of South Africa. In other cases, however, they adopted new cultural forms seemingly without much notice. Changes in the clothing they wore, how they built their homes, how they farmed, how they learned to measure the time of day using clocks, how they learned to work for Europeans for wages and produce crops for the market, the consequences of learning to read and write—each of these might have seemed fairly insignificant at the time it occurred, but over time as these changes accumulated, they formed a new kind of silent, taken-for-granted background for everyday Tswana life. Here we see how power enters culture in the nonagentive mode. And yet the result of these changes was not the total absorption of the Tswana within a transplanted Western colonial culture. On the contrary, the encounter between the Tswana and Europeans also produced new cultural forms, creating a hybrid heritage that eventually contributed to the overthrow of apartheid in South Africa. Thus, the Comaroffs emphasize what they see as one of Gramsci's key insights: hegemony may be powerful but it is never absolute, and there is always the potential for hegemony to be overturned. Hegemonic cultural forms can be unmade, in part, by counterhegemonic ideologies crafted by dominated peoples who draw on traditional cultural forms that have been sidelined as well as by the incorporation of new cultural forms that have been introduced from the outside (Comaroff and Comaroff 1991, 22–25).

What Are Biopower and Governmentality?

The Comaroffs, as we have seen, shared Abu-Lughod's concern that anthropologists develop fresh approaches to power that did not confine it narrowly to dualistic contests within political institutions. They also took note of the pivotal work of French political theorist Michel Foucault for inspiration, observing that " in the wake of Foucault, power has long left the formal bounds of 'political' institutions and diffused and proliferated into hitherto uncharted terrains" (Comaroff and Comaroff [DH6]1991, 17). One of Foucault's key conclusions is that *power is productive*: that is, power may constrain what we do, but its application always makes new things possible as well (e.g., Foucault 1980). One simple example is the way a student of the violin must practice in a disciplined, focused, repetitive—and therefore constraining—manner in order to become competent at making music with the violin. At the same time, subjecting oneself to such practice eventually does build the skills that allow the student to play—perhaps in a virtuoso manner—complex compositions for this instrument.

This example points to another influential concept developed by Foucault: *discipline*. From one perspective, the virtuoso violinist appears to possess the greatest freedom in playing music on the instrument; thanks to training and practice, virtually no score will be too challenging to perform. From another perspective, however, that freedom was produced by the "unfreedom" of practice, a stern form of discipline that restricted the violinist's behavior in numerous ways over many years. Foucault thus argued that the "freedom" of the disciplined subject is not absolute; and that many of the freedoms people in modern societies believe they enjoy are actually the consequence of disciplines to which they have been subject in a variety of areas of social life, such as the military, in schools, in hospitals, and in prisons (Foucault 1977).

Foucault also examined the ways that European thinkers from the late Middle Ages onward had discussed what was necessary to sustain a peaceful, prosperous state. Together with colleagues, he identified the emergence of a new form of power in the nineteenth century, which he called **biopower**. Biopower is preoccupied with the management of bodies, both the bodies of citizens and the social body itself (Hacking 1991, 183). As Colin Gordon summarizes, biopower refers to "forms of power exercised over persons specifically insofar as they are thought of as living beings; a politics concerned with subjects as members of a *population*, in which issues of individual sexual and reproductive conduct interconnect with issues of international policy and power" (1991, 5).

Before the 1600s, according to Foucault, European states were ruled according to different political understandings. At that time, politics was focused on making sure that an absolute ruler maintained control of the state. Machiavelli's famous guide *The Prince* is the best known of a series of handbooks explaining what such an absolute ruler needed to do in order to maintain himself in power. But by the seventeenth century, this approach to state rule was proving increasingly inadequate. Machiavelli's critics began to speak instead about *governing* a state, likening such government to the practices that preserved and perpetuated other social institutions.

The example of household management was a preferred model of government. But running a state as if it were a household meant that rulers would need more information about the people, goods, and wealth that needed to be managed. How many citizens were there? What kinds of goods did they produce and in what quantities? How healthy were they? What could a state do to manage the consequences of misfortunes such as famines, epidemics, and death? In the 1700s, state bureaucrats began to count and measure people and things subject to state control, thereby inventing the discipline of *statistics*.

In this way, according to Foucault, European states began to govern in terms of *biopolitics*, using statistics to inform their political policies. Eventually, a new art appropriate to biopolitical management of the state emerged, which Foucault called governmentality. **Governmentality** uses statistics to govern in a way that promotes the welfare of populations within a state. To exercise governmentality, for example, state bureaucrats

might use statistics to determine that a famine was likely and to calculate how much it might cost the state in the suffering and death of citizens and in other losses. They would then come up with a plan of intervention—perhaps a form of insurance—designed to reduce the impact of famine on citizens to protect economic activity within the state and thereby preserve the stability of the state and its institutions. Importantly, for Foucault, these interventions need to be understood not as directly coercive but rather as persuasive, even seductive, actions upon others' actions, sometimes described as the *conduct of conduct* (Foucault 1991.

Governmentality is at work in the contemporary world, and modern institutions count and measure their members in a variety of ways (Figure 12.4). Although, as Ian Hacking (1991, 183) insists, not all bureaucratic

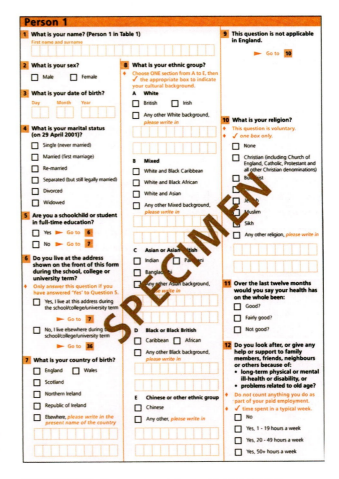

FIGURE 12.4 To govern, a state must know who it is governing. Censuses are one way in which the information a state believes it needs can be collected.

biopower Forms of power preoccupied with bodies, both the bodies of citizens and the social body of the state itself.

governmentality The art of governing appropriately to promote the welfare of populations within a state.

Reforming the Crow Constitution

Anthropologist Kelly Branam Macauley has worked for many years among the Apsáalooke, or Crow, Indian nation in central Montana, and she was able to witness complex negotiations as they struggled in 2001 to reform their constitution. In this passage, Branam Macauley discusses some of the reasons why the constitutional process has been so complex and difficult for Crow people.

With the turmoil facing the Apsáalooke, or Crow, Indian nation in central Montana at the turn of the twenty-first century, including the distrust of their political leaders, a decade of increased chairman decision-making power under "Resolution 90-35," and the lack of large-scale resource development, it is not surprising that the discourse surrounding the 2000 tribal elections included constitutional reform. With the promise of "returning the voice to the tribal council," a new chairman was elected in 2000. In 2001, under this new leadership, the Crow Indian nation accepted a new constitution and a representative democracy. For over 50 years, the Crow Indian nation had been governed under the 1948 Constitution, which maintained a pure democracy system with executive offices of chairman, vice-chairman, secretary, and vice secretary. Why was this system no longer working for the Crow people? Why was a new constitution needed?

For many legal theorists, the importance of constitutions lies in the fact that constitutions outline the relationship the government has to its people. Constitutions restrict governmental power and often ensure citizens' rights. "The theoretical justification for the creation of an independent American nation included, at its center, an assumption that there existed some proper relationship between government and the subjects of government" (Kay 1998, 17). No doubt this is true in other constitutional instances as well. However, when it comes to the unique position of American Indian nations to the U.S. government, it is important to contemplate the meaning of their constitutions. American Indian tribal constitutions exist not only to outline the relationship tribal governments have to their people, but to outline the relationship the tribal government has to the federal government.

In today's global society, having a written form of a polity's rules outlining the ways in which those rules are made, enforced, and maintained is quintessential for national survival. Despite and often because of Indian nations' "domestic dependent nation" (*Cherokee Nation v. Georgia* 1831) status within the U.S. federal framework, more and more Indian nations are reformulating their tribal governing structures. "If tribal communities want to assert greater control over their economic, political, and cultural lives, they will need more effective forms of government. For many communities there is a growing sense of crisis and movement to remake tribal constitutions" (Champagne 2006, 11). Many Indian nations, including the Apsáalooke, have found constitutions crucial to the maintenance and expansion of their sovereignty.

Analysis of the Crow constitution-making processes reveals the ways in which the Crow Indian nation has resisted federal Indian policies. They have fought to maintain their sovereignty and control their political identity. Through this process, "traditional" notions of governance were redefined, district identity became more important, kinship alliances remained crucial to the political process, and the Crow Indian nation took new steps in defining and asserting their sovereignty in relation to the U.S. government. The ways in which Crows have used constitutions to resist federal assimilationist polices may provide an example for other Indian nations who are also trying to exist under the federal sphere yet maintain traditional notions of governance.

Source: Branam Macauley Forthcoming.

applications of such statistical knowledge are evil, and the fact remains that providing the government (or any bureaucratic institution) with detailed vital statistics can be threatening, especially in cases where people are concerned that the state does not have their best interests at heart. After all, states want to tax citizens, vaccinate and educate their children, restrict their activities to those that benefit the state, control their movements beyond (and sometimes within) state borders, and otherwise manage what their citizens do. In the twenty-first century, anthropologists interested in politics are well aware that local affairs cannot be fully understood apart

ANTHROPOLOGY *in Everyday Life*

Anthropology and Advertising

Timothy de Waal Malefyt and Robert J. Morais are anthropologists who work in advertising. Ethnography, and anthropology more generally, has been recently taken up as consumer research methods by advertising agencies, and there are a number of anthropologists who make a living working either for advertising agencies or as researchers. Working in advertising raises a set of ethical issues that are, perhaps, different from the issues raised by academic anthropology. For more on the ethical issues, we present an "In Their Own Words" feature in Chapter 14. Here, Malefyt and Morais present an example of what anthropology offers advertising:

A pharmaceutical corporation was planning to solicit proposals from marketing research companies for a study on diabetics. The research would enable them to better understand four psychologically and behaviorally defined patient segments they were evaluating as targets for a new prescription diabetes medication. The company sought a study that would probe deeply into diabetes sufferers' attitudes, emotions, and behavior and deliver insights that would help it determine which target segment offered the highest market potential and inform a strategy for direct-to-consumer advertising. Several months before the request for a proposal (RFP) was to be issued to research suppliers, the marketing research director responsible for the project invited [Robert] Morais to visit the corporation's headquarters to give a presentation on ethnography, which was the methodology that she believed would be best to achieve her team's goals. About halfway through the presentation, the research director stopped Morais and said she wanted to brief him on what she called the "Portrait" study so that he could begin thinking about how his firm would design the research. As she described the goals of the project in detail, it became clear to Morais that in-depth one-on-one interviews (IDIs) in a focus group research facility, rather than ethnographic research, would be a more appropriate methodology to reach her objectives. Ethnography, he counseled the research director, was not needed for the client's learning needs and it would be an inefficient use of research funds. Morais suggested that after the patient segments representing the most sales potential were identified, ethnography would be an excellent way to learn about their everyday lives as diabetics. He made this recommendation with trepidation, hoping that his company would not lose an opportunity to work with the client, but he felt strongly that IDIs would be a superior research methodology for the client's needs.

The research director and a colleague from the marketing department listened attentively, and a few months later Morais's firm received the RFP. Relieved that his company was being considered despite his methodological challenge, Morais proposed a series of ninety-minute IDIs in a focus room facility. He proffered research techniques drawn from his company's skills as PhD-level psychologists and anthropologists. To underscore the difference in his design from the primarily psychologically oriented approaches that he thought the competition would propose, Morais highlighted several techniques and topics that his firm borrowed from anthropology:

- Mining patients' fundamental definitions of diabetes, wellness, and sickness as if the marketing and marketing research team had no knowledge of these concepts

- Identifying patients' rituals regarding the management and treatment of diabetes

- Discovering patient transformational experiences, exemplified by different attitudinal and emotional states, throughout their diabetes life cycle

- Exploring patients' feelings, if any, about belonging to a diabetics "tribe" and what this means for their attitudes, emotions, and behavior

- Researching myths and beliefs about diabetes treatments

- Exploring beliefs in contrast to empirical thinking regarding diabetes medications

- Learning how interactions with health care professionals impact self-management of diabetes

Morais's company won the assignment. When he asked the client research manager why she and her colleagues chose his firm, she said, "We really liked the anthropology." A senior manager from the advertising agency who was also involved in the RFP review process also mentioned anthropology as the agency's reason for endorsing Morais's firm for the project. Ethnography, often conflated with anthropology in marketing research, was not a factor in the decision.

Source: Malefyt and Morais 2012, 106–07.

from the larger political entities within which they are found, and these often turn out to be one or another nation-state.

How Do Anthropologists Study Politics of the Nation-State?

State societies are not new social forms. Nation-states, however, are a far more recent invention. Prior to the French Revolution, European states were ruled by kings and emperors whose access to the throne was officially deemed to have been ordained by God. After the French Revolution in 1789, which thoroughly discredited the divine right of kings, rulers needed to find a new basis on which to found legitimate state authority. The solution eventually adopted was rooted in political authority in **nations**: groups of people believed to share the same history, culture, language, and even the same physical substance. Nations were associated with territories, as were states, and a **nation-state** came to be viewed as an ideal political unit in which national identity and political territory coincided.

The building of the first nation-states is closely associated with the rise and spread of capitalism and its related cultural institutions during the nineteenth century. Following the demise of European colonial empires and the end of the Cold War, the final decades of the twentieth century witnessed a scramble in which former colonies or newly independent states struggled to turn themselves into nation-states capable of competing successfully in what anthropologist Liisa Malkki (1992) has called a "transnational culture of nationalism."

On one hand, the ideology of the nation-state implies that every nation is entitled to its own state. On the other hand, it also suggests that a state containing heterogeneous populations *might be made into a nation* if all peoples within its borders could somehow be made to adopt a common **nationality**: a sense of identification with and loyalty to the nation-state. As political scientist Benedict Anderson pointed out long ago,

nation-states should be understood as *imagined communities*: that is, as socially and historically constructed communities, associated with geographical territories whose residents have varying origins and backgrounds and lack regular face-to-face contact with one another. However, a shared identity could take shape over time as these heterogeneous residents came to participate in common, territory-wide, cultural practices, such as reading the same newspapers, traveling on shared infrastructure, or transacting business in the same territory-wide economic or bureaucratic institutions. Anderson was especially interested in how residents of a territorial unit such as a European colony, by virtue of their shared experiences, might come to imagine a shared territorial identity that could become the foundation of national identity once the colony gained political independence. However, the willingness or ability for all residents of a nation-state to adopt national identity is far from guaranteed. Groups with other forms of identity that continue to persist within the boundaries of the nation-state are often viewed as obstacles to nationalism. If such groups successfully resist assimilation into the nationality that the state is supposed to represent, their very existence calls into question the legitimacy of the state. Indeed, if their numbers are sufficient, they might well claim that they are a separate nation, entitled to a state of their own.

To head off this possibility, nationalist ideologies typically include some cultural features of subordinate cultural groups. Thus, although nationalist traditions are invented, they are not created out of thin air. That is, those who control the nation-state will try to define nationality in ways that "identify and ensure loyalty among citizens . . . the goal is to create criteria of inclusion and exclusion to control and delimit the group" (Williams 1989, 407). The hope seems to be that if at least some aspects of their ways of life are acknowledged as essential to national identity, subordinated groups will identify with and be loyal to the nation. Following Gramsci, Brackette Williams calls this process a **transformist hegemony** in which nationalist ideologues are attempting to "create purity out of impurity" (1989, 429, 435). Unfortunately, the practices of subordinated groups that are not incorporated into nationalist ideology are regularly marginalized and devalued. Continued adherence to such practices may be viewed as subversive, and practitioners may suffer persecution and even extermination. Other groups, by contrast, may be totally ignored. Ana Maria Alonso has pointed out, for example, that Mexican nationalism is "mestizo nationalism" rooted in the official doctrine that the Mexican people are a hybrid of European whites and the indigenous people they conquered. African slaves were also a part of early colonial

---

nation A group of people believed to share the same history, culture, language, and even physical substance.

nation-state An ideal political unit in which national identity and political territory coincide.

nationality A sense of identification with and loyalty to a nation-state.

transformist hegemony A nationalist program to define nationality in a way that preserves the cultural domination of the ruling group while including enough cultural features from subordinated groups to ensure their loyalty.

Mexican society, but nationalist ideology erases their presence entirely (Alonso 1994, 396).

Nation Building in a Postcolonial World: The Example of Fiji

Nation building involves constructing a shared public identity, but it also involves establishing concrete legal mechanisms for taking group action to influence the state. That is, as John Kelly and Martha Kaplan (2001) argue, nation-states are more than imagined communities; they are also *represented* communities. For this reason, nation building involves more than constructing an image of national unity; it also requires institutions of political representation that channel the efforts of citizens into effective support for the state. But what happens when citizens of a nation-state do not agree about exactly what nation they are building or what kinds of legal and political structures are necessary to bring it about? One answer to these questions can be seen in the South Pacific island of Fiji, which became independent of Britain in 1970 and has experienced a series of political coups since 1987 (see "EthnoProfile 12.2: Fiji").

At independence, the image of the Fijian nation was that of a "three-legged stool," each "leg" being a separate category of voters: "general electors" (a minority of the population including Europeans), "Fijians" (ethnic Fijians, descended from the original inhabitants of the island), and "Indians" (or Indo-Fijians, descendants of indentured laborers brought to Fiji by the British from Bombay and Calcutta in the nineteenth century). Kelly and Kaplan (2001) showed that these three categories have deep roots in the colonial period, where they were said to correspond to separate "races." In the British Empire, race was an accepted way to categorize subordinated peoples, although in many cases—as in the case of the Indo-Fijians—the people so labeled had shared no common identity prior to their arrival in Fiji.

These racial distinctions were concretized in colonial law, and the legal status of the ethnic Fijians was different from the legal status of Indo-Fijians. The status of ethnic Fijians was determined by the Deed of Cession, a document signed by some Fijian chiefs with the British in 1874, which linked ethnic Fijians to the colonial government through their hierarchy of chiefs. The status of Indo-Fijians, by contrast, was determined by the contracts of indenture (*girmit*), which each individual laborer had signed to come to Fiji. Thus, ethnic Fijians were accorded a hierarchical, collective legal identity, whereas the Indo-Fijians had the status of legal individuals, with no legally recognized ties to any collectivity.

EthnoProfile 12.2

Fiji

Region: Oceania

Nation: Fiji

Population: 905,000

Environment: Tropical marine climate, volcanic mountains

Livelihood: Natural resource export, especially sugar; subsistence agriculture; tourism

Political organization: Multiparty nation-state

For more information: Kelly, John D., and Martha Kaplan. 2001. *Represented communities: Fiji and world decolonization*. Chicago: University of Chicago Press.

Inspired by the freedom movement in India in the early twentieth century, Indo-Fijians began to resist racial oppression and struggle for equal rights in Fiji, but their efforts were repeatedly put down by the British. When it became possible for them to vote after 1929, for example, Indo-Fijians lobbied for equal citizenship and the abolition of separate racial voting rolls, and they lost: the voting rolls were divided by race to limit representation for Indo-Fijians in government. At the time of World War II, Indo-Fijians agreed to serve in the armed forces but only if they were treated as equals with white soldiers, and again their efforts were resisted: they spent the war serving in a labor battalion for very low wages, whereas ethnic Fijians joined the Fijian Defense Force. It was primarily Indo-Fijians who pushed for independence in the late 1960s, and once again they engaged in difficult negotiations for equal citizenship and a common voting role—but finally consented to separate race-based voting rolls in 1969 to obtain independence.

Thus, when Fiji's independence became real in 1970, the constitution insisted that races still existed in Fiji and that they had to vote separately. Since then, political parties have generally and increasingly followed racial lines, and the army has remained an enclave of indigenous Fijians. When political parties backed mostly by Indo-Fijian voters won Fiji's 1987 election, the army staged a coup and took over the country after only a month. The constitution that was then installed in 1990 returned to even more naked discrimination against Indo-Fijians with regard to voting rights (Kelly and Kaplan 2001, 77).

The constitution was revised yet again, in a manner that favored chiefly ethnic Fijian interests and seemed guaranteed to prevent parties backed by Indo-Fijian voters from winning control of the government in the 1999 election. To everyone's surprise, parties backing ethnic Fijians lost again. On May 19, 2000, came a second coup. Finally, after new elections in 2001, ethnic Fijians won control of the government. The new government lasted until a December 2006 military takeover. One of the military's demands was an end to the "race-based" voting system, to be replaced by a new "one citizen–one vote" system. However, in April 2009, the president suspended the constitution and appointed himself head of state. In September 2009, the British Commonwealth expelled Fiji for its failure to schedule democratic elections by 2010. An election was finally held in 2014, and Fiji was readmitted to the Commonwealth (Figure 12.5). Although hostility to the opposition has not disappeared, democratic parliamentary elections held in November 2018 were described as "largely credible," according to https://freedomhouse.org/country/fiji/freedom-world/2020

What lessons does this history suggest about nation building in postcolonial states? The issues are many and complex. But Kelly and Kaplan insist that the image of a united Fijian nation projected at independence was severely undermined by legal mechanisms of political representation carried over from the colonial period, particularly the race-based voting rolls. What became apparent in the years after independence was the fact that Indo-Fijians and ethnic Fijians had imagined very different national communities. Indo-Fijians had supported the image of a nation in which all citizens, Indo-Fijian or ethnic Fijian or "general elector," would have equal status, voting on a single roll, working together to build a constitutional democracy. However, "few among the ethnic Fijians have yet come to see themselves as partners with immigrants" (Kelly and Kaplan 2001, 41). Ever since independence, and particularly after each coup, ethnic Fijians worked to construct an image of the Fijian nation based solely on chiefly traditions in which Indo-Fijians had no meaningful place. Thus, Kelly and Kaplan conclude, in Fiji (and in many other parts of the world): "'the nation' is a contested idea, not an experienced reality" (142).

How Does Globalization Affect the Nation-State?

The Fijian history described earlier points to the kinds of movements and mixing of people that were permitted and even encouraged in the age of European colonial empires, and how the consequences of these processes bequeathed a series of challenging problems to postcolonial territories that wanted to transform themselves into nation-states. Even as Fiji and other postcolonial states have been wrestling with these problems from the colonial past, however, ongoing changes in the world have begun to challenge the territorial boundaries that nation-states have struggled to erect around themselves. Since the end of the Cold War in 1989, processes of globalization, abetted by new forms of communication, transportation, and manufacturing, have unleashed flows of wealth, images, people, things, and ideologies across the world. The pressures of these global flows on the boundaries of nation-states have been profound. National governments have struggled, often in vain, to control what their citizens read or watch in the media: satellite services and telecommunications and the Internet elude state-ordered censorship. Nation-states allow migrants or students or tourists to cross their borders because they need their labor or tuition or vacation expenditures; but in so doing, states must be content with the political values or religious commitments or families that these outsiders

FIGURE 12.5 A Fijian citizen contemplates the list of candidates in anticipation of the 2014 national election.

bring with them. Some have argued that weakening the boundaries between nation-states is a good thing, since border restrictions and censorship need to be overcome; but 25 years after the end of the Cold War, the challenges posed by weakened borders have become more apparent. For example, the Schengen Agreement, adopted in 1999 by the European Union, eliminated passport controls between all member states except for Ireland and the United Kingdom, and it was hailed as a positive achievement. Fifteen years later, however, enormous pressure was put on the European Union by waves of refugees escaping economic and political pressures in their home nations: thousands of refugees have died attempting to cross the Mediterranean Sea from points in North Africa. More recently, waves of refugees fleeing the Syrian civil war have passed through Turkey into Greece and then made their way northward by foot, seeking to settle in Germany and other European states that would accept them and offer them asylum. Similar pressures (and similar responses) have been felt in North America on the southern border of the United States. In 2016, Donald Trump ran for President on the promise to build a border wall and to make Mexico pay for it; since his election, his administration has intensified efforts to refuse entry to all undocumented border-crossers, including asylum seekers whose right to enter the country in search of international protection is backed by international and federal law. The Trump administration has also attempted to bar immigrants from certain countries with large Muslim populations. These efforts have been resisted in the courts, with varying degrees of success.

Migrants and refugees themselves often face a dilemma. On one hand, they now form sizeable and highly visible minorities in the countries of settlement, often in the poorer areas of cities. There they find opportunities for economic subsistence and political security, encouraging them to stay. On the other hand, hostility and sometimes violence are directed against them whenever there is a local economic downturn. Many migrants conclude that the possibility of permanent assimilation is unrealistic, which encourages them to maintain ties to their places of origin or to migrant communities elsewhere.

Migration, Trans-Border Identities, and Long-Distance Nationalism

The term *diaspora* is commonly used to refer to migrant populations with a shared identity who live in a variety of different locales around the world, but Nina Glick Schiller and Georges Fouron have pointed out that not all such populations see themselves in the same way. Schiller and Fouron describe different types of "trans-border identities" that characterize different groups of migrants. They prefer to use the term **diaspora** to identify a form of trans-border identity that does not focus on nation building. Should members of a diaspora begin to organize in support of nationalist struggles in their homeland, or to agitate for a state of their own, they become **long-distance nationalists** (Schiller and Fouron 2002, 360–61). "Long-distance nationalism" was coined by political scientist Benedict Anderson to describe the efforts of émigrés to offer moral, economic, and political support to nationalist struggles in their countries of origin. In his original discussion, Anderson emphasized the dangerous irresponsibility of the "citizenshipless participation" of the long-distance nationalists: "while technically a citizen of the state in which he comfortably lives, but to which he may feel little attachment, he finds it tempting to play identity politics by participating (via propaganda, money, weapons, any way but voting) in the conflicts of his imagined *Heimat* [homeland]" (2002, 269–70).

Schiller and Fouron argue, however, that the conditions of globalization have led to new forms of long-distance nationalism that do not correspond to Anderson's original description. They point to the emergence of the **trans-border state**: a form of state "claiming that its emigrants and their descendants remain an integral and intimate part of their ancestral homeland, even if they are legal citizens of another state" (Schiller and Fouron 2002, 357). Trans-border states did not characterize periods of mass emigration in the nineteenth and twentieth centuries. At that time, nations sending emigrants abroad regarded permanent settlement elsewhere as national betrayal. They encouraged emigrants to think of migration as temporary, expecting them eventually to return home with new wealth and skills to build the nation. But in today's global world, political leaders of many states sending emigrants accept the likelihood that those emigrants will settle permanently elsewhere. Some may even insist that emigres retain full membership in the nation-state from which they came, a form of long-distance nationalism that Schiller and Fouron call a **trans-border citizenry**:

---

diaspora Migrant populations with a shared identity who live in a variety of different locales around the world; a form of trans-border identity that does not focus on nation building.

long-distance nationalists Members of a diaspora organized in support of nationalist struggles in their homeland or to agitate for a state of their own.

trans-border state A form of state in which it is claimed that those people who left the country and their descendants remain part of their ancestral state, even if they are citizens of another state.

trans-border citizenry A group made up of citizens of a country who continue to live in their homeland plus the people who have emigrated from the country and their descendants, regardless of their current citizenship.

"Citizens residing within the territorial homeland and new emigrants and their descendants are part of the nation, whatever legal citizenship the emigres may have" (Schiller and Fouron 2002, 358).

Trans-border states and trans-border citizenries are more than symbolic identities: they have become concretized in law. For example, several Latin American countries, including Mexico, Colombia, the Dominican Republic, Ecuador, and Brazil, permit emigrants who have become naturalized citizens in countries such as the United States to retain dual nationality and even voting rights in their country of origin (Figure 12.6). Special government ministries are set up to address the needs of citizens living abroad. This is very different from Anderson's "citizenshipless participation." Schiller and Fouron stress that trans-border states and citizenries spring "from the life experiences of migrants of different classes" and are "rooted in the day to day efforts of people in the homeland to live lives of dignity and self-respect that compel them to include those who have migrated" (2002, 359).

But some trans-border citizenries face difficulties. First, their efforts at nation building are sometimes blocked by political forces in the homeland that do not welcome their contributions. This was the case for Haitians living abroad while Haiti was ruled by the Duvalier family dictatorship and for Cubans living abroad whose efforts have been blocked by the Castro revolutionary government. Second, the states in which immigrants have settled may regard as threatening the continued involvement of trans-border citizens in the affairs of another state. Such involvement has often been seen as even more threatening since terrorists destroyed the World Trade Center and attacked the Pentagon on September 11, 2001. Yet in an era of globalization, attempts to control migration threaten to block the flows of people that keep the global economy going. Moreover, the vulnerability of trans-border citizens in these circumstances often increases the appeal of long-distance nationalism (Schiller and Fouron 2002, 359–60).

The globalizing forces responsible for these changes have undermined previous understandings of what a world made up of nation-states should look like. Indeed, they reveal unacknowledged contradictions and weaknesses of actual nation-states. For example, the existence and strength of trans-border states and citizenries show that some nation-states—especially those sending migrants—are actually what Schiller and Fouron call *apparent states*: they have all the outward attributes of nation-states (government bureaucracies, armies, a seat in the United Nations), but in fact they are unable to meet the needs of their people (Schiller and Fouron 2002, 363). And the existence of apparent states also exposes inconsistencies and paradoxes in the meaning of citizenship in the nation-states where migrants settle.

Schiller and Fouron contrast legal citizenship with what they call substantive citizenship and point out that, for trans-border citizens, the two often do not coincide. **Legal citizenship** is accorded by state laws and can be difficult for migrants to obtain. But even those trans-border citizens who obtain legal citizenship often experience a gap between what legal citizenship promises and the way they are treated by the state. For example, people of color and women who are United States citizens are not treated by the state the same way white male citizens are treated. By contrast, **substantive citizenship** is defined by the actions people take, regardless of their legal citizenship status, to assert their membership in a state and to bring about political changes that will improve their lives. Some trans-border citizens call for the establishment of full-fledged **transnational nation-states.** That is, "they challenge the notion that relationships between citizens and their state are confined within that territory" and work for the recognition of a new political form that contradicts the

FIGURE 12.6 The Dominican Republic permits emigrants who have become naturalized citizens of the United States to vote in Dominican elections. Here, a Dominican woman in New York campaigns in 2004 for a second term for President Hipólito Mejía.

legal citizenship The rights and obligations of citizenship accorded by the laws of a state.

substantive citizenship The actions people take, regardless of their legal citizenship status, to assert their membership in a state and to bring about political changes that will improve their lives.

transnational nation-state A nation-state in which the relationships between citizens and the state extend to wherever citizens reside.

understandings of political theory, but which reflects the realities of their experiences of national identity (Schiller and Fouron 2002, 359).

Anthropology and Multicultural Politics in the New Europe

One of the most interesting things about the early twenty-first century is that Europe—the continent that gave birth to the Enlightenment and colonial empires and (along with North America) to anthropology itself—has become a living laboratory for the study of some of the most complex social and cultural processes to be found anywhere in the world.

During the last half of the twentieth century, the countries of Europe, including Italy, were the target of large waves of migration from all over the world. One venerable working-class Roman neighborhood, only a short walk from the Colosseum, is Rione Monti, which has a fascinating history of its own ("EthnoProfile 12.3: Rione Monti (Rome)"). In 1999, anthropologist Michael Herzfeld (2003) moved into Rione Monti to explore social change in the uses of the past. Herzfeld found that longtime residents of Monti shared a common local culture, which includes use of the *romanesco* dialect rather than standard Italian, and a strong sense of local identity that distinguished them from "foreigners," including diplomats and non-Roman Italians. Their identity survived Mussolini's demolition of part of the neighborhood in the early twentieth

century. They successfully dealt with a local criminal underworld by mastering a refined urban code of politeness. The underworld had faded away by the 1970s, but beginning in the 1990s, residents began to face two new challenges to their community. First, historic Roman neighborhoods became fashionable, and well-to-do Italians began to move into Rione Monti, pushing many workers into cheaper housing elsewhere. Second, in the 1990s, another group of newcomers arrived: immigrants from eastern Europe.

Italy is one of the more recent destinations of immigration into Europe, reversing the country's historical experience as a source, rather than a target, of immigration. However, after Germany, France, and Britain passed laws curtailing immigration in the 1970s, Italy became an increasingly popular destination for immigrants from Africa, Asia, and Latin America; after the end of the Cold War came immigrants from outside the European Union (EU), including eastern Europe. At the time, laws regulating immigration were few, and the country appeared welcoming. But twenty years ago, this began to change, leading Umberto Melotti to observe: "Italy has not historically been a racist country, but intolerant attitudes toward immigrants have increased. To a large extent, this seems to be the result of a long-standing underestimation of the magnitude of the changes and thus poor policy implementation for a lengthy period, in spite of the best intentions officially proclaimed" (Melotti 1997, 91).

Melotti contrasted the distinctive ways in which immigration was understood by the governments of France, Britain, and Germany. According to Melotti, the French project is *ethnocentric assimilationism*: since early in the nineteenth century, when French society experienced a falling birthrate, immigration was encouraged; and immigrants were promised all the rights and privileges of native-born citizens as long as they adopted French culture completely, dropping other ethnic or cultural attachments and assimilating the French language, culture, and character (1997, 75). The British project, by contrast, is *uneven pluralism*: that is, the pragmatic British expect immigrants to be loyal and law-abiding citizens, but they do not expect immigrants to "become British: and they tolerate private cultivation of cultural differences as long as these do not threaten the British way of life (1997, 79–80). Finally, Melotti describes the German project as *the institutionalization of precariousness*, by which he means that despite the fact that Germany has within its borders more immigrants than any other European country, and began receiving immigrants at the end of the nineteenth century, its government continues to insist that Germany is not a country of immigrants.

Immigrants were always considered "guest workers," children born to guest workers are considered citizens of the country from which the worker came, and it remains very difficult for guest workers or their children born in Germany to obtain German citizenship. (This contrasts with France, for example, where children of immigrants born on French soil automatically become French citizens.)

Coming to terms with increasing numbers of Muslims living in countries where Christianity has historically been dominant has been central to cultural debates within Europe for the past quarter century. Although all European states consider themselves secular in orientation (see Asad 2003), the relation between religion and state is far from uniform. France is unusual because of its strict legal separation between religion and state. In Britain, the combination of a secular outlook with state funding of the established Anglican Church has allowed citizens to support forms of religious inclusion that first involved state funding of Catholic schools for Irish immigrants and later involved state funding for Muslim schools for Muslim immigrants (Lewis 1997; Modood 1997). In Germany, where a secular outlook also combines with state-subsidized religious institutions, the state devised curricula for elementary schools designed to teach all students about different religious traditions, including Islam, in ways that emphasize the possibility of harmonizing one's religious faith with one's obligations as a citizen. Perhaps as a result of their own history, many contemporary Germans have had less faith than the British that a civic culture of religious tolerance would automatically lead to harmony without state intervention and less faith than the French in the existence of a separate secular sphere of society from which religion could be safely excluded (Schiffauer 1997).

These are, of course, thumbnail sketches of more complex attitudes and practices. But they illustrate the fact that there is no single "European" approach to the challenges posed by immigration. In a way, each European state, with its own history and own institutions, has been experimenting with different ways of coping with the challenges posed by the arrival of immigrants and refugees, and the results of these experiments have influenced the policies toward outsiders that are taking shape in the twenty-first century. Their responses have been complicated by the structures of the EU, a continent-wide superstate with 28 members. Reconciling the diverse interests and needs of member states has posed enormous challenges for EU members. These challenges have increased even more sharply in recent years, as austerity policies within the EU have threatened the economic viability of states such as Greece, some of whose citizens have responded to the crisis by suggesting that Greece leave the European Union to find financial relief. Similarly, the free movement of EU citizens across state borders has generated anti-immigrant sentiments among some British citizens, which led to the so-called Brexit referendum in the United Kingdom in which voters by a slim majority favored cutting British ties with the EU (as of this writing, in August 2020, Brexit had not yet been fully achieved, despite much political wrangling within the UK, and between the UK and the EU). Finally, radical Islamic Middle Eastern terrorist groups such as ISIS (or the so-called "Islamic State") have managed to perpetrate violent terrorist incidents inside a number of European states, perhaps most notably the attacks in 2015 in Paris, first at the offices of the satirical newspaper *Charli Hebdo* in January, and later coordinated attacks in November on several public venues in Paris including the Bataclan concert hall. These events have further stimulated the growth of right-wing, anti-immigrant and anti-Muslim political movements in many European countries.

Over twenty years ago, Tariq Modood emphasized the need to find ways of supporting European citizenship that allow the "right to assimilate" as well as the "right to have one's 'difference' . . . recognized and supported in the public and the private spheres"; appreciating that "participation in the public or national culture is necessary for the effective exercise of citizenship" while at the same time defending the "right to widen and adapt the national culture" (1997, 20). Modood further suggested that perhaps such tensions "can only be resolved in practice through finding and cultivating points of common ground between dominant and subordinate cultures, as well as new syntheses and hybridities. The important thing is that the burdens of change . . . are not all dependent on one party to this encounter" (1997, 20). Anthropologist John Bowen's field research in France documented the process Modood describes. Bowen has worked among many French Muslims who are not interested in terrorism but who "wish to live fulfilling *and* religious lives in France" (2010, 4). He has paid particular attention to the work of a number of French Muslim religious teachers and scholars, whom he calls "Islamic public actors." Other French Muslims come to them for religious instruction and for advice about how to cope with the difficulties of living in a non-Muslim country. In turn, the Islamic public actors Bowen knew are working to craft solutions that, in their view, are true both to the laws of the French republic and to the norms and traditions of Islam.

FIGURE 12.7 A Turkish bride and groom in Clichy-sous-Bois, a poor suburb of Paris. Islamic and French legal scholars are both working to harmonize French and Islamic marriage practices.

For example, many French Muslims are concerned about how to contract a valid marriage in France. Ever since the French Revolution, France has refused to accept the legality of religious marriages and recognizes only civil marriages contracted at city hall (Figure 12.7). Yet Muslims who want to marry are often confused about whether a "secular" marriage at city hall is appropriate or necessary. Indeed, some Muslims have argued that city hall marriages are un-Islamic because they did not exist at the time of the Prophet Muhammad. But other Muslims, including some of Bowen's consultants, disagree with this position. They argue that there was no need for civil marriages at the time of the Prophet, because in those days, tribal life made it impossible to avoid the obligations of the marriage contract. But things are different today for Muslims in urban France: Bowen's consultants have seen many tragic outcomes when young women who thought they had a valid Muslim marriage were left by their husbands, only to discover that the French state did not recognize their marriage and could offer them no legal redress.

Because this was not the outcome that Islamic marriage was intended to produce, the scholars Bowen knew looked beyond traditional Islamic marriage practices in order to clarify the larger purposes that Islamic marriage was supposed to achieve. They asked if these purposes could be achieved using the French institution of civil marriage. One scholar told Bowen, "I say that if you marry at the city hall, you have already made an Islamic marriage, because all the conditions for that marriage have been fulfilled" (2010, 167). Those conditions include the fact that both Islamic marriages and French civil marriages are contracts; that both require the consent of the spouses; and that the legal requirements imposed on the spouses by French civil marriage further the Islamic goal of keeping the spouses together. When this kind of reasoning is strengthened by appealing to opinions on marriage drawn from the four Sunni schools of law, many Islamic public intellectuals believe that a way can be found to craft acceptable practices for French Muslims in many areas of daily life.

Because Bowen agrees with Modood that accommodation has to go in both directions, he also shows how some French legal scholars are working to craft solutions to the challenges Muslim marriage practices present to French law. Most French judges agree, for example, that Islamic marriages or divorces contracted outside France remain valid when the parties involved move to France. But French judges can refuse to accept international rules for resolving legal conflicts if they decide that the solution would violate French "public order." Bowen found that the concept of "public order" is basic to the French legal system, referring "both to the conditions of social order and to basic values, and it limits the range of laws that a legislator may pass and the decisions that a judge may make" (2010, 173).

Violations of public order may include customs from outside France that are judged to "offend the morality and values" of French law (Bowen 2010, 173). Some French jurists argue that consequences following from Muslim practices of marriage and divorce should not be recognized in France if they violate French and European commitments to the equality of women and men. Other French jurists, however, point to the practical problems that this argument creates: not recognizing the validity of Islamic divorces in France, for example, would mean that a woman divorced according to Islamic law abroad could not remarry if she came to France. Similarly, refusing to recognize polygamous marriage in France would deprive the children of all but a man's first wife of their rights under French and European law. In recent years, Bowen reports, French judges have devised two ways of crafting a solution to these unwelcome consequences. One has been to modify the concept of public order by making so-called practical exceptions for Muslims who emigrate to France. The other is to be more flexible with Muslim marriage and family practices as long as these arrangements involve individuals who are not French citizens. These pragmatic solutions are an improvement over what Bowen calls the "more blunt-instrument approach" associated with the older understanding of public order. Bowen concludes that in France today, Muslim and French jurists alike are both struggling to craft "the legal conditions for common life that are capacious enough to 'reasonably accommodate' people living in different conditions and with differing beliefs, yet unitary enough to retain the hope that such a common life is conceivable" (2010, 178).

Thus, the struggles and dilemmas that faced residents of Rione Monti are widespread in Europe today. But the specifics of each situation, and the cultural resources at people's disposal, have their own particularity. Thus, traditionally left-wing Monti residents resisted attempts by neofascist politicians to get them to turn against immigrant families in the neighborhood. Herzfeld found that the residents of Monti, like other Romans, claimed not to be racists (which accords with Melotti's view of Italians in general) and that they seemed less hostile to immigrants of color than to Ukrainians (Figure 12.8). Local and immigrant Monti residents eventually did find ways to get along with each other (Herzfeld 2009, 231). Indeed, during the years when Herzfeld was doing his ethnography, the mix of residents in Monti was changing in other ways, as young professionals, including professors from the nearby university, began to rent apartments in local buildings. The low-income artisans who had traditionally lived in these buildings were finding, however, that rents were rising even as entire apartment blocks remained empty. Their owners had concluded that it was worth their while to keep their buildings empty until real estate prices rose, even though this precipitated a housing shortage.

Prior to this period, struggles among renters, landlords, and the city government of Rome regarding building permits or over rental rates were common, and these disputes had usually been resolved by negotiations among all interested parties, carried out according to the mostly extralegal rules of the traditional neighborhood "code." As a result, low-income renters had often managed to avoid eviction from their apartments. But in the early years of the twenty first century, the rules changed, in large part because some of the key players changed. A lot of outside money was entering the

FIGURE 12.8 Rione Monti is a neighborhood in central Rome where longtime residents and new immigrants are negotiating new forms of relationships.

Roman real estate market, deployed by businessmen who knew nothing and cared less about whether low-income renters ought to be allowed to stay in buildings in desirable locations.

Still, Monti residents were politically active, and they banded together when threatened with eviction. Herzfeld followed closely the back-and-forth negotiations that ensued when renters in one particular building staged a rent strike, after the building's new owner threatened to evict current residents. In the old days, this sort of action would likely have been quietly resolved according to the neighborhood code; and at first, the strikers were able to get the building's new owner to agree not to evict them. What nobody had counted on, however, was the clout of the wealthy outside buyers who had entered the Roman real estate market.

This new owner sold the building to another company, which then sold it to a third company, whose owners refused to honor the agreement that the original owner had made with the renters. The current owners then tried to sell the building to the city, which refused to pay the price they were asking. "It became clear that nothing further could be done; this company soon thereafter sold the property to yet another firm, one that was developing extensive interest in the neighborhood, and the struggle finally came to an end" (Herzfeld 2009, 297).

A key component contributing to this outcome was a change in the law that reflected struggles over what kinds of rights residents had to their homes. One of Herzfeld's informants, who had been active in Roman city government, explained to him that the power of the city to intervene in struggles against eviction had changed. In the past, the city had respected the view that people had a *social* right to their homes; but these rights were no longer legally protected: "under the national constitution, it was now the owner's rights that were protected. . . . A set of laws, promulgated at the national level by the coalition to which he had belonged at the city level, and reinforced by already existing constitutional guarantees for the rights of property owners, had now effectively undercut any serious prospect of resolving the dispute as an issue of the social right to a home" (Herzfeld 2009, 297). At first, the strikers refused to give up, but their legal position was weak; within a year, they had been evicted. There was much bitterness among those who were forced to leave; and even though all of them eventually did find other places to live, many had to leave Monti, which undermined their sense of community and identity.

The experiences of these Monti residents raise interesting and troubling questions about the rights of longtime residents in a place who discover that under the current regime of global neoliberalism, they apparently possess no rights that international capital is obliged to respect. Herzfeld observes that "the intense attachment to place that aroused my sympathies can also be the source of no less intense forms of cultural fundamentalism and racism" (2009, 301). These responses are not limited to Europe, but can also be found in Bangkok, Thailand, where Herzfeld next carried out fieldwork, following what turned into a 24-year-long battle by residents of an inner-city neighborhood to resist being evicted so that the government might modernize space they occupied (Herzfeld 2016). In May 2018, the remaining residents were finally removed. At that time, Herzfeld observed that the evicted community represented "the best of Thai culture—extraordinary examples of architecture and the everyday life of a community in a single site.. . . They are being sacrificed on the altar of a touristic experience. It's a tragedy for Bangkok and for Thailand" (https://www.reuters.com/article/us-thailand-landrights-property/ancient-fort-community-in-bangkok-loses-25-year-battle-against-bulldozers-idUSKBN1I5005). Herzfeld has insisted that "there is no necessary connection between localism and racism and other forms of intolerance, and in fact what has impressed me throughout both field projects . . . has been the firmness with which some reject the seductions of intolerance in the midst of their own sufferings, even as they recognize the bitterness that drives others in far less attractive directions" (2009, 302). He adds that "none of this will make much sense except in the further context of a consideration of the history of nationalism, both in Italy and elsewhere" (302).

What Happens to Citizenship in a Globalized World?

Our discussion of nationality, nation-states, and nationalism has briefly traced developments from the French Revolution through the spread of European colonial empires through the transformation of colonies into nation-states, ending with the softening of national boundaries that has occurred following post–Cold War processes of globalization. Challenges to national sovereignty—that is, a nation's ability to defend its borders and govern itself—have been accompanied by changes in the meaning of citizenship—the rights and privileges of those persons considered legitimate members of the national population. What might citizenship mean in a twenty-first century globalized world?

How Can Citizenship Be Flexible?

Schiller and Fouron's contrast between formal and substantive citizenship suggests that notions of citizenship that previously seemed straightforward break down in the context of globalization. Another way of addressing these contradictions is suggested by anthropologist Aihwa Ong, who speaks of **flexible citizenship**: "the strategies and effects of mobile managers, technocrats, and professionals seeking both to circumvent *and* benefit from different nation-state regimes by selecting different sites for investment, work, and family relocation (2002, 174). Ong studied diaspora communities of elite Chinese families who played key roles in the economic success of the Pacific Rim in recent years. Although their success is often attributed by outsiders to "Chinese culture," Ong's research questions this simplistic explanation; she documents the ways in which Chinese families responded creatively to opportunities and challenges they have encountered since the end of the nineteenth century, as they found ways to evade or exploit the governmentality of three different kinds of institutions: Chinese kinship and family, the nation-state, and the marketplace.

The break from mainland Chinese ideas of kinship and Confucian filial piety came when Chinese first moved into the capitalist commercial circuits of European empires. Money could be made in these settings, but success required Chinese merchant families to cut themselves off from ties to mainland China and to reinforce bonds among family members and business partners in terms of *guanxi* ("relationships of social connections built primarily upon shared identities such as native place, kinship or attending the same school"; Smart 1999, 120).

The family discipline of overseas Chinese enabled them to become wealthy and provided the resources to subvert the governmentality of the nation-state. The orientation of these wealthy families toward national identity and citizenship, Ong explains, is "market-driven." In Hong Kong, for example, in the years leading up to its return to mainland China in 1997, many wealthy Chinese thought of citizenship not as the right to demand full democratic representation, but as the right to promote familial interests apart from the well-being of society (Ong 2002, 178). None of the overseas Chinese she knew expressed any commitment to nationalism,

flexible citizenship The strategies and effects employed by managers, technocrats, and professionals who move regularly across state boundaries and seek both to circumvent and benefit from different nation-state regimes.

either local or long distance. Quite the contrary. Relying on family discipline and loyalty and buttressed by considerable wealth and strong interpersonal ties, they actively worked to evade the governmentality of nation-states. For example, Chinese from Hong Kong who wanted to migrate to Britain in the 1960s were able to evade racial barriers that blocked other "colored" immigrants because of their experience with capitalism and their reputation for peaceful acquiescence to British rule. When the British decided to award citizenship to some Hong Kong residents in the 1990s, they used a point system that favored applicants with education, fluency in English, and training in professions of value to the economy, such as accountancy and law. These attributes fitted well the criteria for citizenship valued under the government of Margaret Thatcher, while other applicants for citizenship who lacked such attributes were excluded. Citizenship, or at least a passport, could be purchased by those who had the money: "well-off families accumulated passports not only from Canada, Australia, Singapore, and the United States but also from revenue-poor Fiji, the Philippines, Panama, and Tonga which required in return for a passport a down payment of U.S. $200,000 and an equal amount in installments" (Ong 2002, 183) (Figure 12.9).

Although wealthy overseas Chinese families had thus managed to evade or subvert both the governmentality of Chinese kinship and that of nation-states, they remained vulnerable to the discipline of the capitalist market. To be sure, market discipline under globalization was very different from the market discipline typical in the 1950s and 1960s. Making money in the context of globalization required the flexibility to take advantage of economic opportunities wherever and whenever they appeared. Ong described one family in which the eldest son remained in Hong Kong to run part of the family hotel chain located in the Pacific region while his brother lived in San Francisco and managed the hotels located in North America and Europe. Children can be separated from their parents when they are, for example, installed in one country to be educated while their parents manage businesses in other countries on different continents.

These flexible family arrangements are not without costs. "Familial regimes of dispersal and localization . . . discipline family members to make do with very little emotional support; disrupted parental responsibility, strained marital relations, and abandoned children are such common circumstances that they have special terms" (Ong 2002, 190). At the same time, individual family members truly do seem to live comfortably as citizens of the world. A Chinese banker in San Francisco

FIGURE 12.9 Overseas Chinese are to be found in many parts of the world, as here in Kuala Lumpur, Malaysia. They are not always millionaire businesspeople but are shopkeepers and small businesspeople as well.

told Ong that he could live in Asia, Canada, or Europe: "I can live anywhere in the world, but it must be near an airport" (190).

Ong concludes that, for these elite Chinese, the concept of nationalism has lost its meaning. Instead, she says, they seem to subscribe to a **postnational ethos** in which they submit to the governmentality of the capitalist market while trying to evade the governmentality of nation-states, ultimately because their only true loyalty is to the family business (Ong 2002, 190). Such flexible citizenship, however, is not an option for nonelite migrants: "whereas for bankers, boundaries are always flexible, for migrant workers, boat people, persecuted intellectuals and artists, and other kinds of less well-heeled refugees, this . . . is a harder act to follow" (190). Ong concludes that neither the positives nor the negatives associated with the practices of these overseas Chinese merchants should be attributed to any "Chinese" essence; instead, she thinks these strategies are better understood as "the expressions of a habitus that is finely tuned to the turbulence of late capitalism" (191).

What Is Territorial Citizenship?

The forms of citizenship we have considered so far—legal, substantive, or flexible—are best understood in the context of forms of governmentality active in nation-states that are concerned to control and manage the biopower of their populations. But what happens when this form of biopolitics—what we might call a biopolitics of concern and interference—is replaced by what Peruvian anthropologist Marisol de la Cadena calls a biopolitics of abandonment (2015, 158)? The biopolitics of abandonment withdraws governmental resources and management from sections of the citizenry, leaving them to meet their needs as they are able and see fit. From one perspective, this looks like a government refusing to meet its obligations to (at least some of) its citizens, and it is. But recall Foucault's insight that power is productive. In the space left by the withdrawal of the nation-state, it may be possible to develop new forms of citizenship disconnected from the nation-state. Importantly, these new forms do not repudiate the nation-state and all it stands for. Rather, they involve the repurposing of some state forms and practices, such as those connected with citizenship, in terms informed by indigenous understandings that have persisted, often in the spaces where the state and its institutions could not reach.

postnational ethos An attitude toward the world in which people submit to the governmentality of the capitalist market while trying to evade the governmentality of nation-states.

One example of such creativity is a new form of citizenship that is developing among residents of indigenous territories who have been granted full control and authority (or sovereignty) over lands that are located within the boundaries of nation-states. The responsibilities that come with territorial sovereignty may be new to both leaders and residents of indigenous territories and may carry burdens that they are unaccustomed to or unwilling to assume. Juliet S. Erazo has studied the new ways of thinking and acting that have developed in the indigenous territory of Rukullakta, in Ecuador, as its Amazonian Kichwa residents fashion a sense of *territorial citizenship*. According to Erazo (2013), "Negotiating the specific responsibilities and duties associated with territorial citizenship is one of the key sites of enacting sovereignty" (10).

As we saw in Aihwa Ong's study of elite Chinese migrants, Michel Foucault's concept of governmentality has proved extremely helpful in analyzing processes of citizenship formation. Erazo also uses this concept in her analysis of territorial citizenship in Rukullakta, but doing so requires modifying the way governmentality is applied. First, studies of indigenous economic and political development often focus on practices of governmentality issuing from national governments, NGOs, or institutions like the World Bank. By contrast, Erazo (2013) insists that indigenous peoples like the Kichwa of Rukullakta "can also be the agents of governmentality, rationalizing and disciplining their fellow group members while enlisting them in projects of their own rule" (6). Second, many studies often portray governmentality as being exercised in a top-down fashion to manipulate targeted populations in ways that serve the interests of the powerful. By contrast, Erazo argues that this interpretation is too narrow: in Rukullakta, "indigenous leaders' actions have been critical in assuring their members' access to land and development funding" (6). Indigenous territories, therefore, provide a fresh setting in which to examine the operations of governmentality, showing "the ways in which those in governing roles have worked to transform individual subjects (in this case, people who thought of themselves primarily as part of a kinship-based group, occupying family-owned land) into active citizens (in this case, of indigenous territories with collective titles and bureaucratic governments)" (Erazo 2013, 6).

Residents of Rukullakta were able to secure title over their lands in the late 1970s because they agreed to form a ranching cooperative, responding to an offer by the Ecuadorian government that viewed such cooperatives as a means of providing economic development in rural areas. But receiving development aid for this project depended on leaders' abilities to persuade other members of the cooperative to contribute labor by cutting down forests, planting pasture, and caring for the new cattle herds. The negative experiences of many cooperative members during this period led them to resist future attempts by leaders to engage them in demanding collective economic projects. Their resistance shaped the subsequent actions of leaders, who moderated their demands for such active citizen involvement in territorial affairs.

Leaders remain concerned about passing down a strong sense of territorial citizenship to younger generations. One current effort involves a local competition for young women that resembles the beauty pageants that occur throughout Latin America. In Rukullakta, however, candidates are judged on their ability to speak about political challenges currently facing their territory, both in Spanish and in Kichwa. "Pageants are therefore key sites in which leaders invite residents to reflect on what could be done to improve the territory, and to become more involved in territorial governance" (Erazo 2013, 184). At the same time, citizens "work actively to shape leaders in a number of ways inducing demanding conflict resolution services, vocally criticizing leaders whom they think are putting their own interests ahead of those of Rukullakta's members, purposely staying away from some of the meetings and events that leaders ask them to attend, and even punishing leaders as if they were children in public spectacles" (Erazo 2013, 194). In Erazo's view, the joint efforts of Rukullakta's leaders and citizens "have contributed to Rukullakta's ability to remain a viable and resilient political entity for over four decades. However . . . these efforts have also involved new subjectivities, new hierarchies, and new ways of relating to people and nature" (2013, 199).

What Is Vernacular Statecraft?

The processes Erazo identifies among the residents of Rukullakta in Amazonian Ecuador have also been noted by Rudi Colloredo-Mansfeld in his ongoing work in indigenous communities in highland Ecuador (2009). Colloredo-Mansfeld also finds the Foucauldian understanding of governmentality (state-initiated "conduct of conduct" of its subject population) to be inadequate for understanding political change in highland Ecuador in recent decades. Erazo addresses this difficulty by showing how indigenous leaders in Rukullakta have devised their own, local forms of governmentality that they use to encourage community members to act in ways they believe will strengthen indigenous sovereignty. Colloredo-Mansfeld found similar political mechanisms at work in highland communities like Otavalo, where state administrative procedures have been repurposed by local communities. He calls these local practices **vernacular statecraft**.

In describing these local administrative practices as *statecraft*, Colloredo-Mansfeld draws inspiration from James Scott's influential discussion of how modern states operate (Scott 1998). Scott uses the term "statecraft" to describe the forms of top-down management technologies that render local communities "legible" to state manipulation. Such legibility, Scott argues, comes about through practices of "strategic simplification" that focus only on those attributes of a community that are relevant to state designs. When local communities adapt management technologies of the state and put them to work for their own purposes, however, these technologies become instances of what Colloredo-Mansfeld describes as *vernacular* statecraft, which he compares to vernacular architecture: "In vernacular architecture, builders imitate and appropriate standard elements of widely used design, adapting them to local conditions. . . . Translated into political terms, [vernacular statecraft] combines replicable form, local action and an absence of state intervention" (2009, 17).

For Colloredo-Mansfeld, the *absence* of state intervention is key. Most political analyses using concepts of "governmentality" or "statecraft" presume that local communities are targets of an intrusive state. In Latin America, Colloredo-Mansfeld argues, this presumption is not correct, for two main reasons. First, the model of intrusive statecraft presumes that state and local communities can be sharply differentiated from each other. Colloredo-Mansfeld points out, however, that "in the Andes, community and state are impossible to disentangle" (2009, 16). This entanglement goes back to the middle of the sixteenth century, when the indigenous survivors of the Spanish invasion, devastated by disease and labor exploitation, were organized into newly created communities called *reducciones*, at the head of which the Spanish authorities placed local indigenous authorities called *kurakas*. These state interventions remade indigenous culture: "deputized natives, vested in state authority, enabled the sedimentation of government forms as local culture. Bits and pieces of the state steadily accrued as indigenous custom" (2009, 17).

Second, the model of intrusive statecraft presumes that the state is a constant, powerful presence that actively intervenes in local affairs. However, Colloredo-Mansfeld points out that contemporary Latin American states like Ecuador are better known for their *neglect* of indigenous communities than for their intrusive manipulation of them. When states retreat from effective involvement in local communities, those communities may repurpose state management techniques to run their own affairs. Colloredo-Mansfeld detects a "profusion of vernacular structures" in Andean communities; their complexity may be underestimated by outsiders, but all of them "can be treacherous to navigate" (2009, 17).

One feature of Andean vernacular statecraft can be seen in the way Otavalans repurposed the traditional Andean labor practice called a *minga*, or communal work party. Labor mingas go back centuries in the Andes and have often been described as spontaneous voluntary efforts. But Colloredo-Mansfeld found that contemporary minga membership has been joined to *list keeping*, with the result that simply residing in a community is no longer sufficient for being considered a community member. Rather, your name must appear on a communal list, kept by officers of the council, and when a minga is called, these officers note down who shows up. Family members can substitute for one another to remain on the list, and they earn minga points when someone shows up, but families who do not show up will be dropped from the list unless they pay a fine. "The lists cut membership down to discrete moments of community development. Work in past projects may set someone up as a potential participant in the next one, but it does not guarantee it" (2009, 104). As a result, minga participation is not automatic but must be negotiated: "The collective unpaid labor mobilized in a minga is too tightly pledged to the construction of desired services, too carefully tracked by households, and too systematically monitored by community authority to be glibly described as a voluntary, cooperative effort" (2009, 107).

Colloredo-Mansfeld uses the concept of vernacular statecraft to explain how indigenous communities throughout Ecuador are now able to come together to challenge state power. The 1937 Ley de Comuna may have been intended as a way of making indigenous communities legible to the state. But indigenous communities that complied with the law also became more

---

vernacular statecraft The repurposing of state administrative procedures by local communities under circumstances where state institutions are weak, unreliable, or absent.

legible to one another. In Colloredo-Mansfeld's view, the tools of indigenous statecraft have provided the means for indigenous communities to ally with one another regional and national federations, such as the Confederation of Indigenous Nationalities of Ecuador, or CONAIE. "In all this, differences and inequalities are not erased but organized, sometimes in lasting and iniquitous ways, sometimes in passing" (2009, 89). As a result, "When communities arrive at a consensus to act, they frequently mobilize to oppose state policy, rather than speed its implementation. Furthermore, standardized organizational forms allow opposition to scale up quickly" (2009, 7). Colloredo-Mansfeld describes how mingas were called out in 2006 to blockade the northern entrance to the town of Peguche, in support of a nationwide general strike called by CONAIE to protest a proposed free trade treaty between Ecuador and the United States (2009, 186). This use of mingas was controversial, especially among local supporters of the proposed treaty, but this disagreement illustrates precisely how the concerns of contemporary indigenous communities reach beyond their borders: "amid debate and dissent, leaders push for programs at provincial, national, and even international levels, linking residents' interests to wider political projects. To insist on either unanimity of support or individual freedom to opt out of any project at will is to hold indigenous groups to a higher standard than other democracies" (2009, 188). Ten years later, CONAIE is still making its influence felt: when Ecuadorian President Lenín Moreno attempted to lift state fuel subsidies in the fall of 2019, violent demonstrations erupted, calming down only when Moreno agreed to negotiate a new agreement. The leaders of CONAIE have been prominent in both the resistance and the negotiations that followed (https://foreignpolicy.com/2019/11/08/latin-americas-protests-are-likely-to-fail/)

Global Politics in the Twenty-First Century

Although traditional research in political anthropology began among small-scale societies that might at one time have functioned independently of their neighbors, the fact remains that these ethnographic studies were regularly carried out when these societies had been incorporated into European colonial empires. With the breakup of these empires, most colonial territories were transformed into independent nation-states. But as we saw in the case of Fiji, this transformation has been full of tension and struggle, because different segments of the Fijian citizenry had different ideas about what that modern nation-state would look like, and who would be in charge. Even as such struggles to affirm national sovereignty continue in many parts of the world, these struggles have been complicated by global flows of capital, people, images, ideas, and ideologies. National boundaries have softened. In some cases, nation-states have given up claims to sovereignty over some of their citizens; but some of these same citizens, now moving in the same globalized contexts, have found new ways of asserting their own territorial citizenship. Because power is productive, the results may be positive or negative, depending on the specific case. At the end of the second decade of the twenty-first century, however, the globalized world is in a dangerous and unstable condition. While some have been able to benefit enormously from the growth of global capitalism, many others have been left out. As inequalities widen, local leaders and their followers struggle to manage the consequences, with or in spite of the intervention of outside powers. One major consequence has been the increased flows of migrants and refugees seeking to escape the violence. Many long taken-for-granted notions about identity and belonging now seem up for grabs everywhere on Earth.

Chapter Summary

1. Contemporary cultural anthropologists are interested in how cultures change, but they are suspicious of evolutionary schemes that give the impression that social arrangements could not have been—or could not be—other than the way they are. They also point out that no society anywhere is static. The power that human beings have to reproduce or to change their social organization is an important focus of political anthropology.

2. The ability to act implies power. The study of power in human society is the domain of political

anthropology. In most societies at most times, power can never be reduced to physical force, although this is the Western prototype of power. Power in society operates according to principles that are cultural creations. As such, those principles are affected by history and may differ from one society to another.

3. Western thinkers traditionally assumed that without a state, social life would be chaotic, if not impossible. They believed that people were free agents who would not cooperate unless forced to do so.

Anthropologists have demonstrated that power is exercised both by coercive and by persuasive means. They have been influenced by the works of Antonio Gramsci and Michel Foucault. Gramsci argued that coercion alone is rarely sufficient for social control, distinguishing coercive domination from hegemony. Rulers always face the risk that those they dominate may create counterhegemonic accounts of their experience of being dominated, acquire a following, and unseat their rulers. Foucault's concept of governmentality addresses practices developed in Western nation-states in the nineteenth century that aimed to create and sustain peaceful and prosperous social life by exercising biopower over persons who could be counted, whose physical attributes could be measured statistically, and whose sexual and reproductive behaviors could be shaped by the exercise of state power.

4. Nation-states were invented in nineteenth-century Europe, but they have spread throughout the world along with capitalism, colonialism, and eventual political decolonization. Nationalist thinking aims to create a political unit in which national identity and political territory coincide, and this has led to various practices designed to force subordinate social groups to adopt a national identity defined primarily in terms of the culture of the dominant group. When subordinate groups resist, they may become the victims of genocide or ethnic cleansing. Alternatively, the dominant group may try to recast its understanding of national identity in a way that acknowledges and incorporates cultural elements belonging to subordinate groups. If the creation of such an imagined hybrid identity is not accompanied by legal and political changes that support it, however, the end result may be political turmoil, as shown in the recent history of Fiji.

5. The flows unleashed by globalization have undermined the ability of nation-states to police their boundaries effectively. Contemporary migrants across national borders have developed a variety of trans-border identities. Some become involved in long-distance nationalism that leads to the emergence of trans-border states claiming emigrants as trans-border citizens of their ancestral homelands even if they are legal citizens of another state. Some trans-border citizenries call for the establishment of full-fledged transnational nation-states. Struggles of these kinds can be found all over the globe, including in the contemporary states of the European Union.

6. The contrasts between formal and substantive citizenship suggest that conventional notions of citizenship are breaking down in the context of globalization. Diaspora communities of elite Chinese families have developed a strategy of flexible citizenship that allows them to both circumvent and benefit from different nation-state regimes. They seem to subscribe to a postnational ethos in which their only true loyalty is to the family business.

7. In recent decades, nation-states have regularly neglected support for their rural and indigenous citizens. This withdrawal of the state, however, has opened up a space for members of these populations to come up with their own institutional solutions that combine state practices with indigenous practices, even when the populations in question remain within official boundaries of a larger nation-state. Examples from Ecuador alone include the form of territorial citizenship crafted by the Amazonian Kichwa of Rukullakta and the institutions of vernacular statecraft developed by the Otavalans of the Andean highlands.

For Review

1. Define power and the three different kinds of power described by Eric Wolf.
2. What are the different theoretical orientations and subject matters that have interested political anthropology over its history?
3. Explain how power may be understood as physical force or coercion.
4. Compare hegemony and domination.
5. Why is hegemony a useful term for anthropologists?
6. What does the perspective of political anthropology highlight about the history of nationalism in Sri Lanka?
7. What is biopower?
8. Following Foucault, how does governing a state differ from ruling a state?

9. Summarize how kinship affects politics in northern Thailand.

10. What are hidden transcripts? Where do they come from and how do they function?

11. Summarize the argument in the text concerning the powers of the weak, and illustrate your summary with references to the Tswana and Bolivian examples.

12. Summarize the key points concerning multicultural politics in contemporary Europe, with particular attention to the different ways in which the United Kingdom, France, and Germany deal with immigration.

13. How does ethnographic research illuminate the challenges faced by French Muslims who wish to contract a valid marriage?

14. What are everyday forms of peasant resistance? How does James Scott connect them with the political relations of dominant and subordinate categories of people in "Sedaka," Malaysia?

15. What is citizenship? How is citizenship being remade in the context of globalization?

16. How are experiments with territorial sovereignty and vernacular statecraft connected to the challenges of globalization?

Key Terms

biopower 379
diaspora 385
domination 377
flexible citizenship 392
free agency 372
governmentality 379
hegemony 377

hidden transcripts 373
ideology 377
legal citizenship 386
long-distance nationalists 385
nation 382
nationality 382
nation-state 382

political anthropology 370
postnational ethos 393
power 370
substantive citizenship 386
trans-border citizenry 385

trans-border state 385
transformist hegemony 382
transnational nation-state 386
vernacular statecraft 395

Suggested Readings

Arens, W., and Ivan Karp, eds. 1989. *Creativity of power: Cosmology and action in African societies*. Washington, DC: Smithsonian Institution Press. *Contains 13 essays exploring the relationship among power, action, and human agency in African social systems and cosmologies.*

De la Cadena, Marisol. 2015. *Earth beings: Ecologies of practice across Andean worlds*. Durham, NC: Duke University Press. *This rich text has much to offer, including a valuable introduction to the "ontological turn" in contemporary ethnography, and an illustration of how this approach makes possible a powerful reconsideration of the politics of resistance in mid-twentieth-century highland Peru. De la Cadena's original research project involved working with Mariano Turpo, an indigenous activist who had been involved in the successful overthrow of the hacienda system in the 1960s. Originally expecting that their joint reconstruction of his political work would center on an archive of paperwork Turpo had collected over the years, de la Cadena had to change plans when she realized that Turpo's account of this period paid little attention to the papers in his archive and* emphasized instead the active contribution of the earth being Ausangate to which Turpo and his community were inseparably bound. Overall, the text explores changes in who—or what—may count as a political actor in highland Peru, and how such judgments are rooted in alternative (but interpenetrating) assumptions about what really exists in the world in which one lives.

Fogelson, Raymond, and Richard N. Adams, eds. 1977. *The anthropology of power*. New York: Academic Press. *A classic collection of 28 ethnographic essays on the varied ways power is understood all over the world. Also contains two important essays based on case studies.*

Herzfeld, Michael. 2009. *Evicted from eternity: The restructuring of modern Rome*. Chicago: University of Chicago Press. *An extended study of the politics of the new Europe as experienced in one historic neighborhood in Rome.*

Keesing, Roger. 1983. *'Elota's story: The life and times of a Solomon Islands big man*. New York: Holt, Rinehart and Winston. *The autobiography of a Kwaio Big Man, with interpretive material by Keesing. First-rate, very readable, and involving.*

Lewellen, Ted. 2003. *Political anthropology*, 3rd ed. New York: Praeger. *The latest edition of a standard introductory text in political anthropology, covering leading theories, scholars, and problems in the field.*

Vincent, Joan, ed. 2002. *The anthropology of politics.* New York: Wiley–Blackwell. *An excellent collection of texts that illustrate the development of political anthropology over time and showcase important achievements by influential political anthropologists today.*

 Visit our online resource center for further reading, web links, free assessments, flashcards, and videos. www.oup.com/he/ lavenda5e

What can anthropology teach us about sex, gender, and sexuality?

Cultural anthropologists have been interested in sex, gender, and sexuality since the beginnings of anthropology as a discipline, but their preferred approaches to these topics have changed over time, along with broader theoretical developments in the discipline and wider historical shifts in the world. This chapter focuses primarily on perspectives and concepts that have developed since the 1960s and 1970s in Euro-American sociocultural anthropology. However, scholarship and activism on issues surrounding sex, gender, and sexuality extend far beyond the discipline of anthropology. As a result, anthropologists and other social scientists have shared perspectives and borrowed concepts from one another. The result, for sociocultural anthropologists, has been the production of a vast and expanding body of ethnographic research exploring sex, gender, and sexuality both in Euro-American societies and in societies outside the Western world.

CHAPTER OUTLINE

Generations of indigenous women.

LEARNING OBJECTIVES

- Describe the anthropological studies of sex, gender, and sexuality that emerged from twentieth-century feminism.

- Identify the approaches that anthropologists take to study the concepts of sex, gender, and sexuality.

- Analyze how identity is affected and influenced by sex and gender cross-culturally.

- Explain the concept of gender performativity and how ethnographers go about studying gender performativity in different societies.

- Compare how different theorists have approached the concept of "the body" and its connection to sex, gender, and sexuality.

- Articulate the approaches to anthropological studies that examine

connections between the body/bodies and digital technologies.

- Compare how different anthropologists have approached the concept of sexuality and its connection to sex, gender, and sexuality.

- Apply the method of ethnography as a tool for documenting diverse cultural understandings of sex, gender, and sexuality in Mombasa, Nicaragua, and Iran.

How Did Twentieth-Century Feminism Shape the Anthropological Study of Sex, Gender, and Sexuality?

Some anthropologists would argue that twentieth-century feminism was responsible for a series of pivotal transformations in social science scholarship. **Feminism**

feminism   The argument that women and men are equally human and therefore that women are entitled to enjoy the same rights and privileges as men.

argues that women and men are equally human and therefore that women are entitled to enjoy the same rights and privileges as men.

As a social movement in North America, the first wave of feminism emerged in the nineteenth century, sparked by the movement to abolish racial slavery. After women in the United States obtained the right to vote in the early twentieth century, the struggle for women's rights lost momentum. But by the 1960s and 1970s, in the wake of the Civil Rights Movement, a second-wave feminist movement rose up, challenging many remaining forms of inequality between men and women. Second-wave feminists pointed out that even though Western

FIGURE 13.1 Location of societies whose EthnoProfiles appear in Chapter 13.

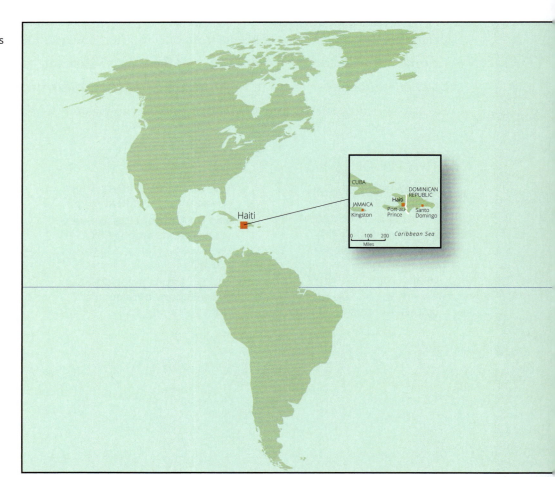

societies were supposed to be democratic, and women now had the right to vote, many domains of social life continued to be organized in terms of **patriarchy**— that is, by the domination of men over women and children.

Feminists coined the term **sexism** (based on an analogy with racism) to describe the systematic sociocultural structures and practices of inequality, derived from patriarchal institutions, that continue to shape relations between women and men. As with racism, sexism was seen to involve more than prejudiced individual beliefs alone; as a result, achieving full equality between women and men was understood to require not only changing beliefs but also dismantling patriarchal institutions and practices.

A rallying cry for many second-wave feminists was that "the personal is political." These feminists confronted the **public/private divide**, a barrier that law and custom had erected between "private" domestic life in the family, conceived as "women's place," and public life, outside the family, conceived as the domain of men.

Feminists pointed out that women were oppressed by domestic forms of patriarchy that were considered "private," and thus understood to be matters beyond the "public" reach of the law. Ostensibly, women's husbands or fathers both looked after women's interests within private, male-headed households and protected women from the harsh effects of the public, male domain. However, women who sought education or employment outside the home, or who lacked husbands or private homes altogether, found themselves at the mercy of hostile public institutions that regularly discriminated against them. At the same time, women who stayed at home were not guaranteed protection because the public/private divide allowed men to evade legal accountability for physically abusing the women living in their private households. Indeed, feminist activism around the issue of spousal abuse spurred second-wave feminists to create a battered-women's movement, which has now become global (Merry 2009).

Feminist struggles in their own societies prompted some anthropologists to rethink many long-held assumptions about the contributions of women to human culture. Feminist anthropologists noted that most ethnographies, including those written by women, were

---

patriarchy The domination of men over women and children.

sexism The systematic sociocultural structures and practices of inequality, derived from patriarchal institutions, that continue to shape relations between women and men (based on an analogy with racism).

public/private divide A barrier that law and custom erected between "private" domestic life in the family, conceived as "women's place," and public life, outside the family, conceived as the domain of men.

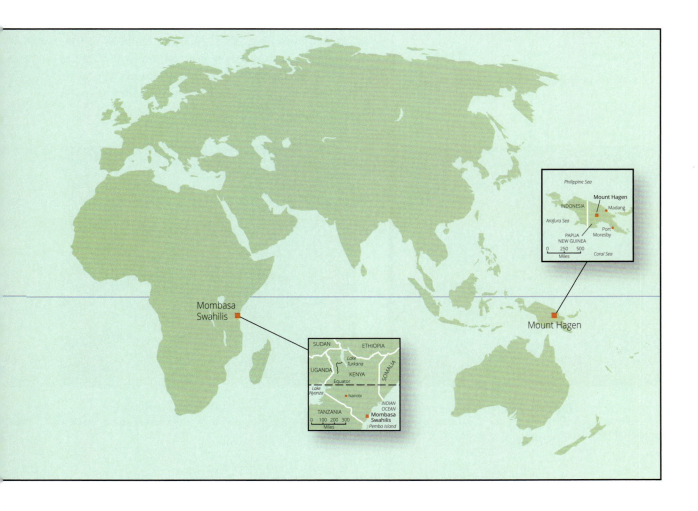

based primarily on the views of male informants, even concerning matters pertaining to women. Thus, most discussions of "the culture" of a group in fact portrayed culture from the viewpoint of men (often high-status men). When women were discussed at all, it was usually in the context of marriage and the family, and the assumption seemed to be that women's cultural roles as wives and mothers followed "naturally" from the biological facts of pregnancy and lactation. However, Margaret Mead's demonstration in the 1930s of the lack of correlation between biological sex and culturally expected behaviors of males and females in society was a well-known exception to this pattern (Figure 13.2). Building on Mead's work, it became commonplace for cultural anthropologists to use the term **sex** to refer to the physical characteristics that distinguish males from females (e.g., body shape, distribution of body hair, reproductive organs, sex chromosomes).

By contrast, they used the term **gender** to refer to the culturally constructed roles assigned to males or females, which varied considerably from society to society. The distinction between sex and gender was an important theoretical breakthrough, and it became widely adopted by anthropologists and other social scientists. At the same time, the sex/gender distinction seemed to take

for granted that even if there seemed to be a demonstrable lack of correlation between physical sex and the content of gender roles, all societies universally distinguished women from men. Such a dual categorization has been called a **gender binary**.

By the 1970s, some feminist anthropologists were concerned that both the gender binary and male domination of females might be universal. For example, many human societies trace descent through women (see Chapter 14), but no persuasive evidence has ever been found to suggest that there have ever been societies organized as *matriarchies*—that is, societies where women as a group dominated men as a group.

In 1974, Sherry Ortner published an article with the title "Is Female to Male as Nature is to Culture?," and her answer to this question was "yes." Her survey of a wide range of ethnographic and historical evidence suggested to her that male dominance was rooted in a universal form of binary thinking that opposed male to female; associated males with culture and females with nature; and valued culture over nature, regardless of the actual activities performed by men and women in a society. At best, women might be seen as *mediating* between culture and nature; but women were always seen as closer to nature than men, perhaps because women's bodies were so obviously bound up with the "natural" processes of pregnancy, childbirth, and lactation.

Ortner's rather pessimistic conclusion was challenged by other feminist anthropologists who adopted Marxian perspectives, looking beyond symbolic systems of culture to consider male domination in the context of wider social, political, and economic processes. Gayle Rubin (1975) argued that these wider processes

sex The physical characteristics that traditionally distinguish males from females (e.g., body shape, distribution of body hair, reproductive organs, sex chromosomes).

gender The culturally constructed roles assigned to males or females, which vary considerably from society to society.

gender binary A dual gender categorization separating all women from all men.

FIGURE 13.2 Cross-cultural research repeatedly demonstrates that physical indicators of sex difference do not allow us to predict the roles that females or males may play in any particular society. In Otavalo, Ecuador, men were traditionally weavers (a), while traditional Tzotzil weavers were women (b).

EthnoProfile 13.1

Mount Hagen

Region: Southeastern Asia

Nation: Papua New Guinea (western highlands)

Population: 75,000 (1960s)

Environment: Forested mountain slopes, grassy plains

Livelihood: Farming, pig raising

Political organization:
Traditionally, some men of influence but no coercive power; today, part of a modern nation-state

For more information:
Strathern, Marilyn. 1972. *Women in between*. London: Academic Press.

British social anthropologist Marilyn Strathern encountered further complexities when, as a second-wave feminist, she first went to Mount Hagen, in New Guinea ("EthnoProfile 13.1: Mount Hagen"). In the 1970s and 1980s, some ethnographers working in New Guinea were suggesting that in New Guinea, as elsewhere, males dominated females in order to control the reproductive powers of women. This interpretation was supported by the views of influential French anthropologist Claude Lévi-Strauss, who claimed that linguistic communication, marriage negotiations, and economic transactions were all forms of exchange controlled by men. Indeed, he argued, women were the most valuable exchange good of all (Figure 13.3).

In *The Gender of the Gift* (1988), Strathern challenged this interpretation, arguing that by imposing Western ideas of this kind on Melanesian cultural practices, Western anthropologists had misunderstood Melanesian gender relations. First, Western anthropologists had assumed that Western notions of *individuality* were universal; that is, that in all human societies, every human individual comes into the world as a self-contained, autonomous being with a unique identity. In Melanesia, however, Strathern argued that persons are not conceived as self-contained, unique entities, but rather as *internally plural*: "the singular person can be imagined as a social microcosm" (1988, 13). This meant, Strathern concluded, that Melanesian persons are better understood as "dividuals" rather than as "individuals." That is, each Melanesian person is seen as being made up of parts contributed by relatives who were responsible for their coming into the world. These components persist and continue to connect them to their kin, over

shaped each society's particular "sex/gender system"; and Eleanor Leacock (1983) argued that cases of male dominance in contemporary societies were less likely to reflect the original human condition than they were to show forms of institutionalized gender inequality influenced by the spread of capitalism. Leacock used ethnographic and historical evidence from North America and South America, Melanesia, and Africa to show how Western capitalist colonization had transformed egalitarian precolonial indigenous gender relations into unequal, male-dominated gender relations.

FIGURE 13.3 Women working a field in Mount Hagen, Papua New Guinea.

the course of a lifetime. Importantly, these kin are both male and female, which means that every internally plural Melanesian "dividual" has some male parts and some female parts. Every Melanesian person is therefore more properly understood as *androgynous*, rather than as either uniquely male or uniquely female. This means that Melanesian **androgyny** will inevitably be misrepresented by any analysis of gender that assumes the existence of a universal gender binary and takes for granted that persons are self-contained unique individuals.

For example, Euro-Americans who accept a gender binary tend to think of women as "naturally" nurturing: they give birth to children and feed their offspring with mother's milk. From a Western analytic perspective, it is precisely this exclusive power of women that men seek to control when they control the exchange of women in marriage. However, Strathern tells us, Melanesians see neither nurturing nor feeding activities to belong exclusively to women. For instance, she cites ethnographic accounts (such as the well-known case of the Trobrianders) in which a pregnant woman's husband is understood to "feed" the fetus growing inside her body with his semen; this is why pregnant women are encouraged to have frequent sexual intercourse with their husbands. Another example involves the initiation rites of people such as the Melanesian Sambia, which traditionally involved ingestion by young male initiates of semen produced by the older men who are initiating them: the semen they ingest nourishes and strengthens the initiates, helping them to grow and mature. Melanesians thus view the breasts of women and the penises of men as analogous organs: both can produce fluids that nourish the young. These androgynous capacities, however, are highlighted and downplayed in different ways in different Melanesian communities and in different sociocultural contexts.

What difference does it make to begin with an understanding of humans as androgynous dividuals, rather than as autonomous individuals divided into two "natural" kinds by a universal gender binary? In Melanesian societies, does it even make sense to talk about such phenomena as "male dominance" or "female submission?" Strathern addressed this question and concluded that even though Melanesians understood gender very differently from Euro-Americans, certain features of traditional Melanesian gender relations nevertheless produced forms of imbalance that tend to favor males over females. In the course of social life, men and women alternated positions of agency with one another, sometimes being seen as responsible for making other persons act, and sometimes being seen as acting in certain ways as a consequence of the actions of others. For this reason, she says, neither men nor women were permanently subjugated to the will of the other gender. Men, however, engaged with other men in the management of large-scale ceremonial exchanges from which women were excluded, but women did not engage in similar kinds of large-scale ritual activities with other women. Strathern concluded: "In a double sense, then, the plurality of men's collective life may lead to men dominating women" (1988, 336). First, men strive for prestige in the context of ceremonial exchanges, but find the recognition of their achievements by women alone to be inadequate. Second, men who support one another in ritual contexts may refuse to condemn a man who individually attempts to dominate a woman to whom he is married, for example, by physically striking her. Women do not experience similar gender solidarity in ritual contexts and cannot count on other women to support them in the same way. Consequently, "the single most effective sanction at the disposal of a Hagen woman is bodily removal of her person" (1988, 337).

Nevertheless, Strathern insists that this kind of interpersonal domination is misunderstood if it is viewed as an effort by males to control females whose reproductive powers they lack. Rather, from a Melanesian perspective, androgynous men are grappling with what she calls "the problem of the multiple person—how both to act and to be the cause of the actions of others, and how thus to ensure that one's actions have indeed taken place" (1988, 336). Strathern's exploration of "the problem of the multiple person" provides a helpful framework for situating more recent discussions of sex, gender, and sexuality that do not presume the existence of a universal gender binary.

Two decades after its initial publication, following much commentary and additional research, Sherry Ortner reconsidered the relations between gender and power. She concluded that "recognizing egalitarianism is not as easy as it looks, that it is a matter of interpretation" (Ortner 2014, 358). Ortner observed that in her original 1974 paper, she had regarded *all* indicators of male privilege as equally significant, and equally entrenched, within "cultures," conceived as systematic, self-contained symbolic systems. By 1996, however, she had come to realize that *not all* gendered distinctions in a particular society were equally significant, and that such inequalities might or might not be embedded in larger social, economic, and political orders. Her understanding of culture had also changed: by the end of the twentieth century, she noted, anthropologists had begun to think differently about "cultures," regarding them "as more disjunctive, contradictory and inconsistent than I had been trained to think" (Ortner 2014, 358) (see Chapter 8).

androgyny A condition in which an individual person possesses both male and female characteristics.

How Do Anthropologists Organize the Study of Sex, Gender, and Sexuality?

In the decades that followed the emergence of second-wave feminism, cross-disciplinary collaboration (and debate) about sex, gender, and sexuality diversified, both theoretically and substantively. One practical consequence has been ongoing discussion about what, in fact, the "field" should be called. Although terms like *feminist anthropology* are still used by some (e.g., Lewin 2006), other scholars prefer to locate their work within the field of *women's studies*. In part, this reflects objections raised in connection with the association of "feminism" with the white, middle-class perspectives of many second-wave feminists; some women of color have preferred to describe their analyses as *womanist* rather than "feminist" to emphasize the distinctiveness of the challenges faced by women who do not enjoy white, middle-class privileges. Many anthropologists and other social scientists have supported the move to combine the study of women, men, sex, gender, and sexuality in an inclusive field called *gender studies*. At the same time, not all women's studies scholars—anthropologists among them—have been convinced that folding women's studies into gender studies was a good move to make. They are concerned that sinking women's studies into gender studies cannot but dilute the attention paid to serious issues that women continue to face. This disagreement remains unresolved, its consequences visible in the many different names given to departments and programs in different universities that specialize in the study of women, men, sex, gender, and sexuality.

In any case, if one thinks of gender identities as parts of a larger "sex/gender system," studying women or men in isolation becomes immediately problematic. In fact, scholarship by anthropologists and other social scientists contributed to the growth of **men's studies** alongside women's studies; and just as women's studies scholars had found that there were many ways of being a woman, so too men's studies scholars identified a range of different ways of being a man, in different places and times; these were called different **masculinities.**

Early efforts to understand masculinities in Western societies stress large-scale structures of domination and subordination, not only of women to men, but of some men to other men. The starkness of earlier approaches has been replaced by more nuanced understandings of how men in different societies engage with ideas and practices concerning masculinity, in our own and other parts of the world. Indeed, recent ethnography shows not only how men's ideas about masculinity vary cross-culturally, but how their views and practices change over time, both in the society itself and in the course of individual lifetimes. Ethnographic studies of issues affecting women far outnumber ethnographic studies of men and masculinities in different societies; but this is changing, leading to new empirical discoveries and theoretical innovations.

One example is the work of Marcia Inhorn, a medical anthropologist whose work in the Middle East began in the 1980s with studies of how Egyptians coped with infertility. At that time, she found that many men were unwilling to accept publicly that they (and not their wives) were responsible for the couple's infertility, and their wives were willing to protect their husbands by not challenging this description. Inhorn also knew that a Muslim husband was traditionally considered justified should he choose to divorce an infertile wife. Nevertheless, she also found that Egyptian men of all social classes rarely exercised this option, remaining for many years in childless marriages with wives whom they loved, and who loved them. Inhorn called this phenomenon *conjugal connectivity*: "In the late 1980s, this was my first evidence that men were changing in the Middle East and . . . changing society with them" (2012, 58) (Figure 13.4).

In subsequent research Inhorn has been able to challenge many stereotypes about Middle Eastern men that became further exaggerated following the September 11, 2001, terrorist attacks in New York City. She observes that these stereotypes are not only the product of Western media and ethnographies written (mostly) by men; they also draw on ideas expressed by Middle Eastern feminist scholars and on negative self-stereotypes that some Middle Eastern men themselves continue to hold. Key features of these stereotypes include the idea that Middle Eastern men all aspire to be family patriarchs who dominate their wives and children; that they are quick to defend family honor to the point of killing individuals, especially women, whom they believe have shamed their family; that they prefer to live together with other men who are related to them in the male line; and, finally, that their female kin "*buy into patriarchy.* To receive the support of men in their natal families, they turn against in-marrying women in a cruel form of intragender patriarchal rivalry" (2012, 49; emphasis in original). This stereotype further insists that Middle Eastern women are estranged from their husbands because their marriages are arranged, because husbands are permitted to have multiple wives, and because wives are expected to produce many children, which in turn requires husbands to display extreme sexual potency. Large patriarchal families are supposed to contribute to "tribalism"—primary loyalty to the tribe over other political entities, such as the state. Tribal conflicts are said to promote violence

---

men's studies/masculinities Research that focuses on the many different ways of being a man that can be identified in different places and times.

FIGURE 13.4 Contemporary practices of conjugal connectivity undermine patriarchal stereotypes about the ways Middle Eastern men relate to their wives and families. This political activist in Bahrain spends time with his wife and children every weekend.

and militarism, which is said to be reinforced by Islam, a religion that is regularly portrayed as promoting gender inequality and encouraging fanaticism to the point of waging *jihad*, or "holy war," against non-Muslims.

Inhorn forcefully rejects this "extremely essentializing and deeply vilifying" composite stereotype of Middle Eastern men (2012, 50). Even if some features of this caricature "may, at times and in certain places, be 'true' to the lives of some men," Inhorn points out that data she has gathered over the past twenty years demonstrate, on the contrary, that "masculinities in the Middle East, as elsewhere, are plural, diverse, locally situated, historically contingent, socially constructed, and performed in ways that require careful empirical inspection" (2012, 50–51). Indeed, her research shows that Middle Eastern men are coming to enact new kinds of masculinity, which she called *emergent masculinities*: "emergent masculinities encapsulate change over the male life course as men age; change over the generations as male youth grow to adulthood; and changes in social history that involve men in transformative social processes (e.g., male labor migration, the rise of companionate marriage, the introduction of computers and the Internet into homes and workplaces)" (Inhorn 2012, 60). Practices of conjugal connectivity are part of emergent masculinities in the Middle East, as are the following:

> Men's desire to date their partners before marriage, men's acceptance of condoms and vasectomy as forms of male birth control, men's desires to live in nuclear family residences with their wives and children, and men's encouragement of daughters' education. All of these masculine practices are, in fact, emerging in the Middle East, but are rarely noticed by scholars or media pundits. (Inhorn 2012, 60)

It is precisely these kinds of emergent masculinities that she has encountered in her work on male infertility in Egypt, Lebanon, and the United Arab Emirates. Inhorn locates her research within the anthropology of science, technology, and medicine, a burgeoning field of anthropology we introduced in Chapter 1, which has taken the anthropological perspective and ethnographic methods into scientific laboratories, medical clinics, and hospitals in order to study the way that new technologies are being adopted by, and reshaping the lives of, people all over the world. Middle Eastern men are no exception, and the focus of anthropologists like Inhorn is on how assisted reproductive technology is becoming entangled with Middle Eastern cultural practices involving gender, religion, and family. We will explore these matters more fully in Chapter 14 (on kinship and marriage) and in Chapter 16 (on medical anthropology).

The concept of emergent masculinities is valuable because it has the potential to undermine toxic and inaccurate gender stereotypes about men, while providing more accurate understandings of how men remake their ways of being men under changing circumstances. Such efforts can also be seen in medical anthropologist Emily Wentzell's work with male patients in the urology ward of a hospital in Cuernavaca, Mexico, between 2007 and 2008. The men Wentzell came to know were facing serious challenges to their ways of being men, as aging and illness interfered with their sexual potency. In the context of the hospital, they were willing, even eager, to talk to her about such issues, which they believed they could not openly discuss with anyone else, certainly not their wives or male doctors. Many of them had to come to terms with whether or not erectile difficulty (and the waning of penetrative sex) was putting their manhood at risk, and they had to decide whether or not they were willing to take medication like Viagra in hopes of putting off that risk. Wentzell's analysis offers a fine-grained examination of what she calls the "concrete mechanics of masculinity" (2013, 184), as she shows how these men tinkered with ways of reformulating and enacting new ways of being men, removing or adding elements to what she calls their *composite masculinities*. She defines composite masculinities as "contingent and fluid constellations of elements that men weave together into masculine selfhoods. These elements are drawn from the entire gamut of men's life worlds: their ideas and emotions, experiences, embodiment, relationships, and context" (2013, 26).

Male sexual potency, and the ability of a man to engage in penetrative sex, has played a central role in traditional understandings of Mexican manhood, which is why the loss of this ability can be so threatening to a Mexican man. At the same time, Mexican masculinity has been negatively stereotyped in ways that compare with the toxic stereotypes of Middle Eastern men described by Inhorn. The Mexican stereotype, however, is rooted in a different culture and history. In Mexico, as elsewhere in Latin America, masculinity is traditionally defined in terms of practices associated with *machismo*—literally, "maleness." These practices include displays of aggression, an obsession with virility, and lack of emotional openness. In Mexico, the origin of this set of masculine traits

---

IN THEIR OWN WORDS

The Consequences of Being a Woman

Bonnie L. Hewlett is an anthropologist who has spent many years working with women in the Central African Republic, women who told her they wanted to tell her their stories. One of these women she calls Blondine. Blondine tells of her marriage.

After Issa [her first husband] left, my second husband, Levi, saw me and wanted to marry me. He spoke so much he had no saliva in his mouth! I loved my second husband Levi. It was a good marriage, but over a long time I came to lose respect for my husband. The most important feeling in a marriage is respect. If you love your husband, you show him respect. But after some time of marriage, if he drank a lot of embacko [moonshine], he hit me. One time my friend heard the fighting and she came and said, "Why are you hitting your wife? Stop this!" After a few years in the marriage, Levi would drink and he'd talk and talk and yell and start fights. Sometimes I'd yell back, but most times I kept quiet until he fell asleep. Levi also neglected me, but not like the first husband, Issa. Levi searched for another wife. He did not ask me. I thought, "This can't be, not yet." If he had asked me before, if he had said, "My wife, can I search for another wife?" and explained to me, I would have said yes. But he married another woman and neglected me. He did not give me money or food and spent most of his nights with his other wife. I was so mad because he did not ask. I hit him. When Levi brought in the second wife, I hit her too. One time a man will look for another wife. Maybe because the other woman is beautiful and he says to himself, "I will marry her." If he tells the first wife, "Is it okay? She can help you with your work," then sometimes it

is good to have two wives. The second wife becomes like a sister and respects the first wife. If they both have a good heart, they work together in the fields and help each other with the work in the house and it is good. But if the second wife is not obedient and respectful, then there is war.

After much hitting and fighting, we tried to reconcile and for awhile we lived together, but when the second wife came, our husband said, "You two wives! Do not fight!!" When she'd come we worked together and prepared food for the family and we'd eat together. But then Levi began to neglect me. He slept too much with the second wife and bought her clothes and shoes and not me. I grabbed him by the neck and said, "My husband! Why do you not sleep with me? Tonight it is my turn!" When he came into the second wife's bedroom one night I grabbed his neck and said, "No! You sleep with me, not her!" If the husband organizes it good, it works so well! But if he does not, if he sleeps three nights with one and two nights with the other it does not work! Even so, when I heard them speak on the bed at night to each other, I listened and it made me so angry! I was jealous. I suffered and because of his neglect I divorced him.

After Levi left, life was so difficult. I was alone with two children.

Source: Hewlett 2013, 163–64.

is traditionally associated with the Spanish conquistadors, whose rape of indigenous women is said to have produced *la raza* (the "race") of Mexicans who possess mixed European and indigenous ancestry. Many of the men Wentzell spoke with agreed that traits associated with *machismo* have been passed on to subsequent generations of Mexican men. At the same time, they were often critical of these traits, either in themselves or in other men (such as their fathers), and were struggling to assert new ways of being Mexican men who were free of such traits. This was especially the case for younger married men, who were revising their ideas about family life and relations with their wives, in response to many of the same globalizing processes that Inhorn detected in the Middle East.

Older men—working-class men in particular—had grown up attempting to perform masculinity in ways that matched the traditional stereotype. This had meant, for many of them, expressing virility by pursuing many women, refusing to be faithful to their wives, drinking alcohol to excess, and working hard. Many believed that as long as they continued to be good providers—taking care of wives and children economically—they were fulfilling their duty as husbands and fathers. Their wives and children did not always agree. And when age and ill health began to undermine their ability to pursue sexual affairs or earn money, they were challenged to reconsider what it meant to be a man.

The older men Wentzell spoke with, however, were not faced with an either-or choice. Instead, they inventoried the various attributes they associated with an acceptable Mexican performance of manhood, and deleted or replaced some attributes in response to the changing circumstances of their lives. For instance, a sixty-eight-year-old man whom Wentzell calls Johnny considered himself to have been both economically and sexually successful, working as a chef in United States and engaging in penetrative sex with many women other than his wife. When Wentzell met him, however, he was in the hospital, facing the surgical removal of his cancerous penis. Prior to the surgery, Johnny was despondent, convinced that his manhood would disappear when his penis was removed. After the surgery, however, his mood was much more positive. He had decided that if he kept the true nature of his surgery a secret, focused on his being able to return to work once he was healthy, and substituted his *memories* of past sexual potency for expectations of future sexual affairs, he could hang on to a viable sense of manhood. Put another way, he was crafting an emerging form of masculinity by tinkering with the composite elements of which it might be constructed (Wentzell 2013, 2).

Johnny's loss of his penis was extreme. But many other older men Wentzell met, experiencing aging, illness, and increasing erectile difficulty, had similar worries about losing their manhood. In their cases, one possible solution might have been drugs like Viagra, Cialis, or Levitra, which, at the time of her research, were being heavily marketed in Mexico as medication to treat what was coming to be called "erectile dysfunction," or ED. Wentzell initially thought that such drugs would have been seized upon by older men for whom sexual potency was central to their composite masculinities. However, many older men were not interested in taking the drugs. Their reasons varied but often included a revised composite masculinity in which the reckless virile behavior of a young man was replaced by "responsible" forms of "mature masculinity," involving closer emotional relationships with wives, children, and grandchildren. In such composite masculinities, memories of past sexual conquests were adequate and did not play a central role in a future focused on mature domesticity.

Wentzell's study focused on composite masculinities, but she points out that the same approach can be taken to *composite femininities*, which she sometimes explored in relation to the wives of some of the men whom she met in the hospital. Johnny's wife Mayra, for example, evaluated his past performance of manhood as a failure: he had been a poor provider, and he had abandoned her to support twelve children and survive a stillbirth on her own while he spent his earnings on other women, enjoying himself in the United States. Viewing Johnny's surgery as just recompense for his past behavior, she "asserted her own composite femininity, which foregrounded piety, responsibility, and the suffering often associated with 'good' womanhood in Roman Catholic contexts.. . . Mayra's mixture of physical caregiving and narrative critique seemed unconsciously strategic, reinforcing their couplehood through the embodied practice of care but putting her in control of the story" (Wentzell 2013, 30). In both these cases, Wentzell demonstrates that individuals' composite gender identity incorporates many features shaped by the historical, economic, political, and sociocultural settings in which they live their lives. This sense of "compositeness" in gender identity has long been of concern to other gender theorists, as we will see later.

How Are Sex and Gender Affected by Other Forms of Identity?

As feminist scholars struggled to debunk supposedly universal "truths" about women, they came to realize that "women" itself is a problematic category. This became clear as comparative research revealed ways that other forms of identity, such as race and class, were deeply entangled with the ways women (and men) came to understand the meaning of gender. For instance, second-wave feminism had been energized by many white, middle-class women whose experiences of women's oppression—being denied professional careers in the public sphere, being confined to roles as wives and mothers—were shaped by race and class privilege. But nonwhite feminists pointed out that nonwhite working-class women experienced oppression very differently—frequently as single mothers forced to work outside the home in dead-end jobs. These differences were the consequence not simply of male domination, but also of structured racial and class oppression, a phenomenon now called **intersectionality**.

To recognize the reality of intersectionality is to recognize that every woman has multiple identities that intersect and complicate each other; taken together, they locate each woman differently (and, sometimes, surprisingly) with respect to other women (or men). Thus, in some settings, a middle-class, African American woman might enjoy class-based privileges denied to a working-class white woman; whereas in other settings, the working-class, white woman's race would allow her privileges that would override the class status of the middle-class, African American woman.

At the same time, it was also becoming increasingly clear that *the content* of a woman's gender identity was often shaped by cultural features used to define different ethnic, religious, or national groups, and to distinguish them from one another. For instance, a woman might feel that submitting to her husband was part of what it meant to be a proper woman in the religious community to which they both belonged, and that to challenge male domination by leaving a husband who physically "chastised" her could call into question both her proper gender identity and her religious identity.

Anthropologists have explored dynamics of intersectionality in different field settings, revealing new patterns that show how gender may become entangled with other forms of identity. For example, Roy Richard Grinker found that male, village-dwelling Lese householders in the Democratic Republic of Congo distinguished themselves from their forest-dwelling Ewe pygmy trading partners using the same unequal gender categories that they used to distinguish themselves from their wives. He made sense of this process by drawing on an observation by Marilyn Strathern concerning the nature of gender symbolism. In *The Gender of the Gift*, Strathern defines gender broadly as "those categorizations of persons, artifacts, event sequences, and so on which draw upon sexual imagery—upon the ways in which the distinctiveness of male and female characteristics make concrete people's ideas about the nature of social relations" (1988, ix). From the point of view of Lese men, Grinker explained, both Efe trading partners and Lese wives were subordinate to Lese men because both categories of persons

had been incorporated into the households of Lese men (Grinker 1994). The Lese are not the only people who make use of gender imagery in this way. Anthropologist Ann Stoler (1997) studied the effects of Dutch colonialism in Indonesia and has compared it with colonialism elsewhere. She has shown that the relationship between white European colonizers and the nonwhite indigenous males they colonized was regularly conceived in terms both of "racial" inequality and of gender inequality. That is, colonizers constructed a "racial" divide between colonizer and colonized that ranked "white" colonial males above "nonwhite" indigenous males. At the same time, by violently punishing any hint of sexual involvement between indigenous males and "white" women, while allowing themselves unrestricted sexual access to indigenous women, white male colonizers "feminized" indigenous males—constructing them as less than fully male because they had been unable to defend either their land or "their women" from more powerful white outsiders. Stoler points out that white male colonizers struggled to shore up these racialized and gendered colonial hierarchies whenever indigenous males organized politically in ways that threatened colonial rule.

Intersectionality can also be seen at work in the history of the Haitian state. Haiti began as a colony of France and achieved its independence following a successful revolt of black slaves against their white colonial masters (see "EthnoProfile 13.2: Haiti"). As Nina Glick Schiller and Georges Fouron (2001) explain, however, "Haiti has

EthnoProfile 13.2

Haiti

Region: Caribbean

Nation: Haiti

Population: 7,500,000

Livelihood: Rough, mountainous terrain, tropical to semi-arid climate. About 80% of the population lives in extreme poverty

Political organization: Multi-party, nation-state

For more information: Farmer, Paul. 1992. *AIDS and accusation: Haiti and the geography of blame.* Berkeley, University of California Press.

---

intersectionality The notion that institutional forms of oppression organized in terms of race, class, and gender are interconnected and shape the opportunities and constraints available to individuals in any society.

its own particular and mixed messages about gender that give to women and men both rights and responsibilities to family and nation" (133). Women appear in official stories about the Haitian Revolution, and some of them are even portrayed as heroines; most, however, are usually portrayed as silent wives and mothers. Moreover, the founders of the Haitian state borrow from their former French masters "a patriarchal idea of family as well as a civil code that gave men control of family life, wealth, and property" (Schiller and Fouron 2001, 134). Women belonged to the Haitian nation, but "state officials and the literate elite envisioned women as able to reproduce the nation only in conjunction with a Haitian man" (134). Until 1987, Haitian women who married foreigners lost their Haitian citizenship. High-status Haitian women are those who are supported economically by their Haitian husbands and who stay home with their children. Schiller and Fouron argue that many Haitians "still believe that to live by these values is to uphold not only family but also national honor" (135) (Figure 13.5).

By contrast, Haitian women who cannot live by these values are accorded low status. On one hand, this means that they are not confined to the domestic sphere. On the other hand, for this very reason, they are assumed to be always sexually available. "Men in Haiti see women alone or in the workplace as willing and able to trade their sexuality for other things they need. Men may ask rather than take, but often they are making an offer that women cannot afford to refuse" (Schiller and Fouron 2001, 139–40). As we will see in Chapter 16, this describes well the structural constraints with which the young Haitian woman

Acéphie Joseph had to contend; options open to women of higher social position were not available to her. To understand why, an exploration of intersectionality—of race and sex, but also of class—provides insights into the connections between all these dimensions of social identity and experiences of social inequality. Issues of social class will be further explored in Chapter 15.

How Do Ethnographers Study Gender Performativity?

As we saw above, anthropologists (and others) who distinguish sex from gender long ago rejected the idea that a person's gendered beliefs or behavior were somehow directly caused by that person's biological sex. However, viewing gendered cultural behavior as the unproblematic consequence of conformity to cultural expectations could not explain how people coped with the complications created by intersectionality. Yet women—and men—regularly manage the contradictions that race, class, gender, and other identities create in the course of everyday life. This success suggested to many observers that it was misleading to think of culturally expected gender "roles" simply as obligations to which individuals learned to *conform*. Instead, these roles looked more like scripts that individuals learned to *perform*; and part of each performance involved deciding which features of which identities to highlight or downplay in any given social interaction. Understanding cultural identity as something people perform compels anthropologists to think of individuals as *agents* who have mastered, and are capable of executing, a range of skills appropriate to the public display of particular identities before particular audiences (Butler [1990] 2006). Thus, displays of gender identity are examples of **gender performativity**; that is, gender is reconceived as something we "perform" or "enact," something we "do," not something we "are" (Figure 13.6).

Put otherwise, no single identity fully captures the inner life of any individual. From the perspective of performativity, culture can also be reconceived less as a set of imposed beliefs and behaviors and more as a set of *resources*—artifacts, actions, and interpretations—that can be deployed by individuals in order to enact before others the identities to which they lay claim. The notion of performativity has been widely applied by anthropologists and others to describe the way humans perform not only gender but also other forms of social identity, such as race or ethnicity (see Chapter 15).

Anthropologist Roger Lancaster explored the performativity of gender and sexual identity in the course of his fieldwork in Managua, Nicaragua, in the 1980s, as he studied the effects of the Sandinista Revolution on the lives of

---

gender performativity The concept that gender is something we "perform" or "enact," something we "do," not something we "are."

FIGURE 13.5 The founders of the Haitian state borrowed from their former French masters an idea of gender that gave men control of family life. Women belonged to the Haitian nation; but until recently, Haitian women who married foreigners lost their Haitian citizenship, and their children would not legally be recognized as Haitian.

FIGURE 13.6 Feminist theorist Judith Butler receives an award in Frankfurt Main, Germany, in 2012.

working people. While he was there, Lancaster learned about *cochones*. *Cochón* could be translated into English as "homosexual," but that would be highly misleading. As Lancaster discovered, working-class Nicaraguans interpret sexual relations between men differently from North Americans; we will explore these matters more fully later in the chapter. At this point, however, we want to discuss how Lancaster's discovery also prompted his recognition of the flexibility and ambiguity surrounding the *performance* of gender and sexuality in Nicaragua.

Lancaster was present one day when his *comadre* Aida brought a new blouse home (see Chapter 14 for a discussion of *compadrazgo*). After she showed it to everyone, her younger brother, Guto, picked it up and used it as a prop in an impromptu performance (1997, 559–60):

> With a broad yet pointed gesture, Guto wrapped himself in the white, frilly blouse, and began a coquettish routine that lasted for 15 or 20 minutes.. . . [He] added a purse and necklace to his ensemble. Brothers, sisters, even his mother, egged on this performance, shouting festive remarks . . . punctuated by whistles, kissing noises. Someone handed Guto a pair of clip-on earrings. With cheerful abandon, he applied a bit of blush and a touch of makeup. His performance intensified, to the pleasure of the audience. After disappearing for a moment into the bedroom, he returned wearing a blue denim skirt. "Hombrote" (Big Guy), he shot in my direction, nuancing his usually raspy voice as if to flirt with me. I was astonished and no doubt my visible surprise was part of the clowning of the evening. "See, Roger," Aida kept remarking, "Look, Guto's a *cochón*, a queer."

What was going on here? When Lancaster later tried to interview those involved, he says, "no one would give

me a *straight* answer" (1997, 560; emphasis in original). One participant laughingly suggested that perhaps Guto was a *cochón*. But Lancaster was puzzled because nothing in Guto's previous behavior, nor in the behavior of others who knew him, had suggested that he claimed or was accorded such an identity. Still, Guto's performance of "femininity" had been extremely skillful.

Lancaster entertained a series of possible, yet contradictory, interpretations of that performance. Was Guto mocking or embracing femininity? Was he engaging in homosexual flirtation with Lancaster, or was he masking same-sex desires by his over-the-top mimicry? Were he and his audience making fun of gender norms, or celebrating them, or simply blowing off steam? Lancaster recalled that he had been drawn into Guto's performance in the role of "straight man," and he speculated that perhaps Guto may have playfully "flirted" with him in an effort to reveal Lancaster's own sexual preferences. At that time, Lancaster had not yet explicitly disclosed his own identity as a gay man, and he wondered whether his friends used Guto's performance to test their suspicions. Still, this seemed an inadequate explanation: "As I was constantly reminded, my own conceptions of homosexuality did not exactly match up with those of my informants. It is not even quite clear to me what would have constituted a 'queer' response on my part . . . when plural others are playing, ambiguities multiply geometrically" (1997, 562).

Even though Lancaster could not provide a definitive explanation of what Guto's performance was all about, he insists that "play is not a trivial thing, and the simultaneously destructive and creative powers of laughter should never be underestimated" (1997, 561). This realization led him to reflect more deeply on what transvestism—the practice of dressing and taking on mannerisms associated with a gender other than one's own—might mean, both in Nicaragua (where cochones traditionally perform during the festival of Carnival in the manner Guto enacted) and perhaps elsewhere in the world (Figure 13.7).

In Lancaster's view, a performance like Guto's involves more that simple cross-dressing. Instead, it displays an awareness of the *ambiguities* that accompany the multiple, intersecting identities that all people juggle in the course of everyday life. For instance, the building blocks of transvestic performance can be found in cases of *reported speech*: when men repeat women's words while mimicking a high-pitched voice; or when women adopt male ways of talking, as did a Nicaraguan woman he knew who, after the death of her husband, told her children, "I am the head of the family now . . . the mother and the father and what I say goes" (Lancaster 1997, 563).

Lancaster uses the term *transvestics* to encompass everything from these everyday forms of gender mimicry to fully

---

transvestism The practice of dressing and taking on mannerisms associated with a gender other than one's own.

FIGURE 13.7 A Nicaraguan cowboy poses with a cross-dressing male during Carnival.

---

fledged performances that cite not only gendered speech but also gendered forms of dress and bodily movement: "no one learns (or unlearns) anything—a gender or a sexuality or an identity or even a meaning—except through some process of physical modeling, sensuous experimentation, and bodily play" (1997, 565). All transvestic performers are not equally skilled, of course, but how their performances are judged varies, depending on context. Lancaster points out that in the context of North American drag balls, the performer may sometimes be evaluated positively by *convincingly* portraying another gender role; but in other contexts, the drag performance fails unless it demonstrates *an ironic parody* of that other gender role.

Lancaster concluded that Guto's performance involved the portrayal of a stock Carnival figure in a manner that was both hostile and affectionate, and that this performance involved "play acting," displaying Guto's enjoyment of "physical abandon, visceral mirth, creative frivolity" (1997, 555–56). He observed that "The pleasures we partook in Guto's performance were very much in the spirit of Carnival, 'the festival of disguises'" (1997, 566). Indeed, cochones are much admired for their transvestic performances, but not all the men who cross-dress in Carnival are cochones, and telling them apart is not easy. As a festival, Carnival involves turning the world upside down, and this involves upending a range of stereotypes about gender, sexuality, race, class, and ethnicity (Lancaster 1997, 566). As our previous discussion of intersectionality shows, we agree with Lancaster that we humans "play our games freely, but we are not free to play them just any way we choose" (1997, 568). Still, to acknowledge the centrality of play to human existence is to acknowledge that "ambiguity lives at the core of identity.. . . Even the most consolidated self retains in the senses a perpetually-available resource for going beyond the self" (1997, 570). Lancaster suggests that play of this kind needs to be understood "as both a human universal and as a base condition of culture" (1997, 568).

This view resonates well with our earlier discussion of play in Chapter 10, and also echoes Strathern's discussion of dividual selves, which will be further explored in Chapter 16.

How Do Anthropologists Study Connections among Sex, Gender, Sexuality, and the Body?

An important trend in sociocultural anthropology in recent decades has been attention to "the body," an object of study that is of obvious relevance to discussions of sex, gender, and sexuality. To understand the growth of interest in the body, it is important to remember that for most of the twentieth century, sociocultural anthropology consistently downplayed human individuals (and their individual bodies) and highlighted structures and patterns that characterized the social groups to which individual humans belonged. Such a strategy could be justified because Euro-American audiences, deeply committed to the cultural value of individualism (especially in the United States), tended to disregard the powerful ways that broader, shared social structures and cultural patterns shaped the life chances of individuals in society. The stress on individualism in Euro-American culture is justified by the taken-for-granted endorsement of the Enlightenment notion of the *social contract*. This view, developed in the writings of political thinkers such as Thomas Hobbes, argued that in the distant past, there was no human society, and individuals lived in a "state of nature," engaged in an ongoing war of "all against all." According to this account, independent human individuals eventually agreed to a social contract in which they would surrender some of their individual liberty in order to create a shared government that would protect the weak from the strong. Anthropologist Marshall Sahlins long ago argued that "The development from a Hobbesian state of nature is the origin myth of Western capitalism" (1976, 53). All the same, the social contract continues to be taken as an unquestioned foundational assumption by many political philosophers and ordinary people in contemporary capitalist societies. As a result, persistently drawing attention to ongoing power-wielding, supra-individual, sociopolitical structures has long been viewed as an important task for historians, anthropologists, and other social scientists.

But individual bodies were never entirely ignored. Anthropologist Mary Douglas famously argued that "The social body constrains the way the physical body is perceived" (1970, 93), and she drew on ethnographic and historical data to show how ritual preoccupations with bodily orifices (e.g., food taboos or menstrual taboos, or restrictions governing sexual intercourse) regularly mirrored preoccupations with the social vulnerabilities faced by a society in relation to its enemies. In recent years, anthropologists have turned to the work of Michel Foucault (Figure 13.8), whose writings highlight the way social power, particularly in modern Western societies, acts on individual bodies. Social institutions like schools and armies regulate the actions of individual bodies in order to render them more efficient in the performance of particular skills or practices. At the same time, modern states depend on statistical information about their populations in order to devise ways of regulating those populations, engaging in what Foucault calls *biopolitics* (see Chapter 12). For example, campaigns to improve the well-being of citizens via medical interventions such as inoculations have allowed

FIGURE 13.8   French philosopher Michel Foucault.

state institutions to increase the numbers of healthy individuals ready for the labor force, or the numbers of healthy recruits eligible to be drafted into the armed forces. Finally, Foucault argues, societies have devised ways of persuading individuals to bring their own bodily activities into conformity with social expectations, a phenomenon he calls "the care of the self." Foucault's theoretical framework has informed work in many areas of anthropological research but has had particular resonance for those scholars—such as Foucault himself—who were concerned with documenting the ways these practices of social intervention and regulation were mobilized to classify and produce particular forms of *sexual* embodiment over time (Foucault 1980, 1990, 1988).

Anthropologists have traditionally understood that human beings are plastic organisms who are open to the molding processes of socialization and enculturation. This resonates with Foucault's understanding of the human body as a *docile* body; that is, a body that is easily taught, or, in Foucault's terms, a body "that may be subjected, used, transformed, and improved" through "disciplinary methods" that apply "an uninterrupted, constant coercion" of bodily activities, making possible "the meticulous control of the operations of the body" (1995, 136, 137). As we observed earlier, however, conceiving of human bodies as nothing more than passive, inert matter that can unresistingly be shaped by sociocultural conditioning raises difficulties. Equally challenging have been liberal Enlightenment views that equate human agency with the exercise of rational deliberation and choice alone. Twenty-five years ago, feminist philosopher Elizabeth Grosz (1995) challenged such views by drawing attention to the experience and forms of consciousness that derived from material processes unique to female bodies, from menstruation through menopause, exploring the implications of these experiences for understanding the connections between sex and embodiment. More recently, theorists in anthropology and elsewhere have drawn attention to the ways in which **affect** (visceral arousal, emotion, or feeling) is not opposed to rational thought but is in fact entwined with thought in processes of human meaning-making.

Some of this research has focused on how individuals experience visceral feelings of desire that are at odds with cultural ideologies about gender and sexuality. One suggestion is that these forms of affect have the potential to disrupt ideologies concerning sexuality, making room for the development of alternative corporeal relations between individuals. Theoretical approaches of this kind offer ways of bringing material bodies back into discussions of sex, gender, sexuality, and human agency, without reducing bodily feelings to genetic or hormonal mechanisms.

Other feminists have explored the connection between the body and technology. Particularly influential in this connection was Donna Haraway's "Cyborg Manifesto" (1991). A **cyborg** is a cybernetic organism, part machine and part living organism.

While cyborgs have long been portrayed as monsters in science fiction, Haraway argued persuasively that all humans—women and men alike—were being increasingly drawn into alliances with machines in the contemporary world, for good and for ill. Haraway recognized the negative side of human–machine connections in cybernetically managed forms of economic production, but she refused to condemn technology as contrary to all the needs and goals of feminists. On the contrary, she argued that thinking in terms of cyborgs could be productive for progressive feminist purposes, particularly as a way of dealing with the conflicts generated by the politics of identity among differently located groups of women. She contrasted the isolating relations promoted by politics based on *identity* (i.e., promoting political solidarity among those who shared the "same" identity) with what she saw as a potentially more promising politics based on *affinity* (i.e., promoting political alliances among those who might claim different

identities, but who nonetheless shared some partial connections regarding some issues that might allow them to bridge their differences). Relations of affinity were a variety of cyborg relations because they joined unlike entities together, but promised political potency that promoted hope. Her model of feminist alliances based on affinity was the set of alliances that produced the hybrid category of *women of color*: although they might be divided by ethnicity or class, all women of color have experienced the consequences of being nonwhite, and have been politically effective by coming together on that basis.

How Do Anthropologists Study Connections between Bodies and Technologies?

As we observed in Chapter 1, Haraway's cyborg thinking helped found the field of science studies and led to the development of *cyborg anthropology*, an area of specialization in which anthropologists focus attention on the proliferating cybernetic connections between humans and machines in contemporary societies. Such connections can be found everywhere today, from computerized management of large informational databases in government and private industry, to online computer gaming, to your personal relationship with your smart phone. Science studies in anthropology are often located within the anthropology of science, technology, and medicine. As we saw earlier, this is the disciplinary location of medical anthropologists like Marcia Inhorn and Emily Wentzell, whose research regularly involves the complex ways that human organisms are entangled with technologies. Furthermore, as the work of Marcia Inhorn shows, to study varieties of assisted reproduction as an anthropologist is simultaneously to study sex, gender, and sexuality; paying attention to the way humans and nonhumans, organisms and tools, as well as the wider social institutions and processes that support them, are regularly brought together in the attempt (frequently successful) to create biological offspring for infertile couples. In the past, medicine and technology were not viewed as having any intrinsic connection to the "natural" biological processes, such as human reproduction, and the failure of this natural process to produce living offspring was understood as equally "natural." Today, however, in all parts of the world, individuals and couples (increasingly, same-sex couples) who want children of their own, but who are unable or unwilling to adopt, may now call on a variety of complex medical technologies and institutions—from sperm banks and egg banks to fertility clinics—that perform procedures like in vitro fertilization for themselves, or for a female surrogate who has agreed, for a fee, to gestate "their" embryo for them. In addition, forms of prenatal

---

affect   Visceral arousal, emotion, or feeling.

cyborg   A cybernetic organism, part machine and part living organism.

testing such as amniocentesis are now standard technological interventions in pregnancies that may be otherwise uncomplicated. (We will explore further some of the consequences of assisted reproduction in Chapter 14, in the context of kinship and relatedness.)

When cyborg thinking asks us to consider connections between "natural" organisms and "cultural" technologies, this inevitably blurs the boundaries between nature and culture. However, close inspection of that which is considered "natural" can also lead to the blurring of boundaries that once seemed clear-cut. As we saw earlier, at one time, anthropologists agreed that "sex," while distinct from culturally shaped "gender," was a "natural" physical attribute clearly visible on the body, to be determined by inspection at birth (i.e., males have penises and females have vaginas) or at puberty (i.e., males grow beards and females grow breasts and start to menstruate). However, this way of classifying bodies, based on the presumption of a "natural" gender binary, turns out to be problematic. For one thing, the determination of the sex of newborns by visual inspection is by no means as straightforward as it may seem. Developmental biologist Anne Fausto-Sterling reports that "about one in a hundred infants is born without a consistent body sex" (2012, 313). That is, infants' patterns of sex chromosomes (XX for females, XY for males) may not correspond to the expected outward appearance of their genitals (an XX baby may have an enlarged clitoris and fused labia, an XY baby may have a tiny penis) or with their internal gonads (i.e., two ovaries for females, two testes for males).

Individuals who possess ambiguous genitalia have been called **intersex**, although many prefer to describe their condition as the result of a **disorder of sexual development**.

Medical scientists are able to identify a number of developmental processes that can produce atypical genitalia in infants, some of which are associated with ongoing risks to the individual's health; however, many newborns with ambiguous genitalia face no such health risks. Still, infants with ambiguous genitalia may cause great anxiety for their parents, which has led to the elaboration of standard medical interventions in the United States soon after the birth of such infants. Decisions are made about the newborn's sex assignment (and the gender in which the child will be reared), and then surgery is performed to bring the external appearance of the infant's genitalia into line with this assignment; sometimes surgery is followed by additional hormonal treatments at puberty. However, many adults who underwent these interventions in childhood have publicly declared that their own personal biographies have been far from "normal." Some have become activists who urge physicians and parents to delay or avoid such surgeries on infants altogether, in order to spare these children the surgical disfigurement and loss

of sexual feeling they experienced (Karkazis 2008). The issues are complex, but one thing is clear: the statistical frequency with which infants with ambiguous genitalia are born means that assigning newborns a sex is far from self-evident or unproblematic, and is powerfully shaped by the cultural expectations and social practices of parents and physicians. This evidence reinforces Judith Butler's well-known insistence that sex is as much a construction of culture as is gender (Butler 1990).

In this context, it is useful to reflect on a phenomenon Roger Lancaster described at the conclusion of his discussion of Guto's performance: namely, Guto's "breasts." Lancaster explained: "After adolescence, Guto, like some other boys in his extended family, had begun to grow small breasts. His older brother Charlie claimed that his own nipples sometimes produced *leche*, milk, as I discovered one day when I encountered him, concentratedly squeezing his nipples and asked him what he was doing" (1997, 572). What could have been responsible for this development? Lancaster could not know, but he speculated that perhaps the growth of breasts on Guto and Charlie might have been stimulated by exposure to pesticides in the countryside, since some pesticides, when they decompose, can affect human bodies the way hormones do. This kind of fleshly malleability, which seems to carry meanings about our sex, gender, or sexuality, is what Lancaster calls "the transvestism of the body" (1997, 572). Guto and his brother managed these bodily changes by undergoing breast reduction surgery shortly before Guto's Carnivalesque performance with Aida's blouse.

How Do Anthropologists Study Relations between Sex, Gender, and Sexuality?

Minimally, **sexuality** refers to the ways in which people experience and value physical desire and pleasure in the context of sexual intercourse.

But contemporary anthropologists are more likely to refer to sexual*ities*, in the plural, to acknowledge the many ways in which sexual desires and pleasures have always been shaped historically by cultural, social, and political structures of the larger societies in which people live. Until recently, as we saw above, many Americans took for granted that biological sex directly determined gendered behavior. These assumptions underlie the view, long popular in

---

intersex/disorder of sexual development Individuals who possess ambiguous genitalia; many who experience this condition prefer to describe it as a disorder of sexual development.

sexuality The ways in which people experience and value physical desire and pleasure in the context of sexual intercourse.

the United States, that "normal" sexuality takes only one form—**heterosexuality**—which involves "natural" sexual attraction, leading to "natural" sexual intercourse, between males and females (i.e., individuals of different sexes).

To emphasize heterosexuality as the only correct form of human sexual expression is to subscribe to an ideology that anthropologists and others call **heteronormativity**: that is, the view that heterosexual intercourse is (and *should be*) the "normal" form that human sexual expression always takes.

For example, heteronormative sexuality has been viewed in Euro-American societies as the appropriate form of sexuality within the nuclear family, formed around a heterosexual married couple who are expected to engage in exclusive sexual relations with one another in order to produce offspring. Claims that the nuclear family is the building block of US society reflect what Foucault would call the biopolitical concern of the state to manage its population of citizens and regulate their reproduction. However, heteronormative thinking about sexuality has been undermined in recent decades, not only by scholarly work on varieties of human sexual expression, but even more by activism by lesbians, gay men, and bisexual and transgender individuals, whose preferred ways of doing gender and enacting sexual expression challenge heteronormative standards. From the perspective of these critics, people who continue to support heteronormativity are perceived to subscribe instead to **heterosexism**, a form of bias (like sexist bias) against all those who are not heterosexual.

Historians of sexuality have demonstrated the recency of heteronormative thinking, and heteronormative sexual classifications, in Euro-American societies. Consider, for example, the concept of heterosexuality and its routine

opposite, **homosexuality**—that is, sexual relations involving two men or two women (i.e., same-sex sexuality).

Many people assume that these terms identify stable forms of sexuality going back deep into the past, but this is not the case. David Halperin observes that the first appearance in print of the word "homosexuality" was in 1869, in German, in a pamphlet urging the German government not to criminalize "homosexual" relations between men; paradoxically, therefore, "'homosexuality' began life as a progay, politically activist coinage" (2014, 481). Before long, however, the term was appropriated by medical specialists called "sexologists" who turned it into a clinical term designating a particular variety of sexual deviance. By the end of the nineteenth century, however, individuals classified as homosexual by the medical authorities began to use the term **gay** to refer to themselves, an affirmative and empowering self-designation that became widespread over the course of the twentieth century.

Although the term "**gay**" may be applied to any person who is sexually attracted to someone of the same sex, it is more commonly used in reference to gay men and the cultures and practices associated with them.

The term **lesbian** did actually emerge in antiquity, but it originally referred to the Greek island of Lesbos, the home of the female poet Sappho, who was reputed to love women rather than men.

The standard use of "lesbian" to describe female same-sex sexuality, however, only began around the turn of the twentieth century. In fact, the terms "homosexuality," "heterosexuality," and **bisexuality** (i.e., sexual attraction to both males and females) were all invented by Euro-American medical researchers in the late nineteenth and early twentieth centuries, and "heterosexuality" did not assume its current meaning as the opposite of "homosexuality" until the 1930s (see Halperin 2014, 458–61). The term **transgender** is even more recent, proposed in the 1960s in an attempt by medical researchers to clarify differences among individuals who, in one way or another, seemed dissatisfied with the sex and gender assignments they had received at birth.

Physicians now recognize *gender identity disorder* or *gender dysphoria* as a formal medical diagnosis, but many persons who claim a transgender identity deny the validity of this diagnosis, arguing that it is based on heteronormative bias. Like individuals diagnosed as "homosexual" in earlier decades, many individuals diagnosed with gender dysphoria insist that their sexuality is not a medical condition to be treated but a valid form of gender variation that requires recognition and support.

In the 1990s, some persons whose gender identities or sexual practices fell outside the range defined by "the heterosexual-homosexual continuum" began to refer to themselves as **queer,** taking back as a badge of pride a term once used to insult non-heterosexuals.

---

heterosexuality The view that "natural" sexual attraction, leading to "natural" sexual intercourse, occurs only between males and females (i.e., individuals of different sexes).

heteronormativity The view that heterosexual intercourse is (and *should be*) the "normal" form that human sexual expression always takes.

heterosexism A form of bias (like sexist bias) against all those who are not heterosexual.

homosexuality The heteronormative opposite of heterosexuality; that is, sexual relations involving two men or two women (i.e., same-sex sexuality).

gay An affirmative and empowering self-designation for individuals medically classified as homosexual, which became widespread over the course of the twentieth century.

lesbian A term used to describe female same-sex sexuality around the turn of the twentieth century; based on the name of the Greek island of Lesbos, the home of the female poet Sappho, who was reputed to love women rather than men.

bisexuality Sexual attraction to both males and females.

transgender A term proposed in the 1960s by medical researchers to classify individuals who, in one way or another, seemed dissatisfied with the sex and gender assignments they had received at birth.

queer A self-identification claimed by some persons whose gender identities or sexual practices fall outside the range defined by "the heterosexual-homosexual continuum."

The status of this term remains controversial, however: some view it as a convenient umbrella term for all those who reject heteronormativity; others, however, use it to signify rejection of *all* categories of gender and sexual classification, including distinctions between lesbian, gay, bisexual, and transgender persons. Recently, the term **nonbinary** has become more widely used by persons who see themselves as neither male nor female. According to the website of the National Center for Transgender Equality, "People whose gender is not male or female use many different terms to describe themselves, with nonbinary being one of the most common. Other terms include genderqueer, agender, bigender, and more. None of these terms mean exactly the same thing—but all speak to an experience of gender that is not simply male or female" https://transequality.org/issues/resources/understanding-non-binary-people-how-to-be-respectful-and-supportive

In the wake of sociopolitical breakthroughs such as the growing legal recognition of same-sex marriage, debates about how to distinguish and label proliferating varieties of sexuality are ongoing. For example, on June 9, 2015, following the highly publicized transition of former male Olympic athlete Bruce Jenner into a woman called Caitlyn, *The New York Times* published an article describing the difficulty of determining statistically the proportion of the US population who might be classified as "transgender" (Miller 2015). Being able to quantify more accurately the proportion of transgender individuals in the US population would have wide-ranging biopolitical effects, for good or for ill: as Miller notes, "knowing more about this population is important for policy-making in health, education, criminal justice, social services, sports, the military and more" (2015, A3). However, the US Census Bureau does not ask about gender identity, and many transgender persons hide their gender identity in order to avoid discrimination (Figure 13.9). At the same time, Miller also noted that "gender identity can be hard to define in a multiple-choice list. There are now more than 50 gender options on Facebook, for instance" (Miller 2015, A3). Similarly, the "Transgender" page on Wikipedia provides several definitions of "transgender" and describes multiple and contradictory ways that people who call themselves transgender might define what that label means (http://en.wikipedia.org/wiki/Transgender; accessed March 28, 2016). In part, the struggle over terminology reflects the desire of some transgender persons to gain public recognition of an identity label of their own choice, as a claim to dignity; at the same time, the proliferation of labels reveals deep disagreements about what that identity might be.

The conclusion seems inescapable that even in Euro-American societies, forms of sexual expression cannot be easily sorted into a handful of unambiguous categories

FIGURE 13.9   Gender identity is complex and can become politicized, as illustrated by battles in the United States over access to public restrooms by transgender people.

in which sex, gender, and sexuality line up in predictable ways. On the contrary, the phenomena we call sex, gender, and sexuality would appear to be fluid and changing, not only over historical time, but also in the biographies of many human individuals, even in the United States. Some scholars speak in terms of a *male-to-female continuum*, along which individuals may plot the development of their own identifications in terms of sex, gender, and sexuality. Others may agree with David Halperin, whose history of the classification of sex, gender, and sexuality in Euro-American societies concludes that "Perhaps the final irony in all this is that the very word sex . . . has had the fine edge of its precise meaning so thoroughly blunted by historical shifts, conceptual muddles, and rearrangements in the forms of sexual life that it now represents that which is most resistant to clear classification, discrimination, and division" (2014, 484).

How Does Ethnography Document Variable Culture Understandings Concerning Sex, Gender, and Sexuality?

In the wake of second-wave feminism and the rise of activism by lesbian, gay, bisexual, and transgender persons, anthropologists have in recent decades produced fresh ethnographic evidence concerning variations in beliefs and practices about sex, gender, and sexuality in the many communities where they carried out fieldwork, both within and outside the Western world. In many cases,

---

Nonbinary   a self-identification claimed by some persons who see themselves as neither male nor female.

the peoples and practices they write about have long histories that predate contact with Euro-American societies, which often came in the form of Western colonialism. As noted above, explorers and settlers often wrote about such practices, which scandalized them and which were officially forbidden by Christian missionaries. One example involves renewed attention to older writings about the cultural and sexual practices of the so-called *berdache*. Until the last decades of the twentieth century, the term "berdache" had been used by anthropologists as a technical term to refer to indigenous (especially Native American) social roles in which men (and sometimes women) were allowed to take on the activities and sometimes the dress of members of the other sex. Sometimes "berdache" has been defined as "male transvestite," but this definition is inadequate because it ignores the fact that a man who took on other aspects of a woman's role might also, as women did, establish sexual relationships with men. Indeed, the term meant "male prostitute" to the early French explorers in the Americas who first used it to describe the men they observed engaging in such behavior. Today, many anthropologists refuse to use the term, as do many contemporary members of indigenous societies who view themselves as modern embodiments of these alternative-gender roles. Some have proposed using terms like *third gender* or *two spirit* instead, although no consensus has yet been achieved. Given our previous discussion, this lack of consensus is hardly surprising.

In the context of globalization in the twenty-first century, Euro-American ideas about sex, gender, and sexuality sometimes mix uneasily with local understandings, even when those local understandings themselves challenge traditional, Western, heteronormative assumptions. The following case studies further illustrate the range of ethnographic findings that continue to challenge taken-for-granted notions about sex, gender, and sexuality.

Female Sexual Practices in Mombasa

Anthropologist Gill Shepherd (1987) showed that traditional patterns of male–female interaction among Swahili Muslims in Mombasa, Kenya, make male and female same-sex relationships in this community intelligible (see "EthnoProfile 13.3: Mombasa Swahilis"; Figure 13.10). In the years when Shepherd did her research, she found that men and women in Muslim Mombasa live in very different subcultures. For women, the most enduring relationship was between mothers and daughters, mirrored in the relationship between an older married sister and a younger unmarried sister. By contrast, relationships between mothers and sons and between brothers and sisters were more distant. Except in the case of young, modern, educated couples, the relationship between husband and wife was often emotionally

distant as well. Because the worlds of men and women overlapped so little, relationships between the genders tended to be one-dimensional. Men and women joined a variety of sex-segregated groups for leisure-time activities such as dancing or religious study. Within these same-sex groups, individuals competed for social rank.

Of the some 50,000 Swahili in Mombasa at the end of the 1980s, Shepherd reckoned that Western observers might classify perhaps 5,000 as "homosexual." The number was misleading, however, because men and women shifted between what Euro-Americans call "homosexuality" and "heterosexuality" throughout their lives. Women were allowed to choose other women as sexual partners only after they had been married, widowed, or divorced. Both men and women were open about their same-sex relationships, and "nobody would dream of suggesting that their sexual choices had any effect on their work capabilities, reliability or religious piety" (Shepherd 1987, 241). Moreover, many women were quite clear about the practical reasons that had led them into sexual relationships with other women. Women with little money were unlikely to marry men who could offer them jewelry, shoes, new dresses, status, or financial security, but a wealthy female lover could offer them all these things. Also, a poor young woman in an unhappy marriage might have no way to support herself if she left her husband unless she had a lesbian lover to rely on.

According to Islamic law, Shepherd was told, a wealthy, high-ranking Muslim woman can only marry a man who is her equal or superior. A marriage of this kind would bring a great deal of seclusion, and her wealth

EthnoProfile 13.3

Mombasa Swahilis

Region: Eastern Africa

Nation: Kenya

Population: 50,000 Swahili among 350,000 total population of city (1970s)

Environment: Island and mainland port city

Livelihood: Various urban occupations

Political organization: Part of a modern nation-state

For more information: Shepherd, Gil. 1987. Rank, gender and homosexuality: Mombasa as a key to understanding sexual options. In *The cultural construction of sexuality*, ed. Pat Caplan, 240–70. London: Tavistock.

FIGURE 13.10 View of Mombasa.

would be administered by her husband. The wealthy partner in a female same-sex relationship, however, would be free of these constraints. "Thus, if she wishes to use her wealth as she likes, and has a taste for power, entry into a lesbian relationship, or living alone as a divorced or widowed woman, are virtually her only options" (Shepherd 1987, 257). Financial independence for a woman offered a chance to convert wealth to power. If she paid for the marriage of other people or provided financial support in exchange for loyalty, a woman could create a circle of dependents. Shepherd pointed out that a few women, some lesbians, had achieved real political power in Mombasa in this way (257).

Still, it was not necessary to be a lesbian to build a circle of dependents. Why did some women follow this route? The answer, Shepherd learned, is complicated. It was not entirely respectable for a woman under 45 or 50 to be unmarried. Some could maintain autonomy by making a marriage of convenience to a man who already lived with a wife and then living apart from him. Many women, however, found this arrangement both lonely and sexually unsatisfying. Living as a lesbian was less respectable than being a second, nonresident wife, but it was more respectable than not being married at all. The lesbian sexual relationship did not reduce the autonomy of the wealthy partner "and indeed takes place in the highly

positive context of the fond and supportive relationships women establish among themselves anyway" (Shepherd 1987, 258).

Shepherd suggested that the reason sexual relationships between men or between women were generally not heavily stigmatized in Mombasa was because social rank took precedence over all other measures of status. Rank was a combination of wealth, the ability to claim Arab ancestry, and the degree of Muslim learning and piety. Rank determined marriage partners as well as relations of loyalty and subservience, and both men and women expected to rise in rank over a lifetime. Although lesbian couples might violate the prototype for sexual relations, they did not violate relations of rank. Shepherd suggested that a marriage between a poor husband and a rich wife might be more shocking than a lesbian relationship between a dominant rich woman and a dependent poor one. It was less important that a woman's lover be a male than it was for her to be a good Arab, a good Muslim, and a person of wealth and influence.

Anthropologists working in Africa have described a range of relations between females (woman marriage, e.g.) that have been likened to European or American models of lesbian relationships, but disputes have arisen about whether such relationships always include an erotic involvement between the female partners. In a survey of this evidence, Wieringa and Black-wood noted that woman marriage could take many forms, some of which were more likely than others to include sexuality between the female partners. Among those where such sexual relations appear more likely are cases like that described by Shepherd "in which a woman of some means, either married (to a man) or unmarried, pays bride-wealth for a wife and establishes her own compound" (Wieringa and Blackwood 1999, 5).

Such evidence is not merely of academic interest. In the contemporary world of intensified global communication and exchange, Western and non-Western same-sex practices are becoming increasingly entangled with one another, leading to the emergence of local movements for "lesbian" and "gay" rights in Africa and elsewhere. In this context, in the late 1990s, the presidents of Zimbabwe, Kenya, and Namibia declared that homosexuality is "un-African." Based on the ethnographic evidence, however, Wieringa and Blackwood (1999) sided with those arguing that on the contrary, it is homophobia that is un-African: "President Mandela from South Africa is a striking exception to the homophobia of his colleagues. The South African constitution specifically condemns discrimination on the basis of sexual orientation" (27).

Male and Female Sexual Practices in Nicaragua

As noted earlier in this chapter, anthropologist Roger Lancaster's fieldwork in Managua, Nicaragua, in the 1980s taught him about *cochones*: men who have sex with other men but whose cultural significance and sexual practices cannot be easily equated with North American "homosexuality." As Lancaster discovered, the views of working-class Nicaraguans about cochones could be properly understood only when considered in the context of broader Nicaraguan ideas about masculinity.

To begin with, a "real man" (or *macho*) is widely admired as someone who is active, violent, and dominant. In sexual terms, this means that the penis is used violently as a weapon to dominate one's sexual partner, who is thereby rendered passive, abused, and subordinate. People in the United States typically think of machismo as involving the domination of women by men, but as Lancaster shows, the system is equally defined by the domination of men over other men. Indeed, a "manly man" in working-class Nicaragua is someone who is the active, dominant, penetrating sexual partner in encounters with women *and* men. The term *cochón* is used to refer to the "passive" male who allows a "manly man" to have sexual intercourse with him in this way.

The Nicaraguans Lancaster knew assumed that men "would naturally be aroused by the idea of anally penetrating another male" (Lancaster 1992, 241). Only the

passive cochón is stigmatized, whereas males who always take the active role in intercourse with other males and females are seen as "normal." At the same time, as we saw earlier, cochones are also much-admired performers during the festival of Carnival. Thus, although Nicaraguans made fun of cochones, they could not imagine cochones being made victims of hate crimes such as gay-bashing. In the United States, by contrast, the active–passive distinction does not exist, and anal intercourse is not the only form that gay male sexual expression may take. Both partners have been considered homosexual, and equally stigmatized by same-sex encounters, and gay-bashing has been a sometimes deadly reality. Perhaps this is because North Americans have *not* traditionally assumed that normal males will naturally be aroused by the idea of sex with another man.

In Nicaragua, Lancaster found that public challenges for dominance were a constant of male–male interaction even when sexual intercourse was not involved. The term *cochón* might be used as an epithet not only for a man who yields publicly to another man but also for cats that do not catch mice or, indeed, anything that somehow fails to perform its proper function. In Lancaster's view, cochones are made, not born: "Those who consistently lose out in the competition for male status . . . discover pleasure in the passive sexual role or its social status: these men are made into cochones. And those who master the rules of conventional masculinity . . . are made into machistas" (Lancaster 1992, 249). These ideas about gender and sexuality created an unanticipated roadblock for Sandinistas who wanted to improve the lives of Nicaraguan women and children. The Sandinista government passed a series of New Family Laws designed to encourage men to support their families economically and to discourage irresponsible sex, irresponsible parenting, and familial dislocation. When Lancaster (1992) interviewed Nicaraguan men to see what they thought of these laws, however, he repeatedly got the following response: "First the interrogative: 'What do the Sandinistas want from us? That we should all become cochónes?' And then the tautological: 'A man has to be a man.' That is, a man is defined by what he is not—a cochón" (274).

The Sandinistas were replaced in 1992 by an administration supported by the US government; and when anthropologist Cymene Howe visited Nicaragua after this change in regime, the country had been politically transformed. Howe carried out ethnographic fieldwork in the late 1990s and early 2000s on women, sexuality, and social change (2013). Nicaraguans she knew were familiar not only with the traditional category of cochón, but also with the category of *cochona*, a "manly woman," although women's same-sex sexuality was less publicly visible than that of men. Howe learned that the partners and girlfriends of cochonas were described as *feminina* or *muy mujer* (very womanly). Not unlike the situation of manly men, feminine women could become involved in sexual relationships with cochonas without losing their status as "normal" women.

At the time of Howe's fieldwork, newer labels like gay, homosexual, and lesbian had also entered the vocabularies of many Nicaraguans she knew, especially activists working to transform public understandings of same-sex sexuality in the country, who were the focus of her research. But their work (and her fieldwork) were hampered by the fact that Nicaragua had passed Latin America's strictest antisodomy law in 1992, targeting both men and women, and it was not repealed until 2007. Under these conditions, the activists Howe studied (and Howe herself) had to be very careful, for there were influential groups, like evangelical Christians, who backed the law and were hostile to their work.

Howe learned that many women who had been revolutionary activists earlier in their lives had transformed themselves into "sexual rights activists," working to protect women who engaged in stigmatized sexual practices from state repression. In post–Cold War, neoliberal economic conditions, these activists sought funding for their work from donors located in North America and Europe. Yet the activists also knew that many of the tactics being urged upon them by their donor allies would not be successful in Nicaragua. The activists' decision to describe their work vaguely, as an attempt to establish "sexual rights," reflects these complications. The activists' work "highlights sexuality as a political object and joins it to rights as a political method, without delineating a particular identity category" (Howe 2013, 13).

As Howe explains, "theirs is not simply a lesbian and gay rights movement. Nicaragua's history of sexuality differs, rather substantially, from many North American and European contexts" (2013, 13). Given these varied constraints and challenges, the activists she knew had to pick and choose among tactics that might further their cause without undermining their efforts. One of the activists' most successful projects was to spread their message using public media like radio and magazines, which protected the identities both of the activists themselves and of those interested in their messages. Perhaps not surprisingly, they ran into difficulties when they attempted to persuade both cochonas and femininas to adopt a lesbian identity. Many cochonas, especially from rural parts of Nicaragua, subscribed to the same distinction between active and passive sexuality as the manly men whom Lancaster knew, and they stoutly refused to recognize any commonality between them and their passive feminina partners. In urban areas, however, where nontraditional understandings of women's same-sex sexuality are gaining ground, Howe concluded that femininas and cochonas were indeed being incorporated into a new,

more expansive sexual category: "in other words, feminine women who would not have been considered gay in the past, now are" (2013, 18).

Transsexuality and Same-Sex Desire in Iran

Afsaneh Najmabadi is a scholar who has investigated the role of gender in the history of Iran. She left Iran as a young woman in the 1960s to study in the United States, where she became a feminist and political activist. She was deeply affected by the consequences of the Islamic Revolution in Iran in 1979; and since that time, her research has explored how gender relations rooted in Iranian history were reworked in the course of the nineteenth century, as Iranian elites developed connections with the West and embarked on a self-conscious process of "modernization." Najmabadi also was interested in how, after the 1979 revolution, Iranians had responded to efforts by the religious authorities to expunge Western influences and to bring Iranian institutions and social practices into conformity with what they determined to be the requirements of Islamic law. She was particularly intrigued when, in 2003, there was a burst of attention in the Iranian and international press concerning what was being calling "the 'trans' phenomenon" (2014, 1). She knew that in the decade prior to the 1979 revolution, Iranian physicians had become involved in hormonal and surgical treatments for persons wishing to change their sex. By 2003, however, journalists seemed both surprised and puzzled that this sort of "progressive" treatment could be possible in an Islamic state; the same state had ruled same-sex sexual relations to be illegal, often equating them with "sodomy," which was punished with the death penalty (2014, 1). After a 25-year absence, Najmabadi returned to Iran in 2005 to carry out ethnographic fieldwork that would explore all these matters more closely.

Najmabadi discovered that the distinctions between sex, gender, and sexuality, developed by Western scholars, did not easily map onto Iranian categories: most Iranians she spoke to did not recognize a distinction between sex and gender, and most also presumed a more or less direct causal link between an individual's sex/gender and the focus of his or her sexual desire: "the indistinction between gender/sex/sexuality . . . regularly disrupts attempts to separate the homosexual from the trans, even as that distinction is regularly invoked" (2014, 8). Iranians had also developed their own version of heteronormativity as a consequence of the "modernization" of Iranian family life: even Muslim theologians she spoke with seemed to take the existence of a heteronormative gender binary for granted (2014, 191). However, Iranian historical and cultural attitudes toward sex/gender/sexuality meant that the status of "trans" persons in contemporary Iranian society did not easily map onto "trans" identities recognized in the West. In Iran, she found that physicians linked "trans" identity with that of "intersex," which itself was associated historically with the category of "hermaphrodite" recognized in Islamic law. Just like infants born with ambiguous external genitalia, therefore, persons who believed that their inner soul or psyche was mismatched with their outer anatomy were considered to be entitled to hormonal and surgical interventions that would "clarify" their "true" sex/gender. This conclusion had been proclaimed lawful in a *fatwa* (or Islamic religious opinion) first issued in the 1960s by none other than Ayatollah Khomeini, leader of the Islamic Revolution in Iran and the highest ranking Shi'a Muslim religious authority in recent Iranian history, whose authority remains unchallenged (2014) (Figure 13.11).

Najmabadi undertook participant-observation in order to learn exactly how trans activists engaged psychological, medical, religious, and governmental authorities on an everyday basis; she also interviewed key figures in these different institutions. Although she expected to encounter rigid attitudes in officials, especially religious authorities, she describes herself as surprised and humbled by how many of them were not interested in denouncing sexual nonconformity, but who in their own ways were working to find humane solutions for affected individuals. The religious endorsement of treatment for "gender dysphoria" has made it possible for Muslim clerics, psychologists, physicians, and government bureaucrats to find some common ground, but it had taken the determined lobbying efforts of trans activists to persuade these officials to make needed changes.

At first, Najmabadi was surprised when trans activists told her that they did not want to "politicize" their cause. What they meant, she found, was that they did not want to turn their activism into a human rights issue that would involve the Iranian parliament passing legislation. Rather, they wanted to make sure that civil servants and others knew who they were and would continue to work with them, regardless of which political faction was in power. Their activism was intended to gain official awareness of the "needs" of trans people; to remove a series of medical, legal, and religious barriers; and to get support and protection from harassment, in order to make "livable lives" for themselves (2014, 12). By such methods, trans activists eventually gained official recognition as members of a "vulnerable" population deserving of state protection (2014, 214). Nevertheless, to become entitled to such protection, they had to pass a series of medical, psychological, and legal examinations designed to prove that they were indeed what they said they were. Once they obtained official certification as trans, they could have their name and sex/gender changed on their national identity papers, complete their sex change treatments, and, if they wished, disappear into the Iranian population.

The high barrier to gaining formal trans certification in Iran points to another difference between Western and Iranian notions about sex, gender, and sexuality. The "filtering" process leading to trans certification was so intense because Iranian authorities wanted to make sure that the applicants they certified were *genuinely* "trans"; put another way, their goal was to *detect and exclude* candidates for trans status who did *not* experience "gender dysphoria" but who, in their view, were trying to mask their sexual attraction to members of their own sex/gender. Indeed, male-to-female trans persons in Iran were constantly suspected of trying to use sex change to hide what was interpreted as their shameful desire to be the passive male partner in sexual relations between

FIGURE 13.11   Iran's first religiously and legally recognized transsexual and her mother.

males. Nevertheless, Najmabadi "never saw the commission exercise the option of turning down an application altogether . . . there seemed to be a general attitude . . . that . . . it was their job to find a socially acceptable 'solution for the problem'" (2014, 18).

As noted earlier, relationships between couples whom Euro-Americans might classify as "gay" or "lesbian" are condemned as immoral and illegal in Iran; such "same-sex players" (as they are called in Persian) are forced to keep their relationships hidden from family and society, which causes them considerable hardship, especially when faced with what Najmabadi calls the Iranian *marriage imperative:* "The adulthood of everyone is bound to marriage. It is almost incomprehensible that someone would wish not to marry" (2014, 124). The pressure of the marriage imperative sometimes led nonheteronormative Iranians, who usually described themselves as "gay" or "lesbian," to wonder if they might be "trans" and ought to consider changing sex. Such thoughts were often prompted by their partners, who wanted to regularize their relationship, and who might threaten to leave them if they did not agree to undergo sex change. Indeed, Najmabadi found attitudes amounting to homophobia among some nonheteronormative couples who insisted that they were not "same-sex players," and who strove to interpret their relationships with their partners in ways

that did not violate hegemonic Iranian understandings of sex/gender/sexuality (2014, 248).

At the same time, some persons who obtained trans certification did not always go on to complete their transition. This might be because they could not afford to pay for the surgery right away. But it might also be because, even though they believed that they truly were trans, they also knew that their families and neighbors would never accept them as such. At bottom, Najmabadi concluded, trans individuals—indeed, all nonheteronormative Iranians—were struggling to find a way to make a "livable" life by exploiting inconsistencies among the various restrictions and opportunities that governed their lives. One postoperative male-to-female trans person she knew "still lives as a man at home; it is very critical for her to remain a man with her family and in the neighborhood everyone knew her as a man.. . . When she is at her boyfriend's house, she explains, she goes into female clothes" (2014, 281). Najmabadi concluded that "what seemed to matter for trans subjecthood was articulated in terms of figuring out how to live livable lives—with families, with partners, in terms of employment, of getting medical and legal changes they wanted, and of what made them comfortable in different spaces of life . . . living livable lives, for some, called for flexibility and the ability to switch back and forth when necessary" (2014, 286).

Chapter Summary

1. Cultural anthropologists have been interested in sex, gender, and sexuality since the beginnings of anthropology as a discipline, and since the 1930s have insisted that biological sex needed to be distinguished from cultural rules for appropriate behavior as a female or a male. Twentieth-century social movements for civil rights, women's rights, and the rights of gay, lesbian, bisexual, and transgender persons called into question the existence of a universal sex and gender binary in all human societies. Some anthropologists argued that sexist patterns in contemporary societies, in the West and elsewhere, were due primarily to the effects of capitalism and colonialism on indigenous societies that had once supported more egalitarian relationships between men and women. Anthropologist Marilyn Strathern provided ethnographic evidence suggesting that Melanesian peoples tended to view males and females as androgynous. These efforts combined with work by scholars in other disciplines to produce an overall rethinking of how sex, gender, and sexuality ought to be understood.

2. The influence of feminism on anthropology initially led to a focus on the roles women played in different

societies, but before long it became clear that women's roles could not be studied apart from the roles of men. Increasing attention to the ways sex, gender, and sexuality are differently enacted in different times and places led to a recognition that masculinities and femininities might be constructed in more than one way, even in a single society. Some anthropologists have used ethnographic data to demonstrate the processes by which new kinds of masculinity can develop over time, as new generations of men in particular societies confront challenges and opportunities that differ from earlier generations, as seen in Marcia Inhorn's discussion of emerging masculinities in the Middle East. Changes in masculinities also emerge over the life cycle, and Emily Wentzell's discussion of composite masculinities illuminates the process whereby Mexican men delete old elements and add new elements of their masculine identities, as they come to terms with the challenges of aging and illness.

3. Women of color developed approaches to sex, gender, and sexuality that went beyond the views of feminists who took the experiences of white, middle-class, Euro-American women as the norm, showing how

(continued)

Chapter Summary (*continued*)

experiences of gender oppression always intersected with other social statuses such as race and social class. Ethnographers have identified patterns of intersectionality in their fieldwork and are able to provide comparative examples from different times and places.

4. Scholars and activists for gay, lesbian, bisexual, and transgender rights developed approaches that showed why gender roles were best understood as performances in which individuals attempted to enact forms of speech and behavior that were considered appropriate in their societies. This made room for individual agency and for recognition that human affect could not be completely contained within any particular set of socially established definitions of sex, gender, or sexuality. The malleability of the human body, shaped by the skills we all learn that enable us to mimic others whose gender or sexuality differs from our own, highlights a range of performance possibilities of gender and sexuality that, as Roger Lancaster argues, can deepen our understanding of what may count as "transvestism."

5. Work in the anthropology of science, technology, and medicine has drawn attention to the ways that humans are increasingly linked to, and dependent on, technologies. These "cyborg" arrangements can be seen in cases of cutting-edge medical technologies that allow infertile couples to produce biological offspring, as shown in Marcia Inhorn's research in the Middle East. But the connection between biology and technology in the production of human bodies that conform to a society's gender binary by means of surgery and hormones also demonstrates a similar kind of "cyborg" connection between biology and technology. Anthropologists and biologists have drawn attention to the high proportion of human infants who are

born with ambiguous genitalia. In the United States, beginning in the 1960s, such infants were assigned a sex by physicians and parents; and surgery, hormone treatments, and other forms of therapy were used to bring such persons into alignment with the American gender binary. Such interventions have become controversial, as adults who were subjected to these interventions as infants have grown up and protested what was done to them. Roger Lancaster persuasively argues that these forms of surgically and hormonally mediated forms of anatomical reshaping may be usefully understood as a "transvestics of the body."

6. Scholars inside and outside anthropology have contributed to attempts to categorize the many categories of sex, gender, and sexuality that people have recognized in different times and places. Historians have provided useful information about the origins of the technical terms relating to sex, gender, and sexuality that are used today by Euro-American scholars and activists. The proliferation of distinct labels over time suggests to some observers that not only is there no gender binary, but that it makes more sense to describe variation in sex, gender, and sexuality in terms of points on a continuum or in terms of gender fluidity.

7. In the context of globalization in the twenty-first century, Euro-American ideas about sex, gender, and sexuality have spread to many parts of the world that traditionally have thought about these phenomena in different ways. Sometimes Euro-American categories mix uneasily with local categories, even as those local understandings themselves challenge traditional Western heteronormative assumptions. Ethnographic studies of sex, gender, and sexuality from Kenya, Nicaragua, and Iran illustrate these kinds of variation and complication.

For Review

1. Explain the public/private divide with reference to gender issues.
2. Why do anthropologists and other scholars distinguish among sex, gender, and sexuality?
3. How does the concept of a "dividual" self challenge universal assumptions about a heteronormative gender binary?
4. Distinguish between composite masculinities and composite femininities.
5. Explain intersectionality, particularly as it relates to issues of sex, gender, and sexuality.
6. What does it mean to say that gender is "performed"?

7. Explain what Donna Haraway means by a cyborg.
8. Explain how gender stereotypes have been used by colonial officials to model the relationship of colonizer to colonized.
9. Why do many contemporary anthropologists use the plural term "sexualities" rather than the singular term "sexuality"?
10. Discuss the history of the term "homosexuality" in western Europe and North America.
11. Using the case studies in the text, discuss how anthropologists analyze human sexual practices.

Key Terms

affect   416

androgyny   406

bisexuality   418

cyborg   416

feminism   402

gay   418

gender   404

gender binary   404

gender performativity   412

heteronormativity   418

heterosexism   418

heterosexuality   418

homosexuality   418

intersectionality   411

intersex/disorder of sexual development   417

lesbian   418

men's studies/ masculinities   407

nonbinary   419

patriarchy   403

public/private divide   403

queer   418

sex   404

sexism   403

sexuality   417

transgender   418

transvestism   414

Suggested Readings

Fausto-Sterling, Anne. 2012. *Sex/gender: Biology in a social world*. New York: Routledge. *Anne Fausto-Sterling is a celebrated developmental biologist whose writings on sex, gender, and sexuality have always located these phenomena in society and history. This brief volume directed at nonspecialists addresses the range of factors that influence sexual differentiation from fertilization through infancy and early childhood, with discussions of human sexuality and child sex differences. As always, Fausto-Sterling combines her scientific learning with critical sensibilities and wit; her guiding principle is "don't get stuck trying to divide nature from nurture."*

Hodgson, Dorothy, ed. 2016. *The gender, culture and power reader*. New York: Oxford University Press. *Dorothy Hodgson is an applied anthropologist who has worked for many years in East Africa, focusing on questions of economic development, politics, and gender. In this volume, she brings together classic essays in feminist anthropology, recent reevaluations of well-known debates in the field, and fresh ethnographic research. Contributions relate gender to power, structure, and agency; examine how persons develop into gendered beings in different cultural settings; and show the way gender is entangled with issues of work and love, labor and violence, and struggles for human rights.*

Karkazis, Katrina. 2008. *Fixing sex: Intersex, medical authority, and lived experience*. Durham, NC: Duke University Press. *Karkazis is a cultural and medical anthropologist and a bioethicist. This book provides an in-depth, non-sensationalistic account of the psychological and biomedical factors that influence the treatment of infants born with ambiguous genitalia. Karkazis reviews the history of these issues from the 1960s to the early twentieth century, considering not only the views of experts and parents but also the opinions of adults who as infants were classified as "intersex," who received surgery, and who, in many cases, have become activists hoping to prevent what happened to them from happening to others.*

Lewin, Ellen, ed. 2006. *Feminist anthropology: A reader*. Hoboken, NJ: Wiley-Blackwell. *Anthropologist Ellen Lewin has selected a series of classic and more recent texts that allow her to trace the origins and development of feminist anthropology. She includes work by feminist ethnographers working inside and outside the United States, all of whom build on insights that, in her view, were "winners in the struggle for legitimacy" in the early years of feminist anthropology.*

Luis, Keridwen N. 2018. *Herlands: Exploring the Women's Land Movement in the United States*. Minneapolis: University of Minnesota Press. *This ethnography documents life in "women's lands"—that is, independent living communities composed entirely of women. Luis's research was multisited, for women's lands can be found around the world, but this book concentrates on ethnography carried out at four women's lands in the United States, supplemented by material collected at events such as the Michigan Womyn's Music Festival and two Landdyke Gatherings, from both hard copy and online publications, and from archival materials. Women's lands are often linked to "lesbian separatism," and the women Luis got to know in these communities were mostly white and mostly lesbian. But life on women's lands is more complex than these terms would suggests. Luis investigates how land-women cope with ongoing issues involving race, class, and capitalism. She examines their complex responses to the notion of trans identity. And she explores the challenges land-women face as they confront "aging and dis/ability in community."*

Stimpson, Catherine, and Gilbert Herdt, eds. 2014. *Critical terms for the study of gender*. Chicago: University of Chicago Press. *This challenging and enlightening collection brings together twenty-one essays by distinguished scholars from a range of disciplines. Each essay addresses a critical key term that figures in the study of sex, gender, and sexuality: Bodies, Culture, Desire, Ethnicity, Globalization, Human Rights, Identity, Justice, Kinship, Language, Love, Myth, Nature, Posthuman, Power, Public/Private, Race, Regulation, Religion, Sex/Sexuality/Sexual Classification, and Utopia.*

 Visit our online resource center for further reading, web links, free assessments, flashcards, and videos. www.oup.com/he/ lavenda5e

Where do our relatives come from and why do they matter?

Because human beings need one another to survive and reproduce, they have invented a variety of ways of creating, maintaining, and dissolving social ties with one another. This chapter focuses primarily on a range of forms of face-to-face **relatedness**, including kinship, marriage, and patterns of family composition, that different human groups have imagined and practiced in different times and places.

LEARNING OBJECTIVES

- Describe the ways that anthropologists create concepts for understanding how human beings organize interdependence.

- Define kinship and the key concepts of marriage, descent, and adoption.

- Identify the roles of lineages in descent systems and the resulting associated cultural patterns.

- Describe adoption as it operates within systems of kinship

cross-culturally, including adoption in Highland Ecuador and the Andes.

- Articulate the anthropological approach to defining marriage and patterns of marriage found around the world, including patterns of residence and number of spouses.

- Analyze the connection between marriage and economic exchange, as demonstrated by transfers of wealth at the time of marriage.

- Describe how anthropologists define family and the different forms of families found cross-culturally, including the nuclear family, polygynous family, extended family, and joint family.

- Examine how families have transformed over time, noting key patterns in divorce, remarriage, migration, and choosing family.

The wives and children of a polygynous family.

How Do Human Beings Organize Interdependence?

Human life is group life. How we choose to organize ourselves is open to creative variation, as we have seen. But each of us is born into a society that was already established when we arrived. Its political, economic, and cultural practices make some social connections more likely than others. Just knowing the kind of social groups a child is born into tells us much about that child's probable path in life. Such human experiences as sexuality, conception, birth, and nurturance are selectively interpreted and shaped into shared cultural practices that anthropologists call **relatedness**. As we will see in this chapter, relatedness takes many forms—friendship, marriage, parenthood, adoption, shared links to a common ancestor, workplace associations, and so on. Furthermore, these intimate everyday relationships are always embedded in and shaped by broader structures of power, wealth, and meaning.

For more than a century, anthropologists have paid particular attention to that form of relatedness believed to be based on shared substance and its transmission (Holy 1996, 171). The shared substance may be a bodily substance, such as blood, semen, genes, or mother's milk. It may be a spiritual substance, such as soul, spirit, nurturance, or love. Sometimes, more than one substance is thought to be shared. Western anthropologists noted that, like themselves, people in many societies believed that those who share a substance were related to each other in systematic ways and that, like the Western societies to which the anthropologists belonged, members of these societies had developed sets of labels for different kinds of relatives, such as *mother* and *cousin*. They also found that people in many parts of the world linked the sharing of substance to conception, the act of sexual intercourse between parents. This collection of similarities was enough to convince early anthropologists that all people base their kinship systems on the biology of reproduction. It was but a short step to conclude that Western beliefs about who counts as relatives are universally valid.

For many decades, kinship studies were based on the assumption that all societies recognize the same basic biological relationships between mothers and fathers, children and parents, and sisters and brothers. But growing ethnographic evidence indicates that quite often people's understanding of their relations to other people is strikingly at odds with these genealogical connections. In other cases, the genealogical connections

relatedness The socially recognized ties that connect people in a variety of different ways.

turn out to form but a small subset of the ways in which people create enduring relationships with one another.

Is there some social glue that ensures social cooperation? In 1968, anthropologist David Schneider argued that North Americans' ideas of kinship generated the feeling of "enduring diffuse solidarity" among all those who understood themselves to be related by ties of blood and sex. In many cases, however, human beings seek to establish (or find themselves belonging to) collectivities organized on regional, national, or global scales. As a result, they come to experience varying degrees of relatedness and solidarity with large numbers of individuals whom they will never meet face to face. As we will see in this chapter, human beings are perfectly capable of establishing and honoring ties of enduring diffuse solidarity that have nothing to do with blood or sex. Sociologist Zygmunt Bauman has argued, in fact, that "all supra-individual groupings are first and foremost processes of collectivization of friends and enemies. . . . More exactly, individuals sharing a common group or category of enemies treat each other as friends" (1989, 152).

Although a common enemy surely has the effect of drawing people together, it is rarely sufficient by itself to produce solidarity that endures. People in all societies have developed patterned social relationships that aim to bind them together for the long term, and some of these reach beyond, and even cut across, ties forged in terms of everyday relatedness. Consider, for example, the way members of Catholic monastic orders, who may neither marry nor bear children, nevertheless refer to one another as *brother*, *sister*, *father*, and *mother*. They also take as the prototype for these interpersonal relationships the formal role obligations of family members. But religious orders in many cases are large, international institutions fitting into the overall global hierarchy of the Catholic Church. Again, the kinds of connections established among members of such institutions reach far beyond the contexts of everyday, face-to-face relatedness.

As we already noted, anthropologists were the first social scientists to recognize that people in different societies classified their relatives into categories that did not correspond to those accepted in European societies. Coming to understand the complexities of different kinds of formal kin relations helped undermine the ethnocentric assumption that European ways of categorizing relatives were a transparent reflection of natural biological ties. Indeed, beginning anthropology students from many backgrounds regularly assume that the way they grew up classifying their kin reflects the universal truth about human relatedness. For this reason, we devote part of this chapter to introducing some findings from kinship studies in anthropology. Learning to distinguish between cross cousins and parallel cousins or considering some of the consequences that follow from tracing descent through women rather than men remain useful exercises that help overcome ethnocentric tendencies.

At the same time, it is important to realize that the different classes of relatives identified in a formal kinship system may or may not be considered important in a particular society. Moreover, even when such kin categories remain important, ties of relatedness to people who are not formally kin may be as important as—or more important than—ties to formal kin. Formal kin ties are supplemented by or replaced by other forms of relatedness in many societies, and these forms of relatedness take a variety of patterns and operate at different scales. This chapter pays particular attention to local, face-to-face forms of relatedness, including friendship, kinship, and adoption.

To recognize the varied forms that institutions of human relatedness can take is to acknowledge fundamental openness in the organization of human interdependence. This openness makes possible the elaboration and extension of ties of relatedness beyond face-to-face contexts. Structures of relatedness with increasingly vast scope tend to emerge when changed historical circumstances draw people's attention to shared aspects of their lives that more intimate forms of relatedness ignore or cannot handle. New shared experiences offer raw material for the invention of new forms of common identity. Recognition of this process led political scientist Benedict Anderson to invent the term **imagined communities** to refer to "all communities larger than primordial villages of face-to-face contact (and perhaps even these)" (1983, 6). Anderson originally applied the concept of "imagined communities" to modern nation-states, but anthropologists were quick to note the range of communities included in his definition and have used the concept successfully to study different forms of human relatedness. The concept of imagined communities is important because it emphasizes that the ties that bind people into *all* supra-individual communities are *contingent*: they have not existed since the beginning of time and they may disappear in the future. Put another way, imagined communities are social, cultural, and historical constructions. They are the joint outcome of shared habitual practices and of symbolic images of common identity promulgated by group members with an interest in making a particular imagined identity endure.

definition might be the relatively "unofficial" bonds that people construct with one another. These tend to be bonds that are personal, affective, and to a varying degree from society to society, matters of choice (Bell and Coleman 1999). A recent work on friendship (Killick and Desai, 2010) argues that friendship evades definition, and that it can best be understood, at least from the perspective of the people who use the term in a particular society, as a relationship that contrasts with other ways of relating to people. One might go fishing with someone because he is your cousin, your friend, or the best fisherman in the area. For many anthropologists, particularly of an older generation, it would have been the kinship category to which attention was to be paid. Killick and Desai (2010) claim that it is essential to retain the analytic distinction between friendship and kinship, "since it is this aspect that appears to be of crucial importance in giving friendship its moral force in so many societies around the world" (Killik and Desai, Kindle location 1%). In other words, when someone from the United States says that her husband is her best friend, she is perfectly aware of the difference between the affinal relationship of husband and wife, and that of the US definition of best friend, and she uses the difference to highlight the kind of relationship she has with her husband.

In contemporary society, social networking programs like Facebook are taking friendship in new and unprecedented directions: what can it mean to have 900 friends? The line between friendship and kinship is often very fuzzy because there may be an affective quality to kinship relations (we can like our cousins and do the same things with them that we would do with friends), sometimes friends are seen after a long time as being related, and some societies have networks of relatedness that can be activated or not for reasons of sentiment, not just for pragmatic reasons. Friendship has been difficult for some anthropologists to study because in the past they have concentrated on trying to find regular, long-term patterns of social organization in societies with noncentralized forms of political organization (Bell and Coleman 1999, 4). Bell and Coleman also note that the importance of friendship seems to be increasing: "In many shifting social contexts, ties of kinship tend to be transformed and often weakened by complex and often contradictory processes of globalization. At the

What Is Friendship?

Anthropologists have devoted surprisingly little attention to **friendship**, and have found that it is no easier to define it than it is to define other such forms of relatedness as kinship or marriage. Nevertheless, a useful

imagined communities Term borrowed from political scientist Benedict Anderson to refer to groups whose members' knowledge of one another does not come from regular face-to-face interactions but is based on shared experiences with national institutions, such as schools and government bureaucracies.

friendship The relatively "unofficial" bonds that people construct with one another that tend to be personal, affective, and often a matter of choice.

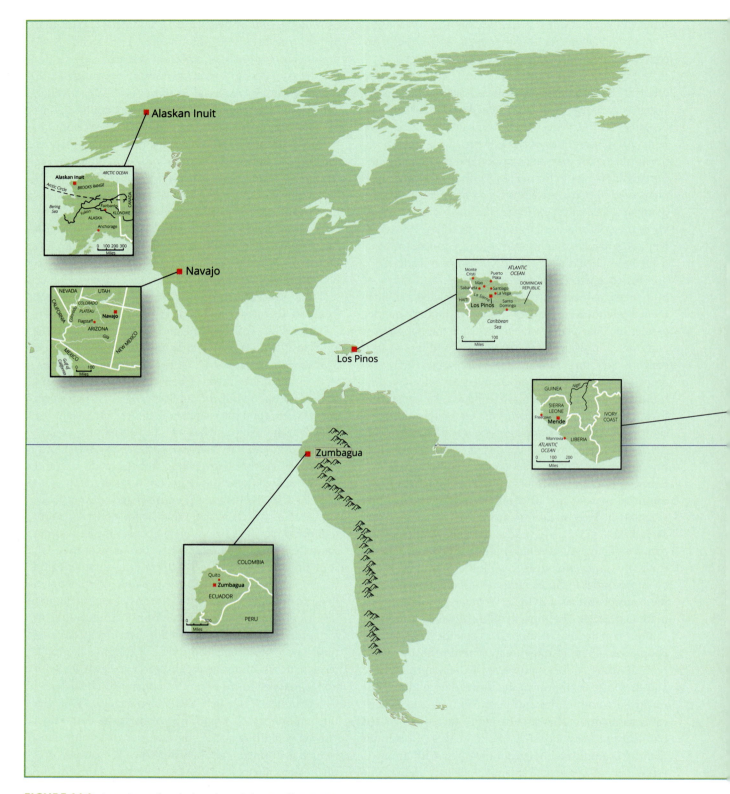

FIGURE 14.1 Locations of societies whose EthnoProfiles appear in Chapter 14.

same time new forms of friendship are emerging" (5). This is illustrated in Rio de Janeiro by Claudia Barcellos Rezende (1999), who observed the ways in which middle-class women and their maids could come to refer to each other as "friends." Within this hierarchical relationship, the distinctions that separated the women were not questioned in themselves, but the "friendship" consisted of affection, care, and consideration that both sets of women valued in their work relationship. It was a way of establishing trust: "What friendship invokes . . . is the affinity that brings these people together as parts of the same social world" (93; see Figure 14.2).

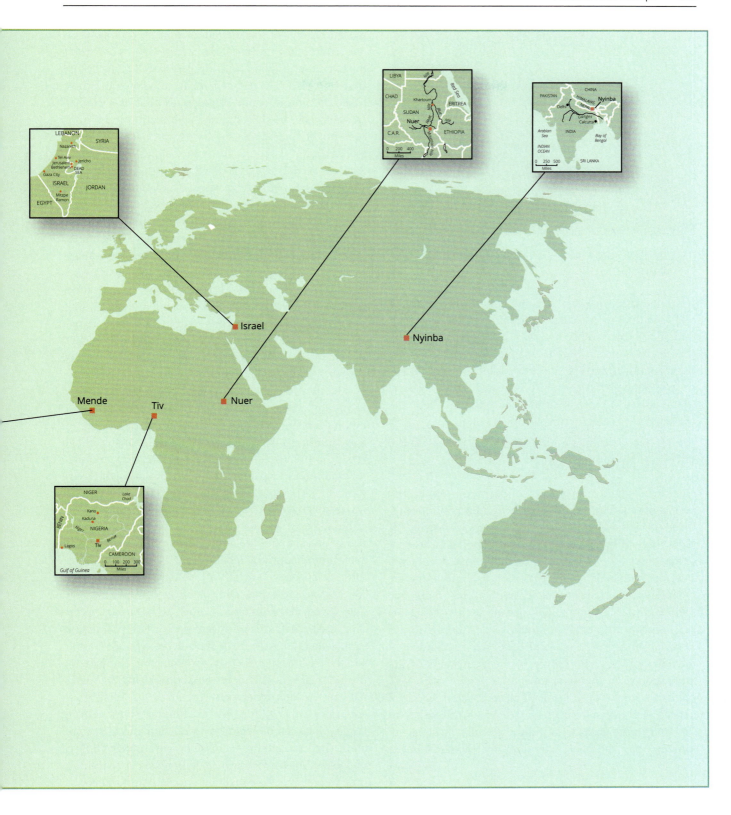

Similarly, Magnus Course directs our attention to the way in which friendship and becoming a real person—*che*—are related among the Mapuche of Chile. The Mapuche are one of the largest indigenous groups in the Americas; there are about one million in Chile and another 40,000 in Argentina. For the Mapuche,

Course asserts, conceptualization of the person is best characterized as "centrifugal"—that is to say that there is an open-ended movement through the life span outward from the kin relations that are "given" at birth to "chosen" friendship relations (Course, 72%). This is how personhood is constituted—one must go beyond

FIGURE 14.2   These two young men in Cameroon were the best of friends.

relations with one's kin that one is born into to those relations that people create through their own volition that allows them to become *che*. This, Course tells us, is the central importance of friendship in the constitution of the Mapuche person: "it is impossible to overestimate the importance of friends, as it is through the activation of the capacity to form relationships with unrelated others that one becomes a true person" (73%).

What Is Kinship?

Our case studies of friendship contrast the relationships people may develop with friends with other relationships based on kin ties. In this part of the chapter, we want to explore more fully how traditional anthropological studies of kinship contribute to our understanding of the organization of human relatedness. People struggle to find ways to preserve certain ties of relatedness over time, reinforcing them with public affirmations and gift exchanges. These practices aim to provide scaffolding for enduring forms of social solidarity that strengthen the agency that group members can exercise jointly in their encounters with other groups. At the same time, as we saw earlier, such publicly acknowledged forms of relatedness can be experienced as a burden from which individuals try to escape.

Anthropologists who study formal systems of **kinship** pay primary attention to those publicly

recognized sets of social relations that are prototypically derived from the universal human experiences of mating, birth, and nurturance. Anthropologists call relationships based on mating **marriage** (discussed below) and those based on birth **descent**. Although nurturance is ordinarily seen to be closely connected with mating and birth, it need not be, and all societies have ways of acknowledging a relationship based on nurturance alone. In the United States, this relationship is called **adoption**.

Although marriage is based on mating, descent on birth, and adoption on nurturance, marriage is not the same thing as mating, descent is not the same thing as birth, and adoption is not the same thing as nurturance. The human experiences of mating, birth, and nurturance are ambiguous. The fascinating thing about systems of relatedness is that different societies choose to highlight some features of those experiences while downplaying or even ignoring others. Europeans and North Americans know that in their societies mating is not the same as marriage, although a valid marriage encourages mating between the married partners. Similarly, all births do not constitute valid links of descent: children whose parents have not been married according to accepted legal or religious specifications do not fit the cultural logic of descent, and many societies offer no positions that they can properly fill. Finally, not all acts of nurturance are recognized as adoption: consider, for example, foster parents in the United States, whose custody of foster children is officially temporary. Put another way, through kinship, a culture emphasizes certain aspects of human experience, constructs its own theory of human nature, and specifies "the processes by which an individual comes into being and develops into a complete (i.e., mature) social person" (Kelly 1993, 521).

Marriage, descent, and adoption are thus selective. One society may emphasize women as the bearers of children and base its kinship system on this fact, paying little formal attention to the male's role in conception. Another society may trace connections through men, emphasizing the paternal role in conception and reducing the maternal role. A third society may encourage its members to adopt not only children but also adult siblings, blurring the link between biological reproduction and family creation. Even though they contradict one another, all three understandings can be justified with reference to the pan-human experiences of mating, birth, and nurturance.

Consider the North American kinship term *aunt*. This term seems to refer to a woman who occupies a unique biological position. In fact, an aunt may be related to a person in one of four different ways: as father's sister, mother's sister, father's brother's wife, or mother's brother's wife. From the perspective of North American kinship, all those women have something in common, and they are all placed into a single kinship category. Prototypically,

---

kinship Social relationships that are prototypically derived from the universal human experiences of mating, birth, and nurturance.

marriage An institution that prototypically involves a man and a woman, transforms the status of the participants, carries implications about sexual access, gives offspring a position in the society, and establishes connections between the kin of the husband and the kin of the wife.

descent The principle based on culturally recognized parent–child connections that define the social categories to which people belong.

adoption Kinship relationships based on nurturance, often in the absence of other connections based on mating or birth.

a person's aunts are women one generation older than he or she is and are sisters or sisters-in-law of a person's parents. However, North Americans may also refer to their mother's best friend as *aunt*. By doing so, they recognize the strengths of this system of classification. By way of contrast, in Chile, *tía*, the Spanish term that translates as "aunt," is regularly used by children to refer to female friends of their parents. Indeed, people well into their early adulthood continue to use the term to refer to women who are taking on the role of "mother," but with whom they are not as intimate as they would be with their own mothers. US university students living with Chilean families frequently use the term *tía* to address the woman who, in English, would be called their "host mother."

Thus, kinship is an idiom. It is a selective interpretation of the common human experiences of mating, birth, and nurturance. The result is a set of coherent principles that allow people to assign one another group membership. These principles normally cover several significant issues: how to carry out the reproduction of legitimate group members (marriage or adoption); where group members should live after marriage (residence rules); how to establish links between generations (descent); and how to pass on positions in society (succession) or material goods (inheritance). Taken together, kinship principles define social groups, locate people within those groups, and position the people and groups in relation to one another both in space and over time.

Kinship practices, rather than written statutes, clarify for people what rights and obligations they owe one another. But the first Westerners who encountered different kinship practices found some of them highly unusual. Western explorers discovered, for example, that some non-Western people distinguished among their relatives only on the basis of *age* and *sex*. To refer to people one generation older than the speaker required only two terms: one applying to men and one applying to women. The man who was married to their mother, or whom they believed to be their biological father, although known to them and personally important to them, was socially no more or less significant than that man's brothers or their mother's brothers. The explorers mistakenly concluded that these people were unable to tell the difference between their fathers and their uncles because they used the same kin term for both. They assumed that terms like *father* and *uncle* were universally recognized kinship categories. However, the people whom the explorers met were no more deluded than English speakers are when they assert that their father's sister and mother's brother's wife are equally their *aunts*.

The categories of feeling these people associated with different kin were as real as, but different from, the emotions Westerners associate with kin. "Just as the word *father* in English means a great deal more than lineal male ancestor of the first ascending generation, *aita* in Basque has many local connotations not reducible to *father*, as we understand the term" (Greenwood and Stini 1977, 333). Because the world of kin is a world of expectations and obligations, it is fundamentally a moral world charged with feeling. In some societies, a man's principal authority figure is his mother's brother, and his father is a figure of affection and unwavering support. A phrase like "God the Father" would not mean the same thing in those societies as it does in a society in which the father has life-and-death control over his children and a mother's brothers are without significant authority.

What Is the Role of Descent in Kinship?

A central aspect of kinship is descent—the cultural principle that defines social categories through culturally recognized parent–child connections. Descent groups are defined by ancestry and so exist in time. Descent involves transmission and incorporation: the transmission of membership through parent–child links and the incorporation of these people into groups. In some societies, descent group membership controls how people mobilize for social action.

Two major strategies are employed in establishing patterns of descent. In the first strategy, the descent group is formed by people who believe they are related to each other by connections made through their mothers and fathers *equally*. That is, they believe themselves to be just as related to their father's side of the family as to their mother's. Anthropologists call this **bilateral descent** (or *cognatic descent*). Two kinds of bilateral kinship groups have been identified by anthropologists. One is made up of people who claim to be related to one another through ties either from the mother's or the father's side to a common ancestor. This *bilateral descent group* is rare. The other kind, called a *bilateral kindred*, is much more common and consists of the relatives of one person or group of siblings.

The second major strategy, **unilineal descent**, is based on the assumption that the most significant kin relationships must be traced through *either* the mother *or* the father. Such descent groups are the most common kind of descent group in the world today, based on a

---

bilateral descent The principle that a descent group is formed by people who believe they are related to each other by connections made through their mothers and fathers equally (sometimes called cognatic descent).

unilineal descent The principle that a descent group is formed by people who believe they are related to each other by links made through a father or mother only.

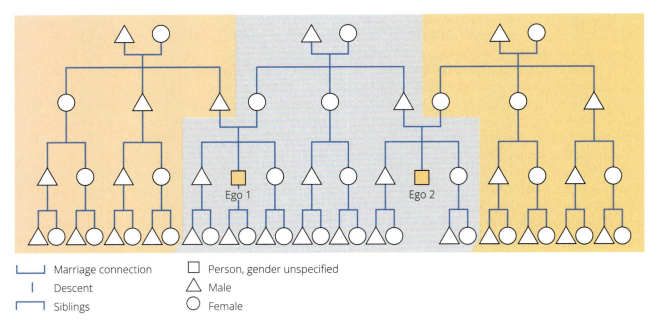

⌐⌐ Marriage connection	☐ Person, gender unspecified
│ Descent	△ Male
⌐─⌐ Siblings	○ Female

FIGURE 14.3 A bilateral kindred includes all recognized relatives on Ego's father's and mother's sides. The dark area in the center indicates where the kindreds of Ego 1 and Ego 2 overlap.

count of the number of societies that continue to employ them. Unilineal descent groups that are made up of links traced through a father are called *patrilineal*; those traced through a mother are called *matrilineal*.

Bilateral Kindreds

The **bilateral kindred** is the kinship group that most Europeans and North Americans know. This group forms around a particular individual and includes all the people linked to that individual through kin of both sexes—people conventionally called *relatives* in English. These people form a group only because of their connection to the central person or persons, known in the terminology of kinship as *Ego* (Figure 14.3). In North American society, bilateral kindreds assemble when Ego is baptized, confirmed, bar or bat mitzvahed, graduated from college, married, or buried. Each person within Ego's bilateral kindred has his or her own separate kindred. For example, Ego's father's sister's daughter has a kindred that includes people related to her through her father and his siblings—people to whom Ego is not related. This is simultaneously the major strength and major weakness of bilateral kindreds. That is, they have overlapping memberships, and they do not endure beyond the lifetime of an individual Ego. But they are widely extended and can form broad networks of people who are somehow related to one another.

A classic bilateral kindred is found among the Ju/'hoansi of the Kalahari Desert in southern Africa (see Chapter 11, "EthnoProfile 11.4: Ju/'hoansi (!Kung)"). Anthropologist Richard Lee points out that for the Ju/'hoansi, every individual in the society can be linked to every other individual by a kinship term, either through males or through females. As a result, a person can expect to find a relative everywhere there are Ju/'hoansi. When they were full-time foragers, the Ju/'hoansi lived in groups that were relatively small (10 to 30 people) but made up of a constantly changing set of individuals. "In essence, a Ju/'hoan camp consists of relatives, friends, and in-laws who have found that they can live and work well together. Under this flexible principle, brothers may be united or divided; fathers and sons may live together or apart. Further, during his or her lifetime a Ju/'hoan may live at many waterholes with many different groups" (2013, 66). A wide range of kinspeople makes this flexibility possible. When someone wanted to move, he or she had kin at many different waterholes and could choose to activate any of several appropriate kin ties.

For the Ju/'hoansi, the bilateral kindred provides social flexibility. However, flexible group boundaries become problematic in at least four kinds of social circumstances: (1) where clear-cut membership in a particular social group must be determined, (2) where social action requires the formation of groups that are larger than individual families, (3) where conflicting claims to land and labor must be resolved, and (4) where people are concerned to perpetuate a particular social order over time. In societies that face these dilemmas, unilineal descent groups are usually formed.

bilateral kindred A kinship group that consists of the relatives of one person or group of siblings.

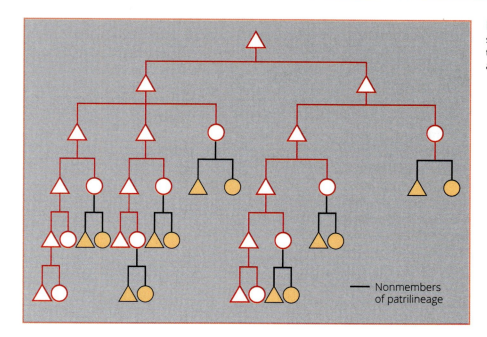

FIGURE 14.4 Patrilineal descent: All those who trace descent through males to a common male ancestor are indicated in white.

— Nonmembers of patrilineage

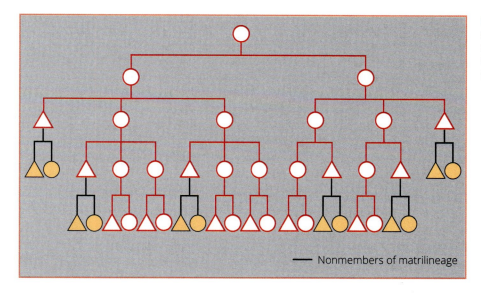

FIGURE 14.5 Matrilineal descent: All those who trace descent through females to a common female ancestor are indicated in white.

— Nonmembers of matrilineage

What Role Do Lineages Play in Descent?

Unilineal descent groups are found all over the world. They are all based on the principle that certain kinds of parent–child relationships are more important than others. Membership in a *unilineal descent group* is based on the membership of the appropriate parent in the group. In patrilineal systems, an individual belongs to a group formed through male sex links, the lineage of his or her father. In matrilineal systems, an individual belongs to a group formed by links through women, the lineage of his or her mother. *Patrilineal* and *matrilineal* do not mean that only men belong to one and women to the other; rather, the terms refer to the principle by which membership is conferred. In a patrilineal society, women and men belong to a **patrilineage** formed by father–child links (Figure 14.4); similarly, in a matrilineal society, men and women belong to a **matrilineage** formed by mother–child connections (Figure 14.5). In other words, membership in the group is, on the face of it, unambiguous. An individual belongs to only one lineage. This is in contrast to a bilateral kindred, in which an individual belongs to overlapping groups.

---

patrilineage A social group formed by people connected by father–child links.

matrilineage A social group formed by people connected by mother–child links.

The *-lineal* in patrilineal and matrilineal refers to the nature of the social group formed. These **lineages** are composed of people who believe they can specify the parent–child links that unite them. Although the abstract kinship diagrams that anthropologists draw include just a few people, lineages in the world vary in size, ranging from 20 or 30 members to several hundred. Before 1949, some Chinese lineages were composed of more than 1,000 members.

Lineage Membership

The most important feature of lineages is that they are *corporate* in organization—that is, a lineage has a single legal personality. As the Ashanti put it, a lineage is "one person" (Fortes 1953). To outsiders, all members of a lineage are equal *in law* to all others. For example, in the case of a blood feud, the death of any opposing lineage member avenges the death of the person who started the feud. Lineages are also corporate in that they control property, especially land, as a unit. Such groups are found in societies where rights to use land are crucial and must be monitored over time.

Lineages are also the main political associations in the societies that have them. Individuals have no political or legal status in such societies except through lineage membership. They have relatives outside the lineage, but their own political and legal status comes through the lineage.

Because membership in a lineage comes through a direct line from father or mother to child, lineages can endure over time and in a sense have an independent existence. As long as people can remember from whom they are descended, lineages can endure. Most lineages have a time depth of about five generations: grandparents, parents, Ego, children, and grandchildren. When members of a group believe that they can no longer accurately specify the genealogical links that connect them but believe that they are "in some way" connected, we find what anthropologists call *clans*.

A **clan** is usually made up of lineages that the society's members believe to be related to each other through links that go back into mythic times. Sometimes the common ancestor of each clan is said to be an animal that lived at the beginning of time. The important point is that lineage members can specify all the generational links back to their common ancestor, whereas clan members ordinarily cannot. The clan is thus larger

EthnoProfile 14.1

Tiv

Region: Western Africa

Nation: Nigeria (northern)

Population: 800,000

Environment: Undulating plain–wooded foothills to sandbanks

Livelihood: Farming

Political organization: Traditionally egalitarian; today, part of a modern nation-state

For more information: Bohannon, Laura, and Paul Bohannon, 1969. *The Tiv of central Nigeria.* 2d ed. London, International African Institute.

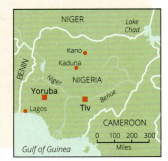

than any lineage and also more diffuse in both membership and the hold it has over individuals.

The Logic of Lineage Relationships

Lineages endure over time in societies in which no other form of organization lasts. Hence, they provide for the "perpetual exercise of defined rights, duties, office and social tasks vested in the lineage" (Fortes 1953, 165). In other words, in the societies where they are found, the system of lineages becomes the foundation of social life.

While lineages might look solid and unchanging, they are often more flexible than they appear. The memories people have of their ancestry are often transmitted in the form of myth or legend. Rather than accurate historical records, they are better understood in Malinowskian terms as mythical charters, justifications from the invisible world for the visible arrangements of the society (see the discussion of myth in Chapter 10).

In showing how this relationship works, Fortes (1953, 165) quotes anthropologists Paul and Laura Bohannan, whose research was among the Tiv of Nigeria (see "EthnoProfile 14.1: Tiv"). The Bohannans observed that Tiv, who had not previously viewed one another as kin, sometimes renegotiated their lineage relationships, announcing publicly that they shared some of the same ancestors. Such changes were plausible to the Tiv because they assumed that traditional lineage relationships determined current social arrangements. If current social arrangements and tradition conflicted, therefore, the Tiv concluded that errors had crept into the tradition. Such renegotiation enabled the

---

lineages The consanguineal members of descent groups who believe they can trace their descent from known ancestors.

clan A descent group formed by members who believe they have a common (sometimes mythical) ancestor, even if they cannot specify the genealogical links.

EthnoProfile 14.2

Nuer

Region: Eastern Africa

Nation: Ethiopia and Sudan

Population: 300,000

Environment: Open grassland

Livelihood: Cattle herding and farming

Political organization: Traditionally, egalitarian tribes, no political offices; today, part of modern nation-states

For more information: Evans-Pritchard, E. E. 1940. *The Nuer.* Oxford: Oxford University Press; and Hutchinson, Sharon. 1996. *Nuer dilemmas.* Berkeley: University of California Press.

Tiv to keep their lineage relationships in line with changing legal and political relationships.

What Are Patrilineages?

By far the most common form of lineage organization is the patrilineage, which consists of all the people (male and female) who believe themselves related to each other because they are related to a common male ancestor by links through men. The prototypical kernel of a patrilineage is the father–son pair. Women members of patrilineages normally leave the lineages when they marry, but they do not relinquish their interest in their own lineages. In a number of societies, they play an active role in the affairs of their own patrilineages for many years.

A classic patrilineal system was found among the Nuer of the Sudan and Ethiopia (see "EthnoProfile 14.2: Nuer"). At the time of his fieldwork in the 1930s, English anthropologist E. E. Evans-Pritchard noted that the Nuer were divided into at least 20 clans. Evans-Pritchard defined *clan* as the largest group of people who (1) trace their descent patrilineally from a common ancestor, (2) cannot marry each other, and (3) consider sexual relations within the group to be incestuous. The clan is divided, or segmented, into lineages that are themselves linked to each other by presumed ties of patrilineal descent. The most basic stage of lineage segmentation is the *minimal lineage,* which has a time depth of three to five generations.

Evans-Pritchard observed that the Nuer kinship system worked in the following way: members of lineages

A and B might consider themselves related because they believed that the founder of lineage A had been the older brother of the founder of lineage B. These two *minimal lineages,* as Evans-Pritchard called them, together formed a *minor lineage*—all those descended from a common father, believed to be the father of the two founders of A and B. Minor lineages connect to other minor lineages by yet another presumed common ancestor, forming *major lineages.* These major lineages are also believed to share a common ancestor and thus form a *maximal lineage.* The members of two maximal lineages believe their founders had been the sons of the clan ancestor; thus, all members of the clan are believed to be patrilineally related.

According to Evans-Pritchard, disputes among the Nuer emerged along the lines created by lineages. Suppose a quarrel erupted between two men whose minimal lineages were in different minor lineages. Each would be joined by men who belonged to his minor lineage, even if they were not in his minimal lineage. The dispute would be resolved when the quarreling minor lineages recognized that they were all part of the same major lineage. Similarly, the minor lineages to one major lineage would ally if a dispute with an opposed major lineage broke out. This process of groups coming together and opposing one another, called **segmentary opposition**, is expressed in kinship terms but represents a very common social process.

Evans-Pritchard noted that lineages were important to the Nuer for political purposes. Members of the same lineage in the same village were conscious of being in a social group with common ancestors and symbols, corporate rights in territory, and common interests in cattle. When a son in the lineage married, these people helped provide the **bridewealth** cattle. If the son were killed, they—indeed, all members of his patrilineage, regardless of where they lived—would avenge him and would hold the funeral ceremony for him. Nevertheless, relationships among the members of a patrilineage were not necessarily harmonious:

> A Nuer is bound to his paternal kin from whom he derives aid, security, and status, but in return for these benefits he has many obligations and commitments. Their often indefinite character may be both evidence of, and a reason for, their force, but it also gives ample scope for disagreement. Duties and rights

---

segmentary opposition A mode of hierarchical social organization in which groups beyond the most basic emerge only in opposition to other groups on the same hierarchical level.

bridewealth The transfer of certain symbolically important goods from the family of the groom to the family of the bride on the occasion of their marriage. It represents compensation to the wife's lineage for the loss of her labor and childbearing capacities.

easily conflict. Moreover, the privileges of [patrilineal] kinship cannot be divorced from authority, discipline, and a strong sense of moral obligation, all of which are irksome to Nuer. They do not deny them, but they kick against them when their personal interests run counter to them. (1951, 162)

Although the Nuer were patrilineal, they recognized as kin people who were not members of their lineage. In the Nuer language, the word *mar* referred to "kin": all the people to whom a person could trace a relationship of any kind, including people on the mother's side as well as those on the father's side. In fact, at such important ceremonial occasions as a bridewealth distribution after a woman in the lineage had been married, special attention was paid to kin on the mother's side. Certain important relatives, such as the mother's brother and the mother's sister, were given cattle. A man's mother's brother was his great supporter when he was in trouble. The mother's brother was kind to him as a boy and even provided a second home after he reached manhood. If he liked his sister's son, a mother's brother would even be willing to help pay the bridewealth so that he could marry. "Nuer say of the maternal uncle that he is both father and mother, but most frequently that 'he is your mother'" (Evans-Pritchard 1951, 162). [1]

What Are Matrilineages?

In matrilineages, descent is traced through women rather than through men. Recall that in a patrilineage, a woman's children are not in her lineage. In a matrilineage, a man's children are not in his. However, certain features of matrilineages make them more than just mirror images of patrilineages.

First, the prototypical kernel of a matrilineage is the sister–brother pair; a matrilineage may be thought of as a group of brothers and sisters connected through links made by women. Brothers marry out and often live with the family of their wives, but they maintain an active interest in the affairs of their lineage. Second, the most important man in a boy's life is not his father (who is not in his lineage) but his mother's brother, from whom he will receive his lineage inheritance. Third, the amount of power women exercise in matrilineages is still being hotly debated in anthropology. A matrilineage is not the same thing as a *matriarchy* (a society in which women rule); brothers often retain what appears to be a controlling interest in the lineage. Some anthropologists claim that the male members of a matrilineage are supposed to run the lineage even though there is more autonomy

for women in matrilineal societies than in patrilineal ones—that the day-to-day exercise of power tends to be carried out by the brothers or sometimes the husbands. A number of studies, however, have questioned the validity of these generalizations. Trying to say something about matrilineal societies in general is difficult. The ethnographic evidence suggests that matrilineages must be examined on a case-by-case basis.

The Navajo are a matrilineal people (see "EthnoProfile 14.3: Navajo"). Traditionally, the basic unit of Navajo social organization is the subsistence residential unit composed of a head mother, her husband, and some of their children with their spouses and children (Witherspoon 1975, 82). The leader of the unit is normally a man, usually the husband of the head mother. He directs livestock and agricultural operations and is the one who deals with the outside world: "He speaks for the unit at community meetings, negotiates with the traders and car salesmen, arranges marriages and ceremonies, talks to visiting strangers, and so on" (82). (Contemporary Navajo women may not be involved in livestock and agricultural operations at all, finding professional and salaried careers outside the residential unit.) He seems to be in charge. But it is the head mother around whom the unit is organized:

[The head mother] is identified with the land, the herd, and the agricultural fields. All residence rights can be traced back to her, and her opinions and wishes are always given the greatest consideration and usually prevail. In a sense, however, she delegates much of her role and prestige to the leader of the unit. If we think of the unit as a corporation, and the leader as its president, the head

[1] Readers interested in what has happened to Nuer kinship and relatedness as a consequence of the seemingly unending civil war in the Sudan should look at Hutchinson 1996 or 2002.

mother will be the chairman of the board. She usually has more sheep than the leader does. Because the power and importance of the head mother offer a deceptive appearance to the observer, many students of the Navajo have failed to see the importance of her role. But if one has lived a long time in one of these units, one soon becomes aware of who ultimately has the cards and directs the game. When there is a divorce between the leader and the head, it is always the leader who leaves and the head mother who returns, even if the land originally belonged to the mother of the leader. (82–83)

Overall, evidence from matrilineal societies reveals some domains of experience in which men and women are equal, some in which men are in control, and some in which women are in control. Observers and participants may disagree about which of these domains of experience is more or less central to Navajo life.

What Are Kinship Terminologies?

People everywhere use special terms to refer to people they recognize as related to them. Despite the variety of kinship systems in the world, anthropologists have identified six major patterns of kinship terminology based on how people categorize their cousins. The six patterns reflect common solutions to structural problems faced by societies organized in terms of kinship. They provide clues concerning how the vast and undifferentiated world of potential kin may be divided up. Kinship terminologies suggest both the external boundaries and the internal divisions of the kinship groups, and they outline the structure of rights and obligations assigned to different members of the society.

What Criteria Are Used for Making Kinship Distinctions?

Anthropologists have identified several criteria that people use to indicate how people are related to one another. From the most common to the least common, these criteria include the following:

- *Generation*. Kin terms distinguish relatives according to the generation to which the relatives belong. In English, the term *cousin* conventionally refers to someone of the same generation as Ego.
- *Gender*. The gender of an individual is used to differentiate kin. In Spanish, *primo* refers to a male cousin and *prima* to a female cousin. In English, cousins are not distinguished on the basis of gender, but *uncle* and *aunt* are distinguished on the basis of both generation and gender.

- *Affinity*. A distinction is made on the basis of connection through marriage, or **affinity**. This criterion is used in Spanish when *suegra* (Ego's spouse's mother) is distinguished from *madre* (Ego's mother). In matrilineal societies, Ego's mother's sister and father's sister are distinguished from one another on the basis of affinity. The mother's sister is a direct, lineal relative; the father's sister is an affine; and they are called by different terms.
- *Collaterality*. A distinction is made between kin who are believed to be in a direct line and those who are "off to one side," linked to Ego through a lineal relative. In English, the distinction of **collaterality** is exemplified by the distinction between mother and aunt or father and uncle.
- *Bifurcation*. The distinction of **bifurcation** is employed when kinship terms referring to the mother's side of the family differ from those referring to the father's side.
- *Relative age*. Relatives of the same category may be distinguished on the basis of whether they are older or younger than Ego. Among the Ju/'hoansi, for example, speakers must separate "older brother" (*!ko*) from "younger brother" (*tsin*).
- *Gender of linking relative*. This criterion is related to collaterality. It distinguishes *cross relatives* (usually cousins) from *parallel relatives* (also usually cousins). Parallel relatives are linked through two brothers or two sisters. **Parallel cousins**, for example, are Ego's father's brother's children or mother's sister's children. Cross relatives are linked through a brother–sister pair. Thus, **cross cousins** are Ego's mother's brother's children or father's sister's children. The gender of either Ego or the cousins does not matter; rather, the important factor is the gender of the linking relative (Figure 14.6).

By the early 1950s, kinship specialists in anthropology had identified six major patterns of kinship terminology, based on how cousins were classified. In recent years, however, anthropologists have become quite skeptical of the value of these idealized models, in large measure because they are highly formalized and do not capture the full range of people's actual practices.

affinity Connection through marriage.

collaterality A criterion employed in the analysis of kinship terminologies in which a distinction is made between kin who are believed to be in a direct line and those who are "off to one side," linked to the speaker by a lineal relative.

bifurcation A criterion employed in the analysis of kinship terminologies in which kinship terms referring to the mother's side of the family are distinguished from those referring to the father's side.

parallel cousins The children of a person's parents' same-gender siblings (a father's brother's children or a mother's sister's children).

cross cousins The children of a person's parents' opposite-gender siblings (a father's sister's children or a mother's brother's children)

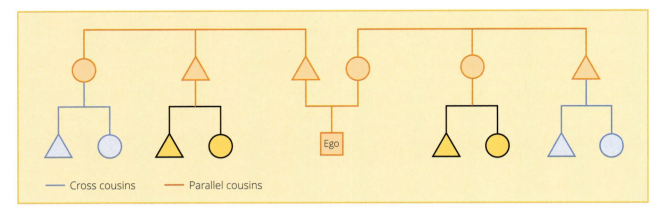

— Cross cousins   — Parallel cousins

FIGURE 14.6 Cross cousins and parallel cousins: Ego's cross cousins are the children of Ego's father's sister and mother's brother. Ego's parallel cousins are the children of Ego's father's brother and mother's sister.

Perhaps the main value to come from formal kinship studies is the fact that they took seriously the ways other people classified their relatives and were able to show the logic that informed such classifications. On the model of language, the set of kinship terms can be derived from a small number of principles that direct our attention to the important categories in a society.

What Is Adoption?

Kinship systems may appear to be fairly rigid sets of rules that use the accident of birth to thrust people into social positions laden with rights and obligations they cannot escape. Social positions that people are assigned at birth are sometimes called **ascribed statuses**, and positions within a kinship system have long been viewed as the prototypical ascribed statuses in any society. Ascribed statuses are often contrasted with **achieved statuses**, those social positions that people may attain later in life, often as the result of their own (or other people's) effort, such as becoming a spouse or college graduate. All societies have ways of incorporating outsiders into their kinship groups, however, which they achieve by converting supposedly ascribed kinship statuses into achieved ones, thus undermining the distinction between them. We use the term *adoption* to refer to these practices, which allow people to transform relationships based on nurturance into relations of kinship.

Adoption in Highland Ecuador

Mary Weismantel is an anthropologist who carried out fieldwork among indigenous farmers living outside the

ascribed statuses Social positions people are assigned at birth.
achieved statuses Social positions people may attain later in life, often as the result of their own (or other people's) effort.

EthnoProfile 14.4

Zumbagua

Region: South America

Nation: Ecuador

Population: 20,000 (parish)

Environment: Andean mountain valley

Livelihood: Farming

Political organization: Peasant village and parish in modern nation-state

For more information: Weismantel, Mary. 2001. *Food, gender, and poverty in the Ecuadorian Andes.* Prospect Heights, IL: Waveland Press.

community of Zumbagua, in highland Ecuador (1995; see "EthnoProfile 14.4: Zumbagua"). The farmers' households were based on lifelong heterosexual relationships, but she discovered that Zumbaguans recognized kin ties that were very different from those found in Euro-American cultures. Most striking was her discovery that every adult seemed to have several kinds of parents and several kinds of children.

In some societies, like that of ancient Rome, people distinguish between Ego's biological father (or *genitor*) and social father (or *pater*); they may also distinguish between Ego's biological mother (or *genetrix*) and social mother (or *mater*). Social parents are those who nurture a child, and they are often the child's biological parents as well. Zumbaguans use the Quichua term *tayta* for both genitor and pater and *mama* for both genetrix and mater. In their society, however, genitor, pater, genetrix, and mater are often entirely different people.

Weismantel learned that this use of kin terms was related to local forms of adoption, most of which occur within the family. In 1991, for example, a young girl named Nancy moved into the household of her father Alfonso's prosperous, unmarried older sister, Heloisa, whom Nancy called *tía* (aunt). By 1993, however, Nancy was calling Heloisa *mama*. Everyone concerned viewed this transition positively, a way of strengthening family solidarity in a difficult economic situation, and no one seemed worried about whether Heloisa was Nancy's natural mother.

People often also adopted children who were not kin. In both cases, however, the bond of adoption was created through nurturing, symbolized by the provision of food. Heloisa became Nancy's adoptive *mama* because she took care of her, fed her. Men in Zumbagua can also become the adoptive *tayta* of children by feeding them in front of witnesses who verbally proclaim what a "good father" the man is. However, the adoptive relationship does not gain recognition unless the adoptive parent continues feeding the child regularly for a long time. Weismantel discovered that the Zumbaguan family consists of those who eat together. The kinship bond results, they believe, because people who regularly eat the same food together eventually come to share "the same flesh," no matter who gave birth to them. Weismantel points out that feeding children is every bit as biological as giving birth to them: it is simply a different aspect of biology.

Indeed, in Zumbagua, a woman's biological tie to her offspring is given no greater weight than a man's biological tie to his. Many Zumbaguans are closer to their adopted family than they are to their biological parents. If genitor and genetrix are young and poor, moreover, they run a very real risk that they will lose their children to adoption by older, wealthier individuals. In other words, enduring kin ties in Zumbagua are achieved, not merely ascribed, statuses.

What Is the Relation between Adoption and Child Circulation in the Andes?

Adoption in Zumbagua, Ecuador, is a regional example of widespread Andean relatedness practices that involve the movement of children from one household to another as they grow up. Anthropologist Jessaca Leinaweaver, who carried out field research in Ayacucho, Peru, calls these patterns *child circulation*. In her view,

child circulation is "a deliberate method of strengthening social ties, building an affective network that will remain key as a child matures into a world of poverty and distinction, and redistributing both the pleasures and constraints of parenting and being a child" (2008, 4). Although there are no official statistics to describe the frequency of child circulation in Andean societies, expressions referring to these practices can be found in indigenous languages as well as in Spanish; and child circulation has been described in the ethnographies of numerous anthropologists working in the Andes. Child circulation appears to have roots in indigenous, kin-based, community structures such as the Inka *ayllu*. In the devastating aftermath of the Spanish conquest, such kin structures were undermined but did not disappear and were reformulated in different ways.

Leinaweaver emphasizes the difference between child circulation and two other forms of child movement recognized in contemporary Peru: child trafficking and adoption. Child trafficking involves "removing children from their natal homes for destinations unknown," a criminal operation that the Peruvian national government opposes (2008, 4). Child circulation is also different from what the Peruvian government calls adoption; that is, state-backed practices whereby children are "legally severed from their natal families before their incorporation into a new and approved family can take place" (2008, 8). This legal definition of adoption is supported by Peru's 1992 Code of the Child and Adolescent. Based on international agreements such as the 1990 United Nations Convention on the Rights of the Child, the 1992 Code states that adoptions in Peru shall be directed by the principle of the "best interests of the child and adolescent" (2008, 52). Leinaweaver does not doubt that Peruvians are sincere when they celebrate and defend children's rights. However, she points out that the "best interests of the child" principle derives from middle-class Western views about what counts as a proper childhood (2008, 53–54). As such, she argues, it does not reflect local, indigenous understandings about children, their rights, and their responsibilities, especially as materialized in practices of child circulation.

The principles underlying child circulation can be found in the widespread Latin American practice of *compadrazgo* (discussed later in this chapter). Leinaweaver and her partner were frequently asked to serve as godparents at important life cycle events for the children of people they knew, and came to understand that this was an accepted way for their friends in Ayacucho to incorporate outsiders into their kin group. Godparents take on new responsibilities, especially financial ones, in relation to their godchildren. At the same time, as one woman with four godchildren told Leinaweaver, becoming a godparent gives people "more family." In this way, *compadrazgo*—like other forms of child circulation "is a key producer of social life" (2008, 8).

Leinaweaver learned about the moral principles associated with child circulation from the life histories of Ayacuchanos who had been circulated as children. They described a child who moved into the homes of a more prosperous relative in order "to accompany" (*acompañar*) that person, particularly when the older relative would otherwise be living alone. A child who "accompanied" an older person in this way would perform chores children usually carried out in poor indigenous households, in return for which they would receive room and board and a small amount of money, which they described as a "tip" or "allowance" rather than a wage. In return, child companions relieved the loneliness of the people they "kept company" while gaining the opportunity to attend better schools and learn more sophisticated urban customs. For poor indigenous families, Leinaweaver argues, child circulation possesses "an unassailable cultural logic" (2008, 4). This logic, however, is often not apparent to Peruvians from higher social classes. For example, one well-to-do woman Leinaweaver knew conceded that circulated children might be treated better than hired servants, but insisted that "they do not treat the godchild like their own child, because they make him do chores, which is wrong. For her, there can only be coddled children or maids; anything between is ambiguous and exploitative. *Acompañar* is uncomfortable or even unacceptable to outside observers (2008, 94).

Despite hardships and loneliness, Leinaweaver's interviewees regularly described their experience of child circulation as necessary for their own self-betterment, or *superación*. Self-betterment is an important goal for children from poor, indigenous families and, Leinaweaver argues, is tightly bound up with institutionalized Peruvian racism, which stigmatizes rural indigenous people for their poverty, illiteracy, and "backward" customs. Many indigenous people accept this devaluation, and use child circulation as a way to offer their children a chance to better themselves by shedding traditional ways and adopting customs associated with Spanish-speaking, middle-class, urban life.

During the 1980s, life in the Peruvian highlands was severely disrupted by the insurgent left-wing movement known as Shining Path (Sendero Luminoso), which began in Ayacucho and became known for its extreme brutality. When the Peruvian army was sent into the highlands to crush Shining Path, indigenous people were frequently targeted by both sides, and entire communities were wiped out. By the 1990s, as the violence lessened, for the first time, orphanages were set up in the Peruvian highlands. Prior to the years of violence,

Leinaweaver suggests, the category of "orphan" as a child whose parents had died would not have made sense for indigenous people, for they would have found homes for such children by means of child circulation. Today, however, in the aftermath of brutal community destruction, indigenous families' capacities to care for or circulate children appear to have been overwhelmed, with the result that many children have ended up in orphanages.

Since the end of the war, many couples from Europe and the United States have sought to adopt the children in Peruvian orphanages. However, the 1992 Peruvian adoption law insists that children may not be adopted unless they have first legally been certified as "abandoned." Leinaweaver found that officials concerned with adoption procedures, especially social workers, took a long time to make sure that any child in an orphanage had truly been abandoned by its parents. The social workers Leinaweaver knew understood that poor indigenous children often ended up in orphanages for reasons other than abandonment. In a country like Peru, where social safety nets for poor people have been seriously undermined by neoliberal economic reforms as well as by war, the orphanage has come to serve as a refuge where many desperate poor parents might "circulate" a child temporarily if, for reasons beyond their control, neither they nor their relations are able to care for that child. As with child circulation more generally, indigenous parents rarely intend to abandon their children permanently, often visiting and eventually taking them back home when their situations stabilize. Nevertheless, relying on an orphanage can be risky for indigenous parents because it "does not provide a site for the child or her parents to reciprocate these immense gifts of food, shelter, care, and education. To use the orphanage is, in this sense, amoral. Where Andean morality is rooted in reciprocity . . . an orphanage only gives" (2008, 80). Orphanages in highland Peru thus offer another early twentieth-century instance of what anthropologist Didier Fassin calls "humanitarian reason" (see Chapter 15).

How Flexible Can Relatedness Be?

Negotiation of Kin Ties among the Ju/'hoansi

Michael Peletz observes that many contemporary kinship studies in anthropology "tend to devote considerable analytic attention to themes of contradiction, paradox and ambivalence" (1995, 343). This is true both of Weismantel's study in Zumbagua and of Richard Lee's analysis of kinship among the Ju/'hoansi. Lee learned that for the Ju/'hoansi "the principles of kinship constitute, not an invariant code of laws written in stone, but instead a whole series of codes, consistent enough to provide structure but open enough to be flexible." He adds: "I found the best way to look at [Ju/'hoansi] kinship is as a game, full of ambiguity and nuance" (2013, 67).

The Ju/'hoansi have what seems to be a straightforward bilateral kindred with alternating generations. Outside the nuclear core of the system, the same terms are used by Ego for kin of his or her generation, his or her grandparents' generation, and his or her grandchildren's generation. Likewise, the same terms are used for Ego's parents' generation and children's generation. These terms have behavioral correlates, which Lee calls "joking" and "avoidance." Anyone in Ego's own generation (except opposite-gender siblings) and in the grandparents' generation or the grandchildren's generation is joking kin. Anyone in Ego's parents' generation or children's generation is avoidance kin, as are Ego's same-gender siblings. Relatives in a joking relationship can be relaxed and affectionate and can speak using familiar forms. In an avoidance relationship, however, respect and reserve are required, and formal language must be used. Many of these relationships may be warm and friendly if the proper respect is shown in public: however, people in an avoidance relationship may not marry one another.

The "game," as Lee puts it, in the Ju/'hoansi system begins when a child is named. The Ju/'hoansi have very few names: 36 for men and 32 for women. Every child must be named for someone: A first-born son should get his father's father's name and a first-born daughter her father's mother's name. Second-born children are supposed to be named after the mother's father and mother. Later children are named after the father's brothers and sisters and the mother's brothers and sisters. It is no wonder that the Ju/'hoansi invent a host of nicknames to distinguish among people who have the same name. Ju/'hoansi naming practices impinge on the kinship system because all people with the same name will claim to be related. A man older than you with your name is called *!kun!a* ("old name"), which is the same term used for *grandfather*. A man younger than you with your name is called *!kuna* ("young name"), the same term used for *grandson*. It does not matter how people are "really" related to others with the same name or even if they are related at all according to formal kinship terminology; the name relationship takes precedence.

But the complications do not end here. By metaphorical extension, anyone with your father's name you call *father*, anyone with your wife's name you call *wife*, and so on. Worse, "a woman may not marry a man with her father's or brother's name, and a man may not marry a woman with his mother's or sister's name" (Lee 2013, 79). Sometimes a man can marry a woman, but because his name is the same as her father's, she can't marry him! Further, you may not marry anyone with the name of one of your avoidance kin. As a result, parents who do not want their children to marry can almost always find a kinship-related reason to block the marriage. Once again, it does not matter what the exact genealogical relationships are.

The name relationship ties Ju/'hoansi society closer together by making close relatives out of distant ones. At the same time, it makes nonsense of the formal kinship system. How is this dilemma resolved? The Ju/'hoansi have a third component to their kinship system, the principle of *wi*, which operates as follows: relative age is one of the few ways the Ju/'hoansi have of marking distinctions. Thus, in any relationship that can be described by more than one kin relationship, the older party chooses the kin term to be used. For example, a man may get married only to discover that his wife's aunt's husband has the same name he has. What will he and his wife's aunt call each other? According to the principle of *wi*, the aunt decides because she is older. If she calls him *nephew* (rather than *husband*), he knows to call her *aunt*.

The principle of *wi* means that a person's involvement with the kinship system is continually changing over the course of his or her lifetime. For the first half of people's lives, they must accept the kin terms their elders choose, whether they understand why or not. After midlife, however, they begin to impose *wi* on their juniors. For the Ju/'hoansi, kinship connections are open to manipulation and negotiation rather than being rigidly imposed from the outside.

Euro-American Kinship and New Reproductive Technologies

Western medicine has developed new reproductive technologies, such as in vitro fertilization, sperm banks, and surrogate motherhood, that are creating challenges not only for law and morality, but also for Western concepts of kinship (Figure 14.7). Marilyn Strathern (1992) observes that in the Euro-American world, kinship is understood as the social construction of natural facts, a logic that both combines and separates the social and natural worlds. That is, Euro-Americans recognize kin related by blood and kin related by marriage, but they also believe that the process—procreation—that brings kin into existence is part of nature. "The rooting of social relations in natural facts traditionally served to impart a certain quality to one significant dimension of kin relations. For all that one exercised choice, it was also the case that these relations were at base non-negotiable" (Strathern 1992, 28).

FIGURE 14.7   In vitro fertilization (IVF), one of the new reproductive technologies, is already having an effect on what it means to be a "natural" parent. Over 1,000 IVF babies gathered in 2003 to celebrate the twenty-fifth anniversary of the birth of the first IVT baby, Louise Brown (center front).

Ties of kinship are supposed to stand for what is unalterable in a person's social world in contrast to what is open to change. Yet the new reproductive technologies make clear that nothing is unalterable: even the world of natural facts is subject to social intervention.

As Janet Dolgin (1995) reports, contemporary ambiguities surrounding kinship in the United States have put pressure on the courts to decide what constitutes biological parenthood and how it is related to legal parenthood. She examined two sets of cases, the first involving the paternal rights of unwed putative fathers and the second focusing on the rights of parties involved in surrogate motherhood agreements. In two cases involving putative unwed fathers, courts reasoned that biological maternity automatically made a woman a social mother but biological paternity did not automatically make a man a social father. Because the men in these two cases had failed to participate in rearing their children, their paternity rights were not recognized. In another case, the biological father had lived with his child and her mother for extended periods during the child's early years and had actively participated in her upbringing. However, the child's mother had been married to another man during this period, and the law proclaimed her legal husband to be the child's father. Although the genitor had

established a supportive relationship with his daughter, the court labeled him "the adulterous natural father," arguing, in effect, that a genitor can never be a pater unless he is involved in an ongoing relationship with the child's mother, something that was clearly impossible because she was already married to someone else.

The surrogacy cases demonstrate directly the complications that can result from new reproductive technologies. The "Baby M" situation was a traditional surrogacy arrangement in which the surrogate, Mary Beth Whitehead, was impregnated with the sperm of the husband in the couple who intended to become the legal parents of the child she bore. Whitehead was supposed to terminate all parental rights when the child was born, but she refused to do so. The court faced a dilemma. Existing law backed Whitehead's maternal rights, but the court was also concerned that the surrogacy agreement looked too much like baby selling or womb rental. The court's opinion focused on Whitehead's attempt to break the surrogacy contract to justify terminating her legal rights, although she was awarded visitation rights.

More complicated than traditional surrogacy, *gestational surrogacy* deconstructs the role of genetrix into two roles that can be performed by two different women. In a key case, the Calverts, a childless married couple, provided egg and sperm that were used in the laboratory to create an embryo, which was then implanted in Anna Johnson's uterus. But when Johnson gave birth to the baby, she refused to give it up. As Dolgin points out, this case "provided a context in which to measure the generality of the assumption that the gestational role both produces and constitutes maternity" (1995, 58). As we have seen, several other court cases emphasized the role of gestation in forming an indissoluble bond between mother and child. In this case, however, the court referred to Anna Johnson "as a 'gestational carrier,' a 'genetic hereditary stranger' to the child, who acted like a 'foster parent'" (59). The court declared the Calverts and the child were a family unit on genetic grounds and ruled that the Calverts were the baby's "natural" and legal parents.

Dolgin notes that in all of these cases, the courts awarded legal custody to those parties whose living arrangements most closely approximated the traditional middle-class, North American two-parent family. "Biological facts were called into judicial play only . . . when they justified the preservation of traditional families" (1995, 63). Biological facts that might have undermined such families were systematically overlooked. Perhaps the clear-cut biological basis of North American kinship is not so clear-cut after all.

Assisted Reproduction in Israel

Similar unanticipated trajectories that derive from our systems of relatedness are being opened by recent biotechnological advances, such as assisted reproduction; these practices are already transforming and complicating traditional understandings of human connectedness in any society that adopts them. For example, studying assisted reproduction in Israel (see "EthnoProfile 14.5: Israel") led Susan Martha Kahn to ask whether Jewish ideas about kinship are or are not usefully understood as "Euro-American," especially since Jews have lived for millennia within the boundaries of many different societies outside Europe and America. Within Israel itself, Euro-American ideas about kinship coexist with other ideas from elsewhere that developed among different Jewish populations long before the state of Israel was founded; moreover, "multiple and often contradictory popular opinions about these matters have always simultaneously coexisted, competed, and conflicted with each other" (Kahn 2000, 161–62). This means that it is important not to equate Jewish ideas about kinship in Israel with "Euro-American kinship thinking" and to recognize that "Jewish" and "Euro-American" conceptual frameworks for imagining kinship make "differing assumptions about genetic relatedness and its role in establishing kinship" (2000, 162–63).

EthnoProfile 14.5

Israel

Region: Middle East

Nation: Israel

Population: 7,150,000

Livelihood: Modern nation-state with diversified economy

Political organization:
Modern representative democracy

For more information:
Kahn, Susan Martha. 2000. *Reproducing Jews: A cultural account of assisted conception in Israel.* Durham, NC: Duke University Press.

As a result, assisted reproduction has played a very different role in Israel than it has played in the United States. First, Israelis in general are pronatalist: they believe they have a duty to produce children, for a variety of historical and political reasons (Kahn 2000, 3). Second, through its national health insurance programs, the Israeli state supports both families and unmarried mothers, and this support includes heavily subsidized access to reproductive technologies for all women, married or not. As one Israeli woman told Kahn, "It is considered much worse to be a childless woman than to be an unmarried mother" (16). Third, Kahn found that most Jews of all backgrounds endorse the idea that Jewishness is passed on to children matrilineally—that is, from one's mother, not from one's father. As a result, "genetic relatedness is a considerably more plastic category in rabbinic thinking about kinship; it can be conceptually erased, made invisible, or otherwise reconfigured" (165).

One consequence of this is that religious authorities agree that "the specific identity and origin of sperm is conceptualized as irrelevant to Jewish reproduction" (Kahn 2000, 166). On one hand, this means that infertile couples are encouraged (and subsidized by the state) to use assisted reproduction. On the other hand, assisted reproduction "has revealed curious and provocative loopholes within the rabbinic imagination of relatedness" that "implicitly allow for and legitimate Jewish children conceived by unmarried Jewish women as well as by infertile Jewish couples who conceive children with reproductive genetic material donated by anonymous non-Jews" (170).

Compadrazgo in Latin America

An important set of kinship practices in Roman Catholic Latin America is *compadrazgo*, or ritual coparenthood. The baptism of a child requires the presence of a godmother and a godfather as sponsors. By participating in this ritual, the sponsors become the ritual coparents of the child. In Latin America, godparents are expected to take an active interest in their godchildren and to help them wherever possible. However, the more important relationship is between the godparents and the parents. They become *compadres* ("coparents"), and they are expected to behave toward each other in new ways.

Sometimes the godparents are already kin; in recent years, for example, Nicaraguans have been choosing relatives living in the United States as compadres (Lancaster 1992, 66). A couple often chooses godparents whose social standing is higher than their own: the owners of the land they farm, for example, or of the factory where they work. Participating together in the baptism changes these unequal strangers into ritual kin whose relationship, although still unequal, is now personalized, friendlier, more open. The parents will support the godparents when that support is needed (politically, e.g.), and the godparents will do favors for the parents. They even call each other *compadre* rather than, say, "Señor López" and "José."

Catherine Allen notes that the bonds of *compadrazgo*, in combination with marriage alliances and kinship, "form constellations of mutual obligation and dependence that shift with time as new compadrazgo relationships are formed, young relatives come of age, and old bonds fall into disuse through death or quarreling. Like kin ties, bonds of compadrazgo can become as much a burden as an asset, and like kin ties they can be ignored or honored in the breach" (1988, 90).

Organ Transplantation and the Creation of New Relatives

Equally curious and provocative are the new kinds of kin ties that have emerged in the United States, following the increasingly widespread use of biomedical and surgical techniques that allow bodily organs to be salvaged from brain-dead individuals and transplanted into the bodies of others. Lesley Sharp reports that professionals who manage the many steps involved in organ transplantation have, until very recently, attempted to keep the families of organ donors from finding out the identities of organ recipients. The rather paternalistic justification given was that keeping people ignorant would

be good for their psychic health. But Sharp reports that donor kin and organ recipients have found ways to find each other and meet face to face, and her research contradicted the fears of the professionals: of 30 recorded cases of such meetings, only 1 failed (2006, 191).

An important outcome of the bringing together of donor kin and organ recipients has been the development of kinship relationships linking donor kin to those who received organs from their relatives. Affected individuals struggle with the question of what Sharp calls "donor ownership": "What rights do surviving kin have to trace the whereabouts of the remains of the lost loved one? Can one, for instance, assert claims of access—or postmortem visiting rights?" (Sharp 2006, 190). Sharp's research showed her that

> donor kin and recipients alike share the understanding that transplanted organs, as donor fragments, carry with them some essence of their former selves, and this persists in the bodies of recipients. The donor then becomes a transmigrated soul of sorts, one that generates compelling dilemmas for involved parties.... At risk here is the further shattering of each person's world; yet, as successful encounters reveal, potentially each party is partially healed in the process. (190)

One example Sharp offers involves Sally and Larry. Both had been involved in activities promoting organ donation and had known each other for several years, before they learned that Sally's son had provided the heart now beating inside Larry's body. When Sharp interviewed them, Sally was in her mid-fifties and a widow; Larry was a dozen years older and married. Right after his transplant surgery, and against the advice of his doctors, Larry had begun trying to find the family of the teenager who had provided his heart, and his wife, "Bulldog," helped him find Sally. Larry and Sally exchanged letters and met three years later. As they got to know one another, Larry, Sally, and Sally's daughter began to use kin terms to refer to one another.

> For example, Larry addresses Sally's daughter as "Sis," and she calls him "Bro." After Larry's own birth mother died, he then began to address Sally as "Mom," and she now calls him "Son." As Sally explained, Larry now sends her a Mother's Day card. These terms have facilitated the establishment of an elaborate joking relationship.... They are mildly troubled by the adulterous overtones of their relationship, one laced, too, I would assert, with the incestuous, given that Larry now harbors part of Charlie inside his body. (Sharp 2006, 188)

Sharp found that, of all kinship statuses, the role of the donor mother was particularly important among those whom she interviewed (Figure 14.8). In this case, emphasizing Sally's role as donor mother helped Sally and Larry deal with the "adulterous" or "incestuous" overtones in their relationship. "In assuming the role

---

compadrazgo Ritual coparenthood in Latin America and Spain, established through the Roman Catholic practice of having godparents for children.

FIGURE 14.8 The families of organ donors and the recipients of those organs have begun to meet face to face in the United States. A heart recipient (center, facing camera) embraces the mother of the young man whose heart he received; his wife (right) and the young man's sister (left) look on.

of donor mother to Larry, she eliminates the discomfort that arises when one considers their proximity in age. In essence, the mother–son bond trumps age" (2006, 190). Interestingly, traditionally North American understandings about "blood" relations extend to Larry but not to his wife: "Today, Sally, Larry, and Bulldog are dear to one another," but "there is no special term of address reserved for Bulldog. . . . Structurally, she is simply 'Larry's wife,' whereas Larry, in embodying Charlie's heart, is now embraced as blood kin" (190).

What Is Marriage?

The forms of relatedness we have just described are intimately connected with another widespread social process—marriage. Marriage and household formation provide significant forms of social support that enable people to take part in wider patterns of social life. In many places, they also facilitate important economic and political exchanges between the kinship groups to which the marriage partners belong. Even when marriage is not connected with lineage or clan relations, marriage patterns provide frameworks for linking previously unrelated people to one another, embedding individuals within groups, and organizing individual emotional commitments and economic activities.

Toward a Definition of Marriage

Getting married involves more than just living together or having sexual relations, and nowhere in the world is marriage synonymous with *mating*. In most societies, marriage also requires involvement and support from the wider

social groups to which the spouses belong—first and foremost from their families. *Marriage* and *family* are two terms anthropologists use to describe how different societies understand and organize mating and its consequences.

A prototypical **marriage** (1) transforms the status of the participants; (2) stipulates the degree of sexual access the married partners are expected to have to each other, ranging from exclusive to preferential; (3) perpetuates social patterns through the production or adoption of offspring; (4) creates relationships between the kin of the partners; and (5) is symbolically marked in some way, from an elaborate wedding to simply the appearance of a husband and wife seated one morning outside her hut.

Ordinarily, a prototypical marriage involves a man and a woman. But what are we to make of the following cases? Each offers an alternative way of understanding the combination of features that define appropriate unions in a particular society.

Woman Marriage and Ghost Marriage among the Nuer

Among the Nuer, as E. E. Evans-Pritchard observed during his fieldwork in the 1930s, a woman could marry another woman and become the "father" of the children the wife bore (see "EthnoProfile 14.2: Nuer"). This practice, which also appears in some other parts of Africa, involves a distinction between *pater* and *genitor*. The female husband (the pater) had to have some cattle of her

---

marriage An institution that prototypically transforms the status of a man and a woman, carries implications about permitted sexual access, gives the offspring a position in society, establishes connections between the kin of the partners, and is symbolically marked.

own to use for bridewealth payments to the wife's lineage. Once the bridewealth had been paid, the marriage was established. The female husband then got a male kinsman, friend, or neighbor (the genitor) to impregnate the wife and to help with certain tasks around the homestead that the Nuer believed could be done only by men.

Generally, Evans-Pritchard (1951) noted, a female husband was unable to have children herself "and for this reason counts in some respects as a man." Indeed, she played the social role of a man. She could marry several wives if she was wealthy. She could demand damage payment if those wives engaged in sexual activity without her consent. She was the pater of her wives' children. On the marriage of her daughters, she received the portion of the bridewealth that traditionally went to the father, and her brothers and sisters received the portions appropriate to the father's side. Her children were named after her, as though she were a man, and they addressed her as *Father*. She administered her compound and her herds as a male head of household would, and she was treated by her wives and children with the same deference shown a male husband and father.

More common in Nuer social life was what Evans-Pritchard called the *ghost marriage*. The Nuer believed that a man who died without male heirs left an unhappy and angry spirit who might trouble his living kin. The spirit was angry because a basic obligation of Nuer kinship was for a man to be remembered through and by his sons: His name had to be continued in his lineage. To appease the angry spirit, a kinsman of the dead man—a brother or a brother's son—would often marry a woman "to his name." Bridewealth cattle were paid in the name of the dead man to the patrilineage of a woman. She was then married to the ghost but lived with one of his surviving kinsmen. In the marriage ceremonies and afterward, this kinsman acted as though he were the true husband. The children of the union were referred to as though they were the kinsman's—but officially they were not. That is, the ghost husband was their pater and his kinsman their genitor.

As the children got older, the name of their ghost father became increasingly important to them. The ghost father's name, not his stand-in's name, would be remembered in the history of the lineage. The social union between the ghost and the woman took precedence over the sexual union between the ghost's surrogate and the woman.

Ghost marriage serves to perpetuate social patterns. Although it was common for a man to marry a wife "to his kinsman's name" before he himself married,

it became difficult, if not impossible, for him to marry later in his own right. His relatives would tell him he was "already married" and that he should allow his younger brothers to use cattle from the family herd so they could marry. Even if he eventually accumulated enough cattle to afford to marry, he would feel that those cattle should provide the bridewealth for the sons he had raised for his dead kinsman. When he died, he died childless because the children he had raised were legally the children of the ghost. He was then an angry spirit, and someone else (in fact, one of the sons he had raised for the ghost) had to marry a wife to *his* name. Thus the pattern continued, as, indeed, it does into the present day.

Why Is Marriage a Social Process?

Like all formal definitions, our definition of marriage is somewhat rigid, especially if we think of marriage as a ritual action that accomplishes everything at a single point in time. However, if we think of marriage as a social process that unfolds over time, we find that our definition allows us to account for a wider range of marriage practices (Figure 14.9). For example, a marriage ritual may join spouses together, but their production of offspring who mature into recognized members of a particular social group takes time and cannot be assured in advance. Traditionally in some societies, a couple were not considered fully married until they had a child. Similarly, marriage set up new relations between the kin of both spouses, called **affinal** relationships (based on *affinity*—i.e., created through marriage). These contrast with descent-based **consanguineal** relationships (from the Latin words for "same blood"). But a married couple's relationships with their affinal kin again develop over time, and whether they get along well and cooperate or become hostile to one another cannot be predicted or controlled when a marriage is first contracted. How successfully the married couple, their children, and their other relatives are able to manage the many challenges that emerge over time (economic transactions such as bridewealth payments, births, deaths, divorces) affects the extent to which they will be able to play important roles in the wider society to which they belong. The lives of all are transformed, though not all at the same time or with the same outcome—shaping the future of the community as a whole.

Sometimes marriages must be contracted within a particular social group, a pattern called **endogamy**. In other cases, marriage partners must be found outside a particular group, a pattern called **exogamy**. In Nuer society, for example, a person had to marry outside his or her lineage. Even in North American society, there is a

---

affinal Kinship connections through marriage, or affinity.

consanguineal Kinship connections based on descent.

endogamy Marriage within a defined social group.

exogamy Marriage outside a defined social group.

FIGURE 14.9 Marriage is a social process that creates social ties and involves more than just the people getting married. This is an elaborate marriage in Rajasthan, India.

preference for people to marry within the bounds of certain groups. People are told to marry "their own kind," which usually means their own ethnic or racial group, religious group, or social class. In all societies, some close kin are off limits as spouses or as sexual partners. This exogamous pattern is known as the *incest taboo*.

Patterns of Residence after Marriage

Once married, a couple must live somewhere. There are four major patterns of postmarital residence. Most familiar to North Americans is **neolocal** residence in which the new couple sets up an independent household at a place of their own choosing. Neolocal residence tends to be found in societies that are more or less individualistic in their social organization.

When the married couple lives with (or near) the husband's father's family, it is called **patrilocal** residence, which is observed by more societies in the contemporary world than any other residence pattern. It produces a characteristic social grouping of related men: a man, his brothers, and their sons, along with in-marrying wives,

all live and work together. This pattern is common in both herding and farming societies; some anthropologists argue that survival in such societies depends on activities that are best carried out by groups of men who have worked together all their lives.

When the married couple lives with (or near) the family in which the wife was raised, it is called **matrilocal** residence, which is usually found in association with matrilineal kinship systems. Here, the core of the social group consists of a woman, her sisters, and their daughters, together with in-marrying men. This pattern is most common among groups practicing extensive agriculture.

Less common, but also found in matrilineal societies, is the pattern known as **avunculocal** residence. Here, the married couple lives with (or near) the husband's mother's brother. The most significant man in a boy's matrilineage is his mother's brother, from whom he will inherit. Avunculocal residence emphasizes this relationship.

Single and Plural Spouses

The number of spouses a person may have varies cross-culturally. Anthropologists distinguish forms of marriage in terms of how many spouses a person may have. **Monogamy** is a marriage form in which a person may have only one spouse at a time, whereas **polygamy** is a marriage system that allows a person to have more than one spouse. Within the category of polygamy are two subcategories: **polygyny**, or multiple wives, and **polyandry**, or multiple husbands. Most societies in the world permit polygyny.

Monogamy   Monogamy is the only legal spousal pattern of the United States and most industrialized nations. (Indeed, in 1896, a condition of statehood for the territory of Utah was the abolition of polygyny, which had been practiced by Mormon settlers for nearly 50 years.) There are variations in the number of times a monogamous

neolocal A postmarital residence pattern in which a married couple sets up an independent household at a place of their own choosing.

patrilocal A postmarital residence pattern in which a married couple lives with (or near) the husband's father.

matrilocal A postmarital residence pattern in which a married couple lives with (or near) the wife's mother.

avunculocal A postmarital residence pattern in which a married couple lives with (or near) the husband's mother's brother (from avuncular, "of uncles").

monogamy A marriage pattern in which a person may be married to only one spouse at a time.

polygamy A marriage pattern in which a person may be married to more than one spouse at a time.

polygyny A marriage pattern in which a man may be married to more than one wife at a time.

polyandry A marriage pattern in which a woman may be married to more than one husband at a time.

person can be married. Before the twentieth century, people in western European societies generally married only once unless death intervened. Today, some observers suggest that we practice *serial monogamy;* we may be married to several different people but only one at a time.

Polygyny Polygynous societies vary in the number of wives a man may have. Islam permits a man to have as many as four wives but only on the condition that he can support them equally. Some Muslim authorities today argue, however, that equal support must be emotional and affective, not just financial. Convinced that no man can feel the same toward each of his wives, they have concluded that monogamy must be the rule. Other polygynous societies have no limit on the number of wives a man may marry. Nevertheless, not every man can be polygynous. There is a clear demographic problem: for every man with two wives, there is one man without a wife. Men can wait until they are older to marry and women can marry very young, but this imbalance cannot be completely eliminated. Polygyny is also expensive because a husband must support all his wives as well as their children (Figure 14.10).

Polyandry Polyandry is the rarest of the three marriage forms. In some polyandrous societies, a woman may marry several brothers. In others, she may marry men who are not related to each other and who all will live together in a single household. Sometimes a woman is allowed to marry several men who are not related, but she will live only with the one she most recently married. Studies of polyandry have shed light on the dynamics of polygyny and monogamy.

The traditional anthropological prototype of polyandry has been found among some groups in Nepal and Tibet, where a group of brothers marry one woman. This is known as *fraternal polyandry.* During one wedding, one brother, usually the oldest, serves as the groom. All brothers (including those yet to be born to the husbands' parents) are married by this wedding, which establishes public recognition of the marriage. The wife and her husbands live together, usually patrilocally. All brothers have equal sexual access to the wife, and all act as fathers to the children. In some cases—notably among the Nyinba of Nepal (Levine 1980, 1988)—each child is recognized as having one particular genitor, who may be a different brother than the genitor of his or her siblings (see "EthnoProfile 14.6: Nyinba"). In other cases, all the brothers are considered jointly as the father, without distinguishing the identity of the genitor.

There appears to be little sexual jealousy among the men, and the brothers have a strong sense of solidarity with one another. Levine (1988) emphasizes this point for the Nyinba. If the wife proves sterile, the brothers may marry another woman in hopes that she may be fertile. All brothers also have equal sexual access to the new wife and are treated as fathers by her children. In societies that practice fraternal polyandry, marrying sisters (or *sororal polygyny*) may be preferred or permitted. In this system, a group of brothers could marry a group of sisters.

According to Levine, Nyinba polyandry is reinforced by a variety of cultural beliefs and practices (1988, 158ff.). First, it has a special cultural value. Nyinba myth provides a social charter for the practice because Nyinba legendary ancestors are polyandrous, and they are praised for the harmony of their family life. Second, the solidarity of brothers

FIGURE 14.10 The wives and children of a polygynous family.

EthnoProfile 14.6

Nyinba

Region: Central Asia

Nation: Nepal

Population: 1,200

Environment: Valleys

Livelihood: Agriculture, herding

Political organization: Traditionally, headmen; today, part of a modern nation-state

For more information: Levine, Nancy. 1988. *The dynamics of polyandry: Kinship, domesticity, and population on the Tibetan border.* Chicago: University of Chicago Press.

is a central kinship ideal. Third, the corporate, landholding household, central to Nyinba life, presupposes polyandry. Fourth, the closed corporate structure of Nyinba villages is based on a limited number of households, and polyandry is highly effective in checking the proliferation of households. Finally, a household's political position and economic viability increase when its resources are concentrated.

The Distinction between Sexuality and Reproductive Capacity Polyandry demonstrates how a woman's sexuality can be distinguished from her reproductive capacity. This distinction is absent in monogamous or purely polygynous systems in which polyandry is not permitted; such societies resist perceiving women's sexual and reproductive capacities as separable (except, perhaps, in prostitution), yet they usually accept such separation for men without question. "It may well be a fundamental feature of the [worldview] of polyandrous peoples that they recognize such a distinction for *both* men and women" (Levine and Sangree 1980, 388). In the better-known polyandrous groups, a woman's sexuality can be shared among an unlimited number of men, but her childbearing capacities cannot be. Indeed, among the Nyinba (Levine 1980), a woman's childbearing capacities are carefully controlled and limited to one husband at a time. But she is free to engage in sexual activity outside her marriage to the brothers as long as she is not likely to get pregnant. As we saw in Chapter 13, Western assumptions about the relationship between sex, gender, and sexuality are not universal.

What Is the Connection between Marriage and Economic Exchange?

In many societies, marriage is accompanied by the transfer of certain symbolically important goods. Anthropologists have identified two major categories of marriage payments, usually called *bridewealth* and *dowry*. **Bridewealth** is most common in patrilineal societies that combine agriculture, pastoralism, and patrilocal marriage, although it is found in other types of societies as well (Figure 14.11). When it occurs among matrilineal peoples, a postmarital residence rule (avunculocal, e.g.) usually takes the woman away from her matrilineage.

The goods exchanged have significant symbolic value to the people concerned. They may include shell ornaments, ivory tusks, brass gongs, bird feathers, cotton cloth, and animals. Bridewealth in animals is prevalent in eastern and southern Africa, where cattle have the most profound symbolic and economic value. In these societies, a man's father, and often his entire patrilineage, give a specified number of cattle (often in installments) to the patrilineage of the man's bride. Anthropologists view bridewealth as a way of compensating the bride's relatives for the loss of her labor and childbearing capacities. When the bride leaves her home, she goes to live with her husband and his lineage. She will be working and producing children for his people, not her own.

Bridewealth transactions create affinal relations between the relatives of the wife and those of the husband. The wife's relatives, in turn, use the bridewealth they receive for her to find a bride for her brother in yet another kinship group. In many societies in eastern and southern Africa, a woman gains power and influence over her brother because her marriage brings the cattle that allow him to marry and continue their lineage. This is why Jack Goody describes bridewealth as "a societal fund, a circulating pool of resources, the movement of which corresponds to the movement of rights over spouses, usually women" (Goody and Tambiah 1973, 17). Or, as the Southern Bantu put it, "cattle beget children" (Kuper 1982, 3).

Dowry, by contrast, is typically a transfer of family wealth, usually from parents to their daughter, at the

---

bridewealth The transfer of certain symbolically important goods from the family of the groom to the family of the bride on the occasion of their marriage. It represents compensation to the wife's lineage for the loss of her labor and her childbearing capacities.

dowry The transfer of wealth, usually from parents to their daughter, at the time of her marriage.

IN THEIR OWN WORDS

Outside Work, Women, and Bridewealth

Judith M. Abwunza took life histories from and interviewed many women among the Logoli of western Kenya about their lives and has allowed many of those women to speak for themselves in her 1997 book, Women's Voices, Women's Power: Dialogues of Resistance from East Africa. *Here, Abwunza introduces us to Alice, a 24-year-old secondary school teacher.*

Alice's father is relatively affluent, as all his children are in school or working, his land is well-kept and fully utilized and the yard has cows, chickens, and goats. Alice's motivation to get a job was that she wanted to assist her family. She said that everyone in the family depends upon her for money, a burden that she finds to be "overwhelming." Alice has been living with her husband, who is also a teacher, since January, 1987. They have seven-month-old twins, a boy and a girl. Uvukwi [bridewealth] discussion has taken place and her in-laws and her relatives have agreed on 23,000 shillings and five cows. A 3,000 shilling "down payment" has been given, and her marriage occurred in January, 1988. Alice discusses her situation in English:

> We live in a house supplied by the school. We have electricity and water and a gas cooker. We have a small house plot in my husband's yard at Bunyore, and six acres in the scheme in Kitale. We hire people to dig there, as we are teaching. So far, we have not sold cash crops. We are only beginning. On the schemes, workers are paid between five and six hundred shillings a month to dig, so it is expensive. There is no need of paying uvukwi. Am I a farm to be bought? It is unfortunate the parents are poor. Parents ought to contribute to the newly married to start them off. But there is nothing we can do; it's a custom. Also uvukwi is not the end of assistance to parents. Some men mistreat after buying, that is paying uvukwi. Some men refuse to help parents any more after uvukwi, think that's enough. On the other hand, if you don't pay uvukwi, the husbands think you are not valued by parents. You are cheap. It's a tug of war.

People who get jobs in Kenya have been to school, these are the elite. They are able to integrate various situations. They are analytical and choosing courses of action. They have developed decision-making skills; this gives access to wage labour. Most women are not this; many men are not. Things have changed for women, but still it is very difficult; they must work very hard. In the old days, customs did not allow men in the kitchen; now they do. It's absurd to see milk boiling over in the kitchen while I'm taking care of the baby and he is reading. A more even distribution of labour is needed. Women need a word of appreciation for their hard work, in the home and caring for children. Here in Maragoli we cannot develop: the population is too high. The government is suggesting that maternity leave will not be given after the fourth child. This is a good thing but it has not been passed yet. I will not be abused in my marriage. I will leave. My job is difficult. Children are beaten, sent from school for fees, for harambee this, harambee that. Seldom do I have my entire class to teach. Some are always missing. I have had to chase them for fees. This is not my role; my job is to teach them, so they may better their lives. I refuse to beat them. I try not to upset them. I want them to learn. But many do not want to. Girls only want to chase boys, and boys the girls. But a few learn. Teaching is difficult.

[Abwunza concludes:] Alice takes a different position from most Logoli women. She complains of having to follow traditional ways in these difficult economic times, even as she adheres to them. Although many people complained about the "high cost" of uvukwi, on no other occasion did women suggest that parents should assist a newly married couple and not follow the custom of uvukwi. Alice's feeling is not typical of Logoli people. It comes about at least in part because Alice's uvukwi is quite high and both she and her husband will have to contribute to its payment, as she says, "at the expense of our own development." She sees that she is caught in a bind. Not following the traditions will place her in a position of being without a good reputation and thus at risk in the community.

Source: Abwunza 1997, 77–78.

time of her marriage. It is found primarily in the agricultural societies of Europe and Asia but has been brought to some parts of Africa with the arrival of religions like Islam that support the practice. In societies where both women and men are seen as heirs to family wealth, dowry is sometimes regarded as the way women receive their inheritance. Dowries are often considered the wife's contribution to the establishment of a new household,

FIGURE 14.11 Dowries take many forms, depending on the cultural preferences of a given group of people. Here is a display of dowry items from Tamil Nadu, India.

to which the husband may bring other forms of wealth. In stratified societies, the size of a woman's dowry often ensures that when she marries she will continue to enjoy her accustomed style of life, and the dowry can be reclaimed by the woman in the event of divorce, to avoid destitution. The goods included in dowries vary in different societies and may or may not include land (Goody and Tambiah 1973). There is perhaps a carryover from the European dowry in the Western practice of the bride's family paying for her wedding.

What Is a Family?

A minimal definition of a **family** would be that it consists of a woman and her dependent children. [2] While some anthropological definitions require the presence of an adult male, related either by marriage or by descent (husband or brother, e.g.), recent feminist and primatological scholarship has called this requirement into question. As a result, some anthropologists prefer to distinguish the **conjugal family**, which is a family based on marriage—at its minimum, a husband and wife (a spousal pair) and their children—from the **nonconjugal family**, which consists of a woman and her children. In a nonconjugal family, the husband/father may be occasionally present or completely absent.

Nonconjugal families are never the only form of family organization in a society and, in fact, cross-culturally are usually rather infrequent. In some large-scale industrial societies including the United States, however, nonconjugal families have become increasingly common. In most societies, the conjugal family is coresident—that is, spouses live in the same dwelling, along with their children—but there are some matrilineal societies in which the husband lives with his matrilineage, the wife and children live with theirs, and the husband visits his wife and children.

What Is the Nuclear Family?

The structure and dynamics of neolocal monogamous families are familiar to North Americans. They are called *nuclear families*, and it is often assumed that most North Americans live in them (although in 2013, only about one half of North American children under the age of 18 did). For anthropologists, a **nuclear family** is made up of two generations: the parents and their unmarried children. Each member of a nuclear family has a series of evolving relationships with every other member: husband and wife, parents and children, and children with each other. These are the lines along which jealousy,

---

family Minimally, a woman and her dependent children.

conjugal family A family based on marriage; at a minimum, a husband and wife (a spousal pair) and their children.

nonconjugal family A woman and her children; the husband/father may be occasionally present or completely absent.

nuclear family A family made up of two generations: the parents and their unmarried children.

---

[2]In the contemporary United States, where many men as well as women are single parents, the view that a man and his children constitute a family is widely shared. This illustrates the ongoing reconfiguration of North American family relations, other features of which are described later.

IN THEIR OWN WORDS

Dowry Too High. Lose Bride and Go to Jail

In some parts of the world, discussions of bridewealth or dowry seem so divorced from reality as to appear "academic." But elsewhere, these topics remain significant indeed. In May 2003, news media all over the world reported the story of a bride in India who called the police when a battle erupted over demands for additional dowry payments at her wedding. The New York Times *reports.*

Nisha Sharma, surrounded by some of the dowry with which her family had intended to endow her.

Noida, India, May 16—The musicians were playing, the 2,000 guests were dining, the Hindu priest was preparing the ceremony and the bride was dressed in red, her hands and feet festively painted with henna.

Then, the bride's family says, the groom's family moved in for the kill. The dowry of two televisions, two home theater sets, two refrigerators, two air-conditioners and one car was too cheap. They wanted $25,000 in rupees, now, under the wedding tent.

As a free-for-all erupted between the two families, the bartered bride put her hennaed foot down. She reached for the royal blue cellphone and dialed 100. By calling the police, Nisha Sharma, a 21-year-old computer student, saw her potential groom land in jail and herself land in the national spotlight as India's new overnight sensation.

"Are they marrying with money, or marrying with me?" Ms. Sharma asked today, her dark eyes glaring under arched eyebrows. In the next room a fresh wave of reporters waited to interview her, sitting next to the unopened boxes of her wedding trousseau.

After fielding a call from a comic-book artist who wanted to bring her act of defiance last Sunday night to a mass market, she said, "I'm feeling proud of myself."

"It Takes Guts to Send Your Groom Packing," a headline in *The Times of India* read.

Rashtriya Sahara, a major Hindi daily, said in a salute, "Bravo: We're Proud of You."

"She is being hailed as a New Age woman and seen as a role model to many," the newspaper *Asian Age* wrote next to a front-page drawing of Ms. Sharma standing in front of red and green wedding pennants while flashing a V sign to cameras and wearing a sash over her blue sari with the words *Miss Anti-Dowry*.

"This was a brave thing for a girl dressed in all her wedding finery to do," said Vandana Sharma, president of the Women's Protection League, one of many women's rights leaders and politicians to make a pilgrimage this week to this eastern suburb of Delhi. "This girl has taken a very dynamic step." India's new 24-hour news stations have propelled Nisha Sharma to Hindi stardom. One television station set up a service allowing viewers to "send a message to Nisha." In the first two days, 1,500 messages came in.

Illegal for many decades in India, dowries are now often disguised by families as gifts to give the newlyweds a start in life. More than a media creation, Ms. Sharma and her dowry defiance struck a chord in this nation, whose expanding middle class is rebelling against a dowry tradition that is being overfed by a new commercialism.

"Advertisements now show parents giving things to make their daughters happy in life," Brinda Karat, general secretary of the All India Democratic Women's Association, a private group, said, referring to television commercials for products commonly given in dowries.

"It is the most modern aspects of information technology married to the most backward concepts of subordination of women," Ms. Karat continued in a telephone interview. Last year, she said, her group surveyed 10,000 people in 18 of India's 26 states. "We found an across-the-board increase in dowry demand," she said.

IN THEIR OWN WORDS

Much of the dowry greed is new, Ms. Karat added. In a survey 40 years ago, she noted, almost two-thirds of Indian communities reported that the local custom was for the groom to pay the bride's family, the reverse of the present dominant custom. According to government statistics, husbands and in-laws angry over small dowry payments killed nearly 7,000 women in 2001.

When Ms. Sharma's parents were married in 1970, "my father-in-law did not demand anything," her mother, Hem Lata Sharma, said while serving hot milk tea and cookies to guests.

For the Sharma family, the demands went far beyond giving the young couple a helping hand.

Dev Dutt Sharma, Nisha's father, said his potential in-laws were so demanding that they had stipulated brands. "She specified a Sony home theater, not a Philips," Mr. Sharma, an owner of car battery factories, said of Vidya Dalal, the mother of the groom, Munish Dalal, 25.

Sharma Jaikumar, a telecommunications engineer and friend of the Sharma family, said as the press mob ebbed and flowed through the house: "My daughter was married recently and there was no dowry. But anyone can turn greedy. What can be more easy money than a dowry? All you have to do is ask."

Source: Brooke 2003.

---

competition, controversy, and affection develop in neolocal monogamous families; sibling rivalry, for example, is a form of competition characteristic of nuclear families that is shaped by the relationships between siblings and between siblings and their parents.

What Is the Polygynous Family?

A polygynous family includes, at a minimum, the husband, all his wives, and their children. Polygynous families are significantly different in their dynamics. Each wife has a relationship with her cowives as individuals and as a group (Figure 14.12). Cowives, in turn, individually and collectively, interact with the husband. These relationships change over time, as the authors (EAS and RHL) were once informed during our fieldwork in Guider, northern Cameroon (see Chapter 15, "EthnoProfile 15.2: Guider"). The nine-year-old daughter of our landlord announced one day that she was going to become Lavenda's second wife. "Madame [Schultz]," she said, "will be angry at first, because that's how first wives are when their husbands take a second wife. But after a while, she will stop being angry and will get to know me and we will become friends. That's what always happens."

The differences in internal dynamics in polygynous families are not confined to the relationships of husband and wives. An important distinction is made between children with the same mother and children with a different mother. In Guider, people ordinarily refer to all their siblings (half and full) as brothers or sisters.

FIGURE 14.12 Cowives in polygynous households frequently cooperate in daily tasks, such as food preparation.

EthnoProfile 14.7

Mende

Region: Western Africa

Nation: Sierra Leone

Population: 12,000,000

Environment: Forest and savanna

Livelihood: Slash-and-burn rice cultivation, cash cropping, diamond mining

Political organization: Traditionally, a hierarchy of local chiefdoms; today, part of a modern nation-state

For more information: Little, Kenneth. 1967. *The Mende of Sierra Leone.* London: Routledge and Kegan Paul.

When they want to emphasize the close connection with a particular brother or sister, however, they say that he or she is "same father, same mother." This terminology conveys a relationship of special intimacy and significance. Children, logically, also have different kinds of relationships with their own mothers and their fathers' other wives—and with their fathers as well.

Where there is a significant inheritance, these relationships serve as the channels for jealousy and conflict. The children of the same mother, and especially the children of different mothers, compete with one another for their father's favor. Each mother tries to protect the interests of her own children, sometimes at the expense of her cowives' children.

Competition in the Polygynous Family   Although the relationships among wives in a polygynous society may be very close, among the Mende of Sierra Leone, cowives eventually compete with each other (see "EthnoProfile 14.7: Mende"). Caroline Bledsoe (1993) explains that this competition is often focused on children: how many each wife has and how likely it is that each child will

obtain things of value, especially education. Husbands in polygynous Mende households should avoid overt signs of favoritism, but wives differ from one another in status. First, wives are ranked by order of marriage. The senior wife is the first wife in the household, and she has authority over junior wives. Marriage-order ranking structures the household but also lays the groundwork for rivalries. Second, wives are also ranked in terms of the status of the families from which they came. Serious problems arise if the husband shows favoritism toward a wife from a high-status family by educating her children ahead of older children of other wives or children of wives higher in the marriage-order ranking.

The level of her children's education matters intensely to a Mende woman because her principal claim to her husband's land or cash, and her expectations of future support after he dies, comes through her children. She depends not only on the income that a child may earn to support her but also on the rights her children have to inherit property and positions of leadership. Nevertheless, education requires a significant cash outlay in school fees, uniforms, books, and so on. A man may be able to send only one child to school, or he may be able to send one child to a prestigious private school only if he sends another to a trade apprenticeship. These economic realities make sense to husbands but can lead to bitter feuds—and even divorce—among cowives who blame the husband for disparities in the accomplishments of their children. In extreme cases, cowives are said to use witchcraft to make their rivals' children fail their exams. To avoid these problems, children are frequently sent to live with relatives who will send them to school. Such competition is missing in monogamous households unless they include adopted children or spouses who already have children from a previous marriage.

Extended and Joint Families

Within any society, certain patterns of family organization are considered proper. In American nuclear families, two generations live together. In some societies, three generations—parents, married children, and grandchildren—are expected to live together in a vertical **extended family**. In still other societies, the extension is horizontal: Brothers and their wives (or sisters and their husbands) live together in a **joint family**. These are ideal patterns, which all families may not be able or willing to emulate.

It is important to emphasize that extended families do not operate the way joint families operate, and neither can be understood as just several nuclear families

---

extended family A family pattern made up of three generations living together: parents, married children, and grandchildren.

joint family A family pattern made up of brothers and their wives or sisters and their husbands (along with their children) living together.

that overlap. Extended and joint families are fundamentally different from a nuclear family with regard to the relationships they engender.

How Are Families Transformed over Time?

Families change over time. They have a life cycle and a life span. The same family takes on different forms and provides different opportunities for the interaction of family members at different points in its development. New households are formed and old households change through divorce, remarriage, the departure of children, and the breakup of extended families.

Divorce and Remarriage

Most societies make it possible for married couples to separate. In some societies, the process is long, drawn out, and difficult, especially when bridewealth must be returned; a man who divorces a wife in such societies, or whose wife leaves him, expects some of the bridewealth back. But for the wife's family to give the bridewealth back, a whole chain of marriages may have to be broken up. Brothers of the divorced wife may have to divorce to get back enough bridewealth from their in-laws. Sometimes a new husband will repay the bridewealth to the former husband's line, thus letting the bride's relatives off the hook.

Divorce in Guider   In other societies, divorce is easier. Marriages in Guider, for example, are easily broken up (see Chapter 15, "EthnoProfile 15.2: Guider"). The Fulbe of Guider prefer that a man marry his father's brother's daughter. In many cases, such marriages are contracted simply to oblige the families involved; after a few months, the couple splits up. In other cases, a young girl (12 or 13 years old) is married to a man considerably her senior, despite any interest she may have had in men closer to her own age. Here too the marriage may not last long. In general, there is enough dissatisfaction with marriage in Guider to make household transformation through divorce quite common.

Among Muslims in Guider, divorce is controlled by men; women are not allowed legally to initiate divorces. A man wanting a divorce need only follow the simple procedure laid down in the Qur'an and sanctioned by long practice in Guider: he appears before two witnesses and pronounces the formula "I divorce you" three times. He is then divorced, and his wife must leave his household.

She may take an infant with her, but any children at the toddler stage or older stay with the father. If she takes an infant, she must return the child to the father's household by the time the child is six to eight years old. In case she was pregnant at the time of the divorce, a woman must wait three months after she is divorced before she can remarry. After this time, the vast majority of women remarry.

Do women in Guider, then, have no power to escape from marriages that are unsatisfactory? Legally, perhaps not. But several conventionally recognized practices allow a woman to communicate her desire for a divorce. She can ask her husband for a divorce, and in some cases he will comply. If he does not or if she is unwilling to confront him directly, she can neglect household duties—burn his food or stop cooking for him entirely or refuse to sleep with him. She can also leave, going to live in the compound of her father or brother.

Grounds for Divorce   Depending on the society, nagging, quarreling, cruelty, stinginess, or adultery may be cited as causes for divorce. In almost all societies, childlessness is grounds for divorce as well. For the Ju/'hoansi, most divorces are initiated by women, mainly because they do not like their husbands or do not want to be married (Lee 2013; Shostak 1981; see Chapter 11, "EthnoProfile 11.4: Ju/'hoansi (!Kung)"). After what is often considerable debate, a couple that decides to break up merely separates. There is no bridewealth to return, no legal contract to be renegotiated. Mutual consent is all that is necessary. The children go with the mother. Ju/'hoansi divorces are cordial, Richard Lee (2013) tells us, at least compared with the Western norm. Ex-spouses may continue to joke with each other and even live next to each other with their new spouses.

Separation among Inuit   Among the northwestern Inuit, the traditional view is that all kin relationships, including marital ones, are permanent (Burch 1970) (see "EthnoProfile 14.8: Alaskan Inuit"). Thus, although it is possible to deactivate a marriage by separating, a marriage can never be permanently dissolved. (Conversely, reestablishing the residence tie is all that's needed to reactivate the relationship.) A husband and wife who stop living together and having sexual relations with each other are considered separated and ready for another marriage. If each member of a separated couple remarried, the two husbands of the wife would become cohusbands; the two wives of the husband, cowives; and the children of the first and second marriages, cosiblings. In effect, a "divorce" among the Inuit results in more, not fewer, connections. Not all contemporary Inuit, especially those who are Christians, continue to follow this practice.

IN THEIR OWN WORDS

Law, Custom, and Crimes against Women

John van Willigen and V. C. Channa describe the social and cultural practices surrounding dowry payments that appear to be responsible for violence against women in some parts of India.

A 25-year-old woman was allegedly burnt to death by her husband and mother-in-law at their East Delhi home yesterday. The housewife, Mrs. Sunita, stated before her death at the Jaya Prakash Narayana Hospital that members of her husband's family had been harassing her for bringing inadequate dowry.

The woman told the Shahdara subdivisional magistrate that during a quarrel over dowry at their Pratap Park house yesterday, her husband gripped her from behind while the mother-in-law poured kerosene over her clothes.

Her clothes were then set ablaze. The police have registered a case against the victim's husband, Suraj Prakash, and his mother.

—Times of India,
February 19, 1988

This routinely reported news story describes what in India is termed a "bride-burning" or "dowry death." Such incidents are frequently reported in the newspapers of Delhi and other Indian cities. In addition, there are cases in which the evidence may be ambiguous, so that deaths of women by fire may be recorded as kitchen accidents, suicides, or murders. Dowry violence takes a characteristic form. Following marriage and the requisite giving of dowry, the family of the groom makes additional demands for the payment of more cash or the provision of more goods. These demands are expressed in unremitting harassment of the bride, who is living in the household of her husband's parents, culminating in the murder of the woman by members of her husband's family or by her suicide. The woman is typically burned to death with kerosene, a fuel used in pressurized cook stoves, hence the use of the term "bride-burning" in public discourse.

Dowry death statistics appear frequently in the press and parliamentary debates. Parliamentary sources report the following figures for married women 16 to 30 years of age in Delhi: 452 deaths by burning for 1985; 478 for 1986 and 300 for the first six months of 1987. There were 1,319 cases reported nationally in 1986 (*Times of India*, January 10, 1988). Police records do not match hospital records for third degree burn cases among younger married women; far more violence occurs than the crime reports indicate.

There is other violence against women related both directly and indirectly to the institution of dowry. For example, there are unmarried women who commit suicide so as to relieve their families of the burden of providing a dowry. A recent case that received national attention in the Indian press involved the triple suicide of three sisters in the industrial city of Kanpur. A photograph was widely published showing the three young women hanging from ceiling fans by their scarves. Their father, who earned about 4000 Rs. [rupees] per month, was not able to negotiate marriage for his oldest daughter. The grooms were requesting approximately 100,000 Rs. Also linked to the dowry problem is selective female abortion made possible by amniocentesis. This issue was brought to national attention with a startling statistic reported out of a seminar held in Delhi in 1985. Of 3000 abortions carried out after sex determination through amniocentesis, only one involved a male fetus. As a result of these developments, the government of the state of Maharashtra banned sex determination tests except those carried out in government hospitals.

Source: van Willigen and Channa 1991, 369–70.

Blended Families   In recent years in the United States, anthropologists have observed the emergence of a new family type: the **blended family**. A blended family is created when previously divorced or widowed people marry, bringing with them children from their previous marriages. The internal dynamics of the new family—which can come to include his children, her children, and their children—may resemble the dynamics of polygynous families, as the relations among the children and their relations to each parent may be complex and negotiated over time.

blended family A family created when previously divorced or widowed people marry, bringing with them children from their previous families.

EthnoProfile 14.8

Alaskan Inuit

Region: North America

Nation: United States (northwestern Alaska)

Population: 11,000 (1960s)

Environment: Arctic: mountains, foothills, coastal plain

Livelihood: Hunting, wage labor, welfare

Political organization:
Traditionally, families; today, part of a modern nation-state

For more information:
Burch, Ernest S. Jr. 1975. *Eskimo kinsmen: Changing family relationships in northwest Alaska.* American Ethnological Society Monograph, no. 59. St. Paul: West.

EthnoProfile 14.9

Los Pinos

Region: Caribbean

Nation: Dominican Republic

Population: 1,000

Environment: Rugged mountain region

Livelihood: Peasant agriculture (tobacco, coffee, cacao) and labor migration

Political organization: Part of a modern nation-state

For more information:
Georges, Eugenia. 1990. *The making of a transnational community: Migration, development, and cultural change in the Dominican Republic.* New York: Columbia University Press.

How Does International Migration Affect the Family?

Migration to find work in another country has become increasingly common worldwide and has important effects on families. Anthropologist Eugenia Georges (1990) examined its effects on people who migrated to the United States from Los Pinos, a small town in the Dominican Republic (see "EthnoProfile 14.9: Los Pinos"). Migration divided these families, with some members moving to New York and some remaining in Los Pinos. Some parents stayed in the Dominican Republic while their children went to the United States. A more common pattern was for spouses to separate, with the husband migrating and the wife staying home. Consequently, many households in Los Pinos were headed by women. In most cases, however, the spouse in the United States worked to bring the spouse and children in Los Pinos there.

This sometimes took several years because it involved completing paperwork for the visa and saving money beyond the amount regularly sent to Los Pinos. Children of the couple who were close to working age also came to the United States, frequently with their mother, and younger children were sent for as they approached working age. Finally, after several years in the United States, the couple who started the migration cycle would often take their savings and return home to the Dominican Republic. Their children stayed in the United States and continued to send money home.

Return migrants tended not to give up their residence visas and therefore had to return to the United States annually. Often they stayed for a month or more to work. This also provided them with the opportunity to buy clothing and household goods at a more reasonable cost, as well as other items—clothing, cosmetics, and the like—to sell to neighbors, friends, and kin in the Dominican Republic (Figure 14.13).

FIGURE 14.13 As migration from the Dominican Republic to the United States has increased, more Dominicans are staying and bringing their families or creating families in the United States. Such celebrations of ethnic pride as Dominican Day in New York have increased in recent years.

IN THEIR OWN WORDS

Survival and a Surrogate Family

What is a family? How are families similar to, and different from, other forms of relatedness? In this excerpt from Gangsters without Borders: An Ethnography of a Salvadoran Street Gang, *anthropologist T. W. Ward addresses these questions from different points of view.*

Youth like José join gangs as a means of survival and self-defense, as a means of constructing an identity of self-worth, and as a way to create a surrogate family. The fact that the gang family can be as dysfunctional as the biological one it replaces—if not much more so—reflects the lack of positive role models and resources available to marginalized youth. As anyone who has studied gang members can attest, adolescents join street gangs in response to hostile neighborhoods, dysfunctional schools, aggressive (bullying) peers, lack of good-paying jobs, and absent, neglectful, or abusive parents or surrogate caretakers. Adolescents also join street gangs as a response to the poverty, racism, and discrimination they experience as the stigmatized and marginalized of society.

Street gangs are part of a deviant subculture, and therefore certain aspects of gang life tend to be shrouded in mystery, which leads to misinformation and misunderstanding. Because they live in a shadow of denial and deception, it is difficult to know what gang members do on a daily basis, much less what they really think and feel. Although partially based on reality, a distorted, stereotypical view of street gangs as highly organized, criminal organizations bent on murder and mayhem has been perpetuated by gang members and law enforcement officials tasked with the attempt to curb their criminal activities. Because it serves their different agendas, these actors have created a mythos about street gangs, which the media is all too eager to report. Despite the vast amount of academic research that has elucidated much of gang life and corrected this distorted view, there is still a large gap between the reality of street gangs and the public perception of what it means to be a gang member.

When I began the research for this book in 1993, like most people I had been conditioned by news, film, and television to believe this stereotype of gang members as tough "street thugs" who enjoy terrorizing others and spend most of their time selling drugs, robbing people, or doing drive-by shootings. Although this is partly true for a small minority of gang members, what I found over the course of eight and a half years of fieldwork was much more complex. Although the violence and criminality of gang life have been well documented and it is well known that some gang members are heavily involved with using and dealing drugs, what is missing from media descriptions of gang life is a holistic perspective that places this behavior in context. The media is not concerned with the fact that there is a great deal of variability of deviance between street gangs and that no two gangs are alike. Likewise, it ignores the enormous variability between individual members and the fact that most gang members are not involved in serious crimes of violence. Furthermore, the popular conception of a gang career does not consider the fact that the vast majority of members eventually retire from their gang and move on to a pro-social life.

For those who have had no direct contact with street gangs, what is least known about them is the flip side of their members' aggression and criminality: namely, the altruism or compassion expressed between homeboys and homegirls and the extent to which their gangs serve as adaptations to hostile environments. Street gangs thrive in the poorest neighborhoods in our urban communities. They are highly complex social organizations that serve multiple functions. Some gangs are like deviant social clubs providing camaraderie, excitement, and entertainment, which are an escape from boredom. Other gangs are like paramilitary organizations that provide protection and opportunity for economic gain and positive "gangster" status. Regardless of the type of gang, most youth join street gangs in their search for a particular quality of life, a sense of self-worth, and a sense of belonging to a group that cares about their welfare and survival.

When gang members speak about their group as a (surrogate) family, they are referring to this aspect of love and concern for one another. For many, the gang temporarily fills a vacuum of love and respect. Although veterans of the gang life admit that their members usually fall far short of this ideology of sharing and caring for "fellow homies," the fact remains that, for many members, the gang replaces the dysfunctional families and communities that have neglected, abused, or abandoned them

IN THEIR OWN WORDS

in one way or another. Most gang members call their gang a family because, at some level of functionality, it serves the essential purposes of caring and survival. As the gang members intuitively know, the core of any family is kinship, and love and compassion are expected byproducts.

In order for the street gang to survive, much less thrive, it must provide some degree of safety and comfort to its members, some sense of status, and some sense of belonging. Otherwise, these disenfranchised youth would seek out some alternative to the gangster life. Generally speaking, the degree to which a gang serves this function of family is the degree to which an individual is committed

to a hard-core version of the gangster life. He or she sees the gang as an acceptable substitute for his or her biological or fictive kin. For the most hard-core of gang members, the gang is the primary family they know or care about. For them, in addition to the questions of survival and status, the heart of the matter with street gangs is the matter of the heart, in terms of solidarity and bonding. The gang as surrogate family gives a person a sense of meaning and purpose in life, however distorted, destructive, or dysfunctional. It took me many years of conversation and observation to understand the complexity of how this played out between gang members over many places and many years.

Georges observes that the absent family member maintained an active role in family life despite the heavy psychological burden of separation. Although he might be working in a hotel in New York, for example, the husband was still the breadwinner and the main decision maker in the household. He communicated by visits, letters, and occasional telephone calls. Despite the strains of migration, moreover, the divorce rate was actually slightly lower in migrant families. In part, this was because the exchange of information between Los Pinos and New York was both dense and frequent, but also because strong ties of affection connected many couples. Finally, "the goal of the overwhelming majority of the migrants [from Los Pinos] I spoke with was permanent return to the Dominican Republic. Achievement of this goal was hastened by sponsoring the migration of dependents, both wives and children, so that they could work and save as part of the reconstituted household in the United States" (Georges 1990, 201). This pressure also helped keep families together.

In recent years, the Internet has come to play an increasingly important role in the lives of families that are separated by migration, education, work, and so on. Daniel Miller and Don Slater (2000) studied Internet use in Trinidad, finding that e-mail and instant messaging have considerably strengthened both the nuclear and the extended families, allowing closer relations between distant parents and children, among siblings, and among other relatives as well. They remark on the experiences of a widow they knew who, depressed after her husband's

death, was convinced by relatives to learn to use e-mail to contact a beloved grandchild who had gone abroad. This experience was so valuable to her that she began to contact other relatives abroad and in Trinidad, that younger members of her family "swear it has given 'new lease of life'" (61). Overall, the use of the Internet offers anthropologists the opportunity to observe how family separation can be moderated and offers people around the world opportunities for relaxed, expansive, and everyday forms of communication that seem to have important effects on family life.

Not all migrants to the United States share the same financial constraints or family pressures. A contrasting case comes from Japanese corporate wives in the United States. Anthropologist Sawa Kurotani, born and raised in Japan and trained and now working in the United States, discusses the situation of middle-class Japanese women who accompany their husbands when the husband's corporate employer sends him to work in the United States for up to five years. Kurotani (2005) observes that, traditionally, domestic management was the job of the wife. In Japan, there is a sharp division of labor and of interest: Husbands and wives know little about the other's world and do not engage in many activities together. But when removed from the social context of work, family, and neighbors that surrounds them in Japan and placed in the position of expatriates living in the United States—a position that some of the women liken to a "long vacation"—a space is opened for changes in family dynamics.

Caring for Infibulated Women Giving Birth in Norway

Female genital cutting has generated enormous publicity—and enormous conflict. Coping with this practice across difference is complex. People in Western societies often have very little grasp of how the operation fits into the cultural practices of those who perform it. Even women from societies with the tradition find themselves on opposing sides: some seek asylum to avoid it, while others are prosecuted because they seek to have it performed on their daughters. Many governments have declared it a human rights violation.

Norway has struggled with these issues since 1991, when it became the home of a large number of refugees from civil war in Somalia (Figure 14.14). Norwegian health care is free, and Norway has one of the lowest infant mortality rates in the world. Nevertheless, despite the efforts of dedicated health care workers to be culturally sensitive, outcomes for Somali women are not always optimal. Medical anthropologist R. Elise B. Johansen tried to find out why (Johansen 2006, 516).

In contemporary Norway, Johansen reports, giving birth is considered a positive, "natural" process that women are expected to be able to handle with minimal medical intervention. As a result, "midwives are preferred to obstetricians, medication and incisions are avoided whenever possible, partners are allowed to be present in the delivery room to support the birthing mother, newborns are immediately placed on the mother's belly, and mothers are encouraged to breast feed immediately" (2006, 521). At the same time, Norwegian health workers believe that giving birth naturally is hard for Norwegian women, because their "natural female essence" is "buried under layers of modernity" (521). Norwegian women nevertheless support natural birth practices out of concern for the health of the child, and they expect to manage the pain of unmedicated labor assisted by nothing more than their own physical stamina. Midwives also usually leave women alone until the expulsion phase of labor begins, a practice connected to their idea of what constitutes a natural delivery: "Women are expected to take charge of their own deliveries. Health workers explained restricted interference as a gesture of respect for women's strength and ability to deliver by themselves," an attitude that is possibly also reinforced by the Norwegian values of independence and privacy (538).

What happens when midwives with these expectations encounter Somali women about to give birth? The high value they place on "natural" birthing has led some to regard African immigrant women as "more natural than most Norwegians" and "in closer contact with their female essence" (Johansen 2006, 521). As a result, health care workers sometimes assume that African women are "naturally" equipped with the skills they need to deliver and care for their babies. Only "modern" Norwegian women require such things as medication or child care instruction.

At the same time, Somali women present a paradox: they are African, but they have been infibulated, and infibulation is thought by most health workers to be "the ultimate expression of female oppression and male dominance" (Johansen 2006, 522). As a result, "infibulated women in the delivery ward present a confusing mixture because 'the natural wild' has culturally constructed genitals" (522). Johansen saw this paradox as "central to understanding the challenges facing health workers in looking after infibulated women during delivery" (522).

Midwives thought of infibulation as a social stigma: it marked infibulated women "as incomplete, disfigured, and oppressed" (Johansen 2006, 523). Johansen concludes that health care workers are at once troubled by infibulation and concerned that this discomfort not interfere with their "professionalism." Their solution is simply *not to speak about infibulation*, a decision that "seems to increase discomfort in both health workers and birthing women. It also reduces the parties' chances of exchanging vital information" (523).

Although the midwives Johansen interviewed knew about infibulation, they had not been formally trained to provide care for infibulated women giving birth because guidelines were not yet available. This lack of training, coupled with the midwives' unwillingness to talk with Somali women about infibulation, had two unfortunate, interconnected effects. First, it made many Somali women unsure about whether they would be properly cared for during their deliveries, adding to their own anxieties about childbirth. Second, it allowed health care workers to draw their own silent, *mistaken* conclusions about the "cultural meaning" of infibulation for Somali women. Midwives assumed without asking, for example, that Somali women would not want to be defibulated—that is, to have the infibulation scar cut to widen the vaginal opening. They further assumed without asking that Somali women would also oppose the use of *episiotomies*—cuts

Kurotani studied corporate wives in three places in the United States where there were substantial but different communities of expatriate Japanese: a place in the Midwest she calls "Centerville," New York City, and the Research Triangle in North Carolina. The three cases were different in important ways, in terms of the availability of Japanese products, Japanese schools and restaurants, and the degree to which the major Japanese

FIGURE 14.14 These Somali women are returned refugees. Political turmoil in their country has led many Somalis to flee to other countries, including Norway.

used to widen the vaginal passage for the child during delivery. Such cuts, which are sewn up afterward, are a standard practice in Western obstetrics.

Since many health care workers assumed that Somali values dictated that Somali women remain infibulated through life, they were concerned that defibulation would violate those values. Why had one midwife chosen to perform three episiotomies to avoid defibulating one Somali woman, even though episiotomies involve cutting through muscular and blood-filled tissue? Had the midwife asked the woman if she preferred defibulation? The surprised midwife replied, "No! Of course she wants to remain the way she is" (Johansen 2006, 526). Because the midwife assumed that Somali women want to remain infibulated and because the midwife wanted to respect this wish, to ask this Somali woman if she wanted defibulation made no sense to the midwife.

Had the midwives actually spoken with Somali women, Johansen reports, much discomfort and misunderstanding could have been avoided on both sides. Midwives would have learned that almost all Somali women *wanted* to be defibulated and *did not want* to be reinfibulated—and that nearly two thirds of their husbands did not want their wives to be reinfibulated either (Johansen 2006, 527). Midwives would also have learned that Somali infibulation practices were different from infibulation practices elsewhere in Africa. As we saw from Boddy's ethnography in Chapter 8, lifelong infibulation is a traditional practice in Sudan. Johansen discovered that "infibulation as practiced in Sudan has been taken to represent infibulation in general, so that the practice of reinfibulation in Sudan is taken as evidence that reinfibulation must also be common in all other societies practicing infibulation. However, as we have seen, this is not always the case" (529).

Johansen's research shows how even attempts to be culturally sensitive can generate a wall of misconceptions. These can circumvent actual conversation with those individuals whose culture is the focus of attention. There is no question that the midwives were trying to do right by the women they attended. Ironically, however, from a Norwegian perspective, to respect the dignity and autonomy of Somali women meant that one left Somali women alone and *did not ask them questions*. In situations like this, medical anthropologists can play an important role as cultural brokers who see situations from a fresh perspective, ease the friction, and help to build a bridge across difference. ∎

corporations provided for the families of their Japanese employees on assignment in the United States. But there were some experiences in common. As Kurotani remarks, "During their long vacation, Japanese corporate wives also experience several profound changes in their lives that, in some cases, permanently change their relation to their domesticity, their family and to Japan. Although the vacation will come to an end sooner or later, its transformative potential goes far beyond wishful thinking in some critical instances" (2005, 182). Not only are husbands and wives thrown together in ways that are unfamiliar to them, but also they are forced to deal with life in the United States and with neighbors, friends, coworkers, teachers, or other parents who defamiliarize the things about everyday life that the Japanese wives had always previously taken for granted.

Many women find that their relationships with their children change as a result of residence in the United States: mothers feel that they have an improved understanding of their children because the isolation and difficulty they faced together have made them more like partners. But a much larger change can occur in the conjugal relationship, beginning in ways that seem trivial—a husband begins to take out the trash and bring the trash bin back from the end of the driveway; a husband begins to cook on the barbecue grill in warm weather. But Kurotani observes that "it was often through everyday practices in and around their home that they begin to renegotiate their domestic relationships" (2005, 189).

One of the consequences of this renegotiation was that male Japanese workers spent more time at home with the family, took on additional responsibilities at home, and often found themselves enjoying both as well as coming to depend on their wife's support. The wives appreciated a greater sense of closeness and egalitarian partnership with their husbands. "Expatriate Japanese husbands and wives in the United States not only depend on each other to share the responsibility of work, but also seek personal support and camaraderie in each other—in many cases, for the first time in their marriage. Once established, this sense of partnership seems to last. To many of my informants, this is 'the best thing' that happened to them during [their stay abroad]" (Kurotani 2005, 191). Although the return to Japan was difficult, and many of the changes the women underwent in the United States had to be put on hold, the changes in the conjugal relationships have called into question the "naturalness" of the division between men's and women's work.

Families by Choice

In spite of the range of variation in family forms that we have surveyed, some readers may still be convinced that family ties depend on blood and that blood is thicker than water. It is therefore instructive to consider the results of research carried out by Kath Weston (1991) on family forms among gays and lesbians in the

San Francisco Bay Area during the 1980s. Weston knew that a turning point in the lives of most gays and lesbians was the decision to announce their sexual orientation to their parents and siblings. If blood truly were thicker than water, this announcement should not destroy family bonds, and many parents have indeed been supportive of their children after the announcement. Often enough, however, shocked parents have turned away, declaring that this person is no longer their son or daughter. Living through—or even contemplating—such an experience has been enough to force gays and lesbians to think seriously about the sources of family ties.

By the 1980s, some North American gays and lesbians had reached two conclusions: (1) that blood ties *cannot* guarantee the "enduring diffuse solidarity" supposedly at the core of North American kinship (Schneider 1968); and (2) that new kin ties *can* be created over time as friends and lovers demonstrate their genuine commitment to one another by creating families of choice. "Like their heterosexual counterparts, most gay men and lesbians insisted that family members are people who are 'there for you,' people you can count on emotionally and materially" (Weston 1991, 113). Some gay kinship ideologies now argue that "whatever endures is real" as a way of claiming legitimacy for chosen families that were not the product of heterosexual marriages. Such a definition of family is compatible with understandings of kinship based on nurturance described earlier in this chapter. Gay and lesbian activists have used this similarity as a resource in their struggles to obtain for long-standing families by choice some of the same legal rights enjoyed by traditional heterosexual families, such as hospital visiting privileges, joint adoption, and property rights (Weston 1995, 99). As legislation in the United States, Canada, Europe, and parts of Latin America has made it possible for LGBT people to marry, these legal rights have followed.

The Flexibility of Marriage

It is easy to get the impression that marriage rules compel people to do things they really do not want to do. Younger people, for example, seem forced by elders to marry complete strangers of a certain kin category belonging to particular social groups; or women appear to be pawns in men's games of prestige and power. Marriage rules, however, are always subject to some negotiation, as illustrated by the marriage practices of the Ju/'hoansi of the Kalahari Desert (see Chapter 11, "EthnoProfile 11.4:

IN THEIR OWN WORDS

Why Migrant Women Feed Their Husbands Tamales

Brett Williams suggests that the reasons Mexican migrant women feed their husbands tamales may not be the stereotypical reasons that outside observers often assume.

Because migrant women are so involved in family life and so seemingly submissive to their husbands, they have been described often as martyred purveyors of rural Mexican and Christian custom, tyrannized by excessively masculine, crudely domineering, rude and petty bullies in marriage, and blind to any world outside the family because they are suffocated by the concerns of kin. Most disconcerting to outside observers is that migrant women seem to embrace such stereotypes: they argue that they should monopolize their foodways and that they should not question the authority of their husbands. If men want tamales, men should have them. But easy stereotypes can mislead; in exploring the lives of the poor, researchers must revise their own notions of family life, and this paper argues that foodways can provide crucial clues about how to do so.

The paradox is this: among migrant workers both women and men are equally productive wage earners, and husbands readily acknowledge that without their wives' work their families cannot earn enough to survive. For migrants the division of labor between earning a living outside the home and managing household affairs is unknown; and the dilemma facing middle-class wives who may wish to work to supplement the family's income simply does not exist. Anthropologists exploring women's status cross-culturally argue that women are most influential when they share in the production of food and have some control over its distribution. If such perspectives bear at all on migrant women, one might be led to question their seemingly unfathomable obsequiousness in marriage.

Anthropologists further argue that women's influence is even greater when they are not isolated from their kinswomen, when women can cooperate in production and join, for example, agricultural work with domestic duties and childcare. Most migrant women spend their lives within large, closely knit circles of kin and their work days with their kinswomen. Marriage does not uproot or isolate a woman from her family, but rather doubles the relatives each partner can depend on and widens in turn the networks of everyone involved. The lasting power of marriage is reflected in statistics which show a divorce rate of 1% for migrant farmworkers from Texas, demonstrating the strength of a union bolstered by large numbers of relatives concerned that it go well. Crucial to this concern is that neither partner is an economic drain on the family, and the Tejano pattern of early and lifelong marriages establishes some limit on the whimsy with which men can abuse and misuse their wives.

While anthropology traditionally rests on an appreciation of other cultures in their own contexts and on their own terms, it is very difficult to avoid class bias in viewing the lives of those who share partly in one's own culture, especially when the issue is something so close to home as food and who cooks it. Part of the problem may lie in appreciating what families are and what they do. For the poor, public and private domains are blurred in confusing ways, family affairs may be closely tied to economics, and women's work at gathering and obligating or binding relatives is neither trivial nor merely a matter of sentiment. Another problem may lie in focusing on the marital relationship as indicative of a woman's authority in the family. We too often forget that women are sisters, grandmothers, and aunts to men as well as wives. Foodways can help us rethink both of these problematic areas and understand how women elaborate domestic roles to knit families together, to obligate both male and female kin, and to nurture and bind their husbands as well.

Source: Williams 1984.

Ju/'hoansi (!Kung). Richard Lee (2013) notes that all first marriages were set up by means of a long-term exchange of gifts between the parents of a bride and groom.

The Ju/'hoansi kinship system is as simple or as complex as people want to make it, and the game of kinship is extended to marriage. A girl may not marry a father, brother, son, uncle, or nephew or a first or second cousin. A girl may also not marry a boy with her father's or brother's name, and a boy may not marry a girl with his mother's or sister's name. In addition, neither a

IN THEIR OWN WORDS

Two Cheers for Gay Marriage

Roger Lancaster is professor of anthropology and director of cultural studies at George Mason University. In this essay from the Anthropology News of September 2004, he discusses some of the issues involved with gay marriage.

Announcing his support for a proposed constitutional amendment to ban same-sex marriages, President Bush pronounced marriage, or more specifically the union of one man and one woman, to be "the most fundamental institution of civilization." Actually, it can hardly be said that monogamous heterosexual marriage is the sole form of union "honored and encouraged in all cultures and by every religious faith," as Bush claims. That's Anthropology 101. Nor can it be said that the idea of gay marriage runs counter to 5,000 years of moral teaching, as spokespersons for the Christian right insist.

What careful scholarship and "millennia of human experience" actually show is that marriage cannot be forever fixed into a one-size-fits-all formula. There's more than one way to live, to love, and to set up home and hearth.

Just What Is Marriage?

Marriage sometimes involves a formal union marked by a public announcement or a ritual—like a wedding. Or it might have the informal character of a union gradually acquired or consolidated over a period of time. What North Americans and Europeans call "common-law marriage" is the prevailing form of union in many parts of Latin America and elsewhere. For these (and other) reasons, anthropologists often avoid using baggage-laden terms like "marriage" when describing the broad sweep of institutions related to affinity, residency and kinship, opting instead for more portable (if off-putting) technical terms like "union" or "alliance."

Just how many forms of same-sex union one discerns across cultures and throughout human history will depend on what one counts as "same sex" and "union." Bonds of same-sex friendship, publicly announced and ritually marked by an officiating authority, amount to something very much like "marriage" in a great number of cultures. So do other forms of same-sex group affiliation, such as orders of nuns, certain priesthoods, the Band of Thebes,

any number of warrior castes, and highly organized groups of women who lived collectively on the Chinese Kwantung delta in the 19th century. Ironically, the very wedding vows that the president wants to "protect" derive from early Greek Christian same-sex commitment ceremonies, as historian John Boswell has shown in his final book, *Same-Sex Unions in Premodern Europe.*

Modern Love

What most Americans think of as "marriage" actually turns out not to be a universal institution, but a relatively recent invention. If you read St Paul or St Augustine, for instance, you'll see that the fathers of the early Christian Church were quite hostile to marriage. Far from celebrating the sexual union of one man and one woman, St Paul recommended celibacy for everyone and only grudgingly accepts marriage as a back-up plan: "Better to marry than to burn."

Although archaic texts sometimes refer to wedding feasts, marriage rituals involving the exchange of vows appear to develop fairly late in medieval Europe. The idea that an officiating authority—a priest—ought to be present during those vows comes later still. Later yet, the Church starts to keep records. And much later, the state becomes involved.

The revolutionary notion that one might marry, not in the political or economic interests of extended kin groups, but voluntarily and out of love, is an idea of distinctly modern vintage—one whose implications our culture continues to digest. And that's where we find ourselves today: in the throes of ongoing changes and contestations.

Social conservatives lament the decline of traditional families, the rise of divorce rates, the spread of cohabiting arrangements, the emergence of new family forms and, perhaps especially, the growing visibility of lesbian and gay relationships. They tap pervasive feelings of unease about the new arrangements. But logically, you can't have love without heartache. You probably can't have the idea that love is the sole legitimate basis for marriage without also having modern divorce rates. (Levelheaded people entered into the spirit of this arrangement in the 1970s, when they began vowing "as long as we both shall love.") All said, these aspects of sexual modernity would seem to follow,

IN THEIR OWN WORDS

more or less logically, from the idea that our relationships, like other contracts in a market economy, ought to be entered into freely. They would seem to follow from the idea that marriage ought to be based on love.

And once you have a modern culture of love, linked to that consummate American right, "the pursuit of happiness," it becomes difficult to justify arbitrarily excluding people from it.

Where Do We Go from Here?

Obviously, who's in and who's out of official kinship really matters. It counts in ways that are more than symbolic. There are real social, economic and health care implications. It's thus important to modernize the official definitions of marriage. But like most members of the gay left, I do worry about the fetishization of marriage and family in US political culture—a phenomenon not notably vented in a single other industrial democracy. Claims about the supposed benefits of marriage, anguish over how to strengthen the family, and endless talk about "individual responsibility" have become panaceas in an era of declining wages, skyrocketing health care costs, vindictive welfare reform and social insecurity in general.

These collective fantasies distill a distinctly neoliberal picture of the world: the family, shored up by monogamous marriage (and sometimes enhanced by "covenant marriage"), is to act as a sort of state within the state, providing for individual members' welfare—precisely at a time when the state has renounced its historic responsibilities for social welfare (as I have shown in *The Trouble with Nature*).

In this skewed and surreal context, advocates of gay marriage sometimes sound more conservative than the conservatives. They sometimes present an astonishingly unrepresentative and unrealistic picture of gay and lesbian relationships. In a recent *Nation* article, Lisa Duggan pulls this quote from "The Roadmap to Equality," published by the Lambda Legal Defense and Education Fund and Marriage Equality in California: "Gay people are very much like everyone else. They grow up, fall in love, form families and have children. They mow their lawns, shop for groceries and worry about making ends meet. They want good schools for their children, and security for their families as a whole."

Frankly, I doubt that this suburban picture of children, school worries, lawnmowers, and domestic bliss really applies to more than a very small minority—perhaps as small as 3 or 4%—of the gay and lesbian community. I certainly want no part of America's deranged culture of lawn care. I also chafe at the idea, floated in the same guide, that denying marriage rights to lesbian and gay couples keeps them in a state of permanent adolescence. . . . I don't feel like a permanent adolescent, and palaver like this makes me deeply ashamed for Lambda Legal Defense.

I've lived with my lover for over 15 years. I'd like some legal recognition of our relationship. I'd like the right to file joint taxes, if married couples are going to have that option, and the right to inherit each other's pensions and social security benefits. But I have no interest in quasi-religious rigmarole or moralizing platitudes. I don't feel that our relationship would benefit from the exchange of vows. And like most sound people of my generation, I'm skeptical of claims about the moral and existential benefits of being "shackled by forgotten words and bonds / And the ink stains that are dried upon some line" (as John Hartford once put it).

We need gay marriage, and we should fight for it. But we also need recognition of the true existent variety of ways people live and love. And everybody—whether they take the plunge or not—ought to have access to basic health care, affordable housing and a decent retirement. A one-size institution won't fit all. We need more options, not less. We need to be as radical as reality about these matters.

Source: Lancaster 2004.

boy nor a girl should marry someone who stands in an avoidance relationship.

Consequently, for the Ju/'hoansi, about three-quarters of a person's potential spouses are off limits. In practice, parents of girls tend to be quite choosy about whom their daughter marries. If they are opposed to a particular suitor, they will come up with a kin or name prohibition to block the match. Because the parents arrange the first marriage, it appears that the girl has very little to say about it. If she has an objection and protests long and hard, however, her parents may well call it off. This clear and insistent assertion of displeasure is not uncommon in the world. Even when a young woman follows the wishes of her parents for her first marriage, that first marriage may not be her last if dissatisfaction persists. Despite the parents' quest to find ideal spouses for their children, close to half of all first marriages among the Ju/'hoansi fail. However, as in many societies, only about 10% of marriages that last five years or longer end in divorce (Lee 2013, 90).

Sometimes the contrast between the formal rules of marriage and the actual performance of marriage rituals can be revealing. Ivan Karp (1990) asks why Iteso women laugh at marriage ceremonies. During his fieldwork, Karp was struck by a paradox. The marriage ritual is taken very seriously by the patrilineal Iteso; it is the moment of creation for a new household, and it paves the way for the physical and social reproduction of Iteso patrilineages. But the ritual is carried out entirely by women who are not consanguineal members of the patrilineage! Despite the seriousness of the occasion and although they are carrying out the ritual for the benefit of a lineage to which they do not belong, Iteso women seem to find the ceremony enormously funny.

To explain this apparently anomalous behavior, Karp suggests that the meaning of the marriage ritual needs to be analyzed from two different perspectives: that of the men and that of the women. The men's perspective constitutes the official (or hegemonic) ideology of Iteso marriage. It emphasizes how marriage brings the bride's sexuality under the control of her husband's lineage. It distinguishes between women of the mother-in-law's generation and women of the wife's own generation. It stresses the woman's role as an agent of reproduction who is equivalent, in a reproductive sense, to the bridewealth cattle.

The women's perspective constitutes an unofficial (or counterhegemonic) ideology. For the men and women of a given lineage to succeed in perpetuating that lineage, they must control women's bodies. But the bodies they must control belong to female outsiders who marry lineage men. These same female outsiders direct the two ritual events crucial to lineage reproduction: marriage and birth. And men of the lineage are not allowed to attend either of these rituals. In sum, female outsiders control the continued existence of a patrilineage whose male members are supposed to control them!

Iteso women, Karp says, can see the irony in this: they are at once controlled and controlling. In the marriage ritual itself, they comment on this paradox through their laughter. In so doing, they reveal two things. First, they show that they know the men are dependent on them. Second, even as the men assert their control over

women's bodies, the women's ritual actions escape the men's control. The official ideology of male control is subverted, at least momentarily, by the women's laughter. Even as they ensure that lineages will continue, they are able to comment on the paradoxical relation of women to men. It should be remembered, however, that all the women could do was comment on those relations; they did not have the power to change them.

Love, Marriage, and HIV/AIDS in Nigeria

While marriages among the Igbo (the third largest ethnic group in Nigeria) used to be arranged, today ideas about romantic love have become increasingly important, and most young people expect to marry for love. Anthropologist Daniel Smith (2006) explored how changes in Igbo ideas about marriage, romance, intimacy, and premarital sex intersect with older ideas about parenthood, gender inequality, and how male extramarital sexual relationships put married women at serious risk for contracting HIV/AIDS from their husbands.

Historically, Igbo marriage was "an alliance between two families rather than a contract between two individuals" (Uchendu 1965, 50) and regularly took several years to accomplish. After marriage, the couple ordinarily lived in the compound of the husband's father, and (although this was changing by the mid-1960s) the bride was expected to be a virgin at marriage. Uchendu mentioned that among Igbo professionals, the trend was toward living in nuclear, neolocal families and marrying for love. By the late 1990s, in a sample of 775 Igbo students, Daniel Smith found that 95% said they expected to choose their marriage partners by themselves; and all 420 university students he surveyed had that expectation (2006, 140). Love was frequently mentioned as a criterion for marriage, but was not the only criterion.

Given that men and women are marrying at a later age, that love is becoming an increasingly important criterion for marriage, and that there is a greater value for male–female intimacy in relationships, Smith points out that premarital sexual relationships are increasingly common. "Sex is being socially constructed as an appropriate expression of intimacy, but also as a statement about a particular kind of modern identity" (D. Smith 2006, 141). Smith adds that premarital romances also tend to support a more egalitarian gender dynamics with regard to expectations of fidelity. During courtship, the couple's relationship is based on their personal emotional connection to each other, and both parties feel that they should be faithful to each other. If they are not, one or the other is likely to break off the relationship. But once courtship is over and a couple marries, the situation changes: "conjugal relationships are much more deeply embedded in larger kinship structures and relationships to extended family and community than premarital relationships" (143). In large part, this is due to the importance of parenthood—married people are supposed to have children. Once they have children, particularly if there is a son, there are few socially acceptable reasons for a couple to divorce. If their personal relationship is a difficult one, family members will try to mediate, but even a broken relationship between husband and wife is not generally sufficient grounds for divorce.

A second important change after marriage and parenthood is a shift away from the individualistic gender dynamics of courtship toward a more traditional pattern of male infidelity. Wives continue to want a faithful husband, but this is unrealistic; a significant proportion of married men have lovers, sometimes several in sequence. "The sad irony is that even as women continue to deploy ideals of intimacy and love to influence their husbands' sexual behavior, these very ideals prevent the negotiation of safe sex" (D. Smith 2006, 145). In the first place, HIV/AIDS has been defined by Igbo people as a disease of immorality spread through reckless sex with prostitutes or other strangers. But married men with lovers do not think they are engaging in reckless or anonymous sex—they know who their lovers are. Even when money changes hands it is not directly for sex; it is understood to be for personal or kinship and family matters—it is for school tuition for the lover's siblings or to assist her parents with a problem in the village. Because men's lovers hardly appear to be stereotypical AIDS carriers, men see no reason to use a condom when they are with them, especially since condoms are supposed to inhibit pleasure. At the same time, for a wife who believes in ideals of love and intimacy marked by sexual fidelity and who expects to have children, to insist that her husband use a condom can be taken by her husband as implying that he (or she!) is unfaithful. Thus, for a wife to try to protect herself undermines exactly what she wants to preserve. "Rather than protecting women, love marriages may contribute to the risk of contracting HIV from their husbands" (153).

Chapter Summary

1. Human life is group life; we depend on one another to survive. All societies invent forms of relatedness to organize this interdependence. People in all societies recognize that they are connected to certain other people in a variety of ways and that they are not connected to some people at all. Anthropologists have traditionally paid closest attention to those formal systems of relatedness called kinship systems. But anthropologists also draw attention to other forms of relatedness, like friendship, that may provide ways of counterbalancing relations with kin. It is important to remember that all forms of relatedness are always embedded in and shaped by politics, economics, and worldviews.

2. To recognize the varied forms that institutions of human relatedness can take is to acknowledge fundamental openness in the organization of human interdependence. New shared experiences offer raw material for the invention of new forms of common identity. Anthropologists now argue that all communities—even face-to-face communities—larger than a single individual are contingent, "imagined" communities. That is, all human communities are social, cultural, and historical constructions. They are the joint outcome of shared habitual practices and of symbolic images of common identity promulgated by group members with an interest in making a particular imagined identity endure.

3. Friendships are relatively "unofficial" bonds of relatedness that are personal, affective, and, to a varying extent from society to society, a matter of choice. Nevertheless, in some societies, friendships may be so important that they are formalized like marriages. Depending on the society, friendships may be developed to strengthen kin ties or to subvert kin ties because friendship is understood as the precise opposite of formal kin ties. This illustrates the ways in which people everywhere struggle to find ways to preserve certain ties of relatedness without being dominated by them.

4. The system of social relations that is based on prototypical procreative relationships is called kinship. Kinship principles are based on but not reducible to the universal human experiences of mating,

(continued on next page)

Chapter Summary *(continued)*

birth, and nurturance. Kinship systems help societies maintain social order without central government. Although female–male duality is basic to kinship, many societies have developed supernumerary sexes or genders.

5. Patterns of descent in kinship systems are selective. Matrilineal societies emphasize that women bear children and trace descent through women. Patrilineal societies emphasize that men impregnate women and trace descent through men. Adoption pays attention to relationships based on nurturance, whether or not they are also based on mating and birth.

6. Descent links members of different generations with one another. Bilateral descent results in the formation of groups called *kindreds* that include all relatives from both parents' families. Unilineal descent results in the formation of groups called *lineages* that trace descent through either the mother or the father. Unlike kindreds, lineages are corporate groups. Lineages control important property, such as land, that collectively belongs to their members. The language of lineage is the idiom of political discussion, and lineage relationships are of political significance.

7. Kinship terminologies pay attention to certain attributes of people that are then used to define different classes of kin. The attributes most often recognized include, from most to least common, generation, gender, affinity, collaterality, bifurcation, relative age, and the gender of the linking relative.

8. Anthropologists recognize six basic terminological systems according to their patterns of classifying cousins. In recent years, however, anthropologists have become quite skeptical of the value of these idealized models because they are highly formalized and do not capture the full range of people's actual practices.

9. By prescribing certain kinds of marriage, lineages establish long-term alliances with one another. Two major types of prescriptive marriage patterns in unilineal societies are a father's sister's daughter marriage system (which sets up a pattern of direct exchange marriage) and a mother's brother's daughter marriage system (which sets up a pattern of asymmetrical exchange marriage).

10. Achieved kinship statuses can be converted into ascribed ones by means of adoption. In Zumbagua, Ecuador, most adults have several kinds of parents and several kinds of children, some adopted and some not. Zumbaguan adoptions are based on nurturance—in this case, the feeding by the adoptive parent of the adopted child.

11. From the complexities of Ju/'hoansi kinship negotiations to the unique features of *compadrazgo* in Latin America to the dilemmas created by new reproductive technologies and organ transplantation, anthropologists have shown clearly that kinship is a form of relatedness, a cultural construction that cannot be reduced to biology.

12. Marriage is a social process that transforms the status of a man and woman, stipulates the degree of sexual access the married partners may have to each other, establishes the legitimacy of children born to the wife, and creates relationships between the kin of the wife and the kin of the husband.

13. Woman marriage and ghost marriage highlight several defining features of marriage and also demonstrate that the roles of husband and father may not be dependent on the gender of the person who fills it.

14. There are four major patterns of postmarital residence: neolocal, patrilocal, matrilocal, and avunculocal.

15. A person may be married to only one person at a time (monogamy) or to several (polygamy). Polygamy can be further subdivided into polygyny, in which a man is married to two or more wives, and polyandry, in which a woman is married to two or more husbands.

16. The study of polyandry reveals the separation of a woman's sexuality and her reproductive capacity, something not found in monogamous or polygynous societies. There are three main forms of polyandry: fraternal polyandry, associated polyandry, and secondary marriage.

17. Bridewealth is a payment of symbolically important goods by the husband's lineage to the wife's lineage. Anthropologists see this as compensation to the wife's family for the loss of her productive and reproductive capacities. A woman's bridewealth payment may enable her brother to pay bridewealth to get a wife.

18. Dowry is typically a transfer of family wealth from parents to their daughter at the time of her marriage. Dowries are often considered the wife's contribution to the establishment of a new household.

19. In some cultures, the most important relationships a man and a woman have are with their opposite-sex siblings. Adult brothers and sisters may see one another often and jointly control lineage affairs.

20. Different family structures produce different internal patterns and tensions. There are three basic family types: nuclear, extended, and joint. Families may change from one type to another over time and with the birth, growth, and marriage of children.

21. Most human societies permit marriages to end by divorce, although it is not always easy. In most societies, childlessness is grounds for divorce.

Sometimes nagging, quarreling, adultery, cruelty, and stinginess are causes. In some societies, only men may initiate a divorce. In very few societies is divorce impossible.

22. Families have developed ingenious ways of keeping together even when some members live abroad for extended periods. Gays and lesbians in North America have created families by choice, based on nurturance, which they believe are as enduring as families based on marriage and birth.

23. Marriage rules are subject to negotiation, even when they appear rigid. This is illustrated by Iteso marriage. The Iteso depend on women from the outside to perpetuate their patrilineages, and the women express their ironic awareness of this fact through ritualized laughter at marriage.

For Review

1. What is relatedness?
2. Define imagined communities.
3. How are friendship and kinship related, yet distinctive?
4. List the major elements of human kinship systems, as presented in the section "What Is Kinship?"
5. Describe the major strategies human beings have used to establish patterns of descent.
6. Compare bilateral kindreds and unilineal descent groups.
7. What is the technical difference anthropologists recognize between a lineage and a clan?
8. Summarize the key points in the text about patrilineages.
9. Summarize the key points in the text about matrilineages.
10. Explain how kinship and politics come together in northern Thai elections.
11. Prepare a chart of the key criteria used to distinguish kin within kinship terminologies, with a brief explanation of each criterion.
12. Explain the differences between ascribed and achieved status.
13. Explain how the flexibility of relatedness is illustrated by the case studies on adoption in Zumbagua, Ju/'hoansi kin ties and naming, Euro-American new reproductive technologies, and *compadrazgo* in Latin America.

14. Summarize the ways in which kinship relations can produce unexpected or contradictory social outcomes.
15. Define marriage and explain each of the five points of the definition given in the text.
16. Explain woman marriage and ghost marriage among the Nuer. Why is it important to distinguish *pater* and *genitor*?
17. What are affinal relationships? What are consanguineal relationships?
18. Distinguish between endogamy and exogamy.
19. Summarize the different kinds of residence human groups adopt after marriage.
20. Describe monogamy, polygyny, and polyandry.
21. Discuss how different marriage patterns reflect variation in social understandings of male and female sexuality.
22. What are the differences between bridewealth and dowry?
23. What is a family?
24. Summarize the major forms of the family that are discussed in the text.
25. Discuss the ways in which families change, as discussed in the text.
26. Describe the effects of international migration on families.

Key Terms

Suggested Readings

Anderson, Benedict. 2006. *Imagined communities: Reflections on the origin and spread of nationalism,* Rev. ed. London: Verso. *Although Anderson's goal is to address the origin of nationalism, his insistence that all human communities—even those based on kinship—are imagined communities marks an important breakthrough for the study of human social forms. It can be read with profit not only in connection with this chapter, but also with the next.*

Bell, Sandra, and Simon Coleman, eds. 1999. *The anthropology of friendship.* Oxford: Berg. *A collection of articles on friendship, with contributions on Europe, Asia, Africa, and South America.*

Bohannan, Paul, and John Middleton. 1968. *Marriage, family, and residence.* New York: Natural History Press. *A classic collection, with important and readable articles.*

Collier, Jane, and Sylvia Yanagisako, eds. 1987. *Gender and kinship: Essays toward a unified analysis.* Stanford: Stanford University Press. *An important collection of work on the connections between gender and kinship.*

Ginsburg, Faye D. 1998. *Contested lives: The abortion debate in an American community.* Updated ed. Berkeley: University of California Press. *A study of gender and procreation in the context of the abortion debate in Fargo, North Dakota, in the 1980s.*

Ginsburg, Faye D., and Rayna Rapp, eds. 1995. *Conceiving the new world order: The global politics of reproduction.* Berkeley: University of California Press. *An important collection of articles by anthropologists who address the ways human reproduction is structured across social and cultural boundaries.*

Hirsh, Jennifer, and Holly Wardlow, eds. 2006. *Modern loves: The anthropology of romantic courtship and companionate marriage.* Ann Arbor: University of Michigan Press. *This collection of essays explores the many ways in which love, marriage, and desire are changing in societies around the world.*

Kahn, Susan Martha. 2000. *Reproducing Jews: A cultural account of assisted conception in Israel.* Durham, NC: Duke University Press. *An exceptionally interesting ethnographic study of the effects of new reproductive technologies on kinship in Israel.*

Lancaster, Roger. 1992. *Life is hard.* Berkeley: University of California Press. *A stunning analysis of machismo in Nicaragua in which sexual practices North Americans consider homosexual are interpreted very differently.*

Sacks, Karen. 1979. *Sisters and wives.* Urbana: University of Illinois Press. *A Marxian analysis of the notion of sexual equality. This book includes very important data and analysis on sister–brother relations.*

Sharp, Lesley. 2006. *Strange harvest: Organ transplants, denatured bodies, and the transformed self.* Berkeley: University of California Press. *In addition to her discussion of posttransplant forms of kinship, Sharp addresses a range of related issues raised by organ transplantation, all of which—as her subtitle indicates—call into question traditional Western notions of natural bodies and autonomous selves.*

Shostak, Marjorie. 1981. *Nisa: The life and words of a !Kung woman.* New York: Vintage. *A wonderful book. The story of a Ju/'hoansi woman's life in her own words. Shostak provides background for each chapter. There is much here on marriage and everyday life.*

Smith, Mary F. [1954] 1981. *Baba of Karo.* Reprint. New Haven, CT: Yale University Press. *A remarkable document: The autobiography of a Hausa woman born in 1877 in what is today northern Nigeria. A master storyteller, Baba provides much information about Hausa patterns of friendship, clientage, adoption, kinship, and marriage.*

Stone, Linda. 2013. *Kinship and gender*, 5th ed. Boulder, CO: Westview. *A recent discussion of human reproduction*

and the social and cultural implications of male and female reproductive roles.

Stone, Linda, ed. 2001. *New directions in anthropological kinship*. Lanham, MD: Rowman & Littlefield. *An excellent collection of articles on kinship.*

 Visit our online resource center for further reading, web links, free assessments, flashcards, and videos. www.oup.com/he/ lavenda5e

What can anthropology tell us about social inequality?

The ethnographic and historical records show that societies in which people enjoy relatively equal relations with one another have flourished in different times and places. But cultural constructions of human differences and the use of such cultural constructions to build societies based on unequal social relations also have a long history. This chapter discusses some key forms of social and cultural inequality in the contemporary world to which anthropologists have devoted attention.

CHAPTER OUTLINE

What Are Naturalizing Discourses?

Class

Caste

Race

Ethnicity

How Do Anthropologists Study Human Rights?

Chapter Summary

LEARNING OBJECTIVES

- Define a naturalizing discourse and how anthropologists use this concept to understand social inequality.
- Describe how anthropologists define class and how class is constructed cross-culturally, including in Indonesia and the United States.

- Describe how anthropologists define caste and how caste is constructed in India.
- Describe how anthropologists define race and how race is constructed cross-culturally, including in Nicaragua.

- Describe how anthropologists define ethnicity and how ethnicity is constructed cross-culturally.
- Apply anthropological concepts to the notion of human rights and how human rights operate universally in a multicultural world.

Local fishermen head out to sea in Labadee, Haiti, as a luxury cruise ship leaves in the background.

What Are Naturalizing Discourses?

In Chapter 12, we observed that most people in the world today come under the authority of one or another nation-state and that all nation-states are socially stratified. *Stratified societies*, you will recall, are societies made up of permanently ranked subgroups in which the higher ranking groups have disproportionately greater access to wealth, power, and prestige than do lower ranking groups. But inequality in the contemporary world may be constructed out of multiple categories arranged in different, and sometimes contradictory, hierarchies of stratification. In Chapter 13, we discussed how some of these categories—sex, gender, and sexuality—intersect with other categories in the production of such hierarchies. In this chapter, we will pay close attention to some additional important social categories involved in the construction of hierarchies of social inequality: class, caste, race, and ethnicity. It is important to emphasize from the outset that *all* of these categories are culturally and historically created. At the same time, many members of the societies anthropologists study—whether their own or other people's—often argue just the opposite, that these categories have always been part of human society. Claims that consider social categories as eternal and unchanging, rather than the result of history or culture, have been called **naturalizing discourses**.

Anthropologists are suspicious of naturalizing discourses for three related reasons. First, they ignore historical evidence showing how present-day arrangements contrast with earlier social arrangements in society. Second, they ignore variations in social arrangements in other present-day societies, which also show that social life may be organized differently. Finally, they direct attention away from current social inequalities, insisting that these inequalities are so deeply rooted that attempting to change them would be impossible.

Anthropologist Brackette Williams (1989) has argued that naturalizing discourses rely on the imaginary reduction, or *conflation*, of identities to achieve persuasive power. For example, forms of identity such as gender or race or caste—and sometimes even class and ethnicity, not to mention kinship and other forms of relatedness—have been described or justified by someone at some time in terms of *shared bodily substance*. Thus, living within the same territory is conflated with having the same ancestors and inheriting the same culture, which is further conflated with eating the same food, or sharing the same blood or the same genes. Culture is reduced to blood, and "the magic of forgetfulness and selectivity, both deliberate and inadvertent, allows the once recognizably arbitrary classifications of one generation to become the given inherent properties of reality several generations later" (Williams 1989, 431).

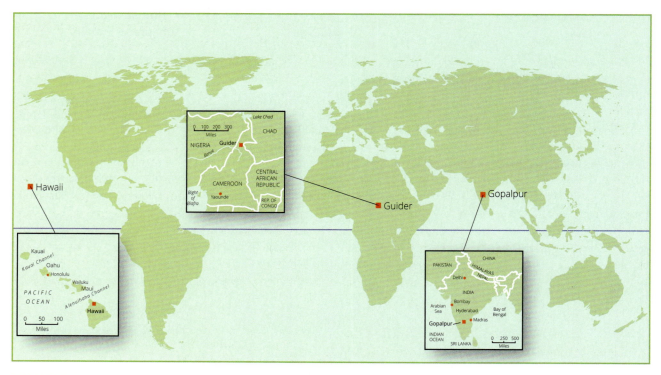

FIGURE 15.1   Location of societies whose EthnoProfiles appear in Chapter 15.

FIGURE 15.2 Social classes often live within easy sight of one another. Here, luxury apartments and squatter settlements rub shoulders in Caracas, Venezuela.

Some of these patterns of inequality, such as class and caste, reach back thousands of years into human history. Others, such as race and ethnicity, are far more recent in origin and are closely associated with changes that began in Europe some 500 years ago. The spread of capitalism and colonialism introduced new forms of stratification into formerly autonomous, egalitarian societies, and these also reshaped forms of stratification that predated their arrival.

Class

In general, **classes** are hierarchically arranged social groups defined on economic grounds. That is, higher-ranked social classes have disproportionate access to sources of wealth in the society, whereas the members of low-ranked classes have much more limited access to wealth (Figure 15.2).

The concept of class has a double heritage in modern anthropology, one stemming from Europe and the other from the United States. European social scientists lived in states with a long history of social class divisions reaching back into the Middle Ages and, in some cases, even into earlier times. In their experience, social classes are well-entrenched and relatively closed groups. In the late 1700s, both the Industrial Revolution and the French Revolution promised to end the oppressive privileges of the ruling class and to equalize everyone's access to wealth. However, class divisions did not wither away in Europe during the nineteenth century; they just changed their contours. Followers of Marx judged that, at best, an old ruling class had been displaced by a new

one: feudal aristocrats had been replaced by bourgeois capitalists. The lowest level in European societies—rural peasants—were partially displaced as well, with the appearance of the urban working class. But the barriers separating those at the top of the class hierarchy from those at the bottom seemed just as rigid as ever.

As we saw in Chapter 11, Marx defines classes in terms of their members' different relations to the means of production. This means that as long as a particular set of unequal productive relations flourishes in a society, the classes defined by these unequal roles in the division of labor will also persist. The French Revolution had triggered the displacement of aristocrats and peasants who had played the key roles in European feudalism. They were replaced by new key classes—industrial entrepreneurs and the industrial working class—who were linked together within the capitalist mode of production. In time, Marx predicted, these industrial workers would become the new "leading class," rising up to oust capitalists when the socialist revolution came.

As Marx was well aware, all those who are linked to the means of production in the same way (e.g., as workers) often do not recognize what they have in common and may therefore fail to develop the kind of solidarity among themselves—the "class consciousness"—that could, in Marx's view, lead to revolution. Indeed, the possibility of peasant- or working-class solidarity in

naturalizing discourses Claims that consider social categories as eternal and unchanging, rather than the result of history or culture.

class A ranked group within a hierarchically stratified society whose membership is defined primarily in terms of wealth, occupation, or other economic criteria.

many of the stratified societies studied by anthropologists is actively undercut by institutions of clientage. According to anthropologist M. G. Smith ([1954] 1981), **clientage** "designates a variety of relationships, which all have inequality of status of the associated persons as a common characteristic" (31). Clientage is a relationship between *individuals* rather than groups. The party of superior status is the patron, and the party of inferior status is the client. Stratified societies united by links of client age can be very stable. Low-status clients believe their security depends on finding a high-status individual who can protect them. For example, clientage is characteristic of *compadrazgo*, or ritual coparenthood relationships, found throughout Latin America. The Latin American societies in which compadrazgo flourishes are class societies, and parents who are peasants or workers often seek landowners or factory owners to serve as *compadres*, or godparents, at the baptism of their children. When the baptism ritual is completed, the parents and godparents of the child now have a new, more relaxed relationship. They call each other "compadre" and can feel freer to seek one another out for support in times of need. Whereas the lower-status biological parents may seek out their higher-status compadres for economic relief, the higher-status individuals might seek out their lower-status compadres for political support.

Class and Gender in Indonesia

In recent years, anthropologists have begun to pay attention to the concerns of the growing middle classes throughout the world. Carla Jones studied the middle class in Indonesia, the world's fourth most populous country and the largest majority Muslim country in the world. Jones notes that market-research companies estimate that the middle-income segment of this population (based on monthly expenditures of approximately US$300) rose from about 19% in the mid-1990s to 30% in 2009 (Jones 2012, 151). Jones (2012) points out that middle-class status in Indonesia is highly gendered: "it is impossible to think of the virtues, thrills, and concerns associated with being middle class in Indonesia without seeing those qualities take form in gendered ways" (146). She tells the story of a friend of hers, whom she calls Ati, who was, like most Javanese women, in charge of her family's income and expenditures but whose husband had forbidden her to allow her small teacher's salary to enter their household, especially for buying food for their four children. Like many middle-class Indonesians whom Jones knew, Ati's husband was concerned with

the level of corruption in Indonesia, as well as the repression of the Suharto government, and believed that money earned from a repressive and corrupt state was itself contaminating and could not be purified. To let that kind of money—and what it purchased—into the private sphere of the household generated anxiety and also put the family at risk. Ati's solution was to use her salary to pay public school fees and to purchase school uniforms for her children. In this way, she returned the tainted money to the state and also complied with her husband's order.

This story suggests that members of the Indonesian middle class do not define themselves in terms of income or money. In fact, citing Ariel Heryano, Jones (2012) notes that they do not even see themselves as members of a class, but rather "as people who are 'educated' or 'developed' and thereby have to pursue a commitment to 'truth, justice, ethics, or beauty' while needing 'to deny their privileged status'" (149). Some scholars argue that consumption is the key element uniting middle-class Indonesians because it is through their consumption patterns that they are able to distinguish themselves from both the lower class and the extremely wealthy.

Indonesian middle-class consumption patterns revolve around women. When the frugal, full-time housewife was seen as the model for middle-class distinction in the 1980s and 1990s, she was seen as domesticating income used for family consumption. But the figure of the housewife also became associated with corruption because she was increasingly seen as a woman who "strained her income-earning husband" through her feminine impulse to consume, corrupting her husband as he strove to satisfy his wife's consumption demands (Jones 2012, 155–56). More recently, the frugal housewife has been replaced by the woman who claims respectability through Muslim piety. But even this image has become tarnished: by consuming the latest elegant Islamic fashions, women are now criticized for pursuing piety as a fashion statement rather than as a religious statement (Jones 2012, 161).

Thus, consumption and femininity are closely linked components in the creation of selves shaped by class. Jones (2012) notes that these Indonesian examples overlap with experiences of middle classes elsewhere (163) and that one might conclude that "the work of linking consumption to feminine pleasure is always political and is a process that rests on irresolvable anxieties" (165). Women, whether housewives, fashionably dressed pious women, or career women, have become symbols of a middle class with an ever-increasing desire for material things, which then increases their share of the burden of proving middle-class respectability.

---

clientage The institution linking individuals from upper and lower levels in a stratified society.

Class and Caste in the United States?

Marx's view of class is clearly different from the hegemonic view of class in the United States. For generations the "American Dream" has been that in the United States individuals may pursue wealth, power, and prestige unhampered by the unyielding class barriers characteristic of "Old World" societies. As a result, many social scientists trained in the United States (including cultural anthropologists) have tended to define social classes primarily in terms of income level and to argue that such social classes are open, porous, and permeable, rather than rigid and exclusionary. Upward class mobility is supposed to be, in principle, attainable by all people, regardless of how low their social origins are. Even poor boys like Abraham Lincoln, born in a log cabin on the frontier, can grow up to be president.

But the promise of the American Dream of equal opportunity for upward class mobility has not been realized by all those living in the United States. In the early twentieth century, both black and white social scientists concluded that an unyielding "color bar" prevented upward class mobility for US citizens with African ancestry. One participant in these studies, a sociologist named W. Lloyd Warner, argued in 1936 that the color bar looked more like the rigid barrier reported to exist between castes in India than the supposedly permeable boundary separating American social classes. That is to say, membership in a **caste** is ascribed at birth, and each ranked caste is closed such that individuals are not allowed to move from one caste into another. Membership in social classes is also ascribed at birth, according to Warner; but unlike castes, classes are not closed, and individual social mobility from one class into another is possible (Sharma 1999, 15; Harrison 1995, 1998; Warner 1936). Warner's distinction between *caste* and *class* became standard for decades in American cultural anthropology.

Is this a plausible contrast? The aspect of caste that impressed Warner was the reported rigidity of the barrier between castes, which seemed much like the barrier separating blacks and whites in the United States. But in 1948, an African American sociologist named Oliver Cromwell Cox rejected an equation between caste and race. Cox pointed out that many authorities on caste in India claimed that Hindu castes were harmoniously integrated within a *caste system* shaped by Hindu religious beliefs about purity and pollution. Most importantly, it appeared that members of low-ranked "impure" castes did not challenge the caste system, although it oppressed them. If this were true, Cox concluded, caste relations were *unlike* race relations in the United States because whites had imposed the color bar by force, and only by

force had they been able to repress black resistance to the injustice of the system. Ursula Sharma (1999) points out, however, that both Warner and Cox were relying on an understanding of Hindu castes that today is considered highly misleading.

Caste

The word **caste** comes from the Portuguese word *casta*, meaning "chaste." Portuguese explorers applied it to the stratification systems they encountered in South Asia in the fifteenth century. They understood that these societies were divided into a hierarchy of ranked subgroups, each of which was "chaste" in the sense that sexual and marital links across group boundaries were forbidden.

Caste in India

The term *caste*, as most Western observers use it, collapses two different South Asian concepts.

The first term, *varna*, refers to the widespread notion that Indian society is ideally divided into priests, warriors, farmers, and merchants—four functional subdivisions analogous to the estates of medieval and early modern Europe (Guneratne 2002; Sharma 1999). The second term, *jati*, refers to localized, named, endogamous groups. Although jati names are frequently the names of occupations (e.g., farmer, saltmaker), there is no agreed-upon way to group the many local jatis within one or the other of the four varnas, which is why jati members can disagree with others about where their own jati ought to belong. In any case, varna divisions are more theoretical in nature, whereas jati is the more significant term in most of the local village settings where anthropologists have traditionally conducted fieldwork. Villagers in the southern Indian town of Gopalpur defined a jati for anthropologist Alan Beals (see "EthnoProfile 15.1: Gopalpur"). They said it was "a category of men thought to be related, to occupy a particular position within a hierarchy of jatis, to marry among themselves, and to follow particular practices and occupations" (Beals 1962, 25). Beals's informants compared the relationship between jatis of different rank to the relationship between brothers. Ideally, they said, members of low-ranking jatis respect and obey members of high-ranking jatis, just as younger brothers respect and obey older brothers.

Villagers in Gopalpur were aware of at least 50 different jatis, although not all were represented in the village. Because jatis have different occupational specialties that

---

caste A ranked group within a hierarchically stratified society that is closed, prohibiting individuals to move from one caste to another.

EthnoProfile 15.1

Gopalpur

Region: Southern Asia

Nation: India

Population: 540 (1960)

Environment: Center of a plain, some fertile farmland and pasture

Livelihood: Intensive millet farming, some cattle and sheep herding

Political organization: Caste system in a modern nation-state

For more information:
Beals, Alan. 1962. *Gopalpur, a south Indian village.* New York: Holt, Rinehart and Winston.

they alone can perform, villagers were sometimes dependent on the services of outsiders. For example, there was no member of the Washerman jati in Gopalpur. As a result, a member of that jati from another village had to be employed when people in Gopalpur wanted their clothes cleaned ritually or required clean cloth for ceremonies.

Jatis are distinguished in terms of the foods they eat as well as their traditional occupations. These features have a ritual significance that affects interactions between members of different jatis. In Hindu belief, certain foods and occupations are classed as pure and others as polluting. In theory, all jatis are ranked on a scale from purest to most polluted (Figure 15.3). Ranked highest of all are the vegetarian Brahmins, who are pure enough to approach the gods. Carpenters and blacksmiths, who also eat a vegetarian diet, are also assigned a high rank. Below the vegetarians are those who eat "clean," or "pure," meat. In Gopalpur, this group of jatis included saltmakers, farmers, and shepherds who eat sheep, goats, chicken, and fish but not pork or beef. The lowest ranking jatis are "unclean" meat eaters, who include stone workers and basket weavers (who eat pork) and leather workers (who eat pork and beef). Occupations that involve slaughtering animals or touching polluted things are themselves polluting. Jatis that traditionally carry out such activities as butchering and washing dirty clothing are ranked below jatis whose traditional work does not involve polluting activities. Hindu dietary rules deal not only with the kinds of food that may be eaten by

different jatis but also with the circumstances in which members of one jati may accept food prepared by members of another. Members of a lower ranking jati may accept any food prepared by members of a higher ranking jati. Members of a higher ranking jati may accept only certain foods prepared by a lower ranking jati. In addition, members of different jatis should not eat together.

In practice, these rules are not as confining as they appear. In Gopalpur, "'food' referred to particular kinds of food, principally rice. 'Eating together' means eating from the same dish or sitting on the same line. . . . Members of quite different jatis may eat together if they eat out of separate bowls and if they are facing each other or turned slightly away from each other" (Beals 1962, 41). Members of jatis that are close in rank and neither at the top nor at the bottom of the scale often share food and eat together on a daily basis. Strict observance of the rules is saved for ceremonial occasions.

The way in which non-Hindus were incorporated into the jati system in Gopalpur illuminates the logic of the system. For example, Muslims have long ruled the region surrounding Gopalpur; thus, political power has been a salient attribute of Muslim identity. In addition, Muslims do not eat pork or the meat of animals that have not been ritually slaughtered. These attributes, taken together, led the villagers in Gopalpur to rank Muslims above the stone workers and basket weavers, who eat pork. All three groups were considered to be eaters of unclean meat because Muslims do eat beef.

Although the interdependence of jatis is explained in theory by their occupational specialties, the social reality is a bit different. For example, saltmakers in Gopalpur are farmers and actually produce little salt, which can be bought in shops by those who need it. It is primarily in the context of ritual that jati interdependence is given

FIGURE 15.3 Gautam Ganu Jadhao, a city worker, removes a cart full of sewage waste from a Bombay neighborhood in July 2005. People like him whose occupations are characterized as polluting are ranked at the bottom of the Hindu caste system.

IN THEIR OWN WORDS

Burakumin: Overcoming Hidden Discrimination in Japan

Tomoe Kawasaki is a college staff member in Japan and identifies herself as a Buraku. Although the Japanese government has passed laws prohibiting discrimination against Burakumin, prejudice remains. On the website globalcompassion.com, which features photos, videos, and writings about our human condition, Tomoe tells her story.

My parents didn't tell me much about Buraku, and they raised me as far away from the Buraku as possible. They didn't want me to suffer any discrimination. Upon taking a class about Buraku issues in college, I started to face my family roots—roots that I was forgetting. I sometimes wrestled with my parents' protective love, and it made me anxious; I wondered if other people would accept me having a Buraku origin. At the same time, it was over-whelmingly joyful for me to learn so much about myself in the contexts of history, culture, and people. Now I often visit my hometown, the Buraku [town] where I lived until the age of 7. Now I am weaving a story that leads to me through the people I was reunited with there. When I took

the plunge and faced my roots, and then leaped further into my past, I found a world so wonderful.

Source: https://masarugoto.com/portfolios/nihon-jin-buraku-min-portraits-of-japans-outcast-people. Consulted August 12, 2020.

Tomoe Kawasaki.

full play. Recall that Gopalpur villagers required the services of a washerman when they needed to ritually clean garments or cloth; otherwise, most villagers washed their own clothing. "To arrange a marriage, to set up the door-way of a new house, to stage a drama, or to hold an entertainment, the householder must call on a wide range of jatis. The entertainment of even a modest number of guests requires the presence of the Singer. The potter must provide new pots in which to cook the food; the Boin from the Farmer jati must carry the pot; the Shepherd must sacrifice the goat; the Crier, a Saltmaker, must invite the guests. To survive, one requires the cooperation of only a few jatis; to enjoy life and do things in the proper manner requires the cooperation of many" (Beals 1962, 41).

How Do Caste and Class Intersect in Contemporary India?

When Beals lived in Gopalpur, he found that there was no direct correlation between the status of a jati on the scale of purity and pollution and the class status of members of

that jati. Beals noted, for example, that the high status of Brahmins meant that "there are a relatively large number of ways in which a poor Brahmin may become wealthy" (1962, 37). Similarly, members of low-status jatis might find their attempts to amass wealth curtailed by the op-position of their status superiors. In Gopalpur, a group of farmers and shepherds attacked a group of stone workers who had purchased good rice land in the village. Those stone workers were eventually forced to buy inferior land elsewhere in the village. In general, however, regardless of jati, a person who wished to advance economically "must be prepared to defend his gains against jealous neighbors. Anyone who buys land is limiting his neigh-bor's opportunities to buy land. Most people safeguard themselves by tying themselves through indebtedness to a powerful landlord who will give them support when difficulties are encountered" (39).

In the past half century, class differentiation has be-come increasingly evident, especially in India's cities. Anthropologist Sara Dickey has worked in urban India for over 30 years, and she has studied how caste and class

IN THEIR OWN WORDS

As Economic Turmoil Mounts, So Do Attacks on Hungary's Gypsies

Ethnic conflict in Europe takes a variety of forms, but one that has a long history is prejudice against Roma, the Gypsies. In April 2009, reporter Nicholas Kulish filed this story with the New York Times.

Jeno Koka was a doting grandfather and dedicated worker on his way to his night-shift job at a chemical plant last week when he was shot dead at his doorstep. To his killer, he was just a Gypsy, and that seems to have been reason enough.

Prejudice against Roma—widely known as "Gypsies" and long among Europe's most oppressed minority groups—has swelled into a wave of violence. Over the past year, at least seven Roma have been killed in Hungary, and Roma leaders have counted some 30 Molotov cocktail attacks against Roma homes, often accompanied by sprays of gunfire.

But the police have focused their attention on three fatal attacks since November that they say are linked. The authorities say the attacks may have been carried out by police officers or military personnel, based on the stealth and accuracy with which the victims were killed.

In addition to Mr. Koka's death, there were the slayings of a Roma man and woman, who were shot after their house was set ablaze last November in Nagycsecs, a town about an hour's drive from Tiszalok in northeastern Hungary. And in February, a Roma man and his 4-year-old son were gunned down as they tried to escape from their home, which was set on fire in Tatarszentgyorgy, a small town south of Budapest.

Jozsef Bencze, Hungary's national police chief, said in an interview on Friday with the daily newspaper *Nepszabadsag* that the perpetrators, believed to be a group of four or more men in their 40s, were killing "with hands that are too confident." Military counterintelligence is taking part in the investigation, Hungarian radio reported, and Mr. Bencze said the pool of suspects included veterans of the Balkan Wars and Hungarian members of the French Foreign Legion.

Experts on Roma issues describe an ever more aggressive atmosphere toward Roma in Hungary and elsewhere in Central and Eastern Europe, led by extreme right-wing parties, whose leaders are playing on old stereotypes of Roma as petty criminals and drains on social welfare

Funeral for Robert Csorba, 27, and his son Robert Jr., 4, in Tatarszentgyorgy, Hungary. The Csorbas were shot dead in February 2009 while fleeing their home, which had been set on fire.

systems at a time of rising economic and political turmoil. As unemployment rises, officials and Roma experts fear the attacks will only intensify.

"One thing to remember, the Holocaust did not start at the gas chambers," said Lajos Korozs, senior state secretary in the Ministry of Social Affairs and Labor, who works on Roma issues for the government. . . .

"In the past five years, attitudes toward Roma in many parts of Eastern Europe have hardened, and new extremists have started to use the Roma issue in a way that either they didn't dare to or didn't get an airing before," said Michael Stewart, coordinator of the Europe-wide Roma Research Network.

The extreme-right party Jobbik has used the issue of what its leaders call "Gypsy crime" to rise in the polls to near the 5% threshold for seats in Hungary's Parliament in next year's election, which would be a first for the party. Opponents accuse the Hungarian Guard, the paramilitary group associated with the party, of staging marches and public meetings to stir up anti-Roma sentiment and to intimidate the local Roma population.

The group held a rally last year in Tiszalok and in 2007 in Tatarszentgyorgy, the town where the father and son were killed in February, an act that some residents deplored while in the same breath complaining about a spate of break-ins in town that they blamed on Roma.

"The situation is bad because of the many Roma," said Eva, 45, a non-Roma Hungarian in Tatarszentgyorgy who declined to give her last name, out of what she said was fear of reprisals. "When the guard was here, for a while they weren't so loud. It helped."

Since the attacks in Tatarszentgyorgy, some local residents have joined their terrified Roma neighbors in nighttime patrols, looking for strange cars armed with nothing but searchlights.

"We are living in fear, all the Roma people are," said Csaba Csorba, 48, whose son Robert, 27, and grandson, also named Robert, were killed by a blast from a shotgun shortly after midnight in the February attack. They were buried together in one coffin, the little boy laid to rest on his father's chest.

The child's death in particular shook Roma here. "It proved to us it doesn't matter whether we are good people or bad people," said Agnes Koka, 32, the niece and goddaughter of Mr. Koka, who relatives said loved to bring candy and fruit to his grandchildren. "It only matters that we are Gypsy," Ms. Koka said.

Source: Kulish 2009.

---

intertwine. Many Indians dream of moving into a higher social class; however, the hurdles poor people face are enormous and involve more than higher income alone. Dickey points out that class status depends not only on economic capital but also on "cultural capital" (how you speak, how you dress, what kind of housing you live in, what kinds of consumer goods you possess) as well as on 'social capital' (whom you know). Being able to amass sufficient amounts of all these kinds of capital is typically beyond the reach of most Indian citizens.

So what makes class mobility possible in India? Dickey contrasts two proposed answers to this question. One proposal, dating from the late twentieth century, argues that class status in India is an individual achievement. Scholars who take this position observed that within any Indian family, there are often stark differences between siblings, in terms of their access both to education and to jobs that provide high incomes. Dickey, however, proposes a second view, arguing that these kinds of differences are better understood as a consequence of choices made by the families of the siblings in question. For example, it is families who decide whether or not they can afford to send one or more of their children to school, because putting a child in school means not only additional expenses but also losing that child as a wage earner. Next, families must decide whether to send their children to government schools or private schools. Government schools cost less, but the education they provide is seen as inferior to that provided in private schools where English is the language of instruction. How many years children attend school is also a family decision, as are further decisions such as whether the family can help pay for university education, and if so, which subjects they are willing to allow their children to study. But even though education opens a lot of doors, education alone cannot ensure that students will be able to acquire all the additional forms of social and cultural capital that might permit their movement into a higher social class.

Against all odds, thanks to family support, luck, and timing, a woman Dickey calls Anjali seems to have successfully moved into a higher social class. Dickey first met Anjali in the city of Madurai in 1985, when Anjali was 7 years old. Her family's caste status was high, but her father worked driving a cycle rickshaw; and even though by Madurai standards they were not considered "poor," their financial situation was precarious. Unlike many girls, Anjali was allowed to attend school, and she did so well that her family allowed her to continue until she graduated from high school. She had hoped to go to university, but her family did not support this expensive ambition. However, when she suggested attending business school, her family did agree to help her. Anjali was also fortunate in being able to find a job that helped pay for her education, and she spent several years juggling work and her studies until she finally obtained her business degree. Shortly thereafter, she persuaded her family to help pay for a course in computer programming, which gave her desirable skills as the Indian tech industry began to grow. With these credentials, Anjali was able to get a job in a small business near home. Spending time with coworkers, she learned how to update her hairstyle and find stylish clothes. Through her work, she made friends with young men as well as young women, something that would have been impossible in earlier generations. As the economic situation in India improved, business loans became available at attractive interest rates. When the firm Anjali worked for decided to move to another part of the city, she persuaded her family to take out such a loan, which allowed her to set up her own firm in the offices of her former employer.

Anjali's family support had made these changes possible, and her parents and siblings benefitted from her increased earning power. But this path to success was not entirely smooth. Her father was injured and unable to continue working. Lacking health insurance, Anjali's family went into debt to pay for his medical treatment, which meant exhausting their savings (including money set aside for her brother's wedding and her own dowry) and pooling their earnings for several years until the debt was paid off. These economic challenges put planning for Anjali's own wedding on hold. Originally Anjali's family had hoped to arrange a marriage for her with either a civil servant with a guaranteed income and pension, or with a business owner. But they knew that securing such a husband would require them to provide a high dowry.

Eventually, Anjali did get married, but by negotiating an "arranged love marriage." Through her work contacts, Anjali had met a man who was the son of a retired civil servant and who owned his own business. They fell in love and wanted to marry, but they did not do so until after their respective families had both approved of the match. Anjali's dowry included not just traditional wealth but the wealth represented by her business. After their marriage, Anjali moved into her husband's extended household. Her husband soon closed his own firm and joined Anjali's prosperous business, where they continued to work together successfully, bringing their young children to the office with them and bringing one of Anjali's younger brothers into the company. After a decade of marriage, Anjali appeared to have successfully moved into a higher social class, and that class status was likely to be perpetuated: both her children were enrolled in a prestigious English-language school in Madurai. But, as Dickey emphasizes, this class mobility depended on her family's support, even as her successes improved their own class standing in the eyes of others.

Beals's study of Gopalpur documented three dimensions of caste relations in India that have become increasingly significant over time. First, Beals describes a rural village in which jati membership mattered most on ritual occasions. In the past 40 years, cultural practices associated with caste in village India have become even more attenuated or have disappeared as increasingly large numbers of Indians have moved to large cities where they are surrounded by strangers whose caste membership they do not know (Sharma 1999, 37). They still use the idiom of purity and pollution to debate the status of particular castes, but otherwise their understanding of caste usually has nothing to do with ritual status.

Second, Beals describes members of middle-ranking jatis in Gopalpur who treated one another as equals outside of ritual contexts. Subrata Mitra points out that "By the 1960s, electoral mobilization had led to a new phenomenon called horizontal mobilization whereby people situated at comparable levels within the local caste hierarchy came together in caste associations" (1994, 61), many of which formed new political parties to support their own interests. Moreover, increased involvement of Indians in capitalist market practices has led to "a proliferation of modern associations that use traditional ties of jati and varna to promote collective economic well-being" (65). For example, a housing trust set up for Brahmins in the Indian state of Karnataka recruits Brahmins from throughout the Karnataka region in an effort to overcome "jati-based division into quarrelling sects of Brahmins" (66). The interests that draw jatis into coalitions of this kind "often turn out to be class interests. . . . This does not mean that caste and class are the same, since commentators note caste as blurring class divisions as often as they express them. Rather it tells us that class and caste are not 'inimical' or antithetical" (Sharma 1999, 68).

Third, Beals showed that middle-ranking jatis in Gopalpur in the 1960s were willing to use violence to block the upward economic mobility of members of a low-ranking jati. Similar behavior was reported in the work of other anthropologists like Gerald Berreman, who did fieldwork in the late 1950s in the peasant village of Sirkanda in the lower Himalayas of North India. Berreman observed that low-caste people in Sirkanda "do not share, or are not heavily committed to, the 'common official values' which high-caste people affect before outsiders. . . . Low-caste people resent their inferior position and the disadvantages which inhere in it" while "high castes rely heavily on threats of economic and physical sanctions to keep their subordinates in line," such that when low-caste people do publicly endorse "common official values," they do so only out of fear of these sanctions (1962, 15–16).

In recent years, a number of low-caste groups in urban India have undertaken collective efforts to lift themselves off the bottom of society, either by imitating the ritual practices of higher castes (a process called "Sanskritization") or by converting to a non-Hindu religion (such as Buddhism or Christianity) in which caste plays no role. According to Dipankar Gupta, this should not surprise us. His research has shown that "castes are, first and foremost, discrete entities with deep pockets of ideological heritage" and that "the element of caste competition is, therefore, a characteristic of the caste order and not a later addition. . . . This implies that the caste system, as a system, worked primarily because it was enforced by power and not by ideological acquiescence" (2005, 412–13).

These challenges have had little effect in changing the negative stereotypes of so-called untouchables held by the so-called clean castes. However, the constitution of India prohibits the practice of untouchability, and the national government has acted to improve the lot of the low castes by regularly passing legislation designed to improve their economic and educational opportunities. In some cases, these measures seem to have succeeded, but violent reprisals have been common. In rural areas, many disputes continue to be over land, as in Gopalpur. However, even worse violence has been seen in urban India, as in 1990, when unrest was triggered by publication of a report recommending increases in the numbers of government jobs and reserved college places set aside for members of low castes. At the end of the twentieth century, relations between low-caste and high-caste Hindus were described as "conflictual rather than competitive in some localities" with "caste violence . . . recognized as a serious problem in contemporary India" (Sharma 1999, 67).

A key element recognized by all anthropologists who use the concept of caste is the endogamy that is enforced, at least in theory, on the members of each ranked group. As van den Berghe (1970) put it, membership in such groups is "determined by birth and for life" (351). Sharma (1999) notes the significance of this link between descent and caste, observing that "in societies where descent is regarded as a crucial and persistent principle (however reckoned, and whatever ideological value it is given) almost any social cleavage can become stabilized in a caste-like form" (85). She suggests the term *castification* to describe a political process by which ethnic or other groups become part of a ranked social order of some kind, probably managed from the top, but which need not develop into a caste system (Sharma 1999, 92–93).

But the principle of descent has also played a central role in the identification and persistence of race, ethnicity, and nation. As noted above, these three categories are all closely bound up with historical developments over the past 500 years that built the modern world. Indeed, these categories are particularly significant in nation-states, and many contemporary nation-states are of very recent, postcolonial origin. Clearly, to make sense of

contemporary postcolonial forms of social stratification, we also need to look more closely at the categories of race and ethnicity.

Race

As we saw in Chapters 1 and 5, the concept of "**race**" developed in the context of European exploration and conquest, beginning in the fifteenth century. Europeans conquered indigenous peoples in the Americas and established colonial political economies that soon depended on the labor of Africans imported as slaves. By the end of the nineteenth century, light-skinned Europeans had established colonial rule over large territories inhabited by darker-skinned peoples, marking the beginnings of a global racial order (see Smedley 1995, 1998; Harrison 1995; Sanjek 1994; Trouillot 1994; Köhler 1978). Some European intellectuals argued at that time that the human species was subdivided into "natural kinds" of human beings called "races" that could be sharply distinguished from one another on the basis of outward phenotypic appearance. All individuals assigned to the same race were assumed to share many other common features, such as language or intelligence, of which phenotype was only the outward index. *Race* was used both to explain human diversity and to justify the domination of indigenous peoples and the enslavement of Africans.

European thinkers, including many early anthropologists, devised schemes for ranking the "races of mankind" from lowest to highest. Not surprisingly, the "white" northern Europeans at the apex of imperial power were placed at the top of this global hierarchy. Darker-skinned peoples, like the indigenous inhabitants of the Americas or of Asia, were ranked somewhere in the middle. But Africans, whom Europeans had bought and sold as slaves and whose homelands in Africa were later conquered and incorporated into European empires, ranked lowest of all. In this way, the identification of races was transformed into **racism**: the systematic oppression of one or more socially defined "races" by another socially defined "race" that is justified in terms of the supposedly inherent biological superiority of the rulers and the supposed inherent biological inferiority of those they rule. It is important to emphasize once

---

race A human population category whose boundaries allegedly correspond to distinct sets of biological attributes.

racism The systematic oppression of one or more socially defined "races" by another socially defined "race" that is justified in terms of the supposedly inherent biological superiority of the rulers and the supposed inherent biological inferiority of those they rule.

again that all the so-called races of human beings are *imagined communities*. As we emphasized in Chapter 5, there are *no* major biological discontinuities within the human species that correspond to the supposed racial boundaries that nineteenth-century European observers thought they had discovered. This means that the traditional concept of biological "race" in Western society is incoherent and biologically meaningless.

Nevertheless, racial thinking persists at the beginning of the twenty-first century, suggesting that racial categories have their origins not in biology but in society. And as we saw in earlier chapters, anthropologists have long argued that race is a culturally constructed social category whose members are identified on the basis of certain selected phenotypic features (e.g., skin color) that all are said to share. The end result is a highly distorted but more or less coherent set of criteria that members of a society can use to assign people they see to one or another culturally defined racial category. Once these criteria exist, members of society can treat racial categories *as if* they reflect biological reality, using them to build institutions that include or exclude particular culturally defined races. In this way, race can become "real" in its consequences, even if it has no reality in biology.

The social category of "race" is a relatively recent invention. Audrey Smedley (1998) reminds us that in the worlds of European classical antiquity and through the Middle Ages, "no structuring of equality . . . was associated with people *because of their skin color*" (693; emphasis in original); and Faye Harrison (1995) points out that "phenotype prejudice was not institutionalized before the sixteenth century" (51). By the nineteenth century, European thinkers (some early anthropologists among them) were attempting to classify all humans in the world into a few, mutually exclusive racial categories. Significantly, from that time until this, as Harrison (1998) emphasizes, "blackness has come to symbolize the social bottom" (612; see also Smedley 1998, 694–95).

White domination of Euro-American racial hierarchies has been a constant, but some anthropologists who study the cultural construction of whiteness point out that even in the United States, "whiteness" is not monolithic, and the cultural attributes supposedly shared by "white people" have varied in different times and places. Some members of white ruling groups in the southern United States, for example, have traditionally distanced themselves from lower-class whites, whom they call "white trash"; and the meaning of whiteness in South

Africa has been complicated by differences of class and culture separating British South Africans from Afrikaners (Hartigan 1997). For that matter, "blackness" is not monolithic either. In Haiti, for example, white French colonists were expelled at independence in 1804, but an internal racial divide has persisted since then between the mass of black Haitians descended from freed slaves and a minority of wealthy, well-educated "mulattos" who originally comprised the offspring of white French fathers and black slave mothers. Throughout Haitian history, this mulatto elite has struggled to distinguish itself from the black majority in the face of outsiders who have steadfastly refused to recognize any difference between the two groups. At times of unrest, however, the US government has regularly supported members of this elite, who have defended their interests by ruthlessly dominating other Haitians, especially the poor (Schiller and Fouron 2001). In the United States, the sharp "caste-like" racial divide between blacks and whites is currently being complicated by new immigrants identified with so-called brown/Hispanic and yellow/Asian racial categories. Harrison and others recognize that racial categorization and repression take different forms in different places.

Colorism in Nicaragua

Anthropologist Roger Lancaster (1992) argues that in Nicaragua, racism exists but that it is "not as absolute and encompassing a racism as that which one encounters in the United States"—although it remains, in his opinion, "a significant social problem" (215). One dimension of Nicaraguan racism contrasts the Spanish-speaking *mestizo* (or "mixed" European and indigenous) majority of the highlands with the indigenous Miskitos and African Caribbeans along the Atlantic coast. The highland mestizos Lancaster knew tended to regard these coastal groups as backward, inferior, and dangerous. These notions were overlaid with political suspicions deriving from the fact that Lancaster's informants were Sandinistas and that some Miskito factions had fought with the Contras against the Sandinistas after the Sandinistas deposed the dictator Anastasio Somoza in 1979.

But Lancaster came to see racism toward the coastal peoples as simply an extension of the pattern of race relations internal to highland mestizo culture that he calls **colorism**: a system of color identities negotiated situationally along a continuum between white and black (Figure 15.4). In colorism, no fixed race boundaries exist. Instead, individuals negotiate their color identity anew in every social situation they enter, with the result that the color they might claim or be accorded changes from situation to situation.

---

colorism A system of social identities negotiated situationally along a continuum of skin colors between white and black.

FIGURE 15.4 This photograph of Brazilian children shows a range of skin tones. In some parts of Latin America, such as Nicaragua and Brazil, such variation is used to create a system of classification based on lightness or darkness of skin tone that assigns people with relatively lighter skin to higher status, a phenomenon that anthropologist Roger Lancaster calls colorism.

Lancaster's informants used three different systems of color classification. The first, or "phenotypic" system, has three categories—*blanco* (white), *moreno* (brown), and *negro* (black)—that people use to describe the various skin tones that can be seen among Nicaraguan mestizos: "Nicaraguan national culture is mestizo; people's physical characteristics are primarily indigenous; and in the terms of this phenotypic system, most people are moreno. In this system, *negro* can denote either persons of African ancestry or sometimes persons of purely indigenous appearance, whether they are culturally classified as Indio or mestizo" (Lancaster 1992, 217).

Lancaster calls the second system Nicaraguans use the "polite" system in which all the colors in the phenotypic system are "inflated." That is, Europeans are called *chele* (a Mayan word meaning "blue," referring to the stereotypically blue eyes of people of European ancestry), morenos are called blanco, and negros are called moreno. Polite terms are used in the presence of the person about whom one is speaking, and Lancaster (1992) was told that it was "a grave and violent offence to refer to a black-skinned person as *negro*" (217). In rural areas, for similar reasons, Indians are called *mestizos* rather than *Indios*.

Lancaster calls the third system of color terms the "pejorative and/or affectionate" system. This system has only two terms, *chele* (fairer skin and lighter hair) and *negro* (darker skin, darker hair). For example, when the less powerful man in an interaction feels he is being imposed on by the more powerful man, the former might express his displeasure by addressing the latter as *chele* or *negro*, both of which would be seen as insulting. Paradoxically,

members of families call one another *negro* or *negrito mio* as affectionate and intimate terms of address, perhaps precisely because these terms are "informal" and violate the rules of polite discourse (Lancaster 1992, 218).

Lancaster (1992) discovered that "Whiteness is a desired quality, and polite discourse inflates its descriptions of people" (219). People compete in different settings to claim whiteness. In some settings, individuals may be addressed as *blanco* if everyone else has darker skin; but in other settings, they may have to yield the claim of whiteness to someone else with lighter skin than theirs and accept classification as *moreno*.

Because it allows people some freedom of maneuver in claiming higher-status color for themselves, Nicaraguan colorism may seem less repressive than the rigid black–white racial dichotomy traditional in the United States. Lancaster points out, however, that all three systems of colorist usage presuppose white superiority and black inferiority. "Africanos, Indios, and lower-class mestizos have been lumped together under a single term—*negro*—that signifies defeat" (Lancaster 1992, 223). Lancaster is not optimistic about the possibilities of successfully overturning this system any time soon in Nicaragua. Similarly, Harrison argues that racial solidarity and rebellion are hard to achieve or sustain in societies like Nicaragua, and she is not optimistic that adoption of a similar system in the United States would improve race relations. On the contrary, she fears that a "more multishaded discourse" would be more likely to contribute to "an enduring stigmatization of blackness" than to "democratization and the dismantling of race" (Harrison 1998, 618–19).

IN THEIR OWN WORDS

On the Butt Size of Barbie and Shani

Dolls and Race in the United States

Anthropologist Elizabeth Chin writes about race and Barbie dolls, based on some hands-on research.

The Shani line of dolls introduced by Mattel in 1991 reduces race to a simulacrum consisting of phenotypical features: skin color, hair, and butt. Ann DuCille . . . has discussed much of their complex and contradictory nature, highlighting two central issues: derriere and hair. According to DuCille's interviews with Shani designers, the dolls have been remanufactured to give the illusion of a higher, rounder butt than other Barbies. This has been accomplished, they told her, by pitching Shani's back at a different angle and changing some of the proportions of her hips. I had heard these and other rumors from students at the college where I teach: "Shani's butt is bigger than the other Barbies' butts," "Shani dolls have bigger breasts than Barbie," "Shani dolls have bigger thighs than Barbie." DuCille rightly wonders why a bigger butt is necessarily an attribute of blackness, tying this obsession to turn-of-the-century strains of scientific racism.

Deciding I had to see for myself, I pulled my Shani doll off my office bookshelf, stripped her naked, and placed her on my desk next to a naked Barbie doll that had been cruelly mutilated by a colleague's dog (her arms were chewed off and her head had puncture wounds, but the rest was unharmed). Try as I might, manipulating the dolls in ways both painful and obscene, I could find no difference between them, even after prying their legs off and smashing their bodies apart. As far as I have been able to determine, Shani's bigger butt is an illusion (see photo). The faces of Shani and Barbie dolls are more visibly different than their behinds, yet still, why these differences could be considered natural indicators of race is perplexing. As a friend of mine remarked acidly, "They still look like they've had plastic surgery." The most telling difference between Shani and Barbie is at the base of the cranium, where Shani bears a

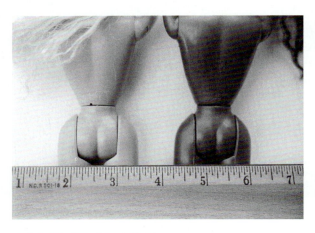

Barbie and Shani from behind.

raised mark similar to a branding iron scar: © 1990 MATTEL INC. Barbie's head reads simply © MATTEL INC. Despite claims of redesign, both Barbie and Shani's torsos bear a 1966 copyright, and although DuCille asserts that Shani's legs are shaped differently than Barbie's, their legs are imprinted with the same part numbers. This all strongly suggests that despite claims and rumors to the contrary, Shani and Barbie are the same from the neck down.

These ethnically correct dolls demonstrate one of the abiding aspects of racism: that a stolid belief in racial difference can shape people's perceptions so profoundly that they will find difference and make something of it, no matter how imperceptible or irrelevant its physical manifestation might be. If I had to smash two dolls to bits in order to see if their butts were different sizes, the differences must be small indeed: holding them next to each other revealed no difference whatsoever—except color—regardless of the positioning (crack to crack or cheek to cheek). With the butt index so excruciatingly small, its meaning as a racial signifier becomes frighteningly problematic. Like the notion of race itself, Shani's derriere has a social meaning that is out of all proportion to its scientific measurement.

Source: Chin 1999, 311–13.

Ethnicity

For anthropologists, ethnic groups are social groups whose members distinguish themselves (and/or are distinguished by others) in terms of **ethnicity**—that is, in terms of distinctive cultural features such as language, religion, or dress. Ethnicity, like race, is a culturally constructed concept. Many anthropologists today would agree with John and Jean Comaroff (1992) that ethnicity is created by historical processes that incorporate distinct social groups into a single political structure under conditions of inequality (55–57; see also Williams 1989; Alonso 1994).

IN THEIR OWN WORDS

The Politics of Ethnicity

Stanley Tambiah reflects on the late twentieth-century upsurge in ethnic conflict that few people predicted because many assumed that ethnic particularisms would disappear within modern nation-states.

The late-twentieth-century reality is evidenced by the fact that ethnic groups, rather than being mostly minority or marginal subgroups at the edges of society, expected in due course to assimilate or weaken, have figured as major "political" elements and major political collective actors in several societies. Moreover, if in the past we typically viewed an ethnic group as a subgroup of a larger society, today we are also faced with instances of majority ethnic groups within a polity or nation exercising preferential or "affirmative" policies on the basis of that majority status.

The first consideration that confirms ethnic conflict as a major reality of our time is not simply its ubiquity alone, but also its cumulative increase in frequency and intensity of occurrence. Consider these conflicts, by no means an exhaustive listing, that have occurred since the sixties (some of them have a longer history, of course): conflicts between anglophone and francophone in Canada; Catholic and Protestant in Northern Ireland; Walloon and Fleming in Belgium; Chinese and Malay in Malaysia; Greek and Turk in Cyprus; Jews and other minorities on the one hand and Great Russians on the other in the Soviet Union; and Ibo and Hausa and Yoruba in Nigeria; the East Indians and Creoles in Guyana. Add, to these instances, upheavals that became climactic in recent years: the Sinhala–Tamil war in Sri Lanka, the Sikh–Hindu, and Muslim–Hindu, confrontations in India, the Chackma–Muslim turmoil in Bangladesh, the actions of the Fijians against Indians in Fiji, the Pathan–Bihari clashes in Pakistan, and last, but not least, the inferno in Lebanon, and the serious erosion of human rights currently manifest in Israeli actions in Gaza and the West Bank. That there is possibly no end to these eruptions, and that they are worldwide has been forcibly brought to our attention by a century-old difference that exploded in March 1988 between Christian Armenians and Muslim Azerbaijanis in the former U.S.S.R.

Most of these conflicts have involved force and violence, homicide, arson, and destruction of property. Civilian riots have evoked action by security forces: sometimes as counteraction to quell them, sometimes in collusion with the civilian aggressors, sometimes both kinds of action in sequence. Events of this nature have happened in Sri Lanka, Malaysia, India, Zaire, Guyana, and Nigeria. Mass killings of civilians by armed forces have occurred in Uganda and in Guatemala, and large losses of civilian lives have been recorded in Indonesia, Pakistan, India, and Sri Lanka.

The escalation of ethnic conflicts has been considerably aided by the amoral business of gunrunning and free trade in the technology of violence, which enable not only dissident groups to successfully resist the armed forces of the state, but also civilians to battle with each other with lethal weapons. The classical definition of the state as the authority invested with the monopoly of force has become a sick joke. After so many successful liberations and resistance movements in many parts of the globe, the techniques of guerrilla resistance now constitute a systematized and exportable knowledge. Furthermore, the easy access to the technology of warfare by groups in countries that are otherwise deemed low in literacy and in economic development—we have seen what Afghan resistance can do with American guns—is paralleled by another kind of international fraternization among resistance groups who have little in common save their resistance to the status quo in their own countries, and who exchange knowledge of guerrilla tactics and the art of resistance. Militant groups in Japan, Germany, Lebanon, Libya, Sri Lanka, and India have international networks of collaboration, not unlike—perhaps more solidary than—the diplomatic channels that exist between mutually wary sovereign countries and the great powers. The end result is that the professionalized killing is no longer the monopoly of state armies and police forces. The internationalization of the technology of destruction, evidenced in the form of terrorism and counterterrorism, has shown a face of free-market capitalism in action unsuspected by Adam Smith and by Immanuel Wallerstein.

Source: Tambiah 1989, 335–49.

The Comaroffs recognize that ethnic consciousness existed in precolonial and precapitalist societies; however, they and most contemporary anthropologists have been more interested in forms of ethnic consciousness that were generated under capitalist colonial domination.

ethnicity A principle of social classification used to create groups based on selected cultural features such as language, religion, or dress. Ethnicity emerges from historical processes that incorporate distinct social groups into a single political structure under conditions of inequality.

EthnoProfile 15.2

Guider

Region: Western Africa

Nation: Cameroon

Population: 18,000 (1976)

Environment: Savanna

Livelihood: Farming, commerce, civil service, cattle raising

Political organization:
Traditionally, an emirate; today, part of a modern nation-state

For more information:
Schultz, Emily. 1984. From pagan to Pullo: Ethnic identity change in northern Cameroon. *Africa* 54(1): 46–64.

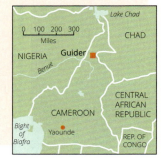

Ethnicity develops as members of different groups try to make sense of the material constraints they experience within the single political structure that confines them. This is sometimes described as a struggle between *self-ascription* (i.e., insiders' efforts to define their own identity) and *other-ascription* (i.e., outsiders' efforts to define the identities of other groups). In the Comaroffs' view, furthermore, the ruling group turns both itself and the subordinated groups into *classes* because all subordinated social groupings lose independent control "over the means of production and/or reproduction" (Comaroff and Comaroff 1992, 56).

One outcome of this struggle is the appearance of new **ethnic groups** and identities that are not continuous with any single earlier cultural group (Comaroff and Comaroff 1992, 56). In northern Cameroon, for example, successive German, French, and British colonial officials relied on local Muslim chiefs to identify for them significant local social divisions and adopted the Muslim practice of lumping together all the myriad non-Muslim peoples of the hills and plains and calling them *Haabe* or *Kirdi*—that is, "pagans." To the extent, therefore, that Guidar, Daba, Fali, Ndjegn, or Guiziga were treated alike

---

ethnic groups Social groups that are distinguished from one another on the basis of ethnicity.

by colonial authorities and came to share a common situation and set of interests, they developed a new, more inclusive level of ethnic identity, like the young man we met in Guider who introduced himself to us as "just a Kirdi boy." This new, postcolonial "Kirdi" identity, like many others, cannot be linked to any single precolonial cultural reality but has been constructed out of cultural materials borrowed from a variety of non-Muslim indigenous groups who were incorporated as "Pagans" within the colonial political order (see Figure 15.5 and "EthnoProfile 15.2: Guider").

The Comaroffs argue that a particular structure of nesting opposed identities was quite common throughout European colonies in Africa. The lowest and least inclusive consisted of local groups, often called "tribes," who struggled to dominate one another within separate colonial states. The middle levels consisted of a variety of entities that crossed local boundaries, sometimes called "supertribes" or "nations." For example, the British administered the settler colony of southern Rhodesia (later to become Zimbabwe) according to the policy of "indirect rule," which used indigenous "tribal" authorities to maintain order on the local level. The effect of indirect rule was thus both to reinforce "tribal" identities where they already existed and to create them where they had been absent in precolonial times. Two such tribal identities, those of the Shona and Ndebele, became preeminent; and each gave rise to its own "(supratribal) nationalist movement."

Both movements joined together in a "patriotic front" to win a war of independence fought against white settlers. This confrontation took place at the highest level of the ethnic hierarchy, which the Comaroffs call "race." At this level, "Europeans" and "Africans" opposed one another, and each group developed its own encompassing ethnic identity. For example, Africans dealing regularly with Europeans began to conceive of such a thing as "African culture" (as opposed to European culture) and "pan-African solidarity" (to counter the hegemony of the European colonizers). Conversely, in the British settler colonies of southern and eastern Africa, European immigrants defined themselves in opposition to Africans by developing their own "settler-colonial order" based on a caricature of aristocratic Victorian English society (Comaroff and Comaroff 1992, 58).

Because ethnic groups are incorporated into the colony on unequal terms (and, if we follow the Comaroffs, in different class positions), it is not surprising to discover that many individuals in colonies attempted to achieve upward mobility by manipulating their ethnicity. Anthropological studies of such attempts at ethnic

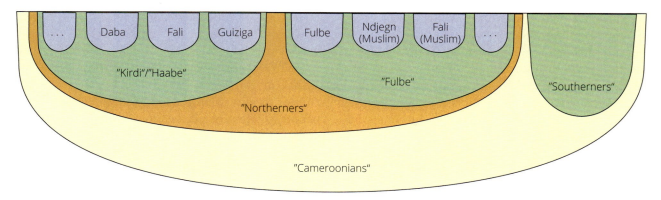

FIGURE 15.5 Nesting identities in northern Cameroon (1976).

mobility constitute, as the Comaroffs (1992) put it, "the very stuff of the ethnography of urban Africa" (63); and one of us (E. A. S.) investigated ethnic mobility in the northern Cameroonian town of Guider.

Guider began as a small settlement of non-Muslim Guidar. In 1830, it was brought into the Muslim Fulbe empire of Yola and remained a Fulbe stronghold under subsequent colonial rule. The Fulbe remained numerically dominant in town until after World War II; by 1958, however, individuals from more than a dozen non-Fulbe groups had migrated to town, primarily from the surrounding countryside. By 1976, 83% of household heads in town were recent migrants, and 74% did not claim Fulbe origins.

In the Comaroffs' terms, all these groups, including the Fulbe, had lost political and economic independence with the coming of colonial rule and, under conditions of inequality, were incorporated by the colonizers as ethnic groups into first the German and later the French colony of Cameroon. The Europeans uniformly admired the political, cultural, and religious accomplishments of the Muslim Fulbe. In their own version of indirect rule, they allowed Fulbe chiefs to administer territories they had controlled prior to colonization and, in some cases, handed over to them additional territories whose residents had successfully resisted Fulbe domination in precolonial times.

In 1976, the local ethnic hierarchy in Guider placed Fulbe at the top and recent non-Muslim, non-Fulfulde-speaking migrants from rural areas at the bottom. But in the middle were numerous individuals and families of Fulfulde-speaking Muslims who could claim, and in some cases be accorded, recognition as Fulbe by others in the town. For example, two young men whom I hired as field assistants first described themselves to me as "100% Fulbe." As I got to know them better, however, I learned that the family of one was Ndjegn and the family of the other was Fali. Neither young man saw anything contradictory about being both Fulbe and Ndjegn or Fulbe and Fali. In fact, each ethnic identity was emphasized in different situations. Ndjegn and Fali ethnicity mattered to them in the domain of family and kinship; these ethnic identities nested within the broader Fulbe ethnicity that mattered in urban public settings, especially high-status ones associated with education and cash salaries.

Indeed, by 1976, Fulbe identity had become an achieved status; it was the ethnicity claimed by the upwardly mobile in Guider. It was therefore possible for people born outside the dominant Fulbe ethnic group to achieve Fulbe status in their lifetimes (Schultz 1984). To do this, they had to be successful at three tasks: they had to adopt the Fulbe language (Fulfulde); the Fulbe religion (Islam); and the Fulbe "way of life," which was identified with urban customs and the traditional Muslim high culture of the western Sudan. Many Fulbe claimed that descent from one or another Fulbe lineage was needed to claim Fulbe identity. Nevertheless, they seemed willing to accept "Fulbeized Pagans" as Fulbe (e.g., by giving their daughters to them as brides) because those people were committed defenders of the urban Fulbe way of life. Those who were "Fulbeizing," however, came from societies in which descent had never been an important criterion of group membership. For these people, ethnic identity depended on the territorial affiliation of the group to which they were currently committed. From their perspective, in becoming Fulbe, they had simply chosen to commit themselves to Fulfulde, Islam, and life in "Fulbe territory," the town.

This example illustrates some of the key attributes often associated with ethnicity: it is fluid, malleable, something that can be voluntarily embraced or successfully ignored in different situations. Ambitious individuals and groups in an ethnically stratified society can manipulate ethnicity as a resource to pursue their interests. When nesting identities are present, people may regularly alternate between different identities in different contexts. Ethnic Fulbeization in northern Cameroon might be described as the formation of a "supertribe." Like the formation of caste alliances in India, it involves the expansion of group boundaries, allowing for the creation of stronger solidarity linkages among more people of different backgrounds. When such expanded alliances actually achieve increased success in political, economic, and social struggles, they may affect the very structures that gave rise to them (as the Shona-Ndebele alliance did in Zimbabwe) (Comaroff and Comaroff 1992, 61).

For dominant groups, however, defense of ethnic identity can be a way of defending privilege. Those who dominate may be threatened rather than flattered by subordinate groups who master elite cultural practices. Members of the dominant ethnic group may stress their cultural superiority and question the eligibility (and even the humanity) of subordinate groups who challenge them. It is at this point that anthropologists like Faye Harrison would argue that ethnicity becomes *racialized*. In her view, race differs from ethnicity precisely because it is used to "mark and stigmatize certain peoples as essentially and irreconcilably different, while treating the privileges of others as normative. This quality of difference, whether constructed through a biodeterminist or culturalist idiom, is what constitutes the social category and material phenomenon of 'race'" (Harrison 1998, 613). Racialization in Western societies would thus bear a family resemblance to castification in South Asian societies.

Harrison argues that by the middle of the nineteenth century, white northern Europeans, connecting their growing colonial power with their whiteness, began to racialize ethnic, religious, or class stereotypes associated with other Europeans (e.g., Irish, Jews, Italians, Poles, Slavs), viewing them as less human or, at any rate, differently human from themselves and attributing this difference to biologically inherited factors (Harrison 1995, 52). Conversely, some racialized ethnic groups, such as the Irish, were able to reverse this process once they moved to the United States, shedding their stigma and *ethnicizing* into just another "ordinary" American ethnic group. Some social scientists might argue, or at any rate hope, that all racialized groups should be able to ethnicize sooner or later. But such a perspective risks ignoring the plight of racialized groups whose status never seems to change. Historians argue, for example, that the Irish were able to ethnicize precisely because they accepted the racialization of African Americans (Allen 1997). Indeed, operating

under material conditions that presuppose white privilege, nonwhite races in the United States "historically have defined layers of the social bottom vis-à-vis several successive waves of immigrants" (Harrison 1995, 49; see also Smedley, 1998, 690).

For these reasons, Harrison (1995) argues that attempts to interpret race relations in the United States as ethnic relations "euphemized if not denied race" by failing to address the social, political, and economic factors responsible for keeping groups like African Americans excluded and stigmatized at the bottom of society (48). Harrison (1998) agrees that African Americans do engage in "ethnicizing practices emphasizing cultural heritage"; but in her view, such practices have never been able to overcome the "caste-like assumptions of the most systematically oppressive racial orders" like that of the United States (613; 1995, 54; see also Sharma 1999, 91).

As we have seen, anthropologists have argued about which technical terms ought to be used to describe which forms of identity under which circumstances. We agree with Ursula Sharma (1999) that social scientists should use a particular term only if it highlights a dimension of social relationships that would otherwise go unnoticed (93). Thus, ethnicity probably needs to be supplemented by the notion of race to distinguish the dehumanizing confinement of certain social groups to the bottom layers of society; and caste's emphasis on endogamy and hierarchical ranking highlights features of social organization that elude the usual scope of race, class, or ethnicity. Anthropologist Pnina Werbner (1997) further builds on these distinctions when she argues that to make progress in analyzing ethnic violence as a social force, practices of "everyday" ethnic identification must be distinguished from racism.

Based on her research on multicultural social relations in Britain, Werbner distinguishes two different social processes, objectification and reification. *Objectification* simply refers to the intentional construction of a collective public identity; it is the process that produces everyday or normal ethnicity. Ethnic identities are distinguished by the fact that they are "evoked situationally . . . highlighted pragmatically, and objectified relationally and contingently" and by the fact that they focus on two key issues: "a demand for ethnic rights, including religious rights, and a demand for protection against racism" (Werbner 1997, 241). Social relations between objectified ethnic groups are based on a "rightful performance" of multiple, shifting, highly valued forms of collective identification, based on religion, dress, food, language, and politics. Interaction between groups that differentiate themselves along such lines ordinarily does not lead to violent confrontations (229). *Reification*, by contrast, is a form of negative racial or ethnic absolutism that encourages the violent elimination of targeted groups and is central to the practice of racism. Reification "distorts and silences"; it is "essentialist in the pernicious sense" (229). It is violence that differentiates racism from everyday ethnicity; and if ethnic confrontation becomes violent, then it turns into a form of racism (234–35). For Werbner (1997), making this distinction is crucial in multiethnic situations because when people fail to distinguish nonviolent forms of everyday ethnicity from racism, they are, in effect, criminalizing valid ethnic sentiments and letting racists off the hook (233).

How Do Anthropologists Study Human Rights?

Concerns about and struggles against social inequality have only taken on more urgency in the context of globalization. In the midst of these struggles, concerns about human rights and their violation have been increasingly heard from all over the world. Anthropologists have been attentive to the spread of this discourse and the issues it raises, some of which we explore here.

Are Human Rights Universal?

Globalization has stimulated discussions about **human rights**: powers, privileges, or material resources to which people everywhere, by virtue of being human, are justly entitled. Rapidly circulating capital, images, people, things, and ideologies juxtapose different understandings about what it means to be human or what kinds of rights people may be entitled to. The context within which human rights discourse becomes relevant is often described as **multiculturalism**: living permanently in settings surrounded by people with cultural backgrounds different from your own and struggling to define with them the degree to which the wider society should accord respect and recognition to the cultural beliefs and practices of different groups. It is precisely in multicultural settings—found everywhere in today's globalized world—that questions of rights become salient and different cultural understandings of what it means to be human, and what rights humans are entitled to, become the focus of contention.

Human-Rights Discourse as the Global Language of Social Justice Discourses about human rights have proliferated in recent decades, stimulated by the

FIGURE 15.6 Women protesting against violence at the Fourth World Conference on Women in Beijing, 1995.

original UN Universal Declaration on Human Rights in 1948 and followed by numerous subsequent declarations. For example, in 1992, the Committee for the Elimination of Discrimination against Women (CEDAW) declared that violence against women was a form of gender discrimination that violated the human rights of women. This declaration was adopted by the UN General Assembly in 1993 and became part of the rights platform at the Fourth World Conference on Women in Beijing, China, in 1995 (Figure 15.6). Anthropologist Sally Merry (2001) observes that this declaration "dramatically demonstrates the creation of new rights—rights which depend on the state's failure to protect women rather than its active violation of rights" and that "the emergence of violence against women as a distinct human rights violation depends on redefining the family so that it is no longer shielded from legal scrutiny" (36–37).

Although CEDAW has proved particularly contentious, other human rights documents have been signed without controversy by many national governments. Signing a human rights declaration supposedly binds governments to take official action to implement changes in local practices that might be seen to violate the rights asserted in the declaration. Human rights discourses are common currency in all societies, at all levels.

human rights Powers, privileges, or material resources to which people everywhere, by virtue of being human, are justly entitled.

multiculturalism Living permanently in settings surrounded by people with cultural backgrounds different from one's own and struggling to define with them the degree to which the cultural beliefs and practices of different groups should or should not be accorded respect and recognition by the wider society.

Because of the wide adoption of human rights discourses throughout the world, some people have come to speak of an emerging "culture of human rights" which has now become "the preeminent global language of social justice" (Merry 2001, 38). As Jane Cowan, Marie-Bénédicte Dembour, and Richard Wilson (2001) write, it is "no use imagining a 'primitive' tribe which has not yet heard of human rights . . . what it means to be 'indigenous' is itself transformed through interaction with human-rights discourses and institutions" (5). These developments mean that anthropologists must take note of the important influence this human rights discourse is having in the various settings where they do their research.

What counts as "human rights" has changed over time, not only because of the action of international bodies like the UN but also because of the efforts of an increasing number of NGOs that have become involved in various countries of the world, many of them deeply committed to projects designed to improve people's lives and protect their rights (Figure 15.7). As Merry (2001) says, these developments "have created a new legal order" (35) that has given birth to new possibilities throughout the world for the elaboration and discussion of what human rights are all about.

In addition, because the "culture of human rights" is increasingly regarded, in one way or another, as the "culture of globalization," it would seem to be a topic well-suited to anthropological analysis in itself. This is because, as we shall see, human rights discourse is not as straightforward as it seems. On the face of things, defending human rights for all people would seem unproblematic. Few people who are aware of the devastation wrought by colonial exploitation, for example, would want to suggest that the victims of that exploitation did not have rights that needed to be protected at all costs. Yet, when we look closely at particular disputes about human rights, the concept no longer seems so simple.

Cowan and her colleagues have noted that there are two major arguments that have developed for talking about the way human rights and culture are related. The first involves the idea that *human rights are opposed to culture* and that the two cannot be reconciled. The second involves the idea that a key universal human right is precisely one's *right to culture*. We will consider each in turn.

Rights versus Culture?   Arguments that pit human rights against culture depend on the assumption that "cultures" are homogeneous, bounded, and unchanging sets of ideas and practices and that each society has only one culture, which its members are obligated to follow. As we saw in Chapter 8, this view of culture has been severely criticized by cultural anthropologists. But it is a view of culture that is very much alive in many human rights disputes because if people have no choice but to follow the rules of the culture into which they were born, international interference with customs said to violate human rights would seem itself to constitute a human rights violation. Outsiders would be disrupting a supposedly harmonious way of life and preventing those who are committed to such a way of life from observing their own culturally specific understandings about rights. Thus, it is concluded, cultures should be allowed to enjoy absolute, inviolable protection from interference by outsiders. This has been the position adopted, for example, by some national governments that have refused to sign the CEDAW declaration that violence against women violates women's human rights. "Many states have opposed this conception of human rights on cultural or religious grounds, and have refused to ratify treaties" (Merry 2001, 37). Nevertheless, as of November 2019, 189 countries had ratified CEDAW (https://treaties.un.org/Pages/ViewDetails.aspx?src=TREATY&mtdsg_no=IV-8&chapter=4&lang=en)

Sometimes representatives of non-Western nation-states may feel free to dismiss rights talk as an unwelcome colonial imposition of ideas that, far from being universal, reflect ethnocentric European preoccupations. But such a dismissal of human rights discourse must be closely examined. In the case of the right of women to protection from violence, for example, Merry points out that although some forms of violence against women may be culturally sanctioned in some societies, there are many forms that violence against women can take even in those societies, and not all of these are accorded the same amount of cultural support. As we saw

FIGURE 15.7 Women's shelters run by NGOs in Afghanistan provide a variety of services. Classmates applaud a fellow student after she stood up to read in a literacy class at one such shelter.

in Chapter 8, practices such as female genital cutting could be justified in the past in some circumstances as an appropriate cultural action, but it is now being questioned and even outlawed in the societies where it was traditional. This suggests that "culture values" cannot be held responsible for everything that people do in any society and that members of the same society can disagree about these matters and sometimes change their minds.

As talk about human rights has become incorporated into local cultural discussions in recent decades, anthropologists are not surprised to discover that the notion undergoes transformation as people try to make sense of what it means in their own local contexts (Cowan et al. 2001, 8). Being forced to choose between rights and culture, however, seems increasingly unviable in a globalizing, multicultural world. In their own anthropological work on these matters, Cowan and her colleagues (2001) are convinced that the rights-versus-culture debate exaggerates cultural differences. Like many cultural anthropologists today, they find that "it is more illuminating to think of culture as a field of creative interchange and contestation" (4). Such a view of culture makes it possible to find points of connection between the defense of certain human rights and the defense of particular cultural values.

Finally, it is worth asking if "culture" is sometimes used as a scapegoat to mask the unwillingness of a government to extend certain rights to its citizens for reasons that have nothing to do with culture. Cowan and colleagues observe that states like Indonesia and Singapore, which position themselves as stout defenders of "Asian values," have welcomed Western industrial capitalism. To reject human rights discourse because it contradicts "Asian values" would, at the very least, suggest "an inconsistent attitude toward westernization," which in turn feeds suspicions that the defense of "Asian values" may be a political tactic designed "to bolster state sovereignty and resist international denunciations of internal repression and political dissent" (Cowan et al. 2001, 6–7).

Rights to Culture?   A second popular argument about the relationship between rights and culture begins from very different premises. This argument does not view universal "human rights" as alien and opposed to "cultures." Instead, it says that all peoples have a universal human right to maintain their own distinct cultures. The *right to culture* has already been explicit in a number of international rights documents.

This argument is interesting because it seems to concede that such things as universal human rights do exist after all. The list of universal rights is simply amended to include the right to one's culture. It draws strength from the idea that cultural diversity is intrinsically valuable and that people should be able to observe their own cultural practices free from outside interference. However, it calls into question the common understanding that people frequently cannot enjoy their full human rights until they are *freed* from the constraints of local cultures. A right to culture, therefore, shows how the very idea of rights and culture is transformed and contested by globalization.

One key issue in the struggle to protect the right to culture is shared by *any* claim to human rights. It concerns the kinds of legal mechanisms needed to ensure protection. The great promise of international documents like the UN Declaration on Human Rights seems to be that people are now free to bring allegations of human rights abuses to an international forum to seek redress. But in fact this is not the case. As human rights activists have discovered, human rights are legally interpreted as *individual* rights, not group rights. This means that people must demand that the *governments of the nation-states in which they are citizens* recognize and enforce the individual rights defended in international documents. International institutions like the UN have been unwilling to challenge the sovereignty of individual nation-states.

The defense of all human rights, including a right to culture, thus depends on the policies of national governments. Some activists see this as a serious contradiction in human rights discourse that undermines its effectiveness. Talal Asad recounts, for example, how Malcolm X argued in the 1960s that African Americans who wanted redress for abuses of their human rights should go directly to the UN and press their case against the government of the United States: "When you expand the civil-rights struggle to the level of human rights, you can then take the case of the black man in this country before the nations in the UN" (quoted in Asad 2003, 141).

In fact, however, this is not the way the system was intended to work. Asad (2003) reminds us that

> *The Universal Declaration of Human Rights* begins by asserting "the inherent dignity" and the "equal and inalienable rights of all members of *the human family*," and then turns immediately to the state. In doing so, it implicitly accepts the fact that the universal character of the rights-bearing person is made the responsibility of sovereign states. (137)

In this legal universe, African Americans (and similarly situated groups in other nation-states) occupied an anomalous position: "they were neither the bearers of national rights nor of human rights" (Asad 2003, 144).

The recognition of the human rights of African Americans thus depended on persuading the *US government* to recognize those rights; the UN might use its persuasive power to urge such changes, but it had no coercive power to force the United States—or any other national government—to come into compliance.

Martin Luther King's strategy, Asad points out, took a very different tack, using arguments drawn from prophetic religious discourse and the discourse of American liberalism. His movement aimed at "mobilizing American public opinion for change," and it was effective at pressing for progressive social change in a way that, among other things, was compatible with the division of labor set forth by the UN Declaration of Human Rights (Asad 2003, 146). In a globalizing world, however, this division of human rights labor—international bodies propose, but nation-states implement—is being challenged. For example, transborder citizenries lack any forum in which their status and their demands are clearly accorded legitimacy. The right-to-culture movement has succeeded in recent years in highlighting such anomalies and eroding the traditionally recognized right of nation-states to determine the kinds of rights their citizens will be accorded (Cowan et al. 2001, 8–9). As in the case of the rights-versus-culture argument, however, the right-to-culture argument can be "called upon to legitimate reactionary projects as easily as progressive ones . . . the uses to which culture can be put in relation to rights are evidently multiple" (Cowan et al. 2001, 10).

Anthropological disciplinary commitments have allowed anthropologists to approach debates about rights and culture in ways that contribute something new to the discussion. These anthropological contributions can be seen in two ways. First, anthropologists have addressed the ways in which human rights discourse can itself be seen as culture. Second, their own struggles with the concept of "culture" allow them to mount a critique of some of the ways that this concept has been mobilized in discussions of human rights.

Are Rights Part of Culture? Anthropological approaches are well suited for investigating the so-called culture of human rights that appears to have emerged in recent years. As in the cultures traditionally studied by anthropologists, the culture of human rights is based on certain ideas about human beings, their needs, and their ability to exercise agency, as well as the kinds of social connections between human beings that are considered legitimate and illegitimate. The entire question of "legitimacy" in human rights discourse points to the central role played by *law*, both as a way of articulating specific human rights and as a tool for defending those

rights. Cowan and colleagues (2001) have drawn on earlier anthropological work in which systems of law were analyzed as cultural systems.

One important source has been the "law and culture" framework developed by anthropologists Clifford Geertz, Laura Nader, and Lawrence Rosen and nonanthropologists like Boaventura de Sousa Santos. In this framework, "law is conceived as a worldview or structuring discourse. . . . 'Facts' . . . are socially constructed through rules of evidence, legal conventions, and the rhetoric of legal actors" (Cowan et al. 2001, 11). Analysts who talk about a "culture of human rights" as the new culture of a globalizing world point out that the key features of the human rights worldview clearly indicate its origins in Western secular discourse. That is, it focuses on the rights of individuals, it proposes to relieve human suffering through technical rather than ethical solutions, and it emphasizes rights over duties or needs (Cowan et al. 2001, 11–12).

In the meantime, most anthropologists would probably agree that anthropology can clarify the idea of a "culture of human rights" (Cowan et al. 2001, 13). An understanding of culture as open, heterogeneous, and supple could be effective in helping us understand how human rights processes work.

How Can Culture Help in Thinking about Rights? To use the culture concept as a tool for analyzing human rights processes means looking for "patterns and relationships of meaning and practice between different domains of social life" that are characteristic of the culture of human rights (Cowan et al. 2001, 13). Since human rights are articulated in legal documents and litigated in courts, one of the most important patterns that become visible in the culture of human rights is the way they are shaped to accommodate the law. Groups and individuals who assert that their human rights have been violated regularly take their cases to courts of law. But this means that to get the courts to take them seriously, they must understand how the law operates. A key feature of this understanding involves a realistic awareness of the kinds of claims that the law pays attention to and the kinds of claims that it dismisses.

Looking at human rights law as culture reveals that only certain kinds of claims are admissible. As we saw above, the culture of human rights as currently constituted is best suited to redress the grievances of individuals, not groups. It also provides technical, not ethical, remedies, and it emphasizes rights over duties or needs. Plaintiffs are therefore likely to have a difficult time if they want to claim that their group rights have been violated, that they want the violator exposed and

ANTHROPOLOGY *in Everyday Life*

Anthropology and Indigenous Rights

Anthropologists are increasingly participating in organizations for the defense of human rights. In particular, they have contributed to the recognition by human rights legal advocates that the collective rights of groups (such as indigenous peoples) deserve as much attention as the rights of individuals. For example, one of the foremost anthropologically oriented organizations involved with human rights is Cultural Survival, founded in 1972 by anthropologists Pia Maybury-Lewis and David Maybury-Lewis (Figure 15.8) and dedicated to helping indigenous people and ethnic minorities deal as equals in their encounters with industrial society, and this includes struggles for indigenous rights (Lutz 2006).

Settings in which indigenous rights are debated and policies are formulated have become sites for ethnographic research, much of it multisited. For example, anthropologist Ronald Niezen began his career in the time-honored fashion of carrying out single-sited research on Islamic reform in Mali. Later he undertook community-based research with the eastern James Bay Crees in northern Quebec, Canada. Nevertheless, he writes, "the James Bay Crees also introduced me to international politics." In 1994, he traveled as an observer delegate with the Grand Council of the Crees to a meeting of the Working Group on Indigenous Populations at the United Nations in Geneva, Switzerland. People on the reservation were also learning via the Internet about the struggles of other indigenous communities for rights and were starting to "see themselves as leading a cause for justice directly analogous to (and without distinguishing among) a variety of liberation movements, including the American civil rights movement and resistance to South African apartheid" (Niezen 2003, xiii).

As his involvement with the James Bay Crees increased, Niezen found that the Crees valued his ability to provide a link between their own aboriginal government and the government of Canada. He was called on to perform many roles in addition to that of participant observer: during the first two years, he found himself acting "as an observer, witness, advocate, author—roles that were pretty much informally developed as needs became felt" (Niezen 2003, xiv). As he moved back and forth from reservation to government meetings, he came to realize that a global movement of indigenous peoples had come into existence and was getting noticed at places such as the United Nations. His earlier research in Mali also became relevant in a new way when, during one of his trips to Geneva, he encountered delegates from West Africa who were coming to identify themselves as indigenous peoples and who were working "to develop human rights standards appropriate to their concerns" (xiv).

Indigeneity is supposed to refer to a primordial identity that preceded the establishment of colonial states. Yet the very possibility that groups from West Africa, Latin America, and North America might come together as indigenous peoples "is predicated upon global sameness of experience, and

FIGURE 15.8 Anthropologists have become increasingly involved in the defense of human rights. David Maybury-Lewis (pictured here with Xavante informants in Brazil) and Pia Maybury-Lewis founded Cultural Survival, an organization dedicated to helping indigenous peoples and ethnic minorities deal as equals in their encounters with industrial society.

is expressed through the mechanisms of law and bureaucracy" (Niezen 2003, 2–3). "Indigenous peoples" is not just a badge of identity, but also a legal term that has been included in international conventions issued by the International Labor Organization.

According to Niezen (2003), it is important to distinguish what he calls *ethnonationalism* from *indigenism*. Ethnonationalism, he believes, describes a movement of people who "have defined their collective identities with clear cultural and linguistic contours and who express their goals of autonomy from the state with the greatest conviction and zeal, sometimes with hatreds spilling over into violence" (8). For example, in Canada, the advocates of sovereignty for Quebec have pushed for an independent French-speaking nation-state (8). Indigenism, by contrast, "is not a particularized identity but a global one, . . . grounded in international networks" (9). What connects specific groups to this identity, whether they live in dictatorships or democratic states, "is a sense of illegitimate, meaningless, and dishonorable suffering" (Niezen 2003, 13; Figure 15.9).

Unlike ethnonationalists, indigenous rights activists do not seek to form breakaway states of their own. Their approach is entirely different: indigenous representatives lobby for their rights before international bodies such as the United Nations, attempting to hold states accountable for abusing their indigenous citizens. In Niezen's (2003) opinion, the strategy "shows some indigenous leaders to be, despite their limited power and resources, some of the most effective political strategists on the contemporary national and international scenes" (16). Their goal is to get nation-states to live up to their responsibilities and promises to indigenous people, which are often explicitly stated in treaties. Thus, they seek affirmation of their rights to land and compensation for past losses and suffering; they seek cultural self-determination and political sovereignty. The goal of indigenous liberation thus involves the recognition of *collective rights*.

Juliet S. Erazo is an activist anthropologist who has become an ally of the Amazonian Kichwa of Rukullakta, "one of the longest-running 'experiments' with territorial sovereignty in Ecuador" (Erazo 2013, xx). She wanted to do research that would be of value to the residents of Rukullakta; and in the early 2000s, they asked her to write a history of their territory, beginning in the 1970s, when a group of local activists in Rukullakta took advantage of development assistance that was being made available to indigenous groups in many parts of Latin America. The goal of the developers was to reduce poverty and political radicalism in rural areas, but the goal of the Rukullakta activists was to form a ranching cooperative as a step toward gaining legal title to a large area of land, which they achieved in 1977. Two decades later, after the end of the Cold War, development organizations were no longer interested in ranching cooperatives, but were willing to fund projects that focused on sustainable development. Indeed, much of the territory that belonged to the Rukullakta cooperative was included in a large region of Amazonian Ecuador set aside as a UN Biosphere Reserve for purposes of conservation. Recognizing these new opportunities, Rukullakta's residents gave up their previous legal designation as a cooperative and highlighted their indigenous identity by renaming themselves the Kichwa People of Rukullakta. They now speak of their lands as an indigenous territory and elect a *kuraka,* or chief. Erazo (2013) emphasizes that these decisions do not reflect a

FIGURE 15.9 Sidney Hill, Tadodaho Chief of the Haudenosaunee, speaking at the United Nations Permanent Forum on Indigenous Issues.

romantic view of their past; rather "they are seeking autochthonous-sounding terms to signify and champion what are indeed very new social relations among indigenous people, and between indigenous governments and outsiders" (xxi).

A key feature of these new social relations has been the spread of neoliberal market ideology, which insists that nation-states lower their budgets for social programs and make investments in productive activities that will earn income on the global capitalist market. This means that leaders of an indigenous territory like Rukullakta are expected to seek funding from international donors, private companies, and other outside sources. Erazo (2013) reports that "leaders have been reminded that if they cannot control the actions of their people and guide them effectively toward the particular development priorities of the time, they could lose access to all sources of financial assistance, and possibly even to the lands" (xxii).

As Erazo observed, leaders must now negotiate with a range of outsiders (and a variety of insiders) to ensure that everyone can be counted on to engage successfully with development projects. Erazo traces the efforts made by Rukullakta's leaders to develop among local people a sense of territorial citizenship that will ensure the viability and continued development of their territory; that is, that will secure a genuine form of territorial sovereignty. She points out that sovereignty is not the same as autonomy: "indigenous leaders in this region have never seen their role as simply securing an area of land for their people so that they could live in isolation. They have also sought to improve their constituents' lives through a variety of projects" (Erazo 2013, xxv). At the same time, territorial residents have found ways to negotiate with their leaders whenever they judge that the demands being made on them are improper or excessive. These negotiations define a form of governmentality "that goes beyond resistance to domination . . . Thus, citizens . . . practice . . . government through distance, shaping the ways in which their leaders can shape them" (Erazo 2013, 7). Erazo concludes that "Negotiating the specific responsibilities and duties associated with territorial citizenship is one of the key sites of enacting sovereignty" (10). ◼

punished, or that the state itself has failed to fulfill its responsibilities toward them. Part of the human rights process therefore involves learning how to craft cases that will fit the laws. This can be tricky if the categories and identities recognized in human rights law do not correspond to categories and identities that are meaningful to the plaintiffs.

Anthropologists have worked with many social groups struggling with national governments to practice their culture freely. These political struggles regularly include claims about distinct and unchanging values and practices. These kinds of arguments for a right to culture are often cases of *strategic essentialism*. That is, the unity and unchanging homogeneity of a particular "culture" is deliberately constructed to build group solidarity and to engage the state in a focused and disciplined way. But the "essentialism" that often comes to dominate discussions of group rights is not entirely a result of the strategies of activists. Once they choose to make their case in a court of law, they become subject to the "essentializing proclivities of the law" (Cowan et al. 2001, 11). Because human rights law recognizes only certain kinds of violations, groups with grievances must tailor those grievances to fit.

According to Merry, for example, groups like the Hawaiian Sovereignty Movement have successfully achieved some of their political goals by making claims based on the requirements of their "traditional culture." But this is because they live in a society that is "willing to recognize claims on the basis of cultural authenticity and tradition but not reparations based on acts of conquest and violation" (Merry 2001, 42–43). Outside the courtroom, many members of indigenous groups think of their culture the way contemporary anthropologists think about culture: there are some common patterns but culture is basically unbounded, heterogeneous, and open to change. The conflict between these two understandings of culture has the potential to reshape their ideas about what their culture is. Groups that enter into the human rights process, thus, are entering into ethically ambiguous territory that is "both enabling and constraining" (Cowan et al. 2001, 11).

Human Rights in Hawaii: Violence against Women

Merry has studied how changing legal regimes in Hawaii over nearly two centuries have reshaped local understandings of Hawaiian culture (see "EthnoProfile 15.3: Hawaii"). Part of her work has addressed the ways "local human rights activists are struggling to create a new space which incorporates both cultural differences and transnational conceptions of human rights" (Merry 2001, 32). Hawaii is a particularly interesting setting for such a study, since for much of the nineteenth century it was located "at the crossroads of a dizzying array of peoples and at the center of a set of competing cultural logics" (44)—in a setting that is very much like the globalized, multicultural settings that are increasingly common today. Over the course of the century, Hawaiian law went through two important periods of "legal transplantation": the first, 1820–1844, involved the adoption of a Christianized Hawaiian law; and the second, 1845–1852, involved the adoption of a secularized Western law. Although these legal transformations involved colonial imposition, they also depended on active collaboration by Hawaiian elites (43–44). Indeed, Merry says that these legal changes are best understood as a process of *transculturation* in which subjugated Hawaiians received and adopted forms of self-understanding imposed by the Christian West, even as the Christian West was modified in response to this reception and adoption. Because the Hawaiians were not passive in this process and tried to make use of Christianity and Western ideas for purposes of their own, the process, Merry argues, was fraught with frustration and failure. Missionaries and rulers who wanted to turn Hawaii into a "civilized" place were forced to try to impose their will in stages, rather than all at once, and the end result still bore many Hawaiian traces that, to their dismay, seemed to evade the civilizing process (Figure 15.10).

This process of cultural appropriation is uncertain: change comes in fits and starts, constantly requiring adjustment as circumstances vary. Merry (2001) argues that human rights discourse is being appropriated by contemporary Hawaiians in much the same way (46–47). In 1991, she studied a feminist program in Hilo, Hawaii, that "endeavors to support women victims of violence and retrain male batterers" (48). This program is based on one originally created in Duluth, Minnesota, and it works closely with the courts. In 1985, the courts adopted the language of rights in dealing with violence against women. This means that the law supports the notion of gender equality and, when husbands are found guilty of battering their wives, calls for separation of the couple. By contrast, Hawaiian couples who participate in the program are often conservative Christians who do not believe in divorce. It might seem that this is a classic example of the conflict between rights and culture, but in fact "local adaptations of the rights model do take place" (47). This was done by tailoring the program's curriculum to local circumstances using

EthnoProfile 15.3

Hawaii

Region: Polynesia

Nation: United States

Population: 1,244,000 (2002 census)

Environment: Tropical Pacific island

Livelihood: Agriculture, industry, tourism, service, state and local government

Political organization: Modern state within United States

For more information: Merry, Sally Engle. 1999. *Colonizing Hawai'i.* Princeton, NJ: Princeton University Press.

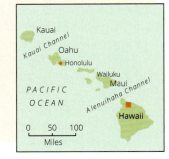

Hawaiian images and examples. Particularly interesting was the way the part of the program designed to teach anger management to batterers was made locally relevant by combining Christian ideas with ideas from Hawaiian activists that connected male anger to the losses they have suffered as a consequence of conquest. Merry visited a similar kind of program in New Zealand based on the same Minnesota model, which had been locally modified for Maori men in a way that linked their anger to Maori experiences of racism and loss. "Although all of these programmes share a similar commitment to a rights-based approach that works in conjunction with the criminal justice system, each has developed a local accommodation of the curriculum, a reframing which takes into account local problems and cultural practices" (Merry 2001, 49).

These examples suggest two important conclusions: first, it is possible to find ways of accommodating the universal discourse of human rights to the particularities of local conditions; second, no single model of the relationship between rights and culture will fit all cases. Moreover, as the culture of human rights becomes better established, it increasingly becomes enmeshed in political and legal institutions that go beyond the local level. As activists become more experienced operating in globalized circumstances, moreover, they are likely to become more sophisticated about making use of these different settings as they

FIGURE 15.10 The Hawaiian Sovereignty Movement has emphasized traditional culture and has taken action more broadly. Here members lead a march protesting the Asian Development Bank.

plan their human rights strategies (Cowan et al. 2001, 21). Struggles over human rights are hardly likely to go away; indeed, along with struggles over global citizenship, they can be seen as the prime struggles of our time (Mignolo 2002). Anthropologists are well positioned to help make sense of these complex developments as they unfold.

What Is the Relationship between Human Rights and Humanitarianism?   Over the course of the twentieth century, political conflicts in many parts of the world have engendered social upheaval and triggered population movements across political borders. However, French anthropologist Didier Fassin (2012) has detected a significant change in the way national governments and international organizations have come to respond to asylum seekers in recent decades. Until the 1980s, the persecution and suffering of asylum seekers had generally been interpreted as human rights violations. After that time, however, political asylum seekers were increasingly lumped together with victims of earthquakes and tsunamis and addressed by a new form of governmentality, which Fassin calls *humanitarianism*, "a mode of governing that concerns the victims of poverty, homelessness, unemployment, and exile, as well as disasters, famines, epidemics and wars—in short, every situation characterized by precariousness" (x).

Humanitarian thinking includes the acknowledgement of a universal humanity, which is central to human rights discourse, but it also emphasizes "humaneness"; that is, "an affective movement drawing humans toward their fellows [which] creates the obligation to provide assistance and attention to others" (Fassin 2012, 2). When the discourse of humanitarianism replaces the discourse of human rights, outside observers are encouraged to regard all crises as equal and to experience empathy for the suffering of victims, rather than indignation at the violation of their human rights. The humanitarian response is to relieve suffering through charitable generosity. However, Fassin points out that this generosity is not as innocent as it may appear: "compassion is a moral sentiment with no possible reciprocity . . . those at the receiving end know quite well that they are expected to show the humility

IN THEIR OWN WORDS

How Sushi Went Global

Talk of "global flows" can seem abstract and divorced from everyday life, but one of the strengths of anthropology is its ability to capture the articulation of the local with the global. As sushi has swept the United States, anthropologist Theodore Bestor looked at the trade in tuna.

A 40-minute drive from Bath, Maine, down a winding two-lane highway, the last mile on a dirt road, a ramshackle wooden fish pier stands beside an empty parking lot. At 6:00 p.m. nothing much is happening. Three bluefin tuna sit in a huge tub of ice on the loading dock.

Between 6:45 and 7:00, the parking lot fills up with cars and trucks with license plates from New Jersey, New York, Massachusetts, New Hampshire, and Maine. Twenty tuna buyers clamber out, half of them Japanese. The three bluefin, ranging from 270 to 610 pounds, are winched out of the tub, and buyers crowd around them, extracting tiny core samples to examine their color, fingering the flesh to assess the fat content, sizing up the curve of the body.

After about 20 minutes of eyeing the goods, many of the buyers return to their trucks to call Japan by cellphone and get the morning prices from Tokyo's Tsukiji market—the fishing industry's answer to Wall Street where the daily tuna auctions have just concluded. The buyers look over the tuna one last time and give written bids to the dock manager, who passes the top bid for each fish to the crew that landed it.

The auction bids are secret. Each bid is examined anxiously by a cluster of young men, some with a father or uncle looking on to give advice, others with a young woman and a couple of toddlers trying to see Daddy's fish. Fragments of concerned conversation float above the parking lot: "That's all?" "Couldn't we do better if we shipped it ourselves?" "Yeah, but my pickup needs a new transmission now!" After a few minutes, deals are closed and the fish are quickly loaded onto the backs of trucks in crates of crushed ice, known in the trade as "tuna coffins." As rapidly as they arrived, the flotilla of buyers sails out of the parking lot—three bound for New York's John F. Kennedy Airport, where their tuna will be airfreighted to Tokyo for sale the day after next.

Bluefin tuna may seem at first an unlikely case study in globalization. But as the world rearranges itself—around silicon chips, Starbucks coffee, or sashimi-grade tuna—new channels for global flows of capital and commodities link far-flung individuals and communities in unexpected new relationships. The tuna trade is a prime example of the globalization of a regional industry, with intense international competition and thorny environmental regulations; centuries-old practices combined with high technology; realignments of labor and capital in response to international regulation; shifting markets; and the diffusion of culinary culture as tastes for sushi, and bluefin tuna, spread worldwide. . . .

Culture Splash

Just because sushi is available, in some form or another, in exclusive Fifth Avenue restaurants; in baseball stadiums in Los Angeles; at airport snack carts in Amsterdam; at an apartment in Madrid (delivered by motorcycle); or in Buenos Aires, Tel Aviv, or Moscow, doesn't mean that sushi has lost its status as Japanese cultural property. Globalization doesn't necessarily homogenize cultural differences nor erase the salience of cultural labels. Quite the contrary, it grows the franchise. In the global economy of consumption, the brand equity of sushi as Japanese cultural property adds to the cachet of both the country and the cuisine. A Texan Chinese-American restauranteur told me, for example, that he had converted his chain of restaurants from Chinese to Japanese cuisine because the prestige factor of the latter meant he could charge a premium; his clients couldn't distinguish between Chinese and Japanese employees (and often failed to notice that some of the chefs behind his sushi bars were Latinos).

The brand equity is sustained by complicated flows of labor and ethnic biases. Outside of Japan, having Japanese hands (or a reasonable facsimile) is sufficient warrant for sushi competence. Guidebooks for the current generation of Japanese global *wandervogel* sometimes advise young Japanese looking for a job in a distant city to work as a sushi chef; U.S. consular offices in Japan grant more than 1,000 visas a year to sushi chefs, tuna buyers, and other workers in the global sushi business. A trade school in Tokyo, operating under the name Sushi Daigaku (Sushi University), offers short courses in sushi preparation so "students" can impress prospective employers with an

IN THEIR OWN WORDS

imposing certificate. Even without papers, however, sushi remains firmly linked in the minds of Japanese and foreigners alike with Japanese cultural identity. Throughout the world, sushi restaurants operated by Koreans, Chinese, or Vietnamese maintain Japanese identities. In sushi bars from Boston to Valencia, a customer's simple greeting in Japanese can throw chefs into a panic (or drive them to the far end of the counter).

On the docks, too, Japanese cultural control of sushi remains unquestioned. Japanese buyers and "tuna techs" sent from Tsukiji to work seasonally on the docks of New England laboriously instruct foreign fishers on the proper techniques for catching, handling, and packing tuna for export. A bluefin tuna must approximate the appropriate *kata*, or "ideal form," of color, texture, fat content, body shape, and so forth, all prescribed by Japanese specifications. Processing requires proper attention as well. Special paper is sent from Japan for wrapping the fish before burying them in crushed ice. Despite high shipping costs and the fact that 50% of the gross weight of a tuna is unusable, tuna is sent to Japan whole, not sliced into salable portions. Spoilage is one reason for this, but form is another. Everyone in the trade agrees that Japanese workers are much more skilled in cutting and trimming tuna than Americans, and no one would want to risk sending botched cuts to Japan.

Not to impugn the quality of the fish sold in the United States, but on the New England docks, the first determination of tuna buyers is whether they are looking at a "domestic" fish or an "export" fish. On that judgment hangs several dollars a pound for the fisher, and the supply of sashimi-grade tuna for fishmongers, sushi bars, and seafood restaurants up and down the Eastern seaboard. Some of the best tuna from New England may make it to New York or Los Angeles, but by way of Tokyo—validated as top quality (and top price) by the decision to ship it to Japan by air for sale at Tsukiji, where it may be purchased by one of the handful of Tsukiji sushi exporters who supply premier expatriate sushi chefs in the world's leading cities.

Source: Bestor 2000.

---

of the beholden rather than express demands for rights" (3–4). Thus, humanitarianism "always presupposes a relation of inequality" (4).

In Fassin's view, these changes are well illustrated by the history of the Sangatte transit center in Calais, France, whose opening (and eventual closure) illustrates "the sidelining of asylum and the advent of humanitarianism . . . the process whereby the refugee issue became subordinate to migration control policy" (Fassin 2012, 141). Beginning in the 1980s, a succession of political crises in various parts of the globe propelled waves of refugees across Europe to Calais, the continental European terminus of the Channel Tunnel, the last barrier in their quest for political asylum in the United Kingdom. By the mid-1990s, however, the British began refusing requests for asylum and sending those who had been rejected back to France. By 1999, the population of suffering asylum seekers in Calais was so large that the French government hired the Red Cross to manage a transit center where they could stay. Many critics of Sangatte referred to it as a "camp," but it was an unusual camp, because it was "not enclosed by barbed wire, and residents were free to come and go as they pleased" (Fassin 2012, 133). In Fassin's view, Sangatte was a paradoxical entity: "a place of indeterminate status, with a humanitarian mission but set up for reasons of security, though which foreigners were supposed to pass but where they were not supposed to stay. . . . Neither guests nor enemies, they enjoyed a furtive hospitality that conferred no rights—and in particular no right of asylum" (136). Residents were advised to return to their countries of origin, but were never informed that they might seek asylum in France, and less than 1% ever did so (Fassin 2012, 140).

In 2002, the Sangatte transit center closed, but asylum seekers did not stop coming to France, and those who did directly experienced the consequences of the subordination of asylum to humanitarianism. Fassin (2012, 141–43) offers the example of a Haitian woman whom he calls Marie. Marie told Fassin that her father had been murdered as a political dissident, after which her mother had been abducted and presumed killed.

After she was gang raped by a group of young men who broke into her house, she and her boyfriend sought political asylum in France. Her first application for asylum was denied (probably, Fassin suggests, because she could not demonstrate that the gang rape had been politically motivated). An appeal was also denied and her case was closed. Marie became an illegal immigrant, hiding with a friend for two years until she was persuaded to see a doctor. The doctor who examined Marie wrote a report requesting that she be allowed to stay in France on medical grounds because of her suicidal depression. However, when the results of Marie's blood tests came back, she was found to be HIV positive, probably as a consequence of the gang rape. Now diagnosed as suffering from advanced AIDS, she was quickly granted residence in France, on humanitarian grounds.

The closure of Sangatte did not bring an end to the crisis posed by refugees living in Calais; with no protection or aid, they subsisted as best they could in public parks or on the beach, vulnerable to harassment by the police. Europe still remains a desirable destination for refugees fleeing violence and suffering in their home countries. But many Europeans continue to associate asylum seekers with terrorism, or with undermining of the welfare state, or see them as a threat to Europe's identity as white and Christian. It is these anxieties, Fassin suggests, that have subordinated asylum to immigration policy. As circulation of individuals within the European Union has become freer, border control has become tighter. It is easier now to turn back asylum seekers at airports, to deport undocumented immigrants, and even to hold them in camps outside Europe itself (2012, 156). Ironically, these policies have been promulgated because "the European space is also a space of the rule of law—and hence of rights, notably human rights" (2012, 155). Perhaps this explains why humanitarianism has become so popular in the contemporary world: it "bridges the contradictions of our world, and makes the intolerableness of its injustices somewhat bearable. Hence, its consensual force" (2012, xi).

But anthropology is more than simply good to think with. Applying anthropological insights in an effort to cope with the challenges humans face in the contemporary world has a long history in our discipline. Drawing on different subfields, different schools of thought within those subfields, and even from disciplines outside anthropology, anthropologists have engaged in a range of significant practical interventions that aim to improve the circumstances under which different communities live. In Chapter 16, we will look at two significant areas of applied anthropology: medical anthropology and development anthropology.

Chapter Summary

1. Because membership in social categories such as class, caste, race, and ethnicity can determine enormous differences in people's life chances, much is at stake in defending these categories and all may be described as if they were rooted in biology or nature, rather than culture and history. Conceptualizing these forms of identity as essences can be a way of stereotyping and excluding, but it has also been used by many stigmatized groups to build a positive self-image and as a strategic concept in struggles with dominant groups. Although strategic essentialism may be successful in such struggles, it also risks repeating the same logic that justifies oppression.

2. The concept of "class" in anthropology has a double heritage: Europeans tended to view class boundaries as closed and rigid, whereas North Americans tended to view them as open and permeable. Class solidarity may be undercut by clientage relations that bind individuals to one another across class boundaries.

3. The stratification system of India has been taken as the prototype of caste stratification, although anthropologists also have applied the concept to social hierarchies encountered elsewhere in the world. Local caste divisions (*jatis*) in village India adhere to rules of purity and pollution defined in terms of the occupations their members perform and the foods they

eat and that govern whom they may marry. Members of jatis of similar rank do not observe most of these distinctions with one another, especially in urban settings. Caste associations in large cities of India use jati ties to promote their members' economic well-being. Contemporary anthropologists reject views of caste in India that portray it as internally harmonious and uncontested by those at the bottom of the hierarchy.

4. The contemporary concept of "race" developed in the context of European exploration and conquest beginning in the fifteenth century as light-skinned Europeans came to rule over darker-skinned peoples in different parts of the world. The so-called races whose boundaries were forged during the nineteenth century are imagined communities; human biological variation does not naturally clump into separate populations with stable boundaries. Despite variations in opinions and practices regarding race over the centuries, a global hierarchy persists in which whiteness symbolizes high status and blackness symbolizes the social bottom.

5. Although ethnic consciousness existed in precolonial and precapitalist societies, contemporary anthropologists have been most interested in forms of ethnicity that were generated under capitalist colonial domination, when different groups were subordinated within a single political structure under conditions of inequality. This process can produce ethnic groups not continuous with any single earlier group and is often characterized by nesting, opposed identities that individuals often manipulate to achieve upward mobility. When dominant ethnic groups feel threatened, they may attempt to stigmatize subordinate groups by "racializing" them.

6. Discussions of human rights have intensified as global flows juxtapose and at least implicitly challenge different understandings of what it means to be human or what kinds of rights people may be entitled to under radically changed conditions of everyday life. But different participants in this discourse have different ideas about the relationship between human rights and culture. Some arguments about human rights include the right to one's culture. But most international human rights documents protect only individual human rights, not group rights. And even those who seek to protect their individual rights are supposed to appeal to the governments of their own nation-states to enforce rights defended in international documents.

7. Some anthropologists argue that a "culture of human rights" has emerged in recent years that is based on certain ideas about human beings, their needs, and their abilities that originated in the West. Some consider this culture of human rights the culture of a globalizing world that emphasizes individual rights over duties or needs and that proposes only technical rather than ethical solutions to human suffering. Anthropologists disagree about the value of such a culture of human rights in contemporary circumstances.

8. Because human rights law recognizes only certain kinds of rights violations, groups with grievances must tailor those grievances to fit the violations that human rights law recognizes. Groups that enter into the human rights process are entering into ethically ambiguous territory that is both enabling and constraining. Debates about women's rights in Hawaii show both that it is possible to accommodate the universal discourse of human rights to local conditions and that no single model of the relationship between rights and culture will fit all cases. Some anthropologists are concerned that a discourse of humanitarianism that responds to human suffering on compassionate grounds is pushing aside a discourse emphasizing human rights and social justice.

For Review

1. What are naturalizing discourses?
2. Summarize the key points in the text's discussion of class.
3. How does caste differ from class?
4. Based on the Gopalpur case study, discuss how caste worked in village India.
5. Describe some of the caste struggles occurring in contemporary India.
6. What is race?
7. Summarize the key arguments in the discussion of race in the textbook.
8. What are the key points in the discussion of colorism in Nicaragua?
9. Summarize the main arguments in the discussion of ethnicity in this chapter.
10. How are ethnicity and race related?
11. What are human rights? How do anthropologists study human rights?
12. Explain strategic essentialism.
13. What is humanitarianism? How does the discourse of humanitarianism differ from human rights discourse? Give examples.

Key Terms

caste 481	colorism 488
class 479	ethnic groups 492
clientage 480	ethnicity 491

human rights 495	multiculturalism 495
naturalizing	race 487
discourses 479	racism 487

Suggested Readings

American Anthropological Association. 1998. Statement on race, http://www.aaanet.org/stmts/racepp.htm.

Anderson, Benedict. 1991. *Imagined communities*, rev. ed. London: Verso. *The classic discussion of the cultural processes that create community ties between people—such as citizens of a nation-state—who have never seen one another, producing the personal and cultural feeling of belonging to a nation.*

Buerger, Catherine, and Richard Ashby Wilson. 2019. The practice of human rights. In *Exotic no more: Anthropology for the contemporary world*, 2nd ed., 291–305. Chicago: University of Chicago Press. *This essay reviews the history of anthropological investigations of human rights issues. The authors argue that the concept of human rights seems straightforward, but in practice it turns out to be quite malleable, called on by various groups to justify very different political claims. They offer examples of the way in which "rights talk" gets translated into terms that local communities find attractive and relevant, even as rights activists must take care to describe local issues in terms that will also be recognized by international donors and media outlets, a process that is complex and challenging.*

Harrison, Faye V. 2019. Unraveling race for the twenty-first century. In *Exotic no more: Anthropology for the contemporary world*, 2nd ed., 77–103. Chicago: University of Chicago Press. *In this essay, Harrison reprises her previous insights about race in anthropology and investigates how notions of race have been reconfigured in the context of globalization. Reviewing recent research in a variety of settings, Harrison reminds us that "North American experiences do not exhaust the discursive and materials structures of racial formation that developed in the past and are still unfolding in the present world."*

Hinton, Alexander Laban. 2002. *Annihilating difference: The anthropology of genocide*. Berkeley: University of California Press. *A recent collection of articles probing the ways in which anthropology can help explain and perhaps contribute to the prevention of genocide. Case studies include Nazi Germany, Cambodia under the Khmer Rouge, Rwanda, Guatemala, and the former Yugoslavia.*

Jenkins, Richard. 2019. Imagined but not imaginary: Ethnicity and nationalism in the early twenty-first century. In *Exotic no more: Anthropology for the contemporary world*, 2nd ed., 105–120. Chicago: University of Chicago Press. *Jenkins reiterates longstanding anthropological insights about ethnicity (and nationality)—the importance of these identities for individuals and the fact that both define imagined communities that are constructs of society and history, rather than given by nature or biology. He also draws attention to the way the growing influence social media and the Internet have enabled forms of extremism that has allowed racism and ethnic abuse to circulate in new ways.*

Malkki, Liisa. 1995. *Purity and exile: Memory and national cosmology among Hutu refugees in Tanzania*. Chicago: University of Chicago Press. *This ethnography chronicles a recent example in Africa of the bloody consequences of nationalist politics and explores the connections between the conditions of refugee resettlement and the development of refugee identities.*

Nash, Manning. 1989. *The cauldron of ethnicity in the modern world.* Chicago: University of Chicago Press. *Nash looks at ethnicity in the postcolonial world and sees more of a seething cauldron than a melting pot. He examines the relations between Ladinos and Maya in Guatemala, Chinese and Malays in Malaysia, and Jews and non-Jews in the United States.*

Sharma, Ursula. 1999. *Caste.* Buckingham, UK: Open University Press. *A brief, up-to-date survey of recent*

anthropological scholarship dealing with caste in south Asia.

Smedley, Audrey. 1998. *Race in North America: Origin and evolution of a worldview,* 2nd ed. Boulder, CO: Westview Press. *This book offers a comprehensive historical overview of the development of the concept of race in North America, beginning in the late eighteenth century. The second edition includes additional coverage of developments in the nineteenth and twentieth centuries. Smedley shows how the concept of "race" is a cultural construct that over time has been used in different ways, for different purposes.*

 Visit our online resource center for further reading, web links, free assessments, flashcards, and videos. www.oup.com/he/ lavenda5e

What is applied anthropology?

It is possible to argue that, from its inception, anthropology always had an applied dimension. After all, it was E. B. Tylor, one of the first professional anthropologists in the late nineteenth century, who described anthropology as a "reformer's science." Since Tylor's day, many anthropologists have been motivated to use research findings from anthropology to propose solutions to practical problems that challenge the people among whom they have worked. As we mentioned in Chapter 1, applied anthropological work ranges widely, from cultural resource management to linguistic revitalization to economic development, and examples of applied work are cited throughout this book. In the twenty-first century, at least half of all new anthropology PhDs will most likely work in settings outside university departments of anthropology; for most, this is likely to be in one or another field of applied anthropology.

In this chapter, we will concentrate on two important areas of applied anthropology: medical anthropology and development anthropology. Each discussion shows how the anthropological perspective, coupled with participant observation as a research method, is able to address practical challenges in everyday life that are often ignored or mischaracterized by other perspectives or methods.

CHAPTER OUTLINE

What Is Medical Anthropology?
What Makes Medical Anthropology "Biocultural"?
How Do People with Different Cultures Understand the

Causes of Sickness and Health?
How Are Human Sickness and Health Shaped by the Global Capitalist Economy?

What Is Development Anthropology?
Chapter Summary

LEARNING OBJECTIVES

- Articulate the characteristics of the field of medical anthropology as one field of applied anthropology.
- Define the concept of biocultural and why this concept is fundamental to the field of medical anthropology.

- Compare how people in different cultures understand the causes of sickness and health.
- Apply the concepts of medical anthropology to health and illness examples in the modern world, such as lead poisoning among Mexican American children.

- Explain the concept of structural violence and the corresponding notions of subjectivity and trauma.
- Analyze examples of ways that human sickness and health are shaped by the global capitalist economy.

A Navajo healer on a reservation in Arizona treats a patient using traditional healing techniques.

What Is Medical Anthropology?

What does it mean to be healthy? What does it mean to be sick? Members of the same society who share understandings of what it means to be healthy are also likely to agree about what symptoms indicate an absence of health. In the United States, many people understand **health** as a state of physical, emotional, and mental well-being, together with an absence of disease or disability that would interfere with such well-being. Anthropologists recognize, however, that what counts as wellness or its opposite is very much shaped by people's cultural, social, and political experiences and expectations. This means that measuring health (or its reverse) in a straightforward way can sometimes be challenging. Increasing numbers of anthropologists now apply insights and practices from the various subfields of anthropology in efforts to understand (and find solutions to) health challenges faced by members of the many communities where they work. This area of specialization is generally called **medical anthropology** (Figure 16.1).

Medical anthropologists have been deeply influenced by (as well as critical of) findings by Western physicians and medical scientists who claim to describe normal human biological functioning, the causes for impairment of such functioning, and the scientifically developed therapies available to cure or manage such impairment. These traditional Western forms of knowledge and practice are often called **biomedicine**, and forms of biological impairment identified and explained within the discourse of biomedicine are those to which medical anthropologists often apply the term **disease**. However, to describe non-Western systems of belief and practice in relation to human health accurately, medical anthropologists have developed a technical vocabulary

FIGURE 16.1   Many people around the world seek help from biomedical practitioners when they feel that they are not healthy. A medical doctor (left) counsels a breast cancer patient in Sudan.

that does not presume the universality of biomedical understandings of health and disease. For example, many medical anthropologists prefer to use the term **suffering** to describe the forms of physical, mental, or emotional distress experienced by individuals who may or may not subscribe to biomedical understandings of disease. Medical anthropologists have often used the term **sickness** to refer to classifications of physical, mental, and emotional distress recognized by members of a particular cultural community. Sometimes, such sicknesses may bear a close resemblance to diseases recognized by scientific biomedicine, but other times, the sickness (and the therapy to relieve it) may be unique to a particular cultural group. Such sicknesses have been called **culture-bound syndromes**. Finally, some medical anthropologists contrast both the biomedical understanding of disease and the local cultural categories of sickness with a suffering person's own understanding of his or her distress, which is called **illness**.

health A state of physical, emotional, and mental well-being, together with an absence of disease or disability that would interfere with such well-being.

medical anthropology The specialty of anthropology that concerns itself with human health—the factors that contribute to disease or illness and the ways that human populations deal with disease or illness.

biomedicine Western forms of medical knowledge and practice based on biological science.

disease Forms of biological impairment identified and explained within the discourse of biomedicine.

suffering The forms of physical, mental, or emotional distress experienced by individuals who may or may not subscribe to biomedical understandings of disease.

sickness Classifications of physical, mental, and emotional distress recognized by members of a particular cultural community.

culture-bound syndromes Sicknesses (and the therapies to relieve them) that are unique to a particular cultural group.

illness A suffering person's own understanding of his or her distress.

What Makes Medical Anthropology "Biocultural"?

The anthropological perspective has always emphasized that human biological adaptations to physical environments are mediated by cultural practices. How this relationship is understood, however, varies among medical anthropologists. Some anthropologists (including some medical anthropologists) are comfortable speaking of both biological and cultural evolution, and they focus on the biological and cultural evolutionary contexts of human sickness and health. This approach tends to accept the traditional Western modernist distinction between

IN THEIR OWN WORDS

American Premenstrual Syndrome [PMS]

Anthropologist Alma Gottlieb explores some of the contradictions surrounding the North American biocultural construction known as PMS.

To what extent might PMS be seen as an "escape valve," a means whereby American women "let off steam" from the enervating machine of the daily domestic grind? To some extent this explanation is valid, but it tells only part of the story. It ignores the specific contours of PMS and its predictable trajectory; moreover it puts PMS in a place that is peripheral to the American vision of womanhood, whereas my contention is that the current understanding of PMS (and, before its creation, of the menstrual period itself) is integral to how we view femininity. Even if it occupies a small portion of women's lives (although some women may see the paramenstruum as occupying half the month), and even if not all women suffer from it, I contend that the contemporary vision of PMS is so much a part of general cultural consciousness that it constitutes, qualitatively, half the female story. It combines with the other part of the month to produce a bifurcated vision of femininity whose two halves are asymmetrically valued.

Married women who suffer from PMS report that during the "normal" phase of the month they allow their husbands' myriad irritating acts to go uncriticized. But while premenstrual, they are hyper-critical of such acts, sometimes "ranting and raving" for hours over trivial annoyances. Unable to act "nice" continually, women break down and are regularly "irritable" and even "hostile." Their protest is recurrent but futile, for they are made to feel guilty about it, or, worse, they are treated condescendingly. "We both know you're going to have your period tomorrow so why don't we just go to bed?" one husband regularly tells his wife at the first sign of an argument, thereby dismissing any claim to legitimate disagreement. Without legitimacy,

as Weber taught us long ago, protests are doomed to failure; and so it is with PMS.

I suggest that these women in effect choose, however unconsciously, to voice their complaints at a time that they know those complaints will be rejected as illegitimate. If complaints were made during the non-premenstrual portion of the month, they would have to be taken seriously. But many American women have not found a voice with which to speak such complaints and at the same time retain their feminine allure. They save their complaints for that "time of the month" when they are in effect permitted to voice them yet by means of hormones do not have to claim responsibility for such negative feelings. In knowing when their complaints will not be taken seriously yet voicing them precisely during such a time, perhaps women are punishing themselves for their critical thoughts. In this way, and despite the surface-level aggression they display premenstrually, women continue to enact a model of behavior doomed to failure, as is consistent with what some feminists have argued is a pervasive tendency among American women in other arenas . . .

So long as American society recreates its unrealistic expectations of the female personality, it is inevitable that there will be a PMS, or something playing its role: a regular rejection of the stringent expectations of female behavior. But PMS masks the protest even as it embodies it: for, cast in a biological idiom, PMS is made to seem an autonomous force that is often uncontrollable . . .; or if it can be controlled, it is only by drugs, not acts of personal volition. Thus women's authorship of their own states of mind is denied them. As women in contemporary America struggle to find their voices, it is to be hoped that they will be able to reclaim their bodies as vehicles for the creation of their own metaphors, rather than autonomous forces causing them to suffer and needing to be drugged.

Source: Gottlieb 1988.

"biology" and "culture" and conceives of both biological and cultural evolution as processes shaped by natural selection on units of "information." Units of biological information are associated with "genes," and biological evolution is measured by changes in gene frequencies over time (in conformity with the modern evolutionary synthesis that is the foundation of contemporary evolutionary biology). Cultural evolution is measured by

changes in the frequencies of particular units of cultural information across space and time, as these are acquired and passed on by means of social learning (Boyd and Richerson 1985; Durham 1991; Richerson and Boyd 2005).

Medical anthropologists who study patterns of sickness and health in different human populations may have training in biological anthropology or medicine and may become skilled in disciplines like *demography*, the statistical study of human populations, or *epidemiology*, which collects information on the distribution of disease in human populations and seeks explanations for such distributions.

Demographic approaches distinguish *epidemic* diseases that spread quickly over a short period of time from *endemic* diseases that are always present in the population. Recently, some medical anthropologists have promoted the concept of **syndemic** to describe the combined effects on a population of more than one disease, the effects of which are exacerbated by poor nutrition, social instability, violence, or other stressful environmental factors. Multiple pathogens exacerbate the disease burden, whereas lack of food, clean water, or other environmental challenges amplifies the suffering of the affected population. Environments where poor people live, characterized by substandard housing and poor sanitation, may simultaneously be breeding grounds for disease-causing organisms. Merrill Singer (2009; Chapters 4 and 5) has explored what happens when individuals are simultaneously infected by HIV/AIDS and another pathogen, such as tuberculosis, hepatitis, or malaria; or when they suffer from HIV/AIDS, together with a noncommunicable condition such as kidney disease or heart problems. A common syndemic condition is what Singer calls "SAVA": substance abuse, violence, and AIDS. To acknowledge syndemic interconnections is to recognize that public health interventions directed at only one component—only HIV/AIDS, only tuberculosis, only substance abuse—will always be inadequate. Multipronged approaches to control and prevention will be required to make progress in addressing the complexity of entanglements that characterize syndemic conditions.

Medical anthropologists who seek to understand human sickness and health in an evolutionary context sometimes use the concept of **adaptation**: an adjustment by an organism (or group of organisms) that helps them cope with environmental challenges of various kinds. Most evolutionary biologists tend to restrict their attention to *biological adaptations*: modifications of anatomical or physiological attributes of individual organisms, produced by natural selection, that better adjust organisms to the environmental settings in which they live. Medical anthropologists are particularly interested

in cases where there is strong evidence that human cultural practices have influenced natural selection on genes that affect human health and hence must be understood as **biocultural adaptations**.

The best-known example of such a biocultural adaptation is that of *sickle-cell anemia*, a serious condition that affects people in the United States with ancestors from Africa, but that also affects many people in India, Saudi Arabia, and Mediterranean countries such as Turkey, Greece, and Italy. As we discussed in Chapter 5, sickle-cell anemia is brought on when an individual is born with two copies of a mutant variant of the gene that codes for hemoglobin, one of the proteins in red blood cells. The mutant variant in question alters the structure of red blood cells, distorting them into a characteristic sickle shape and reducing their ability to carry oxygen. When individuals inherit the mutant variant from both parents, they develop sickle-cell anemia. About 85% of those with two of these mutant variants do not survive to adulthood and, hence, will not pass the mutant variants on to the next generation.

If the mutant hemoglobin variant first appeared in populations of gatherers and hunters, it probably had a low frequency. But once local people began to cultivate plants for food, they cleared large tracts of forest for their fields, creating large, open spaces where rainwater could collect in stagnant pools, providing ideal breeding conditions for mosquitoes. As the population of cultivators grew, so did the number of hosts for the malaria parasite, altering selection pressures via niche construction. Individuals with copies of both the normal and the mutant variants were fitter because they had a greater probability of surviving and reproducing than individuals with copies of two normal variants or of two mutated variants. As a result, the frequencies of the mutant variant increased in the population, despite the fact that a double dose of it was generally lethal.

A second example of the role of cultural practices shaping natural selection on genes that affect human health concerns *lactose intolerance*. Many North Americans of European ancestry have been told for years that cows' milk is nature's perfect food and think nothing of consuming milk well into adulthood. Yet biomedical researchers discovered in the 1960s that many people around the world are unable to digest fresh milk in adulthood. This became particularly obvious when adults in places like South Asia were sickened when they tried to consume powdered fresh milk sent as a form of foreign aid by the US government. It turned out that the milk sugar lactose provoked these digestive upsets. Most human infants are able to absorb lactose because their digestive systems produce the enzyme lactase, but the production of lactase decreases as children grow up.

---

syndemic The combined effects on a population of more than one disease, the effects of which are exacerbated by poor nutrition, social instability, violence, or other stressful environmental factors.

adaptation Adjustments by an organism (or group of organisms) that help them cope with environmental challenges of various kinds.

biocultural adaptations Human cultural practices influenced by natural selection on genes that affect human health.

The Madness of Hunger

Medical anthropologist Nancy Scheper-Hughes describes how symptoms of a rural Brazilian folk ailment can be understood as a form of protest against physical exploitation and abuse.

Among the agricultural wage laborers living in the hillside shantytown of Alto do Cruzeiro, on the margins of a large, interior market town in the plantation zone of Pernambuco, Brazil, and who sell their labor for as little as a dollar a day, socioeconomic and political contradictions often take shape in the "natural" contradictions of angry, sick, and afflicted bodies. In addition to the wholly expectable epidemics of parasitic infections and communicable fevers, there are the more unexpected outbreaks and explosions of unruly and subversive symptoms that will not readily materialize under the health station's microscope. Among these are the fluid symptoms of nervos (angry, frenzied nervousness): trembling, fainting, seizures, hysterical weeping, angry recriminations, blackouts, and paralysis of face and limbs.

These nervous attacks are in part coded metaphors through which the workers express their dangerous and unacceptable condition of chronic hunger and need . . . and in part acts of defiance and dissent that graphically register the refusal to endure what is, in fact, unendurable and their protest against their availability for physical exploitation and abuse. And so, rural workers who have cut sugarcane since the age of seven or eight years will sometimes collapse, their legs giving way under an ataque de nervos, a nervous attack. They cannot walk, they cannot stand upright; they are left . . . without a leg to stand on.

In "lying down" on the job, in refusing to return to the work that has overly determined their entire lives, the cane cutters' body language signifies both surrender and defeat. But one also notes a drama of mockery and refusal. For if the folk ailment nervos attacks the legs and the face, it leaves the arms and hands intact and free for less physically ruinous work. Consequently, otherwise healthy young men suffering from nervous attacks press their claims as sick men on their various political bosses and patrons to find them alternative work, explicitly "sitting down" work, arm work (but not clerical work for these men are illiterate).

The analysis of nervos does not end here, for nervous attack is an expansive and polysemic (having multiple meanings) form of disease. Shantytown women, too, suffer from nervos—both the nervos de trabalhar muito, "overwork" nerves from which male cane cutters suffer, and also the more gender-specific nervos de sofrir muito, the nerves of those who have endured and suffered much. "Sufferers' nerves" attacks those who have endured a recent, especially a violent, tragedy. Widows of husbands and mothers of sons who have been abducted and violently "disappeared" are prone to the mute, enraged, white-knuckled shaking of "sufferers' nerves."

Source: Scheper-Hughes 1994, 236–37.

After this occurs, adults without lactase who consume fresh milk can develop serious intestinal upsets and are said to be "lactose intolerant." So what would explain the fact that not all human adults are lactose intolerant?

Some scientific observers noticed that adults able to absorb lactose successfully appeared to be members of human populations that had a history of keeping dairy herds. As William Durham (1991) observed, this hypothesis "includes the concept of cultural mediation at its very core, since the hypothesized fitness advantage of [lactose absorption genetic variants] would have depended upon the presence of socially transmitted values and beliefs that supported dairying" (241). Subsequent efforts have confirmed this connection, not only for dairying peoples of Europe but also in Africa and elsewhere.

How Do People with Different Cultures Understand the Causes of Sickness and Health?

Anthropologists have long been intrigued by the accounts offered by people with different cultures to explain why people get sick and how (or whether) their sicknesses may be cured. Whereas explanations of some illnesses and their cures resemble biomedicine (e.g., digestive upsets treated with medicinal plants), explanations for other sicknesses may be interpreted as being caused by witchcraft or sorcery or punishment by ancestors for the breaking of taboos. For example,

Lead Poisoning among Mexican American Children

In the summer of 1981, a Mexican American child was treated for lead poisoning in a Los Angeles emergency room. When the child's stomach was pumped, a bright orange powder was found. It was lead tetroxide, more than 90% elemental lead. Lead in that form is not usually found in lead poisoning cases in the United States. When questioned by health professionals, the mother revealed that her child had been given a folk remedy in powdered form—*azarcón*. Azarcón was used to treat an illness called *empacho*, part of the Mexican American set of culturally recognized diseases. Empacho is believed to be a combination of indigestion and constipation.

This case prompted a public health alert that was sent out nationally to clinics and physicians. The alert turned up another case of lead poisoning from azarcón in Greeley, Colorado. A nurse had read about the Los Angeles case and asked if the mother was treating the child for empacho. She was. Additional investigation revealed widespread knowledge of azarcón in both Mexican American communities. The US Public Health Service decided that an anthropological study of azarcón would be useful.

The Public Health Service in Dallas called Dr. Robert Trotter (1987), who had done research on Mexican American folk medicine. Trotter had never heard of azarcón and could not find it in south Texas. But a short time later, he received information from the Los Angeles County Health Department, which had discovered that azarcón was not the only name for the preparation. When he asked for *greta*, he was sold a heavy yellow powder that turned out to be lead oxide with an elemental lead content of approximately 90%. The shop owners said it was used to treat empacho. Here was confirmation that two related lead-based remedies were being used to treat empacho. Trotter discovered that a wholesale distributor in Texas was selling greta to more than 120 herb shops.

Trotter was asked to work in a health education project designed to reduce the use of these lead-based remedies. Because of the complex nature of the problem, he had six different clients with somewhat different needs and responsibilities. The first client was the Public Health Service office in Dallas, which sponsored the first study he did.

The second client was the task force that had been formed to create and implement a health education project in Colorado and California. Task force members wanted to reduce the use of azarcón—but they did not want to attack or denigrate the folk medical system that promoted its use. The goal of the task force became product substitution—to convince people to switch from greta or azarcón to another, harmless remedy for empacho that was already part of the folk medical system.

E. E. Evans-Pritchard's celebrated study of witchcraft, oracles, and magic among the Azande ([1937] 1976) demonstrated how sickness and death (but also healing) could be explained in what Western science would describe as "mystical" terms, although Azande people also acknowledged the role played by material causes recognized in Western biomedicine. For instance, Evans-Pritchard found that Azande people understood the material causation involved when a person trips over a root and cuts his foot in the same way as a Western scientific observer understands it; nevertheless, an Azande person might also invoke witchcraft to explain why the cut failed to heal. (See the discussion of Azande witchcraft in Chapter 10.)

Many people who accept a biomedical approach to sickness and health are perplexed by explanations that involve witchcraft or other nonmaterial causes that cannot be identified in a scientific laboratory. Biomedical accounts accept only material causes for ill health.

In addition, as we saw earlier, biomedicine depends on a Western cultural understanding of the individual human organism as a bounded, self-contained, autonomous **self**. Together, these biomedical understandings define ill-health as disease caused by material entities located *within* individual human bodies. Biomedical therapy likewise is targeted inside individuals, with the goal of curing diseases located *within* their individual bodies. However, findings from medical anthropology repeatedly demonstrate that these assumptions are not universal.

Kinds of Selves

In many parts of the world (including some subgroups in Western societies, such as Charismatic Christians), individual human beings are not understood to possess selves that are self-contained and closed off. As a result, individuals consider themselves vulnerable to penetration by phenomena from outside their skins, including both material entities like microbes and nonmaterial entities like spirits. For instance, Charismatic Christians emphasize the openness of human individuals to God's

---

self The result of the process of socialization/enculturation for an individual.

The Food and Drug Administration (FDA), Trotter's third client, decided it needed basic ethnographic information on the use of greta. The FDA had never considered that lead oxide could be a food additive or a drug, and it needed verifiable data that the compound was being used in this way. As a result of Trotter's research, the FDA concluded that greta was a food additive. It issued a Class I recall to ban the sale of greta as a remedy.

Client number four was the Texas regional office of the Department of Health and Human Services. It needed assistance in creating and carrying out a survey along the United States-Mexico border. Trotter's survey indicated that as many as 10% of the Mexican American households along the border had at one time used greta or azarcón. The survey also turned up several other potentially toxic compounds that were in use.

Trotter's fifth client was the Hidalgo County Health Care Corporation, a local migrant clinic. It needed a survey that would compare the level of greta and azarcón usage in the local population in general with the level of usage among the people who came to the clinic. Trotter found that the two groups did not differ significantly in their knowledge about and use of the two preparations; however, the clinic population was more likely to treat folk illnesses with folk medicines than was the population at large.

The sixth client was the Migrant Health Service. It needed to know whether it was necessary to design a nationwide lead project. Based on the research that Trotter and others did, it became clear that such a major project was not necessary; rather, health projects were targeted and health professionals notified in the areas of high greta and azarcón use only.

Two years after the project began, both greta and azarcón were hard to find in the United States. In addition, the various surveys Trotter carried out led to better screening procedures for lead poisoning. Information on traditional medications is now routinely gathered when lead poisoning is suspected, and several other potentially toxic compounds have been discovered. Health professionals were able to learn about the current use of traditional medications in their areas and about the specific health education needs of their clients.

Trotter brought to the project the skills of the anthropologist; his principal focus was on culture. He took a holistic, comparative approach, and he was willing to innovate, to look for explanations in areas in which investigators from other disciplines had not thought to look. This is typical for medical anthropologists, who struggle with the friction generated when biomedical approaches encounter cultural practices that begin with different assumptions about the way the world works. ■

Holy Spirit, but individuals may be equally open, and therefore susceptible, to attacks by evil spirits or demons—and none of these entities registers on scientific instruments. Charismatic Christians do not feel helpless in their vulnerability, however, because they believe that gifts of the Holy Spirit, such as the power to heal, can be channeled through prayer in certain ritual contexts and directed toward suffering individuals to provide healing. As it happens, many forms of suffering that are explained cross-culturally in terms of spirit possession or witchcraft often resemble mental and emotional disturbances with which Western psychologists and psychiatrists are familiar, but that cannot be reduced to simple material causes. As Thomas Csordas (1988) has written, Charismatic Christians who acknowledge the existence of evil spirits are able to place "'spiritual power' alongside 'illness' as a way to make sense of a frustrating life situation . . . along with the reassurance that an unsettling apparition was not a sign of insanity but the manifestation of an evil spirit" (102) (Figure 16.2).

A self that is open to the wider world—that can be trained to open itself even wider through spiritual discipline—calls into question taken-for-granted assumptions about *bounded selves* bequeathed to us by the European Enlightenment. Postmodern critiques of Enlightenment ideas have also questioned taken-for-granted assumptions about naturally *unified and integrated selves*; these critics regularly insist, on the contrary, that *decentered selves* are the norm rather than the exception. From this perspective, the notion of a bounded,

FIGURE 16.2 Charismatic Christians consider themselves vulnerable to penetration by nonmaterial entities like spirits.

centered, integrated self appears to be an illusion or an effect of powerful political ideologies that work to mask the heterogeneity and contradictory features of individual experience.

Decentered, rather than unified, selves are not just the product of postmodern philosophical theory. Such selves are regularly experienced by aficionados of virtual reality gaming. This was already apparent a decade ago when anthropologist Tom Boellstorff carried out fieldwork in the virtual reality computer program Second Life, whose players created alternative avatars, or *alts*, with which they would sometimes log on. The most common kind of alt was the "social alt," used to try out a different self or an aspect of a resident's self that was not part of the main avatar. Sometimes a player would create several alts, and this did not seem to trouble them as they moved through the virtual world of the game. Here the sense of a single, unified, individual self begins to break down, becoming what Boellstorff calls "dividual" self (2008, 150). This concept was developed by anthropologist Marilyn Strathern (1988) to articulate the divided sense of self taken for granted by people she knew in Papua New Guinea. Recognition of dividual selves in these very different settings, where the decentered experience of self is not viewed as problematic, suggests that individuals with dividual, decentered selves should not be assumed to be suffering from mental or emotional disturbances that require medical intervention.

Self and Subjectivity

At the same time, anthropologists who recognize the uneven and contradictory features of individual self-experience often draw attention to the attempts individuals make, even in the most difficult or bewildering situations, to impose meaning, to make sense of what is happening to them. In recent years, many psychological anthropologists (some of whom also identify as medical anthropologists) have come to speak not of individual self, but of individual **subjectivity**. Veena Das and Arthur Kleinman (2000), for example, define subjectivity as "the felt interior experience of the person that includes his or her positions in a field of relational power" (1). Medical anthropologists have sought to understand individual subjectivity from a variety of perspectives. One approach is *interpretive medical anthropology*, which is based on the anthropological view that culture mediates

human experiences (including experiences of suffering). Interpretive medical anthropology emphasizes that cultural systems, including medical systems, are symbolic systems. This means that beliefs and practices about sickness and health held by people with different cultures could be better understood if they are situated in their own symbolic cultural contexts.

Subjectivity, Trauma, and Structural Violence

To focus on subjectivity in an anthropological analysis is to acknowledge the way in which individuals are to some extent initiating subjects, or *agents* of their own actions. However, subjects are never absolutely free to act as they choose. Our action is circumscribed by various forms of social, economic, and political inequality that we encounter in the societies in which we live. That is, we occupy various *subject positions* in society and are *subject to* the institutional forms of power in which those subject positions are embedded. Predictable institutional relationships shape individual subjectivities that reflect established forms of political power. But social and cultural patterns are sometimes overturned by unpredictable events that leave enduring marks on the subjectivities of individuals who live through them. These kinds of events, from colonial conquest to population displacements to armed conflict and war, regularly produce **trauma**, severe suffering caused by forces and agents beyond the control of individuals. Large-scale violence aims to destroy not only individuals but also the social order. Both individual and cultural factors contribute to trauma and are equally implicated in recovery from trauma, which may take a long time and is not guaranteed. Significantly, traumatic events can have negative health consequences for those who live through them.

This is seen in the research of Mokshika Gaur and Soumendra M. Patniak (2011), who explored understandings of health and nonhealth among the Korwa people of central India. Gaur and Patniak carried out fieldwork in 2002 and 2004 among a group of Korwa people working as wage laborers in stone quarries and road construction, settled in villages around a provincial town. Their initial research questions were designed to investigate Korwa ideas of "health, illness, body, factors affecting the state of health and illness experiences and their own state of health" (Gaur and Patniak 2011, 88). The responses they got revealed a Korwa understanding of health that connected it with their past life of hunting, gathering, and farming in their forested hills of central India. In the 1970s, this group of Korwa had been forcibly evicted from their forest homeland and resettled in

---

subjectivity The felt interior experience of the person that includes his or her positions in a field of relational power.

trauma Events in life generated by forces and agents external to the person and largely external to his or her control; specifically, events generated in the setting of armed conflict and war.

their current villages because of government plans to incorporate their homeland into a forest conservation district, as well as to promote their assimilation into urban Indian society. In their current circumstances, displaced Korwa are persuaded that health is impossible. They say they feel tired, achy, and without energy and complain of "'fever' that doesn't show up on a thermometer" (Gaur and Patniak 2011, 86) (Figure 16.3).

Gaur and Patniak (2011) use the term *experiential health* to describe Korwa understandings of health, which do not easily fit into a biomedical framework: "By experiential health we imply a purely subjective feeling . . . by 'health' [the Korwa] do not merely imply a disease-free bodily state. They consider forest-based life healthy in spite of the fact that they acknowledge their encounters with various diseases before displacement because, barring a few illness episodes, they could 'feel' health for most of their lives" (86). The Korwa word that most closely translates as "health" is *sukh*, "a condition of all around prosperity with bodily health as an integral component. Most of the informants expressed ideas on embeddedness of health in social, economic, and emotional conditions of existence" (Gaur and Patniak 2011, 90). These conditions of existence are connected to their traditional forest home, where Korwa felt protected by family and village deities and where they lived in harmony with natural, social, and supernatural worlds. "By contrast, illness is attributed to disruption, disorderliness, disharmony, and imbalance in relationship with the 'three worlds' that are played out on the body" (91), leading to physical difficulties in carrying out the activities of daily life. As a result, "The Korwa, both young and old, consider the forest their actual 'home' and associate all of their maladies with the new living space" (92).

Gaur and Patniak (2011) compare the Korwa experience with that of people in other parts of the world who have been displaced and resettled, pointing out that the experience of resettlement is not unlike a rite of passage in which the resettled communities "go through a phase of transition, which may last for a number of years . . . and is associated with morbidity, mortality, distress and despair" (87). Tragically, Korwa resettlement has brought poverty and exploitation. "Among the Korwa, displacement has not only demolished their economic livelihood, but has also dismantled the foundational structures of community living, namely mutuality and reciprocity" (94). Under these conditions, people work too hard, lose energy, and feel vulnerable to illness, leading to "a state of nonhealth—a condition of liminality where one is neither healthy (because of loss of economic and emotional well-being) nor ill (as one is able to carry out everyday activities)" (94). Those most affected by this social disintegration are families

FIGURE 16.3 Agriculture has not proven to be successful for displaced Korwa, and many find themselves forced to work as wage laborers or, as here, to prepare and sell firewood.

or individuals in the villages who lack support networks and who are also those who complain most about health problems with no obvious cause. In some cases, Korwa people blame their ill health on the activities of witches. "In the case of the Korwa, we found that women accused of witchcraft are typically those having a marginal existence [who] live in a constant fear for their life and complain of suffering from perpetual aches, weakness, and intermittent fever" (Gaur and Patniak 2011, 95–96).

To alleviate their ill health, Korwa preferred to consult a "full healer" who was "considered capable of curing any illness with his combinative therapy of forest herbs, propitiation of deities, and exorcising of spirits" (Gaur and Patniak 2011, 96). Unfortunately, in the village settings where they now lived, full healers were hard to find. Gaur and Patniak conclude that Korwa experiences of ill-health can be described as instances of *somatization*, where forms of social, political, and economic suffering are experienced as forms of bodily suffering. "Their bodily experiences are situated in the loss of the people–place interface so that the notion of nonhealthy body becomes a trope of their socioeconomic conditions of existence" (98). Nevertheless, Gaur and Patniak insist that it is important to understand Korwa forms of suffering as rooted in their transitional status, not as the result of a fixed state of impoverishment. Such an understanding holds out the hope that, in the future, displaced Korwa may make a "place" for themselves outside the forest and that their current sufferings will abate.

This discussion of the Korwa draws attention to forms of violent disruption of stable ways of life that can produce the experience of trauma among those who survive them. Sometimes, however, the source of human suffering can be located in features of everyday forms of social inequality. Paul Farmer is an anthropologist and medical doctor who has worked since 1983 in Haiti. His activities as a physician have exposed him to extreme

FIGURE 16.4 Dr. Paul Farmer with AIDS patients at Clinique Bon Sauveur. Political and economic forces structure people's risks for various forms of suffering in Haiti and elsewhere.

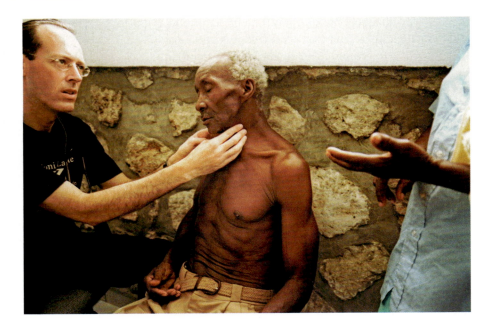

forms of human suffering that are part of everyday life for those at the bottom of Haitian society (Figure 16.4). As he pointed out in 2002, "In only three countries in the world was suffering judged to be more extreme than that endured in Haiti; each of these three countries is currently in the midst of an internationally recognized civil war" (Farmer 2002, 424). But if the suffering of poor Haitians is not the outcome of the traumatic violence of war, it can be described as a consequence of another form of violence: structural violence.

Structural violence is violence that results from the way that political and economic forces structure risk for various forms of suffering within a population. Much of this suffering is in the form of infectious and parasitic disease. But it can also include other forms of extreme suffering such as hunger, torture, and rape (Farmer 2002, 424). Farmer's work highlights the effects of structural violence on the production of individual subjectivity. The operations of structural violence create circumscribed spaces in which the poorest and least powerful members of Haitian society are subjected to highly intensified risks of all kinds, increasing the likelihood that sooner or later they will experience one or more varieties of social suffering.

Farmer's work as a physician allowed him to see firsthand the suffering of poor Haitians he knew, and his work as an anthropologist allowed him to link that suffering to local economic and political structures in Haitian society. Farmer begins by offering the biographies of a young woman named Acéphie Joseph and a

young man named Chouchou Louis. Both died young: the woman of AIDS and the man of injuries inflicted on him in the course of a beating by the police. As Farmer (2002) says, these two individuals "suffered and died in exemplary fashion," and he shows how the combined forces of racism, sexism, political violence, and poverty conspired "to constrain agency" and "crystallize into the sharp, hard surfaces of individual suffering" (425).

Acéphie and Chouchou are individuals, and so it is natural to ask how representative their experiences might be. Farmer's experience among many poor Haitian women with AIDS, including Acéphie, showed "a deadly monotony." The women he interviewed "were straightforward about the nonvoluntary aspect of their sexual activity," driven by poverty to agree to sexual liaisons with Haitian soldiers and other men with a measure of money and power. Similarly, Chouchou was only 1 of more than 3,000 Haitian civilians, most of them poor peasants, who were killed after 1991 by military or paramilitary forces. Thus, Farmer concluded, "the agony of Acéphie and Chouchou was in a sense 'modal' suffering, in Haiti, AIDS and political violence ware two lead causes of death among young adults" (Farmer 2002, 431).

And all this suffering and death was the outcome of structural violence. As Farmer explains, "gender helps explain why Acéphie died of AIDS whereas Chouchou died from torture" (Farmer 2002, 432). Race or ethnicity helps explain why illness is more likely to be suffered by the descendants of enslaved Africans, and social class helps explain why they are more likely to be poor (Figure 16.5). "These grim biographies suggest that the social and economic forces that have helped to shape the AIDS epidemic are, in every sense, the same forces that

structural violence Violence that results from the way that political and economic forces structure risk for various forms of suffering within a population.

FIGURE 16.5 The individual subjectivities of many Haitians have been shaped by the experience of structural violence in the form of AIDS and political violence, two leading causes of death among young people in Haiti. They leave behind other forms of social suffering for their parents and children. Here, the parents of Jean-David Droitdieu, an AIDS victim, holding his orphaned daughter, sit in front of their home and the place of his burial, surrounded by relatives and neighbors.

led to Chouchou's death and to the larger repression in which it was eclipsed. What is more, both were 'at risk' of such a fate long before they met the soldiers who altered their destinies. *They* were both, from the outset, victims of structural violence" (Farmer 2002, 431).

How Are Human Sickness and Health Shaped by the Global Capitalist Economy?

Previous examples show how medical anthropology is capable of contextualizing experiences of sickness and health across the world in terms that go well beyond the experiences of individual illnesses and culture-bound syndromes. As Farmer shows, the structures and processes that shape these wider contexts have the ability to expand or contract the agency of particular individuals and groups who must deal with them. As Singer (2009) emphasizes, the consequences for ill health for those at the bottom of unequal hierarchies are syndemic, interacting with one another in ways that intensify suffering. For these reasons, many medical anthropologists carry out research that shows how individual and local experiences and interpretations of suffering fit into broader historical and political contexts.

The broader contexts that must be considered are first historical. A history of European colonial domination and the institution of racial slavery in places like Brazil and Haiti (and the United States) set the stage for inequalities that would follow, even after colonial empires ended and slavery was abolished (Figure 16.6).

Even where racial slavery was not institutionalized, colonial administrations attempted to organize indigenous groups living within their borders according to hierarchical principles that favored colonizer over colonized, and some colonized groups benefitted more than other groups did. European colonial empires were themselves shaped by the expansion of a globalizing capitalist market in which all colonial powers were enmeshed. European cultural practices of many kinds were imported to the colonies, including European biomedical ideas of health, sickness, and therapy. The breakup of these empires following World War II made increasingly visible the fact that none of the individual groups studied by anthropologists could realistically be represented as ever having lived in isolation from their neighbors.

FIGURE 16.6 Colonial powers brought biomedicine with them and established hospitals like this one in Mozambique in colonial territories, but access to those hospitals was not equal for everyone.

IN THEIR OWN WORDS

Ethical Dilemmas and Decisions

We have already met the authors of this selection in an earlier chapter—Timothy De Waal Malefyt and Robert J. Morais are anthropologists who have spent their careers in advertising and marketing. Here, they dig into the ethics of working in advertising, often with products that have public health consequences. The ethical issues they raise, however, are issues that all anthropologists must confront.

The way we frame ethically questionable situations in marketing depends on where we locate the idea of individual free will, choice, and human agency. We believe that business anthropologists who consider the ethics of their work should assess the impact of their contributions on the target audience, even when the ultimate decision about buying is up to the consumer. This process is not always simple. A good example of this conundrum is direct-to-consumer (DTC) prescription drug advertising. The benefits and liabilities of this multibillion-dollar mode of consumer communication are hotly debated (. . .). Advocates contend that DTC advertising builds awareness among sufferers of underdiagnosed conditions, leads to needed treatment for these conditions, and reminds consumers to take their medication, thereby improving public health. Critics argue that DTC advertising profits mainly pharmaceutical companies, contributes to overmedication, and places physicians in the uncomfortable position of talking their advertising-influenced patients out of medications that they do not need. Given that both sides of the argument have merit and are discussed openly, we believe that the decision to accept or refuse a DTC assignment must be a personal one for the researcher.

Other advertising categories are more or less problematic. Cigarettes are unequivocally harmful to human health, but freedom of speech allows some degree of marketing and advertising of these products. We would not choose to participate in cigarette marketing research because we see no redeeming value in the products, but other anthropologists might argue that these products deserve representation and that consumers can decide for themselves whether to purchase them. Children's sugar laden cereals provide scant nutritional value, but mothers feed them to their children because they feel these cereals are the only food their children will consume in time-compressed mornings. Hard-surface disinfectants protect individuals from contagion, but they may reduce the broader population's resistance to bacteria. Credit cards bring convenience but can result in unmanageable debt. Candy and other junk foods are satisfying when consumed but represent empty calories and contribute to obesity. Some fast-food companies claim their offerings are more nutritious than their competition—for example, grilled versus fried hamburgers. Is the highly salted, fatty beef offered as a healthier option really healthy? Political advertisements can be combative and stress only the truth that is advantageous to one side.

A cigarette campaign that aims to increase smoking or surreptitious surveillance on government projects for war efforts, as in the Camelot affair, are two examples where most anthropologists would refuse cooperation. However, deciding on the degree of ethical responsibility for many consumable categories is difficult. Moreover, we recognize that we are complicit in muddying consumer evaluation of brands when we highlight their positive attributes, such as soda for its taste enjoyment, and downplay its negative dietary impact, or when we stress the most dire consequences of not attending to the pain of tooth sensitivity. At the same time, we have observed that corporate profit and consumer fulfillment are not mutually exclusive, as in a zero-sum game. Many consumers derive pleasure and obtain no deleterious consequences when they drink soda in moderation, some of which is sugar-free, and they protect their teeth when they brush with a toothpaste for sensitivity. Both the buyer and the marketer win. In the end, we feel that consumers usually have access to information that enables them to make an informed choice about the brands they consider. Assuming that a marketing researcher believes that the client's essential claims are valid and that the consumer has enough information available, each of us must weigh the merits in developing advertising that might influence consumers toward potentially detrimental ends. . . .

Human interaction demands that we make judgments every day that have moral and ethical implications. Should we walk by the homeless woman or stop to give her spare change? Is it acceptable to use a hand sanitizer to prevent illness while contributing to the spawning of superbug bacteria in the broader community? Should university professors, well aware that the job market for PhD anthropologists is dismal . . . decrease the size of graduate programs and suggest alternative careers to prospective students?

Are we all above reproach in our responses to questions such as these? Taking this argument further, must anthropologists be advocates for the public good? This is a noble calling, but is it central to the practice of anthropology in the twenty-first century? During anthropology's historical period in the early twentieth century, when the field's objectives were often intertwined with colonial aims and "powerless natives" needed protection, anthropologists could rightly be called upon to play activist roles. We have suggested that business is not an all-powerful force; consumers have the freedom to reject marketing and advertising messages. Other than in cases of malfeasance, consumers do not require advocates. Consequently, we do not believe that advertising and marketing researchers need to take on a protective role for consumers. (. . .)

Ethics are ultimately defined and negotiated in public discourse as well as by individual decision making. We and other practicing anthropologists with whom we are acquainted constitute a community that views ethics as certain appropriate and responsible behavior in the context of our businesses. We value our communal discussions, professional meetings, and informal lunches where we vent frustrations, discuss our concerns, and inform one another of the issues we face. It is, in part, through communities like these that we arbitrate what is ethical and what is not. Our personal values inform our judgments and actions in our business conduct as well. Through both communities and personal experiences, we evolve guidelines for our business conduct. As our stories revealed, we have, at times, felt conflicted. A decision to turn away work is not easy, and we find ourselves more likely to rationalize accepting a client in a gray area than refusing to work on a project on moral grounds. We have boundaries, but we do not pretend that we hold ourselves to a lofty standard of pure truth in advertising. We also accept that some academic anthropologists might find the profit motives of business abhorrent and consumer manipulation repugnant. We hope that they will recognize the ethical considerations most marketing and advertising anthropologists try to abide by in our working lives. We also urge academic anthropologists to embrace cultural relativity and accept that advertising anthropology can be not only a viable career path but also an ethical one.

Source: Malefyt and Morais 2012, 132–33, 134–35.

Newly independent nation-states forged from former colonies regularly contained within their boundaries social groups with varied political and cultural histories, whose relations with one another, and with the state authorities, were complex and sometimes antagonistic. The areas of disagreement often included different opinions about the causes of health and culture for illness.

After World War II, the anthropology of medicine began to turn attention to these wider arenas within which different understandings of sickness and health rubbed up against one another. Inspired by the interpretive cultural anthropology of Clifford Geertz, Charles Leslie and his associates urged that non-Western medical beliefs and practices be understood as cultural systems (Leslie 1976). Leslie wanted to draw attention to the sophisticated "great tradition" medical systems that developed over centuries in the civilizations of South Asia and China, fully fledged alternative medical systems such as Ayurvedic medicine in India. But Leslie also pointed out that Western exploration, colonial expansion, and industrialization had fostered the spread and adoption of Western biomedical systems by people in many non-Western societies around the world. Consequently, it seemed incorrect to continue to regard biomedicine as the exclusive property of "the West." Leslie argued that it was more accurate to consider biomedicine as a particularly high-status form of **cosmopolitan medicine**.

Finally, Leslie also emphasized that wherever cosmopolitan medicine is found, it always coexists with a range of alternative **ethnomedical systems** based on practices of local sociocultural groups—a state of affairs called **medical pluralism**. Under conditions of medical pluralism, people seeking medical care develop *hierarchies of resort*: first, they consult local practitioners whom they know and trust and who treat them with respect; if they fail to receive satisfaction, they will seek out practitioners associated with other ethnomedical systems. Medical pluralism was present in Guider, Cameroon, in 1976 when the authors were living there (Figure 16.7).

---

cosmopolitan medicine A more accurate way to refer to Western biomedical systems adopted by people in non-Western societies around the world.

ethnomedical systems Alternative medical systems based on practices of local sociocultural groups.

medical pluralism The coexistence of ethnomedical systems alongside cosmopolitan medicine.

FIGURE 16.7   Medical pluralism in Guider, 1976. Vendor of traditional medicines in the market.

For example, one husband described the hierarchy of resort that he and his wife had followed when seeking therapy for infertility. First, they had gone to the local biomedical clinic, which had nothing to offer them. Their next visit was to a local Muslim practitioner whose therapy involved copying out key verses from the Qur'an onto a board, washing off the ink with which they had been written, and instructing the patient to drink the ink. This, too, had proved unsatisfactory. When we last spoke, the man said that he and his wife were now thinking of consulting a traditional non-Muslim Fali healer living outside Guider, who had a reputation for success in cases of infertility.

Health, Human Reproduction, and Global Capitalism

Medical anthropologists have drawn attention to a range of factors that affect women's health in relation to childbearing. Many formal studies of *fertility* by government agencies or biomedical authorities have exclusively been concerned with the challenges of population growth in many poorer societies and have pressured families to reduce the number of offspring they produce. Medical anthropologists have been instrumental in drawing attention to the challenges that *infertility* poses for individual women living in societies with particular gender and family structures. In societies like China, where descent is traditionally traced through males, and property and status move through lineages of related men, women who fail to produce sons for their husbands may be regarded as extra mouths to feed and may find themselves

isolated when their husbands die and they have no son to take care of them in old age.

The spread of global capitalism may undermine traditional sources of livelihood and social organization, which in turn erode traditional supports for reproductive health. In many countries, landless peasants who are forced out of the countryside into cities in search of work often live under extraordinarily difficult circumstances that have a serious negative impact on pregnant and nursing women and their children (Scheper-Hughes 1992). As we saw in Chapter 14, new research in the anthropology of science, technology, and medicine has shown how many people now engage in assisted reproduction when challenged by infertility. These technologies have now become components of cosmopolitan medicine, but the ways in which they are integrated into the reproductive practices of people with different cultural understandings about kinship and motherhood vary greatly.

Assisted reproduction, like other forms of assistance to pregnant or birthing mothers, is uneven across the world, a phenomenon described as "stratified reproduction" by Faye Ginsburg and Rayna Rapp (1995). Stratified reproduction occurs when those in favored social strata are supported in their efforts to produce children, whereas those in marginalized social strata are discouraged from doing so. Indeed, these same low-income women are sometimes recruited as caregivers for the children of members of the upper social strata, turning stratified reproduction into a form of structural violence and placing the children of lower-strata parents at greater risk for social suffering.

In 2007–2008, Sydney Spangler engaged in participant observation in a medical dispensary staffed by a nurse-midwife and health aide in a village in south-central Tanzania. A few weeks after her fieldwork in the dispensary began, she found herself being asked by a woman on the verge of delivery for help in putting the woman's mattress on the floor of the sparsely equipped delivery room. When asked, the woman told Spangler that the reason she needed help with the mattress was so that her baby would not fall off the bed if she gave birth before the midwife returned. This woman had just been examined by the nurse-midwife, who had decided the woman was not yet ready to deliver her child, scolded her for being weak, and then left the room to attend to other patients. Spangler (2011) writes, "The woman on the floor, who I'll call Asha, did not deliver alone. To relieve the midwife, I attended the birth—an act that prevents me from knowing what would have happened had I not been present" (480).

For the rest of her fieldwork, Spangler sought to understand how this event could have happened, which led her to explore "the multiple and specific pathways through which [inequality] becomes physically integrated within peoples' bodies" (Spangler 2011, 480). She described these pathways as processes of *social exclusion* that eventually produced in Asha's stressed, neglected body a phenomenon that some epidemiologists and medical anthropologists and others call **embodied inequality**. The physical toll that inequality takes on people like Asha is sometimes explained as being the result of chronic individual stress; other times it is seen as the consequence of weak or absent social networks. But Spangler (2011) finds more persuasive an explanation perspective that locates differential health outcomes in "inequitable distribution of social and material resources" (480) at the level of broader social institutions that produced social exclusion while blaming those excluded for their own suffering (Figure 16.8). **Social exclusion**, in turn, refers to "the processes through which individuals or groups are excluded from material resources and societal belonging . . . on multiple levels of political economy" (481). The social exclusion perspective on embodied inequality dovetails with earlier analyses that focus on the effects of structural violence and the production of syndemics among poor people. Spangler's ethnography traces the entanglements among varying scales of social exclusion for birthing mothers and their families in south-central Tanzania.

In Tanzania, "women face a 1 in 23 chance of dying in their lifetimes from obstetrical causes—versus one in 4,300 for women in industrialized regions" (Spangler 2011, 481). Tanzania is also characterized by medical pluralism, and the value of cosmopolitan biomedicine

FIGURE 16.8 Resource inequality sometimes means inequality in health care. Expectant mothers wait to deliver their babies at the Temeke hospital in Dar-es-Salaam, Tanzania.

is recognized by rich as well as poor, urban as well as rural. According to Spangler, the forms of social exclusion that affect women like Asha can be traced to the late nineteenth and early twentieth centuries, when colonial rulers divided up the resources in what would become Tanzania on unequal terms, enriching themselves and impoverishing indigenous Africans. After independence, these inequalities were inherited by Tanzanian elites who then managed resources in ways that furthered regional inequalities. At the regional level, these inequalities were extended when some groups were allowed to monopolize good farmland while other groups were not. At the local level, some of those with land to farm were provided with resources to improve agricultural production, whereas others were not.

Most socially excluded of all poor rural people were women, who were prevented from owning land and unable to obtain paid work. These forms of social exclusion are further exacerbated by bureaucratic and political corruption that benefit some more than others, with no accountability. Finally, Tanzania has felt the effect of neoliberal capitalist notions of development, which equate citizenship with individual purchasing power in a free market. As a result, citizens who do not succeed in consumerist terms are subjected to further social exclusion. These many layers of social exclusion produced encounters like the one between Asha and the nurse-midwife, where "face-to-face claims on biomedical care collide with enactments of discrimination at multiple levels" (Spangler 2011, 482). The consequences leave

embodied inequality The physical toll that inequality takes on people's bodies.

social exclusion "The processes through which individuals or groups are excluded from material resources and societal belonging . . . on multiple levels of political economy."

women like Asha suffering and deprived of medical attention at the moment of delivery, with lasting traces in their bodies of that suffering and deprivation.

Although delivery is supposed to be free of charge at the public health center, Spangler observed that women who arrived to deliver were expected to provide all the supplies needed by the nurse-midwife for the birth: rubber gloves, blankets, soap, a basin, a razor to cut the umbilical cord, cotton wool, and so forth. It turned out that there was no government requirement that women furnish their own birthing supplies. However, the district had adopted birthing guidelines based on recommendations of the World Health Organization, which included a list of supplies women should have. And "in a setting where nurses were attending deliveries with condoms on their hands for lack of gloves, this list took on a different purpose. Inefficiencies in the national Medical Stores Department (MSD) had been contributing to supply shortages for years" (Spangler 2011, 486). As a result, midwives "improvised" the rule that all women had to provide their own supplies. The positive result was that when women did provide their own supplies, clean deliveries were possible and nobody worried about the transmission of infectious diseases. To be sure, staff members of rural health clinics were overworked, serving large populations with limited supplies, and their comparatively high salaries were often stretched to support relatives. Still, "in an emerging capitalistic system with limited opportunity and few means of accountability, rural health facilities became privatized enterprises for the gain of those who worked there" (Spangler 2011, 487).

The public shaming of poor farmers like Asha and her husband marked them as socially inferior and, by extension, only worthy of inferior treatment at the health center. But the poor women Spangler knew did the best they could to minimize their risk at the time of delivery while attempting to minimize the risk to their families of public humiliation or debt. For nearly half of all women in the district, this meant giving birth at home, which seemed the lesser of the evils. Spangler (2011) was impressed that "some disadvantaged women sought biomedical care despite the hurdles they had to overcome" (492). But her research led her to conclude that the health outcomes they experienced could not be explained only in terms of their individual behavior. On the contrary, she argues that "socioeconomic inequalities make their way into women's bodies through multilevel processes of social exclusion that determine the care they can access—their care-seeking behavior and the treatment they receive" (491). She insists that "approaches that seek to understand differences, focus on the needs of the disadvantaged, and address systematic

power imbalances might lead to health development efforts that serve to disembody inequality" (494).

Medical Anthropology and HIV/AIDS

In 2013, according to the World Health Organization, 34 million people in the world were living with HIV; 54% of eligible people currently receive antiretroviral (ARV) therapy for HIV; and 7 million people with HIV are still waiting for such therapy (http://www.who.int/hiv/en/). Effective ARV therapy for AIDS was first developed in the late 1980s, but these drugs were prohibitively expensive and out of reach for poor people like Acéphie Joseph in places like Haiti. By 2006, however, the situation had changed enormously. In that year, Paul Farmer and his colleague Jim Yong Kim wrote that "in the United States, such therapy has prolonged life by an estimated 13 years—a success rate that would compare favorably with that of almost any treatment for cancer or complications of coronary artery disease" ([2006] 2010, 327). At the same time, they pointed out that the conditions that favored adherence to ARV therapy were not found in parts of the world like Haiti and Africa, where infection rates were highest and the people suffering with HIV/AIDS were poor. Therefore, Farmer and Kim offered advice to the medical community, based on their experiences delivering ARV therapy in Haiti and Rwanda through Partners in Health, the nongovernmental organization (NGO) they founded (328):

- ARVs should be made universally available and free to all those who needed them to ensure that the poor were not excluded.

- Antiretroviral therapy could not succeed unless it was embedded in a solid health-care infrastructure, run by the government: "only the public sector, not nongovernmental organizations, can offer health care as a right" (328).

- More trained health-care providers are needed if antiretroviral therapy is to be successfully delivered to people in poor countries.

- Programs designed to relieve poverty must be instituted if antiretroviral therapy among the poor is to succeed: "Our experience in Haiti and Rwanda has shown us that it is possible to remove many of the social and economic barriers to adherence, but only with what are sometimes termed 'wrap-around services': food supplements for the hungry, help with transportation to clinics, child care, and housing. In many rural regions of Africa, hunger is the main coexisting condition in patients with AIDS or tuberculosis and these consumptive diseases cannot be treated effectively without food supplementation" (328).

FIGURE 16.9 A social worker carrying a crack addict to receive treatment in November 2012. As is the case for poor people living with HIV/AIDS, poor people struggling to recover from drug addiction need food and social connections to survive after treatment. If these supports are not available, their chances for recovery are slim.

Many medical anthropologists have investigated the conditions under which people with AIDS attempt to survive, especially under conditions of poverty. An outstanding example of such work is medical anthropologist João Biehl's long-term ethnographic research project on life with AIDS among the poor and homeless in the city of Salvador de Bahia (2007). Salvador is a city of 2.5 million located on the coast of northeastern Brazil. When Biehl began his ethnographic research in 1995, 70% of the AIDS cases in Bahia state were concentrated in Salvador, a popular tourist destination and a city in which nearly half the population live below the poverty line.

The center of Biehl's participant observation research was Casaah, "house of support" founded in 1992 when

> a group of homeless AIDS patients, former prostitutes, transvestites, and drug users squatted in an abandoned maternity ward in the outskirts of Salvador.
>
> Soon, perhaps surprisingly, Caasah became an NGO and began to receive funding from a World Bank loan disbursed through the Brazilian government. By 1994, eviction threats had ceased and the service had gathered resources for basic maintenance. Caasah had formalized partnerships with municipal and provincial Health Divisions, buttressed by strategic exchanges with hospitals and AIDS NGOs. (Biehl 2007, 15)

But Biehl's ethnography is multisited, however, and his research also took him to local hospitals and government offices and into discussions with physicians, Brazilian politicians, and pharmaceutical representatives. His research was ongoing in 1997 when the Brazilian government made it official policy to guarantee its citizen universal, free access to ARVs. An additional strength of Biehl's ethnography is his discussion of how this came about.

In the mid-1990s, Brazil accounted for 57% of all AIDS cases in Latin America, and HIV was spreading unchecked among poor Brazilians in places like Salvador, in part because the drugs that could treat their condition were too expensive for them to afford. Faced with a health crisis of unimaginable proportions, AIDS patients banded together and organized politically to demand that the state acknowledge that health was a human right and that the cost of drugs should not deprive poor AIDS patients of effective therapy. **Biosociality** is the term medical anthropologists use to describe social identities that are based on a shared medical diagnosis. In recent years, patient groups like those diagnosed with HIV/AIDS have proclaimed a shared biosocial identity and have rallied around this identity to engage in what medical anthropologists call **health activism**, whether to demand that the state provide funding for medications, as in Brazil, or to demand funding for research that would seek a cure for the disease they share. Medical anthropologists describe health activism of this kind as an attempt to assert **biological citizenship** (Petryna 2002), that is, to oblige governments to take notice of their citizens' health needs and to intervene on their behalf (Figure 16.9).

biosociality Social identities based on a shared medical diagnosis.

health activism Political organization around a biosocial identity in order to demand health-related interventions by the state or other organizations.

biological citizenship Government recognition of citizens' health needs and to intervene on their behalf.

FIGURE 16.10 In 2012, AIDS activists in Brazil demonstrate against government measures opposed to HIV/AIDS prevention.

In Brazil, AIDS activists were joined by a number of other actors, such as civil servants, nongovernmental development agencies, and Brazilian pharmaceutical manufacturers; together, they succeeded in challenging the pricing practices of global pharmaceutical companies (Figure 16.10). To begin with, these activists asserted that free and universal access to ARVs was a human right. At the same time, Brazilian pharmaceutical companies were enlisted to reverse engineer and produce generic versions of expensive name-brand drugs. While this was happening, the Brazilian Health Ministry was working to negotiate drug price reductions from the global pharmaceutical companies that sold the name-brand drugs. To the astonishment of many observers, inside and outside Brazil, this strategy worked. ARV prices dropped. The Brazilian government, accepting the argument that health was a human right, agreed that it would supply these drugs to AIDS patients free of charge. Subsequently, Brazil became a model for other poor countries to follow in obtaining ARVs for their afflicted citizens.

The Brazilian success story literally changed the lives of the poor AIDS patients whom Biehl knew. As his ethnographic project extended over the years, many individuals who had expected to die began to develop a new "will to live" once they gained access to ARVs. Many of them eventually were able to stabilize their lives and move on with optimism into the future. Nevertheless, although access to ARVs truly could be life altering for many AIDs sufferers, Biehl also saw how the possibilities for such an outcome were shaped by structural violence. Biological citizenship, he discovered,

> is not an inclusive form of care or citizenship. Many are left out . . . [categorized as] drug addict, prostitute,

beggar, thief. . . . To get that to which they are legally entitled, these individuals must not only identify themselves as belonging to the class of those served but also constantly seek service. To retain services, furthermore, they must behave in particular ways. As a result, they largely remain part of the underground economy and constitute a hidden AIDS epidemic. (Biehl 2007, 49)

Further, even for those who benefitted from this new access to vital drugs, the government policy that made this possible—namely, the agreement to supply expensive ARVs to all citizens free of charge—had troubling consequences. Most obvious was the emergence of a phenomenon that Biehl calls the *pharmaceuticalization of public health*:

> Regional governments have been forced to alter their health budgets drastically to accommodate the growing judicial demands for high-cost medicines by patient groups formed around chronic diseases and rare genetic diseases, for instance. Patients follow the path opened up by AIDS mobilization, with the exception that many groups are now supported by the pharmaceutical industry. (Biehl 2007, 99)

In the meantime, neoliberal economic policies adopted by the Brazilian government meant that funding for other features of the Brazilian health-care infrastructure were disappearing. So were government-sponsored welfare programs that in the past had supported the most destitute AIDs patients as they accessed their medications. Too often, loss of these other supports meant that free medication and a "will to live" was insufficient to ensure survival.

Since the 1990s, access to lifesaving ARV therapy by AIDS sufferers has advanced around the world, and medical anthropologists have been on hand to study what happens when ARV therapy is localized in different cultural and political settings. Whereas some of these settings have been characterized by AIDS activism organized around a newfound biosocial identity, other settings have not. For instance, medical anthropologist Rebecca Marsland found that the way ARV therapy was being localized in rural Tanzania in 2009 was rather different from the Brazilian situation. To begin with, the AIDS sufferers she knew did not organize around their biosocial status. In the rural community where she worked, "biosociality is laid down along already existing networks of family and neighbors, reinforced by shared practices, such as clinic attendance, and the recognition of symptoms in others that have been experienced in one's own body" (Marsland 2012, 473). This meant that advertising one's HIV status could lead to social ostracism by one's family and neighbors. Nor were AIDS patients willing to join a self-help group unless they offered tangible material benefits. One of the women Marsland knew "had little interest in her biological identity—it clearly offered less than the answer she needed to survive" (475).

In addition, AIDS patients in this rural Tanzanian community did not separate their own individual well-being from the well-being of their families, many of whose members' daily lives were difficult although they were not suffering from AIDS. As Marsland (2012) put it, "The demands that a pharmaceutical places on the body cannot always be placed before the hunger and the health of one's family" (482). Peasant farmers in the best of times had to work hard in their fields to feed their families. AIDS patients could afford neither the "healthy" diet recommended at the clinic nor the luxury of lessening their workload—especially because they felt responsible for the well-being of family members and not themselves alone. Marsland's conclusion echoes the messages of Biehl, Farmer, and Kim, and other medical anthropologists familiar with the struggles of disadvantaged AIDS patients: "Life is not possible without ARVs, and yet the recipients of this gift carry the burden that they must ask for more, to make that life worth living" (Marsland 2012, 483).

The Future of Medical Anthropology

Biomedical breakthroughs, many of them mediated by technological innovations and interventions, are welcomed by medical anthropologists who accept that biomedicine is a form of cosmopolitan medicine that ought to be accessible to anyone who might benefit from it, anywhere in the world. But as we saw most dramatically in the case of the spread of ARV therapy for

HIV/AIDS, more than pharmaceuticals are required in many parts of the world if positive health outcomes are to be achieved. Many medical anthropologists would argue that it is their ethical obligation to make clear the forms of structural violence that condemn some people to worse health and earlier death than other people. They also draw attention to the fact that the cultural practices of different peoples cannot be ignored by those with the power to intervene medically in other people's lives. Are the targets of biomedical intervention in agreement with the view that they are, first and foremost, self-contained individuals whose health problems (and their cures) are located within their own skins? Or are their selves dividual, linked first and foremost to kin and family, even at the risk of their own health? Do their ideas of health encompass more than simply bodily well-being, but extend to a larger sense of well-being that can be demolished if the social, economic, and religious supports to which they are accustomed are destroyed by violence or war? Does their own sense of pride and dignity mean that they will keep silent about their health or interpret their illnesses in ways that, however implausible, reaffirm their sense of dignity?

Ethnography, informed by a broad understanding of sickness and health, biomedical and otherwise, is an excellent way to seek answers. As Margaret Lock and Vinh-Kim Nguyen insist, top-down approaches and standardized forms of medical care are problematic, as are attempts to provide pharmaceuticals to poor people who are also in need of food and water. They write, "The work of anthropologists to represent and engage effectively with the impact of biomedical technologies at local sites is indispensable in bringing about some change" (Lock and Nguyen 2010, 364). This view would surely be endorsed by the medical anthropologists whose work we have reviewed in this chapter.

What Is Development Anthropology?

Anthropologist Katy Gardner defines **development** as "planned change," and she immediately asks, "why do anthropologists find it so troublesome?" (2019, 193). Even though anthropologists have talked about planned change since the beginning of our discipline, we have often disagreed about how or whether such change should proceed. This concern can be traced back to E. B. Tylor, who claimed that anthropology was a reformer's

---

development: Planned change intended to improve some state of affairs in society.

science—and what is reform, after all, if not deliberate planned change undertaken in order to improve some state of affairs in society? Gardner observes that those who regard planned change in a positive light share "a belief in progress, in life and society improving over time via processes of modernization, enrichment, emancipation (from what are seen as oppressive traditions), and empowerment, the ability of people to exercise individual agency" (2019, 194). Tylor and other social evolutionary thinkers of his day certainly shared this conviction. They were convinced that over time, human societies were all moving ever upward toward more perfect forms of social design, and that Western industrial societies like their own had moved farther in this direction than any other societies on earth.

How might this unidirectional evolutionary progress be described? Tylor's contemporary Herbert Spencer drew on discoveries in nineteenth-century biology about processes of embryological development in living organisms: how, that is, a single fertilized egg divided to produce a ball of cells that then differentiated into distinct tissues, and how these distinct tissues eventually produced complex organ systems that allowed a new organism to function in the wider world. Spencer explicitly drew an analogy between these biological processes of differentiation and change and the patterns of differentiation and change in human societies, from the simplest small-scale societies of foraging peoples to elaborate hierarchical and technologically sophisticated European industrial societies. He and others believed that these processes of evolutionary progress were rooted in nature and revealed by history. Thus, systematic knowledge about human societies, gathered and organized by objective scientific observers, could reveal the steps required to change less progressive social forms into more progressive social forms. Such knowledge could be used to propose planned, progressive interventions.

Yet, as Gardner says, these views about progress have always raised difficulties. For instance, if progress is an inevitable outcome of history, why does it seem to proceed at different speeds for different groups in different societies? Spencer famously argued that uneven social progress was itself a natural process that would inevitably produce overall social betterment in the future. For Spencer and others, capitalist economic practices were the engine of social progress. Social interventions designed to alter inequitable outcomes produced by the working of capitalism (in the form of social welfare programs for the poor, e.g.) were bound to fail because they went against the grain of history. Spencer and others claimed that the spread of capitalism across the world would bring peace and social advancement. Colonial conquest could therefore be justified as a progressive

effort to bring enlightened advances to peoples mired in static, backward traditions. By contrast, Marx and his followers deeply criticized the fact that the benefits of capitalist economic progress were enjoyed only by a narrow elite. They acknowledged that capitalist expansion of productive forces constituted a significant human achievement. Nevertheless, they argued, progress for all people could only happen after capitalism was overthrown, making way for a new communist order in which capitalism's bountiful productive capacities could be made to work for everyone.

Over time, the inequities resulting from capitalist economic practices became increasingly apparent in the territories colonized by European states. To be sure, colonizers had generated new forms of wealth, built mines and plantations, railroads and ports, schools and hospitals, reshaping the world using powerful forms of technology that many colonized communities had never seen before. Yet the benefits flowing to most colonized people from these ventures were scant. By the middle of the twentieth century, such inequities contributed to the growing demands by colonized peoples for the dismantling of European empires. Independence promised to free the citizens of colonized territories to control their own economic destinies. However, the end of empire and formal freedom did not automatically confer economic or social autonomy, let alone prosperity, to newly independent nation-states. Anthropologists carrying out fieldwork in communities subjected to colonial control, or coping with the consequences of independence, observed first-hand who the winners were and who the losers were. Many were not optimistic: after all, the former colonies of Spain and Portugal in South America had become formally independent of their colonial masters in the nineteenth century, and citizens of these nation-states continued to struggle with poverty and inequality over a hundred years later.

If political independence from colonial domination was insufficient, what would it take for newly independent colonies to progress and achieve Western levels of prosperity? The question was urgent in the 1940s and 1950s, as the period of decolonization coincided with the emergence of the Cold War. Competition was intense between so-called first world capitalist economies and so-called second world communist economies for the allegiance of the new, so-called third world (or nonaligned) nation-states. In 1949, President Harry S Truman proposed that the United States, leader of the "first world," create federal programs aimed at *international development*. Planned change would become explicit policy, with the goals of reducing poverty around the world, strengthening the US economy, and—importantly—working to drive back the threat of communist revolution in poor countries. The threat they feared became real in 1959 when Fidel Castro and his allies overthrew the Batista dictatorship in Cuba and installed a revolutionary communist regime, offering "third world" nations an alternative, potentially attractive, noncapitalist model of social change.

The United States and other Western capitalist countries redoubled their efforts to persuade former colonies to reject the Cuban model, insisting that poor countries could achieve prosperity without rejecting capitalism. In 1960, American economist W. W. Rostow published *The Stages of Economic Growth: A non-communist manifesto*. In this book (still in print in 2019), Rostow argued that the historical development of Britain and the United States, properly understood, illustrated how a nation-state could achieve self-sustaining economic growth by following policies that relied on the workings of the capitalist market. In 1961, the US Foreign Assistance Act was passed, aiming to strengthen the power of the federal government to provide development aid to poor countries. Shortly thereafter, the United States Agency for International Development (USAID) was created "to unite development into a single agency responsible for administering aid to foreign countries to promote social and economic development" (https://www.usaid.gov/who-we-are/usaid-history).

Soon thereafter, anthropologists doing fieldwork in Africa, Asia, and Latin America began to learn about development projects sponsored by USAID and similar organizations. Initially, many anthropologists were suspicious of such projects. Katy Gardner offers two reasons for this suspicion. First, she points out that social and cultural anthropologists in the mid-twentieth century were not interested in studying cultural change. Instead, as we saw in earlier chapters, most anthropologists in North America had adopted the Boasian emphasis on *cultural relativity,* and set about documenting and celebrating the diversity of human cultures. And in Britain, anthropologists rejected unilinear schemes of social evolution in favor of structural-functional theory in which each society was treated as a self-contained, internally harmonious entity with its own distinct culture. We would point out, however, that North American anthropologists had good reasons to be suspicious of schemes of planned cultural improvement. They had just fought long and hard to expose the emptiness of nineteenth-century cultural evolutionary accounts that used unfounded racist presuppositions to explain cultural progress. It was therefore difficult for these anthropologists to imagine schemes of planned change that did not revive these dangerous and discredited perspectives on human societies. They tended to view proposals for planned social change as unwanted meddling by outsiders—such as

missionaries, colonial powers, and businessmen—and the role of the anthropologist was to defend individual cultures from such interference.

For Gardner, the most powerful illustration of cultural relativistic analysis was Marshall Sahlins' classic article describing foraging societies like that of the Dobe Ju'hoansi as examples of "the original affluent society." She writes, "while developers believe in progress and improvement for all, anthropologists such as Sahlins believe in the sanctity of cultural difference, following an ethics of non-interference" (2019, 196). However, as we saw in Chapter 6, some anthropologists in the United States were struggling in 1960s and 1970s to reconsider the value of identifying stages of political or social evolution in ways that did not depend on discredited racist classifications. Distinguishing between bands, tribes, chiefdoms, and states, for example, made sense to some archaeologists seeking categories to describe directional cultural change in human history. But other anthropologists remained skeptical, concerned that categorization of this kind seemed incapable of addressing power relations and historical contingency as significant factors shaping changes in human social forms over time. James Scott's recent discussion, also reviewed in Chapter 6, reiterates this skepticism.

Gardner's second reason for social and cultural anthropologists' initial skepticism toward programs of planned change had to do with the *status of applied anthropology* in the middle of the twentieth century. Although applied anthropology of many kinds is flourishing in the early twenty-first century, matters were quite different fifty years ago. Hence Gardner's observation that "work which is aimed at solving social problems has long been seen by the anthropological elite as a lower form of the discipline, nontheoretical and intellectually stunted, certainly not objective" (2019, 196). In general, anthropologists were expected to observe and describe, but not to actively intervene, in their informants' struggles. As noted, many anthropologists' distaste for applied work was also heavily influenced by the stigma associated with the recent, negative history of projects of planned change instituted by colonial powers.

Is Development Anthropology Possible?

Over the past fifty years, and especially since the end of the Cold War and the intensification of processes of globalization, many anthropologists have revised their evaluation of applied anthropology. Anthropologists—and many of the people with whom they work—have come to question many of their earlier presuppositions about cultural authenticity and cultural change: indeed, many of the ethnographic examples you have read in this book document this transformed perspective. It has become clearer over time that at least some of the so-called targets of planned change do not always view such change as an unwarranted imposition by outsiders. Anthropologists are increasingly likely to encounter people who eagerly wish for "development," like the pregnant women in rural Tanzania who sought the benefits of cosmopolitan medicine from the midwives at their local clinic. As Gardner points out, development is

> not simply a "top down" scheme. Rather, becoming "developed" is something that billions of ordinary people believe in and desire. . . . It is here that the problem arises for anthropology, for . . . the true nature of this past state of un(der)development and the future state of development is fiercely contested and entangled with ethical questions concerning the role of the discipline. (2019, 194–95).

Gardner, who has who has been involved in development anthropology for many years, highlights three distinct orientations that mark changes in the way anthropologists have viewed projects of planned change, and the role anthropologists might play in such projects (2019, 198). The first orientation presumed that "good" development could occur, and that anthropologists might contribute to it by working inside development projects to improve or critique them. The second orientation presumed that development was "bad," and that anthropologists should not only refuse to work on development projects but should actively expose the oppressive nature of such projects. The third and most recent orientation has been neither to praise nor to denounce development, but to examine ethnographically the entangled economic, political, cultural, and social processes that characterize programs of planned change.

Is good development possible? Can anthropologists make it better?

Gardner points out that the first period of anthropologists' involvement with development schemes lasted roughly from the 1960s to the 1980s. Development projects funded by institutions like USAID were first promulgated during these years, based on the presumption that rich countries like Britain or the United States had discovered scientific recipes for successful development that could be exported to poor countries. As Rostow suggested in his book (1971), development was initially conceived as an economic process. Governments of "underdeveloped" nation-states were urged to follow the Western recipe and make necessary "top-down" changes in their country's economic policies and institutions. Foreign aid experts from rich countries could provide scientific advice and financial assistance to get the development process going. The expectation was, however, that foreign aid would eventually be withdrawn as these states achieved self-sustaining economic growth.

The Green Revolution was a classic top-down scheme of planned agricultural change that followed this top-down formula. The scheme was designed in the 1950s and 60s to solve a specific problem: how to make poor countries self-sufficient in food production when their farmers relied on low-yielding varieties of native rice. The solution to this problem was to replace these native varieties with new high-yielding varieties of rice developed in the laboratories of the International Rice Institute in the Philippines. In 1975, the shortcomings of the Green Revolution became apparent to anthropologist Stephen Lansing, while he was carrying out ethnographic research in a village on the Indonesian island of Bali. Lansing was interested in the history of an old temple located on the edge of the rice terraces, but "the local farmers were more interested in talking about its current problems. I learned that in the old days the temple had set an irrigation schedule for all the rice terraces in its vicinity. But as a result of a new agricultural policy called the Green Revolution the temple had lost control of the irrigation schedule, and everyone was planting rice as often as they could, without regard for the temple's irrigation schedules" (Lansing 1995, 75). It turned out that the Green Revolution required farmers not only to adopt new rice varieties, but also to use pesticides and chemical fertilizers, and to re-engineer their traditional irrigation systems in order to be able grow rice all year long. Because of the re-engineered irrigation schedule, water was no longer predictable, and rice crops were devastated by insect pests and diseases. When Lansing came back to Bali in 1979, he learned that many rice farmers had abandoned Green Revolution practices and had returned to regulating irrigation water using the temple's schedule.

In 1983, Lansing returned to carry out further ethnographic research in Bali among village farmers, studying the relationship between the water temples and rice paddy ecology more closely. He paid special attention to the way farmers in the village organized themselves into associations called *subaks,* all of whose members shared water from a single source. He worked particularly closely with one rice farmer who had served as subak head for twenty years, and together they visited many other subaks and water temples, comparing their similarities and differences. Eventually Lansing came to understand the Balinese cultural logic that integrated all the water temples, and the waters they disbursed, with the Temple of the Crater Lake, situated beside a large freshwater lake at the top of Mount Batur. Priests told him that the mountain lake was "a sacred mandala, or cosmic map of waters, fed by springs lying at each of the wind directions, high about the irrigated lands. . . . Each of the springs around the lake is regarded as the origin of waters for a particular hydrological region of central Bali" (1995, 77).

But how does this cultural logic connect to the ecology of rice production and the irrigation schedules traditionally managed by the water temples? Lansing knew that the Balinese rice terraces have been under continuous cultivation for more than a thousand years, without experiencing a loss of productivity or a loss of soil fertility. Irrigation management seemed to play a key role in these outcomes. Each irrigation system consists of an intricate network of diversion dams and tunnels branching off one another at different levels, with a water temple located at each diversion point. In other words, there is a hierarchy, ranging from individual farmer's temples at the lowest level; to a temple for each subak; to a temple for several subaks; to temples at the headwaters of major rivers; and finally, the Temple of the Crater Lake. "Chains of water temples articulate the hydro-logic of each irrigation system . . . the congregation of each temple consists of the farmers who obtain water from the irrigation component 'controlled' by the temple's god" (1995, 85). Individual irrigation networks are themselves interconnected, such that "unused water from the tail end of one irrigation system may be shunted into a different block of terraces, or returned to a neighboring stream" (1995, 87).

But the paddy ecosystem involves more than rice and water: paddies are also home to eels, frogs, fish, dragonflies, and most importantly, ducks, all of which are eaten by farmers. Ducks, which eat grain left over after harvest, also feed on insect pests. Pest infestations may also be controlled by flooding or drying the fields, but that works only if many fields in a large area use this technique at the same time—for instance, all the fields belonging to members of the same subak. Subak organization, it turned out, plays a key role in the coordination of cropping patterns as well as irrigation management and pest control. Farmers meet at the water temple to decide which crops will be grown each season in particular fields, especially during the dry season where fields receive water only once every five days. In this way, the temple works to "optimize water sharing, while establishing a widespread fallow period, so as to reduce pest infestation" (1995, 90).

But the Green Revolution paid no attention to this intricate system of irrigation management, crop rotation, protein production, and pest control, "and the result was an ecological crisis" (1995, 90). For these reasons, many farmers wanted to return to their old system of water management and paddy ecology. "But to foreign consultants at the Bali Irrigation Project, the proposal to return control of irrigation to water temples was interpreted as religious conservatism and resistance to change. The answer to pests was pesticide, not prayers of priests. Or as one frustrated American irrigation engineer said to me, 'These people don't need a high priest, they need a hydrologist!'" (1995, 93). Later research, involving collaboration with a systems ecologist and computer modeling, convinced Lansing that, in fact, the subak system was a *complex adaptive system* that "could have developed through a process of trial-and-error adaptation by the farmers, rather than by deliberate planning by royal engineers or other planners" and that "the temple networks are intrinsically capable of doing a better job of management than either uncoordinated planting (the Green Revolution system of 'every man for himself') or centralized government control" (1995, 99). Lansing's conclusions have been echoed by other anthropologists who also witnessed negative consequences when one-size-fits-all, top-down schemes were imposed on people whose own practices were defined as "backward" and dismissed as irrelevant.

Is development bad? Should anthropologists stay away from it? In the 1950s and 1960s, it was still widely assumed that national governments had a responsibility to invest in programs that promoted the welfare of their citizens. Some anthropologists were hopeful that if they worked as development consultants, they might be able to contribute to social welfare by improving development projects. However, anthropological involvement during the Cold War could be complicated and risky. As we described in Module 3 ("On Ethnographic Methods"), a crucial turning point for many North American anthropologists was Project Camelot, a Cold War proposal recommending that anthropologists and other social scientists be enlisted to collect field data that could be useful to government intelligence agencies. After this plan became known in 1965, the project was cancelled, but it led many anthropologists to conclude that accepting funding from or employment by the US government was unethical. Increasing disillusionment led many anthropologists to conclude that "development can never be changed from within . . . this group of anthropologists regard it as an oppressive discourse, or . . . an 'anti-politics machine' which can only ever enforce the assumed expertise and superiority of the West over the rest" (Gardner 2019, 2000).

What does it mean to describe development as an oppressive *discourse*? In Chapter 9, we explored how linguistic anthropologists define the term "discourse" to refer to stretches of speech longer than a sentence, united by a common theme; we also introduced Bakhtin's notion of "discourse genre," which involves a range of stylistic choices that distinguish different ways of speaking from one another. However, anthropologists who describe development as an "oppressive" discourse are using the term in yet a third way, drawing on the work of Michel Foucault. Foucault's (1969) notion of **discourse** refers to the institutionalized knowledge practices of a society, particularly those associated with people considered "experts." Whether these experts are physicians, or criminologists, or educators, Foucault argued that their knowledge practices are never neutral or objective, but are always shaped by power relations. The challenge, then, is to figure out whose interests are served by the discourse of particular experts.

Arturo Escobar drew on Foucault's understanding of expert discourse in his 1995 book *Encountering Development: The Making and the Unmaking of the Third World*. In Escobar's view, the apparently high-minded efforts of development experts to bring the benefits of modern capitalist prosperity to people in poor countries was a deceptive cover for the continuation of Western domination of former colonies after the colonial era had officially ended. The discourse of development classified countries of the world into "developed" and "underdeveloped," and explained how projects put forward by experts from the developed would bring modern prosperity to the residents of underdeveloped countries. Development experts favored programs like the Green Revolution—putting Western science to work in laboratories to develop new plants that citizens of third world countries would then be induced to grow to become self-sufficient food producers. And development discourse shaped the subjectivities of both the experts in charge (whose superior status it affirmed) and the targets of development projects (whose inferior status was reinforced). Escobar traces the origin of the discourse of development to the discourse of Western development economics which, he believes, reflects "the naturalized hegemony of a certain economic conception of the world . . . inherited by development economics from classical political economy, and elsewhere as 'the Western Economy'—a coherent ensemble of systems of production, power and signification that make up one of the most fundamental pillars of modernity" (Escobar 2012, xii).

What does it mean to describe the "development apparatus" as an "anti-politics machine?" James Ferguson coined this description in a 1994 book based on his analysis of the World Bank-sponsored Thaba-Tseka development project in the African nation of Lesotho. Adopting a Foucauldian position similar to that of Escobar, Ferguson regarded development discourse as a seamless whole capable of absorbing any possible challenge to its account of the world. He showed how development discourse was used by experts to argue that poverty and other social and economic ills in Lesotho could be overcome by *technical* solutions, rather than by *political* solutions that might challenge unequal distributions of wealth and power in the country. Ferguson's analysis was most persuasive during the years when national governments were still viewed as responsible for the welfare of their citizens, and were therefore also the favored recipients of development funding. And even when the projects themselves fail, Ferguson concluded, state institutions involved in development are still able to strengthen their own control over citizens who had been involved in the projects.

Escobar's and Ferguson's deeply pessimistic views of the development apparatus derives from their conviction that the discourse of development is seamless and all-encompassing, making it difficult or impossible to challenge. In Gardner's view, however, Escobar's gloomy conclusions are unwarranted because he presents development as "a monolithic enterprise . . . relying on reports rather than ethnographic evidence from within development projects or institutions, he fails to show how the discourse can and does change from within" (Gardner 2019, 202). Gardner points to the achievements of feminist activists, for example, who have been working in development institutions for many decades, and she insists that this work "has led to real changes . . . even if these might not have gone far enough" (2019, 202).

Concern about governmental misuse of development funds, however, has pushed some aid donors to devise alternative institutional arrangements that might bypass government bureaucracies altogether, delivering aid directly to the communities that need it. The most successful alternative may be NGOs that began to proliferate in the 1980s and 1990s. And as NGOs took over development work, national governments withdrew even further from involvement in social welfare projects for citizens. By the time the Cold War ended, and the international economy began reorganizing along neoliberal lines, state responsibility for the welfare of its citizens was no longer expected. Instead, neoliberal development projects shifted responsibility for development to the shoulders of individual citizens or their local communities, working directly with NGOs or other outside donors.

Anthropologist Paige West (2006) documented this changed approach to development—and the

discourse (according to Michel Foucault) the institutionalized knowledge practices of a society, particular those associated with people considered "experts."

disappointments it engendered—among Gimi people living in the highland New Guinea village of Maimufa. West's ethnography focuses on a conservation-as-development project that began when a large section of traditional Gimi territory was set aside in 1994 as the Crater Mountain Wildlife Management Area. A five-year biodiversity conservation project run mostly by NGOs brought Gimi people together with outside development experts from Australia, the United States, and elsewhere in Papua New Guinea. The outside experts hoped that involving Gimi people in the project would teach them to value biodiversity conservation as well as provide them with marketable wildlife management skills. From the experts' perspective, development would occur as soon as Gimi people became integrated in the capitalist market economy. But it was never made explicit to all Gimi that the development they wanted (access to medicine, technology, and other attributes of modern life) would have to be *paid for by the cash they eventually earned working at jobs conserving wildlife.* Gimi participants, by contrast, expected that that the development benefits they desired *would be directly provided to them immediately,* in exchange for the cooperation and material support they had extended to the conservation experts who set up and ran the biodiversity project. In the end, both parties to this arrangement experienced the collaboration as a failure. The Gimi concluded that "conservation" was their government now, and that this new "government" could not be counted on to look after their welfare.

Gardner tells a similar story about a development project in Bangladesh that attempted to solicit the involvement of residents of villages located around land where a multinational energy company was pumping natural gas. In this case, also, project managers had reconceived "development" as a process in which "communities and groups are supposed to be 'helped to help themselves' but in which very little in the way of real services or amenities are offered. Rather . . . what the households surrounding the gas field want is connection, to the gas supply, to hospitals and schools, and economic growth" (2019, 203). Both the Gimi and Gardner's Bangladeshi interlocutors thus came face to face with what Gardner refers to a "neoliberal ethics of detachment." As we saw in Chapter 12, this ethics emerges from what Marisol de la Cadena describes (echoing Foucault) as a "biopolitics of abandonment."

Should anthropologists regard development projects as targets of anthropological and historical analysis? Gardner's first two orientations toward development by anthropologists are polar opposites: *either* planned change is possible and can be improved by anthropologists working within the system *or* planned

change is bad and anthropologists working within the system become complicit with oppressive practices. Gardner suggests, however, that a third position began to emerge as neoliberal globalization advanced and stabilized. Choosing neither to approve or to denounce development, many anthropologists began "treating development as a field of study like any other, with theoretical implications for the wider discipline and no moral judgment or political agenda on behalf of the anthropologist" (2019, 204). Arguably, the studies by West and Gardner just described both belong in this category. So does work by anthropologist Tania Li (2007), who draws on many years of research in the highlands of Sulawesi, Indonesia.

Li is not an uncritical cheerleader for planned change, but she does not denounce anthropologists and others who become involved in development projects. Having worked as a development consultant, she is convinced that many development experts are not cynical, but are sincerely committed to making local conditions better, even when past efforts at improvement have failed. At the same time, she argues that her experiences have provided no lessons "for how improvement can be improved" (2007, 2). On the one hand, she says, development programmers "must screen out refractory processes to circumscribe an area of intervention in which calculations can be applied" (2007, 2). On the other hand, she finds "an ethnographic appreciation of the complexities of rural relations to be antithetical to the position of expert. . . . I am sometimes asked by anthropologically trained development administrators in Indonesia to provide suggestions about what they should do . . . to provide them with a bridge between my research . . . and the world of projects which they inhabit. Such a bridge eludes me" (2007, 3).

Li's analysis builds on Ferguson's characterization of the development apparatus as an anti-politics machine. Yet she rejects the idea that development discourse is all-powerful, able to contain all objections and explain away all failures. On the contrary, her research suggests that although development *discourse* may indeed be theoretically closed and complete, attempts to implement that discourse in *practice* are regularly frustrated by a range of factors that thwart the enactment of intended changes. One major roadblock Li identifies is "the limited tolerance of elites for interventions that might actually restructure relations in favor of the poor" (2007, 4). In general, however, social life is messy, forms of power are multiple, and different stakeholders in the development process struggle for competing interests and goals.

Drawing on the work of a range of scholars, including Michel Foucault and Antonio Gramsci (see Chapter 12), Li develops a series of concepts to describe the contradictions she sees as inherent to the development process. The first such concept is that of **trustees**, those who consider themselves experts with the knowledge to decide for others what they lack and what they need to improve their lives. "In Indonesia, since the nineteenth century, the list of trustees includes colonial officials and missionaries, politicians and bureaucrats, international aid donors, specialists in agriculture, hygiene, credit and conservation, and so-called nongovernmental organizations (NGOs of various kinds)" (2007, 4). Those performing the role of trustees are engaged in what Foucault defined as *governmentality*, or the conduct of conduct (see Chapter 12). Ideally, trustees use persuasive methods to educate the desires and modify the habits of those members of society whom trustees have identified as needing improvement. To reach their goals, however, trustees must specify systematically and precisely both the nature of the deficiency that needs improvement and the steps to be taken in order to achieve that improvement, a process Foucault calls **problematization**. According to Li, problematization involves a process she calls **rendering technical** in which trustees translate a deficiency and its proposed solution into the technical terms of development discourse. Rendering a deficiency technical clarifies for trustees and their clients how to bring about improvement. Architects of the Green Revolution engaged in this process: they defined the *problem* as getting farmers in countries like Indonesia to produce more rice, and proposed a series of *technical interventions* to achieve that goal: breeding new high-yield varieties of rice which, together with pesticides, fertilizer, and a modified irrigation system, would allow farmers to produce more rice all year long. However, according to Li, the very translation process that renders a deficiency technical simultaneously renders it *nonpolitical*. In line with Ferguson's analysis, Li observes that "For the most part, experts tasked with improvement exclude the structure of political-economic relations from their diagnoses and prescriptions. They focus more on the capacities of the poor than on the practices through which one social group impoverishes another" (2007, 7).

Being able to recast political-economic problems in nonpolitical, technical terms is perhaps the key skill that development experts possess. Yet Li disagrees with

Ferguson and others who insist that rendering technical, by itself, is sufficient to neutralize local political-economic challenges to planned change. On the contrary, she insists that rendering technical "should be seen as a project, not a secure accomplishment. Questions that experts exclude, misrecognize, or attempt to contain do not go away" (2007, 10). This means that any diagnosis of deficiency "is incomplete if key political-economic processes are excluded from the bounded, knowable technical domain" (2007, 18). The result, Li concludes, is that "programs of improvement are shaped . . . by what they exclude" (2007, 4). That is, political-economic relations remain in force even if they are formally ignored, and they are apt to interfere with any program of planned change. Indeed, if the discourse of development is *not* fully imposed, and if excluded political-economic factors *do* reassert themselves, then development experts may find themselves contending with a backlash (not unlike the one Green Revolution experts encountered in Bali when farmers returned to using the water temples to manage irrigation). Drawing on the work of Gramsci and Stuart Hall, Li examines "the conditions under which expert discourse is punctured by a challenge it cannot contain: moments when the targets of expert schemes reveal . . . their own critical analysis of the problems that confront them" (2007, 11). She describes the experiences of a young Indonesian man called Freddy, whose understanding of his situation was transformed as he was buffeted by the contradictions and gaps of an imperfectly imposed program of planned change. This is why Li insists on distinguishing between "the *practice of government* in which a concept of improvement becomes technical . . . and what I call the *practice of politics*—the expression . . . of a critical challenge [that] often starts out as refusal [but] opens up a front of struggle" (2007, 12; emphasis added).

Li puts this analytic frame to work in her account of poor indigenous farmers in highland Sulawesi, Indonesia, whose involvement in a series of development projects over the past twenty years led many of them to outcomes that were contrary to what had been promised. Historically, farmers in the highlands owned seemingly unlimited lands in common. Although they were familiar with the operation of capitalist commodity and labor markets, highlanders did not depend on them. If market prices or wages were not to their liking, they were always able to return to farming for their livelihood. However, highland farmers were unprepared for what happen in 1990, after some of them began to plant commercial tree crops, enclose their fields, and establish individual title to them. Within a few decades, all land once held in common had been privatized. Farmers who had made these changes in the early years prospered;

---

trustees: Those who consider themselves experts with the knowledge to decide for others what they lack and what they need to improve their lives.

problematization: According to Michel Foucault, specifying systematically and precisely both the nature of the deficiency that needs improvement and the steps to be taken in order to achieve that improvement.

rendering technical: The process by which trustees translate a deficiency and its proposed solution into the technical terms of development discourse. However, the very translation process that renders a deficiency and its remedy technical simultaneously renders it nonpolitical.

those who waited too long became landless and destitute, and faced extremely limited economic options. Landless highlanders, by definition, could not return to traditional farming to sustain themselves because they had no land to return to. There was little paid labor available locally, and their lack of Indonesian language skills and social connections elsewhere meant that labor migration was not open to them either. Ever since, they have sunk deeper and deeper into destitution.

If, as Li argues, programs of improvement are shaped by what they exclude, then the crucial exclusion in highland Sulawesi was the fact that capitalist relations produce new forms of poverty as well as new forms of wealth: "policies that promote growth need to anticipate the poverty that is generated—routinely and predictably—alongside growth" (2014, 7, 182). Attention to these new forms of poverty, however, is routinely and predictably brushed aside in the stories development experts tell about how the transition from underdevelopment to development is likely to play out: "the transition narrative . . . counts on growth to solve most of the problem and envisages distribution as a 'safety net' reserved for the residual cases. The hard realities of jobless growth, and the uneven distribution of the costs and rewards of growth, are left out of the account" (2014, 184–5). According to Li, the experience of the highland farmers of Central Sulawesi calls into question not only the expectations of capitalist development experts, but also the understandings of social activists. Capitalist relations were not imposed on the highland farmers; instead, the highlanders wanted to escape poverty and embraced the opportunity to plant and sell crops that promised increased incomes and better lives. Yet those who were squeezed out had nowhere to turn. Li was convinced, however, that only political struggle would change the terms under which the rural poor currently suffer. At the time she published *Land's End*, in 2014, no activist movement had yet emerged that was willing to engage in political struggle change the conditions of rural impoverishment in Central Sulawesi.

The situation Li describes is only one example of the ways in which expectations and disappointments connected with development projects have been described and interpreted through an anthropological lens. We end with another example from Ecuador that, while instructive in its own right, also offers an interesting contrast to other case studies we have described from this part of South America. The indigenous Cofán people living in the rainforests of the Amazon lowlands of northern Ecuador have been well-known around the world for at least fifty years. They became internationally famous as indigenous opponents of big oil when they became plaintiffs in a lawsuit against Texaco for the damages caused by oil production to their traditional lands and to their own health. Texaco arrived in Amazonian Ecuador in the 1960s, and began to build roads, oil wells, and pipelines without first consulting the Cofán or other indigenous residents. The oil that Texaco pumped out of the ground was not intended for the Cofán and their neighbors either, nor were the profits made by its sale. But the pollution left behind from oil spills, waste materials dumped into the soil and water, and the particles in the air left from natural gas flares did remain behind. A Cofán resident of the town of Dureno told anthropologist Michael Cepek, "That's why we say that we say that we already reside inside of that. . . . We already live inside of oil contamination" (2018, 149). Humans, fish in the rivers, and animals in the forest inhale, ingest, and imbibe these toxins when they eat, breathe and drink.

Oil exploration in Cofán territory brought many changes. Although some Cofán people were hired to work for the oil company, most workers were largely poor, Spanish-speaking, non-indigenous Ecuadorians who migrated to the Amazon from other parts of the country, encouraged by the Ecuadorian government. Roads were built and Dureno and other settlements expanded to accommodate the newcomers. Cofán people were increasingly drawn into the cash economy, as activities associated with the oil industry affected the rainforest, reducing the availability of animals and fish on which their traditional subsistence had depended. Members of the community have died of cancer, a disease with which they had been unfamiliar before oil production began in their lands. Dureno families also have suffered from tuberculosis, colds, flu, diarrhea, malaria, dengue fever, urinary tract infections, ulcers, gastritis, and congenital defects (Cepek 2018, 38).

Michael Cepek, who has worked in the Cofán community of Dureno for twenty years, was originally drawn to their community because of their high-profile resistance to the oil industry. Their first successful protest was in 1987, when they heard rumors that Texaco planned to dig a well on their land. Together with support from local Carmelite priests, they confronted the oil company, but were ignored. So members of the community decided to move to the site where the well was to be dug and occupy it. Indigenous and non-indigenous allies joined their occupation or provided supplies or other support, and eventually they planted gardens near the site. Texaco representatives finally agreed to meet with them, and promised them money, cars, and a schoolhouse if they would leave and allow the well to be dug. But in consultation with their allies, they refused. Eventually Texaco backed down. The Cofán were energized by the success of their 1987 action, and it was followed by subsequent successful protests in 1994 and 1998. By that time, an

Ecuadorian environmental organization had become an important ally. As Cepek notes, "the Cofán were the perfect people around whom to organize a symbolically powerful and culturally authentic resistance campaign" (2018, 181). Their success attracted activists and tourists and other indigenous people. "The Cofán were more famous than ever" (2018, 188).

In 1993, Cofán people became involved in a transnational lawsuit seeking damages from Texaco, which had been active in Amazonian Ecuador from 1964 to 1990. But Texaco left Ecuador in 1990 and was bought by Chevron in 2001, so Chevron became the target of the lawsuit. After Chevron left Ecuador In 2007, it was no longer vulnerable to Ecuadorian lawsuits. In 2011, however, an Ecuadorian court decided the case against Chevron in favor of the Cofán and their allies, awarding them almost $19 billion in damages. In 2014, Chevron successfully challenged this award in a US federal court on the grounds that the legal proceedings in Ecuador had been corrupt; a decision was upheld in 2016 by a US court of appeals, even though plaintiffs in Ecuador continue to pursue alternative methods in order to collect the award (Cepek 2018, 12). Still, after so many years, with nothing to show for their involvement in the lawsuit, many Cofán in Dureno do not expect to ever see any kind of settlement from Chevron. In the meantime, they have continued to search for a livelihood that would support their families and their community. And so, in 2013, community leaders decided to allow a Chinese company to carry out seismic testing on Cofán territory, with the goal of opening new oil wells in Cofán territory. This decision was controversial, and cost the Cofán of Dureno the support of environmentalists, who were inclined to interpret their decision as a sign that the Cofán people had lost their culture and sold out to big oil.

But Cepek argues that the environmentalists' interpretation mischaracterizes Cofán culture and misunderstands the reasoning behind the Cofán decision. Fifty years of life in oil has made the Cofán of Dureno increasingly dependent on cash for their livelihood and they are looking for ways to make a future for themselves. They are puzzled, therefore, by outsiders' concern about Cofán cultural purity. Although Cepek sympathizes with the concerns of environmental activists, who were crucial allies of the Cofán in the past, he also understands why Cofán people are disillusioned with such activists today: "They make a living through their work, but they have never been able to offer significant economic resources to the Cofán. . . . People wonder why the activists do not share more of their wealth with the community. Perhaps they are just liars, people think. . . . Outsiders often seem sad rather than happy when the people of Dureno acquire money" (2018, 193).

In 2013, a new generation of Cofán leaders in Dureno decided that their survival as a community depended on finding a way to make their peace with the oil industry. Their successful protests had kept the oil companies out of their territory since the 1990s. Twenty years later, however, their territory was surrounded on all sides by oil wells. They were still contending with the pollution oil left behind, but no compensation seemed forthcoming, and many felt that the time for successfully protesting the oil industry was past. Moreover, if they refused to allow drilling on their territory, they knew that the oil companies had developed diagonal drilling techniques that would allow them to tap into Cofán oil reserves from outside their territorial boundaries, without needing Cofán permission. The oil would be extracted, but residents of the territory would receive nothing. So sentiment grew that perhaps it made sense to allow this Chinese company to look for oil on their land in return for benefits to the community. A young Cofán leader in Dureno, Eduardo Mendua, was elected as Dureno's president in 2011. He is a successful Cofán businessman who served in the Ecuadorian army, speaks Spanish, and he built a wide network of supporters inside Ecuador (including Rafael Correa, the President at the time) and outside Ecuador (including Canadian indigenous peoples who are involved in petroleum production).

According to Cepek, "Eduardo has no trouble articulating Correa's ideas with long-standing Cofán values to create a hybrid vision for Dureno's development . . ." (2018, 209). Eduardo has no love for the oil companies, but he argues that their technologies have improved greatly in recent decades. With the support of the President of Ecuador, Eduardo insisted on major compensation for the right to drill in Dureno, including allowing only two wells and insisting that they be located far from human settlements. Aware that the oil reserves would run out in a few decades, Eduardo also argued that the benefits received from the new agreement would protect the forest and allow the community to ensure its future livelihood by investing in high-end ecotourism (2018, 212). This plan was resisted by some older members who had opposed oil decades before, but Eduardo argued that this new agreement was really for them, for it would allow them to actually receive compensation for their suffering while they were still alive. In Cepek's view, President Correa had offered the Cofán both a carrot and a stick. The stick was the current government unwillingness to tolerate protests or other interference in oil production. "Correa's carrot was increased participation in development. . . . Most Cofán people no longer believe they can say no to oil, but they do believe they can say how it will be extracted. Perhaps they are naïve, but . . . Correa's administration convinced them that negotiations bear real fruit" (2018, 219-20).

Cepek collected many stories about how Cofán experiences with the petroleum industry had brought them suffering. Many people in Dureno became ill and some have died, often of cancer. Yet not everyone has died, and Cepek knew many Cofán people who retain a zest for life and are eagerly making plans for an improved future that includes cooperation with the oil industry. This does not mean that they have sold out or lost their culture. Contemporary Cofán people continue to hunt in the forest, but they also store hunted meat in electric freezers. They may work as oil company guards, but they may also be practicing shamans; Cepek's adoptive father Alejandro has been both. Borrowing from Bruno Latour, Cepek concludes that oil is "a 'quasi-object' . . . a material thing . . . wrapped up with people's words, thoughts and actions . . . never stable . . . too unwieldy and volatile to have a fixed essence" (2018, 234). Oil has become part of everyday life for Cofán people, remaking but not replacing their cultural identity. Cepek points to recent anthropological studies of Amazonian ontology, described as "multinatural" rather than "multicultural" (see Chapter 10). That is, humans and non-humans are understood to share the same (human, cultural) interiority even though they appear to one another as beings with different, outward material natures. This multinaturalism is most fully realized when hunters encounter prey in the forest. Cepek observes that oil transformed the forest encounters of Cofán hunters: "Even lone Cofán hunters had to contend with the violent newcomers who had populated their land" (2018, 237). They might still encounter nonhumans with cultural subjectivities. But they were also increasingly likely to encounter the sounds of helicopters, forest workers, road builders, and the barking dogs of non-indigenous Spanish-speaking settlers who threatened them in different ways. Nevertheless, "oil did not destroy them" (2018, 245). Instead, they have drawn on multiple experiences and cultural resources from many places to work out new ways of being Cofán.

What Is the Future of Applied Anthropology?

This chapter has introduced only two of many areas in which anthropologists have applied their biocultural insights in order to bring about improvement in the lives of the people with whom they work. Medical anthropology and development anthropology are growing, vibrant fields—but similar vitality is evident in work being pursued by anthropologists in different subfields of our discipline, such as the anthropology of education, the anthropology of work, the anthropology of immigrants and refugees, and newer areas of specialization such as the anthropology of homelessness. Anthropologists do not necessarily only work as academic consultants; in some cases, as we saw earlier in this chapter, anthropologists have founded their own NGOs, such as *Partners in Health*. Other anthropologists, like Juliet Erazo, welcome the possibility of working as activist anthropologists alongside people who can use their skills, allied with indigenous groups or other marginalized populations whose goals they hope to further.

Yet the experience of the Cofán with environmental activists shows how tricky such alliances may prove over time, when people's circumstances change, and their goals diverge from those of their activist allies. As the case studies in this chapter illustrate, it is no longer the case that the role of anthropologists is straightforwardly to defend nonwestern peoples from the penetration of the capitalist market. As we enter the third decade of the twenty-first century, processes of globalization have stabilized. Flows of wealth, people, commodities, ideologies, and images have become parts of the lives of all people everywhere, for good and for ill. Even as the effects of these global processes are beginning to trigger backlashes, however, it is unlikely that the processes will be radically transformed any time soon. Responses, in any case, are unlikely to restore communities and social practices that have been undermined, especially when the resources to support such practices and communities (such as rainforest and oceans) have been destroyed or vastly altered.

Furthermore, the flows and the backlashes they provoke are beyond the ability of any single community, or any individual nation-state, to manage on its own. And so the building of fresh alliances across many former and present boundaries becomes necessary and unavoidable if current challenges—like rainforest destruction or the spread of extractive industries like oil—are to be managed with any success. In this context, it is useful to be reminded that the people with whom anthropologists work today have all been incorporated into the capitalist market, for good and for ill. Moreover, many of them find that they like at least some of what the market brings them, like cosmopolitan medicine or high-quality education or markets for their products or access to the Internet. The people anthropologists work with all over the world want many of the same things for themselves, their families, and their communities that Western experts (including anthropologists!) possess—indeed, that better-off citizens in their own societies possess. Social media bring indigenous leaders into contact with other indigenous peoples around the world, allowing them to share valuable lessons from each other's experiences.

Increasingly they are making their voices heard in international settings like the United Nations (see Chapter 15). Applied anthropological work is likely to become only more relevant with the passage of time, as all of us, anthropologists and nonanthropologists, humans and nonhumans, struggle together to respond to the challenges posed by life in the Anthropocene.

Chapter Summary

1. Medical anthropology is the fastest-growing applied specialty within anthropology today. Medical anthropologists have shown that notions of health and disease, as defined by Western scientific biomedicine, are not adequate for understanding many forms of sickness recognized in other societies, let alone the illness experiences of individuals. Its successes demonstrate how the anthropological perspective, coupled with participant observation as a research method, is able to address matters of illness and health that are often ignored or mischaracterized by other perspectives or methods.

2. Medical anthropology is a biocultural field because it places human sickness and health in biological and cultural evolutionary contexts. As anthropologists, medical anthropologists have long insisted that culture mediates human adaptations to their environments; hence, all human adaptations to environments are biocultural in nature. Furthermore, what counts as a biocultural adaptation or maladaptation depends on biological, environmental, and cultural contexts. Many medical anthropologists carry out their work with a focus on biological and environmental processes also studied by demographers. They trace epidemic patterns of sickness in health that spread across populations as well as those that are confined within particular populations. Some of them highlight the way that a combination of more than one disease, together with other environmental challenges such as poverty, drug use, and violence, can create syndemics. Others show how cultural mediation of human adaptations can produce disease or sickness because of interactions among biological, environmental, and cultural factors. Examples are sickle-cell anemia and lactose intolerance.

3. People in many societies explain sickness as the consequence of such factors as witchcraft, sorcery, or punishment by ancestors. Western biomedicine rejects such explanations, in part because biomedicine regards human organisms as autonomous, self-contained, harmoniously unified entities and recognizes only material causes for diseases occurring within human bodies. However, not even everyone in Western societies accepts Western biomedical views about selves and the causes of human suffering. Groups like Charismatic Christians understand the cause of certain forms of suffering to be evil spirits that penetrate the body. Biomedicine has also considered the experience of a divided self a sign of mental disturbance, but this phenomenon turns out to be a benign and regular experience, not only of people in some non-Western societies, but also of Western Internet users who interact in online environments such as Second Life.

4. Interpretive medical anthropology focuses on how people with particular cultural beliefs and practices make sense of their suffering. They tend to speak not of autonomous, self-contained selves but instead of subjectivity, the inner experience of people shaped by fields of power in which they are embedded. The study of illness narratives is a form of interpretive medical anthropology that allows outside observers, such as biomedical specialists, to understand the perspectives of individual experiences of illness shaped by nonbiomedical beliefs and practices. Some illness narratives show that people may interpret the cause of their suffering in ways that have nothing to do with biomedical factors, but much to do with social beliefs shared by members of their society.

5. Human subjectivity, and interpretations of suffering, is sometimes shaped by the experience of trauma, the intense physical and social dislocation, including violence and war. The Korwa of India, who were moved out of their traditional homeland in the forest and resettled in villages by the Indian government and are currently living as exploited laborers, insist that they cannot be healthy away from their traditional homeland. Population displacement may be understood as a stage in a rite of passage; but the intermediate, liminal stage may take a very long time as displaced groups struggle to turn their new residence into a familiar place where they feel comfort and hope for the future. Until that happens, displaced people, especially those with few social supports, may experience ongoing forms of experiential nonhealth that biomedicine cannot detect.

6. Structural violence describes institutional forms of inequality that make certain groups more likely to fall victim to disease and suffering than other groups. Medical anthropologist Paul Farmer described how structural violence in Haiti in the 1980s made it more likely for the poor than the rich to suffer heavy burdens of disease and more likely for poor women to die of HIV/AIDS and poor men to die of violence at the hands of the Haitian military. The conditions Farmer describes recall the syndemics described by medical anthropologists like Merrill Singer.

7. The structural violence identified by Farmer is shaped by the history and spread of the global capitalist economy, beginning with the formation of European colonial empires some five centuries ago. Western biomedical practices that spread under colonialism lost their original affiliation with the West and were transformed, turning them into cosmopolitan medical practices, which rubbed up against other alternative medical systems (including sophisticated non-Western systems such as Ayurvedic medicine in South Asia) in colonies and postcolonial nation-states. The result was a condition of medical pluralism. Under contemporary conditions of medical pluralism, people in most parts of the world have the option of consulting specialists in different medical systems according to a hierarchy of resort.

8. Many medical anthropologists have devoted attention to women's reproductive health. Although many health experts have traditionally been concerned with women's fertility, medical anthropologists have often paid attention to women worried about infertility. Many point to the ways that the spread of global capitalism has undermined traditional health-care support for pregnant women and their infants; these changes have often also promoted forms of stratified reproduction. Forms of assisted reproduction that originated in Western biomedicine have now spread across the world. For poor women in states like Tanzania, structural violence can create forms of social exclusion that produce embodied inequality in the bodies of women exposed to stress and neglect when they deliver their babies. Some decide they will be better off giving birth at home rather than face the cash expenses and the risk of public humiliation and neglect if they attempt to give birth at the local health center.

9. Many medical anthropologists have been involved in working on various aspects of the HIV/AIDS epidemic. Paul Farmer's early work in Haiti occurred before effective ARV therapy for AIDS was developed. Once ARVs were available, however, they remained out of reach for poor people. Farmer and his colleagues at Partners in Health found ways to ensure that poor AIDS patients took their medications as prescribed, ways that included forms of social and nutritional support. In places like Brazil, people diagnosed with HIV/AIDS banded together on the basis of their shared biosocial identity and, together with allies, demanded that the Brazilian government acknowledge their right to health and therefore to ARV therapy. Pressure on the government to acknowledge the biological citizenship of Brazilian citizens with HIV/AIDS pushed the government to negotiate successfully with international pharmaceutical companies to bring down the cost of ARVs. This made a dramatic difference in the lives of many poor HIV/AIDS patients who otherwise would have died. Unfortunately, although the Brazilian government agreed to pay for ARVs for all citizens, neoliberal economic pressures undermined other aspects of the governmental health and welfare infrastructure, leading to the pharmaceuticalization of public health. The kinds of support structures necessary for successful ARV therapy among the poor were disappearing, with tragic results.

10. Biosociality and its consequences play out differently for HIV/AIDS patients in rural Tanzania than in Brazil. In rural Tanzania, biosocial identity for people with HIV/AIDS overlaps with family or neighborhood identities, and the government is unresponsive to health activism. As in Brazil, however, neoliberal economic reforms have gutted national welfare and health-care programs for the poor.

11. Biomedical breakthroughs are improving people's life chances all over the globe, as is shown by the success of ARV therapy for people with HIV/AIDS. But pharmaceuticals alone are insufficient positive health outcomes to be achieved, even for people with HIV/AIDS. The delivery of effective and appropriate health care still requires attention to structural violence and the cultural particularities of people in different places, who have their own local understandings of why they are ill and what will make them better. Imposing a top-down, one-size-fits-all biomedical solution will meet with failure, not success. This is where medical

(continued on next page)

Chapter Summary *(continued)*

anthropologists and their work will continue to make important contributions.

12. Development is used by anthropologists and others to refer to planned change. Anthropologists have long felt that their knowledge could be used for human betterment, but they have had difficulty signing on to programs of planned change. Partly this is because such plans are rooted in forms of thinking that reflect nineteenth-century racist accounts of human evolutionary progress that were entangled with Western imperialism. Following the end of European empires, the citizens of new nations were eager to gain the benefits they had been promised by colonizers, but which had reached very few of them.

13. The end of European colonial empires overlapped with the Cold War, which followed the end of World War II. Leaders of Western capitalist nations like the United States began to promote international development as a way to reduce poverty around the world while simultaneously driving back the threat of communist revolutions in poor countries. Following the communist revolution in Cuba in 1959, the United States and other capitalist countries redoubled their efforts, arguing that they had a recipe for economic growth that poor countries could adopt that would lead them to the kind of development enjoyed in Britain and the United States. Foreign aid programs administered by agencies like USAID funded these development efforts. Anthropologists were not much involved, however, in part because their research was designed to undermine unilinear schemes of social evolution and celebrate the diversity of human cultures, and in part because many of them were unconvinced of the value of applied anthropology. Many viewed such programs as forms of unwanted interference by outsiders.

14. In the past fifty years, anthropologists' attitudes to applied anthropology changed, and development anthropology seemed worthwhile to many of them. More and more people around the world wanted to become "developed," and some anthropologists believed they could use their expert knowledge to make development programs better. However, other anthropologists, witnessing failed development interventions, concluded that the entire development discourse was deceptive,

allowing the governments of poor societies to benefit from foreign aid even when the targets of development remained poor. In their view, anthropologists ought not to become involved in development projects or they too would be complicit in oppression. Proponents of this second view, such as Arturo Escobar and James Ferguson, have borrowed the concept of discourse from the work of Michel Foucault. Ferguson has argued that the purpose of development discourse is to convert political challenges into problems with technical—and non-political—solutions.

15. Increasing numbers of anthropologists interested in development have adopted a third position, which is to take development projects as objects for ethnographic study, neither praising such projects nor denouncing them, but trying to figure out how they operate, why they succeed or fail. Tania Li has taken this approach. She agrees that development discourse may formally sweep away political issues, but her ethnography of development shows that attempts to implement that discourse in practice is regularly frustrated by a range of factors. When this happens, development discourse is no longer able to ignore political issues, and those targeted with development may mount political challenge against the authorities or agencies who are attempting to persuade them to adopt new forms of planned change.

16. Tania Li's conclusion is that development programs are shaped by what they exclude. They may exclude local politics, or they may exclude effects of development that are different from, or additional to, what the people participating in planned change have been promised. In Central Sulawesi, Li concluded that farmers who eagerly embraced development had not been told that new forms of economic growth also produces new forms of poverty. Planners think about this in abstract terms, assuming that the market will absorb displaced labor. But in Central Sulawesi, in concrete terms, this did not happen; and those who were squeezed out had no where to turn.

17. Today, many indigenous people throughout the world seek to improve the lives of their families and communities. But what that means in practice is not always clear. Fifty years ago, the Cofán of Amazonian Ecuador and their neighbors

confronted oil companies that drilled wells and polluted their soil, water, and air. In the 1980s and 1990s, they were able to mount protests against the oil company that kept them out of Cofán territory. Together with allies they became plaintiffs in a lawsuit demanding billions of dollars in damages from the oil company. But twenty years after the lawsuit was filed, they still have not seen any monetary awards, even though an Ecuadorian court ruled in their favor. They have become disillusioned with activists and lawyers who promised much, but whose actions have not led to any material improvement in their daily lives. And so they are working with new allies to forge a future for themselves and their community.

18. In the fifty years since the oil company first arrived in Cofán territory, more and more oil wells, and more and more people, have moved into the forest near their lands, transforming the environment. Despite suffering as a result, there are still Cofán people living today who want to make a better life for their families and communities, given

the options available to them. A new generation of Cofán leaders have become better informed about the world beyond their territory. Some Cofán have partnered with the Ecuadorian government to let oil drilling begin again on their land, but with generous compensation and possibilities of developing tourism that would preserve the forest. These actions have cost them the support of environmental activists, but they believe their recent negotiations with the government are more realistic, given the way their world has changed—changes that outsiders often do not understand.

19. Applied anthropology has become very important in the twenty-first century. But it remains troublesome. Both development experts and activist allies may be frustrated when the people whom they believe they are helping reject their assistance, choosing to follow a path of their own as they find ways, in a globalized world, to pick and choose from what the world offers as they try to build a better future. Applied anthropologists will surely be allies in this process.

For Review

1. What is medical anthropology?

2. How do anthropologists use the term *suffering* and why do they use it?

3. What are culture-bound syndromes?

4. What makes medical anthropology "biocultural"?

5. Explain the concept of syndemic.

6. How is sickle-cell anemia a biocultural adaptation?

7. Explain the different forms the self can take.

8. What are illness narratives? Give examples.

9. What is trauma? Using case material from this chapter, explain why this phenomenon is important for anthropologists to understand.

10. What is structural violence? Explain how the Haitian case studies in the text are examples of structural violence.

11. Describe medical pluralism and give examples.

12. How can stratified reproduction turn into a form of structural violence? How does Spangler's case study of giving birth in Tanzania illustrate social exclusion and structural violence?

13. Define the terms *biosociality* and *biological citizenship*. How do anthropologists use these concepts to analyze the history of HIV/AIDS in Brazil?

14. What is development? What is development anthropology?

15. What are the three orientations toward development identified by Katy Gardner?

16. What is development discourse? What does it mean to refer to development as an anti-politics machine?

17. Tania Li describes how development projects work using the concept of problematization, which, she says, involves "rendering technical." What is rendered "technical" in the course of problematization?

18. Tania Li says that development projects are defined by what they exclude. What does she mean? Give examples.

19. The Cofán of Amazonian Ecuador resisted oil drilling on their land for decades before deciding very recently that they would allow drilling on their land. What was the reasoning behind this decision?

Key Terms

adaptation   514

biocultural
    adaptations   514

biological citizenship   527

biomedicine   512

biosociality   527

cosmopolitan
    medicine   523

culture-bound
    syndromes   512

development   529

discourse (according to
    Michel Foucault)   534

disease   512

embodied
    inequality   525

ethnomedical
    systems   523

health   512

health activism   527

illness   512

medical
    anthropology   512

medical pluralism   523

problematization
    (according to Michel
    Foucault)   536

rendering technical   536

self   516

sickness   512

social exclusion   525

structural violence   520

subjectivity   518

suffering   512

syndemic   514

trauma   518

trustees   536

Suggested Readings

Edmonds, Alexander. 2010. *Pretty modern: Beauty, sex, and plastic surgery in Brazil.* Durham, NC: Duke University Press. *A powerful, accessible study of beauty in Brazil: cultural definitions of beauty, how to become beautiful, and how to stay beautiful. Not just about plastic surgery, this is an ethnography about the medicalization of beauty, sex, class, and hope.*

Farmer, Paul. 2013. *To repair the world: Paul Farmer speaks to the next generation.* Berkeley: University of California Press. *This volume is an edited collection of public speeches given by Paul Farmer between 2001 and 2013, some of them commencement addresses in which he discusses issues that have been central to his work in medical anthropology, including equity of access to health care, the future of medicine, and health, human rights, and social justice.*

Good, Byron, Michael M. J. Fischer, Sarah S. Willen, and Mary-Jo DelVeccio Good, eds. 2010. *A reader in medical anthropology.* Malden, MA: Wiley-Blackwell. *This excellent edited collection offers excerpts from key texts in medical anthropology, from early anthropological research on health-related topics to topics that interest contemporary medical anthropologists such as: illness narratives, governmentalities and biological citizenship, the consequences of biotechnology, global health and medicine, and the health consequences of sociopolitical changes accompanying*
the end of colonialism and the expansion of neoliberal globalism.

Lock, Margaret, and Vinh-Kim Nguyen. 2010. *The anthropology of biomedicine.* Malden, MA: Wiley-Blackwell. *This volume introduces biomedicine from the perspective of anthropology. The authors explain how notions of a universal human biology produced by biomedical science are regularly ill suited for coping with issues of health and illness shaped by local understandings of health, illness, and human bodies. They also address some of the ways that biomedical technologies such as assisted reproduction and organ transplantation can actually work to increase global health inequalities rather than improve them.*

Singer, Merrill, and Hans Baer. 2012. *Introducing medical anthropology: A discipline in action,* 2nd ed. Lanham, MD: AltaMira Press. *The latest edition of an introduction to critical medical anthropology, a perspective that locates human suffering in particular social settings within a historical and political, as well as a biocultural, context. This approach situates illness and health within larger contexts characterized by inequalities of various kinds. The authors argue that medical anthropology is concerned with health issues across time and space, and in demonstrating the way social and cultural relationships, not biology alone, influence health and illness.*

   Visit our online resource center for further reading, web links, free assessments, flashcards, and videos. www.oup.com/he/lavenda5e

Glossary

acclimatization: A change in the way the body functions in response to physical stress.

Acheulean tradition: A Lower Paleolithic stone-tool tradition associated with *Homo erectus* and characterized by stone bifaces, or "hand axes."

achieved statuses: Social positions people may attain later in life, often as the result of their own (or other people's) effort.

adaptation: (1) The mutual shaping of organisms and their environments; (2) the shaping of useful features of an organism by natural selection for the function they now perform.

adaptations: Adjustments by an organism (or group of organisms) that help them cope with environmental challenges of various kinds.

adoption: Kinship relationships based on nurturance, often in the absence of other connections based on mating or birth.

affect: Visceral arousal, emotion, or feeling.

affinal: Kinship connections through marriage or affinity.

affinity: Connection through marriage.

affluence: The condition of having more than enough of whatever is required to satisfy consumption needs.

agriculture: The systematic modification of the environments of plants and animals to increase their productivity and usefulness.

agroecology: The systematically modified environment (or constructed niche) that becomes the only environment within which domesticated plants can flourish.

alleles: All the different forms that a particular gene might take.

anagenesis: The slow, gradual transformation of a single species over time.

analogy: Convergent, or parallel, evolution, as when two species with very different evolutionary histories develop similar physical features as a result of adapting to a similar environment.

anatomically modern human beings: Hominin fossils assigned to the species *H. sapiens* with anatomical features similar to those of living human populations: short and round skulls, small brow ridges and faces, prominent chins, and light skeletal build.

androgyny: A condition in which an individual person possesses both male and female characteristics.

Anthropocene: A new geological epoch that marks the point at which human activities became decisive in shaping the climate and the environment on earth.

anthropology: The study of human nature, human society, and the human past.

anthropomorphism: The attribution of human characteristics to nonhuman animals.

applied anthropologists: Specialists who use information gathered from the other anthropological specialties to solve practical cross-cultural problems.

applied anthropology: The subfield of anthropology in which anthropologists use information gathered from the other anthropological specialties to propose solutions to practical problems.

aptation: The shaping of any useful feature of an organism, regardless of its origin.

archaeological record: All material objects constructed by humans or near-humans revealed by archaeology.

archaeology: A cultural anthropology of the human past involving the analysis of material remains left behind by earlier societies.

archaic *Homo sapiens*: Hominins dating from 500,000 to 200,000 years ago that possessed morphological features found in both *Homo erectus* and *Homo sapiens*.

art: "Play with form producing some aesthetically successful transformation-representation" (Alland 1977, 39).

artifacts: Objects that have been deliberately and intelligently shaped by human or near-human activity.

ascribed statuses: Social positions people are assigned at birth.

assemblage: Artifacts and structures from a particular time and place in an archaeological site.

assumptions: Basic, unquestioned understandings about the way the world works.

australopithecus: The genus to which taxonomists place most early hominins showing skeletal evidence of bipedalism.

avunculocal: A postmarital residence pattern in which a married couple lives with (or near) the husband's mother's brother (from avuncular, "of uncles").

band: The characteristic form of social organization found among foragers. Bands are small, usually no more than 50 people, and labor is divided ordinarily on the basis of age and sex. All adults in band societies have roughly equal access to whatever material or social valuables are locally available.

bifurcation: A criterion employed in the analysis of kinship terminologies in which kinship terms referring to the mother's side of the family are distinguished from those referring to the father's side.

bilateral descent: The principle that a descent group is formed by people who believe they are related to each other by connections made through their mothers and fathers equally (sometimes called *cognatic descent*).

bilateral kindred: A kinship group that consists of the relatives of one person or group of siblings.

biocultural adaptations: Human cultural practices influenced by natural selection on genes that affect human health.

biocultural organisms: Organisms (in this case, human beings) whose defining features are codetermined by biological and cultural factors.

biological anthropology (or physical anthropology): The specialty of anthropology that looks at human beings as biological organisms and tries to discover what characteristics make them different from other organisms and what characteristics they share.

biological citizenship: Government recognition of citizens' health needs, and of the government's obligation to intervene on their behalf.

biomedicine: Western forms of medical knowledge and practice based on biological science.

biopower: Forms of power preoccupied with bodies, both the bodies of citizens and the social body of the state itself.

biosociality: Social identities based on a shared medical diagnosis.

biostratigraphic dating: A relative dating method that relies on patterns of fossil distribution in different rock layers.

bipedalism: Walking on two feet rather than four.

bisexuality: Sexual attraction to both males and females.

blades: Stone tools that are at least twice as long as they are wide.

blended family: A family created when previously divorced or widowed people marry, bringing with them children from their previous families.

bloodwealth: Material goods paid by perpetrators to compensate their victims for their loss.

bridewealth: The transfer of certain symbolically important goods from the family of the groom to the family of the bride on the occasion of their marriage. It represents compensation to the wife's lineage for the loss of her labor and childbearing capacities.

broad-spectrum foraging: A subsistence strategy based on collecting a wide range of plants and animals by hunting, fishing, and gathering.

caste: A ranked group within a hierarchically stratified society that is closed, prohibiting individuals to move from one caste to another.

catastrophism: The notion that natural disasters, such as floods, are responsible for the extinction of species, which are then replaced by new species.

chiefdom: A form of social organization in which a leader (the chief) and close relatives are set apart from the rest of the society and allowed privileged access to wealth, power, and prestige.

chromosomes: Sets of paired bodies in the nucleus of cells that are made of DNA and contain the hereditary genetic information that organisms pass on to their offspring.

cladogenesis: The birth of a variety of descendant species from a single ancestral species.

clan: A descent group formed by members who believe they have a common (sometimes mythical) ancestor, even if they cannot specify the genealogical links.

classes: Ranked groups within a hierarchically stratified society whose membership is defined primarily in terms of wealth, occupation, or other economic criteria.

clientage: The institution linking individuals from upper and lower levels in a stratified society.

cline: A pattern of gradually shifting frequency of a phenotypic trait from population to population across geographic space.

coevolution: The dialectical relationship between biological processes and symbolic cultural processes in which each makes up an important part of the environment to which the other must adapt.

collaterality: A criterion employed in the analysis of kinship terminologies in which a distinction is made between kin who are believed to be in a direct line and those who are "off to one side," linked to the speaker by a lineal relative.

colorism: A system of social identities negotiated situationally along a continuum of skin colors between white and black.

commodity exchanges: Impersonal economic exchanges typical of the capitalist market in which goods are exchanged for cash and exchange partners need have nothing further to do with one another.

common ancestry: Darwin's claim that similar living species must all have had a common ancestor.

communicative competence: A term coined by anthropological linguist Dell Hymes to refer to the mastery of adult rules for socially and culturally appropriate speech.

communitas: An unstructured or minimally structured community of equal individuals found frequently in rites of passage.

compadrazgo: Ritual coparenthood in Latin America and Spain, established through the Roman Catholic practice of having godparents for children.

comparison: A characteristic of the anthropological perspective that requires anthropologists to consider similarities and differences in as wide a range of human societies as possible before generalizing about human nature, human society, or the human past.

complex societies: Societies with large populations, an extensive division of labor, and occupational specialization.

composite tools: Tools such as bows and arrows in which several different materials are combined (e.g., stone, wood, bone, ivory, antler) to produce the final working implement.

concentrations of particular artifacts: Sets of artifacts indicating that particular social activities took place at a particular area in an archaeological site when that site was inhabited in the past.

conjugal family: A family based on marriage; at a minimum, a husband and wife (a spousal pair) and their children.

consanguineal: Kinship connections based on descent.

consumption: The using up of material goods necessary for human survival.

continuous variation: A pattern of variation involving polygeny in which phenotypic traits grade imperceptibly from one member of the population to another without sharp breaks.

cosmopolitanism: Being at ease in more than one cultural setting.

cosmopolitan medicine: A more accurate way to refer to Western biomedical systems adopted by people in non-Western societies around the world.

cranial capacity: The size of the braincase.

cranium: The bones of the head, excluding the jaw.

cross cousins: The children of a person's parents' opposite-gender siblings (a father's sister's children or a mother's brother's children).

crossing over: The phenomenon that occurs when part of one chromosome breaks off and reattaches itself to a different chromosome during meiosis; also called *incomplete linkage.*

cultural anthropology: The specialty of anthropology that shows how variation in the beliefs and behaviors of members of different human groups is shaped by sets of learned behaviors and ideas that human beings acquire as members of society—that is, by culture.

cultural hybridization (or hybridity): Cultural mixing.

cultural imperialism: The idea that some cultures dominate others and that domination by one culture leads inevitably to the destruction of subordinated cultures and their replacement by the culture of those in power.

cultural relativism: Understanding another culture in its own terms sympathetically enough so that the culture appears to be a coherent and meaningful design for living.

culture: Sets of learned behavior and ideas that human beings acquire as members of society. Human beings use culture to adapt to and transform the world in which they live.

culture-bound syndromes: Sicknesses (and the therapies to relieve them) that are unique to a particular cultural group.

culture shock: The feeling, akin to panic, that develops in people living in an unfamiliar society when they cannot understand what is happening around them.

cyborg: A cybernetic organism, part machine and part living organism.

cyborg anthropology: A form of anthropological analysis based on the notion of animal–machine hybrids, or cyborgs. It offers a new model for challenging rigid social, political, or economic boundaries that have been used to separate people by gender, sexuality, class, and race, boundaries proclaimed by their defenders as "natural."

Denisovans: A population of Pleistocene hominins known only from ancient DNA recovered from three tiny 41,000-year-old fossils deposited in Denisova Cave, Russian Siberia. Denisovans and Neandertals are thought to share a common ancestor that left Africa 500,000 years ago. Parts of the Denisovan genome resemble the genomes of modern humans from New Guinea.

dentition: The sizes, shapes, and number of an animal's teeth.

descent: The principle based on culturally recognized parent–child connections that define the social categories to which people belong.

development: Planned change intended to improve some state of affairs in society.

development anthropology: Efforts by governments and nongovernmental organizations (NGOs) to improve the quality of life of marginalized populations.

dialectic of fieldwork: The process of building a bridge of understanding between anthropologists and informants so that each can begin to understand the other.

diaspora: Migrant populations with a shared identity who live in a variety of different locales around the world; a form of trans-border identity that does not focus on nation building.

digital heritage: Digital information about the past available on the Internet. It can include a range of materials from digitized documents and photographs to images of artifacts to video and sound recordings.

discontinuous variation: A pattern of phenotypic variation in which the phenotype (e.g., flower color) exhibits sharp breaks from one member of the population to the next.

discourse: A stretch of speech longer than a sentence united by a common theme.

discourse (according to Michel Foucault) the institutionalized knowledge practices of a society, particular those associated with people considered "experts."

disease: Forms of biological impairment identified and explained within the discourse of biomedicine.

diurnal: Describes animals that are active during the day.

DNA (deoxyribonucleic acid): The structure that carries the genetic heritage of an organism as a kind of blueprint for the organism's construction and development.

domestication: Human interference with the reproduction of another species, with the result that specific plants and animals become more useful to people and dependent on them.

domination: Coercive rule.

dowry: The wealth transferred, usually from parents to their daughter, at the time of her marriage.

Early Stone Age (ESA): The name given to the period of Oldowan and Acheulean stone-tool traditions in Africa.

ecological niche: Any species' way of life: what it eats and how it finds mates, raises its young, relates to companions, and protects itself from predators.

economic anthropology: The part of the discipline [of anthropology] that debates issues of human nature that relate directly to the decisions of daily life and making a living (Wilk 1996, xv).

egalitarian social relations: Social relations in which no great differences in wealth, power, or prestige divide members from one another.

embodied inequality: The physical toll that inequality takes on people's bodies.

enculturation: The process by which human beings living with one another must learn to come to terms with the ways of thinking and feeling that are considered appropriate in their respective cultures.

endogamy: Marriage within a defined social group.

essentialism: The belief, derived from Plato, in fixed ideas, or "forms," that exist perfect and unchanging in eternity. Actual objects in the temporal world, such as cows or horses, are seen as imperfect material realizations of the ideal form that defines their kind.

ethnic groups: Social groups that are distinguished from one another on the basis of ethnicity.

ethnicity: A principle of social classification used to create groups based on selected cultural features such as language, religion, or dress. Ethnicity emerges from historical processes that incorporate distinct social groups into a single political structure under conditions of inequality.

ethnoarchaeology: The study of the way present-day societies use artifacts and structures and how these objects become part of the archaeological record.

ethnocentrism: The opinion that one's own way of life is natural or correct and, indeed, the only true way of being fully human.

ethnography: An anthropologist's written or filmed description of a particular culture.

ethnology: The comparative study of two or more cultures.

ethnomedical systems: Alternative medical systems based on practices of local sociocultural groups.

ethnopragmatics: The study of language use that relies on ethnography to illuminate the ways in which speech is both constituted by and constitutive of social interaction.

evidence: What is seen when a particular part of the world is examined with great care. Scientists use two different kinds of evidence: material and inferred.

evolution: A characteristic of the anthropological perspective that requires anthropologists to place their observations about human nature, human society, or the human past in a temporal framework that takes into consideration change over time.

evolutionary niche: Sum of all the natural selection pressures to which a population is exposed.

evolutionary theory: The set of testable hypotheses that assert that living organisms can change over time and give rise to new kinds of organisms, with the result that all organisms ultimately share a common ancestry.

exaptation: The shaping of a useful feature of an organism by natural selection to perform one function and the later reshaping of it by different selection pressures to perform a new function.

excavation: The systematic uncovering of archaeological remains through removal of the deposits of soil and other material covering them and accompanying them.

exogamy: Marriage outside a defined social group.

extended family: A family pattern made up of three generations living together: parents, married children, and grandchildren.

fact: A widely accepted observation, a taken-for-granted item of common knowledge. Facts do not speak for themselves but only when they are interpreted and placed in a context of meaning that makes them intelligible.

family: Minimally, a woman and her dependent children.

features: Nonportable remnants from the past, such as house walls or ditches.

feminism: The argument that women and men are equally human and therefore that women are entitled to enjoy the same rights and privileges as men.

feminist archaeology: A research approach that explores why women's contributions have been systematically written out of the archaeological record and suggests new approaches to the human past that include such contributions.

fieldwork: An extended period of close involvement with the people in whose language or way of life anthropologists are interested, during which anthropologists ordinarily collect most of their data.

fitness: A measure of an organism's ability to compete in the struggle for existence. Those individuals whose variant traits better equip them to compete with other members of their species for limited resources are more likely to survive and reproduce than individuals who lack such traits.

flexible citizenship: The strategies and effects employed by managers, technocrats, and professionals who move regularly across state boundaries and seek both to circumvent and to benefit from different nation-state regimes.

formal models: Mathematical formulas used to predict outcomes of particular kinds of human interactions under different hypothesized conditions.

framing: A cognitive boundary that marks certain behaviors as "play" or as "ordinary life."

free agency: The freedom of self-contained individuals to pursue their own interests above everything else and to challenge one another for dominance.

friction: The awkward, unequal, unstable aspects of interconnection across difference.

friendship: The relatively "unofficial" bonds that people construct with one another that tend to be personal, affective, and often a matter of choice.

gay: An affirmative and empowering self-designation for individuals medically classified as homosexual, which became widespread over the course of the twentieth century.

gender: The cultural construction of beliefs and behaviors considered appropriate for each sex.

gender archaeology: Archaeological research that draws on insights from contemporary gender studies to investigate how people come to recognize themselves as different from others, how people represent these differences, and how others react to these claims.

gender binary: A dual gender categorization separating all women from all men.

gender performativity: The concept that gender is something we "perform" or "enact," something we "do," not something we "are."

gene: Portion or portions of the DNA molecule that code for proteins that shape biological traits.

gene flow: The exchange of genes that occurs when a given population experiences a sudden expansion because of in-migration of outsiders from another population of the species.

gene frequency: The frequency of occurrence of the variants of particular genes (i.e., of alleles) within the gene pool.

gene pool: All the genes in the bodies of all members of a given species (or a population of a species).

genetic drift: Random changes in gene frequencies from one generation to the next because of a sudden reduction in population size as a result of disaster, disease, or the out-migration of a small subgroup from a larger population.

genetics: The scientific study of biological heredity.

genome: The sum total of all the genetic information about an organism, carried on the chromosomes in the cell nucleus.

genotype: The genetic information about particular biological traits encoded in an organism's DNA.

genus: The level of the Linnaean taxonomy in which different species are grouped together on the basis of their similarities to one another.

gift exchanges: Noncapitalist forms of economic exchange that are deeply embedded in social relations and always require a return gift.

globalization: Reshaping of local conditions by powerful global forces on an ever-intensifying scale.

governmentality: The art of governing appropriately to promote the welfare of populations within a state.

grammar: A set of rules that aim to describe fully the patterns of linguistic usage observed by speakers of a particular language.

grave goods: Objects buried with a corpse.

Great Chain of Being: A comprehensive framework for interpreting the world, based on Aristotelian principles and elaborated during the Middle Ages in which every kind of living organism was linked to every other kind in an enormous, divinely created chain. An organism differed from the kinds immediately above it and below it on the chain by the least possible degree.

health: A state of physical, emotional, and mental well-being, together with an absence of disease or disability that would interfere with such well-being.

health activism: Political organization around a biosocial identity to demand health-related interventions by the state or other organizations.

hegemony: The persuasion of subordinates to accept the ideology of the dominant group by mutual accommodations that nevertheless preserve the rulers' privileged position.

heteronormativity: The view that heterosexual intercourse is (and *should be*) the "normal" form that human sexual expression always takes.

heterosexism: A form of bias (like sexist bias) against all those who are not heterosexual.

heterosexuality: The view that "natural" sexual attraction, leading to "natural" sexual intercourse, occurs only between males and females (i.e., individuals of different sexes).

heterozygous: Describes a fertilized egg that receives a different particle (or allele) from each parent for the same trait.

hidden transcripts: Private accounts of their oppression and alternatives to it developed by dominated groups outside the public political arena. These hidden accounts contrast with the views dominated peoples express in public political contexts that do not challenge the legitimacy of the dominant political order.

historical archaeology: The study of archaeological sites associated with written records; frequently the study of post-European contact sites in the world.

holism: A characteristic of the anthropological perspective that describes, at the highest and most inclusive level, how anthropology tries to integrate all that is known about human beings and their activities.

hominins: Humans and their immediate ancestors.

Homo erectus: The species of large-brained, robust hominins that lived between 1.8 mya and 0.4 mya.

Homo habilis: The species of large-brained, gracile hominins 2 million years old and younger.

homology: Genetic inheritance resulting from common ancestry.

homoplasy: Convergent, or parallel, evolution, as when two species with very different evolutionary histories develop similar physical features as a result of adapting to a similar environment.

homosexuality: The heteronormative opposite of heterosexuality; that is, sexual relations involving two men or two women (i.e., same-sex sexuality).

homozygous: Describes a fertilized egg that receives the same particle (or allele) from each parent for a particular trait.

human agency: The way people struggle, often against great odds, to exercise some control over their lives.

human rights: Powers, privileges, or material resources to which people everywhere, by virtue of being human, are justly entitled.

hypotheses: Statements that assert a particular connection between fact and interpretation.

icon: A sign that looks like that which it represents.

ideology: A worldview that justifies the social arrangements under which people live.

illness: A suffering person's own understanding of his or her distress.

imagined communities: Term borrowed from political scientist Benedict Anderson to refer to groups whose members' knowledge of one another does not come from regular face-to-face interactions but is based on shared experiences with national institutions, such as schools and government bureaucracies.

index: A sign that points to, or is beside, or is causally linked to that which it signifies.

informants: People in a particular culture who work with anthropologists and provide them with insights about their way of life. Also called respondents, teachers, or friends.

institutions: Complex, variable, and enduring forms of cultural practices that organize social life.

intersectionality: The notion that institutional forms of oppression organized in terms of race, class, and gender are interconnected and shape the opportunities and constraints available to individuals in any society.

intersex/disorder of sexual development: Individuals who possess ambiguous genitalia; many who experience this condition prefer to describe it as a disorder of sexual development.

intrusions: Artifacts made by more recent populations that find their way into more ancient strata as the result of natural forces.

isotopic dating: Dating methods based on scientific knowledge about the rate at which various radioactive isotopes of naturally occurring elements transform themselves into other elements by losing subatomic particles.

joint family: A family pattern made up of brothers and their wives or sisters and their husbands (along with their children) living together.

kinship: Social relationships that are prototypically derived from the universal human experiences of mating, birth, and nurturance.

labor: The activity linking human social groups to the material world around them; from the point of view of Karl Marx, labor is therefore always social labor.

language: The system of arbitrary symbols used to encode one's experience of the world and of others.

language ideology: A marker of struggles between social groups with different interests, revealed in what people say and how they say it.

law of crosscutting relationships: A principle of geological interpretation stating that where old rocks are crosscut by other geological features, the intruding features must be younger than the layers of rock they cut across.

law of superposition: A principle of geological interpretation stating that layers lower down in a sequence of strata must be older than the layers above them; and, therefore, that objects embedded in lower layers must be older than objects embedded in upper layers.

legal citizenship: The rights and obligations of citizenship accorded by the laws of a state.

lesbian: A term used to describe female same-sex sexuality around the turn of the twentieth century; based on the name of the Greek island of Lesbos, the home of the female poet Sappho, who was reputed to love women rather than men.

liminality: The ambiguous transitional state in a rite of passage in which the person or persons undergoing the ritual are outside their ordinary social positions.

lineages: The consanguineal members of descent groups who believe they can trace their descent from known ancestors.

linguistic anthropology: The specialty of anthropology concerned with the study of human languages.

linguistic competence: A term coined by linguist Noam Chomsky to refer to the mastery of adult grammar.

linguistic relativity principle: A position, associated with Edward Sapir and Benjamin Whorf, that asserts that language has the power to shape the way people see the world.

linguistics: The scientific study of language.

linkage: An inheritance pattern in which unrelated phenotypic traits regularly occur together because the genes responsible for those co-occurring traits are passed on together on the same chromosome.

locus: A portion of the DNA strand responsible for encoding specific parts of an organism's biological makeup.

long-distance nationalists: Members of a diaspora organized in support of nationalist struggles in their homeland or to agitate for a state of their own.

macroevolution: A subfield of evolutionary studies that focuses on long-term evolutionary changes, especially the origins of new species and their diversification across space and over millions of years of geological time.

magic: A set of beliefs and practices designed to control the visible or invisible world for specific purposes.

maladaptation: An adjustment by an organism (or group of organisms) that *undermines* the ability to cope with environmental challenges of various kinds.

mandible: The lower jaw.

market exchange: The exchange of goods (trade) calculated in terms of a multipurpose medium of exchange and standard of value (money) and carried out by means of a supply–demand–price mechanism (the market).

marriage: An institution that prototypically transforms the status of a man and a woman, carries implications about permitted sexual access, gives the offspring a position in society, establishes connections between the kin of the partners, and is symbolically marked.

material culture: Objects created or shaped by human beings and given meaning by cultural practices.

matrilineage: A social group formed by people connected by mother–child links.

matrilocal residence: A postmarital residence pattern in which a married couple lives with (or near) the wife's mother.

means of production: The tools, skills, organization, and knowledge used to extract energy from nature.

medical anthropology: The specialty of anthropology that concerns itself with human health—the factors that contribute to disease or illness and the ways that human populations deal with disease or illness.

medical pluralism: The coexistence of ethnomedical systems alongside cosmopolitan medicine.

meiosis: The way sex cells make copies of themselves, which begins like mitosis, with chromosome duplication and the formation of two daughter cells. However, each daughter cell then divides again without chromosome duplication and, as a result, contains only a single set of chromosomes rather than the paired set typical of body cells.

Mendelian inheritance: The view that heredity is based on nonblending, single-particle genetic inheritance.

men's studies/masculinities: Research that focuses on the many different ways of being a man that can be identified in different places and times.

metacommunication: Communication about the process of communication itself.

metaphor: A form of figurative or nonliteral language that violates the formal rules of denotation by linking expressions from unrelated semantic domains.

microevolution: A subfield of evolutionary studies that devotes attention to short-term evolutionary changes that occur within a given species over relatively few generations of ecological time.

Middle Stone Age (MSA): The name given to the period of Mousterian stone-tool tradition in Africa, 200,000 to 40,000 years ago.

mitosis: The way body cells make copies of themselves. The pairs of chromosomes in the nucleus of the cell duplicate and line up along the center of the cell. The cell then divides, each daughter cell taking one full set of paired chromosomes.

mode of production: A specific, historically occurring set of social relations through which labor is deployed to wrest energy from nature by means of tools, skills, organization, and knowledge (Wolf 1982, 75).

modes of exchange: Patterns according to which distribution takes place: reciprocity, redistribution, and market exchange.

monogamy: A marriage pattern in which a person may be married to only one spouse at a time.

monumental architecture: Architectural constructions of a greater-than-human scale, such as pyramids, temples, and tombs.

morphology: (1) The physical shape and size of an organism or its body parts; (2) in linguistics, the study of the minimal units of meaning in a language.

mosaic evolution: A phenotypic pattern that shows how different traits of an organism, responding to different selection pressures, may evolve at different rates.

Mousterian tradition: A Middle Paleolithic stone-tool tradition associated with Neandertals in Europe and southwestern Asia and with anatomically modern humans in Africa.

multiculturalism: Living permanently in settings surrounded by people with cultural backgrounds different from one's own and struggling to define with them the degree to which the cultural beliefs and practices of different groups should or should not be accorded respect and recognition by the wider society.

multisited fieldwork: Ethnographic research on cultural processes that are not contained by social, ethical, or national boundaries in which the ethnographer follows the process from site to site, often doing fieldwork at sites and with persons who traditionally were never subjected to ethnographic analysis.

mutation: The creation of a new allele for a gene when the portion of the DNA molecule to which it corresponds is suddenly altered.

myths: Stories that recount how various aspects of the world came to be the way they are. The power of myths comes from their ability to make life meaningful for those who accept them. The truth of myths seems self-evident because they effectively integrate personal experiences with a wider set of assumptions about the way society, or the world in general, must operate.

nation: A group of people believed to share the same history, culture, language, and even physical substance.

nationality: A sense of identification with and loyalty to a nation-state.

nation building (or nationalism): The attempt made by government officials to instill into the citizens of a state a sense of nationality.

nation-state: An ideal political unit in which national identity and political territory coincide.

nativism: A return to the old ways; a movement whose members expect a messiah or prophet who will bring back a lost golden age of peace, prosperity, and harmony.

naturalizing discourses: Claims that consider social categories as eternal and unchanging, rather than the result of history or culture.

natural selection: A two-step, mechanistic explanation of how descent with modification takes place: (1) every generation, variant individuals are generated within a species as a result of genetic mutation; and (2) those variant individuals best suited to the current environment survive and produce more offspring than other variants.

Neandertals: An archaic species of *Homo* that lived in Europe and western Asia from 130,000 to 35,000 years ago.

neoclassical economics: A formal attempt to explain the workings of capitalist enterprise, with particular attention to distribution.

Neolithic: The "New Stone Age," which began with the domestication of plants 10,300 years ago.

neolocal: A postmarital residence pattern in which a married couple sets up an independent household at a place of their own choosing.

niche construction: When organisms actively perturb the environment in ways that modify the selection pressures experienced by subsequent generations of organisms.

nocturnal: Describes animals that are active during the night.

nonbinary A self-identification claimed by some persons who see themselves as neither male nor female

nonconjugal family: A woman and her children; the husband/father may be occasionally present or completely absent.

nonisotopic dating: Dating methods that assign age in years to material evidence but not using rates of nuclear decay.

norm of reaction: A table or graph that displays the possible range of phenotypic outcomes for a given genotype in different environments.

nuclear family: A family pattern made up of two generations: the parents and their unmarried children.

numerical (or "absolute") dating: Dating methods based on laboratory techniques that assign age in years to material evidence.

objectivity: The separation of observation and reporting from the researcher's wishes.

occupational specialization: Specialization in various occupations (e.g., weaving or pot making) or in new social roles (e.g., king or priest) that is found in socially complex societies.

Oldowan tradition: A stone-tool tradition named after the Olduvai Gorge (Tanzania), where the first specimens of the oldest human tools (2–2.5 mya) were found.

omnivorous: Eating a wide range of plant and animal foods.

oracles: Invisible forces to which people address questions and whose responses they believe to be truthful.

orthodoxy: "Correct doctrine"; the prohibition of deviation from approved mythic texts.

orthopraxy: "Correct practice"; the prohibition of deviation from approved forms of ritual behavior.

paleoanthropology: The search for fossilized remains of humanity's earliest ancestors.

pangenesis: A theory of heredity suggesting that an organism's physical traits are passed on from one generation to the next in the form of multiple distinct particles given off by all parts of an organism, different proportions of which get passed on to offspring via sperm or egg.

parallel cousins: The children of a person's parents' same-gender siblings (a father's brother's children or a mother's sister's children).

participant observation: The method anthropologists use to gather information by living as closely as possible to the people whose culture they are studying while participating in their lives as much as possible.

patriarchy: The domination of men over women and children.

patrilineage: A social group formed by people connected by father–child links.

patrilocal: A postmarital residence pattern in which a married couple lives with (or near) the husband's father.

phenotype: The observable, measurable, overt characteristics of an organism.

phenotypic plasticity: Physiological flexibility that allows organisms to respond to environmental stresses, such as temperature changes.

phonology: The study of the sounds of language.

phyletic gradualism: A theory arguing that one species gradually transforms itself into a new species over time, yet the actual boundary between species can never be detected and can only be drawn arbitrarily.

pidgin: A language with no native speakers that develops in a single generation between members of communities that possess distinct native languages.

play: A framing (or orienting context) that is (1) consciously adopted by the players; (2) somehow pleasurable; and (3) systemically related to what is nonplay by alluding to the nonplay world and by transforming the objects, roles, actions, and relations of ends and means characteristic of the nonplay world.

pleiotropy: The phenomenon whereby a single gene may affect more than one phenotypic trait.

political anthropology: The study of social power in human society.

polyandry: A marriage pattern in which a woman may be married to more than one husband at a time.

polygamy: A marriage pattern in which a person may be married to more than one spouse at a time.

polygeny: The phenomenon whereby many genes are responsible for producing a phenotypic trait, such as skin color.

polygyny: A marriage pattern in which a man may be married to more than one wife at a time.

polymorphous: Describes alleles that come in a range of different forms.

population genetics: A field that uses statistical analysis to study short-term evolutionary change in large populations.

postcranial skeleton: The bones of the body, excluding those of the head.

postnational ethos: An attitude toward the world in which people submit to the governmentality of the capitalist market while trying to evade the governmentality of nation-states.

power: Transformative capacity; the ability to transform a given situation.

pragmatics: The study of language in the context of its use.

prehensile: The ability to grasp, with fingers, toes, or tail.

priest: A religious practitioner skilled in the practice of religious rituals, which he or she carries out for the benefit of the group.

primatology: The study of nonhuman primates, the closest living relatives of human beings.

principle of independent assortment: A principle of Mendelian inheritance in which each pair of particles (genes) separates independently of every other pair when germ cells (egg and sperm) are formed.

principle of segregation: A principle of Mendelian inheritance in which an individual gets one particle (gene) for each trait (i.e., one-half of the required pair) from each parent.

problematization: (According to Michel Foucault), specifying systematically and precisely both the nature of the deficiency that needs improvement and the steps to be taken in order to achieve that improvement.

prototypes: Examples of a typical instance, element, relation, or experience within a culturally relevant semantic domain.

public/private divide: A barrier that law and custom erected between "private" domestic life in the family, conceived as "women's place," and public life, outside the family, conceived as the domain of men.

punctuated equilibrium: A theory claiming that most of evolutionary history has been characterized by relatively stable species coexisting in an equilibrium that is occasionally punctuated by sudden bursts of speciation, when extinctions are widespread and many new species appear.

queer: A self-identification claimed by some persons whose gender identities or sexual practices fall outside the range defined by "the heterosexual-homosexual continuum."

races: Social groupings that allegedly reflect biological differences.

raciolinguistics: Theorizing race and language together by "drawing on diverse methods of linguistic analysis to ask and answer critical questions about the relation between languages, race, and power across diverse ethnoracial contexts and societies" (Alim 2016a, 3).

racism: The systematic oppression of one or more socially defined "races" by another socially defined "race" that is justified in terms of the supposed inherent biological superiority of the rulers and the supposed inherent biological inferiority of those they rule.

reciprocity: The exchange of goods and services of equal value. Anthropologists distinguish three forms of reciprocity: *generalized*, in which neither the time nor the value of the return is specified; *balanced*, in which a return of equal value is expected within a specified time limit; and *negative*, in which parties to the exchange hope to get something for nothing.

redistribution: A mode of exchange that requires some form of centralized social organization to receive economic contributions from all members of the group and to redistribute them in such a way as to provide for every group member.

reflexivity: Critically thinking about the way one thinks, reflecting on one's own experience.

regional continuity model: The hypothesis that evolution from *Homo erectus* to *Homo sapiens* occurred gradually throughout the entire traditional range of *H. erectus*.

relatedness: The socially recognized ties that connect people in a variety of different ways.

relations of production: The social relations linking the people who use a given means of production within a particular mode of production.

relative dating methods: Dating methods that arrange material evidence in a linear sequence, each object in the sequence being identified as older or younger than another object.

religion: "Ideas and practices that postulate reality beyond that which is immediately available to the senses" (Bowen 2008).

rendering technical: The process by which trustees translate a deficiency and its proposed solution into the technical terms of development discourse. However, the very translation process that renders a deficiency and its remedy technical simultaneously renders it nonpolitical.

replacement model: The hypothesis that only one subpopulation of *Homo erectus*, probably located in Africa, underwent a rapid spurt of evolution to produce *Homo sapiens* 200,000 to 100,000 years ago. After that time, *H. sapiens* would itself have multiplied and moved out of Africa, gradually populating the globe and eventually replacing any remaining populations of *H. erectus* or their descendants.

revitalization: A conscious, deliberate, and organized attempt by some members of a society to create a more satisfying culture in a time of crisis.

rite of passage: A ritual that serves to mark the movement and transformation of an individual from one social position to another.

ritual: A repetitive social practice composed of a sequence of symbolic activities in the form of dance, song, speech, gestures, or the manipulation of objects; set off from the social routines of everyday life; adhering to a culturally defined ritual schema; and closely connected to a specific set of ideas that are often encoded in myth.

science: The invention of explanations about what things are, how they work, and how they came to be that can be tested against evidence in the world itself.

science studies: Research that explores the interconnections among sociocultural, political, economic, and historic conditions that make scientific research both possible and successful.

scientific theory: A coherently organized series of testable hypotheses used to explain a body of material evidence.

secularism: The separation of religion and state, including a notion of secular citizenship that owes much to the notion of individual agency developed in Protestant theology.

sedentism: The process of increasingly permanent human habitation in one place.

segmentary opposition: A mode of hierarchical social organization in which groups beyond the most basic emerge only in opposition to other groups on the same hierarchical level.

self: The result of the process of socialization/enculturation for an individual.

semantics: The study of meaning.

seriation: A relative dating method based on the assumption that artifacts that look alike must have been made at the same time.

sex: Observable physical characteristics that distinguish two kinds of humans, females and males, needed for biological reproduction.

sexism: The systematic sociocultural structures and practices of inequality, derived from patriarchal institutions, that continue to shape relations between women and men (based on an analogy with racism).

sexual dimorphism: The observable phenotypic differences between males and females of the same species.

sexuality: The ways in which people experience and value physical desire and pleasure in the context of sexual intercourse.

sexual practices: Emotional or affectional relationships between sexual partners and the physical activities they engage in with one another.

shaman: A part-time religious practitioner who is believed to have the ability to contact invisible powers directly on behalf of individuals or groups.

sherds: Pieces of broken pots.

sickness: Classifications of physical, mental, and emotional distress recognized by members of a particular cultural community.

site: A precise geographical location of the remains of past human activity.

social exclusion: "The processes through which individuals or groups are excluded from material resources and societal belonging … on multiple levels of political economy" (Spangler 2011, 481).

socialization: The process by which human beings as material organisms, living together with other similar organisms, cope with the behavioral rules established by their respective societies.

social organization: The patterning of human interdependence in a given society through the actions and decisions of its members.

social stratification: A form of social organization in which people have unequal access to wealth, power, and prestige.

sodalities: Special-purpose groupings that may be organized on the basis of age, sex, economic role, and personal interest.

species: A distinct segment of an evolutionary lineage. Different biologists, working with living and fossil organisms, have devised different criteria to identify boundaries between species.

species selection: A process in which natural selection is seen to operate among variant, related species within a single genus, family, or order.

state: A stratified society that possesses a territory that is defended from outside enemies with an army and from internal disorder with police. A state, which has a separate set of governmental institutions designed to enforce laws and to collect taxes and tribute, is run by an elite that possesses a monopoly on the use of force.

status: A particular social position in a group.

stereoscopic vision: A form of vision in which the visual field of each eye of a two-eyed (binocular) animal overlaps, producing depth perception.

stratum: Layer; in geological terms, a layer of rock and soil.

structural violence: Violence that results from the way that political and economic forces structure risk for various forms of suffering within a population.

subjectivity: "The felt interior experience of the person that includes his or her positions in a field of relational power" (Das and Kleinman 2000, 1).

subsistence strategies: Different ways that people in different societies go about meeting their basic material survival needs.

substantive citizenship: The actions people take, regardless of their legal citizenship status, to assert their membership in a state and to bring about political changes that will improve their lives.

suffering: The forms of physical, mental, or emotional distress experienced by individuals who may or may not subscribe to biomedical understandings of disease.

surplus production: The production of amounts of food that exceed the basic subsistence needs of the population.

survey: The physical examination of a geographical region in which promising sites are most likely to be found.

symbol: Something that stands for something else. A symbol signals the presence of an important domain of experience.

syncretism: The synthesis of old religious practices (or an old way of life) with new religious practices (or a new way of life) introduced from outside, often by force.

syndemic: The combined effects on a population of more than one disease, the effects of which are exacerbated by poor nutrition, social instability, violence, or other stressful environmental factors.

syntax: The study of sentence structure.

taphonomy: The study of the various processes that objects undergo in the course of becoming part of the fossil and archaeological records.

taxon: Each species, as well as each group of related species, at any level in a taxonomic hierarchy.

taxonomy: A classification; in biology, the classification of various kinds of organisms.

testability: The ability of scientific hypotheses to be matched against nature to see whether they are confirmed or refuted.

trans-border citizenry: A group made up of citizens of a country who continue to live in their homeland plus the people who have emigrated from the country and their descendants, regardless of their current citizenship.

trans-border state: A form of state in which it is claimed that those people who left the country and their descendants remain part of their ancestral state, even if they are citizens of another state.

transformational evolution: Also called *Lamarckian evolution*, it assumes essentialist species and a uniform environment. Each individual member of a species transforms itself to meet the challenges of a changed environment through the laws of use and disuse and the inheritance of acquired characters.

transformist hegemony: A nationalist program to define nationality in a way that preserves the cultural domination of the ruling group while including enough cultural features from subordinated groups to ensure their loyalty.

transgender: A term proposed in the 1960s by medical researchers to classify individuals who, in one way or another, seemed dissatisfied with the sex and gender assignments they had received at birth.

transnational nation-state: A nation-state in which the relationships between citizens and the state extend to wherever citizens reside.

transvestism: The practice of dressing and taking on mannerisms associated with a gender other than one's own.

trauma: Events in life generated by forces and agents external to the person and largely external to his or her control; specifically, events generated in the setting of armed conflict and war.

tribe: A society that is generally larger than a band, whose members usually farm or herd for a living. Social relations in a tribe are still relatively egalitarian, although there may be a chief who speaks for the group or organizes certain group activities.

trustees: Those who consider themselves experts with the knowledge to decide for others what they lack and what they need to improve their lives.

uniformitarianism: The notion that an understanding of current processes can be used to reconstruct the past history of the earth, based on the assumption that the same gradual processes of erosion and uplift that change the Earth's surface today had also been at work in the past.

unilineal descent: The principle that a descent group is formed by people who believe they are related to each other by links made through a father or mother only.

Upper Paleolithic/Late Stone Age (LSA): The name given to the period of highly elaborate stone-tool traditions in Europe in which blades were important; 40,000 to 10,300 years ago.

variational evolution: The Darwinian theory of evolution, which assumes that variant members of a species respond differently to environmental challenges. Those variants that are more successful ("fitter") survive and reproduce more offspring, who inherit the traits that made their parents fit.

vernacular statecraft: The repurposing of state administrative procedures by local communities under circumstances where state institutions are weak, unreliable, or absent.

witchcraft: The performance of evil by human beings believed to possess an innate, nonhuman power to do evil, whether or not it is intentional or self-aware.

worldviews: Encompassing pictures of reality created by the members of societies.

References

Abu El-Haj, Nadia. 2007. The genetic reinscription of race. *Annual Review of Anthropology* 36:283–300.

Abu-Lughod, Lila. 2016. The romance of resistance: Tracing transformations of power through Bedouin women. *In The gender, culture, and power reader*, ed Dorothy Hodgson, 36–44. New York: Oxford University Press.

Abusharaf, Rogaia Mustafa. 2000. Female circumcision goes beyond feminism. *Anthropology News* 41(March):17–18.

Abwunza, Judith M. 1997. *Women's voices, women's power: Dialogues of resistance from East Africa*. Peterborough, ON: Broadview Press.

Adams, Robert. 1981. *Heartland of cities*. Chicago: University of Chicago Press.

Adams, Robert, and Hans Nissen. 1972. *The Uruk countryside*. Chicago: University of Chicago Press.

Adovasio, J. M., J. D. Gunn, J. L. Donahue, and R. Stuckenrath. 1978. Meadowcraft Rockshelter, 1977: An overview. *American Antiquity* 43:632–51.

Advocates for Indigenous California Language Survival. 2010. Master-apprentice program. http://www.aicls.org (accessed April 10, 2010).

Agar, Michael. 1996. *The professional stranger*, 2nd ed. San Diego, CA: Academic Press.

Ahearn, Laura. 2017. *Living Language: An introduction to linguistic anthropology, 2nd ed*. Malden, MA: Wiley Blackwell.

Aiello, Leslie C. 1986. The relationships of the tarisiiformes: A review of the case for the haplorhini. *In Major topics in primate and human evolution*, ed. B. Wood, L. Martin, and P. Andrews, 47–65. Cambridge, UK: Cambridge University Press.

Aiello, Leslie. 1993. The fossil evidence for modern human origins in Africa: A revised view. *American Anthropologist* 95:73–96.

Akmajian, Adrian, Ann K. Farmer, Lee Bickmore, Richard A. Demers, and Robert M. Harnish. 2017. *Linguistics: An Introduction to Language and Communication*, 7 ed. Cambridge, Mass.: MIT Press.

Alim, H. Samy. 2016a. Introducing raciolinguistics: Racing language and languaging race in hyperracial times. *In Raciolinguistics: How language shapes our ideas about race*, ed. H. Samy Alim, John R. Rickford, and Arnetha Ball, 1–30. New York: Oxford University Press.

Alim, H. Samy. 2016b. Who's afraid of the transracial subject? *In Raciolinguistics: How language shapes our ideas about race*, ed. H. Samy Alim, John R. Rickford, and Arnetha Ball, 33–50. New York: Oxford University Press.

Alim, H. Samy, John R. Rickford, and Arnetha Ball, eds. 2016. *Raciolinguistics: How language shapes our ideas about race*. New York: Oxford University Press.

Alim, H. Samy, and Geneva Smitherman. 2012. *Articulate while black: Barack Obama, language, and race in the U.S*. New York: Oxford University Press.

Alland, Alexander. 1977. *The artistic animal*. New York: Doubleday Anchor.

Allen, Catherine J. 1988. *The hold life has: coca and cultural identity in an Andean community*. Washington, D.C.: Smithsonian Institution Press.

Allen, Theodore. 1997. *The invention of the white race*. London: Verso.

Allentuck, Adam. 2015. Temporalities of human-livestock relationships in the late prehistory of the southern levant. *Journal of Social Archaeology* 15(1):94–115.

Alonso, Ana María. 1994. The politics of space, time, and substance: State formation, nationalism, and ethnicity. *Annual Review of Anthropology* 23:379–405.

Alverson, Hoyt. 1977. Peace Corps volunteers in rural Botswana. *Human Organization* 36(3):274–81.

Alverson, Hoyt. 1990. *Guest editorial in Cultural anthropology: A perspective on the human condition*, ed. Emily Schultz and Robert Lavenda, 42–43, 2nd ed. St. Paul, MN: West.

Anderson, Benedict. 1983. *Imagined communities*. London: Verso

Anderson, Benedict. 2002. The new world disorder. *In The anthropology of politics*, ed. Joan Vincent, 261–70. Malden, MA: Blackwell.

Anderson, Richard L. 1990. *Calliope's sisters: A comparative study of philosophies of art*. Englewood Cliffs, NJ: Prentice Hall.

Appadurai, Arjun. 2002. Grassroots globalization and the research imagination. *In The anthropology of politics*, ed. Joan Vincent, 271–84. Malden, MA: Blackwell.

Arensburg, B. O. 1989. New skeletal evidence concerning the anatomy of Middle Palaeolithic population in the Middle East: The Kebara skeleton. *In The human revolution*, ed. P. Mellars and C. B. Stringer, 165–71. Princeton, NJ: Princeton University Press.

Armstrong Oma, Kristin. 2010. Between trust and domination: Social contracts between humans and animals. *World Archaeology* 42:175–78.

Arnold, Jeanne E. 1995. Social inequality, marginalization, and economic process. *In Foundations of social inequality*, ed. T. Douglas Price and Gary M. Feinman. New York: Plenum.

Arsuaga, Juan-Luis, Ignacio Martinez, Ana Gracia, José-Miguel Carretero, and Eudald Carbonell. 1993. Three new human skulls from the Sima de los Huesos, Middle Pleistocene site in Sierra de Atapuerca, Spain. *Nature* 362(April 8):534–37.

Asad, Talal. 2003. *Formations of the secular: Christianity, Islam, modernity*. Palo Alto, CA: Stanford University Press.

Asfaw, B., T. White, O. Lovejoy, B. Latimer, S. Simpson, and G. Suwa. 1999. *Australopithecus garhi: A new species of early hominid from Ethiopia. Science* 284(5414):629–35.

Aschenbach, Joel. 2019. Enigmatic skull suggests our human species reached Europe 210,000 years ago. *Washington Post*, July 10, 2019 at 12:00 p.m. CDT

Ashton N, Lewis SG, De Groote I, Duffy SM, Bates M, Bates R, et al. 2014. Hominin Footprints from Early Pleistocene Deposits at Happisburgh, UK. PLoS ONE 9(2): e88329. https://doi.org/10.1371/journal.pone.0088329

Aufderheide, Patricia. 1993. Beyond television. *Public Culture* 5:579–92.

Autobiografías campesinas. 1979. Vol. 1. Heredia, Costa Rica: Editorial de la Universidad Nacional.

Baer, Hans, Merrill Singer, and Ida Susser. 2003. *Medical anthropology and the world system*, 2nd ed. Westport, CT: Praeger.

Bakhtin, M. M. 1981. *The dialogic imagination: Four essays*, ed. Michael Holquist, trans. Michael Holquist and Caryl Emerson. Austin: University of Texas Press.

Barker, John. 2016. *Ancestral lines: The Maisin of Papua New Guinea and the fate of the rainforest*. Toronto: University of Toronto Press.

Bar-Yosef, O. 1989. Geochronology of the Levantine Middle Paleolithic. *In The human revolution*, ed. P. A. Mellars and C. Stringer, 586–610. Princeton, NJ: Princeton University Press.

Bar-Yosef, Ofer, and Mordechai Kislev. 1989. Early farming communities in the Jordan Valley. *In Foraging and farming: The evolution of plant exploitation*, ed. David Harris and Gordon Hillman, 632–42, vol. 13 of *One World Archaeology*. London: Unwin Hyman.

Bar-Yosef, Ofer, and Steven L. Kuhn. 1999. The big deal about blades: Laminar technologies and human evolution. *American Anthropologist* 101(2):322–28.

Barkow, Jerome, Leda Cosmides, et al. 1992. *The adapted mind: Evolutionary psychology and the generation of culture*. Oxford: Oxford University Press.

Barras, Colin. 2017. *Our common ancestor with chimps may be from Europe, not Africa PLoS One*, DOI: 10.1371/journal.pone.0177127

Bascom, William. 1969. *The Yoruba of southwestern Nigeria*. New York: Holt, Rinehart and Winston.

Basham, Richard. 1978. *Urban anthropology*. Palo Alto, CA: Mayfield.

Bateson, Gregory. 1972. A theory of play and fantasy. *In Steps to an ecology of mind*, ed. Gregory Bateson, 177–93. New York: Ballantine Books.

Bauman, Zygmunt. 1989. *Modernity and the Holocaust*. Ithaca, NY: Cornell University Press.

Baxter, P. T. W., and Uri Almagor, eds. 1978. *Age, generation and time*. New York: St. Martin's Press.

Beals, Alan. 1962. *Gopalpur, a south Indian village*. New York: Holt, Rinehart and Winston.

Bearder, Simon K. 1987. Lorises, bushbabies, and tarsiers: Diverse societies in solitary foragers. *In Primate societies*, ed. Barbara Smuts, Dorothy Cheney, Robert Seyfarth, Richard Wrangham, and Thomas Struhsaker, 11–24. Chicago: University of Chicago Press.

Begun, David. 2018. *The Real Planet of the Apes: A New Story of Human Origins*. Princeton: Princeton University Press.

Belfer-Cohen, Anna. 1988. *The Natufian settlement at Hayonim Cave*. PhD diss. Jerusalem: Hebrew University.

Belfer-Cohen, Anna. 1991. The Natufian in the Levant. *Annual Review of Anthropology* 20:167–86.

Bell, Sandra, and Simon Coleman. 1999. The anthropology of friendship: Enduring themes and future possibilities. *In The anthropology of friendship*, ed. Sandra Bell and Simon Coleman, 1–19. Oxford: Berg.

Bender, Barbara. 1977. Gatherer–hunter to farmer: A social perspective. *World Archaeology* 10:204–22.

Benefit, Brenda, and Monte L. McCrossin. 1995. Miocene hominoids and hominid origins. *Annual Review of Anthropology* 24:237–56.

Berger, L. R., D. J. de Ruiter, et al. 2010. *Australopithecus sediba*: A new species of *Homo-like* australopith from South Africa. *Science* 328:195–204.

Berger, Richard L. 1988. Unity and heterogeneity within the Chavín Horizon. *In Peruvian prehistory*, ed. R. Keatinge, 99–144. Cambridge, UK: Cambridge University Press.

Berman, Judith C. 1999. Bad hair days in the Paleolithic: Modern (re)constructions of the cave man. *American Anthropologist* 101(2):288–304.

Bermúdez de Castro, J. M., J. L. Arsuaga, E. Carbonell, A. Rosas, I. Martinez, and M. Mosquera. 1997. A hominid from the Lower Pleistocene of Atapuerca, Spain. *Science* 276(5317):1392–95.

Bernard, H. R. 2011. *Research methods in anthropology*, 5th ed. Thousand Oaks, CA: Sage.

Berreman, Gerald D. 1962. *Behind many masks: Ethnography and impression management in a Himalayan village*. Lexington, KY: Society for Applied Anthropology.

Bestor, Theodore C. 2000. How sushi went global. *Foreign Policy* (November–December), 54–63.

Biehl, João. 2007. *Will to live: AIDS therapies and the politics of survival*, Princeton, NJ: Princeton University Press.

Bigenho, Michelle. 2002. *Sounding indigenous: Authenticity in Bolivian music performance*. New York: Palgrave.

Binford, Lewis R., and Chuan Kun Ho. 1985. Taphonomy at a distance: Zhoukoudian, "the cave home of Beijing Man"? *Current Anthropology* 26(4):413–29.

Bird, M. I., L. K. Ayliffe, et al. 1999. Radiocarbon dating of "old" charcoal using a wet oxidation, stepped-combustion procedure. *Radiocarbon* 41:127–40.

Blackwood, Evelyn, and Saskia E. Wieringa. 1999. Preface. *In Female desires: Same sex relations and transgender practices across cultures*, ed. Evelyn Blackwood and Saskia E. Wieringa, ix–xiii. New York: Columbia University Press.

Bledsoe, Caroline. 1993. The politics of polygyny in Mende education and child fosterage transactions. *In Sex and gender hierarchies*, ed. Barbara Diane Miller, 170–92. Cambridge, UK: Cambridge University Press.

Boaz, Noel T. 1995. Calibration and extension of the record of Plio-Pleistocene Hominidae. *In Biological anthropology: The state of the science*, ed. Noel T. Boaz and Linda Wolfe, 23–47. Bend, OR: International Institute for Human Evolutionary Research.

Boaz, Noel T., and Linda Wolfe, eds. 1995. *Biological anthropology: The state of the science*. Bend, OR: International Institute for Human Evolutionary Research.

Boddy, Janice. "The Normal and the Aberrant in Female Genital Cutting: Shifting Paradigms." *Hau: Journal of Ethnographic Theory* 6, no. 2, 2016: 41–69.

Boddy, Janice. 1997. Womb as oasis: The symbolic context of Pharaonic circumcision in rural northern Sudan. *In The gender/sexuality reader*, ed. Roger Lancaster and Micaela De Leonardo, 309–24. New York: Routledge.

Boellstorff, Tom. 2008. *Coming of age in Second Life. An anthropologist explores the virtually human*. Princeton, NJ: Princeton University Press.

Boesch-Achermann, H., and C. Boesch. 1994. Hominization in the rainforest: The chimpanzee's piece of the puzzle. *Evolutionary Anthropology* 3(1):9–16.

Bogin, Barry. 1995. Growth and development: Recent evolutionary and biocultural research. *In Biological anthropology: The state of the science*, ed. Noel T. Boaz and Linda Wolfe. Bend, OR: International Institute for Human Evolutionary Research.

Bohannon, Laura, and Paul Bohannon, 1969. *The Tiv of central Nigeria*, 2nd ed. London, International African Institute.

Bökönyi, Sandor. 1989. Definitions of animal domestication. In *The walking larder: Patterns of domestication, pastoralism, and predation*, ed. Juliet Clutton-Brock, 22–27, vol. 14 of *One World Archaeology*. London: Unwin Hyman.

Bolnick, Deborah A., Jennifer A. Raff, Lauren C. Springs, Austin W. Reynolds, and Aida Miró-Herrans. 2016. "Native American Genomics and Population Histories." In *Annual Review of Anthropology*, 319–94.

Borman, Randy. 1999. Cofán: Story of the forest people and the outsiders. *Cultural Survival Quarterly* 23(2):48–50.

Boquet-Appel, J. P. and Degioanni, A. 2013. Neanderthal Demographic Estimates, *Current Anthropology*, 54:8 (202–213).

Boskovic, Aleksander, and Thomas Hylland Eriksen. 2010. *Other People's Anthropologies: Ethnographic Practice on the Margins*. Oxford: Berghahn Books.

Bourgois, Philippe. 1995. *In search of respect: Selling crack in El Barrio*. New York: Cambridge University Press.

Bowen, John. 2008. *Religions in practice: An approach to the anthropology of religion*, 4th ed. Needham Heights, MA: Allyn & Bacon.

Bowen, John R. 2010. *Can Islam be French? Pluralism and pragmatism in a secularist state*. Princeton, NJ: Princeton University Press.

Bowie, Fiona. 2006. *The anthropology of religion: An introduction*, 2nd ed. Malden, MA: Blackwell.

Boyd, Robert, and Peter J. Richerson. 1985. *Culture and the evolutionary process*. Chicago: University of Chicago Press.

Bradburd, Daniel. 1998. *Being there: The necessity of fieldwork*. Washington, DC: Smithsonian Institution Press.

Brain, C. K. 1985. Interpreting early hominid death assemblages: The rise of taphonomy since 1925. *In Hominid evolution: Past, present, and future*, ed. P. V. Tobias, 41–46. New York: Alan R. Liss.

Brain, C. K., and A. Sillen. 1988. Evidence from the Swartkrans Cave for the earliest use of fire. *Nature* 336:464–66.

Branam, Kelly M. Forthcoming. *Constitution making: Law, power, and kinship in Crow Country*. Forthcoming. Albany, NY: SUNY Press.

Bräuer, Günter. 1989. The evolution of modern humans: A comparison of the African and non-African evidence. *In The human revolution*, ed. P. A. Mellars and C. Stringer, 123–54. Princeton, NJ: Princeton University Press.

Brenneis, Donald, and Ronald Macaulay, eds. 1996. *The matrix of language: Contemporary linguistic anthropology*. Boulder, CO: Westview Press.

Brooke, James. 2003. Dowry too high: Lose bride and go to jail. *New York Times*, May 17.

Brooks, Allison, and J. N. Leith Smith. 1991. Politics and problems: Gorilla and chimp conservation in Africa. *Anthro Notes* 13(1 Winter):14.

Brooks, Allison, and John Yellen. 1992. Decoding the Jul/huasi past. *Symbols* September:24–31.

Brown, Keri A., and Terence A. Brown. 2013. Biomolecular archaeology. *Annual Review of Anthropology* 42:159–74.

Brown, P., T. Sutinka, M. Morwood, et al. 2004. A new small-bodied hominin from the Late Pleistocene of Flores, Indonesia. *Nature* 431:1055–61.

Browne, Malcolm. 1994. Asian fossil prompts new ideas on evolution. *New York Times*, February 24.

Brunet, M., et al. 2002. A new hominid from the upper Miocene of Chad, central Africa. *Nature* 418:145–51.

Bruno, Maria C. 2009. Practice and history in the transition to food production. *Current Anthropology* 50(5):703–06.

Burch, Ernest. 1970. Marriage and divorce among the North Alaska Eskimos. *In Divorce and after*, ed. Paul Bohannan, 152–81. Garden City, NY: Doubleday.

Burch, Ernest S. Jr. 1975. *Eskimo kinsmen: Changing family relationships in northwest Alaska*. American Ethnological Society Monograph, no. 59. St. Paul: West.

Burling, Robbins. 2005. *The talking ape: How language evolved*. New York: Oxford University Press.

Butler, Judith. [1990]2006. *Gender trouble: feminism and the subversion of identity (Routledge Classics, 36)*. New York: Routledge.

Cann, R. L., M. Stoneking, and A. C. Wilson. 1987. Mitchondrial DNA and human evolution. *Nature* 325:31–36.

Carneiro, Robert. 1970. A theory of the origin of the state. *Science* 169:733–38.

Cartmill, M. 1972. Arboreal adaptations and the origin of the order Primates. *In The functional and evolutionary biology of primates*, ed. R. Tuttle, 97–122. Chicago: Aldine–Atherton.

Cary, Annette. 2017. Tribes return ancient Kennewick Man to the ground. *Tri City Herald*, https://www.tri-cityherald.com/news/local/article133780309.html

Cavalli-Sforza, L. L., and Marcus W. Feldman. 1981. *Cultural transmission and evolution: A quantitative approach*. Princeton, NJ: Princeton University Press.

Caryl, Christian. 2009. Reality check: Human Terrain Teams. *Foreign Policy*. September 8. http://www.foreignpolicy.com/articles/2009/09/08/reality_check_human_terrain_teams

Cepek, Michael L. *Life in oil: Cofán survival in the Petroleum fields of Amazonia*. Austin: University of Texas Press.

Chase, Arlen F., Diane Z. Chase, et al. 2012. Geospatial revolution and remote sensing LiDAR in Mesoamerican archaeology. *Proceedings of the National Academy of Sciences USA* 109:12916–21.

Chase, Philip G. 1989. How different was Middle Palaeolithic subsistence? A zooarchaeological perspective on the Middle to Upper Palaeolithic transition. *In The human revolution*, ed. P. A. Mellars and C. Stringer, 321–37. Princeton, NJ: Princeton University Press.

Chauchat, Claude. 1988. Early hunter–gatherers on the Peruvian coast. *In Peruvian prehistory*, ed. R. Keatinge, 41–66. Cambridge, UK: Cambridge University Press.

Chen F., Welker F., Shen C.-C., Bailey S.E., Bergmann I., Davis S., Xia H., Wang H., Fischer R. Freidline S.E., et al. 2019. A late Middle Pleistocene Denisovan mandible from the Tibetan Plateau. *Nature* 569: 409–412.

Cheney, D. L., R. M. Seyfarth, B. B. Smuts, and R. W. Wrangham. 1987. The study of primate societies. In *Primate societies*, ed. Barbara Smuts, Dorothy Cheney, Robert Seyfarth, Richard Wrangham, and Thomas Struhsaker, 1–10. Chicago: University of Chicago Press.

Cheverud, James M. 2004. Darwinian evolution by the natural selection of heritable variation: Definition of parameters and application to social behaviors. *In The origins and nature of sociality*, ed. Robert W. Sussman and Audrey R. Chapman, 140–60. New York: Aldine de Gruyter.

Chin, Elizabeth. 1999. Ethnically correct dolls: Toying with the race industry. *American Anthropologist* 101(2):305–21.

Chiu, Lynn, and Scott F. Gilbert. "The Birth of the Holobiont: Multi-Species Birthing Through Mutual Scaffolding and Niche Construction." *Biosemiotics* 8, 2015: 191–210.

Chomsky, Noam. 1957. *Syntactic structures*. Cambridge, MA: MIT Press.

Chomsky, Noam. 1965. *Aspects of the theory of syntax*. Cambridge, MA: MIT Press.

Clarke, Ronald J. 1985. *Australopithecus and early Homo* in southern Africa. In *Ancestors: The hard evidence*, ed. E. Delson, 171–77. New York: Alan R. Liss.

Clottes, Jean. 2016. *What is Paleolithic Art?* Chicago. University of Chicago Press.

Colloredo-Mansfeld, Rudi. 1999. *The native leisure class: Consumption and cultural creativity in the Andes*. Chicago: University of Chicago Press.

Colloredo-Mansfeld, Rudi. 2009. *Fighting like a community: Andean civil society in an era of Indian uprisings*. Chicago: University of Chicago Press.

Colwell-Chanthaphonh, Chip. 2009. The archaeologist as world citizen: On the morals of heritage preservation and destruction. *In Cosmopolitan archaeologies*, ed. Lynn Meskell, 140–65. Durham, NC: Duke University Press.

Comaroff, Jean. 1985. *Body of power, spirit of resistance: The culture history of a South African people*. Chicago: University of Chicago Press.

Comaroff, Jean and John Comaroff. 1991. *Of revelation and revolution*. Chicago: University of Chicago Press.

Comaroff, John and Jean Comaroff. 1992. *Ethnography and the historical imagination*. Boulder, CO: Westview.

Condry, Ian. 2001. Japanese hip-hop and the globalization of popular culture. *In Urban life: Readings in the anthropology of the city*, ed. George Gmelch and Walter Zenner, 357–87. Prospect Heights, IL: Waveland Press.

Conkey, Margaret W. 1993. "Humans as Materialists and Symbolists: Image Making in the Upper Paleolithic." D. Tab Rasmussen (ed), 95–118. Boston: Jones and Bartlett.

Conkey, Margaret W., and Joan M. Gero. 1991. Tensions, pluralities, and engendering archaeology: An introduction to women and prehistory. *In Engendering archaeology*, ed. Margaret Conkey and Joan Gero, 3–30. Oxford: Blackwell.

Conklin, William J., and Michael E. Moseley. 1988. The patterns of art and power in the Early Intermediate period In *Peruvian prehistory*, ed. R. Keatinge, 145–63. Cambridge, UK: Cambridge University Press.

Cords, Marina. 1987. Forest guenons and patas monkeys: Male–male competition in one-male groups. *In Primate societies*, ed. Barbara Smuts, Dorothy Cheney, Robert Seyfarth, Richard Wrangham, and Thomas Struhsaker, 98–111. Chicago: University of Chicago Press.

Counihan, Carole M. 2004. *Around the Tuscan table: Food, family, and gender in twentieth-century Florence*. New York: Routledge.

Course, Magnus. 2011. *Becoming Mapuche: Person and Ritual in Indigenous Chile*. Urbana, IL: University of Illinois Press,

Cowan, Jane, Marie-Bénédicte Dembour, and Richard A. Wilson. 2001. Introduction. In *Culture and rights: Anthropological perspectives*, ed. Jane Cowan, Marie-Bénédicte Dembour, and Richard A. Wilson, 1–26. Cambridge, UK: Cambridge University Press.

Cox, Oliver Cromwell. 1948. *Caste, class, and race: a study in social dynamics*. Garden City, NY: Doubleday.

Crehan, Kate. 2002. *Gramsci and cultural anthropology*. Berkeley: University of California Press.

Csordas, Thomas J. 1988. Elements of charismatic persuasion and healing. *Medical Anthropology Quarterly* 2, no. 2: 121–142.

Daly, Mary. 1978. *Gyn/Ecology: The metaethics of radical feminism*. Boston: Beacon Press.

Daniel, E. Valentine. 1997. Suffering nation and alienation. *In Social suffering*, ed. Arthur Kleinman, Veena Das, and Margaret Lock, 309–58. Berkeley: University of California Press.

Das, Veena, and Arthur Kleinman. 2000. Introduction. *In Violence and subjectivity*, ed. Veena Das, Arthur Kleinman, Mamphela Ramphele, and Pamela Reynolds, 1–18. Berkeley: University of California Press.

Daston, Lorraine. 1999. Objectivity and the escape from perspective. *In The science studies reader*, ed. Mario Biagioli, 110–23. New York: Routledge.

Day, M. H. 1985. Pliocene hominids. *In Ancestors: The hard evidence*, ed. E. Delson, 91–93. New York: Alan R. Liss.

Day, M. H. 1986. Bipedalism: Pressures, origins, and modes. *In Major topics in primate and human evolution*, ed. B. Wood,

L. Martin, and P. Andrews, 188–202. Cambridge, UK: Cambridge University Press.

Deacon, Terrence. 1997. *The symbolic species: The co-evolution of language and the brain*. New York: W. W. Norton.

Deacon, Terrence. 2003. The hierarchic logic of emergence: Untangling the interdependence of evolution and self-organization. *In Evolution and learning: The Baldwin effect reconsidered*, ed. Bruce H. Weber and David J. Depew, 273–308. Cambridge, MA: MIT Press.

Defleur, A., O. Dutour, H. Valladas, and V. Vandermeersch. 1993. Cannibals among the Neanderthals. *Nature* 362:214.

Defleur, A., T. D. White, P. Valensi, L. Slimak, and E. Cregut-Bonnoure. 1999. Neanderthal cannibalism at Moula-Guercy, Ardeche, France. *Science* 286:128–31.

De Heinzelin, J., J. D. Clark, T. White, W. Hart, P. Renne, G. Woldegabriel, Y. Beyene, and E. Vrba. 1999. Environment and behavior of 2.5-million-year-old Bouri hominids. *Science* 284(5414):625–9.

De la Cadena, Marisol. 2015. *Earth beings: Ecologies of practice across Andean worlds*. Durham, NC: Duke University Press.

Dembo, Mana, Davorka Radovcic, Heather Garvin, and Myra Laird. 2016. The evolutionary relationships and age of *Homo naledi*: An assessment using dated Bayesian phylogenetic methods. *Journal of Human Evolution* 97:17–26.

De León, Jason. *The Land of Open Graves: Living and Dying on the Migrant Trail*. Berkeley: University of California Press, 2015.

de Meer, K., R. Bergman, and J. S. Kusner. 1993. Differences in physical growth of Aymara and Quechua children living at high altitude in Peru. *American Journal of Physical Anthropology* 90:59–75.

DeMoule, Jean-Paul. 2012. Rescue archaeology: A European view. *Annual Review of Anthropology* 41:611–26.

Deng, Francis Madeng. 1972. *The Dinka of the Sudan*. New York: Holt, Rinehart and Winston.

Department of Communications, Information Technology, and the Arts. 2005. *Return of indigenous cultural property program*. Canberra: Government of Australia. http://arts.gov.au/sites/default/files/pdfs/national-coordination-framework-101109.pdf [No longer available].

Depew, David J., and Bruce H. Weber. 1989. The evolution of the Darwinian research tradition. *Systems Research* 6(3):255–63.

de Waal, Frans. 1989. *Peacemaking among primates*. Cambridge, MA: Harvard University Press.

DeWalt, K., and B. DeWalt. 2002. *Participant observation*. Walnut Creek, CA: AltaMira Press.

Diamond, Jared. 1997. *Guns, germs, and steel: The fates of human societies*. New York: Norton.

Diamond, Jared. 2005. *Collapse: How societies choose to fail or succeed*. New York: Viking.

Dibble, Harold L. 1989. The implications of stone tool types for the presence of language during the Lower and Middle Palaeolithic. *In The human revolution*, ed. P. A. Mellars and C. Stringer, 415–32. Princeton, NJ: Princeton University Press.

Dickey, Sara. 2010. Anjali's alliance: Class mobility in urban India. *In Everyday life in south Asia* 2nd ed, eds. Diane P. Mines, and Sarah E. Lamb, 192–205. Bloomington: Indiana University Press.

Dillehay, Thomas D. 2000. *The settlement of the Americas*. New York: Basic Books.

Dirks, Paul H. G. M., Lee R. Berger, Eric M. Roberts, and Jan D. Kramers., et al 2015. Geological and taphonomic context for the new hominin species *Homo naledi* from the Dinaledi Chamber, South Africa. *eLife* 4:e09561.

Dolgin, Janet. 1995. Family law and the facts of family. *In Naturalizing power*, ed. Sylvia Yanagisako and Carol Delaney, 47–67. New York: Routledge.

Dominguez-Rodrigo, M., T. R. Pickering, et al. 2005. Cut-marked bones form Pliocene archaeological sites at Gona, Ethiopia: Implications for the function of the world's earliest stone tools. *Journal of Human Evolution* 48:109–121.

Dominguez-Rodrigo, M., T. R. Pickering, et al. 2010. Configurational approach to identifying the earliest hominin butchers. *Proceedings of the National Academy of Sciences USA* 107:20929–34.

Doretti, Mercedes, and Clyde Snow. 2009. Forensic anthropology and human rights: The Argentine experience. *In Hard evidence: Case studies in forensic anthropology*, 2nd ed., ed. Dawnie Wolfe Steadman, 303–20. Upper Saddle River, NJ: Prentice Hall.

Douglas, Mary. 1970. Introduction. *In Witchcraft confessions and accusations*, ed. Mary Douglas, vi–xxxviii. London: Tavistock.

Douglas, Mary, and Baron Isherwood. 1979. *The world of goods: Towards an anthropology of consumption*. New York: W. W. Norton.

Downey, Greg, and Daniel Lende. 2012. Neuroanthropology and the encultured brain. *In The encultured brain: An introduction to neuroanthropology*, ed. D. Lende and G. Downey, 23–66. Cambridge, MA: MIT Press.

Drewal, Margaret Thompson. 1992. *Yoruba ritual: Performers, play, agency*. Bloomington: Indiana University Press.

Dunsworth, Holly, and Leah Eccelston. 2015. The evolution of difficult childbirth and helpless hominin infants. *Annual Review of Anthropology* 44:55–69.

Duranti, Alessandro. 1994. *From grammar to politics: Linguistic anthropology in a western Samoan village*. Berkeley: University of California Press.

Durham, William H. 1991. *Coevolution: Genes, culture, and human diversity*. Stanford, CA: Stanford University Press.

Duveau, Jérémy, Gilles Berillon, Christine Verna, Gilles Laisné, and Dominique Cliquet. 2019. The composition of a Neandertal social group revealed by the hominin footprints at Le Rozel (Normandy, France). Proceedings of the National Academy of Sciences (PNAS) first published September 9, 2019 https://doi.org/10.1073/pnas.1901789116

Eckert, Penelope, and Sally McConnell-Ginet. 1992. Think practically and look locally: Language and gender as community-based practice. *Annual Review of Anthropology* 21:461–90.

Eldredge, Niles. 1985. *Time frames: The rethinking of Darwinian evolution and the theory of punctuated equilibria*. New York: Simon & Schuster.

Eldredge, Niles, and Ian Tattersall. 1982. *The myths of human evolution*. New York: Columbia University Press.

Elliot, Alison. 1981. *Child language*. Cambridge, UK: Cambridge University Press.

Erazo, Juliet S. 2013. *Governing indigenous territories: Enacting sovereignty in the Ecuadorian Amazon*. Durham, NC: Duke University Press.

Errington, Shelly. 1998. *The death of authentic primitive art and other tales of progress*. Berkeley: University of California Press.

Escobar, Arturo. 1992. Culture, economics, and politics in Latin American social movements theory and research. *In The making of social movements in Latin America*, ed. Arturo Escobar and Sonia Alvarez, 62–85. Boulder, CO: Westview Press.

Escobar, Arturo. 2012. *Encountering development*. Revised edition. Princeton, NJ: Princeton University Press.

Evans-Pritchard, E. 1940. *The Nuer*. Oxford: Oxford University Press.

Evans-Pritchard, E. E. 1951. *Kinship and marriage among the Nuer*. Oxford: Oxford University Press.

Evans-Pritchard, E. E. 1963. *Social anthropology and other essays*. New York: Free Press.

Evans-Pritchard, E. E. (1937) 1976. *Witchcraft, oracles, and magic among the Azande*, abridged ed., prepared by Eva Gillies. Oxford: Oxford University Press.

Fagan, Brian. 1990. *The Journey from Eden*. London: Thames & Hudson.

Fagan, Brian. *In the Beginning: An Introduction to Archaeology*. New York: Harper Collins, 1991.

Fagan, Brian, and Christopher DeCorse. 2005. *In the beginning: An introduction to archaeology*, 11th ed. New York: HarperCollins.

Fagen, Robert. 1981. *Animal play behavior*. New York: Oxford University Press.

Fagen, Robert. 1992. Play, fun, and the communication of well-being. *Play and Culture* 5(1):40–58.

Fagen, Robert. 2005. Play, five gates of evolution, and paths to art. *In Play: An interdisciplinary synthesis*, vol. 6, ed. F. F. McMahnon, Donald E. Lytle, and Brian Sutton-Smith. Play and Culture Studies. Lanham, MD: University Press of America.

Falk, D., et al. 2009. LB1's virtual endocast, microcephaly and hominin brain evolution. *Journal of Human Evolution*, 57:597–607.

Farmer, Paul. 1992. *AIDS and accusation: Haiti and the geography of blame.* Berkeley, University of California Press.

Farmer, Paul. 2002. On suffering and structural violence: A view from below. *In The anthropology of politics*, ed. Joan Vincent, 424–37. Malden, MA: Blackwell.

Farmer, Paul. 2003. *Pathologies of power: Health, human rights, and the new war on the poor.* Berkeley: University of California Press.

Farmer, Paul, and Jim Yong Kim. (2006)2010. AIDS in 2006: Moving toward one world, one hope? *In A reader in medical anthropology: Theoretical trajectories, emergent realities,* eds. Byron Good, Michael M. J. Fischer, Sarah S. Willen, and Mary-Jo DelVecchio Good, 327–330. Malden, MA: Wiley-Blackwell.

Fassin, Didier. 2009. Another politics of life is possible. *Theory, Culture & Society* 26:44–60.

Fassin, Didier. 2012. *Humanitarian reason: a moral history of the present times.* Berkeley: University of California Press.

Fausto-Sterling, Anne. 2012. *Sex/gender: Biology in a social world.* New York: Routledge.

Fedigan, Linda M. 1986. The changing role of women in models of human evolution. *Annual Review of Anthropology* 15:25–66.

Feibel, Craig S., Neville Agnew, Bruce Latimer, Martha Demas, Fiona Marshall, Simon A. C. Waane, and Peter Schmid. 1995. The Laetoli hominid footprints—A preliminary report on the conservation and scientific restudy. *Evolutionary Anthropology* 4(5):149–54.

Ferguson, James. 2002. The anti-politics machine. *In The anthropology of politics*, ed. Joan Vincent, 399–408. Malden, MA: Blackwell.

Fernandez, James W. 1990. Guest editorial. In *Cultural anthropology: A perspective on the human condition*, 2nd ed., Emily Schultz and Robert Lavenda. St. Paul, MN: West.

Fernandez-Jalvo, Y., J. C. Diez, I. Cáceres, and J. Rosell. 1999. Human cannibalism in the Early Pleistocene of Europe (Gran Dolina, Sierra de Atapuerca, Burgos, Spain). *Journal of Human Evolution* 37:407–36.

Field, Les. 2004. Beyond "applied" anthropology. *In A companion to the anthropology of American Indians,* ed. Thomas Biolsi, 472–89. Malden, MA: Blackwell.

Firth, Raymond. (1936) 1984. *We, the Tikopia.* Reprint. Stanford, CA: Stanford University Press.

Fleagle, John. 1995. "Origin and radiation of anthropoid primates." *In Biological anthropology: The state of the science*, ed. Noel T. Boaz and Linda Wolfe, 1–21. Bend, OR: International Institute for Human Evolutionary Research.

Fleagle, John G. 2013. *Primate adaptation and evolution*, 3rd ed. Amsterdam: Elsevier/Academic Press.

Floating on the air, followed by the wind. 1973. Film distributed by Indiana University Instructional Support Services, Gunter Pfaff (cinematographer) and Ronald A. Simons (psychiatric consultant). East Lansing: Michigan State University.

Foley, Douglas. 1989. *Learning capitalist culture: Deep in the heart of Tejas.* Philadelphia: University of Pennsylvania Press.

Foley, Robert. 1995. *Humans before humanity.* Oxford, UK: Blackwell.

Forge, Anthony. 1967. The Abelam artist. *In Social organization: Essays presented to Raymond Firth*, ed. Maurice Freedman, 65–84. London: Cass.

Fortes, Meyer. 1953. The structure of unilineal descent groups. *American Anthropologist* 55:25–39.

Foucault, Michel. [1969] 2002. *The archaeology of knowledge.* Translated by A. M. Sheridan Smith. New York: Routledge.

Foucault, Michel. 1977. *Discipline and punish: The birth of the prison.* New York: Vintage Books.

Foucault, Michel. 1980. *Power/Knowledge: Selected interviews and other writings.* New York: Pantheon.

Foucault, Michel. 1988. *Technologies of the Self: A Seminar with Michel Foucault.* Amherst: University of Massachusetts Press.

Foucault, Michel. 1990. *The history of Sexuality: An introduction.* New York: Vintage.

Foucault, Michel. 1991. Governmentality. *In The Foucault effect: Studies in governmentality*, ed. Graham Burchell, Colin Gordon, and Peter Miller, 87–104. Chicago: University of Chicago Press.

Flannery, Tim F. *Europe : a Natural History.* New York: Atlantic Monthly Press, 2018.

Freeman, Leslie G. 1981. The fat of the land: Notes on paleolithic diet in Iberia. *In Omnivorous primates*, ed. Robert S. O. Harding and Geza Teleki, 104–65. New York: Columbia University Press.

Fried, M. H. 1967. *The evolution of political society.* New York: Random House.

Fu, Q, et al 2016. The Genetic History of Ice-age Europe, *Nature*, vol 534, 200–05.

Fuentes, Agustín. 2012. Ethnoprimatology and the anthropology of the human–primate interface. *Annual Review of Anthropology* 41:101–47.

Fuentes, A., M. Wyczalkowski and K.C. MacKinnon. 2010. Niche construction through cooperation: a nonlinear dynamics contribution to modeling facets of the evolutionary history in the genus *Homo. Current Anthropology*, 51:435–444.

Fuss, Jochen; Spassov, Nikolai; Begun, David R; Böhme, Madelaine. 2017. "Potential hominin affinities of Graecopithecus from the Late Miocene of Europe". PLOS One. 12 (5): e0177127. Bibcode:2017PLoSO..1277127F. doi:10.1371/journal. pone.0177127. PMC 5439669. PMID 28531170.

Gallivan, Martin, and Danielle Moretti-Langholtz. 2007. Civic engagement at Werowocomoco: Reasserting Native narratives from a Powhatan place of power. *In Archaeology as a Tool of Civic Engagement*, ed. Barbara J. Little and Paul A. Shackel, 47–66. Lanham, MD: AltaMira Press.

Gamble, Clive. 1994. *Timewalkers.* Cambridge, MA: Harvard University Press.

Gardner, H. 2000. *Intelligence reframed: Multiple intelligences for the 21st century.* New York: Basic Books.

Gardner, Katy. 2019. Anthropology and development. *In Exotic no more: Anthropology for the contemporary world. 2nd edition*, ed. Jeremy MacClancy, 193–207. Chicago: University of Chicago Press.

Gaur, Mokshika and Soumendra M. Patniak. 2011. "Who is healthy among the Korwa?": Liminality in the experiential health of the displaced Korwa of Central India. *Medical Anthropology Quarterly* 25:85–102.

Geertz, Clifford. 1960. *The religion of Java.* New York: Free Press.

Geertz, Clifford. 1973. *The interpretation of cultures.* New York: Basic Books.

Geismar, Haidy. 2015. Anthropology and heritage regimes. *Annual Review of Anthropology* 44:71–85.

Gelles, David. 2019. Jane Goodall Keeps Going, With a Lot of Hope (and a Bit of Whiskey). https://www.nytimes. com/2019/09/12/business/jane-goodall-corner-office. html?searchResultPosition=1

Gentner, Dedre, and Susan Goldin-Meadow. 2003. *Whither Whorf? In Language in mind: Advances in the study of language and thought*, ed. Dedre Gentner and Susan Goldin-Meadow, 3–14. Cambridge, MA: MIT Press.

Georges, Eugenia. 1990. *The making of a transnational community: Migration, development, and cultural change in the Dominican Republic.* New York: Columbia University Press.

Geraads, D. et al. 2013. *The rodents from the late Middle Pleistocene hominid-bearing site of J'bel Irhoud, Morocco, and their chronological and paleoenvironmental implications. Quat. Res. 80,* 552–561 (2013)

Gero, Joan M. 1991. Genderlithics: Women's roles in stone tool production. *In Engendering archaeology*, ed. Margaret Conkey and Joan Gero, 163–93. Oxford: Blackwell.

Giddens, Anthony. 1979. *Central problems in social theory.* Berkeley: University of California Press.

Giemsch, Liane, and Susanne C. Feine. 2015. Interdisciplinary investigations of the late glacial double burial from Bonn-Oberkassel. *Hugo Obermaier Society for Quaternary Research and Archaeology of the Stone Age: 57th Annual Meeting in Heidenheim, April 7–11, 2015, 36–37.*

Gierliński, Gerard D; Niedźwiedzki, Grzegorz; Lockley, Martin G; et al. 2017. "Possible hominin footprints from the late Miocene (c. 5.7 Ma) of Crete?". *Proceedings of the Geologists' Association*. *128* (5–6): 697–710. *doi:10.1016/j.pgeola.2017.07.006*

Ginsburg, Faye, and Rayna Rapp. 1995. *Conceiving the new world order: The global politics of reproduction*. Berkeley: University of California Press.

Gokhman, David, Nadav Mishol, Marc de Manuel, Marques-Bonet, Yoel Rak, Liran Carmel et al. 2019. Reconstructing Denisovan Anatomy Using DNA Methylation Maps. *Cell* 179(1):180–192.e10 DOI:https://doi.org/10.1016/j. cell.2019.08.035

Goodman, M., D. A. Tagle, D. H. A. Fitch, W. Bailey, J. Czelusniak, B. F. Koop, P. Benson, and J. L. Slighton. 1990. Primate evolution at the DNA level and a classification of the hominoids. *Journal of Molecular Evolution* 30:260–66.

Goody, Jack, and Stanley Tambiah. 1973. *Bridewealth and dowry*. Cambridge, UK: Cambridge University Press.

Gordon, Colin. 1991. Governmental rationality: An introduction. *In The Foucault effect: Studies in governmentality*, ed. Graham Burchell, Colin Gordon, and Peter Miller, 1–52. Chicago: University of Chicago Press.

Gottlieb, Alma. 1988. American premenstrual syndrome: A mute voice. *Anthropology Today* 4(6).

Gould, Stephen J. 1987. *Time's arrow, time's cycle*. Cambridge, MA: Harvard University Press.

Gould, Stephen J. 1996. *Full house: The spread of excellence from Plato to Darwin*. New York: Harmony Books.

Gould, S. J. 2002. *The structure of evolutionary theory*. Cambridge, MA: Harvard University Press.

Gould, Stephen J., and N. Eldredge. 1977. Punctuated equilibria: The tempo and mode of evolution reconsidered. *Paleobiology* 3:115–51.

Gould, Stephen J., and Elisabeth Vrba. 1982. Exaptation—A missing term in the science of form. *Palaeobiology* 8:4–15.

Gramsci, Antonio. 1971. *Selections from the prison notebooks*, Trans. Q. Hoare and G. N. Smith. New York: International Publishers.

Gravlee, Clarence. 2013. Race, biology, and culture: Rethinking the connections. *In Anthropology of race*, ed. John Hartigan, 2–41. Santa Fe, NM: School for American Research.

Green, Richard E., Johannes Krause, Adrian W. Briggs, et al. 2010. A draft sequence of the Neandertal genome. *Science* 328(5979):710–722.

Greenwood, David, and William Stini. 1977. *Nature, culture, and human history*. New York: Harper & Row.

Greska, L. P. 1990. Developmental responses to high-altitude hypoxia in Bolivian children of European ancestry: A test of the developmental adaptation hypothesis. *American Journal of Human Biology* 2:603–12.

Grinker, Roy Richard. 1994. *Houses in the rainforest: Ethnicity and inequality among farmers and foragers in Central Africa*. Berkeley: University of California Press.

Grosz, E. A. 1995. *Volatile bodies: toward a corporeal feminism*. St. Leonards, NSW: Allen & Unwin.

Gumert, Michael D., Agustín Fuentes, et al. 2011. *Monkeys on the edge: Ecology and management of long-tailed macaques and their interface with humans*. Cambridge, UK: Cambridge University Press.

Guneratne, Arjun. 2002. Caste and state. *In South Asian folklore: An encyclopedia*, ed. Peter Claus and Margaret Mills. New York: Garland.

Gupta, Akhil, and James Ferguson. 1997. Discipline and practice: "The Field" as site, method, and location in anthropology. *In Anthropological locations: Boundaries and grounds of a field science*, ed. Akhil Gupta and James Ferguson, 1–46. Berkeley: University of California Press.

Gupta, Dipankar. 2005. Caste and politics: Identity over system. *Annual Review of Anthropology* 34:409–27.

Guthrie, R. D. 2005. *The Nature of Paleolithic Art*. Chicago. University of Chicago Press

Hacking, Ian. 1991. How should we do the history of statistics? *In The Foucault effect: Studies in governmentality*, ed. Graham Burchell, Colin Gordon, and Peter Miller, 181–96. Chicago: University of Chicago Press.

Hage, Ghassan. 2015. "*Alter-Politics. Ĉritical Anthropology and the Radical Imagination*. Carleton, Victoria, Australia: Melbourne University Press. Kindle edition.

Hager, Lori D., ed. 1997. *Women in human evolution*. London: Routledge.

Haile Selassie, Y., G. Suwa, and T. D. White. 2004. Late Miocene teeth *from Middle Awash, Ethiopia, and early hominid dental evolution. Science* 303:1503–5.

Haile Selassie, Y. 2001. Late Miocene hominids from Middle Awash. *Nature* 412:178–81.

Halperin, David M. 2014. Sex/Sexuality/Sexual Classification. *In Critical terms for the study of gender*, eds. Catherine R. Stimpson, and Gilbert Herdt, 449–486. Chicago.: University of Chicago Press.

Halperin, Rhoda H. 1994. *Cultural economies: Past and present*. Austin: University of Texas Press.

Handelman, Don. 1977. Play and ritual: Complementary frames of metacommunication. *In It's a funny thing, humour*, ed. A. J. Chapman and H. C. Foot, 185–92. London: Pergamon.

Hanks, William. 1996. *Language and communicative practices*. Boulder, CO: Westview Press.

Hann, Chris, and Keith Hart. 2011. *Economic anthropology: History, ethnography, critique*. Malden, MA: Polity Press.

Haraway, Donna. 1989. *Primate visions*. New York: Routledge.

Haraway, Donna. "A Cyborg Manifesto: Science, Technology, and Socialist-Feminism in the Late Twentieth Century." *In Simians, Cyborgs, and Women: the Reinvention of Nature*, New York: Routledge. 1991.

Haraway, Donna J. 2008. *When species meet*. Minneapolis: University of Minnesota Press.

Harding, Susan. "Religion: It's Not What it Used to be." *In Exotic No More: Anthropology for the Contemporary World*, Jeremy MacClancy (ed), 43–60. Chicago: University of Chicago Press. 2019.

Harmand, Sonia, Jason Lewis, Craig S. Feibel, and Christopher Lepre. 2015. 3.3 million-year-old stone tools from Lomekwi 3, West Turkana, Kenya. *Nature* 521:310–15.

Harris, David. 1989. An evolutionary continuum of people-plant interaction. *In Foraging and farming: The evolution of plant exploitation*, ed. David Harris and Gordon Hillman, 1–30, vol. 13 of *One World Archaeology*. London: Unwin Hyman.

Harrison, Faye. 1995. The persistent power of "race" in the cultural and political economy of racism. *Annual Review of Anthropology* 24:47–74.

Harrison, Faye. 1998. Introduction: Expanding the discourse on "race." *American Anthropologist* 100(3):609–31.

Hartigan, John Jr. 1997. Establishing the fact of whiteness. *American Anthropologist* 99(3):495–504.

Hartigan, John. 2013. Knowing race. *In Anthropology and Race*, ed. John Hartigan, 3–20. Santa Fe, NM: School for Advanced Research Press.

Harvati, Katerina, et al. 2019. Apidima Cave fossils provide earliest evidence of *Homo sapiens* in Eurasia. *Nature* 571:500–4.

Hawks, J., and L. R. Berger. 2016. The impact of a date for understanding the importance of *Homo naledi. Transactions of the Royal Society of South Africa* 71:125–28.

Hayden, Brian. 1995. Pathways to power: Principles for creating socioeconomic inequities. *In Foundations of social inequity*, ed. T. D. Price and G. Feinman, 15–85. New York: Plenum Press.

Henry, Donald. 1989. *From foraging to agriculture: The Levant and the end of the ice age*. Philadelphia: University of Pennsylvania Press.

Herrnstein, Richard, and Charles Murray. 1994. *The bell curve*. New York: Free Press.

Hershkovitz, I., et al. 2018. The Earliest Modern Humans Outside Africa, *Science* 359:456–459.

Herskovits, Melville. 1973. *Cultural relativism*. New York: Vintage Books.

Herzfeld, Michael. 2003. Competing diversities: Ethnography in the heart of Rome. *Plurimundi* 3(5):147–54.

Herzfeld, Michael. 2009. *Evicted from eternity: The restructuring of modern Rome*. Chicago: University of Chicago Press.

Herzfeld, Michael. 2016. *Siege of the spirits: Community and polity in Bangkok*. Chicago: University of Chicago Press.

Hess, David J. 1997. *Science studies: An advanced introduction*. New York: New York University Press.

Hewlett, Bonnie L. 2013. *Listen, here is a story*. New York: Oxford University Press.

Hingham, T. F. G., R. N. Jacobi, et al. 2006. AMS Radiocarbon dating of ancient bone using ultrafiltration. *Radiocarbon* 48:179–95.

Hingham, T. et al. 2014. The Timing and Spatiotemporal patterning of Neanderthal Disappearance. *Nature* 512:306–09.

Hill, Jane, and Judith Irvine, eds. 1992. *Responsibility and evidence in oral discourse*. Cambridge, UK: Cambridge University Press.

Hillman, Gordon. 1989. Late Paleolithic plant foods from Wadi Kubbaniya in Upper Egypt: Dietary diversity, infant weaning, and seasonality in a riverine environment. *In Foraging and farming: The evolution of plant exploitation*, ed. David Harris and Gordon Hillman, 207–39, vol. 13 of *One World Archaeology*. London: Unwin Hyman.

Hinton, Leanne. 1998. Language loss and revitalization in California: Overview. *In Making sense of language*, ed. Susan Blum, 216–22. New York: Oxford University Press.

Hockett, C. F. 1966. The problems of universals in language. *In Universals of language*, ed. J. H. Greenberg, 1–29. Cambridge, MA: MIT Press.

Hodder, Ian. 1982. *Symbols in action*. Cambridge, UK: Cambridge University Press.

Hodder, Ian. 1990. *The Domestication of Europe*. Oxford. Basil Blackwell.

Hodder, Ian. 2006, *The Leopard's Tale: Revealing the Mysteries of Çatalhöyük*. London: Thames & Hudson.

Hodder, Ian. 2010. Probing religion at Çatalhöyük: An interdisciplinary experiment. *In Religion in the emergence of civilization: Çatalhöyük as a case study*, ed. Ian Hodder, 1–31. Cambridge, UK: Cambridge University Press.

Hodder, Ian. *Entangled: An Archaeology of the Relationships Between Humans and Things*. Chichester: John Wiley & Sons, 2012.

Hoffman, M. 1991. *Egypt before the pharaohs: The prehistoric foundations of Egyptian civilization*, rev. ed. Austin: University of Texas Press.

Hoffman, D. L. *et al.* 2018. U-Th Dating of Carbonate crusts Reveals Neandertal Origin of Iberian Cave Art. *Science*, 359:912–15.

Holbraad, Martin, and Morten Axel Pedersen. *The Ontological Turn: An Anthropological Exposition*. Cambridge: Cambridge University Press, 2017.

Holm, John. 1988. *Pidgins and Creoles*, vol. 1, *Theory and Structure*. Cambridge, UK: Cambridge University Press.

Holmes, Seth. 2013. Fresh fruit, broken bodies: Migrant farmworkers in the United States. Berkeley: University of California Press.

Holy, Ladislav. 1996. *Anthropological perspectives on kinship*. London: Pluto Press.

Honeychurch, William, and Cheryl A. Makarewicz. 2016. The archaeology of pastoral nomadism. *Annual Review of Anthropology* 45:341–59.

Howe, Cymene. 2013. *Intimate activism: The struggle for sexual rights in postrevolutionary Nicaragua*. Durham, NC: Duke University Press.

Hublin, J.-J. *et al.* 2017. *New fossils from Jebel Irhoud, Morocco and the pan-African origin of Homo sapiens*. Nature http://dx.doi.org/10.1038/nature22336 *Nature* volume 546, pages 289–292 (08 June 2017).

Hublin, J., F. Spoor, M. Braun, F. Zonneveld, and S. Condemi. 1996. A late Neandertal associated with Upper Palaeolithic artifacts. *Nature* 381:224–26.

Hultkrantz, Åke. 1992. *Shamanic healing and ritual drama: Health and medicine in native North American religious traditions*. New York: Crossroads.

Hunter, David, and Phillip Whitten. 1976. *Encyclopedia of anthropology*. New York: Harper & Row.

Hutchinson, Sharon. 1996. *Nuer dilemmas*. Berkeley: University of California Press.

Hutchinson, Sharon. 2002. Nuer ethnicity militarized. *In The anthropology of politics*, ed. Joan Vincent, 39–52. Malden, MA: Blackwell.

Hymes, Dell. 1972. On communicative competence. *In Sociolinguistics: Selected readings*, ed. J. B. Pride and J. Holmes, 269–93. Baltimore, MD: Penguin.

Inda, Jonathan Xavier, and Renato Rosaldo. 2002. Introduction: A world in motion. *In The anthropology of globalization*, ed. Jonathan Xavier Inda and Renato Rosaldo. Malden, MA: Blackwell.

Ingold, Tim. 1983. The significance of storage in hunting societies. *Man* 18:553–71.

Ingold, Tim. 1994. General introduction. *In Companion encyclopedia of anthropology*, ed. Tim Ingold, xiii–xxii. London: Routledge.

Ingold, Tim. "Prospect." *In Biosocial Becomings: Integrating Social and Biologial Anthropology*, Tim Ingold, and Gisli Palson (eds), 1–21. Cambridge: Cambridge Univeristy Press. 2013.

Ingold, Tim, and G. Pálsson, eds. 2013. *Biosocial Becomings: Integrating Social and Biological Anthropology*. Cambridge, UK: Cambridge University Press.

Inhorn, Marcia Claire. 2012. *The new Arab man: emergent masculinities, technologies, and Islam in the Middle East*. Princeton, NJ: Princeton University Press.

Isaac, Glynn L., and Diana C. Crader. 1981. To what extent were early hominids carnivorous? An archaeological perspective. *In Omnivorous primates*, ed. Robert S. O. Harding and Geza Teleki, 37–103. New York: Columbia University Press.

Isbell, William H. 1988. City and state in middle horizon Huari. *In Peruvian prehistory*, ed. R. Keatinge, 164–89. Cambridge, UK: Cambridge University Press.

Jablonka, Eva., and Marion J. Lamb. *Evolution in Four Dimensions: Genetic, Epigenetic, Behavioral, and Symbolic Variation in the History of Life*. Cambridge, MA: MIT Press, 2005.

Jablonski, N. 2004. The evolution of human skin and skin color. *Annual Review of Anthropology* 33: 585–623.

Jablonski, N., and G. Chaplin. 2000. The evolution of skin coloration. *Journal of Human Evolution* 39: 57–106.

Jakobson, R. "Linguistics and Poetics." *In Style in Language*, T. Sebeok (ed), 350–77. Cambridge: MIT Press. 1960.

Jarman, M. R., G. N. Bailey, and H. N. Jarman, eds. 1982. *Early European agriculture: Its foundations and development*. Cambridge, UK: Cambridge University Press.

Johansen, R. E. 2006. Care for infibulated women giving birth in Norway: An anthropological analysis of health workers' management of a medically and culturally unfamiliar issue. *Medical Anthropology Quarterly* 20(4):516–44.

Johanson, Donald, and Maitland A. Edey. 1981. *Lucy: The beginnings of humankind*. New York: Simon & Schuster.

Johnson, M. 1999. *Archaeological theory: An introduction*. Oxford, UK: Blackwell.

Jolly, Alison. 1985. *The evolution of primate behavior*, 2nd ed. New York: Macmillan.

Jolly, Alison. 2004. *Lords and lemurs*. Boston: Houghton Mifflin.

Jones, Carla. 2012. Women in the middle: Femininity, virtue, and excess in Indonesian discourses of middle classness. In ed. Rachel Heiman, Carla Freeman, et al., *The global middle classes: Theorizing through ethnography*, 145–68. Santa Fe, NM: School for Advanced Research Press.

Jones, J. S. 1986. The origin of *Homo sapiens*: The genetic evidence. *In Modern trends in primate and human evolution*, ed. B. Wood, L. Martin, and P. Andrews, 317–30. Cambridge, UK: Cambridge University Press.

Jourdan, Christine. 1991. Pidgins and Creoles: The blurring of categories. *Annual Review of Anthropology* 20:187–209.

Joyce, Rosemary A. 2008. *Ancient bodies, ancient lives: Sex, gender, and archaeology*. New York: Thames & Hudson.

Judson, Sheldon, and Marvin E. Kauffman. 1990. *Physical geology*. Englewood Cliffs, NJ: Prentice Hall.

Kahn, Susan Martha. 2000. *Reproducing Jews: A cultural account of assisted conception in Israel*. Durham, NC: Duke University Press.

Kapferer, Bruce. 1983. *A celebration of demons*. Bloomington: Indiana University Press.

Karkazis, Katrina. 2008. *Fixing sex: Intersex, medical authority, and lived experience*. Durham, NC: Duke University Press.

Karp, Ivan. 1990. Guest editorial. *In Cultural anthropology: A perspective on the human condition*, ed. Emily Schultz and Robert Lavenda, 74–75, 2nd ed. St. Paul, MN: West.

Karp, Ivan, and Martha B. Kendall. 1982. Reflexivity in field work. *In Explanation in social science*, ed. P. Secord. Los Angeles: Sage.

Keane, Webb. 2003. Semiotics and the social analysis of material things. *Language and Communication* 23:409–35.

Keatinge, Richard W. 1988. A summary view of Peruvian prehistory. *In Peruvian prehistory*, ed. R. Keatinge, 303–16. Cambridge, UK: Cambridge University Press.

Keesing, Roger. 1982. *Kwaio religion: The living and the dead in a Solomon Island society*. New York: Columbia University Press.

Keesing, Roger. 1992. *Custom and confrontation: The Kwaio struggle for cultural autonomy*. Chicago: University of Chicago Press.

Kelly, John D., and Martha Kaplan. 2001. *Represented communities: Fiji and world decolonization*. Chicago: University of Chicago Press.

Kelly, Raymond. 1993. *Constructing inequality: The fabrication of a hierarchy of virtue among the Etoro*. Ann Arbor: University of Michigan Press.

Killick, Evan, and Amit Desai. 2010. Introduction: Valuing friendship. *In The ways of friendship: Anthropological perspectives*, eds. Amit Desai, and Evan Killick, Oxford: Berghahn Books.

Kimbel, William H., Donald C. Johanson, and Yoel Rak. 1994. The first skull and other new discoveries of *Australopithecus afarensis* at Hadar, Ethiopia. *Journal of Human Evolution* 31:549–61.

Kipp, R. S., and E. M. Schortman. 1989. The political impact of trade in chiefdoms. *American Anthropologist* 91:370–85.

Kirksey, S. Eben, and Stefan Helmreich. 2010. The emergence of multispecies ethnography. *Cultural Anthropology* 25:454–76.

Kitcher, P. 1982. *Abusing science*. Cambridge, MA: MIT Press.

Klein, Richard G. 2009. *The human career: Human biological and cultural origins*, 3rd ed. Chicago: University of Chicago Press.

Köhler, G. 1978. *Global apartheid*. New York: Institute for World Order.

Kondo, Dorinne K. 1990. *Crafting selves: Power, gender, and discourses of identity in a Japanese workplace*. Chicago: University of Chicago Press.

Krause, J., C. Lalueza-Fox, L. Orlando, W. Enard, R. E. Green, H. A. Burbano, J.-J. Hublin, et al. 2007. The derived FOXP2 variant of modern humans was shared with Neandertals. *Current Biology* 17:1–5.

Krings, M., H. Geisert, R. W. Schmitz, H. Krainitzki, and S. Pääbo. 1999. DNA sequence of the mitochondrial hypervariable region II from the Neandertal type specimen. *Proceedings of the National Academy of Sciences* 95:5581–5.

Krings, M., A. Stone, R. W. Schmitz, H. Krainitzki, M. Stoneking, and S. Pääbo. 1997. Neandertal DNA sequences and the origin of modern humans. *Cell* 90:19–30.

Kuhn, Thomas. 1979. Metaphor in science. *In Metaphor and thought*, ed. Andrew Ortony, 409–19. Cambridge, UK: Cambridge University Press.

Kulish, Nicholas. 2009. As economic turmoil mounts, so do attacks on Hungary's Gypsies. *New York Times*, April 26.

Kumar, Nita. 1992. *Friends, brothers, and informants: Fieldwork memories of Banares*. Berkeley: University of California Press.

Kuper, Adam. 1982. *Wives for cattle: Bridewealth and marriage in southern Africa*. London: Routledge and Kegan Paul.

Kuper, Adam. 1999. *Culture: The anthropologist's account*. Cambridge, MA: Harvard University Press.

Kurotani, Sawa. 2005. *Home away from home: Japanese corporate wives in the United States*. Durham, NC: Duke University Press.

Labov, William. 1972. *Language in the inner city: Studies in the black English vernacular*. Philadelphia: University of Pennsylvania Press.

Lahr, Marta, and Robert Foley. 1994. Multiple dispersals and modern human origins. *Evolutionary Anthropology* 3(2):48–60.

Lahr, M. M., and R. Foley. 2004. Human evolution writ small. *Nature* 431:1043–44.

Lakoff, George, and Mark Johnson. 1980. *Metaphors we live by*. Berkeley: University of California Press.

Laland, Kevin. 2017. *Darwin's Unfinished Symphony: How Culture Made the Human Mind*. Princeton and Oxford: Princeton University Press.

Laland, Kevin, and M. J. O'Brien. 2010. Niche construction theory and archaeology. *Journal of Archaeological Method and Theory* 17: 303–322.

Lalueza-Fox, C., M. Lourdes Sampietro, D. Caramelli, et al. 2005. Neandertal evolutionary genetics: Mitochondrial DNA data from the Iberian Peninsula. *Molecular Biology and Evolution* 22:1077–1081.

Lalueza-Fox, C., M. Lourdes Sampietro, D. Caramelli, et al. 2007. A Melanocortin 1 Receptor allele suggests varying pigmentation among Neanderthals. *Science* 318:1453–5.

Lalueza-Fox, Carlos, Antonio Rosas, Almudena Estalrrich, et al. 2010. *Genetic evidence for patrilocal mating behavior among Neandertal groups Proceedings of the National Academy of Sciences USA* 108(1):250–253.

Lancaster, Roger. 1992. *Life is hard: Machismo, danger, and the intimacy of power in Nicaragua*. Berkeley: University of California Press.

Lancaster, Roger. 1997. Guto's Performance: Notes on the transvestism of everyday life. *In The Gender/Sexuality Reader: Culture, History, Political Economy*, eds. Roger Lancaster, and Michaela Di Leonardo, 559–573. New York: Routledge.

Lancaster, Roger. 2004. Two cheers for gay marriage. *Anthropology News* 45(6):21–24.

Landau, M. 1984. Human evolution as narrative. *American Scientist* 72:262–68.

Lansing, John Stephen. 1995. *The Balinese*. Fort Worth, TX: Harcourt Brace College Publishers.

Larkin, Brian. 2002. Indian films and Nigerian lovers: Media and the creation of parallel modernities. *In The anthropology of globalization*, ed. Jonathan Xavier Inda and Renato Rosaldo, 350–78. Malden, MA: Blackwell.

Lassiter, Luke Eric. 2004. Music. *In A companion to the anthropology of American Indians*, ed. Thomas Biolsi, 196–211. Malden, MA: Blackwell.

Lassiter, Luke E., Clyde Ellis, and Ralph Kotay. 2002. *The Jesus road: Kiowas, Christianity, and Indian hymns*. Lincoln: University of Nebraska Press.

Latour, Bruno. 1987. *Science in action: How to follow scientists and engineers through society*. Cambridge, MA: Harvard University Press.

Latour, Bruno, and Steve Woolgar. 1986. *Laboratory life: The construction of scientific facts*, Princeton, NJ: Princeton University Press.

Leacock, E. 1983. Interpreting the origins of gender inequality: Conceptual and historical problems. *Dialectical Anthropology* 7(4):263–84.

Leakey, M. G., C. S. Feibel, I. McDougall, and A. C. Walker. 1995. New four-million-year-old hominid species from Kanapoi and Allia Bay, Kenya. *Nature* 376:565–71.

Leakey, M. G., F. Spoor, F. Brown, et al. 2001. New hominin genus from eastern Africa shows diverse Middle Pliocene lineages. *Nature* 410:433–40.

Lederman, Rena. 2005. Unchosen grounds: Cultivating cross-subfield accents for a public voice. *In Unwrapping the sacred bundle*, ed. Daniel Segal and Sylvia Yanigisako, 49–77. Durham, NC: Duke University Press.

Lee, R. B. 1974. Male–female residence arrangements and political power in human hunter–gatherers. *Archaeology of Sexual Behavior* 3:167–73.

Lee, Richard B. 2013. *The Dobe Ju/'hoansi*, 4th ed. [Belmont, CA]: Wadsworth Cengage Learning

Lee, Richard B., and Irven DeVore, eds. 1968. *Man the hunter*. Chicago: Aldine.

LeGros Clark, W. E. 1963. *The antecedents*, 2nd ed. New York: Harper & Row.

Leighton, Donna Robbins. 1987. Gibbons: Territoriality and monogamy. *In Primate societies*, ed. Barbara Smuts, Dorothy Cheney, Robert Seyfarth, Richard Wrangham, and Thomas Struhsaker, 135–45. Chicago: University of Chicago Press.

Leinaweaver, Jessaca B. *The Circulation of Children: Kinship, Adoption, and Morality in Andean Peru*. Durham: Duke University Press, 2008.

Leonard, W. R., R. L. Leatherman, J. W. Carey, and R. B. Thomas. 1990. Contributions of nutrition versus hypoxia to growth in rural Andean populations. *American Journal of Human Biology* 2:612–26.

Lerner, I. M., and W. J. Libby. 1976. *Heredity, evolution, and society*, 2nd ed. San Francisco: W. H. Freeman.

Leslie, Charles M. 1976. *Asian medical systems: A comparative study*, Berkeley: University of California Press.

Leslie, Paul W., and Michael Little. 2003. Human biology and ecology: Variation in nature and the nature of variation. *American Anthropologist* 105(1):28–37.

Levine, Nancy. 1980. Nyinba polyandry and the allocation of paternity. *Journal of Comparative Family Studies* 11(3):283–88.

Levine, Nancy. 1988. *The dynamics of polyandry: Kinship, domesticity, and population on the Tibetan border*. Chicago: University of Chicago Press.

Levine, Nancy, and Walter Sangree. 1980. Women with many husbands. *Journal of Comparative Family Studies* 11(3).

Levins, Richard, and Richard Lewontin. 1985. *The dialectical biologist*. Cambridge, MA: Harvard University Press.

Lévi-Strauss, Claude. 1967. *Structural anthropology*, trans. Claire Jacobson and Brooke Grundfest Schoepf. New York: Doubleday Anchor.

Lewellen, Ted C. 2003. *Political Anthropology: An Introduction 3rd ed.* Westport, Conn.: Praeger Paperback.

Lewin, Roger. 1989. *Human evolution*, 2nd ed. Boston: Blackwell Scientific Publications.

Lewin, Ellen, ed. 2006. *Feminist anthropology: A reader.* Hoboken, NJ: Wiley-Blackwell.

Lewis, I. M. 1967. *A pastoral democracy: A study of pastoralism and politics among the northern Somali of the Horn of Africa.* Oxford: Oxford University Press.

Lewis, Philip. 1997. Arenas of ethnic negotiations: Cooperation and conflict in Bradford. *In The politics of multiculturalism in the new Europe: Racism, identity, and community,* ed. Tariq Modood and Pnina Werbner, 126–46. London: Zed Books.

Lewis-Williams, J. D. 1984. Ideological continuities in prehistoric southern Africa: The evidence of the rock art. *In Past and present in hunter–gatherer studies,* ed. C. Schrire, 225–52. New York: Academic Press.

Lewontin, Richard. 1972. The apportionment of human diversity. *Evolutionary Biology* 6:381–98.

Lewontin, Richard. 1982. *Human diversity.* New York: Scientific American Books.

Lewontin, Richard. 1983. Introduction. *In Scientists confront creationism,* ed. Laurie R. Godfrey, xxiii–xxvi. New York: Norton.

Lewontin, R. 1991. *Biology as ideology: The doctrine of DNA.* New York: Harper Perennial.

Li, Tania. 2007. *The will to improve : governmentality, development, and the practice of politics.* Durham: Duke University Press.

Li, Tania. 2014. *Land's end.* Durham, NC: Duke University Press.

Lieberman, Daniel E., and Dennis M. Bramble. 2007. The evolution of marathon running. *Sports Medicine* 37(4–5):288–90.

Lienhardt, Godfrey. 1961. *Divinity and experience.* Oxford: Oxford University Press.

Linke, Uli. 1997. Gendered difference, violent imagination: Blood, race, nation. *American Anthropologist* 99(3):559–73.

Little, Barbara J., and Paul A. Shackel, eds. 2007. *Archaeology as a tool of civic engagement.* Walnut Creek, CA: AltaMira, 47–66.

Little, Kenneth. 1967. *The Mende of Sierra Leone.* London: Routledge and Kegan Paul.

Little, Michael. 1995. Adaptation, adaptability, and multidisciplinary research. *In Biological anthropology: The state of the science,* ed. Noel T. Boaz and Linda Wolfe. Bend, OR: International Institute for Human Evolutionary Research.

Livingstone, F. B. 1958. Anthropological implications of sickle cell gene distribution in West Africa. *American Anthropologist* 60:533–62.

Livingstone, F. B. 1964. On the nonexistence of human races. *In The concept of race,* ed. M. F. Ashley-Montagu, 46–60. New York: Collier.

Lock, Margaret M. and Vinh-Kim Nguyen. 2010. *An anthropology of biomedicine.* Malden, MA: Wiley-Blackwell.

Longino, Helen E. 1990. *Science as social knowledge.* Princeton, NJ: Princeton University Press.

Lordkipanidze, David, Marcia S. Ponce de Leon, et al. 2013. A complete skull from Dmanisi, Georgia, and the evolutionary biology of early *Homo. Science* 342:326–31.

Lovejoy, A.O. (1936) 1960. *The Great Chain of Being.* New York: Harper Torchbooks.

Luhrmann, T. M. 2012. *When God talks back: Understanding the American evangelical relationship with God.* New York: Vintage Books.

Luis, Keridwen N. 2018. *Herlands: Exploring the Women's Land Movement in the United States.* Minneapolis: University of Minnesota Press.

Lutz, Ellen. 2006. Fighting for the right rights. *Cultural Survival Quarterly* 30(4):3–4.

Mahler, Sarah. *Culture as Comfort.* Boston, MA: Pearson, 2012.

Malefyt, Timothy de Waal, and Robert J. Morais. 2012. *Advertising and anthropology: Ethnographic practice and cultural perspectives.* London: Berg Publishers.

Malinowski, Bronislaw. 1944. *A scientific theory of culture and other essays.* Oxford: Oxford University Press.

Malinowski, Bronislaw. (1926) 1948. *Magic, science, and religion, and other essays.* New York: Doubleday Anchor.

Malkki, Liisa. 1992. National geographic: The rooting of peoples and the territorialization of national identity among scholars and refugees. *Cultural Anthropology* 7(1):24–44.

Mann, Alan E. 1981. Diet and human evolution. *In Omnivorous primates,* ed. Robert S. O. Harding and Geza Teleki, 10–36. New York: Columbia University Press.

Marcus, George. 1995. Ethnography in/of the world system: The emergence of multi-sited Ethnography. *Annual Review of Anthropology* 24:95–117.

Marks, Jonathan. 1995. *Human biodiversity.* New York: Aldine.

Marks, Jonathan. 2009. *Why I am not a scientist: Anthropology and modern knowledge.* Berkeley: University of California Press.

Marks, Jonathan. 2011. *The alternative introduction to biological anthropology.* New York: Oxford University Press.

Marks, Jonathan. 2013. The nature/culture of genetic facts. *Annual Review of Anthropology* 42:247–67.

Marsland, Rebecca. 2012. (Bio)Sociality and HIV in Tanzania. *Medical Anthropology Quarterly* 26:470–85.

Martin, R. D. 1986. Primates: A definition. *In Major topics in primate and human evolution,* ed. B. Wood, L. Martin, and P. Andrews, 1–31. Cambridge, UK: Cambridge University Press.

Martin, R. D. 1993. Primate origins: Plugging the gaps. *Nature* 363(May 20):223–34.

Marx, Karl. 1963. *The 18th brumaire of Louis Bonaparte.* New York: International Publishers.

Mauss, Marcel. (1950) 2000. *The gift: The form and reason for exchange in archaic societies.* New York: W. W. Norton.

Mayr, Ernst. 1982. *The growth of biological thought.* Cambridge, MA: Harvard University Press.

McAnany, Patricia A., and Norman Yoffee, eds. 2009. *Questioning collapse: Human resilience, ecological vulnerability, and the aftermath of empire.* New York: Cambridge University Press.

McCoid, Catherine Hidge, and LeRoy D. McDermott. 1996. Toward decolonizing gender: Female vision in the Upper Paleolithic. *American Anthropologist* 98(2):319–26.

McCorriston, Joy, and Frank Hole. 1991. The ecology of seasonal stress and the origins of agriculture in the Near East. *American Anthropologist* 93:46–69.

McHenry, Henry. 1985. Implications of postcanine megadontia for the origin of *Homo. In Ancestors: The hard evidence,* ed. E. Delson, 178–83. New York: Alan R. Liss.

McHenry, Henry, and L. R. Berger. 1998. Body proportions in *Australopithecus afarensis* and *A. africanus* and the origin of the genus *Homo. Journal of Human Evolution* 35:1–22.

McKinnon, S., and S. Silverman, eds. 2005. *Complexities: Beyond Nature and Nurture.* Chicago: University of Chicago Press.

McPherron, S. P., Z. Alelseged, et al. 2010. Evidence for stone-tool-assisted consumption of animal tissues before 3.39 million years ago at Dikika, Ethiopia. *Nature* 466:857–60.

Meadow, Richard H. 1989. Osteological evidence for the process of animal domestication. *In The walking larder: Patterns of domestication, pastoralism, and predation*, ed. Juliet Clutton-Brock, 80–90. London: Unwin Hyman.

Mellars, Paul. 1996. *The Neandertal legacy*. Princeton, NJ: Princeton University Press.

Mellars, Paul, and Christopher Stringer. 1989. Introduction. *In The human revolution*, ed. P. A. Mellars and C. Stringer, 1–14. Princeton, NJ: Princeton University Press.

Melotti, Umberto. 1997. International migration in Europe: Social projects and political cultures. *In The politics of multiculturalism in the new Europe: Racism, identity and community*, ed. Tariq Modood and Pnina Werbner, 73–92. London: Zed Books.

Meltzer, David J. 2015. Pleistocene overkill and North American mammalian extinctions. *Annual Review of Anthropology* 44:33–53.

Mendez, Fernando L., G. David Poznik, Sergi Castellano, and Carlos D. Bustamante. 2016. The divergence of Neandertal and modern human Y chromosomes. *The American Journal of Human Genetics* 98(4):728–34.

Merry, Sally Engle. 1999. *Colonizing Hawai'i*. Princeton, NJ: Princeton University Press.

Merry, Sally Engle. 2001. Changing rights, changing culture. *In Culture and rights: Anthropological perspectives*, ed. Jane Cowan, Marie-Bénédicte Dembour, and Richard A. Wilson, 31–55. Cambridge, UK: Cambridge University Press.

Merry, Sally. 2003. Human-Rights Law and the Demonization of Culture. *Anthropology Newsletter* 44(2), February.

Merry, Sally Engle. 2009. legal transplants and cultural translation: Making human rights in the vernacular. *In Human rights: an anthropological reader*, ed. Mark Goodale, 265–302.

Meskell, Lynn, ed. 2009. *Cosmopolitan archaeologies*. Durham, NC: Duke University Press.

Meyer, M., Q. Fu, et al. 2014. A mitochondrial genome sequence of a hominin from Sima de los Huesos. *Nature* 505:403–406.

Mielke, James H., Lyle W. Konigsberg, and John H. Relethford. 2011. *Human biological variation*. New York: Oxford University Press.

Mignolo, Walter D. 2002. The many faces of cosmopolis: Border thinking and critical cosmopolitanism. *In Cosmopolitanism*, ed. Carol Breckenridge, Sheldon Pollock, Homi Bhaba, and Dipeesh Chakrabarty, 157–87. Durham, NC: Duke University Press.

Miller, Claire Cain. 2015. The Search for the Best Estimate of the Transgender Population. *New York Times*, 2015, 3.

Miller, Daniel. 1995. Consumption and commodities. *Annual Review of Anthropology* 24:141–61.

Miller, Daniel. 1998. Coca-Cola: A black sweet drink from Trinidad. *In Material cultures: Why some things matter*, ed. Daniel Miller, 169–88. Chicago: University of Chicago Press.

Miller, Daniel. 2005. *Materiality*. Durham, NC: Duke University Press.

Miller, Daniel. 2010. *Stuff*. Cambridge, UK: Polity Press.

Miller, Daniel, and Don Slater. 2000. *The Internet: An ethnographic approach*. Oxford: Berg.

Milton, Katherine. 1993. Diet and primate evolution. *Scientific American* 269(2):86–93.

Miracle, Andrew. 1991. Aymara joking behavior. *Play and Culture* 4(2):144–52.

Mitchell-Kernan, Claudia. 1972. On the status of black English for native speakers: An assessment of attitudes and values. *In Functions of language in the classroom*, ed. C. Cazden, V. John, and D. Hymes, 195–210. New York: Teachers College Press.

Mitra, Subrata. 1994. Caste, democracy and the politics of community formation in India. *In Contextualizing caste: Post–Dumontian approaches*, ed. Mary Searle-Chatterjee and Ursula Sharma, 49–71. Oxford: Blackwell Publishers/Sociological Review.

Modood, Tariq. 1997. Introduction: The politics of multiculturalism in the new Europe. *In The politics of multiculturalism in the new Europe: Racism, identity, and community*, ed. Tariq Modood and Pnina Werbner, 1–25. London: Zed Books.

Molnar, S. 1992. *Human variation: Races, types, and ethnic groups*, 3rd ed. Englewood Cliffs, NJ: Prentice Hall.

Molnar, Stephen. 2001. *Human variation*. New York: Prentice Hall.

Moore, Sally Falk. 2005. Comparisons: Possible and impossible. *Annual Review of Anthropology* 34:1–11.

Morbeck, Mary Ellen. 1997. Life history, the individual and evolution. *In The evolutionary female: A life-history perspective*, ed. Mary Ellene Morbeck, Alison Galloway, and Adrienne Zihlman, 3–14. Princeton, NJ: Princeton University Press.

Morey, D., ed. 2010. *Dogs: Domestication and the development of a social bond*. Cambridge, UK: Cambridge University Press.

Morgan, Lewis Henry. (1877) 1963. *Ancient society*. Cleveland, OH: Meridian Books.

Morgan, Marcyliena. 1995. Theories and politics in African American English. *Annual Review of Anthropology* 23:325–45.

Morgan, Marcyliena. 1997. Commentary on Ebonics. *Anthropology Newsletter* 38(3):8.

Morgan, Marcyliena. 2002. *Language, discourse, and power in African American culture*. Cambridge, UK: Cambridge University Press.

Morris, Craig. 1988. Progress and prospect in the archaeology of the Inca. *In Peruvian prehistory*, ed. R. Keatinge, 233–56. Cambridge, UK: Cambridge University Press.

Morwood, M., et al. 2004. Archaeology and age of a new hominin from Flores in eastern Indonesia. *Nature* 431:1087–91.

Mounier, Aurélien and Marta Mirazón Lahr. 2019. Deciphering African late middle Pleistocene hominin diversity and the origin of our species. *Nature Communications* volume 10, Article number: 3406 (2019) https://www.nature.com/articles/s41467-019-11213-w

Najmabadi, Afsaneh. 2014. *Professing selves: transsexuality and same-sex desire in contemporary Iran*. Durham, NC: Duke University Press.

Nielsen, Rasmus, Joshua M. Akey, Mattias Jakobsson, Jonathan K. Pritchard, Sarah Tishkoff, and Eske Willerslev. 2017. Tracing the peopling of the world through genomics. Nature. 2017 Jan 18; 541(7637): 302–310. doi: 10.1038/nature21347

Niezen, Ronald. 2003. *The origins of indigenism: Human rights and the politics of identity*. Berkeley: University of California Press.

Nishida, Toshisada, and Mariko Hiraiwa-Hasegawa. 1987. Chimpanzees and bonobos: Cooperative relationships among males. *In Primate societies*, ed. Barbara Smuts, Dorothy Cheney, Robert Seyfarth, Richard Wrangham, and Thomas Struhsaker, 165–77. Chicago: University of Chicago Press.

Nissen, H. 1988. *The early history of the ancient Near East, 9000–2000 B.C.* Chicago: University of Chicago Press.

Nixon, Ron. 2007. DNA tests find branches but few roots. *New York Times*, November 25.

Ochs, Elinor. 1986. Introduction. In *Language socialization across cultures*, ed. Bambi Schieffelin and Elinor Ochs, 1–13. Cambridge, UK: Cambridge University Press.

Odling-Smee, F. J. 1994. Niche construction, evolution and culture. *In Companion encyclopedia of anthropology: Humanity, culture, and social life*, ed. Tim Ingold. London: Routledge.

Odling-Smee, F. John, Kevin L. Laland, and Marcus W. Feldman. 2003. *Niche construction: The neglected process in evolution*. Princeton, NJ: Princeton University Press.

Olsen, Bjørnar, Michael Shanks, et al. 2012. *Archaeology: The discipline of things*. Berkeley: University of California Press.

Omohundro, John. 2000. *Careers in anthropology*. New York: McGraw-Hill.

Ong, Aihwa. 2002. The Pacific shuttle: Family, citizenship, and capital circuits. *In The anthropology of globalization*, ed. Jonathan Xavier Inda and Renato Rosaldo, 172–97. Malden, MA: Blackwell.

Ortner, Sherry. 1973. On key symbols. *American Anthropologist* 75(5):1338–46.

Ortner, S. 1974. Is female to male as nature is to culture? *In Woman, culture, and society*, ed. M. Z. Rosaldo and L. Lamphere. Stanford, CA: Stanford University Press.

Ortner, Sherry. 2014. So, is female to male as nature is to culture? *In Anthropology in theory: issues in epistemology*, eds. Henriettta Moore, and Todd Sanders, 357–362.

Ortony, Andrew. 1979. Metaphor: A multidimensional problem. *In Metaphor and thought*, ed. Andrew Ortony, 1–18. Cambridge, UK: Cambridge University Press.

Oyama, S., P. Griffiths, and R. Gray, eds. 2001. *Cycles of contingency: Developmental systems and evolution.* Cambridge, MA: MIT Press.

Oxnard, C., P. J. Obendorf, and B. J. Kefford. 2010. Post-cranial skeletons of hypothyroid cretins show a similar anatomical mosaic as *Homo floresiensis. PLoS ONE* 5(9):e13018. doi:10.1371/journal.pone.0013018

Pagels, Hans. 1985. *Perfect symmetry.* New York: Simon & Schuster, Inc.

Pálsson, Gisli. "Ensembles of Biosocial Relations." *In Biocultural Becomings: Integrating Social and Biological Anthropology,* Tim Ingold, and Gisli Pálsson (eds), 22–41. Cambridge, UK: Cambridge,Univrsity Press. 2013a.

Pálsson, Gisli. 2013b. Retrospect. *In Biosocial Becomings: Integrating Social and Biological Anthropology,* eds Tim Ingold and G. Pálsson. Cambridge: Cambridge University Press. Pp. 229–248.

Parkin, David. 1990. *Guest editorial in Cultural anthropology: A perspective on the human condition,* ed. Emily Schultz and Robert Lavenda, 290–91, 2nd ed. St. Paul, MN: West.

Parsons, Jeffrey R., and Charles M. Hastings. 1988. The late intermediate period. *In Peruvian prehistory,* ed. R. Keatinge, 190–229. Cambridge, UK: Cambridge University Press.

Peletz, Michael. 1995. Kinship studies in late twentieth-century anthropology. *Annual review of anthropology* 24, 343–372.

Pennington, Renee. 1992. Did food increase fertility: Evaluation of !Kung and Herero history. *Human Biology* 64:497–501.

Petryna, Adriana. 2002. *Life exposed: Biological citizens after Chernobyl.* Princeton, NJ: Princeton University Press.

Pigliucci, Massimo, and Gerd Müller. 2010. *Evolution, the extended synthesis.* Cambridge, MA: MIT Press.

Pineda, Rosa Fung. 1988. The late preceramic and initial period. *In Peruvian Prehistory,* ed. R. Keatinge, 67–96. Cambridge, UK: Cambridge University Press.

Plotkin, Henry. 2003. *The imagined world made real.* New Brunswick, NJ: Rutgers University Press.

Polanyi, Karl. 1977. *The livelihood of man.* New York: Academic Press.

Polanyi, Karl. "The Economy as Instituted Process." *In Trade and Market in the Early Empires,* Karl Polanyi, C Arensberg, and H. Pearson (eds), the Free Press: Glencoe. 1957.

Pollock, Anne. 2012. *Medicating race: Heart disease and durable preoccupations with difference,* Durham, NC: Duke University Press.

Potts, Richard. 1993. Archaeological interpretations of early hominid behavior and ecology. *In The origin and evolution of humans and humanness,* ed. D. Tab Rasmussen, 49–74. Boston: Jones & Bartlett.

Potts, Rick. 1996. *Humanity's descent.* New York: William Morrow.

Potts, Richard. 2012. Evolution and environmental change in early human prehistory. *Annual Review of Anthropology* 41:151–67.

Preston, Douglas. 2013. The El Dorado machine. *The New Yorker,* 34 ff.

Preucel, Robert W. 2010. *Archaeological semiotics.* Malden, MA: Wiley-Blackwell.

Price, T. Douglas. 1995. Social inequality at the origins of agriculture. *In Foundations of social inequality,* ed. T. Douglas Price and Gary M. Feinman. New York: Plenum Press.

Price, T. Douglas and Gary M. Feinman. 2001. *Images of the past,* 3rd ed. Mountain View, CA: Mayfield.

Price, T. Douglas, and Anne Birgitte Gebauer, eds. 1995. *Last hunters, first farmers.* Santa Fe, NM: SAR Press.

Rabinow, Paul. 1977. *Reflections on fieldwork in Morocco.* Berkeley: University of California Press.

Radhakrishnan, Sindhu, Michael A. Huffman, et al. 2013. *The macaque connection: Cooperation and conflict between humans and macaques.* New York: Springer.

Rasmussen, Morten, Sarah L. Anzick, et al. 2014. The genome of a Late Pleistocene human from a Clovis burial site in western Montana. *Nature* 506:225–29.

Rasmussen, Morten, Martin Sikora, Anders Albrechtsen, et al. 2015. The ancestry and affiliations of Kennewick Man. *Nature* 523:455–58.

Raymond, J. Scott. 1988. A view from the tropical forest. *In Peruvian prehistory,* ed. R. Keatinge, 279–300. Cambridge, UK: Cambridge University Press.

Reeves, Edward, Billie DeWalt, and Kathleen DeWalt. 1987. The International Sorghum/Millet Research Project. *In Anthropological praxis,* ed. Robert Wolfe and Shirley Fiske, 72–83. Boulder, CO: Westview Press.

Reichel-Dolmatoff, Gerardo. 1971. *Amazonian cosmos: The sexual and religious symbolism of the Tukano indians.* Chicago: University of Chicago Press.

Relethford, John. 2001. *Genetics and the search for modern human origins.* New York: Wiley.

Relethford, John. *Fundamentals of Biological Anthropology.* Mountain View, California: Mayfield, 1996.

Renfrew, Colin, and Paul Bahn. 2004. *Archaeology: Theories, methods and practice,* 4th ed. London: Thames & Hudson.

Renfrew, Colin, and Paul Bahn. 2008. *Archaeology: Theories, methods and practice,* 5th ed. London: Thames & Hudson.

Rezende, Claudia Barcellos. 1999. Building affinity through friendship. *In The anthropology of friendship,* ed. Sandra Bell and Simon Coleman, 79–97. Oxford: Berg.

Rice, Dan Stephen, and Prudence M. Rice. 1993. Lessons from the Maya. *In Talking about people,* ed. William Haviland and Robert J. Gordon, 81–91. Mountain View, CA: Mayfield. First published in *Latin American Research Review* 19(3):7–34, 1984.

Richerson, Peter, and Robert Boyd. 2005. *Not by genes alone: How culture transformed human evolution.* Chicago: University of Chicago Press.

Richerson, Peter, Robert Boyd, and Joseph Henrich. 2003. Cultural evolution of human cooperation. *In Genetic and cultural evolution of cooperation,* ed. Peter Hammerstein, 357–88. Cambridge, MA: MIT Press.

Rick, John W. 1988. The character and context of highland preceramic society. *In Peruvian prehistory,* ed. R. Keatinge, 3–40. Cambridge, UK: Cambridge University Press.

Richter, D. et al. 2017. The Age of the Hominin Fossils from Jebel Irhoud, Morocco, and the Origins of the Middle Stone Age. *Nature* 546: 293–96.

Rightmire, G. Philip. 1990. *The Evolution of Homo erectus.* Cambridge, UK: Cambridge University Press.

Rightmire, G. Philip. 1995. Diversity within the genus *Homo. In Paleoclimate and evolution, with emphasis on human origins,* ed. Elisabeth Vrba, George Denton, Timothy Partridge, and Lloyd Burckle, 483–92. New Haven, CT: Yale University Press.

Rindos, David. 1984. *The origins of agriculture: An evolutionary perspective.* New York: Academic Press.

Roberts, D.F. 1968. Genetic effects of population size reduction. *Nature* 220:1084–88.

Rogers, A. R., D. Iltis, and S. Wooding. 2004. Genetic variation at the MCIR locus and the time since loss of human body hair. *Current Anthropology* 45:105–7.

Romero, Simon. 2009. Protestors gird for long fight over opening Peru's Amazon. *New York Times,* June 12.

Rosas, A., C. Martinez-Maza, M. Bastir, et al. 2006. Paleobiology and comparative morphology of a late Neandertal simple from El Sidron, Asturias, Spain. *Proceedings of the National Academy of Sciences* 103:15266–71.

Rose, Kenneth. 1994. The earliest primates. *Evolutionary anthropology,* 3(5):159–73.

Rostow, W. W. 1971. *The stages of economic growth; a non-communist manifesto.* Cambridge [Eng.]: University Press.

Rothwell, Norman V. 1977. *Human Genetics.* Englewood Cliffs, NJ: Prentice-Hall.

Rouhani, Shahin. 1989. Molecular genetics and the pattern of human evolution: Plausible and implausible models. *In The human revolution,* ed. Robert S. O. Mellars and C. Stringer, 47–61. Princeton, NJ: Princeton University Press.

Rubin, Gayle. 1975. The traffic in women: On the "political economy" of sex. *In Toward an anthropology of women,* ed. Rayna Reiter, New York: Monthly Review Press.

Rubin, Jeffrey W. 1997. *Decentering the regime: Ethnicity, radicalism, and democracy in Juchitán, Mexico.* Durham, NC: Duke University Press.

Ruvolo, Maryellen, and David Pilbeam. 1986. Hominoid evolution: Molecular and palaeontological patterns.

In Major topics in primate and human evolution, ed. B. Wood, L. Martin, and P. Andrews, 157–60. Cambridge, UK: Cambridge University Press.

SAGA (Support for African/Asian Great Apes). 2005. http://www. saga-jp.org (accessed August 24, 2006).

Sahlins, Marshall. 1972. *Stone Age economics*. Chicago: Aldine.

Sahlins, Marshall. 1976. *Culture and practical reason*. Chicago: University of Chicago Press.

Sanjek, Roger. 1994. The enduring inequalities of race. *In Race*, ed. Stephen Gregory and Roger Sanjek, 1–17. New Brunswick, NJ: Rutgers University Press.

Sapir, Edward. 1921. *Language*. New York: Harvest/HBJ.

Sapir, Edward. (1933) 1966. *Culture, language, and personality*, ed. David Mandelbaum. Berkeley: University of California Press.

Saussure, Ferdinand de. 2013. *Course in general linguistics*. HardPress Publishing.

Scheper-Hughes, Nancy. 1992. *Death without weeping: The violence of everyday life in Brazil*. Berkeley: University of California Press.

Scheper-Hughes, Nancy. 1994. Embodied knowledge: Thinking with the body in critical medical anthropology. *In Assessing cultural anthropology*, ed. Robert Borofsky, 229–42. New York: McGraw-Hill.

Schiffauer, Werner. 1997. Islam as a civil religion: Political culture and the organisation of diversity in Germany. *In The politics of multiculturalism in the new Europe: Racism, identity, and community*, ed. Tariq Modood and Pnina Werbner, 147–66. London: Zed Books.

Schiller, Nina Glick, and Georges Fouron. 2001. *Georges woke up laughing: Long-distance nationalism and the search for home*. Durham, NC: Duke University Press.

Schiller, Nina Glick, and Georges Fouron. 2002. Long-distance nationalism defined. *In The anthropology of politics*, ed. Joan Vincent, 356–65. Malden, MA: Blackwell.

Schneider, David. 1968. *American kinship: A cultural account*. Englewood Cliffs, NJ: Prentice-Hall.

Schultz, Emily. 1984. From pagan to Pullo: Ethnic identity change in northern Cameroon. *Africa* 54(1):46–64.

Schultz, Emily. 1990. *Dialogue at the margins: Whorf, Bakhtin, and linguistic relativity*. New Directions in Anthropological Writing. Madison: University of Wisconsin Press.

Schultz, Emily. 2009. Resolving the anti-antievolutionism dilemma: A brief for relational evolutionary thinking in anthropology. *American Anthropologist* 111(2):224–37.

Schwartz, Jeffrey H., and Ian Tattersall. 2015. Defining the genus *Homo*. *Science* 349:391–92.

Schwartzman, Helen. 1978. *Transformations: The anthropology of children's play*. New York: Plenum Press.

Scott, James. 1987. *Weapons of the weak*. New Haven, CT: Yale University Press.

Scott, James C. 1990. *Domination and the arts of resistance*. New Haven, CT: Yale University Press.

Scott, James C. 1998. *Seeing like a state: how certain schemes to improve the human condition have failed*. New Haven: Yale University Press.

Scott, James. 2017. *Against the Grain: A deep history of the earliest states*. New Haven: Yale University Press.

Semaw, S. 2000. The world's earliest stone artifacts form Gona, Ethiopia: Their implications for understanding stone technology and patterns of human evolution between 2.6–1.5 million years ago. *Journal of Archaeological Science* 27:1197–1214.

Semaw, S., J. Renne, J. W. K. Harris, et al. 1997. 2.5-million-year-old stone tools from Gona, Ethiopia. *Nature* 385:333–36.

Senut B., et al. 2001. First hominid from the Miocene (Lukeino Formation, Kenya). *Comptes Rendus Des Seances de l'Academie Des Sciences* 332:137–44.

Service, Elman. 1962. *Primitive social organization*. New York: Random House.

Shanks, Michael, and Christopher Tilley. 1987. *Social theory and archaeology* Oxford: Polity Press.

Shapin, Steven. 2010. *Never pure: Historical studies of science as if it was produced by people with bodies, situated in time, space, culture, and society, and struggling for credibility and authority*. Baltimore, MD: Johns Hopkins University Press.

Sharma, Ursula. 1999. *Caste*. Buckingham, UK: Open University Press.

Sharp, Lesley. 2006. *Strange harvest: Organ transplants, denatured bodies, and the transformed self*. Berkeley: University of California Press.

Sheehan, Elizabeth A. 1997. Victorian clitoridectomy: Isaac Baker Brown and his harmless operative procedure. *In The gender/sexuality reader*, ed. Roger Lancaster and Micaela De Leonardo, 324–34. New York: Routledge.

Shepherd, Gil. 1987. Rank, gender, and homosexuality: Mombasa as a key to understanding sexual options. *In The cultural construction of sexuality*, ed. Pat Caplan, 240–70. London: Tavistock.

Shipman, Pat. 1984. Scavenger hunt. *Natural History* (April):22–27.

Shostak, Marjorie. 1981. *Nisa: The life and words of a !Kung woman*. New York: Vintage.

Silverstein, Michael. 1976. Shifters, linguistic categories, and cultural description. *In Meaning in anthropology*, ed. Keith Basso and Henry Selby, 11–55. Albuquerque: University of New Mexico Press.

Silverstein, Michael. 1985. The functional stratification of language and ontogenesis. *In Culture, communication, and cognition: Vygotskian perspectives*, ed. James Wertsch, 205–35. Cambridge, UK: Cambridge University Press.

Silverstein, Michael. 1993. Metapragmatic discourse and metapragmatics function. *In Reflexive language: Reported speech and metapragmatics*, ed. John Lucy, 33–58. New York: Cambridge University Press.

Simons, Elwyn L. 1985. Origins and characteristics of the first hominids. *In Ancestors: The hard evidence*, ed. E. Delson, 37–41. New York: Alan R. Liss.

Simons, Elwyn, and D. Tab Rasmussen. 1994. A whole new world of ancestors: Eocene australopithecines from Africa. *Evolutionary Anthropology* 3(4):129–39.

Singer, Merrill. 1998. The development of critical medical anthropology: Implications for biological anthropology. *In Building a new biocultural synthesis*, ed. Alan H. Goodman and Thomas L. Leatherman, 93–123. Ann Arbor: University of Michigan Press.

Singer, Merrill. 2009. *Introduction to syndemics: A critical systems approach to public and community health*. San Francisco, CA: Jossey-Bass.

Singer, Natasha. 2007. Is looking your age now taboo? *New York Times*, March 1, E1, E3.

Sjovold, Torstein. 1993. Frost and found. *Natural History* 4:60–64.

Slobin, Dan. 1987. Thinking for speaking. *Proceedings of the Berkeley Linguistics Society* 13:435–44.

Slobin, Dan. 2003. Language and thought online: Cognitive consequences of linguistic relativity. *In Language in mind: Advances in the study of language and thought*, ed. Dedre Gentner and Susan Goldin-Meadow, 157–91. Cambridge, MA: MIT Press.

Smart, Alan. 1999. Expressions of interest: Friendship and Guanzi in Chinese societies. *In The anthropology of friendship*, ed. Sandra Bell and Simon Coleman, 119–36. Oxford: Berg.

Smedley, Audrey. 1995. *Race in North America: Origin and evolution of a worldview*. Boulder, CO: Westview Press.

Smedley, Audrey. 1998. "Race" and the construction of human identity. *American Anthropologist* 100(3):690–702.

Smith, Andrea. 1994. For all those who were Indian in a former life. *Cultural Survival Quarterly* (Winter):71.

Smith, Bruce. 1995a. *The emergence of agriculture*. New York: Scientific American Library.

Smith, Bruce. 1995b. The origins of agriculture in the Americas. *Evolutionary Anthropology* (5):174–84.

Smith, Daniel Jordan. 2006. Love and the risk of HIV: Courtship, marriage, and infidelity in Southeastern Nigeria. *In Modern loves: the anthropology of romantic courtship and companionate marriage*, eds. Jennifer S. Hirsch, and Holly Wardlow, Ann Arbor: University of Michigan Press.

Smith, Gavin A., and R. Brooke Thomas. 1998. What could be: Biocultural anthropology for the next generation. *In Building a new biocultural synthesis*, ed. Alan H. Goodman and Thomas

L. Leatherman, 451–73. Ann Arbor: University of Michigan Press.

Smith, M. G. (1954) 1981. Introduction. *In Baba of Karo,* by Mary Smith. New Haven, CT: Yale University Press.

Smith, Wilfred Cantwell. 1982. *Towards a world theology.* Philadelphia: Westminster.

Sonntag, Selma K. 2002. *The local politics of global English.* Lanham, MD: Lexington Books.

Spangler, Sydney. 2011. "To open oneself is a poor woman's trouble": Embodied inequality and childbirth in South-Central Tanzania. *Medical Anthropology Quarterly* 25:479–98.

Spector, Janet D. 1993. *What this awl means.* St. Paul: Minnesota Historical Society Press.

Spencer, Jonathan. 2000. On not becoming a "Terrorist": Problems of memory, agency, and community in the Sri Lankan conflict. *In Violence and subjectivity,* ed. Veena Das, Arthur Kleinman, Mamphela Ramphele, and Pamela Reynolds, 120–40. Berkeley: University of California Press.

Stammbach, Eduard. 1987. Desert, forest and montane baboons: Multilevel societies. *In Primate societies,* ed. Barbara Smuts, Dorothy Cheney, Robert Seyfarth, Richard Wrangham, and Thomas Struhsaker, 112–20. Chicago: University of Chicago Press.

Stanley, Steven M. 1981. *The new evolutionary timetable.* New York: Basic Books.

Starn, Orin. 1999. *Nightwatch: The making of a movement in the Peruvian Andes.* Durham, NC: Duke University Press.

Steiner, Christopher. 1994. *African art in transit.* Cambridge, UK: Cambridge University Press.

Stewart, Charles, and Rosalind Shaw. 1994. *Syncretism/anti-syncretism.* London: Routledge.

Stewart, Kelly J., and Alexander H. Harcourt. 1987. Gorillas: Variation in female relationships. *In Primate Societies,* ed. Barbara Smuts, Dorothy Cheney, Robert Seyfarth, Richard Wrangham, and Thomas Struhsaker, 155–64. Chicago: University of Chicago Press.

Stocks, Anthony. 2005. Too much for too few: Problems of indigenous land rights in America. *Annual Review of Anthropology* 34:85–104.

Stoler, Ann L. 1997. Making empire respectable: The politics of race and sexual morality in twentieth-century colonial cultures. *In Situated lives,* ed. Louise Lamphere, 373–99. New York: Routledge.

Strathern, Marilyn. 1972. *Women in between.* London: Academic Press.

Strathern, Marilyn. 1988. *The gender of the gift.* Berkeley: University of California Press.

Strathern, Marilyn. 1992. *Reproducing the future: Anthropology, kinship, and the new reproductive technologies.* New York: Routledge.

Strier, Karen. 1997. An American primatologist abroad in Brazil. *In Primate encounters: Models of science, gender, and society,* ed. Shirley Strum and Linda Fedigan, 194–207. Chicago: University of Chicago Press.

Strier, Karen. 2007. *Primate behavioral ecology.* Boston, MA: Pearson Allyn and Bacon.

Stringer, Christopher. 1989. The origin of early modern humans: A comparison of the European and non-European evidence. *In The human revolution,* ed. P. A. Mellers and C. Stringer, 232–44. Princeton, NJ: Princeton University Press.

Stringer, Chris. 2012. *Lone survivors: How we came to be the only humans on earth.* New York: Holt.

Stringer, Chris. 2015. Human evolution: The many mysteries of *Homo naledi. eLife* 4:e10627.

Stringer, Chris, and Peter Andrews. 2005. *The complete world of human evolution.* London: Thames & Hudson.

Struhsaker, T., and L. Leland. 1987. Colobines: Infanticide by adult males. *In Primate Societies,* ed. Barbara Smuts, Dorothy Cheney, Robert Seyfarth, Richard Wrangham, and Thomas Struhsaker, 83–97. Chicago: University of Chicago Press.

Strum, Shirley, Donald G. Lindburg, and David Hamburg, eds. 1999. *The new physical anthropology: Science, humanism, and critical reflection.* Upper Saddle River, NJ: Prentice Hall.

Suplee, Curt. 1997. Find may rewrite America's prehistory. *Washington Post,* February 11, A2.

Susman, Randall L., Jack T. Stern, Jr., and William L. Jungers. 1985. Locomotor adaptations in the Hadar hominids. *In Ancestors: The hard evidence,* ed. E. Delson, 184–92. New York: Alan R. Liss.

Sussman, Robert. 1991. Primate origins and the evolution of angiosperms. *American Journal of Physical Anthropology* 23:209–23.

Sussman, Robert W., and Paul A. Garber. 2004. Rethinking sociality: Cooperation and aggression among primates. *In The origins and nature of socialit,* ed. Robert W. Sussman and Audrey R. Chapman, 161–90. New York: Aldine de Gruyter.

Swanson, Heather Anne, Marianne Elisabeth Lien, and Gro B. Ween, eds. 2018. *Domestication Gone Wild: Politics and Practices of Multispecies Relations.* Durham, NC: Duke University Press.

Tambiah, Stanley J. 1989. The politics of ethnicity. *American Ethnologist* 16(2):335–49.

Tattersall, Ian. 1998. *Becoming human: Evolution and human uniqueness.* San Diego: Harcourt, Brace.

Tattersall, Ian. 2009. *The fossil trail,* 2nd ed. New York: Oxford University Press.

Tattersall, Ian. 2012. *Masters of the planet: The search for our human origins.* New York: Palgrave Macmillan.

Tattersall, Ian, and Rob DeSalle. 2011. *Race? Debunking a scientific myth.* College Station: Texas: A & M Press.

Taylor, Julie. 1987. Tango. *Cultural Anthropology* 2(4):481–93.

Templeton, Alan R. 1993. The "Eve" hypothesis: A genetic critique and reanalysis. *American Anthropologist* 95:51–72.

Thackeray, J. Francis. 2015. Estimating the age and affinities of *Homo naledi. South African Journal of Science* 111(11–12).

Thalmann, O. 2013. Complete mitochondrial genomes of ancient canids suggest a European origin of domestic dogs. *Science* 342:871–74.

Thayer, Zaneta, and Amy L. Non. "Anthropology Meets Epigenetics: Current and Future Directions." *American Anthropologist* 117, 2015: 722–35.

Thorne, Alan G., and Milford H. Wolpoff. 1992. The multiregional evolution of humans. *Scientific American* (April):76–83.

Trigger, Bruce. 1993. *Early civilizations: Ancient Egypt in context.* Cairo: American University in Cairo Press.

Trinkaus, Erik. 1984. Neanderthal public morphology and gestation length. *Current Anthropology* 25:508–14.

Trotter, Robert. 1987. A case of lead poisoning from folk remedies in Mexican American communities. *In Anthropological praxis,* ed. Robert Wolfe and Shirley Fiske, 146–59. Boulder, CO: Westview Press.

Trouillot, Michel-Rolph. 1991. Anthropology and the savage slot: The poetics and politics of otherness. *In Recapturing anthropology,* ed. Richard Fox, 17–44. Santa Fe, NM: SAR Press.

Trouillot, Michel-Rolph. 1994. Culture, color and politics in Haiti. *In Race,* ed. Stephen Gregory and Roger Sanjek, 146–74. New Brunswick, NJ: Rutgers University Press.

Tsing, Anna Lowenhaupt. 2005. *Friction: An ethnography of global connection.* Princeton, NJ: Princeton University Press.

Turner, Victor. 1969. *The ritual process.* Chicago: Aldine.

Tylor, E. B. (1871) 1958. *Primitive culture.* New York: Harper & Row.

Uchendu, Victor. 1965. *The Igbo of southeast Nigeria.* New York: Holt, Rinehart and Winston.

Underwood, J. H. 1979. *Human variation and human microevolution.* Englewood Cliffs, NJ: Prentice Hall.

Valentine, Bettylou. 1978. *Hustling and other hard work.* New York: Free Press.

Valentine, Charles. 1978. Introduction. *In Hustling and other hard work,* by Bettylou Valentine, 1–10. New York: Free Press.

van den Berghe, Pierre. 1970. Race, class, and ethnicity in South Africa. *In Social stratification in Africa,* ed. Arthur Tuden and Leonard Plotnikov, 345–71. New York: Free Press.

Van Gennep, Arnold. 1960. *The rites of passage.* Chicago: University of Chicago Press.

van Willigen, John, and V. C. Channa. 1991. Law, custom, and crimes against women. *Human Organization* 50(4):369–77.

Vaughan, James. 1973. Engkyagu as artists in Marghi society. *In The traditional artist in African societies,* ed. Warren d'Azevedo, 162–93. Bloomington: Indiana University Press.

Vaughan, James. 2006. *The Mandara Margi: A society living on the verge.* http://www.indiana.edu/~margi/

Verdery, Katherine. 2018. *My Life as a Spy: Investigations in a Secret Police File.* Durham, NC: Duke University Press.

Villmoare, Brian, William H. Kimbel, and Chalachew Seyoum. 2015. Early *Homo* at 2.8ma from Ladi-Geraru, Afar, Ethiopia. *Science,* doi: 10.1126/science.aaa1343.

Vincent, Joan. 2002. Introduction. *In The anthropology of politics,* ed. Joan Vincent, 1–13. Malden, MA: Blackwell.

Voloshinov, V. N. (1926) 1987. Discourse in life and discourse in art. *In Freudianism,* ed. and trans. I. R. Titunik, in collaboration with Neil H. Bruss, 93–116. Bloomington: Indiana University Press.

Vrba, Elisabeth, George Denton, et al., eds. 1995. *Paleoclimate and evolution, with emphasis on human origins,* 524–531. New Haven, CT: Yale University Press.

Wade, Peter, Carlos López Beltrán, Eduardo Restrepo, and Ricardo Ventura Santos. 2014a. Introduction: Genomics, race mixture, and nation in Latin America. *In Mestizo genomics: Race mixture, nation, and science in Latin America,* ed. Peter Wade, Carlos López Beltrán, Eduardo Restrepo, and Ricardo Ventura Santos, 1–30. Durham, NC: Duke University Press.

Wade, Peter, Carlos López Beltrán, Eduardo Restrepo, and Ricardo Ventura Santos, eds. 2014b. *Mestizo genomics: Race mixture, nation, and science in Latin America.* Durham, NC: Duke University Press.

Walker, Alan. 1993. The origin of the genus *Homo. In The origin and evolution of humans and humanness,* ed. D. Tab Rasmussen. Sudbury, MA: Jones & Bartlett.

Walker, Alice. *Possessing the Secret of Joy.* New York: Pocket Books, 1992.

Wallace, Anthony F. C. 1966. *Religion: An anthropological view.* New York: Random House.

Wallace, A. F. C. 1972. *The death and rebirth of the Seneca.* New York: Vintage.

Wallerstein, Immanuel. 1974. *The modern-world system: Capitalist agriculture and the origins of the European world-economy in the sixteenth century.* New York: Academic Press.

Wallmann, Joel. 1992. *Aping language.* Cambridge, UK: Cambridge University Press.

Walsh, Michael. 2005. Will indigenous languages survive? *Annual Review of Anthropology* 34:293–315.

Ward, Thomas W. 2013. *Gangsters without borders: an ethnography of a Salvadoran street gang.* New York; Oxford: Oxford University Press.

Warner, W. Lloyd. 1936. American caste and class. *American Sociological Review* 42(2):237–57.

Washburn, Sherwood, and C. S. Lancaster. 1968. The evolution of hunting. *In Man the hunter,* ed. R. Lee and I. DeVore, 293–303. Chicago: Aldine.

Waters, Michael R., Steven L. Forman, Thomas A. Jennings, et al. 2011. The Buttermilk Creek Complex and the origins of Clovis at the Debra L. Friedkin Site, Texas. *Science* 331:1599–1603.

Weatherford, Jack. 1988. *Indian givers: How the Indians of the Americas transformed the world.* New York: Fawcett.

Webster, D. 1975. Warfare and the evolution of the state: A reconsideration. *American Antiquity* 40:471–75.

Weiner, Annette. 1980. Stability in banana leaves: Colonization and women in Kiriwina, Trobriand Islands. *In Women and colonization: Anthropological perspectives,* ed. Mona Etienne and Eleanor Leacock, 270–93. New York: Praeger.

Weiner, Annette. 1988. *The Trobrianders of Papua New Guinea.* New York: Holt, Rinehart, and Winston.

Weiner, Annette. 1990. *Guest editorial in Cultural anthropology: A perspective on the human condition,* ed. Emily Schultz and Robert Lavenda, 392–3, 2nd ed. St. Paul, MN: West.

Weinker, Curtis. 1995. Biological anthropology: The current state of the discipline. *In Biological anthropology: The state of the science,* ed. Noel T. Boaz and Linda Wolfe. Bend, OR: International Institute for Human Evolutionary Research.

Weismantel, Mary. 1995. Making kin: Kinship theory and Zumbagua adoptions. *American Ethnologist* 22(4):685–709.

Weismantel, Mary. 2001. *Food, gender, and poverty in the Ecuadorian Andes.* Prospect Heights, IL: Waveland Press.

Wenke, Robert J. 1999. *Patterns in prehistory,* 4th ed. Oxford: Oxford University Press.

Wenke, Robert J., and Deborah I. Olszewski. er2007. *Patterns in prehistory: Humankind's first three million years,* 5th ed. New York: Oxford University Press.

Wentzell, Emily A. 2013. *Maturing masculinities : aging, chronic illness, and Viagra in Mexico.* Durham, NC: Duke University Press.

Werbner, Pnina. 1997. Introduction: The dialectics of cultural hybridity. *In Debating cultural hybridity: Multi-cultural identities and the politics of anti-racism,* ed. Pnina Werbner and Tariq Modood. 1–28. London: Zed Books.

West, Paige. 2006. *Conservation is our government now: The politics of ecology in Papua New Guinea.* Durham, NC: Duke University Press.

West-Eberhard, Mary Jane. 2003. *Developmental plasticity and evolution.* Oxford: Oxford University Press.

Weston, Kath. 1991. *Families we choose: Lesbians, gays, kinship.* New York: Columbia University Press.

Weston, Kath. 1995. Forever is a long time: Romancing the real in gay kinship ideologies. *In Naturalizing power,* ed. Sylvia Yanagisako and Carol Delaney, 87–110. New York: Routledge.

White, Leslie. 1949. *The science of culture.* New York: Grove Press.

White, T. D., B. Asfaw, Y. Beyene, Y. Haile-Selassie, C. O. Lovejoy, G. Suwa, and G.

White, T. D., G. Suwa, and B. Asfaw. 1994. *Australopithecus ramidus,* a new species of early hominid from Aramis, Ethiopia. *Nature* 371:306–12.

White, Tim D., Gen Suwa, William K. Hart, Robert C. Walter, Giday WoldeGabriel, Jean de Heinzelin, J. Desmond Clark, Berhane Asfaw, and Elisabeth Vrba. 1993. New discoveries of *Australopithecus* at Maka in Ethiopia. *Nature* 366(November 18):261–65.

Whitten, Patricia L. 1987. Infants and adult males. *In Primate societies,* ed. Barbara Smuts, Dorothy Cheney, Robert Seyfarth, Richard Wrangham, and Thomas Struhsaker, 343–57. Chicago: University of Chicago Press.

Whorf, Benjamin Lee. 1956. *Language, thought, and reality.* Cambridge, MA: MIT Press.

Wieringa, Saskia, and Evelyn Blackwood. 1999. Introduction. *In Female desires: Same sex relations and transgender practices across cultures,* ed. Evelyn Blackwood and Saska Wieringa, 1–38. New York: Columbia University Press.

Wilk, Richard. 1996. *Economies and cultures: Foundations of economic anthropology.* Boulder, CO: Westview Press.

Wilk, Richard, and Lisa Cliggett. 2007. *Economies and cultures: Foundations of economic anthropology.* Boulder, CO: Westview Press.

Williams, Brackette F. 1989. A class act: Anthropology and the race to nation across ethnic terrain. *Annual Review of Anthropology* 18:401–44.

Williams, Brett. 1984. Why migrant women feed their husbands tamales: Foodways as a basis for a revisionist view of Tejano family life. *In Ethnic and regional foodways in the United States,* ed. Linda Keller Brown and Kay Mussell. 113–127. Knoxville: University of Tennessee Press.

Wilson, Allan C., and Rebecca L. Cann. 1992. The recent African genesis of humans. *Scientific American* (April):68–73.

Wilson, David Sloan. 2002. *Darwin's cathedral: Evolution, religion and the nature of society.* Chicago: University of Chicago Press.

Wilson, E. O. 1980. *Sociobiology: The new synthesis.* Cambridge, MA: Harvard University Press.

Wimsatt, William C., and J. C. Schank. 1988. Two constraints on the evolution of complex adaptations and the means for their avoidance. *In Evolutionary progress,* ed. M. Nitecki, 231–73. Chicago: University of Chicago Press.

Witherspoon, Gary. 1975. *Navajo kinship and marriage.* Chicago: University of Chicago Press.

Wittfogel, Karl. 1957. *Oriental despotism: A comparative study of total power.* New Haven, CT: Yale University Press.

Wolcott, Harry F. 1999. *Ethnography: A way of seeing.* Walnut Creek, CA: AltaMira Press.

Wolf, Eric. 1982. *Europe and the people without history.* Berkeley: University of California Press.

Wolf, Eric. 1994. Facing power: Old insights, new questions. *In Assessing cultural anthropology*, ed. Robert Borofsky, 218–28. New York: McGraw–Hill.

Wolfe, Linda. 1995. Current research in field primatology. *In Biological anthropology: The state of the science*, Noel T. Boaz and Linda Wolfe, 149–67. Bend, OR: International Institute for Human Evolutionary Research.

Woodward, V. 1992. *Human heredity and society*. St. Paul, MN: West.

Woolard, Kathryn A. 1998. Introduction: Language ideology as a field of inquiry. *In Language ideologies: Practice and theory*, ed. Bambi Schieffelin, Kathryn Woolard, and Paul V. Kroskrity, 3–47. New York: Oxford University Press.

Wrangham, Richard. 2009. *Catching fire: How cooking made us human*. New York: Basic Books.

Yuval-Davis, Nira. 1997. Ethnicity, gender relations, and multiculturalism. *In Debating cultural hybridity: Multicultural identities and the politics of anti-racism*, ed. Pnina Werbner and Tariq Modood, 193–208. London: Zed Books.

Zeder, Melinda A. 2016. Domestication as a model system for niche construction theory. *Evolutionary Ecology* 30:325–48.

Zeder, Melinda A., and Bruce D. Smith. 2009. A conversation on agricultural origins. *Current Anthropology* 50(5):681–91.

Zimmer, Carl. 2019a. A skull bone discovered in Greece may alter the story of human prehistory. *New York Times*, https://www.nytimes.com/2019/07/10/science/skull-neanderthal-human-europe-greece.html

Zimmer, Carl. 2019b. Scientists Find the Skull of Humanity's Ancestor, on a Computer. *New York Times*, https://www.nytimes.com/2019/09/10/science/human-ancestor-skull-computer.html

Credits

Chapter 1

Chapter 1 Opening Photo (p. 2): Anthony Asael/Art in All of Us/Getty Images1.1: PORNCHAI KITTIWONGSAKUL/AFP/Getty Images; **Figure 1.2 (p. 8):** OUP; **Figure 1.3a (p. 10):** courtesy of Agustín Fuentes; **Figure 1.3b (p. 10):** courtesy of Robert H. Lavenda; **Figure 1.4 (p. 12):** courtesy of Arjun Guneratne; **Figure 1.5 (p. 15):** Stanford News Service; **Figure 1.6 (p. 16):** EAAF/AFP/Getty Images; **Figure 1.7 (p. 18):** courtesy of Andrea Wiley

Module 1

Figure M1.1 (p. 23): Photo by COLLART Hervé/Sygma via Getty Images; **Figure M1.2 (p. 25):** Bettmann/Contributor/Getty Images; **Figure M1.3a (p. 26):** Richard T. Nowitz/Corbis Documentary/Getty Images; **Figure M1.3b (p. 26):** DSC-800 by TheBigTouffe/CC BY 2.0; **Figure M1.4 (p. 27):** JIM WATSON/AFP/Getty Images; **Figure M1.5a (p. 30):** courtesy of Robert H. Lavenda; **Figure M1.5b (p. 30):** courtesy of Jon Marks

Chapter 2

Chapter 2 Opening Photo (p. 32): Don Johnston_BI/Alamy Stock Photo; **Figure 2.1 (p. 34):** OUP; **Figure 2.2 (p. 35):** OUP; **Figure 2.3 (p. 38):** OUP; **Figure 2.4 (p. 39):** Bettmann/Contributor/Getty Images; **Figure 2.5 (p. 40):** © Keren Su/Corbis Documentary/Getty Images; **Figure 2.6 (p. 41):** Wellcome Library, London (CC BY 4.0); **Figure 2.7 (p. 43):** ANIMALS ANIMALS © Ardea/David Chapman; **Figure 2.8 (p. 45):** From Steven M. Stanley, The New Evolutionary Time Table: Fossils, Genes and the Origin of the Species, Basic Books, 1984.; **Figure 2.9 (p. 46):** OUP; **Figure 2.10 (p. 47):** OUP; **Figure 2.11 (p. 48):** Courtesy of EAAF; **Figure 2.12 (p. 50):** Martin Schoeller/National Geographic; **Figure 2.13 (p. 51):** OUP; **Figure 2.14 (p. 52):** OUP; **Figure 2.15 (p. 53):** OUP; **Figure 2.16 (p. 54):** From Lewontin, R.C. "The Organism As Subject and Object of Evolution," Scientia 118: 65–82 (1983); **Figure 2.17 (p. 54):** From Lewontin, R.C. "The Organism As Subject and Object of Evolution," Scientia 118: 65–82 (1983); **Figure 2.18 (p. 55):** ANIMALS ANIMALS © Johnny Johnson

Chapter 3

Chapter 3 Opening Photo (p. 62): Avalon/Bruce Coleman Inc/Alamy Stock Photo; **Figure 3.1a (p. 64):** Rko/Kobal/Shutterstock; **Figure 3.1b (p. 64):** UNIVERSAL/WING NUT FILMS/THE KOBAL COLLECTION; **Figure 3.2 (p. 66):** OUP; **Figure 3.3 (p. 67):** [with text: Relethford 1996, 175; with credits: from The Human Species, Third Edition, by John Relethford, p. 175. Copyright © 1997 Mayfield Publishing Company]; **Figure 3.4 (p. 67):** Noel Rowe/alltheworldsprimates.org; **Figure 3.5 (p. 69):** Noel Rowe/alltheworldsprimates.org; **Figure 3.6 (p. 70):** from The Human Career by Richard G. Klein. Copyright © 2009 by the University of Chicago. Reproduced by permission of the publisher, the University of Chicago Press; **Figure 3.7 (p. 70):** © David Parsons/iStock; **Figure 3.8 (p. 71):** Noel Rowe/alltheworldsprimates.org; **Figure 3.9a (p. 71):** Noel Rowe/alltheworldsprimates.org; **Figure 3.9b (p. 71):** Noel Rowe/alltheworldsprimates.org; **Figure 3.10 (p. 72):** Noel Rowe/alltheworldsprimates.org; **Figure 3.11 (p. 74):** Noel Rowe/alltheworldsprimates.org; **Figure 3.12 (p. 74):** © Christine Eichin/iStock; **Figure 3.13 (p. 74):** ©Steve Bloom/SteveBloom.com; **Figure 3.14 (p. 75):** Noel Rowe/alltheworldsprimates.org; **Figure 3.15 (p. 78):** After Klein 2009, 95; **Figure 3.16 (p. 79):** OUP; **Figure 3.17 (p. 80):** Martin D. Robert. Primate Origins and Evolution: A Phylogenetic Reconstruction. © 1990 R. D. Martin. Reprinted by permission of Princeton University Press; **Figure 3.18 (p. 80):** Courtesy of the Peabody Museum of Natural History, Yale University; **Figure 3.19 (p. 81):** OUP; **Figure 3.20 (p. 81):** OUP

Module 2

Figure M2.1 (p. 85): Martin M303/Shutterstock; **Figure M2.2 (p. 86):** Drawn by OUP, based on Renfrew and Bahn 2004, 128; **Figure M2.3 (p. 87):** OUP; **Figure M2.4 (p. 88):** [with text:] Adapted from Renfrew and Bahn 2005, 132. [with credits:] adapted from Archaeology by Renfrew and Bahn; **Figure M2.5 (p. 90):** Courtesy Professor A.J. Timothy Jull; **Figure M2.6 (p. 91):** Drawn by Simon S. S. Driver using information from Bannister & Smiley in "Geochronology," Tuscon 1955. From "Archaeology: Theories, Methods and Practice" by Colin Renfrew and Paul Bahn, Thames & Hudson, London and New York.; **Figure M2.7a (p. 94):** Photo by David Boyer/National Geographic/Getty Images; **Figure M2.7b (p. 94):** © Roger Ressmeyer/Corbis/VCG/Getty Images

Chapter 4

Chapter 4 Opening Photo (p. 96): Xinhua/Alamy Stock Photo; **Figure 4.1 (p. 99):** OUP; **Figure 4.2 (p. 101):** Adapted from Human Evolution, Second Edition, by Roger Lewin, Blackwell Publishers. Reprinted by permission of the publisher.; **Figure 4.3 (p. 103):** OUP; **Figure 4.4 (p. 104):** Courtesy David L. Brill; **Figure 4.5 (p. 104):** John Reader/Science Source; **Figure 4.6**

(p. 106): John Reader/Science Source; **Figure 4.7 (p. 106):** Courtesy David L. Brill; **Figure 4.8 (p. 107):** [from Primate Adaptation and Evolution by John G. Fleagle. Copyright © 1988 by Academic Press. Reproduced by permission of the publisher. Illustration by Stephen Nash.]; **Figure 4.9 (p. 107):** Courtesy David L. Brill; **Figure 4.10a (p. 108):** Pascal Goetgheluck/Science Source; **Figure 4.10b (p. 108):** Pascal Goetgheluck/Science Source; **Figure 4.11 (p. 109):** Pascal Goetgheluck/Science Source; **In Their Own Words (p. 105):** AP Photo/Sebastian John; **Figure 4.12 (p. 111):** John Reader/Science Source; **Figure 4.13 (p. 112):** © Kristie Cannon-Bonventre/AnthroPhoto; **Figure 4.14a (p. 113):** F.E. Grine, SUNY, Stony Brook; **Figure 4.14b (p. 113):** F.E. Grine, SUNY, Stony Brook; **Figure 4.15 (p. 115):** OUP; **Figure 4.16 (p. 116):** © National Museums of Kenya, Nairobi; **Figure 4.17 (p. 116):** John Reader/Science Source; **Figure 4.18 (p. 117):** from F. Bordes, The Old Stone Age, Weidenfield & Nicolson, 1968.; **Figure 4.19 (p. 119):** OUP; **Figure 4.20 (p. 120):** Pascal Goetgheluck/Science Source; **Figure 4.21 (p. 122):** OUP; **Figure 4.22 (p. 123):** Rudi Von Brile/PHOTOEDIT; **In Their Own Words (p. 124):** Image #39441, American Museum of Natural History; **Figure 4.23 (p. 125):** from F. Bordes, The Old Stone Age, Weidenfield & Nicolson, 1968.; **Figure 4.24 (p. 128):** OUP; **Figure 4.25a (p. 129):** Day, Michael H. Guide to Fossil Man University of Chicago Press. Fig 86 (p. 244); **Figure 4.25b (p. 129):** Day, Michael H. Guide to Fossil Man University of Chicago Press. Fig 87 (p. 247).; **Figure 4.26 (p. 131):** from F. Bordes, The Old Stone Age, Weidenfield & Nicolson, 1968.; **Figure 4.27 (p. 131):** from F. Bordes, The Old Stone Age, Weidenfield & Nicolson, 1968.; **Figure 4.28 (p. 133):** Image #39686, American Museum of Natural History, Library; **In Their Own Words (p. 135):** From Catherine Hodge McCoid and LeRoy D. McDermott, "Toard Decolonizing Gender: Female Vision in the Upper Paleolithic," Reproduced by permission of the American Anthropological Association from American Anthropologist, volume 98, Issue 2, pages 319-326, June 1996. Not for sale or futher reproduction.; **Figure 4.29 (p. 137):** LIONEL BONAVENTURE/AFP/Getty Images; **Figure 4.30 (p. 138):** AP Photo/The Daily Oklahoman, Chad Love

Chapter 5

Chapter 5 Opening Photo (p. 144): David Grossman/Alamy Stock Photo; **In Their Own Words (p. 148):** STEVE GSCHMEISSNER/SCIENCE PHOTO LIBRARY; **Figure 5.1 (p. 152):** mauritius images GmbH/Alamy Stock Photo; **Figure 5.2 (p. 154):** Sebastian Kaulitzki/Alamy Stock Photo; **Figure 5.3 (p. 155):** Monkey Business Images/Shutterstock; **Figure 5.4 (p. 157):** OUP; **Figure 5.5 (p. 166):** Maher Attar/Contributor/Sygma/Getty Images

Chapter 6

Chapter 6 Opening Photo (p. 170): Edward Karaa/Alamy Stock Photo; **Figure 6.1 (p. 173):** OUP; **Figure 6.2 (p. 174):** Leopold Nekula/Contributor/Sygma/Getty Images; **Figure 6.3a (p. 175):** Courtesy Dr. Payson D. Sheets; **Figure 6.3b (p. 175):** Courtesy Dr. Payson D. Sheets; **Figure 6.4 (p. 176):** University of California Archaeological Survey; **Figure 6.5 (p. 177):** Courtesy of the Museum Applied Science Center for Archaeology; the University of Pennsylvania Museum; **Figure 6.6 (p. 178):** Courtesy of Mark Muñiz; **Figure 6.7 (p. 180):** OUP; **Figure 6.8 (p. 181):** Morley Read/Alamy Stock Photo; **Figure 6.9 (p. 183):** David Mercado/Reuters; **Figure 6.10 (p. 186):** © PILAR OLIVARES/Reuters/Alamy Stock Photo; **Figure 6.11 (p. 187):** Natalie Fobes/Corbis Documentary/Getty Images; **Figure 6.12 (p. 188):** Smithsonian Institution; **Figure 6.13a (p. 189):** REUTERS/Muzammil Pasha/Alamy Stock Photo; **Figure 6.13b (p. 189):** REUTERS/Sayed Salahuddin; **Figure 6.14 (p. 192):** Michael Melford/National Geographic/Getty; **Figure 6.15 (p. 194):** The Natural History Museum/Alamy Stock Photo; **Figure 6.16 (p. 196):** courtesy of Robert H. Lavenda; **Figure 6.17 (p. 198):** © Trojandog | Dreamstime.com

Chapter 7

Chapter 7 Opening Photo (p. 202): Jan Wlodarczyk/Alamy Stock Photo; **Figure 7.1 (p. 205):** OUP; **Figure 7.2 (p. 206):** © Igorj | Dreamstime.com; **Figure 7.3 (p. 208):** Offset; **Figure 7.4 (p. 208):** © Penny Tweedie/Alamy; **Figure 7.5 (p. 209):** from The Emergence of Agriculture by Bruce Smith. Copyright © 1995 by Scientific American Library. Used with permission of W. H. Freeman and Company.; **Figure 7.6 (p. 210):** from David Harris and Gordon Hillman, Foraging and Farming: The Evolution of Plant Exploitation, One World Archaeology, Vol. 13, 1989, Unwin Hyman. Reprinted with permission from Routledge.; **Figure 7.7 (p. 212):** OUP; **Figure 7.8 (p. 213):** OUP; **Figure 7.9 (p. 215):** OUP; **Figure 7.10 (p. 216):** Courtesy Pictures of Record; **Figure 7.11 (p. 219):** View of the Round Tower at Jericho, 8000 BC (photo)/Israel/Ancient Art and Architecture Collection Ltd./The Bridgeman Art Library; **Figure 7.12 (p. 219):** OUP; **Figure 7.13 (p. 221):** © AnthroPhoto; **Figure 7.14a (p. 222):** © Dhuss/iStock.com; **Figure 7.14b (p. 222):** STRINGER/AFP/Getty Images; **Figure 7.15 (p. 223):** © Corbis/VCG/Getty Images; **Figure 7.16 (p. 224):** OUP; **Figure 7.17 (p. 226):** Jose Fuste Raga/Corbis Documentary/Getty Images; **Figure 7.18 (p. 226):** mbrand85/Shutterstock; **Figure 7.19 (p. 227):** Bettmann/Contributor/Getty Images; **Figure 7.20 (p. 229):** © NASA; **Figure 7.21 (p. 234):** J Marshall - Tribaleye Images/Alamy Stock Photo; **Figure 7.22 (p. 235):** British Museum, London, UK/Bridgeman Images.; **Figure 7.23 (p. 235):** © Keren Su/Corbis

Documentary/Getty Images; **Figure 7.24 (p. 236):** little_monster/Stockimo/Alamy Stock Photo

Chapter 8

Chapter 8 Opening Photo (p. 240): Cultura RM Exclusive/Philip Lee Harvey/Getty Images; **Figure 8.1 (p. 244):** courtesy of Robert H. Lavenda; **Figure 8.2 (p. 245):** OUP; **Figure 8.3 (p. 246):** courtesy of Daniel Lavenda; **Figure 8.4 (p. 249):** OUP; **Figure 8.5 (p. 250):** Images of Africa Photobank/Alamy Stock Photo; **Figure 8.6 (p. 251):** Ariadne Van Zandbergen/Alamy Stock Photo; **Figure 8.7 (p. 256):** TonyV3112/iStock; **Figure 8.8 (p. 257):** Library of Congress/Contributor/Corbis Historical/Getty Images

Module 3

Figure M3.1 (p. 260): OUP; **Figure M3.2 (p. 265):** Rudi Von Brile/PHOTOEDIT; **Figure M3.3a (p. 266):** Courtesy Michelle Bigenho; **Figure M3.3b (p. 266):** Courtesy Michelle Bigenho; **Figure M3.4 (p. 267):** Courtesy Ryan Cook; **Figure M3.5 (p. 268):** Courtesy Dan Bradburd; **Figure M3.6 (p. 270):** JayKay57/iStock

Chapter 9

Chapter 9 Opening Photo (p. 276): ken biggs/Alamy Stock Photo; **Figure 9.1 (p. 279):** KRAZY KAT: DISTRIBUTED BY KING FEATURES SYNDICATE, WORLD RIGHTS RESERVED; **Figure 9.2 (p. 282):** OUP; **Figure 9.3 (p. 284):** Courtesy of Robert H. Lavenda; **Figure 9.4 (p. 287):** [with figure: Geertz 1960; with credits: reprinted with permission of The Free Press, a division of Simon & Schuster, from The Religion of Java, by Clifford Geertz. Copyright © 1960 by The Free Press.]; **Figure 9.5 (p. 287):** © Fintastique | Dreamstime.com; **Figure 9.6 (p. 289):** Courtesy of Robert H. Lavenda; **Figure 9.7 (p. 291):** Radio Australia is the Australian Broadcasting Corporation's (ABC) international radio service; **Figure 9.8 (p. 294):** Monkey Business Images/Shutterstock; **Figure 9.9 (p. 296):** AP Photo/Wisconsin State Journal, Joseph W. Jackson III; **Figure 9.10 (p. 299):** From California Indian Library Collections, Ethnic Studies Library, University of California, Berkeley

Module 4

Figure M4.1 (p. 303): OUP

Chapter 10

Chapter 10 Opening Photo (p. 306): mauritius images GmbH/Alamy Stock Photo; **Figure 10.1 (p. 309):** Courtesy of Robert H. Lavenda; **Figure 10.2 (p. 310):** OUP; **Figure 10.3 (p. 312):** Owen Franken/Corbis Documentary/Getty Images; **Figure 10.4 (p. 313):** Defense Dept. photo by Cherie A. Thurlby; **Figure 10.5 (p. 314):** Express Newspapers via AP Images; **Figure 10.6 (p. 316):** Courtesy Michelle Bigenho; **Figure 10.7**

(p. 317): Aflo Co. Ltd./Alamy Stock Photo; **Figure 10.8 (p. 319):** Courtesy Justin Kerr/KERR ASSOCIATES; **Figure 10.9a (p. 324):** Anders Ryman/Alamy Stock Photo; **Figure 10.9b (p. 324):** Photo by Meredith H. Keffer, © 2014 The Harvard Crimson, Inc. All rights reserved. Reprinted with permission.; **Figure 10.10 (p. 326):** © Bronwyn8 | Dreamstime.com; **Figure 10.11 (p. 326):** REUTERS/Goran Tomasevic/Alamy Stock Photo; **Figure 10.12a (p. 328):** takepicsforfun/Shutterstock.com; **Figure 10.12b (p. 328):** © iStock/Rawpixel Ltd; **Figure 10.13 (p. 331):** © Abbas/Magnum Photos; **Figure 10.14 (p. 332):** ALBERTO PIZZOLI,ALBERTO PIZZOLI/AFP/Getty Images; **Figure 10.15 (p. 338):** © B&C Alexander/ArcticPhoto

Chapter 11

Chapter 11 Opening Photo (p. 342): Frank Bienewald/LightRocket via Getty Images; **Figure 11.1 (p. 346):** OUP; **Figure 11.2a (p. 348):** public domain; **Figure 11.2b (p. 348):** after Peruvian Prehistory: An Overview of Pre-Inca and Inca Society, ed. Richard W. Keatinge, Cambridge (Cambridge University Press, 1988); **Figure 11.3 (p. 351):** courtesy of Robert H. Lavenda; **Figure 11.4 (p. 355):** Philip Gould/Corbis/VCG/Getty Images; **Figure 11.5 (p. 355):** Bettmann/Contributor/Getty Images; **Figure 11.6 (p. 359):** © Steve Allen | Dreamstime.com; **Figure 11.7 (p. 361):** Marjorie Shostak/AnthroPhoto; **Figure 11.8 (p. 362):** Photo by Eric LAFFORGUE/Gamma-Rapho via Getty Images; **Figure 11.9 (p. 364):** Cold Cold; **Figure 11.10 (p. 366):** Macduff Everton/Corbis Documentary/Getty Images

Chapter 12

Chapter 12 Opening Photo (p. 368): MANDEL NGAN/AFP via Getty Images; **Figure 12.1 (p. 371):** OUP; **In Their Own Words (p. 374):** AP Photo/Karel Navarro; **Figure 12.2 (p. 376):** © Stuart Franklin/Magnum Photos; **Figure 12.3 (p. 377):** Courtesy of Robert H. Lavenda; **Figure 12.4 (p. 379):** Source: Office for National Statistisc licensed under the Open Government License v.2.0; **Figure 12.5 (p. 384):** PETER PARKS/AFP/Getty Images; **Figure 12.6 (p. 386):** REUTERS/Chip East CME/Alamy Stock Photo; **Figure 12.7 (p. 389):** © Alexandra Boulat/VII; **Figure 12.8 (p. 390):** Courtesy of Robert H. Lavenda; **Figure 12.9 (p. 393):** © Tanawat Pontchour | Dreamstime.com

Chapter 13

Chapter 13 Opening Photo (p. 400): photo courtesy of Red Works Photography, www.redworks.ca; **Figure 13.1 (p. 402):** OUP; **Figure 13.2a (p. 404):** © Owen Franken/CORBIS/Getty Images; **Figure 13.2b (p. 404):** © Lena Wurm/Alamy Stock Photo; **Figure 13.3 (p. 405):** photo by Education Images/UIG via Getty Images; **Figure 13.4 (p. 408):** photo by Linda Davidson/The Washington Post via Getty Images; **Figure 13.5 (p. 412):** photo by

David Turnley/Corbis/VCG via Getty Images; **Figure 13.6** (p. 413): dpa picture alliance archive/Alamy Stock Photo; **Figure 13.7 (p. 414):** © Thornton Cohen/Alamy Stock Photo; **Figure 13.8 (p. 415):** INTERFOTO/Alamy Stock Photo; **Figure 13.9 (p. 419):** photo by Sara D. Davis/Getty Images; **Figure 13.10 (p. 421):** Jan Butchofsky/Getty; **Figure 13.11 (p. 424):** photo by Kaveh Kasemi/Getty Images

Chapter 14

Chapter 14 Opening Photo (p. 428): Courtesy of Robert H. Lavenda; **Figure 14.1 (p. 432):** OUP; **Figure 14.2 (p. 434):** Courtesy of Robert H. Lavenda; **Figure 14.3 (p. 436):** OUP; **Figure 14.4 (p. 437):** OUP; **Figure 14.5 (p. 437):** OUP; **Figure 14.6 (p. 442):** OUP; **Figure 14.7 (p. 446):** © AP Photo/Alastair Grant; **Figure 14.8 (p. 449):** © AP Photo/Mike Wintroath; **Figure 14.9 (p. 451):** © Galen Rowell/CORBIS/Getty Images; **Figure 14.10 (p. 452):** Courtesy of Robert H. Lavenda; **Figure 14.11 (p. 455):** © Dinodia Photos/Alamy; **Figure 14.12 (p. 457):** Courtesy of Robert H. Lavenda; **Figure 14.13 (p. 461):** © David Grossman/Alamy Stock Photo; **Figure 14.14 (p. 465):** © AP Photo/Radu Sigheti, Pool

Chapter 15

Chapter 15 Opening Photo (p. 476): © Lawrence Weslowski Jr | Dreamstime.com; **Figure 15.1 (p. 478):** OUP; **Figure 15.2 (p. 479):** Pablo Corral V/Corbis/VCG/Getty Images; **Figure 15.3 (p. 482):** Shawn Baldwin; **In Their Own Words (p. 483):** © Masaru Goto; **In Their Own Words (p. 484):** REUTERS/Karoly Arvai (HUNGARY); **Figure 15.4 (p. 489):** Stephanie Maze/Corbis Documentary/Getty Images; **In Their Own Words (p. 490):** from Elizabeth Chin, "Ethnically Correct Dolls: Toying with the Race Industry," American Anthropologist 101(2), 1999. Reprinted by permission of the American Anthropological Association. Not for sale or further reproduction; **Figure 15.5 (p. 493):** OUP; **Figure 15.6 (p. 495):** AP Photo/Mike Fiala; **Figure 15.7 (p. 496):** REUTERS/Lucy Nicholson (AFGHANISTAN SOCIETY EDUCATION); **Figure 15.8 (p. 499):** Crawford/AnthroPhoto; **Figure 15.9 (p. 500):** UN Photo/Eskinder Debebe; **Figure 15.10 (p. 503):** REUTERS/Anthony P.

Chapter 16

Chapter 16 Opening Photo (p. 510): ERIKA LARSEN/National Geographic Creative; **Figure 16.1 (p. 512):** ASHRAF SHAZLY/AFP/Getty Images; **Figure 16.2 (p. 517):** Photo by Lannis Waters/Palm Beach Post/ZUMA Press. © Copyright 2006 by Palm Beach Post.; **Figure 16.3 (p. 519):** Courtesy of Mokshika Gaur; **Figure 16.4 (p. 520):** © Gilles Peress/Magnum Photos; **Figure 16.5 (p. 521):** © Mikce Stocke/Sun-Sentinel/ZUMAPRESS.com; **Figure 16.6 (p. 521):** ERIC LAFFORGUE/Alamy Stock Photo; **Figure 16.7 (p. 524):** Courtesy of Robert H. Lavenda; **Figure 16.8**

(p. 525): ROBERTO SCHMIDT/AFP/Getty Images; **Figure 16.9 (p. 527):** FABIO TEIXEIRA/ESTADAO CONTEUDO (Agencia Estado via AP Images); **Figure 16.10 (p. 528):** © ANDRE LESSA/dpa/Corbis

Text Credits

Chapter 1

In Their Own Words (p. 9): Courtesy of James W. Fernandez; **In Their Own Words (p. 20):** Courtesy of SUNY Plattsburgh Career Development Center

Chapter 2

In Their Own Words (p. 56): Selected excerpts from pages 112–114 from Biology as Ideology by R. C. Lewontin. Copyright © 1991 by R. C. Lewontin and the Canadian Broadcasting Corporation. Reprinted by permission of Harper-Collins Publishers.

Chapter 3

In Their Own Words (p. 68): Flannery, Tim, 2018, Europe: A Natural History, New York: Atlantic Monthly Press 154–156. **In Their Own Words (p. 73):** Strier, 2011, p. 675 from Strier, K.B. 2011. Conservation. In Campbell, C.J., Fuentes, A.F., MacKinnon, K.C., Panger, M., Bearder, S., and Stumpf, R. (eds): Primates in Perspective, 2nd Edition, Oxford University Press, NY, pp. 664–675

Chapter 4

In Their Own Words (p. 105): From LUCY: THE BEGINNINGS OF HUMANKIND by Donald Johanson and Maitland A. Edey. Copyright © 1981 by Donald Johanson and Maitland A. Edey. Reprinted with the permission of Simon & Schuster, Inc. All rights reserved. **In Their Own Words (p. 124):** from Judith C. Berman's "Bad Hair Days in the Paleolithic: Modern (Re) Constructions of the Cave Man?" Reproduced by permission of the American Anthropological Association from American Anthropologist, Volume 101, Issue 2, pages 288–304, June 1999. Not for sale or further reproduction **In Their Own Words (p. 135):** From Catherine Hodge McCoid and LeRoy D. McDermott, "Toward Decolonizing Gender: Female Vision in the Upper Paleolithic," Reproduced by permission of the American Anthropological Association from American Anthropologist, volume 98, Issue 2, pages 319–326, June 1996. Not for sale or further reproduction.

Chapter 5

Table 5.1 (p. 149): The Human Species, Third Edition, by John Relethford. Copyright © 1997 Mayfield Publishing Company

Chapter 6

In Their Own Words (p. 190): From Jean-Paul DeMoule, "Rescue archaeology: A European view," Annual Review of Anthropology 41: 611–626, 2012. Used with permission.

Chapter 7

In Their Own Words (p. 223): From *Indian Givers* by Jack Weatherford. Copyright © 1988 by Jack McIver Weatherford. Reprinted by permission of Crown Publishers, a division of Random House, Inc. **In Their Own Words (p. 231):** Courtesy of Dan Rice and Prudence Rice

Chapter 8

In Their Own Words (p. 243): Courtesy of Ivan Karp; **In Their Own Words (p. 245):** Courtesy of Hoyt Alverson **In Their Own Words (p. 247):** From Sally Engle Merry's "Human Rights Law and the Demonization of Culture (And Anthropology Along The Way). Reproduced by permission of the American Anthropological Association from *PoLAR: Political and Legal Anthropology Review*, volume 26, Issue 1, pages 55–76, May 2003. Nor for sale or for further reproduction.

Chapter 9

Table 9.1 (p. 297): Adapted from Hinton, Leanne. 1998. "Language loss and Revitalization in California: Overview." International Journal of the Sociology of Language 132: pg. 83–85. **In Their Own Words (p. 285):** Courtesy of David Parkin; **In Their Own Words (p. 293):** From Marcyliena Morgan, "Theories and Politics in African-American English," Annual Review of Anthropology 23:325–345, 1995. Permission conveyed through the Copyright Clearance Center.

Chapter 10

In Their Own Words (p. 315): From Julie Taylor, "Tango," Cultural Anthropology 2:4, 1987. Reprinted by permission of the American Anthropological Association. Not for sale or further reproduction; **In Their Own Words (p. 323):** Patricia Aufderheide, "Latin American Grassroots Video: Beyond Television," in Public Culture, Volume 5, no. 3, pp. 579–592. Copyright, 199 All rights reserved. Republished by permission of the copyright holder and present publisher, Duke University Press. www.dukeupress.edu; **In Their Own Words (p. 335):** Cultural Survival, Inc. From Andrea Smith, "For All Those Who Were Indians in a Former Life," Cultural Survival Quarterly, Vol. 17, No. 4, Winter 1994. Used with permission of the publisher; **In Their Own Words (p. 337):** From Custom and Confrontation by Roger M. Keesing. Copyright © 1992 by the University of Chicago. Reproduced by permission of the publisher, the University of Chicago Press.

Chapter 11

In Their Own Words (p. 350): From *Autobiografías Campesinas*, 1979, Vol. 1, Heredia, Costa Rica: Editorial della Universidad Nacional, translated from Spanish by Robert Lavenda; **In Their Own Words (p. 356):** From *Crafting Selves: Power, Gender, and Discourses of Identity in a Japanese Workplace* by Dorinne K. Kondo. Copyright © 1990 by the University of Chicago. Reproduced by permission of the publisher, the University of Chicago Press **In Their Own Words (p. 358):** From *Questioning Collapse: Human Resilience, Ecological Vulnerability, and the Aftermath of Empire* ed. by Patricia A. McAnany and Norman Yoffee. Copyright © 2010 Cambridge University Press. Reprinted with permission from the publisher **In Their Own Words (p. 363):** From *African Art in Transit* by Christopher Steiner, 1994, Cambridge University Press. Reprinted with permission from the publisher.

Chapter 12

In Their Own Words (p. 374): "Protestors Gird for Long Fight over Peru's Amazon" by Simon Romero © 2009 by The New York Times Co. Reprinted with permission; **In Their Own Words (p. 380):** "Reforming the Crow Constitution" by Kelly Branam. Reprinted by permission of author.

Chapter 13

In Their Own Words (p. 409): From Hewlett, *Listen, Here is a Story*. Copyright 2013 by Oxford University Press. Reprinted by permission of the Publisher.

Chapter 14

In Their Own Words (p. 428): From Judith M. Abwunza, *Women's Voices, Women's Power: Dialogues of Resistance from East Africa*, Copyright © Broadview Press (University of Toronto Press Higher Education Division), 1997. Published Feb. 1997. Reproduced with permission of the publisher; **In Their Own Words (p. 454):** From "Dowry too high. Lose bridge and go to jail," by James Brooke. Copyright © 2003 by The New York Times Co. Reprinted with permission; **In Their Own Words (p. 456):** Reproduced by permission of the Society of Applied Anthropology from John van Willigen and V. C. Channa, "Law, Custom, and Crimes Against Women," *Human Organization* 50(4) 1991, 369–370; **In Their Own Words (p. 457):** Ward, *Gangsters without Borders: An Ethnography of a Salvadoran Street Gang*. Copyright © 2013. By permission of Oxford University Press, USA; **In Their Own Words (p. 460):** "Two Cheers for Gay Marriage" by Roger N. Lancaster. Reproduced by permission of the American Anthropological Association

Chapter 15

Chapter 16

Index